We Are Veterans of Change

Perhaps the hardest working word in 2008 was 'change'.

While no one can predict whether '09 will deliver change we can believe in, pocket change or worse – no change at all – our year-round research indicates that music biz entrepreneurs like you, are optimistic about the future of live, original music & the growing success of independent artists & releases.

Yes, it seems 8+ years of music industry upheaval & turmoil has made all of us in the music business seasoned veterans of change – more flexible, more creative and already building new communities and opportunities.

At MRG we've been busy enhancing & expanding our products & programs to keep you marketing & selling your music more successfully in a continually changing marketplace.

In the Atlas print edition, we've added articles to help expand your worldview. Enjoy these insights and get other in-depth coverage of industry issues & trends delivered to your in-box monthly by subscribing to the free AtlasPlugged newsletter on the homepage of: www.MusiciansAtlas.com.

As always, the annual print edition features thousands of detailed listings of performance & promotion contacts selected from our vast online database to keep you connected to an industry that's in constant flux.

Of course you'll always have the freshest contact info plus tools that make it easy to book more gigs and sell more music when you subscribe to the AtlasOnline. It's the ultimate music biz machine packed with 40% more contacts than the print edition with new listings & updates added every day. Interactive tools make it easy to plan tours, coordinate promotional campaigns, track merch & record sales & so much more.

We've waived the activation fee for our loyal Atlas readers; sign up today at www.MusiciansAtlas.com/MA2009 & you'll see just how easy your music biz can be – for as little as $9.95/mo!

One thing that never changes is our commitment to helping indie artists and releases overcome obstacles & succeed.

On pages 8-13 meet the artists participating in this year's Atlas Artist Spotlight program. They will be promoted in print & online promotion campaigns to thousands of industry decision makers including Film, TV & Gaming music supervisors, music press, booking agents, festival & club talent buyers, publishers & radio programmers.

To learn what the Atlas Artist Spotlight can do for your career go to MusiciansAtlas.com/Spotlight.

And, in the centerfold, meet the winners, finalists & judges of the 8th annual Independent Music Awards. Culled from thousands of submissions from around the globe, this year's honorees represent every level of experience - from seasoned recording artists to acts on the rise. The IMAs is a unique program that helps indie artists and releases reach nearly 20 million music fans via strategic partnerships and active promotions that deliver yearlong marketing, broadcast, distribution & performance opportunities.

Go to IndependentMusicAwards.com to hear & view the IMA winners & finalists & vote for your favorites at the IMA Vox Populi Jukebox. The winners of this Vox Pop poll will also receive promotion and marketing support throughout 2009.

New categories added to the 9th IMAs include honors for Love Song, Story Song, Concept Album & Eclectic Album. Stay up to date with all the deadlines & new program details when you sign up for the IMA buzz after you vote at the Vox Pop jukebox.

MRG has lots of changes & innovations in the works that we'll be rolling out in 2009, including exciting live performance opportunities. And, by the time you read this, we will be settled in our spankin' new office space. After more than a decade of working out of an attic – Music Resource Group is re-locating our world headquarters to a spacious 4500 square foot loft. Truly change we can believe in!

As always, we wish you great success...

- Music Resource Group

Martin Folkman
PUBLISHER

Jude Folkman
EDITOR IN CHIEF

Lauren Veteri
MANAGING EDITOR

Donna Zukowski
PRODUCTION MANAGER

Joelle Batelli
Robert Fontana
Samantha Galligan
Theresa McMillan
Alisha Miranda
James Potter
Michael Shelley
EDITORS

Adam Bird
Theresa McMillan
SALES

Smay Vision
COVER, GATEFOLD, ARTICLES & ARTIST SPOTLIGHT DESIGN

Color Optics, Inc.
PRINT PRODUCTION

Music Resource Group

The Musician's Atlas is published annually by:

Music Resource Group, LLC
32 Ann Street
Clifton, NJ 07013
p: 973-767-1800
f: 973-767-1844
e: info@musiciansatlas.com
www.MusiciansAtlas.com

ISBN#: 0-9669368-9-2

FACTORY DIRECT
CD·DVD
MANUFACTURING
recision Disc is proud to be offering a growing line of no-plastic
nd low-plastic CD packaging alternatives. We call them our
Eco" products, which are printed on FSC certified recycled stock
sing vegetable-based inks and waterless print technology. Visit
s at www.predisc.com to learn more and get a quote online.
PRECISION disc

contents

Meet this year's IMA winners in a special gatefold. The IMA section begins on page 224.

FROM THE PAGES OF THE atlas plugged eNEWSLETTER

DOWN THE BLOCK - A NEW MUSIC RENAISSANCE

I live in Nashville, the Music City. If you walk into any coffee shop, bar, or restaurant, you'll find musicians and songwriters hanging out and talking about the business. Lots of Horatio Alger dreaming here, combined with full court creative push, because people are serious about trying to make things happen.

One of the reality checks I've noticed of late is the economy. A lot of my friends are saying things have been slow this year – first due to the price of gas...now with the global fiscal crisis – the result is that less artists are going on the road, less people driving long distances to gigs and clubs hurting. I've noticed it myself, it seems this year my "take" has remained the same, while my expenses, in food, gas, and lodging, has risen.

Anyway, if guys like me or bands like you were previously only barely making enough to scrape by after gas and hotel costs, maybe we all need to take a deep breath and refocus. Maybe it will cause people to collaborate with a wider variety of folks in their hometowns, and go outside of their musical comfort zone as a result. Out of this dynamic, there is sure to be some unexpected surprises, experimentation, magical meeting of the minds.

Clubs are going to hurt, in the short term, and some may fall by the wayside. My guess is there will be a survival of the fittest dynamic, and creative venues will hang on and strengthen. Artists will also be forced to be a bit choosy about gigs out of town, in terms of quality and quantity, which could provide a little necessary length between gigs in certain markets, to make shows a bit more special.

And when local scenes start prospering again, there will be new local media to cover those scenes, followed by new low-band or Internet radio to do what radio did back in the day – serve the community. I've already seen a resurgence of good independent record stores, in the wake of the major chains going under or cutting inventory.

So, the reality of our current economy could be the best thing to happen to music in a long time.

Lately, I've been all over a book called Deep Economy, by Bill McKibben, an illustrious thinker and essayist for more than 20 years. Move over Deepak, Eckhart, and my pal Noam Chomsky, this book is something. It's all about the battle between more and better which for many of us have become almost opposites.

McKibben puts forward a new way to think about the things we buy, food we eat, energy we use, and the money that pays for it all. Our purchases, he says, need not be at odds with the things we truly value. McKibben's animating idea is that we need to move beyond "growth" as the paramount economic ideal and pursue prosperity in a more local direction, with cities, suburbs, and regions producing more of their own food, generating more of their own energy, and even nurturing more of their own culture and entertainment.

Since this is a music article, here's McKibben's paradigm extended into our CD-selling, live-show-playing world. Because of the propensity of "more" in the music business, we've seen the erosion of the pioneering musical spirit that takes root in the local, the immediate, and the intimate.

So, yeah, while we may whine during late nite bull sessions about the fact that we're not all becoming millionaires, like back in the 60s, the truth is music making is about making music and historically the financial rewards have been on a much smaller scale than the 'record amounts' of the past 30 years or so.

Sure, some major talents like the Beatles, et. al, benefited, became millionaires and reached untold scores of listeners. Sure, it's cool to have easy access to artists from Africa and Brazil and France and such, to broaden our sense of the world. And I don't blame any modern artists for taking advantage of this development, doing great work within the parameters of what they were given.

I often wonder though, why we're so complicit in allowing the corporate structure to own our stories, own our music, own our souls.

If you go back 100 years, before phonograph records, communities were "alive with the sound of music". Families had at least a couple people who played an instrument or sang a bit at home and musicians shared their tunes at local shindigs, county fairs, whatever. People passed songs to one another that reflected the experiences and emotions of that locale, which makes perfect sense (I must say, the very best artists today do recreate this).

The record industry was new and there were lots of great regional scenes based around jazz, blues, folk idioms and more. Soul music sounded a little bit different, dependent on whether it came from Chicago, Philly, New York, Detroit, Memphis, or New Orleans, for example. Radio was weirdly diverse and reflected the communities where the artists lived and made their music.

As more and more money changed hands, things tightened up, via the consolidation and monopolization of labels, radio, print media, and record store chains. The standard became a more homogenous music that could be pumped into generic ears, from coast to coast, even internationally. Sure, regional scenes like Stax or Motown went national or international back in the day. But, the difference is, the music grew out of the communities and then was shared with the world – as opposed to being created from the get-go with some sort of nebulous global market in mind.

Re-generated neighborhoods will enable artists to get back to a more 'localized' scene that connects directly to the people. That's a powerful thing - it cuts out the middleman and you're not competing with Django, Elvis, Miles, and everyone else who ever recorded, when you're standing two feet away from your audience. This is the totality of what art with a sane dose of commerce can be, instead of some faux universality.

Bands will get hip to the fact that it is extremely difficult to literally compete with millions of songs around the globe (from the limitless back catalogues, as well as new releases) on a seemingly but not really level playing field such as that prescribed by digital downloads. So the way to sustain one's self as an artist, will increasingly rely on taking it directly to the people.

The language and the rhythms of the community will become more relevant again, as artists literally riff off each other in ways they never imagined, because they will be staying a little closer to home, collaborating.

Once people aren't driving thirty miles to see a movie or vacationing eight states away, they'll discover local talent, and forge more meaningful relationships with artists that they see up close, interact with, buy their music, etc. – a true renaissance vs. a virtual connection. Think Paris in 50s. New York in the 60s. Kingston in the 70s. Only better, because it'll be just down the block from you, within walking distance, no matter where you live.

Feel free to shoot me a question – **doughoekstra@yahoo.com**.
You can also visit **www.doughoekstra.com** or **www.myspace.com/doughoekstra**.

Doug Hoekstra's music has garnered years of praise from critics, djs, and fans throughout the US & Europe. In addition to live discs, eps, and other oddities, he's released six full-length works, earning him Nashville Music Award, Independent Music Award, and NARAS nominations. His short fiction and non-fiction has appeared in numerous literary journals, and he was nominated for the Pushcart Prize for his tale "The Blarney Stone" (2006). Hoekstra's first-full length collection of prose, "Bothering the Coffee Drinkers," was published in 2006 to rave reviews and earned a Bronze Medal for Best Short Fiction in the 2007 Independent Publisher Awards (IPPYs).

ARTIST SPOTLIGHT

 = SONICBIDS EPK™ (ELECTRONIC PRESS KIT)

CELESTIAL DAWN

LOCATION: Montreal, CAN
WEBSITE: www.celestialdawn.com
CONTACT: Jason Davidson
EMAIL: dawnmetal@yahoo.com
www.sonicbids.com/celestialdawn
GENRE: Hard Rock, Metal
LATEST RELEASE: *Disorder*
LABEL: Self Released

REGIONS TOURED: Quebec, Ontario, Eastern US

CAREER HIGHLIGHTS: Playing Chicago Classic Metalfest 4, signing with Insanity Records, Germany (RIP), featured on the Metal File, Chom FM.

INFLUENCES: Iron Maiden, Metallica, Ozzy, a wide range of the Hard Rock and Metal worlds.

3 KISSES

LOCATION: Brenham, TX
WEBSITE: www.3kisses.com
CONTACT: Tish Meeks
EMAIL: tish@3kisses.com
www.sonicbids.com/3kisses
GENRE: Texas Party Punk
LATEST RELEASE: *American Breakdown*
LABEL: Rat Pak Records

REGIONS TOURED: Northeast & Southeast US

CAREER HIGHLIGHTS: Performed for over 300,000 people live at Susan G. Komen Race for the Cure events across Texas. Multiple performances at Dewey Beach Music Fest, Texas Rockfest, SXSW, Rock Solid Pressure Showcase, Hawgs of Texas Biker Rally, Millennium Music Conference, GoGirls Music Fest. Performance on ABC's 'Wife Swap' for over 10 million television viewers. Live performances on FOX Houston, FOX Austin, ABC Houston and NBC San Antonio.

INFLUENCES: Bowling For Soup, Social Distortion, Joan Jett, The Ramones, Primus, and more.

LEON

LOCATION: Union, NJ
WEBSITE: www.nealsight.com
CONTACT: Lisa Neal
EMAIL: nealsight@comcast.net
www.sonicbids.com/leon3
GENRE: Jazz, Smooth Jazz, R&B, Soul, Ero Jazz
LATEST RELEASE: *All For Love*
LABEL: Nealsight Records LLC.
INFLUENCES: My musical style was influenced by many of the great singers and players from the 50's, 60's and 70's. Nat King Cole, Steve Wonder, Bobby Blue Bland, Peabo Bryson, James Brown, Sammy Davis Jr., Little Jimmy Scott, to name a few. Players like Charlie Christian, Charles Parker, Miles Davis, Wes Montgomery, Grant Green, Joe Pass, George Benson, Oscar Peterson, Thelonious Monk ...man there are so many great people!

CARBON 9

LOCATION: Los Angeles, CA
WEBSITE: www.carbon9.com
CONTACT: Stacey Quinealty
EMAIL: stacey@carbon9.com
GENRE: Extreme Alternative Rock
LATEST RELEASE: *The Bull*
LABEL: WorldSound Records
REGIONS TOURED: Southwest & Midwest US

CAREER HIGHLIGHTS: Los Angeles Music Awards – Best Modern Rock Band, Most Outstanding Live Performance. All Access Music Awards – Best Hard Rock Group, Best Live Show, People's Choice Award, Best Live Performance, Best Male Vocalist, Best Guitarist. Universal Studios – Performer of the Year.

INFLUENCES: Trent Reznor, Pantera, "Society in General".

D. BURTON

LOCATION: Oakland, CA
WEBSITE: www.myspace.com/theyaysfinest
CONTACT: D. Burton
EMAIL: dburtonsofly@yahoo.com
www.sonicbids.com/dburton
GENRE: R&B, Pop
LATEST RELEASE: *Never Hurt You*
LABEL: Self Released
REGIONS TOURED: Everywhere

CAREER HIGHLIGHTS: Working with legendary producer "Easy Mo Bee". Working with Oakland's hit master, producer A.R. Fuller Music. Nominated for 2007 "Best Unsigned Artist of the Year". Featured in Performer magazine. Receiving approval of my craft from legendary producer Neil James. Selected as a showcase artist for the Global Gaming Expo 2007 in Las Vegas. Spotlighted Artist on mvyradio.com. Spotlighted Artist on iRadio LA. Meeting and working with American Idol Participants during season 4.

INFLUENCES: Motown, Stax, Kenny Chesney, Brooks & Dunn, Aerosmith, Bon Jovi, Jay-Z, Nas, Common, KRS-one, Kanye West, Wyclef.

EVOKA

LOCATION: Winston-Salem, NC
WEBSITE: www.evokamusic.com
CONTACT: Bryan Ledbetter
EMAIL: info@evokamusic.com
GENRE: Alternative Rock
LATEST RELEASE: *Cries From The Castlegate Empire*
LABEL: Self Released
REGIONS TOURED: East Coast US

CAREER HIGHLIGHTS:
Featured in HM Magazine, Relevant Magazine and on XM Satellite Radio. Charted in top 200 on CMJ charts. Charted #70 in 2007 CRW Rock Chart. Licensed music to MTV Real World and Road Rules, Subway Restaurants TV & Radio Ads. ESPN Radio Ads.

INFLUENCES: Led Zeppelin, Pink Floyd, Johnny Cash, Elbow, Doves, T-Rex.

TO LEARN MORE ABOUT THESE ARTISTS, VISIT:

MusiciansAtlas.com/spotlight

KARLUS TRAPP

LOCATION: New York, NY
WEBSITE: www.karlustrapp.com
CONTACT: Karlus Trapp
EMAIL: ktrapp1@si.rr.com
GENRE: Rock, Pop, Reggae, World
LATEST RELEASE: *Wow*
LABEL: Self Released
REGIONS TOURED: Northeast US, Latin and Central America

CAREER HIGHLIGHTS: Opened for Richie Havens, played with drum legend Anton Fig in group "The Pipes", touring in Central and Latin America for the USO. Songs from 'Wow' being used on *General Hospital.* Wrote song for Japanese TV Commercial. Finalist in 2007 John Lennon Songwriting Contest.

INFLUENCES: Music of New Orleans, Music of the 60's, Bob Marley, Little Feat, Jimi Hendrix, Joni Mitchell, King Sunny Ade and his African Beats.

KEITH AND RENEE

LOCATION: Winnipeg, Manitoba, CAN
WEBSITE: www.keithandrenee.com
CONTACT: Tim Sullivan
EMAIL: tim_sullivan@dkcnews.com
www.sonicbids.com/keithandrenee
GENRE: Pop, Rock
LATEST RELEASE: *Revolution*
LABEL: KAR Music Group
REGIONS TOURED: NYC, Boston, LA, Chicago, Toronto, Winnipeg, Calgary

CAREER HIGHLIGHTS: Nominated for a Western Canadian Music Award alongside Nelly Furtado, Jann Arden and Sarah McLachlan. Music placements in Degrassi, Canadian Idol and AT&T Commercials. Performed in Dubai and Kenya in the summer of 2008. Showcased at Musexpo, NXNE, Canadian Music Week, NACA, London Calling. Currently performing a 70-date high school tour sponsored in part by 'Free the Children' and 'O Ambassadors' (Oprah's Angel Network). 3 Album Releases; *Novice (2001), Simple Stuff (2004) and Revolution (2007).*

INFLUENCES: Crowded House, Sheryl Crow, The Beatles, Melissa Etheridge, Indigo Girls.

LOVE YOU LONG TIME

LOCATION: Los Angeles, CA
WEBSITE: www.myspace.com/loveyoulongtime
CONTACT: Stefanie Reines
EMAIL: stefanie@intrzn.com
www.sonicbids.com/loveyoulongtime
GENRE: Electro Hip-Pop
LATEST RELEASE: *Party To The People*
LABEL: Self Released
REGIONS TOURED: CA, OR, WA, ID, MT, UT, AZ, NV

CAREER HIGHLIGHTS: Playing Warped Tour '08 in LA and having Soul Glow Activatur (Family Force 5) come on stage and dance during set. Signing a management deal with INTRZN MGMT (Stefanie Reines from Drive Thru Records and Chris O'Connor from Westaspenmerch.com).

INFLUENCES: Justin Timberlake, Chromeo, Justice, Michael Jackson, Robyn, Family Force 5, The Aquabats.

KILL KRINKLE CLUB

LOCATION: Dublin, Ireland
WEBSITE: www.myspace.com/killkrinkleclub
CONTACT: Justin Commins
EMAIL: killkrinkleclub@gmail.com
www.sonicbids.com/killkrinkleclub
GENRE: Pop, Electro, Folk
LATEST RELEASE: *The Bloody Murder Of Krinkle EP* (iTunes Release)
REGIONS TOURED: Ireland, London, Canada, Sweden

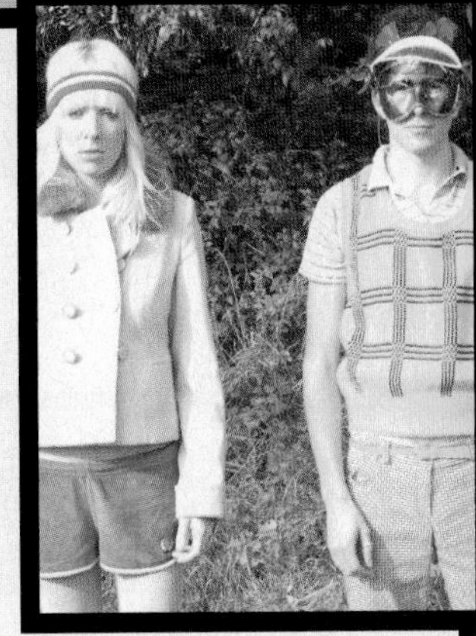

CAREER HIGHLIGHTS: The Halifax Pop, Canada with Islands, Holy Fuck. Swedish National Radio P3 and NSD Newspaper interview and features. Chicago's Venuszine magazine's Band Of The Month for May 08.

INFLUENCES: The beating heart in our collecting ribcage! David Lynch, The Beach Boys, Leonard Cohen, 80's pop, Haruki Murakami, The National, endless hours of reading, The Beatles, Hot Chip, children's books.

LAZLO HOLLYFELD

LOCATION: Buffalo, NY
WEBSITE: www.lazlohollyfeld.com
CONTACT: Scott Molloy / Chris Gangarossa
EMAIL: lazlo@lazlohollyfeld.com
www.sonicbids.com/lazlohollyfeld
GENRE: Indie Rock, Post-Rock, Instrumental
LATEST RELEASE: *Elimination*
LABEL: Self Released
REGIONS TOURED: Full US

CAREER HIGHLIGHTS: Live performances with India Arie, Mogwai and Bonobo. Multiple night stands at the Boom Boom Room in San Francisco. Several performances during the past 2 SXSW Festivals in Austin. Various commercial licensing agreements with shows airing on Discovery Channel and several independent documentary and film works.

INFLUENCES: Tortoise, Phillip Glass, Stereolab, Arcade Fire, DJ Shadow, Radiohead.

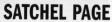

 = SONICBIDS EPK™ (ELECTRONIC PRESS KIT)

MAYORS OF SUPER AWESOME TOWN

LOCATION: Cincinnati, OH
WEBSITE: www.myspace.com/mayorsofsuperawesometown
CONTACT: Don Peteroy and Jack Curley
EMAIL: themayorsofsuperawesometown@gmail.com
www.sonicbids.com/mayorsofsuperawesometown
GENRE: Geek Rock
LATEST RELEASE: *Bald Lang Syne EP*
REGIONS TOURED: Midwest, Northeast and Southeast US

INFLUENCES: They Might Be Giants, Ben Folds, Barenaked Ladies, Lincoln, Weezer.

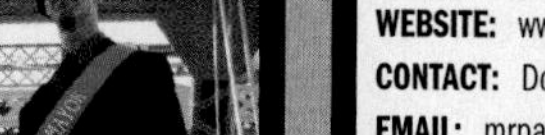

SATCHEL PAGE

LOCATION: New York, NY
WEBSITE: www.myspace.com/satchelpage
CONTACT: Dominique Deleon
EMAIL: mrpage@themrpage.com
www.sonicbids.com/satchelpage
GENRE: Hip-Hop, Rap, New Wave
LATEST RELEASE: *The Underground EP*
LABEL: Jet Records
REGIONS TOURED: New York, Boston, Wash D.C.

CAREER HIGHLIGHTS: Opened for Fabolous and Busta Rhymes in concert. Gold Album credit on 8Ball and MJG's Living Legends and Method Man's Tical D: The Prequel.

INFLUENCES: Classic cinema, design, shape and form. Classic Hip Hop, innovative people, travel, new ideas.

STARCODE

LOCATION: New York, NY
WEBSITE: www.starcode.com
CONTACT: Michele Larsen
EMAIL: mllarsen@tmo.blackberry.net
www.sonicbids.com/starcode
GENRE: Rock
LATEST RELEASE: *TBD* (2009)
REGIONS TOURED: Northeast, East Coast US, Bosnia, Germany, former Yugoslavia

CAREER HIGHLIGHTS: MP3 Music & Technology tour with Fono, Tonic, and Goo Goo Dolls. Feature on Billboard.com, opening for Belly.

INFLUENCES: Dead, The Kinks, Stone Temple Pilots, Afghan Whigs, Mingus.

STIFF TRIXY

LOCATION: Paris, TX
WEBSITE: www.stifftrixy.com
CONTACT: Josh Allen
EMAIL: info@stifftrixy.com
GENRE: Rock
LATEST RELEASE: *It's Not All Just Black and White*
LABEL: Second City Records
REGIONS TOURED: Full US, Costa Rica, Asia

CAREER HIGHLIGHTS: Tours with Adema, playing with Alice Cooper, Black Sabbath, Queensryche and Shadows Fall at the Locobazooka Festival. Apearing on CBS Channel 11 Morning News twice. Appearing in Urban Mainstream Magazine, playing with the Romantics, appearing in Skratch Magazine and on a Skratch Magazine compilation disc.

INFLUENCES: The Beatles, Chuck Berry, Poison, Cinderella, Candlebox, Black Sabbath, Faster Pussycat, Hanoi Rocks, Motley Crue, AC/DC, The Allman Brothers Band, .38 Special, Lynyrd Skynyrd, The Band, CCR, The Black Crowes, The Marshall Tucker Band, David Alan Coe, Hank Williams, Hank Williams Jr., Elvis, Prince, The Used, Tesla, Hair metal.

MATTHEW POP

LOCATION: New York, NY
WEBSITE: www.myspace.com/matthewpop
CONTACT: Matthew Pop
EMAIL: matthewpop1@yahoo.com
GENRE: Pop, Rock
LATEST RELEASE: *Hopeless Melodic*
LABEL: Self Released
REGIONS TOURED: US & Canada

CAREER HIGHLIGHTS: Song, "Get It On" featured on MTV's The Real World: Philadelphia 2004 and 2005. POP finalist in the John Lennon Songwriting Contest, Opened up Regina Spektor's 2006 tour in Montreal. Completed a highly-regarded 5 week tour of the US including Toronto in 2008.

INFLUENCES: The Beatles, The Replacements, Superdrag, Elvis Costello, The Pixies, Weezer, New Order.

LAUREN JANE BOWMAN

LOCATION: New York, NY
WEBSITE: www.myspace.com/laurenjanebowman
CONTACT: Lauren Bowman
EMAIL: wwangelww6@aol.com
GENRE: Pop, Alternative, Rock
LATEST RELEASE: *Dangerous Angel*
REGIONS TOURED: Check website for details on upcoming shows.

CAREER HIGHLIGHTS: Every song I write and feeling I get on stage.

INFLUENCES: God, my parents, Madonna, Bob Dylan, Alanis Morisette, Queen, A Perfect Circle, Red Hot Chili Peppers, Rihanna, Led Zeppelin, Evanescence.

TEJAS SINGH

LOCATION: New York, NY
WEBSITE: www.myspace.com/tejassingh
CONTACT: Zach Diaz
EMAIL: zachdiaz42@gmail.com
www.sonicbids.com/tejassingh
GENRE: Singer-Songwriter
LATEST RELEASE: *A Brief History*

CAREER HIGHLIGHTS: Regular performances at NYC hot spots Rockwood Music Hall, The Bitter End, and The National Underground.

INFLUENCES: Ben Harper, John Mayer, Ray LaMontagne, Tracy Chapman, Dave Matthews.

THE PARLOTONES

LOCATION: South Africa/UK
WEBSITE: www.parlotones.com
CONTACT: Raphael Domalik
EMAIL: raphael@sovent.co.uk
www.sonicbids.com/theparlotones
GENRE: Rock
LATEST RELEASE: *A World Next Door*
LABEL: Sovereign Entertainment
REGIONS TOURED: Europe, Africa

CAREER HIGHLIGHTS: Biggest selling rock band in South Africa, performed at Live Earth, Coke Fest and V Fest. Key acknowledgements include Best Rock Album 2006 at South African Music Awards. Best Music Act - People's Choice awards 2008, Best Band - You Awards 2007, FHM Readers Choice 2007, Best Video MK Awards 2007, Best Video nomination Resfest 2007. The Parlotones latest album is already platinum in South Africa and is due for release in UK/Europe and US in the new year.

INFLUENCES: 80's British Alternative scene

THE SHOW

LOCATION: Pittsburgh, PA
WEBSITE: www.myspace.com/comeseetheshow
CONTACT: William Endler
EMAIL: theshowmail@aol.com
GENRE: Alternative, Indie Rock
LATEST RELEASE: *Here's To Your Jigsaw*
LABEL: Self Released
REGIONS TOURED: Northeast & Midwest US, Canada
CAREER HIGHLIGHTS: Having our first shows sold out to 525+ people in Pittsburgh. Landing several TV appearances on college stations as a result of the anticipation of the band containing three well-locally and regionally known solo artists that were unlikely to be found in the same band together. Being able to tour after just six months together, doing the entire Northeast from Cleveland to New York City to Boston and Buffalo down to DC and Baltimore and down to Nashville, and many places in between. Having thousands of paid preorders lined up for our debut album over 3 months before it's due for release. Getting to do a UK tour in April/May 2009 after only 18 months together.

INFLUENCES: The Verve, The Shins, Oasis, Built To Spill, Bob Dylan, Rolling Stones, Sub Pop, The Cure, Green Day, R.E.M., DCFC, 238, Helio Sequence, Jealous Sound, Guster, Divinyls.

NEIL C. YOUNG

LOCATION: UK
WEBSITE: www.introducingtheincredible.com
CONTACT: Neil C. Young
EMAIL: charlyneil@gmail.com
GENRE: Jazz
LATEST RELEASE: *Chick(pea) Soup*
LABEL: Ence/Isolation Network Inc.
REGIONS TOURED: UK, France, Germany, Austria, Sweden, Finland, Texas, California, Wisconsin, Illinois

INFLUENCES: John Scofield, George Benson, Bill Frisell, Martin Taylor, Larry Carlton, Keith Jarrett, Herbie Hancock.

TELETEXTILE

LOCATION: Brooklyn, NY
WEBSITE: www.teletextile.com
CONTACT: Pamela Martinez
EMAIL: pamalucha@gmail.com
www.sonicbids.com/teletextile
GENRE: Indie Art Rock
LATEST RELEASE: *Care Package*
LABEL: Self Released
REGIONS TOURED: East Coast, Mid Atlantic, Southern US

CAREER HIGHLIGHTS: Receiving a compliment about our music from one of the mentioned influences.

INFLUENCES: Salvador Dali, Jim Henson, Sigur Ros, Bjork, Nick Drake, Broken Social Scene,William Basinski, Michel Gondry, house parties, late night talks, much more.

ARTIST SPOTLIGHT

(EPK icon) = **SONICBIDS EPK™ (ELECTRONIC PRESS KIT)**

SCRAPING FOR CHANGE

LOCATION: San Francisco, CA
WEBSITE: www.scrapingforchange.com
CONTACT: Sterling Selover
EMAIL: sterlin@scrapingforchange.com
(EPK) www.sonicbids.com/scrapingforchange
GENRE: Rock, Alternative, Pop
LATEST RELEASE: *19*6*3*
LABEL: Self Released
REGIONS TOURED: CA, AZ, NV, Indonesia

CAREER HIGHLIGHTS: Scraping for Change played at the Playboy Mansion in May, 2007. They followed this show by taking a summer tour throughout Indonesia in July and August of 2007 to play in the largest music festival of the year, "Soundrenaline." The average attendance at each festival show was 50,000+. Their song "Crazy Mary" climbed to the #1 spot on the Top 40 Charts of Prambors Radio right above Kanye West's "Stronger," and various other acts including Yellowcard, Sum41, Jordin Sparks, Shiny Toy Guns and more!

INFLUENCES: Foo Fighters, Smashing Pumpkins, Incubus, Red Hot Chili Peppers, Guns N Roses, Tom Petty, Green Day, Coheed and Cambria, AFI, Nirvana, 30 Seconds To Mars, Linkin Park.

UNIVERSOL

LOCATION: Central Jersey
WEBSITE: www.killahproduckt.com
CONTACT: Rob Young
EMAIL: team_radiowreck@hotmail.com
(EPK) www.sonicbids.com/universol
GENRE: Hip-Hop, Rap
LATEST RELEASE: *www.KILLAHPRODUCKT.com*
LABEL: Radio Wreck Records
REGIONS TOURED: NYC, CT, NJ, Philly, VA, MD, Atlanta, Miami, Seattle

CAREER HIGHLIGHTS: Semifinalist in DiscMakers Independent World Series. Featured on New York's Hot 97 radio as part of DJ Envy's mobile mixtape. Nominated for the Most Original Male Artist in 2007 and 2008 in the Underground Music Awards. Nominated for Street Album of the Year by Justo's MixTape Awards in 2008 for his latest compilation "Concrete Music".

INFLUENCES: Wu-Tang, Outkast, Rakim, Jay-Z, Slick Rick, Michael Jackson, James Brown, Stevie Wonder.

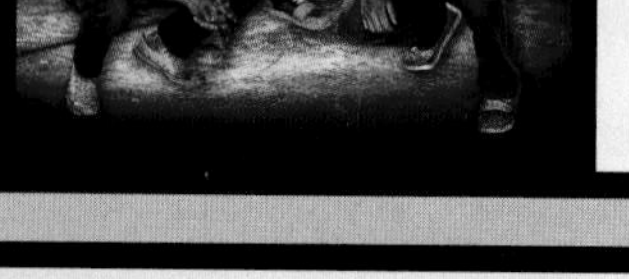

THE GOOD LUCK JOES

LOCATION: Milwaukee, WI
WEBSITE: www.thegoodluckjoes.com
CONTACT: Ken K.
EMAIL: kk@thirdwardrecords.com
GENRE: Pop Rock
LATEST RELEASE: *Why Everything Goes Wrong*
LABEL: Third Ward Records LLC
REGIONS TOURED: Full US

CAREER HIGHLIGHTS: Too many to name.

INFLUENCES: All genres, from Alt to Pop to Rock to Soul.

STEALING DECEMBER

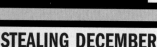

LOCATION: Newark, DE
WEBSITE: www.stealingdecember.com
CONTACT: Michael A. Ristano Sr.
EMAIL: marfgr@aol.com
(EPK) www.sonicbids.com/stealingdecember
GENRE: Rock
LATEST RELEASE: *Put It To Flame*
LABEL: Won't Believe The Chaos Records
REGIONS TOURED: NC, OH, GA, TN, KY, PA, WI, IL, CA, DE, MD, VA, NY, FL, IN

CAREER HIGHLIGHTS: National Tour with Papa Roach and Hed pe., Playing with: Boys Like Girls, Paramore, Stroke 9, Valencia. Playing at the famed Viper Room on the Sunset Strip.

INFLUENCES: Blink 182, Goo Goo Dolls, Led Zeppelin, Motley Crue, Our Lady Peace, Pearl Jam, Smashing Pumpkins, SR 71, and Butch Walker.

THE KRIMS

LOCATION: Fargo, ND
WEBSITE: www.myspace.com/thekrims
CONTACT: Eusabius Burgard
EMAIL: thekrims@yahoo.com
GENRE: Astro Honky Tonk
LATEST RELEASE: *Lusk*
LABEL: Self Released
REGIONS TOURED: Upper Midwest, West Coast, Rocky Mt. regions

CAREER HIGHLIGHTS: Being known for relentless touring, opening for Grand Funk Railroad, Nazrath, Brian Howe (Bad Company), to name a few.

INFLUENCES: The Black Crowes, Tom Petty, The Doors, Pantera, Johnny Cash, Skynyrd, Willie Nelson, Black Sabbath, KISS.

KATYA

LOCATION: Los Angeles, CA
WEBSITE: www.katyamusic.com
CONTACT: Katya
EMAIL: katya@katyamusic.com
(EPK) www.sonicbids.com/katya
GENRE: Rock n Roll
LATEST RELEASE: *Rock Lives!*
LABEL: Self Released
REGIONS TOURED: CA

CAREER HIGHLIGHTS: International radio airplay, licensed to MTV, performed at the Angels Stadium of Anaheim, performed at the E World Entertainment red carpet event, having six nationally known guests on debut album (John Philip Shenale, Stephen Perkins, Jerry Peterson, Adam Cohen, Paulo Gustavo, Gonzo Sandoval), endorsed by legendary John Carruthers of Guitars Carruthers, TKL cases, Get'Em Get'Em wear & Venice amplifiers.

INFLUENCES: Jimi Hendrix, The Doors, Janis Joplin, Rush, Led Zeppelin, David Bowie.

TO LEARN MORE ABOUT THESE ARTISTS, VISIT:

MusiciansAtlas.com/spotlight

MUY CANSADO

LOCATION: Boston, MA
WEBSITE: www.muycansado.com
CONTACT: Chris Mulvey
EMAIL: muycansado@gmail.com
www.sonicbids.com/muycansado
GENRE: Rock, Indie, Punk
LATEST RELEASE: *Stars & Garters*
LABEL: Precious Gems The Label
REGIONS TOURED: South, Midwest & Northeast US

CAREER HIGHLIGHTS: Touring the South & Midwest in Summer 08.

INFLUENCES: Pixies, The Beatles, Talking Heads, Bob Dylan, Velvet Underground, Tom Waits, David Bowie.

WAYNE NICHOLSON

LOCATION: Halifax, NS, CAN
WEBSITE: www.waynenicholson.com
CONTACT: Wayne Nicholson
EMAIL: wnicholson@ns.sympatico.ca
GENRE: Rock
LATEST RELEASE: *Playin' It Cool*
LABEL: Loggerhead
REGIONS TOURED: Major venues in Eastern and Western Canada

CAREER HIGHLIGHTS: Opened for Tina Turner, Foreigner, James Cotton, and The Allman Brothers.

INFLUENCES: 60's and 70's rock.

BIG REENO

LOCATION: Fargo, ND
WEBSITE: www.bigreeno.com
CONTACT: William Johnson
EMAIL: william@hustleproofrecords.com
GENRE: Hip Hop, Rap, R&B, Soul
LATEST RELEASE: *My Emotions* [SINGLE]
LABEL: Hustle Proof Records
REGIONS TOURED: ND, MN

CAREER HIGHLIGHTS: "My Emotions" #1 most requested song in Fargo, ND & Moorhead MN. Shared the stage with Hip Hop elites such as Ill Bill, Sean Price, Big Left & Ruste Juxx.

INFLUENCES: Marvin Gaye, Chaka Khan, Notorious B.I.G., 2pac, Common, Jay-Z, Nas & P. Diddy.

THE FOUNDATION BAND

LOCATION: Sacramento, CA
WEBSITE: www.dafoundationband.com
CONTACT: John Allen
EMAIL: johnallen@ix.netcom.com
www.sonicbids.com/johnallenandthefoundationband
GENRE: Jazz, Fusion
LATEST RELEASE: *New Music, Old Legacy*
LABEL: Digital Futures
REGIONS TOURED: France, Cuba, San Francisco Bay Area, Northern CA, Los Angeles, San Jose area

CAREER HIGHLIGHTS: Honorable mention in Billboard song contest. MIDEM festival participant. Music used in movie soundtrack. Founders of the Samuel C Allen Memorial Scholarship Foundation. Will soon have a jazz history book published entitled The Content of Their Character.

INFLUENCES: Jeff Lorber, Joe Sample, Herbie Hancock, Chick Corea.

SABLE

LOCATION: Earth
WEBSITE: www.sablecountry.com
CONTACT: Charles E. Million
EMAIL: maxmillion1@earthlink.net
www.sonicbids.com/sable
GENRE: Rock
LATEST RELEASE: *Drop Of Rain* [SINGLE]
LABEL: American Eagle Recordings
REGIONS TOURED: US, Europe, Mexico

CAREER HIGHLIGHTS: Three consecutive nationally charting US singles. Radio play in 15 countries outside US. Nationally aired video tribute to US Troops. Performing at the 2008 CMA Music Fair in Nashville, TN. USO tours for US troops in Turkey, Greece, Italy and Spain.

INFLUENCES: John Mellencamp, Pat Green, Keith Urban.

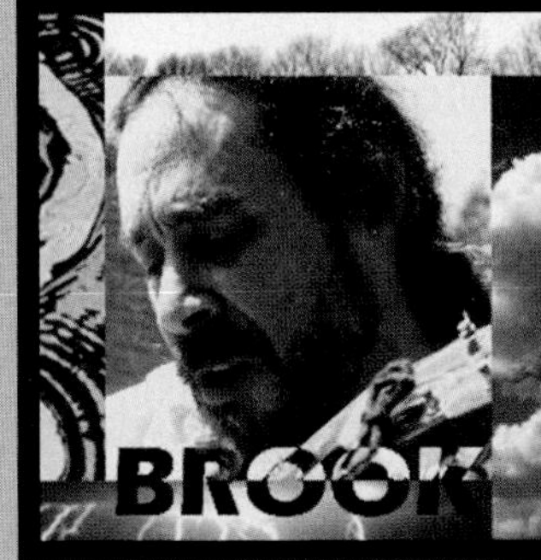

MAGIC BROOK

LOCATION: Oakland, CA
WEBSITE: www.magicbrook.com
CONTACT: Brook
EMAIL: brook@magicbrook.com
www.sonicbids.com/brook
GENRE: Contemporary Instrumental, Acoustic, Progressive Folk
LATEST RELEASE: *The Source*
LABEL: Melusine Records
REGIONS TOURED: Germany, Netherlands, Mid Atlantic US, New England, CA, CO

CAREER HIGHLIGHTS: Guitarist with Bo Diddley and Chuck Berry, Opie Bellas, has worked with players like Laurie Lewis, Michealle Gorllitz, October 2007, hit top 10 in Chicago blues on BroadJam 2 weeks in a row. K&K Artist of the Month. Featured Artist at the Zihuateneo International Guitar Festival 2006. Played Berklee Jazz Festival.

INFLUENCES: Vocally & songwriting: Keb Mo, Taj Mahal, Omar Faruk Tekbilek, Oliver Mtukudzi, Nusrat Ali Khan, Otis Redding, Joe Williams, Eddie Jefferson, Van Morrison, Nora Jones. Michael Hedges, Andy McKee, Viki Genfan, John Renborne, John Fahay, Tomatito, with currents from Mississippi John Hurt, John Hammond Jr., Blind Lemon Jefferson, Django Rheinhardt, acoustic John McLaughlin, Kenny Burrell, Jim Hall, Eric Clapton, BB King, Freddie King, Albert King, Otis Span, Taj Mahal, McCoy Tyner, Ruben Gonzales, Paul Desmond, The Fourth Way, Chopin nocturnes, and Schubert's song cycles.

associations

A2IM (American Assoc. of Independent Music)
29 W 17th St., 10th Fl.
New York, NY 10011
p: 212-937-8975
www.a2im.org
contact: Rich Bengloff
ext: 212-937-8975 x200
e: rich.bengloff@a2im.org
Non-profit represents broad coalition of indie labels in issues related to fair trade, legislation & access to media. Membership contact: Jim Mahoney, 212-937-8975 x201; jim.mahoney@a2im.org

Academy of Country Music
5500 Balboa Blvd., Ste. 200
Encino, CA 91316
p: 818-788-8000
f: 818-788-0999
e: info@acmcountry.com
www.acmcountry.com
contact: Anna Grigorian
ext: 818-788-8000 x216
e: annag@acmcountry.com
Promotes Country music worldwide thru a televised awards show, seminars & showcases.

AFM (American Federation of Musicians)
1501 Broadway, Ste. 600
New York, NY 10036
p: 212-869-1330
f: 212-764-6134
e: info@afm.org
www.afm.org
contact: Diane Depiro
ext: 212-869-1330 x1238
e: ddepiro@afm.org
booking: Honore Stockley
ext: 315-422-0900 x104
e: honore@afm.org
Represents USA & Canadian musicians & assists w/ contracts, copyrights, insurance & health care. LA office: Carol Sato, 213-251-4510; Canadian office: Liana White, 416-391-5161. Holds some showcases.

AFTRA (American Federation of TV & Radio Artists)
5757 Wilshire Blvd., Ste. 9
Los Angeles, CA 90036
p: 323-634-8100
f: 323-634-8246
e: losangeles@aftra.com
www.aftra.org/locals/losangeles.htm
contact: Harry Mar
ext: 323-634-8219
e: hmar@aftra.com
Nat'l org w/ reg'l offices represents the rights of artists in recording, radio & TV. Involved in royalties, pay scales, copyright & immigration issues. For showcases, contact: Roxanne Brown, 323-634-8240; rbrown@aftra.com. AFTRA San Diego merged w/ AFTRA Los Angeles. Other locations:
Bethesda: Justin Purvis, 301-657-2560 x231, jpurvis@aftra.com
Cleveland: Cathy Nowlin, 216-781-2255 x11; cnowlin@aftra.org
Dallas: TJ Jones, 214-363-8300; dallas@aftra.com
Denver: Julie Crane, 720-932-8228; jcrane@aftra.com
Nashville: Dometra Bowers, 615-327-2944; dbowers@aftra.com
New York: Evelyn LaRoca, 212-532-2242; elaroca@aftra.com
Philadelphia: Michelle Dooley, 215-732-0507; mdooley@aftra.com
Pittsburgh: John Haer, 412-281-6767; jhaer@aftra.com
Seattle: Ina Novak, 206-282-2506; inovak@aftra.com.

The Agents' Assoc.
54 Keyes House, Dolphin Sq.
London, SW1V 3NA UK
p: 44-207-834-0515
f: 44-207-821-0261
e: association@agents-uk.com
www.agents-uk.com
contact: Gordon Poole
Largest trade org of its kind represents agents that specialize in Rock, Pop, Cabaret, cruises & corporate events.

AIR (Australian Independent Record Label Assoc.)
437 Spencer St.
West Melbourne,
Victoria 3003
Australia
p: 61-73-257-1838
f: 61-73-257-0087
e: info@air.org.au
www.air.org.au
contact: Stuart Watters
e: stu@air.org.au
Non-profit org supports Australia's Indie artists & labels.

American Composers Forum
332 Minnesota St., Ste. E-145
St. Paul, MN 55101
p: 651-228-1407
f: 651-291-7978
e: mail@composersforum.org
www.composersforum.org
contact: Wendy Collins
ext: 651-251-2824
Supports Classical & Electronic composers, performers & presenters. No unsolicited material.

Americana Music Association
411 E Iris Dr., Ste. D
Nashville, TN 37204
p: 615-386-6936
f: 615-386-6937
e: info@americanamusic.org
www.americanamusic.org
contact: Danna Strong
e: danna@americanamusic.org
Trade org advocates for genre-related issues. See site for submissions info for annual music conference.
See Ad On Page 19

AMRA (American Mechanical Rights Agency)
149 S Barrington Ave., Ste. 810
Los Angeles, CA 90049
p: 310-440-8778
f: 310-440-0059
e: info@amermechrights.com
www.amermechrights.com
contact: Sindee Levin, Esq.
e: amracalif@aol.com
Issues mechanical & synch licenses. Registers copyrights worldwide & collects mechanical & performance royalties for songwriters, composers & publishers.

Archive of Contemporary Music
54 White St.
New York, NY 10013
p: 212-226-6967
f: 212-226-6540
e: arcmusic@inch.com
www.arcmusic.org
contact: Bob George
Non-profit preserves & provides info about popular music since 1950. Collection includes recordings, books, photos, films & memorabilia from around the world. Board members include David Bowie, Lou Reed, Keith Richards, Jelly Bean Benitez & Paul Simon. Annual showcase opportunities.

ASCAP (American Society of Composers, Authors & Publishers)
1 Lincoln Plaza
New York, NY 10023
p: 212-621-6000
f: 212-724-9064
e: info@ascap.com
www.ascap.com
contact: Alison Toczylowski
Performing rights org licenses & distributes royalties to over 330,000 members. Offers grants & scholarships, workshops, awards, insurance programs, financial services & showcases. Other locations:
Atlanta: *Phil Skinner, 800-505-4052; glcs@ascap.com*
Chicago: *Shawn Murphy, 773-394-4286; smurphy@ascap.com*
Los Angeles: *323-883-1000*
Miami: *Karl Avanzini, 305-673-3446; kavanzini@ascap.com*
Nashville: *Connie Bradley, 615-742-5000*
Puerto Rico: *Anna Rosa Santiago, 787-707-0782; asantiago@ascap.com.*
No unsolicited material.
See Ad On Page 14

Austin Songwriters Group
PO Box 2578
Austin, TX 78768
p: 512-203-1972
e: info@austinsongwritersgroup.com
www.austinsongwritersgroup.com
contact: Lee Duffy
Provides members w/ performance opps. & exposure to the music biz. Monthly meetings feature song pitching, critique sessions & showcases. Produces the Summer Songwriter Conference & the Austin Songwriters Symposium annually.

Black Rock Coalition
PO Box 1054
Cooper Stn.
New York, NY 10276
www.blackrockcoalition.org
contact: Darrell McNeill
e: brcmembersinfo@aol.com
booking: LaRonda Davis
e: ldavis@blackrockcoalition.org
Promotes black musicians, songwriters, producers & engineers outside the mainstream.

The Blues Foundation
49 Union Ave.
Memphis, TN 38103
p: 901-527-2583
f: 901-529-4030
e: jay@blues.org
www.blues.org
contact: Joe W. Whitmer
ext: 901-527-2583 x11

e: joe@blues.org
Non-profit is umbrella for 140+ affiliated Blues orgs spanning the globe. Produces The Blues Music Awards (formerly W.C. Handy Awards), Lifetime Achievement Awards, the Hart Fund & The Int'l Blues Challenge.

BMI
(Broadcast Music Inc.)
320 W 57th St.
New York, NY 10019
p: 212-586-2000
f: 212-582-5972
e: newyork@bmi.com
www.bmi.com
contact: Phil Graham
e: pgraham@bmi.com
PRO for songwriters & publishers collects licensing fees & distributes royalties for copyrighted music; represents 375,000 musicians throughout North America & Europe; provides grants, scholarships, workshops & career development seminars all year. Check site for showcase opportunities. Other locations:
Atlanta: *Catherine Brewton, 404-261-5151; cbrewton@bmi.com*
London: *Brandon Bakshi, 44-207-486-2036; london@bmi.com*
Los Angeles: *Barbara Cane, 310-659-9109; bcane@bmi.com*
Miami: *Delia Orjuela, 310-289-6345; dorjuela@bmi.com*
Nashville: *Jody Williams, 615-401-2000; nashville@bmi.com*
See Ad On Opposite Page

BMR
British Music Rights
British Music House,
26 Berners St.
London, W1T 3LR UK
p: 44-207-306-4446
f: 44-207-306-4449
e: britishmusic@bmr.org
www.bmr.org
contact: Sarah Coward
e: sarah.coward@bmr.org
booking: Anika Daughton
ext: 44-207-306-4445
e: anika.daughton@bmr.org
Umbrella org represents rights of British composers & publishers. For showcases, contact Anika Daughton 44-207-306-4445; anika.daughtonm@bmr.org. No unsolicited material.

Boston Musicians Assoc.
130 Concord Ave.
Belmont, MA 02478
p: 617-489-6400
f: 617-489-6962
e: info@bostonmusicians.org
www.bostonmusicians.org
contact: Barbara Owens
e: btowens@bostonmusicians.org
BMA is local 9-535 of the AFM & serves 1700 members. No unsolicited material.

Brazilian Composers Union
Rua Visconde de Inhauma, 107
Rio de Janeiro, RJ CEP 20091-007 Brazil
p: 55-212-223-3233
f: 55-212-516-8291
e: ubc@ubc.org.br
www.ubc.org.br
contact: Marisa Gandelman
e: marisa.gandelman@ubc.org.br
booking: Gustavo Gonzalez
e: gustavo@ubc.org.br
Deals w/ performance rights of musical works & defends the copyrighted works of its members. Email material to: gustavo@ubc.org.br.

British Underground
60-62 Clapham Rd.
London, SW9 0JJ UK
p: 44-207-840-5514
e: info@britishunderground.net
www.britishunderground.net
contact: Crispin Parry
e: crispin@britishunderground.net
Helps emerging artists & labels access the int'l music industry w/ UK showcase stages in the USA, Japan & Europe. Hosts the annual Bootleg BBQ at SXSW. Send CDs.

Cascade Blues Assoc.
PO Box 14493
Portland, OR 97293
p: 503-223-1850
f: 503-223-1850
e: cbastaff@cascadeblues.org
www.cascadeblues.org
contact: Greg Johnson
Non-profit preserves & promotes Blues & Roots music in northwest North America. Sponsors showcases at the Annual Muddy Awards, Willamette Delta Showcase & Waterfront Blues Festival. No unsolicited material.

CCMA
(Canadian Country Music Assoc.)
626 King St. W, Ste. 203
Toronto, ON M5V 1M7
Canada
p: 416-947-1331
f: 416-947-5924
e: country@ccma.org
www.ccma.org
contact: Brandi Mills
ext: 416-947-1331 x211
e: bmills@ccma.org
booking: Alannah Cruickshank
ext: 416-947-1331 x210
e: acruickshank@ccma.org
Non-profit furthers the interests of the Canadian Country music industry. Holds showcases during CMW. No unsolicited material.

Central Carolinas Songwriters Assoc.
131 Henry Baker Rd.
Zebulon, NC 27597
p: 919-269-6240
f: 919-662-7176
e: ccsa_raleigh@yahoo.com
www.ccsa-raleigh.com
contact: Tony Dickens
e: dawnstyle@hotmail.com
Monthly critique sessions, networking, performance opps. & musician collaborator programs that caters to the local area. No unsolicited material or out-of-state members.

Central Oregon Songwriters Assoc.
2191 NE Shepard Rd.
Bend, OR 97701
p: 541-389-3045
e: cosanewsletter@bendcable.com
http://cosa4u.tripod.com
contact: Rick Miller
Monthly group motivates members to write, market & improve their skills as songwriters. Holds a "Song of the Month" & "Song of the Year" contests, songwriters workshops & publishes a newsletter. Members songs are also in rotation on a local radio station.

Chicago Songwriters Collective
406 Bluebird Ave.
Bolingbrook, IL 60440
p: 312-827-7206
e: info@chicagosongwriters.com
www.chicagosongwriters.com
contact: Greg Steele
e: g.steele@steeleweb.com
Promotes songwriting, storytelling, composing & lyric writing with info & gigs in & around Chicago. Material to: 743 Prescott Ct., Naperville, IL 60563.

CISAC
(Confederation of Societies of Authors & Composers)
20-26 Blvd. du Parc
Neuilly-sur-Seine, 92200
France
p: 33-15-562-0850
f: 33-15-562-0860
e: cisac@cisac.org
www.cisac.org
contact: Martial Bernard
ext: 33-15-562-0850 x62
e: martial.bernard@cisac.org
Numbers 217 authors' societies from 114 countries & indirectly represents 2.5 million+ creators w/in all the artistic repertoires No unsolicited material.

CMA USA
(Country Music Association)
1 Music Cir. S
Nashville, TN 37203
p: 615-244-2840
f: 615-726-0314
e: communications@cmaworld.com
www.cmaworld.com
contact: Dana Davis
e: membership@cmaworld.com
Genre-specific org w/ members from 38 countries promotes Country music worldwide. Annual Country Music Awards & CMA Fest. No unsolicited material.

CMC
(Creative Musicians Coalition)
PO Box 6205
Peoria, IL 61601
p: 309-685-4843
f: 309-685-4878
e: aimcmc@aol.com
www.creativemusicianscoalition.com
contact: Ron Wallace
Represents Indie artists & labels worldwide, along w/ sister org, Music Discovery Network, helps members market, distribute & network. No unsolicited material.

CMRRA
(Canadian Music Reproduction Rights Agency)
56 Wellesley St. W, #320
Toronto, ON M5S 2S3
Canada
p: 416-926-1966
f: 416-926-7521
e: inquiries@cmrra.ca
www.cmrra.ca
contact: Caroline Rioux
ext: 416-926-1966 x234
e: crioux@cmrra.ca
Non-profit music licensing agency represents most copyright owners doing business in Canada. No unsolicited material.

Colorado Music Association
1490 Lafayette St., Ste. 104B
Denver, CO 80218
p: 720-570-2280
f: 720-570-2290
e: info@coloradomusic.org
www.coloradomusic.org
contact: Barb Dye
e: president@coloradomusic.org
Networking resource for CO musicians, songwriters, agents, managers, publicists, promoters, attorneys, bookers, etc. Presents showcases, monthly panels, email newsletter & provides members w/ UPC symbols for indie CD & DVDs. Send CD, one sheet & promo photo. Must provide email address.

Connecticut Songwriters Assoc.
PO Box 511
Mystic, CT 06355
p: 860-572-9285
e: info@ctsongs.com
www.ctsongs.com
contact: Bill Pere
e: bill@billpere.com
Reg'l group helps original songwriters w/monthly networking events, showcases & critiques. Sponsors the CT Songwriting Conference, New England Music Expo & CSA Pro Workshop series.

DMA
(Denver Musicians Association)
1165 Delaware St.
Denver, CO 80204
p: 303-573-1717
f: 303-573-1945
e: info@dmamusic.org
www.dmamusic.org
contact: Pete Vriesenga
e: pvriesenga@aol.com
Reg'l support group for area Folk, Jazz, Rock, orchestral musicians & composers. Promotes live music & holds concerts/showcases in the park. Snail mail promos.

EFWMF
(European Forum of Worldwide Music Festivals)
Jan Frans Willemsstraat 10a
Boechout, B-2530

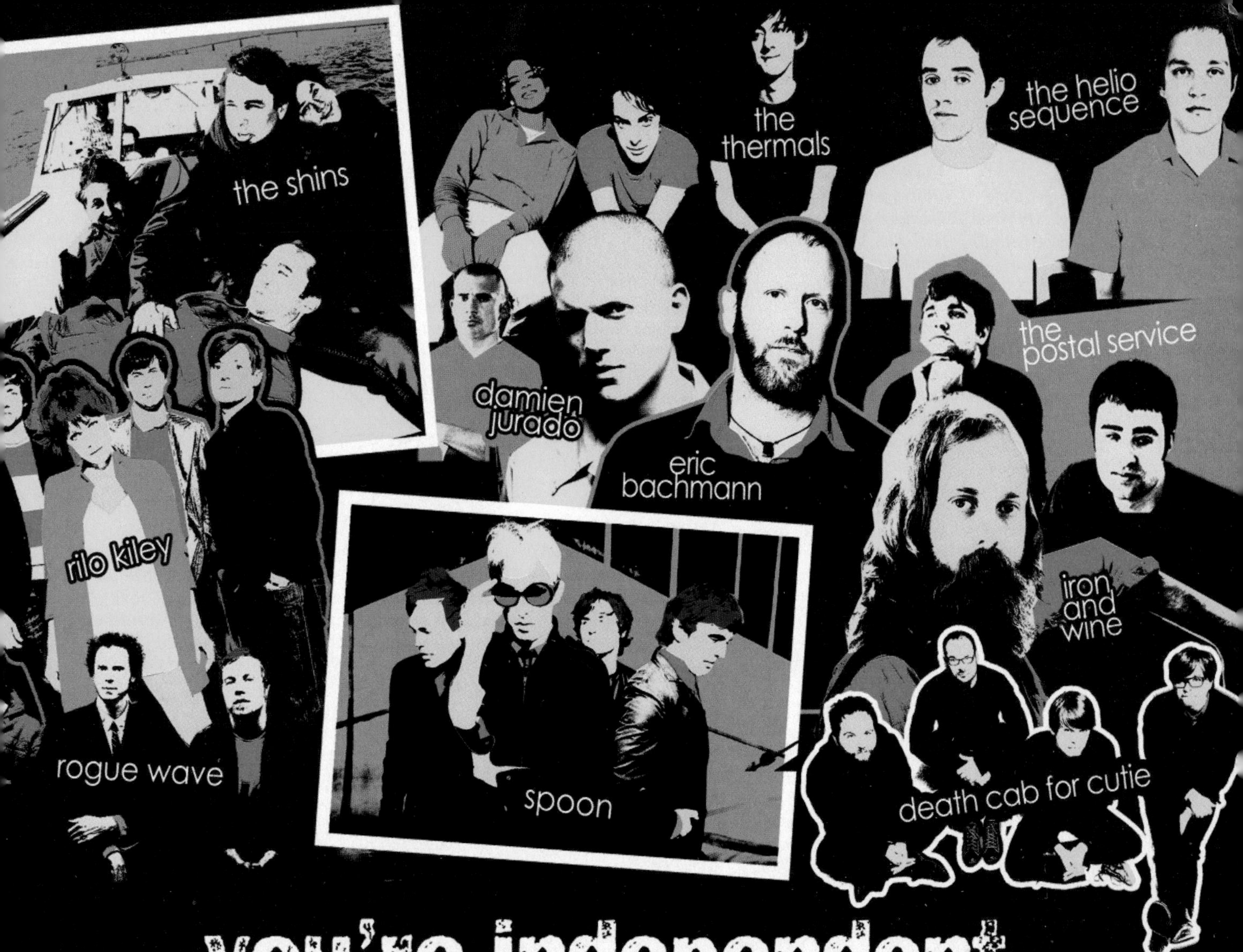

Belgium
p: 32-3-455-6944
f: 32-3-454-1162
e: info@efwmf.org
www.efwmf.org
contact: Patrick DeGroote
Represents promoters of World, Ethnic, Trad. & Roots festivals in 15 countries.
No unsolicited material.

Export Incentives
PO Box 4115
Wagstaffe, NSW 2257
Australia
p: 61-24-360-2811
f: 61-24-360-2911
e: wbc@exportgrants.com.au
www.exportgrants.com.au
contact: Warren Cross
Australia's leading consultants on export grants, licensing & copyrights. Central Coast Office: 28 Wagstaffe Ave, Wagstaffe NSW 2257.

FACTOR - Foundation to Assist Canadian Talent on Records
30 Commercial Rd.
Toronto, ON M4G 1Z4
Canada
p: 416-696-2215
e: general.info@factor.ca
www.factor.ca
contact: Krista Culp
e: krista.culp@factor.ca
Non-profit group provides funding to the Canadian indie record industry. Holds showcases at NXNE & CMW. Complete application on site.

The Folk Alliance
510 S Main, 1st Fl.
Memphis, TN 38103
p: 901-522-1170
f: 901-522-1172
e: fa@folk.org
www.folk.org
contact: Louis Meyers
e: louis@folk.org
Supports broad definition of contemporary & trad. Folk music including Americana, S/S, Children's, Jam, Blues, & World. Offers workshops, networking & prime annual conference & showcase.
No unsolicited material.
See Ad On Page 177

French Music Export Office North America
161 W 54th St., Ste. 1403
New York, NY 10019
p: 212-757-1217
f: 212-315-2691
e: usa@french-music.org
www.french-music.org
contact: Robert Singerman
Sponsored by French Gov't to expand French music export sales & int'l media interest. Also showcases for French artists touring in North America. Must be a French label or an American label licensing from French labels or a SACEM artist to submit.

GAP (Global Alliance of Performers)
19924 Aurora Ave. N, Ste. 101
Seattle, WA 98133
p: 206-264-5072
e: info@gap.org
www.gap.org
Non-profit org increases public awareness of social & environmental concerns.
No unsolicited material.

GoGirlsMusic.com
PO Box 16940
Sugar Land, TX 77496
p: 281-541-0981
e: info@gogirlsmusic.com
www.gogirlsmusic.com
contact: Madalyn Sklar
e: madalyn@gogirlsmusic.com
Online community of indie women musicians promotes & empowers its members thru online network, events, showcases & conferences. Must be a GoGirls Elite Member to submit & must have a least 1 female in the group to be a member.
See Ad On Page 22

Gospel Music Assoc.
1205 Division St.
Nashville, TN 37203
p: 615-242-0303
f: 615-254-9755
www.gospelmusic.org
contact: Megan Ledford
ext: 615-242-0303 x238
e: megan@gospelmusic.org
Promotes Gospel music & provides resources for artists & writers. Sponsors showcases at the GMA Music Awards, GMA Music Week, GMA in the Rockies & The GMA Academy.

House Ear Institute
2100 W 3rd St.
Los Angeles, CA 90057
p: 213-483-4431
f: 213-483-8789
e: info@hei.org
www.hei.org
contact: Marilee Potthoff
e: soundpartners@hei.org
Non-profit org to advance hearing science thru research & education, focusing on the impact of sound overexposure for music pros.
No unsolicited material.

IBMA
2 Music Cir. S, Ste. 100
Nashville, TN 37203
p: 615-256-3222
f: 615-256-0450
e: info@ibma.org
www.ibma.org
contact: Jill Crabtree
e: jill@ibma.org
Trade org promotes Bluegrass music w/ resources, awards, showcases, workshops, seminars & annual Bluegrass Fan Fest in early Oct.

IMRO (Irish Music Rights Organization)
Copyright House, Pembroke Row, Lower Baggot St.
Dublin, 2 Ireland
p: 35-31-661-4844
f: 35-31-676-3125
e: info@imro.ie; membership@imro.ie
www.imro.ie
contact: Manus Hanratty
Administers performance rights in Ireland on behalf of its members. Also sponsors showcases.
No unsolicited material.

Indie Managers Assoc.
554 N Frederick Ave., Ste. 218
Gaithersburg, MD 20877
f: 240-597-1330
e: info@indiemanagers.com
www.indiemanagers.com
contact: Jeremy Rwakaara
Networking opps. for managers & helps link them w/ artists seeking representation. Holds an annual conference & publishes a mgmt. manual.

Indie Pool
118 Berkeley St.
Toronto, ON M5A 2W9
Canada
p: 416-424-4666; 888-88-INDIE
f: 416-424-4265
e: mail@indiepool.com
www.indiepool.com
contact: Glendon Tremblay
e: glendon@indiepool.com
Provides Canadian musicians w/ mfg., distrib., merchandising, web services, bar codes & directories.

International Entertainment Buyers Assoc.
PO Box 128376
Nashville, TN 37212
p: 615-251-9000
f: 615-251-9001
e: info@ieba.org
www.ieba.org
contact: Tiffany Davis
Networking system for talent buyers & sellers hosts an annual convention w/ artist showcase. Must be a member to submit for performance opps.
No unsolicited material.

International Fan Club Org.
PO Box 40328
Nashville, TN 37204
p: 615-371-9596
f: 615-371-9597
e: 4info@ifco.org
www.ifco.org
contact: Loudilla Johnson
e: ifco@ifco.org
More than 200 official fan clubs & the artists they follow are affiliated w/ IFCO. Largely, though not exclusively involved w/ the Country music genre.

International Festivals & Events Association
2603 Eastover Terr.
Boise, ID 83706
p: 208-433-0950
f: 208-433-9812
www.ifea.com
contact: Beth Peterson
ext: 208-433-0950 x1
e: beth@ifea.com
Networking for the festival & events industry has an annual convention & expo.
No unsolicited material.

Just Plain Folks
5327 Kit Dr.
Indianapolis, IN 46327
p: 317-513-6557
e: jpfolkspro@aol.com
www.justplainfolks.org
contact: Brian Austin Whitney
Online music community offers forums, news & message boards for members in 100 countries. Hosts showcases in N America & Europe & produces largest awards program - 200 categories in 180 genres.

Kerrville Music
3876 Medina Hwy.
Kerrville, TX 78028
p: 800-435-8429
f: 830-257-8680
e: info@kerrville-music.com
www.kerrvillefolkfestival.com
contact: Dalis Allen
e: dalis@kerrvillefolkfestival.com
Non-profit org promotes original & trad. Folk, S/S, Americana, Roots, Country, Jazz and related styles. Produces Kerrville Folk Festival & annual Wine & Music Fest. Contact before sending promos to: PO Box 291466, Kerrville, TX 78029.
No unsolicited material.

LAWIM (Los Angeles Women in Music)
11664 National Blvd., #280
Los Angeles, CA 90064
p: 213-243-6440
f: 213-244-1260
e: info@lawim.com
www.lawim.com
contact: Judy Lamppu
ext: 818-831-3905
e: jlamppu@socal.rr.com
booking: Harriet Schock
ext: 323-934-5691
e: harriet@harrietschock.com
Non-profit org holds mixers, panels, workshops, seminars & showcases/ fundraisers at various CA locations. Submission policies vary by event, see site for info.

LIFEbeat - The Music Industry Fights AIDS
630 9th Ave., Ste. 1010
New York, NY 10036
p: 212-459-2590
f: 212-459-2892
e: info@lifebeat.org
www.lifebeat.org
contact: John Cannelli
ext: 212-459-2590 x101
e: jcannelli@lifebeat.org
booking: Sarah Peters
e: speters@lifebeat.org
Non-profit org mobilizes the music industry to raise awareness & funds to teach US youths about HIV/AIDS prevention. Their Nat'l Tour Outreach Program supplies touring acts with free materials to distribute at their shows. Contact John Atanasio, Mngr.: 212-459-2590 x111; jatanasio@lifebeat.org.

Los Angeles Music Network
PO Box 2446
Toluca Lake, CA 91610
p: 818-769-6095
e: info@lamn.com
www.lamn.com
contact: Naddi Zschiesche
e: naddi@lamn.com
Promotes communication among record executive thru panels, seminars, get-togethers & monthly LAMN Jam. Publishes network news &

THE
AMERICANA
MUSIC
ASSOCIATION
95626663

provides job listings.
No unsolicited material.

MMF Australia
32 Martin Pl., Level 5
Sydney, NSW 2000
Australia
p: 61-28-223-3567
f: 61-28-223-3555
e: rferguson@imf.com.au
www.imf.com.au
contact: John Walker
e: jwalker@imf.com.au
Represents artist managers & offers funding for litigation & assistance in facilitating settlements.
USA Branch: PO Box 444, Village Stn., New York, NY 10014 ph: 212-213-878; email: info@mmfus.com, url: www.mmfus.com. contact: Barry Bergman, barrybergman@earthlink.net.
No unsolicited material.

Music Cares - Map Fund
817 Vine St., Ste. 219
Hollywood, CA 90038
p: 323-993-3197; 888-627-6271
f: 323-993-3198
e: musicares@grammy.com
www.grammy.com/musicares
contact: Harold Owens
e: harold@grammy.com
Non-profit charity arm of Grammys; helps musicians & industry pros recover from drug & alcohol abuse. Regional Offices: ***Nashville:*** *615-327-0050* ***New York:*** *212-245-7840*
No unsolicited material.

Musicians On Call
1133 Broadway, Ste. 630
New York, NY 10010
p: 212-741-2709
f: 212-741-3465
e: info@musiciansoncall.org
www.musiciansoncall.org
contact: Katy Brown
ext: 615-936-3768
e: katy.brown@musiciansoncall.org
Members volunteer to perform for hospitalized patients & their families. Over 65,000 performances to date.

N.A.M.E. (National Assoc. of Mobile Entertainers)
PO Box 144
Willow Grove, PA 19090
p: 215-658-1193
f: 215-658-1194
e: name@nameentertainers.com
www.nameentertainers.com
contact: Bruce Keslar
e: bruce@nameentertainers.com
Publishes bi-monthly National Entertainer Mag & holds an annual conference. Sponsors Mobile Beat Vegas Show.
No unsolicited material.

NACA (National Assoc. for Campus Activities)
13 Harbison Way
Columbia, SC 29212
p: 803-732-6222
f: 803-749-1047
e: memberservices@naca.org; info@naca.org
www.naca.org
contact: Gordon Schell
e: gordons@naca.org
College booking outfit presents artists to college talent buyers at 7 reg'l & nat'l showcase. Must be paying member to be considered.

NAMM (National Assoc. of Music Merchants)
5790 Armada Dr.
Carlsbad, CA 92008
p: 760-438-8001
f: 760-438-7327
e: info@namm.org
www.namm.org
contact: Melanie Ripley
ext: 760-438-8007
e: melanier@namm.org
Produces 2 annual tradeshows (Anaheim, CA, Jan; Nashville, TN, July) for music instrument retailers, manufacturers & distrib. Performance opps.
No unsolicited material.

NARAS (National Academy of Recording Arts & Sciences)
3402 Pico Blvd.
Santa Monica, CA 90405
p: 310-392-3777
f: 310-392-3090
e: losangeles@grammy.com
www.grammy.com
contact: Robert Accatino
e: roberta@grammy.com
Over 14,000 musician, songwriter, producer, engineer & industry members. Services include showcase, education & networking programs, publications, legislative advocacy & the Grammys. Other locations:
Atlanta: *Michele Rhea Caplinger, 404-816-1380; michele.caplinger@grammy.com*
Austin: *Theresa Jenkins, 512-328-7997; texas@grammy.com*
Chicago: *Pera Healy, 312-786-1121; chicago@grammy.com*
Memphis: *Jon Hornyak, 901-525-1340; memphis@grammy.com*
Miami: *Neil Crilly, 305-672-4060; neilc@grammy.com*
Nashville: *Susan Stewart, 615-327-8030; susans@grammy.com*
New York: *Elizabeth Healy, 212-245-5440; newyork@grammy.com*
Philadelphia: *Dawn Frisby Byers, 215-985-5411; dawn.frisbybyers@grammy.com*
San Francisco: *Merl Saunders, Jr., 415-749-0779; sanfrancisco@grammy.com*
Seattle: *Ben London, 206-834-1000 x1; benl@grammy.com*
Washington, DC: *Shannon Emamali, 202-662-1341; washingtondc@grammy.com.*
No unsolicited material.

NARIP (National Assoc. of Record Industry Professionals)
PO Box 2446
Toluca Lake, CA 91610
p: 818-769-7007
e: info@narip.com
www.narip.com
contact: Amy Lewis
e: amy@narip.com
Promotes communication & goodwill among record executives thru seminars, conferences, brunches, cocktail mixers, etc.
No unsolicited material.

NARM (National Assoc. of Recording Merchandisers)
9 Eves Dr., Ste. 120
Marlton, NJ 08053
p: 856-596-2221
www.narm.com
contact: Evelyn Dichter
e: dichter@narm.com
Promotes the interests of music retailers & hosts conferences & conventions.
No unsolicited material.

Nashville Songwriters Assoc. International
1710 Roy Acuff Pl.
Nashville, TN 37203
p: 800-321-6008; 615-256-3354
f: 615-256-0034
e: nsai@nashvillesongwriters.com
www.nashvillesongwriters.com
contact: Bart Herbison
booking: Sheree
ext: 800-321-6008 x222
e: sheree@nashvillesongwriters.com
World's largest non-profit songwriter trade association. Services include quarterly song evaluations, newsletter, discounts, Reg'l workshops & online songwriter workshops. Sponsors showcases at the Tin Pan South Annual Songwriters Festival.
No unsolicited material.

Network Europe
PO Box 1519
Nijmegen, 6501 BM
The Netherlands
p: 31-24-323-9322
f: 31-24-323-2762
e: info@networkeurope.net
www.networkeurope.net
contact: Rob Berends
e: networkeurope@networkeurope.net
Members include: agents, promoters, bookers & talent buyers in Europe. Submits talent to showcases & festivals like EuroSonic & Popkomm. Also hosts its own showcases at festivals.
No unsolicited material.

Nielsen Soundscan - The Nielsen Company
1 N Lexington Ave., 14th Fl.
White Plains, NY 10601
p: 914-684-5500
f: 914-328-0234
e: sales@soundscan.com
www.soundscan.com
contact: Trudy Lartz
e: trudy.lartz@nielsen.com
The standard for tracking music retail sales & digital download offers an independent tracking package for small labels to track sales of their product in over 15,000 stores in 100 cities.
No unsolicited material.

NMPA (National Music Publishers Assoc.)
101 Constitution Ave. NW, Ste. 705E
Washington, DC 20001
p: 202-742-4375
f: 202-742-4377
e: pr@nmpa.org
www.nmpa.org
contact: David M. Israelite
Represents more than 600 music publishers & works to interpret copyright law, educate the public about licensing & safeguard the interests of its members.

Percussive Arts Society
32 E Washington, Ste. 1400
Indianapolis, IN 46204
p: 317-974-4488
f: 317-974-4499
e: percarts@pas.org
www.pas.org
contact: Jon Feustel
e: jfeustel@pas.org
Int'l non-profit org promotes the use of percussion thru a network of performers, teachers, students & manufacturers. Annual convention held in Oct/Nov.

RAINN (Rape, Abuse & Incest National Network)
2000 L St. NW, Ste. 406
Washington, DC 20036
p: 800-656-HOPE
f: 202-544-3556
e: info@rainn.org
www.rainn.org
contact: Chelsea Bowers
ext: 202-544-3064
e: chelseab@rainn.org
Nation's largest anti-sexual assault org operates the Nat'l Sexual Assault Hotline & has programs to prevent sexual assault, help victims & ensure that rapists are brought to justice. Tori Amos is founding member & advisory board chair.

Red Hot Organization
112 Madison Ave., 4th Fl.
New York, NY 10016
p: 212-343-0043
f: 212-343-3645
e: info@redhot.org
www.redhot.org
contact: Jonah Eller-Isaacs
e: jonah@redhot.org
Leading music industry org helps fund AIDS research & prevention projects worldwide thru sales of their CD compilation series.
No unsolicited material.

Reggae Ambassadors Worldwide Street
911 N Marine Corps Dr.
Tumon Bay, Guam 96913
p: 671-646-9180
www.reggaeambassadors.org
contact: Tom Pearson
e: tap@kuentos.guam.net
Roughly 1500+ members in 55 countries participate in or appreciate Reggae music. Hosts a bi-annual conference.

Rhythm & Blues Foundation
100 S Broad St., Ste. 620

Philadelphia, PA 19110
p: 215-568-1080
f: 215-568-1026
e: info@rhythmblues.org
www.rhythmblues.org
contact: Tina Wise
e: twise@rhythmblues.org
Non-profit service org preserves R&B music. Provides financial support, medical assistance & educational outreach w/ various grants & programs to support R&B & Motown artists of the 40s-70s.

RIAA (Recording Industry Assoc. of America)
1025 F St. NW, 10th Fl.
Washington, DC 20004
p: 202-775-0101
f: 202-775-7253
www.riaa.com
contact: Brigette Tenor
e: btenor@riaa.com
Members create, manufacture & distribute more than 90% of all recordings produced & sold in the USA. Strives to protect artistic freedom, combat record piracy & expand market opps.

Rochester Music Coalition
PO Box 26378
Rochester, NY 14626
p: 585-235-8412
e: info@rochestermusiccoalition.org
www.rochestermusiccoalition.org
contact: Linda Fullerton
Non-profit group comprised of reg'l club owners, radio stations, studios, promoters, musicians & fans to strengthen the area scene.

Rock For Choice
433 S Beverly Dr.
Beverly Hills, CA 90212
p: 310-556-2500
f: 310-556-2509
e: nbakody@feminist.org
www.feminist.org
contact: DuVergne Gains
e: dgains@feminist.org
Supports reproductive rights w/ benefit concerts & recordings.

Rock For Health
PO Box 230397
Boston, MA 02115
p: 215-801-9527
e: info@rockforhealth.org
www.rockforhealth.org
contact: Jasmine Hagans
e: jasmine@rockforhealth.org
Known as "The voice of the musician in the health care industry", this group advocated & informs artists about health care options.

Rock the Vote
1505 22nd St. NW
Washington, DC 20037
p: 202-223-1520
f: 202-223-0973
e: info@rockthevote.com
www.rockthevote.com
contact: Jeff Ayeroff
Dedicated to protecting freedom of expression & helping young people affect change in their communities thru voter registration & issues advocacy. No unsolicited material.

SESAC
55 Music Sq. E
Nashville, TN 37203
p: 615-320-0055
f: 615-329-9627
www.sesac.com
contact: Jocelyn Harms
e: jharms@sesac.com
booking: Diana Akin
e: dakin@sesac.com
Collects royalties for affiliated songwriters & publishers. Uses state of the art tech for tracking public performances of members' music. Showcases at SXSW. Other locations: ***Los Angeles:*** *Alex Perez, 310-393-9671; aperez@sesac.com* ***New York:*** *Linda Lorence, 212-586-3450; llorence@sesac.com* ***Miami:*** *Kenny Cordova, 305-534-7500. No unsolicited material.*
See Ad On This Page

SMPA (The Swiss Music Promoters Assoc.)
PO Box 146
Herisau, CH-9101
Switzerland
p: 41-71-220-8440
f: 41-71-220-8442
e: info@smpa.ch
www.smpa.ch
contact: Stefan Breitenmoser
e: stefan.breitenmoser@smpa.ch
Concert & festival organizers in Switzerland are members & make up approximately 80% of concert tickets sold annually. Services include financing, taxes & fees, permits, security, PR, catering & public transportation. No unsolicited material.

SOCAN (Society of Composers, Authors & Music Publishers of Canada)
41 Valleybrook Dr.
Toronto, ON M3B 2S6
Canada
p: 800-557-6226; 416-445-8700
f: 416-445-7108
e: socan@socan.ca
www.socan.ca
contact: Rick MacMillan
ext: 416-442-3815
e: macmillanr@socan.ca
Licenses music performed in Canada, collects fees & distributes royalties to composers, songwriters, lyricists & publishers whose works are broadcast or performed publicly. Many performance opps. No unsolicited material.

Songsalive!
PO Box 135
Castle Hill, NSW 1765
Australia
p: 61-29-294-2415
f: 61-28-850-7778
e: sydney@songsalive.org
www.songsalive.org
contact: Roxanne Kiely
booking: Russell Neal
ext: 61-41-182-7571
e: russellneal57@hotmail.com
Supports & promotes songwriters worldwide. Provides workshops, annual CD sampler, song camps, showcases, retreats & panel nites. For USA Songsalive! contact: Gilli Moon, 310-442-9294; usa@songsalive.com. Must be a Songsalive! member to be considered for all programs.

Songwriters Association of Canada
26 Soho St., Ste. 340
Toronto, ON M5T 1Z7
Canada
p: 416-961-1588; 866-456-SONG
f: 416-961-2040
e: sac@songwriters.ca
www.songwriters.ca
contact: Don Quarles
e: don@songwriters.ca
Nat'l arts org for Canadian composers, lyricists & songwriters. Must be a member to submit for showcases.

The Songwriters Guild of America
1560 Broadway, Ste. 408
New York, NY 10036
p: 212-768-7902
f: 212-768-9048
e: corporate@songwritersguild.com
www.songwritersguild.com
contact: Mark Saxon
e: ny@songwritersguild.com

Provides creative & financial services & activities & sponsors showcases. Other locations in: **CA:** *Kitty Wright, 323-462-1108; membership@songwritersguild.com* **TN:** *Kitty Martin, 615-742-9945; membership@songwritersguild.com. Full membership for published songwriters only.*

Songwriters Hall of Fame
330 W 58th St., Ste. 411
New York, NY 10019
p: 212-957-9230
f: 212-957-9227
e: info@songhall.org
www.songhall.org
contact: April Anderson
e: aanderson@songhall.org
booking: Peter Bliss
e: pbliss@songhall.org
Org sponsors programs for aspiring songwriters including showcases, workshops & website forums. Holds elections for songwriting inductees.

SoundExchange
1121 14th St. NW, Ste. 700
Washington, DC 20005
p: 202-640-5858
f: 202-640-5859
e: info@soundexchange.com
www.soundexchange.com
contact: Neeta Ragoowansi
e: neeta@soundexchange.com
Non-profit PRO collects & distributes performance royalties for non-interactive digital audio transmissions of the sound recordings on behalf of recording artists & sound recording copyright owners, featured & non-featured artists. Also provides advocacy services for artists & copyright owners to ensure the fair compensation for the use of copyrighted sound recordings. Recording artists & indie labels, register w/ SoundExchange to collect any royalties that may be owed to you for use of your records by digital services such as XM & Sirius Radio, Yahoo, AOL, Muzak & Music Choice, among others.

South By Southeast
9904 N Kings Hwy.
Myrtle Beach, SC 29572
p: 843-272-4050
f: 843-497-3643
e: southxsoutheast@aol.com
www.southbysoutheast.org
contact: Jeffrey L. Roberts
e: jrontheporch@yahoo.com
booking: Seth Funderburk
ext: 843-455-6499
Non-profit/charitable org for Myrtle Beach, SC area music lovers & educators to preserve & promote American music not usually heard in traditional venues. Uses events to generate funds to support public education music projects. Not associated w/ SXSW. Sponsors some showcases. Send material to: PO Box 7691, Myrtle Beach, SC 29572.

Sweet Relief Musicians Fund
65 S Grand Ave., #209
Pasadena, CA 91105
p: 888-955-7880; 626-792-2858
f: 626-792-2899
e: info@sweetrelief.org
www.sweetrelief.org
contact: Joanne Klabin
Pays medically-related expenses for qualified, financially needy or older musicians who have serious medical conditions or are unable to work.

Tennessee Songwriters Assoc. International
PO Box 2664
Hendersonville, TN 37077
p: 615-969-5967
e: asktsai@aol.com
www.tnsai.com
contact: Jim Sylvis
e: tunechaser@aol.com
Weekly meetings, newsletter, critique sessions, workshops, Living Legend Series & annual awards show. Features pitch-a-pro night & pro rap Q&A. Must be a member to pitch a song or have it critiqued.

Texas Folk Music Foundation
3876 Medina Hwy.
Kerrville, TX 78028
p: 800-435-8429
f: 830-257-8680
e: info@kerrville-music.com
www.tfmf.org
contact: Theresa Tod
Opportunities include The New Folk Concerts for emerging songwriters, & management seminar. Promo address: PO Box 291466, Kerrville, TX 78029.

Texas Music Office
PO Box 13246
Austin, TX 78711
p: 512-463-6666
f: 512-463-4114
www.governor.state.tx.us/music; www.enjoytexasmusic.com
contact: Stephen Ray
e: music@governor.state.tx.us
Clearing house & promo office for the Texas music industry. Makes referrals from artists to venues. Sponsors Music Industry Boot Camps. Send material to: State Insurance Bldg., Ste. 3.410, 1100 San Jacinto Blvd., Austin, TX 78701.

Urban Music Assoc. of Canada (UMAC)
675 King St.
Ste. 210
Toronto, ON M5V 1M9
Canada
p: 416-916-2874
f: 416-504-7343
e: umacgoturb@gmail.com
www.umac.ca; www.umacunited.com
contact: Will Strickland
booking: Gail Phillips
Non-profit org is dedicated to building the domestic & int'l profile of Canadian Urban music. Offers workshops, seminars & artist showcases in addition to their nationally televised signature event, the Canadian Urban Music Awards. Email before sending material.

Victory Music
PO Box 2254
Tacoma, WA 98401
e: victory@nwlink.com
Supports acoustic music in the NW USA by nurturing musical growth & creativity. Lists artist showcases on site event calendar & publishes Victory Review Mag. No unsolicited material.

Women In Music
New York, NY
www.womeninmusic.org
contact: Evangelia Livanos
ext: 215-292-4264
e: synergymgt@gmail.com
Supports & cultivates the talents of women in the industry w/ panels, showcases & networking events in NYC.

World Music Institute
49 W 27th St., Ste. 930
New York, NY 10001
p: 212-545-7536
f: 212-889-2771
www.worldmusicinstitute.org
contact: Robert H. Browning
ext: 212-545-7536 x15
e: robert@worldmusicinstitute.org
booking: Isabel Soffer
e: isabel@worldmusicinstitute.org
Presents World music shows in NYC, arranges USA tours & sells World CDs on site. Sponsors Globalfest. Call before sending material.

Yourope (The European Festival Assoc.)
Adlerbergstrasse 13
St. Gallen, CH-9000
Switzerland
p: 41-71-223-4101
f: 41-71-223-4109
e: yourope@yourope.org
www.yourope.org
contact: Christof Huber
Dedicated to strengthening the festival scene in Europe. Focus on working conditions, safety, environmental awareness & exchange of performing talent across borders.

booking agents

100 Proof Entertainment
PO Box 742016
Dallas, TX 75374
p: 214-597-2426
www.100proofentertainment.com
contact: April Samuels
e: booking@100proofentertainment.com
venues: Clubs, Festivals, Corporate Events
regions: Reg'l TX
genres: Rock, Pop, Acoustic, Punk
No unsolicited material.

A&M Entertainment
13280 NW Frwy., Ste. F-328
Houston, TX 77040
p: 516-620-1216
f: 516-620-1212
e: info@amentertainment.com
www.amentertainment.com
contact: Keetria Gardner-Chamber
e: keetria@amentertainment.com
venues: Clubs, College, Festivals, Events
regions: Int'l
genres: All Styles
No unsolicited material.

A.M. Only
55 Washington St., Ste. 658
Brooklyn, NY 11201
p: 718-237-2428
f: 718-237-2429
www.amonly.com
contact: Paul Morris
ext: 718-237-2428 x13
e: paul@amonly.com
venues: Festivals, Clubs thru Arenas
regions: USA
genres: Rock, Hip-Hop, Electronica, Industrial
No unsolicited material.

A.P.A. (Agency For The Performing Arts)
405 S Beverly Dr.
Beverly Hills, CA 90212
p: 310-888-4200
f: 310-888-4242
www.apa-agency.com
contact: Jim Gosnell
e: jgosnell@apa-agency.com
venues: Clubs thru Arenas
regions: USA, Int'l
genres: All Styles
Offices in Nashville & NYC. No unsolicited material.

Ace Productions
PO Box 428
Portland, TN 37148
p: 615-325-3340
e: aceaaron1@aol.com
www.aceproductions.com
contact: Jimmy Case
venues: Festivals, Clubs, Arenas
regions: Reg'l-Int'l
genres: Country, Rockabilly, Bluegrass, Gospel, Nostalgia
Call before sending material.

ACTS Nashville
1103 Bell Grimes Ln.
Nashville, TN 37207
p: 615-254-8600
f: 615-254-8667
www.actsnashville.com
contact: Lee Shields
e: lee@actsnashville.com
venues: Clubs, Festivals, Fairs, Arenas, Casinos, Events
regions: Nat'l, Int'l
genres: Country, R&B, Rap, Rock, Nostalgia
Call before sending material.

Adams & Green Entertainment
2011 Masters Ln.
Missouri City, TX 77459
p: 281-835-6400
f: 281-835-6004
e: info@entertainmenthouston.com
www.entertainmenthouston.com
contact: Bob Messer
e: bob@entertainmenthouston.com
venues: Festivals, Events
regions: southwest TX
genres: Country, Rock, Swing, Latin, Reggae, Top 40, Jazz, R&B
Promos to: PO Box 17376, Sugar Land, TX 77496. No unsolicited material.

The Agency Group (LA)
1880 Century Park E, Ste. 711
Los Angeles, CA 90067
p: 310-385-2800
f: 310-385-1221
e: lindakordeck@theagencygroup.com
www.theagencygroup.com
contact: Andy Somers
e: andysomers@theagencygroup.com
regions: USA, Int'l
genres: Rock, Pop, Latin, Urban, Country, R&B
Offices in NY, Toronto, London & Scandinavia. CDs from artists w/ representation only.

Am-Can Int'l Talent
9615 Macleod Tr. S
Calgary, AB T2J 0P6
Canada
p: 403-259-4516 x234
f: 403-259-5447
e: ranchmans@ranchmans.com
www.amcantalent.com
contact: Wendy Daniels
e: wendy@ranchmans.com; amcantalent@amcantalent.com
venues: Clubs, Casinos, Festivals: Ranchman's Dance Hall & Cookhouse
regions: USA, Canada
genres: Country, Country Rock, Alt. Country, Rock, Pop
Only reps Canadian acts in the above genres w/ presence on country or rock radio.

American Artists
315 S Beverly Dr., Ste. 407
Beverly Hills, CA 90212
p: 310-277-7877
f: 310-277-9697
e: ethan@americanartists.net
www.americanartists.net
contact: Phil Hache
ext: 310-277-7877 x107
e: phil@americanartists.net
venues: Colleges, Festivals, Clubs thru Arenas
regions: USA, Int'l
genres: Rock, Country, R&B, Swing
No unsolicited material.

American Mgmt.
19948 Mayall St.
Chatsworth, CA 91311
p: 818-993-9943
f: 818-993-6459
www.muzbiz2000.com
contact: Jim Wagner
e: jrwagner@earthlink.net
venues: Clubs, Events, Fairs, Cruises
regions: USA, Int'l
genres: Rock, Country, Big Band, Pop
No unsolicited material.

American Promotions
2507 Fifth St. Rd.
Log Cabin Office, Main Fl.
Huntington, WV 25701
p: 304-634-5156
f: 304-7523-1718
e: talentbuyers@hotmail.com
contact: Rick Widdifield
venues: Colleges, Clubs
regions: Huntington, WV & Nashville, TN
genres: Dance, Funk, Top 40, Rock, Jazz, Blues, Country
DVD submissions preferred. Email first.

American Talent Agency
173 Main St.
Ossining, NY 10562
p: 914-944-9500
f: 914-944-9555
e: info@americantalentagency.com
www.americantalentagency.com
contact: Peter Seitz
ext: 914-944-9500 x111
e: peter@americantalentagency.net
venues: Clubs thru Arenas
regions: Int'l
genres: R&B, Hip-Hop, Latin, Gospel, Pop
No unsolicited material.

Artist Representation & Management
1257 Arcade St.
St. Paul, MN 55106
p: 651-483-8754
f: 651-776-6338
www.armentertainment.com
contact: John Domagall
e: jd@armentertainment.com
venues: Festivals, Events, Clubs thru Arenas
regions: Int'l
genres: 80's, 90's, Rock, Country, Blues, Metal
Send full kits.

Artists Worldwide
3921 Wilshire Blvd., Ste. 619
Los Angeles, CA 90010
p: 213-368-2112
f: 213-368-2110
e: artistsworldwide@aol.com
www.artists-worldwide.com
contact: Chuck Bernal
venues: Festivals, Clubs, Arenas
regions: Int'l
genres: Rock, Punk, Metal
No unsolicited material.

Associated Booking
501 Madison Ave., Ste. 603
New York, NY 10022
p: 212-874-2400
f: 212-769-3649
e: musicbiz@mindspring.com
www.abcbooking.com
contact: Oscar Cohen
venues: Casinos, Festivals, Events, Clubs thru Arenas
regions: USA, Int'l
genres: Blues, R&B, Jazz, Pop, Reggae
No unsolicited material.

Austin Universal Entertainment
1701 Directors Blvd., Ste. 350
Austin, TX 78744
p: 512-452-6856
f: 512-452-7257
e: info@aueonline.com
www.aueonline.com
contact: Greg Henry
ext: 512-452-6856 x12
e: greg@aueonline.com
venues: Clubs, Theaters, Festivals, Fairs
regions: USA, Int'l
genres: Country, Americana
No unsolicited material.

Backstreet Booking
700 W Pete Rose Way, Lobby

B, 3rd Fl., Ste. 1, PO Box 18
Cincinnati, OH 45203
p: 513-542-9544
f: 513-542-9545
e: info@backstreetbooking.com
www.backstreetbooking.com
contact: Jim Sfarnas
ext: 513-542-9544 x1
e: jimbb@backstreetbooking.com
venues: Clubs, Theaters, PACs, Festivals
regions: N America, Europe
genres: Prog, Fusion, Jazz, Rock, Jam, Metal
Call before sending material.

Beachfront Bookings
PO Box 13218
Portland, OR 97213
p: 503-281-3874
www.beachfrontbookings.com
contact: Tam Martin
e: tammartin@aol.com
venues: Colleges, Clubs, Theaters, Festivals, Cruises
regions: North America
genres: Folk, AC, Jazz, Blues
Specializes in female artists. No unsolicited material.

Bennett Morgan & Associates
1022 Rte. 376
Wappingers Falls, NY 12590
p: 845-227-6065
f: 845-227-4002
www.bennettmorgan.com
contact: Bennett Morgan
e: ben@bennettmorgan.com
venues: Clubs, Halls, PACs
regions: USA, Int'l
genres: Jazz
Call before sending material.

The Berkeley Agency
2608 9th St., #301
Berkeley, CA 94710
p: 510-843-4902
e: mail@berkeleyagency.com
www.berkeleyagency.com
contact: Jim Cassell
e: jim@berkeleyagency.com
venues: Clubs, College, Festivals, PACs, Corporate
regions: USA, Int'l
genres: Latin, Jazz, Blues
No unsolicited material.

BFG Communications
11 E 44th St., 18th Fl.
New York, NY 10017
p: 212-763-0022
f: 212-763-0023
contact: Philippa Murphy
ext: 212-763-0022 x275
e: pmurphy@bfgcom.com
Books touring bands for corporate clients.

Big Beat Productions
1515 University Dr., #108
Coral Springs, FL 33071
p: 954-755-7759
f: 954-755-8733
e: talent@bigbeatproductions.com
www.bigbeatproductions.com
contact: Richard Lloyd
e: rlloyd@bigbeatproductions.com
venues: Clubs, Theaters, Festivals, PACs, Cruises
regions: USA, Int'l
genres: All Styles

Bignote Ent.
87 Tuscany Springs Way NW
Calgary, AB T3L 2N4 Canada
p: 403-668-0880
f: 403-668-7441
www.bignote.net
contact: Jim Samuelson
e: jim@bignote.net
venues: Theatres, Festivals, Special Events, Clubs
regions: North America
genres: Roots, Jazz, World, Pop
Contact before sending material.

Bigshot Touring Artists
3257 SE Hawthorne Blvd.
Ste. C
Portland, OR 97204
p: 503-731-8700
f: 503-731-0920
e: info@bigshottouring.com
www.bigshottouring.com
contact: Kevin French
e: kevin@bigshottouring.com
venues: Clubs, Theaters
regions: USA
genres: Rock, Indie Rock
San Francisco office: 415-646-6010. Label-supported artists email w/ request to submit CD. NO CALLS or links. Will contact if interested.

BigWaveBuz Entertainment
PO Box 3207
Stamford, CT 06905
p: 914-779-6087
f: 603-699-6517
e: info@bigwavebuz.com
contact: David Backer
e: backerent@aol.com
venues: Clubs, Theaters, Fairs, Festivals, Social Functions
regions: Nat'l, Europe
genres: Blues, Oldies, Rock
Also does management & promotion. Send bio, 8x10 photo & CD w/ original music. No tapes or MP3's.

The Billions Corp.
3522 W Armitage Ave.
Chicago, IL 60647
p: 312-997-9999
f: 312-997-2287
www.billions.com
contact: David Viecelli
e: boche@billions.com
venues: Clubs, Festivals, Corporate Events
regions: USA, Int'l
genres: Rock, Pop
No unsolicited material.

Billy Deaton Talent
1214 16th Ave. S
Nashville, TN 37212
p: 800-767-4984; 615-321-0600
f: 615-321-0182
www.billydeaton.com
contact: Billy Deaton
e: billydeaton@aol.com
venues: Fairs, Festivals, Clubs, Theaters, PACs
regions: USA, Int'l
genres: Country, Bluegrass, Gospel
Include photos w/ CD.

Black Label Promotions
1105 Oregon St.
Green Bay, WI 54303
p: 920-602-7625
e: info@blacklabelpromotions.com
www.blacklabelpromotions.com
contact: Kenda Brunette
e: kenda@blacklabelpromotions.com
venues: Clubs, Festivals, Events
regions: WI, IL, MI, MN
genres: Rock, Country, Acoustic

The Bobby Roberts Co.
PO Box 1547
Goodlettsville, TN 37070
p: 615-859-8899
f: 615-859-2200
e: info@bobbyroberts.com
www.bobbyroberts.com
contact: Brian Jones
e: brian@bobbyroberts.com
venues: Festivals, Corporate, Casinos, Clubs thru Arenas
regions: USA, Int'l
genres: Country, Pop, Rock
No unsolicited material.

Booking Entertainment
275 Madison Ave.
6th Fl.
New York, NY 10016
p: 800-4ENTERTAINMENT
f: 212-645-0333
e: agents@bookingentertainment.com
www.bookingentertainment.com
contact: Steve Einzig
ext: 212-645-0555 x25
e: steve@bookingentertainment.com
venues: College, Festivals, Events, Clubs thru Arenas
regions: USA, Int'l
genres: Rock, Pop, Jazz, R&B
No unsolicited material.

The Brad Simon Org.
155 W 46th St., 5th Fl.
New York, NY 10036
p: 212-730-2132
f: 212-730-2895
e: info@bsoinc.com; officemgr@bso.com
www.bsoinc.com
contact: Brad Simon
ext: 212-730-2132 x11
e: brad@bsoinc.com
venues: Clubs thru Arenas, Schools, Events
regions: USA, Int'l
genres: Jazz, Blues, World
Email: artistinquiry@bsoinc.com before sending material.

The Breen Agency
3811 Bedford Ave., Ste. 206
Nashville, TN 37215
p: 615-777-2227
f: 615-321-4656
e: info@thebreenagency.com
www.thebreenagency.com
contact: David Breen
e: david@thebreenagency.com
venues: Clubs, Festivals, Theaters, Churches, Colleges
regions: USA
genres: Christian
Email before sending material.

C&B Booking
1050 Cranberry Rd.
Gardners, PA 17324
p: 717-421-9125
e: cnbbooking@yahoo.com
www.myspace.com/cbbooking
contact: Jim Fetzer
venues: Cafes, Clubs
regions: PA, NY, & DE
genres: Rock, Alt., Urban, Hardcore, Acoustic, Pop, Techno

Cantaloupe Music Prod.
157 W 79th St., Ste. 4A
New York, NY 10024
p: 212-724-2400
f: 212-724-7957
e: inquiry@cantaloupeproductions.com
www.cantaloupeproductions.com
contact: Ellen Azorin
venues: Festivals, College, Museums, Events
regions: USA, Int'l
genres: Brazilian, Jazz, World, Blues, Classical

Carlini Group
445 Park Ave., 9th Fl.
New York, NY 10022
p: 212-714-7722
f: 212-202-7579
e: info@carlinigroup.com
www.carlinigroup.com
contact: Charles Carlini
venues: Clubs, PACs, Festivals
regions: Int'l
genres: Jazz, Pop, Rock, Blues, World, Latin
London office: 44-207-084-6330. Submit via Sonicbids.

Carnelian Agency
2328 Iron St.
Bellingham, WA 98225
p: 360-752-9829
f: 360-752-3282
www.carnelianagency.com
contact: Teri Cruzan
e: tericruzan@carnelianagency.com
venues: Clubs, College, Festivals, Events
regions: USA
genres: Rock, Alt., Reggae, Tribute, Hip-Hop
Unsigned artists submit thru Sonicbids.

CEG (Central Ent. Group)
166 5th Ave., 4th Fl.
New York, NY 10010
p: 212-921-2190
f: 212-921-8761
e: booking@cegtalent.com
www.cegtalent.com
contact: Michael Schweiger
ext: 212-921-2190 x11
e: michael@cegtalent.com
venues: Clubs, Concert Halls
regions: USA, Int'l
genres: DJs, Rap, R&B, Top 40, Dance
No unsolicited material.

Celebrity Talent Agency
111 E 14th St., Ste. 249
New York, NY 10003
p: 212-539-6039
e: makingator@msn.com
www.celebritytalentagency.com
contact: Mark Green
e: markg@celebritytalentagency.com
venues: Clubs thru Arenas
regions: USA, Europe
genres: Jazz, R&B, Hip-Hop, Gospel

Circle Agency
2276 N 69th St.
Milwaukee, WI 53213
p: 414-453-9181
e: circleagency@earthlink.net
www.circleagency.bravehost.com

contact: June Lehman
venues: Clubs, PACs, Series, Colleges, Festivals, Events
regions: North America, Asia, Australia, Europe
genres: Americana, Folk, Blues, Alt. Country, Roots
Represents premier Americana artists w/ proven track record. Email before sending material.

Class Act Ent.
PO Box 160236
Nashville, TN 37216
p: 615-262-6886
f: 615-262-2974
www.classactentertainment.com
contact: Mike Drudge
e: mike@classactentertainment.com
venues: Festivals, Churches, PACs, Clubs
regions: Int'l
genres: Americana, Folk, Bluegrass, Country, Roots
No unsolicited material.

Columbia Artists Management
1790 Broadway
New York, NY 10019
p: 212-841-9500
f: 212-841-9744
e: info@cami.com
www.cami.com
contact: Tim Fox
ext: 212-841-9735
venues: Theaters, PACs
regions: USA, Int'l
genres: All Styles
No unsolicited material.

Concert Ideas
73 Ratterman Rd.
Woodstock, NY 12498
p: 800-836-2000; 845-679-6000
f: 845-679-9022
e: info@concertideas.com
www.concertideas.com
contact: Harris Goldberg
e: harrisg@concertideas.com
venues: Colleges
regions: USA
genres: Rock, Pop, Urban, Country
No unsolicited material.

Concerted Efforts
PO Box 600099
Newtonville, MA 02460
p: 617-969-0810
f: 617-969-6761
e: concerted@concertedefforts.com
www.concertedefforts.com
contact: Chris Colbourn
e: chris@concertedefforts.com
venues: Clubs thru Arenas
regions: USA, Int'l
genres: Blues, Soul, Jazz, Gospel, Folk, S/S, Rock, World
Only touring artists w/ labels. No unsolicited material.

Creative Artists Agency
2000 Ave. of the Stars
Los Angeles, CA 90067
p: 424-288-2000
f: 424-288-2900
e: caaccmadmin@caa.com
www.caaccm.com; www.caatouring.com
contact: Michael Mand
e: mmandasst@caa.com
venues: Clubs, Festivals, Arenas
regions: USA, Int'l
genres: All Styles
No unsolicited material.

Creative Entertainment Group
505 8th Ave., Ste. 805
New York, NY 10018
p: 212-634-0427
f: 212-634-0432
e: info@cegmusic.com
www.cegmusic.com
contact: Howie Schnee
ext: 212-634-0427 x6
e: howie@cegmusic.com
venues: Clubs, Theatres, Festivals, Cruises
regions: NY, NJ, MA, LA, CA
genres: Rock, Funk, Jazz
No unsolicited material.

The Crow Agency
2007 SE 11th Ave.
Portland, OR 97214
p: 920-251-6834
f: 503-236-6120
e: thecrowagency@gmail.com
www.thecrowagency.com
contact: Krist Krueger
venues: Clubs, Colleges, Festivals
regions: North America
genres: Indie, Rock, Acoustic, Experimental, Pop
No unsolicited material.

Cuthbertson Ent. & Events
40 Havenbrook Blvd.
Toronto, ON L6H 4R9
Canada
p: 416-496-8200
f: 416-496-8900
www.cuthbertsonevents.com
contact: Larry Cuthbertson
e: cuthbertsonevents@rogers.com
venues: Corporate Events
regions: North America
genres: Tribute, Legends, Rock n Roll, Jazz, World, Instrumental, Classical
No unsolicited material.

D. Bailey Mgmt.
4520 W Village Dr., Ste. C
Tampa, FL 33624
p: 813-960-4660
f: 813-960-4662
e: info@dbaileymanagement.com
www.dbaileymanagement.com
contact: Dennis Bailey
ext: 813-960-4660 x1
e: dennis@dbaileymanagement.com
venues: Clubs, Conventions, Colleges, Events
regions: southeast USA
genres: Pop, R&B, Funk, Jazz, Reggae, Variety Rock
Contact before submitting to: PO Box 273358, Tampa, FL 33688.

Dark Sky Productions
215 Chelmsford St., Ste. 7
Chelmsford, MA 01824
e: othniel77@yahoo.com
www.myspace.com/othniel77
contact: Anderson Mar
regions: New England
genres: Punk, Alt., Rock, Metal, Country, Women
Also runs Punk, Metal & Goth Fest in Worcester, MA. No booking thru MySpace.

Davis McLarty Agency
708 S Lamar Blvd., Ste. D
Austin, TX 78704
p: 512-444-8750
f: 512-416-7531
e: info@davismclarty.com
www.davismclarty.com
contact: Davis McLarty
e: davis@davismclarty.com
venues: Clubs, Festivals, Colleges
regions: USA
genres: Alt. Country, Roots, Blues, Americana
No unsolicited material.

Degy Booking Int'l
6 Industrial Way W., Ste. E
Eatontown, NJ 07724
p: 732-263-1000
f: 732-544-5600
e: info@degy.com
www.degy.com/degybooking/
contact: Ari Nisman
e: ari@degy.com
venues: Clubs thru Arenas, Festivals, Colleges
regions: USA, Int'l
genres: Rock, Blues, Pop, Bluegrass, World, Soul
Promos to: PO Box 3036, West End, NJ 07740.

Devil Dolls Booking
360 Wisconsin Ave., Ste. 301
Long Beach, CA 90814
p: 562-434-0692
f: 562-434-0693
www.devildollsbooking.com
contact: Deborah Toscano
e: deborah@devildollsbooking.com
venues: Clubs
regions: North America
genres: Punk, Ska, Emo, Hardcore, Psychobilly
No unsolicited material.

Do It Booking
PO Box 522016
Salt Lake City, UT 84152
p: 801-466-8374
f: 801-466-8376
www.doitbooking.com
contact: Margie Alban
e: margie@doitbooking.com
venues: All-Ages Venues
regions: USA
genres: Indie, Pop, Alt., Punk
Contact before sending material.

Down the Road Entertainment
425 Sprucewood Ln.
Glenwood Springs, CO 81601
p: 970-945-7930
e: downroad@comcast.net
contact: Tony Grifasi
venues: Clubs, Arenas, Colleges
regions: USA, Int'l
genres: Rock, Bluegrass, S/S

Elysian Artist Agency
37321 Cypress Ave.
Burney, CA 96013
p: 303-832-7679
f: 303-281-7871
e: info@elysianartists.com
www.myspace.com/elysianartists
contact: Jeremy Walker
venues: Theatres, Clubs
regions: USA, Int'l
genres: All Styles
Offices in Denver, San Francisco & Austin. Electronic submissions only.

Earthtone Music/ Fantasma Tours West
8306 Wilshire Blvd., Ste. 981
Beverly Hills, CA 90211
p: 323-650-4488
f: 323-983-8687
www.earthtone-music.com
contact: Richard Rees
e: rich@earthtone-music.com
venues: Clubs thru PACs
regions: USA, Int'l
genres: Rock, Pop, Acoustic
No unsolicited material.

East Coast Ent.
PO Box 11283
Richmond, VA 23230
p: 804-355-2178
f: 804-353-3407
www.eastcoastentertainment.com
contact: Lee Moore
venues: Colleges, Festivals, Clubs thru Arenas, Events
regions: USA, Int'l
genres: Rock, Acoustic, Pop, Latin, Jazz, R&B, Funk
No unsolicited material.

Ellis Industries
234 Shoreward Dr.
Great Neck, NY 11021
contact: Matt Galle
ext: 917-470-9109
e: xstandx@aol.com
venues: Clubs, Festivals
regions: USA
genres: Rock, Alt., Indie

Entertainment Services Int'l
6400 Pleasant Park Dr.
Chanhassen, MN 55317
p: 952-470-9000
f: 952-474-4449
www.esientertainment.com
contact: Randy Erwin
e: randy@esientertainment.com
venues: Corporate, Casinos, Fairs, Festivals, Clubs, Theatres
regions: USA, Int'l
genres: Classic Rock
Nat'l acts only.

Entourage Talent Associates
236 W 27th St., 8th Fl.
New York, NY 10001
p: 212-633-2600
www.entouragetalent.com
contact: Wayne Forte
e: booking@entouragetalent.com
venues: Clubs thru Arenas, Festivals, Corporate
regions: USA, Int'l
genres: Rock, Pop, S/S, Jazz
Mark pkg. for rep or client support.

Family Productions
3983 S McCarran Blvd., #186
Reno, NV 89502
p: 775-358-1150
f: 773-358-1152
e: info@fpaagency.com
www.fpaagency.com
contact: Tony Servidio
e: tonyservidio@aol.com
venues: Clubs thru Arenas
regions: USA
genres: Urban, Pop, Reggae
Send w/ ATTN: Daniel.

Fat City Artists
1906 Chet Atkins Pl., Ste. 502
Nashville, TN 37212
p: 615-320-7678

f: 615-321-5382
www.fatcityartists.com
contact: Rusty Michael
venues: Clubs thru PACs, Festivals, Events
regions: USA
genres: Nostalgia, Country, Bluegrass, Blues, R&B, World, Folk, Funk, Gospel, Jazz
No unsolicited material.

FATA Booking
2601 S Alder St.
Philadelphia, PA 19148
p: 215-468-5101
f: 215-468-5124
e: fatabooking@gmail.com
www.fatabooking.com
contact: Eva Alexiou
venues: Clubs, Festivals, Colleges
regions: North America
genres: Emo, Rock, Punk
Works w/ buzz bands & estab. Indies. Send CDs only.

First Row Talent
6220 Lemona Ave., Ste. 8
Van Nuys, CA 91411
p: 818-994-9544
f: 818-994-9547
e: firstrowtalent@aol.com
www.myspace.com/firstrowtalent
contact: John Finberg
venues: Clubs, Theaters
regions: USA, Int'l
genres: Mainly Metal

Fleet Team Booking
1808 S Carpenter St.
Chicago, IL 60608
p: 312-455-1350
f: 773-442-0224
e: fleetteam@gmail.com
www.fleetteambooking.com
contact: Scott Comeau
e: scott@fleetteambooking.com
venues: Clubs, Theaters, Colleges, Festivals
regions: North America
genres: Punk, Indie Rock, Hip-Hop
Works w/ estab acts & buzz bands. No unsolicited material.

Fleming & Associates
543 N Main St.
Ann Arbor, MI 48104
p: 734-995-9066
f: 734-662-6502
e: contact@flemingartists.com
www.flemingartists.com
contact: Jim Fleming
e: jim@flemingartists.com
venues: Clubs thru Arenas, Festivals
regions: USA, Int'l
genres: Acoustic, Rock, Folk, Alt. Country, Roots, Indie, S/S
Artists must have 2 yrs Nat'l touring & sustained ticket sales in 3+ markets. No unsolicited material.

Flowerbooking
1532 N Milwaukee Ave.
Ste. 201
Chicago, IL 60622
p: 773-289-3400
f: 773-289-3434
e: info@flowerbooking.com
www.flowerbooking.com
contact: Tim Edwards
e: tim@flowerbooking.com
venues: Clubs, Festivals, Colleges, Arenas
regions: North America
genres: Indie Rock, Pop
Send current CD & press clips. No calls.

FMMusic
215 S Walnut St.
Muncie, IN 47305
p: 765-286-0949
e: follymoonmusic@hotmail.com
venues: Doc's Music Hall & The Locker Room Bar/Grill
regions: midwest thru southeast USA

Forsyth Agency
415 Evergreen Ave., Ste. 102
Pittsburgh, PA 15209
p: 412-822-7747
f: 412-822-7873
e: info@forsythagency.com
www.forsythagency.com
contact: Scott Forsyth
e: scott@forsythagency.com; scott@opusoneproductions.com
venues: Clubs, Festivals
regions: USA, Int'l
genres: Jazz, Avant-Garde, Rock, Jam
Call for permission to submit.

Fruition Artist Agency
PO Box 3721
Brentwood, TN 37024
p: 615-377-9177
f: 615-377-9178
e: info@fruitionartistagency.com
www.fruitionartistagency.com
contact: Carla Archuletta
venues: Ministry Events, Concerts, Festivals
regions: USA, Int'l
genres: CCM
Submit via New Artist Inquiry Form online.

GAMI/Simonds
42 County Rd.
Morris, CT 06763
p: 860-567-2500
f: 925-396-7046
e: gamisim@worldnet.att.net
www.gamisim.com
contact: Laurelle Favreau
venues: Concert Halls, PACs
regions: USA, Int'l
genres: World, Jazz, Flamenco, Classical
Also provides immigration services for USA tours. No unsolicited material.

Gen-X Entertainment Int'l
PO Box 140
Cedar, MN 55011
p: 763-413-9611
f: 763-413-9610
e: genxinc@aol.com
www.genxentertainment.us
contact: Tim Murphy
venues: Clubs thru Arenas
regions: USA, Int'l
genres: Rock, Tribute
No unsolicited material.

Gigmasters
73 Redding Rd., Ste. 7
Redding, CT 06896
p: 866-342-9794
f: 203-587-1128
e: info@gigmasters.com
www.gigmasters.com
contact: Kevin Kinyon
ext: 203-587-1134 x225
e: kkinyon@gigmasters.com
venues: Clubs, Festivals
regions: USA, Int'l
genres: Blues, Bluegrass, Christian, Country, Covers, Jazz, Punk, Rock, Swing

Ginny Davis Entertainment
PO Box 420944
San Diego, CA 92142
p: 619-886-1628
www.ginnydavisentertainment.com
contact: Ginny Davis
e: ginny@ginnydavisentertainment.com
venues: Clubs, Casinos, Special Events & Radio
regions: USA, Int'l
genres: Jazz, Blues, R&B, Rockabilly, Rock
Books reg'l talent for area gigs & radio voice-over work.

GOA (Greg Oliver Agency)
1710 General George Patton Dr., Ste. 104
Brentwood, TN 37027
p: 615-790-5540
f: 615-376-4515
e: info@goa-inc.com
www.goa-inc.com
contact: Greg Oliver
e: greg@goa-inc.com
venues: Clubs thru Arenas, Festivals, Churches, Colleges
regions: USA
genres: Christian
Also contact Stephen Garrett: stephen@goa-inc.com. No unsolicited material.

Golden Land Concerts & Connections
118 E 28th St., Rm. 304
New York, NY 10016
p: 212-683-7816
f: 212-213-2033
e: concerts@goldenland.com
www.goldenland.com
contact: Moishe Rosenfeld
e: goldenland@aol.com
venues: Clubs, Colleges, Houses of Worship, PACs, Festivals, Corporate
regions: USA, Int'l
genres: Klezmer, Jazz, Middle Eastern, World
Contact before sending material.

Gravatt Entertainment
1701 Fall Hill Ave., Ste. 104A
Fredericksburg, VA 22401
p: 540-361-4448
f: 540-361-4462
e: bookit@gravattentertainment.com
www.gravattentertainment.com
contact: Wil Gravatt
e: wil@gravattentertainment.com
venues: Clubs, Theaters, Festivals, Private Events
regions: DC Metro Area
genres: All Styles
Send audio/video footage, photos & bio w/CD. DC office: 202-470-2631.

Great American Talent
PO Box 2476
Hendersonville, TN 37077
p: 615-452-7878
f: 615-452-7887
e: info@gatalent.com
www.gatalent.com
contact: Sheila Futch
e: sheila@gatalent.com
venues: Clubs, Theaters, Casinos, Festivals, Fairs
regions: Nat'l, Int'l
genres: Country, Cajun
No unsolicited material.

Great American Talent
PO Box 2476
Hendersonville, TN 37077
p: 615-452-7878
f: 615-452-7887
e: info@gatalent.com
www.gatalent.com
contact: Sheila Futch
e: sheila@gatalent.com
venues: Clubs, Theaters, Casinos, Festivals, Fairs
regions: Nat'l, Int'l
genres: Country, Cajun
No unsolicited material.

Green Light Talent Agency
PO Box 3172
Beverly Hills, CA 90212
p: 323-655-4407
f: 323-655-8078
e: greentunes@aol.com
contact: Andrew Greif
venues: Clubs, Arenas, Festivals
regions: Int'l
genres: R&B, Funk, Rap, Pop
No unsolicited material.

Ground Control Touring
20 Jay St., Ste. 838
Brooklyn, NY 11201
p: 718-218-8203
f: 718-679-9261
www.groundcontroltouring.com
contact: Eric Dimenstein
e: eric@groundcontroltouring.com
venues: Clubs, Festivals, Arenas
regions: USA
genres: All Styles
Estab. touring bands or acts w/ representation or a nat'l buzz. NC office: 919-932-9165. No unsolicited material.

H2O Artist Agency
2422 Waterscape Tr.
Snellville, GA 30078
p: 770-736-5363
www.h2oartistagency.com
contact: Scott Huie
e: booking@h2oartistagency.com
venues: Churches, Clubs, Auditoriums, Theatres, Arenas
regions: Int'l
genres: CCM
Specializes in cutting-edge Christian artists concert tours. No unsolicited material.

Harmony Artists
8455 Beverly Blvd., Ste. 400
Los Angeles, CA 90048
p: 323-655-5007
f: 323-655-5154
e: contact_us@harmonyartists.com
www.harmonyartists.com
contact: Jerry Ross
e: jross@harmonyartists.com
venues: Clubs, Festivals, Fairs, Casinos, PACs
regions: Nat'l, Int'l

genres: R&B, Latin, Blues, Bluegrass, Jazz, Swing
Specializing in nat'l headliners, nostalgia & tribute acts.

Hello! Booking
11623 E Laketowne Dr.
Albertville, MN 55301
p: 651-647-4464
f: 763-463-1264
e: info@hellobooking.com
www.hellobooking.com
contact: Eric Roberts
ext: 651-647-4464 x1
e: eric@hellobooking.com
venues: Clubs, Festivals
regions: USA
genres: Bluegrass, Country, Rock, Folk, Pop, Jazz, Hip-Hop
Send CDs, press kit & tour history to: PO Box 252, Albertville, MN 55301.

Helter Skelter
Plaza 535 Kings Rd.
London, England SW10 0SZ
UK
p: 44-207-376-8501
f: 44-207-376-8336
e: info@helterskelter.co.uk
www.helterskelter.co.uk
contact: Nigel Hassler
e: nigel.hassler@helterskelter.co.uk
venues: Clubs, Festivals
regions: Europe, Australia, Singapore, South Africa
genres: All Styles
Label acts or acts w/ mgmt.

High Road Touring
751 Bridgeway, 3rd Fl.
Sausalito, CA 94965
p: 415-332-9292
f: 415-332-4692
e: info@highroadtouring.com
www.highroadtouring.com
contact: Zachary Cepin
e: submit@highroadtouring.com
venues: Clubs thru Arenas
regions: North America
genres: Rock, Americana, Folk, Pop, Alt. Country, S/S
Mail CD & press kit or email submit@highroadtouring.com.

Highway Key Touring & Promotion
PO Box 4160
Key West, FL 33041
p: 773-743-9546
f: 270-626-1899
www.hwykey.com
contact: Casey Scott
e: cscott@hwykey.com
venues: Clubs, Festivals, Special Events, TV, Radio
regions: Worldwide
genres: Blues, Roots, Rock, Alt. Country, Folk
Formerly Magnolia Entertainment
Send bio, pics & CD.

HM Live
1305 W 80th, Ste. 2B #3
Cleveland, OH 44102
p: 216-631-6916
f: 216-631-6598
e: info@hmconcerts.com
www.hm-live.com
contact: Neil Sheehan
e: neil@hmmgmnt.com
venues: Clubs, Theaters, Festivals, Colleges
regions: USA, Int'l
genres: All Styles
Works w/ rising talent.

Hollywood Concerts
6520 Costello Ave.
Valley Glen, CA 91401
p: 818-780-5525
e: hollywoodconcert@aol.com
www.hollywoodconcerts.com
contact: Mike Giangreco
regions: southern CA

ICM (Int'l Creative Management)
10250 Constellation Blvd.
Los Angeles, CA 90067
p: 310-550-4000
f: 310-550-4100
e: contemporary@icmtalent.com
www.icmtalent.com
contact: Steve Levine
e: slevine@icmtalent.com
venues: Clubs thru Arenas
regions: USA, Int'l
genres: Rap, Rock, Pop, S/S, R&B, Jazz, Folk, World
Offices in NY: 212-556-5600 & London: 44-207-432-0800.
No unsolicited material.

Inland Empire Touring
292 Ainslie St., #1F
Brooklyn, NY 11211
p: 718-218-7350
f: 718-218-7354
e: info@inlandempiretouring.com
www.inlandempiretouring.com
contact: Robin Taylor
venues: Clubs, Theatres
regions: North America
genres: Rock, Indie Rock
Works w/ rising Indie talent.
No unsolicited material.

Int'l Booking Dept.
Bodenseestr 91
Munich, 81243 Germany
p: 49-89-834-2410
f: 49-89-834-2288
e: info@ibdbooking.de
www.ibdbooking.de
contact: Sabine Waltz
e: sabine@ibdbooking.de
venues: 100-5000 cap venues & festivals
regions: Europe, Japan
genres: Reggae, Hip-Hop, Rock, Punk, Ambient
No unsolicited material.

Int'l College Bookings & Theatrical Productions
19 Pierce Ave., Ste. C
Fitchburg, MA 01420
p: 978-203-6108
f: 978-203-6159
www.icbtalent.com
e: booking@icbtalent.com
venues: Colleges
regions: USA
genres: All Styles

Int'l Music Network
278 Main St.
Gloucester, MA 01930
p: 978-283-2883
f: 978-283-2330
e: info@imnworld.com
www.imnworld.com
contact: Scott Southard
e: scott@imnworld.com
venues: Clubs thru Arenas
regions: USA, Int'l
genres: Jazz, World, Pop, Roots, Bluegrass
Polished & top-tier talent.
No unsolicited material.

Intrepid Artists
1300 Baxter St., Ste. 405
Charlotte, NC 28204
p: 704-358-4777
f: 704-358-3171
e: staff@intrepidartists.com
www.intrepidartists.com
contact: Rick Booth
venues: Clubs, Festivals
regions: Reg'l-Int'l
genres: Zydeco, Blues, Roots, Jazz, Jam, Bluegrass
Works w/ polished talent.
Contact before sending material.

J. Chriss & Co.
300 Mercer St., Ste. 3J
New York, NY 10003
p: 212-353-0855
f: 212-353-0094
e: info@jchriss.com
www.jchriss.com
contact: Joel Chriss
e: jchriss@aol.com
venues: Clubs, Festivals, PACs, Halls, Theaters, Colleges
regions: USA, Int'l
genres: Jazz, Blues
A-list & polished talent.
No unsolicited material.

Jackson Artists
7251 Lowell Dr., Ste. 200
Overland Park, KS 66204
p: 913-384-6688
f: 913-384-6689
e: jacksonartists@msn.com
contact: Dave Jackson
venues: Grandstand Shows, Clubs, Halls, Hotels
regions: USA
genres: Country, Pop, Jazz, R&B, Big Band, Reggae
Prefers live videos & recordings.
Call before sending material.

Jay Siegan Presents
1655 Polk St., Ste. 1
San Francisco, CA 94109
p: 415-447-4730
f: 415-447-4230
e: info@jaysieganpresents.com
www.jaysieganpresents.com
contact: Sean Burke
e: sean@jaysieganpresents.com
regions: SF Bay Area
genres: All Styles
Email w/ all pertinent details.
No unsolicited material.

Jeff Roberts & Assoc.
3050 Business Park Cir.
Ste. 301
Goodlettsville, TN 37072
p: 615-859-7040
f: 615-851-7023
www.jeffroberts.com
contact: Jeff Roberts
e: jeff@jeffroberts.com
venues: Colleges, Festivals, Conventions, Churches
regions: USA
genres: CCM, Rock
No unsolicited material.

Jim Wadsworth Prod.
2213 Bellfield Ave.
Cleveland Heights, OH 44106
p: 216-721-5624
f: 216-721-6533
www.jwpjazz.com
contact: Jim Wadsworth
e: jwadsworth@aol.com
venues: Clubs, Festivals, PACs
regions: USA, Int'l
genres: Jazz, World, Folk
Works w/ top & polished talent.
Call before sending material.

JL Entertainment
511 Ave. of Americas, Ste. 230
New York, NY 10011
p: 212-647-8795
f: 323-462-9099
e: ny@jlentertainment.com
www.jlentertainment.com
contact: Jeremy Larner
ext: 213-387-8800
e: jeremy@jlentertainment.com
venues: Clubs, Arenas, Events
regions: USA, Int'l
genres: Hip-Hop, R&B, Reggae, Rock, Jazz, Funk
Works w/ buzz bands & estab. acts. LA office: 323-462-9000.
No unsolicited material.

Keith Case & Assoc.
1025 17th Ave. S, 2nd Fl.
Nashville, TN 37212
p: 615-327-4646
f: 615-327-4949
e: claire@keithcase.com
www.keithcase.com
contact: Keith Case
e: keith@keithcase.com
venues: Clubs thru PACs
regions: USA, Int'l
genres: Bluegrass, Roots, S/S
Works w/ top-tier talent & some polished new comers.
Submissions by referral only.

The Kenmore Agency
59 Park St., Ste. 2
Beverly, MA 01915
p: 978-232-1295
f: 978-232-1299
www.thekenmoreagency.com
contact: Matt Pike
ext: 978-232-1295 x1
e: mattpike@thekenmoreagency.com
venues: Clubs, Theaters
regions: USA
genres: Rock, Punk, Metal
No unsolicited material.

Kiss the Sky
80 E 3rd St., #3
New York, NY 10003
p: 646-301-4754
e: info@kisstheskyinc.com
www.kisstheskyinc.com
contact: Caroline Tully
e: caroline@kisstheskyinc.com
venues: All Types
regions: USA
genres: Alt., Indie, Blues

Leave Home Booking
1400 S Foothill Dr., Ste. 34
Salt Lake City, UT 84108
p: 801-582-4111
f: 801-582-4112
e: info@leavehomebooking.com
contact: Stormy Shepherd
venues: Clubs thru Arenas
regions: USA, Int'l
genres: Punk, Rock
Female fronted agency works w/ major indies & buzz bands w/ DIY touring experience.
No unsolicited material.

Libertalia Ent.
18627 Brookhurst St., #396
Fountain Valley, CA 92708
p: 714-849-3342
f: 714-849-6885
e: info@libertalia.us
www.libertalia.us

contact: James Harding
e: james@libertalia.us
venues: Clubs, Theatres, Festivals
regions: USA, Int'l
genres: Punk, Rock, Indie, Blues, Americana

Live Nation (CA)
PO Box 429094
San Francisco, CA 94142
p: 415-371-5500
www.livenation.com
contact: Lee Smith
venues: Clubs thru Arenas, Festivals
regions: USA, Int'l
genres: All Styles
Presents buzz bands & A-list artists.
No unsolicited material.

LiveTourArtists
1451 White Oaks Blvd.
Oakville, ON L6H 4R9
Canada
p: 866-400-1003; 905-844-0097
f: 905-844-9839
e: info@livetourartists.com
www.livetourartists.com
contact: Doug Kirby
ext: 866-400-1003 x223
e: doug@livetourartists.com
venues: Clubs, Schools, Theaters, Festivals, PACs
regions: North America, Int'l
genres: AC, Rock, Punk, Blues, Country, Family, Folk
Outside N America: 905-844-0097. Include contact info & DVD.

Lucky Artist Booking
745 W Katella Ave.
Orange, CA 92867
p: 714-997-9141
f: 714-997-4655
www.luckyartistbooking.com
contact: Angie Dunn
e: angiemdunn@gmail.com
venues: Clubs, Festivals, Churches, PACs, Skateparks
regions: North America
genres: Rock, Alt., Punk, Pop
Acts w/ touring history mail CDs w/ kit.
No MySpace links or tapes.

Lustig Talent Enterprises
PO Box 770850
Orlando, FL 32877
p: 407-816-8960
f: 407-816-8959
www.lustigtalent.com
contact: Richard Lustig
e: lustig@lustigtalent.com
venues: Clubs thru Arenas, Festivals, Colleges
regions: USA, Int'l
genres: Classic Rock, Tribute, Pop, Country, Blues, R&B
No unsolicited material.

M.O.B. Agency
6404 Wilshire Blvd., Ste. 505
Los Angeles, CA 90048
p: 323-653-0427
f: 323-653-0428
e: mobster411@verizon.net
www.mobagency.com
contact: Mitch Okmin
venues: Clubs thru Arenas
regions: USA, Int'l
genres: Rock, Alt.
Estab. & buzz acts w/ tour history.
No unsolicited material.

Mach Turtle Productions
PO Box 5223
Playa Del Rey, CA 90296
p: 310-714-6224
f: 305-768-6224
contact: Jamie Murray
e: machturtleprods@yahoo.com
venues: Small & Mid-size
regions: western US
genres: Surf, Instrumental
Send CD, photo & bio.

Mad Mission Agency
2 Wing Hill Rd.
Williamsburg, MA 01096
p: 413-268-3398
f: 413-268-3820
www.madmissionagency.com
contact: Lori Peters
e: lori@madmissionagency.com
venues: Festivals, Clubs, Colleges
regions: North America, UK
genres: Folk, S/S, Indie, Spoken Word, Americana
Works w/ polished touring acts.
No unsolicited material.

Magnetized Prod.
9456 154th St.
Surrey, BC V3R 9E1 Canada
p: 604-597-0650
www.myspace.com/magnetizedproductions
contact: Clyde Hill
e: clydedhill@yahoo.com
venues: Cheers Nightclub, Red Room, The Waldorf Hotel
regions: Vancouver, BC
genres: All Styles

MaineStream Music
2 Greenwood Dr.
Kennebunk, ME 04043
p: 207-985-6790
f: 207-985-8447
e: mainestrm@aol.com
www.mainestreammusic.com
contact: Jody Cyr
venues: Clubs thru Arenas
regions: USA
genres: Blues, Alt., Classic Rock, Country, Tribute
Contact before sending material.

MarsJazz Booking Agency
1006 Ashby Pl.
Charlottesville, VA 22901
p: 434-979-6374
f: 434-979-6179
www.marsjazz.com
contact: Reggie Marshall
e: reggie@marsjazz.com
venues: Clubs thru Arenas, Festivals, Schools, Churches
regions: Int'l
genres: Jazz
No unsolicited material.

Mascioli Ent.
2202 Curry Ford Rd., Ste. E
Orlando, FL 32806
p: 407-897-8824
f: 407-897-8828
www.masciolientertainment.com
contact: Paul Mascioli
ext: 407-897-8824 x104
e: paul@masciolientertainment.com
venues: Clubs thru Arenas
regions: Reg'l-Int'l
genres: Country, Jazz, Rock
No unsolicited material.

Maurice Montoya Music Agency
1133 Broadway, Ste. 1608
New York, NY 10010
p: 212-229-9160
f: 212-229-9168
www.mmmusicagency.com
contact: Maurice Orlando Montoya
e: maurice@mmmusicagency.com
venues: Blue Note Jazz Club, Lincoln Ctr., Hollywood Bowl
regions: USA, Int'l
genres: Jazz, Afro-Cuban, Brazilian, Pop
No unsolicited material.

MaxC Talent Group
535 Pierce St., #1216
Albany, CA 94706
p: 510-525-4837
f: 510-559-3672
www.maxctalentgroup.com
contact: Max Cooperstein
e: maxc@maxctalentgroup.com
venues: Clubs thru Arenas, Churches
regions: USA, Int'l
genres: Blues, Jazz
Polished & estab. talent.
Call before sending material.

Metro Talent Group
4514 Chamblee Dunwoody Rd., Ste. 333
Atlanta, GA 30338
p: 770-395-1000
f: 770-395-1095
e: mail@metrotalentgroup.com
www.metrotalentgroup.com
contact: Cass Scripps
ext: 770-395-1000 x1
e: cass@metrotalentgroup.com
venues: Clubs thru Arenas
regions: USA
genres: Rock, Pop, S/S
No unsolicited material.

Midnight Special Productions
PO Box 916
Hendersonville, TN 37077
p: 615-822-6713
f: 615-824-3830
www.bestdamnshows.com
contact: Marty Martel
e: martymartel@bestdamnshows.com
venues: Clubs thru Arenas
regions: Int'l
genres: Country, Pop, Classic Rock

Milestone Agency
Dallas, TX
p: 972-977-8663
f: 877-822-0643
www.milestoneagency.com
e: booking@milestoneagency.com; magency1@gmail.com
venues: Clubs, Colleges, Festivals
regions: USA
genres: Rock, Pop
Email for permission to sumbit.

Monterey Int'l
200 W Superior, Ste. 202
Chicago, IL 60654
p: 312-640-7500
f: 312-640-7515
www.montereyinternational.net
contact: Ron Kaplan
e: ron@montereyinternational.net
venues: Clubs thru Arenas
regions: Int'l
genres: Blues, Jazz, World, Rock, Pop, Latin, Alt., R&B
Estab. & polished touring talent.
Contact before sending material.

More Music Group
397 Little Neck Rd., 3300 Bldg., Ste. 305
Virginia Beach, VA 23452
p: 757-463-1940
f: 757-463-3769
e: info@moremusicgroup.com
www.moremusicgroup.com
contact: Joe Guida
e: jguida@moremusicgroup.com
venues: Clubs, Colleges, Festivals, Parties
regions: USA
genres: Pop, Rock, Country, Folk, Jazz, Latin, R&B, Top 40
A-list & polished touring talent. For nat'l, college, corp & festival bookings contact: Michael Jones, mjones@moremusicgroup.com; Melissa Boyle, mboyle@moremusicgroup.com.

Music Group Ent.
5001 5th St. NW, Ste. A
Washington, DC 20011
p: 404-822-4138
e: info@mgentonline.com
www.mgentonline.com
contact: Mya Richardson
e: seeking_mya@hotmail.com
venues: Clubs
regions: FL & NYC
genres: Neo Soul, R&B, Pop, Rock, Jazz, Alt, Dance
Currently no Hip-Hop.

musiclocker one worldwide ent.
151 Vose Ave., Ste. A1
South Orange, NJ 07079
p: 917-584-6698
e: musiclocker1@yahoo.com
contact: Michael Locker
venues: Clubs, Theatres, Colleges, Festivals
regions: Local-Int'l
genres: All Styles
Contact before sending material.

Muzik Management/ Productions
25904 Freedom Rd.
Chester, AR 72934
p: 479-369-2221
f: 479-369-4118
www.muzikmgt.com
contact: Dick Renko
e: drenko@muzikmgt.com
venues: Clubs, PAC's, Festivals, Events
regions: USA, Int'l
genres: Folk, Pop, Children's
No unsolicited material.

Nancy Fly Agency
PO Box 90306
Austin, TX 78709
p: 512-288-2023
f: 512-288-2744
www.nflyagency.com
contact: Nancy Fly
e: nfly@nflyagency.com
venues: Clubs, Festivals, Theaters
regions: North America
genres: Americana, Blues, Roots Rock, World
Nat'l Roots & Americana artists w/ proven show history submit

EPKs only. No CDs.
Call before sending material.

New City Talent
PO Box 147
Kennedy, AL 35574
p: 205-662-4826;
205-596-4371
f: 205-596-4375
e: office@newcitytalent.com
www.newcitytalent.com
contact: Randall Wilds
e: randall@newcitytalent.com
venues: Concert Halls, Churches
regions: Nat'l
genres: Southern Gospel, Christian Country

NoBetta Booking
34 Benton Ct.
Staten Island, NY 10306
e: booking@nobetta.com
www.myspace.com/nobettabooking
contact: Keith Profeta
e: keith@nobetta.com
venues: Colleges, Clubs
regions: northeast USA
genres: Rock, Metal, Alt.
Bands must draw 50+ fans to a show. Email before submitting.

Noteworthy Prod.
124 1/2 Archwood Ave.
Annapolis, MD 21401
p: 410-268-8232
f: 410-268-2167
www.mcnote.com
contact: McShane Glover
e: mcshane@mcnote.com
venues: Clubs, Festivals, Theaters, Schools
regions: North America
genres: Acoustic, S/S, Celtic, Bluegrass, Blues
Polished talent only.
No unsolicited material.

Olympic Productions
4501 Interlake Ave. N, Ste. 7
Seattle, WA 98103
p: 206-634-1142
www.iwantaband.com
contact: Ed Hartman
e: edrums@aol.com
venues: Clubs, Festivals
regions: USA
genres: World, Rock, Pop, Urban, Jazz, Latin, Caribbean
Email before sending material.

On Queue Performing Artists
PO Box 145
Cooperstown, NY 13326
p: 607-547-9494
f: 607-547-9494
e: info@onqueueartists.com
www.onqueueartists.com
contact: Sandra Peevers
e: sandra@onqueueartists.com;
sandy@telenet.net
venues: PACs, Festivals, Clubs, Colleges, Museums, Theaters
regions: USA, Int'l
genres: World, Roots, Jazz
No unsolicited material.

Ozark Talent
718 Schwarz Rd.
Lawrence, KS 66049
p: 785-760-3143
e: oztalent@aol.com
contact: Steve Ozark
venues: Clubs, Theaters, Festivals, Colleges
regions: Int'l
genres: All Styles
Send CD w/ tour & promo plans.

Pacific Talent
PO Box 19145
Portland, OR 97280
p: 503-228-3620
f: 503-228-0480
e: inbox@pacifictalent.com
www.pacifictalent.com
contact: Andy Gilbert
e: andy@pacifictalent.com
venues: Corporate Events, Festivals, Conventions
regions: northwest USA
genres: Jazz, Blues, R&B, Rock, Funk, Disco
Call before sending material.

Paradigm
360 Park Ave. S, 16th Fl.
New York, NY 10010
p: 212-897-6400
f: 212-764-8941
e: music-newyork@paradigmagency.com
www.paradigmagency.com
contact: Marty Diamond
venues: Clubs, Stadiums, Theaters, Arenas, Festivals
regions: USA, Int'l
genres: Rock, Pop, Hip-Hop
Works w/ top acts & buzz bands.
No unsolicited material.

Piedmont Talent
PO Box 680006
Charlotte, NC 28216
p: 704-399-2210
f: 704-399-2261
e: info@piedmonttalent.com
www.piedmonttalent.com
contact: Steve Hecht
e: steve@piedmonttalent.com
venues: Clubs, Festivals
regions: Reg'l, USA
genres: Acoustic, World, Jazz, Blues
Estab. & polished touring bands.
No unsolicited material.

Pinnacle Ent.
30 Glenn St.
White Plains, NY 10603
p: 914-686-7100
e: pinnacle@pinnacleentertainmentinc.com
contact: John Dittmar
venues: Clubs thru Arenas
regions: USA, Int'l
genres: Hard Rock, Pop, Rock
Must have label representation.

Pistol Booking
140 S. Dixie Hwy Ste. 612
Hollywood, FL 33020
p: 954-304-4395
www.pistolbooking.com
contact: Brian Kurtz
e: brian@pistolbooking.com
venues: Clubs
regions: USA
genres: Rock, Pop, Indie

Platform Booking
1905 W 2nd Ave. H
Spokane, WA 99201
f: 509-328-9694
e: platformbooking@gmail.com
www.myspace.com/rockcoffee
contact: Patrick Kendrick
e: patrickrockcoffee@gmail.com
venues: Clubs
regions: Spokane, WA
genres: All Styles
Mail submissions or via MySpace.

Premiere Artists Group
12230 Forest Hill Blvd.
Ste. 200
Wellington, FL 33414
p: 561-792-2177
f: 561-383-5301
e: info@premiereartistsgroup.com
www.premiereartistsgroup.com
contact: Sondra Chaikin
ext: 561-792-2177 x2001
e: sondra@premiereartistsgroup.com
venues: Colleges, Clubs, Festivals, Theaters, Arenas
regions: USA, Int'l
genres: Underground, Urban
Send 2 CDs of Hip-Hop or Electronic only, press &/or promo materials & cover letter.

Pretty Polly Prod.
397 Moody St.
Waltham, MA 02453
p: 781-894-9600
f: 781-894-9696
e: info@prettypolly.com
www.prettypolly.com
contact: Howard Cusack
e: howie@prettypolly.com
venues: Colleges, Clubs
regions: USA
genres: Pop, Rock, S/S, Soul, Reggae, Blues, R&B, Hip-Hop
No unsolicited material.

Pyramid Entertainment Group
377 Rector Pl., Ste. 21-C
New York, NY 10280
p: 212-242-7274
f: 212-242-6932
e: info@pyramid-ent.com
www.pyramid-ent.com
contact: Sal Michaels
ext: 212-242-7274 x7
e: smichaels@pyramid-ent.com
venues: Clubs thru Arenas
regions: Int'l
genres: Urban, Jazz, Gospel
No unsolicited material.

Rainbow Talent Agency
146 Round Pond Ln.
Rochester, NY 14626
p: 585-723-3334
f: 585-720-6172
e: rtalent@frontiernet.net
www.rainbowtalentagency.com
contact: Carl Labate
e: carl@rainbowtalentagency
venues: Theaters, Casinos, Colleges, Festivals
regions: USA
genres: Alt., Classic Rock, Jazz, Nostalgia, R&B
No unsolicited material.

Real Good Music
14461 E Rincon Valley Dr.
Vail, AZ 85641
p: 520-647-3851
f: 520-647-3069
www.rgmbooking.com
contact: Pat Garrett
ext: 520-250-6607 (cell)
e: rgmgarrett@cs.com;
pat@rgmbooking.com
venues: Clubs, Festivals
regions: North America
genres: Folk Rock, World, Folk
No unsolicited material.

Red Entertainment Agency
16 Penn Plaza, Ste. 824
New York, NY 10001
p: 212-563-7575
f: 212-563-9393
e: info@redentertainment.com
www.redentertainment.com
contact: Carlos Keyes
e: carloskeyes@redentertainment.com
venues: Clubs thru Arenas
regions: USA, Int'l
genres: Rock, Jazz, Gospel, R&B, Pop, Latin, Hip-Hop
Must include CD, photo & live performance DVD.

Red Ryder Entertainment
1532 N Milwaukee Ave.
Ste. 207
Chicago, IL 60622
p: 773-384-0050
f: 773-384-0070
www.rryder.com
contact: Erik Selz
e: erik@rryder.com
venues: Clubs thru Arenas
regions: USA
genres: Rock, Jazz, Indie, Folk, World
Email EPKs. No calls.

The Roots Agency
177 Woodland Ave.
Westwood, NJ 07675
p: 201-263-9200
f: 201-358-8784
e: info@therootsagency.com
www.therootsagency.com
contact: Tim Drake
e: tim@therootsagency.com
venues: Clubs, Theaters
regions: USA, Int'l
genres: Acoustic, Folk, Blues, Jazz, Pop Rock, Dance, World
No unsolicited material.

The Rosebud Agency
PO Box 170429
San Francisco, CA 94117
p: 415-386-3456
e: info@rosebudus.com
www.rosebudus.com
contact: Mike Kappus
e: mikek@rosebudus.com
venues: Clubs thru PACs
regions: USA, Int'l
genres: Blues, S/S, Jazz, Folk, World, Rock, Gospel, R&B

Savoy Music
512 F NE 81st St., #307
Vancouver, WA 98665
p: 503-245-2321
www.savoymusicinternational.com
contact: Stephen Gordon
e: gordoom@aol.com
venues: Clubs thru PACs
regions: Int'l
genres: Roots, Blues
No unsolicited material.

Simon Says Booking
131 W Main St., #7
Orange, MA 01364
p: 978-544-5110
f: 978-544-5112
www.simonsaysbooking.com
contact: Phil Simon
e: phil@simonsaysbooking.com
venues: Clubs, Festivals, Schools
regions: USA
genres: Jazz, Rock, Funk, World, Alt. Country, Roots, Bluegrass
Email before sending material.

The Siren Music Co.
PO Box 12110

Portland, OR 97212
p: 503-238-4771
www.sirenmusiccompany.com
contact: December Carson
e: december@sirenmusiccompany.com
venues: Clubs, Festivals
regions: USA
genres: Americana, Roots, Alt. Country
Call before sending material.

SMG Artists
108 Glenray Ct.
New Freedom, PA 17349
p: 717-227-0060
f: 717-227-0066
www.smgartists.com
contact: Larry Kosson
e: larry@smgartists.com
venues: PACs, Universities
regions: North America
genres: All Styles
See site before sending material.

Sophie K. Ent.
262 W 38th St., Ste. 1605
New York, NY 10018
p: 212-268-9583
f: 212-302-6690
www.sophiek.com
contact: Kate Magill
e: kate@sophiek.com
venues: Colleges, Clubs, Festivals
regions: USA
genres: Rock, Celtic Rock
Only call on Fri.
No unsolicited material.

Spectrum Talent Agency
520 W 43rd St., Ste. 16E
New York, NY 10036
p: 212-268-0404
f: 212-268-1114
www.spectrumtalentagency.com
contact: Marc Katz
e: marc@spectrumtalentagency.com
venues: Clubs thru Arenas
regions: USA, Int'l
genres: Pop, R&B, Dance, Hip-Hop
No unsolicited material.

St. John Artists
1233 S Commercial St.
PO Box 619
Neenah, WI 54957
p: 920-722-2222
f: 920-725-2405
www.stjohn-artists.com
contact: Jon St. John
e: jon@stjohn-artists.com
venues: Clubs, Festivals, Fairs, Corporate
regions: midwest USA
genres: Pop, Cover, Rock
Midwest-region bands only send CD or video & promo material.

Stars & Artists Entertainment SW
99 S Cameron St.
Harrisburg, PA 17101
p: 717-236-4500; 215-338-5094
f: 717-307-3300
e: gmail@starsandartists.com
www.starsandartists.com
contact: Joseph Marrero
e: josephmarrero@starsandartists.com
venues: Clubs thru Arenas
regions: USA
genres: Urban, Pop, Jazz, Funk, Gospel
NJ location: 717-236-4500.
No unsolicited material.

Sueflayy Presents
Santa Monica, CA 90403
p: 310-422-4015
www.sueflayypresents.com
contact: Sue Flayy
venues: Clubs
regions: Los Angeles
genres: All Styles
Include last 2 LA venues played (when, where & draw).

Sybarite Productions
402 Park Ave., #3
Brooklyn, NY 11205
p: 917-312-8002
www.sybariteproductions.net
contact: Dinna Alexanyan
e: dinna@sybariteproductions.net
venues: Clubs
regions: USA
genres: Hip-Hop, R&B, Funk, Neo Soul, Dancehall
No unsolicited material.

Tantrum Management
3341 W Berteau Ave.
Chicago, IL 60618
p: 773-588-8825
f: 773-244-7105
www.tantrummanagement.com
contact: Matt Suhar
e: mattsuhar@sbcglobal.net
venues: Clubs thru Arenas
regions: USA, Int'l
genres: Rock, Jazz, Celtic, S/S, Hip-Hop, Punk, Country, DJs
Email before sending material.

Tempest Ent.
245 W 25th St., Ste. 3B
New York, NY 10001
p: 212-645-1702
f: 212-691-8348
www.tempestentertainment.com
contact: Lian Calvo Serrano
e: lian@tempestentertainment.com
venues: Clubs, Festivals
regions: USA, Int'l
genres: World, Latin
Contact before sending material.

Third Coast Artists Agency
2021 21st Ave. S, Ste. 220
Nashville, TN 37212
p: 615-297-2021
f: 615-297-2776
e: info@tcaa.biz
www.tcaa.biz
contact: Mike Snider
e: mike@tcaa.biz
venues: Clubs, Churches, Amphitheaters, Colleges
regions: USA
genres: CCM
CDs only; will contact if interested.

TLC Booking Agency
37311 N Valley Rd.
Chattaroy, WA 99003
p: 509-292-2201
f: 509-292-2205
e: tlcagent@ix.netcom.com
www.tlcagency.com
contact: Tom Lapsansky
venues: Clubs, Theaters
regions: USA
genres: Rock, Pop, DJs

Top Notch Talent
PO Box 250
Gladeville, TN 37071
p: 615-547-0341
f: 615-547-0342
contact: Reggie Mac
e: reggietnt@bellsouth.net
venues: Clubs thru Arenas
regions: Int'l
genres: Country
Include lyric sheet.

Tree Lawn Artists
8331 Germantown Ave.
Philadelphia, PA 19118
p: 215-248-5296
f: 215-974-7773
e: info@treelawn.org
www.treelawn.org
contact: Eric Hanson
venues: Clubs thru PACs
regions: USA, Int'l
genres: Jazz, S/S, World, R&B, Pop, Rock
Email before sending material.

Triangle Talent
10424 Watterson Tr.
Louisville, KY 40299
p: 502-267-5466; 800-467-SHOW
f: 502-267-8244
e: info@triangletalent.com
www.triangletalent.com
contact: David Snowden
venues: Clubs, Fairs, Festivals
regions: PA, OH, WI, IA, MI, KY, UT, TN, OK, WY
genres: Rock, Country, Dance, Blues, Jazz, Pop
For club bookings, contact: Tom Nutgrass at nutgrass@triangletalent.com.
No unsolicited material.

Ujaama Talent Agency
501 7th Ave., Ste. 312
New York, NY 10018
p: 212-629-4454
f: 212-629-4484
www.ujaamatalent.com; www.ujaamaonline.com
contact: Erskine Isaac
e: eisaac@ujaamatalent.com
venues: Clubs thru Arenas
regions: USA, Int'l
genres: Urban
No unsolicited material.

Union Artists Group
214 Woodhaven Dr.
Union, SC 29379
p: 864-427-6464
f: 864-427-6463
www.unionartistsgroup.com
contact: Billy Messer
e: billy@unionartistsgroup.com
venues: Clubs thru Theaters
regions: USA
genres: Hip-Hop, Top 40, Rock
Email before sending material.

Universal Attractions
145 W 57th St., 15th Fl.
New York, NY 10019
p: 212-582-7575
f: 212-333-4508
e: info@universalattractions.com
www.universalattractions.com
contact: Jeff Epstein
venues: Clubs thru Arenas
regions: USA, Int'l
genres: R&B, Soul, Funk, Hip-Hop
No unsolicited material.

Unknown Legends Artists
PO Box 2781
Hot Springs, AR 71914
p: 501-620-3596
www.unknownlegendsbooking.com
contact: David Hughes
e: dhughes@hotsprings.net
venues: Clubs thru Halls
regions: AR, Nat'l
genres: Classic Rock, Alt., Blues, Country, CCM
Include photos, CDs, bios, set list, list of venues played, press clippings & contact info.

Unlimited Myles
6 Imaginary Pl.
Matawan, NJ 07747
p: 732-566-2881
f: 732-566-8157
www.unlimitedmyles.com
contact: Myles Weinstein
e: myles@unlimitedmyles.com
venues: Clubs, Theaters, PACs
regions: USA, Int'l
genres: Jazz
No unsolicited material.

Utopia Artists
217 Sycamore Dr.
Wofford Heights, CA 93285
p: 760-376-4411
f: 775-854-9101
e: utopiaartists@aol.com
www.marstalent.com
contact: Walter Stewart
e: wstwart@mchsi.com
venues: Clubs, Arenas, College, Package Tours
regions: USA
genres: All Styles
No unsolicited material.

Variety Artists Int'l
793 Higuera, #6
San Luis Obispo, CA 93401
p: 805-545-5550
f: 805-545-5559
e: info@varietyart.com
www.varietyart.com
contact: Bob Engel
venues: Clubs thru Arenas
regions: USA, Int'l
genres: Rock, Folk, Pop, Rap, Jazz, Oldies
No unsolicited material.

Vision Int'l
PO Box 201
Highland, MD 20777
p: 301-854-0888
f: 301-854-0999
e: info@visionintl.com
contact: Armand Sadlier
e: armand@visionintl.com
venues: Clubs, Festivals, Theatres, Casinos, Colleges
regions: N America, Europe
genres: Rock, Pop, Jam, Blues, Jazz
No unsolicited material.

William Morris Agency
150 El Camino Dr.
Beverly Hills, CA 90212
p: 310-859-4000
f: 310-859-4440
www.wma.com
contact: Ron Opaleski
ext: 310-859-4430
e: ro@wma.com
venues: Colleges, Clubs, Arenas
regions: USA, Int'l
genres: All Styles
Offices in NY, TN, FL, London & China.
No unsolicited material.

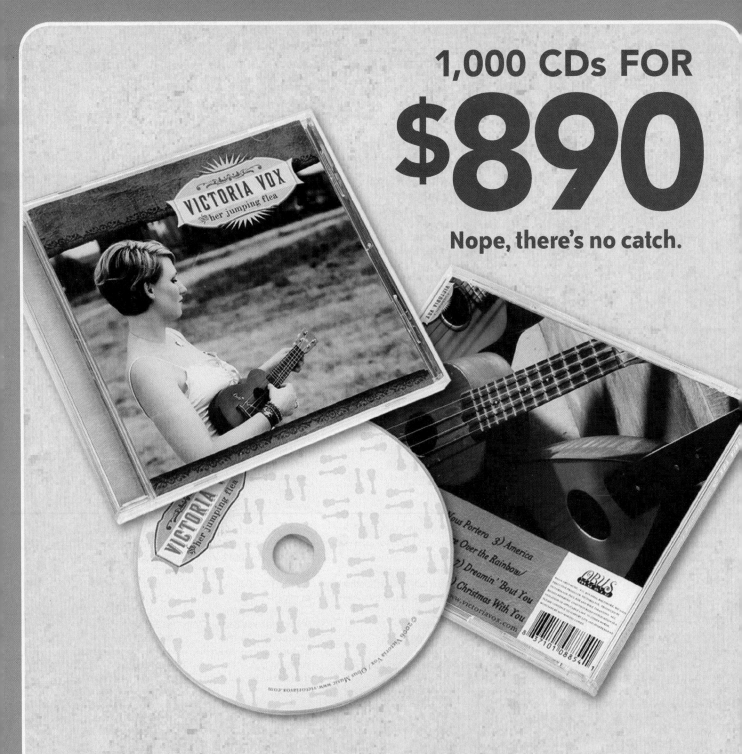

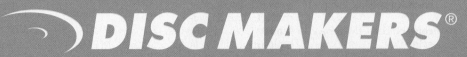

clubs

Alabama

Auburn/ Montgomery

1048 Jazz & Blues
1104 E Fairview Ave.
Montgomery, AL 36106
p: 334-834-1048
e: manager@1048jazzandblues.com
www.1048jazzandblues.com
contact: Doug Gurny
call: evenings
genres: Acoustic, Jazz, Blues, Rock, Punk, Funk, Alt., Folk, Reggae
capacity: 100
pa: Yes
stage: 14 x 12
Jazz & Blues club open to all styles of original music, has 8 shows/wk. Locals play 4 nites & Nat'ls play 2; Jazz on Sun. Usu. 1 act/nite; many opps. for new acts. Send promos: PO Box 6407, Montgomery, AL 36106.

Billy's Bar & Grill
2012 Cahaba Rd.
Mountain Brook, AL 35223
p: 205-879-2238
e: info@billysbarandgrill.com
www.billysbarandgrill.com
contact: Wes Humphries
e: wes@billysbarandgrill.com
genres: All Styles
capacity: 151
pa: Yes
stage: floor space
Pub books area bands Thu-Sat. 3hr set w/ breaks; 21+ after 10pm. Email or snail mail kit.

The Bottletree
3719 3rd Ave. S
Birmingham, AL 35222
p: 205-533-6288
www.thebottletree.com
contact: Tina Pilgrim
e: tina@thebottletree.com
genres: All Styles
advance: 2 months
capacity: 300
pa: Yes **sound eng:** Yes
stage: 12 x 14
Rustic vegan eatery by day/indie-friendly club by nite serves up to 3 original Local-Nat'l acts & some DJs up to 7 nites to 18+. Also contracts acts for residencies. Prefers email; Nat'l acts email: leah@secrethistoryproductions.com. Locals & openers email: bottletreevenue@gmail.com. No unsolicited mail.

Brothers Bar
206 Pelham Rd. S
Jacksonville, AL 36265
p: 256-435-6090
e: info@mybrothersbar.net
www.mybrothersbar.net
contact: Dan Nolen
p: 404-876-8436
e: booking@mybrothersbar.net
genres: Rock
College-town landmark hosts Local-Touring bands. Also books other hot spots, The Nick & Smith's Olde Bar in Atlanta.

Café Firenze
110 Inverness Plaza
Birmingham, AL 35242
p: 205-980-1315
www.myspace.com/cafefirenze
contact: Yance MacLeroy
p: 205-222-1414
genres: All Styles
advance: 1-2 months
capacity: 350+
stage: large
open mics: Sun **sign in:** 7pm
Cafe hosts wide variety of Local-Int'l acts for 21+ crowd. 1-2 bands fill 4hrs w/ breaks for door on wknds & varied payment on wkdys. Mail kit.

Capone's 4th & 23rd
401 23rd Ave.
Tuscaloosa, AL 35401
p: 205-248-0255
www.myspace.com/393894593
contact: Ronnie Pennington
e: ronnie@4thand23rd.net
call: Thu daytime
genres: Jazz, Blues, Bluegrass, Funk
advance: 1-3 months
capacity: 250
Converted warehouse books 1 Reg'l/Touring act Thu-Sat nites. Mail kit & follow up in 2 wks.

Carver Theatre
1631 4th Ave. N
Birmingham, AL 35203
p: 205-254-2731
www.jazzhall.com
contact: Evelyn
p: 205-254-2731 x21
e: tours@jazzhall.com
call: M-F 9am-5pm
genres: Jazz
capacity: 508
pa: Yes **sound eng:** Yes
stage: 39 x 31.5
All ages theatre books Local-Int'l acts Tue-Sun & can also be rented. Snail mail promos or email booking requests.

Cave 9
2237 Magnolia Ave. S
Birmingham, AL 35205
e: cave9rock@aol.com
www.cave9.com
e: hugsandhighfivesbooking@gmail.com
genres: Punk, Hardcore, Metal, Indie Rock
capacity: 250
pa: Yes **sound eng:** Yes
Volunteer-run, all ages, DIY venue books up to 5 original Local-Int'l acts Thu-Sun. Bands split the door; sets run 30min. Club is seeking donations due to tax problems. Hardcore & Metal acts contact Mike: xmikeparsonsx@gmail.com. All booking done via email; No Calls.

High Note Lounge/ Rock-n-Horse
414 Richard Arrington Blvd.
Birmingham, AL 35233
p: 205-251-7625
www.myspace.com/samshighnote
contact: Sam Pilato
p: 205-985-4549
e: samap2@charter.net
call: Tue & Wed 6-9pm; Thu-Sat 7-9pm
genres: Jazz, Hip-Hop, Rap, Emo, Rock, Metal, Hardcore, Punk, Blues, Bluegrass, Classical, Electronic
advance: 3 months
capacity: 340
pa: Yes **sound eng:** Yes
stage: 15 x 30
Books Reg'l & Touring bands & DJs any nite of the wk. 1-2 acts play for 100% of door minus prod. costs. Must draw a crowd. Contact via myspace.com/highnotex3. No unsolicited mail.

Marty's
1813 10th Ct. S
Birmingham, AL 35205
p: 205-939-0045
www.martysbar.com
contact: Marty Eagle
call: Mon-Sat 11pm
genres: Rock, Blues, Folk, Jazz
advance: 2+ months
capacity: 75 **stage:** small
Music bar books original Local-Reg'l acts & DJs 6 nites. 1 band plays 3-4hrs w/ breaks for the door; some double shows w/ 2 acts. Mail press kit to venue.

Mellow Mushroom
2230 University Blvd.
Tuscaloosa, AL 35401
p: 205-758-0112
www.mellowmushroom.com
contact: Alex Freeman
p: 205-758-0439
e: ttownshroom@yahoo.com
call: M-F after 8pm
genres: All Styles
advance: 2 months
capacity: 500
pa: Yes **sound eng:** Yes
stage: 10 x 20
open mics: Tue S/S
Original music venue w/ steady patronage hosts Local-Int'l acts & DJs Tue-Sat & some Mon for 19+ crowd. 1-2 acts play from 10:30pm-1:30am & til 3am on Fri-Sat for flat fee or fee & 80% of door.

The Nick
2514 10th Ave. S
Birmingham, AL 35205
p: 205-252-3831
www.thenickrocks.com
contact: Dan Nolan
p: 404-876-8436
e: nolenreevesmusic@mindspring.com
call: M-F 11am-5pm
genres: Alt., Rock, Punk, Country, Americana, Alt. Country
advance: 1-2 months
capacity: 250
pa: Yes **sound eng:** Yes
Area's prime 21+ spot presents polished Reg'l & Touring talent nitely. 2+ original acts play 45-50min. Promos: Nolen-Reeves Music, 1574 1/2 Piedmont Rd., Atlanta, GA 30324; follow up 1 wk later w/ email or call. Also books Smith's Olde Bar in Atlanta, GA & Brother's Bar in Jacksonville, FL.

Sundilla Acoustic Concert Series
450 Thach Ave.
Auburn, AL 36830
p: 334-741-7169
e: sundilla@mindspring.com
www.sundilla.org
contact: Bailey Jones
e: baileyjones@mindspring.com
genres: Folk, Bluegrass, S/S, Blues, Alt. Country, Acoustic
advance: 6-12 months
capacity: 110
pa: Yes **stage:** 20 x 10
12 concert/yr series books Reg'l-Int'l acts Fri-Mon. Featured act plays two 45min sets for 80-90% of door. Prefers email, but may mail kit to: PO Box 3367, Auburn, AL 36831.

War Eagle Supper Club
2061 S College St.
Auburn, AL 36832
p: 334-821-4455
www.wareaglesupperclub.com
contact: John Brandt
e: jpbrandt@mindspring.com
call: M-F 10am-12pm; 1-3pm
genres: Rock, Blues, Alt., Country, Reggae
advance: 6-9 months
capacity: 500
pa: Yes **sound eng:** Yes
stage: 24 x 12
Renowned college bar 40mi

from Columbus, GA presents Local-Int'l bands Fri-Sat. Original acts must be estab. 1 act plays 60-90min. Mail press kit to venue; incl. CD or DVD (no cassettes), bio, pics & press clips along w/ contact info & honest approx. of area draw.

Workplay Theatre
500 23rd St. S
Birmingham, AL 35233
p: 205-879-4773
e: info@workplay.com
www.workplay.com
contact: Todd Coder
e: todd@workplay.com
call: M-F 9am-6pm
genres: All Styles
advance: 2-4 months
capacity: 400
pa: Yes **sound eng:** Yes
stage: 20 x 32
Intimate room w/ sunken floor & wrap-around balconies books 2 original Local-Int'l acts 4-5 nites. Sets run 30-105min. Offers full video & audio recording, artist mgt. & CD/DVD prod. Some all ages shows; DJs spin occasionally.

Zydeco
2001 15th Ave. S
Birmingham, AL 35205
p: 205-933-1032
www.zydecobirmingham.com
contact: Layne
e: laynef@zydecobirmingham.com
genres: All Styles
advance: 6-8 weeks
capacity: 600
pa: Yes **sound eng:** Yes
stage: 23 x 12
open mics: Wed 9:30pm
All ages ent. complex books original Local-Nat'l acts & DJs up to 7 nites for 18+ crowd. Opener plays 45+min, headliner 90+ & are paid % of door. Also does some booking for Exit/In, Bourbon Street Blues & Boogie Bar, The Legacy & Jupiter Bar & Grill.

Huntsville

Brick Deli & Tavern
112 Moulton St. E
Decatur, AL 35601
p: 256-355-8318
www.brickdeli.com
contact: Tina Hall
e: delifolk@hotmail.com
call: M-F after 4pm
genres: Rock, Bluegrass, Blues, New Age
advance: 3-6 months
capacity: 150 **stage:** 10 x 16
Local-Reg'l music Wed-Sat nites. 21+ at nite only.

Crossroads Café
115 Clinton Ave. E
Huntsville, AL 35801
p: 256-533-3393
www.crossroadsmusic.biz
contact: Jeff Goltz
e: jeffgoltz@yahoo.com
call: M-F after 8pm
genres: Roots, Zydeco, Rockabilly, Rock, Bluegrass, Blues, Alt., Jam, Punk
advance: 2 months
capacity: 650
pa: Yes **sound eng:** Yes
stage: 12 x 25
open mics: Mon
Popular bar books original Nat'l groups & DJs w/ Reg'l openers on wknds for 21+; 1-2 acts perform. Some Local wkdy acts.

Mobile

The Soul Kitchen
219 Dauphin St.
Mobile, AL 36602
p: 251-433-5958
e: solkitchen@aol.com
www.soulkitchenmobile.com
contact: Brad Young
genres: All Styles
advance: 6 months
capacity: 1000; 250
pa: Yes **sound eng:** Yes
stage: 24 x 20
Cookin' music room, popular w/ U of AL students & area hipsters hosts Local-Int'l bands & DJs 2-4 nites. 1-3 acts play for mostly 18+ crowd & keep 85% of merch sales; some all ages shows. Snail mail kits.

Greater AL

Cowboy's
4657 S Oates St.
Dothan, AL 36301
p: 334-793-6937
e: cowboysofdothan@aol.com
www.cowboysofdothan.com
contact: Ron Bedford
call: M-F midday
genres: Country, Oldies, Southern Rock
advance: 3-4 months
capacity: 525
pa: Yes **sound eng:** Yes
stage: 23 x 40
Country-focused 21+ niteclub near FL & GA borders features 1-3 Local-Nat'l acts 3 nites for flat fee; bands play from 9pm-2am or later. Snail mail kits.

Arizona

Flagstaff

Applesauce Tea House
213 S San Francisco St.
Flagstaff, AZ 86001
p: 928-214-7028
www.myspace.com/applesauceteahouse1
contact: Jessica
genres: Most Styles
advance: 3 months
capacity: 170
open mics: Mon
All ages music venue/tea house books Local-Int'l acts Thu-Sat; No Hardcore or Metal. 2 acts play for % of door. Use MySpace for booking. No unsolicited mail.

Charly's Pub & Grill at Weatherford Hotel
23 N Leroux St.
Flagstaff, AZ 86001
p: 928-779-1919
e: weathtel@weatherfordhotel.com
www.weatherfordhotel.com
contact: Henry Taylor
genres: Rock, Reggae, Blues, Celtic, Bluegrass, Pop
advance: 6+ months
capacity: 100 **stage:** 12 x 15
open mics: Tue 9pm-1am
Historic room has Local-Nat'l acts Thu-Sat for 21+ college crowd. Featured band or soloist plays 9pm-1am for % of door vs flat fee.

Future Studios
30 Hozoni Dr.
Sedona, AZ 86336
p: 928-282-9139
www.futurestudios.org
contact: Mycenay
e: booking@futurestudios.org
call: Mon-Sat 8am-5pm
genres: World, Folk, S/S, New Age
advance: 2+ weeks
capacity: 150
pa: Yes **sound eng:** Yes
stage: 24 x 20
A/V prod. studio wired for Internet broadcast & social activist venue 30mi from Flagstaff, is open to all ages. Books Local-Int'l acts w/ positive message up to 7 nites. 1-2 original acts play 45min for % of door. Merch split is 90/10. Mail press kit to: PO Box 4779, Sedona, AZ 86340.

Lyzzard's Lounge
120 N Cortez St.
Prescott, AZ 86301
p: 928-778-2244
www.lyzzards.com
contact: Joseph
e: jpurcell@cableone.net
genres: Rock, Blues, Punk, Ska
advance: 3-4 months
capacity: 210
pa: Yes
stage: 9 x 12
Touring acts & Locals play 21+ retro bar Fri-Sat. 1 or more acts play 4-5hrs from 9:30pm-1:30am. Snail mail kits.

Monte Vista Cocktail Lounge
100 N San Francisco St.
Flagstaff, AZ 86001
p: 928-779-6971
www.hotelmontevista.com
contact: Johnny Swoope
e: booking@hotelmontevista.com
genres: Rock, Rockabilly, Hip-Hop, Punk, Electronic
advance: 1-2 months
capacity: 250
pa: Yes **sound eng:** Yes
stage: 20 x 8
Lounge in lower level of historic & haunted Hotel Monte Vista, hosts Local-Int'l bands Thu-Sat; DJs spin wkly. Up to 3 acts play 45+min sets for flat fee. Touring bands get free room. Use email for booking.

Orpheum Theater
15 W Aspen Ave.
Flagstaff, AZ 86001
p: 928-556-1580
e: orpheumtheater@yahoo.com
www.orpheumpresents.com
contact: Art Babbott
e: info@orpheumpresents.com
call: M-F noon
genres: All Styles
advance: 3 months
capacity: 750
pa: Yes **sound eng:** Yes
stage: 26 x 30
Premier PAC books Local-Int'l acts & some DJs up to 7 nites. 2-3 original acts play 75min for flat fee; sometimes % of door. Merch split is 80/20. Prefers email or may send EPK. No unsolicited mail or calls. No booking thru MySpace.

Phoenix

Alice Cooper's Town
101 E Jackson St.
Phoenix, AZ 85004
p: 602-253-7337
e: music@alicecooperstown.com
www.alicecooperstown.com
contact: Leslie Criger
p: 602-253-7337 x205
e: lesliec@alicecooperstown.com
genres: Rock, Blues, Alt.
advance: 1-2 months
capacity: 900
pa: Yes
stage: 20 x 20
21+ ent. complex presents mostly Local-Reg'l Acoustic acts Wed-Thu, full bands Fri-Sat. 3-6 acts play 45-60min for % of door. Mail press kit to venue or email EPK & wait for response. No Calls.

Big Fish Pub & Grub
1954 E University Dr.
Tempe, AZ 85281
p: 480-449-FISH
www.myspace.com/azbigfish
contact: Jyoti Dietrich
genres: Metal, Rock, Indie, Punk, Blues, Hip-Hop, R&B, Neo Soul, Funk
advance: 3 months
capacity: 190
pa: Yes **sound eng:** Yes
stage: medium
open mics: Sun 4-8pm
21+ dive bar w/ charm is a haven for Local-Nat'l acts & DJs up to 7 nites. 2-5 acts play 45-120min sets for % of door. No Country. Contact via MySpace.

Cave Creek Coffee Co. & Wine Purveyors
6033 E Cave Creek Rd.
Cave Creek, AZ 85327
p: 480-488-0603
f: 480-595-9868
www.cavecreekcoffee.com
contact: Todd & Rose
e: todd@cavecreekcoffee.com
genres: Acoustic, S/S, Folk, Americana
advance: 2 months
capacity: 225
pa: Yes **sound eng:** Yes
open mics: Thu 7:30pm
Cozy room books low volume Local-Nat'l acts for % of door or flat fee up to 6 nites. Featured act plays 7-10pm for all ages. Send promos to: PO Box 4650, Cave Creek, AZ 85327.

Chasers
8005 E Roosevelt Rd.
Scottsdale, AZ 85257
p: 480-945-4985
www.myspace.com/chasersliveaz
contact: Jason Olsen
p: 480-540-7914
call: Wed evenings
genres: All Styles
capacity: 300
pa: Yes **sound eng:** Yes
open mics: Mon
Dive bar presents 1-2 Local-Int'l acts Thu-Sat for 40min sets; some all ages shows.

Clubhouse Music Venue
1320 E Broadway Rd.
Tempe, AZ 85282
p: 480-968-3238
www.clubhousemusicvenue.com

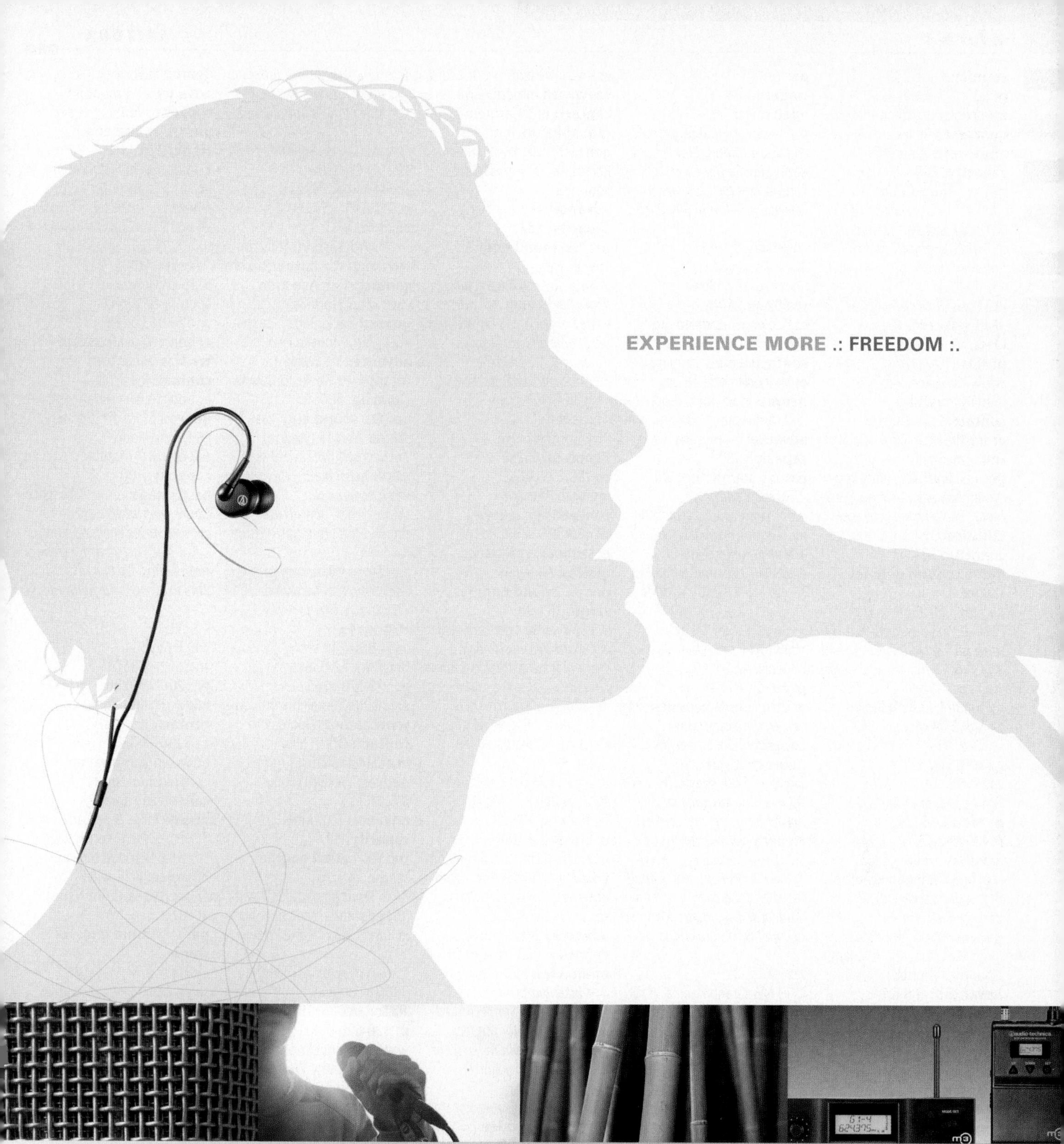
EXPERIENCE MORE .: FREEDOM :.

contact: Eugenia
p: 602-703-8967
e: clubhousegigs@hotmail.com
genres: All Styles
advance: 3-4 months
capacity: 550
pa: Yes **sound eng:** Yes
Club w/ 2 stages hosts 5-9 original Local-Nat'l bands up to 7 nites; many all ages shows. Email w/ link to EPK preferred.

Hollywood Alley
2610 W Baseline Rd.
Mesa, AZ 85202
p: 480-820-7117
www.myspace.com/hollywoodalley
contact: Ross Wincek
e: srossw@msn.com
call: email only
genres: Rock, Alt., Emo, Pop, World, Acoustic, Grunge, Punk, Metal, Funk, Prog., Jazz, Soul
advance: 3 months
capacity: 300
pa: Yes **sound eng:** Yes
stage: 20 x 10
Rocking club 20mi from Phoenix presents Reg'l, Nat'l & some Int'l acts nitely. 3 original acts play 45min sets to 21+ for % of door. Prefers EPKs, but may mail kit to: 29 Shades Crest Rd., Hoover, AL 35226.

Last Exit
1425 W Southern Ave.
Tempe, AZ 85282
p: 480-557-6656
f: 480-557-6570
www.lastexitlive.com
contact: Brannon Kleinlein
e: booking@lastexitlive.com
call: M-F after noon
genres: Rock, Alt., Emo, Indie, Americana, Punk, Jam, Country, Acoustic
advance: 1-2 months
capacity: 350
pa: Yes **sound eng:** Yes
stage: 17 x 17
open mics: Tue Acoustic
Rockin' bar books mostly original Local-Reg'l acts & some Nat'l bands 5-6 nites. 2-3 bands play 60-90min for % of door. Prefers EPKs.

Mama Java's Coffeehouse
3619 E Indian School Rd.
Phoenix, AZ 85018
p: 602-840-5282
www.mamajavascoffeehouse.com
contact: Patrick McKay
e: mckays@mamajavascoffeehouse.com
genres: Acoustic, S/S, Pop, Indie
capacity: 100
pa: Yes
stage: 10 x 4
open mics: Tue
Showcases original performers on stage 4-6 nites. Low volume Reg'ls play for flat fee & some Touring acts for % of door. 1-2 acts play 45-90min for all ages.

Modified Arts
407 E Roosevelt St.
Phoenix, AZ 85004
p: 602-462-5516
e: booking@modified.org
www.modified.org
contact: Kimber Lanning
e: kimber@modified.org
genres: Indie Rock, Prog, Jazz, Americana, Experimental
advance: 3+ months
capacity: 150
pa: Yes **sound eng:** Yes
All ages art gallery & performance space presents non-mainstream, original Local-Int'l acts up to 7 nites w/ up to 4 acts/bill. Use email or mail kit. No copyrighted music w/ BMI.

The Paisley Violin
1028 NW Grand Ave.
Phoenix, AZ 85007
p: 602-254-7843
e: cafepaisley@thepaisley.com
www.thepaisley.com
contact: Gina or Derrick
genres: Alt., Jazz, S/S
capacity: 60 **stage:** 10 x 5
All ages cafe/art gallery & hipster hang presents original Reg'l & a few Touring acts Thu-Sat. Up to 5 bands play 8:30-11pm for tips & maybe a small fee or % of the door. Also a few outdoor shows. Prefers MySpace or email w/ link to online kit.

PHiX
1113 NW Grand Ave.
Phoenix, AZ 85007
p: 602-252-7449
www.inimi.net
contact: Lee Berger
e: leros@inimi.net
call: Afternoons; prefers email
genres: All Styles
advance: 3 months
capacity: 250
pa: Yes **sound eng:** Yes
stage: 18 x 16
All-ages warehouse arts ctr. books 1-5 Local & Touring acts 4 nites for 50% of door. Accepts EPK, or send promos: PO Box 45449, Phoenix, AZ 85064 & follow up via email.

Rhythm Room
1019 E Indian School Rd.
Phoenix, AZ 85014
p: 602-265-4842
e: rhythm@rhythmroom.com
www.rhythmroom.com
contact: Bob Corritore
call: M-F 9am-5pm
genres: Rock, Roots, Blues, Rockabilly, Bluegrass, Jazz, Soul, S/S
advance: 1+ months
capacity: 282
pa: Yes **sound eng:** Yes
stage: varies
Premier Roots & Blues club books Reg'ls-Int'ls 4-7 nites & some Locals. Acts play 45+min sets. Some all ages shows. Promos: 8221 E Garfield, #L115, Scottsdale, AZ 85257.

The Sets
93 E Southern Ave.
Tempe, AZ 85282
p: 480-829-1822
www.thesets.com
contact: Kim LaRowe
p: 480-894-8339
e: setsbooking@cox.net
genres: All Styles
pa: Yes **sound eng:** Yes
stage: 25 x 15
Massive complex houses 5 venues & features live music nitely. Original Local-Nat'l acts & some DJs play mostly all ages shows. Email or mail kits w/ ATTN: Kim LaRowe. Booker also does shows all around the valley.

Steel Horse Saloon
1818 W Bell Rd., #100
Phoenix, AZ 85023
p: 602-942-8778
e: info@steelhorsesaloon.com
www.steelhorsesaloon.com
contact: Debey Scheller
genres: Blues, Rock
advance: 2-3 months
capacity: 200 **stage:** 10 x 8
open mics: Mon 9pm
21+ biker bar books Local & Reg'l bands Fri-Sun. Featured act plays 4 sets for flat fee. Email, contact via MySpace or mail press kit to venue.

The Trunk Space
1506 NW Grand Ave.
Phoenix, AZ 85007
p: 602-256-6006
e: thetrunkspace@yahoo.com
www.thetrunkspace.com
contact: JRC
genres: Avant-Garde, Experimental, Underground, Anti-Folk, Americana
advance: 3 months
capacity: 150
pa: Yes **sound eng:** Yes
All-ages art gallery features music Mon-Sat on irregular basis. Up to 5 original Local & Touring acts play for 50% of door. Email w/ info & link first; no calls or kits will be responded to w/o initial email.

Upper Deck Sports Grill
4224 N Craftsman Ct.
Scottsdale, AZ 85251
p: 480-941-9333
e: info@upperdecksportsgrill.com
www.upperdecksportsgrill.com
contact: Tom Anderson
call: Mon 11am-3pm
genres: Rock, Retro, Classic Rock, Alt., Modern Pop
advance: 3-5 weeks for Locals; 5-10 weeks for Nat'ls
capacity: 300; 90
pa: Yes **sound eng:** Yes
stage: 25 x 15 (wedge)
1-2 acts perform several sets; mostly Local bands, monthly Reg'ls & some Nat'l acts are showcased w/ few all ages shows. Mail press kit to venue.

Tucson

Arizona Folklore Preserve
56 Folklore Tr.
Hereford, AZ 85615
p: 520-378-6165
e: folklore@email.arizona.edu
www.arizonafolklore.com
contact: Dolan Ellis
e: dolan@dolanellis.net
genres: Western, Folk, S/S, Blues
advance: 6 months
capacity: 60
pa: Yes **sound eng:** Yes
stage: 24 x 10
Rural venue presents Reg'l-Nat'l acts w/ cultural content monthly. Send CDs w/ promo..

Boondocks Lounge
3306 N 1st Ave.
Tucson, AZ 85719
p: 520-690-0991
www.boondockslounge.com
contact: Cathy Warner
genres: Blues, R&B, Rock
advance: 3+ months
capacity: 227
pa: Yes **sound eng:** Yes
stage: 10 x 12
Friendly bar w/ loyal regulars presents Reg'ls Sat-Sun. Featured act plays 3hrs for mature 21+ crowd. Mail kit.

Club Congress
The Hotel Congress
311 E Congress St.
Tucson, AZ 85701
p: 520-622-8848
www.hotelcongress.com
contact: David Slutes
e: congressbooking@yahoo.com
genres: Indie Rock, World, S/S
advance: 3-4 months
capacity: 400
pa: Yes **sound eng:** Yes
stage: 22 x 15
Eclectic club in historic hotel has up to 4 Local-Int'l acts & DJs up to 7 nites; some all ages shows. Prefers links to music.

Javalinas
9136 E Valencia Rd., #160
Tucson, AZ 85747
p: 520-663-5282
e: bonnie@javalinas.com
www.javalinas.com
contact: Joe Schill
e: booking@javalinas.com
genres: S/S, Folk, Country, Jazz, Indie Rock
advance: 7 months
capacity: 100
pa: Yes **stage:** corner floor space
Coffee shop w/ indoor & outdoor stages books original Local-Nat'l acts 4 nites; some cover bands. Up to 4 acts fill 2hrs to all ages crowd for tips.

Plush
340 E 6th St.
Tucson, AZ 85705
p: 520-798-1298
www.plushtucson.com
contact: Kris Kerry
p: 520-798-1302
e: kwkerry@msn.com; kris@plushtucson.com
call: prefers email
genres: Indie, Americana, Rock, S/S, Blues, Alt. Country, R&B, Jazz, Underground Hip-Hop
advance: 8-12 weeks
capacity: 80 (front room); 400 (back room)
pa: Yes **sound eng:** Yes
stage: 25 x 12
Original music venue w/ 2 stages & some outdoor shows feat. Local-Int'l bands & DJs nitely for 21+ partying crowd. Up to 4 acts play 45+min. Email w/ dates needed, link to website or press kit & info on previous area gigs.

The Rialto Theatre
318 E Congress St.
Tucson, AZ 85701
p: 520-740-1000
www.rialtotheatre.com
contact: Curtis McCrary
p: 520-740-0126 x5
e: b00king@rialtotheatre.com
genres: All Styles
advance: 2+ months
capacity: 1440
pa: Yes **sound eng:** Yes
stage: 40 x 60
Historic all ages room books acts w/ a draw; original

Touring acts & Locals-Reg'ls as openers nitely for flat fee & 80% merch sales; DJs welcome. Prefers email; No unsolicited mail, EPKs or calls.

The Rock
136 N Park Ave.
Tucson, AZ 85719
p: 520-629-9211
e: rocktucson@aol.com
www.rocktucson.com
contact: Kent VanStelle
p: 520-272-4165
genres: All Styles
advance: 1+ months
capacity: 650
pa: Yes **sound eng:** Yes
stage: 12 x 25
Rockin' club w/rich history near U of AZ avail. for rent w/a few shows booked in-house. Email or mail kits to PO Box 77387, Tucson, AZ 85703. Hard to reach by phone.

Vaudeville
110 E Congress St.
Tucson, AZ 85701
p: 520-622-3535
www.vaudevillecabaret.com
contact: Brent
genres: All Styles
advance: 1-2 months
capacity: 150
pa: Yes **sound eng:** Yes
stage: 11 x 14
21+ club w/ artsy vibe books up to 4 original Local-Nat'l acts up to 7 nites for 80% of door. Contact via MySpace.

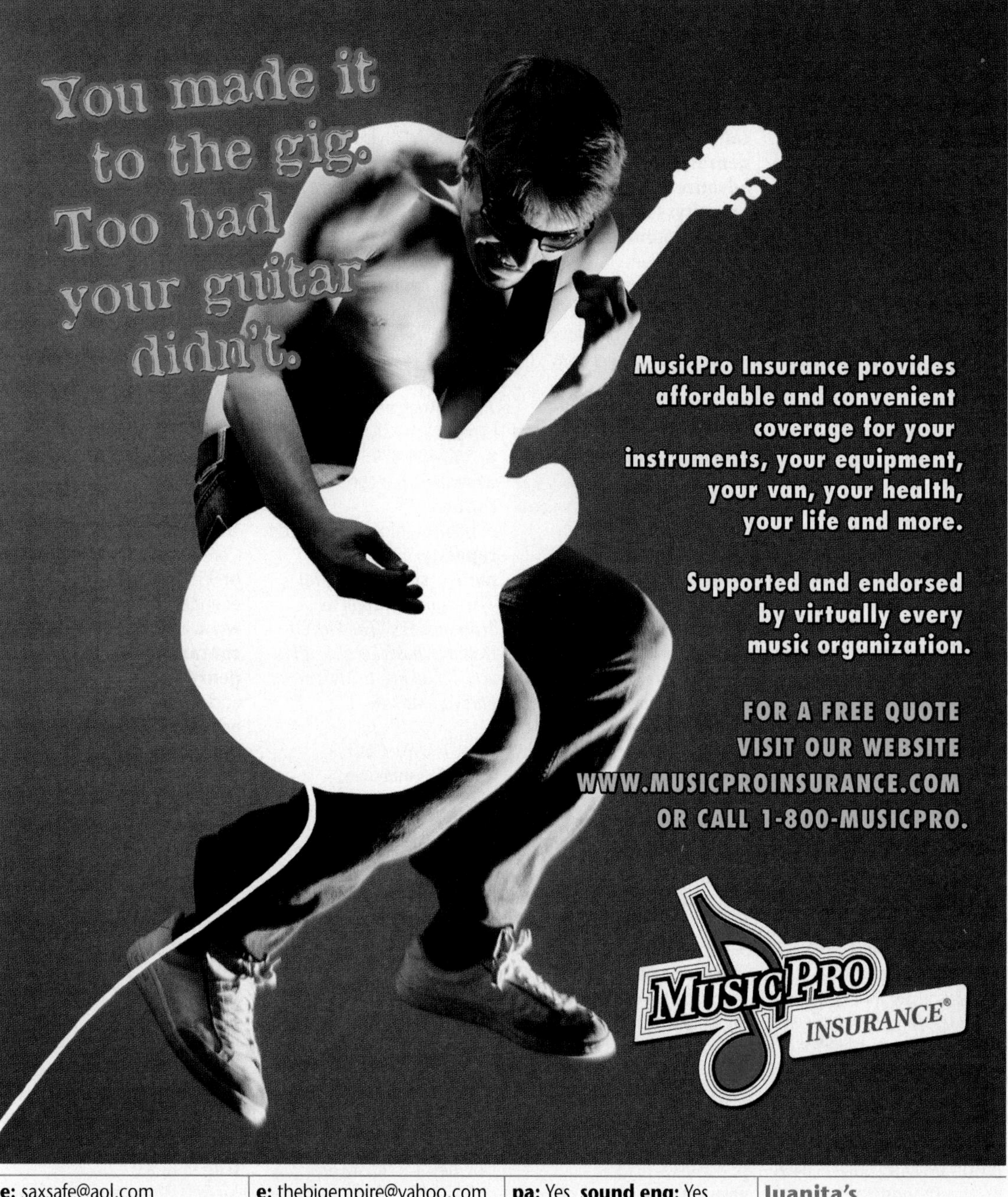

You made it to the gig. Too bad your guitar didn't.
MusicPro Insurance provides affordable and convenient coverage for your instruments, your equipment, your van, your health, your life and more.
Supported and endorsed by virtually every music organization.
FOR A FREE QUOTE VISIT OUR WEBSITE WWW.MUSICPROINSURANCE.COM OR CALL 1-800-MUSICPRO.
MusicPro INSURANCE®

Arkansas

Fayetteville

Arsaga's Crossover
1852 Crossover, Ste. 2
Fayetteville, AR 72703
p: 479-527-0690
www.arsagas.com
contact: Jon Allen
p: 479-799-6552
e: arsagasbooking@gmail.com
call: prefers email
genres: Jazz, Acoustic, S/S, Folk
advance: 3 months
capacity: 150 **stage:** 10 x 10
open mics: 3rd Wed of mo
All ages espresso café & wi-fi hotspot presents original Local & Touring acts Fri & Sat, playing two 45-50min sets for drink sales after initial $200 is made. Mail press kit to venue.

George's Majestic Lounge
519 W Dickson St.
Fayetteville, AR 72701
p: 479-527-6618
e: saxsafe@aol.com
www.georgesmajesticlounge.com
contact: Brian Crowne
genres: All Styles
advance: 3 months
capacity: 350; 700
pa: Yes **sound eng:** Yes
stage: 27 x 16 (plus 8 x 8 addition); 12 x 22 (outdoor)
Popular 21+ music room w/ 2 stages presents up to 5 Local & Touring acts 5-7 nites.

Little Rock

Club 2720
2720 Albert Pike Rd.
Hot Springs, AR 71913
p: 501-760-2505
e: 2720@comcast.net
www.2720nightclub.com
contact: Ron Schultz
e: thebigempire@yahoo.com
genres: All Styles
pa: Yes **sound eng:** Yes
10,000 sq. ft. dance club boasting advanced niteclub experiences in area. Live music Fri-Sat & world-class DJs spinning regularly; shows are 21+. Mail press kit to venue.

Downtown Music & Records
211 W Capitol Ave.
Little Rock, AR 72201
p: 501-376-1819
e: downtownshows@yahoo.com
www.downtownmetal.com
contact: Ronnie Dobbule
call: prefers email
genres: Metal, Hardcore, Punk, Rock, Rap, Country
advance: 1 month
capacity: 300
pa: Yes **sound eng:** Yes
Original Local-Int'l acts play it loud Tue-Sat for devoted all ages crowd. 3 acts play 40min sets. Prefers email or EPK, but may mail kit to: 211 W Capitol Ave., Little Rock, AR 72201.

Flying Saucer
323 President Clinton Ave.
Little Rock, AR 72201
p: 501-372-8032
www.beerknurd.com
contact: Mac
call: M-F 10am-2pm
genres: Acoustic
advance: 3 months
capacity: 100 **stage:** small
Popular brewery w/ 200 beer varieties features Area Acoustic bands playing three 1hr sets every Fri & Sat to 21+ for flat fee. Snail mail kits.

Juanita's Cantina Ballroom
1300 S Main St.
Little Rock, AR 72202
p: 501-374-3271
e: management@juanitas.com
www.juanitas.com
contact: Erin Hurley
p: 501-374-3660
e: erin@greengrassent.com
call: M-F 11am-4pm
genres: Rock, Country, Jam, Bluegrass, Reggae
advance: 2 months
capacity: 300
pa: Yes **sound eng:** Yes
stage: 24 x 18 **in-house:** Organ
Celebrated 18+ venue books Local & Touring acts Tue-Sat. Up to 3 acts play 30-90min sets & keep 80% merch sales; some all ages shows. Email or snail mail press kit. Also books

Sound Stage
1008 Oak St.
Conway, AR 72032
p: 501-514-2561
www.soundstageshows.homestead.com
contact: Brandon Lohnes
e: maneatmanrecords@yahoo.com
call: email only
genres: All Styles
advance: 1-3 months
capacity: 350
pa: Yes **sound eng:** Yes
Reg'l & Touring acts & DJs perform nitely at nitespot 33mi from Little Rock. 3-4 acts play 45-90min for all ages. Prefer emails w/ links but accepts snail mail.

Sticky Fingerz Rock-n-Roll Chicken Shack
107 S Commerce St.
Little Rock, AR 72201
p: 501-372-7707
www.stickyfingerz.com
contact: Chris King
p: 501-372-1151
e: cking@stickyfingerz.com
call: M-F 2-5pm
genres: Rock, Jazz, Reggae, Americana, Alt., R&B, Hip-Hop
advance: 2 months
capacity: 300
pa: Yes **sound eng:** Yes
stage: 14 x 18
Premier music bar books Nat'l & Reg'l bands & DJs Tue-Sat. 2-3 acts on bill split % of door & flat fee. Snail mail kits w/ phone #, will call if interested.

Vino's
923 W 7th St.
Little Rock, AR 72201
p: 501-375-8468; 501-375-8466
e: vinos@vinosbrewpub.com
www.vinosbrewpub.com
contact: Samantha Allen
p: 501-744-4387
e: samanthaxvinos@gmail.com
genres: Alt., Metal, Punk, Alt. Country, Hip-Hop
advance: 2+ months
capacity: 500
pa: Yes **sound eng:** Yes
stage: 24 x 20
Pizza joint popular for live music, presents original Local-Int'l acts & DJs up to 7 nites. 4 bands play 40min sets for all ages. Email or call for booking.

West End Smokehouse & Tavern
215 N Shackleford Rd.
Little Rock, AR 72211
p: 501-224-7665
e: patrick@westendsmokehouse.net
www.westendsmokehouse.net
contact: Andy Rose
e: andy@westendsmokehouse.net
call: M-F 6pm-2am
genres: Rock, Alt.
advance: 2-3 months
capacity: 450
pa: Yes **sound eng:** Yes
stage: medium
Smoked-filled popular hang books Local-Touring acts Fri-Sat for 21+. 1 act plays two 90min sets or 2-3 acts play 30-60min each.

California

Fresno

Audie's Olympic/ Club Fred
1426 N Van Ness Ave.
Fresno, CA 93728
p: 559-233-FRED
www.myspace.com/clubfredmusic
contact: Audie Pardon
e: audiesolympic@yahoo.com
genres: All Styles
advance: 2-3 months
capacity: 185
pa: Yes **sound eng:** Yes
stage: 23 x 24
open mics: Tue **sign in:** 9pm
Now under new ownership & booking original Local-Int'l bands 6 nites. Up to 4 acts play 30-75min for flat fee or % of door; DJs spin wkly. Email, use MySpace or mail promos: PO Box 4639, Fresno, CA 93744.

Downtown Brew
1119 Garden St.
San Luis Obispo, CA 93401
p: 805-543-1843
www.downtownbrewingco.com
contact: Korie Newman
e: korie@downtownbrew.com
genres: All Styles
advance: 2 months
capacity: 450
pa: Yes **sound eng:** Yes
stage: 24 x 15
Central CA pourhouse known for wide spectrum of live music hosts 2-3 Local-Int'l acts & Touring DJs 4 nites. Openers play 40min sets & headliners 75-90min for 21+ crowd; rare all ages shows. Prefers email.

Los Angeles

The Airliner
2419 N Broadway
Los Angeles, CA 90031
p: 323-221-0771
www.myspace.com/theairlinerclub; myspace.com/booktheairliner
contact: Eli
p: 323-707-7212
call: prefers MySpace
genres: All Styles
capacity: expanding
pa: Yes **sound eng:** Yes
stage: small; medium & large
Cavernous, aeronautically-themed 18+ hot spot hosts 5-15 polished Local-Int'l acts & DJs nitely on 3 stages. Contact via Myspace. No unsolicited mail.

Alex's Bar
2913 E Anaheim St.
Long Beach, CA 90804
p: 562-434-8292
www.alexsbar.com
contact: Alex
e: bookinginfo@alexsbar.com
capacity: 178
pa: Yes **sound eng:** Yes
The filming location for Tenacious D's "The Pick Of Destiny," hosts Local-Nat'l acts. Email link to MySpace or PureVolume page.

The Alley Club
140 W Wilshire Ave.
Fullerton, CA 92832
p: 714-738-6934
e: staff@thealleyclub.com
www.thealleyclub.com
e: booking@thealleyclub.com
genres: Rock, Punk, Metal, Ska, Screamo, Hardcore
capacity: 550
pa: Yes **sound eng:** Yes
stage: 30 x 24
Books Local-Nat'l groups. No booking thru MySpace.

The Anarchy Library
13250 Woodruff Ave.
Downey, CA 90242
p: 562-803-9134
www.theanarchylibrary.com
e: booking@theanarchylibrary.com; metalmonday@hotmail.com
genres: Punk, Rockabilly, Psychobilly, Ska, Indie, Rock, Reggae, Metal, Hardcore
advance: 2+ months
Punk powerhouse 13mi SE of downtown Los Angeles, hosts up to 5 mostly Local acts for 21+ devotees Fri-Sat & some Sun. Metal, Rock, Hard Rock & Hardcore bands email metalmonday@hotmail.com; all others email booking@theanarchylibrary.com; incl. links to music & dates you aren't avail. in next 2-3 mos.

Angel's Roadhouse
32464 Dunlap Blvd.
Yucaipa, CA 92399
p: 909-795-0665
www.myspace.com/angelsroadhouse
contact: Wayno
p: 310-367-7782
e: wayno1@dslextreme.com
call: Tue-Sat evenings
genres: Metal, Punk, Alt., Rockabilly, Psychobilly
advance: 1-3 months
capacity: 650+
pa: Yes **sound eng:** Yes
stage: 20 x 25
21+ concert venue 72mi E of L.A. hosts 4-6 mostly original Local-Touring acts Fri-Sun. Bands play 45min for the door. Send kits first.

Angel's Sports Bar
1650 E 6th St.
Corona, CA 92879
p: 951-371-9738
e: angelsbar@aol.com
www.myspace.com/angelsbar
contact: Brad
genres: Metal, Punk, Alt., Rockabilly, Psychobilly
advance: 1-3 months
capacity: 200
pa: Yes **sound eng:** Yes
stage: 16 x 20
21+ Rock bar hosts mostly original Local-Touring acts Fri & Sat.

The Baked Potato
3787 Cahuenga Blvd.
Studio City, CA 91604
p: 818-980-1615
www.thebakedpotato.com
e: jazzboss@roadrunner.com
genres: Jazz, Blues
advance: 2 months
capacity: 85
pa: Yes **sound eng:** Yes
stage: 12 x 9
No frills 21+ venue 13mi NW of L.A., is frequented by label execs & books 1-2 polished Local-Reg'l artists nitely for 90min sets. Email for booking.

Blue Cafe
210 Promenade N
Long Beach, CA 90802
p: 562-983-7111
e: lbbluecafe@aol.com
www.thebluecafe.com
contact: Cat Borga
p: 562-489-2230
e: h2ventures@hotmail.com
call: Tue-Sat 8-10pm
genres: All Styles
advance: 1 month
capacity: 500
pa: Yes **sound eng:** Yes
stage: 25 x 15; 10 x 15
Music room 25mi S of L.A., presents mostly original Local-Int'l acts & some DJs 6 nites. 2-4 bands play 75min. Also books 2nd location in Huntington Beach. Prefers email. No unsolicited mail. See web for submission details.

Cafe Boogaloo
1238 Hermosa Ave.
Hermosa Beach, CA 90254
p: 310-318-2324
www.boogaloo.com
contact: Steven Roberts
e: sroberts@boogaloo.com
call: Tue noon-6pm
genres: Blues, Zydeco, Soul, R&B, Americana
advance: 2-4 months
capacity: 138
pa: Yes **sound eng:** Yes
stage: 15' radius
Blues eatery books original Local-Int'l artists Tue-Sun. Usu. 1 act plays two 75min sets for 21+. Prefers emailed music.

Canter's Kibitz Room
419 N Fairfax Ave.
Los Angeles, CA 90036
p: 323-651-2030
www.cantersdeli.com
contact: Eric Thatcher
e: pirates@eldiablosfunhouse.com
call: Tue-Fri after 8pm
genres: Rock, Acoustic, Jazz, Blues, S/S
advance: 1 month
capacity: 69
pa: Yes **sound eng:** Yes
stage: 8 x 12 **in-house:** Piano
open mics: Sun
Landmark lounge in a deli presents 2-3 polished original Local-Int'l bands nitely for 21+. Bands play from 10pm-1:30am & are paid w/ drinks & food. Prefers snail mail, but may email or use: myspace.com/piratesoffairfax.

Canyon Club
28912 Roadside Dr.
Agoura Hills, CA 91301
p: 818-879-5016
e: info@canyonclub.net
www.canyonclub.net
contact: Lance Sterling
e: lance@canyonclub.net
call: Tue-Sat noon-6pm
genres: All Styles
capacity: 1270
pa: Yes **sound eng:** Yes
stage: 24 x 65
Mostly all ages venue 35mi N of L.A., books Local & Touring bands. Opener plays 45min, headliner 90. 21+ after 11pm.

The Cat Club
8911 Sunset Blvd.

West Hollywood, CA 90069
p: 310-657-0888
www.myspace.com/thecatclub
contact: Dessica
call: Mon-Thu 12-4pm
genres: Acoustic, Rock, Blues, Punk, Alt., Indie, S/S
advance: 1 month
capacity: 150
pa: Yes **sound eng:** Yes
stage: small
Leather-clad venue, owned by former Stray Cat member, Slim Jim Phantom, books Local-Reg'l bands nitely for 21+. 5-6 acts play 35-45min for% of door. ALL booking thru MySpace.

Catalina Jazz Club
6725 Sunset Blvd.
Hollywood, CA 90028
p: 323-466-2210
e: catjazz@sbcglobal.net
www.catalinajazzclub.com
contact: Manuel Santiago
call: M-F 2:30-10pm
genres: Jazz
advance: 3-6 months
capacity: 200
pa: By Request
sound eng: To hire
stage: 22 x 13
All ages supperclub showcases top-tier Local-Int'l artists 6 nites. Featured act plays 75-90min. Merch splits 85/15. Email links or mail kits.

Chain Reaction
1652 W Lincoln Ave.
Anaheim, CA 92801
p: 714-635-6067
f: 714-633-4569
e: chainreactionbooking@yahoo.com
www.allages.com
contact: Andy
genres: Hard Rock, Ska, Pop, Alt., Punk
advance: 3 months
capacity: 400
pa: Yes **sound eng:** Yes
stage: 15 x 20
Alcohol-free all ages club books popular Local & some Touring acts nitely. 5 bands play original 25-30min sets. Email or snail mail kit.

The Coach House
33157 Camino Capistrano
San Juan Capistrano, CA 92675
p: 949-496-8930
e: info@thecoachhouse.com
www.thecoachhouse.com
contact: Adam Spriggs
p: 714-545-3460
e: adam@thecoachhouse.com
call: M-F 9am-6pm
genres: Indie Rock, Jam, Rock, Reggae, Blues
advance: 2-3 months
capacity: 500
pa: Yes **sound eng:** Yes
stage: 32 x 16
All ages venue 55mi SE of L.A. books 3-5 known Local-Int'l bands & DJs 4 nites. Nat'ls split merch 80/20. Also books Key Club in L.A., Morongo &The Galaxy. Email or mail press kit w/ ATTN: Adam, Galaxy Concert Theater, 3503 S Harbor Blvd., Santa Ana, CA 92704.

The Coffee Gallery Backstage
2029 N Lake Ave.
Altadena, CA 91001
p: 626-398-7917
www.coffeegallery.com
contact: Bob Stane
p: 626-794-2902
e: bstane@earthlink.net
call: M-F 10-11:00am; 4-5:30pm
genres: Folk, S/S, Americana, Blues, Bluegrass, Roots
advance: 2 months
capacity: 45
pa: Yes **sound eng:** Yes
stage: 6 x 12
Prime all-ages listening room 15mi from L.A., presents 1-2 polished original Local-Int'l acts nitely. Great sound, stage & lights. Opener plays 30min, headliner plays up to 2hrs & takes % of door.

The Derby
4500 Los Feliz Blvd.
Los Angeles, CA 90027
p: 323-663-8979
e: thederby@clubderby.com
www.clubderby.com
e: booking@clubderby.com
genres: Swing, Dance, Rock, Big Band, Indie, Solo Acoustic, Country, Honky-Tonk
capacity: 550
pa: Yes **sound eng:** Yes
stage: 31 x 25; 302 sq. ft.
Classic dance hall & serious swing joint hosts up to 6 Local-Int'l developing/polished acts on 2 stages for trendy, all ages clientele up to 7 nites.

Detroit Bar
843 W 19th St.
Costa Mesa, CA 92627
p: 949-642-0600
e: info@detroitbar.com
www.detroitbar.com
contact: Chris Fahey
e: booking@detroitbar.com; chris@detroitbar.com
genres: Alt., Pop, Hip-Hop, Indie, New Wave, Electro
advance: 3 months
capacity: 222
pa: Yes **sound eng:** Yes
stage: 15 x 22
Prime hipster music club 42mi from L.A. w/ veteran booker, presents original Local & Touring bands & DJs 4 nites. 2-3 acts play 30-60min sets for 21+. Accepts EPKs only. No unsolicited mail or calls.

The Doll Hut
107 S Adams St.
Anaheim, CA 92802
p: 714-533-1286
e: thedollhut@yahoo.com
www.myspace.com/newhut
contact: Michee
genres: Rockabilly, Psychobilly, New Old School Punk
advance: 2-3 months
capacity: 100
pa: Yes **sound eng:** Yes
stage: 10 x 13
Legendary 21+ roadhouse books 3-4 Local-Nat'l bands nitely. Acts play 30-45min for% of door. Mail press kit to venue or contact via MySpace.

Dragonfly
6510 Santa Monica Blvd.
Los Angeles, CA 90038
p: 323-466-6111
www.thedragonfly.com
contact: Anthony Belanger
e: bands@thedragonfly.com
call: M-F 11am-4pm
genres: Rock, Alt., Emo, Punk
advance: 1 month
capacity: 400
pa: Yes **sound eng:** Yes
stage: 20 x 15
Cool 21+ niteclub spotlights 4 Local-Int'l bands every Tue-Wed, DJs Thu-Sat. Payment is % of door for 40min sets. Email or contact via MySpace.

El Rey Theatre
5515 Wilshire Blvd.
Los Angeles, CA 90036
p: 323-936-6400
e: booking@theelrey.com
www.theelrey.com
contact: Goldenvoice
e: concerts@goldenvoice.com
genres: Alt., S/S, World, Funk, Punk, Country, Rock, Electronic
advance: 1-4 months
capacity: 771 (GA)
pa: Yes **sound eng:** Yes
stage: 26 x 17
Prime Art Deco venue boasting top sound & lights features 2-4 Local acts w/ buzz & top Touring bands nitely; DJs also.

Fais Do-Do
5257 W Adams Blvd.
Los Angeles, CA 90016
p: 323-931-4636

e: info@faisdodo.com
www.faisdodo.com
e: booking@faisdodo.com
genres: Most Styles
advance: 1-2 months
capacity: 300
pa: Yes **sound eng:** Yes
stage: 12 x 7 (plus extensions)
open mics: 1-2/month
Eclectic music club w/ Cajun menu showcases Local-Int'l acts & DJs up to 7 nites for 21+; some all ages shows. 3-6 acts play 30+ min. Merch split can be up to 85/15. No Hard Rock or Gangsta Rap. Mail kit or email link to music.

Genghis Cohen
740 N Fairfax Ave.
Los Angeles, CA 90046
p: 323-653-0640
www.genghiscohen.com
contact: Jay Tinsky
p: 310-578-5591
e: jaytinsky@comcast.net
call: anytime
genres: Acoustic, S/S, Country
advance: 2 months
capacity: 62
pa: Yes **sound eng:** Yes
stage: 8 x 12
Venerable all ages listening room showcases polished Reg'l & estab. Touring talent 6 nites for % of door. 3-5 acts play 45min sets. Also books Molly Malone's. Prefers EPKs, but accepts snail mail kits w/ ATTN: J.T. Presents.

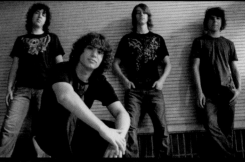

The Gig in Hollywood
7302 Melrose Ave.
Hollywood, CA 90046
p: 323-936-4440
www.liveatthegig.com
contact: Marsha Kersadis
p: 323-936-4440 x4
e: marsha@livefromthegig.com
call: M-F 8-11pm
genres: Rock, Pop, Indie, Gothic, Industrial, Alt., Country, Metal, Punk
advance: 1-2 months
capacity: 188
pa: Yes **sound eng:** Yes
stage: 17 x 18
Prime 21+ listening room showcases original Local & Touring bands nitely. Up to 4 acts play 40min for% of door. Prefers EPKs but snail mail kits w/ ATTN: Booking. Allow 1 wk.

The Good Hurt
12249 Venice Blvd.
Los Angeles, CA 90066
p: 310-390-1076
www.goodhurt.net
contact: Alec Ziegler
p: 818-324-3883
e: booking@goodhurt.net
call: M-F noon-7pm
genres: Rock, Electronic, Reggae
advance: 2 months
capacity: 300
pa: Yes **sound eng:** Yes
stage: 20 x 20
21+ niteclub boasts 2 stages w/ full sound & books original Local-Int'l bands & DJs nitely.

4-5 acts play 40min for% of door. New bands should email first. No unsolicited mail.

Harvelle's
1432 4th St.
Santa Monica, CA 90401
p: 310-395-1676
e: info@harvelles.com
www.harvelles.com
contact: Cezin
p: 310-395-1676 x3
e: cezin@harvelles.com
genres: Soul, Jazz, Blues, Afro-Cuban Jazz, R&B
advance: 1-2 months
capacity: 150
pa: Yes **sound eng:** Yes
stage: 15 x 9
Renowned Blues room showcases original Reg'l-Int'l Touring acts nitely. 1 act plays 9:30pm-1:30am w/ breaks. Also books new Harvelle's location in Redondo Beach, CA. Mail kit or call.

Hogue Barmichaels
3950 Campus Dr.
Newport Beach, CA 92660
p: 949-261-6270
www.hoguebarmichaels.com
contact: Jason
e: booking@hoguebarmichaels.com
genres: All Styles
advance: 2-4 weeks
capacity: 300
pa: Yes **sound eng:** Yes
stage: 22 x 15
Sushi sports bar 44mi SE of L.A., books Local-Int'l bands & DJs 5-7 nites for% of door. 4-7 acts play 25-45min sets. All ages Sun-Thu; Fri-Sat is 18+. Prefers booking form thru website, but may snail mail kit.

House of Blues Sunset Strip
8430 Sunset Blvd.
West Hollywood, CA 90069
p: 323-848-5100
http://hob.com/venues/clubvenues/sunsetstrip
contact: Paul McGuigan
p: 310-598-4041
e: paulmcguigan@livenation.com
call: M-F 10am-6pm
genres: Alt., Blues, Emo, Country, Rock, Punk, Latin, Pop, Hip-Hop
advance: 6-8 weeks
capacity: 1000
pa: Yes **sound eng:** Yes
stage: 30 x 20
Celebrated 18+ room books estab. artists & polished up & comers nitely. 2-3 acts play 30-90min for flat fee & sometimes % of door; some all ages shows. Merch splits 80/20. Snail mail or email kits.

Joint
8771 W Pico Blvd.
Los Angeles, CA 90035
p: 310-275-2619
www.myspace.com/thejoint
genres: Rock, Alt., Pop
advance: 1-2 months
capacity: 80
pa: Yes **sound eng:** Yes
Out-of-the-way, recently renovated bar hosts 4-6 Local & Reg'l bands w/ local draw nitely for % of door. Books thru MySpace or snail mail.

Key Club
9039 Sunset Blvd.
West Hollywood, CA 90069
p: 310-274-5800
www.keyclub.com
contact: Carrie Istad
p: 310-274-5800 x248
e: carrie@keyclub.com
call: M-F 10am-6pm
genres: Indie Rock, Hip-Hop, Alt., Rock, Metal
advance: 2-3 months
capacity: 600
pa: Yes **sound eng:** Yes
stage: 24 x 27
Multi-level hot spot books acts w/ buzz & some DJs nitely for all ages. 3-5 acts play 30-90min sets. Promos: 9041 Sunset Blvd., W Hollywood, CA 90069.

Knitting Factory
7021 Hollywood Blvd.
Ste. 209
Hollywood, CA 90028
p: 323-463-0204
www.knittingfactory.com
contact: Chris Diaz
e: cdiaz@knitmedia.com
call: prefers email
genres: Rock, Hip-Hop, Electronica, Alt., Punk, Americana, Rock en Espanol
advance: 2-3 months
capacity: 525; 300; 100
pa: Yes **sound eng:** Yes
stage: 28 x 16 (main); 25 x 16 (front); 13 x 11 (AlterKnit)
West coast arm of illustrious NYC venue, presents nitely new music showcases w/ cutting-edge bands & few DJs. 3-6 Local-Int'l acts perform 30+min sets on 3 stages & keep 85% merch sales. Some all ages shows. Send email w/ link to music.

Kulak's Woodshed
5230-1/2 Laurel Canyon Blvd.
North Hollywood, CA 91607
p: 818-766-9913
www.kulakswoodshed.com
contact: Paul Kulak
e: paulkulak@earthlink.net
genres: Acoustic, S/S
advance: 2 months
capacity: 50
sound eng: Yes
stage: 8 x 10
open mics: Mon
Scrappy & notable listening room showcases fine Acoustic talent for all ages. 2-3 Local-Int'l artists play Thu-Sat. Email or mail press kit to venue.

The Lighthouse Cafe
30 Pier Ave.
Hermosa Beach, CA 90254
p: 310-376-9833
e: info@thelighthousecafe.net
www.thelighthousecafe.net
contact: C.J. Chiappinelli
e: booking@thelighthousecafe.net; lighthousebooking@gmail.com
call: email only
genres: Jazz, Reggae, Rock, Blues, Funk
advance: 1-2 months
capacity: 200
pa: Yes **sound eng:** Yes
stage: medium
Historic Jazz landmark presents diverse Reg'l & Touring bands nitely & tribute acts Fri & Sat; Sun Jazz brunch. Up to 5 acts play 55min-3hrs for flat fee. Few DJs spin. Prefers EPKs; No unsolicited mail.

Live at the Lounge
1014 Hermosa Ave.
Hermosa Beach, CA 90254
p: 310-372-1193
www.liveatthelounge.com
contact: Jay Tinsky
p: 310-578-5591
e: jaytinsky@comcast.net
genres: Acoustic
advance: 2-3 weeks
capacity: 104
pa: Yes **sound eng:** Yes
stage: 12 x 20
Devoted listening room hosts 3-4 acts Fri & Sat for flat fee. Currently booking 90min revue show wknds for 18+ crowd. Also books Genghis Cohen & Molly Malone's. Promos: J.T. Presents, 740 N Fairfax Ave., Los Angeles, CA 90046.

McCabe's Guitar Shop
3101 Pico Blvd.
Santa Monica, CA 90405
p: 310-828-4497
f: 310-453-4245
e: mccabesconcerts@gmail.com
www.mccabes.com
contact: Lincoln Meyerson
p: 310-828-8037
call: M-F
genres: Folk, Acoustic, S/S, Rock, Jazz, Alt., Americana, Indie
advance: 1-2 months
capacity: 150
pa: Yes **sound eng:** Yes
stage: 17 x 10
Venerable shop & showcase presents 1-2 original Local & Touring acts w/ buzz 2-3 nites on wknds for 75-90min; must draw 50+. Prefers email, but may mail kit w/ ATTN: Lincoln; call to follow up.

Molly Malone's
575 S Fairfax Ave.
Los Angeles, CA 90036
p: 323-935-1577
e: booking@mollymalonesla.com
www.mollymalonesla.com
contact: Jay Tinsky
p: 310-578-5591
e: jaytinsky@comcast.net
genres: Rock, Country, S/S, Alt., Celtic
advance: 1-2 months
capacity: 125-150
pa: Yes **sound eng:** Yes
stage: 12 x 20
Music industry hang presents live acts w/ buzz nitely for 45min sets; some DJs & cover acts. Payment is % of door. Also books Genghis Cohen & Live at the Lounge. Prefers email but may mail kit to: J.T. Presents, 740 Fairfax Ave., Los Angeles, CA 90046.

Mr. B
1333 N Hollywood Way
Burbank, CA 91505
p: 818-845-1800
www.mrbjazz.com
contact: Gina B.
p: 818-541-1522
e: ginabbooking@yahoo.com
genres: Jazz, Acoustic, Blues, Rock, Alt. Pop - No Loud acts
advance: 1-2 months
capacity: 150 **pa:** Yes
stage: 10 x 10 **in-house:** Piano
Lounge books original Local-Int'l bands Tue-Fri. Featured act plays 60-90min for all ages. Prefers email for booking; incl. phone number.

Mr. T's Bowl
5621-1/2 N Figueroa St.
Los Angeles, CA 90042
p: 323-256-7561
e: mrtsbowl@gmail.com
http://mrtsbowl.tripod.com
contact: Arlo
call: M-F after 7pm
genres: All Styles
advance: 2-3 months
capacity: 150
pa: Yes **sound eng:** Yes
No more bowling but still a fave 21+ hang & a cool gig for original Local-Int'l bands. 4-5 acts play 30-45min nitely for% of door on wknds; no cover during the wk. Month-long Mon residencies & Sat theme nites. Also books Old Towne Pub in Pasadena. Email link to music first.

Paladino's
6101 Reseda Blvd.
Tarzana, CA 91335
p: 818-342-1563
www.paladinosclub.com
contact: Jimmy D. Prod.
p: 818-719-0091
e: jimmydrocks@aol.com
genres: All Styles
advance: 2 months
capacity: 350
pa: Yes **sound eng:** Yes
stage: large **in-house:** Drums
Back-to-the-basics venue 24mi NW of L.A. & w/ great sound books 3-5 Local-Int'l bands & DJs nitely for 21+; cover bands on wknds. Opener plays 45+min, headliner plays 70-90min. Email or call first.

The Roxy Theatre
9009 W Sunset Blvd.
West Hollywood, CA 90069
p: 310-278-9457
e: theroxy@mac.com
www.theroxyonsunset.com
contact: Scott Reifman
e: scottrox@mac.com
call: M-F noon-5pm
genres: All Styles
advance: 45 days
capacity: 500; 125 (upstairs)
pa: Yes **sound eng:** Yes
stage: 35 x 25; 6 x 9 plus 4.5 x 2 addition
Sunset Strip landmark w/ 2 stages presents top acts & buzz bands nitely for % of door. Local sets run 30-45min, Touring acts 45-60. 3-5 bands play mostly all ages shows. Email or mail press kit to venue.

Safari Sam's
5214 Sunset Blvd.
Los Angeles, CA 90027
p: 323-666-7267
e: info@safari-sams.com
www.safari-sams.com
e: booking@safari-sams.com
call: prefers email
genres: Indie, Rock, Pop, Punk, Experimental
advance: 8-10 weeks
capacity: 500
pa: Yes **sound eng:** Yes
stage: 12 x 16
Popular themed niteclub books Local-Int'l acts & DJs up to 7 nites. 3-5 acts play 30-60min for all ages. Send kit or link.

Silverlake Lounge
2906 Sunset Blvd.
Los Angeles, CA 90026
p: 323-666-2407
www.foldsilverlake.com
contact: Scott Sterling
e: fold@sbcglobal.net
genres: Rock, Alt., Acoustic, Psychedelic, Experimental
advance: 1-4 months
capacity: 176
pa: Yes **sound eng:** Yes
stage: 15 x 20
Anything goes at this Fri-Mon Latino drag-queen hangout & Tue-Thu Rock club. 2-3 original Local-Int'l acts play 45-60min for 21+. Bookings often avail. last min. Also book Tangier, Bordello & El Sid. Promos: The Fold c/o Scott Sterling, 3835 1/2 Tracy St., Los Angeles, CA 90027.

Spaceland
1717 Silver Lake Blvd.
Los Angeles, CA 90026
p: 323-661-4380
e: info@spaceland.tv
www.clubspaceland.com
contact: Jennifer Tefft
p: 213-985-4333
e: booking@spaceland.tv
call: prefers email
genres: All Styles
advance: 3 months
capacity: 260
pa: Yes **sound eng:** Yes
stage: 14 x 20
Prime club showcases indie heroes & buzz bands to fans & industry nitely for 21+. 3-4 mostly original acts play 45min; DJs spin sometimes. Prefers email w/ link to music; No attachments. May also mail kit to: 2658 Griffith Park Blvd., #391, Los Angeles, CA 90039.

The Talking Stick
1411-C Lincoln Blvd.
Venice, CA 90291
p: 310-450-6052
www.thetalkingstick.net
contact: Rich Braaksma
e: richlymade@gmail.com
genres: All Styles
advance: 3 days - 3 months
capacity: 70
pa: Yes **sound eng:** Yes
stage: medium floor space
open mics: Wed
Laid back cafe recently relocated 17mi W of L.A. & now hosts mostly original Reg'l & some Touring talent Mon-Sat. 3 acts play 45-60min from 7-9:45pm for tips.

Temple Bar
1026 Wilshire Blvd.
Santa Monica, CA 90401
p: 310-393-6611
e: info@templebarlive.com
www.templebarlive.com
contact: Dexter Story
e: booking@templebarlive.com
call: M-F 11am-6pm
genres: Latin, Hip-Hop, S/S, Soul, Funk, World, Indie Rock
advance: 6-12 weeks
capacity: 300
pa: Yes **sound eng:** Yes
stage: 22 x 14
Multicultural, hippie bar w/ a pinch of soul books 3 diverse original bands & DJs nitely. Local-Int'l acts play 45min sets for 21+. Also books Zanzibar, Little Temple & Townhouse. Email or mail kit w/ ATTN: Temple Bar Booking. Incl. band name, style, links to MySpace & YouTube, L.A. performance history, # of draw & how you promote shows in L.A.

Troubadour
9081 Santa Monica Blvd.
West Hollywood, CA 90069
p: 310-276-6168
www.troubadour.com
contact: Lena Lux
p: 310-276-6168 x4
e: lenatroub@yahoo.com
call: Tue, Wed, Fri after 3pm
genres: Rock
advance: 2 months
capacity: 450
pa: Yes **sound eng:** Yes
stage: 15 x 31
Legendary all ages club presents original music & DJs nitely w/ 15-90min sets. Local acts must present L.A. gig history & ensure 50+ paying customers. Mail promos w/ ATTN: Booking, 618 N Doheny Dr., 2nd Fl., West Hollywood, CA 90069.

Vinotéque
4437 Sepulveda Blvd.
Culver City, CA 90230
p: 310-482-3290
e: info@vinotequela.com
www.vinotequela.com
contact: Alex Shteyman
p: 310-482-3490
e: alex@vinotequela.com
call: M-F after 2pm
genres: Jazz, Acoustic
advance: 6 months
capacity: 70; 50 (outdoors)
pa: Yes **sound eng:** Yes
stage: 13 x 7 **in-house:** Piano
open mics: Tue **sign in:** 7pm
Previously Synergy Cafe & Lounge, this new winebar 13mi from L.A., is friendly to Local acts & also hosts Reg'l-Int'l acts & DJs Tue-Sun for all ages. 1-2 acts play 60-90min for tips.

The Viper Room
8852 Sunset Blvd.
West Hollywood, CA 90069
p: 310-358-1881
www.viperroom.com
contact: Mike DuCharme
e: booking@viperroom.com
call: M-F 9am-5pm
genres: Alt., Rock, Indie
advance: 1-2 months
capacity: 200
pa: Yes **sound eng:** Yes
stage: 16 x 14 **in-house:** Drums
Uber-cool 21+ industry hang showcases estab. & cutting edge acts & DJs nitely. Sets run 30-45min; 3-4 mostly original Local-Int'l acts on a bill. Use email; No booking done via mail or MySpace.

Whisky-A-Go-Go
8901 Sunset Blvd.
West Hollywood, CA 90069
p: 310-652-4202
e: mail@whiskyagogo.com
www.whiskyagogo.com
contact: Celina Denkins
p: 310-652-4202 x14
e: celina@whiskyagogo.com
call: M-F After 10:30am
genres: Mainly Rock
advance: 2 months
capacity: 450
pa: Yes **sound eng:** Yes
stage: 20 x 30
Famed Rock club presents acts on the way up or down for all ages nitely. 5-9 acts play 30-40min for % of door. Most nites, bands pre-sell 50 tix; 75+ for wknd. Merch splits 80/20 for soft goods; 100% for CDs. Prefers link to music, but may mail press kit to venue w/ ATTN: Celina Denkins.

The Wiltern
3790 Wilshire Blvd.
Los Angeles, CA 90010
p: 213-388-1400
e: frontoffice@livenation.com
www.wiltern.com
contact: Greg Siegel
p: 310-598-4100
e: gregsiegel@livenation.com
genres: All Styles
capacity: 2300
pa: Yes **sound eng:** Yes
stage: large
Large theater books mostly Nat'l & Int'l talent up to 7 nites/wk. Some Local-Reg'l openers. Promos: ATTN: Greg Sigel, 9601 Wilshire Blvd., Ste. 800, Beverly Hills, CA 90210.

Zen Sushi
2609 Hyperion Ave.
Los Angeles, CA 90027
p: 213-675-6666

www.myspace.com/zensushiclub
contact: Abel Silva
e: abel@humblegraphics.com
call: M-F 10:30am-5pm
genres: Rock, Alt., Pop, Funk, Punk, Country, Jazz
advance: 6 weeks
capacity: 350
pa: Yes **sound eng:** Yes
stage: medium
Popular Japanese eatery & indie hot spot, features Reg'l & Touring bands & DJs on 2 stages nitely. 2-3 acts play 45min to 21+ crowd. Promos: 3175 S Hoover St. #479, Los Angeles, CA 90007.

Sacramento

Blue Lamp
1400 Alhambra Blvd.
Sacramento, CA 95816
p: 916-455-3400
www.bluelamp.com
contact: Ed Stoner
e: booking@bluelamp.com
call: daytime
genres: Alt., Rock, R&B, Blues, Country, Reggae, Indie
advance: 1-2 months
capacity: 100
pa: Yes **sound eng:** Yes
stage: 10 x 14
open mics: Mon 9pm
Recently relocated SF staple, books Local-Int'l acts 5 nites to 21+ crowd; DJs spin 2 nites. 3-4 original bands play 20-40min for % of door. Merch splits 85/15. Prefers booking by email.

Constable Jack's
515 Main St.
Newcastle, CA 95658
p: 916-663-9385
www.constablejacks.com
contact: Tim Looper
e: tlooper4@aol.com
genres: Blues, Rock, Celtic, Americana, Hawaiian
capacity: 100
pa: Yes **sound eng:** Yes
Popular venue & restaurant features Local-Nat'l acts.

The Distillery
2107 L St.
Sacramento, CA 95816
p: 916-443-8815
www.myspace.com/savethedistillery
contact: Jim Barr
p: 916-441-6442
call: M-F evenings
genres: Alt., Rock, Punk, Hip-Hop
advance: 2 months
capacity: 170
pa: Yes **sound eng:** Yes
Steakhouse w/ corner for Local & some Touring bands Thu-Sat for 21+. 2-4 original acts play 30-45min for % of door.

G Street Pub
228 G St.
Davis, CA 95616
p: 530-758-3154
e: gnetline@hotmail.com
www.gstreetpub.com
contact: Rodney Williams
genres: Alt., Rock, Hip-Hop
advance: 1-2 months
capacity: 250
pa: Yes **sound eng:** Yes
open mics: Tue
Original music room 17mi W of Sacramento, books Local-Reg'l acts for regulars & walk-in crowd. Up to 3 acts play 1hr sets. Email for booking.

Harlow's
2708 J St.
Sacramento, CA 95816
p: 916-441-4693
e: harlows@harlows.com
www.harlows.com
contact: Peter Torza
p: 916-441-4693 x11
genres: Salsa, Dance, Rock, Alt., R&B, Soul, Blues, Jazz
advance: 2-3 months
capacity: 400; 150-200
pa: Yes **sound eng:** Yes
stage: 30 x 20
Post-modern eatery w/ 21+ dancing crowd books 1-3 Local-Touring acts & DJs 5-7 nites for flat fee. Also hosts Jazz acts in upstairs Momo Lounge. Snail mail kit to venue w/ ATTN: Peter or Danny.

Luna's Cafe
1414 16th St.
Sacramento, CA 95814
p: 916-441-3931
e: artangelss1@netzero.com
www.lunascafe.com
contact: Natalie Gordon
genres: Acoustic, S/S, Jazz, Folk, Pop, Alt., Latin, Rock
advance: 2-3 months
capacity: 40
pa: Yes
stage: 6 x 8
All ages listening room showcases original music Wed, Fri, Sat & some Mon & Tue. Up to 3 acts play 45min for % of door. Prefers to book in person; call before mailing kits.

Moody's Bistro & Lounge
10007 Bridge St.
Truckee, CA 96161
p: 530-587-8688
e: talktous@moodysbistro.com
www.moodysbistro.com
contact: JJ Morgan
e: jj@moodysbistro.com
genres: Jazz
advance: 2-3 months
capacity: 75-100
Jazz bar features Local & Touring acts Wed-Sat.

Old Ironsides
1901 10th St.
Sacramento, CA 95811
p: 916-442-3504; 916-443-9751
e: ironsides@rcip.com
www.theoldironsides.com
contact: Jerry Perry
p: 916-448-2582
e: jerry@alivenkicking.com
call: Afternoons
genres: Pop, Rock, Indie, Emo, Prog, Punk, Alt. Country, Rockabilly, Jam, Funk, Electro Pop
advance: 6-8 weeks
capacity: 150
pa: Yes **sound eng:** Yes
stage: 10 x 12
open mics: Wed
Original music venue books Local-Int'l bands Thu-Sat & some Sun & Mon. 3-4 acts play 45-60min sets for % of door to 21+ hipsters. Email or mail press kit to venue w/ ATTN: Jerry Perry c/o Old Ironsides.

The Palms Playhouse
13 Main St.
Winters, CA 95694
p: 530-795-1825
e: palms@yolo.com
www.palmsplayhouse.com
contact: Dave Fleming
p: 530-795-1824
call: M-F 11am-4pm
genres: Americana, Celtic, Blues, Folk, Roots
advance: 1-3 months
capacity: 220
pa: Yes **sound eng:** Yes
stage: 20 x 15
Original 21+ music venue features mostly Nat'l acts, some Reg'ls, few Locals 2-3 nites. 1 act plays two 1hr sets. Prefers EPK, or MySpace. No unsolicited mail or calls.

Torch Club
904 15th St.
Sacramento, CA 95814
p: 916-443-2797
www.torchclub.net
contact: Marina Texeira
e: marina@torchclub.net; marinatexeira@sbcglobal.net
call: Mon, Wed & Fri:10am-noon
genres: Blues, Reggae, Funk, Americana, R&B
advance: 2-3 months
capacity: 97
pa: Yes
stage: 12 x 8
open mics: Wed 5:30pm
Blues joint popular w/ diverse music fans, showcases original Local & some Touring groups Tue-Sun. 2 acts play 2hrs each for 21+. Prefers MySpace for booking.

San Diego

4th & B
345 B St.
San Diego, CA 92101
p: 619-231-4343
e: jrforthandb@yahoo.com
www.4thandbevents.com
contact: Candace Mandracia
p: 619-525-1926
e: candace.mandracia@hobconcerts.com
call: M-F 10am-5pm
genres: Rock, Blues, Hip-Hop, Alt., Jam
advance: 2 weeks
capacity: 1500
pa: Yes **sound eng:** Yes
stage: 35 x 35
Premier 21+ concert venue now booking thru House of Blues, features original USA & Int'l talent & some Touring DJs.

710 Beach Club
710 Garnet Ave.
San Diego, CA 92109
p: 858-483-7844
www.710beachclub.com
contact: Tim Crowley
e: tim@710bc.com
call: prefers email
genres: Rock, Reggae, Hip-Hop, World Beat, Jam, Funk, Dance, Jazz
advance: 1-2 months
capacity: 230
pa: Yes **sound eng:** Yes
Formerly Blind Melon's, books Local-Int'l bands & DJs up to 7 nites. Up to 4 acts on a bill play 40-120min. Also owns (doesn't book) Winston's in San Diego. Email kit; No unsolicited mail.

Belly Up Tavern
143 S Cedros Ave., Ste. T
Solana Beach, CA 92075
p: 858-481-8140
www.bellyup.com
contact: Eric Milhouse
p: 858-481-8771
e: booking@bellyup.com
genres: Rock, Alt., Roots, Soul, Blues, Reggae, Country, Hip-Hop, Pop
advance: 2-3 months
capacity: 600
pa: Yes **sound eng:** Yes
stage: 30 x 20
Legendary club in funky setting 30min from San Diego, presents Local-Int'l acts Tue-Sun & some DJs. Shows are well-attended w/ great sound & sight lines. 2-3 acts play 30-90min. Acts keep 100% music merch sales; 80% on swag. Sister club in Aspen, CO also books music. Prefers links to music w/ bio.

Canes Bar & Grill
3105 Ocean Front Walk
San Diego, CA 92109
p: 858-488-1780
www.canesbarandgrill.com
contact: Pamela Johnsen
p: 858-488-1780 x302
call: M-F 11:30am-5:30pm
genres: Rock, Alt., Reggae, Metal, S/S
advance: 1-3 months
capacity: 900
pa: Yes **sound eng:** Yes
stage: 32 x 16
Hidden hot spot books Local & Touring acts 3 nites for 21+. 3-4 original bands play 30-90min; DJs spin monthly. Email EPK or snail mail kit w/ ATTN: Booking. Also owns McMurphy's Tavern & Sandson Grill.

The Casbah
2501 Kettner Blvd.
San Diego, CA 92101
p: 619-232-HELL
www.casbahmusic.com
contact: Tim Mays
e: tenmanbren@aol.com
call: Wed noon-2:30pm
genres: All Styles
advance: 2-3 months
capacity: 225
pa: Yes **sound eng:** Yes
stage: 12 x 20
Prime music room boasting top sound presents mostly estab. original Nat'l bands & acts w/ buzz nitely to 21+; some DJs. 3-4 acts play 40min. Prefers email; incl. contact info & tentative booking dates; allow 3-6 wks for review.

Epicentre
8450 Mira Mesa Blvd.
San Diego, CA 92126
p: 858-271-4000
e: info@epicentre.org
www.epicentreconcerts.com
contact: Jerry Figueroa
p: 858-271-4000 x21
call: M-F 2-6pm
genres: Punk, Alt., Rock, Indie
advance: 2 months
capacity: 525
pa: Yes **sound eng:** Yes
stage: 12 x 20 **in-house:** Drums
open mics: In the summer
All ages underground music

club presents Local & Nat'l acts 3-4 nites. 4-5 bands play 30min; quality recording avail. Email or mail press kit to venue or contact thru MySpace.

Humphrey's Concerts By the Bay
2241 Shelter Island Dr.
San Diego, CA 92106
p: 619-226-4033
e: concerts@humphreysconcerts.com
www.humphreysconcerts.com
contact: Mitzi Stone
e: mitzi@humphreysconcerts.com
call: M-F 10am-6pm
genres: Rock, Jazz, Blues, Folk, World
advance: 6 months
capacity: 1390
pa: Yes **sound eng:** Yes
stage: 48 x 24
Outdoor theatre presents top original acts 5-6 nites May-Oct for all ages. 1-2 acts play 90min for flat fee. Indoor lounge hosts polished Reg'ls. Merch splits 75/25. Promos: 4875 N Harbor Dr., 5th Fl., San Diego, CA 92106, but contact via email first.

Jimmy Love's
672 5th Ave.
San Diego, CA 92101
p: 619-595-0123
www.jimmyloves.com
contact: Dennis Huls
p: 619-595-0123 x1 x7
e: dennishuls@jimmyloves.com
genres: Jazz, R&B, Disco, Top 40, Blues, Swing
advance: 1 month
capacity: 600
pa: Yes **sound eng:** Yes
stage: 20 x 10
Upscale dinnerclub in hosts live music nitely. 1-2 acts play 45-60min for flat fee.

Patricks II
428 F St.
San Diego, CA 92101
p: 619-233-3077
www.patricksII.com
contact: Mario Matranga
genres: Blues, Soul, Rock
advance: 1-2 months
capacity: 85
pa: Yes
stage: 15 x 8
Original Local-Int'l acts play 50min sets nitely for flat fee in 21+ Irish pub.

Soma
3350 Sports Arena Blvd.
San Diego, CA 92110
p: 619-226-7662
e: info@somasandiego.com
www.somasandiego.com
e: booking@somasandiego.com
genres: Hardcore, Emo, Punk, Pop Punk, Rock, Gothic, Death Metal, Ska, Metal
capacity: 2300; 1200
pa: Yes **sound eng:** Yes
stage: 42 x 24 w/ drum riser
Legendary Hardcore & Punk venue w/ 2 state-of-the-art stages & 3 dressing rooms. Local & Reg'l acts who draw 80-100 on small stage may open for Nat'l acts. Large 18 & under audience. No racist tattoos/weapons/drugs/alcohol/gang clothing allowed.

Tio Leo's Lounge
5302 Napa St.
San Diego, CA 92110
p: 619-542-1462
e: info@tioleos.com
www.tioleos.com
contact: Rod
genres: Rock, Blues, Country, Rockabilly, Swing, Alt.
advance: 2 months
capacity: 200
pa: Yes **sound eng:** Yes
stage: 45 x 22
Popular Mexican eatery & music lounge features Local & Touring talent mostly Fri-Sat. Up to 3 original bands play 45min sets to 21+. Email or snail mail kit w/ ATTN: Booking.

Whiskey Girl
600 5th Ave.
San Diego, CA 92101
p: 619-236-1616
www.thewhiskeygirl.com
contact: Dave Schiffman
e: schiffmand@hotmail.com
call: M-F after 4pm
genres: Rock, Blues, Jazz, Soul, Reggae, Alt., Hip-Hop
advance: 1 month
capacity: 300
pa: Yes **sound eng:** Yes
stage: Fits 5-6 pieces
Bar books Local thru Nat'l acts 5 nites for a flat fee. Send promos ATTN: Ent. Dept.

Winstons
1921 Bacon St.
San Diego, CA 92107
p: 619-222-6822
www.winstonsob.com
contact: Teddy Wigler
p: 619-223-8609
e: ted@twigler.com
genres: All Styles
advance: 1-2 months
capacity: 300
pa: Yes **sound eng:** Yes
stage: 28 x 20
Popular speakeasy books original Reg'l & Touring bands Mon-Sat & DJs up to 7 nites for 21+. Full PA & lights spotlight up to 5 bands w/ 75 min sets. Also owns 710 Beach Club in San Diego. Prefers email, but may contact by any means; incl. CD, bio, photo, links & past shows.

San Francisco

19 Broadway
19 Broadway Ave.
Fairfax, CA 94930
p: 415-459-1091
e: nineteenbroadway@yahoo.com
www.19broadway.com
contact: Amelie Kindler
p: 415-485-0375 x2
call: Mon, Wed & Fri 12-5pm
genres: Rock, Reggae, Funk, Hip-Hop, Jazz, Blues, Roots
advance: 6-12 weeks
capacity: 250
pa: Yes **sound eng:** By Request
stage: 20 x 10 **in-house:** Drums
open mics: Mon
Prime niteclub just outside SF, books original bands nitely, some Touring DJs. Local/Reg'ls gig Mon-Thu; Touring acts on wknds. Up to 3 acts; sets run 45min. Use online form for booking. No unsolicited mail.

330 Ritch
330 Ritch St.
San Francisco, CA 94107
p: 415-902-3125; 415-541-9574
e: info@330ritch.com; popscenesf@gmail.com
www.330ritch.com; www.popscene-sf.com
contact: Scott
e: scott@330ritch.com
genres: Pop, Soul, R&B, House, Rock, Indie, Brit-Pop, New Wave, Mod, Hip-Hop
advance: 2-3 months
capacity: 300
pa: Yes **sound eng:** Yes
stage: 18 x 12
Official venue of SPIN mag, hosts varied bands & DJs. Popscene holds residency on Thu nites for 18+ w/ house DJs, some Touring bands & DJs. No unsolicited mail. Use email for Popscene booking.

924 Gilman
924 Gilman St.
Berkeley, CA 94701
p: 510-525-9926
www.924gilman.org
contact: Jay, Carlos or Pete
p: 510-524-8180
call: Tue 7-9pm
genres: Punk, Emo, Grindcore, Alt., Rock

advance: 3 months
capacity: 250
pa: Yes **sound eng:** Yes
stage: 20 x 11
Influential all ages, non-profit Punk club books Local & Touring bands Fri-Sun. 4 original acts play 30min for % of door. Solo acts booked in cafe, contact myspace.com/924gilmancommunity. No intolerant lyrics or major label acts. Send promo w/ lyrics to Alt. Music Foundation, PO Box 1058, Berkeley, CA 94701. Wait 3-4 wks to call.

Ashkenaz
1317 San Pablo Ave.
Berkeley, CA 94702
p: 510-525-5054; 510-525-5099
www.ashkenaz.com
contact: Kristen Sbrogna
p: 510-525-5099 x2
e: kristen@ashkenaz.com
call: Mon & Wed
genres: World, Roots
advance: 2-3 months
capacity: 300
pa: Yes **sound eng:** Yes
stage: 26 x 18
All ages non-profit cultural diversity ctr. presents skilled Local-Int'l talent up to 6 nites. 1-2 original acts play 60-90min for % of door.

Beach Chalet Brewery & Restaurant / The Park Chalet Garden Restaurant
1000 Great Hwy.
San Francisco, CA 94121
p: 415-386-8439
www.beachchalet.com
contact: Lara Trupelli
p: 415-753-5260
e: lara@beachchalet.com
call: Tue-Thu 9am-5pm
genres: Jazz, Blues, R&B, Surf, Instrumental, Acoustic, Light Rock, Alt.
advance: 6-8 weeks
capacity: 200
stage: 10 x 12 (floor space)
Eatery w/ a view features Local & Nat'l acts up to 5 nites. Band plays three 5hr sets w/ breaks for flat fee & food/drinks. Electronic submissions preferred. Incl. bio, gig history & avail. dates.

Bimbo's 365 Club
1025 Columbus Ave.
San Francisco, CA 94133
p: 415-474-0365
e: info@bimbos365club.com
www.bimbos365club.com
contact: Toby Suckow
call: M-F 9am-5pm
genres: Indie Rock, Jazz, Hip-Hop, Electronica
advance: 1-2 months
capacity: 685
pa: Yes **sound eng:** Yes
stage: 29 x 23
High class vintage ballroom showcases top-notch Touring acts & Local-Reg'l openers on 2 stages 4-6 nites. 2 acts play 60-90min for mostly 21+; 18+ events 1/mo. Call for booking.

Biscuits & Blues
401 Mason St.
San Francisco, CA 94102
p: 415-292-2583
e: info@biscuitsandblues.com
www.biscuitsandblues.com
contact: Steven Suen
p: 415-215-6737
e: steven@biscuitsandblues.com
call: M-F 11am-8pm
genres: Blues, R&B, Americana, Roots, Zydeco, New Orleans Jazz
advance: 2-12 months
capacity: 110
pa: Yes **sound eng:** Yes
stage: 15 x 25
Reg'l & Touring bands play in candlelit setting w/ clear sound 2-3 nites. 1 original act plays 80min for all ages. House sells merch for $1/sale or artist sells for 100%. Email & wait for reply before sending kit.

The Bistro
1001 B St.
Hayward, CA 94541
p: 510-886-8525
e: bookingagent@the-bistro.com
www.the-bistro.com
contact: Victor Krolj
e: vicbistro@the-bistro.com
call: M-F mornings
genres: Alt., Jazz, Blues, Rock, Acoustic
advance: 2-3 months
capacity: 80
pa: Yes
stage: 14 x 8 **in-house:** Piano
open mics: 3/mo **sign in:** 7pm
Café books original Reg'l & Touring bands nitely. 1-2 acts play 1hr sets for % of bar. Email for booking.

Blakes on Telegraph
2367 Telegraph Ave.
Berkeley, CA 94704
p: 510-848-0886
e: info@blakesontelegraph.com
www.blakesontelegraph.com
contact: Gary
e: kidgloveentertainment@hotmail.com
genres: Rock, Blues, Alt.
advance: 1-4 months
capacity: 220
pa: Yes **sound eng:** Yes
stage: 15 x 12
College hang known for fostering up & comers books 3-4 original Local-Int'l bands 4 nites for % of door. Acts play 45-75min to 18+. Acoustic Mon; new acts play Wed. No unsolicited mail; email first.

Boom Boom Room
1601 Fillmore St.
San Francisco, CA 94115
p: 415-673-8000
e: mail@boomboomblues.com
www.boomboomblues.com
contact: Frank
p: 415-673-8067
call: M-F after 2pm
genres: Blues, R&B, Funk, Jazz, Soul, Boogie, Electronica, House
advance: 1-6 months
capacity: 200+
pa: Yes **sound eng:** Yes
stage: 12 x 17
Funky original music showcase w/ top sound presents Nat'l headliners, acts w/ buzz & some Touring DJs Tue-Sun. 1-2 acts play 90min. Also books the Frequinox Fest., & New Orleans Jazzfest. Prefers EPK sent to alex@boomboomblues.com, but accepts snail mail.

The Bottom of Hill
1233 17th St.
San Francisco, CA 94107
p: 415-621-4455
e: email@bottomofthehill.com
www.bottomofthehill.com
contact: Ursula Rodriguez
e: booking@bottomofthehill.com
genres: Rock, Alt., Punk
advance: 8 weeks
capacity: 325
pa: Yes **sound eng:** Yes
stage: 10 x 15
Fully-equipped club presents top Local-Int'l acts 6-7 nites to 21+; some all ages shows. New acts w/ buzz fill 2 opening slots & play 40min, headliner plays 60. Prefers online submissions; No unsolicited mail.

Brain Wash Cafe
1122 Folsom St.
San Francisco, CA 94103
p: 415-255-4866
e: contact@brainwash.com
www.brainwash.com
contact: Jeff
p: 415-861-3663
e: booking@brainwash.com
genres: Alt., Jazz, Rock, Blues, Folk
advance: 5 months
capacity: 100
pa: Yes
stage: small
open mics: Tue **sign in:** 7pm
All ages cafe & laundromat presents Local-Int'l acts w/ following Tue & Fri-Sun. 3 original bands play 1hr sets. Prefers EPKs.

Broadway Studios
435 Broadway
San Francisco, CA 94133
p: 415-291-0333
e: info@broadwaystudios.com
www.broadwaystudios.com
contact: Francesca Valdez
e: booking@broadwaystudios.com
call: Tue-Fri
genres: House, Techno, R&B, Swing, Blues, Jazz, Soul, Rock
advance: 6-8 weeks
capacity: 365
pa: Yes **sound eng:** Yes
stage: 30 x 20 **in-house:** Piano
open mics: Wed **sign in:** Call
State-of-the-art ent. complex w/ dance floor books Local-Int'l bands & DJs for all ages shows up to 3 nites. Up to 3 acts play 60min for flat fee or % of door.

Café Du Nord
2170 Market St.
San Francisco, CA 94114
p: 415-861-5016
www.cafedunord.com
contact: Guy Carson
call: M-F 10am-5pm
genres: Rock, Electronic, Indie, Acoustic
advance: 2 weeks - 4 mo
capacity: 250
pa: Yes **sound eng:** Yes
stage: 17 x 11
Former speakeasy, now 21+ celebrated showcase, presents 2-4 original Local-Int'l acts & DJs nitely. Local openers get 30min sets; Touring up to 2hrs. Some all ages shows. Can rent Swedish American Hall above club for Acoustic shows. Use online booking form. No unsolicited mail.

DNA Lounge
375 11th St.
San Francisco, CA 94103
p: 415-626-1409
e: manager@dnalounge.com
www.dnalounge.com
contact: Gene Maze
p: 415-626-2654
e: booking@dnalounge.com; gene@dnalounge.com
call: daytime
genres: Most Styles
advance: 3 months
capacity: 700
pa: Yes **sound eng:** Yes
stage: 20 x 18
Hi-tech 21+ club boasts excellent sound & viewpoints. Shows incl. everything from live Local & Touring bands & DJs to plays & burlesque. 3-4 acts play 30-90min during the wk for flat fee or backend; Promoter parties on wknds. No Country or Classical. Prefers email for booking.

Edinburgh Castle Pub
950 Geary St.
San Francisco, CA 94109
p: 415-885-4074
www.castlenews.com
contact: Marcella Gries
e: marcellagries@gmail.com
genres: Indie, Math Rock, Noise, Experimental, Electronic
advance: 1-3 months
capacity: 100
pa: Yes **sound eng:** Yes
Original Local & Touring acts & DJs w/ SF following booked up to 4 nites. Up to 3 acts play 40min sets. Email or drop off submissions only.

El Rio
3158 Mission St.
San Francisco, CA 94110
p: 415-282-3325
e: elriosf@mindspring.com
www.elriosf.com
genres: Rock, Punk, Country, Acoustic, Salsa, World, Alt., Hip-Hop, R&B
advance: 1-12 months
capacity: 98
pa: Yes **sound eng:** Yes
Bay Area bands play 21+ neighborhood bar w/ flair up to 4-5 nites for % of door. 2-4 original acts play 30-45min sets. Booking done thru website.

Elbo Room
647 Valencia St.
San Francisco, CA 94110
p: 415-552-7788
www.elbo.com
contact: Matt Shapiro
e: mattshapiro@mac.com; matt@elbo.com
call: M-F afternoons
genres: Rock, Garage, Punk, Rockabilly, Soul, Hip-Hop, Metal, World, Reggae, Indie, Dance
advance: 2-3 months
capacity: 325
pa: Yes **sound eng:** Yes
stage: 20 x 17
Elegant room draws hip crowd 6-7 nites for original Local & Touring bands & DJs. Up to 4 acts play 30-90min for 21+. Email or mail press kit to venue.

The Fillmore
1805 Geary Blvd.

San Francisco, CA
94115
p: 415-346-6000
www.thefillmore.com
contact: Michael Bailey
p: 415-371-5525
e: booking@bgp.com
genres: All Styles
advance: 3 months
capacity: 1150
pa: Yes **sound eng:** Yes
stage: 32 x 20
Legendary all ages venue presents top Touring & emerging talent nitely. Up to 3 original acts play 45-60min sets for flat fee & 70% merch. Also books Warfield Theatre. Call or email for booking.

Freight & Salvage Coffee House

1111 Addison St.
Berkeley, CA 94702
p: 510-548-1761
e: info@freightandsalvage.org
www.freightandsalvage.org
e: folk@freightandsalvage.org
call: Mon-Sat noon-6pm
genres: Americana, Celtic, World, Jazz, S/S, Folk, Blues, Bluegrass, Rockabilly, Cajun
advance: 3-6 months
capacity: 238
pa: Yes **sound eng:** Yes
stage: 30 x 10
open mics: Tue
Premier non-profit listening room showcases Local-Int'l Traditional music 5-7 nites for all ages. Featured act plays two 45min sets for % of door. Email for booking, No unsolicited mail.

Grant & Green

1371 Grant Ave.
San Francisco, CA 94133
p: 415-693-9565
www.myspace.com/grantandgreensf
contact: Scott Rootenberg
e: scottbooksbands@yahoo.com
genres: Alt., Rock, Blues, Reggae, Ska
advance: 1 day - 2 months
capacity: 100
pa: Yes
stage: 10 x 14
Pub books Local-Int'l acts 4 nites for 21+. Up to 3 acts play mostly original tunes w/ 40-60min sets for a flat fee. Email w/ band name & 'booking' in subject.

Great American Music Hall

859 O'Farrell St.
San Francisco, CA 94109
p: 415-885-0750
e: info@gamh.com
www.musichallsf.com
contact: Dana Kamian
p: 415-255-0333
e: dana@slims-sf.com
call: M-F 10am-6pm
genres: Rock, Experimental, S/S, Funk, Rap
advance: 4-6 weeks
capacity: 500
pa: Yes **sound eng:** Yes
stage: 20 x 10
City's oldest niteclub hosts 2 Local-Int'l acts & DJs 2-7 nites for all ages. Headliner plays 90min & opener plays 45min usu. for flat fee. Also books Slim's & is avail. to rent.

The Hotel Utah

500 4th St.
San Francisco, CA
94107
p: 415-546-6300
www.thehotelutahsaloon.com
contact: Keith
e: keith@hotelutah.com
call: M-F 10am-4pm
genres: All Styles
advance: 2-3 months
capacity: 150
pa: Yes **sound eng:** Yes
stage: 9 x 19 **in-house:** Piano
Popular 21+ room books original Local-Int'l acts for % of door. 3-4 acts play 30-45min sets nitely; some 18+ shows. Email thru site for booking & incl. link to music, bio & recent tour or show history; No attachments or unsolicited mail.

Jupiter

2181 Shattuck Ave.
Berkeley, CA 94704
p: 510-843-8277
www.jupiterbeer.com
contact: Alain Grissette
e: jupiterbands@hotmail.com
genres: Jazz, Brazilian, S/S, Afro-Cuban Soul
advance: 1-2 months
capacity: 150
pa: Yes **sound eng:** Yes
stage: floor space
Popular beerhouse books original Local-Int'l acts Tue-Sun (summer) & Tue-Sat (winter) for flat fee & food. Single act fills 3hrs.

The Last Day Saloon

120 5th St.
Santa Rosa, CA
95401
p: 707-545-5876
www.lastdaysaloon.com
contact: Dave Daher
e: daher1@pacbell.net; davedaher@hotmail.com
call: M-F 11am-4pm
genres: Rock, Blues, R&B, Americana, Jam, Latin, Reggae
advance: 2-4 months
capacity: 600
pa: Yes **sound eng:** Yes
Newly-renovated 21+ niteclub 55mi N of SF, has state-of-the-art sound system & hosts original Local-Int'l acts Tue-Sat for flat fee & % of door. Local & Touring acts must draw 100 on wkdys & 300 on wknds. Locals must also submit list of past area gigs. Email mp3s or music link or snail mail.

Lou's Pier 47

300 Jefferson St.
Fisherman's Wharf
San Francisco, CA 94133
p: 415-771-LOUS
e: louspier47@yahoo.com
www.louspier47.com
contact: Garrett Meyers
p: 415-771-LOUS x5
call: 1st Tue/mo 10am-12pm
genres: Blues
advance: 3 months
capacity: 150
pa: Yes
stage: 8 x 10
Supperclub presents top Local talent & some Touring acts nitely. 2 acts play 4hrs w/ breaks for flat fee; 3 acts on Sat. 65+ bands/mo. 21+ after 8pm. Mail press kit to venue w/ ATTN: Booking. Incl. photo, bio & contact info.

McNear's Mystic Theatre

23 Petaluma Blvd. N
Petaluma, CA 94952
p: 707-765-2121
e: info@mystictheatre.com
www.mystictheatre.com
contact: Sheila Groves
p: 800-853-6683
e: notablet@aol.com
genres: S/S, Folk, Jazz, Rock, Pop, Jam
capacity: 550 **stage:** 30 x 20
Located 39mi N of SF & lauded as the area's premier music venue. 1-4 Reg'l-Int'l buzz bands perform up to 7 nites. Email or call before mailing.

Oakland Metro

630 3rd St.
Oakland, CA 94607
p: 510-763-1146
e: oaklandopera@yahoo.com
www.oaklandmetro.org
contact: Tom Dean
e: tom@oaklandopera.org
genres: Indie Rock, Pop, Emo, Jazz, Experimental
advance: 6-18 weeks
capacity: 600+
pa: Yes **sound eng:** Yes
stage: 16 x 12
Artist-run, non-profit black box theater books original Local-Int'l bands 3 nites. Up to 3 acts play 60-90min for all ages. Promos: 1734 Campbell St., Oakland CA 94607.

Peri's Silver Dollar

29 Broadway Blvd.
Fairfax, CA 94930
p: 415-459-9910
www.home.earthlink.net/~mikebtl
contact: Mike
p: 415-721-4086
e: perisbooking@earthlink.net
call: prefers email
genres: Rock, Blues, Country, Alt., Americana, Rockabilly
advance: 1-3 months
capacity: 150
pa: Yes
stage: 10 x 20
open mics: Mon **sign in:** 9pm
Mostly Local & some Touring bands play cool pub w/ large heated patio. Up to 3 acts play 1hr sets for % of bar wknites, % of bar & door wknds. Prefers email.

Pier 23 Cafe

Pier 23 on the Embarcadero
San Francisco, CA 94111
p: 415-362-5125
e: mac@pier23cafe.com
www.pier23cafe.com
contact: Ben Thompson
e: booking@pier23cafe.com
genres: Jazz, Salsa, R&B, Reggae, New Orleans Jazz
advance: 2 months
capacity: 250
Eatery presents Local-Int'l acts nitely for 21+ dancing crowds. Cover bands Sun & Touring DJs 2-3/wk. 1 act fill 3.5hrs.

The Plough & Stars
116 Clement St.
San Francisco, CA 94118
p: 415-751-1122
e: sfplough@aol.com
www.theploughandstars.com
contact: Séan Heaney
genres: Irish, Folk, Bluegrass, Rockabilly
advance: 2-3 months
capacity: 100
pa: Yes **sound eng:** Avail.
Top Irish pub presents original Local-Int'l bands 6 nites. Up to 3 acts play 45min sets for 21+. EPKs preferred.

Red Devil Lounge
1695 Polk St.
San Francisco, CA 94109
p: 415-921-1695
www.reddevillounge.com
contact: Sean Burke
p: 415-447-4730
e: booking@jaysieganpresents.com
call: M-F 10am-6pm
genres: Alt., Pop, Indie, Gothic, World, Urban, Funk, Soul, Punk
advance: 1-3 months
capacity: 290
pa: Yes **sound eng:** Yes
stage: 15 x 14 **in-house:** Piano
Musician-run club books Local & Touring talent Wed-Sat for 21+. 1-4 acts play 45min sets for % of door. Also promotes & books all around SF area. Promos: Jay Siegan Presents, ATTN: Sean Burke, 1655 Polk St., Ste. 1, San Francisco, CA 94109.

Slim's
333 11th St.
San Francisco, CA 94103
p: 415-255-0333
e: slims@slims-sf.com
www.slims-sf.com
contact: Dana Kamian
call: M-F 10:30am-6pm
genres: All Styles
advance: 1+ months
capacity: 430
pa: Yes **sound eng:** Yes
stage: 25 x 15 **in-house:** Some
Sister club to Great American Music Hall & celebrated all ages room w/ super sight lines, books Local-Int'l talent & DJs nitely; 2-3 acts play 30-90min. Merch split is 80/20 for soft, 100% for hard. Snail mail kits.

The Starry Plough
3101 Shattuck Ave.
Berkeley, CA 94705
p: 510-841-2082; 510-841-0188
www.starryploughpub.com
contact: Matt "Smitty" Smith
p: 510-841-1424
e: starryploughbooking@yahoo.com
genres: Rock, Traditional Irish, Country, Americana, Roots, Folk, Indie Pop
advance: 2-3 months
capacity: 200
pa: Yes **sound eng:** Yes
open mics: Tue
Popular 21+ Irish pub presents original & trad. Local-Touring acts that can & fill the dance floor Thu-Sat. 2-3 acts play 45-60min. Prefers EPK or email, but may mail kit: Incl. genre, venues played, when last played, draw of last show, expected draw & links; allow 6 wks before/after gig; promoters approach w/ full bill; No booking via MySpace.

Stork Club
2330 Telegraph Ave.
Oakland, CA 94612
p: 510-444-6174
e: storkcluboakland@yahoo.com
www.storkcluboakland.com
contact: Joann Rawkmom
genres: Punk, Rock, Country, Experimental, Electronic, Pop
advance: 2 months
capacity: 300
pa: Yes **sound eng:** Yes
stage: 10 x 17
Frequented Punk dive features mostly Local & some Touring Bands & DJs 5-6 nites. 3-4 original acts generally split the door. Bands play 30-45min & members must be 21+. Email or mail press kit to venue. Increase chances of being booked by first putting together your own bill.

Sweetwater Saloon
32 Miller Ave.
Mill Valley, CA 94941
p: 415-388-2820
e: booking@sweetwatersaloon.com
www.sweetwatersaloon.com
contact: Becky Steere
p: 415-388-7769
e: becky@sweetwatersaloon.com
call: M-F 9am-5pm
genres: R&B, Blues, Folk, Jazz, Rock, Roots, Bluegrass
advance: 4-6 weeks
capacity: 220
pa: Yes **sound eng:** Yes
stage: 14 x 16
open mics: Mon
Legendary music room recently moved down the street but still just 14mi N of San Francisco. 1-2 original acts play 1hr nitely for % of door. Recording of set avail. Other location near by in Larkspur, CA. Prefers email or EPK, but contact by any means; incl. draw & venues played; wait 4-6 wks for response.

Thee Parkside
1600 17th St.
San Francisco, CA 94107
p: 415-252-1330
www.theeparkside.com
contact: Audra Morse
p: 415-824-9054
e: dinoandluigi@gmail.com
call: M-F noon-6pm
genres: Garage Rock, Punk, Rockabilly, Rock, Indie, Metal, Pop-Punk, Hardcore, Electro
advance: 1-3 months
capacity: 250
pa: Yes **sound eng:** Yes
stage: 30 x 15
Fun club books mostly original Local-Int'l acts nitely. Hosts 21+ & all ages shows incl. Sun matinees. 3-5 acts play 30+min. Prefers EPKs.

Uptown Nightclub
1928 Telegraph Ave.
Oakland, CA 94612
p: 510-451-8100
www.uptownnightclub.com
contact: Larry
e: gm@uptownnightclub.com
call: no calls
genres: Rock, Metal, Indie, Country, Jazz, Electronic
advance: 8 weeks
capacity: 250
pa: Yes **sound eng:** Yes
stage: 15 x 20
Room adjoining hip bar hosts 3 original Local-Int'l bands 4 nites for 21+. Prefers emailed links to music, but may mail kit or use MySpace. No Calls.

Yoshi's Oakland
510 Embarcadero W
Oakland, CA 94607
p: 510-238-4205
e: info@yoshis.com
www.yoshis.com
contact: Peter Williams
p: 510-238-4555
e: peter@yoshis.com
call: M-F 9am-5pm
genres: Jazz, Blues, Latin, World, Alt. Pop, Americana
advance: 6 months
capacity: 310
pa: Yes **sound eng:** Yes
stage: 20 x 20
Prime all ages showcase boasts great acoustics & sight lines. Top Reg'l & Touring bands gig nitely. Featured original act plays 70min; merch splits 85/15. Mail basic kits.

San Jose/Santa Cruz

The Agenda Lounge
399 S 1st St.
San Jose, CA 95113
p: 408-287-3991
e: info@agendalounge.com
www.agendalounge.com
contact: Mondo Millan
p: 408-327-9571
genres: Jazz, Roots, Funk, R&B, Salsa, Hip-Hop, Reggae, Dance
advance: 1 month
capacity: 250
pa: Yes **sound eng:** Yes
stage: 15 x 30; 20 x 30
Area's premier 21+ dance hall & Jazz lounge presents 1-2 acts & Touring DJs Fri & Sat. Sets are 75-120min w/ break. Promos: PO Box 2410, San Jose, CA 95109.

The Catalyst
1011 Pacific Ave.
Santa Cruz, CA 95060
p: 831-425-7799
e: thomas@catalystclub.com
www.catalystclub.com
contact: Gary Tighe
call: M-F 11am-2pm
genres: Rock, Reggae, Punk, Hip-Hop, Alt., World, Beat
advance: 2-6 months
capacity: 800
pa: Yes **sound eng:** Yes
stage: 28 x 18
Prime all ages club features top Local-Int'l artists nitely. 3 acts & DJs play 45-60min for flat fee. Promos: PO Box 8545, Santa Cruz, CA 95061.

J.J.'s Blues Club
3439 Stevens Creek Blvd.
San Jose, CA 95117
p: 408-243-6441
www.jjsblues.net
contact: Johnnie Perkins
p: 408-391-1477
e: jomipe@aol.com
genres: Blues, Jazz, R&B
advance: 3-4 months
capacity: 109
pa: Yes **sound eng:** Yes
stage: 12 x 15 **in-house:** Drums
open mics: Mon 7pm
Cozy 21+ listening room showcases primarily Reg'l & Nat'l artists on the Blues circuit nitely. 2 acts play from 7 or 9pm-close for % of register. Snail mail or email kits.

Kuumbwa Jazz Center
320-2 Cedar St.
Santa Cruz, CA 95060
p: 831-427-2227
e: kuumbwa@kuumbwajazz.org
www.kuumbwajazz.org
contact: Tim Jackson
e: tim@montereyjazzfestival.org
call: M-F 9am-5pm
genres: Jazz, Experimental, World, Folk
advance: 2-12 months
capacity: 200
pa: Yes **sound eng:** Yes
stage: 8 x 10
Refined non-profit listening room showcases legends & polished newcomers up to 4 nites. Featured act plays 75min or two 1hr sets of original material for all ages. Acts get flat fee vs % of door. Mail kit.

Moe's Alley
1535 Commercial Way
Santa Cruz, CA 95065
p: 831-479-1854
e: booking@moesalley.com
www.moesalley.com
contact: Bill Welch
p: 831-426-8435
e: bill@moesalley.com
call: Tue-Thu 10am-6pm
genres: Blues, Americana, Jam, World, Swing
advance: 6-8 weeks
capacity: 250
pa: Yes **sound eng:** Yes
stage: 13 x 20
Premier room w/ full prod. showcases top Reg'l & Touring talent for 21+. 1-2 original acts play 75min sets 5-7 nites. Mail promos w/ ATTN: Bill Welch, PO Box 3601, Santa Cruz, CA 95063. No mp3s.

The Mountain Winery
14831 Pierce Rd.
Saratoga, CA 95070
p: 408-741-2822
www.mountainwinery.com
contact: Jodi Goodman
p: 415-371-5500
e: jodigoodman@livenation.com
genres: Rock, Country, Folk, Blues, Soul, Oldies
advance: 9-12 months
capacity: 2236
pa: Yes **sound eng:** Yes
stage: large
Winery just W of San Jose, presents Local openers & Touring talent May-Oct for all ages until 10:30pm. Booking thru Live Nation. Call or email first before mailing kit w/ ATTN: Jodi Goodman, 260 5th St., San Francisco, CA 94103.

Santa Barbara

Majestic Ventura Theater
26 S Chestnut St.
Ventura, CA 93001
p: 805-653-0721
www.venturatheater.net
contact: Loanne Wullaert
e: loannew@aol.com
call: Mon-Sat 11am-5:30pm
genres: Punk, Alt., Reggae, S/S, Metal, Blues, Jazz, World,

Hip-Hop
advance: 1+ months
capacity: 1200
pa: Yes **sound eng:** Yes
stage: 40 x 30
Restored theatre w/ cool vibe located btwn Santa Barbara & L.A., hosts Touring pros & some Reg'ls for all ages shows. 2-6 acts play 30-90min 2-7 nites. Merch splits 80/20. Popular stop btwn L.A. & San Francisco. Email or mail kit.

SOhO Restaurant & Music Club
1221 State St., Ste. 205
Santa Barbara, CA 93101
p: 805-962-7776
www.sohosb.com
contact: Gail Hansen
p: 805-899-2176
e: gigs@sohosb.com
genres: World, Blues, Funk, Rock, Country, Jazz, Acoustic
advance: 2 months
capacity: 300
pa: Yes **sound eng:** Yes
stage: 20 x 8 **in-house:** Piano
Classy room books mostly original Local-Int'l bands nitely for 21+; some all ages shows. Up to 3 acts play 3hrs. Also hosts special Jazz, World & Acoustic nites. Call or email first before mailing promos w/ show history to venue; will respond if interested. No unsolicited mail.

Velvet Jones
423 State St.
Santa Barbara, CA 93101
p: 805-965-8676
e: velvet@velvet-jones.com
www.velvet-jones.com
contact: Craig Jenkins
call: M-F after 1pm
genres: Punk, Reggae, Hard Rock
advance: 1-2 months
capacity: 299
pa: Yes **sound eng:** Yes
stage: 14 x 17
21+ live music venue & dance club books Local-Nat'l acts Tue-Sat. Up to 5 bands play 40min for % of door. Must be able to sell 50 tix for wkdy & 75 for wknd slot. Email w/ link to music.

Colorado

Aspen

Belly Up Aspen
450 S Galena St.
Aspen, CO 81611
p: 970-544-9800
e: info@bellyupaspen.com
www.bellyupaspen.com
contact: Erik Newson
p: 970-544-8089
e: booking@bellyupaspen.com
call: M-F 10am-6pm
genres: All Styles
capacity: 450
pa: Yes **sound eng:** Yes
Accessories, Drums, Keyboards
Notable all ages concert venue in ski resort area hosts mostly major acts & DJs up to 7 nites/wk. Email for booking.

Boulder

The b.side Lounge
2017 13th St.
Boulder, CO 80302
p: 303-473-9463
e: bside@thebsidelounge.com
www.thebsidelounge.com
contact: Molly
e: molly@thebsidelounge.com
genres: Jazz, Rock, Electronic
advance: 2-3 months
capacity: 200
pa: Yes **sound eng:** Yes
Inviting new lounge offers original Local-Int'l acts in back room & DJs in front room Wed-Sun for 21+ college scene. Prefers emailed link to music; No unsolicited mail or calls.

Boulder Theater
2032 14th St.
Boulder, CO 80302
p: 303-786-7030
www.bouldertheater.com
contact: Kirk Peterson
p: 303-998-9422
e: kpeterson@bouldertheater.com
call: M-F 10am-6pm
genres: Jazz, Americana, World, Folk, Bluegrass, Rock
advance: 3-6 months
capacity: 1000
pa: Yes **sound eng:** Yes
stage: 42 x 28
Movie theater venue books Reg'l-Int'l acts 5-6 nites. Up to 4 acts play 70min for flat fee vs door & 80% merch. Monthly Jazz series unites rising & estab. artists. Many all ages shows.

Chautauqua Aud.
900 Baseline Rd.
Boulder, CO 80302
p: 303-440-7666
e: info@chautauqua.com
www.chautauqua.com
contact: Julie Pomerantz
p: 303-442-3282 x632
e: julie@chautauqua.com
call: Tue 10am-12pm
genres: World, Folk, Jazz, S/S, Acoustic
advance: 6 months
capacity: 1300
pa: Yes **sound eng:** Yes
stage: 70 x 35 **in-house:** Piano
Historic all ages venue books original Reg'l-Int'l acoustic acts. Opener plays 30-45min headliner plays 90min for flat fee. Summer series booked by Nobody in Particular Presents.

Conor O'Neill's
1922 13th St.
Boulder, CO 80302
p: 303-449-1922
www.conoroneills.com
contact: Bridget Fisher
e: bridget@conoroneills.com
genres: All Styles
advance: 2-3 months
capacity: 250 **stage:** small
open mics: Tue 8pm **sign in:** 7pm
Irish pub books Local & Reg'l acts Wed-Sat. Bands play from 10pm-1am to 21+ crowd for flat fee. Email or mail kit. No calls.

Fox Theatre
1135 13th St.
Boulder, CO 80302
p: 303-447-0095
www.foxtheatre.com
contact: Sarah Finger
p: 303-447-0095 x20
e: sfinger@foxtheatre.com
call: M-F 10am-6pm
genres: Rock, Bluegrass, Reggae, Punk
advance: 4-6 weeks
capacity: 625
pa: Yes **sound eng:** Yes
stage: 18 x 24
Former cinema w/ good sound books 2-5 original Reg'l-Int'l acts up to 7 nites for 30-90min sets; merch splits 85/15. Some all ages shows. Email for booking; No unsolicited mail.

Oskar Blues
303 Main St.
Lyons, CO 80540
p: 303-823-6685
e: info@oskarblues.com
www.oskarblues.com
contact: Dave McIntyre
p: 303-746-0915
e: dave@oskarblues.com
genres: Blues, Rock, Bluegrass, Folk, Jam, Americana, Country
capacity: 100
Basement music room features 1-2 original, Local-Nat'l acts mostly Sat-Sun & some Thu-Sat for 21+ crowd.

Wildflower Pavilion
500 W Main St.
Lyons, CO 80540
p: 303-823-0848
www.wildflowerpavilion.com
contact: Craig Ferguson
p: 800-624-2422 x101
e: planet@bluegrass.com
genres: S/S, Folk, Bluegrass, Acoustic, Rock
advance: 1-2 months
capacity: 300
pa: Yes **sound eng:** Yes
stage: medium
Up to 2 original Local-Int'l bands play 90min sets for 90% merch & a flat fee. Headliner gets guarantee plus % of door. Use EPK or snail mail.

Denver

Aztlan Theater
974 Santa Fe Dr.
Denver, CO 80204
p: 303-573-0188
contact: Tim Correa
call: M-F 12-6pm
genres: Alt., Hard Rock, Ska, Goth
advance: 1-2 months
capacity: 1000
pa: Yes **sound eng:** Yes
stage: 30 x 45 **in-house:** Avail
Hall for rent w/ large stage & projection screen hosts top Local-Nat'l bands for all ages Fri & Sat. Up to 5 acts play 45+min sets. Prefers fax or call.

Bluebird Theater
3317 E Colfax Ave.
Denver, CO 80206
p: 303-377-1666
www.bluebirdtheater.net
contact: Scott Campbell
p: 720-931-8708
genres: Rock, Alt., Country, Blues, Punk, Metal, Indie
advance: 1-3 months
capacity: 500
pa: Yes **sound eng:** Yes
Prime music venue features 1-5 Touring & some Reg'l acts play 30-120min up to 7 nites. Some all ages shows & Touring DJs. Now booking thru AEG Live. Also books Ogden Theatre. Accepts EPKs or mail promos: 930 W 7th Ave., Denver, CO 80204.

Cervante's Masterpiece Ballroom
2637 Welton St.
Denver, CO 80205
p: 303-297-1772
www.cervantesmasterpiece.com
contact: Jay Bianchi
e: jbird@quixotes.com
genres: Jam, Hip-Hop, Reggae, Indie Rock
advance: 1 week - 3 months
capacity: 700
pa: Yes **sound eng:** Yes
Hot multi-level music club hosts wide variety of music for 18+ crowd 5+ nites/mo. 2-3 acts play 90+min sets & take 80% of merch sales. Snail mail or email kits.

Climax Lounge
2217 Welton St.
Denver, CO 80201
p: 303-292-5483
www.climaxlounge2217welton.com
contact: Christian
e: climaxlounge2217@yahoo.com
genres: Ska, Psychobilly, Punk, Rock
advance: 3 weeks
capacity: 280
pa: Yes **sound eng:** Yes
stage: small
All ages haven for mostly Local-Reg'l acts & DJs; some Nat'l's. 5-6 bands play 45min 1-2 nites. Email or mail kit.

Gothic Theatre
3263 S Broadway
Englewood, CO 80113
p: 303-788-0984
e: info@gothictheatre.com
www.gothictheatre.com
contact: Steve Schalk
e: steve@gothictheatre.com
call: M-F 10am-5pm
genres: Rock, Punk, Metal, Hardcore, Jam, Alt. Country
advance: 2 months
capacity: 999
pa: Yes **sound eng:** Yes
stage: 25 x 18
16+ club not too far from U of Denver, books original Local-Int'l bands 3-4 nites in remodeled '20s movie palace. 3-4 acts play 30-120min sets. No longer associated w/ NIPP.

Herb's
2057 Larimer St.
Denver, CO 80205
p: 303-299-9555
www.herbsbar.com
contact: Laura Newman
genres: Jazz, Blues, Funk, Rock, Hip-Hop
advance: 3+ months
capacity: 120
pa: Yes **sound eng:** Yes
Local-centric room has open booking Fri & Sat; live Hip-Hop Sun. Featured act plays to 21+ after 10:30pm.

Herman's Hideaway
1578 S Broadway
Denver, CO 80210
p: 303-777-5840
www.hermanshideaway.com
contact: M.P.
p: 303-777-2535
e: booking@hermanshideaway.com
call: M-F afternoons

genres: Rock, Pop, Alt., Rockabilly, Reggae
advance: 6-12 weeks
capacity: 500
pa: Yes sound eng: Yes
stage: 35 x 15
Large listening room presents mostly Local groups Wed-Sat. 2-4 acts play 45-90min sets. Books bands from Wed 'New Talent Showcase.' Use online booking form, email or mail press kit to venue w/ ATTN: Mike Roth.

Lincoln's Roadhouse
1201 S Pearl St.
Denver, CO 80210
p: 303-777-3700
www.lincolnsroadhouse.com
contact: Jim Bob Housley
e: jimbob80210@yahoo.com
call: Wed
genres: Blues, Rockabilly, S/S, Rock, Country, Cajun, Jam
advance: 3-4 months
capacity: 150 stage: 10 x 10
Frequented by bikers, this 21+ tour stop features Local-Nat'l acts Thu-Sun. 1-2 acts fill 9pm-1am w/ breaks for flat fee. No Heavy Metal. Prefers mailed hard copies.

Lion's Lair
2022 E Colfax Ave.
Denver, CO 80206
p: 303-320-9200
e: info-co@nipp.com
www.nipp.com
contact: Matthew
e: booking@nipp.com
call: Mon & Wed 2-8pm
genres: Country, Punk, Alt., Rock, Metal, Industrial
advance: 2-4 months
capacity: 130
pa: Yes sound eng: Yes
stage: 20 x 25 (wedge)
open mics: Tue 8pm-close
Mainstay of Punk culture, this 21+ dive bar presents Local & Touring bands 4-5 nites. Up to 3 acts play original 30-60min sets for % of door. Mail promos to: NIPP, 1633 York St., Denver, CO 80206.

Little Bear Saloon
28075 Main St.
Evergreen, CO 80439
p: 303-674-9991
e: littlebearsaloon@yahoo.com
www.littlebearsaloon.com
contact: Cody Swanson
genres: Most Styles
advance: 2-3 months
capacity: 375
pa: Yes sound eng: Yes
stage: 12 x 18
Formerly a church, now a wild, rustic, but intimate 21+ mountain bar hosting Local-Nat'l acts Tue-Sun; some Mon gigs; some days w/ multiple shows. Sat & Sun all ages shows during the day til 7pm. 1-3 acts fill 3hrs. No Heavy Metal. Mail kit to: PO Box 1366, Evergreen, CO 80437.

Mercury Cafe
2199 California St.
Denver, CO 80205
p: 303-294-9281
www.mercurycafe.com
contact: Marilyn Megenity
p: 303-294-9240
e: marilyn@mercurycafe.com
call: Mon & Thu after 2pm
genres: Jazz, Swing, Tango, Irish, Cajun, Folk, Soloists - No Loud Acts
advance: 1-6 months
capacity: 400; 100; 100
pa: Yes sound eng: Yes
stage: large
open mics: Wed sign in: By 8pm
Dance hall w/ several performance spaces books 3 mostly original Local-Int'l acts for all ages. Call first.

Ogden Theater
935 E Colfax Ave.
Denver, CO 80206
p: 720-224-9200
www.ogdentheater.net
contact: Don Strafburg
genres: All Styles
advance: 6 weeks
capacity: 1600
pa: Yes sound eng: Yes
Historic venue books top Reg'l-Int'l acts & some Locals 4 nites for 16+ crowd unless noted. 2-5 original acts play 30-120min for flat fee & 80% merch. Also books Bluebird Theater & Larimer Lounge. Prefers email, but may mail press kit to venue or call. No booking thru MySpace.

Oriental Theatre
4335 W 44th Ave.
Denver, CO 80212
p: 303-455-2124
e: info@theorientaltheater.com
www.theorientaltheater.com
contact: Jay Bianchi
e: jbird@quixotes.com
genres: All Styles
advance: 1+ months
capacity: 738
pa: Yes sound eng: Yes
Books eclectic Local & Touring acts w/ draw for 21+ crowd. Prefers Sonicbids EPK.

Shag
610 Main St.
Frisco, CO 80443
p: 970-668-9930
e: shaginfriscocolorado@gmail.com
contact: Clint Jester
genres: All Styles
advance: 2 weeks
capacity: 300
stage: floor space
Formerly Chill & now under new ownership, books 1-2 Local-Int'l acts. Will be making upgrades to venue soon. Mail press kit to: PO Box 5235, Frisco, CO 80443 or email.

Snake Pit
608 E 13th Ave.
Denver, CO 80203
p: 303-831-9788
e: denverpit@yahoo.com
www.myspace.com/snakepitdenver
contact: Ethan Rubin
call: M-F after 6pm
genres: All Styles
advance: 3-4 weeks
capacity: 225 stage: 30 x 12
1-2 original Reg'l acts play 1hr sets & Touring DJs spin nitely for 21+. Will sometimes book live Electronic acts. Prefers email or mailed kit to venue w/ ATTN: Travis, Josh or Ethan.

The Soiled Dove Underground
7401 E 1st Ave.
Denver, CO 80230
p: 303-830-9214
e: booking@soileddove.com
www.soileddove.com
contact: Rhett Lee
p: 303-226-1555 x117
e: rhett@soileddove.com
call: M-F 9am-5pm
genres: Rock, Jazz, Blues, Country, Acoustic
advance: 1-4 months
capacity: 350
pa: Yes sound eng: Yes
stage: 17 x 23
Original 18+ music room w/ tiered seating & a half-round stage features Local-Int'l bands 2-3 nites; some all ages shows. 1-2 original acts play 75-120min sets & keep 90% merch. Send EPKs or mail kit to: Soiled Dove Booking, 538 E 17th Ave., Denver, CO 80203.

Swallow Hill Music Association
71 E Yale Ave.
Denver, CO 80210
p: 303-777-1003
e: info@swallowhillmusic.org
www.swallowhillmusic.org
p: 303-777-4415
genres: Americana, Acoustic, Celtic, Folk, Blues, Bluegrass
advance: 3-6 months
capacity: 300; 95; 50 (café)
pa: Yes sound eng: Yes
open mics: 2nd Wed of mo
Folk music assoc. hosts Reg'l-Int'l talent on 2 stages 2-5 nites from Thu-Sat & some Sun. 1-2 original acts play 30-85min sets for all ages.

Three20South
320 S Main St.
Breckenridge, CO 80424
p: 970-547-5320
e: info@three20south.com
www.three20south.com
call: prefers email
genres: All Styles
advance: Up to 1 year
capacity: 350
pa: Yes sound eng: Yes
stage: 22 x 14
Formerly Sherpa & Yeti's, now new owners have vowed to create the best live music venue in the region w/ top notch Local-Int'l acts & DJs. 1-2 original bands play 10pm-2am for 21+ crowd. Use online booking form, email or mail press kit to: PO Box 606, 320 S Main St., Breckenridge, CO 80424.

Toad Tavern
5302 S Federal Cir.
Littleton, CO 80123
p: 303-795-6877
www.toadtavern.com
contact: Mark Fundermeier
p: 303-690-3361
e: mark@toadtavern.com
genres: All Styles
advance: 2 months
capacity: 300
pa: Yes sound eng: Yes
stage: 15 x 20 in-house: Drums
open mics: Tue 8pm
sign in: 7:30pm contact: Kyle
Spacious 21+ bar 13mi S of Denver, held grand re-opening w/ new stage this yr. Features Local-Reg'l bands 4-5 nites; Nat'l act 1 nite/mo. Up to 4 original bands play 45min-4hrs for % door. Prefers email.

Ziggies
4923 W 38th Ave.
Denver, CO 80212
p: 303-455-9930
e: email@ziggiessaloon.com
www.ziggieslivemusic.com
contact: Carla Jordan
e: booking@ziggieslivemusic.com
genres: Blues, Funk, Groove, Rock, R&B, Swing, New Jazz
advance: 4-5 months
capacity: 100
pa: Yes sound eng: Yes
stage: Fits 8 piece act
open mics: Thu 8:30pm Acoustic & S/S
Well-worn music venue books Local-Nat'l bands nitely for 21+. 1-2 acts play 1hr sets for % of door + flat fee. No Rap, Hip-Hop or Country. Prefers audition at Wed Open Jam or use online booking form. If emailing, incl. pdf, link to music & contact info; when mailing, incl. contact info.

Fort Collins

Aggie Theatre
204 S College Ave.
Ft. Collins, CO 80524
p: 970-482-8300
e: kyle@aggietheatre.com
www.aggietheatre.com
contact: Scoo Leary
e: scoo@aggietheatre.com
call: M-F 11am-5pm
genres: Rock, Hard Rock, Funk, Jam, Hip-Hop, Country
advance: 2-3 months
capacity: 650
pa: Yes sound eng: Yes
stage: 25 x 20
Premier music venue books up to 4 Local-Touring acts & DJs 3-6 nites for 18+. Merch split is 85/15. No Tribute or Oldies acts. Email for booking.

Avogadro's Number
605 S Mason St.
Ft. Collins, CO 80524
p: 970-493-5555
e: avos@frii.com
www.avogadros.com
contact: Rob Osborne
p: 970-482-1756
genres: Acoustic, Bluegrass, Jazz, Rock
advance: 2-3 months
capacity: 100+
pa: Yes sound eng: Yes
stage: 12 x 12
open mics: Tue sign in: 7pm
Eatery books original, mostly Local/Reg'l acts Thu-Sun for % of door.

Greater CO

Fly Me to the Moon Saloon
132 E Colorado Ave.
Telluride, CO 81435
p: 970-728-6666
e: flymetothemoonsaloon@yahoo.com

www.flymetothemoonsaloon.com
contact: Thomas Fortier
call: M-F 10am-4pm
genres: All Styles
advance: 3 months
capacity: 200
pa: Yes **sound eng:** Yes
stage: 16 x 12 **in-house:** Drums
Historical subterranean venue known as 'The Basement' w/ spring-loaded dance floor is under new ownership. Decent tour stop btwn Denver & Vegas hosts 1 Local-Int'l act & some Touring DJs up to 3 nites. Bands play min of two 1 hr sets; some all ages shows. Email or mail press kit to: PO Box 566, Telluride, CO 81435.

Connecticut

Bridgeport/ Fairfield County/ Stamford

Acoustic Cafe
2926 Fairfield Ave.
Bridgeport, CT 06605
p: 203-335-3655
www.acousticafe.com
contact: Chris Morgan
e: acousticcafemail@yahoo.com
genres: Jam, Acoustic, Blues, Acid Jazz/Fusion, Rock, Bluegrass, Hip-Hop
advance: 2-5 months
capacity: 100
pa: Yes **sound eng:** Yes
stage: 16 x 12
open mics: Tue **sign in:** Call at 6pm
Popular listening room under new ownership, draws diverse crowds w/ up to 5 original Local-Int'l acts nitely; some all ages shows. Prefers email w/ as much info as possible, but can mail kit; follow up w/ email. No Calls.

Arch St. - Greenwich Teen Ctr.
100 Arch St.
Greenwich, CT 06830
p: 203-629-5744
e: info@archstreet.org
www.archstreet.org
contact: Kyle Silver
p: 203-618-1642
e: kyle@archstreet.org; kylesilver@aol.com
genres: Punk, Ska, Hardcore, Acoustic, Rock, Reggae, Hip-Hop
advance: 1-2 months
capacity: 544
All ages non-profit teen ctr. 6mi W of Stamford, books mostly Reg'l & some Local & Touring acts wknds. 5-6 original acts play 45min sets. Promos: PO Box 1339, Greenwich, CT 06830.

Cousin Larry's
1 Elm St.
Danbury, CT 06810
p: 203-730-0035
www.myspace.com/larrysdanbury
contact: Anthony Yacobellis
e: subrosaparty@gmail.com
call: M-F after noon
genres: All Styles
advance: 1+ months
capacity: 100
pa: Yes **sound eng:** Yes
stage: 15 x 12
open mics: Mon **sign in:** 9pm
Small 21+ bar w/ excellent sound & run by musicians is 30mi N of Stamford. Local-Int'l acts & DJs gig up to 7 nites. 3-4 acts play 30-45min for %. No profanity. Email or mail kit w/ ATTN: Anthony Yacobellis, Sub Rosa Party, 174 Lake Pl. S, Danbury, CT 06810.

Levitt Pavilion for the Performing Arts
10 Jesup Rd.
Westport, CT 06880
p: 203-226-7600
e: levitt@westportct.gov
www.levittpavilion.com
contact: Freda Welsh
call: M-F 8:30am-4:30pm
genres: Blues, Folk, Rock, Jazz, Blues, Big Bands, Classical
advance: 6-12 months
capacity: 2500
pa: Yes **sound eng:** Yes
stage: 30 x 40
Outdoor showcase for original estab. & emerging talent presents free shows nitely for all ages from mid-Jun to Aug & a few ticketed benefits w/ Nat'l acts. Featured acts play 90min for flat fee. Promos: 260 S Compo Rd., Westport, CT 06880.

The Maxx
94 Railroad St.
New Milford, CT 06776
p: 860-354-0047; 860-210-2165
e: maxx@youthagency.org
www.themaxxclubonline.com
contact: Luke
pa: Yes **sound eng:** Yes
Teen center w/ large built-in audience hosts Local-Nat'l acts. 5 bands gig for a % of the door. Admission only allowed if between the ages of 14-20.

SoNo Caffeine
133 Washington St.
South Norwalk, CT 06854
p: 203-857-4224
www.sonocaffeine.com/navpage.html
contact: John Stuart
e: johnstuartmktg@aol.com
genres: S/S
capacity: 100
pa: Yes **sound eng:** Yes
stage: small
Showcase for original Reg'l talent Wed & Thu. Single act plays 2hrs for flat fee. Email for booking.

Toquet Hall Teen Ctr.
58 Post Rd. E
Westport, CT 06880
p: 203-341-1155
e: toquethall@hotmail.com
www.toquethall.org
contact: Kevin Godburn
call: Afternoons
genres: Rock, Indie, Ska, Reggae, Pop, Electronic, Rap, Country, Acoustic, Hip-Hop
advance: 1-3 months
capacity: 200
pa: Yes **sound eng:** Yes
stage: 15 x 25
open mics: Yes
Teen ctr. 10mi W of Bridgeport books Local-Int'l acts & DJs Fri-Sat from Sep-Jun. 3-5 bands play 30-45min. Shows vary during Jul & Aug. Only H.S. kids are allowed in. No Hardcore or Metal. Email or mail press kit to venue.

Trackside
15 Station Rd.
Wilton, CT 06897
p: 203-834-2888
e: info@trackside.org
www.trackside.org
contact: Britton Billik
e: brittonbillik@mac.com
genres: Pop, Rock, Alt.
advance: 3-5 months
capacity: 400
pa: Yes **sound eng:** Yes
Former house converted into venue, hosts original Local-Int'l bands on Fri & Sat nites. Up to 5 acts play 45min sets for a flat fee. Email or snail mail kits.

Hartford

Billy Wilson's Ageing Still
57 Broadway
Norwich, CT 06360
p: 860-887-8733
contact: Joe Manfredi
call: Mon & Wed 3-5pm
genres: S/S, Folk, Acoustic Rock
advance: 2-3 months
capacity: 75
pa: By Request
stage: small
Small acoustic acts gig Thu-Sat in 21+ pub. Single act plays two 1hr sets for flat fee. Mail or drop off kit to venue.

Black-Eyed Sally's BBQ & Blues
350 Asylum St.
Hartford, CT 06103
p: 860-278-7427
e: sally@blackeyedsallys.com
www.blackeyedsallys.com
contact: James
e: james@blackeyedsallys.com
genres: Blues, Rock, Roots, S/S, Acoustic
capacity: 250
pa: Yes **sound eng:** Yes
stage: 15 x 22
BBQ joint books 1-2 mostly original Local-Int'l artists Fri-Sat for flat fee vs % door. Matt Zeiner hosts Acoustic Showcase on Thu 9pm w/ 3 S/S acts.

The Half Door Pub
270 Sisson Ave.
Hartford, CT 06105
p: 860-232-PUBS
e: thehalfdoor@hotmail.com
www.thehalfdoor.com
contact: Spiro
genres: Irish, Pop, Rock, Bluegrass
advance: 1+ months
capacity: 85+ **stage:** 10 x 15
21+ Irish pub books mostly original Reg'l & some Touring talent Wed, Fri & Sat. 1 act plays 2 sets from 10pm-close. Email or mail press kit to venue.

Hungry Tiger Cafe
120 Charter Oak St.
Manchester, CT 06040
p: 860-649-1195
e: info@thehungrytiger.com
www.thehungrytiger.com
contact: Don Denley, Jr.
genres: Rock, Blues, R&B, Folk
advance: 3 months
capacity: 180
pa: Yes **sound eng:** Yes
stage: 25 x 7
Popular revamped music room 9mi E of Hartford lights up w/ 1 polished Local-Touring band & possible opener nitely for two 75min sets; some DJs & cover acts. Most shows 21+. Mail press kit & follow up w/ a call.

Sounding Board Coffeehouse
Universalist Church
433 Fern St.
West Hartford, CT 06107
p: 203-272-8404
e: bshall@folknotes.org
www.folknotes.org
contact: Janet Steucek
p: 860-635-7685
e: folkie43@sbcglobal.net
genres: Folk, Blues
advance: 6-12 months
capacity: 200
pa: Yes **sound eng:** Yes
stage: Yes
Original Locals-Nat'ls booked Sat from Sep-May at volunteer-run venue. 1-2 acts play two 45min sets for all ages. Also hosting shows at The First Church of Christ Congregational, in West Hartford. Prefers email, but may mail promos to: Janet, 668 Main St., Cromwell, CT 06416.

Sully's Pub
2071 Park St.
Hartford, CT 06106
p: 860-231-8881
e: sully@sullyspub.com
www.sullyspub.com
contact: Robert Salter
e: rob@sullyspub.com

genres: Rock, Funk, Jam, Hip-Hop, Reggae
advance: 1-3 months
capacity: 125; 200 (outdoors)
pa: Yes **sound eng:** Yes
stage: 12 x 8
open mics: Mon - Tue Acoustic; Sun Electric
Dimly lit bar fills as up to 4 original Local-Int'l artists & DJs hit the stage Thu-Sun. Always booking Locals w/ buzz. Send music link & bio, or mail kit; follow up via email in a few wks.

Szechuan Tokyo
1245 New Britain Ave.
West Hartford, CT 06110
p: 860-561-0180
e: jazz@asianfusion.net
www.asianfusion.net
contact: Paul Lewis
e: paul@asianfusion.net
genres: Jazz
advance: 4 months
capacity: 180
pa: Yes **sound eng:** Yes
stage: 20 x 12
Sushi haven features top tier Local-Int'l talent Thu-Sun for all ages. 1 act plays for flat fee & generous % of door. Snail mail only; No EPKs.

The Vanilla Bean Café
450 Deerfield Rd.
Pomfret, CT 06258
p: 860-928-1562
www.thevanillabeancafe.com
contact: Maria Sangiolo
e: maria@thevanillabeancafe.com
genres: Folk, Bluegrass, Blues, Americana
advance: 4-6 months
capacity: 90
pa: Yes **sound eng:** Yes
stage: 12 x 8 floor space
open mics: 1st Fri of month
All ages coffeehouse midway btwn Hartford, Providence & Worcester, has great acoustics & presents original Local-Touring acts Sat. 1-2 acts play two 45-50min sets w/ 20min break for 90% of door; shows webcast live. Prefers email first for booking. No Calls.

Webster Theatre/ Webster Underground
31 Webster St.
Hartford, CT 06114
p: 860-525-5553
e: webstertheater@gmail.com
www.webstertheatre.com
contact: Rick Bober
p: 860-246-8001
genres: Rock, Hard Rock, Metal, Punk, Emo, Jam
advance: 6+ weeks
capacity: 1250; 200
pa: Yes **sound eng:** Yes
stage: 32 x 21
Restored theatre presents 4-6 Local-Int'l acts nitely. Opener plays 20-35min, headliner plays 1+hrs. Merch splits 80/20. Also books Locals & Touring Indies in 200-cap Webster Underground. Email or mail kit.

New Haven

Bank Street Cafe
637-639 Bank St.
New London, CT 06320
p: 860-444-1444
www.bankstreetcafe.com
contact: Jeff Mullen
p: 860-434-6365
e: lnmullen@aol.com
call: evenings
genres: R&B, Blues, Metal, Rock-a-Billy, Country, Rock
advance: 6-8 weeks
capacity: 170
pa: Yes **sound eng:** Yes
stage: 14 x 16 **in-house:** Piano
Bar w/ excellent, rebuilt sound system has Local & Touring acts Fri-Sat. Up to 3 acts play 50min or two 75min sets for 21+. Mostly original acts w/ some cover bands. No Hip-Hop. Snail mail kits. No EPKs.

Bar
254 Crown St.
New Haven, CT 06511
p: 203-495-8924
e: info@barnightclub.com
www.barnightclub.com
contact: Rick Omonte
e: rickomonte@aol.com
genres: Noise, Avant Garde, Free Folk, Weird, Psych, Rock
advance: 1-3 months
capacity: 250
pa: Yes **sound eng:** Yes
Popular & trendy pizza eatery w/ backroom stage & dance floor near Yale campus, hosts 1-2 Local & some cutting-edge Touring acts Sun nites for flat fee. Mail CD or email links; follow up w/ email. No Calls.

Cafe Nine
250 State St.
New Haven, CT 06510
p: 203-789-8281
www.cafenine.com
contact: Paul Mayer
e: book9live@aol.com
call: M-F 10am-noon
genres: All Styles
advance: 2-3 months
capacity: 125
pa: Yes **sound eng:** Yes
stage: 13 x 11
Old-time Rock-n-Roll/Honky Tonk books mostly original Local-Int'l acts Mon-Sat & some Sun; some early shows. 2-4 acts play 40-90min. Prefers emails & EPKs; no unsolicited mail.

Oasis Pub
16 Bank St.
New London, CT 06320
p: 860-447-3929
e: oasispub@gmail.com
www.myspace.com/oasispub
contact: Sean Murray
call: M-F after 7pm
genres: Rock, Alt., Reggae, Jam
advance: 1-2 months
capacity: 150
pa: Yes **sound eng:** Yes
stage: 12 x 10 **in-house:** Drums
Stage in heart of downtown music scene books Local-Int'l bands & DJs up to 5 nites. Up to 3 original acts play 45min for 100% of door. Prefers mailed press kit, email or EPK. May also contact thru MySpace. Incl. link to EPK, description of sound, influences, bands opened for/played w/ & gig history.

The Space
295 Treadwell St., Bldg. H
Hamden, CT 06514
p: 203-288-6400
e: info@thespace.tk
www.thespace.tk
contact: Noah Goldman
e: spacebooking@yahoo.com
call: Tue & Wed noon-5pm
genres: Indie Rock, Folk, Pop/Punk, Hard Rock, Ska
advance: 6-10 weeks
capacity: 150
pa: Yes
stage: 20 x 10
open mics: Tue **sign in:** 7pm
All ages original music room 7mi N of New Haven btwn an arts collective & a sticky floor Rock venue, presents Local-Nat'l bands Thu-Sat plus Fri matinee. Up to 5 acts play 30-60min sets. Prefers Sonicbids EPK; incl. link to MySpace or PureVolume.com, avail. dates, phone number, expected draw in the area, etc.

Toad's Place
300 York St.
New Haven, CT 06511
p: 203-624-8623
www.toadsplace.com
contact: Hollis Martin
p: 203-562-5589 x11
e: hollis@toadsplace.com
call: M-F
genres: All Styles
advance: 6 weeks
capacity: 750
pa: Yes **sound eng:** Yes
stage: 25 x 30
Renowned club books Local-Int'l acts 3-4 nites. Headliner w/ 3-4 openers play mostly all ages shows w/ some 21+; some Touring DJs. Contact thru MySpace, or mark kits w/ ATTN: Toad's Place Booking.

Delaware

Dover

Arena's Deli
149 Rehoboth Ave.
Rehoboth Beach, DE 19971
p: 302-227-1272
www.arenasdeliandbar.com
contact: Kim Stude
e: kim@arenasdeliandbar.com
call: M-F after 5pm
genres: Rock, Acoustic, Reggae, Punk, Classic Rock
advance: 2 months
capacity: 150 **stage:** 10 x 10
Beachtown eatery hosts area acts Fri & Sat nites & some wkdys. Send press kit to venue.

Bottle & Cork
1807 Hwy. 1
Dewey Beach, DE 19971
p: 302-227-3888 x134
www.deweybeachlife.com
contact: Vikki Walls
e: vwalls@dweybeachlife.com
call: M-F 9am-5pm
genres: Rock, Country
advance: 4-5 months
capacity: 800
pa: Yes **sound eng:** Yes
stage: 36 x 18
Hip club books Reg'l & estab. Touring talent Tue-Fri & Sun from May-Oct. Up to 4 acts play 45min to 21+. Split on Nat'l merch sales. Closed during the winter season. Email first.

Dogfish Head
320 Rehoboth Ave.
Rehoboth Beach, DE 19971
p: 302-226-2739
e: dogfish@dogfish.com
www.dogfish.com
contact: Chris Lausch
p: 302-645-7644
e: dogfishmusic@dogfish.com
call: M-F 2-5pm
genres: Pop, Rock, Americana, Blues, Rockabilly, Jazz, Bluegrass
advance: 2 months
capacity: 250
pa: Yes **sound eng:** Yes
stage: 15 x 20
Famed brewpub books Local-Int'l bands Fri & Sat nites; some all ages shows. 1-2 original acts play from 10pm-12:30am for flat fee & buyout. Prefers link to MySpace, but may mail press kit to venue.

Jazz & Blues Dine-Around
14 Victoria Sq.
Rehoboth Beach, DE 19971
p: 302-227-1339; 800-808-1924
contact: Sydney Arzt
e: sydsblues@yahoo.com
call: M-F 10am-5pm
genres: Jazz, Blues, R&B, Soul
advance: 3 months
capacity: 200
pa: Yes **sound eng:** Yes
stage: varies
open mics: Thu: May-Sep
sign in: 8pm **contact:** Ed Shockley
Formerly Sydney's Blues & Jazz. Renamed, but still books original Local-Int'l talent 3-6 nites for all ages. 1 act plays two 75min sets for flat fee. Merch splits 90/10. Prefers email.

northbeach
125 McKinley St. & The Bay
Dewey Beach, DE 19971
p: 302-226-8673
www.deweybeachlife.com
contact: Vikki Walls
p: 302-227-1209
e: vwalls@deweybeachlife.com
genres: All Styles
advance: 3 months
capacity: 800
pa: Yes **sound eng:** Yes
stage: medium
Dance club w/ 2 separate levels books DJs & Local-Touring acts from May-Sep. Excellent surround sound & lights. Up to 3 acts play 45min sets for flat fee; 21+ after 9pm. Also books Rusty Rudder & Bottle & Cork. Email first for policy. No unsolicited mail.

W.T. Smithers
140 S State St.
Dover, DE 19901
p: 302-674-8875
e: manager@wtsmithers.us
www.wtsmithers.us
contact: Jason Thomas
genres: Folk, Rock, Pop, Punk
capacity: 200
open mics: Tue & last Thu/mo
Original Locals & Reg'ls gig Tue & some Sat for flat fee in popular restaurant/bar. Featured act plays from 10pm-1am. Mail press kit to venue.

Wilmington

The East End Cafe
270 E Main St.
Newark, DE 19711

p: 302-738-0880
www.eastend-cafe.com
contact: Nick Green
genres: All Styles
advance: 4 months
capacity: 200
pa: Yes **sound eng:** Yes
stage: 13 x 14
open mics: Sun 7:30pm
Original Reg'l & Touring acts gig nitely in all ages dive bar blocks from U of MD campus; some Nat'ls & Local cover acts. 4+ bands fill 4hrs for the door. Tue is Hip-Hop Nite w/ DJs. Prefers MySpace, but may contact by any means.

Iron Hill Brewery
710 S Madison St.
Wilmington, DE 19801
p: 302-472-2739
www.ironhillbrewery.com
contact: Greg
e: gregb@ironhillbrewery.com
genres: Rock
pa: Yes
stage: floor space
Live Local-Reg'l music. Use email or mail press kit to venue.

J.B. McGinnes Pub
519 E Basin Rd.
New Castle, DE 19720
p: 302-322-4766
www.myspace.com/gatorsbar
contact: Brian
call: M-F after 9pm
genres: Alt.
advance: 2 months
capacity: 278
pa: Yes **sound eng:** Yes
Party bar, formerly Gator's, books 1-2 Local-Reg'l bands 10pm-12:30am Fri & Sat for all ages.

Just Mugs Saloon
780 Pulaski Hwy.
Bear, DE 19701
p: 302-328-5945
e: justmugs@comcast.net
www.justmugssaloon.com
contact: Liz
call: mornings
genres: Country, Southern Rock
advance: 2 months
capacity: 299 **stage:** 15 x 30
'The Area's Hottest Country Bands' play Fri-Sat & 1 Thu/mo. 1 act plays to 21+ crowd for flat fee. Mail press kit.

Kelly's Logan House
1701 Delaware Ave.
Wilmington, DE 19806
p: 302-652-9493
www.loganhouse.com
contact: Drew Davis
e: drew@loganhouse.com
call: prefers email
genres: Alt., Rock, Pop, Acoustic, R&B
advance: 2 months
capacity: 250
pa: Yes **sound eng:** Yes
stage: 15 x 20
1-2 Reg'l & some Touring artists play two or three 45-75min sets for flat fee Tue-Sat at 21+ Irish pub; Acoustic acts Tue-Thu, full bands Fri-Sat, sometimes Thu. Use Sonicbids or snail mail kits.

Mojo 13
1706 Philadelphia Pike
Wilmington, DE 19809
p: 302-798-5798
www.mojothirteen.com
contact: Jerad
p: 610-909-7066
capacity: 165-200
pa: Yes **sound eng:** Yes
21+ venue supports the alt.-music community in DE & beyond w/ original Local-Int'l acts. Prefers booking thru MySpace. No unsolicited mail.

District of Columbia

9:30 Club
815 V St. NW
Washington, DC 20001
p: 202-265-0930
e: human@930.com
www.930.com
contact: Lisa White
e: booking@930.com
call: M-F noon-7pm
genres: Eclectic
advance: 3-4 months
capacity: 1200
pa: Yes **sound eng:** Yes
stage: 30 x 20
Prime SRO club w/ balcony & great sight lines books top-tier original Local-Int'l talent 4-7 nites. Bands & some DJs play mostly all ages shows for flat fee & % of door. 80/20 merch split; 90/10 on hard goods. Mail submission & allow 6 wks.

The Black Cat
1811 14th St. NW
Washington, DC 20009
p: 202-667-4490
f: 202-667-4527
e: info@blackcatdc.com
www.blackcatdc.com
contact: Vicki
p: 202-667-4527
call: Mon-Thu noon-4pm
genres: Indie Rock, Alt., Punk, Experimental
advance: 2 months
capacity: 600 (main); 150 (backstage)
pa: Yes **sound eng:** Yes
stage: 2 stages
All ages institution w/ 2 stages books top original Local-Nat'l talent nitely. 2-3 bands play 45min sets. See site for submission details. Promos: ATTN: Vicki, PO Box 73338, Washington, DC 20056. Wait 3 wks, then call.

Blues Alley
1073 Wisconsin Ave. NW
Washington, DC 20007
p: 202-337-4141
f: 202-337-7946
www.bluesalley.com
contact: Bob Israel
p: 301-704-4314
genres: Jazz, Blues
advance: 1 year
capacity: 130
pa: Yes **sound eng:** Yes
stage: 16 x 16 (expandable)
Lauded intimate all ages supperclub w/ sparkling sound books original Local-Int'l bands nitely. Featured act plays 90min sets. Promos: PO Box 3616, Washington, DC 20007.

Bohemian Caverns
2001 11th St. NW
Washington, DC 20001
p: 202-299-0800
e: vickey@mahoganydc.com
www.bohemiancaverns.com
contact: Omrao Brown
e: omrao@mahoganydc.com; booking@mahoganydc.com
genres: Jazz, World, Reggae, Blues, Soul
advance: 1 month
capacity: 120
pa: Yes **sound eng:** Yes
stage: Fits 8 piece act
open mics: Wed **sign in:** 8pm
Pricey Jazz club, formerly the legendary Crystal Caverns, presents 1 polished Local-Touring act Mon-Sat; some Sun; 21+, 13+ w/ guardian. Act plays 90min for flat fee. Great sound, some obstructed views. DJs spin upstairs in Club Liv for mostly upscale urban pros. Mail press kit or send email.

DC9
1940 9th St. NW
Washington, DC 20001
p: 202-483-5000
f: 202-483-0666
e: info@dcnine.com
www.dcnine.com
contact: Bryan Deily
e: booking@dcnine.com
genres: All Styles
advance: 2 months
capacity: 250
pa: Yes **sound eng:** Yes
stage: 100 sq. ft.
Bi-level 21+ niteclub books Local-Touring bands & DJs; 3-4 acts on a bill. Mail press kit to venue w/ ATTN: Booking. Use website form for any questions.

Felix & The Spy Lounge
2406 18th St. NW
Washington, DC 20009
p: 202-483-3549
f: 202-483-6165
e: nwaskewich@yahoo.com
www.thefelix.com
contact: Alan Popovsky
genres: Funk, Big Band, Ska, Jazz, Rock
advance: 1 month
capacity: 200 **stage:** floor space
Retro-swanky venue w/ fine food & James Bond decor attracts sophisticated 21+ crowd & Local-Nat'l artists on Sat; DJs spin 4 nites. Featured act plays 4hrs for flat fee. Mail press kit to venue & incl. photo, CD & upcoming area gigs.

Five
1214 B 18th St. NW
Washington, DC 20036
p: 202-331-7123
e: info@fivedc.com
www.fivedc.com
contact: Jeff Duke
call: Wed noon-4pm; Thu-Sat after 10:30pm
genres: All Styles
advance: 2 months
capacity: 600
pa: To rent **sound eng:** To hire
stage: 8 x 20 (expandable)
Local-Int'l acts play & DJs w/ a buzz spin Wed-Sun at this 18+ multi-level club w/ great sound. Up to 9 acts keep things varied. Email or snail mail kits.

Madam's Organ
2461 18th St. NW
Adams Morgan
Washington, DC 20009
p: 202-667-5370
e: madamsorgan@gotham-city.net
www.madamsorgan.com
contact: Amy
genres: Blues, Bluegrass, R&B, Acoustic, Reggae, Funk
advance: 4-5 months
capacity: 399
pa: Yes **sound eng:** Yes
stage: 10 x 10
Beloved & quirky music & soul food joint features mostly original Local-Reg'l acts Sun-Thu; Touring acts Fri & Sat. 1 act plays three 60-80min sets w/ two 30min breaks from 10pm-2:30am for 21+. Mail kit to venue. No Calls.

Millennium Stage/ Kennedy Ctr for the Performing Arts
2700 F St. NW
Washington, DC 20566
p: 202-416-8043
www.kennedy-center.org
contact: Diana Ezerins
e: dmezerins@kennedy-center.org
call: M-F 10am-6pm
genres: Jazz, American Roots, World Roots
advance: 3 months
capacity: 2000; 5000
pa: Yes **sound eng:** Yes
stage: 24 x 24
Stage in Kennedy Ctr. foyer features free, no tix required, multi-genre performances nitely from 6-7pm. 1 act plays to all ages for flat fee. Band keeps 70% merch sales if house sells, 80% if band sell. Shows are webcast & archived. Email or send promo w/ dates avail. to: PO Box 101510, Arlington, VA 22210.

Rock & Roll Hotel
1353 H St. NE
Washington, DC 20002
p: 202-388-ROCK
e: rockandrollhoteldc@gmail.com
www.rockandrollhoteldc.com
contact: Steve Lambert
e: steve@rockandrollhoteldc.com
call: M-F 9am-5pm
genres: All Styles w/ focus on Rock, Indie, Dance & Underground
advance: 8 months
capacity: 400
pa: Yes **sound eng:** Yes
Alt./chic bi-level club books 2-3 hip & original Local faves thru estab. Touring bands play 35-40min sets; shows are all ages. Sound & sight lines lacking. Email MP3s or links to music only w/ DC proper show history, expected draw, Local support ideas & promo capability; booker will request hard copy if needed.

Twins Jazz
1344 U St. NW, 2nd Fl.
Washington, DC 20009
p: 202-234-0072
www.twinsjazz.com
contact: Kelly Tesfaye
e: bookings@twinsjazz.com
call: Wed-Sun after 6pm
genres: Jazz
advance: 3 months
capacity: 100
pa: Yes **sound eng:** Yes
open mics: Sun **sign in:** 8pm
Popular all ages venue features

Local-Int'l Jazz Tue-Sun. 1 act plays two 45-60min sets for % of door on wkdys; flat fee wknds. Sound person on select evenings. Prefers EPKs; No booking thru MySpace.

Velvet Lounge
915 U St. NW
Washington, DC 20001
p: 202-462-3213
e: velvetloungedc@gmail.com
www.velvetloungedc.com
contact: Scott Verrastro
call: M-F after 8pm
genres: Experimental, Rock, Avant Garde, Jazz, Punk, Reggae, Hardcore, Folk, Bluegrass, Indie, Hip-Hop, Electronica
advance: 2-4 months
capacity: 110
pa: Yes **sound eng:** Yes
stage: 16 x 16
Local-Int'l bands & some DJs play up to 7 nites in eclectic lounge. 3 original acts play 45 min to mostly 18+; Sat & Sun all ages matinees. Locals get % of door & Touring acts get flat fee. Prefers email w/ phone #, music link, press, gig history, bands played w/ & expected draw. May also mail press kit to venue; will contact if interested.

The Zoo Bar Café
3000 Connecticut Ave. NW
Washington, DC
20008
p: 202-232-4225
www.zoobardc.com
contact: Steve McKinney
e: crazed4278@mypacks.net
genres: Blues
advance: 2-3 months
capacity: 75-100
stage: medium
No cover beer & burger joint across from the Nat'l Zoo popular w/ families & college crowd features Local-Reg'l acts Fri-Sat for 21+. 1 act plays three 45min sets for flat fee. Call or email first.

Florida

Jacksonville/ Gainesville

Common Grounds
210 SW 2nd Ave., Ste. A
Gainesville, FL 32601
p: 352-372-7320
e: info@commongroundslive.com
www.commongroundslive.com
contact: Nigel Hamm
e: nigel@commongroundslive.com
call: M-F noon-4pm
genres: Rock, Alt., Punk, Ska, Folk
capacity: 200
pa: Yes **sound eng:** Yes
stage: 27 x 17
Former coffeehouse features Local up & comers & estab. Touring acts 3 nites. 3 original bands play 30min sets for 18+. Call first for booking.

Durty Nelly's Irish Pub
208 W University Ave.
Gainesville, FL 32601
p: 352-374-9567
www.durtynellysgnv.com
contact: Joel Tynes
genres: Irish, Celtic, Folk, S/S, Punk, Rock, Bluegrass
advance: Up to 2 months
capacity: 126
pa: Yes **stage:** 6 x 12
Local or Touring band every Thu-Sat for 21+; some Sun & Mon shows. 1-2 acts play three 40min sets. Snail mail kit.

European St. Listening Room
1704 San Marco Blvd.
Jacksonville, FL 32207
p: 904-398-1717
www.hackingcat.com
contact: Andy Zarka
p: 904-399-1740
e: andy@hackingcat.com
genres: S/S, Americana
advance: 2-3 months
capacity: 75
pa: Yes **sound eng:** Yes
stage: 12 x 18
Intimate all ages space features a Nat'l or Int'l act every Thu from 8:30-10:30pm; acts are paid a flat fee vs % of door.

Freebird Live
200 N 1st St.
Jacksonville Beach, FL 32250
p: 904-246-2473
www.freebirdlive.com
contact: Tim Hall
p: 904-399-8839
e: tim@jaxlive.com
call: prefers email
genres: All Styles
advance: 6-8 weeks
capacity: 700
pa: Yes **sound eng:** Yes
stage: 18 x 18
Famed 2-story Skynyrd-themed club w/ state-of-the-art sound & lights, books top Local-Int'l acts & DJs. Up to 4 original acts play 45-120min for all ages. Merch splits 90/10. Email music link 6-8 wks from desired date. No unsolicited mail.

Fuel
1037 Park St.
Jacksonville, FL 32204
p: 904-425-3835
e: jrw@fuelin5pts.com
www.fuelin5pts.com
contact: Jim Webb
e: booking@fuelin5pts.com
genres: Rock, Alt., Punk, Metal, Indie
advance: 2 months
capacity: 300+
pa: Yes **sound eng:** Yes
stage: 20 x 20
Rockin' all ages venue & cafe presents 3+ original Local-Nat'l acts & DJs playing 30-60min sets most nites. Nat'l merch split on soft goods is 85/15. Snail mail press kit to venue.

Jack Rabbits
1528 Hendricks Ave.
Jacksonville, FL 32207
p: 904-398-7496
www.jackrabbitsonline.com
contact: Tim Hall
p: 904-399-8839
e: tim@jaxlive.com
call: prefers email
genres: Rock, Punk, Jazz, Alt., Jam, Alt. Country
advance: 6-8 weeks
capacity: 299
pa: Yes **sound eng:** Yes
stage: 20 x 12
Mostly all ages Alt. Rock room still packs them in for Local-Touring rising buzz bands. Up to 6 original acts play original tunes for 30-120min. Also books Freebird Live. Email music, links & dates first before mailing kit to: 1650-302 Margaret St #195, Jacksonville, FL 32204.

Mill Top Tavern
19-1/2 St. George St.
St. Augustine, FL 32084
p: 904-829-2329
www.milltop.com
contact: Don Oja-Dunaway
call: Wed-Mon
genres: Americana, Rock, Folk, Grassroots, S/S
advance: 6-24 months
capacity: 70-80
pa: Yes
open mics: Sun 5pm-close
Musician-friendly tavern books Local-Int'l acts w/ up to 3 shows from 1pm-close, incl. big name drop-ins. Up to 3 acts play 3-4hr sets. Day bands gets % of drinks + tips & nite bands keep flat fee. Call first; No unsolicited mail.

Murray Hill Theatre
932 Edgewood Ave. S
Jacksonville, FL 32205
p: 904-388-7807
e: thehill@usa.net
www.murrayhilltheatre.com
contact: Tom Rosmanith
p: 904-388-3179
call: Tue-Thu
genres: CCM, Pop, Rock, Rap
advance: 2-3 months
capacity: 700
pa: Yes **sound eng:** Yes
stage: 20 x 30
All ages niteclub books original faith-based music up to 6 nites. Locals open for Touring acts. 4 acts play 25min. Wknd & some select midwk all ages shows. $100 staging fee for Reg'l Touring & smaller Nat'l acts. Email or snail mail kit w/ ATTN: Booking; incl. pastoral reference, lyrics, link to music or EPK.

The Pit
14003 Beach Blvd.
Jacksonville, FL 32250
p: 904-223-9850
e: jaxpit@jaxrock.com
www.myspace.com/brewsterspit
contact: Amii
call: email only
genres: Most Styles
advance: 2-3 months
capacity: 300
pa: Yes **sound eng:** Yes
stage: 20 x 12
Newly remodeled w/ expanded stage & sound, this rockin' club hosts Local & Touring acts up to 7 nites w/ focus on underground music. 3-6 acts play 20-40min for % of door or flat fee for guaranteed draw. No Country, Rap or Hip-Hop. Prefers EPK or contact thru MySpace; incl. alt. dates, contact info, genre, bands played w/ or wish to play w/; will contact if dates are avail. No unsolicited mail or calls.

TSI
333 E Bay St.
Jacksonville, FL 32202
p: 904-424-3531
www.clubtsi.com
contact: Brendon Clark
e: booking@clubtsi.com
genres: Indie, Garage, Rock
advance: 1-2 months
capacity: 250
pa: Yes **sound eng:** Yes
Premiere underground niteclub books original Local-Nat'l bands Fri nites & some Mon & Wed. No Hardcore, Pop-Punk or Radio Rock. Email music links.

Miami/ Ft. Lauderdale

Alligator Alley
1321 E Commercial Blvd.
Oakland Park, FL 33334
p: 954-771-2220
www.alligatoralleyflorida.com
contact: Kilmo
e: kilmo@alligatoralleyflorida.com
call: Tue-Fri after 6pm
genres: All Styles
advance: Up to 3 months
pa: Yes **sound eng:** Yes
stage: 20 x 12
State-of-the-art musician-owned hall, hosts mostly Jazz & Blues acts & Touring DJs. Up to 5 original Local-Int'l acts/bill; some shows all ages. Email link to artist website & contact phone number; no large attachments like sound files or EPKs.

Cheers
941 E Cyprus Creek Rd.
Ft. Lauderdale, FL 33334
p: 954-771-6337
e: cheersftl@aol.com
www.cheersfoodandspirits.com
contact: Shawn Chase
e: chaser1@bellsouth.net
call: M-F after noon
genres: Classic Rock, Blues, Jam, Acoustic
advance: 1-3 months
capacity: 250
pa: Yes **sound eng:** To hire
stage: 16 x 16
open mics: Mon **sign in:** 9pm
Popular late nite books mostly Local & some Touring-Nat'l acts Wed-Mon. Featured act plays five 45min sets w/ 30min breaks usu. for flat fee. Mostly 21+ w/ some 18+ shows. Must be able to draw. Email for booking; see MySpace for info.

Churchill's Pub
5501 NE 2nd Ave.
Miami, FL 33137
p: 305-757-1807
www.churchillspub.com
contact: David Daniels
e: david@churchillspub.com
call: M-F afternoons
genres: Rock, World, Metal, Folk
advance: 1-2 months
capacity: 150; 350
pa: Yes **sound eng:** Yes
stage: 14 x 8; 24 x 12
open mics: Wed 9:30pm
Launching pad for original Local talent also books Reg'l & Touring acts. 3+ acts play for 18+ crowd. Books 'Acoustic Nite' after open mic w/ 3 acts. Snail mail or email kit.

Cruzan Amphitheatre
601-7 Sansbury's Way
West Palm Beach, FL 33411
p: 561-795-8883

www.soundadviceamp.com
contact: Randy McElrath
p: 954-626-7881
genres: All Styles
advance: 2 months
capacity: 19,000
pa: Yes **sound eng:** Yes
Formerly Sound Advice Amphitheatre, new Live Nation venue hosts top Reg'l & Nat'l acts wkly for all ages; busier during summer season. Prefers email for booking.

Culture Room
3045 N Federal Hwy.
Ft. Lauderdale, FL 33306
p: 954-564-1074
e: cultureroom@yahoo.com
www.cultureroom.net
contact: Greg Aliferis
p: 954-561-4880
call: afternoons
genres: Rock, Alt.
capacity: 550
pa: Yes **sound eng:** Yes
stage: 30 x 20
Celebrated Rock club features original Local & Nat'l artists 5 nites. Up to 5 acts perform 40-90min sets. Merch splits 80/20. Label scouts rumored to frequent shows. Promos: PO Box 11021, Ft. Lauderdale, FL 33339.

Dada
52 N Swinton Ave.
Delray Beach, FL 33444
p: 561-330-3232
e: walterdada@msn.com
www.dada.closermagazine.com
contact: Kristen Kelly
e: krissiness@gmail.com
genres: Jazz, Indie Pop, Rock, Punk, Acid Jazz, Reggae, Folk
advance: 1-2 months
capacity: 150
pa: Yes
open mics: Tue 10pm
Eatery books Local/Reg'l bands Thu-Sun. Featured act plays two 1hr sets for flat fee. Email or snail mail kit.

Jazid
1342 Washington Ave.
Miami Beach, FL 33139
p: 305-673-9372
e: jazid@jazid.net
www.jazid.net
contact: Daniel Wohlstein
call: email only
genres: Jazz, R&B, Soul, Funk, Reggae, Rock, Latin
advance: 1 month
capacity: 300
pa: Yes
Long-running South Beach room hosts original Local-Int'l bands nitely for 21+; cover acts on Thu. 3 acts play 45min for 20% of bar sales. For booking, use MySpace, email, or mail press kit to: 1205 Lincoln Rd., #218, Miami Beach, FL 33139.

The Octopus Garden
1942 Hollywood Blvd.
Hollywood, FL 33020
p: 954-924-9631
www.myspace.com/octopusgardenbar
contact: Rose
genres: Rock
capacity: 199
21+ Rock club books Local & Reg'l acts for a flat fee. Snail mail kits; No emails.

Purdy Lounge
1811 Purdy Ave.
Miami Beach, FL 33139
p: 305-531-4622
e: purdylounge@gmail.com
www.purdylounge.com
contact: Steve
genres: Rock
advance: 1 month
capacity: 200
stage: large floor space
Niteclub books up to 3 mostly original Locals, Wed & some Tue. Touring acts sometimes booked; bands play 1-2 sets; up to 1hr/set for meal & merch sales. Also books The Bar. Email or snail mail kit.

Respectable Street
518 Clematis St.
West Palm Beach, FL 33401
p: 561-832-9999
www.respectablestreet.com
contact: Steve Rullman
e: steev@thehoneycomb.com
genres: Indie Rock, Alt., Punk
advance: 3 months
capacity: 450 **stage:** 16 x 20
Music club books mostly original Reg'l & Touring bands w/ draw wkly. Up to 3 acts play 45-120min; Touring DJs spin Wed. Email or send kit to: 1810 Camodiana Rd., West Palm Beach, FL 33401.

Revolution
200 W Broward Blvd.
Ft. Lauderdale, FL 33312
p: 954-727-0950
e: info@jointherevolution.net
www.jointherevolution.net
contact: Jeff John
p: 954-449-1033
genres: All Styles
advance: 6 weeks
capacity: 1100
pa: Yes **sound eng:** Yes
stage: 40 x 20
Niteclub books 2-4 acts on 2 stages 3-4 nites; DJs on Sat. Local-Reg'ls booked in-house; Nat'ls booked thru House of Blues. Prefers email, but may mail press kit to: 100 Nugent Ave., Ste. 1, Ft. Lauderdale, FL 33312.

Tobacco Road
626 S Miami Ave.
Miami, FL 33130
p: 305-374-1198
e: tobaccoroad626@yahoo.com
www.tobacco-road.com
contact: Mark Weiser
p: 786-399-7447
e: mark@entertainmentmiami.com
genres: All Styles
advance: 2-8 weeks
capacity: 300; 500-2000
pa: Yes **sound eng:** Yes
Oldest bar in Miami w/ 4 stages & outdoor concert areas hosts Local-Int'l acts nitely for 21+ crows; 1 all ages show/yr. Acts play three 1hr sets. Solo, duo & bands welcome. Also books Titanic Microbewery, Finnigans River, Christabelle's Quarter & CocoWalk. Prefers EPKs, but may mail promos to: Mark Weiser Prod., 640 S Miami Ave., Miami, FL 33130.

Van Dyke Cafe
846 Lincoln Rd.
Miami Beach, FL 33139
p: 305-534-3600
e: info@graspagroup.com
www.thevandykecafe.com
contact: Randy Singer
e: randy@randysinger.com
call: M-F after 8pm
genres: Jazz, Brazilian, R&B, Soul, Rock, Funk, Reggae, Americana
advance: 2 months
capacity: 80
pa: Yes
Music lounge has Local & Nat'l acts nitely. Featured artist plays three 1hr sets for flat fee.

Orlando

AKA Lounge
68 E Pine St., 2nd Fl.
Orlando, FL 32801
p: 407-839-3707
e: akadino711@aol.com
www.akalounge.com
call: Tue-Sun
genres: Punk, Blues, S/S, Rock, Pop, Dance, Techno, Hip-Hop, Folk
Artsy club hosts Local-Nat'l acts & DJs for a 21+ crowd.

Backbooth
37 W Pine St.
Orlando, FL 32801
p: 407-999-2570
www.backbooth.com
contact: Chris Anderson
e: booking@backbooth.com
genres: All Styles
advance: 1-2 months
capacity: 350
pa: Yes **sound eng:** Yes
stage: 15 x 17
Orlando hotspot hosts Local acts, Nat'l headliners & DJs nitely. 2-5 bands play 30-45min for % of door. Shows all ages or 18+. Email for booking.

Copper Rocket Pub
106 Lake Ln.
Maitland, FL 32751
p: 407-645-0069
www.copperrocketpub.com
contact: Michelle
call: prefers MySpace
genres: Rockabilly, Rock, Country
advance: 2 months
capacity: 120
pa: Yes **sound eng:** Yes
stage: 15 x 8
European style hang books mostly Locals on Fri-Sat & Honky Tonk on Sun for the door. 2-3 acts play 1hr sets to 21+ crowd; some 18+ shows. No Rap. Prefers MySpace for booking.

Hard Rock Cafe/ Hard Rock Live
6050 Universal Blvd.
Orlando, FL 32819
p: 407-351-LIVE
www.hardrock.com
contact: Colleen Flynn
p: 407-370-5900
e: colleen_flynn@hardrock.com
call: M-F 9am-6pm
genres: Rock, Pop, Hip-Hop, Country
capacity: 1853 (seated); 2800 (general admission main floor); 600 (reserved balcony)
pa: Yes **sound eng:** Yes
stage: 50' wide
All-ages theme restaurant chain books top Local & Touring performers up to 7 nites. Located in Universal Citywalk & caters to tourists. Electronic submissions only.

The Haven
6700 Aloma Ave.
Winter Park, FL 32792
p: 407-673-2712
e: havenlounge@aol.com
www.thehavenrocks.com
contact: Dave Himes
e: havenbooking@bellsouth.net
genres: Rock, Rap, Country, Blues, Jazz
advance: 1-3 months
capacity: 350
pa: Yes **sound eng:** Yes
stage: 24 x 16 **in-house:** Drums
Specializes in all types of live music w/ Local-Nat'l bands; most shows are age 18+. Snail mail press kit to venue.

House of Blues Orlando/BB Blues Bar
1490 E Buena Vista Dr.
Lake Buena Vista, FL 32830
p: 407-934-2583
http://hob.com/venues/clubvenues/orlando
contact: Jim Mallonee
p: 407-934-2014
e: jmallonee@hob.com
genres: Country, Rock, Gospel, Urban, Jazz, Blues
capacity: 2100
pa: Yes **sound eng:** Yes
Celebrated music chain presents polished Local-Int'l talent nitely for mostly all ages. 2-5 acts play mostly original material. Also books Myrtle

Beach location. Promos: PO Box 22804, Lake Buena Vista, FL 32830. No Calls.

Orlando Island Oasis
2716 Forsyth Rd.
Winter Park, FL 32792
p: 407-657-6047
www.soundinoff.com/oasis
contact: Anita
p: 321-460-6766
capacity: 383
pa: Yes **sound eng:** Yes
21+ dive bar & home to the Orlando scene books area & Touring acts Fri-Sat for % of door. Mail press kit w/ ATTN: Anita, 1265 Pine Ave., Orlando, FL 32824.

The Peacock Room
1321 N Mills Ave.
Orlando, FL 32803
p: 407-228-0048
e: peacockroom@aol.com
www.thepeacockroom.com
contact: Tania Bernard
e: tatankab@aol.com
genres: Rock, Indie, Acoustic, Heavy Rock
advance: Up to 3 months
capacity: 187
pa: Yes **sound eng:** Yes
stage: 16 x 6
Hip 21+ venue books Tue-Sat w/ up to 3 original Local-Nat'l bands 3 nites to fill 4 hrs. Prefers email or MySpace contact.

The Social
54 N Orange Ave.
Orlando, FL 32801
p: 407-246-1419
e: bookings@thesocial.org
www.thesocial.org
contact: Michael McRaney
e: michaeldmc@mac.com
call: M-F noon-6pm
genres: All Styles
advance: 3-4 months
capacity: 400
pa: Yes **sound eng:** Yes
stage: 30 x 12
Top spot for Nat'l acts & Reg'ls w/ buzz nitely. 2-3 mostly original acts play 30-60min sets for all ages. Nat'ls play for flat fee; 80% merch split. Sound system hailed for depth & detail. Prefers email, but may contact via MySpace or mail kits to: PO Box 3007, Orlando, FL 32802. No Calls.

Underground Bluz
12261 University Blvd.
Orlando, FL 32817
p: 407-482-4141
www.ucf.undergroundbluz.com
contact: Paul Mahoney
e: paulwmahoney@gmail.com
genres: Blues, Rock, Jazz, Fusion, Dance, Reggae, S/S, Folk, Bluegrass, Acoustic, Funk
advance: 3 months
capacity: 55
pa: Yes
open mics: Tue & Wed
Premium beer & winebar hosts polished Local-Reg'l acts up to 7 nites. Bands play 45min to 21+ for door after fees. Also books Metropolitan Orlando location. MySpace links preferred.

Pensacola

Flora Bama Lounge
17401 Perdido Key Dr.
Pensacola, FL 32507
p: 850-492-3048
e: info@florabama.com
www.florabama.com
contact: Donna Slater
p: 850-393-1798
e: florabamadonna@yahoo.com
genres: Rock, Country, Blues, Jazz
capacity: 200
pa: Yes **sound eng:** Yes
open mics: Mon: Mar-Sep
Party spot w/ eclectic regular crowd boasts indoor & outdoor stages & features Local acts up to 7 nites & some Nat'ls for flat fee. All ages during the day. Snail mail or email kit.

Handlebar
319 N Tarragona St.
Pensacola, FL 32501
p: 850-434-9060
www.myspace.com/thehandlebar
contact: Sue Lamar
p: 850-432-7332
call: M-F 11am-3pm
genres: All Styles
advance: 1-2 months
capacity: 375
pa: Yes **sound eng:** Yes
stage: 18 x 20
Tavern books 2-3 original Local & Reg'l acts Fri-Sat for % of door after costs. Sets are 45-60min; 60+min for headliners. Holds some all ages shows outside, but mainly 18+ to enter. Promos: 4390 N 9th Ave., Pensacola, FL 32503.

Tallahassee

Bradfordville Blues Club
7152 Moses Ln.
Tallahassee, FL 32309
p: 850-906-0766
e: comments@bradfordvilleblues.com
www.bradfordvilleblues.com
contact: Gary Anton
e: ganton@comcast.net
call: M-F 10am-6pm
genres: Blues, Zydeco, Rockabilly
advance: 4 months
capacity: 120
pa: Yes **sound eng:** Yes
stage: 9 x 18
Atmospheric juke joint showcases serious Blues for mature all ages crowd. Estab. original Reg'l & Touring artists booked Fri-Sat. Featured band plays two 75min sets for flat fee. Email or snail mail kit.

The Engine Room
809 Railroad Ave.
Tallahassee, FL 32310
p: 850-222-8090
e: engineroomsounds@gmail.com
www.engineroomsounds.com
contact: Truewill Mashburn
p: 850-212-3403
call: M-F 10am-6pm
genres: All Styles
advance: 1-4 months
capacity: 500
pa: Yes **sound eng:** Yes
stage: 20 x 13
Formerly The Beta Bar, newly renovated music mecca presents polished, original Local-Nat'ls 6-7 nites. 3-5 acts play 30-40min. Bands keep 80-100% merch sales. Caters to locals w/ some all ages shows. Prefers emailed link to music, but may mail press kit to venue.

Floyd's Music Store
666-1 W Tennessee St.
Tallahassee, FL 32304
p: 850-222-3506
e: info@floydsmusicstore.com
www.floydsmusicstore.com
contact: John Robertson
genres: Rock
advance: 1 month
capacity: 500
pa: Yes **sound eng:** Yes
Although not a music store, this venue sells the all ages crowd on hot Touring & Local Rock groups primarily Fri-Sat. Merch split is 90/10. Books mostly thru MySpace.

Tampa/ St. Petersburg

Bourbon St. Nightclub
4331 US Hwy. 19
New Port Richey, FL 34652
p: 727-843-0686
e: info@clubbourbonstreet.com
www.clubbourbonstreet.com
contact: Gregory F. Serio
call: M-F 10am-2pm
genres: Blues, Alt., Rock, Jazz, Reggae, Jam, Country, Metal, Hip-Hop
advance: 2-3 months
capacity: 900
pa: Yes **sound eng:** Yes
stage: 20 x 30
10,000 sq. music venue features up to 8 Local-Nat'l acts & DJs 3-5 nites; sets are 30-120min; some all ages shows. Complete w/ theatrical curtain & 2 dressing rms. Artists keep 80% merch. Use booking form on website.

Emerald Bar
550 Central Ave.
St. Petersburg, FL 33701
p: 727-898-6054
e: emeraldbar@gmail.com
www.myspace.com/emeraldbar
contact: Crissy
call: Mon 4-9:30pm; Thu after 10pm; Fri after 9pm
genres: Most Styles
advance: 1-2 months
capacity: 70
pa: Yes **sound eng:** To hire
stage: floor space
Bar w/ art gallery books Local-Nat'l bands & DJs for 45min sets Fri & Sat nites; some Thu shows. 3 original acts play for the door to 21+ crowd. No Hip-Hop. Call or mail kit w/ ATTN: Crissy. No EPKs.

Ford Amphitheater
4802 US Hwy. 301 N
Tampa, FL 33610
p: 813-740-2446
e: info@fordamp.com
www.fordamp.com
contact: Danny Wilde
e: dannywilde@livenation.com
genres: All Styles
capacity: 20,000
pa: Yes **sound eng:** Yes
stage: 3 stages
All ages Live Nation outdoor venue books Locals & Reg'ls on 2 stages; Touring bands play main stage for flat fee. 35-45 shows/yr. Mail kit to venue.

Jannus Landing Courtyard
16 2nd St. N
St. Petersburg, FL 33701
p: 727-896-2276
www.jannuslandingconcerts.com
contact: John "Jack" Bodziak
e: jackbodz@aol.com
genres: Rock, Pop, Americana, Jazz, Reggae
advance: 4-6 weeks
capacity: 1500
pa: Yes **sound eng:** Yes
stage: 48 x 20
Mostly all ages outdoor stage presents estab. Nat'l & polished original acts. 2+ acts play 45-90min. Mail press kit w/ ATTN: Jack, 220 1st Ave. N, St. Petersburg, FL 33701.

New World Brewery
1313 E 8th Ave.
Tampa, FL 33605
p: 813-248-4969
www.myspace.com/newworldbrewery
e: newworldbooking@gmail.com
genres: All Styles
advance: 1-2 months
capacity: 200
pa: Yes **sound eng:** Yes
stage: 20 x 20
Celestially-themed bar books up to 4 original Reg'l & Nat'l acts for % of door 3-4 nites. Acts perform 20-90min for 21+ crowd. Prefers MySpace for booking. No Calls.

The Orpheum
1902 Republica de Cuba Ave.
Ybor City, FL 33605
p: 813-248-9500
www.statemedia.com
contact: Dave Drake
e: davetwopercent@gmail.com
call: Mon-Wed 1pm-3am
genres: Rock, Urban, Electro, Alt.
advance: 1-3 months
capacity: 200
pa: Yes **sound eng:** Yes
stage: 14 x 24
Original Local-Int'l bands gig 4 nites for mostly all ages in popular bar w/ great sound. 3-6 acts play 30-60min sets for % door. Email or snail mail kit.

Palm Pavilion Grill & Bar
10 Bay Esplanad
Clearwater Beach, FL 33767
p: 727-446-2642
www.palmpavilion.com
contact: Jimmy James
p: 813-913-3353
e: jimmyj1@aol.com
genres: Pop, Rock
1-2 Local-Touring bands gig daily in summer & wknds during off-season at this busy tourist resort. Email for booking.

Pegasus Lounge
10008 N 30th St.
Tampa, FL 33612
p: 813-971-1679
www.pegasusniteclub.com
contact: Julie
e: julie.bible@verizon.net
genres: All Styles

capacity: 200
pa: Yes **sound eng:** Yes
stage: large
Dive bar is at the forefront of Local scene, hosts 75-80 original acts/mo. 3-5 acts play for % of door Tue & Thu-Sun. Most shows are 18+; Sun all ages. Check calendar for avail. dates, then call.

Ringside Cafe
2742 4th St. N
St. Petersburg, FL 33704
p: 727-894-8465
www.myspace.com/ringsidecafe
contact: Mitch Gray
call: Tue-Sat 7pm-2am
genres: Blues, Rock, Jazz
advance: 6 months
capacity: 150
Popular all ages Blues spot hosts polished Local & some Touring bands nitely. Featured act plays 4hrs w/ breaks, usu. for flat fee. Call or mail press kit to venue w/ ATTN: Mitch. No booking via MySpace.

Sacred Grounds Coffeehouse
4819 E Busch Blvd., #104
Tampa, FL 33617
p: 813-983-0837
e: sacredgroundstampa@yahoo.com
www.sacredgroundstampa.com
contact: Karen
e: sacredgroundsbooking@gmail.com
genres: Pop, Rock, Acoustic, Folk, Americana, Classical, Jazz, Blues
advance: 2 weeks - 6 months
capacity: 50
pa: Yes
stage: 6 x 8
open mics: Mon **sign in:** 8pm
Local-Int'l acts gig 3-4 nites from Wed-Sun at this upbeat performance space located near U of South FL. Up to 4 acts play 45-60min mostly for tips; sometimes % of door. Prefers email or MySpace contact; No Calls.

Skipper's Smokehouse
910 Skipper Rd.
Tampa, FL 33613
p: 813-971-0666
www.skipperssmokehouse.com
contact: Tom White
p: 831-971-0666 x27
e: tom@skipperssmokehouse.com
call: Tue-Thu noon-4pm
genres: Blues, Roots, Zydeco, Reggae, Bluegrass, World Alt. Country, Jam
advance: 3 months
capacity: 700
pa: To rent **sound eng:** To hire
stage: 24 x 16
Celebrated Blues club books Local-Int'l talent Tue-Sun for 21+ crowd; Grateful Dead cover band Thu. 1-2 mostly original acts play from 9pm-midnite. Prefers press kits snail mailed.

The State Theatre
687 Central Ave.
St. Petersburg, FL 33701
p: 727-895-3045
e: info@statetheatreconcerts.com
www.statetheatreconcerts.com
contact: Mark A.
e: booking@statetheatreconcerts.com
call: prefers email
genres: Hard Rock, Reggae, Americana, Country, Ska, Pop, Punk, Hardcore, Jazz, Blues
advance: 4-6 weeks
capacity: 705
pa: Yes **sound eng:** Yes
stage: 24 x 19 **in-house:** To rent
Top all ages venue w/ awesome acoustics presents original Local-Int'l acts & DJs 3 nites. 3 bands play 45+min & keep 80% merch sales. Most shows all ages, some 18+. Prefers email.

Tampa Bay PAC
1010 N W.C. McInnes Pl.
Tampa, FL 33602
p: 813-222-1000
e: comments@tbpac.org
www.tbpac.org
contact: Jeanne Piazza
p: 813-222-1017
e: jeanne.piazza@tbpac.org
genres: All Styles
advance: 6-52 weeks
capacity: 100; 150; 300; 1042; 2610
pa: Yes **sound eng:** Yes
Massive PAC hosts Local-Int'l talent 6 nites for mostly all ages. Up to 4 mostly original acts play 45+min sets; Bands keep 65-75% of merch sales. Email or snail mail kit w/ ATTN: Jeanne Piazza.

Yeoman's Road Pub
236 E Davis Blvd.
Tampa, FL 33606
p: 813-251-2748
e: yeomanspub@hotmail.com
www.myspace.com/yeomansdi
contact: Doug
genres: Rock, Jazz, Blues, Reggae
advance: 6 weeks
capacity: 145
pa: Yes
stage: 12 x 18
open mics: Tue 9pm-2am
Bohemian English pub books original Reg'l & Nat'l acts 2 nites for % of door. Featured act plays 4hrs w/ breaks to 21+.

Greater FL

Rockstarz
3557 Fowler St.
Fort Myers, FL 33901
p: 239-332-7625
www.myspace.com/rockstarzbar
contact: Alan Silverberg
e: silverberg8@comcast.net
genres: Alt., Rock, Metal
advance: 2 months
capacity: 225
pa: Yes **sound eng:** Yes
stage: 20 x 20
Seated halfway btwn Miami & Tampa w/ a 'Rock club feel' & a great PA. Books up to 4 Local-Nat'l bands Wed-Sun w/ 45min sets. Snail mail only; No EPKs

Georgia

Athens

40 Watt
285 W Washington St.
Athens, GA 30601
p: 706-549-7871
www.40watt.com
contact: Velena Vego
e: fortywatt@athens.net
call: Thu 2-6pm
genres: Indie, Alt. Country, Pop, Hip-Hop
advance: 2 months
capacity: 800
pa: Yes **sound eng:** Yes
stage: large
Home of Athens scene, showcases polished rising Locals, known Touring bands & DJs up to 3 nites/wk. 3 original acts play 1hr set for 18+. Wait 3 wks to call after mailing kit.

Caledonia Lounge
256 W Clayton St.
Athens, GA 30601
p: 706-549-5577
www.caledonialounge.com
contact: Bryant
e: booking@caledonialounge.com
genres: Punk, Rock, Indie
21+ venue hosts live music up to 5 nites. All booking done thru email & MySpace. No email attachments.

Farm255
255 W Washington St.
Athens, GA 30601
p: 706-549-4660
e: info@farm255.com
www.farm255.com
contact: Aaron Burns
p: 240-994-6315
e: music@farm255.com
call: M-F before 3pm
genres: All Styles
advance: 1-2 months
capacity: 250
pa: Yes
stage: 14 x 8
Farm-fresh eatery hosts Local & Touring acts Wed-Sun for % of bar. 1-2 bands play 1hr sets & are responsible for promotion. Email EPK or link.

Flicker Theater & Bar
263 W Washington St.
Athens, GA 30601
p: 706-546-0039
www.myspace.com/flickerbar
contact: Clint
e: flickerbooking@yahoo.com
genres: S/S, Acoustic, Instrumental, Bluegrass
advance: 1-2 months
capacity: 100
pa: Yes **sound eng:** Yes
stage: 10 x 12 **in-house:** Piano
Intimate 21+ performance space welcomes indies & 1st-time performers. Mostly Local acts play 2.5hrs 4 nites. Email or mail kit to venue.

The Georgia Theatre
215 N Lumpkin St.
Athens, GA 30601
p: 706-353-3405
www.georgiatheatre.com
contact: Scott Orvold
e: scotto@georgiatheatre.com
call: Tue noon-5pm
genres: All Styles
advance: 3-4 months
capacity: 850
pa: Yes **sound eng:** Yes
stage: 25 x 25
Spacious venue books Local-Int'l acts & DJs 5- 6 nites for 18+ crowd. Up to 3 artists play 60-90min sets. Bands keep 80% soft merch sales, 100% on hard. Assists w/ booking for several other venues. Prefers EPKs; No unsolicited mail.

The Melting Point
295 E Dougherty St.
Athens, GA 30601
p: 706-254-6909
www.meltingpointathens.com
contact: Troy Aubrey
p: 706-354-6107
e: troy@foundryent.com
genres: Most Styles
advance: 1-4 months
capacity: 250-300
pa: Yes **sound eng:** Yes
stage: 15 x 10
Fully-loaded w/ sound & interactive, the best newcomer on the Athens scene presents up to 3 Local-Touring buzz bands Tue-Sat for 18+. Merch split is 85/15. Sets are 60-75min. No Rap, Pop or Punk. Email or mail kit: PO Box 1186, Athens, GA 30603.

Nuçi's Space
396 Oconee St.
Athens, GA 30601
p: 706-227-1515
www.nuci.org
contact: Will Kiswer
e: will@nuci.org
genres: All Styles
advance: 1 month
capacity: 200
pa: Yes **sound eng:** Yes
stage: medium
Unique non-profit health & music resource ctr. supports indies by providing treatment for depression & booking occasional shows Fri-Sat. Bands play for merch; shows mostly all ages. Prefers email, but may contact via MySpace.

Tasty World
312 E Broad St.
Athens, GA 30601
p: 706-543-0797
e: tastyworld@mindspring.com
www.tastyworld.net
contact: Murphy Wolford
call: Wed-Thu 3-6pm
genres: Rock, Alt., Country, Rockabilly, Bluegrass, Jazz, Punk
advance: 6-8 weeks
capacity: 330
pa: Yes **sound eng:** Yes
stage: 16 x 16
Bi-level niteclub features diverse Reg'l-Nat'l acts & DJs 6 nites for 18+. 3 acts play 40-60min for % of door. Prefers email.

Atlanta

The 7 Venue
5975-A Fairburn Rd.
Douglasville, GA 30135
p: 770-942-4224
e: info@the7venue.com
www.the7venue.com
genres: Metal, Emo, Punk, Indie, Rock
capacity: 800; 450
pa: Yes **sound eng:** Yes
stage: Yes
Venue 20min outside of Atlanta, features 3 stages: large, medium & Acoustic stage. Hosts Local-Nat'l acts. Books thru MySpace.

Andrews Upstairs
56 E Andrews Dr., Ste. 13
Atlanta, GA 30305
p: 404-467-1600
e: info@andrewsupstairs.com

www.andrewsupstairs.com
contact: Kevin Greene
p: 404-869-1132
e: kevin@eastandrews.com; kgreene@eastcoast entertainment.com
call: M-F 10am-7pm
genres: Pop, Hip-Hop, Country
advance: 6 weeks for Locals
capacity: 400
pa: Yes **sound eng:** Yes
stage: 10 x 20
Upscale 21+ venue books Local & Touring talent 3-4 nites. 1-2 acts play 90-120min. Nat'l merch split is 80/20; Locals keep 100%. Prefers EPKs or drop off/mail press kit to venue before 5pm; wait 3 wks to call.

Apache Cafe
64 3rd St. NW
Atlanta, GA 30308
p: 404-876-5436
e: image@mindspring.com
www.apachecafe.info
contact: Ace
e: booking@apachecafe.info
genres: Jazz, Funk, R&B, Hip-Hop, Rock, Soul, Latin
advance: 1 month
capacity: 300
pa: Yes **sound eng:** Yes
stage: 12 x 21
open mics: Tue MC Battle; Wed S/S, R&B & Vocalists
Artsy hang features up to 3 original Local & Touring acts & DJs Wed-Sat. Many 18+ nites, some 21+. Prefers EPKs.

Blind Willie's
828 N Highland Ave.
Atlanta, GA 30306
p: 404-873-2583
www.blindwilliesblues.com
contact: Eric King
p: 404-525-7844
genres: Blues, S/S, Americana
advance: 4-5 months
capacity: 150
pa: Yes **sound eng:** Yes
stage: 12 x 14
Celebrated Blues room showcases Local-Touring talent Mon-Sat & some Sun. Single original act plays 50-90min sets for 21+. Mail press kit w/ ATTN: Eric King, 443 Euclid Terr., Atlanta, GA 30307. Only demos in genres listed.

Cafe 290
290 Hilderbrand Dr.
Atlanta, GA 30328
p: 404-256-3942
www.cafe290atlanta.com
contact: John Scatena
genres: Jazz, R&B
advance: 1 month
capacity: 250
pa: Yes **sound eng:** Yes
stage: medium
open mics: Sun **sign in:** 9pm
Dingy all ages listening room features mostly prime Reg'l Jazz up to 7 nites; some Local & Nat'l acts. Featured original act plays two or three 1hr sets for 18+. Mail press kit to venue.

Center Stage Atlanta
3474 W Peachtree St.
Atlanta, GA 30309
p: 404-885-1365
www.centerstage-atlanta.com
contact: Lucy Lawler
p: 404-885-1365 x107
e: lucy@rivalentertainment.com
genres: All Styles
capacity: 1100
pa: Yes **sound eng:** Yes
Formerly Earthlink Live, mostly all ages venue boasts premier sound & lights. Books top tier original Local-Int'l bands & DJs for flat fee. Email Brandon: brandon@rivalentertainment.com or mail kit w/ ATTN: Brandon Mize.

Crimson Moon Cafe
24 N Park St.
Dahlonega, GA 30533
p: 706-864-3982
www.thecrimsonmoon.com
contact: Dana Marie LaChance
p: 404-374-1026
e: gigs@thecrimsonmoon.com
call: Sun-Thu 10am-7pm
genres: Acoustic, Folk, S/S, Bluegrass, Trad. Folk, Pop, Blues, Jazz, Country, Gospel
advance: 1-4 months
capacity: 95
pa: Yes **sound eng:** Yes
stage: 8 x 9
open mics: 1st & 3rd Mon
Supper club hosts mostly Nat'l & some Local-Reg'l acts Fri-Mon. 1-2 bands play 45-70min to all ages. Payment is a flat fee & 80-90% of door after back-end costs split point incl. guarantee, meals & 10% promoters profit. Email or snail mail w/ billing name & dates requested in subject & incl. web links, awards, credits, shared stage w/, etc.

The Earl
488 Flat Shoals Ave.
Atlanta, GA 30316
p: 404-522-3950
e: info@badearl.com
www.badearl.com
contact: Patrick Hill
e: wordproductions2@ gmail.com; booking@badearl.com
call: M-F noon-5pm
genres: Underground, Rock, Funk
advance: 2 months
capacity: 300
pa: Yes **sound eng:** Yes
stage: medium
No frills indie Rock haven w/ some DJs presents Reg'l-Int'l bands 4 nites for 21+. 3 acts play 30-40min for% of door. Touring bands must hook up w/ Locals. Prefers email w/ link to MySpace or Sonicbids or mail to: Word Prod., 356 Atlanta Ave., #3, Atlanta, GA 30315.

Eddie's Attic
515-B N McDonough St.
Decatur, GA 30030
p: 404-377-4976
e: info@eddiesattic.com
www.eddiesattic.com
contact: Eddie Owen
e: booking@eddiesattic.com
call: email only
genres: Acoustic, S/S, Folk, Rock, Bluegrass
advance: 2+ months
capacity: 150
pa: Yes **sound eng:** Yes
stage: 13' off corner
open mics: Mon Open Mic Songwriting Competition
Long-running Acoustic listening room & launching pad presents original Local-Touring talent nitely; most shows all ages. Up to 5 acts play 45min sets. See Artist Info on website first. Prefers email w/ EPK or links to music, but may mail press kit to venue w/ ATTN: Booking. Follow up w/ email. No Calls.

The Five Spot
1123 Euclid Ave.
Atlanta, GA 30307
p: 404-223-1100
www.fivespot-atl.com
contact: Abbey Swanson
e: fivespotbooking@yahoo.com
call: email only
genres: Jazz, Funk, Blues, Reggae, Hip-Hop, Electronica
advance: Up to 3 months
capacity: 200
pa: Avail **sound eng:** To hire
stage: 18 x 15
open mics: Tue 9pm
Deli-style eatery hosts Local-Int'l acts nitely for all ages; 1-3 mostly original bands play 1-3hrs. Prefers EPKs but may snail mail hard copy to venue.

Lenny's
486 Decatur St. SE, Ste. 13
Atlanta, GA 30312
p: 404-577-7721
www.lennysbar.com
contact: Bean
e: beansummer@gmail.com
genres: All Styles
advance: 2-3 months
capacity: 450+
pa: Yes **sound eng:** Yes
stage: 34 x 10
An integral part of Atlanta's Local scene & ideal venue for new bands to cut their chops. Reg'l-Int'l acts & DJs play 5 nites for 90% of door minus $150 for prod. costs. 5 original acts play 30min to 21+. Email or use website booking form; No unsolicited packages.

The Loft
1032 Broadway
Columbus, GA 31901
p: 706-596-8141
www.theloft.com
e: booking@theloft.com
genres: Most Styles
advance: 2-3 months
capacity: 250
pa: Yes **sound eng:** Yes
stage: 20 x 14 (wedge)
open mics: Wed 8pm
21+ listening room below Earthlink Live perfectly designed to pack in bodies for DJ-spun dancing or live shows under impressive light display. Presents Local-Int'l artists 3 nites. 2 acts play two 70min sets. Full recording capabilities avail. No Metal or Hip-Hop. Prefers email, but may mail press kit to: PO Box 19, Columbus, GA 31901.

The Masquerade
695 North Ave. NE
Atlanta, GA 30308
p: 404-577-8178
e: masq@masq.com
www.masq.com
contact: Tim Sweetwood
e: tim@masq.com
genres: Rock, Punk, Electronic, Hip-Hop, Alt.
advance: 2-3 months
capacity: 1200
pa: Yes **sound eng:** Yes
stage: large
Premier all-ages venue housed in a turn-of-the-century mill, features top Local-Int'l acts 6 nites. 4 bands play 45-90min sets. Prefers email w/ link to music, tour history & dates wanted; call few wks later to follow up

The RedLight Cafe
553 Amsterdam Ave.
Atlanta, GA 30306
p: 404-874-7828
www.redlightcafe.com
contact: Bill Hoover
e: rlcbill@hotmail.com
call: Wed after 7pm
genres: Bluegrass, Alt., Acoustic, Jazz, Rock
advance: 2 months
capacity: 150
pa: Yes **sound eng:** Yes
stage: 12 x 12
open mics: Wed **sign in:** 7pm
Promising original Local-Int'l talent showcased up to 6 nites to 18+ crowd. Difficult to reach, but try to email or call.

Sambuca
3102 Piedmont Rd.
Atlanta, GA 30305
p: 404-237-5299
www.sambucarestaurant.com
genres: Jazz, Big Band
advance: 2-3 months
capacity: 350
pa: Yes **sound eng:** Yes
Upscale all ages supper club presents polished Local-Int'l acts nitely at 7pm. 1 act plays 4-5hrs w/ breaks for flat fee. Other locations in Dallas, Houston & Denver. Local & 1st-timers, call mgmt. for booking. Nat'ls call corporate: 972-458-0800.

Smith's Olde Bar
1578 Piedmont Ave.
Atlanta, GA 30324
p: 404-875-1522
www.smithsoldebar.com
contact: Dan Nolen
p: 404-876-8436
e: nolenreevesmusic@ mindspring.com
call: Mon, Tue, Thu & Fri noon-5pm; Wed noon-3pm
genres: Americana, Rock, Jam, Acoustic, Pop
advance: 1-10 months
capacity: 300
pa: Yes **sound eng:** Yes
stage: medium
Legendary listening room w/ killer sound hosts top Local-Touring buzz bands nitely. Up to 4 mostly original acts play 45-50min for diverse crowd of 21+. Major acts get flat fee & Local-Reg'l acts get% of door. Also books The Nick in Birmingham & Brother's Bar in Jacksonville, AL. Promos: Nolen/Reeves Music, 1574 1/2 Piedmont Ave., Atlanta, GA 30324.

The Star Bar
437 Moreland Ave.
Atlanta, GA 30307
p: 404-681-9018
www.starbar.net
contact: Bryan Malone
p: 404-681-5740
e: starbarbooking@hotmail.com
call: Mon, Tue & Fri 2-6pm
genres: Rockabilly, Garage,

Punk, Rock
advance: 3 months
capacity: 250
pa: Yes **sound eng:** Yes
stage: 18.5 x 9.5
No frills 21+ bar features diverse Local-Int'l bands up to 7 nites. 3 original acts play 45min for the door. Promos: PO Box 6019, Atlanta, GA 31107.

Swayze's
2543 Bells Ferry Rd., Ste. 650
Marietta, GA 30066
p: 770-590-0111
e: swayzesvenue@aol.com
www.swayzesvenue.com
contact: Lee Satterfield
call: Fri 3-5pm
genres: Punk, Hardcore, Metal, Indie Rock, Ska, Emo, Folk, Instrumental, Americana, Experimental, S/S, Alt. Country
advance: 3+ months
capacity: 200
pa: Yes **sound eng:** Yes
stage: 25 x 20
Smoke-free mom & pop club just outside Atlanta, has original live music 3-7 nites. 3-6 Local-Int'l acts play 25-30min sets. Use MySpace for booking; No unsolicited mail, email or calls.

Variety Playhouse
1099 Euclid Ave.
Atlanta, GA 30307
p: 404-524-7354
e: variety@mindspring.com
www.varietyplayhouse.com
contact: Lisa
e: lisa@variety-playhouse.com
genres: Roots, Alt., Jazz, Americana, World
advance: 2 months
capacity: 750-1000
pa: Yes **sound eng:** Yes
stage: 36 x 27
Flexible & intimate all ages hall presents top Reg'l & Touring acts 3-4 nites, mostly Fri-Sat. 2-3 original acts play 30-90min; few tribute acts. Merch splits 80/20. EPK or mail promo to: PO Box 5253, Atlanta, GA 31107.

The Venue
425 N Hamilton St.
Dalton, GA 30720
p: 706-280-9254
www.myspace.com/thevenuega
contact: Susie Roberson
e: reisus2@yahoo.com
call: evenings
genres: All Styles
advance: 2-6 months
capacity: 350
pa: Yes **sound eng:** Yes
stage: 20 x 20
Punk haven welcomes 4-5 Local-Int'l acts of varying styles 3-4 nites for all ages crowds of youngsters & college students. Bands play 30-45min. Snail mail kits.

Greater GA

The Jinx
127 W Congress St.
Savannah, GA 31401
p: 912-236-2281
www.thejinx.net
e: booking@thejinx.net
pa: Yes **sound eng:** Yes
Formerly The Velvet Elvis; premier area live music venue hosts eclectic blend of polished Local-Nat'l acts & DJs 6 nites. Snail mail or email.

Sector 7G
631 Ellis St.
Augusta, GA 30901
p: 706-432-0401
www.myspace.com/sector7g
genres: Rock, Indie, Punk, Hardcore, Metal
pa: Yes **sound eng:** Yes
stage: Yes
All ages Rock venue & recording studio w/ good sound & lighting presents Local-Touring bands for a % of door & 100% merch. Shows booked by Reg'l promoters only: myspace.com/jams; myspace.com/over9000augusta; myspace.com/remedybookingcompany. No calls, emails, pkgs or booking at MySpace.

The Sentient Bean
13 E Park Ave.
Savannah, GA 31401
p: 912-232-4447
www.myspace.com/kelli_rose
contact: Travis
e: sentientbooking@gmail.com
genres: Most Styles
advance: 3 months
capacity: 100
pa: Yes
stage: 10 x 11
open mics: 3rd Sun of mo
Edgy coffeehouse stone's throw from SC, hosts eclectic blend of Local-Int'l polished & developing acts 3-5 nites. 1-3 bands play 45+min for tips or % of door. No Heavy Metal. Use form at sentientbean.com/performers/submit.

Whiskey River
4570 Pio Nono Ave.
Macon, GA 31206
p: 478-788-3000
e: info@whiskeyriver.tv
www.whiskeyriver.tv
contact: Brad Majors
p: 478-788-3000 x212
e: riverhousemedia@yahoo.com
genres: S/S, New Country, Rock, Pop
advance: 6 months
capacity: 995
pa: Yes **sound eng:** Yes
Housed in well-adorned ent. complex, this cavernous 21+ venue boasts top sound, lighting & polished Local-Nat'l acts Wed-Sat. Featured act plays 45min for flat fee. Prefers email & EPKs. No unsolicited mail, MySpace contact or calls.

Idaho

Boise

The Bouquet
1010 Main St.
Boise, ID 83702
p: 208-345-6605
www.thebouquet.net
e: booking@thebouquet.net
call: no calls
genres: Rock, Alt., Punk, Indie Rock, Bluegrass, S/S
advance: 6 months
capacity: 375
pa: Yes **sound eng:** Yes
stage: 20 x 10
Renovated Rock club w/ new owners, books Local-Int'l acts & DJs for 21+ crowd; mostly Reg'ls. 1-2 original acts play 1hr sets. Use MySpace for booking; No Calls.

Common Ground Cafe
303 E Colorado St.
McCall, ID 83638
p: 208-634-2846
e: commongroundcafe@hotmail.com
www.commongroundcafe.net
contact: Brian Thomas
genres: Americana, Jazz, World, Alt. Country, Jam, Rock
advance: 3 months
capacity: 300
pa: Yes **sound eng:** Yes
stage: 20 x 12
Cool coffeehouse/CD store, features 1-3 original Reg'l-Touring artist every Fri 6-10pm w/ breaks for all ages; also some outdoor shows. Promos: PO Box 797, McCall, ID 83638.

Knitting Factory Concert House
416 S 9th St.
Boise, ID 83702
p: 208-367-1212
e: info@bigeasyconcerts.com
http://bo.knittingfactory.com
contact: Chris Moore
p: 208-343-8883
genres: Punk, Alt., Hip-Hop, Rock, Alt. Country
capacity: 1000
pa: Yes **sound eng:** Yes
stage: 32 x 40
Once The Big Easy, now re-branded & revamped as a state-of-the-art live music venue. Up to 5 original Touring & Reg'l acts w/ a following play mostly all ages shows. Merch splits 70/30. WA venue also renamed.

Neurolux
111 N 11th St.
Boise, ID 83702
p: 208-343-0886
e: info@neurolux.com
www.neurolux.com
contact: Allen Ireland
genres: Alt., Punk, Rock, Country
advance: 1 month
capacity: 250
pa: Yes **sound eng:** Yes
stage: 20 x 15
Lounge books original Local-Int'l bands up to 7 nites. 1-3 original bands play 1hr sets. Email or snail mail kits; follow-up w/ email.

Tom Grainey's
109 S 6th St.
Boise, ID 83702
p: 208-345-2505
e: tomgraineys@gmail.com
www.boiseevents.net/tomgraineys
contact: Bryan Crew
genres: Alt., Folk, Blues, Reggae, Roots
advance: 1-3 months
capacity: 150; 230
pa: Yes **sound eng:** Yes
stage: 15 x 10
Mainstay Irish-style pub above J.T. Toads, w/ great sound & dance floor hosts Local-Touring bands Wed-Sat for 21+. Email or mail press kit w/ CD, bio & photo to: PO Box 1404, Boise, ID 83702.

The Venue
521 W Broad St.
Boise, ID 83702
p: 208-919-0011
www.myspace.com/boisevenue
contact: Brandy Morris
e: booking@boisevenue.com
genres: Punk, Emo, Metal, Hardcore, Indie Rock, Pop
advance: 2-3 months
capacity: 400
pa: Yes **sound eng:** Yes
stage: large
Loud, all ages, non-profit & booze-free showcase hosts mostly original Touring bands 3-5 nites. Acts play 30-45min for flat fee & % of door. Must be able to draw. Email first for booking.

Greater ID

John's Alley
114 E 6th St.
Moscow, ID 83843
p: 208-883-7662
e: johnsalley@turbonet.com
www.alleyvault.com
contact: Brian Jordan
p: 208-882-7531
call: M-F noon-5pm
genres: Jam, Rock, Reggae, Funk, Punk, Country
advance: 3-6 months
capacity: 350
pa: Yes **sound eng:** Yes
stage: 28 x 12
open mics: Every other Tue
Up to 5 original Reg'l-Nat'l artists gig several nites/wk in cool college town bar. Promos: ATTN: Brian, PO Box 8992, Moscow, ID 83843.

Whiskey Jacques
251 N Main St.
Ketchum, ID 83340
p: 208-726-5297
e: whiskeyjacques@yahoo.com
www.whiskeyjacques.com
contact: Thatcher Marsted/Kristin Derrig
call: Mon & Fri 11am-4pm
genres: Rock, Jazz, Funk, Country, Jam
advance: 2 months
capacity: 362
pa: Yes **sound eng:** Yes
Rustic tavern 153mi E of Boise, books even mix of original & cover bands 4 nites for 21+. 1 Reg'l-Nat'l act plays 3hrs; some Locals occasionally. Mail kit w/ ATTN: Booking, PO Box 6720, Ketchum, ID 83340.

Illinois

Bloomington/Champaign

Canopy Club
708 S Goodwin Ave.
Urbana, IL 61801
p: 217-344-2263
www.canopyclub.com
contact: Mike Armintrout
e: mikea@jaytv.com
call: M-F daytime
genres: Rock, Alt., Jam, Pop, Jazz, World, R&B
advance: 4-8 weeks
capacity: 750
pa: Yes **sound eng:** Yes
stage: 20 x 40 **in-house:** Drums
Niteclub showcases Local-Touring acts & DJs up to 7 nites for 18+. Mon is Locals nite.

Cowboy Monkey
6 Taylor St.

Champaign, IL 61820
p: 217-398-2688
e: info@cowboy-monkey.com
www.cowboy-monkey.com
contact: Ward Gollings
call: email only
genres: Rock, Rockabilly, Country, Folk, Bluegrass, Salsa, Jazz, Blues, Acoustic
advance: 4-8 weeks
capacity: 120
pa: Yes **sound eng:** Yes
stage: 12 x 16
open mics: Tue **sign in:** 10pm
Music bar hosts up to 4 mostly Local-Reg'l bands, DJs & some Touring talent. Prefers email w/ 'Booking' or 'Ward' in subject.

Fat Jack's
511 N Main St.
Bloomington, IL 61701
p: 309-821-9222
e: fatjacksinc@hotmail.com
www.fatjacksinc.net
contact: Tyler Holloway
call: M-F 9am-5pm
genres: All Styles
advance: Up to 1 year
capacity: 397+
pa: Yes
stage: 15 x 11; 15 x 11; small
Crowded bar w/ 4 rooms & 3 stages books mostly area bands Sat & some Fri. Single act plays 4-5hrs for mixed 21+ crowd; more bands play during local fests. Also owns Maggie Miley's in Normal. Prefers hard copies dropped off at bar.

Friend's & Co.
509 Van Buren Ave.
Charleston, IL 61920
p: 217-345-2380
www.myspace.com/friendsdungeon
contact: Michael G.
e: friendsandco.booking@yahoo.com
genres: Punk, Alt. Country, Rock, Jazz, Metal
advance: 1+ months
capacity: 150
pa: Yes **sound eng:** Yes
stage: 12 x 17
open mics: Wed **sign in:** 8pm
Perfect midway tour stop btwn St. Louis, Chicago or Indy. Original music club books 2-4 Reg'l & some Touring talent up to 5 nites. Accepts EPKs or mail to: PO Box 182, Charleston, IL 61920; No Calls.

Highdive
51 Main St.
Champaign, IL 61820
p: 217-356-2337
e: info@thehighdive.com
www.thehighdive.com
contact: Ward Gollings
e: kimward5@insightbb.com
call: email only
genres: All Styles
advance: 4-8 weeks
capacity: 425
pa: Yes **sound eng:** Yes
stage: 20 x 16
Prime music venue w/ great sight lines & sound, books Local-Touring estab. acts, buzz bands. Up to 4 acts play 30-45min of mostly original tunes for 19+; all ages w/ guardian. Touring acts must be able to draw 100-400+. Also books Cowboy Monkey for smaller draws. Snail mail or email kit.

Chicago

The Abbey Pub
3420 W Grace St.
Chicago, IL 60618
p: 773-478-4408
www.abbeypub.com
contact: Sean Duffy
e: booking@abbeypub.com
call: M-F after 5pm
genres: Irish, Folk, Pop, Rock, Celtic, Hip-Hop
advance: 2 months
capacity: 550
pa: Yes **sound eng:** Yes
stage: 25 x 20; 8 x 8
open mics: Tue
Celtic hot spot draws original Local-Int'l touring bands & DJs nitely on 2 stages for 21+. Up to 3 acts play 45min; some shows 18+. Also books The Pony, Otto's Niteclub & Underground. Prefers EPKs, but area up & comers may mail kits w/ ATTN: Sean Duffy & incl. info, past & future shows, etc. For smaller pub stage, send ATTN: Sean Kelly.

Andy's Jazz Club
11 E Hubbard St.
Chicago, IL 60611
p: 312-642-6805
e: info@andysjazzclub.com
www.andysjazzclub.com
contact: Chris
genres: Jazz, Blues, Motown
capacity: 150
pa: Yes **sound eng:** Yes
stage: Yes
One of Chicago's best known Jazz clubs. Local-Int'l acts play to 18+ crowd. Sun jam sessions are all ages. Use email for booking; No unsolicited mail.

B.L.U.E.S.
2519 N Halsted St.
Chicago, IL 60657
p: 773-528-1012
e: info@chicagobluesbar.com
www.chicagobluesbar.com
contact: Jennifer Littleton
e: parties@chicagobluesbar.com
call: evenings
genres: Blues, R&B
advance: 2+ months
capacity: 100
pa: Yes **sound eng:** Yes
stage: 12 x 10
Long-running 21+ Blues room presents mostly polished Local acts up to 7 nites. Up & comers play 'No Cover' Sun shows; some Touring acts. Payment is a flat fee & 1hr sets can continue well into the nite. Send CD w/ bio & photo w/ ATTN: Jennifer.

Beat Kitchen
2100 W Belmont Ave.
Chicago, IL 60618
p: 773-281-4444
www.beatkitchen.com
contact: Derron Swan
p: 773-278-6600 x1
e: derron@housecallent.com
genres: Rock, Alt. Country
advance: 6-8 weeks
capacity: 200
pa: Yes **sound eng:** Yes
stage: 20 x 18
Back room stage hosts original, mostly Local-Reg'l & some Touring talent up to 7 nites. Up to 5 acts play 20-60min for mostly 21+; some all ages shows. Email kit & links to john@housecallent.com or mail to venue w/ ATTN: House Call Ent., c/o Subterranean. Follow up w/ email after 3-5 wks.

Big Cities Lounge
905 E State St.
Rockford, IL 61104
p: 815-965-6026
www.bigcitieslounge.com
contact: Nino
call: M-F after 4pm
genres: Blues
advance: 2-3 months
capacity: 100
pa: Yes **sound eng:** Yes
stage: small **in-house:** Drums
Mostly Reg'l acts play Blues club every Fri & Sat nites & some wkdays. Mail promos.

Bill's Blues Bar
1029 Davis St.
Evanston, IL 60201
p: 847-424-9800
www.billsbluesbar.com
contact: Bill Gilmore
e: billsblues9800@sbcglobal.net
call: M-F 10am-6pm
genres: Blues, Folk, Jazz, Rock, Hip-Hop
advance: 4-8 weeks
capacity: 200
pa: Yes **sound eng:** Yes
stage: 10 x 12 **in-house:** Piano
open mics: Sun S/S Nite
Popular listening room 18mi outside of Chicago, hosts mostly original Local-Touring talent up to 6 nites. Featured act play up to 3hrs for 21+. Email link to music or mail kit to club.

Buddy Guy's Legends
754 S Wabash St.
Chicago, IL 60605
p: 312-427-1190
www.buddyguys.com
contact: Brian Fadden
call: M-F before 5pm
genres: Blues
advance: 2+ months
capacity: 400
pa: Yes **sound eng:** Yes
stage: 20 x 10
Popular club/eatery books Local-Nat'l Touring acts Tue-Sun for 21+. Up to 3 original bands play 45-75min for flat fee. Buddy & other celebs often sit in. Mail kit w/ ATTN: Brian Fadden.

C.J. Arthur's
1168 Wilmette Ave.
Wilmette, IL 60091
p: 847-256-8870
e: cjarthurs@sbcglobal.net
www.cjarthurs.com
contact: Cindy Falzer
genres: Jazz, Blues, Rock, Pop, Bluegrass, Funk
advance: 2-6 months
capacity: 150+
pa: Yes **sound eng:** To hire
stage: floor space
All ages eatery 18mi outside Chicago, books Locals on Mon-Tue; Reg'l-Int'l acts on wknds. Featured act plays up to 3 sets from 90+min for % of sales. Email or snail mail kits.

Champs Rock Room
6501 W 79th St.
Burbank, IL 60459
p: 708-233-0181
contact: Sherry
genres: Rock, Metal
advance: 3 weeks
capacity: 150
pa: Yes **sound eng:** Yes
stage: medium
Popular bar & loud Rock club books Local-Nat'l bands on wknds. 4-5 mostly original acts play 40min for % of door. No more all ages nites; 21+ only.

Chicago City Limits
1712 Wise Rd.
Schaumburg, IL 60193
p: 847-524-9910
e: cclarnie@sbcglobal.net
www.chicagocitylimits.net
contact: Joey Demarco
p: 630-620-1154
e: joey@unitedtalentco.com
genres: Alt., Rock, 80s Metal
advance: 2 months
capacity: 400
pa: Yes **sound eng:** Yes
stage: 30 x 22
Suburban Chicago sports club hosts Local-Reg'l bands Fri-Sat & Acoustic Nite on Tue. Doesn't book Nat'l acts.

Darkroom
2210 W Chicago Ave.
Chicago, IL 60622
p: 773-276-1411
e: contact@darkroombar.com
www.darkroombar.com
contact: Arunas Ingaunis
p: 773-276-1411 x3
e: arunas@darkroombar.com; amyteri@darkroombar.com
genres: Downtempo, House, Rock, Reggae, Hip-Hop, Funk, New Wave, Disco, Electronic, Indie, Soul
advance: 2-3 months
capacity: 221-350
pa: Yes **sound eng:** Yes
stage: 18 x 16
Artsy bar presents original Local-Touring artists Sun & Thu & some Wed & Fri for 21+ crowd. Up to 4 acts & DJs play 35-45min sets. Prefers mailed kit, but may email link to music.

Double Door
1572 N Milwaukee Ave.
Chicago, IL 60622
p: 773-489-3160
e: phil@doubledoor.com
www.doubledoor.com
contact: Nate Arling
e: nate@doubledoor.com
call: M-F noon-5pm
genres: Rock, Alt., Blues, Country, Pop
advance: 1-5 months
capacity: 550
pa: Yes **sound eng:** Yes
stage: 20 x 16
Hotspot w/ top sound & sight lines books original Local-Touring talent & DJs for 21+. Up to 4 acts play 30+min sets nitely. 90/10 split on soft goods. Email EPK first; email follow-up 1 wk later. Must get permission to mail kit to: 1321 N Milwaukee Ave., Ste. #425, Chicago, Il 60622. Also books downstairs in Dirt Room for Acoustic acts Sun-Mon: contact Jesse, jesse@doubledoor.com.

Durty Nellie's
180 N Smith St.
Palatine, IL 60067
p: 847-358-9150
e: info@durtynellies.com

www.durtynellies.com
contact: Duff Rice
e: duff@duffentertainment.com
genres: Alt., Pop, Rock, Heavy Metal, Urban, Blues
advance: 2+ months
capacity: 750; 1000
pa: Yes **sound eng:** Yes
stage: large **in-house:** Drums
open mics: Mon
Bi-level venue 30mi from Chicago books up to 3 Local-Touring bands Mon-Sat for 18+; Sun afternoon all ages shows. Merch split is 80/20. Also books other venues incl. The Cubby Bear in Lincolnshire & in Wrigleyville. Email or mail kit; follow up w/ email.

The Elbo Room
2871 N Lincoln Ave.
Chicago, IL 60657
p: 773-549-5549
e: info@elboroomchicago.com
www.elboroomchicago.com
contact: Brian Bender
p: 773-549-5549 x2
e: brian@elboroomchicago.com
call: M-F 1-7pm
genres: Pop, Rock, Alt.
advance: 3-4 months
capacity: 200
pa: Yes **sound eng:** Yes
stage: 16 x 9
Prime 21+ Alt. music club w/ devoted college/post-college crowd books mostly original Local-Touring buzz bands nitely. 4-5 acts play 30-60min sets for the door. Prefers email, but may mail press kit to venue; allow 2-3 wks; call to follow up.

Empty Bottle
1035 N Western Ave.
Chicago, IL 60622
p: 773-276-3600
e: brucef@emptybottle.com
www.emptybottle.com
contact: Pete Toalson
e: pete@emptybottle.com
call: M-F 1-6pm
genres: Rock, Alt., Indie, World, Jazz, Hip-Hop
advance: 1 month
capacity: 400
pa: Yes **sound eng:** Yes
stage: 20 x 20
Chic dive bar hosts Touring bands up to 7 nites; Jazz showcased Wed. 3 acts play 45min sets. Also books Logan Square Aud. & Open End Gallery. Mail press kit to venue; wait 2 wks for review.

Fitzgerald's
6615 W Roosevelt Rd.
Berwyn, IL 60402
p: 708-788-2118
e: fitzpublicity@earthlink.net
www.fitzgeraldsnightclub.com
contact: Bill Fitzgerald
p: 708-788-2118 x23
e: billfitzberwyn@yahoo.com
call: M-F noon 5:30pm
genres: Americana, Roots, Jazz, Rock, Blues, Zydeco, Country, Folk, Bluegrass
advance: 30-45 days
capacity: 400; 225 (seated)
pa: Yes **sound eng:** Yes
stage: 18 x 12 **in-house:** Piano
open mics: Tue 9pm (Side Bar)
Roadhouse 12mi outside of Chicago, books Local-Touring acts 6 nites for 21+. 1-2 acts play 30-120min & keep 90% merch sales if house runs table. EPKs preferred, incl. past Chicago area gigs & local contacts.

Flatlander's
200 Village Green
Lincolnshire, IL 60069
p: 847-821-1234
e: russ@flatlanders.com
www.flatlanders.com
contact: Brenden Lynch
e: brenden@flatlanders.com
genres: All Styles
advance: 3 months
capacity: 300
pa: Yes **sound eng:** Yes
stage: small **in-house:** Drums
open mics: Mon 10:30pm
21+ brew pub 30+mi outside of Chicago books mostly Local/Reg'l bands Fri & Sat. 1-2 acts play from 10pm-1am for flat fee vs door or just a flat fee. Snail mail or email kits.

Green Dolphin St.
2200 N Ashland Ave.
Chicago, IL 60614
p: 773-395-0066
e: info@jazzitup.com
www.jazzitup.com
contact: Gabriel Segura
p: 815-463-9024
e: music@jazzitup.com
genres: Jazz, R&B
advance: 3 months
capacity: 350
pa: Yes **sound eng:** Yes
stage: 25 x 16 **in-house:** Piano
Swanky supper club books well-known, original Local-Int'l acts Tue-Sat for 21+ crowd. 1 act plays 2-3 sets for a flat fee. Email or mail press kit to venue.

Green Mill Jazz Club
4802 N Broadway
Chicago, IL 60640
p: 773-878-5552
e: greenmill@comcast.net
www.greenmilljazz.com
contact: David Jemilo
genres: Jazz
advance: 3 months
capacity: 178
pa: Yes **sound eng:** Yes
stage: 12 x 10
Listening room in former speakeasy books original Reg'l & Touring acts nitely for serious jazzhounds. 1-3 acts play for 21+ crowd. Snail mail kits.

Heartland Cafe
7000 N Glenwood Ave.
Chicago, IL 60626
p: 773-465-8005
www.heartlandcafe.com
contact: Brettly K.
e: brettly@heartlandcafe.com
call: email only
genres: Americana, S/S, Reggae, Ska, Latin, World, Acoustic Rock, Pop, Country
advance: 2-8 months
capacity: 200
pa: Yes **sound eng:** Yes
stage: 20 x 15
open mics: Wed **sign in:** 9pm
Lauded listening room hosts 2-5 polished, original Local-Int'l acts Thu-Sat w/ some Nat'l & Reg'l shows on wkdys. Some all ages shows. Live radio broadcast Sat 9-10am on WLUW. Also books Heartland Studio Theater, No Exit Cafe & Red Line Tap. Prefers Sonicbids EPK; email follow up.

Hideout
1354 W Wabansia Ave.
Chicago, IL 60622
p: 773-227-4433
: 773-227-3650
e: hideoutinn@aol.com
www.hideoutchicago.com
contact: Michelle DeBois
call: M-F 2-6pm
genres: Rock, Pop, Folk, Alt. Country, Blues, Dance, Experimental, Hip-Hop
advance: 2-3 months
capacity: 150
pa: Yes **sound eng:** Yes
stage: 15 x 10 **in-house:** Piano
Popular warehouse hangout books original Local-Int'l acts 5 nites. 2-3 bands play 45-60min for % of door after expenses. Email links or small MP3s. No unsolicited mail.

Jazz Showcase
806 S Plymouth Ct.
Chicago, IL 60605
p: 312-360-0234
e: jazzshowcase@jazzshowcase.com
www.jazzshowcase.com
contact: Wayne Segal
call: M-F 10am-6pm
genres: Jazz
capacity: 199
pa: Yes **sound eng:** Yes
stage: 15 x 10 **in-house:** Piano
Landmark listening room, recently relocated to new location, presents polished original Local-Touring artists up to 7 nites.

Joe's Bar
940 W Weed St.
Chicago, IL 60622
p: 312-337-3486
e: joesbarmusic@yahoo.com
www.joesbar.com
contact: Ed Warm
call: Afternoons
genres: Urban, Rock, Pop
advance: 3 months
capacity: 1000
pa: Yes **sound eng:** Yes
stage: 46 x 16
Multi-room venue mostly books original Local-Int'l talent several nites/mo. 2-3 acts play Thu-Sat. Accepts press kits electronically or mailed to venue; allow 1 mo. for review.

Katerina's
1920 W Irving Park Rd.
Chicago, IL 60613
p: 773-348-7592
www.katerinas.com
contact: Katerina Carson
genres: Jazz, Funk, Latin, Blues
pa: Yes
Club books polished talent up to 6 nites for 3hr sets w/ 2 breaks. Use snail mail or online form.

Kingston Mines Chicago Blues Center
2548 N Halsted St.
Chicago, IL 60614
p: 773-477-4646
e: anne@kingstonmines.com
www.kingstonmines.com
contact: Laura Gennaro
p: 815-439-3436
e: info@kingstonmines.com
call: mornings
genres: Blues
advance: 3 months
capacity: 402
pa: Yes **sound eng:** Yes
stage: 20 x 30; 20 x 15
Landmark venue pairs rising Local talent w/ estab. Touring acts on 2 stages nitely. 2-3 acts play two to four 1hr sets for flat fee; all ages w/ guardian. Mail press kit to venue. Accepts EPKs at anne@kingstonmines.com.

Kryptonite
308 W State St.
Rockford, IL 61103
p: 815-965-0931
www.kryptonitebar.com
contact: Chris Wachowiak
e: chris@kryptonitebar.com
advance: 2 months
capacity: 200
open mics: Thu
Bar books live Reg'l acts 2-4 nites. For 1st time booking, email w/ info, expected draw & link to music.

Logan Square Aud.
2539 N Kedzie Blvd.
Chicago, IL 60647
p: 773-252-6179
e: info@lsachicago.com
www.lsachicago.com
contact: Saul Osacky
e: saulosacky@yahoo.com
genres: All Styles
advance: 2 months
capacity: 750
pa: Yes **sound eng:** Yes
stage: 24 x 16
All ages theater w/ state-of-the-art sound & lights books original Local-Int'l bands & DJs up to 7 nites. 4-5 acts play 45min for flat fee to 18+. Mail kit.

Lonie Walker's Underground Wonder Bar
10 E Walton St.
Chicago, IL 60611
p: 312-266-7761
e: wondermail@aol.com
www.undergroundwonderbar.com
contact: John Collins
genres: Blues, Jazz, S/S, Rock, Reggae, Funk
capacity: 70
open mics: Mon **sign in:** 8pm
Artist-run late nite music room famed for legendary jam sessions, presents top Local-Touring artists nitely for 21+ from 8pm-4am. 2-3 acts play for flat fee.

Martyrs'
3855 N Lincoln Ave.
Chicago, IL 60613
p: 773-404-9494
www.martyrslive.com
contact: Bruce Krippner
p: 773-404-9494 x52
e: bruce@martyrslive.com
genres: Rock, Alt., Country
advance: 1-3 months
capacity: 400
pa: Yes **sound eng:** Yes
stage: 30 x 20
Top music dive w/ great sound & views draws loyal following for estab. Touring acts & buzz bands & some DJs. 3 original acts play 45-90min for 21+. Email link to music only; No hard kits or attachments.

Mary's Place
602 N Madison St.

Rockford, IL 61107
p: 815-962-7944
www.marysplacebar.com
contact: Jack
call: Sat after 6pm
genres: Rock, Alt. Country, Jam, Jazz
advance: 2+ weeks
capacity: 100+
pa: Yes **sound eng:** Yes
stage: 15 x 10
open mics: Tue & Thu Open Stage 9:30pm-2am; Wed Open Turntables 10:30pm-2am
Music bar 88mi outside of Chicago, books original Local-Touring bands Fri & Sat for 21+. 1-2 acts play for door & small % of bar.

Metro
3730 N Clark St.
Chicago, IL 60613
p: 773-549-0203
e: metro@metrochicago.com
www.metrochicago.com
contact: Chris Baronner
p: 773-549-4140 x215
e: chrisb@metrochicago.com
call: M-F 10am-6pm
genres: Rock, Punk, Hip-Hop, Alt., Dance
advance: 2-4 months
capacity: 1100
pa: Yes **sound eng:** Yes
stage: 30 x 25
Launch pad for up & coming acts books original Local-Touring bands up to 7 nites; mostly all ages shows. 3-4 bands play 30-60min. Merch splits 80/20. Also has bands in basement room, Smart Bar & co-owns The Double Door. Prefers mailed kit w/ CD; wait 4-6 wks for email response.

Mojoe's Rock House
7537 W 159th St.
Tinley Park, IL 60477
p: 708-444-0588
e: mojoescoffeehouse@gmail.com
www.myspace.com/mojoesrockhouse
contact: Marc Bernal
genres: Rock, Hardcore, Metal
capacity: 400; 150-200
pa: Yes
open mics: Tue **sign in:** 9pm
Formerly Mojoe's Coffee House, venue 26mi from Chicago, now showcases hard rockin' Local-Reg'l talent w/ some Nat'l-Int'l acts. 4-6 acts play for $2/head after 20; signed Nat'ls get flat fee. Email for booking & put dates avail. in subject line; no booking thru MySpace.

Nite Cap
5007 W Irving Park Rd.
Chicago, IL 60641
p: 773-282-8654
e: nitecaplounge@gmail.com
www.nitecaplive.com
contact: Scott Davidson
p: 773-909-0303
e: rebelbookings@yahoo.com
call: M-F noon-6pm
genres: All Styles mainly Hardcore & Metal
advance: 2-3 months
capacity: 275
pa: Yes **sound eng:** Yes
stage: 15 x 10
Underground Metal club books Local & Touring acts & DJs Fri-Sat & some other nites. 3-4 bands play 35-45min to 21+ crowd. Use myspace.com/rebelbookings if contacting thru MySpace.

No Exit Cafe
6970 N Glenwood Ave.
Chicago, IL 60626
p: 773-743-3355
www.heartlandcafe.com
contact: Brettly K.
e: brettly@heartlandcafe.com
call: email only
genres: Jazz, Folk, Americana, S/S
advance: 2-3 months
capacity: 125
pa: Yes
Hip hang in ent. complex books original Local-Touring bands up to 3 nites; some all ages shows. Also books other performance spaces inside complex. Prefers Sonicbids. No contact thru MySpace & no calls.

Old Town School of Folk Music
4544 N Lincoln Ave.
Chicago, IL 60625
p: 773-728-6000
www.oldtownschool.org
contact: Colleen Miller
p: 773-728-6000 x3345
e: cmiller@oldtownschool.org
call: M-F 9am-5pm
genres: Folk, Alt., Alt. Blues, Country, World, S/S, Jazz
advance: 4-6 months
capacity: 425
pa: Yes **sound eng:** Yes
stage: 30 x 15
open mics: 1st Fri of month
School w/ full music store presents eclectic original Local-Int'l acts 3-4 nites for all ages. Up to 3 original acts play 30-90min. Prefers email; No unsolicited mail.

Otto's Niteclub & Underground
118 E Lincoln Hwy.
DeKalb, IL 60115
p: 815-758-2715
www.ottosdekalb.com
contact: John Ugolini
e: kickstandproductions@gmail.com
genres: Indie, Rock, Punk, Metal, Jam
advance: 2 months
capacity: 325; 650 (upstairs)
pa: Yes **sound eng:** Yes
stage: 20 x 12 & 2nd stage
open mics: Wed **sign in:** 8pm
Popular 21+ college hang 60+mi outside of Chicago w/ full lighting books 2-3 original Local-Touring estab. acts, buzz bands & DJs Thu-Sat & some other nites on 2 stages. Prefers email w/ bio & link or snail mail kit w/ ATTN: Booking.

Red Line Tap
7006 N Glenwood Ave.
Chicago, IL 60626
p: 773-274-5463
www.heartlandcafe.com
contact: Brettly K.
e: brettly@heartlandcafe.com
call: email only
genres: Rock, Pop, Punk, S/S, Americana, Bluegrass, Jazz, Blues, Country, Alt. Country, Metal, Rockabilly, Psychobilly
advance: 2-8 months
capacity: 150
pa: Yes **sound eng:** Yes
stage: 20 x 30
open mics: Thu **sign in:** 8pm
Smaller stage in Heartland Cafe complex hosts 3-5 Local-Touring acts up to 7 nites. Also books other performance spaces inside complex. Prefers Sonicbids. No contact thru MySpace; No calls.

Reggies Music Joint
2105 S State St.
Chicago, IL 60616
p: 312-949-0120
www.reggieslive.com
contact: Brendan Joyce
p: 312-949-1025
e: brendan@reggieslive.com; ellediablo@hotmail.com
genres: All Styles
advance: 1-2 months
capacity: 101-200
pa: Yes **sound eng:** Yes
stage: 17 x 11
Little sister to next door's Reggie's Rock Joint, books 3-5 mostly original Local-Nat'l acts nitely for 45+min sets. Incl. music, short bio & full contact info.

Rosa's Lounge
3420 W Armitage Ave.
Chicago, IL 60647
p: 773-342-0452
www.rosaslounge.com
contact: Tony Mangiullo
e: tony@rosaslounge.com
call: M-F 1-5pm; prefers email
genres: All Styles of Blues
advance: 2-3 months
capacity: 100
pa: Yes **sound eng:** Yes
stage: 20 x 10
open mics: Thu **sign in:** 8pm
Listening room showcases original Local-Int'l acts 3 nites for 21+. Usu. 1 but up to 3 acts play two 45-75min sets. Email first w/ links. Promos may then be sent w/ ATTN: Tony, 4064 N Lincoln Ave., #359, Chicago, IL 60618.

Schubas Tavern
3159 N Southport Ave.
Chicago, IL 60657
p: 773-525-2508
www.schubas.com
contact: Matt Rucins
e: rucins@schubas.com
call: M-F 2-5pm
genres: Rock, Alt., Country, S/S, Funk, Roots
advance: 3 months
capacity: 125; 200 (SRO)
pa: Yes **sound eng:** Yes
stage: 22 x 13
Music staple for emerging Reg'l talent & estab. Touring acts books 3 original bands nitely playing 45min. Excellent sight lines; monthly all ages shows. Mail CD & contact info only to venue; no full kits.

Smart Bar
3730 N Clark St.
Chicago, IL 60613
p: 773-549-0203
www.smartbarchicago.com
contact: James Amato
p: 773-549-0203 x226
e: james@smartbarchicago.com
call: M-F 10am-6pm
genres: Dance, Electronic, House, Goth, Drum n Bass
capacity: 400
pa: Yes **sound eng:** Yes
The Metro's downstairs hot spot boasts large dance floor & all the trimmings. 1-4 original Local-Touring acts & DJs urge 21+ crowds to shed their inhibitions nitely. Snail mail kit w/ ATTN: James Amato.

Smoke Daddy
1804 W Division St.
Chicago, IL 60622
p: 773-772-6656
e: info@thesmokedaddy.com
www.thesmokedaddy.com
contact: Brian
call: M-F after 4pm
genres: Blues, Jazz, Rockabilly, Western Swing
advance: 3 months
capacity: 62
pa: Yes
stage: 10 x 8
Popular BBQ/music joint presents Local-Reg'l acts nitely for all ages. 1 act plays 45min; 2 sets on wkdy & 3 on wknd. Prefers snail mailed press kit.

Subterranean
2011 W North Ave.
Chicago, IL 60647
p: 773-278-6600
e: derron@housecallent.com
www.subt.net
contact: John Benetti
e: john@housecallent.com
genres: All Styles
advance: 6 weeks
capacity: 375; 100 (for DJs)
pa: Yes **sound eng:** Yes
stage: 23 x 15
open mics: Mon Acoustic; Tue Urban
Popular 3-story club features original Local-Int'l bands & DJs nitely in separate rooms. Upstairs offers elevated stage w/ good sight lines. Up to 5 acts play 25-120min; some all ages shows as well as 18+ & 21+. Also books Beat Kitchen, Wicker Park Summerfest & Belmont Art Music Fest. Prefers EPKs, but may mail press kit to venue.

Two Way Street Coffee House
1047 Curtiss St.
Downers Grove, IL 60515
p: 630-969-9720
e: booking@twowaystreet.org
www.twowaystreet.org
contact: Dave Humphreys
p: 930-968-5526
e: dave@twowaystreet.org
call: M-F 10am-2pm
genres: Folk, Roots, Americana, S/S, Acoustic Rock
advance: 4-6+ months
capacity: 65
pa: Yes **sound eng:** Yes
stage: 4 x 8
open mics: Last Thu of month (College & HS only); 4 Fri/year (all ages)
Volunteer-run all ages listening room 19mi outside of Chicago, showcases native & Touring talent Fri. Featured act performs two 45min sets for 90% of door. Prefers email w/ 'Booking' & artist's name in subject line. May also mail kit w/ ATTN: Booking. See site for details. Limited spots, so be patient for a response.

Uncommon Ground
3800 N Clark St.
Chicago, IL 60613
p: 773-929-3680
e: info@uncommonground.com
www.uncommonground.com

contact: David Chavez
e: bookings@uncommonground.com
genres: All Styles except Loud Acts
advance: 4-12 weeks
capacity: 30
pa: Yes **sound eng:** Yes
stage: 8 x 6
open mics: Mon **sign in:** 7pm
Acoustic all ages listening room presents polished original Local-Touring talent nitely. 3 acts play 45min sets for door minus $10 for sound. Email w/ desired dates & link to EPK; no MP3s. Live recording avail. Also books 2nd location on Devon Ave.

Underground Lounge
952 W Newport Ave.
Chicago, IL 60657
p: 773-327-2739
e: ulchicago@sbcglobal.net
www.ulchicago.com
contact: Don Ridge
call: Mon-Thu 1-5pm
genres: Rock, Pop, Jazz
advance: 4-6 weeks
capacity: 150
pa: Yes **sound eng:** Yes
stage: 20 x 20
Basement Rock club books mostly Local acts or Reg'l-Nat'ls w/ local following 2-3 nites. All band members must be 21+. Prefers EPKs; incl. previous Chicago gigs & wknd draw.

The Velvet Lounge
67 E Cermak Rd.
Chicago, IL 60616
p: 312-791-9050
www.velvetlounge.net
contact: Dan Melnick
p: 773-682-7455
e: danielmelnick@gmail.com
genres: Jazz
pa: Yes **sound eng:** Yes
Listening room books original Local-Int'l acts up to 6 nites for the door. Prefers email, but may call for booking.

Vic Theatre
3145 N Sheffield Ave.
Chicago, IL 60657
p: 773-472-0449
e: victheater@aol.com
www.victheatre.com
contact: Nick Miller
p: 312-266-6262
e: contactjam@jamusa.com
genres: Rock, Alt., Metal, Jam
advance: 1-4 months
capacity: 1400
pa: Yes **sound eng:** Yes
stage: 44 x 29
Original music venue books top Nat'ls & some Reg'ls 6+ nites/mo on any nite; some DJs. Mostly all ages shows. Email, call or use online booking form.

Greater IL

The Rock Island Brewing Co.
1815 2nd Ave.
Rock Island, IL 61201
p: 309-793-1999
e: ribco@ribco.com
www.ribco.com
contact: Terry Tilka
p: 309-793-0085
e: talent@ribco.com
call: M-F 10am-5pm
genres: All Styles
advance: 2 months
capacity: 320; 2000
pa: Yes **sound eng:** Yes
stage: 20 x 20 (indoor); large outdoor stage
open mics: Tue 9pm-1am
Popular Quad city venue near Moline & Davenport, IA presents mostly Reg'l-Int'l talent. 1-2 acts play 1hr sets. 21+ w/ rare all ages shows outdoors. Mail kit.

Stagger Inn Again
104 E Vandalia Ave.
Edwardsville, IL 62025
p: 618-656-4221
www.myspace.com/staggerinnagain
contact: Tim Early
call: Tue-Thu & Sat
genres: Jam, Rock, Reggae, R&B, Alt., Blues, Bluegrass, S/S, Acoustic
advance: 2 months
capacity: 200
pa: Yes **sound eng:** Yes
stage: 15 x 8
open mics: Wed & Sun 9pm-1am
Bar/eatery 2mi E of Southern Illinois U, features 2 original Reg'l & Nat'l bands 3 nites. Thu & Sat are Acoustic; Fri turns it up. Call or mail kit.

Indiana

Bloomington

Bear's Place
1316 E 3rd St.
Bloomington, IN 47401
p: 812-339-3460
www.bearsplacebar.com
contact: Dan Coleman
e: junebugjenkins@gmail.com
genres: Rock, Jazz, Blues
advance: 1-2 months
capacity: 150
pa: Yes **sound eng:** Yes
Tavern books up to 3 Local-Reg'l acts for 45min sets Wed & some Fri nites; occasional Touring bands & DJs.

The Bluebird
216 N Walnut St.
Bloomington, IN 47404
p: 812-336-3984
www.thebluebird.ws
contact: Dave Kubiak
e: dkubiak@hotmail.com
call: M-F 1-5pm
genres: All Styles
advance: 1-6 months
capacity: 700
pa: Yes **sound eng:** Yes
stage: 24 x 24
Prime music club features up to 3 Local-Touring artists & DJs up to 6 nites for a 21+ crowd. Email for booking.

Jake's
419 N Walnut St.
Bloomington, IN 47404
p: 812-332-0402
www.jakesnightclub.com
contact: Dave Kubiak
p: 812-336-3984
e: dkubiak2515@hotmail.com
call: M-F 1-5pm
genres: Alt., Rock, Jam
advance: 1-2 months
capacity: 800
pa: Yes **sound eng:** Yes
stage: 30 x 15
21+ niteclub presents 2 Local-Int'l acts & DJs for flat fee plus % of door. Also books The Bluebird. Mail press kit to venue.

JoeyG's
218 E Main St.
Madison, IN 47250
p: 812-273-8862
www.houseohits.com/joeygs
contact: Joey G.
e: joeyg@houseohits.com
genres: Blues, Rock, Americana, S/S
advance: Up to 3 months
capacity: 67; 80 (SRO)
pa: Yes **sound eng:** Yes
stage: 15 x 15
open mics: Wed **sign in:** 4pm
Eatery books Reg'l & house bands from 9:30pm-1:30am nitely; Touring acts gig monthly. Prefers original music. Also owns House O' Hits next door & consigns Local CDs. Snail mail or email kit.

Rhino's Youth Center
331 S Walnut St.
Bloomington, IN 47401
p: 812-333-3430
e: rhinos@bloomington.in.us
www.rhinosyouthcenter.org
contact: Tim Pritchett
p: 812-333-3430 x2
call: M-F noon-6pm
genres: Alt., Punk, Rap, Funk, Ska, Hip-Hop
advance: 1-2 months
capacity: 440
pa: Yes **sound eng:** Yes
stage: 30 x 25
Non-profit all ages club books Local HS & College bands Fri & Sat & Nat'ls 2-3 nites/mo. Locals get % of door & Nat'ls get flat fee. 3 acts gig 30-45min for all ages. Email or mail promos: PO Box 1727, Bloomington, IN 47402.

Evansville

1123 First Ave.
1123 1st Ave.
Evansville, IN 47711
www.1123club.com
contact: K.C.
e: booking@1123club.com
genres: Punk, Metal, Emo, Ska
capacity: 300
pa: Yes **sound eng:** Yes
Loud all ages club on KY border, books original bands Fri & Sat. Up to 4 acts play 30-60min sets. Local/Reg'l openers; some wkly shows for signed Nat'l acts. Email link to music, but prefers mailed kit to venue; incl. CD, name, location, style/influences, dates avail.

Penny Lane Coffeehouse
600 SE 2nd St.
Evansville, IN 47713
p: 812-421-8741
www.pennylanecoffee.com
contact: Heidi Krause
e: heidi.pennylanecoffee@gmail.com
genres: S/S, Celtic, Folk, Rock, Reggae
capacity: 60
pa: Yes **sound eng:** Yes
All ages room books Reg'l & some Touring talent Fri & Sat for tips. Email link to music. No unsolicited mail or calls.

Indianapolis/Richmond

8 Seconds Saloon
111 N Lynhurst St.
Indianapolis, IN 46224
p: 317-486-1569
e: 8secondssaloon@comcast.net
www.8secondssaloon.com
contact: Loren Hadenfeldt
p: 715-232-9300
e: loren@dagenentertainment.com
call: M-F 10am-5:30pm
genres: Country, Dance
advance: 4-6 months
capacity: 1500
pa: Yes **sound eng:** Yes
Gritty cowboy hangout books Local-Nat'l bands 2/wk. 1-2 mostly original acts play three 1hr sets for 21+. Back room, Tremors, plays Rock & Hip-Hop. Promos: N-4762 Hwy 25, Menomonie, WI 54751.

Barley Island Brewing Co.
639 Conner St.
Noblesville, IN 46060
p: 317-770-5280
e: barleyisland@sbcglobal.net
http://barleyisland.tripod.com
contact: Michael Smith
e: headies737@hotmail.com
genres: Rock, Blues, Jam, Bluegrass, Country
advance: 2-3 months
capacity: 150 **stage:** medium
open mics: Sun 6-10pm
Family-friendly brewpub 23mi outside of Indy, books Local & Reg'l acts Fri-Sat for flat fee & extra bonus for good draw; some Nat'l acts. 1-2 bands play for 3hrs w/ 1hr break. After 10pm is 18+ or w/ an adult. Email or snail mail kit.

Birdy's Bar & Grill
2131 E 71st St.
Indianapolis, IN 46220
p: 317-254-8971
e: birdysbarandgrill@juno.com
www.birdyslive.com
contact: Jeff Sample
p: 317-254-8979
genres: All Styles
Haven for indie talent hosts up to 6 polished Local-Int'l acts nitely for 21+ hipster crowd. Email music links or snail mail kit to venue w/ ATTN: Jeff Sample.

Doc's
215 S Walnut St.
Muncie, IN 47305
p: 765-286-0949
www.docsmusichall.com
contact: Mike Martin
e: hillbilly_martin@hotmail.com
genres: Rock, Alt. Country, Jam
advance: 3-6 months
capacity: 300
pa: Yes **sound eng:** Yes
stage: 12 x 15
open mics: Wed 9pm-3am
Music hall books up to 4 Local & Touring bands & DJs 3 nites. Original acts play from 10pm-2am for 10% of bar or 80% of door for 21+ crowd. Also books The Locker Room in Muncie, IN. Use email or mail kit to venue.

The Emerson Theater
4634 E 10th St.
Indianapolis, IN 46201
p: 317-357-0239
www.emersontheater.com
contact: Josh Russell

e: booking@emersontheater.com
call: email only
genres: Rock, Hard Rock, Punk, Hip-Hop, Metal, Hardcore
advance: 2 months
capacity: 400
pa: Yes **sound eng:** Yes
stage: 25 x 25
Alcohol-free all ages venue books loud original acts mostly Fri-Sat for % of door. Touring acts play w/ Local opener. Up to 4 acts on Fri & 5 on Sat play 30min sets. No Jazz, Country or Pop. No unsolicited packages; all booking done via email.

Friends of Bob
106 Main St.
Battle Ground, IN 47920
p: 765-567-2478
e: fofbob@comcast.net
www.friends-of-bob.org
contact: Richard Fudge
call: M-F 4-8pm
genres: Roots, S/S, World, Rock, Alt.Country
advance: 2-6 months
capacity: 230; 340; 1200
pa: Yes **sound eng:** Yes
Non-profit co-op nestled btwn Chicago & Indy books original Touring talent monthly around town; some all ages shows. 2 original acts play 45 & 90min sets for flat fee & % of door. Prefers email, but may mail kit to: Box 59 at venue address.

The Jazz Kitchen
5377 N College Ave.
Indianapolis, IN 46220
p: 317-253-4900
e: info@thejazzkitchen.com
www.thejazzkitchen.com
contact: David Allee
e: david@thejazzkitchen.com
call: email only
genres: Jazz
advance: 3 months
capacity: 140
pa: Yes **sound eng:** Yes
stage: large
Prime Jazz hot spot presents mostly original Local-Touring talent for 21+. Featured act plays two 90min sets for flat fee & % of door; merch splits 80/20. Email or mail press kit to venue. No Calls.

Knickerbocker Saloon
113 N 5th St.
Lafayette, IN 47901
p: 765-423-2234
e: info@knickerbockersaloon.com
http://knickerbockersaloon.com.b1.hostkarma.com
contact: Jeff Hamann
e: booking@knickerbockersaloon.com
call: M-F 11am-1pm
genres: Blues, Roots Rock, R&B, Rockabilly, Jam, Electronic Rock
advance: 2-3 months
capacity: 150
pa: Yes **sound eng:** Yes
A favorite music bar 78mi+ outside of Indianapolis, features Local-Reg'l acts Thu-Fri for 21+; Featured act plays 2 sets for flat fee. Use email or mail press kit to venue for booking.

Locals Only
2449 E 56th St.
Indianapolis, IN 46220
p: 317-255-4013
e: info@localsonlyindy.com
www.localsonlyindy.com
e: booking@localsonlyindy.com
genres: Experimental, Rock
advance: 5-6 months
capacity: 220
pa: Yes **sound eng:** Yes
stage: 20 x 15
open mics: Sun 7pm, Wed 8pm, Tue 8:30pm
Clearing house for local arts scene books original Local-Nat'l bands Thu-Sat & some other nites for 21+. Up to 3 acts play 30-90min for door; Nat'ls get flat fee. Email or snail mail kit.

Madame Walker Theatre
617 Indiana Ave.
Indianapolis, IN 46202
p: 317-236-2099
www.walkertheatre.com
contact: Cynthia Bates
e: mwtcpresident@aol.com
call: M-F 9am-5pm
genres: Jazz, Gospel, World, Classical, R&B
advance: Up to 4 years
capacity: 930 (theatre); 350
pa: Yes **sound eng:** Yes
stage: 28 x 40 **in-house:** Piano
Non-profit theatre books Reg'l & Nat'l acts & DJs wkly. 1-2 acts play 2-4hrs for flat fee.

Melody Inn
3826 N Illinois St.
Indianapolis, IN 46208
p: 317-923-4707
www.melodyindy.com
contact: Dave Brown
e: picwizard@earthlink.net
genres: All Styles
advance: 2 months
capacity: 100
pa: Yes
stage: 8 x 18
open mics: Mon **sign in:** 9pm
Premier 21+ venue books original Local-Int'l acts up to 7 nites for % of door. 3-4 acts play 45min sets. Snail mail kit w/ CD, bio & contact info.

Mickey's Irish Pub
13644 N Meridian St.
Carmel, IN 46032
p: 317-573-9746
e: pubmickeys@aol.com
www.mickeysirishpub.com
contact: Bill Adkins
genres: Rock, Blues, Dance
advance: 4-6 weeks
capacity: 300+
pa: Yes
stage: 9 x 30
Prime area Rock room 16mi outside of Indianapolis, books Local-Touring artists Fri & Sat for 21+. 1 act plays three 1hr sets w/ 30min break from 9pm-1am for 100% of door + flat fee. Mail press kit to venue.

Music Mill
3720 E 82nd St.
Indianapolis, IN 46240
p: 317-841-1850
e: info@themusicmillvenue.com
www.themusicmillvenue.com
contact: Jake Schockman
genres: Most Styles
advance: 2-5 months
capacity: 750
pa: Yes **sound eng:** Yes
stage: 45 x 25
open mics: Tue 9pm-12am
State-of-the-art 21+ club books polished Touring acts & DJs for a flat fee. Emerging Local-Reg'l acts submit via Sonicbids & are selected for monthly Sonicbids showcase, playing for the door. 2-3 acts play 45min-3hrs. No unsolicited mail.

Radio Radio
1119 E Prospect St.
Indianapolis, IN 46203
p: 317-251-6957; 317-955-0995
e: roni@futureshock.net
www.futureshock.net
contact: Tufty
e: tufty@futureshock.net
call: M-F 11am-7pm
genres: All Styles
advance: 3+ weeks
capacity: 250
pa: Yes **sound eng:** Yes
stage: 20 x 14
Stylish 21+ venue books original Local-Int'l acts & DJs (no Hip-Hop). Up to 3 acts play 45-60min for 100% of door. Promos: FutureShock, ATTN: Tufty, 6323 N Ferguson St., Indianapolis, IN 46220.

Slippery Noodle Inn
372 S Meridian St.
Indianapolis, IN 46225
p: 317-631-6974
www.slipperynoodle.com
contact: Carol Yeagy
e: headnoodle@slipperynoodle.com
call: Mon-Wed 2-7pm
genres: Blues
advance: 4-5 months
capacity: 600
pa: Yes **sound eng:** Yes
stage: large
Local landmark showcases Local-Nat'l artists nitely for 21+ crowd. 1-2 acts play three 60-70min sets. Also runs recording label, Slippery Noodle Sound. Accepts EPKs; No unsolicited mail.

The Verve
677 Wabash Ave.
Terre Haute, IN 47807
p: 812-234-9536
e: verveat677@aol.com
www.theverve.biz
contact: Connie Wrin
genres: Rock, Alt.
advance: 1-3 months
capacity: 200
pa: Yes **sound eng:** Yes
stage: 12 x 20
Club 1 block from Iowa State U campus, books Reg'l & some Touring acts Thu-Sat. Featured act play several sets for 21+.

The Vogue Nightclub
6259 N College Ave.
Indianapolis, IN 46220
p: 317-259-7029
e: mail@thevogue.ws
www.thevogue.ws
contact: Matt Schwegman
e: matt@thevogue.ws
genres: Rock, Reggae, Jam, Country, Alt.
advance: 3 months
capacity: 1000
sound eng: Yes
Niteclub books mostly original Touring acts several nites w/ some Reg'l openers. Up to 3 acts play 45min sets for 21+. Nat'l Touring acts email & openers submit via Sonicbids.

South Bend/ Ft. Wayne

Bean Counters Coffee House
8413 Kennedy Ave.
Highland, IN 46322
p: 219-838-3333
e: beancounterscoffeehouse@live.com
www.myspace.com/beancounterscoffeehouseandmusic
contact: Sean Repay
genres: Most Styles
capacity: 106
pa: Yes **sound eng:** Yes
open mics: Mon 7pm
All ages Internet cafe 32mi from Chicago, hosts up to 5 original Local-Int'l acts nitely; some 21+ shows. Acts play 20-45min for % of door after drawing 50 heads. No Metal or Hardcore.

Cheers Lounge
103 S Dixie Way
South Bend, IN 46637
p: 574-277-8407
www.myspace.com/therealcheerslounge
contact: Drew
genres: Metal, Indie Rock, Hard Rock, Punk
capacity: 250
pa: Yes **sound eng:** Yes
open mics: Thu
Mixed crowd gathers for Reg'l rockin' acts Wed-Sat in small club w/ great acoustics.

Front Porch Music
505 E Lincoln Way
Valparaiso, IN 46383
p: 219-464-4700
www.frontporchmusic.com
contact: Chad Clifford
e: fpm@frontporchmusic.com
genres: Americana, S/S, World
advance: 6 months
capacity: 72
pa: Yes **sound eng:** Yes
stage: 10 x 10 **in-house:** Piano
open mics: Thu **sign in:** 7pm
Music dealer & all ages coffeehouse 52mi from Chicago, showcases Reg'l & Nat'l talent Fri & Sat; wkly all ages shows. 1-2 acts fill 90+min for % of door from Sep-Jun.

Galveston SteakHouse & Blues Room
10 Commerce Sq.
Michigan City, IN 46360
p: 219-879-5555
e: admin@thegalvestonsteakhouse.com
www.thegalvestonsteakhouse.com
contact: Jiorgios Karayannis
e: galvestonsteak@sbcglobal.net
call: Tue 5pm
genres: Blues, R&B, Funk, Rock, Soul, Motown
advance: 6 months
capacity: 100 **stage:** 13 x 11
open mics: Sun **sign in:** 7pm
Club 60mi outside of Chicago, books Reg'l & occasional Nat'l bands Sat for 21+ crowd. Featured act plays 4hrs for a flat fee. Mail press kit to venue.

Iowa

Cedar Rapids

The Busted Lift
180 Main St.
Dubuque, IA 52001

p: 563-584-9712
e: info@thebustedlift.com
www.thebustedlift.com
contact: Aaron Hefel
e: booking@180main.com; counterproduction@mchsi.com
genres: Celtic, Alt., Rockabilly, Folk, Reggae, Blues, Hip-Hop, Punk, Metal
advance: 3 months
capacity: 224
pa: Yes **sound eng:** Yes
stage: 16 x 20
open mics: Wed 9pm-1am
Irish pub halfway btwn Cedar Rapids & Madison WI features mostly original Local-Touring bands Fri-Sat & many wkday shows for all ages. Featured act plays several sets for fee vs door. Email for booking. No unsolicited mail.

Checkers Tavern
3120 6th St. SW
Cedar Rapids, IA 52404
p: 319-364-9927
e: chekerstav@aol.com
www.checkerstavern.com
contact: PJ Harrington
genres: Blues
advance: 3-4 months
capacity: 70
pa: Yes
Racing-themed bar presents original Reg'l-Int'l Blues every Sun. Single act plays 60-90min for flat fee.

Cocktails & Co.
1625 Blairs Ferry Rd.
Marion, IA 52302
p: 319-377-1140
e: cocktailsandco@aol.com
www.cocktails-company.com
contact: Justin Crippen
e: cocktailsoffice@aol.com
genres: Most Styles
advance: 2-4 months
capacity: 200-250
stage: floor space
21+ tavern books Reg'ls w/ following & a few Nat'ls 3-4 nites. 1-2 acts play 4hrs w/ breaks from 9pm-1am for % of door after costs. Wed is Acoustic Nite. No Country or Heavy Metal. Call or snail mail kit.

CSPS
1103 3rd St. SE
Cedar Rapids, IA 52401
p: 319-364-1580
e: info@legionarts.org
www.legionarts.org
contact: F. John Herbert
p: 319-364-1580 x20
e: john@legionarts.org
genres: Folk, World, Jazz, Experimental, Lite Rock
advance: 2 weeks - 8 months
capacity: 70-175
pa: Yes **sound eng:** Yes
stage: 25 x 30; 8 x 12 (platform)
open mics: Monthly
Non-profit, all ages arts ctr. showcases original Local-Int'l talent 3-4 nites in 1891 Czech hall. 1-2 acts play 2hrs for flat fee + % of door. Merch split is 85/15. Send promo pack & follow up via email.

Spicoli's Rock Garden
3555 University Ave.
Waterloo, IA 50701
p: 319-287-5747
www.thereverb.net
contact: Cody
e: thereverbbooking@aol.com
call: Mon & Thu 2-4pm
genres: Rock, Metal
advance: 6 weeks
capacity: 400
pa: Yes **sound eng:** Yes
open mics: Tue
Previously The Reverb in Cedar Falls, this relocated, revamped club heats things up w/ Local & Touring talent 3 nites. 3 acts play 40+min for door minus expenses or flat fee. Mostly 18+; some all ages & 21+. Prefers EPK, but may call or mail press kit to: PO Box 512, Cedar Falls, IA 50613. Allow 3-4 wks for review.

Des Moines

Blues On Grand
1501 Grand Ave.
Des Moines, IA 50312
p: 515-244-3092
www.bluesongrand.com
contact: Jeff Wagner
e: drdoubt@bluesongrand.com
genres: Blues
capacity: 144
pa: Yes **sound eng:** Yes
Prime music bar books original 1-2 Local & Touring bands Tue-Sat for the door. Call or email.

The House of Bricks
525 E Grand Ave.
Des Moines, IA 50309
p: 515-727-4370
e: thehouseofbricks@aol.com
www.thehouseofbricks.com
contact: J.C. Wilson
p: 515-280-1388
genres: All Styles
advance: 2 months
capacity: 275
pa: Yes **sound eng:** Yes
stage: 26 x 14
Mosh-friendly club w/ excellent acoustics books mostly Reg'l & some Touring bands 4 nites. Up to 5 acts play 1hr sets to all ages crowd. Prefers email for booking. Contact before mailing kit.

Java Joe's
214 4th St.
Des Moines, IA 50309
p: 515-288-5282
e: info@javajoescoffeehouse.com
www.javajoescoffeehouse.com
contact: Amy Brehm
p: 515-953-9591
genres: Americana, Celtic, Alt., Acoustic, Jazz, Folk, Bluegrass
advance: 2 weeks
capacity: 60; 75 (theater)
pa: Yes **sound eng:** Yes
stage: 12 x 8; larger stage for theater
open mics: 2nd Wed of mo
Under new ownership & now booking Local-Int'l acts & DJs for all ages several nites/wk. Also hosts live music & prod. in neighboring theater space on larger stage. 1-2 acts fill 2hrs for tips. Use email or mail press kit to venue for booking.

Ritual Café
1301 Locust St., Ste. D
Des Moines, IA 50309
p: 515-288-4872
e: ritualcafe@aol.com
www.ritualcafe.com
genres: All Styles
advance: 1-3 months
capacity: 50
pa: Yes
stage: 10 x 10
open mics: 1 Thu/mo 7pm
Coffeehouse hosts 1-2 original Local-Int'l acts Thu-Sat for diverse crowd. Acts play 90-120min for 100% of door, which is set by the act. Prefers EPK or hard copy demos sent to venue w/ ATTN: Ritual Cafe.

Val Air Ballroom
301 Ashworth Rd.
West Des Moines, IA 50265
p: 515-223-6152
e: info@valairballroom.com
www.valairballroom.com
contact: Chris Cardani
e: chris@valairballroom.com
genres: All Styles
advance: 3-6 months
capacity: 2775
stage: 2 stages; main stage is adjustable 24 x 40
Vintage all ages venue has mostly top Touring acts 4-5 nites/mo; few Local-Reg'ls. 3 acts play 90min sets & keep 80% merch sales. Prefers email, but may mail kit or call.

Vaudeville Mews
212 4th St.
Des Moines, IA 50309
p: 515-243-3270
e: info@vaudevillemews.com
www.vaudevillemews.com
contact: Ladd Askland
e: booking@vaudevillemews.com
genres: Indie Rock, Pop, Folk, Alt. Country, Punk
advance: 3 months
capacity: 230
pa: Yes **sound eng:** Yes
stage: 15 x 14
Artsy all ages venue books original acts & DJs up to 7 nites. Up to 5 Local-Int'l acts play 30-60min sets. Email before mailing promos.

Iowa City

the industry.
211 Iowa Ave.
Iowa City, IA 52240
p: 319-337-9107
e: industrybooking@gmail.com
www.theindustryic.com
contact: Jason Parris
p: 563-271-7054; 319-331-6912
e: jason@ribco.com
call: M-F 9am-5pm
genres: All Styles
advance: 6 weeks
capacity: 550; 250 (upstairs)
pa: Yes **sound eng:** Yes
stage: 36 x 18
Formerly Que Bar, premier live music venue is attracting attention w/ top notch Local-Int'l acts & DJs for 19+ crowd. 2-4 bands play mostly Thu-Sat til 1:45am on 2 levels/stages. Features back door load-in, band parking & large green room. Prefers email, but may call or mail press kit to: PO Box 2531, Iowa City, IA 52244.

Iowa City Yacht Club
13 S Linn St.
Iowa City, IA 52240
p: 319-337-6464
e: iwannarock@iowacityyachtclub.org
www.iowacityyachtclub.org
contact: Scott Kading
call: no calls
genres: Rock, Jam, Roots, Blues, Reggae, Bluegrass
advance: 3 months
capacity: 250
pa: Yes **sound eng:** Yes
stage: small
Local-Touring bands play original tunes 5 nites in cool basement club/BBQ joint w/ decent sound; few Tribute acts booked. 21+ after 10pm. 2-3 acts play 2hrs for % of door. Prefers MySpace or email; No Calls.

The Mill
120 E Burlington St.
Iowa City, IA 52240
p: 319-351-9529
e: info@icmill.com
www.icmill.com
contact: Trevor Lee Hopkins
e: booking@icmill.com
call: M-F noon-2pm
genres: Americana, Roots, Folk, S/S, Indie Rock
advance: 2-3 months
capacity: 290
pa: Yes **sound eng:** Yes
stage: 12 x 15
open mics: Mon
Int'lly-known ctr. of Americana music community, presents top Reg'l & Touring artists up to 7 nites. 1-2 original acts play 50-60min; mostly all ages.

The Picador
330 E Washington St.
Iowa City, IA 52240
p: 319-354-4788
e: info@thepicador.com
www.thepicador.com
contact: Doug Roberson
e: doug@thepicador.com
call: M-F 5-7pm
genres: Indie Rock, Punk, Hardcore, Insurgent Country, Garage Rock, Electronica, Ska, House, Techno, Rockabilly
advance: 2-3 months
capacity: 375
pa: Yes **sound eng:** Yes
stage: 30 x 15
19+ music room, books Local-Int'l acts & DJs up to 7 nites; all ages 5-9pm. 3-5 original acts play 45-60min sets. Always on the lookout for new Locals. Email, mail kit or contact thru MySpace.

Quad Cities

The Blue Shop
320 N 4th St.
Burlington, IA 52601
p: 319-758-9553
www.theblueshop.com
contact: David Hazell
e: hazellislands@hotmail.com
call: M-F 10am-1pm
genres: Blues, Jazz, Space, Int'l, Folk
advance: 6 months
capacity: 125
pa: Yes **sound eng:** Yes
stage: 10 x 14
All ages BYOB joint books original Local-Int'l acts & DJs 1-2 nites. Featured act plays two 45-90min sets; some shows w/ 2-3 bands. Prefers email, but may mail promos w/ ATTN: Booking, PO Box 843, Burlington, IA 52601.

Redstone Room
129 Main St.
Davenport, IA 52801
p: 563-326-1333
www.redstoneroom.com

contact: Santo Pullella
e: santo@rivermusicexperience.org
call: M-F 8am-5pm
genres: All Styles
advance: 6-12 weeks
capacity: 250+
pa: Yes **sound eng:** Yes
stage: 20 x 19 x 24; 8 x 8 x 6
State-of-the-art non-profit room has Local-Int'l acts 5+ nites for few all ages shows. 1-2 original acts play 1hr; some Tribute acts. 80/20 merch split. Great stop btwn Madison, Des Moines, St. Louis, Chicago. Prefers online booking form w/ attached EPK, but may email or mail kit.

Greater IA

Rebels
600 16th Ave.
Council Bluffs, IA 51501
p: 712-396-0189
www.myspace.com/rebelsrocks
e: booking@rebelsrocks.com
genres: All Styles
advance: 1-2 months
capacity: 250
pa: Yes **sound eng:** Yes
stage: 6 x 12
All ages youth ctr. a few mi from Omaha, NE books positive Local-Int'l acts Fri & Sat. 3-5 original acts play 45min for flat fee. Call or mail kit to: 338 Fleming Ave., Council Bluffs, IA 51503.

Surf Ballroom
460 N Shore Dr.
Clear Lake, IA 50428
p: 641-357-6151
e: thesurf@surfballroom.com
www.surfballroom.com
contact: Shane Cooney
e: swc@surfballroom.com
genres: Blues, Bluegrass, Country, Jazz, Metal, Punk, Rock, Christian
advance: 6+ months
capacity: 2100
pa: Yes **sound eng:** Yes
Historic venue known as last stop 'before the music died' books Nat'l acts a few nites/mo w/ Reg'l openers. Opener plays 1hr, headliner 90min for % vs flat fee; some all ages shows. Merch split is 80/20. Prefers mailed kit No unsolicited mail, email or booking via MySpace.

Kansas

Kansas City/Topeka

Boobie Trap Bar
1417 SW 6th St.
Topeka, KS 66606
p: 785-232-9008
e: boobietrapbar@cox.net
www.boobietrapbar.com
contact: Brian Chambers
call: email only
genres: All Styles
advance: 1+ months
capacity: 90
pa: Yes **sound eng:** Yes
open mics: Thu **sign in:** 9pm
The louder, the better at this all ages joint. Venue features Local-Nat'l acts Tue-Sat for % of door. 3-4 bands play 45-60min sets. Prefers emailed music links or snail mail.

Classic Bean
2125 SW Fairlawn Plaza Dr.
Topeka, KS 66614
p: 785-271-5005
www.classicbean.com
contact: JJ
genres: Acoustic, Folk, Rock, Jazz, Bluegrass
advance: 2-4 months
capacity: 100
All ages coffeehouse books Local-Reg'l bands Fri & Sat for tips. No large or loud groups. Snail mail kits.

Danny's Bar & Grill
13350 College Blvd.
Lenexa, KS 66210
p: 913-345-9717
e: nathan@dannysbandg.com
www.dannysbarandgrill.com
contact: Jason
e: jevolve@hotmail.com
genres: Acoustic, Rock
advance: 6-8 weeks
capacity: 199
pa: Yes **sound eng:** Yes
stage: small
Bar books mostly original Local-Nat'l bands Sat & acoustic acts Wed. Up to 3 acts play 3hrs to 21+ crowd; DJs on Fri. 2nd location in Kansas City, KS, 913-328-0247. Email, mail kit to venue or contact via MySpace.

Longhorns Saloon
1115 Moro St.
Manhattan, KS 66502
p: 785-776-8770
e: longhorns@longhornssaloon.com
www.longhornssaloon.com
contact: Patrick Shannon
p: 785-564-1551
e: patrick@longhornssaloon.com
call: M-F 8pm-2am
genres: Country
advance: 2-6 months
capacity: 350
pa: Yes **sound eng:** Yes
stage: 30 x 20
open mics: Wed 10pm
Popular 18+ club 58mi outside of Topeka, books original Reg'l-Nat'l acts & few Local bands that can keep em' dancing 1-2 nites. 2 acts play 1-2hrs for flat fee or % of door. Promos: 1202 Deep Creek Rd., Manhattan, KS 66502.

Lawrence

Abe & Jake's Landing
8 E 6th St.
Lawrence, KS 66044
p: 785-841-5855
www.abejakes.com
contact: Ryan Lantz
e: abejakes@gmail.com
call: M-F 10am-4pm
genres: Rock, Country, Jam, Hip-Hop, Bluegrass
advance: 2 months
capacity: 950
pa: Yes **sound eng:** Yes
Top midwest venue w/ huge stage attracts baby acts, DJs & A-list talent 1-2 nites. Up to 3 acts play 45-60min sets; some all ages shows. Merch splits 80/20. Mail promos to venue w/ ATTN: Booking; will contact if interested.

The Bottleneck
737 New Hampshire St.
Lawrence, KS 66044
p: 785-842-LIVE
e: music@thebottlenecklive.com
www.thebottlenecklive.com
contact: Julia Peterson
genres: Hip-Hop, Rap, Jazz, Blues, Reggae, Rock, Pop, Bluegrass, Heavy Metal
advance: 3+ months
capacity: 450
pa: Yes **sound eng:** Yes
stage: 20 x 24
open mics: Mon **sign in:** 3pm
Legendary dive w/ great views draws area hipsters & Touring bands w/ buzz. Up to 4 acts usu. play 45min for mostly all ages shows; DJs spin 2/wk. Some 18+ shows. Prefers EPKs, but may mail press kit to w/ ATTN: Brett, The Bottleneck, 123 W 8th St., Ste. 309, Lawrence, KS 66044. No Calls.

Fatso's Public House & Stage
1016 Massachusetts St.
Lawrence, KS 66044
p: 785-865-4055
e: fatsos@sunflower.com
www.myspace.com/fatsoslawrence
contact: Gavin Smith
call: Afternoons
genres: All Styles mainly Jam
advance: 6+ weeks
capacity: 400
pa: Yes **sound eng:** Yes
stage: 16 x 20 **in-house:** To rent
Downtown club books Local-Touring bands & DJs up to 4 nites for 18+ crowd. Acts play til 1:45am for negotiable payment. Prefers EPKs.

Gaslight Tavern & Coffeehouse
317 N 2nd St.
Lawrence, KS 66044
p: 785-856-4330
e: info@gaslighttavern.com
www.gaslighttavern.com
e: bookings@gaslighttavern.com
call: email only
genres: Bluegrass, Americana, Reggae, Folk, Electronic, Metal, Hip-Hop, Indie, Punk, Jazz, Blues
advance: 1-3 months
capacity: 140
pa: Yes **sound eng:** Yes
stage: small (indoor); medium
Local & Touring bands & DJs booked up to 7 nites in cozy clubhouse or patio bar. 2-3 acts play 1hr sets. Prefers MySpace but can email or mail press kit.

The Granada
1020 Massachusetts St.
Lawrence, KS 66044
p: 785-842-1390
e: thegranada@gmail.com
www.thegranada.com
contact: Mike Logan
genres: Rock, Hip-Hop, Country, Bluegrass, Jam
advance: 2-6 months
capacity: 700
pa: Yes **sound eng:** Yes
stage: 18 x 32
Renovated historic theater books Reg'l & Nat'l acts Fri-Sat; Locals may open. Up to 4 acts play original 1hr sets & DJs spin on off nites; some all ages shows. Bands take 80% merch. Call or email for booking.

Jackpot Music Hall
943 Massachusetts St.
Lawrence, KS 66044
p: 785-832-1085
www.thejackpotsaloon.com
contact: Justin Nicholson
p: 785-843-2846
e: replaybooking@hotmail.com
call: Mon, Wed & Fri 2-8pm
genres: All Styles
advance: 3 months
capacity: 265
pa: Yes **sound eng:** Yes
stage: 13 x 15
Original Local-Touring bands gig several nites; DJs spin Fri in hip music hall. 3 acts play for % of door. Also books Replay Lounge in Lawrence. Must have a major or known indie label release or be represented by a booking agent. Email w/ MP3s or EPK, then call only if necessary. May also mail press kit to venue.

Jazzhaus
926-1/2 Massachusetts St.
Lawrence, KS 66044
p: 785-749-3320
e: info@jazzhaus.com
www.jazzhaus.com
contact: Rick McNeely
p: 785-749-3320 x3
e: rick@jazzhaus.com
genres: Blues, Jazz, Funk, Reggae, Rock
advance: 2-3 months
capacity: 225
pa: Yes **sound eng:** Yes
Cool 21+ niteclub features original, polished Local-Touring acts up to 5 nites. Featured act plays 60-75min. Call or email.

Replay Lounge
946 Massachusetts St.
Lawrence, KS 66044
p: 785-749-7676
www.replaylounge.com
contact: Justin Nicholson
p: 785-838-4510
e: replaybooking@hotmail.com
call: Mon, Wed & Fri 2-8pm
genres: Rock, Punk
advance: 2 months
capacity: 150; 400+
pa: Yes **sound eng:** Yes
stage: 9 x 9; outdoor patio
Funky pinball & music bar books original Local-Touring bands & DJs on recognized label or working w/ known agents only. Touring bands paired w/ Local act nitely for 18+; Sun all ages. 2-3 bands play 30-45min sets for % of door on indoor & outdoor stages. Prefers EPK, but may mail press kit to venue.

Wichita

Cotillion Ballroom
11120 W Kellogg St.
Wichita, KS 67209
p: 316-722-4201
e: info@thecotillion.com
www.thecotillion.com
contact: Richard Leslie
e: richard@thecotillion.com
call: Mon-Sat 9:30am-5:30pm
genres: Rock, Blues, Latin, R&B, Jam, Alt.
advance: 2-4 months
capacity: 2000
pa: To rent **sound eng:** To hire
Circular & domed facility hosts top original Touring acts w/ some Local-Reg'l openers for all ages. 2-4 bands fill 3hrs; house takes 20% merch sales. Mail or email press kit.

Kirby's Beer Store
3227 E 17th St. N
Wichita, KS 67208
p: 316-239-7990
www.kirbysbeerstore.com
contact: Steve Schroeder
e: stevekirbys@cox.net
genres: Rock, Bluegrass, Ska, Punk
advance: 6 weeks
capacity: 50
pa: Yes **sound eng:** Yes
stage: 10 x 12
Wild little venue w/ a punch is good for some xtra cash if passing thru the area. Books Local-Touring bands 4-5 nites for tips. 2 acts play 1hr sets for 21+. Email, call or mail kit.

Kentucky

Covington

Mad Hatter
620 Scott St.
Covington, KY 41011
p: 859-291-2233
e: info@madhatterclub.com
www.madhatterclub.com
contact: Frank Huelefeld
e: frank@madhatterclub.com
genres: Punk, Rock, Metal, Hip-Hop, Pop
advance: 3-6 months
capacity: 440
pa: Yes **sound eng:** Yes
Original music club 8mi outside of Cincinnati, OH has emerging Local-Touring bands 4-5 nites. 3-5 acts play 45-75min. Shows 18+ w/ some 21+ & all ages. Nat'l acts get flat fee & openers % of door. Touring acts should pair up w/ Local band from Links page on venue site.

Madison Theater
730 Madison Ave.
Covington, KY 41011
p: 859-491-2444
e: info@madisontheateronline.com
www.madisontheateronline.com
contact: Esther Johnson
e: madisontheater@insightbb.com
call: M-F 1-7pm
genres: Rock, Americana, Roots, Jazz, Blues
advance: 2-3 months
capacity: 1200
pa: Yes **sound eng:** Yes
stage: 20 x 30
Restored theatre just 1mi from Cincinnati, OH w/ top sound & views, presents polished Local-Touring talent for all ages; some 18+ shows. 3-5 acts play 60-90min. Nat'ls get flat fee, Locals get % of door. Mail press kit to: PO Box 1018, Covington, KY 41012.

Southgate House
24 E 3rd St.
Newport, KY 41071
p: 859-431-2201
www.southgatehouse.com
contact: Rick McCarty
e: sghbooking@gmail.com
genres: Rock, Folk, Alt., Punk, Electronic, Jazz, Roots
advance: 2-3 months
capacity: 600 (ballroom); 75
pa: Yes **sound eng:** Yes
stage: 35 x 15 **in-house:** Piano
open mics: Mon **sign in:** 9pm
Reported to be haunted & the coolest original music spot in the greater Cincinnati area, presents polished Local-Touring bands & DJs nitely on 2 stages. 3 bands play 45min; some all ages shows. Prefers email, but may mail press kit to venue.

Lexington

Common Grounds Coffeehouse
343 E High St.
Lexington, KY 40507
p: 859-233-9761
e: jimd@qx.net
www.commongroundsoflexington.com
contact: Eric Rupple
e: ericr@qx.net
call: M-F 9am-10pm
genres: Acoustic
advance: 1-2 months
pa: Yes
open mics: Mon **sign in:** 8pm
Local & some Reg'l acts play 1hr sets Fri-Sat for all ages. 2 acts/bill. Also books The Hub in Danville & Main & Maple in Nicholasville. Prefers email w/ music link.

The Dame
156 W Main St.
Lexington, KY 40507
p: 859-226-9204
e: dameonmain@yahoo.com
www.dameky.com
contact: Nick Sprouse
genres: All Styles
advance: 1 month
capacity: 390
pa: Yes **sound eng:** Yes
stage: 22 x 20
open mics: Every other Mon
Music hall books 2-3 Local & Nat'l bands Mon-Sat. Openers play 30min; headliners 90. Email link to music or EPK.

Louisville

Bluegrass Brewing Co.
3929 Shelbyville Rd.
Louisville, KY 40207
p: 502-899-7070
www.bbcbrew.com
contact: Melissa Purvis
e: mel@bbcbrew.com
genres: Most Styles
advance: 1-2 months
capacity: 300
pa: Yes **sound eng:** To hire
stage: 12 x 16 (expandable)
City's oldest brewpub hosts 1-2 Local-Int'l acts Fri-Sat for 21+ crowd. Opener plays 1hr & headliner jams for 2hrs for the door after any prod. costs. No Hip-Hop or Rap. Email link to music; no packages or calls.

The Brick House
1101 S 2nd St.
Louisville, KY 40203
p: 502-213-0428
www.brickhouse.cc
e: booking@brickhouse.cc
genres: Punk, Rock, Hip-Hop
advance: 1 month
capacity: 125 **stage:** 20 x 15
open mics: Wed
Non-profit, DIY community ctr. run by volunteers. No alcohol, drugs or tobacco on premises. Works w/ Food Not Bombs & runs radio stn. WXBH 92.7 in Louisville which airs Open Mic. Local-Int'l bands gig Fri & Sat for % of door.

Coyote's Music & Dance Hall
166 W Jefferson St.
Louisville, KY 40202
p: 502-589-3866
www.cityblocklouisville.com
contact: Eric Weigel
p: 502-561-7050 **call:** M-F
e: emweigel@aol.com
genres: Country, Rock, Pop, Blues
capacity: 1250
pa: Yes **sound eng:** Yes
stage: 24 x 36
Popular honky tonk hosts some Local-Nat'l acts. 21+ except Wed 18+ college nites. Snail mail kit.

Dutch's Tavern
3922 Shelbyville Rd.
Louisville, KY 40207
p: 502-895-9004
www.myspace.com/dutchs_tavern
contact: John Lang
call: M-F 11am-2pm
genres: Alt., Pop, Rock
advance: 3 months
capacity: 100
pa: Yes **stage:** small
The 'Ville's oldest venue books Locals & Reg'ls 4-6 nites & Mon Hip-Hop battles. Contact via MySpace for booking.

Headliners Music Hall
1386 Lexington Rd.
Louisville, KY 40206
p: 502-584-8088
www.headlinerslouisville.com
contact: Mike Pollard
e: mikepollardemail@yahoo.com
call: M-F 10:30am-3pm
genres: Alt., Country, Rock, Blues, Celtic
capacity: 800
pa: Yes **sound eng:** Yes
stage: 20 x 25
Original music club presents polished Reg'l & estab. Touring acts 4-7 nites. Up to 6 acts on a bill; some all ages shows. Use email for booking.

Phoenix Hill Tavern
644 Baxter Ave.
Louisville, KY 40204
p: 502-589-4957
e: pht@phoenixhill.com
www.phoenixhill.com
contact: Kim Donze
e: kim@phoenixhill.com
genres: Rock, Blues, Metal, Alt., Indie, Acoustic, Country, Swing
advance: 2 months
capacity: 500; & smaller room
pa: Yes **sound eng:** Yes
stage: 20 x 13.5; 2 others
Ent. complex/21+ club presents top Reg'l talent Wed-Sat & Touring bands monthly. 3-8 acts play 1-4hrs for flat fee. Books a Thu "Audition Nite" for this venue & Jim Porter's Good Time Emporium where Locals open for Nat'l acts. Prefers EPKs. No unsolicited mail.

The Rudyard Kipling
422 W Oak St.
Louisville, KY 40203
p: 502-636-1311
e: homeagin@digicove.com
www.therudyardkipling.com
contact: Ken Pyle
call: Mon-Sat after 10am; prefers email
genres: Folk, Celtic, Acoustic Rock, Blues, Jazz, Reggae, World
advance: 2-4 months
capacity: 150; 75
pa: Yes **sound eng:** Yes
stage: 10 x 16 **in-house:** Piano
Popular niteclub books mostly original Local-Reg'l acts w/ a following Fri-Sat; 21+ after 9pm. Must be able to draw 75-150 fans to headline. Nat'ls should have Local support. Up to 4 acts play one or two 40-45min sets for full door. Snail mail kit.

Stevie Ray's Blues Bar
230 E Main St.
Louisville, KY 40202
p: 502-582-9945
www.stevieraysbluesbar.com
contact: Todd Webster
e: justtodd2002@yahoo.com
genres: Blues, Funk, Soul, R&B, Jazz, Rock, Acoustic
advance: 4+ months
capacity: 200
pa: Yes **sound eng:** Yes
stage: 12 x 20
open mics: Mon **sign in:** 8pm
City's premier live music venue books top Touring acts & Local acts Mon-Sat. 2-3 mostly original acts play for 21+ crowd. Mail press kit to venue.

Louisiana

Baton Rouge/ Lafayette

Blue Moon Saloon
215 E Convent St.
Lafayette, LA 70501
p: 337-234-2422
e: info@bluemoonpresents.com
www.bluemoonpresents.com
contact: Mark Falgout
e: mark@bluemoonpresents.com
genres: Creole, Cajun, Zydeco, Blues, Bluegrass, Swamp Pop, Jazz
advance: 1-2 months
capacity: 450
pa: Yes **sound eng:** Yes
Cajun roadhouse presents well-known Reg'l & Touring acts Wed-Sat. Up to 3 original acts play for all ages crowd. Mail press kit to venue w/ ATTN: Performance Submissions.

The Caterie
3617 Perkins Rd.
Baton Rouge, LA 70808
p: 225-383-4178
www.thecaterie.com
contact: Darrin Dominguez
e: booking@thecaterie.com
genres: Alt., Rock
advance: 1 month
capacity: 150
pa: Yes **sound eng:** Yes
stage: medium
Local-Reg'l bands play for 18+ college crowd 6 nites. Up to 3 acts play 30-60min sets. No Metal or Screamo. Contact via MySpace.

Chelsea's Cafe
2857 Perkins Rd.
Baton Rouge, LA 70808
p: 225-387-3679
www.chelseascafe.com
contact: David Remmetter
e: dave@chelseascafe.com
genres: Rock, Funk, Jazz, Americana, Jam, Folk, Country
advance: 1-2 months

capacity: 300
pa: Yes **sound eng:** Yes
stage: 20 x 10
A new location for this original music room & college hang near Louisiana State U, showcases polished Local-Touring artists Tue-Sat. Featured act fills 1-2hrs. No Rap or Metal. Email for booking.

Click's
5124 Corporate Blvd.
Baton Rouge, LA 70808
p: 225-925-0806
e: baton@clicks.com
www.clicks.com
contact: Mike
call: prefers MySpace
genres: Hard Rock, Rock
advance: 10 days - 1 month
capacity: 420
pa: Yes **sound eng:** Yes
stage: 20 x 20
open mics: Wed **sign in:** 9pm
Large pool-hall has original Local bands & Nat'l Touring acts for 18+ crowd up to 5 nites. Bands play from 10:30pm-close. Mail press kit to venue or contact thru MySpace.

Grant Street Dance Hall
113 W Grant St.
Lafayette, LA 70501
p: 337-237-8513
www.grantstreetdancehall.com
contact: Casey Phillips
p: 310-246-3442
e: booking@wagatailpresents.com
genres: Rock, Alt., Blues, Zydeco, Cajun, Jazz, Country, R&B, Hip-Hop
advance: 2 months
capacity: 750
pa: Yes **sound eng:** Yes
stage: 14 x 46
Prime Honky Tonk books 2-3 top tier Local-Int'l acts 4-5 nites for 1+hrs to 18+. Email link to music, recent draw/history in Lafayette, avail. dates not w/in 2 wks of another gig. No unsolicited mail.

North Gate Tavern
136 W Chimes St.
Baton Rouge, LA 70802
p: 225-346-6784
www.myspace.com/northgatetavern
contact: Dustin
e: hackandslasher@hotmail.com
genres: Alt. Country, Acoustic, Indie, Punk, Emo, Post-Hardcore
capacity: 200+
pa: Yes **sound eng:** Yes
Original music hang books 1-2 polished Locals & Reg'ls & a rare Nat'l Thu-Sat for 40-60min sets for college crowd. Email music link or use MySpace.

Phil Brady's Bar & Grill
4848 Government St.
Baton Rouge, LA 70806
p: 225-927-3786
www.philbradys.org
contact: Joe Hall
genres: R&B, Zydeco, Rock, Blues, Soul, Funk
advance: 60-75 days
capacity: 190
pa: Yes **sound eng:** Yes
stage: 40 x 10
Hole-in-the wall Blues club presents Reg'l & Nat'l artists to 18+ crowd Thu-Sat. Up to 3 acts fill 3hrs. Snail mail kit or call.

Red Star Bar
222 Laurel St.
Baton Rouge, LA 70801
p: 225-346-8454
e: frank@redstarbar.com
www.redstarbar.com
contact: Frank McMains
e: frank@redstarbar.com
call: M-F after 4pm
genres: Indie Rock, Pop, Country, Folk
advance: 2 months
capacity: 175
pa: Yes **sound eng:** Yes
Original music room popular w/ LSU students, may host Reg'l & Touring talent Thu-Sat. 1-2 acts play 1hr sets for % of door. Accepts EPKs.

The Texas Club
456 N Donmoor Ave.
Baton Rouge, LA 70806
p: 225-928-4656
e: texasclub@aol.com
www.thetexasclub.com
contact: Mark Rogers
e: mark@thetexasclub.com
genres: Country, Rock, Blues
advance: 2-3 months
capacity: 1100
pa: Yes **sound eng:** Yes
stage: 30 x 25
Top 18+ music room books Nat'l & polished Reg'ls monthly for flat fee vs % of door & 85% merch after sales tax. 2-4 acts play 1-2hr sets. Mon-Sat are open for booking. Email or snail mail kit; follow up 2 wks later.

The Varsity Theatre
3353 Highland Rd.
Baton Rouge, LA 70802
p: 225-383-7018
e: mark@varsitytheatre.com
www.varsitytheatre.com
contact: Chris Lundgren
e: chris@varsitytheatre.com
call: M-F 1-3pm
genres: Rock, Blues, Techno, Country, Pop, Reggae
advance: 3 months
capacity: 810
pa: Yes **sound eng:** Yes
stage: 28 x 18
City's only mid-size venue hosts Reg'ls & Touring bands up to 5 nites for 18+ crowd. Email or mail press kit to venue.

New Orleans

Banks Street Bar & Grill
4401 Banks St.
New Orleans, LA 70119
p: 504-486-0258
www.banksstreetbar.com
contact: Richard Fendley
e: bankstreetbar@bellsouth.net
genres: Zydeco, Rock, Blues, R&B, New Orleans, Funk, Jazz
advance: 1+ months
capacity: 150
pa: Yes **sound eng:** Yes
stage: 10 x 15 (floor space)
Funky joint showcases mostly Reg'l acts nitely. 1 bands plays three 1hr sets. Sun Jazz showcase. Mail kit to venue email music link.

Carrollton Station
8140 Willow St.
New Orleans, LA 70118
p: 504-865-9190
e: info@carrolltonstation.com
www.carrolltonstation.com
contact: Eric Orlando
genres: Rock, Blues, Roots, New Orleans, S/S, Country
advance: 2 months
capacity: 100
pa: Yes **sound eng:** Yes
stage: 16 x 14
open mics: Tue Acoustic 9pm
Hip neighborhood joint hosts 1-2 top Local acts Thu-Sat for 18+ crowd. Bands play from 10pm-2am & usu. get % of door.

Checkpoint Charlie's
501 Esplanade Ave.
New Orleans, LA 70116
p: 504-281-4847
e: igorscheckpointcharlie@hotmail.com
www.myspace.com/checkpoints
contact: Angelo Manis
genres: Alt. Rock, Jazz, Blues, R&B, Country
advance: 1-2 months
capacity: 350
pa: Yes **stage:** medium
open mics: Tue **sign in:** 9pm
Hipsters, bikers & college kids mingle at this 24hr bar, laundromat & showcase for Local-Int'l acts nitely. Up to 6 acts play for % of till or door if they charge a cover for 21+ crowd. Prefers MySpace but can mail press kit to venue.

Circle Bar
1032 St. Charles Ave.
New Orleans, LA 70130
p: 504-588-2616
e: circlebarinfo@cox.net
www.myspace.com/thecirclebar
contact: Jason Songe
e: jason@liveneworleans.com
genres: Punk, Rock, Country, Blues
advance: 1 month
capacity: 50
pa: Yes **stage:** floor space
Music fans pack bar for original Reg'l & Nat'l bands nitely; few DJs. Up to 3 acts play from 10pm-1am for % of bar Mon-Fri or % of door & tips on wknds. Prefers contact via MySpace, but may email or snail mail kit.

Contemporary Arts Center
900 Camp St.
New Orleans, LA 70130
p: 504-528-3805
e: info@cacno.org
www.cacno.org
contact: Jay Weigel
e: jweigel@cacno.org
call: M-F 10am-5pm
genres: Jazz, Electronic, New Music, Hip-Hop
advance: 6-12 months
capacity: 250; 2000
pa: Yes **sound eng:** Yes
stage: 45 x 30 **in-house:** Piano
Non-profit presents all ages performances 4-8 nites/mo., focusing on cutting edge & New Orleans music. 1-2 original bands play 2hr sets for flat fee. Merch splits 80/20. No Pop. Contact before mailing promo.

D.B.A.
618 Frenchman St.
New Orleans, LA 70116
p: 504-942-3731
e: dbaneworleans@yahoo.com
www.drinkgoodstuff.com
genres: Blues, Jazz, Soul New Orleans
Beer enthusiasts' bar books original Local & Touring talent nitely for mixed crowd. Call or contact mgmt. thru site. No booking via MySpace.

The High Ground
3612 Hessmer Ave.
Metairie, LA 70002
p: 504-388-6665
www.thehighgroundvenue.com
contact: Jay
e: jay@thehighgroundvenue.com
genres: Rock, Metal, Ska, Electronic, Hardcore, Punk
advance: 2 months
capacity: 600
pa: Yes **sound eng:** Yes
stage: 14 x 24
2-story club w/ bottom floor music & top floor for merch & lounge, books Local-Int'l bands & DJs up to 7 nites. 4 original acts play 30-40min for all ages. Email link to MySpace.

House of Blues/New Orleans
225 Decatur St.
New Orleans, LA 70130
p: 504-310-4971
e: chris.recinos@hob.com
http://hob.com/venues/clubvenues/neworleans
contact: Sonny Schneidau
call: M-F 10am-6pm
genres: Blues, Rock, Hip-Hop, Country, Jazz
advance: 1-2 months
capacity: 1000; 400
pa: Yes **sound eng:** Yes
Home of renowned music chain showcases hosts top Local-Touring talent up to 7 nites on 2 stages. 2-3 acts play 90min sets for 18+ crowd; some all ages shows. Merch splits 75/25. Email for booking.

The Howlin' Wolf
907 S Peters St.
New Orleans, LA 70130
p: 504-522-WOLF; 504-529-5844
e: info@thehowlinwolf.com
www.thehowlinwolf.com
contact: Stu Schayot
p: 504-529-5844 x3
e: stu@thehowlinwolf.com
call: M-F 11am-5pm
genres: Rock, Funk, Jam, Punk, Metal, Hip-Hop, Jazz
advance: 2 months
capacity: 1300; 600 (seated)
pa: Yes **sound eng:** Yes
stage: 30 x 25
Premier, no frills club presents original Local-Int'l acts up to 7 nites for flat fee plus % of door. Up to 4 acts play 45min sets for 18+ crowd. Prefers email for booking. No unsolicited mail.

Maple Leaf Bar
8316 Oak St.
New Orleans, LA 70118
p: 504-866-9359
www.myspace.com/themapleleafbar
contact: Hank Staples III
call: M-F 3-5pm
genres: R&B, Folk, Funk, Jazz, Blues, New Orleans
advance: 1-2 months
capacity: 450
pa: Yes **sound eng:** Yes
stage: 12.5 x 15 **in-house:** Piano
open mics: 1st Wed of month

Low key spot near Tulane & Loyola, draws loyal 21+ crowd & books hi-caliber original Local-Touring acts 3 nites; house acts Thu & Sun. 1 act plays 2-4hrs sets; 2 acts on wknd. Mail press kit to venue.

Mid City Lanes/ Rock 'n' Bowl
4133 S Carrollton Ave.
New Orleans, LA 70119
p: 504-482-3133
e: info@rocknbowl.com
www.rockandbowl.com/index.htm
contact: John Blancher
e: john@rocknbowl.com
call: evenings
genres: Blues, R&B, Zydeco, Swing, Rockabilly, Rock, Soul
advance: 1-2 months
capacity: 500
pa: Yes **sound eng:** Yes
stage: 15 x 25
Vintage bowling alley hosts mostly Local-Reg'l acts w/ some Touring bands Tue-Sat. 1-2 acts play 60-90min for flat fee vs door. Crowd is 18+ Rockabilly bunch; all ages w/ guardian. Email; No unsolicited pkgs.

Old Point Bar
545 Patterson St.
New Orleans, LA 70114
p: 504-364-0950
e: info@oldpointbar.com
www.oldpointbar.com
contact: Chad
call: M-F before 11am
genres: Jazz, Blues
capacity: 200
pa: Yes **sound eng:** Yes
stage: 10 x 12 **in-house:** Piano
21+ hang attracts students, hipsters & polished Local-Nat'l bands Thu-Sun. Featured act plays 1hr for % of bar. Call for booking.

One Eyed Jacks
615 Toulouse St.
New Orleans, LA 70130
p: 504-569-8361
e: elmatadorlounge@earthlink.net
www.oneeyedjacks.net
contact: Bailey Smith
p: 504-569-9100
e: bailsmith@gmail.com
genres: Rock, Indie, Roots
advance: 2-3 months
capacity: 450+
pa: Yes **sound eng:** Yes
stage: 25 x 20
Prime music venue w/ full stage & VIP area, hosts edgy & original Local-Touring talent Fri & Sat. 2-3 original acts play 1hr sets for 18+. Call or email for booking.

Republic New Orleans
828 S Peters St.
New Orleans, LA 70130
p: 504-528-8282
e: info@republicnola.com
www.republicnola.com
contact: Scott Simoneaux
p: 504-250-0081
e: booking@republicnola.com
call: M-F noon-8pm
genres: All Styles of Indie
advance: 1+ months for Locals; 3-9 months for Nat'ls
capacity: 1000
pa: Yes **sound eng:** Yes
stage: 20 x 17
Dance club/live music venue where The Howlin' Wolf once stood, books Local-Nat'l acts & DJs 1-2 nites for 18+. 2-3 bands play 60-90min usu. for flat fee + % after split point. Locals play 1/wk usu. on Fri; Nat'ls play 2/mo usu. Sun-Wed. Prefers email or mailed CD & contact info; or thru MySpace.

Ruby's Roadhouse
840 Lamarque St.
Mandeville, LA 70448
p: 985-626-9748
www.rubysroadhouse.com
contact: Fred Holland
genres: Blues, Zydeco, R&B, Roots
advance: 3-6 months
capacity: 200
pa: Yes **sound eng:** Yes
stage: 20 x 10
open mics: Monthly
Historic local joint w/ dancing 21+ crowd, features Reg'l acts w/ four 45min sets mostly Fri-Sat for flat fee vs door. Mail press kit to venue.

Snug Harbor
626 Frenchmen St.
New Orleans, LA 70116
p: 504-949-0696
e: info@snugjazz.com
www.snugjazz.com
contact: Jason Patterson
p: 504-309-5299
e: jason@snugjazz.com
call: Mon-Sat 11am-5pm
genres: Jazz
advance: 1-2 months
capacity: 90
pa: Yes **sound eng:** Yes
stage: 10 x 15
Prime all ages Jazz club presents original Reg'l & Touring talent nitely for flat fee. Featured act plays two 90min sets. Promos: 628 Frenchmen St., New Orleans, LA 70116.

Sweet Lorraine's
1931 St. Claude Ave.
New Orleans, LA 70116
p: 504-945-9654
e: info@sweetlorrainesjazzclub.com
www.sweetlorrainesjazzclub.com
contact: Paul Sylvester
genres: Jazz, Blues, R&B
capacity: 200
pa: Yes **sound eng:** Yes
21+ venue w/ one of the best sound systems around, presents Local-Nat'l acts. Voted it 1 of 10 best Jazz clubs in USA.

Tipitina's Uptown
501 Napoleon Ave.
New Orleans, LA 70115
p: 504-895-8477
e: getinfo@tipitinas.com
www.tipitinas.com
contact: Bill Taylor
call: M-F 10am-5pm
genres: Funk, Rock, Soul, Jazz, Country, World, Latin, Hip-Hop, Alt., Prog.
advance: 2-3 months
capacity: 800
pa: Yes **sound eng:** Yes
stage: 16 x 28 **in-house:** Drums
Top original talent showcased Fri-Sun & some Thu at this Holy Grail of venues. 2-4 acts play 75min to 18+; few all ages shows, cover bands & DJs. Locals consider it a major breakthru to play here; Nat'l acts consider it an honor. Bands keep 80% merch sales on soft goods; 100% on hard. Email link to music or mail press kit to venue w/ ATTN: Lindsay Adler.

Maine

Bangor/Bar Harbor

103 Ultra Lounge
103 Park St.
Orono, ME 04473
p: 207-866-7700
e: info@eye9d
www.myspace.com/103ultralounge
p: 207-773-1398
genres: Rock, Jam, Reggae, Ska, Metal, Punk, Hip-Hop
advance: 2 months
capacity: 500
pa: Yes **sound eng:** Yes
stage: 54 x 14
All ages club near college campus, books up to 4 original Local-Int'l acts & DJs w/ draw 1-2 nites. Also books The Station in Portland. Booking thru www.myspace.com/eye9d. No unsolicited mail.

Carmen Verandah
119 Main St.
Bar Harbor, ME 04609
p: 207-288-2766; 207-288-2886
e: info@carmenverandah.com
www.carmenverandah.com
contact: Chris
genres: Funk, Rock, Blues, Dance, Reggae, Ska, Jazz
advance: 2-3 months
capacity: 200
pa: Yes **sound eng:** Yes
stage: 10 x 10
Bar w/ large dance floor books Reg'ls Fri/Sat & Jazz Sun afternoons. Open Apr-Nov. Send promos to: PO Box 10, Bar Harbor, ME 04609. Incl. photo & bio & follow up via email; no calls.

Gilbert's Pub
12 Bay View St.
Camden, ME 04843
p: 207-236-4320
e: gilbertsmusic@gmail.com
www.myspace.com/gilbertspub
contact: Stacey
call: evenings
genres: Rock, Blues, Funk, Country, Reggae, Irish, Folk
advance: 1-2 months
capacity: 166
open mics: Mon **sign in:** 9:30pm
Features Local & few Touring acts Thu-Sat to 21+. Featured act plays three 45min sets for flat fee. Larger tourist walk-in crowd during summer. Booking: PO Box 1315, Camden, ME 04843.

The Lompoc Cafe & Brew Pub
36 Rodick St.
Bar Harbor, ME 04609
p: 207-288-9392
e: info@lompoccafe.com
www.lompoccafe.com
contact: James Pike
genres: All Styles
advance: 2-3 months
capacity: 150
pa: Yes **sound eng:** Yes
stage: 15 x 20 (floor space)
open mics: Thu 9:30pm
Pub hosts low-volume Local-Reg'ls & growing number of Touring acts Fri & Sat. 1-3 acts play from 9:30pm-1am to 21+ crowd. Mail press kit to venue.

Unity Centre for the Performing Arts
42 Depot St.
Unity, ME 04988
p: 207-948-SHOW
www.unitymaine.org/theater
contact: John Sullivan
e: show@unitymaine.org
genres: S/S, Folk, Rock, Blues, Celtic, World
advance: 3-6 months
capacity: 200
pa: Yes **sound eng:** Yes
Theatre housed in 100-yr-old barn hosts 1-2 original Reg'l & Nat'l acts; some all ages shows. Email or snail mail kit.

Portland/Augusta

The Asylum
121 Center St.
Portland, ME 04101
p: 207-772-8274
www.myspace.com/portlandasylum
contact: Justin Hendrickson
p: 207-232-9767
e: justin@portlandasylum.com
genres: Rock, Folk Rock, Jam, Hip-Hop, S/S, Reggae, Metal
advance: 2-3 months
capacity: 800
pa: Yes **sound eng:** Yes
stage: 24 x 20
Great sound & showcases Local-Touring bands 5-7 nites for 21+. 2-3 acts/bill. Openers play 45min & headliners longer. Snail mail kit.

Bath Youth Meetinghouse & Skatepark
26 Summer St.
Bath, ME 04530
p: 207-443-8900
www.bathskatepark.com
contact: Claire Berkowitz
call: M-F 2-9pm
advance: 2 months
capacity: 150
pa: Yes **sound eng:** Yes
stage: 12 x 18
Teen ctr. hosts all ages shows w/ mostly Local-Reg'l bands 1-2 nites/mo. for 50% of door minus fee for sound. Fill out booking form on website.

The Big Easy
55 Market St.
Portland, ME 04101
p: 207-775-2266
www.bigeasyportland.com
contact: Derek Lombardi
e: bigeasybooking@gmail.com
genres: Pop, Folk, Reggae
advance: 3 months
capacity: 200
pa: Yes **sound eng:** Yes
stage: 20 x 12
open mics: Mon Hip-Hop
Bar mixes Local-Int'l bands & DJs nitely. Up to 3 mostly original acts play several sets for % of door; flat fee for Nat'ls. Few Sun all ages matinees

The Big Kahuna Cafe
270 Main St.
Bridgton, ME 04009
p: 207-647-9031

e: thebigkahunacafe@ime.net
www.thebigkahunacafe.com
genres: Blues, Folk, Bluegrass, Country, S/S, Jazz
pa: Yes **sound eng:** Yes
open mics: Thu
Venue in historic Masonic Hall, books Local-Nat'l acts Fri-Sat for 21+ crowd in summer; opens mid-May. Featured band plays two 45min sets.

Boothbay Harbor Opera House
86 Townsend Ave.
Boothbay Harbor, ME 04538
p: 207-633-6855
e: info@boothbayoperahouse.com
www.boothbayoperahouse.com
contact: Cathy Sherrill
genres: Rock, Blues, World, Country, Jazz, Pop, Classical
advance: 3-12 months
capacity: 350+
stage: 2 levels: 24 x 12; 2nd level 16' deep
Restored opera house books Reg'l & Touring acts 1-5 nites/wk. Send CD, printed materials, contact info & avail. dates to: PO Box 800, Boothbay Harbor, ME 04538.

Bray's Brewpub & Eatery
Rtes. 302 & 35
Naples, ME 04055
p: 207-693-6806
www.braysbrewpub.com
contact: Rob Prindall
e: braysbrewpub@adelphia.net
call: M-F after 10am
genres: Bluegrass, Blues, Country, Rock
capacity: 150
open mics: Sun 8pm
Victorian farmhouse has low volume Local & Reg'ls Thu-Sun. Featured act plays several sets for flat fee. Mailing address: PO Box 548, Naples, ME 04055.

Bubba's Sulky Lounge
92 Portland St.
Portland, ME 04101
p: 207-828-0549
www.bubbassulkylounge.com
contact: Mark Griffiths
e: mark.griffiths@tylertech.com
genres: All Styles
advance: 1-6 months
capacity: 300
pa: Yes **sound eng:** Yes
stage: 12 x 12
Bar w/ character to spare books Local & Reg'l bands & DJs w/ following Fri-Sat & most Thu. Bands play from 9pm-1am for % of door to 21+ crowd.

The Gold Room
512 Warren Ave.
Portland, ME 04103
p: 207-221-2343
www.thegoldroommaine.com
contact: Jim Grutello
p: 207-205-0705
e: jim@portlandsportscomplex.com
capacity: 500
Venue in sports complex hosts Local-Nat'l acts Sat for 21+ crowd. Snail mail kit.

Gritty McDuff's
396 Fore St.
Portland, ME 04101
p: 207-772-BREW
e: grittys@grittys.com
www.grittys.com
contact: Nate Drinkwater
p: 207-772-2739 x4
genres: Blues, Rock, Folk
advance: 2 months
capacity: 192 **stage:** 12 x 15
Brewpub books Local-Reg'l & some Touring bands Thu & Sat. Act supplies PA & plays for flat fee.

Inn on the Blues
7 Ocean Ave.
York Beach, ME 03910
p: 207-351-3221
e: info@innontheblues.com
www.innontheblues.com
contact: Joe Lipton
genres: All Styles
advance: 6-8 months
capacity: 150
pa: Yes **sound eng:** Yes
stage: 6 x 10
open mics: Sun **sign in:** 7pm
Resort area cafe has mostly Local-Reg'l acts playing from 9:30pm-12:30am; more frequent in summer. 1 act plays to mostly 21+ w/ some all ages events. Promos: PO Box 700, York Beach, ME 03910.

Mainely Brews
1 Post Office Sq.
Waterville, ME 04901
p: 207-873-2457
www.mainelybrews.com
contact: Luke Duplessis
e: luke.duplessis@umit.maine.edu
genres: All Styles
advance: 2 months
capacity: 200
pa: Yes **stage:** 10 x 10
open mics: Mon 8:30pm
Pub books Local & some Touring talent & DJs Wed-Sat & some Sun; all ages til 10pm. 1 act plays 4hrs w/ breaks from 9pm-1am. Snail mail kit.

Midnight Blues Club
2 Silver St.
Waterville, ME 04901
p: 207-877-8300
e: pm@3clubs.com
www.midnightbluesclub.net
contact: Chuck Noe
p: 207-934-5535
genres: Blues, Rock
advance: 2-3 months
capacity: 100; 200 (upstairs)
pa: Yes **stage:** 12 x 15
open mics: Wed & Thu 6pm
Club w/ full lights hosts Local-Reg'l talent Wed-Sat. 2 acts play four 40min sets for 21+ crowd. Touring acts booked 1 Sun/mo. Sister restaurant upstairs has live Rock & Acoustic area acts. Also helps book many other venues. Snail mail kit.

Space Gallery
538 Congress St.
Portland, ME 04101
p: 207-828-5600
www.space538.org
contact: Ian Paige
e: bookings@space538.org
genres: Indie Rock, Hip-Hop, Experimental, Folk, Jazz
advance: 8-10 weeks
capacity: 300
pa: Yes **sound eng:** Yes
Artist-run art community w/ emphasis on non-commercial music, hosts 2-3 original Touring acts w/ Reg'l openers to play 30-60min sets 7-9 nites/mo for % of door. Mostly 18+ w/ some all ages shows. Prefers email w/ link to music & band info; no unsolicited mail, calls or requests via MySpace!

The Station
272 St. John St.
Portland, ME 04102
p: 207-773-3466
e: info@eye9d
www.myspace.com/thestationlive
p: 207-773-1398
genres: Rock, Metal, Hip-Hop, Acoustic
advance: 2 months
capacity: 700
pa: Yes **sound eng:** Yes
stage: 24.5 x 18
3-5 original Local-Int'l bands play 30-90min sets Fri-Sat at this all ages venue. Booking thru www.myspace.com/eye9d.

Maryland

Baltimore/Annapolis

49 West Coffeehouse
49 West St.
Annapolis, MD 21401
p: 410-626-9796
e: info@49westcoffeehouse.com
www.49westcoffeehouse.com
contact: Brian Calahan
call: evenings
genres: Jazz, Blues, Folk, S/S, Classical, Ambient, Bluegrass
advance: Up to 1 year
capacity: 40 seats
All ages art space hosts mostly original Local & Reg'l music nitely w/ some early shows. 1 act plays 1hr sets from 8:30-12am w/ breaks for 100% of door.

The 8x10
10 E Cross St.
Baltimore, MD 21230
p: 410-625-2000
www.the8x10.com
contact: Abigail Janssens
e: booking@the8x10.com
call: M-F after 11am
genres: All Styles
advance: 3 months
capacity: 300
pa: Yes **sound eng:** Yes
stage: 20 x 20
open mics: Mon **sign in:** 7pm
Fave music club packs a wallop w/ great sound, views & dance floor. 2-5 mostly original Local-Touring acts w/ local draw gig 6 nites; most shows all ages. Snail mail press kit to venue; No Calls!

An die Musik LIVE!
409 N Charles St.
Baltimore, MD 21201
p: 888-221-6170; 410-385-2638
e: scc@andiemusik.com
www.andiemusiklive.com
contact: Henry Wong
e: henry@andiemusik.com
genres: Jazz, Classical
advance: 3 months
capacity: 75
pa: Yes **stage:** 10 x 30
Concert hall books Local-Int'l acts 7 nites. 1 acts plays for 60-90 min. Email submissions.

Andy's
337 1/2 High St.
Chestertown, MD 21620
p: 410-778-6779
e: info@andys-ctown.com
www.andys-ctown.com
contact: Andy
e: andy-s@baybroadband.net
call: M-F after 2pm
genres: Bluegrass, Newgrass, Pop, Rock, Alt. Country
advance: 3 months
capacity: 150+
pa: Yes **sound eng:** By Request
stage: 10 x 8
open mics: Last Wed of month
sign in: Email fordo1@aol.com
Lounge 47mi from Annapolis, offers original Local-Touring acts for 21+. Featured act plays 45+min Fri-Sat for flat fee vs door. No Trad Folk, Rap, or Metal. Prefers EPK, but may mail to: 337 High St., PO Box 166, Chestertown, MD 21620.

Austin Grill
919 Ellsworth Dr.
Silver Spring, MD 20910
p: 240-247-8969
www.austingrill.com
contact: Don Perrone
e: donp@austingrill.com
genres: Folk, S/S, Country, Alt. Country, Indie Rock, Rock
advance: 1-2 months
capacity: 250
pa: Yes **sound eng:** Yes
open mics: Tue **sign in:** 9pm
All ages Tex-Mex eatery features Local act w/ two 1hr sets Tue-Sun; S/S on Tue w/ 3+ acts. Other locations in DC, MD & VA. Broadcasts some gigs on local MHz TV. Prefers email, or snail mail press kit.

Baldwin's Station
7618 Main St.
Sykesville, MD 21784
p: 410-795-1041
www.baldwinstation.com
contact: Joyce Sica
p: 410-922-5210
e: uptownconcerts@gmail.com
call: M-F before 9pm
genres: Acoustic, Folk, Jazz, S/S, World
advance: Up to 1 year
capacity: 73
pa: Yes **sound eng:** Yes
stage: 8 x 8 (small raised wedge)
Upscale eatery S of Baltimore, features Local-Int'l acts w/ an audience. 1 act plays two 45min sets for all ages. Joyce/Uptown Concerts also books Cellar Stage in Baltimore. For promos: PO Box 1503, Randallstown, MD 21133.

Bushwaller's
209 N Market St.
Frederick, MD 21701
p: 301-695-6988
www.pages.frederick.com/dining/bushwallers.htm
contact: Rob Casey
p: 703-548-7800 **call:** M-F
e: rob@jamesturner.com
genres: Rock, Alt., Irish Folk, Acoustic
advance: 1-3 months
capacity: 220 **stage:** floor space
open mics: Thu
Irish pub 49mi from Baltimore, hosts mostly area acts Wed-Sun for 21+. Featured act fills 3-4hrs w/ breaks for flat fee. Promos: 1431 Duke St., Alexandria, VA 22316; no EPKs.

Cancun Cantina
7501 Old Telegraph Rd.
Hanover, MD 21076
p: 410-761-6188
e: management@cancuncantina.com
www.cancuncantina.com
contact: Greg Therres
p: 410-828-9400
e: greg@starleigh.com
genres: Country, Rock
advance: 1-12 months
capacity: 500
pa: Yes **sound eng:** Yes
stage: 2 stages
Dance club presents Local-Int'l bands Fri & Sat & some wknites. 1 Country act plays inside & 1 Top 40 act plays outside deck. 4hr set for flat fee. For deck booking, send press kit to: 205 E Joppa Rd., Ste. 106, Baltimore, MD 21286.

Cat's Eye Pub
1730 Thames St.
Baltimore, MD 21231
p: 410-276-9866
e: catseyepub@hotmail.com
www.catseyepub.com
contact: Ana Marie Cushing
p: 410-664-0009
genres: Zydeco, Blues, Irish, Rock, Bluegrass, Roots Rock, Jazz, Country, Reggae
advance: 3+ months
capacity: 110
pa: Limited **stage:** 10 x 12
Popular Irish bar w/ atmosphere books Locals-Nat'ls nitely & Sat & Sun afternoons. 1 act plays 4hrs for flat fee, tips & a few drinks. Email or snail mail kit.

Charm City Art Space
1729 Maryland Ave.
Baltimore, MD 21201
e: mike@headcold.net
www.ccspace.org
genres: Metal, Punk, Indie, Folk, Avant Garde
pa: Yes **stage:** floor space
Small volunteer-run PAC, in basement of record store down the street from local art college, hosts Local-Nat'l acts. Bands keep % of door. There are 15 different promoters, each w/ a different email to contact depending on style of music. See www.ccspace.org/index.php?action=booking for the list. Send promo w/ lyrics, requested date(s) & contact info.

Fletcher's
701 S Bond St.
Baltimore, MD 21231
p: 410-558-1889
www.fletchersbar.com
contact: Paul Manna
p: 410-323-7772
e: paul@24-7booking.com
genres: Rock
advance: 2 months
capacity: 325
pa: Yes **sound eng:** Yes
Prime all ages Rock club presents 3-4 original Local-Int'l bands 4-5 nites; DJs downstairs. Showcases many indie label acts. Mon nite spotlights Local talent. Bands play 40min sets for % of door. Prefers email, but may mail press kit to venue; no calls.

Leadbetters Tavern
1639 Thames St.
Baltimore, MD 21231
p: 410-675-4794
e: leadbetterstavern@gmail.com
www.leadbetterstavern.com
contact: Donna A. Thomas
p: 443-838-4558
e: donnaathomas@gmail.com
call: M-F after 3pm
genres: Acoustic, Blues, Folk, Rock, Rockabilly
advance: 2-3 months
capacity: 75
pa: Yes **stage:** small floor space
open mics: Mon **sign in:** 9pm
Historic Fells Point dive hosts Local-Reg'l music 5-9pm & 9:30pm-1:30am nitely for 21+. Acts play for % of bar. 3-4 piece bands max due to small space. Email or mail press kit w/ CD, bio & type of music to venue.

Lexington Market
400 W Lexington St.
Baltimore, MD 21201
p: 410-685-6169
e: info@lexingtonmarket.com
www.lexingtonmarket.com
contact: Darlene Hudson
e: dhudson@lexingtonmarket.com
genres: Jazz, Blues, Reggae, Pop, R&B
advance: 2 months
capacity: 1000
pa: Yes **sound eng:** Yes
stage: large **in-house:** Keyboard
Large & popular farmers' market hosts free live bands noon-2pm Fri & Sat. 1 Reg'l or Touring band plays 2hrs for flat fee to 18+. Great for merch sales & driving crowd to evening performance. Snail mail kit.

The Mudd Puddle
124 S Carroll St., #1
Frederick, MD 21701
p: 301-620-4323
www.myspace.com/frederickmuddpuddle
contact: Donna
call: prefers MySpace
genres: All Styles
advance: 1 month
capacity: 150
pa: Yes **stage:** floor space
Coffeehouse w/ very artsy atmosphere hosts Local-Int'l acts. Shows are never more than $5 & bands get % of door. Proud of treating bands quite well. 4 acts play Fri & Sat to all ages crowd w/ 30min sets; 45min for headliners. Use MySpace for booking inquiries; no unsolicited mail.

Ottobar
2549 N Howard St.
Baltimore, MD 21218
p: 410-662-0069
e: info@theottobar.com
www.theottobar.com
contact: Todd Lesser
e: booking@theottobar.com
genres: Indie, Rock, Punk, Hip-Hop, Garage, Metal, S/S
advance: 8-12 weeks
capacity: 450
pa: Yes **sound eng:** Yes
stage: 21 x 4
All ages venue books mid-level Nat'l bands w/ Local & Reg'l openers & DJs 5-7 nites. 4 original acts play 30min for % of door. Only acts w/ past area gigs considered. Use email only.

Rams Head On Stage
33 West St.
Annapolis, MD 21401
p: 410-268-4545
e: annapolis@ramsheadtavern.com
www.ramsheadonstage.com
contact: Kris Stevens
p: 410-295-9761
e: kris@ramsheadtavern.com; booking@ramsheadtavern.com
genres: Jazz, Country, Folk, Rock, Pop, Blues, Zydeco
advance: 9 months
capacity: 250
pa: Yes **sound eng:** Yes
stage: 18 x 10 **in-house:** Piano
Prime music spot has polished Reg'l & Touring talent up to 7 nites. 1 original act plays 90-120min for flat fee & 80% of merch. 21+ w/ all ages on wknds before 5pm. Other MD locations in Savage, Crownsville & Baltimore. Send EPK or mail kit.

Recher Theatre
512 York Rd.
Towson, MD 21204
p: 410-337-7178
e: info@rechertheatre.com
www.rechertheatre.com
contact: Paul Manna
p: 410-323-7772
e: paul@24-7booking.com
genres: Rock, Metal, Blues, Reggae, S/S, World, Indie, Jazz
advance: 2-3 months
capacity: 750
pa: Yes **sound eng:** Yes
stage: medium
Great mid-Atlantic tour stop hosts estab. & rising, original talent for all ages. Locals star on Sun & keep all merch sales. 4 bands play 40min for % of door. Email only; no unsolicited mail or calls.

The Sidebar Tavern
218 E Lexington St.
Baltimore, MD 21202
p: 410-659-4130
www.sidebartavern.com
contact: Matty Pants
e: sidebarbooking@gmail.com
genres: Punk, Hardcore, Rock, Hip-Hop
advance: 2 months
capacity: 90
pa: Yes **sound eng:** Yes
Mainly a Punk & Hardcore venue, books Local-Int'l acts 6 nites. Shows are all ages.

Sonoma's Bar & Grille
7284 Cradlerock Way
Columbia, MD 21045
p: 410-381-7220
www.sonomasbar.com
contact: Greg Therres
p: 410-828-9400
e: gtherres@aol.com; greg@starleigh.com
genres: All Styles
advance: 1-3 months
capacity: 250
pa: Yes **sound eng:** Yes
stage: 15 x 50
Live music bar books mostly Baltimore/DC-area Alt. Rock bands & few DJs up to 6 nites. Featured act plays 3 sets for 21+ crowd. Also books other venues. Promos: 205 E Joppa Rd., Ste. 106, Baltimore, MD 21286; no EPKs.

Greater MD

Seacrets
117 W 49th St.
Ocean City, MD 21842
p: 410-524-4900
www.seacrets.com; www.seacretslive.com
contact: Skip Dixxon
p: 410-524-4900 x202
e: skip.dixxon@irieradio.com
genres: Most Styles
advance: 6 months
capacity: 5120
pa: Yes **sound eng:** Yes
stage: 5 stages
open mics: Wed, winter-fall
Venue w/ 6 performance areas hosts 5 bands Fri-Sat & 3 bands Mon-Thu; mostly cover acts. 17 bars in massive complex! 21+ after 9pm. Bands may be broadcast on Seacrets' own 98.1 FM & web TV stns. Also offers HD-DVD authoring for bands. No Heavy Metal. Mail press kit to venue.

Massachusetts

Boston

Abbey Lounge
3 Beacon St.
Somerville, MA 02143
p: 617-441-9631
www.abbeylounge.com
contact: Mike Feudale
e: abbeyloungebooking@yahoo.com
call: M-F 9am-5pm
genres: Rock, Alt., Blues, Punk, Garage
advance: 3 months
capacity: 112
pa: Yes **sound eng:** Yes
stage: 12 x 16 **in-house:** Drums
Nominated 'City's Best Live Venue' & books Local-Int'l acts Wed-Sat on 2 stages. 4 bands play 30-45min sets. Stripped down bands & solo acts play Pub Stage, while full bands play Main Stage. Email press kit & wait 4 wks to follow up; no unsolicited mail.

Alchemist Lounge
435 S Huntington Ave.
Jamaica Plain, MA 02130
p: 617-477-5741
www.alchemistlounge.com
contact: Lyndon Fuller
e: lyndon.fuller@alchemistlounge.com
genres: Blues, Jazz, Alt.
pa: Yes **sound eng:** Yes
stage: floor space
Very eclectic mix of Local-Nat'l music for 21+; never a cover. Email EPK w/ band name in subject & incl. link to music, size of mailing list & contact info; allow 4-6 wks for review; may also mail press kit to venue w/ ATTN: Booking; will contact if interested; no calls.

The All Asia
334 Mass Ave.
Cambridge, MA 02139
p: 617-497-1544
e: allasiabar@gmail.com
www.allasiabar.com
contact: Marc
e: marc@allasiabar.com
genres: Acoustic, Folk, Indie, Pop, Power Pop, Blues, Bluegrass, Funk, R&B, Soul

capacity: 100
pa: Limited
open mics: Wed **sign in:** 8:45pm
Grub & music room books 2 Local shows nitely. Bands must bring mics & stands.

Amazing Things Arts Center
160 Hollis St.
Framingham, MA 01702
p: 508-405-2787
e: info2@amazingthings.org
www.amazingthings.org
contact: Michael Moran
e: mmoran@amazingthings.org
call: Tue-Sat 1-7pm
genres: Jazz, Bluegrass, World, Folk, Country, Rock, Blues, Classical
capacity: 180
pa: Yes **sound eng:** Yes
stage: 12 x 24
Community non-profit books wide mix of original Local-Int'l talent up to 7 nites. 1-2 acts play two 45min sets for all ages. Merch splits 85/15. Also books 450-seat Civic League 15 nites/yr. EPKs preferred, but may also mail to: PO Box 3310, Framingham, MA 01701.

Atwood's Tavern
877 Cambridge St.
Cambridge, MA 02139
p: 617-864-2792
e: atwoodstavern@gmail.com
www.atwoodstavern.com
contact: Ryan
e: booking@atwoodstavern.com
genres: Roots, Blues, Bluegrass, Jazz
capacity: 85
pa: Yes
21+ music venue hosts original Local-Nat'l acts up to 7 nites. No full-sized drum sets allowed; bring brushes or bundles. Email w/ music samples for booking; no calls.

Bill's Bar
5 1/2 Lansdowne St.
Boston, MA 02215
p: 617-421-9678
e: info@billsbar.com
www.billsbar.com
contact: Lionel Brown
e: promo@onslaught entertainment.com; booking@onslaught entertainment.com
call: email only
genres: Rock, Metal, Indie, Reggae, Hip-Hop
advance: 2-3 months
capacity: 247
pa: Yes **sound eng:** Yes
3-5 Local-Reg'ls & some Touring acts gig 30-90min Thu-Sat at music bar w/ super sight lines. Some all ages shows Sat-Sun. Email booker for 18+ Fri-Sat gigs & use online booking form for 21+ Thu gigs. No unsolicited mail or calls.

Bull Run Restaurant
215 Great Rd.
Shirley, MA 01464
p: 978-425-4311
e: bullrun@bicnet.net
www.bullrunrestaurant.com
contact: George Tocci
p: 718-935-9019
call: M-F 11am
genres: S/S, Folk, Country, Americana, Blues, Rock, Jazz
advance: 6 months
capacity: 75; 300
pa: Yes **sound eng:** Yes
stage: 12 x 8; 30 x 15
Busy inn 40mi from Boston, books Locals-Int'l acts most Fri & Sat in 3 spaces. Books via Sonicbids or email.

Cantab Lounge & Club Bohemia
738 Massachusetts Ave.
Cambridge, MA 02139
p: 617-354-2685
www.cantab-lounge.com
contact: Geoff Bartley
e: geoffbartley@pobox.com
genres: Rock, R&B, Blues, Soul, Jam, Funk, Dance, Jazz, Folk, Bluegrass
advance: Up to 6 months
capacity: 150; 100 **stage:** 15 x 10
open mics: Mon S/S; Tue Bluegrass
Old school 21+ music joint w/ Club Bohemia downstairs, books Touring Folk, S/S on Mon & Touring Bluegrass acts Tue. 1-3 acts play 30-90min sets; notable open mics. For Club Bohemia booking, send promos to: 276 Washington St., #374, Boston, MA 02108.

The Center for Arts in Natick (TCAN)
14 Summer St.
Natick, MA 01760
p: 508-647-0097
e: info@natickarts.org
www.natickarts.org
contact: David Lavalley
p: 508-647-0097 x204
genres: Folk, Jazz, Rock, Blues, World, Country, Pop
capacity: 275
pa: Yes **sound eng:** Yes
stage: 12 x 20 **in-house:** Piano
open mics: Most Mon
Non-profit all ages arts ctr. in renovated firehouse 23mi from Boston, presents an original Touring act w/ Local opener every Fri & Sat. Mail press kit to venue w/ ATTN: Bookings.

Club Lido
1290 N Shore Rd.
Revere, MA 02151
p: 781-289-3080
www.clublido.com
contact: Brian
e: office@clublido.org
genres: Reggae, Latin
advance: 1-3 months
capacity: 1350; 600; 300
pa: Yes **sound eng:** Yes
Niteclub minutes from Boston, presents mostly Reg'l-Int'l talent on 3 stages. Up to 4 acts play 45min on Wed, Fri-Sun. Pay varies but drinks are free. Also books Roxy in Boston & Providence, RI. Email for booking.

Club Passim
47 Palmer St.
Cambridge, MA 02138
p: 617-492-5300
www.clubpassim.org
contact: Matt Smith
p: 617-492-5300 x3
e: matt@clubpassim.org
genres: Acoustic, Folk, S/S, Blues
advance: 4-5 months
capacity: 125
pa: Yes **sound eng:** Yes
stage: 12 x 6 **in-house:** Keyboard
open mics: Tue **sign in:** 6:30pm
Notable non-profit music room showcases polished original Touring talent & Reg'ls w/ a buzz to all ages. 1-2 acts play from 8-10:30pm for % of door. Snail mail or email kit.

Copperfield's Bar & Down Under Pub
98 Brookline Ave.
Boston, MA 02215
p: 617-247-8605; 617-499-6907
e: copperfieldsfenway@ hotmail.com
www.copperfieldsboston.com
contact: Ed Leary
p: 617-499-6945
e: bands@copperfieldsboston.com
genres: Alt., College Rock
advance: 2 months
capacity: 140; 300
pa: Yes **sound eng:** Yes
stage: 2 stages
Popular bar books original Reg'l bands for college crowd Fri-Sat in 2 rooms for door. Up to 4 bands in each room play 40min sets to 21+.

Fusion 5
105 Washington St.
Foxboro, MA 02035
p: 508-543-0599
www.myspace.com/clubfusion5
contact: Jimmy
genres: Rock
advance: 4 months
capacity: 400
pa: Yes **sound eng:** Yes
open mics: Wed
Sports bar books Local-Reg'l acts & DJs Fri-Sat for 21+. Contact thru MySpace; no unsolicited mail.

Great Scott
1222 Commonwealth Ave.
Boston, MA 02134
p: 617-566-9014
www.greatscottboston.com
contact: Carl Lavin
e: allstonsubmissions@gmail.com
call: email only
genres: Indie Rock
advance: 1 month
capacity: 240
pa: Yes **sound eng:** Yes
stage: 18 x 10
Packs in the college crowd up to 7 nites. 3-4 original Local-Nat'l acts play 40min for % of door; 21+ Fri/Sat, 18+ Sun-Thu. Email link to press kit; no calls or unsolicited packages.

The Grog
13 Middle St.
Newburyport, MA 01950
p: 978-465-8008
e: enjoy@thegrog.com
www.thegrog.com
contact: Joey Newman
e: joeygrogmusic@hotmail.com
genres: Blues, R&B, Dance, Rockabilly, Rock, Jazz
advance: 1-9 months
capacity: 130
pa: Yes **sound eng:** Yes
stage: 15 x 8
contact: Julie Dougherty/ Paul Prue/Bob Kramer/ Chad Verbeck
Popular eatery presents 1-2 Local-Reg'l & some Nat'l acts Thu-Sun for 21+; original music on Thu. Sun nite Blues Party. Bands play 2-3 sets for a flat fee w/ incentive program for first timers. Email or mail kit.

Harpers Ferry
158 Brighton Ave.
Allston, MA 02134
p: 617-254-9743
www.harpersferryboston.com
contact: Mike Delehanty
p: 617-254-7380
e: booking@ harpersferryboston.com
genres: Rock, Funk, Indie, Roots, Reggae, Hip-Hop
advance: 2-3 months
capacity: 400
pa: Yes **sound eng:** Yes
stage: 24 x 15
Longstanding Rock club w/ great sight & sound, hosts up to 5 Local-Int'l acts nitely for college crowd; usu. paid % of door. Send link to music & press kit; no calls.

Jacques Cabaret/ Underground
79 Broadway
Boston, MA 02116
p: 617-426-8902
e: jacquesunder@aol.com
www.jacquescabaret.com/ JacquesUnderground
contact: John Surette
genres: Alt., Goth, Industrial, Rock
advance: 1 month
capacity: 117
pa: Yes **sound eng:** Yes
stage: 18 x 10
Drag acts upstairs nitely & Local-Nat'l bands downstairs Fri-Sat. Up to 4 bands play 40min for % of door. Snail mail or email kit.

Johnny D's
17 Holland St.
Somerville, MA 02144
p: 617-776-2004
www.johnnyds.com
contact: Dana Westover
p: 617-776-7450
e: dana@johnnyds.com
call: M-F noon-6pm
genres: Blues, Roots, Folk, S/S, Int'l, Rock, Rockabilly, Zydeco, Bluegrass, Celtic
advance: 2-3 months
capacity: 310
pa: Yes **sound eng:** Yes
Highly praised 21+ club books Reg'l & Nat'l talent Tue-Sun; Jazz brunch Sat-Sun. 1-2 acts play several sets. Call or email link to music, gig history, estimated draw, label info, discography, radio play & why you can draw in Boston; contact before mailing. No unsolicited mail.

Lizard Lounge
1667 Massachusetts Ave.
Cambridge, MA 02138
p: 617-547-0759; 617-547-1228
e: info@lizardloungeclub.com
www.lizardloungeclub.com
contact: Billy Beard
p: 617-499-6992
e: bookagig@ lizardloungeclub.com
genres: Most Styles
advance: 2 months
capacity: 105
pa: Yes **sound eng:** Yes
stage: 15 x 15 (floor space)
open mics: Mon **sign in:** 7:30pm
Harvard hang, hosts original low-volume Reg'l & Touring artists Tue-Sat. Early show 'Soul Low' features 1 act

playing 1hr for free. Late show: up to 3 acts play for % of door. Email link to music & indicate "Acoustic" or "Electric" in subject; allow 6 wks for a response. No unsolicited mail.

Lucky Dog Music Hall
89 Green St.
Worcester, MA 01604
p: 508-363-1888
www.luckydogmusic.com
contact: Erick Godin
e: nineftsix@aol.com
call: Tue & Wed noon-5pm
genres: All Styles
advance: 1-3 months
capacity: 235
pa: Yes **sound eng:** Yes
stage: 22 x 10 **in-house:** Backline
open mics: Wed
Famed Rock club 45+mi from Boston, hosts estab. & buzz bands Wed-Sat. 2-6 acts play 20-120min for 21+. New Local bands use email to play Wed open mic; others may mail kit to venue.

Matt Murphy's Pub
14 Harvard St.
Brookline, MA 02445
p: 617-232-0188
www.mattmurphyspub.com
contact: Jason Waddleton
e: jason@mattmurphyspub.com
genres: Reggae, Jazz, Hip-Hop
advance: 3 months
capacity: 70
pa: Yes **stage:** 10 x 8
open mics: Mon 11pm
Serves up original Local bands for mixed 21+ crowd. Featured acts plays two 1hr sets for flat fee Thu-Tue; SRO. In-house record label, Pub Records, puts live recordings online & on CD release. All booking via email.

McFadden's
148 State St.
Boston, MA 02109
p: 617-227-5100
www.mcfaddensboston.com
contact: Dan
e: diannello@mcfaddenssalloon.com
genres: Reggae, Rock
capacity: 277
pa: Yes **sound eng:** Yes
Features state-of-the-art technology w/ interesting interior design. Original Local-Reg'l acts & DJs play for 21+. Email or mail press kit to venue.

Middle East
472/480 Massachusetts Ave.
Cambridge, MA 02139
p: 617-864-3278
e: booking@mideastclub.com
www.mideastclub.com
contact: Kevin Hoskins
e: kevin@mideastclub.com
genres: Rock, Punk, Pop, Ska, Rockabilly, Surf, Hip-Hop, Electronica, Goth, Industrial, World, Blues, Metal
advance: 6-8 weeks
capacity: 200; 575; 75; 60
pa: Yes **sound eng:** Yes
stage: 4 stages
open mics: Mon **sign in:** 10pm
Influential showcase for original talent, presents polished Local-Int'l artists nitely. 3-4 acts on 4 stages perform for 30-60min; first timers get % of door; some all ages shows. No Hardcore or Agressive Metal. Email links w/ band name in subject line or snail mail ATTN: Upstairs Booking. Allow 6-8 wks, then follow up w/ email.

Midway Café
3496 Washington St.
Jamaica Plain, MA 02130
p: 617-524-9038
e: info@midwaycafe.com
www.midwaycafe.com
contact: David Balerna
call: M-F after 9pm
genres: Rock, Rockabilly, Alt., Blues, World
advance: 6-8 weeks
capacity: 90
pa: Yes **sound eng:** Yes
stage: 15 x 12
Volume-constricted music club showcases polished Reg'l bands, some Touring acts 5 nites for 21+. Up to 4 acts play 45min for door after expenses. No Metal or Hardcore. Mail press kit to venue.

Milky Way Lounge & Lanes
403 Centre St.
Jamaica Plain, MA 02130
p: 617-524-3740
e: info@milkywayjp.com
www.milkywayjp.com
contact: Dan Shea
p: 617-524-3740 x22
e: dan@milkywayjp.com
genres: Rock, Jazz, Reggae, Afro-Latin, Hip-Hop
advance: 1 month
capacity: 200
pa: Yes **sound eng:** Yes
stage: 25 x 20
open mics: Last Mon/mo 8pm
Bowling alley/club presents quirky original Local-Touring bands nitely for 21+. 2-4 acts play 45min sets for 80-90% of door. Prefers email, but may mail press kit to venue.

Narrows Center
16 Anawan St.
Fall River, MA 02721
p: 508-324-1926
www.ncfta.org
contact: Patrick Norton
p: 508-324-1926 x6
e: bookings@ncfta.org
genres: Americana, Roots, Folk, S/S
capacity: 280
pa: Yes **sound eng:** Yes
stage: 12 x 24
open mics: Wed **sign in:** 6:45pm
Volunteer-run space in old mill bldg w/ church pew seating & great acoustics, hosts top Touring acts w/ some polished Local-Reg'l openers 5-10 nites/mo. Shows are all ages; 1-2 acts on a bill; 54mi from Boston. Mail press kit to venue.

O'Briens Pub
3 Harvard Ave.
Allston, MA 02134
p: 617-782-6245
e: info@obrienspubboston.com
www.obrienspubboston.com
contact: Carl Lavin
e: allstonsubmissions@gmail.com
genres: Rock, Alt., Punk, Metal, Jam
advance: 1-2 months
capacity: 80
pa: Yes **sound eng:** Yes
stage: 15 x 12
Dive bar w/ character books loud area bands & some Touring acts nitely for 21+. 3-5 bands play 45min for % of door. Also books Great Scott. Email link to press kit or website only; no calls.

The Palladium
261 Main St.
Worcester, MA 01608
p: 508-797-9696
e: palladiumemail@aol.com
www.thepalladium.net
contact: Josh Smith
genres: Heavy Metal, Pop, Punk, Rock, R&B, Acoustic
advance: 2-3 months
capacity: 2160 **stage:** 60 x 30
Packed all ages Rock room w/ supersonic sound, lures big name Metal/Hardcore acts & some Reg'l openers. Up to 3 acts play mostly original sets. Mail press kit to venue w/ ATTN: Josh. Call 2 wks later to follow up. No unsolicited emails.

The Plough & Stars
912 Massachusetts Ave.
Cambridge, MA 02139
p: 617-576-0032
www.ploughandstars.com
contact: Jim Seery
e: jim@ploughandstars.com
genres: All Styles
capacity: 80
pa: Yes **sound eng:** Yes
stage: floor space
Local bands play nitely for 21+. Snail mail kit w/ ATTN: Jim.

Ryles Jazz Club
212 Hampshire St.
Cambridge, MA 02139
p: 617-876-9330
e: info@thejazzagency.com
www.ryles.com
contact: Frank Vardaros
p: 617-593-9192
call: M-F 10am-6pm
genres: Jazz, Funk, World, Latin, Swing
advance: 3 months
capacity: 313
pa: Yes **sound eng:** Yes
stage: 8 x 32
Mostly all ages niteclub presents top tier Reg'l & Touring talent. Original act plays three 50min sets Tue-Sun. Prefers kit w/ CD or EPK sent w/ ATTN: Frank, The Jazz Agency, 1209 Saxon Blvd, Ste. 7, Orange City, FL 32763; allow 8wks for review.

T.T. The Bear's Place
10 Brookline St.
Cambridge, MA 02139
p: 617-492-0082
www.ttthebears.com
contact: Randi Millman
p: 617-492-0082 x1
e: booking@ttthebears.com
genres: Pop, Indie, Garage, Electronic, Roots Rock
advance: 2 months
capacity: 300
pa: Yes **sound eng:** Yes
stage: 17 x 10
Prime 18+ music room features 4 Local-Int'l bands nitely. Openers get 45min, headliner 1+hrs. New band nites most Sun & Tue. Prefers MySpace for booking. Mail promos to venue only if you've played at least 3 times at smaller local venues. Wait 3 wks, then email or call.

Toad
1912 Massachusetts Ave.
Cambridge, MA 02140
p: 617-497-4950; 617-876-9180
e: bookagig@toadcambridge.com
www.toadcambridge.com
contact: Billy Beard
e: ltbookings@comcast.net
genres: Americana, Roots, Blues, Rock, Indie Pop, Folk, S/S, Jazz
advance: 2-3 months
capacity: 62
pa: Yes **stage:** 10 x 6
Prime no cover music club hosts Local-Touring bands nitely for 21+; many 2-show nites. Up to 2 acts play 1hr sets for flat fee. No Punk, Metal or Loud. Also books Lizard Lounge. Prefers emailed links to music; will contact if interested. No unsolicited mail or calls.

Union Street
107 Rear Union St.
Newton Centre, MA 02459
p: 617-964-6684
e: manager@unionst.com
www.unionst.com
contact: Stephen DeSousa
e: stephen@unionst.com
capacity: 150
pa: Yes
Local & Reg'l bands upstairs on wknds. All shows 21+ & start at 10pm. Email for booking.

Wally's Café
427 Massachusetts Ave.
Boston, MA 02118
p: 617-424-1408
e: information@wallyscafe.com
www.wallyscafe.com
contact: Lloyd Poindexter
call: Mon-Sun 2pm-2am
genres: Jazz, Blues, Latin
advance: 2 months
capacity: 99
pa: Yes **sound eng:** Yes
stage: 8 x 5 **in-house:** Piano
Old school Jazz joint & "training ground" features live Reg'ls nitely for flat fee, often w/ students from Berklee College. Prefers email, or call for booking.

Western MA

The Basement
21 Center St.
Northampton, MA 01060
p: 413-586-2632
e: info@iheg.com
www.iheg.com/basement_main.asp
contact: John Sanders
p: 413-586-2632 x108
e: john@iheg.com
genres: Jazz, Celtic, Rock, Americana
advance: 2-3 months
capacity: 50
pa: Yes **sound eng:** Yes
Iron Horse venue books polished, original Reg'ls up to 6 nites. Also books Iron Horse & Calvin Theatre. No unsolicited material.

Calvin Theater
19 King St.
Northampton, MA 01060
p: 413-586-2632
e: info@iheg.com
www.iheg.com
contact: John Sanders
p: 413-586-2632 x108

e: john@iheg.com
call: M-F 10am-5pm
genres: Alt., S/S, Reggae, Ska, Jazz, Rock, Folk, Blues
advance: Up to 1 year
capacity: 1355
pa: Yes **sound eng:** Yes
stage: large
All ages restored theater books mostly original Nat'l acts w/ some Local-Reg'l openers. 1-2 acts play 90min sets. Call before mailing press kit to: 78 Main St., #514, Northampton, MA 01060.

Club Helsinki
284 Main St.
Great Barrington, MA 01230
p: 413-528-3394
e: info@clubhelsinkiweb.com
www.clubhelsinkiweb.com
contact: Deborah McDowell
p: 413-528-6308
e: booking@clubhelsinkiweb.com
genres: R&B, Soul, Jazz, Country, Fusion, Blues
advance: 2-4 months
capacity: 90
pa: Yes **sound eng:** Yes
stage: large **in-house:** Drums
open mics: Tue Open Stage 7pm
Prime original music showcase books Local openers for top Reg'l & Nat'l performers up to 5 nites for 21+. Sets run 45-60min. Email or mail press kit.

Dream Away Lodge
1342 County Rd.
Becket, MA 01223
p: 413-623-8725
e: dreamawaylodge@aol.com
www.myspace.com/thedreamawaylodge
contact: Daniel Osman
genres: S/S, Rock, Folk, Blues
advance: 3 months
capacity: 60+ **stage:** floor space
Venerable inn - a must for Dylan junkies - showcases Reg'l & few Touring acts Fri/Sat for dinner & tips; more often in summer. Featured act plays from 8:30-12am for all ages. Great stop on the NYC/New England circuit. Snail mail or email kit.

The Elevens
1 Pearl St.
Northampton, MA 01060
p: 413-586-9155
www.elevensmusic.com
contact: John Reilly
e: jreils87@comcast.net
genres: Rock, Pop, S/S
advance: 2 months
capacity: 200
pa: Yes **sound eng:** Yes
stage: 22 x 12
Haven for indie bands traveling the NYC/Boston circuit.

1-3 Local-Int'l acts gig up to 4 nites for 21+ crowd. Mail kit or email links; follow up in 3 wks.

Iron Horse
20 Center St.
Northampton, MA 01060
p: 413-584-0610
e: info@iheg.com
www.iheg.com
contact: John Sanders
p: 413-586-2632 x108
e: john@iheg.com
genres: S/S, Blues, Hip-Hop, Americana, Jazz, Rock, Funk
advance: 1-4 months
capacity: 170
pa: Yes **sound eng:** Yes
stage: medium **in-house:** Drums
Premier original music venue showcases top tier Touring talent & DJs up to 7 nites. Reg'ls w/ a buzz snag some opening slots. 2-3 bands play 1hr to 14+ crowd. Merch split is 80/20. Promos: 78 Main St., #514, Northampton, MA 01060.

Montague Bookmill
440 Greenfield Rd.
Montague, MA 01351
p: 413-367-9206
e: info@montaguebookmill.com
www.montaguebookmill.com
contact: Gregg Cornish
p: 413-367-9666
e: gregg@montaguebookmill.com
genres: All Styles
advance: 2 months
capacity: 50 **stage:** floor space
Used bookstore just N of Northampton & Amherst, presents Local-Int'l acts 1-2 nites playing for 90% of door or $50 (whichever is greater). 1-2 acts play for all ages. Use email for booking or mail press kit to: PO Box 954, Montague, MA 01351.

North Quabbin Ctr.
6 Old Main St. on the Common
New Salem, MA 01355
p: 978-544-5200
e: info@1794meetinghouse.org
www.1794meetinghouse.org
contact: Program Committee
genres: Low Volume, Acoustic
advance: 2+ months
capacity: 200 **stage:** large
Non-profit listening room in historic bldg. w/ great acoustics & full lights, 24mi from Northampton, hosts original Local-Touring artists 3 nites/wk from late May-Sep for all ages. 1-2 acts split 50-66% of door. Mail press kit to venue.

Pearl St. Nightclub
10 Pearl St.
Northampton, MA 01060
p: 413-584-7810; 413-584-7771
e: info@iheg.com
www.iheg.com
contact: John Sanders
p: 413-586-2632
e: john@iheg.com
call: M-F 10am-5pm
genres: S/S, Americana, Ska, Rap, Rock
advance: 1-4 months
capacity: 300; 700 (bar)
pa: Yes **sound eng:** Yes
stage: medium
Iron Horse venue books buzz bands & estab. acts 4 nites for 14+ crowd. 2-6 acts w/ local draw play original sets; headliner gets 75-90min. Call before sending press kits to: 78 Main St., #514, Northampton, MA 01060.

Waterfront Tavern
920 Main St.
Holyoke, MA 01040
p: 413-532-2292
www.waterfronttavern.com
contact: Anna Rigali
e: waterfronttavern@hotmail.com
call: Tue after 9am
genres: Rock, R&B, Blues
advance: 1-2 months
capacity: 800
pa: To rent **sound eng:** To hire
stage: large L-shaped
Mostly Local bands w/ some Reg'l-Int'l acts & DJs gig 3 nites for flat fee + door. 1 act plays 3 sets w/ breaks from 9:30pm-1am for 21+. Equal mix of original & cover bands.

Greater MA

Outerland
17 Airport Rd.
Edgartown, MA 02539
p: 508-693-1137
e: info@outerlandmv.com
www.outerlandmv.com
contact: Whitney Dailey
p: 508-693-1137 x12
e: whitney@outerlandmv.com
call: M-F noon-5pm
genres: Rock, Reggae, Blues, Roots, Americana, S/S
capacity: 700
sound eng: Yes
stage: 24 x 20
Prime 18+ island venue on Martha's Vineyard books original, estab. acts & buzz bands w/ local draw from Apr-Jan for natives & tourists; few all ages shows. Touring acts play main stage & smaller Acoustic bands at 'The Dock.' No Metal or Hardcore. Prefers EPKs or link to music w/ no attachments; snail mail accepted reluctantly: PO Box 2098, Edgartown, MA 02539.

Michigan

Detroit/Ann Arbor

313.Jac/Jacoby's
624 Brush St.
Detroit, MI 48226
p: 313-962-7067
www.staticrecords.com
contact: Sue Static
p: 313-886-7860
call: afternoons
genres: Acoustic, Indie Rock
advance: 1-2 months
capacity: 75-100
pa: Yes **stage:** small
Showcase for area bands & emerging Touring acts interested in gig swaps. Original bands gig Fri & Sat for 21+. Call or email booker before sending material to: ATTN: Static/313.jac shows, 17215 Mack, Detroit, MI 48224.

AJ's Music Cafe
240 W Nine Mile Rd.
Ferndale, MI 48220
p: 248-399-3946
e: ajamesoneil@gmail.com
www.ajsmusiccafe.com
contact: Branden Reeves
call: prefers MySpace
genres: Acoustic, Indie
capacity: 115
sound eng: By Request
open mics: Mon-Thu 8pm
Formerly Xhedos Cafe, but still booking Local-Nat'l acts for 70% of door on wknds. Bands must draw 30-100. Email, call or contact via MySpace.

Alvin's
5756 Cass St.
Detroit, MI 48202
p: 313-633-6326
www.myspace.com/alvinsdetroit
contact: Jason Berry
p: 734-623-9962
e: jmberry3@comcast.net
call: M-F noon-4pm
genres: Rock, Punk, Blues, Alt., Pop, Jam, Jazz, Hip-Hop, R&B, Electronic, Country
advance: 2 months
capacity: 300
pa: Yes **sound eng:** Yes
stage: 20 x 12
Now under new ownership, 18+ landmark venue near Wayne State U, hosts Local-Touring acts & some DJs nitely. 2-4 original bands play 1hr sets; some all ages shows. Also books Blind Pig in Ann Arbor. Mail kit or email music link.

The Ark
316 S Main St.
Ann Arbor, MI 48104
p: 734-761-1800
e: theark@theark.org
www.theark.org
contact: Anya Siglin
p: 734-761-1800 x22
call: Tue, Wed & Fri by 11am
genres: Folk, S/S, Country, Americana, Bluegrass, Celtic, Roots, World, Blues
advance: 2-3 months
capacity: 400
pa: Yes **sound eng:** Yes
Prime non-profit Acoustic listening room hosts original polished & estab. Local-Touring artists 5-7 nites. 1-2 acts perform 45min sets for all ages Merch splits 90/10. Also books Ann Arbor Folk Fest, Power Ctr., Michigan Theater & Hill Aud. Promos: 1955 Pauline Blvd., Ste. 200, Ann Arbor, MI 48103; follow up in 8 wks.

Baker's Keyboard Lounge
20510 Livernois Ave.
Detroit, MI 48221
p: 313-345-6300
www.bakerskeyboardlounge.com
contact: John Colbert
e: bakerslounge@sbcglobal.net
call: Tue-Sun 11am-5pm
genres: Jazz, Quartets, Big Band
advance: 2 months
capacity: 110
pa: Yes **sound eng:** Yes
stage: large **in-house:** Piano
open mics: Sun, Mon & Tue
History radiates from this prime all ages showcase for original Reg'l & Touring talent & monthly cover bands. Featured act plays three 40min sets 5-6 nites. Send email or EPK.

The Belmont
10215 Joseph Campau St.
Hamtramck, MI 48212
p: 313-871-1966
e: contactus@thebelmontbar.com
www.thebelmontbar.com
contact: Melody Beatons
e: booking@thebelmontbar.com; belmontpr@yahoo.com
genres: Rock, Punk, Country, Rockabilly, Psychobilly, Funk
capacity: 200 **stage:** 16 x 12
3-5 mostly original Local-Reg'ls acts gig up to 6 nites at this eclectic 18+ bar; few Touring acts. Bands play 30-45min & divide door minus $50; some get flat fee. Email link to site w/ mp3s, past gigs & avail. dates; no unsolicited mail.

The Blind Pig
208 S 1st St.

Ann Arbor, MI 48104
p: 734-996-8555
www.blindpigmusic.com
contact: Jason Berry
p: 734-623-9962
e: jmberry3@comcast.net
call: M-F noon-4pm
genres: Rock, Blues, Alt., Pop, Jam, Hip-Hop, Electronic
advance: 2 months
capacity: 400
pa: Yes **sound eng:** Yes
stage: 20 x 12
open mics: Tue **sign in:** Call
Notable 18+ launch pad supports rising stars & estab. Touring acts nitely. 2-4 original acts play 1hr for college crowds; some opening slots for Locals & some all ages shows. No Country. Also books Alvin's in Detroit. Mail kit to venue or email link.

Cadieux Café
4300 Cadieux Rd.
Detroit, MI 48224
p: 313-882-8560
e: cadieuxcafe@yahoo.com
www.cadieuxcafe.com
contact: Ron Devos
genres: Jazz, Rock, Groove, Americana
advance: 1-2 months
capacity: 100
pa: Yes **sound eng:** Yes
stage: 10 x 10
open mics: 1st Sun of month
21+ Belgian eatery & US's only feather bowling venue, books up to 3 mostly Local & Reg'l acts Tue-Sun.

Clutch Cargo's
65 E Huron St.
Pontiac, MI 48342
p: 248-333-0649
e: info@clutchcargos.com
www.clutchcargos.com
contact: Amir Daiza
e: amirdaiza@gmail.com
genres: Metal, Punk, Latin, Rockabilly, Electronic, Funk
advance: 1+ months
capacity: 400; 1200; 1500
pa: Yes **sound eng:** Yes
Top original music venue w/ dance floor 30mi from Detroit, features polished DJs & known Touring bands up to 5 nites for 18+; some all ages shows. Merch split is 70/30.

Conor O'Neill's
318 S Main St.
Ann Arbor, MI 48104
p: 734-665-2968
www.conoroneills.com/annarbor
contact: Caroline King
e: caroline@conoroneills.com; cking@conoroneills.com
call: M-F 9am-5pm
genres: Bluegrass, Jazz, Southern Rock, Irish
advance: 2 months
capacity: 250; **stage:** floor space
Irish pub books Reg'l & Touring acts up to 3 nites; some DJs. 1 act plays several sets from 9:30pm-close for flat fee to 21+ crowd. 2nd location in Boulder, CO: 303-449-1922. Snail mail kit.

Elbow Room
6 S Washington St.
Ypsilanti, MI 48198
p: 734-483-6374
www.ypsielbow.com
contact: Damon
genres: Punk, Hardcore, Electro, Alt. Country, Metal, Indie Rock, Emo, Avant Jazz
capacity: 128
pa: Yes **sound eng:** Yes
Dive bar 35mi from Detroit, books original Local-Reg'l bands w/ following Tue-Sun; some Nat'l-Int'l acts & DJs. 3 bands play 30min for % of door. Use online booking form.

Emerald Theatre
31 N Walnut St.
Mt. Clemens, MI 48043
p: 586-913-1920
e: info@emeraldtheatre.com
www.emeraldtheatre.com
contact: Derek Jendza
e: derek@emeraldtheatre.com
genres: Alt., Rock, Alt. Country, Rap, Jazz, Country
advance: 2 months
capacity: 1700
pa: Yes **sound eng:** Yes
stage: 35 x 24
open mics: Wed **sign in:** 9pm
Hi-tech niteclub 25mi+ from Detroit hosts original Local-Nat'l acts 1-2 nites. 4-5 bands play from 7-11:30pm; mostly all ages shows. Smaller Rock Room has wkly open mic. Mail press kit to venue.

The Firefly Club
637 S Main St.
Ann Arbor, MI 48104
p: 734-665-9090
www.fireflyclub.com
contact: Susan Chastain
e: susan@fireflyclub.com
call: Wed mornings
genres: Jazz, Blues, Swing, Latin, Acoustic
advance: 1-3 months
capacity: 250
pa: Yes **sound eng:** Yes
in-house: Drums, Piano
Suave listening room w/ great acoustics, showcases Reg'l & Touring artists nitely for discerning audience. 1-2 acts perform 3-4 sets.

Heidelberg
215 N Main St.
Ann Arbor, MI 48104
p: 734-663-7758
e: theclubabove@yahoo.com
www.heidelbergrestaurant.net
contact: Michael Holloway
e: clubabovebooking@hotmail.com
call: M-F 9am-5pm
genres: All Styles
advance: 2 months
capacity: 250
pa: Yes **stage:** 40 x 20
'The Club Above' books Local-Touring bands & DJs for 18+ college crowd. Up to 3 acts play 1-2hrs from 10pm-2pm for 100% of door. Use email or mail kit to venue.

I-Rock Nightclub
16350 Harper Ave.
Detroit, MI 48224
p: 313-881-7625
e: irocknightclub@hotmail.com
www.irocknightclub.com
contact: Ted Jankowski
call: Thu 1-3pm
genres: Rock, Alt., Metal, Classic Rock
advance: 4-5 months
capacity: 850
pa: Yes **sound eng:** Yes
Long-running Rock haven books Local-Touring bands that play it loud up to 4 nites for 18+; some all ages shows. 2-4 original acts play 30-60min for % of door. Call, email or mail kit w/ ATTN: Booking; will contact if interested.

The Magic Bag
22920 Woodward Ave.
Ferndale, MI 48220
p: 248-544-1991; 248-544-3030
e: info@themagicbag.com
www.themagicbag.com
contact: Jeremy Haberman
genres: Rock, Jam, Garage, Alt. Country, Jazz
advance: 2-3 months
capacity: 400; 300 (seated)
pa: Yes **sound eng:** Yes
Cool venue w/ full stage & lights presents Local-Int'l acts w/ a draw up to 5 nites for flat fee or % of door. Live recording avail.

Majestic Theater/ The Magic Stick
4140 Woodward Ave.
Detroit, MI 48201
p: 313-833-9700
e: majestic@majesticdetroit.com
www.majesticdetroit.com
contact: Phil Childers
p: 313-833-9700 x202
e: philc@majesticdetroit.com
genres: All Styles
advance: 2-3 months
capacity: 1000 (theatre); 550
pa: Yes **sound eng:** Yes
stage: medium & large
Premier live music venue presents 3-5 top Local-Int'l acts & DJs 3-5 nites on 2 stages & deck areas. Shows are mostly all ages; some 18+. Openers play 20-30min; headliners, 45-75min. Snail mail kit.

The Modern Exchange
12219 Dix-Toledo Rd.
Southgate, MI 48195
p: 734-284-2547
www.themodernexchange.com
genres: Mainly: Rock, Indie, Metal, Punk, Hardcore
advance: 6 weeks
capacity: 250
pa: Yes **sound eng:** Yes
stage: 16 x 25
Vintage clothing/record store & cafe hosts cutting-edge Local-Int'l bands & DJs nitely in large concert space w/ great sound, lights & mixing avail. Matinee showcase on Sun. 3-5 original acts play 30-45min to all ages for % of door. Book via MySpace.

New Way Bar
23130 Woodward Ave.
Ferndale, MI 48220
p: 248-541-9870
www.myspace.com/newwaybar
contact: Tina Kourtesis
p: 248-867-2657
call: prefers MySpace
genres: Rock, Blues, Hip-Hop, Indie Rock, Metal, Country, Jazz, Acoustic
advance: 2 months
capacity: 200
pa: Yes **sound eng:** Yes
open mics: Mon
Local-friendly music bar books Touring acts as well. 3 bands play 1hr up to 6 nites. Hip-Hop on Tue. Use MySpace for booking.

Old Miami
3930 Cass Ave.
Detroit, MI 48201
p: 313-831-3830
www.myspace.com/oldmiami
contact: Julie Flynn
call: Thu after 8pm
genres: All Styles
advance: 2-4 months
capacity: 150; 600 (outdoors)
pa: Yes **sound eng:** Yes
stage: 2 stages
"CBGB of the midwest" hosts original Reg'ls & some Touring acts & DJs 6 nites. 3-4 acts play 45min to 21+ for 100% of door. Outdoor stage requires $100 deposit & 11pm curfew, but is well-attended. Call or snail mail kit.

PJ's Lager House
1254 Michigan Ave.
Detroit, MI 48226
p: 313-961-4668
www.myspace.com/lagerhouse
contact: Jeremy Cybulski
e: lagerhousebooking@yahoo.com
genres: Punk, Pop, Alt., Indie Rock, Alt. Country
advance: 3 months
capacity: 150
pa: Yes **sound eng:** Yes
stage: small
Nitty gritty bar hosts Reg'l acts on the rise & some Touring talent Mon-Sat. 3 acts play 45min. Use email, MySpace or mail kit to venue; follow up in 2-3 wks.

Small's Bar
10339 Conant St.
Hamtramck, MI 48212
p: 313-873-1117

e: mjmdet@aol.com
www.smallsbardetroit.com
contact: Mike
e: smallsbooking@aol.com
genres: Indie, Rock, Pop, Folk, Garage, Alt. Country, Experimental
advance: 2+ months
capacity: 200
pa: Yes **sound eng:** Yes
stage: 45 x 20
Original music bar w/ top sound & lights books Local-Touring bands w/ buzz mostly Thu-Sat. 3-4 acts play 40-60min for 21+; some all ages shows. Prefers email w/ name, band name, link to music, Detroit venues played, bands played w/; Touring acts also incl. dates. May also call or mail press kit to venue w/ ATTN: Booking. No booking via MySpace.

St. Andrews Hall/ The Shelter
431 E Congress St.
Detroit, MI 48226
p: 313-961-MELT
www.standrewshall.com
contact: Josh Newman
p: 248-538-4545
e: joshnewman@livenation.com
call: M-F 10am-4pm
genres: Punk, Rock, Emo, Hardcore, Pop, Hip-Hop
advance: 4-6 weeks
capacity: 818 (hall); 226 (shelter)
pa: Yes **sound eng:** Yes
stage: 20 x 18; 15 x 12
Live Nation venue books Local openers & estab. Nat'l acts & DJs up to 7 nites. 3-5 original bands play on 2 stages for % of door & 80% merch. Sets run 30-90min. Many all ages shows. Prefers calls, but may contact via MySpace or mail press kit to venue; no unsolicited email or EPKs.

Grand Rapids/ Lansing

Billy's Lounge
1437 Wealthy St. SE
Grand Rapids, MI 49506
p: 616-459-5757
e: thebar@billyslounge.com
www.billyslounge.com
contact: Rick Tipton
e: booking@billyslounge.com; ricktipton@hotmail.com
call: M-F 3pm
genres: Blues, Jazz, R&B, Rock, Funk, Folk, Reggae
advance: 3-6 months
capacity: 250
pa: Yes **sound eng:** Yes
open mics: Mon & Tue 8pm
Speakeasy books up to 3 Local-Int'l bands Thu-Sat for 21+. Email for booking.

Eccentric Cafe & Beergarden
355 E Kalamazoo Ave.
Kalamazoo, MI 49007
p: 269-382-2338; 269-382-2332
e: entertainment@bellsbeer.com
www.bellsbeer.com
contact: Amy Hoffman
p: 269-382-2332 x27
e: bellsbooking@gmail.com
genres: Blues, Jazz, Jam, Bluegrass, Rock, Celtic, Rockabilly, Funk, Roots
advance: 2-3 months
capacity: 94; 800 (outdoors)
pa: Limited **stage:** 25 x 7
Chill brewpub books original Local & Touring bands up to 3 nites for 21+. Featured act plays three 45min sets. Snail mail or email kit.

The Grass Cup Cafe
4607 60th St.
Holland, MI 49423
p: 616-355-1994
e: grasscupcafe@excite.com
www.grasscup.com
contact: Angie Anderson
genres: Acoustic
advance: 1 month
capacity: 80
pa: Yes **stage:** small
open mics: Thu **sign in:** 6pm
Coffee house 29mi from Grand Rapids, hosts original area artists only performing for % of door. Up to 4 acts fill 3hrs playing for all ages Thu-Sat. Snail mail or email kit.

Green Door Blues Bar & Grille
2005 E Michigan Ave.
Lansing, MI 48912
p: 517-482-6376
www.greendoorlive.com
contact: Jenny Costigan
e: jenny@greendoorlive.com
call: M-F 3-7pm
genres: Blues, Bluegrass
advance: 4-6 months
capacity: 238
pa: Yes **sound eng:** Yes
stage: 35 x 15
Local-Reg'l bands gig nitely at neighborhood Blues joint; very few Nat'l acts. Featured band plays 4 sets for 21+. Bluegrass on Mon. Mail press kit to venue.

The Intersection
133 Grandville Ave. SW
Grand Rapids, MI 49503
p: 616-451-8232
e: robharley@sectionlive.com
www.sectionlive.com
contact: Scott Hammontree
p: 616-451-8232 x226
e: scott@sectionlive.com
genres: Rock, Punk, Country, R&B, Folk, Jam, Blues, Metal
advance: 1-4 months
capacity: 900
pa: Yes **sound eng:** Yes
stage: 18 x 32
Packed all ages music venue w/ full sound & lights, books top Touring bands & buzz acts w/ local draw nitely. Up to 6 original bands & DJs play 30-120min; cover acts every other wk. Bands keep 80-85% merch sales, 100% for first timers. Email or mail press kit to venue.

The Machine Shop
3539 S Dort Hwy.
Flint, MI 48507
p: 810-715-2650
www.themachineshop.info
contact: Kevin Zink
e: zinkbros@charter.net
genres: Rock, Metal, Industrial
advance: 1-3 months
capacity: 550
pa: Yes **stage:** 32 x 15
Great loud music club 56mi from Lansing, books original Local-Touring bands 2 nites for 18+ w/ up to 3 acts on a bill. Check MySpace for opening slots for Nat'l acts; use email for booking.

Mac's Bar
2700 E Michigan Ave.
Lansing, MI 48912
p: 517-484-6795
e: oldmacsbar@yahoo.com
www.macsbar.com
contact: Chuck Mannino
e: sciencebooking@gmail.com
call: M-F 2:30-3pm
genres: Underground, Rock, New Wave, Metal
advance: 2-3 months
capacity: 200
pa: Yes **sound eng:** Yes
stage: 15 x 12
Top dive showcase for cutting-edge Local-Int'l bands & DJs. 3 original acts play 30min up to 6 nites for mostly 18+; few all ages shows. Shoot your own music video at the bar. Email or snail mail kit. Allow 2 wks for review; follow up via email; no booking via MySpace.

Old Hat Brewery
114 N Main St.
Lawton, MI 49065
p: 269-624-6445
http://oldhatbeer.com
contact: Tom Fuller
e: oldhatbooking@gmail.com
genres: Rock, Americana, Bluegrass, Blues, Jazz
advance: 2+ months
capacity: 100
pa: Yes **sound eng:** Yes
stage: 15 x 12
Music-friendly brewpub hosts Reg'l & Touring talent Fri-Sat for all ages. 1 original acts fills 3hrs for flat fee. Email or mail press kit to venue.

Skelletones
Grand Rapids, MI 49503
Closing Jan 18, 2009.

Greater MI

Acorn Theater
107 Generations Dr.
Three Oaks, MI 49128
p: 269-756-3879
www.acorntheater.com
contact: David Fink
e: acorntheater@aol.com
call: Thu-Sun daytime
genres: Jazz, Folk, S/S, World, Cabaret, Rock, Country, Classical, Opera
advance: 3-9 months
capacity: 250
pa: Yes **sound eng:** Yes
stage: 20 x 10
in-house: Piano, Pipe Organ
Intimate all ages space 70min from Chicago & 78mi from Kalamazoo, presents Local-Int'l talent a few times/mo. Locals mostly play on Fri & Sat for 45min. Prefers hard copies, but accepts EPKs; incl. contact info.

Minnesota

Duluth

Amazing Grace Bakery & Cafe
394 S Lake Ave.
Duluth, MN 55802
p: 218-723-0075
e: info@amazinggracebakery.com
www.amazinggracebakery.com
contact: Lori Hatten
p: 218-724-0752
e: lori@amazinggracebakery.com
genres: Acoustic, Folk, S/S
advance: 2-3 months
capacity: 75
pa: Yes **sound eng:** Yes
stage: 14 x 10 **in-house:** Piano
Acoustic showcase presents original Local-Int'l artists 2-4 nites. 1 act plays two 45min sets for all ages. Prefers hard copies.

Beaner's Central
324 N Central Ave.
Duluth, MN 55807
p: 218-624-5957
www.beanerscentral.com
contact: Jason Wussow
p: 218-724-7129
e: wussow1@msn.com
genres: Folk, Prog., Bluegrass, Americana, Reggae, Jazz, Rock, Cabaret, Celtic, Alt. Country
advance: 2-6 months
capacity: 100
pa: Yes **sound eng:** Yes
stage: 12 x 14
open mics: Wed 7-11pm
Area's premier all ages listening room books original Local-Int'l talent 3-4 nites. Up to 3 acts play for % of door for 25-90min; capable of recording shows. Snail mail kit; 1st time booking, use online form.

Fitger's Brewhouse
600 E Superior St.
Duluth, MN 55802
p: 218-279-2739
e: brew@brewhouse.net
www.brewhouse.net
contact: Tim Nelson
e: timn@brewhouse.net
genres: Roots, Blues, S/S, Acoustic
advance: 2-3 months
capacity: 100
pa: Yes **stage:** 8 x 3
Classic brewpub books original Local-Touring acts Tue-Sat. 1 act plays 3hrs for flat fee. Also books for Burrito Union. Prefers Sonicbids.

Mankato

Buster's Bar
1325 Madison Ave.
Mankato, MN 56001
p: 507-389-8999
e: info@bustersbar.com
www.bustersbar.com
contact: Dustin
e: booking@bustersbar.com
genres: Mainly Rock
advance: 2-4 weeks
capacity: 401
stage: 20 x 30
Bar & grill features a polished Reg'l or Nat'l Fri-Sat for a flat fee. Lots of Tribute acts.

The Coffee Hag
329 N Riverfront Dr.
Mankato, MN 56001
p: 507-387-5533
www.myspace.com/thecoffeehag
contact: Jenn Melby
e: thecoffeehag@hotmail.com
genres: Folk, Alt., Rock, Jazz, Blues
advance: 2-3 months
capacity: 65 **stage:** 6 x 6
Popular all ages cafe 84mi SW of St. Paul books 1-2 original Reg'l & Touring acts Fri & Sat, playing 1-2hrs for tips. Covers may be mixed into set; No Tribute acts. Mail press kit to venue.

Minneapolis/St. Paul

318 Cafe
318 Water St.
Excelsior, MN 55331
p: 952-401-7902
www.three-eighteen.com
contact: Elli Rader
e: booking@three-eighteen.com
call: No calls
genres: Eclectic, Rock, Folk, Jazz, Bluegrass, Reggae, World, Pop, Blues
advance: 2 months
capacity: 60 **pa:** Yes
contact: Matt Muller
e: mattmuller@embarqmail.com
Wine bar by nite just west of Minneapolis, features 1-2 original Local-Nat'l acts 3-4 nites for % of door. Email for booking or open mic info; no mail or calls.

400 Bar
400 Cedar Ave. S
Minneapolis, MN 55454
p: 612-332-2903
e: westbank@400bar.com
www.400bar.com
contact: Bill Sullivan
call: M-F after 6pm
genres: Rock, Folk, Funk Alt. Country, R&B, Techno
capacity: 275
pa: Yes **sound eng:** Yes
stage: 20 x 15
Nitely hot spot near U of MN, showcases rising Local-Nat'l indie talent. Up to 3 acts/nite; few all ages shows.

7th St. Entry
29 N 7th St.
Minneapolis, MN 55403
p: 612-332-1775; 612-338-8388
www.first-avenue.com
contact: Sonia Grover
e: sonia@first-avenue.com
call: M-F noon-5:30pm
genres: Rock, Alt., Funk, Afro-Caribbean
advance: 6-8 weeks
capacity: 250
pa: Yes **sound eng:** Yes
stage: 15 x 10
Entry point to MN scene, books 2-4 polished original Local-Int'l bands nitely for all ages. New bands showcase Wed nites. Also books legendary club, First Ave. Email booking form on site.

Anodyne Coffeehouse
4301 Nicollet Ave. S
Minneapolis, MN 55409
p: 612-824-4300
www.anodynecoffeehouse.com
contact: Theresa Lien
e: anodynemusic@earthlink.net
genres: S/S, Folk, Blues, Jazz
advance: 3+ months
capacity: 70
pa: Yes **sound eng:** Yes
open mics: 1st Fri of month
All ages coffee joint hosts original Local-Nat'l acts. 1 act plays 2 sets Fri/Sat for flat fee & tips. Sign up at tcmusic.net, then email booker.

Artists' Quarter
408 St. Peters St.
St. Paul, MN 55102
p: 651-292-1359
e: artistsquarter@gmail.com
www.mnjazz.com
contact: Kenny Horst
p: 651-292-1354
call: Mon-Sat 7pm-1am
genres: Jazz
advance: 6-12 weeks
capacity: 135
pa: Yes **sound eng:** Yes
stage: 20 x 20
in-house: Drums, Piano
Prime spot for dates & jazzbos, features original top-notch Local-Touring talent. Tue is 21+, otherwise 18+. Snail mail kit. No unsolicited emails.

Big V's
1567 University Ave. W
St. Paul, MN 55104
p: 651-645-8472
e: hollandusa@gmail.com
www.myspace.com/bigvs
contact: Joe Holland
p: 612-331-0002
e: bigvsbooking@gmail.com
call: M-F 2-6pm
genres: Rock, Punk, Garage, Hardcore, Hip-Hop, Experimental
advance: 2-3 months
capacity: 150
pa: Yes **sound eng:** Yes
stage: 15 x 8
Spirited bar presents Reg'l & Touring bands Wed-Sat. Up to 4 acts play for % of door; Local bands play for free. Email MySpace link for booking; no requests thru MySpace.

Blue Fox Bar & Grill
3833 N Lexington Ave.
Arden Hills, MN 55126
p: 651-483-6000
www.bluefoxgrill.com
contact: Gene Wenger
p: 651-484-2095
genres: Rock, Funk, Rock, Swing, Alt., 80s, Pop, Country
advance: 4-6 months
capacity: 292
stage: 20 x 10
open mics: 2nd & 4th Tue/mo
Suburban St. Paul party spot books mostly Local-Reg'l up-tempo acts Fri & Sat. 1 band plays three 1hr sets for % of door after prod. costs. No calls!

Bunker's Music Bar & Grill
761 Washington Ave.
Minneapolis, MN 55401
p: 612-338-8188
www.bunkersmusic.com
contact: James Klein
p: 612-332-3904
e: james@blueskyartists.com
call: M-F 10am-6pm
genres: Blues, R&B, Funk, Reggae, Roots, Americana
advance: 1-3 months
capacity: 299
pa: Yes **sound eng:** Yes
stage: medium wedge
Joint attracts mostly older, working class crowd for Sun-Thu house bands & some Local-Touring acts Fri & Sat. 1-2 acts play 9-1am. Snail mail kit.

Cabooze
917 Cedar Ave.
Minneapolis, MN 55404
p: 612-338-6425
e: information@cabooze.com
www.cabooze.com
contact: James Martin
p: 612-379-0500
e: taco@ecompanypro.com
call: M-F 9am-5pm
genres: Rock, Alt., Blues, Reggae, Zydeco, Jam
advance: 45-75 days
capacity: 1044
pa: Yes **sound eng:** Yes
Recently renovated 18+ roadhouse books Reg'l & Touring acts up to 7 nites. 2-3 original bands play 30-120min & keep 80% soft merch sales, 100% hard. Great sight lines & acoustics. Email booker or mail promos w/ ATTN: James 'Taco' Martin, PO Box 581486, Minneapolis, MN 55458.

Cedar Cultural Ctr,
416 Cedar Ave. S
Minneapolis, MN 55454
p: 612-338-2674
e: tickets@thecedar.org
www.thecedar.org
contact: Bill Kubeczko
p: 612-338-2674 x100
genres: World, S/S, Folk
advance: 6-8 months
capacity: 450
pa: Yes **sound eng:** Yes
stage: 18 x 10
open mics: 1 Wed/month
Non-profit cultural ctr. presents polished indie & major artists 3 nites from Sep-Jun. 1-2 original Local-Int'l acts play to all ages.

Club 3 Degrees
113 N 5th St.
Minneapolis, MN 55403
p: 612-781-8488
e: info@club3degrees.com
www.club3degrees.com
contact: Rick Narvaez
e: nationalartists@club3degrees.com
genres: Christian
advance: 2+ months
capacity: 1500
pa: Yes **sound eng:** Yes
stage: 30 x 24
Tri-level club hosts Local-Int'l Christian groups & DJs 3 nites. 3-5 acts play 45-90min for all ages. Check booking info on site before submitting; promos to: 510 1st Ave. N, Ste. 302, Minneapolis, MN 55403.

The Dakota Jazz Club
1010 Nicollet Mall
Minneapolis, MN 55403
p: 612-332-1010
e: dakotajazz@aol.com
www.dakotacooks.com
contact: Craig
genres: Jazz
advance: 2 months
capacity: 140
pa: Yes **sound eng:** Yes
stage: 20 x 12 **in-house:** Piano
Niteclub hosts top Reg'l-Int'l artists nitely for all ages. Featured act performs three 1hr original sets. Snail mail kits.

The Dinkytowner Cafe
412 1/2 14th Ave. SE
Minneapolis, MN 55414
p: 612-362-0437
e: info@dinkytowner.com
www.dinkytowner.com
contact: Dan Kane
e: dinkytownercafe@yahoo.com
genres: Alt., Electronica, Dance, Hip-Hop, Rock, Punk
advance: 1-2 months
capacity: 296
pa: Yes **sound eng:** Yes
stage: medium
College hang books an average of 5 Local-Touring acts & DJs nitely w/ 30min sets; some Nat'l acts. Sun all ages show from 4-10pm. Prefers email for booking.

Dunn Bros
1569 Grand Ave.
St. Paul, MN 55105
p: 651-699-2636
e: info@dunnbrosgrand.com
www.dunnbrosgrand.com
contact: Luann Hinderaker
p: 651-698-0618
e: music@dunnbrosgrand.com
genres: S/S, Jazz, Celtic, Rock, Folk, Blues
advance: 3-4 months
capacity: 150
pa: Yes **stage:** 10 x 12
open mics: 1st & 4th Sun
Retro coffee shop hosts Acoustic Reg'l artists nitely for all ages. Featured act gigs 2hrs for $20, drinks, 1lb of coffee & tips. Prefers email, or snail mail kit.

Famous Dave's BBQ & Blues
3001 Hennepin Ave. S
Minneapolis, MN 55408
p: 612-822-9900
www.famousdaves.com/musicclu.cfm
contact: Paul Metsa
p: 612-788-6815
e: metsa@black-hole.com
call: evenings
genres: Blues, Zydeco, Roots, Latin, Country, Reggae, Salsa, Rock, Alt.
pa: Yes **sound eng:** Yes
BBQ franchise's only music club serves up Local & Touring bands nitely for all ages. Featured act plays 2-3 sets for the door. Mail press kit to venue; will contact if interested.

Fine Line Music Café
318 1st Ave. N
Minneapolis, MN 55401
p: 612-338-8100
www.finelinemusic.com
contact: Kim King
p: 612-338-8100 x203
e: finelinebooking@gmail.com
call: M-F 11am-5pm
genres: All Styles
advance: 3 months
capacity: 570-800
pa: Yes **sound eng:** Yes
stage: 24 x 16
Celebrated venue w/ full lights & sound presents up & coming Locals & name Touring acts nitely. Up to 4 acts & DJs play from 9pm-2am for flat fee vs backend. Shows are mostly 18+ or 21+. Use email or MySpace for booking. No unsolicited mail.

First Avenue
701 1st Ave. N
Minneapolis, MN 55403
p: 612-338-8388
e: info@first-avenue.com
www.first-avenue.com
contact: Nate Kranz
e: nate@first-avenue.com
call: M-F noon-5:30pm
genres: Rock, Hip-Hop, House, Jazz, Blues
advance: 6 months
capacity: 1500; 250
pa: Yes **sound eng:** Yes
stage: 30 x 20
Venerable mother club to 7th St. Entry, showcases polished Reg'l & Touring acts nitely in 2 rooms. 2-4 acts play 45min for 18+; some all ages & 21+ shows. Bands keep 80% merch

sales in large room & 100% in small room. Also books other area venues. Email or mail promos: PO Box 52110, Minneapolis, MN 55402.

Kitty Cat Klub
315 14th Ave. SE
Minneapolis, MN 55414
p: 612-331-9800
e: kittycatklub@mac.com
www.kittycatklub.net
contact: Ryan
e: booking@kittycatklub.net
genres: Rockabilly, Swing, Jazz, S/S, Blues, Reggae, Electronic, Ambient, Dance
advance: 2-3 months
capacity: 325
pa: Yes **sound eng:** Yes
stage: 20 x 15
Eclectic club caters to campus crowd w/ original Local & Touring acts & DJs nitely. 1-3 acts play 45-60min for 21+ crowd. Prefers email for booking.

Lee's Liquor Lounge
101 N Glenwood Ave.
Minneapolis, MN 55403
p: 612-331-0002
www.leesliquorlounge.com
contact: Joe Holland
e: booking@leesliquorlounge.com
call: M-F afternoons
genres: Country, Americana, Roots Rock, Rockabilly, Punk
advance: 2-3 months
capacity: 300
pa: Yes **sound eng:** Yes
stage: 18 x 7
Tavern w/ interesting regulars, presents original Reg'l-Int'l talent. Up to 4 acts keep patrons entertained up to 5 nites. Prefers EPKs, but may snail mail.

Medina Entertainment Ctr.
500 Hwy. 55
Medina, MN 55340
p: 763-478-6661
e: medinarec@aol.com
www.medinaentertainment.com
contact: Bob Roskob
genres: Oldies, Country, Big Band, R&B, Rock, Cajun, Alt.
advance: 1+ months
capacity: 1600
stage: 33 x 25 **in-house:** Piano
Former ballroom, now w/ in-house bowling & dining spot 29mi from Twin Cities, presents polished Reg'l & some Touring acts 5 nites for flat fee or % of door. Audience & bands skew older. 1-2 acts & DJs play til 1am. Mail press kit to venue.

Minnesota Music Cafe
499 Payne Ave.
St. Paul, MN 55130
p: 651-776-4699
www.minnesotamusiccafe.com
contact: Billy Larson
e: billyraggsband@yahoo.com
genres: Blues, Rock, Jazz, R&B
advance: 5 months
capacity: 350
pa: Yes **sound eng:** Yes
stage: medium
Venue w/ huge dance floor & top lights/sound presents polished Reg'l & Nat'ls nitely; cover bands Thu-Sun. Featured act plays 9pm-1am w/ breaks to 21+ crowd. No Heavy Metal. Email or mail press kit to venue.

The Narrows
3380 Shoreline Dr.
Navarre, MN 55392
p: 952-471-3352
e: thenarrowssaloon@questoffice.net
www.thenarrowssaloon.com
contact: Jim Anderst
genres: Blues, R&B
advance: 4-6 months
capacity: 300
pa: Yes **sound eng:** Yes
stage: 16 x 12
Music room 28mi from city, features a Local-Reg'l act 5 nites. Acts play three 1hr sets to 21+ for flat fee. Mail kit to venue.

Nomad World Pub
501 Cedar Ave. S
Minneapolis, MN 55454
p: 612-338-6424
e: info@nomadpub.com
www.nomadpub.com
contact: Matt Perkins
p: 952-270-9432
e: booking@nomadpub.com
call: M-F 10am-5pm
genres: Rock, S/S, Reggae, Jazz, World, Hip-Hop, Bluegrass, Indie, Acoustic
advance: 2-3 months
capacity: 271
pa: Yes **sound eng:** Yes
stage: 20 x 15 **in-house:** Piano
Notable showcase w/ 2nd venue in Milwaukee, draws eclectic crowds for original Reg'l-Touring bands & DJs. Up to 4 original acts play Tue-Sun for 21+ crowd; some 18+ shows. Mail press kit to venue.

O'Gara's Garage
164 Snelling Ave. N
St. Paul, MN 55104
p: 651-644-3333
www.ogaras.com
contact: Nicholas Hensley
e: angrymen@comcast.net
genres: Indie, Alt. Country, Hip-Hop
advance: 2 months
capacity: 700
pa: Yes **sound eng:** Yes
stage: 25 x 15
Family-owned pub books mostly original Local-Int'l acts for % of door; busier schedule in winter. 2-5 acts play 75min sets nitely. Prefers email, but may mail press kit w/ ATTN: Nicholas Hensley, 2051 Ford Pkwy., St. Paul, MN 55116.

Red Carpet
11 5th Ave. S
St. Cloud, MN 56301
p: 320-251-4047
e: troy@redcarpetnightclub.com
www.redcarpetnightclub.com
contact: Troy Rahn
p: 320-251-4047 x4
e: redcarpetbooking@yahoo.com
call: Wed-Fri 11am-8pm
genres: Pop, Alt., Americana
advance: 75 days
capacity: 576
pa: Yes **sound eng:** Yes
stage: 20 x 12
Niteclub for college crowd, 76mi from city, showcases Reg'l & some Nat'l bands Wed-Sat. 1 act plays 3 sets. Prefers email, but may contact via MySpace; no EPKs, unsolicited mail or calls.

Red Sea
316 Cedar Ave. S
Minneapolis, MN 55454
p: 612-333-3349
www.esoundman.com
contact: Eric Bare
p: 612-333-1555
e: esoundman@earthlink.net
call: M-F 3-9pm
genres: Reggae, Rock, Jazz, Funk, Hip-Hop, Dancehall, African, Punk
advance: 4-8 weeks
capacity: 200; 30
pa: Yes **sound eng:** Yes
stage: 14 x 16
open mics: Tue **sign in:** 10pm
Venue near campus showcases original Local-Touring acts up to 7 nites. 3-5 acts play 45-60min for 18+ & keep % of box office on progressive pay-out scale. Prefers EPK or link to MySpace for booking, but may mail promos to: 320 Cedar Ave. S, Ste 300, Minneapolis, MN 55454.

The Rock Nightclub
2029 Woodlynn Ave.
Maplewood, MN 55109
p: 651-770-7822
e: info@therocknightclub.com
www.therocknightclub.com
contact: Brian
e: booking@therocknightclub.com
call: M-F 9am-5pm
genres: Rock, Hip-Hop, Metal
advance: 1-2 months
capacity: 700
pa: Yes **sound eng:** Yes
stage: 18 x 30
Prime 18+ club w/ good sound & sight lines books Local-Nat'l bands 5 nites. Up to 4 acts play 1hr for flat fee or 80% of door; some all ages shows. Mail press kit to venue.

Station 4
201 E 4th St.
St. Paul, MN 55101
p: 651-298-0173
www.station-4.com
contact: Dawn
e: dawn@station-4.com; station4booking@yahoo.com
genres: All Styles
capacity: 600
pa: Yes **sound eng:** Yes
open mics: Wed
Seedy Rock club spotlights original Local-Int'l bands nitely. 3-9 original acts play 40-60min w/ some all ages shows. Prefers email for booking.

Triple Rock Social Club
629 Cedar Ave. S
Minneapolis, MN 55454
p: 612-333-7399
e: info@triplerocksocialclub.com
www.triplerocksocialclub.com
contact: Brian
p: 612-333-7499
e: brian@triplerocksocialclub.com
genres: Punk, Alt. Country, Hip-Hop, Indie, Metal
advance: 1-4 months
capacity: 350
pa: Yes **sound eng:** Yes
stage: 20 x 15
Cool Punk bar books original Reg'l & Touring bands up to 5 nites. 2-5 acts on a bill; some all ages shows, usu. Sun matinee. Prefers EPKs or email link to music.

Trocaderos Nightclub
107 3rd Ave. N
Minneapolis, MN 55401
p: 612-465-0440
e: mail@trocaderos.com
www.trocaderos.com
contact: Scott Cronin
genres: Rock, R&B, Latin, Swing, Reggae, Salsa, Country
Posh venue w/ 3 levels, hosts polished Local-Nat'l acts & DJs up to 7 nites for 30+ bohemian crowd. Email or snail mail kit.

The Turf Club
1601 University Ave.
St. Paul, MN 55104
p: 651-647-0486
e: booking@turfclub.net
www.turfclub.net
contact: Ryan
e: ryan@turfclub.net
genres: Alt., Rock, Rockabilly, Jazz
advance: 6 weeks
capacity: 300
pa: Yes **sound eng:** Yes
in-house: Full backline
Hip spot showcases original bands nitely. 3 Local-Int'l acts play 45-60min & usu. get % of door. Mail press kit to venue.

Uptown Bar & Cafe
3018 Hennepin Ave. S
Minneapolis, MN 55408
p: 612-823-4719
www.uptownbarandcafe.com
contact: Brian McDonough
e: brianpmbooking@gmail.com
genres: Rock, Indie, Metal, Jazz, Hip-Hop
advance: 6-8 weeks
capacity: 300
pa: Yes **sound eng:** Yes
Tavern specializing in Local music books up to 4 original Local-Int'l acts Tue-Sat & some Sun-Mon. Bands play 35min to 21+ crowd. Prefers email.

Greater MN

Acoustic Cafe
77 Lafayette St.
Winona, MN 55987
p: 507-453-0394
e: info@theacoustic.com
www.theacoustic.com
contact: Nate Gill
e: musicmanager@theacoustic.com
genres: Acoustic, S/S, Americana, Blues, Folk, Country, Bluegrass
advance: 2-6 months
capacity: 100
pa: Yes **stage:** 7 x 14
Local fave 30mi N of La Crosse on border of WI where Local-Touring bands gig for all ages Fri-Sat. 1 act plays 2 sets from 8-10:30pm w/ 15min break for flat fee & tips. 2nd location in Eau Claire, WI. Accepts press kits or links to music.

Jammers Nightclub & Bluenote Ballroom
11328 Bemidji Rd. NE
Bemidji, MN 56601
p: 218-759-1565
e: jammers@paulbunyan.net
www.myspace.com/nightclubinbemidji
contact: Dawn Eve
call: afternoons
genres: Blues, Jazz, Funk, Rock, Country, Folk, Reggae, Punk
advance: 2-8 weeks
capacity: 500; 200 (winter)
pa: Yes **sound eng:** Yes

stage: 12 x 10; 4 x 8
Mostly Reg'ls perform 2 nites at this shabby-chic ballroom that's 'open to jammers.' 1+ acts play to 21+ crowd w/ some all ages shows. Good stop-point btwn Reg'l fests & casinos. Mail press kit to venue.

Mississippi

Hattiesburg

Tal's Music Emporium
9 Old Rawl Springs Rd.
Hattiesburg, MS 39402
p: 601-268-9512
contact: Nikki
p: 601-660-5963
genres: Alt., Rock, Blues, Country
advance: 1 month
capacity: 150
pa: Yes **stage:** 20 x 10
Area's premier 21+ music room presents Local bands & DJs up to 4 nites. Up to 3 acts fill 4hrs. Some Reg'l & Nat'l acts booked. Call or mail press kit to venue.

The Thirsty Hippo
211 S Main St.
Hattiesburg, MS 39401
p: 601-583-9188
www.thirstyhippo.com
contact: Brad Newton
e: brad@thirstyhippo.com
call: M-F after 5pm
genres: Rock, Ska, Latin, Jazz, Blues
advance: 1-2 months
capacity: 125
pa: Yes **sound eng:** Yes
stage: floor space
open mics: Wed **sign in:** 10pm
Laid-back club presents polished Reg'l & Touring bands 3 nites for 18+. 1-2 original acts play 60-90min sets. Prefers email w/ music link.

Jackson

Fenian's Pub
901 E Fortification St.
Jackson, MS 39202
p: 601-948-0055
e: fenians@bellsouth.net
www.fenianspub.com
contact: Damon Hogben
call: M-F 4pm
genres: Folk, Bluegrass, Celtic, Acoustic, Americana, Blues, Soul
advance: 2 months for Locals; more for Nat'l
capacity: 150
pa: Yes **stage:** 8 x 5
open mics: Tue **sign in:** 4:30pm
Original Reg'l & some Nat'l talent play for flat fee in trad'l Irish bar. Single act, plays 3hrs set 6 nites; all ages til 9:30pm. Prefers hard copies sent to venue.

Hal & Mal's
200 S Commerce St.
Jackson, MS 39201
p: 601-948-0888
www.halandmals.com
contact: Charly Abraham
p: 601-355-7685
e: charly@halandmals.com
genres: Rock, Americana, Jazz, Bluegrass, Country Rock, Blues
advance: 1 month
capacity: 150; 200; 7000
pa: Yes **sound eng:** Yes
stage: 20 x 20; 10 x 10
Brewery offers some live music w/ Local-Int'l acts. 1-3 acts play 45min sets for 21+. Merch splits 85/15. Snail mail kit.

Martin's
214 S State St.
Jackson, MS 39201
p: 601-354-9712
www.martinslounge.net
contact: Chris Rybolt
p: 601-668-8464
e: ryboltproductions@comcast.net
genres: Jam, Southern Rock, S/S, Acoustic, Rock, Indie
advance: 1+ months
capacity: 250
pa: Yes **sound eng:** Yes
stage: 22 x 12
Bar & grill has Local-Touring acts & DJs gig Thu-Sat for 21+ college crowd; solo acts play Wed. Up to 3 acts play 45+min from 10:30pm-1:30am for 90% of door; some get flat fee. Prefers email w/ EPK or link to music, but may mail kit to venue.

Oxford/Tupelo

Ground Zero Blues Club
0 Blues Alley
Clarksdale, MS 38614
p: 662-621-9009
e: groundzerogm@cableone.net
www.groundzerobluesclub.com
contact: Roger Stolle
e: roger@cathead.biz
call: email only
genres: Mississippi Blues
advance: 3 months
capacity: 200
pa: Yes **sound eng:** Yes
stage: small
open mics: Thu **sign in:** 7pm
Notable 21+ room co-owned by Morgan Freeman, is known for real-deal Mississippi Blues. Local acts Wed-Thu. Wknd acts play four 45min sets for flat fee & % of door. Promos: GZBC, Roger Stolle, 252 Delta Ave., Clarksdale, MS 38614.

The Library
120 S 11th St.
Oxford, MS 38655
p: 662-234-1411
e: thelibrarymusic@yahoo.com
contact: John Desler
call: M-F after 1pm
genres: Blues, Country, Alt., Rock, Rap, Jam
advance: 4 months
capacity: 800
pa: Yes **sound eng:** Yes
stage: 40 x 20
Largest music venue in Oxford caters to college crowds & books some original Local-Int'l artists Wed-Sat. 1 acts plays 90-120min for flat fee or % of door. Send promos w/ ATTN: John Desler, PO Box 42, Oxford, MS 38655.

Proud Larry's
211 S Lamar Blvd.
Oxford, MS 38655
p: 662-236-0050
www.proudlarrys.com
contact: Scott Caradine
e: scott@proudlarrys.com
call: M-F
genres: All Styles
advance: 2-3 months
capacity: 325
pa: Yes **sound eng:** Yes
stage: 20 x 25
Down-home venue hosts mostly original Reg'l & Touring bands 4+ nites. 2 acts play 1+hr sets; some 18+ & 21+ shows. Also helps book The Library. Mail kit to venue.

Ricks Café
319B Hwy. 182 E
Starkville, MS 39759
p: 662-324-7425
www.rickscafe.net
contact: Rick Welch
e: rick@rickwelch.com
call: Mon-Tue 1-4pm
genres: All Styles
advance: 4-6 months
capacity: 800
pa: Yes **sound eng:** Yes
stage: 16 x 32
18+ tavern books 1-2 Local-Int'l acts 2-3 nites. Bands play 10pm-midnite wkdys & 9pm-1am Fri-Sat. Merch splits 90/10. Prefers email.

Missouri

Columbia

Blue Fugue
120 S 9th St.
Columbia, MO 65201
p: 573-815-9995
e: bluefugue@hotmail.com
www.myspace.com/thebluefugue
contact: Scott Meiner
genres: Rock, Punk, Country, Jazz, Reggae, R&B, S/S, World
advance: 1 year
capacity: 247
pa: Yes **sound eng:** Yes
stage: 20 x 15
open mics: Mon **sign in:** 6pm
Bar w/ character showcases original Local-Nat'l bands Mon, Wed & Fri-Sat. 4 bands play 50min sets for 18+ crowd.

Blue Note
17 N 9th St.
Columbia, MO 65201
p: 573-874-1944
e: booking@thebluenote.com
www.thebluenote.com
contact: Richard King
e: richard@thebluenote.com
call: M-F afternoons
genres: Rock, Hip-Hop, Jam, Country
advance: 2-3 months
capacity: 850
pa: Yes **sound eng:** Yes
stage: 22 x 16
College town venue btwn St. Louis & KC, books Local-Int'l bands & DJs nitely for all ages. 2-4 acts play 45-75min. Merch splits 80/20.

Mojo's
1013 Park Ave.
Columbia, MO 65201
p: 573-875-0588
e: manager@mojoscolumbia.com
www.mojoscolumbia.com
contact: Peter McDevitt
p: 573-847-1944
e: petermcdevitt@thebluenote.com
call: M-F noon-7pm
genres: Blues, Roots, Indie Rock, Jam, Punk, Country
advance: 2-3 months
capacity: 250
pa: Yes **sound eng:** Yes
stage: 16 x 12
open mics: Tue 8pm
Original music room presents Local-Int'l acts 5-7 nites for all ages. Up to 3 acts play 45-75min sets usu. for % of door. Merch splits 80/20. Also books The Blue Note. Email link to website; No MP3s or unsolicited mail.

Kansas City

B.B.'s Lawnside BBQ
1205 E 85th St.
Kansas City, MO 64131
p: 816-822-7427
www.bbslawnsidebbq.com
contact: Lindsay Shannon
e: lindsay@bbslawnsidebbq.com
genres: Blues, Jazz
advance: 3 months
capacity: 154 **in-house:** Piano
Serves up finger lickin' good Local & prime Touring artists Wed-Sun for all ages. 1-2 acts play 1hr sets. Email for booking.

Beaumont Club
4050 Pennsylvania Ave.
Kansas City, MO 64111
p: 816-561-2560; 816-561-2668
e: kcbeaumont@aol.com
www.kcclubs.com/beaumont.cfm
contact: Jon Lunkwicz
genres: Country, Rock, Americana, Pop
advance: 1-5 months
capacity: 1000+
pa: Yes **sound eng:** Yes
Dancehall books original Nat'ls w/ some Reg'l or Int'l artists 4 nites/wk. 2 acts play 60-90min; some all ages shows.

Blayney's
421 Westport Rd.
Kansas City, MO 64111
p: 816-561-3747
www.blayneys.com
contact: Dick Schulte
e: barbiz77@hotmail.com
call: M-F 9am-noon
genres: Blues, Jazz, Swing, Motown, R&B
advance: 2 months
capacity: 220
pa: Yes **stage:** 17 x 10
Prime Blues showcase attracts even mix of original & cover talent Tue-Sat. Up to 3 top notch Local-Touring acts fill 4+hrs for 21+ crowd. Also books Irish Tavern upstairs.

Blue Room
1600 E 18th St.
Kansas City, MO 64108
p: 816-474-2929
www.americanjazzmuseum.org
contact: Gerald Dunn
p: 816-474-8463 x217
e: gdunn@kcjazz.org
call: Mon, Thu & Fri 5-11pm
genres: Jazz, R&B, Blues
advance: 2-3 months
capacity: 150
pa: Yes **sound eng:** Yes
Stage inside Jazz museum presents Reg'l & Nat'l talent 4 nites for all ages. Single act plays 45-75min set & keep 90% on hard merch, 70% on soft. Email or mail press kit w/ ATTN: Gerald Dunn, American Jazz Museum, 1616 E 18th St., Kansas City, MO 64108.

Davey's Uptown Ramblers Club
3402 Main St.
Kansas City, MO 64111

p: 816-753-1909
www.daveysuptown.com
contact: Michele Markowitz
genres: Rock, Country, Alt. Country, Indie Rock, Jazz
advance: 2 months
capacity: 350
pa: Yes **sound eng:** Yes
stage: 18 x 12
Prime indie showcase presents original Local-Touring acts & DJs for hip 21+ crowd 5-6 nites. 2-3 acts fill 2-5hrs for% of door. Call or snail mail press kit.

Jardine's
4536 Main St.
Kansas City, MO 64111
p: 816-561-6480
e: carriebrockman@gmail.com
www.jardines4jazz.com
contact: Beena
e: jazz4beena@gmail.com
call: M-F 10am-4pm
genres: Jazz
advance: 6 months
capacity: 115
pa: Yes **stage:** 10 x 30
Sublime listening room showcases exceptional Local-Int'l artists nitely. Up to 3 acts play 1hr; all ages before 9pm. Email or snail mail press kit.

Plaza III
4749 Pennsylvania Ave.
Kansas City, MO 64112
p: 816-753-0000
e: banquetsplaza3@accessus.net
www.plazaiiisteakhouse.com
contact: Belinda Hoyer
e: bhoyer@haddadgroup.com
genres: Jazz, Blues
advance: 1-2 months
capacity: 150
stage: large
Supperclub books mostly Reg'l & some Touring artists Fri & Sat for all ages. Featured act plays from 5-11pm for flat fee.

Westport Coffeehouse
4010 Pennsylvania Ave.
Kansas City, MO 64111
p: 816-756-3222
www.westportcoffeehouse.com
contact: Pam Ptacek
p: 816-756-3221
e: pam@baretv.com
call: M-F afternoons
genres: Acoustic Rock, Jazz, Folk, S/S
advance: 3 months
capacity: 60; 125 **pa:** Yes
stage: 14 x 20
All ages listening room showcases Local-Int'l bands Fri & Sat. 1-2 acts play 45min for flat fee. Rent downstairs theater space & keep the door. Email or mail press kit to venue.

The Riot Room
4048 Broadway
Kansas City, MO 64111
p: 816-442-8179
e: robbie@theriotroom.com
www.theriotroom.com
contact: Tim
e: tim@theriotroom.com; booking@theriotroom.com
Formerly Hurricane, this local hang w/ circular bar attracts crowds w/ plenty of quality live music. Email for booking.

Springfield

Nathan P. Murphy's
218 S Campbell Ave.
Springfield, MO 65806
p: 417-863-1909
www.drbobsbluesshow.com
contact: Bob Martin
genres: Blues, Jazz, Rock
advance: 3-4 months
capacity: 279
pa: Yes **sound eng:** Yes
stage: 20 x 10
1-2 Reg'ls & Nat'ls bands gig for 100% of door Thu-Sat to 18+. Openers play 45min; headliners play 90+min. Mail press kit to venue.

The Outland
326 South Ave.
Springfield, MO 65806
p: 417-863-9779
www.myspace.com/springfieldoutland
contact: Jason McGill
call: prefers MySpace
genres: Mainly Indie Rock
advance: 1 month
capacity: 200
pa: Yes **sound eng:** Yes
stage: 15 x 10
open mics: Tue **sign in:** 10pm
Welcoming 21+ dive hosts emerging Local-Touring bands; some all ages shows. 3 acts play 50min usu. for the door. Upstairs Ballroom books more polished acts on a larger stage. Contact via MySpace or snail mail kit.

The Outland Ballroom
324 South Ave.
Springfield, MO 65806
p: 417-869-7625
www.downtownlivemusic.com
contact: Kevin Willis
e: kevin@downtownlivemusic.com
genres: All Styles
advance: 1 month
capacity: 325
pa: Yes **sound eng:** Yes
stage: 24 x 16
Area's top spot for Reg'l buzz bands & Nat'l Touring acts books mostly original acts for 21+ gigs. 3-6 acts play 45min sets. Downstairs is the smaller, darker, Outland, booking up & coming Local-Touring acts for all ages nitely. Prefers email.

St. Louis

B.B.'s Jazz, Blues & Soups
700 S Broadway
St. Louis, MO 63102
p: 314-436-5222
e: carolatbbs@aol.com
www.bbsjazzbluessoups.com
contact: John May
e: johnmayatbbs@aol.com
call: M-F after 11am
genres: Jazz, Blues, Reggae
advance: 3-6 months
capacity: 200
pa: Yes **sound eng:** Yes
stage: 16 x 12
Blues room fills in w/ estab. Local-Nat'l acts. Sets are 45-90min of originals for% of door. Featured act gigs Sun-Wed; 2 bands Thu-Sat. Email for booking.

Blueberry Hill
6504 Delmar Blvd.
St. Louis, MO 63130
p: 314-727-4444
www.blueberryhill.com
contact: Pat Hagin
p: 314-726-6161
e: phagin@thepageant.com
call: M-F 10am-5pm
genres: Roots, Rock, R&B, Jazz, Reggae
advance: 2-3 months
capacity: 350
pa: Yes **sound eng:** Yes
stage: 18 x 10
Kitschy burger & music joint, has Reg'ls open for Nat'ls 2-5 nites. 1-2 acts play original music 9pm-12am in The Duck Room; mostly 21+ w/ some all ages. Also books for sister club, The Pageant. Mail kit w/ ATTN: Pat Hagin, 6161 Delmar Blvd., St. Louis, MO 63112.

Broadway Oyster Bar
736 S Broadway
St. Louis, MO 63102
p: 314-621-8811
e: oysterbar@hotmail.com
www.broadwayoysterbar.com
contact: John Johnson
p: 314-621-8813
call: M-F 9am-5pm
genres: All Styles
advance: 2-3 months
capacity: 350
pa: To rent **sound eng:** To hire
stage: medium
Funky Cajun eatery/Blues club books Reg'l & Nat'l acts nitely w/ Local openers; Mon all Locals. Up to 4 acts play two 1hr sets on patio rain or shine; some larger showcases & Battle of the Bands. All ages shows upon request. Prefers email, but may mail press kit to venue.

Cicero's
6691 Delmar Blvd.
St. Louis, MO 63130
p: 314-862-0009
www.ciceros-stl.com
contact: Jay Mumma
p: 314-862-5999
e: jaymumma@gmail.com
call: Mon, Wed & Fri 1pm-12am
genres: Pop, Rock, Funk, Jam
advance: 3-4 months
capacity: 250
pa: Yes **sound eng:** Yes
stage: 20 x 10
open mics: Mon **sign in:** 8:30pm
Indie showcase presents original Local-Nat'l bands & DJs nitely. 2-3 acts play 1+hr sets for all ages. Venue street team hangs band flyers. Booking ONLY done at www.sonicbids.com/ciceros.

The Creepy Crawl
3524 Washington Ave.
St. Louis, MO 63103
p: 314-531-3885
e: creepy@creepycrawl.com
www.creepycrawl.com
contact: Jeff
e: booking@jpconcerts.com
genres: Punk, Metal, Alt., Emo, Indie Rock
advance: 6-8 weeks
capacity: 450
stage: 13.5 x 18
Underground all ages club in new location books all Rock styles nitely. 5-9 acts play 30min for flat fee. Only accepts EPKs.

Focal Point Arts Ctr.
2720 Sutton Blvd.
Maplewood, MO 63143
p: 314-781-4200
www.thefocalpoint.org
contact: Judy Stein
p: 314-726-4707
e: j_c_stein@yahoo.com
call: M-F after 5pm
genres: Americana, Cajun, S/S, Celtic, Acoustic, Blues, Swing
advance: 4-6 months
capacity: 140
Non-profit arts ctr. spotlights original & traditional Local & Touring talent on wknds.; some shows on other days. Featured act plays 45min. Promos: PO Box 430157, Maplewood, MO 63143.

Hammerstone's
2028 S Ninth St.
St. Louis, MO 63104
p: 314-773-5565
e: lhammerstone@earthlink.com
www.hammerstones.net
contact: Lyn Hammerstone
genres: Blues, Jazz, R&B
advance: 3 months
capacity: 100
pa: Yes **stage:** medium
Eatery books original Local & Reg'l bands nitely w/ daytime music Sat & Sun. 1 act plays 9pm-1am w/ breaks for 21+.

Jazz at The Bistro
3536 Washington Blvd.
St. Louis, MO 63103
p: 314-289-4030
www.jazzstl.org
contact: Bob Bennett
p: 314-289-4032
e: bob@jazzstl.org
call: Tue-Fri 9am-5pm
genres: Jazz
advance: 1 year
capacity: 150
pa: Yes **sound eng:** Yes
stage: 10 x 20
Non-profit all ages listening room presents 1-2 original Local acts Fri-Sat & Touring artists Wed-Sat for 75min sets. Promos: 3547 Olive St., Ste. 212, St. Louis, MO 63103.

Off Broadway
3509 Lemp Ave.
St. Louis, MO 63118
p: 314-773-3363
www.offbroadwaystl.com
contact: Steve Pohlman
e: stevepohlman@yahoo.com; steve@offbroadwaystl.com
genres: All Styles
advance: 3 months
capacity: 325
pa: Yes **sound eng:** Yes
stage: 20 x 12 **in-house:** Drums
Welcoming niteclub w/ crisp acoustics, books Locals to open for Reg'l & Touring acts nitely for% of door. 1-3 acts play 45-90min. See site for FAQs.

Sheldon Concert Hall
3648 Washington Blvd.
St. Louis, MO 63108
p: 314-533-9900
www.thesheldon.org
contact: Paul Reuter
e: preuter@thesheldon.org
genres: Folk, Jazz, Classical
advance: 6+ months for Nat'ls; Locals vary
capacity: 712
pa: Yes **sound eng:** Yes
stage: 24 x 18
Performance space w/ excellent acoustics presents mostly Nat'ls w/ some polished Reg'l & Int'l talent Sep-May for all ages shows;

Locals play thru summer. 1, sometimes 2 original acts play 30+min & keep 85% merch. Use email for booking. No unsolicited pkgs.

Venice Cafe
1903 Pestalozzi St.
St. Louis, MO 63118
p: 314-772-5994
e: thevenicecafe@yahoo.com
www.thevenicecafe.com
contact: Chad Taylor
call: M-F noon-5pm
genres: Americana, Reggae, Rock, World, Blues
advance: 2 months
capacity: 75-100
open mics: Mon **sign in:** 9pm
Colorful & intimate space hosts mainly Local & Reg'l bands Wed-Sat w/ some Nat'ls. 1 act plays 90min set. Snail mail kit.

Way Out Club
2525 S Jefferson
St. Louis, MO 63104
p: 314-664-7638
www.thewayoutclub.com
contact: Sherri Danger
e: yourhomeawayfrom@aol.com
call: Mon-Wed after 5pm
genres: Most Styles
advance: Up to 1 month
capacity: 250
stage: 15 x 15
World-renowned, transgender-friendly 21+ club & launching pad for original Reg'l talent & some Touring bands. 2-3 acts play 1hr sets Wed-Sat & some Mon-Tue. No Jazz or Blues. Up-and-comers featured on jukebox & released on small label. Also hosts show on KDHX 88.1 for female groups. Snail mail or contact via MySpace.

Montana

Billings

Alberta Bair Theater
2801 3rd Ave. N
Billings, MT 59103
p: 406-256-6052; 877-321-2074
www.albertabairtheater.org
contact: William Wood
p: 406-256-8915 x203
e: woody@albertabairtheater.org
genres: World, Classical, Country
capacity: 1400
pa: Yes **sound eng:** Yes
PAC books about 10 shows/yr w/ top Touring acts. Most booking done at performing arts conferences. Mailing address: PO Box 1556, Billings, MT 59103.

Carlin Martini Bar
2501 Montana Ave.
Billings, MT 59101
p: 406-245-2500
e: ssmontana@bresnan.net
www.clubcarlin.com
contact: Suzy
e: suzy@thecarlin.com
genres: Jazz
advance: 3 months
capacity: 235
pa: Yes **sound eng:** Yes
stage: 16 x 12
Niteclub books Local Dance, Hip-Hop & Top Hits DJs 2-4 nites, Reg'l Jazz acts some Thu & some Touring groups. Featured act plays 2 sets for flat fee. Promos: 2407 Montana Ave., Billings, MT 59101.

Bozeman

The Filling Station
2005 N Rouse Ave.
Bozeman, MT 59715
p: 406-587-5009
www.myspace.com/thefillingstationpresentz
contact: Grant Gilmore
p: 406-209-3556
e: comlbproductions@aol.com
call: M-F after 5:30pm
genres: Rock, Country, Blues, Punk, Folk, Alt., Jam, Rockabilly
advance: Up to 6 months
capacity: 190
pa: Yes **stage:** 20 x 15
21+ Rock club housed in VFW hall books original Local-Int'l acts & DJs up to 7 nites; busier in summer. Up to 5 acts play 45-60min for % of door. Most booking done via MySpace; no unsolicited mail.

The Haufbrau
22 S 8th Ave.
Bozeman, MT 59715
p: 406-587-4931
contact: Don Frye
p: 406-580-4973
genres: Acoustic, Rock
advance: 2 months
capacity: 96
pa: Yes **stage:** 6 x 6
open mics: Sun & Mon
Pub books low volume original Local & Reg'l solo acts Fri-Sat & house bands Tue-Thu for college crowds. Featured act plays three 45-60min sets for flat fee. Also helps out w/ booking for The Filling Stn. Mail press kit to venue.

Zebra Cocktail Lounge
321 E Main St.
Bozeman, MT 59715
p: 406-585-8851
e: info@zebracocktaillounge.com
www.zebracocktaillounge.com
contact: Brett Cline
call: M-F noon-5pm
genres: Funk, Reggae, Hip-Hop, Techno, Punk
advance: 3-4 months
capacity: 250
pa: Yes **sound eng:** Yes
stage: 10 x 20
Niteclub w/ 3 spaces books mostly original Reg'ls & some Nat'ls Thu-Sat. Live, multi-track recording avail. Prefers email, or snail mail; no booking via MySpace or calls.

Missoula

The Loft
424 N Higgins Ave.
Missoula, MT 59802
www.myspace.com/theloftmissoula
contact: Damon Metzner
p: 503-231-1530
e: damon@mikethrasherpresents.com
genres: Most Styles
advance: 1-2 months
capacity: 200
pa: Yes **sound eng:** Yes
stage: 12 x 10
Cool, original music lounge books polished Local-Touring acts & DJs up to 7 nites; shows are 18+. No Punk or Metal. Email EPKs for booking or mail hard copy to: Diatribe9 Prod., 1820 45th Ave. SE, Portland, OR 97215.

The Other Side
1805 Regent St.
Missoula, MT 59803
p: 406-543-3405
e: figzag@graffiti.net
www.theothersidemusic.net
contact: Damon Metzner
e: diatribe_nine@hotmail.com
genres: All Styles
advance: 1-2 months
capacity: 550
pa: Yes **sound eng:** Yes
stage: 15 x 24
Area's primary 21+ Rock club, books notable & original Nat'l acts that can make the most of venue's large stage, dance floor, lights & sound. Payment is door vs flat fee. Email for booking.

Sean Kelly's
130 W Pine St.
Missoula, MT 59801
p: 406-542-1471
www.seankellys.com
contact: Paul Rudd
e: rudd@seankellys.com
call: M-F after 2pm
genres: Blues, Rock, R&B
advance: 3 months
capacity: 100
pa: Yes **stage:** 15 x 10 (corner)
open mics: Mon **sign in:** Call
Popular pub books original Reg'ls & some Touring bands up to 3 nites. Featured band plays three 1hr sets on elevated corner stage. Email for booking.

Nebraska

Lincoln

Duffy's Tavern
1412 O St.
Lincoln, NE 68508
p: 402-474-3543
e: duffstuffonline@yahoo.com
www.myspace.com/duffystavern
contact: Dub Wardlaw
p: 402-304-6939
e: duffysmusic@gmail.com
genres: Punk, Country, Rock, Hardcore, Blues, Alt. Country
advance: 2-3 months
capacity: 255
pa: Yes **sound eng:** Yes
stage: 20 x 20
Lauded 21+ club books mostly midwestern acts, some Touring talent & DJs Sun & Wed. 2-3 acts play 35-45min for % of door or maybe a flat fee; few all ages shows before 9pm. Email or mail press kit to venue w/ ATTN: Dub.

Duggan's Pub
440 S 11th St.
Lincoln, NE 68508
p: 402-477-3513
www.myspace.com/dugganspub
contact: Jack Gross
call: M-F 10:30am-4pm
genres: Blues, Bluegrass, Rock, Acoustic, Classic Rock, Indie, Hardcore, Country Swing
advance: 2 months
capacity: 280
stage: 17 x 30
open mics: Mon & Wed 9pm
Up to 4 Local-Touring acts gig 4hrs Tue & Thu-Sun for door at rare 19+ indie Rock showcase w/ accommodating ownership. Call or mail press kit to venue.

Knickerbockers
901 O St.
Lincoln, NE 68508
p: 402-476-6865
e: mail@knickerbockers.net
www.knickerbockers.net
contact: Chris Kelley
call: Tue-Fri after 5pm
genres: Mainly Rock
advance: 2 months
capacity: 400
stage: 18 x 16
Bar books Local-Int'l bands 5 nites. 3-6 acts play 1hr for all ages on wknds & 18+ M-F. Merch splits 85/15. Email or mail press kit to venue.

Uncle Ron's Wild West Saloon
340 W Cornhusker Hwy.
Lincoln, NE 68521
p: 402-474-2332
e: uncr@msn.com
www.unclerons.com
contact: Ron
call: M-F 11am-1pm
genres: All styles of Country
advance: 2-3 months
capacity: 850
pa: Yes **sound eng:** Yes
stage: 24 x 32
Themed niteclub w/ mechanical bull, shots bar & scantily-clad women also books top-notch original Local-Int'l acts Thu-Sat for 21+. Featured act plays 45min. Prefers email, but may call or contact via MySpace.

Zoo Bar
136 N 14th St.
Lincoln, NE 68508
p: 402-435-8754
e: info@zoobar.com
www.zoobar.com
contact: Peter
p: 402-617-1526
e: booking@zoobar.com
genres: Blues, Zydeco, Rockabilly, Reggae
advance: 3-4 months
capacity: 125
pa: Yes **sound eng:** Yes
stage: 10 x 12
Famed Blues bar showcases Local-Int'l acts Tue-Sat. 1-2 acts play 9pm-1am & early Jazz show Wed 6-9pm for 21+ crowd. Contact by any means.

Omaha

Barley Street Tavern
2735 N 62nd St.
Omaha, NE 68134
p: 402-408-0028
www.barleystreet.com
contact: Jef Parker
e: bookings@barleystreet.com
call: M-F 8:30-9pm
genres: Folk, Jazz, Blues, Pop, Acoustic, Indie, Rock, Experimental, Ambient, Noise
advance: 3 months
capacity: 70
stage: 16 x 8
open mics: Mon **sign in:** 8pm
The place to catch original Local bands Mon-Sat in the area; some Reg'ls & Nat'ls booked. 3-4 acts will fill 3hrs & split cash sales. No Punk or Rap. Mail press kit or email music links.

Bushwackers
7401 Main St.
Ralston, NE 68127
p: 402-593-9037

www.jmmbushwackers.com
contact: Dave Waterman
e: manager@jmbushwackers.com
genres: Country
advance: 3-6 months
capacity: 780
pa: Yes **stage:** 24 x 18
Large 21+ venue w/ full lights, books Local & Touring acts Fri & Sat; 3 shows/nite. 1 band plays 1hr sets for flat fee & sliding scale. Has a buzz as accommodating tour stop. Mail bio & CD or DVD to venue w/ ATTN: Dave.

The Chrome Lounge
8552 Park Dr.
Omaha, NE 68127
p: 402-339-8660
www.chromelive.com
contact: Scott
genres: Rock n Roll, Blues, Roots
advance: 4 months
capacity: 350
pa: Yes **sound eng:** Yes
stage: large
open mics: Thu 9pm
Drinking & music spot for motorheads, books Local & Nat'l bands for wknd gigs; some Nat'l acts on wkdys. Usu. 1, but up to 4 acts play from 9pm-1am for flat fee to 21+ crowd. Email or snail mail kit.

The Dubliner Pub
1205 Harney St.
Omaha, NE 68102
p: 402-342-5887
e: dublinerpub@aol.com
www.dublinerpubomaha.com
contact: Frank Vance
call: M-F 10am-noon
genres: Celtic, Irish
advance: 11 months
capacity: 90 **stage:** 8 x 10
Original Local-Int'l acts gig 2 nites in Irish spot for 21+. Single act plays three 45min sets for a flat fee. Mail press kit to venue.

The Hideout Lounge
322 S 72nd St.
Omaha, NE 68114
p: 402-504-4434
www.myspace.com/hideoutloungeomaha
contact: Steve Rewak
p: 402-612-1228
e: srewak@cox.net
genres: Rock, Metal, Indie, Hip-Hop, Blues, Acoustic
advance: 1 month
capacity: 175
pa: Yes **sound eng:** Yes
stage: 15 x 21
open mics: Tue 9pm
Formerly Shea Riley's, this dive bar features mostly original Local-Reg'l acts Fri-Sat for 21+ crowd. 3+ bands play 45min from 9pm-1am for % of door. Draw 25+ & get door minus $55; draw 50+ & keep 100% of door.

Manhattan Club
15244 W Maple Rd.
Omaha, NE 68116
p: 402-493-3009
e: info@manhattanomaha.com
www.manhattanomaha.com
contact: Jake Biel
e: manhattanclub@cox.net
advance: 2 months
capacity: 223 **stage:** 20 x 10
Only the area's hottest bands grace this 21+ stage; some Nat'l acts. 1 act plays three 45min sets 3 nites. Mail kit to venue.

McKenna's Blues, Booze & BBQ
7425 Pacific St.
Omaha, NE 68114
p: 402-393-7427
e: info@mckennasbbb.com
www.mckennasbbb.com
contact: Kyron O'Brien
genres: Blues, Reggae, Jazz, Rock, Alt., Indie
advance: 3-4 months
capacity: 120
pa: Yes **sound eng:** Yes
stage: medium
21+ roadhouse presents 1-3 original Local-Reg'l acts for 3hrs Fri & Sat. Mail press kit to venue.

Mick's Music & Bar
5918 Maple St.
Omaha, NE 68104
p: 402-502-2503
e: question@micksomaha.com
www.micksomaha.com
contact: Mick
e: booking@micksomaha.com
genres: Rock, Jazz, S/S, Indie, Acoustic
capacity: 100
pa: Yes **sound eng:** Yes
stage: 10 x 10
Hip club supports Local & Touring Acoustic solo & small groups nitely. 2 original acts play 90min to 21+ for % of door. Only accepts emailed music link.

Murphy's Lounge
4727 S 96th St.
Omaha, NE 68127
p: 402-339-7170
e: terry@murphysomaha.com
www.murphysomaha.com
contact: Terry O'Halloran
e: blueterryo@aol.com
genres: Blues, Reggae, Ska, Rock, Alt.
capacity: 230
pa: Yes **sound eng:** Yes
stage: 15 x 30
Local-Touring bands play two 75min sets for 21+ Thu-Sat. Email link to press kit or mail promo to: 1311 S 90th St., Omaha, NE 68124.

O'Leavers Pub
1322 S Saddle Creek Rd.
Omaha, NE 68106
p: 402-556-1238
www.oleavers.com
contact: Brendan
e: oleaversbooking@gmail.com
genres: Rock
advance: 2 months
capacity: 150
stage: floor space
Laid-back bar books original Local-Nat'l bands Wed-Sat for 21+. Up to 3 acts play 45min & split door. Email or snail mail kit.

The Roxbury
10841 Q St.
Omaha, NE 68144
p: 402-339-9791
e: omaharox@msn.com
www.clubroxbury.com
contact: Mike
genres: Most Styles
advance: 2 months
capacity: 800+
pa: Yes **sound eng:** To hire
stage: 12 x 24
It's always party nite at this twin-room niteclub. Original Local-Nat'l bands play 1hr for mostly all ages crowd; some 18+ & 21+ shows. No Hip-Hop. Prefers email or snail mail kit.

Nevada

Las Vegas

Beauty Bar
517 Fremont St.
Las Vegas, NV 89101
p: 702-598-1965
www.beautybar.com
contact: Bree Blumstein
e: bree@beautybar.com
advance: 2 weeks for Locals; 1 month for others
capacity: 100; 400 (outdoors)
pa: Yes **sound eng:** Yes
stage: 15 x 24
open mics: 3rd Sun/mo MC Nite
Hip hang w/ late 50's decor, books Local-Touring bands & DJs; some cover bands. 2-4 acts play 30-45min for 21+ crowd. Other locations w/ music in San Diego, CA & Austin, TX. Contact via MySpace.

Bunkhouse Saloon
124 S 11th St.
Las Vegas, NV 89101
p: 702-384-4536
www.bunkhouselv.com
contact: Keith Fox
p: 702-429-0661
e: booking@bunkhouselv.com; manager@bunkhouselv.com
genres: Rock, Garage, Punk, Alt. Country, Rockabilly, Surf, 60s Soul, Indie Rock
pa: Yes **sound eng:** Yes
Formerly Peyton Place, now a western wonderland, draws mixed crowd for Local & Touring acts on wknds & various wkdys. Up to 4 original acts play for % of bar sales or % of door. No Rap or Hip-Hop. Email or contact thru MySpace.

Cheyenne Saloon
3103 N Rancho Dr.
Las Vegas, NV 89130
p: 702-645-4139
www.myspace.com/thecheyennesaloonlv
contact: Brittney Stalbaum/ Mark Hornsby
genres: Rock, Hard Rock, Punk, Garage, Hardcore, Metal, Reggae, Rockabilly
advance: 3 months
capacity: 250
pa: Yes **sound eng:** Yes
stage: 20 x 12
open mics: Sun **sign in:** 8pm
Premier Rock club books Local-Reg'l acts 5 nites, Nat'l acts monthly to 21+. 2-5 bands play 30-60min for % of door. Also books The Icehouse. Use MySpace, call, or mail press kit to venue.

Dive Bar
3035 E Tropicana Blvd., Ste. E
Las Vegas, NV 89121
p: 702-435-7526
e: info@vegasdivebar.com
www.vegasdivebar.com
contact: Nate
p: 702-806-8207
e: nate@vegasdivebar.com
genres: Rock, Punk, Rockabilly, Metal, Funk
capacity: 200
pa: Yes **sound eng:** Yes
stage: 10 x 8
open mics: Mon Acoustic
Rock club books Local-Nat'l bands nitely to 21+ crowd. Up to 4 acts play 30-60min for possible flat fee. Prefers contact via MySpace, but may email or snail mail kit; call 2 wks later.

Double Down Saloon
4640 Paradise Rd.
Las Vegas, NV 89169
p: 702-791-5775
www.doubledownsaloon.com
contact: Moss
e: doubledownsaloon@gmail.com
genres: Punk, Garage, Lo-Fi, Surf
advance: 2-3 months
capacity: 150
pa: Yes **stage:** small
24hr dive bar w/ attitude, books 4-6 original acts 4-5 nites. Local-Int'l bands play 45min sets for flat fee. Bring mics & stands. Email links to music or mail kit w/ email address to venue; no calls. Strict about genres booked.

House of Blues/ Las Vegas
3950 Las Vegas Blvd. S
Las Vegas, NV 89119
p: 702-632-7600
http://hob.com/venues/clubvenues/lasvegas
contact: Max McAndrews
e: mmcandrew@hob.com
call: M-F 10am-7pm
genres: Rock, Country, 70s, 80s, Urban
advance: 2-3 months
capacity: 1800
pa: Yes **sound eng:** Yes
stage: 45 x 22
Themed music chain books 1-4 Reg'l polished bands 3 nites/wk & top Touring talent a few nites/mo. Prefers EPK to hbeverstein@hob.com, or snail mail kit.

Lucille's Smokehouse BBQ
2245 Village Walk Dr.
Henderson, NV 89074
p: 702-257-7427
www.lucillesbbq.com
contact: Don McGreevy
p: 702-616-9966
e: dmcgreevy@cox.net
call: M-F
genres: Blues
pa: Yes **sound eng:** Yes
stage: small
Chain restaurant 15mi outside of Vegas, serves up Local-Reg'l Blues Fri & Sat. Featured act plays 7-11pm for flat fee. Promos: The Las Vegas Agency, 2850 Skowhegan Dr., Ste. 3, Henderson, NV 89074.

Sand Dollar Blues Nightclub & Lounge
3355 W Spring Mountain Rd.
Las Vegas, NV 89102
p: 702-871-6651
www.sanddollarblues.com
contact: Pat McKnight
e: pat@sanddollarblues.com
genres: Blues, Rock
advance: 1-3 months
capacity: 180
pa: Yes **sound eng:** Yes
stage: 15 x 20
open mics: Weekly
A true-blue oasis in a sea of glitz,

this top-rated listening room attracts 1-2 Local-Touring bands to play & hang. Email for booking.

Reno

Abby's Hwy. 40
424 E 4th St.
Reno, NV 89512
p: 775-322-9422
www.abbyshighway40.com
contact: Donnie Schwartz
e: info@abbyshighway40.com
genres: Light Rock, Blues, Jam, Funk
advance: 2 months
capacity: 100
pa: Yes **sound eng:** Yes
stage: 20 x 10
Lively bar features 1-3 original & some cover Reg'l bands Fri & Sat for 21+ crowd.

Comma Coffee
312 S Carson St.
Carson City, NV 89701
p: 775-883-2662
www.commacoffee.com
contact: Jen Scaffidi
p: 775-721-1150
genres: Jazz, Blues, Hardcore, Indie Rock, Punk
advance: 3 months; 5 months for outdoor shows
capacity: 100 **pa:** Yes
stage: small floor space
open mics: 1st Fri of month 8pm; Open Jazz Wed
All ages cafe 32mi from Reno, books Local-Nat'l acts for tips & meals; occasionally get % of door. Mosh-worthy acts only booked on summer outdoor stage. Up to 3 original bands fill 30-120min. All booking done via website; read policy first.

Great Basin Brewing Co.
846 Victorian Ave.
Sparks, NV 89432
p: 775-355-7711
www.greatbasinbrewingco.com
contact: Paul Ganzer
e: paul@greatbasinbrewingco.com
call: Wed-Sat after 4pm
genres: All Styles
advance: 6 weeks
capacity: 300; 2000 outdoors
pa: Yes **sound eng:** Yes
stage: 25 x 12; 30 x 30 outdoors
Busy brewpub books original Locals, DJs & some Touring acts Fri-Sat & some on other nites; cover bands & all ages shows in summer. Up to 3 bands play all nite starting from 9pm. Email or snail mail kit.

Java Jungle
246 W 1st St.
Reno, NV 89501
p: 775-329-4484
www.myspace.com/javajunglevino
contact: Ty Martin
e: ty-martin@sbcglobal.net
call: evenings
genres: Acoustic, Jazz
capacity: 50
pa: Yes **stage:** floor space
open mics: Mon **sign in:** 7:30pm
Coffeehouse books some Reg'l Acoustic performers, but is better-known for open mic. Mail press kit to venue.

New Oasis
2100 Victorian Ave.
Sparks, NV 89431
p: 775-772-2475
www.newoasisrenosparks.com
contact: Karen
e: karen01nv@aol.com
genres: Most Styles
advance: 1 month
capacity: 1000
pa: Yes **sound eng:** Yes
stage: large **in-house:** Drums
All ages venue reopened Nov '07, hosts big indie & small major label artists a few times/mo; Locals booked as openers. 3-4 acts play 45-50min for % of door; merch split is 90/10. No Hardcore Rap or Hip-Hop. Mail press kit to venue.

Reno Music Project at Maytan Music Center
777 S Center St.
Reno, NV 89501
p: 775-530-2940
e: info@renomusicproject.com
www.renomusicproject.com
contact: Todd South
call: afternoons
genres: Most Styles
advance: 2-3 months
capacity: 150
pa: Yes **sound eng:** Yes
stage: 20 x 10
open mics: Fri **sign in:** 7pm
Lauded music listening room w/ pro sound & backline, features original Local-Int'l artists Fri-Sat for all ages. 2-3 acts play 1hr sets for tips. Free live recording for featured & showcase performers. No Hip-Hop or Straight Edge Punk. Prefers email; see detailed policy on website first.

Satellite Cocktail Lounge
188 California Ave.
Reno, NV 89509
p: 775-786-3536
www.myspace.com/satellitereno
contact: Ryan Goldhammer
p: 775-232 7877
e: scrapbookmedia@gmail.com
genres: All Styles
advance: 2 months
capacity: 140
pa: Yes **sound eng:** Yes
stage: 15 x 10 (wedge)
open mics: 1st Fri of month
Hipster hang has Local & Touring bands & DJs 2-4 nites. 2-4 acts play 30+min to 21+ crowd. Promos: 830 Casa Loma Dr., Reno, NV 89503 or send EPK or use MySpace. Follow up via email.

The Underground
555 E 4th St.
Reno, NV 89512
p: 775-786-2582
e: contact@renounderground.com
www.renounderground.com
contact: Remi Jourdan
e: booking@renounderground.com
genres: All Styles
advance: 2-3 months
capacity: 250+
pa: Yes **sound eng:** Yes
open mics: Thu Open Mic/Open Table & Jam 10pm
Rockin' spot btwn major tour destinations w/ 2 stages, mixes Local bands, DJs & Touring acts 5 nites; some all ages shows. 3 acts play 45min sets. Prefers email, but may snail mail.

The Zephyr Lounge
1074 S Virginia St.
Reno, NV 89502
p: 775-324-9853
www.myspace.com/the_zephyr_lounge
contact: Nick Tuesday
genres: Rock, Jazz, Funk
advance: 30-45 days
capacity: 115
pa: Yes **sound eng:** Yes
stage: small
open mics: Mon 10pm
Popular local dive hosts Local-Reg'l acts & DJs up to 7 nites & Touring bands Fri & Sat. 2-3 acts play 45min to 21+ crowd for 100% of door. Prefers calls.

New Hampshire

Laconia

Black Cat Café
17 Veterans Sq.
Laconia, NH 03246
p: 603-528-3233
e: info@blackcatcafe.com
www.blackcatcafe.com
contact: Kenny O'Rourke
e: kinney@blackcatcafe.com
genres: Jazz, Acoustic, Blues, Folk, Bluegrass
advance: 1 month
capacity: 35+; **stage:** floor space
Homey eatery books low volume Local-Reg'l acts Thu-Fri for all ages. Featured performer fills 3hrs for flat fee. Send EPK.

Lebanon Opera House
51 N Park St.
Lebanon, NH 03766
p: 603-448-0400
e: info@lebanonoperahouse.org
www.lebanonoperahouse.org
contact: Heather Clow
e: lebanon.opera.house@verizon.net
call: mornings after 9am
genres: S/S, Folk, Rock, World, Jazz
advance: 6-12 months
capacity: 800
pa: Yes **sound eng:** Yes
stage: 28 x 50
Intimate hall w/ great sight & sound, hosts 2-3 eclectic shows/wk featuring Nat'l & Int'l talent Oct-May, about half are produced in-house. Promos: PO Box 384, Lebanon, NH 03766.

Patrick's Pub
18 Weirs Rd. (Rts. 11 & 11B)
Gilford, NH 03249
p: 603-293-0841
e: info@patrickspub.com
www.patrickspub.com
contact: Paul Costley
p: 603-624-4022
e: druma32@aol.com
genres: Rock, Blues, Pop
advance: 3-6 months
capacity: 300 **stage:** 12 x 14
All ages eatery has Local & Reg'l acts Wed-Sat yr-round & Sun in summer. Featured act plays 3hrs for mature crowd out for fun. Mail press kit to venue.

Manchester/ Portsmouth

The Barley House
132 N Main St.
Concord, NH 03301
p: 603-228-6363
e: info@thebarleyhouse.com
www.thebarleyhouse.com
contact: Matt Weeks
call: email only
genres: Jazz, Blues, Funk, Folk, Jam, Indie Rock, Hip-Hop
advance: 2-3 months
capacity: 85; 300
stage: 15 x 9
Irish tavern 17mi from Manchester, books mostly Local & Reg'l acts Fri-Sat. Featured act plays 3hrs for flat fee & meals. Email w/ link to music.

Blue Mermaid
409 The Hill
Portsmouth, NH 03801
p: 603-427-2583
e: thebluemermaid@cs.com
www.bluemermaid.com
contact: Chad A. Verbeck
p: 603-721-9152
e: nugaverbs@yahoo.com
call: M-F after 5pm
genres: Rock, Blues, Jazz, Folk, Indie Rock, Bluegrass, Country, Reggae, S/S
advance: 1-3 months
capacity: 50 **stage:** 8 x 14
open mics: Wed **sign in:** 8pm
Caribbean eatery features original Reg'l bands in the lounge Fri & Sat. Featured act plays 2-3 sets (3hrs) for 100% of door. Mail press kit to venue.

Boardwalk Inn & Cafe
139 Ocean Blvd.
Hampton Beach, NH 03842
p: 603-929-7400
www.boardwalkinns.com
contact: Jim Trainor
e: jt@boardwalkinns.com
genres: Rock
advance: 3+ months
capacity: 100+; 100+
pa: Yes **sound eng:** Yes
open mics: Tue
21+ beach party spot 14mi from Portsmouth, books Local/Reg'l acts in 2 rooms Fri & Sat during off season; nitely in the summer. Featured act fills 4hrs for flat fee. Mail press kit to venue.

Bourbons At Muddy Rivers Smokehouse
21 Congress St.
Portsmouth, NH 03801
p: 603-430-9582
www.muddyriver.com
contact: Gerri
e: gerri@muddyriver.com
genres: Rock, Pop, Punk, Americana
advance: 1-3 months
capacity: 125
pa: Yes **sound eng:** Yes
stage: 20 x 12
BBQ & music joint midway btwn Boston & Portland, hosts 1-2 Local-Touring acts Fri-Sat for the door after prod. costs ($100).

Chubb Theatre at the Capitol Ctr. for the Arts
44 S Main St.
Concord, NH 03301
p: 603-225-1111
e: friends@ccanh.com
www.ccanh.com
contact: Ric Waldman
p: 603-225-1111 x103
e: rwaldman@ccanh.com
genres: S/S, Rock, Blues, Jazz
advance: 3-12 months
capacity: 1310

pa: Yes **sound eng:** Yes
stage: 39 x 25
Restored space w/ state-of-the-art sound, books well-known Touring acts a few nites/wk. Featured act plays 75-90min sets for flat fee or guarantee plus % of door. Also avail. to rent.

Dover Brick House
2 Orchard St.
Dover, NH 03820
p: 603-749-3838
www.doverbrickhouse.com
contact: Rex
p: 603-591-3689
e: rex@doverbrickhouse.com
genres: Rock, Hip-Hop, Metal, Reggae, Funk, Blues, Jazz, Punk
capacity: 120; 110
pa: Yes **sound eng:** Yes
stage: 20 x 15
Bar's upstairs music room books up to 6 original Local-Nat'l bands Tue-Sun. Great sound & sight lines. Email link to website w/ music, press kit & upcoming & previous bookings; no unsolicited mail.

Hampton Beach Casino Ballroom
169 Ocean Blvd.
Hampton Beach, NH 03843
p: 603-929-4022
e: info@casinoballroom.com
www.casinoballroom.com
contact: Fred Schaake
genres: Rock, Country, S/S, Blues, Pop
advance: 6-8 weeks
capacity: 2200; 1800 (seated)
pa: Yes **sound eng:** Yes
stage: 42 x 24
Summertime 21+ venue books mostly original Nat'l acts up to 4 nites w/ some Local-Reg'l openers Mar-Nov; several all ages shows. Mail press kit to: PO Box 1209, Hampton Beach, NH 03843.

Harlow's Pub
3 School St.
Peterborough, NH 03458
p: 603-924-6365
e: info@harlowspub.com
www.harlowspub.com
contact: Dave Szehi
p: 603-924-7554
call: Mon, Wed & Fri
genres: Rock, Funk, Reggae, Jazz, Jam, Blues, Latin, Americana
advance: 6 months
capacity: 110
pa: Yes
stage: 10 x 10
open mics: Wed
NH Mag's 'Best Rural Pub' books Reg'l & some Touring acts Fri & Sat for door & meals. Band plays 2.5hrs for 21+ crowd.

La Bec Rouge
73 Ocean Blvd.
Hampton Beach, NH 03842
p: 603-926-5050
e: labec@labecrouge.com
www.labecrouge.com
contact: Tracey Dewhurst
e: tracey@labecrouge.com
genres: Rock, Soft Rock, Acoustic, Reggae
capacity: 100; 100; 100
stage: small
Seaside party spot 16+mi from Portsmouth, hosts area bands nitely in 3 spaces. Up to 3 acts play matinee or evening sets; all ages in restaurant area; 21+ in pub & summer-only outdoor deck.

Mark's Showplace
390 S River Rd.
Bedford, NH 03110
p: 603-668-7444
e: info@marksshowplace.com
www.marksshowplace.com
contact: Nicole Silverman
e: marksshowplace@aol.com
call: email only
genres: Rock, Alt., Metal
advance: 3-6 months
capacity: 250
pa: Yes **sound eng:** Yes
Gentlemen's club 7mi from Manchester, has 2 Local-Nat'l acts & Tribute bands 2-3 nites for hard rockin' 21+ crowd. Bands get free billiards & admission to gentlemen's club. Email for booking; no unsolicited mail or calls.

Mason's Barley Pub
328 Central Ave.
Dover, NH 03820
p: 603-742-4226
www.barleypub.com
contact: Rob Boyk
e: entertainment@barleypub.com
genres: Jazz, Bluegrass, Rock, Funk, Reggae, S/S
advance: 3-4 months
capacity: 110
pa: Yes **sound eng:** Yes
stage: 12 x 12
Relaxed beer joint 12mi from Portsmouth, is loved by patrons & bands of all stripes. Locals & Reg'ls gig Tue-Wed & Sat-Sun. Featured act plays 1 or 2 sets for % of door. Email only.

Meadowbrook Musical Arts Center
72 Meadowbrook Ln.
Gilford, NH 03249
p: 603-293-4700
e: info@meadowbrook.net
www.meadowbrook.net
contact: Bridget Harding
p: 603-293-4700 x206
genres: Rock, Pop, Country, Blues, S/S
advance: 3-4 months
capacity: 3200-6400; 250; 150
pa: Yes **sound eng:** Yes
stage: 90 x 45 & 60 x 45 (pavilion); 24 x 24 (second stage); 20 x 16 (center stage)
Premier summer concert venue books top Touring artists mid-Jun to mid-Sep w/ Reg'ls playing pre- & post-concert sets on 2nd stage. Covers acts play during Oct-May winter series. Promos: PO Box 7296, Gilford, NH 03247.

Michael Timothy's
212 Main St.
Nashua, NH 03060
p: 603-595-9334
e: michaeltimothys@verizon.net
www.michaeltimothys.com
contact: Michael Buckley
p: 603-595-9412
genres: Jazz, Acoustic
advance: Up to 1 year
capacity: 40-150
stage: floor space
Wine bar 18mi from Manchester, has mostly Local-Reg'l acts Wed & Fri-Sun. Featured act plays 3-4hrs for flat fee; merch sales not allowed. Acoustic on Wed & Sun. Mail press kit to venue.

Milly's Tavern
500 Commercial St.
Manchester, NH 03101
p: 603-625-4444
e: info@millystavern.com
www.millystavern.com
contact: Peter Telge
e: petertelge@millystavern.com
genres: All Styles
advance: 10-12 weeks
capacity: 450
pa: Yes **sound eng:** Yes
stage: 50 x 20
open mics: Tue **sign in:** 7:30pm
4-6 Reg'l acts, DJs & some Touring bands play 45min for door after costs Tue-Sun; all ages Sun. Non-negotiable $150 fee required to cover house expenses; must supply door person. See website for detailed policy; email for avail. dates.

New England Revival Coffeehouse
Calvary Fellowship Church,
60 Bailey Ave.
Manchester, NH 03109
p: 603-625-9550
e: booking@nerch.org
www.nerch.org
contact: Doug MacCormack
p: 603-623-7900 x444 (daytime); 603-232-0350 (evenings)
e: doug@nerch.org
genres: CCM, Christian Folk, Popular Rock, Gospel
advance: 6-7 months
capacity: 175
pa: Yes **sound eng:** Yes
stage: 16 x 25
Christian community-based venue hosts Local-Int'l artists 1st & 3rd Fri/mo for donations. Acts fill 60-75min w/ 2 shorter sets or 1 longer set. 3-camera video prod. of show broadcasts on local cable TV. Email or call before you submit.

The Press Room
77 Daniel St.
Portsmouth, NH 03801
p: 603-431-5186
www.pressroomnh.com
contact: Bruce Pingree
call: Thu 1:30-3pm
genres: Jazz, Blues, R&B, Folk, Rock, S/S
advance: 3-6 months
capacity: 85; 85 (upstairs)
pa: Yes **sound eng:** Yes
stage: 20 x 8 **in-house:** Piano
Popular 21+ pub spotlights mostly original Local-Int'l acts on 2 floors up to 7 nites. 1 act plays 4hrs for flat fee vs % of door. Jazz on Sun & Mon has Touring talent. Snail mail kit.

The Sad Cafe
148 Plaistow Rd., Rte. 125
Plaistow, NH 03865
p: 603-382-8893
www.thesadcafe.com
contact: Linda
e: bookings@thesadcafe.com
genres: Family-Friendly
advance: Up to 3 months
capacity: 220
pa: Yes **sound eng:** Yes
stage: 20 x 13
Non-profit all ages venue presents mostly original Local-Reg'l acts Fri-Sun during school yr & nitely in summer. Up to 6 acts play 30-35min sets for merch sales & CD of their set. All ages bands are welcome. No Rap, Thrash or Death Metal. Prefers email or contact via MySpace, but may call.

Spring Hill Tavern at The Dolphin Striker
15 Bow St.
Portsmouth, NH 03801
p: 603-431-5222
www.dolphinstriker.com
contact: Ray Brandin
call: M-F after 5pm
genres: Blues, Funk, Rock, Folk, S/S, Jazz, Americana
capacity: 110
stage: 15 x 12
Local & some Reg'l low-volume talent play nitely at cozy pub. Featured act plays 3-4hrs for flat fee. Call for booking.

The Stone Church Music Club
5 Granite St.
Newmarket, NH 03857
p: 603-659-6321
www.thestonechurch.com
contact: Chris Hislop
p: 603-659-0066
e: chris@thestonechurch.com
genres: Rock, Folk, Jazz, Reggae, Bluegrass, Hardcore, Funk, Blues
advance: 1-2 months
capacity: 192
pa: Yes **sound eng:** Yes
stage: 20 x 10
Landmark venue books up to 3 original Local-Int'l bands for 1+hr sets Wed-Sun. Some shows are seated; some all ages shows. Prefers EPKs, but may snail mail kit to venue; no calls.

Tupelo Music Hall
2 Young Rd.
Londonderry, NH 03053
p: 603-437-5100
e: info@tupelohall.com
www.tupelohall.com
contact: Scott Hayward
p: 603-490-7909
e: booking@tupelohall.com
genres: Most Styles
advance: 3-6 months
capacity: 240
pa: Yes **sound eng:** Yes
stage: 22 x 14 **in-house:** Piano
open mics: 1st Thu/mo 7pm
All ages listening room books 1-2 original top Touring talent w/ some Reg'l openers. Nat'l acts play 75-120min. Also books a featured act for open mic. Merch splits 85/15. No Hard Rock or Punk. Prefers email w/ link to EPK.

Washington St. Cafe
Keene Recreation Ctr.
312 Washington St.
Keene, NH 03431
www.ci.keene.nh.us/wscafe
contact: Eli Rivera
e: erivera@ci.keene.nh.us
genres: Rock, Alt.
pa: Yes **sound eng:** Yes
Teen ctr. books monthly high energy bills w/ up to 4 Reg'l & Nat'l bands. Prefers Sonicbids EPKs, or snail mail kit w/ ATTN: Eli Rivera, 11 Washington St., Keene, NH 03431.

New Jersey

Central

Asbury Lanes
209 4th Ave.
Asbury Park, NJ 07712
p: 732-776-6160
e: asburylanes@asburylanes.com

www.asburylanes.com
contact: Layney
p: 732-233-4269
e: layney@asburylanes.com
call: afternoons & evenings
genres: Punk, Indie, Dance, Rockabilly, Psychobilly, Rock, Country, Alt. Country
advance: 1-3 months
capacity: 350
pa: Yes **sound eng:** Yes
stage: 14 x 15
Original Local-Int'l acts & Touring DJs perform in revamped vintage bowling alley run by local musicians & artists. 3-4 acts play 30-60min on circular stage set in middle of lanes. 18+ & some all ages shows are Wed-Sat w/ some matinees & Sun-Tue shows. Mail press kit or send EPK.

The Brighton Bar
121 Brighton Ave.
Long Branch, NJ 07740
p: 732-229-9676
www.brightonbar.com; www.cojackproductions.com
contact: Jack Monahan
p: 732-229-7258
e: jacko@cojackproductions.com
genres: Indie Rock, Pop, Punk, Jazz
advance: 4-6 weeks
capacity: 250
pa: Yes **sound eng:** Yes
Oldest Rock club in NJ, w/ a "Wall of Fame" to prove it, filters only the best talent thru mainstay booker. Local-Touring bands perform mostly Wed-Sun for 18+. Local promos: Co. Jack, 139 Brighton Ave., Apt. 2-Side, Long Branch, NJ 07740; Nat'l acts: 7 Lane St., Long Branch, NJ 07740.

Count Basie Theatre
99 Monmouth St.
Red Bank, NJ 07701
p: 732-224-8778
e: info@countbasietheatre.org
www.countbasietheatre.org
contact: Numa Saisselin
p: 732-224-8778 x105
call: M-F 9am-5pm
genres: Rock, Pop, Jazz, World, Country, S/S
advance: 3-12 months
capacity: 1543
pa: Yes **sound eng:** Yes
stage: 84 x 26; 43' proscenium
Fully restored theatre presents mostly Local acts 2-3 nites w/ some Reg'l & few Nat'l acts; 125-150 total bands/yr. 1-2 acts plays 90+min for flat fee; some all ages shows. Merch split is 75/25. Mail press kit to venue c/o Programming Dept.

The Court Tavern
124 Church St.
New Brunswick, NJ 08901
p: 732-545-7265
www.myspace.com/thecourttavern
contact: Andy Diamond
e: newjersey2320@hotmail.com
genres: Rock, Punk, Reggae, Groove
advance: 1-2 months
capacity: 170
pa: Yes **sound eng:** Yes
stage: 8 x 20
open mics: Mon **sign in:** 10pm
Authentic Rock club near Rutgers U, books Reg'l & Touring acts Fri-Sat. 3-4 original acts play 35+min sets. Email music links or snail mail kit. No plastic wrap on CDs; no cassettes.

The Downtown
8 W Front St.
Red Bank, NJ 07701
p: 732-741-2828
e: info@thedowntownnj.com
www.thedowntownnj.com
contact: Chris Masi
e: chris@thedowntownnj.com
genres: Rock, Soul, Blues, Reggae
capacity: 150; 148 (upstairs)
pa: Yes **sound eng:** Yes
stage: large
open mics: Sun 9pm
Recently renovated cafe reopened Mar 21, 2008 & now hosting Locals-Nat'ls Mon-Sat downstairs & some acts Thu-Sat upstairs; all shows 21+. 1 act plays 3hrs w/ breaks from 10pm-1:30am for flat fee. Send EPK or snail mail kit.

Espresso Joe's
50 W Front St.
Keyport, NJ 07735
p: 732-203-9499
e: events@espresso-joes.com
www.espresso-joes.com
contact: Sonny Han
e: sonny@espresso-joes.com
genres: Acoustic, Folk, Soft Rock, Blues, Bluegrass
advance: 3 months
pa: Yes
open mics: Wed
Gourmet coffeehouse welcomes 2-3 mostly Local-Reg'l Acoustic acts favoring original music 2 nites. Email or mail press kit to venue w/ ATTN: DEMO.

Joey Harrison's Surf Club
1900 Ocean Ave.
Ortley Beach, NJ 08751
p: 732-830-8000
www.surfclubnj.com
contact: Tony Pallagrosi
p: 732-539-2632
e: pallagrosi_antonio@comcast.net
genres: Oldies, Alt., Pop, Rock, Reggae
capacity: 1400
pa: Yes **sound eng:** Yes
stage: 26 x 17
Famed Jersey Shore club books variety of polished original & cover acts. Up to 4 Local-Int'l acts play for 21+; some 18+ shows. Locals keep 100% of merch sales. Email or call. No unsolicited mail.

KatManDu
Rte. 29, 50 Riverview Plaza
Trenton, NJ 08611
p: 609-393-7300
www.katmandutrenton.com
contact: Joe Surdo
e: bands@katmandutrenton.com
genres: Modern Rock, Pop, Top 40
advance: 6-12 months
capacity: 1000; 1500 (outdoor)
pa: Yes **sound eng:** Yes
stage: 12 x 16; 20 x 16
in-house: Backline, Drums
21+ niteclub in tropical-themed complex, books Reg'l original & cover bands & DJs 2-4 nites on indoor & outdoor stages; very few all ages shows. 1 act plays 3hrs for a flat fee. Use email or mail press kit to venue w/ ATTN: Booking, 50 Riverview Exec. Pk., Trenton, NJ 08611.

Rahway Cafe & Stage
1433 Main St.
Rahway, NJ 07065
p: 732-943-7660
e: rahwaycafeandstage@yahoo.com
www.rahwaycafeandstage.com
contact: Eric Finley
genres: All Styles
capacity: 600
pa: Yes **sound eng:** Yes
stage: 16 x 24
New, fully-equipped, multi-purpose art space is now open & booking Local-Int'l acts & DJs up to 4 nites. 6 acts play 30min for all ages. Prefers email.

The Saint
601 Main St.
Asbury Park, NJ 07712
p: 732-775-9144
e: bookings@thesaintnj.com
www.thesaintnj.com
contact: Scott Stamper
p: 732-776-8913
e: saintnj601@aol.com
call: M-F afternoon
genres: All Styles
advance: 6-8 weeks
capacity: 150
pa: Yes **sound eng:** Yes
stage: 16 x 14
Laid back 18+ club is a local fave & showcases original Reg'l & Touring talent 5-7 nites. 4 acts play 35-45min for % of door. All ages wknd matinees presented by Jerseyshows.com. CD & DVD recordings of your set avail. for purchase. Prefers email, but contact by any means. If mailing, address to: The Saint, c/o Asbury Music Co., PO Box 427, Belmar, NJ 07719.

Starland Ballroom
570 Jernee Mill Rd.
Sayreville, NJ 08872
p: 732-238-5500
e: info@starlandballroom.com
www.starlandballroom.com
contact: Adam Weiser
p: 732-238-1996
e: aweiser@aeglive.com
call: M-F 10am-6pm
genres: Rock, Alt., Punk, Metal, Pop
advance: Weeks - months
capacity: 2000
pa: Yes **sound eng:** Yes
stage: 40 x 32
Macro-scale sound system put to use by lively mix of big name Nat'l acts w/ Local & Reg'l openers. 3-4 acts play 30-90min. Some all ages shows make this a must play tour stop. Prefers email or MySpace contact.

Stone Pony
913 Ocean Ave.
Asbury Park, NJ 07712
p: 732-502-0600
www.stoneponyonline.com
contact: Kyle Brendle
e: stoneponybooking@yahoo.com; ponyrocks89@yahoo.com
genres: Rock, Alt., Blues, Metal
advance: 3 months
capacity: 800
pa: Yes **sound eng:** Yes
stage: 30 x 14
Nostalgic breeding ground & world famous Rock club, books original Reg'l & Nat'l talent nitely w/ Local openers. 3-6 acts play 40min; some all ages shows. Email only for booking: Local-Reg'ls use stoneponybooking@yahoo.com, Nat'l acts use ponyrocks89@yahoo.com; no unsolicited mail.

Triumph Brewing Co.
138 Nassau St.
Princeton, NJ 08542
p: 609-924-7855
www.triumphbrewing.com
contact: Lauren K. Palena
p: 609-924-7855 x263
e: lauren@triumphbrew.com
genres: Indie, Rock, Pop, Alt., Folk, Acoustic, Latin, Jazz, Blues
advance: 2-3 months
capacity: 350
21+ brewpub spotlights mostly original Local-Reg'l bands Thu-Sat w/ some Nat'ls. 1-2 acts play 70-80min. Also books New Hope, PA location. Prefers email but may mail press kit to: 287 S Main St., Ste. 16, Lambertville, NJ 08530.

North

Bergen PAC
30 N Van Brunt St.
Englewood, NJ 07631
p: 201-816-8160
www.bergenpac.org
contact: Mark Green
p: 201-816-8160 x19
e: mgreen@bergenpac.org
call: M-F 9am-5pm
genres: Jazz, Rock, R&B, Pop, Americana, Latin, Children's
advance: 2-4 months
capacity: 1367
pa: Yes **sound eng:** Yes
stage: 33 x 28
Just outside NYC & features 1-2 Local & indie openers & 1 estab. major act for all ages shows. CD press kit preferred; accepts EPKs if small.

Cornerstone
84 Broadway
Hillsdale, NJ 07642
p: 201-666-8688
e: info@thecornerstonenj.com
www.thecornerstonenj.com
contact: George Manousos
genres: Solo Acoustic
advance: 1-2 months
capacity: 100 **stage:** floor space
Formerly Bourbon St. Saloon, club presents Local & Reg'l solo Acoustic acts Fri-Sat for 21+. 1 act plays 3hrs for flat fee. Snail mail kit.

The Cup
1410 E Elizabeth Ave.
Linden, NJ 07036
e: webmaster@cupcomplex.com
www.cupcomplex.com
contact: Dan
genres: Alt., Loud Rock
advance: 6-8 weeks
capacity: 250
pa: Yes **sound eng:** Yes
stage: 15 x 15
Bi-level ent. complex books Reg'l bands Fri-Sat; 3 acts play 45min sets. No all ages shows. Snail mail kit; no calls.

Dingbatz
620 Van Houten Ave.
Clifton, NJ 07013

p: 973-471-1145
e: info@dingbatznj.com
www.dingbatznj.com
contact: Donna Mae
call: prefers MySpace
genres: Rock, Alt., Punk, Metal, Indie Rock
advance: 2 months
pa: Yes **sound eng:** Yes
open mics: Wed
Rock dive books 2-5 original Local-Touring bands 3-4 nites for 21+; some Sun all ages matinees. Openers play 30min & headliners 1hr. Must stay the entire nite to get paid. Contact via MySpace.

Fitzgerald's Harp'n Bard
363 Lakeview Ave.
Clifton, NJ 07011
p: 973-772-7282
www.myspace.com/fitzgeraldsharpnbard
contact: Melissa
genres: All Styles
advance: 2 months
capacity: 120
pa: Yes
Irish pourhouse hosts Local-Int'l acts Thu-Sat for 21+. 1 band plays 3 sets from 9pm-1am for flat fee. Mail press kit to venue.

The Goldhawk
936 Park Ave.
Hoboken, NJ 07030
p: 201-420-7989
e: info@thegoldhawk.com
www.thegoldhawk.com
contact: Fran Azzarto
e: thepeoplesopenmic@yahoo.com
genres: Folk, S/S, Jazz
capacity: 80
pa: Yes **sound eng:** Yes
stage: 8 x 4
open mics: Tue
Original music room books pro Local & Touring acts 3-5 nites. 1-2 acts play 2hrs for % of door. No full drum kits. Email for booking; no unsolicited mail.

Loop Lounge
373 Broadway
Passaic, NJ 07055
p: 973-365-0807
www.thelooplounge.com
contact: Matt Giaquinto
e: matt@thelooplounge.com
genres: All Styles
advance: 2+ months
capacity: 250
pa: Yes **sound eng:** Yes
stage: 16 x 12 **in-house:** Drums
21+ dance club w/ 2 just outside NYC up & coming Reg'l & Touring bands Fri for % of door. Up to 5 original acts play 30+min sets. Bring cymbals, snare & foot pedal for in-house drum kit. Prefers EPK, but may mail press kit to venue.

Mainstage
222 Wanaque Ave.
Pompton Lakes, NJ 07444
e: mainstagenj@hotmail.com
www.myspace.com/mainstagenj
genres: Rock, Metal, Hardcore, Punk, Emo, Indie
advance: 1-2 months
pa: Yes **sound eng:** Yes
All ages Rock venue w/ strong scene books original Local-Int'l bands 5-6 nites. Sets are 45min.

Maxwell's
1039 Washington St.
Hoboken, NJ 07030
p: 201-653-1703
www.maxwellsnj.com
contact: Todd Abramson
e: telstarrec@aol.com
genres: Rock, Country, Alt., Folk
advance: 1-2 months
capacity: 200
pa: Yes **sound eng:** Yes
Famed music showcase draws hip NYC crowd & their Jersey cousins for polished Local-Int'l acts 4-5 nites; some all ages shows. Up to 4 acts on a bill. Email or mail submission to venue & allow 1 mo. for demo review.

Mexicali Live
1409 Queen Anne Rd.
Teaneck, NJ 07666
p: 201-833-0011
e: mexicalilive@hotmail.com
www.mexicalilive.com
contact: Rob Ortiz
p: 908-876-3884
e: rob@createavibe.com
genres: Most Styles
advance: 2+ months
capacity: 300
pa: Yes **sound eng:** Yes
stage: 12 x 20
Formerly Mexicali Blues Cafe, this indie-friendly 18+ club w/ top notch sound & good eats, hosts original Local-Int'l acts 2-5 nites. No Punk or Metal. Contact bookings@createavibe.com.

NJPAC
1 Center St.
Newark, NJ 07102
p: 973-642-8989
e: production@njpac.org
www.njpac.org
contact: Evan White
p: 973-297-5803
e: ewhite@njpac.org
genres: Rock, World, S/S, Reggae, Jazz, Classical, Pop, Dance, Hip-Hop, R&B
advance: 6-24 months
capacity: 250; 514; 2750
pa: Yes **sound eng:** Yes
Hi-tech all ages venue w/ multiple performance areas features 1-2 known original Touring acts playing 90-120min for flat fee. Local acts can apply online for 'Chase Sounds of the City' on Thu which features free shows in the theater square from Jul-Sep. New bands email performance schedules for consideration. No unsolicited mail or calls; no booking via MySpace.

Orphan Annie's
1255 Valley Rd.
Stirling, NJ 07980
p: 908-647-0138
e: oannies99@aol.com
www.oannies.com
contact: Rick Romano
p: 908-772-5526
genres: Rock, Blues, Alt., R&B
advance: 6-8 weeks
capacity: 150 **stage:** 12 x 20
Party bar w/ mixed crowd books mostly original Local-Int'l acts 5 nites, cover bands monthly. Bands must be 21+. Snail mail kit w/ ATTN: Rick Romana or audition in Sun Open Jam.

Outpost in the Burbs
40 S Fullerton Ave.
Montclair, NJ 07042
p: 973-744-6560
e: stevecutaia@outpostintheburbs.org
www.outpostintheburbs.org
contact: Steve Cutaia
e: outpostconcerts@outpostintheburbs.org
genres: Americana, World, Folk, Bluegrass, Blues, S/S
advance: 2-6 months
capacity: 250; 700; 1500
pa: Yes **sound eng:** Yes
Non-profit community org 12mi W of NYC, hosts estab. & rising talent 20-24 nites/yr at 3 venues for mature, attentive audiences. Opener plays 20min, headliner gets 90min. Payment is flat fee; headliner also gets % of door. Merch splits 90/10. Email for booking.

Sanctuary Concerts
240 Southern Blvd.
Chatham, NJ 07928
p: 973-376-4946
e: boxoffice@sanctuaryconcerts.org
www.sanctuaryconcerts.org
contact: Scott Sheldon
e: scott@sanctuaryconcerts.org
genres: Acoustic, Folk, Bluegrass, Blues, World
advance: 6-12 months
capacity: 425
stage: 30 x 20
Church concert series books original Local-Int'l acts for 2 Sat shows/mo from Sep-May. 2 bands play 45min sets for flat fee plus % of door over split point. Mail full CD (no print materials) to: 361 N Fullerton Ave., Montclair, NJ 07043.

Trumpets
6 Depot Sq.
Montclair, NJ 07042
p: 973-744-2600
e: trumpets@verizon.net
www.trumpetsjazz.com
contact: Enrico Granafei
e: enrimus@aol.com
genres: Jazz
advance: 2 months
capacity: 128
stage: 20 x 10 **in-house:** Piano
Jazz supperclub showcases rising talent & top recording artists Tue-Sun. Featured act performs 3 sets for all ages. Mail promos w/ ATTN: Enrico, Trumpets, PO Box 1561, Montclair, NJ 07042.

Van Gogh's Ear
1017 Stuyvesant Ave.
Union, NJ 07083
p: 908-810-1844
www.vangoghsearcafe.com
contact: Sarah Perara
e: sarahvangogh@yahoo.com
genres: Acoustic, Jazz, Blues
advance: 1-2 months
capacity: 70
pa: Yes **stage:** floor space
open mics: 1st & 3rd Tue/mo
Artsy coffeehouse features Local-Reg'l acts Sun & Acoustic acts 1st & 3rd Tue after open mic. Acts play 1hr for tips to 18+ crowd. Email, use MySpace or send kit; will contact if interested.

The Wellmont Theatre
5 Seymour St.
Montclair, NJ 07042
e: info@bowerypresents.com
www.wellmonttheatre.com
contact: Jaime
e: jaime@bowerypresents.com
p: 212-375-1200
genres: Rock, Pop, Folk, S/S
advance: 1-8 months
capacity: 2500
Recently remodeled historic theatre 12mi W of NYC, brings top Local-Int'l acts to perform for eager all ages crowd. Prefers email for booking; no unsolicited mail.

South

Appel Farm Arts & Music Center
457 Shirley Rd.
Elmer, NJ 08318
p: 856-358-2472
www.appelfarm.org
contact: Sean Timmons
p: 856-358-2472 x111
e: perform@appelfarm.org
genres: Pop, Rock, Folk, Blues, Country
advance: 3-12 months
capacity: 50; 240; 2400; 10,000 (festival)
pa: Yes **sound eng:** Yes
stage: 3 stages
Multi-level, all ages music ctr. open Oct-June. Mostly Nat'ls play theatre & annual fest; Locals open or play gallery. Send promos: PO Box 888, Elmer, NJ 08318.

Buckalew's
101 N Bay Ave.
Beach Haven, NJ 08008
p: 609-492-1065
e: buckalews@comcast.net
www.buckalews.com
contact: Allan Menegus
p: 609-292-1065 x101
call: Tue-Sat noon-5pm
genres: All Styles
advance: 6 months
capacity: 260; **stage:** floor space
Landmark 21+ tavern hosts developing & polished Local-Reg'l acts & a few Nat'ls nitely in summer; 2 nites off-season; mostly cover bands. 1 act plays for 4hrs w/ breaks. Contact before sending materials.

The Captain's Inn
307 E Lacey Rd.
Forked River, NJ 08731
p: 609-693-2210
www.myspace.com/captainsinntikibar
contact: Alex
call: M-F after 5pm
genres: Rock, Pop, Blues, Folk, S/S, Acoustic, Reggae, New Country
capacity: 300
pa: Yes
Bar hosts 2 Local/Reg'l acts Fri-Sun from Memorial Day to Labor Day & 1 Local/Reg'l act Thu-Fri & Sun in off-season. Acts are paid a flat fee & perform for all ages. Mail press kit to venue.

New Mexico

Albuquerque

Atomic Cantina
315 Gold Ave. SW
Albuquerque, NM 87102
p: 505-242-2200
e: booking@atomiccantina.com
www.atomiccantina.com
contact: Leonard

e: atomiccantina@hotmail.com
genres: Punk, Rock, Indie Rock, Alt., Rockabilly, Swing
advance: 2 months
capacity: 166
pa: Yes **sound eng:** Yes
stage: 10 x 18
Laid back bar books 3-4 original Local & Touring bands for 30-45min sets up to 6 nites. All band members must be 21+. Email links or EPKs.

Caravan East
7605 Central Ave. NE
Albuquerque, NM 87108
p: 505-265-6994
www.caravaneast.com
contact: Charlie Walton
e: ctokool@aol.com
call: M-F evenings
genres: Country
advance: 6-8 weeks
capacity: 800
pa: Yes **sound eng:** Yes
stage: large
Prime Country niteclub books Local-Int'l acts Tue-Sun. 2 bands fill 5hrs w/ original music for flat fee to 21+. Mail promos to club.

Cowboys
9800-4 Montgomery Blvd. NE
Albuquerque, NM 87111
p: 505-299-4559
e: cowboys1@cowboysabq.com
www.cowboysabq.com
contact: Ron Cowdrey
call: Tue-Fri noon-5pm
genres: Country
advance: 6 months
capacity: 560
pa: Yes **sound eng:** Yes
stage: 17 x 36
Roadhouse presents Local & Touring acts Thu-Sat for 21+. 1-2 original bands play for flat fee & % of door. Email or call; No EPKs.

El Rey Theater/ Puccini's Golden West Saloon
620-624 Central Ave. SW
Albuquerque, NM 87102
p: 505-242-2353
e: elreytheater@qwestoffice.net
www.elreytheater.com
contact: Mark Frederick/ Mike Fleming
genres: Alt., Rock, Metal, Reggae, Blues, Punk
advance: 2 months
capacity: 700 (theater)
pa: To rent **sound eng:** Yes
stage: large
The saloon has burned to the ground & is currently taking donations for rebuilding it. The historic theater is still open & presents 3-4 Local-Nat'l acts Fri & Sat. Bands play 30-45min sets to 21+; some all ages shows. Merch split for Nat'l acts only. Also books The Stove in Albuquerque & Santa Ana Star Ctr. Prefers email for booking, but may mail press kit to venue. No contact thru MySpace.

Launchpad
618 Central Ave. SW
Albuquerque, NM 87102
p: 505-764-8887
e: info@launchpadrocks.com
www.launchpadrocks.com
contact: Joe Anderson
e: bookinglp@gmail.com
genres: Alt., Punk, Metal, Funk, Roots
advance: 10 weeks
capacity: 300
pa: Yes **sound eng:** Yes
stage: 20 x 20
Prime venue books original Local-Nat'l acts nitely; some all ages shows. 3 bands play 40min sets. Merch split is 90/10. Also owns Sunshine Theater. Prefers email, but may snail mail kit. No calls.

Outpost Performance Space
210 Yale Blvd. SE
Albuquerque, NM 87106
p: 505-268-0044
e: mail@outpostspace.org
www.outpostspace.org
contact: Tom Guralnick
genres: Jazz, Acoustic, World, Experimental, Folk, Blues, Americana
advance: Up to 6 months
capacity: 175
pa: Yes **sound eng:** Yes
All ages non-profit ctr. books Local-Int'l acts 3 nites for 45min sets & flat fee. Mail full kits to: PO Box 4543, Albuquerque, NM 87196.

Santa Fe

The Adobe Bar at Taos Inn
125 Paseo Del Pueblo Sur
Taos, NM 87571
p: 575-758-2233
www.taosinn.com/adobe_bar.html
contact: Nic Knight
p: 575-758-2233 x191
e: entertainment@taosinn.com
call: Sat-Tue 4-11pm
genres: Jazz, Flamenco, Blues, Bluegrass, Americana, Folk, Rock, World
capacity: 100 **stage:** 8 x 10
open mics: Mon 6:45pm
Prime spot in historic Inn 69mi from Santa Fe, features a polished Local-Touring act nitely for all ages. 1 act perform 2 original 90min sets for flat fee. Email for booking; No requests via MySpace.

Cowgirl Bar & Grill
319 S Guadalupe
Santa Fe, NM 87501
p: 505-982-2565
e: cowgirlbbq@comcast.net
www.cowgirlsantafe.com
contact: Christina Aguilar
call: Mon-Thu 9-11am
genres: Americana, Alt. Country, Blues, Bluegrass
advance: 2 months
capacity: 75-100
pa: Yes
stage: floor space
Eatery popular w/ locals, tourists & press, features Local & Touring acts Wed-Sun for 21+; Nat'ls on outdoor stage in spring/summer; DJs on Tue. Single original act plays three 1hr sets or two 90min sets from 9:30pm-1am w/ breaks. Email or mail press kit to venue.

El Farol
808 Canyon Rd.
Santa Fe, NM 87501
p: 505-983-9912
www.elfarolsf.com
contact: Stephen Jacobs
e: steve@elfarolsf.com
genres: Latin Fusion, Latin, Latin Jazz, Blues, R&B
advance: 2 months
capacity: 85; **stage:** 6 x 12; 4 x 6
Cantina w/ 2 stages & walk-in crowd in summer, offers original Local-Reg'l acts Fri-Sat. Featured act plays three 1hr sets for flat fee or the door. 21+ after 10pm. Snail mail or email kit.

El Paseo Bar & Grill
208 Galisteo St.
Santa Fe, NM 87501
p: 505-992-2848
www.elpaseobar.com
contact: Matt Chavez
p: 505-992-0281
e: coldestbeer@hotmail.com
genres: Jazz, Blues, Bluegrass, Rock, Reggae, Latin
advance: 3 months
capacity: 100
pa: Yes **stage:** 10 x 12
open mics: Tue
Area hot spot dishes up original Reg'l & Touring artists Fri-Sat for the door; featured act plays two 90min sets. Call for booking.

Santa Fe Brewing Co. Pub & Grill
35 Fire Pl.
Santa Fe, NM 87508
p: 505-424-9637
e: pubandgrillsfbc@aol.com
www.santafebrewing.com
contact: Justin Young
p: 505-660-9600
e: justin@santafebrewing.com
genres: Rock, Blues, Country-Western, Reggae, Alt., Roots, World Beat, Jazz
capacity: 300; 700 (outdoors)
pa: Yes **sound eng:** Yes
stage: 16 x 24
Free Reg'ls & a few ticketed shows w/ Touring acts 5 nites on 2 stages. Mail kit to: 3957 Agua Fria St., Santa Fe, NM 87507; follow up w/ email.

Second Street Brewery
1814 2nd St.
Santa Fe, NM 87505
p: 505-982-3030
e: info@secondstreetbrewery.com
www.secondstreetbrewery.com
contact: Tom
call: M-F noon-6pm
genres: Blues, Rock, Folk, S/S, Pop, Jazz
advance: 2-3 months
capacity: 90; **stage:** floor space
All ages brewpub books Local-Nat'l acts Wed-Sat for three 1hr sets. 1-2 acts play for flat fee. Mail press kit to venue.

New York

Buffalo

Broadway Joe's
3051 Main St.
Buffalo, NY 14214
p: 716-837-3650
www.bjoes.com
contact: Sam
e: sam@bjoes.com
call: Mon-Wed 10am-2pm
genres: Rock, Indie, Metal, Hip-Hop, Jam, Reggae, Jazz
advance: 6-8 weeks
capacity: 250
pa: To rent **sound eng:** To hire
stage: 15 x 12
open mics: Tue **sign in:** 9pm
Music club near SUNY campus, books up to 4 Local-Int'l acts & DJs up to 6 nites to 18+ crowd. Prefers email, or snail mail kit.

Lafayette Tap Room
391 Washington St.
Buffalo, NY 14203
p: 716-854-2466
www.lafayettetaproombbq.com
contact: Mark
p: 716-852-3730
e: marc@lafayettetaproombbq.com
genres: Blues, Western
advance: 1-2 months
capacity: 300-400
pa: Yes **sound eng:** Yes
stage: 16 x 12; 12 x 12
Blues haven now under new mgmt., books 1-2 top-notch Reg'l & Touring artists Wed-Sat; some Sun matinees & few all ages shows. Sponsors Washington St. Blues Fest in Jun & has state-of-the-art recording studio. Prefers mailed hard copies to venue.

Merlin's
727 Elmwood Ave.
Buffalo, NY 14222
p: 716-886-9270
e: merlinsbooking@gmail.com
www.merlinsbuffalo.com
contact: Curt Rotterdam
p: 716-602-2464
genres: Rock, Alt.
advance: 3-4 weeks
capacity: 100
pa: Yes **sound eng:** Yes
stage: 25 x 15
Dive/sports bar books original Local bands Thu-Sat for % of door. 3 acts play 45min to mostly older 21+ crowd; bands must be 21+. Touring acts must have 2 Local openers. Also helps book Nietzsche's in Buffalo & The Buffalo Infringement Fest. Promos: 574 Bird Ave., Apt. 2, Buffalo, NY 14222. No booking via Myspace.

Mohawk Place
47 E Mohawk St.
Buffalo, NY 14203
p: 716-855-3931
www.mohawkplace.com
contact: Bill Nehill
e: garofalo12@aol.com
genres: Punk, Indie Rock, Alt. Country, Experimental, Garage, Funk, Blues
advance: 3-4 months
capacity: 250
pa: Yes **sound eng:** Yes
stage: 20 x 12
Area's top indie music bar draws eclectic 18+ crowd of music lovers & Local-Touring buzz bands 3-7 nites. 3 acts play 1hr of original tunes for % of door; sometimes flat fee. Mail press kit to venue.

Nietzsche's
248 Allen St.
Buffalo, NY 14201
p: 716-886-8539
www.nietzsches.com
contact: Joe Rubino
call: Mon-Thu 1-4pm
genres: Alt., Reggae, Jazz, Americana, S/S
capacity: 300
pa: Yes **sound eng:** Yes
stage: 2 stages **in-house:** Piano
open mics: Mon 10pm S/S

Venerable 21+ hotspot & launching pad presents mostly original Reg'ls & Nat'ls nitely on 2 stages. Up to 6 acts play for % of door. Calls preferred, but may mail press kit to venue w/ ATTN: Nietzsche's Booking.

Pearl Street
76 Pearl St.
Buffalo, NY 14202
p: 716-856-2337
www.pearlstreetgrill.com
contact: Roy Bakos
e: royb@pearlstreetgrill.com
call: anytime
genres: Rock, R&B, Jazz, Blues, Zydeco, Reggae, World Beat
advance: 2+ months
capacity: 500
stage: 28 x 14; 60 x 20 (upstairs)
Brewpub hosts bands & DJs in basement cellar on Fri & Sat; few all ages shows. Mail press kit to venue w/ ATTN: Roy or Bill; or use email for booking.

Roxy's
884 Main St.
Buffalo, NY 14202
p: 716-885-3464
e: roxysgirlsrock@aol.com
www.myspace.com/roxysbuffalo
contact: Julia
genres: Indie, Rock, Dance
pa: Yes **sound eng:** Yes
Busy gay/lesbian bar hosts DJs, indie musicians & occasional mega-Rock stars.

Spot Coffee
227 Delaware Ave.
Buffalo, NY 14202
p: 716-332-2299
e: spottalk@spotcoffee.com
www.spotcoffee.com
contact: Ted
e: tgetman@spotcoffee.com
genres: All Styles
advance: 1-2 months
capacity: 150 **stage:** 15 x 10
2-room java joint puts Local musicians on stage. 1 act plays 45min-3hrs Thu for $50. Prefers email, but may call or mail press kit to venue. 2nd location at 765 Elmwood (716-332-4564) plans on hosting music in early '09.

Capital District

Bayou Cafe
79 N Pearl St.
Albany, NY 12207
p: 518-462-9033
www.bayoucafe.com
contact: Ralph
e: rspill@bayoucafe.com
call: evenings
genres: Rock, Blues, Jazz, Zydeco
pa: Yes **sound eng:** Yes
open mics: Wed **sign in:** 9pm
Hip nitespot hosts Local-Reg'l acts & DJs Fri-Sat. Bring press kit in person to Wed Open Mic.

Caffé Lena
47 Phila St., PO Box 245
Saratoga Springs, NY 12866
p: 518-583-0022
www.caffelena.org
contact: Sarah Craig
e: sarah@caffelena.org
call: Tue-Thu 9am-5pm
genres: Folk, Americana, Jazz, S/S, Roots
advance: 5-6 months
capacity: 85
pa: Yes **sound eng:** Yes
stage: 10 x 10 **in-house:** Piano
open mics: Thu **sign in:** 7pm
Famed all ages Acoustic room hosts rising talent & estab. recording acts Wed-Sun. Featured act plays two 45min sets of original material for % of door. Prefers email; read booking info on website first.

Gaffney's
16 Caroline St.
Saratoga Springs, NY 12866
p: 518-587-7359
e: crazybake@earthlink.net
www.gaffneysrestaurant.com
contact: Arthur Gonick
e: arthursound1@earthlink.net
call: email only
genres: Acoustic, S/S
advance: 1 year
pa: Yes
open mics: Tue **sign in:** 9pm
Casual eatery 30+mi from Albany, presents 1-3 Local-Reg'l Acoustic acts Thu-Sat for flat fee; seasonal shows Wed & Sun. Hosts S/S Series on Thu. Prefers email for booking; no calls.

Northern Lights
1208 Rte.
146 N Country Commons
Clifton Park, NY 12065
p: 518-371-0012
www.northernlightslive.com
contact: J. Kip Finck
e: kip@northernlightslive.com
call: M-F noon-6pm
genres: Rock, Alt., Country, Jam, Reggae, Folk, Metal
advance: 3-6 months
capacity: 1000
pa: Yes **sound eng:** Yes
stage: 30 x 19
Nestled in a strip mall, this prime 2-stage Rock club w/ clean sight lines, presents polished indie acts & top shelf Nat'ls 3-6 nites. Mostly 16+ & all ages w/ guardian; some 21+. Merch splits 80/20 for Nat'ls. Prefers email or call first.

Tess's Lark Tavern
453 Madison Ave.
Albany, NY 12210
p: 518-463-9779
e: larktavern@gmail.com
www.larktavern.com
contact: Alex
call: M-F 10am-2pm
genres: Funk, Reggae, Soul, Hip-Hop, Jam, Rock, Jazz, Blues, Latin, Indie
open mics: Wed 8pm
Bar/eatery w/ eclectic patronage books 1 Local-Reg'l act Mon & Fri-Sat. Email or call for booking.

Valentine's
17 New Scotland Ave.
Albany, NY 12208
p: 518-432-6572
e: howard@valentinesalbany.com
www.valentinesalbany.com
contact: Howard Glassman
e: kranepoop@aol.com
call: Fri 1-5pm
genres: Rock, Alt., Punk, Hardcore, Country, Jam, S/S
advance: 6 weeks
capacity: 120; 250
pa: Yes **sound eng:** Yes
stage: 10 x 20; 20 x 40 (upstairs)
Music club presents original Local-Nat'l bands on 2 stages for 18+. Up to 5 acts play 30-90min for the door. Touring acts hook up w/ Locals to be considered. Email or call before 5pm; No booking thru mail or MySpace.

Hudson Valley

The Back Door
58 Depew Ave.
Nyack, NY 10960
p: 845-358-2600
e: backdoorcafe@gmail.com
www.backdoorcafe.org
contact: Ed Willock
p: 845-596-6553
genres: All Styles
advance: 2 months
capacity: 400
pa: Yes **sound eng:** Yes
stage: 24 x 18
Cultural space geared toward teens, books original Local-Reg'l acts for all ages. 5 acts play 25min for % of door. Absolutely no alcohol or profanity. Shows on 2nd & last Fri/mo. Bands are selected on 1st come, 1st serve basis. Fill out online form or attend meeting on Tue 7pm.

Cabaloosa
58 Main St.
New Paltz, NY 12561
p: 845-255-3400
www.cabaloosa.com
contact: Mike
e: cabaloosabookings@cabaloosa.com
genres: Acoustic, Jazz, Rock, Alt.
advance: 2 months
capacity: 100-250
pa: Avail. to rent **stage:** small
18+ bar located below Oasis Cafe in small ent. complex, hosts mostly Reg'l bands Sat. 1-4 bands fill 10pm-3am for % of door. Snail mail kit or send email.

The Chance Theater
6 Crannell St.
Poughkeepsie, NY 12601
p: 845-471-2490
e: info@thechancetheater.com
www.thechancetheater.com
contact: Abby Puka
p: 845-471-1966
e: chancecomplex@aol.com
call: M-F noon-5pm
genres: Rock, Hip-Hop, Reggae, Metal, Punk, Alt.
advance: 2-5 months
capacity: 748
pa: Yes **sound eng:** Yes
stage: 20 x 30
Premier music venue hosts 5-7 live acts & DJs 2-3 nites for 16+ crowd; w/ adult if underage. Locals play 30min & keep $2/tix. Headliners play 1-2hrs. All new bands must attend Music Industry Nite, usu. held once/mo.; bring press kit & 2 copies of demo. No unsolicited mail.

Cubbyhole Coffee House
44 Raymond Ave.
Poughkeepsie, NY 12603
p: 845-483-7584
contact: Lee Brown
call: M-F 6pm-midnite
genres: Folk, Acoustic, Rock
open mics: Tue Acoustic 8:30pm
Cozy spot near Vassar College puts Local-Nat'l acts on small stage.

Oasis Cafe
58 Main St.
New Paltz, NY 12561
p: 845-255-2400
www.cabaloosa.com
contact: Matt
e: oasisbookings@hotmail.com
call: Mon before 2pm
genres: Most Styles
advance: 2 months
capacity: 100
open mics: Wed
Stage in small upstate ent. complex, hosts mostly Reg'l bands Thu-Sat for 21+. 1-2 original acts play three 1hr sets for % of door. Also books for 18+ venue, Cabaloosa, also in complex. No Loud acts. Prefers email; No booking thru MySpace.

Rosendale Cafe
434 Main St.
Rosendale, NY 12472
p: 845-658-9048
www.rosendalecafe.com
contact: Mark Morganstern
e: dorsey1156@yahoo.com
genres: Jazz, Blues, Folk, Latin, World
advance: 2 months
pa: Yes
open mics: Tue
Hosts eclectic music Sat & Sun; many Nat'ls & smaller Local names. 1 act/wknd plays for mix crowd. Use website form or mail press kit to: PO Box 436, Rosendale, NY 12472.

Tarrytown Music Hall
13 Main St.
Tarrytown, NY 10591
p: 914-631-3390
e: info@tarrytownmusichall.org
www.tarrytownmusichall.org
contact: Bjorn Olsson
p: 914-631-8390
e: bjorn@tarrytownmusichall.org
genres: All Styles
capacity: 843 **stage:** 32 x 28
Non-profit hall boasts excellent acoustics. Emerging artists may open for Nat'ls. Hosts up to 4 shows/wk. Prefers mailed press kit to: PO Box 686, Tarrytown, NY 10591.

Towne Crier Cafe
130 Rte. 22
Pawling, NY 12564
p: 845-855-1300
e: mailing@townecrier.com
www.townecrier.com
contact: Phil Ciganer
call: Fri-Sun 5pm-1am
genres: Folk, Jazz, Blues, Celtic, Bluegrass, World
advance: 3-4 months
capacity: 140
pa: Yes **sound eng:** Yes
stage: 26 x 16 (2 wedges)
open mics: Wed **sign in:** 5pm
Prestigious listening room off beaten path, pairs polished Local-Reg'l openers w/ Nat'l-Int'l headliners Wed, Fri-Sun & some other nites. Bands play two 45-50min sets for all ages w/ great sight lines. Sign up for open mic to audition for gig. No unsolicited mail, email or calls.

Turning Point
468 Piermont Ave.
Piermont, NY 10968
p: 845-359-1089
e: turning@turningpointcafe.com
www.turningpointcafe.com
contact: John McAvoy
call: Wed-Fri 10:30am-1:30pm

& evenings
genres: Rock, Jazz, Zydeco, Blues, Folk
advance: 3-4 months
capacity: 70
pa: Yes **sound eng:** Yes
stage: 18 x 10
All ages listening room presents original polished Touring talent Wed-Sun & some Mon-Tue. 1-2 mostly Acoustic acts, play w/ some Local openers.

Tuscan Café
5 South St.
Warwick, NY 10990
p: 845-987-2050
e: cafe@warwick.net
www.tuscancafe.net
contact: Brendan McManus
genres: Punk, Hardcore, Ska, Acoustic, Indie Rock, Grindcore
advance: 2 months
capacity: 65
pa: Yes **sound eng:** Yes
open mics: Thu **sign in:** 8pm
All ages coffee shop & vegetarian eatery, is nice pit stop btwn NYC & upstate that serves beer & wine has free wi-fi & vegetarian food. 5-6 acts play 30-45min on Fri & Sat for % of door. Contact via website or thru: www.myspace.com/caterwaulrecords.

Long Island

The Crazy Donkey
1058 Rte. 110
Farmingdale, NY 11735
p: 631-753-1975
e: info@thecrazydonkey.com
www.thecrazydonkey.com
e: loadedrockshows@gmail.com
genres: Rock, Country, Hip-Hop, Blues
advance: 1 month
capacity: 850
pa: Yes **sound eng:** Yes
stage: 24 x 28
All ages venue, books Local to Nat'l acts up to 7 nites. Email for booking; incl. band name, MySpace link, genre, contact name, email, phone number & ages of bands members; may also use online booking form.

Da Funky Phish
1668 Union Blvd.
Bay Shore, NY 11706
p: 631-665-8550
e: kingphish@dafunkyphish.com
www.dafunkyphish.com
contact: Craig
e: dafunkyph@aol.com
genres: Funk, Ska, Jazz, Jam, Punk, Emo, Rock
advance: 2-3 months
capacity: 200
pa: Yes **sound eng:** Yes
stage: 12 x 15
open mics: Tue **sign in:** 9pm
Jammin' club w/ quadraphonic sound, books Local & some Touring acts Wed-Sun. Sets run 45-60min w/ 2-3 acts on a bill. Call first before sending promo.

Patti & Johnny's
139 Nassau Blvd.
West Hempstead, NY 11552
p: 516-486-9543
www.myspace.com/pjs_westhempstead
contact: Barbara
genres: All Styles
advance: 1 month
capacity: 150
Bar books wide variety of Local & Reg'l acts Fri-Sat for 21+. 3 acts play 1hr for % of door. Must bring own door person. Call or email first.

Stephen Talkhouse
161 Main St.
Amagansett, NY 11930
p: 631-267-3117
e: info@stephentalkhouse.com
www.stephentalkhouse.com
contact: Peter Honerkamp
genres: Blues, Reggae, Folk, Funk, Rock, Pop, Country, Hip-Hop, Indie, Ska
advance: 3-4 months
capacity: 150
pa: Yes **sound eng:** Yes
stage: 14 x 24
Upscale listening room features top Touring artists & polished Reg'l talent nitely for 21+. 2 acts play 90min & house donates 10% of artist merch sales to charity. Email or snail mail kit.

Village Pub South
198 Broadway Ave.
Amityville, NY 11701
e: villagepubsouth@gmail.com
www.myspace.com/cookstavern44
contact: Mike Versandi
genres: Rock, Metal, Punk
advance: 2+ weeks
capacity: 150
pa: Yes **sound eng:** Yes
stage: 20 x 20 **in-house:** Backline
open mics: Tue **sign in:** 7pm
LI's unofficial home of new Rock, from popular to the esoteric, books Reg'l & Touring acts 5 nites to 16+ crowd; some all ages shows. 5-8 acts play 25-60min sets. Even mix of original & cover music. Now under new ownership & prefers booking via MySpace; may also mail kit to venue, email or call.

The Wave
380 E Main St.
Patchogue, NY 11772
p: 631-475-4315
e: thewavevenue@yahoo.com
www.myspace.com/wavevenue
contact: John Curcio, Jr./Daniel O'Brien
p: 631-664-1055
e: dobrien07881gmail.com
capacity: 100; 300 (The Oasis)
Church-run all ages venue books Local-Int'l acts. Mail press kit to venue for booking.

New York City

169 Bar
169 E Broadway
New York, NY 10002
p: 212-473-8866
www.169barnyc.com
contact: Charles
e: astrochuck@hotmail.com
genres: Acoustic, Rock, Indie, Funk, R&B, Jazz, Swing, Latin, Bluegrass, World, Bebop, Alt.
advance: 2 months for weekends; less for weekdays
capacity: 74
pa: Yes **sound eng:** Yes
stage: 15 x 15
Candlelit dive bar w/ stereo room mics & 4 cameras for A/V recording to DVD or CD. Up to 8 original acts & DJs play 30+min nitely for tips or % of door. Must use house drum kit, but may add to it; brushes or bundles preferred. Sun-Tue: must be able to draw 10+; Wed & Thu: 15+; Fri & Sat: 20+. No Hip-Hop. Read full policy on MySpace before contacting; no unsolicited mail.

55 Bar
55 Christopher St.
New York, NY 10014
p: 212-929-9883
e: contact@55bar.com
www.55bar.com
contact: Scott Ellard
e: scott@55bar.com
call: email only
genres: Jazz, Blues
advance: 2 months
capacity: 75
pa: Yes **stage:** corner area
Prohibition-era dive bar books accomplished Local-Int'l talent nitely. 2 original acts play two 1hr sets each for all ages. Mail kit or email w/ links to music.

92YTribeca
200 Hudson St.
New York, NY 10023
p: 212-601-1000
www.92y.org
contact: Jack "Skippy" McFadden
e: skippy92y@gmail.com
genres: Rock, Indie, Alt., World, Jewish
advance: 2-3 months
capacity: 350
pa: Yes **sound eng:** Yes
Secular niteclub in Jewish cultural ctr., presents polished live performances & DJs 5-6 nites. Swag splits 85/15. Email or mail press kit to venue.

ABC No Rio
156 Rivington St.
New York, NY 10002
p: 212-254-3697
e: abc@abcnorio.org
www.abcnorio.org
contact: Melanie
p: 212-254-3697 x11
e: punk@abcnorio.org
call: Wed 2-4pm
genres: Punk, Hardcore
All ages collective w/ political agenda hosts Punk/Hardcore Sat matinees & wkly improv music series. No major label, sexist, racist or homophobic acts considered. Mail in demo, lyrics & desired dates; follow up w/ phone or email 2 wks later.

Ace of Clubs
9 Great Jones St.
New York, NY 10012
p: 212-677-6963
e: aceofclubsnyc2@yahoo.com
www.aceofclubsnyc.com
contact: Bill Harris
p: 212-677-6924
e: aceofclubsnyc@yahoo.com
genres: Rock, Funk, Metal, Avant-Garde, Acoustic
advance: 1-2 months
capacity: 175
stage: 21 x 15
6 nites of original music in this streamlined 21+ venue which favors Locals but welcomes Nat'ls. 2-6 acts overseen by top soundman allowing 45-90min sets for % of door. Formerly Acme Underground. Email link to site; no attachments or kits.

Alphabet Lounge
104 Ave. C
New York, NY 10009
p: 212-780-0202
www.alphabetnyc.com
contact: Suzanne G.
p: 212-633-2024
e: alphabetloungenyc@hotmail.com
genres: Most Styles
advance: 2-3 months
capacity: 100
pa: Yes **sound eng:** Yes
Hip lounge has some bands Thu-Sat. Up to 4 acts play 40min. No Hip-Hop or Metal. Email music link & incl. NYC draw.

The Annex
152 Orchard St.
New York, NY 10002
p: 212-673-3410
e: theannexnyc@yahoo.com
www.theannexnyc.com
contact: Joady
e: joady_annex@yahoo.com
pa: Yes **sound eng:** Yes
L.E.S. venue w/ great sound system, books Local-Nat'l bands & DJs to a 21+ crowd. Bands play for 45min.

Arlene's Grocery
95 Stanton St.
New York, NY 10002
p: 212-995-1652
www.arlenesgrocery.net
contact: Julia
p: 212-358-1633
e: julia@arlenesgrocery.net
call: M-F 2-7pm
genres: Rock, Pop, Alt., Blues, Punk
advance: 2 months
capacity: 150
pa: Yes **sound eng:** Yes
stage: 19 x 15 **in-house:** Drums
Hip 21+ music club w/ top notch sound, showcases Local-Int'l acts nitely for fans & industry. 5 mostly original bands play 45min & split 80% of door. 16-track live recording avail. Email links to music or mail press kit w/ ATTN: Julia; will contact if interested.

B.B. King Blues Club & Grill (NYC)
237 W 42nd St.
New York, NY 10036
p: 212-997-4144
e: info@bbkingblues.com
www.bbkingblues.com
contact: Toffer Christensen
call: M-F 11am-7pm
genres: Blues, Rock, R&B, Hip-Hop, Reggae
advance: 1-3 months
capacity: 1000; 500 (seated)
pa: Yes **sound eng:** Yes
stage: 30 x 16
Top all ages music chain hosts notable Local-Int'l bands on 2 stages. Up to 4 acts/nite; openers play 30min, headliner 70-90. Merch splits 70/30.

Banjo Jim's
700 E 9th St.
New York, NY 10009
p: 212-777-0869
www.banjojims.com
e: booking@banjojims.com
genres: Americana, Roots, Country, Bluegrass, Jazz, Folk, S/S, World, Klezmer
advance: 1-5 months
capacity: 74

pa: Yes **sound eng:** Yes
stage: 16 x 8
in-house: Drums, Piano
open mics: Sat **sign in:** 2:30pm
One of the city's best kept secrets, this quirky music venue w/ all ages shows, has 4 original Local-Int'l acts play 1-3hrs for tips. Books primarily thru email.

Barbès
376 9th St.
Brooklyn, NY 11215
p: 718-965-9177
e: barbes@earthlink.net
www.barbesbrooklyn.com
contact: Oliver Conan
e: oconan@barbesbrooklyn.com
genres: Jazz, Latin, French, World, Blues
capacity: 60 **pa:** Yes
Live World music every nite in a modest performance space. No Rock or loud acts. Prefers email w/ music links.

Birdland
315 W 44th St.
New York, NY 10036
p: 212-581-3080
www.birdlandjazz.com
genres: Jazz
advance: 1 year
capacity: 140
pa: Yes **sound eng:** Yes
stage: large **in-house:** Yes
open mics: Mon 10pm-1am
Premier niteclub features top tier Nat'l talent nitely. Featured act will play for the wk; 2 shows: 8:30pm & 11pm. Shows are all ages & some are webcast. No unsolicited booking inquiries.

The Bitter End
147 Bleecker St.
New York, NY 10012
p: 212-673-7030
e: info@bitterend.com
www.bitterend.com
contact: Ken Gorka
call: Mon-Thu 2-5pm
genres: All Styles
advance: 8 weeks
capacity: 217
pa: Yes **sound eng:** Yes
stage: 24 x 18
Legendary 18+ listening room showcases gifted Local-Int'l performers nitely; some all ages shows. Up to 6 mostly original acts play 45-50min for door. Some shows webcast.

Black Betty
366 Metropolitan Ave.
Brooklyn, NY 11211
p: 718-599-0243
www.blackbetty.net
contact: Bud
e: budrico@hotmail.com
genres: Most Styles
advance: 2 months
capacity: 100
pa: Yes **stage:** small
Local-Touring bands & DJs play 3 nites/wk; some Nat'l acts. 1-2 acts play two 40min sets for 21+ crowd. No Hip-Hop.

Blue Note
131 W 3rd St.
New York, NY 10012
p: 212-475-8592
e: club@bluenote.net
www.bluenote.net
contact: Christian
p: 212-475-0049
e: christian@bluenote.net
call: M-F 11am-7pm
genres: Jazz
advance: 3 months
capacity: 250
pa: Yes **sound eng:** Yes
Legendary club books 1-2 estab. artists Tue-Sun. Rising stars gig Mon; all ages shows. Merch splits 70/30. No unsolicited mail.

Bowery Ballroom
6 Delancey St.
New York, NY 10002
p: 212-533-2111
e: info@boweryballroom.com
www.boweryballroom.com
contact: Johnny Beach
p: 212-260-4700
genres: All Styles
advance: 2 months
capacity: 575
pa: Yes **sound eng:** Yes
stage: large
Prime mid-sized venue provides great sound & sight lines. 2-5 cutting edge & estab. musicians & DJs play 6 nites. Opener plays 45min, headliner 90. Some 16+, 18+ & 21+ shows. Promos: 156 Ludlow St., 5th Fl., New York, NY 10002; no calls or emails.

Canal Room
285 W Broadway
New York, NY 10013
p: 212-941-8100
e: info@canalroom.com
www.canalroom.com
contact: Sheryl Witlen
e: booking@canalroom.com
genres: All Styles
advance: 3 months
capacity: 450
pa: Yes **sound eng:** Yes
stage: 10 x 20
Posh 21+ lounge is prime spot for music industry showcases, record release parties, etc. Boasts top of the line sound & lighting. 3 Local-Int'l acts & DJs play 45min. Prefers email; call if necessary.

Central Park Summerstage
830 5th Ave.
New York, NY 10021
p: 212-360-2777
e: info@summerstage.org
www.summerstage.org
contact: Erika Elliott
e: talent@summerstage.org
genres: All Styles
capacity: 4000
pa: Yes **sound eng:** Yes
All ages summer music series at Rumsey Playfield, pairs polished Reg'ls w/ estab. Touring talent. Accepts promos Nov-Jan; send w/ ATTN: Programming.

Cornelia St. Cafe
29 Cornelia St.
New York, NY 10014
p: 212-989-9319
e: info@corneliastreetcafe.com
www.corneliastreetcafe.com
contact: Poul Weis
e: music@corneliastreetcafe.com; music_corneliastcafe@yahoo.com
genres: Jazz, S/S, Ethnic
advance: 2-3 months
capacity: 50-60
pa: Yes **sound eng:** Yes
stage: 10 x 8
Prime listening room features original Local-Int'l talent nitely. 3 acts play 75min for all ages. Email EPK or link to website or MySpace. 'Songwriter's Beat' is 3rd Wed/mo & hosted by Valerie Ghent: email songwriter@corneliastreetcafe.com or mail promos to PO Box 20086, West Village Sta., NYC NY 10014.

Crash Mansion
199 Bowery
New York, NY 10002
p: 212-982-0740
e: info@crashmansion.com
www.crashmansion.com
contact: Andrew Gerardi
e: booking@crashmansion.com
call: M-F 11am-6pm
genres: Rock, Pop, R&B, Punk, Hardcore, Alt., Jazz
advance: 4-6 weeks
capacity: 500
pa: Yes **sound eng:** Yes
stage: 15 x 9
Spacious music club w/ unexpected intimacy, presents estab. & rising Local-Nat'l acts nitely for 21+. Up to 5 original bands play 45+min for % of door. Email links, w/ 6 mo. NY gig history & bio; no calls.

Cutting Room
19 W 24th St.
New York, NY 10010
p: 212-691-1900
e: thecuttingroomcontact@gmail.com
www.thecuttingroomnyc.com
contact: Peter Abraham
p: 212-691-7775
e: cuttingroompeter@gmail.com
call: M-F 1-6pm
genres: Jazz, Rock, S/S, Pop, Blues
advance: 2-3 months
capacity: 100; 250 w/o seats
pa: Yes **sound eng:** Yes
stage: 17 x 22 **in-house:** Backline
Hip music room showcases estab. & new talent 5 nites for 60% of door. 3-5 Reg'l & Touring acts play 40-60min for all ages. Mail press kit to venue or call; allow 1 mo for review.

The Delancey
168 Delancey St.
New York, NY 10002
p: 212-254-9920
e: georgie_seville@yahoo.com
www.thedelancey.com
e: delanceybooking@gmail.com
call: M-F afternoons
genres: Rock, Indie Rock
capacity: 200
pa: Yes **sound eng:** Yes
in-house: Backline, Drums
3-level club hosts 3-4 Local-Nat'l bands downstairs to 21+ crowd; DJs on the main floor. Email for all booking.

Dinosaur Bar-B-Que
646 W 131st St.
New York, NY 10027
p: 212-694-1777
e: dino@dinosaurbarbque.com
www.dinosaurbarbque.com
contact: Jason Rosen
e: dinosaurbbqbooking@yahoo.com
genres: Soul, Funk, Blues
advance: 3 months
capacity: 150 **pa:** Yes
stage: floor space
Chain w/ Local-Reg'l music Fri & Sat at 10pm. Featured act fills 3hrs for flat fee to all ages. Other locations in Rochester & Syracuse. Snail mail kit or use email.

Don Hill's
511 Greenwich St.
New York, NY 10013
p: 212-219-2850
e: info@donhills.com
www.donhills.com
contact: Nicki Camp
p: 212-539-3694
e: nickicamp@hotmail.com
call: M-F 2-5pm
genres: Metal, Dance, Rock, Hip-Hop, Reggae
advance: 6 weeks
capacity: 299
pa: Yes **sound eng:** Yes
stage: 22 x 17 **in-house:** Backline
Original Rock showcase presents Local-Int'l bands nitely for % of door; some DJs spin; Must draw 30+. Send EPK or snail mail.

Duplex
61 Christopher St.
New York, NY 10014
p: 212-255-5438
www.theduplex.com
contact: Thomas Honeck
p: 212-989-3015
e: thomas@theduplex.com
call: M-F midday
genres: S/S
advance: 1 month
capacity: 70
pa: Yes **sound eng:** Yes
stage: 13 x 16
open mics: Nitely Singers 9pm-4am; Fri-Sat Late Nite
2-3 shows nitely in upstairs cabaret room; 2nd piano bar strictly for show tunes entitled "Mostly Sondheim" every Fri. Acts are paid % of door. Email or snail mail kit; No in-person solicitations or calls.

Enzo's Jazz At The Jolly Hotel Madison Towers
22 E 38th St.
New York, NY 10016
p: 212-802-0600
e: enzoc@worldnet.att.net
www.jollymadison.com/amenities_enzo.htm
contact: Enzo Capua
call: No calls
genres: Jazz, Blues, Soul - Singers only
advance: 3 months
capacity: 50
pa: Yes **stage:** floor space
Offers creme de la creme of the Jazz world w/ a rare opp. to catch world-class Touring artists in intimate setting. Sets are 8pm & 9:30pm on Wed & Fri. Featured act plays for flat fee. Email first describing your music style & career.

Europa
98 Meserole Ave.
Brooklyn, NY 11222
p: 718-383-5723
e: europa@europaclub.com
www.europaclub.com
contact: Scott Long
e: booking@europaclub.com
advance: 2-3 months
capacity: 550
pa: Yes
in-house: Drums
Polish venue w/ decent lighting & focus on original indie music; some all ages nites. Experienced bookers keep this club hoppin'. Email EPK for booking.

Fillmore New York at Irving Plaza
17 Irving Pl.
New York, NY 10003
p: 212-777-6817
e: info@irvingplaza.com
www.irvingplaza.com
contact: Sean McDonough
p: 917-421-5156
e: seanmcdonough@livenation.com
genres: All Styles
advance: 2-3 months
capacity: 1000
pa: Yes **sound eng:** Yes
stage: large
Nat'l & developing acts w/ draw fill opening slots at top 16+ concert venue; some DJs booked. Also books Blender Theater. EPKs or promos: 220 W 42nd St., 11th Fl., New York, NY 10036.

Fontana's
105 Eldridge St.
New York, NY 10002
p: 212-334-6740
www.fontanasnyc.com
contact: Deannie
e: bandsatfontanas@yahoo.com
genres: All Styles, mainly Rock
advance: 2 months
pa: Yes **sound eng:** Yes
stage: 10 x 15
Cavernous subterranean bar w/ cool vibe, presents mostly original Local-Int'l acts & DJs. 3-5 bands plays 45min to 21+ crowd. Prefers email or contact thru MySpace; no calls.

Galapagos Art Space
16 Main St.
Brooklyn, NY 11201
p: 718-222-8500
e: info@galapagosartspace.com
www.galapagosartspace.com
p: 718-384-4586
e: booking@galapagosartspace.com
genres: Indie, Hip-Hop, Rock, Dance, Acoustic, Jazz, World
advance: 2 months
pa: Yes **sound eng:** Yes
Recently relocated to DUMBO section, but still books eclectic acts Tue-Sun w/ emphasis on Local talent. 4 original acts play 45-60min for 60% of door. Prefers email or snail mail.

Garage
99 7th Ave. S
New York, NY 10014
p: 212-645-0600
e: charlie@garagerest.com
www.garagerest.com
contact: David Coss
e: garagebooking@aol.com
call: email only
genres: Jazz, Blues
advance: 6 months
capacity: 200+
pa: Yes **stage:** 10 x 8
Eatery presents 2 live Jazz shows every nite; payment is in tips. Use email for booking.

Gizzi's Cafe
16 W 8th St.
New York, NY 10011
p: 212-260-9700
e: info@gizzisny.com
www.gizzisny.com
contact: Mike McHugh
e: newcenturybooking@yahoo.com
call: No calls
genres: Acoustic, Jazz, S/S, Folk, Country, Bluegrass, R&B
advance: 6-8 weeks
capacity: 35
pa: Yes **stage:** small
open mics: Thu **sign in:** 7pm
Books Local Acoustic acts Wed & wknds for all ages. 3 acts play 45min for tips. Stage can hold trios or less. Also does booking for a new venue, The Nat'l Underground & some booking for other larger NYC venues. Snail mail kit; no calls.

Groove
125 MacDougal St.
New York, NY 10012
p: 212-254-9393
e: info@clubgroovenyc.com
www.clubgroovenyc.com
contact: Rich Brownstein
e: rich@clubgroovenyc.com
genres: R&B, Soul, Funk
advance: 6 weeks
capacity: 150
pa: Yes **sound eng:** Yes
stage: medium
Live music nitely; Locals gig before house band Sat nites. 2 bands play for a flat fee to 21+ crowd. Also books Cafe Wah. Email or mail press kit to venue.

Hank's Saloon
46 3rd St.
Brooklyn, NY 11217
p: 718-625-8003
www.hankssaloon.com
e: hanksbooking@gmail.com
call: M-F after 11am
genres: Country, Punk, Honky-Tonk, Bluegrass
Bklyn Country bar features Regulars & Touring acts Thu-Sat. Email or mail press kit to venue.

Iridium
1650 Broadway
New York, NY 10019
p: 212-582-2121
e: info@iridiumjazzclub.com
www.iridiumjazzclub.com
contact: Jim Eigo
p: 845-986-1677
e: jazzpromo@earthlink.net
genres: Jazz, Latin Jazz, World, Cabaret, Vocalists
advance: 4-6 months
capacity: 175
pa: Yes **sound eng:** Yes
Major 21+ Jazz club features top notch sound, live recording & great sight lines. Hosts world-class & rising stars nitely. Offers short residencies from Thu-Sun & some early shows. Featured act plays 2 shows: 8:30 & 10:30pm. Prefers email.

Jalopy
315 Columbia St.
Brooklyn, NY 11231
p: 718-395-3214
e: jalopy@speakeasy.net
www.www.jalopy.biz
contact: Lynette Wiley
genres: Acoustic Trad.
advance: 2-3 months
capacity: 74
pa: Yes **sound eng:** Yes
stage: raised
Hot all ages theater, music school & listening room is packed w/ vintage gear & quirky, stellar talent. Up to 3 Local-Touring acts play 45-90min for the door & some free brews. No unsolicited pkgs.

Jazz Standard
116 E 27th St.
New York, NY 10016
p: 212-576-2232
e: jzstandard@aol.com
www.jazzstandard.com
contact: Seth Abramson
p: 212-253-2263
call: M-F 10am-6pm
genres: Jazz, Blues, World
advance: 4-6 months
capacity: 130
pa: Yes **sound eng:** Yes
stage: large
Cool room w/ great sound & sight lines, cooks up top notch Nat'l acts nitely. Featured original act plays two 1hr sets on wkdys, 3 sets on wknds; some all ages shows. Call or email first for booking; no unsolicited mail.

Joe's Pub
425 Lafayette St.
New York, NY 10003
p: 212-539-8500
e: bookings@joespub.com
www.joespub.com
contact: Shanta Thake
p: 212-539-8540
e: sthake@publictheater.org
genres: Jazz, World, Americana, Country
advance: 2-4 months
capacity: 161
pa: Yes **sound eng:** Yes
stage: 14.5 x 10.5
Intimate all ages showcase features name talent & rising stars. Original Local-Int'l bands & some DJs gig nitely. 2-3 acts play 1hr for % of door. No unsolicited mail; email first.

Kenny's Castaways
157 Bleecker St.
New York, NY 10012
p: 212-979-9762; 212-979-0104
e: info@kennyscastaways.net
www.kennyscastaways.net
contact: Maria Kenny
genres: Alt., Rock, R&B, Acid Jazz, Folk, Acoustic
advance: 2 months
capacity: 250
pa: Yes **sound eng:** Yes
open mics: Last Wed of month
Showcase for emerging talent features original Local & Touring artists nitely. 4-6 acts play 45min sets to 21+ crowd. Great sound & views. Prefers email w/ link.

Knitting Factory Main Space/ The Tap Bar/Old Office
74 Leonard St.
New York, NY 10013
p: 212-219-3006
e: bookers@knittingfactory.com
www.knittingfactory.com
contact: Chantelle Hulton
p: 212-219-3006 x530
e: chantelle@knittingfactory.com
genres: All Styles
advance: 3-4 months
capacity: 400; 200; 100
pa: Yes **sound eng:** Yes
Illustrious all ages performance space fills 3 stages w/ top tier Touring artists, unusual bands & DJs nitely. 2-4 original acts play 30-60min sets. Email music links; no unsolicited mail.

Lakeside Lounge
162 Ave. B
New York, NY 10009
p: 212-529-8463
e: info@lakesidelounge.com
www.lakesidelounge.com
contact: Eric
genres: Rock, Country, Garage
advance: 1 month
capacity: 155
pa: Yes **sound eng:** Yes
stage: small corner
E Village hillbilly music club, books up & coming & some Touring bands up to 7 nites for 21+. Featured original act plays 1hr set on small corner stage for tips & drinks. Bands MUST use backline. Email link to music.

Lenox Lounge
288 Lenox Ave.
New York, NY 10037
p: 212-427-0253
e: info@lenoxlounge.com
www.lenoxlounge.com
contact: Danny Mixon
p: 212-636-9262
call: M-F noon-5pm
genres: Jazz, R&B, Blues
advance: 1 month
capacity: 80 **pa:** Yes
stage: floor space
open mics: Sun 7-11pm
Legendary club draws everyone 21+ from the college crowd & locals to tourists for top Reg'l & some Touring talent 6 nites. Featured act plays three 1hr sets for flat fee. Mail press kit to venue w/ ATTN: Danny.

The Living Room
154 Ludlow St.
New York, NY 10002
p: 212-533-7235
e: info@livingroomny.com
www.livingroomny.com
contact: Jennifer Gilson
call: M-F 2-6pm
genres: S/S, Folk, Rock
advance: 1-2 months
capacity: 125
pa: Yes **sound eng:** Yes
stage: 21 x 11
L.E.S. Acoustic listening room features up-&-comers & estab. acts nitely. 3-6 original acts play 45+min sets for tips. Also hosts acts upstairs in Googie's Lounge. Snail mail kit or send music links; no mp3s or attachments.

The Lucky Cat
245 Grand St.
Brooklyn, NY 11211
p: 718-782-0437
e: info@theluckycat.com
www.theluckycat.com
contact: Anthony Roman
call: email only
genres: Funk, Soul, World, S/S, Country, Bluegrass, Jazz, Indie Rock, Americana
advance: 1 month
capacity: 150
stage: medium
open mics: Tue 7pm
Socially-conscious, artist-driven venue books Local-Int'l acts nitely for artsy all ages crowd. 3 acts play 45-90min for door minus cost of doorman if house provides; if no cover, bands get % of take; some other arrangements are made. New acts may audition at open mic. No Hardcore Punk or Metal. Mail CD or press kit to venue or email link to music; no MP3s - use www.yousendit.com for big files. No Calls.

Lyceum
227 4th Ave.

Brooklyn, NY 11215
p: 866-469-2687
www.brooklynlyceum.com
e: booking@gowanus.com; pd@gowanus.com
genres: All Styles
capacity: 300; 300
pa: Yes **sound eng:** To hire
stage: floor space
open mics: Thu **sign in:** 8pm
Also known as Public Bath #7, performance space books original acts, rents out to cover bands & DJs & offers recording services. Up to 6 Local-Int'l acts play 30min-2.5hrs for all ages. No Heavy Metal. Email or call for dates or mail press kit to venue.

Mercury Lounge
217 E Houston St.
New York, NY 10002
p: 212-260-4700
e: info@bowerypresents.com
www.mercuryloungenyc.com
contact: Jay Belin
p: 212-375-1200
e: jaybelin@bowerypresents.com
genres: Rock, Alt., S/S, Pop
advance: 1 month
capacity: 250
pa: Yes **sound eng:** Yes
stage: 30 x 10
One of downtown's best spots for bands on the rise. Up to 5 cutting-edge Local-Touring artists gig nitely for % of door. Great sound & following. Snail mail kit ATTN: Jay Belin; No MP3s.

Merkin Concert Hall
129 W 67th St.
New York, NY 10023
p: 212-501-3340
e: info@kaufman-center.org
www.kaufman-center.org
contact: Jeff Shreve
p: 212-501-3345
e: jshreve@kaufman-center.org
call: M-F 10am-6pm
genres: Jazz, World, Eclectic, Classical, Klezmer
advance: 1 year
capacity: 449
pa: Yes **sound eng:** Yes
stage: 57 x 35 **in-house:** Piano
Premier all ages venue for small ensembles provides intimate scale, excellent acoustics & views. Diverse shows has original cutting-edge Local-Nat'l acts Sat-Thu. Books in Feb for Sep. Mail press kit to venue.

Metropolitan Room
34 W 22nd St.
New York, NY 10010
p: 212-206-0440
www.metropolitanroom.com
contact: Lennie Watts
p: 212-206-0440 x14
genres: Jazz, Cabaret, Folk
Club features Local-Int'l acts for all ages. Use email for booking.

Music Hall of Williamsburg
66 N 6th St.
Brooklyn, NY 11211
p: 718-486-5400
e: info@bowerypresents.com
www.musichallofwilliamsburg.com
contact: Josh Moore
p: 212-375-1200
e: josh@bowerypresents.com
call: M-F 11am-7pm
advance: 5+ weeks
capacity: 550
pa: Yes **sound eng:** Yes
stage: 30 x 18
Formerly Northsix, renovated venue w/ upstairs balconies added - basically the Bowery in Brooklyn. Built to minimize harsh sonic reflections & has unimpeded sight lines. Features original Local-Int'l bands & some DJs for 16+. Also books Mercury Lounge, Bowery Ballroom & Terminal 5.

Nokia Theatre
1515 Broadway
New York, NY 10036
p: 212-930-1940
e: nokiainfo@nokiatheatrenyc.com
www.nokiatheatrenyc.com
p: 212-930-5180
genres: All Styles
capacity: 2100
stage: large
Formerly Astor Plaza movie theatre, excellent acoustics & surreal lighting enhance the intimate setting of this 3-tiered Times Square venue. Hosts about 2 shows/wk w/ mostly Nat'l-Int'l acts & Touring DJs as openers. Up to 3 acts play for 16+ crowd. Call AEG for booking: 212-930-5180.

Paddy Reilly's Music Bar
519 2nd Ave.
New York, NY 10016
p: 212-686-1210
www.myspace.com/paddysopenmic
contact: Steve Duggan
call: Mon, Thu & Sat after 8pm
genres: Irish Rock, Celtic, Bluegrass, Folk, Rock
advance: 1 month
capacity: 74 **stage:** 6 x 6
open mics: Wed **sign in:** 6:30pm
Trad. Irish pub features Local & Touring artists up to 7 nites. 1 act plays 30min-3hrs to 21+ crowd. Email or call first.

Parkside Lounge
317 E Houston St.
New York, NY 10002
p: 212-673-6270
e: parksideny@aol.com
www.parksidelounge.com
contact: Jenny Davis
p: 609-972-5486
call: M-F afternoons
genres: Latin, Bluegrass, S/S, Rock, Punk, Folk, Hip-Hop
capacity: 75
pa: Yes **sound eng:** Yes
open mics: Sat **sign in:** 5pm
Popular laid-back retro bar books mostly Local-Reg'l bands nitely for 21+; very few Nat'ls. 2-5 original acts play 45-90min. No Metal or Rap. Email, call or mail kit to venue.

Pete's Candy Store
709 Lorimer St.
Brooklyn, NY 11211
p: 718-302-3770
e: andy@petescandystore.com
www.petescandystore.com
contact: Jacob Silver
e: booking@petescandystore.com
call: email only
genres: Indie, S/S, Jazz, Rock, Folk
advance: 2 months
capacity: 50
pa: Yes **stage:** 10 x 5
open mics: Sun **sign in:** 5-8pm
Williamsburg bar has 3 rooms (total cap. 120) & books 3 original bands nitely for 45min sets to hot-n-hip 21+ crowd. Email MP3s/link to music or mail press kit to venue w/ removed shrinkwrap; will contact if interested; Do not follow up.

Pianos
158 Ludlow St.
New York, NY 10002
p: 212-505-3733
www.pianosnyc.com
contact: Zachary Waldman
e: booking@pianosnyc.com
call: email only
genres: Indie Rock, Avant-Garde, S/S
advance: 3 months
capacity: 150
Piano store turned live music room w/ great sound & views features original Local-Int'l bands nitely. 3-4 acts play 45min & keep 70% of door. Prefers email w/ link to music; no MP3s or calls.

R-Bar
218 Bowery
New York, NY 10012
p: 212-334-0484
e: info@rbarnyc.com
www.rbarnyc.com
contact: Lee Sobel
p: 718-783-1776
e: lee@lofientertainment.com; leesobel@aol.com
genres: All Styles
advance: 2-3 months
sound eng: Yes
Party club favors its female patrons & features live music Wed-Sat. 3-5 Local-Int'l bands & DJs play for % of door. Mail promos w/ ATTN: Lee Sobel, 250 Washington Ave. # 1C, Brooklyn, NY 11205.

Rebel
251 W 30th St.
New York, NY 10001
p: 212-695-2747
e: info@rebelnyc.com
www.rebelnyc.com
contact: Saraphine
call: M-F 10am-6pm
genres: Dance, Goth, Rock, Pop, Jazz, Blues, Hip-Hop
advance: 2 months
capacity: 400
pa: Yes **sound eng:** Yes
Formerly Downtime, 18+ multi-level club w/ dance floor, VIP Room & video screen books Local-Int'l bands up to 4 nites. Mail kit w/ ATTN: Saraphine, PO Box 2407, New York, NY 10116.

Red Lion
151 Bleecker St.
New York, NY 10012
p: 212-260-9797
e: redlion@verizon.net
www.redlionnyc.com
contact: David Sheridan
genres: Jazz, Bluegrass, S/S, Rock
advance: 1 month
capacity: 1175
pa: Yes **sound eng:** Yes
Stylish Village hangout has 3 Local-Int'l acts & 1 DJ nitely. Email or mail press kit to venue w/ ATTN: David.

Rockwood Music Hall
196 Allen St.
New York, NY 10002
p: 212-477-4155
e: info@rockwoodmusichall.com
www.rockwoodmusichall.com
genres: S/S, Acoustic, Folk
NYC smallest fine showcase where many A-list Local stars work out new material. Featured act plays for tips from 21+ crowd. Email links to website, MySpace or EPK & incl. band name in subject; No attachments; Touring acts incl. dates. No unsolicited mail.

Rodeo Bar
375 3rd Ave.
New York, NY 10016
p: 212-683-6500
e: info@rodeobar.com
www.rodeobar.com
contact: Jack Grace
p: 212-591-0261
e: booking@rodeobar.com
genres: Alt. Country, Rockabilly, Bluegrass, Country, Western Swing
advance: Up to 6 months
capacity: 200
pa: Yes **sound eng:** Yes
stage: 15 x 10
open mics: Sun 6-9pm
City honky tonk presents urban & some traveling cowboys nitely. 1-2 acts play 3+ sets of original music for all ages. Prefers email, but may call or mail press kit to venue w/ ATTN: Booking.

S.O.B.'s
204 Varrick St.
New York, NY 10014
p: 212-243-4940
e: sobs@sobs.com
www.sobs.com
contact: Larry Gold
e: lgold@sobs.com
genres: Salsa, Latin, Hip-Hop, R&B, Reggae, Alt., Brazilian, Caribbean, Haitian
advance: 1-3 months
capacity: 450
pa: Yes **sound eng:** Yes
stage: 12 x 24; **in-house:** Backline
Marquee club features original Local & world-class talent Mon-Sat. Acts play 1-2hrs. Promos: 200 Varick St., Basement, New York, NY 10014.

Sidewalk Cafe
94 Ave. A
New York, NY 10009
p: 212-473-7373
e: info@sidewalkmusic.net
www.sidewalkmusic.net
contact: Ben Krieger
p: 917-447-4686
call: Mon noon-3pm
genres: Antifolk, S/S, Edge Pop, Jazz, Rock
advance: 1-2 months
capacity: 125
pa: Yes **sound eng:** Yes
stage: 18 x 10
open mics: Mon **sign in:** 7:30pm
All ages breeding ground for Antifolk movement, showcases performers w/ social messages nitely. 4-5 original acts play 45min for tips. Prefers email, but may mail press kit to venue.

Snitch
59 W 21st St.
New York, NY 10010
p: 212-727-7775
e: info@snitchbar.com

www.snitchbar.com
contact: Dave
e: dave@snitchbar.com
genres: Rock, Hip-Hop
advance: 1 month
capacity: 115
pa: Yes **sound eng:** Yes
Primarily Rock bar w/ stage & in-house sound engineer, books Local-Int'l acts Mon-Sat w/ some cover bands thrown in. 3-5 acts play 30min for 21+. Email or mail press kit.

Sound Fix Lounge
110 Bedford Ave.
Brooklyn, NY 11211
p: 718-388-8087
www.soundfixrecords.com
contact: Tammy
e: tammy@soundfixrecords.com
genres: Acoustic, Indie, Alt., Folk, Experimental
advance: 2 months
capacity: 110
pa: Yes **sound eng:** Yes
stage: 12 x 6
open mics: Mon **sign in:** 6:30pm
Hip original music club w/ video projection screen books low-volume Local-Int'l acts.4-5 bands play 30-45min for tips. Brushes only if using drums. Email for booking.

Southpaw
125 5th Ave.
Brooklyn, NY 11217
p: 718-230-0236
e: southpaw@spsounds.com
www.spsounds.com
contact: Todd Abramson
e: telstarrec@aol.com
genres: Alt., Hard Rock, Hip-Hop
advance: 1-3 months
capacity: 400
pa: Yes **sound eng:** Yes
stage: 18 x 16
Stellar original bands journey to this posh venue w/ blast-friendly sound & fans are following. Polished Reg'l & Touring bands entertain 5-6/wk. 3-4 acts play 45-60min sets for 18+. Prefers link to MySpace but may mail kit; wait 3-4 wks for response.

Sputnik
262 Taaffe Pl.
Brooklyn, NY 11205
p: 718-398-6666
www.barsputnik.com
contact: Euripides Pelekanos
e: bookings@barsputnik.com
genres: Blues, Folk, Rap, Bluegrass, Punk, Hip-Hop
pa: Yes **sound eng:** To hire
open mics: Fri Turntables
sign in: Call or email
p: 917-331-5655
e: sepahbodi@gmail.com
Ultra-hip club books Local-Nat'l bands & DJs most nites for 21+ dancers. Email or snail mail kit.

Studio B
259 Banker St.
Brooklyn, NY 11222
p: 718-389-1880
e: rrstudiob@gmail.com
www.clubstudiob.com
contact: Chris Love
e: chrislove.studiob@gmail.com
genres: Varies
advance: 6-8 weeks
capacity: 650
pa: Yes **sound eng:** Yes
stage: 17 x 20
New full service 19+ niteclub in the Greenpoint/Williamsburg area features live Local-Int'l acts as well as DJs, but sporadic hrs. House takes 10% merch sales. Use email for booking.

Sullivan Hall
214 Sullivan St.
New York, NY 10012
p: 212-477-2782
www.sullivanhallnyc.com
contact: Mike Maietta
p: 212-634-0427 x7
e: mike@cegmusic.com
call: M-F 1-7pm
genres: Acoustic, Rock, Jam, Funk, Alt.
advance: 4-6 weeks
capacity: 345
pa: Yes **sound eng:** Yes
stage: 20 x 20
Previously The Lion's Den, this 18+ venue hosts up to 5 original Local-Int'l acts w/ local draw nitely, playing 40min for % of polled draw. Promos: 505 8th Ave., Rm. 805, New York, NY 10018.

Sweet Rhythm
88 7th Ave. S
New York, NY 10014
p: 212-255-3626
www.sweetrhythmny.com
contact: James
genres: Jazz, Blues, Salsa, Reggae, Flamenco, World
Formerly Sweet Basil, eclectic Jazz niteclub showcases Nat'l & up-&-coming talent nitely. Snail mail kit w/ ATTN: Music. Incl. current CD, photos, press & contact info; will contact if interested.

Swing 46
349 W 46th St.
New York, NY 10036
p: 212-262-9554
e: info@swing46.com
www.swing46.com
contact: Judith
genres: Swing, Jump, Blues, Big Band, Jazz
advance: 2 months
capacity: 160
pa: Yes **sound eng:** Yes
stage: 25 x 10
Retro supperclub w/ dance floor features 1 Local-Int'l act nitely playing three 45-60min sets for 18+; all ages w/ guardian. Email or mail press kit to venue.

The Tank
279 Church St.
New York, NY 10013
p: 212-563-6269
e: info@thetanknyc.org
www.thetanknyc.org
contact: Tanya Mueller
e: music@thetanknyc.org
genres: Rock, Hip-Hop, Electronica, Indie, Jazz, Blues, Experimental, Country
advance: 1-3 months
capacity: 74
pa: Yes **sound eng:** Yes
stage: floor space
Focuses on experimental music & the art scene, also books up & coming artists of all genres. Local-Nat'l acts gig Thu-Sun; DJs on Sat nite. Up to 3 acts play 45 min for a % of the door. Use email for booking or mail to: PO Box 2026, New York, NY 10013.

Terminal 5
610 W 56th St.
New York, NY 10019
p: 212-582-6600
e: info@bowerypresents.com
www.terminal5nyc.com; www.eventsitenyc.com
p: 212-375-1200
genres: Rock, Hard Rock, Pop
advance: 1-8 months
capacity: 2800-3998
pa: Yes **sound eng:** Yes
Formerly Club Exit, now extravagant all ages multi-level event site w/ hi-tech sound & lighting & unobstructed sight lines. Mostly original Local-Int'l acts & DJs play up to 7 nites. Prefers email for booking; no unsolicited mail.

Terra Blues
149 Bleecker St.
New York, NY 10012
p: 212-777-7776
e: terrablues@aol.com
www.terrablues.com
genres: Blues, Acoustic, Roots, Americana
advance: 3 months
capacity: 150
pa: Yes **sound eng:** Yes
stage: 20 x 40
Crowded & in the heart of NYU campus, this true blue room attracts stellar veterans & rising stars nitely. 2 original acts play 1hr for flat fee to 21+ crowd.

Trash Bar
256 Grand St.
Brooklyn, NY 11211
p: 718-599-1000
www.thetrashbar.com
contact: Walter
p: 718-326-2353
e: booking@thetrashbar.com
call: Mon-Thu noon-4pm
genres: Rock
advance: 1-2 months
capacity: 220
pa: Yes **sound eng:** Yes
stage: 30 x 30 **in-house:** Drums
Rockin' dive presents Local & Touring acts nitely in back room for 21+. 4-5 bands play 40min for % of door minus costs. Wait 2 wks to follow up.

Triad Theatre & Lounge
158 W 72nd St., 2nd Fl.
New York, NY 10023
p: 212-362-2590
e: triadnyc@yahoo.com
www.triadnyc.com
contact: Peter Martin
p: 212-877-7176
call: Mon-Thu 4-9pm
genres: Pop, Rock, S/S, Jazz, Blues, Cabaret
advance: 1-4 months
capacity: 130
pa: Yes **sound eng:** Yes
stage: 20 x 12
Flexible space w/ excellent sound hosts Local & Touring talent 3-4 nites for all ages. 1-2 bands perform 50-90min for % of door. Late nite music series upstairs.

Underground Lounge
955 W End Ave. @ 107th
New York, NY 10025
p: 212-531-4759
e: info@theundergroundnyc.com
www.theundergroundnyc.com
e: booking@theundergroundnyc.com
genres: Pop, Folk, Soul, Indie
open mics: Sun Songwriters
Original indie acts & DJs up to 7 nites. All shows are free. Email for booking.

Union Hall
702 Union St.
Brooklyn, NY 11215
p: 718-638-4400
e: unionhallny@aol.com
www.unionhallny.com
contact: Skippy
e: unionhall@gmail.com
genres: Indie Rock, S/S
advance: 2 months
capacity: 100
pa: Yes **sound eng:** Yes
stage: 11 x 14
Large 2-story space w/ Bocci courts & indie Rock shows up to 7 nites in the basement. 3 acts play 45min for % to 21+. Email for booking.

Union Pool
484 Union Ave.
Brooklyn, NY 11211
p: 718-609-0484
e: unionpoolbooking@yahoo.com
www.myspace.com/unionpool
advance: 1-2 months
capacity: 150
pa: Yes **sound eng:** Yes
Cool indie Rock venue books Local-Int'l acts. 3 bands play for a % of the door to a 21+ crowd. Mail promos w/ ATTN: Booking.

Village Vanguard
178 7th Ave. S
New York, NY 10014
p: 212-255-4037
e: email@villagevanguard.com
www.villagevanguard.com
contact: Lorraine Gordon
call: Sun-Fri 3:30-5:30pm
genres: Jazz
advance: 6-12 months
capacity: 125
pa: Yes **sound eng:** Yes
stage: 12 x 18
Still the mecca for serious jazzbos, presents estab. name acts that draw crowds; big band on Mon. Sultry sound system highlights a top notch act for Tue-Sun residency w/ 75min shows. All ages allowed w/ cover. Mail press kit to venue.

Webster Hall
125 E 11th St.
New York, NY 10003
p: 212-353-1600
www.websterhall.com
contact: Rachel Perry
p: 212-375-1200
e: rachel@bowerypresents.com
genres: Electronic, Trance, Techno, Gothic, Rock, Pop
advance: 1-3 months
capacity: 3000
pa: Yes **sound eng:** Yes
stage: 25 x 40
Historic multi-level venue w/ top sound & lights books cutting-edge live acts & DJs several nites. Featured original act plays 1+hrs & may have 1-2 openers. Shows well-promoted. Call or email for booking.

Rochester/Syracuse

The ABC Cafe
308 Stewart Ave.
Ithaca, NY 14850
p: 607-277-4770
www.theabccafe.com
contact: Shad

e: booking@theabccafe.com
genres: Folk, S/S, Jazz, Bluegrass, Trip-Hop, Eclectic
advance: 1 month
capacity: 60
pa: Yes
open mics: Every other Tue
All ages eatery near Cornell campus, features mostly Locals & Touring acts w/ draw for after dinner gigs & Sun brunch. Up to 5 shows/wk.

The Bug Jar
219 Monroe Ave.
Rochester, NY 14607
p: 585-454-2966
e: mediacontacts@bugjar.com
www.bugjar.com
contact: Rob Ferardo
e: liveshows@bugjar.com; robferardo@hotmail.com
genres: All Styles
advance: 2 months
capacity: 200
pa: Yes **sound eng:** Yes
stage: small
Books diverse Local-Int'l talent up to 4 nites. 3 acts play 1hr sets for door; some all ages shows. Mail press kit to venue.

Castaways
413 Old Taughannock Blvd.
Ithaca, NY 14850
p: 607-272-1370
www.castawaysithaca.com
contact: Eliot Rich
p: 607-229-0310
e: castawaysbookings@gmail.com
call: Wed-Fri noon-4pm
genres: Rock, Punk, Jam, Reggae, Ska, Country
advance: 3 months
capacity: 400
pa: Yes **sound eng:** Yes
stage: 16 x 28
Area's only club w/ full lighting system, books Local & some Touring bands & DJs Thu-Sun for all ages shows. 2-4 acts play 30-90min & split the door. Prefers EPKs; No unsolicited mail.

Chapter House
400 Stewart Ave.
Ithaca, NY 14850
p: 607-277-9782
www.chapterhouseithaca.com
contact: Jon
call: M-F after 4pm
genres: Indie, Bluegrass, Americana, Desert Rock, Blues, Rockabilly
Mostly Locals & some Touring acts play Sat nites. Call first.

Cyber Cafe West
176 Main St.
Binghamton, NY 13905
p: 607-723-2456
www.cybercafewest.com
contact: Jeff Kahn
e: jeff@cybercafewest.com
genres: Folk, Jazz, S/S, Blues, Rock
advance: 1 year
capacity: 90
pa: Yes **sound eng:** Yes
stage: 16 x 12
All ages coffeehouse books Reg'l & some Touring bands & DJs 5 nites. Featured act plays 9pm-midnite for % of door.

Dinosaur Bar-B-Que
246 W Willow St.
Syracuse, NY 13202
p: 315-476-4937
e: dino@dinosaurbarbque.com
www.dinosaurbarbque.com
contact: Scott Sterling
e: ssarmie1@twcny.ri.com
call: Wed evenings
genres: Blues, Zydeco, R&B, Americana, Roots, Rockabilly
advance: 3-4 months
capacity: 150
pa: Yes **sound eng:** Yes
stage: medium
open mics: Tue **sign in:** 9pm
Top area Blues club presents mostly original Reg'l & Touring acts 6 nites. 1 act plays from 10pm-2am for flat fee; 21+ at nite. Also books for Rochester location. Other location in NYC. Mail press kit or use email.

The Haunt
702 Willow Ave.
Ithaca, NY 14850
p: 607-275-3447
www.thehaunt.com
contact: Tony Kent
p: 607-277-2726
e: booking@thehaunt.com
call: Tue-Fri 11am-4pm
genres: Alt., Rock, Goth, Industrial, Heavy Metal, Jam, Reggae, Punk
advance: 3 months
capacity: 550
pa: Yes **sound eng:** Yes
stage: 24 x 12
Long-running music club hosts Local-Int'l talent Thu-Sat; all ages wknd matinees. 3 bands play 45min sets for % of door. Email or snail mail kit.

High Fidelity
170 East Ave.
Rochester, NY 14604
p: 585-325-6490
www.highfidelityrochester.com
contact: Joe
e: booking@highfidelityrochester.com
genres: Rock, Groove/Funk, Dub, Roots, Jazz
advance: 2-3 months
capacity: 275
pa: Yes **sound eng:** Yes
stage: 22 x 20
Great live music venue w/ DJs. 2-3 Local-Int'l acts play 90min for 21+; rare all ages shows. Email before mailing press kit.

Lost Dog Cafe Ithaca
106-112 S Cayuga St.
Ithaca, NY 14850
p: 607-277-9143
e: nick@lostdogcafe.net
www.lostdogcafe.net
contact: Sprocket
e: sprocketrages@yahoo.com
genres: S/S, Indie, Hip-Hop, Jazz, Latin
advance: 1-2 months
capacity: 100
pa: Yes
Funky & delish' cafe features original Local-Int'l artists Tue-Sat from 10pm-1am. Acts receive 100% of door. 2nd spot in Binghampton. Email or snail mail promo w/ ATTN: Sprocket.

Maxie's Supper Club & Oyster Bar
635 W State St.
Ithaca, NY 14850
p: 607-272-4136
e: maxie@maxies.com
www.maxies.com
contact: Todd Parlato
e: todd@maxies.com
genres: Roots, Blues, Jazz, Bluegrass
advance: 2-3 months
capacity: 50
pa: Yes; **stage:** floor space
Popular Cajun spot near Cornell U, has Local-Reg'l bands every Tue & Sun from 6-10pm; few Nat'l bands. 1 act plays 2.5hrs for flat fee. Snail mail kit w/ ATTN: Todd.

The Night Eagle Cafe
200 State St.
Binghamton, NY 13901
p: 607-843-7378
e: info@nighteaglecafe.org
www.nighteaglecafe.org
contact: Ken Millett
p: 607-217-7334
e: bookings@nighteaglecafe.org
genres: Americana, Jazz, Celtic, S/S, Acoustic
advance: 4 months
pa: Yes **sound eng:** Yes
open mics: 1st & 3rd Wed of month 7:30-11pm
Recently relocated, this stage draws Reg'l & estab. world-class performers mostly on wknds for all ages; some Mon & Wed shows. Email or mail press kit w/ ATTN: Ken Millet, PO Box 446, Oxford, NY 13830. Incl. bio, photo, list of venues played, CD or link to music, avail. dates & contact info.

The Nines
311 College Ave.
Ithaca, NY 14850
p: 607-272-1888
www.theninesithacany.com
contact: George
e: theninesithacany@gmail.com
call: Tue 3-5pm; Wed & Thu 6-8pm
genres: Funk, Ska, Rock, Jam, Roots, Reggae, Jazz, Bluegrass
advance: 2-3 months
capacity: 175
pa: Yes **sound eng:** Yes
stage: medium
open mics: Sun 9pm
Firehouse turned collegetown eatery, books Reg'l & few Touring bands Wed-Sat from 10pm-1am for 18+. Opener plays 1hr, headliner 2hrs for 100% door after sound expenses. Prefers email, but may call.

Penny Arcade
4785 Lake Ave.
Rochester, NY 14612
p: 585-267-5576
e: thepennyarcade@bluegirlonline.com
www.myspace.com/thepennyarcade
contact: Andrew Haines
e: scorpionbooking@hotmail.com
call: M-F daytime
genres: Rock, Ska, Alt., Reggae, Pop, Jam, Metal, Country, Jazz
advance: 1-6 months
capacity: 850
pa: Yes **sound eng:** Yes
stage: 28 x 18 (8 x 8 riser)
Area's prime Rock room books original Local & Touring acts & DJs w/ a draw 6-7 nites. Out-of-towners w/o label muscle should hook up w/ Local act. Be prepared to pre-sell tix & play for door after expenses. 4-6 acts play 30+min sets. Prefers email, but contact by any means.

Rongovian Embassy
1 W Main St.
Trumansburg, NY 14886
p: 607-387-3334
www.rongo.com
contact: Mike Barry
e: rongomike@yahoo.com
call: Tue-Thu 1-4pm
genres: Folk, Rock, Jazz, Jam, Blues, Country, Fusion, Funk
advance: 2-3 months
capacity: 220
pa: Yes **sound eng:** Yes
Area staple w/ hippie vibe near many colleges, hosts variety of music Fri-Sat for all ages shows. 1-2 bands gig for % of door. Email, call or mail promos: 1 W Main St., PO Box 993, Trumansburg, NY 14886.

Water St. Music Hall/ Club at Water St.
204 N Water St.
Rochester, NY 14604
p: 585-546-3887
www.waterstreetmusic.com
contact: Catherine Bauer
e: cat@waterstreetmusic.com
call: M-F 10am-3pm
genres: All Styles
advance: 2-6 months
capacity: 500; 1100
pa: Yes **sound eng:** Yes
stage: 20 x 30; 12 x 20
Area's largest concert hall, presents small & large shows w/ full lights & sound on 2 stages. Top Touring acts & Reg'l buzz bands play original music 2-6 nites; under 16 w/ adult. Email link to website, tour history & interested dates. Local & upcoming Touring acts use MySpace or email dave@waterstreetmusic.com. May also mail press kit to venue w/ ATTN: Booking.

Westcott Community Ctr.
826 Euclid Ave.
Syracuse, NY 13210
p: 315-478-8634
e: info@westcottcc.org
www.westcottcc.org
contact: Lisa Jackson
call: M-F 9am-5pm
genres: All Styles
pa: Yes **sound eng:** Yes
Community ctr. hosts Local-Reg'l acts for all ages. Call for booking.

North Carolina

Asheville

Barley's Taproom & Pizzeria
42 Biltmore Ave.
Asheville, NC 28801
p: 828-255-0504
www.barleystaproom.com
contact: Pat Huss
p: 828-281-3910
e: barleysashv@hotmail.com
call: M-F 9am-5pm
genres: Jazz, Bluegrass
advance: 2-3 months
capacity: 390
pa: Yes **sound eng:** Yes
stage: 15 x 10
Tavern books polished Reg'ls & Nat'ls Tue & Sun for all ages crowd. Single original act plays 2 sets for flat fee. Other locations in Knoxville, TN:

865-521-0092 & Greenville, SC: 864-232-3706.

Club Hairspray
38 N French Broad Ave.
Asheville, NC 28801
p: 828-258-2027
e: clubhairspray@charterinternet.com
www.clubhairspray.com
contact: Lynn Moody
genres: Pop, Alt., Indie Rock, Blues, Jazz, Hard Rock
advance: 3 months
capacity: 151
pa: Yes **sound eng:** By Request
stage: small
open mics: 1st & 4th Tue 8pm
Unusual club attracts eclectic 21+ crowd for Local & Reg'l bands that play 1-2hr sets 1-3 nites from Fri-Sun. Snail mail kit or email.

The Grey Eagle
185 Clingman Ave.
Asheville, NC 28801
p: 828-232-5800
e: info@thegreyeagle.com
www.thegreyeagle.com
contact: Brian Landrum
e: booking@thegreyeagle.com
call: Mon-Thu 1-5pm
genres: Folk, Rock, Jazz, Bluegrass, Acoustic, S/S
advance: 2-3 months
capacity: 550
stage: 18 x 30
Notable listening room presents original Local-Nat'l recording acts for all ages shows. 1-2 acts perform 1hr sets. Email if you'd like to open for an artist on calendar. No unsolicited mail.

Jack of the Wood
95 Patton Ave.
Asheville, NC 28801
p: 828-252-3445
e: jackworking@mac.com
www.jackofthewood.com
contact: Celene DeLoach
e: jackmusic@bellsouth.net
call: Mon, Wed & Fri afternoons
genres: Bluegrass, Celtic, Alt. Country, Rockabilly, Roots
advance: 1-5 months
capacity: 180
pa: Yes **sound eng:** Yes
stage: 14 x 12
Celtic pub books original Local acts Wed, Thu & Sun for all ages. Reg'l-Int'l talent Wed, Fri & Sat. Single act plays 4hrs for flat fee vs door after expenses. Merch split is 80/20. Promos: 40 Wall St., Asheville, NC 28801.

Orange Peel Social Aid & Pleasure Club
101 Biltmore Ave.
Asheville, NC 28801
p: 828-225-5851
e: info@theorangepeel.net
www.theorangepeel.net
contact: Bryan Benson
p: 865-523-2665
e: bbenson@acentertainment.com
call: M-F 9am-5pm
genres: All Styles
advance: 1-6 months
capacity: 942
pa: Yes **sound eng:** Yes
stage: 36 x 28
Premier music hall features Touring bands & DJs 3-4 nites. Opener plays 45min, headliner 90-180min to 18+ for flat fee; Merch splits 75/25. Locals email booking@theorangepeel.net. Reg'l-Nat'l acts email or send kit to: 505 Market St., 7th Fl., Knoxville, TN 37902.

Town Pump Tavern
135 Cherry St.
Black Mountain, NC 28711
p: 828-669-4808
e: info@townpumpmusic.com
www.townpumpmusic.com
contact: Dan Johnston
call: M-F
genres: Blues, Rock, Americana, Honky-Tonk, Bluegrass, Roots
advance: 2 months
capacity: 110
pa: Yes **sound eng:** Yes
stage: 10 x 12
open mics: Wed 9pm; Sun Open Acoustic 9pm
Books original Local-Nat'ls 6 nites for 18+ locals & tourists. 1 act plays 2-3hrs for 100% of door. Mail press kit to venue.

Tressa's Downtown Jazz & Blues
28 Broadway
Asheville, NC 28801
p: 828-254-7072
e: tressas@aol.com; tressas@charter.net
www.tressasdowntownjazzandblues.com
contact: Tressa Thornton
call: Mon noon-2pm
genres: Jazz, Blues, Swing, Latin, R&B, Funk
advance: 6 months
capacity: 150
pa: Yes
stage: 7 x 14 **in-house:** Piano
Casual but classy niteclub books Local-Reg'l artists 6 nites. Featured act plays 3hrs for 21+. Snail mail kit.

Westville Pub
777 Haywood Pub
Asheville, NC 28806
p: 828-225-9782
www.westvillepub.com
contact: Greg Turner
e: bookthepub@yahoo.com
genres: Blues, Reggae, Rock, Bluegrass, Country, Folk
advance: 1-2 months
capacity: 125
pa: Yes **sound eng:** To hire
open mics: Mon 7:30pm
Local-Nat'l play 9pm-midnite Thu-Sat for % of door. Email first.

Chapel Hill/ Raleigh/Durham

The Berkeley Cafe
217 W Martin St.
Raleigh, NC 27601
p: 919-821-0777
e: lakeboonee@bellsouth.net
www.berkeleycafe.net
contact: Marianne Taylor
p: 919-376-9532
e: mtaylormusic@aol.com
call: M-F noon-5pm
genres: Rock, Blues, Country Drum n Bass, Hip-Hop, Jam, Rockabilly, Newgrass, Roots, Americana, Country, Alt.
advance: 2 months
capacity: 300
pa: Yes **sound eng:** Yes
stage: 20 x 30
open mics: Wed 9pm
Trendy all ages spot has Local-Touring bands 4 nites; 1-3 acts fill 90-180min. Also hosting shows for the Shuttered Hideaway Music Hall. Send Sonicbids EPK or use MySpace.

Blue Bayou Club
106 S Churton St.
Hillsborough, NC 27278
p: 919-732-2555
e: contact@bluebayouclub.com
www.bluebayouclub.com
contact: Gary Lee
genres: Blues, Jazz
advance: 1 month
capacity: 100
pa: Yes **sound eng:** Yes
stage: medium
open mics: Tue 8pm
Cajun-themed 21+ bar 14mi from Durham, books fun Local-Touring bands Thu-Sat. Up to 2 acts gig from 9pm-1am. Mail press kit to venue for booking.

The Brewery
3009 Hillsborough St.
Raleigh, NC 27607
p: 919-838-6788
www.brewerync.com
contact: Tom Taylor
e: tom@brewerync.com
genres: Rock, Alt., Indie, Reggae, Bluegrass, Metal
Landmark private club stays on the cutting edge w/ up to 6 mostly Local-Reg'l bands 5-7 nites for all ages; some Nat'l acts. Email for booking.

Cat's Cradle
300 E Main St.
Carrboro, NC 27510
p: 919-967-9053
e: thecat@catscradle.com
www.catscradle.com
contact: Derek Powers
e: derek@catscradle.com
call: Wed 1:30-4:30pm
genres: Alt., Bluegrass, Rock, Punk, Folk, Hip-Hop
advance: 1-2 months
capacity: 615
pa: Yes **sound eng:** Yes
stage: 22 x 25
First-rate listening room pairs Reg'ls w/ Touring acts 6 nites for all ages. Up to 3 original acts & DJs play for flat fee vs door; monthly cover bands. Most shows all ages; some 21+. Email or snail mail kit.

The Cave
452-1/2 W Franklin St.
Chapel Hill, NC 27516
p: 919-968-9308
e: info@caverntavern.com
www.caverntavern.com
contact: Mr. Mouse
p: 919-370-7056
call: Tue & Thu 2-5pm
genres: Most Styles
advance: 2 months
capacity: 87
pa: Yes
stage: medium
open mics: 1st Tue of mo 9pm
Smokey 21+ music club has original Local-Touring bands nitely. 3 acts play 45min for door. No Hip-Hop, Metal or Hardcore. Snail mail kit.

Deep South the Bar
430 S Dawson St.
Raleigh, NC 27601
p: 919-844-1515
www.deepsouthentertainment.com
contact: Christian Dysart
p: 919-624-1180
e: christian@deepsouthentertainment.com
call: M-F 1-7pm
genres: Acoustic
advance: 1 month
capacity: 100
pa: Yes
House concert setup books original Acoustic music Sun. 1-2 acts play two 1hr sets for the door vs % of bar sales. Promos: Deep in the Triangle Series, PO Box 17737, Raleigh, NC 27619.

Lighthouse Convention Center
326 Tryon Rd.
Raleigh, NC 27603
p: 919-661-6902
www.lgma.info
contact: Dr. James Layton
p: 919-661-6902 x101
e: jim@lgma.info
call: afternoons
genres: Gospel, Folk, Bluegrass Gospel
advance: 1 year
capacity: 946
pa: Yes **sound eng:** Yes
stage: 20 x 40
Largest local Gospel assoc. hosts Local-Reg'l & some Nat'l acts Fri; few Sat shows. 2 groups play 45min for % of love offering. Snail mail kit.

The Lincoln Theatre
126 E Cabarrus St.
Raleigh, NC 27601
p: 919-821-4111
e: info@lincolntheatre.com
www.lincolntheatre.com
contact: Mark Thompson
p: 919-828-4444
e: booking@lincolntheatre.com
call: Mon-Thu 1-5pm
genres: Rock, Pop, Country, Metal, Jazz
advance: 2-3 months
capacity: 800
pa: Yes **sound eng:** Yes
stage: 21 x 25
Renovated movie house presents Local-Nat'l acts nitely; most shows all ages. 2-4 bands play 75min sets; DJs spin wkly. Merch splits 80/20. Good views & state-of-the-art sound & lights. Promos: 805 N West St., Raleigh, NC 27603.

Local 506
506 W Franklin St.
Chapel Hill, NC 27516
p: 919-942-5506
e: info@local506.com
www.local506.com
contact: Glenn Boothe
e: booking@local506.com
call: no calls
genres: Rock, Country, Indie
advance: 2-4 months
capacity: 250
pa: Yes **sound eng:** Yes
stage: 16 x 24
Members-only venue presents original Reg'l acts & DJs up to 7 nites & Touring acts 1-2 nites. Acts play 45min to 18+ crowd. Only use email for booking.

Nightlight
405 1/2 W Rosemary St.
Chapel Hill, NC 27516
p: 919-933-5550

e: nightlightbooking@gmail.com
www.nightlightclub.com
contact: Jenks Miller
call: prefers email
genres: Noise, Experimental, Avant-Garde, Rock, Alt., Indie
advance: 6-8 weeks
capacity: 100
pa: Yes
stage: 10 x 10
open mics: Sun **sign in:** 8pm
Former Rock club 14mi from Durham now all ages cafe/bookstore, hosts original Reg'l & Touring acts & DJs Mon-Sat. 3-4 original acts play for 2/3 of door. Bands w/ more than 2 singers must supply sound, mics & cords. Send press kit w/ email address & bio w/ ATTN: Jenks. No contact thru MySpace or calls.

Open Eye Café
101 S Greensboro St.
Carrboro, NC 27510
p: 919-968-9410
www.openeyecafe.com
contact: Scott Conary
e: scott@openeyecafe.com
genres: S/S, Acoustic Rock, Folk, World, Jazz, Celtic
advance: 3-6 months
capacity: 100 **stage:** 10 x 7
All ages winebar w/ great vibe books Reg'l & Touring bands Thu-Sat for tips. Act plays 90min w/ some openers. Email or snail mail kit.

Pittsboro General Store Café
39 West St.
Pittsboro, NC 27312
p: 919-542-2432
e: info@generalstorecafe.com
www.thegeneralstorecafe.com
contact: Joyce Remick
e: joyce@thegeneralstorecafe.com
genres: Blues, Bluegrass, Acoustic, Jazz, World, Roots
advance: 2 months
capacity: 117
pa: Yes **sound eng:** Yes
Popular eatery showcases Local-Reg'l & some Touring performers Thu-Sat for all ages. Mail press kit w/ ATTN: Joyce Remick, GSC, PO Box 1651, Pittsboro, NC 27312.

The Pour House Music Hall
224 S Blount St.
Raleigh, NC 27601
p: 919-821-1120
e: tpourhouse@aol.com
www.the-pour-house.com
contact: Eric Mullen
genres: All Styles
advance: 12 weeks
capacity: 350
pa: Yes **sound eng:** Yes
stage: 19 x 15
Popular pub hosts Nat'l-Int'ls w/ estab. Local-Reg'l openers; mostly 21+ w/ some 18+ shows. 2-6 original acts per bill. See faqs at site.

Reservoir
100-A Brewer Ln.
Carrboro, NC 27510
p: 919-933-3204
e: reservoirbar@hotmail.com
www.reservoirbar.net
contact: Wes Lowder
genres: Rock, Country, Hip-Hop
advance: 1 month
capacity: 80
pa: Yes **sound eng:** Yes
stage: floor space
Bar in college town, primarily books Local-Int'l Rock bands. Up to 3 acts play 45min sets for tips. Email MySpace link or send CD for booking.

Charlotte

The Alley Cat
314 N College St.
Charlotte, NC 28202
p: 704-375-8765
e: info@thealleycat.com
www.thealleycat.com
contact: Kevin Mitchell
e: kevinm@thealleycat.com
genres: Rock
advance: 2-5 months
capacity: 900
pa: Yes **sound eng:** Yes
stage: 24 x 14
Rock venue w/ mostly 21+ shows features original music Wed & Fri; cover acts play Fri-Sat. Locals booked on wknds, Reg'ls on Wed. Up to 3 acts play 1-2hrs for flat fee. Send kit. No Calls. Do not follow up, will call if interested.

Amos' Southend
1423 S Tryon St.
Charlotte, NC 28203
p: 704-377-6874
www.amossouthend.com
contact: John
call: Tue-Fri 1-8pm
genres: Rock, Alt., Country, Reggae, Jam
advance: 3-6 months
capacity: 1500
pa: Yes **sound eng:** Yes
stage: 20 x 24
Popular music room hosts 3 Local-Nat'l acts for flat fee vs door. Some all ages shows & Tribute acts. Merch splits 80/20.

Double Door Inn
1218 Charlottetowne Ave.
Charlotte, NC 28204
p: 704-376-1446
www.doubledoorinn.com
contact: Micah
e: micah@carolinalivemusic.com
genres: Blues, Roots Rock, Zydeco, Rockabilly, Jazz, Fusion, Funk, Country, Bluegrass, Americana, Soul
advance: 2-3 months
capacity: 175
pa: Yes **sound eng:** Yes
stage: 15 x 15
Music club hosts original Local-Nat'l names Mon-Sat. 1-2 acts play two 75min sets for mostly 21+ shows. Send EPK or snail mail kit.

The Evening Muse
3227 N Davidson St.
Charlotte, NC 28205
p: 704-376-3737
www.eveningmuse.com
contact: Lea Kuhlmann
e: lea@eveningmuse.com
call: email only
genres: S/S, Rock, Folk, Blues, Indie Rock, Americana
advance: 10 weeks
capacity: 120
pa: Yes **sound eng:** Yes
stage: 12 x 20
open mics: 1st Wed of mo
All ages listening room hosts polished Reg'l & Touring bands 5+ nites. 2-4 bands play 45min of original tunes for % of door. Touring acts w/ Local openers moved to top of pile. Email & incl. band name & dates in subject line or mail press kit to venue w/ ATTN: Booking. Email follow-up 4 wks later.

Midtown Sundries at Lake Norman
18665 Harborside Dr.
Cornelius, NC 28031
p: 704-896-9013
e: info@midtownsundries.com; soniclounge@midtownsundries.com
www.midtownsundries.com
call: M-F before 11am; after 2pm
genres: Dance, Acoustic, Rock, Blues, Country, Jam
advance: 1-3 months
capacity: 500
pa: Yes
stage: 20 x 12
Family dining chain books area bands Sat-Sun for flat fee. Also hosts televised performances of area talent in Sonic Lounge; details at MySpace pg.

The Milestone Club
3400 Tuckaseegee Rd.
Charlotte, NC 28208
p: 704-398-0472
e: neal@solidgoldempire.com
www.themilestoneclub.com
contact: Phillip Shive
e: afterbirthcasserole@gmail.com
call: prefers email
genres: Most Styles
advance: 2 months
capacity: 170
pa: Yes **sound eng:** Yes
stage: 14 x 12
Underground music haven, hosts Local-Int'l bands Thu-Sun. 3 original acts play 35-50min. Only books acts w/ marquee value. No Nu-Metal or Gangsta styles. Email only for booking. No unsolicited mail, MySpace messages or calls.

Tremont Music Hall/ The Casbah
400 W Tremont Ave.
Charlotte, NC 28203
p: 704-343-9494
www.tremontmusichall.com
contact: Dave Ogden
e: booking@tremontmusichall.com
genres: All Styles
advance: 1-2 months
capacity: 1000; 325
pa: Yes **sound eng:** Yes
stage: 19 x 24
Premier venue books lauded & rising bands 5 nites. Nat'ls play 5-15 shows/mo. 3 Reg'l up & comers gig 30+min in smaller Casbah Fri & Sat. Merch splits 90/10. Email or mail promos to: PO Box 9480, Charlotte, NC 28299.

Greensboro/ Winston-Salem

The Blind Tiger
2115 Walker Ave.
Greensboro, NC 27403
p: 336-272-9888
e: theblind@theblindtiger.com
www.theblindtiger.com
contact: Doc
genres: Rock, Blues, Reggae, Bluegrass, Hardcore, Alt., Americana, Folk
capacity: 350
pa: Yes
open mics: Mon
Bar w/ full lights has DJs & mainly Local-Reg'l & some Nat'l bands nitely. Up to 5 bands play 60-90min for 21+.

Boone Saloon
489 W King St.
Boone, NC 28607
p: 828-264-1811
www.boonesaloon.com
contact: Matt Johnston
e: boonesaloon@yahoo.com
call: M-F 10am-5pm
genres: Reggae, Bluegrass, Jam, Hip-Hop, Funk Fusion, Cuban
advance: 3 months
capacity: 150
pa: Yes **sound eng:** Yes
stage: 16 x 15
Campus area hotspot near TN border & 100+mi from Winston, Salem & Asheville, book original Local-Touring bands & DJs w/ a draw. Featured act fills 3hrs, Wed, Thu & Sat for 21+. Prefers email, but may mail press kit to venue; will contact if interested. No Calls.

Somewhere Else Tavern
5713 W Friendly Ave.
Greensboro, NC 27410
p: 336-292-5464
www.myspace.com/somewhereelsetavern
contact: Burley Hayes
p: 336-273-8928
e: somewhereelsemusic@yahoo.com
call: M-F after 8pm
genres: Acoustic, Americana, Rock
advance: 2-3 months
capacity: 250
pa: Yes **sound eng:** Yes
stage: medium
All ages club books original Local-Reg'l acts 2-5 nites. 5-15 bands play for % of door. Use MySpace for booking.

The Sound Vent
120 W Main St.
Thomasville, NC 27360
p: 336-476-9523
www.soundvent.com
e: booking@soundvent.com
capacity: 99
21+ venue books Local & Reg'l acts. Email EPK or links; follow up on MySpace.

The Werehouse
211 E 3rd St.
Winston-Salem, NC 27101
p: 336-722-3016
e: werehousewerehouse@yahoo.com
www.thewerehouse.com
call: email only
genres: All Styles
advance: 2 months
capacity: 221
pa: Yes **sound eng:** Yes
stage: 20 x 24
All ages community arts ctr. presents original Reg'ls & some Touring acts & DJs 1-2 nites. 3 bands play 35-45min for % of

door. Prefers emailed link to music; no attachments. May also mail press kit to venue w/ ATTN: Music Booking; incl. statement of intent, preferred dates & times, anticipated requirements. See website for details. Must give written permission if registered w/ licensing org.
No MySpace messages or calls.

Wilmington

The Rusty Nail
1310 S 5th Ave.
Wilmington, NC 28401
p: 910-251-1888
www.myspace.com/rustynailnc
contact: Sandy
call: prefers MySpace
genres: Jazz, Blues, Bluegrass, Rock, Metal, Americana
advance: 2-6 months
capacity: 99
pa: Yes **sound eng:** By Request
stage: 10 x 20
open mics: Wed Acoustic
Bar w/ state-of-the-art recording facility showcases Reg'l talent & some Nat'l bands for all ages. Solo act plays four 45min sets. Hosts Cape Fear Blues Society wkly jams each Tue & 1st Sat/mo. Jams serve as auditions for booking gigs. Prefers contact via MySpace or snail mail kit; call to follow up.

The Soapbox
255 N Front St.
Wilmington, NC 28401
p: 910-251-8500
e: info@soapbox laundrolounge.com
www.soapboxlaundrolounge .com
contact: Brent Watkins
e: booking@soapbox laundrolounge.com
genres: Rock, Country, Jam, Hip-Hop, Blues, Jazz, Metal
advance: 6 months
capacity: 350; 125
pa: Yes **sound eng:** Yes
open mics: Wed **sign in:** 9pm
Largest area venue has 3 stages. Up to 6 Local-Int'l acts & DJs play 20-90min sets up to 7 nites for all ages. Email or mail press kit to venue.

Greater NC

The Pit Surf Shop & Boardrider's Grill
1209 S Croatan Hwy.
Kill Devil Hills, NC 27948
p: 252-480-3128
www.pitsurf.com
contact: Ben Sproul
p: 252-480-3128 x7
e: ben@pitsurf.com
call: prefers email
genres: Rock, Jam, Acoustic, Punk, Hard Rock, Reggae
advance: 6 weeks - 1 year
capacity: 300
pa: Yes **sound eng:** Yes
stage: 16 x 15
Top hangout/surfshop on Outer Banks has 1-2 original Local-Int'l bands & DJs 2-3 nites. Acts play 1-2hrs for small flat fee vs 100% of door after expenses. 21+ w/ all ages Mon, Wed & Fri in summer, some Fri & Sat in fall/spring. Prefers email w/ MP3 & list of venues headlined w/ crowd over 150; may also mail press kit w/ ATTN: Ben, PO Box 2920, Kill Devil Hills, NC 27948.

North Dakota

Bismark

The Light Club
3200 N 11th St.
Bismarck, ND 58503
p: 701-258-5683
www.clubradiolive.com
contact: Kurt Chaffee
p: 701-400-2706
e: kchaffee.newsong@ midconetwork.com
genres: CCM, Rock, Acoustic, Hardcore, Emo, Punk, Urban
advance: 3 months
capacity: 600
pa: Yes **sound eng:** Yes
stage: 24 x 20
All ages, youth-based Christian venue books Local-Int'l bands & DJs Fri & Sat. 2-4 acts play 45-60min. Prefers email for booking. Has own FM stn. & record label to offer one-stop recording, airing & performing.

Fargo

M & J Brand Saloon
817 Main Ave.
West Fargo, ND 58078
p: 701-282-3059
contact: Pat Hewitt
call: Tue after 6pm
genres: Country, Rock
advance: Up to 3 months
capacity: 250 **stage:** 20 x 15
Reg'l bands play 21+ casino lounge Thu-Sat for flat fee. 1 act plays from 9:30pm-1:20am. Snail mail kit.

The Nestor
1001 NP Ave. N
Fargo, ND 58103
p: 701-232-2485
www.thenestortavern.com
contact: Bryan Grog
e: bryangrog@hotmail.com
genres: Jam, Metal, Jazz, Alt., Bluegrass, Punk, Country
advance: 2-3 months
capacity: 170
pa: Yes **sound eng:** Yes
stage: small
Area's top music bar presents original Local-Touring bands for 21+ gigs Fri-Sat. 2-3 bands w/ positive attitude play for flat fee. Openers play 45min; headliners play 90min. Email or mail press kit to venue.

Rick's Bar
2721 Main Ave. W
Fargo, ND
58103
p: 701-232-8356
www.ricks-bar.com
contact: Spike
call: M-F after 4:30pm
genres: Rock
advance: 6-12 months
capacity: 250 **stage:** medium
Lively bar hosts Local & Touring acts Wed-Sat. Featured act plays 40min. Call for booking.

The Venue At The Hub
2525 9th Ave. S
Fargo, ND 58103
p: 701-232-6767
e: info@thehubfargo.com
www.thehubfargo.com
contact: Jade Nielson
p: 701-298-0071
e: jade@jadepresents.com
genres: All Styles
advance: 1-3 months
capacity: 1500
pa: Yes
stage: 36 x 28
Club inside recently remodeled, state-of-the-art ent. complex features up to 3 polished Local-Touring acts nitely; some all ages shows. Promos: Jade Presents, 3014 26th Ave. SW, Fargo, ND 58103.

Windbreak Saloon
3150 39th St. SW
Fargo, ND 58104
p: 701-282-5507
www.thewindbreak.com
contact: Gary Bitzer
p: 218-287-2037
e: gary@bitzeragency.com
call: M-F 8am-6pm
genres: Country, Rock, Pop
advance: 2 months
capacity: 260
Casino bar books Reg'l bands Wed-Sun. 1 act plays three 1hr sets. Email or mail press kit to: Bitzer Agency, 2703 12th Ave. S, Moorhead, MN 56560.

Ohio

Akron

Cedar's Lounge
23 N Hazel St.
Youngstown, OH 44503
p: 330-743-6560
www.myspace.com/ cedarslounge
contact: Pete Drivere
call: prefers MySpace
genres: Punk, Alt., Rock, Alt. Country, Jazz
advance: 2-3 months
capacity: 200
pa: Yes **sound eng:** Yes
stage: 30 x 15
Long-running indie music club 50mi from Akron, books polished Local-Touring bands Fri-Sat & some Wed & Sun for 18+. Up to 4 original bands play 45-60min for door minus sound or flat fee. Prefers contact thru MySpace, or snail mail kit w/ ATTN: Pete, Mara or Chris.

The Lounge
370 Paul Williams St.
Akron, OH 44311
p: 330-535-LIVE
www.theloungeniteclub.com
contact: Frank
call: evenings
genres: Blues, Rock
advance: 6 weeks
capacity: 150
pa: Yes
Formerly Daily Double, music room hosts Local-Reg'l bands Fri-Sat; few Nat'ls. Featured act performs for 4hrs for flat fee to 21+ crowd. Mail kit to venue.

Sadie Rene's
7200 Whipple Ave. NW
North Canton, OH 44720
p: 330-499-8246
www.sadierenes.com
contact: Michael Murphy
e: bookings@sadierenes.com
call: Wed & Sun after 3pm
genres: Rock, Alt., Metal
advance: 4+ weeks
capacity: 233
pa: Yes **sound eng:** Yes
stage: 20 x 15
open mics: Tue; fall-spring
Rockin' 18+ bar 23mi from Akron, books mostly Local-Reg'l bands Wed & Fri-Sun. Up to 3 acts play 1hr for % of door.

Cincinnati

Annie's Ent. Complex
4343 Kellogg Ave.
Cincinnati, OH 45226
p: 513-321-2572
www.anniesentertainment.com
contact: Bill Georgeton
e: events@ anniesentertainment.com
call: M-F noon-5pm
genres: Mainly Metal & Rock
advance: Up to 5 months
capacity: 1100; 3500
pa: Yes **sound eng:** Yes
stage: 35 x 25
Large complex features indoor stage & outdoor pavilion for 18+ (21+ for dance nites). 2-3 acts/bill. Nat'ls gig 90-120min sets Sat for flat fee. Locals mostly open or play on Fri for 30-45min; DJs welcomed. Merch splits 80/20. Mail press kit to venue.

Arlin's Bar & Restaurant
307 Ludlow Ave.
Cincinnati, OH 45220
p: 513-751-6566
contact: Margie Fantelli
call: Mon 9:30am-12pm
genres: Eclectic
advance: 1 month
capacity: 160
pa: Yes
stage: floor space
open mics: First 2 Thu mo
21+ bar books Local bands & DJs on wknds. Featured act plays 45-60min for flat fee. Send CD promos to venue.

Arnold's Bar & Grill
210 E 8th St.
Cincinnati, OH 45202
p: 513-421-6234
www.arnoldsbarandgrill.com
contact: Abe Bates
p: 513-421-3123
genres: Jazz, Blues, Acoustic, Swing, Cajun
capacity: 49; 90
City's oldest bar books Local-Touring bands Thu-Sat for 21+. Up to 2 bands fill 2hrs.

The Blue Note
4520 W 8th St.
Cincinnati, OH 45238
p: 513-921-8898
e: bluenotecincinnati@ yahoo.com
www.bluenotecincinnati.com
genres: Rock, Alt., College, Acoustic
capacity: 249
pa: Yes **sound eng:** Yes
Hole-in-the wall bar w/ mostly indifferent staff books 2-4 original Local-Nat'l acts Wed-Sun for 21+. Thu College Nite is 18+. Send kit or use MySpace.

Bogart's
2621 Vine St.
Cincinnati, OH 45219
p: 513-872-8800
e: info@bogarts.com

www.bogarts.com
contact: Amy Dahlhoff
p: 513-421-9000
call: M-F 9am-5pm
genres: Pop, Rock, Jazz, R&B, Country, Metal, Punk, Blues
advance: 6 weeks
capacity: 1464
pa: Yes **sound eng:** Yes
Live Nation venue books USA & Int'l estab. & rising talent 3-7 nites. Up to 3 acts play 45+min sets, merch splits 85/15. Local/Reg'ls enroll in band challenges for consideration.

Brick Street
36 E High St.
Oxford, OH 45056
p: 513-523-1335
www.brickstreetbar.com
contact: Lara Pavloff
e: brickstreetbar@gmail.com
genres: Rock, Alt., Pop, Country
capacity: 850
pa: Yes **sound eng:** Yes
stage: medium
Bar right off Miami U of OH campus books original Local & Touring acts Thu-Sat & cover bands Wed. DJs spin b/w sets. Prefers EPKs or email before mailing kit to venue.

The Mad Frog
1 E McMillan St.
Cincinnati, OH 45219
p: 513-784-9119
www.themadfrog.net
contact: Bryan Billhimer
e: madfrogbooking@gmail.com
genres: Reggae, Hip-Hop, Blues, Rock, Jazz
advance: 2 months
capacity: 500
pa: Yes **sound eng:** Yes
stage: 20 x 18
Prime 18+ music club presents original estab. artists & buzz bands nitely. Up to 4 acts play 40min sets.

Rohs Street Cafe
245 W McMillian St.
Cincinnati, OH 45219
p: 513-328-7647
www.rohsstreetcafe.com
contact: Vern Leong
e: booking@rohsstreetcafe.com
call: email only
genres: Jazz, Rock, Acoustic, Bluegrass
advance: 2 months
capacity: 200+
pa: Yes
sound eng: Yes
Coffeehouse features Local-Nat'l acts Thu-Sat. 2 acts play 45-60min for 100% of door. Prefers email or snail mail kits.

The Stadium Bar
16 S Poplar
Oxford, OH 45056
p: 513-523-4661
www.myspace.com/stadiumbar
contact: Matt Hughes
e: thestadiumclub@aol.com
call: Mon, Wed & Fri 12-4pm
genres: Pop, Rock, Alt., Hip-Hop
advance: 4/mo+
capacity: 350
pa: Yes **sound eng:** Yes
open mics: Wed **sign in:** 9pm
College bar near Miami U, books 1-2 Reg'l & Touring bands Thu-Sat for 18+.

Cleveland

The Agora Theatre & Ballroom
5000 Euclid Ave.
Cleveland, OH 44103
p: 216-881-2221
e: info@clevelandagora.com
www.clevelandagora.com
contact: Andrea Sweazy
p: 216-881-2221 x101
e: book@clevelandagora.com
call: M-F 10am-5:30pm
genres: Rock, Alt., Hardcore, Emo, Country, Jazz, Blues, Acoustic, S/S
advance: 1-4 months
capacity: 500; 2000
pa: Yes **sound eng:** Yes
stage: 2 large stages
Prime concert venue w/ 2 stages books estab. Nat'l acts thru agencies for mostly all ages. Polished original Local-Reg'l acts & DJs may fill opening slots in smaller room. 3-5 acts/bill. Contact via email.

Barking Spider
11310 Juniper Rd.
Cleveland, OH 44106
p: 216-421-2863
www.barkingspidertavern.com
contact: Martin Juredine
call: M-F 2-5pm
genres: Americana, Jazz, Gospel, Rock, New Age, Blues, Folk, Reggae
advance: 1 week - 6 months
capacity: 100
pa: Yes **sound eng:** Yes
stage: 20 x 6 **in-house:** Piano
open mics: 1st & 4th Tue
Popular 21+ hole-in-the-wall music room near campus presents original Local-Nat'l acts nitely for mixed crowd. Opener plays 1hr; headliner fills 10pm-12:30am. Popular open mic. Mail kit to venue.

Beachland Ballroom & Tavern
15711 Waterloo Rd.
Cleveland, OH 44110
p: 216-383-1124
e: music@beachlandballroom.com
www.beachlandballroom.com
contact: Mark Leddy
call: M-F noon-5pm
genres: Alt., Rock, Roots, Folk, Alt. Country, World, Punk
advance: 3 months
capacity: 150; 550
pa: Yes **sound eng:** Yes
stage: medium (Tavern); large
Notable original music showcase hosts estab. Touring & buzz bands w/ local draw up to 7 nites for all ages. Polished Local-Reg'ls may play Local shows or fill opening slots. Openers play 30-40min; headliner 60-90min. Email or mail full press kit to venue; will contact if interested.

Fat Fish Blue!
21 Prospect Ave. E
Cleveland, OH 44115
p: 216-875-6000
e: fun@fatfishblue.com
www.fatfishblue.com
contact: Steve Zamborsky
e: steve@fatfishblue.com
genres: Blues, Jazz, R&B
advance: 6 months
capacity: 250
pa: Yes **sound eng:** Yes
stage: 14 x 12
Cajun-themed all ages party spot features a Local-Touring band Wed-Sun. Featured band plays 3hrs for % of door. Email or mail press kit to venue. No Calls.

The Grog Shop
2785 Euclid Heights Blvd.
Cleveland Heights, OH 44106
p: 216-321-5588
e: grogkat@yahoo.com
www.grogshop.gs
contact: Kathy Simkoff
e: kathy@grogshop.gs
call: M-F noon-6pm
genres: Indie Rock, Punk, Alt. Country, Emo, Hip-Hop
advance: 1-3 months
capacity: 400
pa: Yes **sound eng:** Yes
stage: 20 x 20
Popular all ages club books estab. & rising talent nitely. 3 bands play 30-60min nitely. Also books for B Side & Liquor Lounge. Send EPK or snail mail kit; call 2wks later.

Hi-Fi Concert Club
11729 Detroit Ave.
Lakewood, OH 44107
p: 216-521-8878
e: thehificlub@aol.com
www.hificoncertclub.com
contact: Jim Maler
call: M-F 2-7pm
genres: Rock, Alt., S/S, Americana, Metal
advance: 1 month
capacity: 300
pa: Yes **sound eng:** Yes
Top indie label acts & new artists gig up to 7 nites in rocking 18+ venue. Locals usu. keep 100% of door. Up to 3 acts play 45-60min. Prefers link to EPK; allow 2-4 wks, follow up via email or phone.

Maple Grove
14832 Pease Rd.
Maple Heights, OH 44137
p: 216-475-4224
www.maplegrovebar.com
contact: Nick Summa
e: nicksumma@earthlink.net
genres: Rock, Indie Rock, Alt.
capacity: 70
pa: Yes **sound eng:** Yes
2-3 Local-Nat'l acts gig Fri & Sat in multi-level music hall 'built by rockers for rockers.' Thu & 1st Fri/mo Live Band Karaoke. 21+, incl. bands. Snail mail or use online form.

Nighttown
12387 Cedar Rd.
Cleveland, OH 44106
p: 216-795-0550
e: info@nighttowncleveland.com
www.nighttowncleveland.com
contact: Jim Wadsworth
p: 216-721-5624
e: jwadsworth@aol.com
call: M-F 10am-6pm
genres: Jazz, Folk, World
advance: 2 weeks - 6 mo
capacity: 100
pa: Yes **sound eng:** Yes
stage: 12 x 12
Niteclub near campuses, draws diverse crowds & top artists. Featured original Touring act or polished Reg'l gig nitely for all ages; may host Locals on wknds. Acts play two 60-75min sets w/ break & keep 80% of merch sales. Only Nat'l-Int'ls - mail bio & full CD to: Jim Wadsworth Prod., 2213 Bellfield Ave., Cleveland Heights, OH 44106.

Peabody's Down Under
2045 E 21st St.
Cleveland, OH 44115
p: 216-776-9999
e: clevelandbooking@gmail.com
www.peabodys.com
contact: Chris Zitterbart
e: chris.z@peabodys.com
call: M-F 11am-6pm
genres: Metal, Rock, Hip-Hop
advance: 1-2 months
capacity: 750
pa: Yes **sound eng:** Yes
stage: 27 x 19
Top concert club books Reg'l & Touring acts nitely & hosts Band Battles. Large main room w/ good sight lines hosts Nat'l & Locals w/ draw; cave-like Pirates Cove offers smaller stage & outdoor patio; upstairs Rockstar bar is intimate. Mostly all ages shows w/ rare 18+ DJ nite. 3-7 bands play 30min. Merch split is 90/10 for Touring acts. Call first.

Phantasy Nite Club
11802 Detroit Ave.
Lakewood, OH 44107
p: 216-228-6300
e: phantcleve@sbcglobal.net
www.phantasyconcertclub.net
contact: Michelle DeFrasia
call: M-F 10am-5pm
genres: Rock, Alt., Acoustic, Electronic, Goth, College, Rockabilly, Metal
advance: 6 weeks
capacity: 350
pa: Yes **sound eng:** Yes
stage: 19 x 19
Multi-room ent. complex features mainly 3-5 original Reg'l bands Fri & Sat for 40-50min sets. Club is 18+ w/ some shows 16+; theater is all ages. Contact via email only.

Columbus

Alrosa Villa
5055 Sinclair Rd.
Columbus, OH 43229
p: 614-885-9125
www.alrosavilla.com
contact: Rick Cautela
p: 614-895-1966
e: alrosarick@aol.com
call: M-F 11am-5pm
genres: Rock, Metal, Reggae, Hip-Hop, R&B, Punk, Jam
advance: 1-3 months
capacity: 800
pa: Yes **sound eng:** Yes
stage: 23 x 50
Area's prime Rock room w/ full sound & lights & dark past, hosts top bands on their way up & down 6 nites w/ Local openers & DJs. Up to 5 acts play 45-60min sets; some all ages shows. Merch splits 80/20. Email booking inquiries.

Billiard Club Pub 161
911 E Dublin-Granville Rd.
Columbus, OH 43229
p: 614-885-9299
www.myspace.com/bcpool
contact: Clint Barnette

e: clint221159@sbcglobal.net
genres: Rock, Dance, S/S
advance: 2 months
capacity: 300-600
pa: Yes **sound eng:** Yes
stage: medium
open mics: Tue **sign in:** 9pm
Pool room/Rock club books 4 original Local-Touring Acoustic acts on Tue; louder bands gig Fri & Sat for 18+. Must sell 15+ tix at $5 ea. Openers play 35-45min; headliner, 90. Bands must be 18+. Prefers email.

Brew-Stirs French Quarter
6118 Busch Blvd.
Columbus, OH 43229
p: 614-433-9366
www.brew-stirs.com
contact: Sandy
call: M-F after 11am
genres: All Styles
capacity: 400
pa: Yes **sound eng:** Yes
Lively New Orleans-themed complex features Local-Reg'l bands & DJs Thu-Sat. 1-2 acts play to all ages. Jose's Cabana upstairs books music on Sat. Snail mail or drop off kit.

Dick's Den
2417 N High St.
Columbus, OH 43202
p: 614-268-9573
contact: Ron Yednock
call: Mon after 9pm
genres: Jazz, Blues, Folk, Bluegrass, Funk, Soul, R&B
advance: 3 months
capacity: 84
pa: Yes
stage: 8 x 10
open mics: Tue 11pm
Top 21+ dive bar/listening room draws students & jazzbos for top tier Reg'l & Touring artists Thu-Sun. Featured act plays 10pm-2am for 100% of door. Mail press kit to venue.

The Distillery
1896 N High St.
Columbus, OH 43201
p: 614-291-3448
www.cringe.com/bs
contact: Tony Painter
p: 614-279-2016
e: bsienna@aol.com
call: evenings
genres: Alt., Punk, Ska, Hip-Hop, Appalachia Rock
advance: 1 month
capacity: 250
pa: Yes **sound eng:** Yes
stage: 14 x 14
Club below deli serves up estab. Touring acts 3 nites & rising Local/Reg'l talent looking for a foothold nitely; mostly all ages. Up to 4 bands play 30-45min sets for % of door. Prefers email.

Frog Bear & Wild Boar
343 N Front St.
Columbus, OH 43215
p: 614-621-9453
www.frogbearbar.com
contact: Dave Allsbrooks
e: dallsbrooks@yahoo.com
genres: All Styles
advance: 2 months
capacity: 1500
pa: Yes **sound eng:** Yes
stage: large; medium
Spacious 21+ venue w/ indoor & outdoor stages for Local-Int'l acts. 2 bands play Thu-Fri; 1 act plays Sat. Few all ages shows. Also books Skye Bar. Email or mail press kit to venue.

Gatsby's
151 N Hamilton Rd.
Gahanna, OH 43230
p: 614-476-0088
e: gatsbys1@aol.com
www.gatsbys1977.com
contact: Doug
genres: Rock, Acoustic
capacity: 70
21+ bar books Local & Reg'l bands Fri & Sat nites for flat fee. Send promos to club.

High Five
1227 N High St.
Columbus, OH 43201
p: 614-421-2998
www.highfivebar.com
e: booking@highfivebar.com
genres: Rock, Hip-Hop, Jazz, Blues, Folk, S/S, Punk, Metal, Noise, Experimental
advance: 2 months
capacity: 200
pa: Yes **sound eng:** Yes
stage: 12 x 15
3-4 original Reg'l & Touring bands & DJs play popular 18+ downtown dive w/ dance floor Tue-Sun. All booking done online. No unsolicited mail.

Mustard Seed Café
18 W Main St.
West Jefferson, OH 43162
p: 614-572-8608
e: mustardseed202@aol.com
www.myspace.com/themustardseedcafe
contact: Susan Vargo
genres: Christian-based
advance: 2 months
capacity: 200
pa: Yes
stage: 22 x 18
All ages Christian music club 19mi from Columbus, has Local-Reg'l bands Wed-Sat; some Nat'l acts. 2 bands play 30+min for % of door or offering. Snail mail kit.

Newport Music Hall
1722 N High St.
Columbus, OH 43201
p: 614-294-1659
www.promowestlive.com
contact: Adam Vanchoff
p: 614-461-LIVE (5483)
call: M-F 10am-5pm
genres: Alt., Prog., Jam, Punk
capacity: 1000-1700
pa: Yes **sound eng:** Yes
Former movie palace now prime concert spot has top Reg'l-Touring acts w/ some Local showcases; mostly all ages. Also books The LC, House of Crave & The Basement. Snail mail kit.

Oldfield's on High
2590 N High St.
Columbus, OH 43202
p: 614-784-0477
www.myspace.com/oldfields1
contact: Lance James
p: 614-560-4570
e: lance_james123@yahoo.com
genres: All Styles
advance: 4 months
capacity: 200
pa: Yes **sound eng:** Yes
stage: 15 x 20
open mics: Mon 10pm
Popular dive showcase near campuses, hosts mostly original area talent & some Touring bands & DJs nitely. 1-2 bands fill 3hrs for 21+ & keep % of bar. Mail press kit to venue.

On the Rocks
5815 Karric Sq. Dr.
Dublin, OH 43016
p: 614-717-9215
www.otr-bar.com
contact: Jeff
e: booking@otr-bar.com
call: email only
genres: Rock, Blues
advance: 2 months
capacity: 150
Original Local & Reg'l bands gig Tue-Sat in relaxed joint. 1 act plays 3hrs w/ breaks to 21+. Best bet is to email.

Ravari Room
2661 N High St.
Columbus, OH 43202
p: 614-263-4058
www.ravariroom.com
contact: Jeff Stewart
p: 614-261-4686
call: M-F after 3pm
genres: All Styles
advance: Up to 6 months
capacity: 300
pa: Yes **sound eng:** Yes
stage: 18 x 15
Popular 21+ club near Ohio State U campus, draws blue hairs to blue collars, punks to suits for original Local-Touring bands & DJs mostly Thu-Fri but up to 5 nites. 3-4 acts play 45-60min sets. Prefers email, but may mail press kit to venue.

Ruby Tuesday
1978 Summit St.
Columbus, OH 43201
p: 614-291-8313
www.rubytuesdaylive.com
contact: Scott Farthingham
p: 614-284-9551
e: sfotheri@columbus.rr.com
genres: All Styles
advance: 2 months
capacity: 200
pa: Yes **sound eng:** Yes
stage: 20 x 10
open mics: Tue 9:30pm
Hang that started the chain, near one of the world's largest campuses, books up to 3 Reg'l & Touring bands Mon-Sat for 100% of door minus sound. Shows are 21+. Good sound & elevated stage. Call for booking.

Scarlet & Grey Cafe
2203 N High St.
Columbus, OH 43201
p: 614-291-2347
www.scarletandgreycafe.com
contact: Jen or Helen
p: 614-354-9832 (Helen)
e: booking@scarletandgreycafe.com
genres: Rock
capacity: 100
pa: Yes **sound eng:** Yes
open mics: Mon Acoustic
Bar near campus, books 2-5 original Local bands for 2 shows Thu-Sat. Shows start at 10pm w/ some early all ages shows 6-9pm. Touring bands must hook up w/ Locals. Acts play 1hr & get paid after drawing 10. Email or contact via MySpace & incl. contact info & website.

Skully's Music Diner
1151 N High St.
Columbus, OH 43201
p: 614-291-8856
e: skullys@columbus.rr.com
www.skullys.org
contact: Angelo Palma
call: email only
genres: Indie, Hip-Hop, Metal
advance: 4-5 months
capacity: 800
pa: Yes **sound eng:** Yes
stage: 35 x 15
18+ dance club books original Local-Int'l acts Mon, Tue, Fri & Sat. 3-4 acts play 45min from 10:30pm-2am. Use email or snail mail kit w/ 3-4 song CD.

The Thirsty Ear
1200 W 3rd Ave.
Columbus, OH 43212
p: 614-299-4987
www.thethirstyear.com
contact: Dan Koloskus
p: 614-299-4775
e: dan@thethirstyear.com
genres: Blues, Folk, Roots, Rock, S/S
advance: 2-4 weeks
capacity: 126
pa: Yes **sound eng:** Yes
stage: 12 x 15
open mics: Wed Acoustic
Music room books original Reg'l bands Tue-Sun for 21+ crowd; some cover acts. Act plays three 1hr sets. Touring bands need local draw or airtime on WCBE.

Woo Doggie's Grill
5257 Westpointe Plaza Dr.
Columbus, OH 43228
p: 614-876-2147
www.woodoggies.net
contact: Ronnie Boggs
genres: Acoustic
pa: Yes **sound eng:** Yes
open mics: Thu
1 Local or Touring act gigs Wed-Sat at 21+ bar &. Mail or drop off promo to venue. No booking via MySpace or calls.

Dayton

The Attic
2852 Wilmington Pike
Kettering, OH 45419
p: 937-297-9634
www.theatticclub.com
contact: Elizabeth Kilby
e: elizabeth@theatticclub.com
call: email only
genres: Family-Friendly
advance: 3-4 months for Locals; 1 month for Nat'ls
capacity: 771
pa: Yes **sound eng:** Yes
stage: 24 x 30
Faith-based teen club hosts Local & Touring bands for secular crowd. 5 acts play 20-35min sets Fri-Sat. Nat'ls keep 85% merch sales. No Praise or Worship. Also books The Cellar. Email or mail press kit w/ short bio, music samples, info about fan base & past shows in the Dayton area to: Attic Booking, 2720 Ferncliff Ave., Dayton, OH 45420. No calls.

Canal Street Tavern
308 E 1st St.
Dayton, OH 45402

p: 937-228-2450
www.canalstreettavern.com
contact: Mick Montgomery
e: mickcst@ameritech.net
call: M-F noon-3pm
genres: All Styles
advance: 1-3 months
capacity: 200
pa: Yes **sound eng:** Yes
stage: 30 x 16 **in-house:** Piano
Intimate Alt. music club presents known Touring acts w/ Local & Reg'l openers Wed-Sun. Either 1 headliner & opener or 3-4 Locals perform for 18+. Mail kit to: Canal St. Concerts, 118 Green St., Dayton, OH 45402. Wait 1-2 wks after submitting, then call or email to follow up. EPKs accepted only after establishing interest.

The Cellar
5238 Cobblegate Dr.
Moraine, OH 45439
p: 937-395-9186
www.thecellar.org
contact: Elizabeth Kilby
e: elizabeth@theatticclub.com
call: email only
genres: All Styles
advance: 1-2 months
capacity: 704
pa: Yes
stage: 24 x 30
Up to 3 Local bands gig 30min Fri & Sat for merch money at teen hang w/ skate park & 2 dance floors. Prefers email, but may mail promos to: Harvest Youth Ministries, 3101 Indian Ripple Rd., Beavercreek, OH 45440. No Calls.

Crosswalk Coffee
118 E Main St.
Eaton, OH 45320
p: 937-456-9955
e: info@crosswalkcoffee.net
www.crosswalkcoffee.net
contact: Tevi Tarler
p: 937-456-9300
genres: Acoustic-based
advance: 6-8 months
capacity: 50
pa: Yes
stage: floor space
open mics: Thu 7-10pm
All ages music venue midway b/w Dayton & Indianapolis showcases Local-Reg'l bands Fri. Featured act plays 8pm-11pm w/ breaks for tips. Snail mail press kit for booking.

The Dublin Pub
300 Wayne Ave.
Dayton, OH 45410
p: 937-224-7822
e: info@dubpub.com
www.dubpub.com
contact: Steve Tieber
e: stieber@dubpub.com
genres: Irish, Celtic Rock, Rock
advance: 2-6 months
capacity: 150; 50 (outdoors)
Popular spot serves up polished Reg'l & Touring bands Thu-Sat. 1-2 acts play three 45-50min sets. Mail promos to club.

Oregon Express
336 E 5th St.
Dayton, OH 45402
p: 937-223-9205
www.myspace.com/oregonexpress
contact: Joe Bavaro
e: jsus84@aol.com
call: M-F 9:30am-5pm
genres: Most Styles
advance: 3-4 months
capacity: 250
pa: Yes **sound eng:** Yes
stage: 15 x 12 (wedge)
open mics: Thu Blues 9pm
Prime Reg'l showcase w/ some Nat'l acts has awkward stage but loyal following & reputable pizza. Up to 3 bands gig from 10pm-1:30am Tue-Sat for 21+. No Country or Jazz. Email or mail press kit to venue.

The Trolley Stop
530 E 5th St.
Dayton, OH 45402
p: 937-461-1101
e: trolleystopdayton@yahoo.com
www.trolleystopdayton.com
contact: Marty
e: mrfirstcall@hotmail.com
genres: Jazz, Blues, Alt., Newgrass, Rock n' Roll, Acoustic
advance: 2 months
capacity: 80
stage: 10 x 12
open mics: Thu **sign in:** 9pm
Lively 21+ Acoustic showcase supports Local & some Reg'l-Touring bands Thu-Sat. Featured act plays 9:30pm-1:30am for flat fee.

Toledo

Headliners
4500 N Detroit Ave.
Toledo, OH 43612
p: 419-697-5300
e: headliners@versogroup.com
www.headlinerstoledo.com
contact: Jonathan Anderson
p: 419-698-4020
e: janderson@versogroup.com
call: M-F 10am-5pm
genres: Metal, Pop, Alt., Punk, Hip-Hop, Country, Jam, Blues, Southern Rock
advance: 3-4 weeks
capacity: 650; 800; 1750
pa: Yes **sound eng:** Yes
stage: 14 x 22; 12 x 16; 24 x 32
Ent. complex w/ 3 stages books original Local & Touring bands 3-4 nites. Mostly all ages. Also books Frankie's. Email or mail promos: Verso Group, ATTN: Headliners Booking, 146 Main, Toledo, OH 43605.

Howard's Club H
210 N Main St.
Bowling Green, OH 43402
p: 419-352-3195
www.howardsclubh.com
contact: Jim Gavarone
e: groovy@howardsclubh.com
call: email only
genres: All Styles
advance: 3-4 months
capacity: 500
pa: Yes **sound eng:** Yes
stage: 16 x 20
Prime music club w/ awesome sound in college town only presents top-notch Touring acts & buzz bands w/ local draw that will keep the bar busy Wed-Sat for 18+; some all ages shows. Most shows headliner & opener(s) play from 10pm-2am for door minus $65 for sound. Send enticing email w/ ATTN: Booking w/ band name in subject & incl. music links, tour history, expected draw & fee. No unsolicited mail or calls.

Oklahoma

Oklahoma City

The Conservatory
8911 N Western Ave.
Oklahoma City, OK 73114
p: 405-607-4805
e: info@conservatoryokc.com
www.conservatoryokc.com
contact: Gianni
call: prefers MySpace
genres: Indie Rock, Metal, Hardcore, Hip-Hop, Rock
advance: 3 months
capacity: 240
pa: Yes **sound eng:** Yes
stage: 20 x 12
All ages original music club books Local-Int'l bands & DJs Mon-Sat. 3 bands play 40min sets. Prefers MySpace message.

The Deli
309 White St.
Norman, OK 73069
p: 405-329-3534
e: thedeli@cox.net
www.thedeli.us
contact: Lori Treisa
call: M-F noon-3pm
genres: All Styles
advance: 6-8 weeks
capacity: 100
pa: Yes **sound eng:** Yes
stage: 30 x 10
Busy 21+ bar 19mi from OK City, books a mix of Touring & Reg'l acts nitely. Up to 3 mostly original acts play 45+min for the door. Email for booking.

Galileo Bar & Grill
3009 Paseo Dr.
Oklahoma City, OK 73103
p: 405-415-7827; 405-525-4152 (office)
www.myspace.com/galileobarandgrill
contact: Sandi Burden
e: galileook@aol.com
call: M-F after 5pm
genres: Acoustic, Folk, Indie
advance: 2-3 months
capacity: 80-100
pa: Yes
stage: small
open mics: Thu 9pm
Original Reg'l & some Touring bands perform Fri & Sat for 21+ restaurant crowd; all ages show on Tue. 1-2 acts play 9pm-1:30am for % of door. Prefers press kit mailed to club.

VZD's
4200 N Western Ave.
Oklahoma City, OK 73118
p: 405-524-4203
www.vzds.com
contact: Chad Bleakley
p: 405-524-4200
e: chadb1@cox.net
call: prefers email
genres: Alt., Country, Rock, Jam, R&B
advance: 3 months
capacity: 200
pa: Yes **sound eng:** Yes
stage: 20 x 14
Bar & grill is a mainstay for live music hosting prime Local-Nat'l acts w/ buzz Fri-Sat & some DJs. 1-2 original acts play 45min to 21+ crowd for % of door. Mail press kit to venue w/ ATTN: Chad Bleakley.

Wormy Dog Saloon
311 E Sheridan Ave.
Oklahoma City, OK 73104
p: 405-601-6276
e: philip@wormydog.com
www.wormydog.com
contact: Chuck T.
e: chuck@wormydog.com
call: email only
genres: TX & Alt. Country, Red Dirt, Americana
advance: 2-3 months
capacity: 700
pa: Yes **sound eng:** Yes
stage: 20 x 20
21+ wild west showcase w/ 2 floors books 1-2 Local-Int'l acts Wed-Sat. Opener gets 1hr & headliner plays 90min. Prefers email, but may mail press kit to venue w/ ATTN: Bookings.

Tulsa

Arnie's Bar
318 E 2nd St.
Tulsa, OK 74120
p: 918-583-0797
www.arniesbar.com
contact: JoAnn Armstrong
e: joann@arniesbar.com
genres: Rock, Celtic
advance: 4 months
capacity: 100 **stage:** floor space
Beloved Irish hole-in-the-wall books 1 Local/Reg'l band Fri-Sat for the door; featured act plays 10pm-2am.

Brady Theater
105 W Brady St.
Tulsa, OK 74103
p: 918-582-7239
e: info@bradytheater.net
www.bradytheater.com
contact: Jennifer Sorrels
p: 405-721-8066
e: jennifer@dcfconcerts.com
call: M-F 9:30am-5:30pm
genres: All Styles
capacity: 2800
pa: Yes **sound eng:** Yes
stage: large
Vintage all ages theater, now under original mgmtpresents 2 or more Reg'l & Touring acts for flat fee; some Local openers. Email preferred for booking. Mail press kit to: 6957 NW Expy., #316, Oklahoma City, OK 73132.

Cain's Ballroom
423 N Main St.
Tulsa, OK 74103
p: 918-584-2306
e: info@cainsballroom.com
www.cainsballroom.com
contact: Chad Rodgers
e: booking@cainsballroom.com
call: M-F 10am-noon; 1-4pm
genres: Rock, Jazz, Blues, CCM, Alt., Gospel, Americana, Urban, Folk, Acoustic
advance: 4-6 months
capacity: 1711; 325
pa: Yes **sound eng:** Yes
stage: 45 x 25; 20 x 12
Famed all-ages venue has Reg'ls open for top Nat'ls 4 nites/wk. 2-3 acts & DJs fill 4hrs for flat fee; Nat'l merch splits 75/25. Adjacent club, Bob's, books up to 4 Rock, Folk, Jazz or Acoustic acts. Prefers email for booking, but may also mail press kit.

Gray Snail Saloon
1334 E 15th St.

Tulsa, OK 74120
p: 918-587-7584
www.myspace.com/graysnailsaloon
contact: Rob Mason
e: onerob@cox.net
call: Fri afternoons
genres: Rock, Pop, Alt.
advance: 3 months
capacity: 300; 340 (outdoors)
stage: 35 x 13; 10 x 8 (outdoor)
Large 21+ venue w/ biker vibe books Reg'ls up to 7 nites. 1 act performs 45-60min for flat fee.

The Otherside
6904 S Lewis Ave.
Tulsa, OK 74136
p: 918-488-0100
e: theothersidetulsa@yahoo.com
www.myspace.com/theothersideclub
pa: Yes **sound eng:** Yes
Books many Nat'l acts that come thru Tulsa & Locals as well. Also books The Pink Eye.

The Pink Eye
1539 E 11th St.
Tulsa, OK 74120
p: 918-853-7283
e: info@fatlipmusic.com
www.myspace.com/thepinkeye
contact: Tieson
genres: Rock, Underground, Hardcore, Punk, Metal, Rap, Indie Rock, Emo
advance: 2 months
capacity: 150
pa: Yes **sound eng:** Yes
stage: 10 x 20
All ages original music club books Local-Int'l acts & some DJs 6 nites. Bands play 30min for% of draw after costs. Also books several other Reg'l venues. Prefers MySpace for booking.

Oregon

Eugene

John Henry's
77 W Broadway
Eugene, OR 97401
p: 541-342-3358
e: info@johnhenrysclub.com
www.johnhenrysclub.com
contact: Keith Martin
p: 541-345-9315
e: keith@johnhenrysclub.com
genres: All Styles
advance: 2 months
capacity: 329
pa: Yes **sound eng:** Yes
stage: 18 x 14
Music club w/ great sound, hosts 3-4 Local-Touring bands & DJs Mon, Tue, Fri & Sat for 40min sets. Known artists gig early; late shows Fri, Mon & Tue feature 4 acts. Must be 21+ to gig. Prefers link to music, but may also contact via MySpace; see web for detailed policy. No unsolicited mail.

Peacock Tavern
125 SW 2nd St.
Corvallis, OR 97333
p: 541-754-8522
e: peacockbar-grill@comcast.net
www.myspace.com/peacockbargrill
contact: Stephanie Mather
call: prefers MySpace
genres: All Styles
advance: 2-3 months
capacity: 350; 400
pa: Yes **sound eng:** Yes
Lively bar books Local-Touring Wed, Fri & Sat. Bands play from 9:30pm-1:30am for 100% of door to 21+ crowd. Use MySpace or snail mail kit.

Sam Bond's Garage
407 Blair Blvd.
Eugene, OR 97402
p: 541-343-2635; 541-431-6603 (office)
www.sambonds.com
contact: Peter Wild
e: bondsbooking@hotmail.com
genres: Americana, Alt., Groove, Bluegrass, Rock, Acoustic, Irish, Celtic
advance: 2 months
capacity: 125
pa: Yes **sound eng:** Yes
Quirky pub/performance space presents 1-2 Local & Touring acts nitely for% of door. Sets run 1hr; some all ages shows. Email for booking.

WOW Hall
291 W 8th Ave.
Eugene, OR 97401
p: 541-687-2746
e: info@wowhall.org
www.wowhall.org
contact: Calyn Kelly
e: booking@wowhall.org
call: M-F noon-5pm
genres: All Styles
advance: 2 months
capacity: 500; 250
pa: Yes **sound eng:** Yes
stage: 20 x 16
All ages non-profit venue showcases 1-4 polished original Local-Int'l acts 4-7 nites & split the door. Sets run 45-60min; merch splits 80/20. Email or snail mail kit.

Portland/Salem

The Aladdin Theater
3017 SE Milwaukee Ave.
Portland, OR 97202
p: 503-234-9694; 503-233-1994
e: tom@aladdin-theater.com
www.aladdin-theater.com
contact: Mark Adler
e: crackadler@aol.com
genres: Americana, World, Loud Rock, Alt., Jazz, Folk, Country, Classical, Blues
advance: 2-5 months
capacity: 620
pa: Yes **sound eng:** Yes
stage: 26 x 10
Notable all ages stage hosts mostly original Reg'l openers & Nat'l headliners 4-5 nites for 90min sets. Email link to music or mail promo to: 3116 SE 11th Ave., Portland, OR 97202.

Ash Street Saloon
225 SW Ash St.
Portland, OR 97204
p: 503-226-0430
www.myspace.com/ashstreetsaloon
contact: Heather
p: 503-226-0430 x1
e: ashstreetsaloon@aol.com
genres: Mainly Punk & Alt.
advance: 2-3 months
capacity: 350
pa: Yes **sound eng:** Yes
stage: 18 x 12
open mics: Mon 4:30pm
Destination Rock & burger bar presents original Local & Touring bands for 30-60min sets for% of door up to 7 nites. Show recording avail. Prefers links to music or snail mail kit.

Berbati's Pan
231 SW Ankeny St.
Portland, OR 97204
p: 503-248-4579
www.berbati.com
contact: Anthony Sanchos
p: 503-248-4579 x3
e: booking@berbati.com
genres: Rock, Reggae, Punk, Urban, Electronic, Folk, Metal
advance: 2-4 months
capacity: 600
pa: Yes **sound eng:** Yes
stage: 20 x 15
Club showcases up & coming Reg'l & Touring talent nitely. 2-3 original bands or DJs play 45min to 21+. Prefers email w/ links to music & bio. Details for Touring bands on site.

Boon's Treasury
888 Liberty St. NE
Salem, OR 97301
p: 503-399-9062
e: boons@mcmenamins.com
www.mcmenamins.com
contact: Jan Haedinger
p: 503-257-4155
e: jhaedinger@aol.com
genres: Blues, Rock, Funk, Folk, Country
Part of the McMenamins chain, family-style pub features 1 original Local-Reg'l band Wed-Sat for 21+ crowd. Use email.

Buffalo Gap
6835 SW Macadam Ave.
Portland, OR 97219
p: 503-244-7111
www.thebuffalogap.com
contact: Matthew Kendall
e: gapbooking@gmail.com
call: Mon 2-6pm
genres: Americana, Jazz, Rock, Folk, Pop
advance: 2-3 months
capacity: 75
pa: Yes
stage: small
open mics: Wed 8:30pm
Cozy saloon books Local-Nat'l acts Wed-Sat. 1-2 artists play up to three 45min sets for flat fee &% of sales. Email link to EPK, MySpace or website first.

Candlelight Cafe
2032 SW 5th St.
Portland, OR 97201
p: 503-222-3378
contact: Shawn Thompson
genres: Blues, R&B, Funk
advance: 4-5 months
capacity: 110
pa: Yes **sound eng:** To hire
stage: floor space
Listening room showcases top Local-Touring talent nitely. Featured act plays 3 sets from 9:30pm-1:30am; resident acts Sun-Thu. Send promos to venue.

Crystal Ballroom
1332 W Burnside Ave.
Portland, OR 97209
p: 503-225-0047
www.danceonair.com
contact: Jimi Biron
p: 503-225-0047 x225
e: jimib@hq.mcmenamin.com
genres: Alt., Psychedelic, Hardcore, Latin, Hip-Hop, S/S, Punk, Rock, Folk, Reggae
advance: 3 months
capacity: 340-1500
pa: Yes **sound eng:** Yes
stage: 30 x 16
Prime 3-tiered concert facility w/ full lights & sound presents mostly original estab. Touring acts & Reg'l buzz bands. 3 acts play 30-60min sets; monthly all ages shows. Also books Lola's. Read booking FAQs on site first.

Dante's
1 SW 3rd Ave.
Portland, OR 97204
p: 503-226-6630
www.danteslive.com
contact: Frank Faillace
e: dantesbooking@qwest.net
call: prefers email
genres: All Styles
advance: 1-3 months
capacity: 400; 600
pa: Yes **sound eng:** Yes
stage: 26 x 15
Mix of top area talent, notable Touring acts & DJs gig nitely. Up to 4 acts are backed by full lights & sound attracting diverse crowd of punks & pros. Also books Devil's Point & Tiger Bar. Email preferred for booking.

Doug Fir Lounge
830 E Burnside St.
Portland, OR 97214
p: 503-231-9663
e: booking@dougfirlounge.com
www.dougfirlounge.com
contact: Alicia Rose
p: 503-943-6197

e: alicia@dougfirlounge.com
genres: All Styles
capacity: 299
pa: Yes **sound eng:** Yes
stage: 20 x 15
Local-Touring bands & DJs gig nitely at popular niteclub. 2-3 acts play 40-60min to 21+ crowd. Mail press kit w/ CD, photo & bio to club w/ ATTN: Booking. Follow up in 6 wks to booking@dougfirlounge.com.

Eden Hall
6645 Gleneden Beach Loop Rd.
Gleneden Beach, OR 97388
p: 541-764-3826
www.edenhall.com
contact: John
e: john@edenhall.com
genres: All Styles
advance: 1 year
capacity: 200
pa: Yes **sound eng:** Yes
stage: 20 x 28
All ages performance space 60mi+ from Salem, boasts state-of-the-art sound & lights. A Reg'l or Touring act stars Sat for 45min show. Email before mailing promos to: Box 190, Gleneden Beach, OR 97388.

Gemini
456 N State St.
Lake Oswego, OR 97034
p: 503-636-9445
e: geminibng@aol.com
www.myspace.com/geminibarngrill
contact: Lea
genres: Blues, R&B, Rock, Roots, Reggae, Indie Pop
advance: 2+ months
capacity: 250
pa: Yes
stage: large
Recently renovated tavern w/ dance floor puts mostly original Local-Nat'l acts on stage Wed-Sat for 21+ crowd. Featured act plays 9:30pm-1:30am for flat fee. Bands bring own mic stands. Mail press kit to venue.

Ike Box
299 Cottage St. NE
Salem, OR 97301
p: 503-581-6154
www.ikebox.com
contact: Andrew
e: booking@ikebox.com
genres: All Styles
advance: 1 month
capacity: 500
pa: Yes **sound eng:** Yes
All ages venue 45+ mi from Portland, has 3-6 original acts play for % of door; sets run 30min; great acoustics. Email for booking; No unsolicited mail.

Jimmy Mak's
221 NW 10th St.
Portland, OR 97209
p: 503-295-6542
e: jmak@jimmymaks.com
www.jimmymaks.com
contact: Jimmy Makarounis
e: booking@jimmymaks.com
call: M-F noon-3pm
genres: Jazz, Be-Bop
advance: 3 months
capacity: 175
pa: Yes
stage: medium
Lauded listening room spotlights polished Reg'ls & world class Touring acts Mon-Sat for 21+ crowd. 1 act plays two 90min sets for % of door. Email or call for booking.

LaurelThirst Public House
2958 NE Glisan St.
Portland, OR 97232
p: 503-232-1504
e: laurelthirstbookings@msn.com
http://mysite.verizon.net/res8u18i/laurelthirstpublichouse
contact: Lewi Longmire
p: 503-236-2455
call: M-F 2-5pm; prefers email
genres: Country, Acoustic, Folk, Roots Rock, Americana
advance: 2 months
capacity: 100
stage: 5 x 5
Cozy tavern known for great Local-Reg'l bands draws diverse 21+ crowd. Up to 3 original area acts play for 100% of door after costs. No Touring acts. Prefers emailed link to music, but may mail press kit to venue or call booker. No EPKs.

Lola's Room
1332 W Burnside Ave.
Portland, OR 97209
p: 503-225-0047
www.danceonair.com
contact: Jimi Biron
p: 503-225-0047 x225
e: jimib@hq.mcmenamin.com
genres: All Styles
advance: 3 months
capacity: 340
pa: Yes **sound eng:** Yes
stage: 15 x 20
Part of the McMenamin's chain, Crystal Ballroom's blossoming kid sister presents Reg'l & Touring bands & DJs nitely to pack the dance floor. 3 acts play 40min for 21+ crowd. Prefers email w/ link to music.

The Mississippi Pizza Pub & Atlantis Lounge
3552 N Mississippi Ave.
Portland, OR 97227
p: 503-288-3231
www.mississippizza.com
contact: Sunny Jaynes
p: 503-888-4480
e: booking@mississippipizza.com
call: M-F 9am-5pm
genres: Blues, Folk, S/S, Jazz, Acoustic, World, Rock, Hip-Hop, Electronic
advance: 1-3 months
capacity: 120
pa: Yes **sound eng:** By Request
stage: 10 x 20
All ages listening room books original Local & Touring artists nitely. Sun-Wed reserved for groups that can draw 35+. Fri-Sat are for draws of 65+. Up to 4 acts play for 100% of door. See booking policy on website first. Prefers EPK or email, but may mail press kit to venue. Incl. link to EPK &/or MySpace, expected draw, dates wanted & promo strategy; wait 2 wks to follow up.

Mt. Tabor Legacy
4811 SE Hawthorne Blvd.
Portland, OR 97215
p: 503-235-8021
e: mttaborlegacy@comcast.net
www.mttaborlegacy.com
contact: Kate
call: prefers email
genres: All Styles
advance: 2-4 months
capacity: 526; 88
pa: Yes **sound eng:** Yes
stage: 12 x 6 (main); 8 x 12
Sweat-soaked theater spotlights original Local-Int'l bands nitely for 21+. 3-4 acts play 40min for % of door. Only email links to music or mail to: 10430 SW Meier Dr., Tualatin, OR 97062.

Roseland Theater/Grill
8 NW 6th Ave.
Portland, OR 97209
p: 503-221-0288; 503-224-2038
www.doubletee.com
contact: David Leiken
e: dtl@doubletee.com
genres: Alt., Blues, Hardcore, Pop, S/S
advance: 3-6 months
capacity: 1350 (theatre); 400
pa: Yes **sound eng:** Yes
stage: 36 x 24; 30 x 16
Original Reg'l & Touring buzz bands w/ Local openers in both theater & grill for all ages. Merch splits 80/20. Promos: Doubletee Concerts, 10 NW 6th Ave., Portland, OR 97209.

White Eagle Saloon
836 N Russell St.
Portland, OR 97227
p: 503-282-6810
e: generalinfo@mcmenamins.com
www.mcmenamins.com/index.php?loc=55
contact: Tony Cameron
p: 503-225-0047 x241
e: tonyc@mcmenamins.com
genres: Rock n Roll, Jazz, Roots, Blues, Folk
advance: 3 months
capacity: 115
sound eng: Yes
stage: small
open mics: Sun 8pm
2-3 Local & Touring bands gig nitely at historic Rock 'n Roll saloon/hotel for 21+ crowd. Wkdy sets run 8:30pm-1:30am; 9:30pm-2am wknds. Part of McMenamins chain. Prefers call from agent or manager, but may email. No unsolicited mail.

Pennsylvania

Allentown

Crocodile Rock
520 W Hamilton St.
Allentown, PA 18101
p: 610-434-4600
e: info@crocodilerockcafe.com
www.crocodilerockcafe.com
contact: Joe Clark
p: 610-434-4600 x4 x1
e: rocklord2000@aol.com
call: M-F after noon
genres: All Styles
advance: 4-6 weeks
capacity: 2300
pa: Yes **sound eng:** Yes
stage: 30 x 24
Multi-room niteclub features 2-5 Local-Nat'l bands & DJs up to 5 nites. Stan Levinstone Presents books Nat'ls: slevinstone@aol.com, 201-803-7871; 201-803-1828 (cell).

Deer Head Inn
5 Main St.
Delaware Water Gap, PA 18327
p: 570-424-2000
www.deerheadinn.com
contact: Dennis Carrig
e: jazz@deerheadinn.com
genres: Jazz, Blues
advance: 2 months
capacity: 120 **stage:** small
Historic inn & lauded showcase for top-notch talent 40+mi from Allentown & 70+mi from NYC, is now under new mgmt. Local-Int'l acts gig Wed-Sun for mostly 35+ affluent audience. Featured act plays 3-4hrs w/ breaks for door minus $2/head up to 9:30pm & minus $1 after. Prefers kit mailed to venue.

The FunHouse
5 E 4th St.
Bethlehem, PA 18015
p: 610-868-5311
www.funhousepub.com
contact: Tina Kowalski
call: Thu-Sat 9pm-2am
genres: Jazz, Blues, Alt., Rock, Punk, Acoustic, Ska
advance: 1-3 months
capacity: 55 **stage:** floor space
open mics: Every other Mon
Party spot for Lehigh campus books mostly original Locals-Nat'ls 6 nites for 21+; some cover bands on Sat. 1-3 acts perform from 10:30pm-2am for 100% of door. Mail kit to venue.

Godfrey Daniels
7 E 4th St.
Bethlehem, PA 18015
p: 610-867-2390
www.godfreydaniels.org
contact: Mike Space
e: artisticcommittee@godfreydaniels.org
genres: Americana, Folk, Bluegrass, S/S
advance: 6-9 months
capacity: 100
stage: 5 x 13
open mics: Sun (monthly)
Acclaimed all ages listening room & popular stop on the Folk circuit, books polished Local-Touring artists Thu-Sat. Up to 2 original bands play 45min for guarantee & % of door. No Garage, Rock or Punk. Email or call first.

The Sterling Hotel
343 W Hamilton St.
Allentown, PA 18101
p: 610-433-3480
e: sterlinghotel@enter.net
www.myspace.com/sterlinghotel
contact: Skip Horn
p: 610-704-8719
genres: All Styles
advance: 3 months
capacity: 700
pa: Yes **sound eng:** Yes
stage: 30 x 21; 20 x 22
open mics: Thu **sign in:** 8pm
Hotel boasts 'largest original music venue on E Coast.' 1-10 Local & Touring bands & DJs gig 30min-3hrs Wed-Sat & some Sun for % of door. 2 rooms & 3rd DJ Dance room. Most shows all ages til 11pm, then 21+. Call or contact thru MySpace & incl. genre, expected draw, age range of band & crowd, how often you play Lehigh Valley & specify dates.

Harrisburg/ Lancaster/York

The Abbey Bar
50 N Cameron St.
Harrisburg, PA 17101
p: 717-221-1080
www.abcbrew.com/abbey
genres: Rock
advance: 2 months
capacity: 350
pa: Yes **sound eng:** Yes
stage: 20 x 20
Musicbar books Local-Touring acts usu. on wknds. 2-4 acts play for 45-60min. Snail mail kit w/ ATTN: Mike.

The Chameleon
223 N Water St.
Lancaster, PA 17603
p: 717-299-9684
e: lizard@chameleonclub.net
www.chameleonclub.net
contact: Gregg Barley
call: M-F 10am-2pm
genres: Rock, Pop, Alt., S/S, Jam
advance: 1-2 months
capacity: 700
pa: Yes **sound eng:** Yes
stage: 20 x 15
Premier all ages venue en route to DC, Philly & NYC, brings original Touring & buzz bands 4+ nites. Jam nites fit up to 3 acts; Rock nites, 5. Mail bio, pic & CD w/ 3 songs. Will contact if interested; No Calls.

The Depot
360 W Cottage Pl.
York, PA 17401
p: 717-891-2036
e: thedepot@yorkhost.com
www.theyorkdepot.com
contact: Kimon Kanellakis
e: kimon@yorkhost.com
call: M-F after 3pm
genres: Rock, Country, Hip-Hop, Blues, Jazz
advance: 1 month
capacity: 320
pa: Yes **sound eng:** Yes
stage: 10 x 20
Formerly Murph's Other Bar, is near York College & somewhat of a indie/Punk scene. Books Local & Reg'l groups Fri & Sat. Accepts EPKs but can mail promos to: 360 W Cottage Pl., York, PA 17401.

Dragonfly Club
234 N 2nd St.
Harrisburg, PA 17101
p: 717-232-6940
e: info@dragonflyclub.com
www.dragonflyclub.com
e: booking@dragonflyclub.com
genres: Metal, Urban, Reggae, Rock, Jam, Country
advance: 3 months
capacity: 600; 300
stage: 20 x 36
Area's largest club books Local-Reg'l bands & DJs; some all ages shows. Hard to contact.

Gingerbread Man
312 Market St.
Harrisburg, PA 17110
p: 717-221-8400
contact: Matt Pfarr
call: M-F after 5pm
genres: Blues, Rock, Hip-Hop, Techno, Alt.
advance: 1-2 months
capacity: 195
pa: Yes **sound eng:** Yes
stage: small & medium
Eatery w/ 2 stages - formerly City Bar & Grill - features Local-Reg'l acts Fri-Sat. 1-2 bands play from 9:30-1:30am for flat fee or % of door. No Country. Call or snail mail kit w/ ATTN: Matt.

Gullifty's Underground
1104 Carlisle Rd.
Camp Hill, PA 17011
p: 717-761-6692
www.gulliftys.net
contact: Matt Eisenhower
e: matt@gulliftys.net
genres: Rock, Pop, Jam, Blues, Acoustic
advance: 45-60 days
capacity: 300
pa: Yes **sound eng:** Yes
stage: 16 x 30
Stage below eatery showcases Reg'l & Touring bands Tue & Thu-Sat. 2-3 acts play 45min for 21+ crowd. Acoustic nite Thu. Send EPK or snail mail.

Rumors Night Club
252 Enola Rd.
Enola, PA 17025
p: 717-421-9125
www.myspace.com/rumorsnightclubenola
e: cnbbooking@yahoo.com
call: M-F noon-5pm
genres: All Styles
advance: 2-3 months
capacity: 200 **stage:** floor space
Books 2-4 Local-Int'l acts Thu & Sat. Original acts mostly on Thu to 16+; cover bands on Sat. Use Sonicbids or snail mail.

Tourist Inn
671 W Market St.
Hellam, PA 17406
p: 717-755-7629
www.touristinn.net
contact: Duane Markle
p: 717-424-2518
e: tirocks@comcast.net
genres: Rock, Country, Blues, Pop
advance: 1+ months
capacity: 400
pa: Yes **sound eng:** Yes
stage: 30 x 20
Bike-friendly bar 6mi from York books Reg'l & some Touring bands mostly Fri & Sat. Headliner plays two or three 45min sets. Prefers call or snail mail kit w/ ATTN: Duane.

Philadelphia

Brittingham's Irish Pub
640 E Germantown Pike
Lafayette Hill, PA 19444
p: 610-828-7351
www.brittinghams.com
contact: Mike Allan
e: mwa640inc@yahoo.com
call: M-F after 10:30am
genres: Irish, Rock
advance: 3-6 months
capacity: 300
pa: Avail. to rent
stage: 10 x 15
Vintage spot hosts Reg'l & Touring bands Thu-Sun. Featured act plays 3 sets from 9pm-1am. Call first.

Chris' Jazz Cafe
1421 Sansom St.
Philadelphia, PA 19102
p: 215-568-3131
e: info@chrisjazzcafe.com
www.chrisjazzcafe.com
contact: Alan McMahon
e: wamcmahon@earthlink.net
call: prefers email
genres: Jazz
advance: 4 months
capacity: 150
pa: Yes **sound eng:** Yes
stage: large
open mics: Tue **sign in:** 8pm
Awarded Best Jazz Club 2007 by Philadelphia Mag, venue showcases top & cutting-edge talent 6 nites for all ages. Featured act performs two 75min sets for % of door on wkdys; 2 acts play for flat fee on wknds. Snail mail or email kit.

Electric Factory
421 N 7th St.
Philadelphia, PA 19123
p: 215-569-9400
www.electricfactory.info
contact: Geoff Gordon
e: geoffgordon@livenation.com
call: M-F 10am-6pm
genres: All Styles
advance: 2-3 months
capacity: 2250-2500
pa: Yes **sound eng:** Yes
stage: 44 x 28
Spacious concert hall pairs original Reg'l openers w/ top Touring acts 2-3 nites. 2-3 acts play 45-60min sets; most shows all ages. Merch split is 70/30. Promos: Live Nation, 111 Presidential Blvd., Ste. 111, Bala Cynwyd, PA 19004.

Fergie's Pub
1214 Sansom St.
Philadelphia, PA 19107
p: 215-928-8118
www.fergies.com
contact: Raphael
e: booking@fergies.com
genres: Americana, Irish, Blues, Bluegrass, Jazz, Rock, Folk, S/S, Indie Rock
advance: 3 months
capacity: 65
pa: Yes
stage: floor space
open mics: Mon 9:30pm
Cozy 21+ watering hole has mostly original Reg'l, some Touring bands & DJs Wed & Fri-Sun. Up to 3 acts plays low volume sets from 10pm-2am for flat fee. Prefers EPKs.

The Fillmore At Theater of Living Arts (TLA)
334 South St.
Philadelphia, PA 19147
p: 215-922-2599
www.theateroflivingarts.net
contact: Brian Dilworth
p: 215-569-9400
e: briandilworth@livenation.com
genres: Rock, Hip-Hop, Country, Reggae, Groove, S/S
advance: 2-3 months
capacity: 950
pa: Yes **sound eng:** Yes
stage: large
Live Nation hall presents original Touring artists w/ Local openers Wed-Sat. 2-3 acts perform 90-120min sets; mostly all ages. Merch split is 70/30. Promos: Live Nation, 111 Presidential Blvd., Ste. 111, Bala Cynwyd, PA 19004.

The Fire
412 W Girard Ave.
Philadelphia, PA 19123
p: 267-671-9298
e: thefire@iourecords.com
www.iourecords.com/thefire
contact: Derek Dorsey
p: 215-627-6078
call: M-F 1-6pm
genres: All Styles
advance: 2 months
capacity: 150
pa: Yes **sound eng:** Yes
stage: 15 x 12
open mics: Mon 8:30pm
21+ joint w/ live recording capability, presents original Reg'l & Nat'l acts 6-7 nites. 2-4 bands play 30-60min sets for % of door; Fri is all ages. Also runs I.O.U. Records & Fresh Produce Studio & helps book other Philly clubs. Use online booking form or mail press kit to venue.

Johnny Brenda's
1201 N Frankford Ave.
Philadelphia, PA 19125
p: 215-739-9684
e: info@johnnybrendas.com
www.johnnybrendas.com
contact: Brandy
e: booking@johnnybrendas.com
genres: Rock, Metal, Country
advance: 6 months
capacity: 250
pa: Yes **sound eng:** Yes
stage: 16 x 10
Primarily 21+ Indie Rock venue books mostly estab. acts w/ Local bands as openers 3-5 nites. 3 original acts play 40min for flat fee & % of door. Email contact info, MySpace link, brief band history & ability to draw in Philly; will contact if interested.

The Khyber
56 S 2nd St.
Philadelphia, PA 19106
p: 215-238-5888
e: the_khyber@thekhyber.com
www.thekhyber.com
contact: Justin Cohen
p: 215-389-9890
e: justin@heydayentertainment.com
genres: All Styles
advance: 6 weeks
capacity: 220
pa: Yes **sound eng:** Yes
stage: 12 x 14
Area's haven for scenesters showcases Touring acts & buzz bands nitely. 2-4 acts play 30-90min for 21+. Also books North Star Bar. Prefers EPK, but may mail promos w/ ATTN: Justin Cohen, Heyday Ent., 1619 E Passyunk Ave., Philadelphia, PA 19148.

Kimmel Center for the Performing Arts
260 S Broad St., Ste. 901
Philadelphia, PA 19102
p: 215-790-5800
e: info@kimmelcenter.org
www.kimmelcenter.org
contact: Christine Volpe
p: 215-670-2340
genres: Jazz, Pop, Folk, World, R&B, Reggae, Blues
advance: 1 year
capacity: 650; 2500
pa: Yes **sound eng:** Yes
stage: large **in-house:** Organ

Non-profit presents mostly original music w/ polished USA & Int'l performers up to 7 nites for all ages. Merch must be sold by gift shop.

The M Room
15 W Girard Ave.
Philadelphia, PA 19123
p: 267-687-1667
www.themanhattanroom.com
contact: Joe Lekkas
e: joe@villagegreen productions.net
call: M-F noon-6pm
genres: Indie, Electronic, Rock, Alt., DIY Hip-Hop
advance: 6 weeks
capacity: 200
pa: Yes
sound eng: Yes
Prime indie showcase has Touring acts & buzz bands nitely. 2-4 acts play 30-60min. Prefers email, but may mail press kit ATTN: Joseph Lekkas, Village Green Prod., 827 E Girard Ave., Philadelphia, PA 19125.

MilkBoy Main Stage
2 E Lancaster Ave.
Ardmore, PA 19003
p: 610-645-5269
e: info@milkboycoffee.com
www.milkboycoffee.com
contact: Tommy Joyner
e: booking@milkboycoffee.com
genres: Rock, S/S
advance: 2 months
capacity: 200
pa: Yes **sound eng:** Yes
open mics: Mon; Tue 6pm
Rock venue specializes in polished Reg'l bands Fri-Sat; Also books MilkBoy Acoustic Cafe. 2-4 acts play 30-45min for %. Email for booking.

Millcreek Tavern
4200 Chester Ave.
Philadelphia, PA 19104
p: 215-222-1255
www.millcreektavernphilly.com
contact: Ben Morgan
e: booking@ millcreektavernphilly.com
genres: Rock
advance: 6-8 weeks
capacity: 350
pa: Yes
sound eng: Yes
stage: 12 x 18
21+ dive bar/music club w/ good stage & sound books 3-5 original Local-Touring bands Thu & Fri; some shows w/o cover & some all ages. Openers perform 30-40min sets; headliner play longer for mix of college kids, hipsters & wary regulars. Snail mail kit.

North by Northwest
7165 Germantown Ave.
Philadelphia, PA 19119
p: 215-248-1000
e: nxnwphl@comcast.net
www.nxnwphl.com
contact: Bill Ingram
genres: All Styles
advance: 6 weeks
capacity: 300
pa: Yes **sound eng:** Yes
stage: 20 x 15
Celebrated live music showcase for Reg'l & Touring talent Thu-Sat. Opener plays 1hr, headliner 2hrs. Email or snail mail kit.

North Star Bar
2639 Poplar St.
Philadelphia, PA 19130
p: 215-787-0488
e: joe@ heydayentertainment.com
www.northstarbar.com
contact: Andrew
p: 215-389-9890
e: andrew@ heydayentertainment.com
genres: All Styles of Rock
advance: 6 weeks
capacity: 280-300
pa: Yes **sound eng:** Yes
stage: 12 x 18
Lauded club w/ raised stage & great sound books polished acts & buzz bands for 21+ crowd up to 7 nites; some shows all ages Sun-Wed. Up to 4 original Local-Touring acts play 40min sets. Some bands have reported clashes w/ staff. Also books The Khyber in Philly. Prefers EPKs, but may mail to: Heyday Ent., 1619 E Passyunk Ave., Philadelphia, PA 19148.

Ortlieb's Jazzhaus
847 N 3rd St.
Philadelphia, PA 19123
p: 215-922-1035
www.ortliebsjazzhaus.com
contact: Kevin Mayberry
e: kevin@ortliebsjazzhaus.com
genres: Bebop, Hard Bop, Jazz, Vocals, Blues
advance: 2 months
capacity: 90-100
pa: Yes
Notable dark, listening room & jazzbo hang showcases top-notch Local-Int'l talent nitely for 21+; DJs may spin. Featured act fills 4hrs w/ breaks for flat fee. Email or snail mail kit.

Painted Bride Art Ctr.
230 Vine St.
Philadelphia, PA 19106
p: 215-925-9914
e: info@paintedbride.org
www.paintedbride.org
contact: Lenny Seidman
p: 215-925-9914 x16
e: lenny@paintedbride.org
call: prefers email
genres: World, Jazz
advance: 9-12 months
capacity: 250
pa: Yes **sound eng:** Yes
stage: 56 x 28
Intimate PAC/gallery showcases original Local-Int'l Jazz & World talent Fri-Sat & some Sun from Sep-Jun for all ages. Featured act plays 90min for flat fee & sometimes %. Merch split is 80/20. Email first; No unsolicited mail.

Penn's Landing - Great Plaza
121 N Columbus Blvd.
Philadelphia, PA 19106
p: 215-928-8801
e: lc@pennslandingcorp.com
www.pennslandingcorp.com
contact: Keeya Davis
e: kbd@pennslandingcorp.com
call: M-F 10am-5pm
genres: All Styles
advance: 6 months
pa: Yes **sound eng:** Yes
Premier waterfront destination holds Fest Pier Concert Series (booked by Live Nation) headlined by Nat'l acts. Also Multicultural & Jazz series at Great Plaza at Penn's Landing, booked locally by non-profit org. Acts play 4 nites/wk from Jun-Sep for all ages. Prefers mailed press kit, but may email or contact via MySpace. No Calls.

Phila Funk Live
8 N Preston St.
Philadelphia, PA 19104
p: 215-222-2714
e: contactus@philafunklive.com
www.philafunklive.com
contact: Michael Davis
genres: All Styles
advance: 3 months
capacity: 500
pa: Yes **sound eng:** Yes
All ages venue w/ Local-Nat'l bands Fri-Sun. 5 original acts play for 50% of door after $600. Opener play 30min & headliner, 45. Films bands' sets w/ pro video & audio equip. to post online. Must use backline.

Puck
1 Printers Alley
Doylestown, PA 18901
p: 215-348-9000
e: music@pucklive.com
www.pucklive.com
contact: Jesse Lundy
p: 610-642-0292
e: ptinfo@ pointentertainment.com
genres: Rock, Blues, Jazz, Folk, Roots
advance: 2 weeks - 6 mo
capacity: 156
pa: Yes **sound eng:** Yes
stage: 10 x 14
open mics: Wed 7:30pm
Music showcase 35mi+ from Philly, books Local-Touring talent 4 nites for 21+; all ages Sun. Cover acts considered. Up to 3 acts play on inside stage or outside patio w/ 30min or 1-2 long sets. Mail kit to venue.

The Rusty Nail Tavern
2580 Haverford Rd.
Ardmore, PA 19003
p: 610-649-6245
e: thenail1@comcast.net
www.thenail1.com
contact: Chris
call: M-F 11am-4pm
genres: Rock, Alt., Indie, Pop
pa: Yes **sound eng:** Yes
Popular bar features 1-4 Local-Int'l bands Wed-Sat for 21+. Broadcasts a live radio show every Sat. Email or call for booking; leave phone number in msg.

Steel City Coffee House
203 Bridge St.
Phoenixville, PA 19460
p: 610-933-4043
e: steelcitycoffee@aol.com
www.steelcitycoffeehouse.com
contact: Barron Chandler
e: bookingsteelcity@aol.com
advance: 3-4 months
capacity: 92
open mics: Tue Acoustic 7-10pm; Thu 7:30-10:30pm
Laid-back snackery w/ salon-like ambiance host Local-Nat'l concerts Wed, Fri, Sat & other nites for all ages. Prefers Sonicbids link; incl. website w/ music, previous venues played, normal draw, normal cover charge & whether act is opener, co-bill or headliner. No unsolicited mail, calls or MySpace messages.

Tin Angel
20 S 2nd St.
Philadelphia, PA 19106
p: 215-928-0978; 610-891-9766
www.tinangel.com
contact: Larry Goldfarb
e: lawrencemgoldfarb@ gmail.com
call: Jan & Jul only
genres: Rock, Pop, Acoustic
capacity: 115
pa: Yes **sound eng:** Yes
Lauded upscale Acoustic listening room showcases original Local-Int'l artists for mostly 21+ shows. ONLY books in Jan & Jul. Prefers email, but may call during that time. No unsolicited mail.

Trocadero Theatre/ The Balcony
1003 Arch St.
Philadelphia, PA 19107
p: 215-922-LIVE
e: trocadero@thetroc.com
www.thetroc.com
contact: Jen Corsilli
p: 215-922-6888
call: prefers MySpace
genres: Indie Rock, Rock, Alt., World, Americana, Metal, Punk, Hip-Hop, Latin
advance: 5-24 weeks
capacity: 1200; 225
pa: Yes **sound eng:** Yes
stage: 28 x 30
Former burlesque theatre w/ top sound, lights & stage, features 2-6 original estab. artists, buzz bands 6 nites. Most shows are all ages. Prefers MySpace for booking: www.myspace.com/cybeletroc. Incl. band name, brief description, link, contact info & avail. dates. Promoters need 2-3 bands in line-up before contacting.

World Cafe Live
3025 Walnut St.
Philadelphia, PA 19104
p: 215-222-1400
e: talent@worldcafelive.com
www.worldcafelive.com
contact: Karl Mullen
p: 215-222-1400 x2934
e: karl@worldcafelive.com
genres: All Styles
advance: 4-8 weeks
capacity: 300-650; 120-200
pa: Yes **sound eng:** Yes
stage: large
open mics: Mon **sign in:** 6pm
Local & Touring bands gig nitely at renowned music hall w/ 3-tier seating & 2 stages. Events incl. 'MySpace Acoustic Mon' noon-2pm & 'Free At Noon Fri.' 2 original acts play upstairs & 2 downstairs. Prefers email, but may mail press kit to venue. Incl.: name of artist, links, preferred dates & area draw; No attachments.

Pittsburgh

31st Street Pub
3101 Penn Ave.
Pittsburgh, PA 15201
p: 412-391-8334
e: webmaster@31stpub.com
www.31stpub.com
contact: Joel Greenfield

call: Wed-Fri 3-9pm
genres: Garage, Punk, Rockabilly, Ska, Rock
advance: Up to 2 months
capacity: 225
pa: Yes **sound eng:** Yes
stage: medium
Cutting-edge 21+ Rock room books original Local-Int'l acts w/ draw up to 7 nites. 3 acts play 45-60min for door after prod. costs. 1st time acts must draw or hook up w/ previously booked bands. Call or send press kit to venue.

Club Café Live
56-58 S 12th St.
Pittsburgh, PA 15203
p: 412-431-4950
e: feedback@clubcafelive.com
www.clubcafelive.com
contact: Michael Sanders
p: 412-821-0472
e: sanders@opusoneproductions.com
genres: All Styles
advance: 1-2 months
capacity: 150
pa: Yes **sound eng:** Yes
stage: medium wedge
Premier 'wired' niteclub w/ 2nd fl recording facility, hosts original Locals-Nat'ls nitely. 1-2 acts play for flat fee or % of door to 21+ crowd. Prefers EPKs, but may mail press kit to: Opus One Prod., 415 Evergreen Ave., #102, Pittsburgh, PA 15209.

Eclectic Etceteras Coffee House
118 Erie St.
Edinboro, PA 16412
p: 814-734-2909
www.eecoffeehouse.com
contact: Renee Thayer
e: renee@eecoffeehouse.com
call: M-F 9am-5pm
genres: Acoustic
advance: 1 month
capacity: 50
pa: Yes
Showcase 100mi from Pittsburgh, 80+mi from Youngstown, OH & 2hrs from Buffalo, NY, books top Local & Touring artists Fri & Sat for all ages. 1 act plays two 45min sets of original tunes for 10% of sales.

Gooski's
3117 Brereton St.
Pittsburgh, PA 15219
p: 412-681-1658
http://groups.myspace.com/gooskis
contact: Marcus Visco
genres: Indie Rock, Ska, Punk
advance: 6 weeks
capacity: 250 **stage:** medium
Prime dive bar w/ rockin' jukebox allows original Reg'l & Touring bands to play it loud Sat. 2 acts play 2hr sets for door. No Hardcore.

Hard Rock Cafe/ Pittsburgh
5 Station Square Dr.
Pittsburgh, PA 15219
p: 412-481-7625
www.hardrock.com
contact: Roy Smith
e: pittsburgh_sales@hardrock.com
genres: Country, Rock, Blues, Jazz, Metal
advance: 3 months
capacity: 375
pa: Yes **sound eng:** Yes
stage: 12 x 24
This Int'l Rock chain location books eclectic, polished Local-Touring bands for 21+. 2-3 bands w/ local draw gig 40-75min for % of door usu. Fri-Sat Mail press kit to venue.

Make Your Mark ARTspace & Coffeehouse
6736 Reynolds St., Point Breeze
Pittsburgh, PA 15206
p: 412-365-2117
www.myspace.com/makeyourmarkartspace
contact: Maree Gallagher
e: trcreativeservices@yahoo.com
call: email only
genres: Solo Acoustic, Folk, Americana, Blues, Jazz
advance: Booking Feb-Mar
capacity: 50; 70-75
stage: floor space
Seasonal all ages Acoustic spot hosts original Local/Reg'ls & some Nat'ls for Sat nite gigs from late spring to early fall. Opener plays 30min; headliner 90min for tips, food & drink. Booker is also a Reg'l promoter. Send email w/ links only.

Moondog's
378 Freeport Rd.
Blawnox, PA 15238
p: 412-828-2040
www.moondogs.us
contact: Ron Esser
p: 412-403-1777; 412-828-9842
e: moonesser@aol.com
genres: All Styles
advance: 4-6 weeks
capacity: 200
pa: Yes **sound eng:** Yes
stage: medium
open mics: Wed 8pm
Crowded joint just outside Pittsburgh, has up to 3 polished Local-Int'l acts 6 nites for 21+. Most original bands play 45+min for % of door. Also books Syria Shrine Ctr.; Liberty Park; & Pittsburgh Blues Fest. Snail mail kit.

Mr. Small's Funhouse
400 Lincoln Ave.
Millvale, PA 15209
p: 412-821-4447
www.mrsmalls.com
contact: Michael Sanders
p: 412-821-0472
e: submissions@opusoneproductions.com
genres: All Styles
advance: 2-4 mo (Nat'ls); 3-6 weeks (Locals)
capacity: 650
pa: Yes **sound eng:** Yes
stage: 24 x 25
Original music venue only 5min from Pittsburgh, books up to 5 Local-Int'l acts & some DJs up to 7 nites. Also houses recording studio & skatepark. No unsolicited mail from Local bands; email first.

Mullaney's Harp & Fiddle
2329 Penn Ave.
Pittsburgh, PA 15222
p: 412-642-6622
www.harpandfiddle.com
contact: David Regan
e: davidregan@harpandfiddle.com
genres: Irish
advance: 8-12 months
capacity: 161
pa: Yes
stage: small
Local & Touring acts gig Fri & Sat & some other nites for flat fee at this popular authentic Irish pub w/ rowdy patrons. 1 act plays 9pm-1am w/ breaks for 21+. Snail mail kits.

Rex Theatre
1602 E Carson St.
Pittsburgh, PA 15203
p: 412-381-6811
www.rextheatre.com
contact: Chris Theoret/ Bill Ferchak
call: M-F after 8pm
genres: Alt., Country, Americana, S/S, Acoustic, Jazz
advance: 6 weeks
capacity: 400
pa: Yes **sound eng:** Yes
stage: 24 x 20
open mics: Mon Acoustic 9pm
Former movie palace w/ bar, hi-tech light/sound & projection, hosts original Reg'l & Touring acts Tue-Sat. Up to 3 acts play 45-60min. New bands audition at Acoustic Open Stage. Estab. & Nat'l acts call.

Shadow Lounge
5972 Baum Blvd.
Pittsburgh, PA 15206
p: 412-363-8277
www.shadowlounge.net
contact: Justin Strong
e: jstrong@7thmovement.net; bookings@7thmovement.net
call: M-F 10am-4pm
genres: Jazz, Soul, R&B, Alt., Pop, Rock, Acoustic, Hip-Hop
advance: 3 months
capacity: 120
pa: Yes **sound eng:** Yes
stage: 21 x 9
open mics: Tue & Wed 9pm
Unusual all ages space presents original Reg'l & Touring talent 5-7 nites. 3-4 bands play 30-45min sets for 100% of their door after house fees. Vibrant freestyle & spoken word scene. Email or EPKs only for booking. No unsolicited mail or calls.

Smiling Moose
1306 E Carson St.
Pittsburgh, PA 15203
p: 412-431-4668
www.smiling-moose.com
contact: Scarfo
e: elscarfo@comcast.net
genres: Punk, Metal, Rock
advance: 1 month
capacity: 150
pa: Yes **sound eng:** Yes
21+ 2-level venue books Locals-Int'l acts Thu-Sun. 3 bands play 45min sets. Email link to MySpace for booking.

Scranton/ Wilkes-Barre

Brews N Bytes Cafe & Eatery
20 Lower Mulberry St.
Danville, PA 17821
p: 570-275-8666
e: brewsnbytes@verizon.net
www.brewsnbytes.com
contact: Jason Perez
call: prefers email
genres: All Styles
advance: 1-3 months
capacity: 40
pa: Yes **sound eng:** Yes
stage: 8 x 4 (wedge)
open mics: Fri & Sat 6pm
All ages cyber cafe 56mi from Wilkes-Barre, hosts mostly original Local-Touring acts for Fri & Sat gigs. Featured act performs 2+hrs for pay & grub. Prefers email w/ music or links.

Sarah Street Grill
550 Quaker Alley
Stroudsburg, PA 18360
p: 570-424-9120
www.sarahstreetgrill.com
contact: Dave Lapoint
p: 570-424-9120 x7 x0
e: dave@sarahstreetgrill.com
genres: Most Styles
advance: 6 months
capacity: 250
pa: Yes **sound eng:** Yes
stage: 20 x 15
open mics: Wed 9:15pm
Eatery 46mi from Scranton, hosts mostly original Local & Touring bands 6 nites for the door. 1-2 acts play 10pm-1:45am; cover material must be creative. New bands audition Thu for pay. No Hard Rock or Extreme. Check FAQs on site.

Tuesday Tunes
226 E Independence St.
Shamokin, PA 17872
p: 570-648-0193
www.myspace.com/tuesdaytunesstore
contact: Jessica Herman
e: tuesdaytunesbooking@gmail.com
call: Tue-Fri noon-6pm
genres: Punk, Hardcore, Screamo, Grindcore, Alt., Rock, Acoustic, Post-Hardcore, Pop-Punk, Power Pop, Metal
advance: 6 months
capacity: 500
pa: Yes **sound eng:** Yes
All ages club books Local-Int'l bands up to 7 nites. 4-7 original acts play 30min sets. Email or snail mail kit.

State College

Acoustic Brew Concert Series
PO Box 1090
Lemont, PA 16851
p: 814-571-5182
www.acousticbrew.org
contact: Mel DeYoung
p: 814-238-8048
e: bookings@acousticbrew.org
genres: S/S, Bluegrass, Celtic, Acoustic Blues
advance: 5 months
capacity: 100-400
pa: Yes **sound eng:** Yes
Selective, non-profit Acoustic series, showcases top-notch Local-Touring talent w/ polished openers at various all ages area stages every Sat, Sep-Jun. Opening act plays 20min for flat fee; headliner plays 45min & must have strong local appeal. Only books opening acts. Prefers Sonicbids EPKs, See site before emailing kit.

Bullfrog Brewery/ Jeremiah's Listening Room
231 W 4th St.
Williamsport, PA 17701
p: 570-326-4700
www.bullfrogbrewery.com
contact: Steven Koch
e: skoch18@aol.com
genres: Jazz, Americana, Blues, Rock, Reggae, Fusion, Roots, Celtic, Funk, Jam, Acoustic
advance: Up to 6 months
capacity: 230; 100 (upstairs)
pa: Yes
18+ brewpub features a Local-Touring band Wed & Fri-Sun from 10:30pm-1:30am. Jazz bands play Wed & Sun; Acoustic acts gig monthly upstairs. PA is ltd; best to bring your own. Mail press kit to venue; email follow-up.

Cafe 210 West
210 W College Ave.
State College, PA 16801
p: 814-237-3449
www.statecollege.com/mcc/cafe210
contact: JR Mangan
genres: Most Styles
advance: 3-4 months
capacity: 150
pa: Yes **sound eng:** Yes
stage: medium
Bar under new ownership near Penn State, seeks Local & Touring acts for Thu-Sat. Single act plays two or three 45min sets. No Metal. Mail or drop off press kit to venue.

The Saloon
101 Heister St.
State College, PA 16801
p: 814-234-1344
www.dantesinc.com/saloon.htm
contact: Jen Hoag
e: jennifer@dantesinc.com
genres: Rock, Rap, Alt., Jam
advance: 3 months
capacity: 250
pa: Yes **sound eng:** Yes
stage: 18 x 12
Popular college pub books Local-Reg'l acts nitely for 21+. Act plays 3hrs w/ breaks. Also books Jazz at Bar Bleu. Send EPK or snail mail kit.

Rhode Island

Newport

Captain Nick's Rock & Roll Bar
34 Ocean Ave.
Block Island, RI 02807
p: 401-466-5670
e: captainnicks@hotmail.com
www.captainnicks.com
contact: Marc Scortino
genres: All Styles
advance: 5+ months
capacity: 300
pa: Yes **sound eng:** Yes
stage: 25 x 25
Club off coast of RI, hosts Reg'l & Touring bands nitely May-Oct. 1 act plays two 75min sets for flat fee. Most play 2 nite stints. No booking calls; mail & email only. Mailing address: PO 280, Block Island, RI 02807.

Newport Blues Cafe
286 Thames St.
Newport, RI 02840
p: 401-841-5510
e: bluesman@newportblues.com
www.newportblues.com
contact: Jim Quinn
genres: Blues, R&B, Rock, Classic Rock
advance: 3-4 months
capacity: 300
pa: Yes **sound eng:** Yes
stage: 26 x 14; 12 x 22
New York style Blues club attracts top Reg'l-Int'l talent nitely in summer & 3 nites in winter. Opener plays 70-75min, headliner plays 75-90min from 9:30pm-1am. Merch split is 80/20. Usually 21+.

Ocean Mist
895 Matunuck Beach Rd.
South Kingstown, RI 02879
p: 401-782-3740
www.oceanmist.net
contact: Kevin Finnegan
p: 401-782-4799 x6
e: bookings@oceanmist.net
call: afternoons
genres: Reggae, Blues, Rock, Ska, Hip-Hop, Alt.
advance: 2-3 months
capacity: 300
pa: Yes **sound eng:** Yes
stage: medium
open mics: Wed 9:30pm
Beach bar near U of RI, books 1-2 Local-Nat'l bands 4 nites in summer & 3 nites in winter. Some all ages matinees, but mostly 21+. Mail kit to venue.

Wheel House Tavern
294 Great Island Rd.
Narragansett, RI 02882
p: 401-284-0246
e: info@wheelhousetavern.com
www.wheelhousetavern.com
contact: Chris B.
e: wheelhousebooking@gmail.com
genres: Rock, Jazz, Funk, Reggae, Blues, Bluegrass
advance: 6 weeks
capacity: 200
pa: Yes **sound eng:** Yes
stage: 20 x 12
Bar books Local-Reg'l act Thu-Sat for 18+ or 21+. Wed is audition nite. Snail mail kit; No unsolicited calls.

Providence

AS220
115 Empire St.
Providence, RI 02903
p: 401-831-9327
www.as220.org
contact: Meredith Stern
e: booking@as220.org
call: no calls
genres: Punk, Indie Rock, Metal, Folk, Jazz, Electronica, Country, R&B
advance: 2 months
capacity: 200
pa: Yes **sound eng:** Yes
stage: 28 x 11
open mics: 2nd Sun of mo 6pm
All ages non-profit showcases original area bands, DJs & some Reg'l-Touring acts nitely. Up to 5 acts play 35min sets. Use booking form on website; No Calls.

The Blackstone
1005 Main St., Unit 1112
Pawtucket, RI 02860
p: 401-726-2181
e: info@blackstoneclub.com
www.blackstoneclub.com
contact: Marion Davis
genres: Rock, Funk, Blues, Reggae, Ska, Punk, Jazz
capacity: 560
pa: Yes **sound eng:** Yes
Club books 3-4 Local-Int'l bands Tue-Sun for 40-60min. Supports promising RI & MA artists & estab., label-backed acts. All booking via online form.

Blackstone River Theatre
549 Broad St.
Cumberland, RI 02864
p: 401-725-9272
www.riverfolk.org
contact: Russell Gusetti
e: russell@riverfolk.org
genres: Celtic, Folk, Ethnic, Blues, Jazz, S/S, Children's
advance: 6 months
capacity: 165
stage: 16 x 12
Non-profit cultural arts ctr. w/ excellent acoustics books low volume Local-Int'l acts most wknd nites. 1-2 bands play two 50min sets. Prefers hard copy promos, but may use email.

Bovi's Tavern
287 Taunton Ave.
East Providence, RI 02914
p: 401-434-9670
contact: John Bovi
genres: Jazz, R&B, Rock, Blues
advance: 2-3 months
capacity: 250
Friendly eatery books original Local & Reg'ls Mon, Fri & Sat. Featured act plays 2 sets.

Cat's at KC's Tap
530 Broadway
Pawtucket, RI 02860
p: 401-722-0150
e: web@volumeproductions.com
www.kcstap.com
contact: Kevin Cummings
e: kegman1968@comcast.net
call: Mon-Thu after 2pm
genres: Hard Rock, Metal
capacity: 200
pa: Yes **sound eng:** Yes
Club books 2-5 hard rockin' Local & Nat'l acts up to 7 nites. Crowd & bands must be 21+. Email & put 'Want To Book At Cat's' in subject line or call.

Chan's
267 Main St.
Woonsocket, RI 02895
p: 401-765-1900
www.chanseggrollsandjazz.com
contact: John Chan
genres: Jazz, Blues, Cabaret
advance: 6 months
capacity: 125
stage: 15 x 20
open mics: Last Wed of mo
All ages supperclub features original Nat'l acts Fri/Sat; some Local-Reg'l opps. Featured act plays a show at 8pm & 10pm. Call first for booking; No unsolicited mail or email.

The Living Room
23 Rathbone St.
Providence, RI 02908
p: 401-521-5200
www.myspace.com/livingroomri
contact: Aaron Jaehnig
e: thetroublewithmusic@gmail.com
call: Wed & Fri 4-7pm
genres: Rock, Alt., Hardcore, Techno, Jazz, Funk, Blues, Hip-Hop
advance: 1-3 months
capacity: 600
pa: Yes **sound eng:** Yes
stage: 25 x 20
Original Local-Int'l bands play up to 6 nites at popular all ages venue. Line-ups confirmed on Fri 4-7pm. MySpace preferred.

The Stone Soup Coffee House
St. Paul's Church, 50 Park Pl.
Pawtucket, RI 02860
p: 401-457-7147
e: stone@soup.org
www.stonesoupcoffeehouse.com
contact: Barbara Wahlberg
e: booking@soupsoupcoffeehouse.com
call: email only
genres: Folk, Americana, Acoustic, Celtic, Reggae, Latin
advance: 8-12 months
capacity: 230
pa: Yes **sound eng:** Yes
stage: 15 x 40
Non-profit all ages listening room presents 1-2 original Local & Touring acts Sat from Sep-May. Headliners play two 45min sets, openers 20-25min. Prefers Sonicbids or email w/ link to website or MySpace. No unsolicited mail or calls.

Tazza Caffe & Lounge
250 Westminster St.
Providence, RI 02903
p: 401-421-3300
e: mcorso@tazzacaffe.com
www.tazzacaffe.com
contact: Mike
e: tazzabooking@gmail.com
genres: Jazz, Funk, World, S/S, World, Hip-Hop, Blues
advance: 8-12 weeks
capacity: 200
pa: Yes **sound eng:** Yes
open mics: Sun **sign in:** 7pm
Sophisticated spot hosts cool mix of original Local-Int'l acts Tue-Sun. 1 featured act/nite. Only books via email.

South Carolina

Charleston

The Music Farm
32 Ann St.
Charleston, SC 29403
p: 843-722-8904; 843-853-FARM
e: info@musicfarm.com
www.musicfarm.com
contact: Marshall Lowe
p: 843-577-7414
e: marshall@allinent.com
genres: All Styles
advance: 2 months
capacity: 750-1000
pa: Yes **sound eng:** Yes
stage: 40 x 20
Legendary room presents mostly top Reg'l & Nat'l acts up to 4 nites; few opps. for Locals. 2 original acts perform two 2.5hr sets; most shows are all ages. Merch split is 80/20. Mail press kit w/ ATTN: Marshall, 49 Immigration St., #102, Charleston, SC 29403.

The Pour House
1977 Maybank Hwy.
Charleston, SC 29412
p: 843-571-4343
www.charlestonpourhouse.com
contact: Alex Harris
e: alex@charlestonpourhouse.com
genres: Reggae, Rock, Jam, Hip-Hop
advance: 2-3 months
capacity: 450
pa: Yes **sound eng:** Yes
All ages venue books original Local-Int'l acts Tue-Sun. 1-2 bands play for flat fee; shows webcast. Use online form or send music links.

Village Tavern
1055 Johnnie Dodds Blvd.
Ste. 100
Mount Pleasant, SC 29464
p: 843-884-6311
www.village-tavern.com
contact: Trey Lofton
p: 843-822-2501
e: trey@village-tavern.com; treylofton@bellsouth.net
call: Tue & Thu noon-2pm
genres: Rock, Alt., Alt. Country, Psychobilly, S/S, Bluegrass, Hip-Hop
advance: 2-3 months
capacity: 200
pa: Yes **sound eng:** Yes
stage: 16 x 12
18+ hot spot has Reg'l & Touring bands perform 5-7 nites. 2-3 acts play 45-60min; some all ages shows. Prefers email; No calls or MySpace.

The Windjammer
1008 Ocean Blvd.
Isle of Palms, SC 29451
p: 843-886-8948
e: windjammer@comcast.net
www.the-windjammer.com
contact: Bobby Ross
p: 843-886-8596 x102
call: email only
genres: Rock
advance: 2 weeks - 6 mo
capacity: 550
pa: Yes **sound eng:** Yes
stage: 25 x 13
Resort bar books Touring bands 2-5 nites during summer & Fri & Sat after Labor Day. 2 acts play 45-90min for % of door. Email & put band name in subject; incl. link or 64kbps mp3 if there's no music on site. No unsolicited calls or mail.

Columbia

The Art Bar
1211 Park St.
Columbia, SC 29201
p: 803-929-0198
www.artbarsc.com
contact: Tim Bedford
e: booking@artbarsc.com
call: prefers email
genres: Indie Rock, Art Rock, Alt., Punk
advance: 1+ months
capacity: 260
pa: Yes **sound eng:** Yes
stage: medium
Colorful hang books Locals & some Touring acts Sat for % of door; DJs on Fri. Two bands play 45-60min for 21+ crowd. Emails preferred for booking.

Bentley's Bar & Grill
114 Glassmaster Rd.
Lexington, SC 29072
p: 803-359-3335
www.bentleysbarandgrill.com
contact: Chris Schumpert
genres: Acoustic, Classic Rock, Rock, 90s
advance: 6 months
capacity: 100 **stage:** small
open mics: Wed 6:30pm
Formerly Buckets Cafe, Local & Reg'l bands play for all ages Thu-Sat. Featured act plays three 1hr sets for flat fee. No Hard Rock or Metal. Mail or drop off kit to venue.

Bill's Music Shop & Pickin' Parlor
710 Meeting St.
West Columbia, SC 29169
p: 803-796-6477
www.billsmusicshop.com
contact: Bill Wells
e: wwells5939@aol.com
call: Tue-Thu 10am-2pm
genres: Bluegrass, Folk, Acoustic Blues, Gospel
advance: 6-8 months
capacity: 250
pa: Yes **sound eng:** Yes
stage: 12 x 20
Music shop doubles as Acoustic venue & books exceptional players for wknd concert series Sep-Apr. Fri open stage is yr-round.

New Brookland Tavern
122 State St.
West Columbia, SC 29169
p: 803-791-4413
e: info@newbrooklandtavern.com
www.newbrooklandtavern.com
contact: Mike Lyons
p: 803-414-9070
e: newbrooklandtavern@hotmail.com
call: M-F 2-7pm
genres: All Styles
advance: 3 months
capacity: 300
pa: Yes **sound eng:** Yes
stage: 16 x 16
Award-winning music venue hosts Local-Int'l acts up to 7 nites. 3-4 bands play 30-60min for door split based on draw. Sponsors 'New Music Nites' for Local talent (unpaid) to audition for headlining spots. Link to music preferred, or snail mail.

Greenville/ Spartanburg

Acoustic Seen At Coffee Underground
1 E Coffee St.
Greenville, SC 29601
p: 864-298-0494
www.acousticseen.com
contact: Ray Guenthner
p: 864-963-8688
e: dryridge@mindspring.com
genres: Folk, S/S, Acoustic
advance: 3-6 months
capacity: 60
pa: Yes **sound eng:** Yes
stage: 8 x 12
open mics: Wed Songwriters
Listening room hosts original Local-Reg'l bands w/ following Fri-Sat for all ages. 1 act plays two 45min sets for % of door. Promos: Dry Ridge Prod., Box 53, Simpsonville, SC 29681.

The Gathering Spot
103 N Main St., Ste. 101
Greenville, SC 29601
p: 864-271-4972
www.myspace.com/thegatheringspot
contact: Danny Morgan
call: M-F after 10pm
genres: Rock, Alt., Acoustic
advance: 6-8 weeks
capacity: 187
stage: 35 x 30
Great stop b/w Charlotte & Atlanta, books some Local-Nat'l acts & DJs for 21+; regular Battle of the Bands. Act plays 3hrs w/ break for flat fee.

Gottrocks
200 Eisenhower Dr.
Greenville, SC 29607
p: 864-235-5519
www.myspace.com/gottrocks
contact: Charles Floyd
genres: All Styles
advance: 2 months
capacity: 450
pa: Yes **sound eng:** Yes
stage: 17 x 25
Area's prime original music club features Local-Nat'l acts Fri-Sat & some wkdys for 21+. Up to 4 bands play from 9pm-1:45am. Mail press kit to venue.

Ground Zero
3059 Howard St.
Spartanburg, SC 29303
p: 864-948-1661
e: gzsc@aol.com
www.myspace.com/groundzerorocks
contact: Mick Minchow
genres: Alt., Metal, Punk
advance: 1-2 months
capacity: 1100; 300
pa: Yes **sound eng:** Yes
stage: 30 x 30; 18 x 10
open mics: Wed
sign in: Call on Mon
Premiere all ages Rock club showcases mostly original Nat'l acts, some Reg'l & Int'l bands & some DJs up to 6 nites on 2 stages. 3 acts play 40min sets for flat fee vs door. Email & put BOOKING in subject line.

The Handlebar
304 E Stone Ave.
Greenville, SC 29609
p: 864-233-6173
e: handlebar@handlebar-online.com
www.handlebar-online.com
contact: John Jeter
call: Mon 1-6pm
genres: Rock, Roots, Americana, Jazz, Reggae
advance: 2 months
capacity: 520
pa: Yes **sound eng:** Yes
stage: 26 x 28
Listening room presents Reg'ls 3 nites & Touring acts 4, from Mon-Sat. Email if able to draw at least 200. No unsolicited mail; see details on web.

Nu-Way Lounge
373 E Kennedy St.
Spartanburg, SC 29302
p: 864-582-9685
www.myspace.com/nuwayrestaurantlounge
contact: Marc Higgins
p: 864-590-8883
e: marc2407@bellsouth.net
advance: 3 months
capacity: 240
pa: Avail. to rent
stage: corner floor space
open mics: 1st Thu of mo
sign in: Call
Popular 21+ dive books mostly original Local-Reg'l bands w/ some Nat'ls acts Tue & Fri; some Sat. Featured act plays from 10:15pm-1:30am w/ breaks for flat fee. Prefers email w/ ATTN: Marc.

Sylvia Theater
27 N Congress St.
York, SC 29745
p: 803-684-5590
e: info@sylviatheater.com
www.sylviatheater.com
p: 803-684-5333
e: theater@sylviatheater.com
genres: All Styles
advance: 3+ months
capacity: 200
pa: Yes **sound eng:** Yes
stage: large
open mics: 1st Fri of mo
New acts are welcomed at this all ages venue w/ great acoustics. Guaranteed quality toe-tapping Fri-Sat. Band plays 2hr set from 9-11pm & club takes 50% door til purchaser reaches $400. Merch split is 80/20. Mail press kit to venue w/ ATTN: Talent Coord.

Myrtle Beach

Aroma Underground
600 D Pamplico Hwy.
Florence, SC 29505
p: 843-413-9020
e: aroma@aromaunderground.com
www.aromaunderground.com
contact: Cyprian
call: mornings
genres: Acoustic, Folk, Indie
advance: 2-3 months
capacity: 100
pa: Yes **sound eng:** Yes
stage: 10 x 8
All ages stop b/w Columbia & Myrtle Beach, feat. Local-Reg'l acts Fri & Sat. Band plays 2hrs for flat fee. Shows are webcast on site. Email for booking.

Hard Rock Cafe/ Myrtle Beach
1322 Celebrity Cir.
Myrtle Beach, SC 29577
p: 843-946-0007
www.hardrock.com
contact: Bridget Bain-Grasse
e: myrtle_beach_sales@hardrock.com
genres: Rock, Alt., Classic Rock
capacity: 500
sound eng: To hire
Themed all ages chain located 27mi S of NC border, books mostly Local-Reg'l & some Nat'l acts 1-2 nites. Featured act plays 3hrs for flat fee. Email or mail press kit to venue.

House of Blues/ Myrtle Beach
4640 Hwy. 17 S
North Myrtle Beach, SC 29582
p: 843-272-3000
http://hob.com/venues/clubvenues/myrtlebeach
contact: Jim Mallonee
p: 407-934-2014
e: jmallonee@hob.com
genres: Rock, Pop, Blues, Jazz
advance: 3 months
capacity: 2200
pa: Yes **sound eng:** Yes

stage: 50 x 24
Top Reg'l & Nat'l bands gig 5-7 nites in famed all ages music room. 1-4 acts play 75min & keep 75% of merch sales. No unsolicited mail.

South Dakota

Rapid City

Back Porch & B&B Bar
703 N Main St.
Spearfish, SD
57783
p: 605-642-2134
e: backporchbar@hotmail.com
www.myspace.com/bbbackporch99
contact: Leland Ruzicka
call: Mon-Sun 10am-1pm
genres: Rock, Alt.
advance: 6-9 weeks
capacity: 300
pa: Yes
stage: Fits 4 piece act
21+ biker bar books Reg'l-Int'ls Fri & Sat. During Sturgis Rally, bands play nitely. Single act plays from 9:30pm-1:30am w/ breaks for flat fee. Local DJs spin Wed. Mail CD & posters.

Firehouse Brewing Co.
610 Main St.
Rapid City, SD
57701
p: 605-348-1915
e: firehousebrewing@rushmore.com
www.firehousebrewing.com
contact: Bob Fuchs
call: M-F after 2pm
genres: Rock, Blues, Folk, Jazz
advance: 3-4 months
capacity: 110 **stage:** small
Brewpub hosts Local-Reg'l bands Jun-Aug. Featured band plays 4hrs for flat fee. Booking begins in Jan; snail mail kit.

The Flat Iron
745 N River St.
Hot Springs, SD 57747
p: 605-745-5301
e: hagenproperties@msn.com
www.flatiron.bz
contact: Georgia
call: M-F 8am-5pm
genres: Acoustic
advance: 2 months
capacity: 30; 60-70
stage: floor space
open mics: Fri **sign in:** 6:30pm
Coffee bar hosts low volume Acoustic Reg'l's & some Nat'l's Fri-Sat. Featured act plays 2hrs for fee, tips & possible free room in attached guesthouse. Prefers emails w/ bios & links, or snail may kit.

Saloon No. 10
657 Main St.
Deadwood, SD 57732
p: 800-952-9398
e: info@saloon10.com
www.saloon10shop.com
contact: John Duerkop
p: 920-687-8800
e: johnduerkop@fortunetalent.com
call: M-F after 10am
genres: Rock, Blues
advance: 2 months
capacity: 300
pa: Limited
stage: medium
Historic 21+ old west bar & casino features a Local or Touring act from 9pm-1:30am 3-6 nites; busier during summer. Mostly cover bands perform for flat fee & lodging. Email, call or mail kit to: PO Box 205, Appleton, WI 54912.

Sioux Falls

American Legion Hall
Renner Rd.
Renner, SD 57055
p: 605-332-1309
contact: Paul Bangasser
genres: All Styles
capacity: 140
pa: Yes
stage: floor space
Bands pay $200 upfront to rent room for shows. Call for info.

Black Sheep Coffeehouse
1007 W 11th St.
Sioux Falls, SD 57104
p: 605-339-7207
e: blacksheepcoffee@midconetwork.com
contact: John Berkness
e: johnny.blacksheepcoffeehouse@midconetwork.com
call: M-F early mornings
genres: Acoustic, Folk, Jazz**advance:** 1 month
capacity: 76 **stage:** floor space
Intimate all ages venue for Local-Nat'l artists Fri & Sat. 1-4 act play 45-120min. No Hard Rock. Email links or snail mail kit.

Nutty's North
805 N West Ave.
Sioux Falls, SD 57104
p: 605-767-0264
e: info@nuttys.com
www.nuttys.com
contact: Jered Johnson
p: 605-357-7377
e: jered@pepperentertainment.com
call: M-F 8am-7pm
genres: Rock, Blues, Metal, Punk, Indie, Hip-Hop
advance: Quarterly
capacity: 300
pa: Yes **sound eng:** Yes
stage: 20 x 16
Popular niteclub presents original Local-Touring bands & DJs 3-4 nites/wk; shows are mostly Thu-Sat. 2-4 bands play to all ages; merch splits 80/20. Send EPKs, or mail kit to: Pepper Ent., 122 S Phillips Ave., Ste. 200, Sioux Falls, SD 57104.

Pro's Bar & Grill at Prairie Inn
912 N Dakota St.
Vermillion, SD 57069
p: 605-624-2657
www.prairieinnsd.com
contact: Brett
e: lisa@prairieinnsd.com
genres: All Styles
advance: 1 month
capacity: 400 **stage:** floor space
College town hotspot may book Reg'l acts for all ages. Featured act plays 3hrs. Call or snail mail kit.

Tennessee

Chattanooga

Charles & Myrtle's Coffeehouse
105 McBrien Rd.
Chattanooga, TN 37411
p: 423-892-4960
www.christunity.org
contact: Andrew Kelsey
p: 423-892-3109
e: andrewk166@aol.com
call: M-F after 6pm
genres: S/S, Acoustic, Folk, Bluegrass, Jazz, Blues
advance: 1-2 months
capacity: 80
pa: Yes **sound eng:** Yes
City's only smoke & alcohol-free venue for original Acoustic music, books Local-Int'ls on Sat. Act plays from 8-10pm for all ages. Great stop on circuit b/w Atlanta, Nashville & Asheville. Email or mail kit.

Pokey's
918 Sahara Dr.
Cleveland, TN 37312
p: 423-476-6059
www.pokeyville.com
contact: Steve "Pokey" Clark
genres: Rock, Blues, Alt., Country, Reggae
advance: 2-3 months
capacity: 250
pa: Yes
stage: 20 x 12
Pub books Reg'l bands Tue & Thu-Sat for 21+. Featured act plays 90min. Snail mail kit.

Johnson City

Down Home
300 W Main St.
Johnson City, TN 37604
p: 423-929-9822
www.downhome.com
genres: Americana, S/S, Roots Rock, Folk, Bluegrass, Blues, Acoustic, Jazz
advance: 2-3 months
capacity: 150
pa: Yes **sound eng:** Yes
stage: 25 x 8
open mics: Wed 9pm
Premier all ages listening room books original Reg'l & Touring acts Wed-Sat. 4-5 acts play 30-45min for % of door. Snail mail kit & call to follow up; No EPKs.

The Hideaway
235 E Main St.
Johnson City, TN 37604
p: 423-926-3896
www.myspace.com/ahideaway
contact: Tarvo
genres: Indie Rock, Punk, Southern Rock, Garage, Hip-Hop, Emo, Metal
advance: 1-2 months
capacity: 150
pa: Yes **sound eng:** Yes
open mics: Thu
College town hang 90mi+ from Knoxville, TN & Charlotte, NC, presents original Local-Nat'l bands nitely. 1-4 bands play for 18+ crowd. Use MySpace or mail promo: PO Box 837, Johnson City, TN 37605.

Knoxville

Barley's Taproom & Pizzeria
200 E Jackson Ave.
Knoxville, TN 37915
p: 865-521-0092
www.barleystaproom.com
contact: Robby Dubov
p: 865-525-1336
e: jdubov@aubreys.info
genres: Rock, Jam, Ska, Dance
capacity: 250
pa: Yes **sound eng:** Yes
stage: 15 x 10
Former hardware & feed store has Reg'l & some Touring talent up to 6 nites. Featured band plays several sets. No Calls.

The Bijou Theatre
803 S Gay St.
Knoxville, TN 37902
p: 865-523-4211
e: info@knoxbijou.com
www.knoxbijou.com
contact: Ted Heinig
p: 865-523-2665 x109
e: booking@knoxbijou.com
call: M-F 9am-6pm
genres: Americana, Jazz, Rock, Blues, Country, Alt., Bluegrass
advance: 2-6 months
capacity: 750
pa: Yes **sound eng:** Yes
stage: 35 x 30
Non-profit all ages historic theater w/ great acoustics, books mostly original Local-Int'l acts 2-3 nites. 2-3 acts play 75-120min sets. Bands keep 75% merch if house sells; 80% on soft goods; 90% on hard. Also books other venues. Promos: AC Ent., ATTN: Bijou Booking, 507 Gay St., Ste. 1100, Knoxville TN 37902.

Brackins Blues Club
112 E Broadway Ave.
Maryville, TN 37804
p: 865-983-9800
www.brackinsbar.com
contact: Mark Brackins
e: cuzwecaninc@earthlink.net
call: Wed 9am-2pm
genres: Blues, Jam, Rock
advance: 6-7 months
capacity: 100-120
pa: Yes **sound eng:** Yes
stage: 16 x 12
open mics: Mon Acoustic 8pm
Bikers & Blues bar books mostly Touring acts Thu-Sat for 21+. 1 band plays three 1+hr sets from 9pm-1am. Mail kit to venue.

Pilot Light
106 E Jackson Ave.
Knoxville, TN 37915
p: 865-524-8188
e: ask@thepilotlight.com
www.thepilotlight.com
contact: Jason
e: booking@thepilotlight.com
call: Tue 10am-2pm
genres: All Styles
advance: 6-8 weeks
Up to 5 original Local & Nat'l bands gig Wed-Sat at small, music-centric 18+ venue. No Contemp. Jazz or Jam. Prefers email; No unsolicited mail.

Preservation Pub
28 Market Sq.
Knoxville, TN 37902
p: 865-524-2224
www.preservationpub.com
contact: Virginia Prater
e: booking@preservationpub.com
call: email only
genres: All Styles
advance: 2 months
capacity: 150
pa: Yes **sound eng:** Yes
stage: 12 x 12
open mics: Tue **sign in:** 7pm
Locally-acclaimed 21+ venue w/ diverse patrons, presents

Local & some Touring talent Mon-Sat. Featured act plays two 90min sets for flat fee. Prefers emailed link to music w/ specified dates; or snail kit w/ ATTN: Virginia Prater.

Sassy Ann's
820 N 4th Ave.
Knoxville, TN 37917
p: 865-525-5839
www.sassyanns.com
contact: Vicki Vinson
e: boogedymama@comcast.net
call: email only
genres: Indie
advance: 1-3 months
capacity: 150
pa: Yes **sound eng:** Yes
stage: 15 x 15
open mics: Wed 9pm
Club books TN & Touring artists Fri for 21+. 3 act plays 1hr for the door. Prefers email for booking, but may mail press kit to venue. No Calls.

The Valarium
1213 Western Ave.
Knoxville, TN 37921
p: 865-522-2820
e: contact@thevalarium.com
www.thevalarium
p: 865-523-2665
e: info@acentertainment.com
genres: Rock, Alt. Jam, Pop, Hip-Hop, Country
Prime music hall books nice mix of Local-Int'l acts; some all ages shows. All scheduled shows from the venue, Blue Cats, will be held here til they relocate. Also books many other venues.

Memphis

Center For Southern Folklore
119 S Main St.
Memphis, TN 38103
p: 901-525-3655
e: store@southernfolklore.org
www.southernfolklore.com
contact: Judy Peiser
e: queenbee@southernfolklore.org
genres: Blues, Urban, Alt., Neo Soul, Jazz, Country, Bluegrass, Gospel, S/S, Rock, Rockabilly, World
advance: 3-4 months
capacity: 200; 50
pa: Yes
Most live acts are booked Apr-Oct & play on Fri & Sat; some Thu & Sun. Featured act plays two or three 45min sets for family-friendly crowd & typically split door. Prefers Sonicbids EPK or snail mail.

Hard Rock Cafe/ Memphis
315 Beale St.
Memphis, TN 38103
p: 901-529-0007
www.hardrock.com
contact: Julien Salley
e: memphis_sales@hardrock.com
call: M-F 9am-6pm
advance: 4 months
capacity: 470
pa: Yes **sound eng:** Yes
stage: medium
This branch of the famed Int'l music chain features 2-3 Local-Int'l acts Fri-Sat for 18+ crowd. Bands fill 10pm-2am for % of door. Mail press kit to venue or use email for booking.

Hi Tone Café
1913 Poplar Ave.
Memphis, TN 38104
p: 901-278-8663
e: hitonecafe@hotmail.com
www.hitonememphis.com
contact: Dan Holloway
genres: Garage, Punk, Emo, Alt. Country, Pop, Funk
advance: 6-8 weeks
capacity: 500
pa: Yes **sound eng:** Yes
stage: 20' wide
Popular music club features Touring acts, Local stars & DJs up to 6 nites. 2-3 bands play 45min for door after costs. Accepts EPKs or snail mail.

Java Cabana
2170 Young Ave.
Memphis, TN 38104
p: 901-272-7210
www.javacabanacoffeehouse.com
contact: Mary Burns
e: mary@javacabanacoffeehouse.com
call: prefers email
genres: Acoustic, S/S, Jazz
advance: 1 month
capacity: 50
pa: Yes
stage: floor space
open mics: Thu 7:30pm
Quirky all ages coffeehouse presents Reg'l & some Touring acts Fri-Sat & other nites. 1-2 acts play for tips & divide 3hrs w/ break. Email or snail mail kit.

Murphy's
1589 Madison Ave.
Memphis, TN 38104
p: 901-726-4193
www.murphysmemphis.com
contact: Amy Brooks
e: murphysbooking@comcast.net
call: M-F before 8pm
genres: Americana, Rock, Pop, Punk
advance: 1-3 months
capacity: 120
pa: Yes **sound eng:** Yes
stage: 15 x 15
Classic pub books original Local-Int'l bands 2-5 nites. 2-4 acts play 30-60min sets & split the door after $50 for sound expenses. Nat'l acts need Local support.

New Daisy Theatre
330 Beale St.
Memphis, TN 38103
p: 901-525-8981
e: michael.glenn@attworld.net
www.newdaisy.com
contact: Roach Jones
p: 870-735-3575
e: roachpromos2001@yahoo.com
genres: All Styles
advance: 2-3 months
capacity: 1000
pa: To rent **sound eng:** To hire
stage: 28 x 22
Historic movie house presents cutting-edge talent up to 7 nites. Up to 5 Reg'l & Touring bands play 30-45min for all ages; some 21+ shows. Nat'ls get flat fee & % of door w/ 80% merch. Email or snail mail kit.

Newby's
539 S Highland St.
Memphis, TN 38111
p: 901-452-8408
www.newbysmemphis.com
contact: Todd Adams
e: toddnewbys@gmail.com; todd@newbysmemphis.com
call: M-F 9am-6pm
genres: All Styles
advance: 1-8 months
capacity: 600
pa: Yes **sound eng:** Yes
stage: 25 x 25
Crowded music & pool spot for 18+ college crowd, presents Local-Touring bands 3-4 nites. Up to 2 acts play 45-60+min sets for flat fee or % of door. Mail press kit to venue.

Rum Boogie Café
182 Beale St.
Memphis, TN 38103
p: 901-528-0150
www.rumboogie.com
contact: Wesley Smith
p: 901-525-3891
call: M-F 9am-5pm
genres: Blues, Acoustic, Jam, Funk, Alt., Rock, Alt. Country
advance: 1 month
capacity: 250
pa: Yes **sound eng:** Yes
stage: 12 x 20
21+ music spot is fave w/ tourists & locals. 1-2 stellar Local acts gig nitely; Reg'ls & Nat'ls monthly. Acts play 1hr for flat fee. Also books other Beale St. venues. Email or mail kit to: River City Mgt. Group, 168 Beale St., Upstairs, Memphis, TN 38103.

The Stage Stop
2951 Cela Ln.
Memphis, TN 38128
p: 901-382-1576
e: thestagestop@aol.com
www.myspace.com/thestagestop
contact: Nita Makaris
p: 901-382-1577
call: Tue-Thu after 9pm
genres: Rock, Blues, Alt.
advance: 1-2 months
capacity: 250
pa: Yes **sound eng:** Yes
stage: 30 x 20
Long-running 18+ club features mostly Local-Reg'ls w/ some Nat'l bands Fri & Sat. Up to 4 acts play 1+hrs for a flat fee. Mail press kit to venue or call.

Young Avenue Deli
2119 Young Ave.
Memphis, TN 38104
p: 901-278-0034; 901-274-7080
www.youngavenuedeli.com
contact: Tiger
e: tiger@youngavenuedeli.com
genres: Rock, Americana, Roots, Electronic, Jazz, World
advance: 6 weeks
capacity: 500
pa: Yes **sound eng:** Yes
stage: 16 x 18
Offbeat 21+ venue serves hip clientele w/ cutting-edge Local & Touring artists nitely. 3 acts play original 45-60min sets. Mail press kit to venue; will contact if interested.

Nashville

12th & Porter
114 12th Ave. N
Nashville, TN 37203
p: 615-734-1981
www.12thandporterlive.com
contact: Justin Roddick
p: 615-254-7250
e: justin@12thandporterlive.com
genres: Indie, Americana, Blues, Country, Rock, Alt. Country
advance: 5-6 weeks
capacity: 250
pa: Yes **sound eng:** Yes
Top 18+ music room & industry showcase w/ killer sound, is under new ownership & recently renovated. Excellent balcony views look down on 1-3 original up & comers plus estab. recording acts 6-7 nites. Books thru MySpace.

3rd & Lindsley
818 3rd Ave. S
Nashville, TN 37210
p: 615-259-9891
e: mail@3rdandlindsley.com
www.3rdandlindsley.com
contact: Ron Brice
e: ron@3rdandlindsley.com
call: M-F 10am-5pm
genres: Blues, Americana, R&B, Rock, Alt., Prog, S/S
advance: 6 weeks
capacity: 300
pa: Yes **sound eng:** Yes
stage: 400 sq. ft.
Prime music room w/ good sound & views, draws top area session players & estab. Reg'l & Touring talent nitely. 2 acts play 45-60min sets. Mail press kit to venue.

The 5 Spot
1006 Forrest Ave.
Nashville, TN 37206
p: 615-650-9333
www.myspace.com/the5spotnashville
contact: Todd Sherwood
e: the5spotnashville@gmail.com
call: M-F 2-4pm
genres: Rock
advance: 2 months
capacity: 150
pa: Yes **sound eng:** Yes
Mostly original Local-Int'l acts play on great stage w/ decent sound system. 3-7 acts play 45min to 21+ for %.

The Basement
1604 8th Ave. S
Nashville, TN 37203
p: 615-254-8006
www.thebasementnashville.com
contact: Mike Grimes
p: 615-254-1604
e: mike@slowbar.com
genres: Indie Rock, Country, Rock, Alt., Pop, Blues, Jazz, Acoustic
advance: 1-2 months
capacity: 150
pa: Yes **sound eng:** Yes
stage: 15 x 20
Spare music room below Grimey's Record Shop, presents 3+ original Local-Nat'l acts Mon-Sat for 21+. No Metal. Use form or email music links; will contact if interested. No unsolicited mail.

The Bluebird Cafe
4104 Hillsboro Rd.
Nashville, TN 37215
p: 615-383-1461
e: blubirdcaf@aol.com
www.bluebirdcafe.com
contact: Amy Kurland

call: M-F 10:30am-5pm
genres: Americana, S/S, Blues, Country
advance: 2 months
capacity: 100
pa: Yes **sound eng:** Yes
stage: 9 x 12
open mics: Mon 6-9pm
Premier Acoustic listening room tends to sell out as legends & emerging stars entertain w/ 2 shows nitely for all ages. 2 original acts play 1-2hrs for % of door. Barbara Cloyd books emerging talent for no-pay early shows Tue-Sat. Mail press kit & follow up via phone or email.

The Boro Bar & Grill
1211 Greenland Dr.
Murfreesboro, TN 37130
p: 615-895-4800
www.myspace.com/theboro
contact: Boro Booking
e: bookingtheboro@hotmail.com
genres: Pop, Rock, Jazz, Blues, Metal, Acoustic
advance: 6-8 weeks
capacity: 100+ **stage:** 20 x 10
Popular dive bar near college campus & 30mi from Nashville, books original Reg'ls & some Nat'ls Fri-Sat for 21+. Up to 3 acts play 45min sets for door. Prefers EPKs, or can snail mail.

Douglas Corner Cafe
2106 A 8th Ave. S
Nashville, TN 37204
p: 615-298-1688
e: douglascorner@bellsouth.net
www.douglascorner.com
contact: Mervin Louque
genres: S/S, Country, Rock, Blues, Americana
advance: 2-4 months
capacity: 150
pa: Yes **sound eng:** Yes
stage: 20 x 20
open mics: Tue **sign in:** 2-6pm
Notable S/S showcase presents area talent & Touring buzz bands 6 nites for % of door. Up to 3 acts play original tunes for 18+; sets run 45-60min. Prefers press kit w/ CD sent to venue.

The End
2219 Elliston Pl.
Nashville, TN 37203
p: 615-321-4457
www.myspace.com/theendnashville
contact: Bruce Fitzpatrick
call: M-F 1-5pm
genres: Rock, Alt. Country, Indie, Punk, Heavy Metal
advance: 2 months
capacity: 175
pa: Yes **sound eng:** Yes
stage: 20 x 10
No frills Rock venue w/ impressive past, boasts cutting-edge Local-Nat'l talent. 2-4 original acts & DJs play 45min Tue-Sat to 18+ crowd of hipsters, slackers & old rockers. Snail mail kits.

Exit/In
2208 Elliston Pl.
Nashville, TN 37203
p: 615-321-3340
e: info@exitin.com
www.exitin.com
contact: Jason
e: jexitin@hotmail.com; bookin@exitin.com
genres: Rock, Country, Metal, Jam
advance: 6 months
capacity: 450
pa: Yes **sound eng:** Yes
stage: 32 x 18
Landmark original music club presents 2-3 top-tier Local acts & Touring indies nitely to 18+. Sets run 45-70min; merch splits 80/20. Promos: Great Big Shows, 209 10th Ave. S, Ste. 313, Nashville, TN 37203.

The Family Wash
2038 Greenwood Ave.
Nashville, TN 37206
p: 615-226-6070
e: info@familywash.com
www.familywash.com
contact: Jamie Rubin
e: booking@familywash.com
genres: Rock, Country, Jazz, Pop, Loud
advance: 3+ months
capacity: 100
pa: Yes **sound eng:** Yes
Former laundromat showcases all ages shows w/ 1-2 top original Local-Int'l bands playing Tue-Sat for tips. Snail mail or email kit; will respond if interested.

French Quarter Cafe
823 Woodland St.
Nashville, TN 37206
p: 615-227-3100
e: info@frenchquartercafe.com
www.frenchquartercafe.com
contact: Dennis Lacour
p: 615-668-9545
e: booking@frenchquartercafe.com
genres: Blues, Alt. Country, Country, S/S, Rock n Roll, Americana, Swing, Jazz
advance: 1-2 months
pa: Yes **sound eng:** Yes
stage: 2 stages
open mics: Tue & Thu
New Orleans-themed eatery w/ up to 4 Reg'l bands Tue-Sat playing 1hr sets for % of door to all ages. Use email for booking.

Layla's Bluegrass Inn
418 Broadway
Nashville, TN 37203
p: 615-726-2799
www.laylasbluegrassinn.com
contact: Layla Vartanian
genres: Country, Bluegrass, Rockabilly
advance: 1-2 months
capacity: 85
pa: Yes
stage: 15 x 15
Saloon hosts some Touring acts for 21+. 3 bands each play 2-4hrs. Send kit w/ photo, CD &/or DVD, bio & contact info.

Mercy Lounge/ Cannery Ballroom
1 Cannery Row
Nashville, TN 37203
p: 615-251-3020
www.mercylounge.com
contact: John Bruton
p: 615-248-9494
e: jbruton@comcast.net
genres: Rock, Alt. Country, Indie, Jam
advance: 1-6 months
capacity: 500; 100
pa: Yes **sound eng:** Yes
stage: large
Not the best acoustics, but still considered an asset to Nashville 21+ indie scene. 2-3 Local-Int'l bands & DJs play 30-120min up to 6 nites. Also host shows in larger Cannery Ballroom. Prefers EPK for booking.

The Muse/ Kung Fu Coffeehouse
835 4th Ave. S
Nashville, TN 37210
p: 615-251-0190
e: themusebooking@yahoo.com
www.themusenashville.com
contact: Logan Cheek
genres: Metal, Punk, Alt., Folk, Pop
advance: 1-6 months
capacity: 300
pa: Yes **sound eng:** Yes
stage: 18 x 12
Eclectic venue books Local-Nat'l acts up to 7 nites for all ages. 3-8 original acts play 30-120min for % of door; Nat'ls get flat fee. Prefers email w/ a MySpace link or snail mail.

Rippy's Smokin' Bar & Grill
429 Broadway
Nashville, TN 37203
p: 615-244-7477
e: mb520w@yahoo.com
www.rippysbbq.com
contact: Brandon
e: rippysbbq@yahoo.com
advance: 2-3 months
capacity: 400
pa: Yes
stage: 10 x 13
Mainstay downtown hosts 2 Local-Int'l acts nitely for all ages. Booked bands mixed in w/ house acts. Shows are from 6:30-10pm & 10:30pm-2am.

Robert's Western World
416 Broadway
Nashville, TN 37203
p: 615-244-9552
e: robertswestworld@aol.com
www.robertswesternworld.com
contact: Jesse Lee Jones
p: 615-244-1028
call: M-F 9am-5pm
genres: Traditional Country
advance: 1 month
capacity: 360
pa: Yes
stage: 16 x 12 **in-house:** Drums
All ages club/bootshop, beloved by hip locals, industry & tourists, showcases polished Reg'l & Touring talent 16 hrs/day, every day. 4-6 acts play up to 4hr sets for tips. Send EPKs; No unsolicited mail.

The Station Inn
402 12 Ave. S
Nashville, TN 37203
p: 615-255-3307
e: jt@stationinn.com
www.stationinn.com
contact: Lin Barber
p: 615-352-5467
e: annlinsib@yahoo.com
genres: Bluegrass, Roots
advance: 2-3 months
capacity: 175
pa: Yes **sound eng:** Yes
stage: 10 x 20
Renowned 21+ room books top-notch Reg'l & Touring acts up to 7 nites. 1-2 bands play 1hr sets for flat fee. Email or snail mail kit w/ ATTN: Lin & Ann.

Texas

Austin

Antone's Night Club
213 W 5th St.
Austin, TX 78701
p: 512-320-8424
www.antones.net
contact: David Cotton
p: 512-835-5997
e: cottonaustin@aol.com
call: M-F 2-7pm
genres: Blues, Funk, Cajun, Rock
advance: 1-2 months
capacity: 600
pa: Yes **sound eng:** Yes
stage: 28 x 14
All ages Austin landmark features polished Local-Int'l talent 5-7 nites. 2-3 acts play original 1hr sets. Send EPKs or mail kit to: 12824 Council Bluff Dr., Austin, TX 78727; wait several wks to follow up.

Artz Rib House
2330 S Lamar Blvd.
Austin, TX 78704
p: 512-442-8283
e: info@artzribhouse.com
www.artzribhouse.com
contact: Art
e: ribhouserecords@austin.rr.com
genres: S/S, Folk, Bluegrass
advance: 2-3 months
capacity: 100
pa: Limited
stage: small
Locals-Nat'ls play original music at low volume in popular all ages rib joint up to 7 nites. Featured act plays 2-3 sets for tips & cash. Email for booking.

Austin Music Hall
208 Nueces St.
Austin, TX 78701
p: 512-263-4146
e: info@directevents.net
www.austinmusichall.com
e: booking@directevents.net
genres: Alt., Americana, Urban, Rock
advance: 1-2 months
capacity: 4400; 2300
stage: 54 x 32
Prime all ages concert space presents original buzz bands & estab. Touring acts & DJs. Up to 3 acts play 3-4hrs w/ breaks. Merch split 80/20. Also books The Backyard & La Zona Rosa. Promos to ATTN: Booking Dept, 13101 Hwy 71 W, Austin, TX 78738.

The Backyard
13101 Hwy. 71 W
Austin, TX 78738
p: 512-263-4146
e: info@directevents.net
www.thebackyard.net
contact: Brooke Roeder
e: booking@directevents.net
genres: All Styles
advance: Starts in Nov
capacity: 5000 (GA)
pa: Yes **sound eng:** Yes
Lauded outdoor amphitheater presents 1-4 original Local-Nat'l headliners & DJs Mar-Oct for all ages. Accepts EPKs.

BB Rovers Cafe & Pub
12101 Jollyville Rd.
Austin, TX 78759
p: 512-335-9504
www.bbrovers.com
contact: David Dunn
e: ddunn1@austin.rr.com
genres: Acoustic, Folk, S/S

capacity: 50
pa: Yes
stage: floor space
open mics: Sun 7pm
Mainly original Local bands & some Reg'ls play Sat-Sun for all ages in intimate music venue. 'Songwriters Showcase' on Tue at 7:30pm. Promos to: 12636 Research Blvd. Ste. 101B.

Botticelli's South Congress
1321 S Congress Ave.
Austin, TX 78704
p: 512-916-1315
www.myspace.com/botticellissouthcongress
contact: Matt Botticelli
e: matthewbotticelli@yahoo.com
genres: Country, Zydeco, S/S, Alt. Country, Bluegrass, Jazz
advance: 2 months
capacity: 120
pa: Yes **sound eng:** Yes
stage: 20 x 15
Formerly Beck's on Congress, all ages eatery now presents Local-Touring artists & DJs Tue-Sat. 1-2 acts fill 8-10:30pm w/ breaks for $100 + 5% of sales during time slot. Snail mail kit or email music link.

Broken Spoke
3201 S Lamar Blvd.
Austin, TX 78704
p: 512-442-6189
www.brokenspokeaustintx.com
contact: James M. White
e: jamesmwhitespoke@aol.com
call: M-F 9-11am
genres: Country, Honky-Tonk
advance: 3-4 months
capacity: 661
pa: Yes **sound eng:** Yes
stage: 20 x 12
Authentic all ages Honky Tonk hall spotlights polished original TX talent Tue-Sat for all ages. Acts play 9pm-1am w/ breaks for % of door. Email or mail press kit to venue.

Cactus Cafe
U of TX, 2247 Guadalupe St.
Austin, TX 78705
p: 512-475-6515
e: cactus@mail.utexas.edu
www.utexas.edu/student/txunion/ae/cactus
contact: Griff Luneburg
genres: Acoustic, S/S, Eclectic
advance: 2 months
capacity: 154
pa: Yes **sound eng:** Yes
stage: 10 x 14
open mics: Mon **sign in:** 7pm
Notable on-campus Acoustic room books original Locals-Int'ls 6 nites. 1 act plays two 40+min sets or 2 acts play 30-90min to all ages. Promos: PO Box 7338, Austin, TX 78713.

Carousel Lounge
1110 E 52nd St.
Austin, TX 78723
p: 512-452-6790
www.carousellounge.net
contact: Nicki Mebane
p: 512-407-9647
e: nickimebane@grandecom.net
call: daytime
genres: Roots, Country, Western Swing, Americana, Rockabilly, Punk, Alt., Rock, Jazz
advance: 1-2 months
capacity: 129
pa: Yes
stage: 7 x 10 **in-house:** Piano
Circus-themed dive bar w/ mixed 21+ crowd books Locals-Touring acts Tue-Sat. 2-6 acts play 45-60min for 100% of door if they supply doorman. Snail mail kit or use email.

Cedar St. Courtyard
208 W 4th St.
Austin, TX 78701
p: 512-495-9669
www.cedarstreetaustin.com
contact: Rob Pate
e: robpate@hotmail.com
call: Wed-Fri after 2pm
genres: Jazz, Blues, Funk
advance: 2 months
capacity: 500
pa: Yes **sound eng:** Yes
stage: 30 x 20
Popular bar for 21+ crowd brings in Local & Touring acts nitely. 2 bands gig 2-3hrs for flat fee. Mostly original, but some cover acts. Send EPK or snail mail kit.

Central Market Cafe
4001 N Lamar Blvd.
Austin, TX 78756
p: 512-206-1000
e: urcma5@heb.com
www.centralmarket.com
contact: Sean Hopper
p: 512-206-1000 x1070
e: s0616n@heb.com
genres: R&B, World, Jazz, Blues, Country, Funk, Acoustic, Soul, Latin, Pop
advance: 3 months
capacity: 600
pa: Yes **sound eng:** Yes
stage: 20 x 20
Popular eatery features original Locals-Nat'ls Fri-Sun for all ages. Acts play from 6:30-9pm w/ break. Bands must be able to draw; if so, email or mail kit.

Cheatham Street Warehouse
119 Cheatham St.
San Marcos, TX 78666
p: 512-353-3777
e: bandbooking@cheathamstreet.com
www.cheathamstreet.com
contact: Kent Finlay
e: finlay@cheathamstreet.com
call: M-F after 4:30pm
genres: Rock, S/S, Country, Blues, Americana, Folk
advance: 1-6 months
capacity: 300
pa: Yes **sound eng:** Yes
stage: 15 x 25
open mics: Wed Songwriters
18+ Honky Tonk music hall nurtures mostly original Local-Nat'l acts up to 7 nites. 1-2 bands fill up to 3hrs for 100% of door. Snail mail or use EPKs.

Cypress Creek Cafe
320 Wimberley Sq.
Wimberley, TX 78676
p: 512-847-2515
e: info@cypresscreekcafe.com
www.cypresscreekcafe.com
contact: Bruce Calkins
e: cafe@austin.rr.com
genres: Blues, Jazz, Reggae, Rock, Folk
capacity: 1000
pa: Yes
Popular 21+ eatery showcases 1 polished Reg'l or estab. Touring band in back room or outdoor stage Wed-Sat.

The Elephant Room
315 Congress Ave.
Austin, TX 78701
p: 512-473-2279
www.elephantroom.com
contact: Mike Mordecai
p: 512-477-7777 x1
e: mike@bbabooking.com
call: M-F noon-3pm
genres: Jazz
advance: 2-3 months
capacity: 150
pa: Yes
stage: 20' across
Premier 21+ listening room has original Local act nitely for fee. Sets are 4hrs w/ a break. Email or mail press kit to venue.

Elysium
705 Red River St.
Austin, TX 78701
p: 512-748-5842
e: elysiumaustin@aol.com
www.elysiumonline.net
contact: John Wickham
p: 512-478-2979 x2
e: elysium_nightclub@yahoo.com
call: afternoons
genres: Goth, Industrial, Electronic, Synth Pop, Rock, Alt.
advance: 1-2 months
capacity: 550
pa: Yes **sound eng:** Yes
stage: 20 x 24
Haven for area's Alt. & Goth scenes, books Local & some Touring bands for flat fee plus % of door. Up to 3 acts play 40min sets Thu-Fri for 21+. Use MySpace or mail promos: PO Box 270091, Austin, TX 78727.

Emo's
603 Red River Rd.
Austin, TX 78701
p: 512-477-3667
www.emosaustin.com
contact: Joe Holzheimer
e: emosjohio@gmail.com
genres: Punk, Indie, Emo, Electronica, DIY Hip-Hop
advance: 2-3 months
capacity: 300; 1000
pa: Yes **sound eng:** Yes
stage: 3 stages
Popular all ages club books original Local & Touring bands nitely on 3 stages. 3-4 acts play 45-90min sets for % of door minus expenses. Prefers email or EPK. No unsolicited mail.

Flamingo Cantina
515 E 6th St.
Austin, TX 78701

p: 512-494-9336
e: angela@flamingocantina.com
www.flamingocantina.com
contact: Angela Gillen
e: booking@flamingocantina.com
call: M-F noon-6pm
genres: Reggae, World, Alt., Funk, Dub, Rock, Punk, Pop
advance: 1-3 months
capacity: 300
pa: Yes **sound eng:** Yes
stage: 10 x 18
Tropical themed 18+ club books original Local-Int'l acts Wed-Sat; some all ages shows. Up to 4 bands play 45-60min for% of door. Mail press kit to venue.

Flipnotics Coffeespace Cafe
1601 Barton Springs Rd.
Austin, TX 78704
p: 512-441-3547
e: flipnotics@sbcglobal.net
www.flipnotics.com
contact: Mark Kamburis
genres: Folk, S/S, Jazz, Country, Acoustic Rock, Funk, Roots, Reggae
advance: 1-3 months
capacity: 40; 145 (outside)
pa: Yes
stage: 8 x 8
open mics: Sun 8pm
All ages Acoustic showcase for Local-Int'l talent. 2-3 acts play 90min of original material nitely. Promos: 2121 S Lamar, Ste. 204, Austin, TX 78704.

Friends Bar
208 E 6th St.
Austin, TX 78701
p: 512-320-8193
e: info@friendsbar.com
www.friendsbar.com
contact: Hooman M.
p: 512-589-7878
call: mornings
genres: Blues, Rock
advance: 1-2 months
capacity: 200
pa: Yes
stage: small
Club books mostly Local bands nitely Fri-Sat for 21+ crowd. 1-2 acts play from 7pm-2am. Int'l bands booked during SXSW. Email or mail press kit to: PO Box 639, Austin, TX 78767.

Ginny's Little Longhorn
5434 Burnet Rd.
Austin, TX 78756
p: 512-458-1813
e: ginnyslittlelonghorn@musicroom.org
www.ginnyslittlelonghorn.com
contact: Sharon Lusk
genres: Traditional Country
advance: 1-2 months
capacity: 68
pa: Yes
stage: 12 x 12
18+ Honky Tonk books Local & some Touring acts Tue-Sun. Featured act plays 4hrs w/ breaks for tips. Prefers press kit mailed to venue.

Hanovers Draught Haus
108 E Main St.
Pflugerville, TX 78660
p: 512-670-9617
www.myspace.com/hanoversbar
contact: Mo Ontiveros
genres: Americana, Alt., Country, Blues
advance: 6 months
capacity: 254
pa: Yes **sound eng:** Yes
stage: 20 x 10
open mics: Wed 8pm
Venue books Local-Reg'l talent Tue, Fri, Sat & some Sun. Featured act plays 3.5hrs for% of door. Prefers original material. Booking thru MySpace.

Hole in the Wall
2538 Guadalupe St.
Austin, TX 78705
p: 512-477-4747
e: info@holeinthewallaustin.com
www.holeinthewallaustin.com
contact: Singer Mayberry
e: holeinthewallbooking@yahoo.com
genres: Indie Rock, Garage, Alt. Country, Roots Rock, Blues, Folk, Americana
capacity: 196
pa: Yes **sound eng:** Yes
stage: 12 x 4; 12 x 15
Popular music spot w/ eclectic crowd, presents mostly Local & few Nat'l up & comers wkly. Up to 5 bands play 1hr for% of bar & tips. Prefers EPKs or links to MySpace but accept snail mail.

Jovita's
1619 S 1st St.
Austin, TX 78704
p: 512-447-7825
www.jovitas.com
contact: Joyce DiBona
e: dibonastudio@yahoo.com
call: M-F 9am-5pm
genres: Country, Rockabilly, Blues, Folk, Rock
advance: 1-3 months
capacity: 250+
pa: Yes **sound eng:** Yes
stage: 15 x 10
Funky Mexican eatery presents original Local-Reg'l acts 6 nites; some Nat'l-Int'l artists & cover acts. 2-3 acts play 2hrs for all ages. Prefers EPK or MySpace.

La Zona Rosa
612 W 4th St.
Austin, TX 78701
p: 512-263-4146
e: booking@directevents.net; jmckay@austin.rr.com
www.lazonarosa.com
contact: Tracee Crump
p: 512-263-4240
e: tracee@directevents.net
call: M-F 9am-5pm
genres: Southern Rock, Alt., Hip-Hop, Jazz, Funk, Rock
advance: 2-3 months
capacity: 1200 **stage:** 32 x 25
Eclectic venue w/ 2 pro stages hosts known Touring bands & rising stars 3-4 nites. 2-3 original acts play 1hr sets for all ages. Also books Antones. Promos: Direct Events, 13101 Hwy 71 W, Austin, TX 78738.

Lucky Lounge
209-A W 5th St.
Austin, TX 78701
p: 512-479-7700
www.theluckylounge.com
contact: Will Muntz
e: daddybigz@theluckylounge.com
genres: Rock, Blues, Folk, Acoustic
advance: 1-2 months
capacity: 250
pa: Yes **sound eng:** Yes
stage: medium
Swanky bar features Local-Reg'l bands & DJs Tue-Sat. 1-2 acts play 90-120min w/ break for% of sales to hip 21+ crowd.

Lucy's
141 E Hopkins St.
San Marcos, TX 78666
p: 512-558-7399
e: lucyssanmarcos@hotmail.com
www.lucyssanmarcos.com
contact: John Jansky
p: 210-372-9943
e: skytravel@satx.rr.com
call: M-F 9am-6pm
genres: Punk, Rock, Hip-Hop, Indie
advance: 4-6 weeks
capacity: 400
pa: Yes **sound eng:** Yes
stage: 20 x 15
open mics: Mon 9:30pm
Cool club packs them in for Reg'l buzz bands & estab. Touring acts up to 7 nites. 2-4 acts play for all ages. Promos: 14310 Auberry Dr., Helotes, TX 78023.

Momo's
618 W 6th St., Ste. 200
Austin, TX 78701
p: 512-479-8848
e: paul@momosclub.com
www.momosclub.com
contact: David Cotton
p: 512-835-5997
e: cottonaustin@aol.com
call: M-F afternoons
genres: Rock, S/S, Funk, Blues, Country
advance: 1-2 months
capacity: 320
pa: Yes **sound eng:** Yes
stage: 15 x 12
Vegas-styled 18+ lounge w/ great sound & sight lines, presents mostly Local acts nitely w/ some Touring talent. 3-4 original acts perform 1-2hrs for 80% of door. Accepts EPKs or mail w/ ATTN: Paul Oveisi, Momo's Club, 801 W 5th St., Ste. 601, Austin, TX 78703; incl. phone number.

Mozart's Coffee Roasters
3825 Lake Austin Blvd.
Austin, TX 78703
p: 512-477-2900
e: mozarts@austin.rr.com
www.mozartscoffee.com
contact: Jack Ranstrom
p: 512-698-5834
e: jack@mozartscoffee.com
call: M-F noon-4pm
genres: Jazz, S/S, Folk, World, Christian, Acoustic
advance: 1-2 months
capacity: 400 **stage:** 8 x 8
Scenic cafe serves up original Acoustic talent; area & a few Touring acts gig Wed-Sun. Featured act plays 3hrs w/ breaks for $50. Christian music on Mon. Prefers email, but may mail press kit to venue.

Nutty Brown Cafe & Amphitheatre
12225 Hwy. 290 W
Austin, TX 78737
p: 512-301-4648
www.nuttybrown.com
contact: Mike Farr
e: bigdaddyfarr@yahoo.com
genres: Rock, Country, Alt. Country, Blues
capacity: 120; 3000
pa: Yes
stage: 2 large outdoor stages
Country eatery features Local-Reg'l bands Fri & Sat; Nat'l & Int'l acts on any avail. nite. Openers play 8-9:30pm, headliners 9:30-11:30pm. Snail mail kit.

Ole Moulton Bank
101 Main St.
Moulton, TX 77975
p: 361-596-7499
www.olemoultonbank.com
contact: Jim Mendenhall
e: zoom@olemoultonbank.com
genres: Americana, Country, Folk, Rock, Blues, Bluegrass, Zydeco, Polka
advance: 2 months
capacity: 85
pa: Yes **sound eng:** Yes
stage: medium
open mics: Thu 6:30pm
A great gig b/w gigs from the creators of Houston's Dan Electro's Guitar Bar, this showcase for original guitar-based acts is midway b/w Houston & San Antonio & 60mi from Austin. Polished Local-Int'l acts gig 4 nites for 21+. 1-2 acts fill 2hrs for 100% of door. Mail press kit to venue.

The Parish Room
214 E 6th St.
Austin, TX 78701
p: 512-479-0474
e: shemakesithappen@gmail.com
www.theparishroom.com
contact: Brynn Scott
e: booking@theparishroom.com
call: email only
genres: All Styles
advance: 1-12 months
capacity: 425
pa: Yes **sound eng:** Yes
stage: 24 x 26
Formerly The Mercury, lively room presents original Local-Int'l acts & DJs up to 7 nites for eclectic fans. 2-3 acts play 45min; acts keep 80-85% merch sales. Also books Roux Lounge downstairs. Email EPK & MySpace link w/ past gigs, draw/bar sales numbers & press; or mail press kit to venue. No MySpace contact or calls.

Red Eyed Fly
715 Red River St.
Austin, TX 78701
p: 512-474-1084
e: contact@redeyedfly.com
www.redeyedfly.com
contact: Heath Macintosh
p: 512-474-1084 x1
call: Mon, Wed & Fri 2-8pm
genres: Rock, Roots
advance: 1-2 months
capacity: 450
pa: Yes **sound eng:** Yes
stage: 20 x 20
open mics: Mon
Ultra cool original indie music venue books TX talent plus some Nat'l acts nitely. 4 bands play 40min on covered outdoor stage to 18+ & split% of door. Use email or snail mail kit w/ ATTN: Heath. No booking via MySpace.

Ruta Maya
3601 S Congress Ave., Ste. D-200
Austin, TX 78704
p: 512-707-9637

e: events@rutamaya.net
www.rutamaya.net
contact: Austin Daze
p: 512-924-9864
e: rutabook@gmail.com
genres: Country, Swing, Hip-Hop, Rock, Folk, S/S
advance: 4+ months
capacity: 100+
pa: Yes sound eng: Yes
stage: medium
open mics: Tue 9pm-1am
All ages coffeehouse presents mostly polished Reg'l, some Touring artists & DJs nitely. Up to 3 acts play 90-150min for % of door. Prefers EPKs, but may mail press kit to: 2213 S 3rd Ave., Austin, TX 78704. For Sun-Wed bookings, email events@rutamaya.net.

Saxon Pub
1320 S Lamar Blvd.
Austin, TX 78704
p: 512-448-2552
e: saxonpub@yahoo.com
www.thesaxonpub.com
contact: David Cotton
p: 512-835-5997
e: cottonaustin@aol.com
genres: Americana, Roots Rock, Bluegrass, Blues, Country
advance: 3-6 months
capacity: 150
pa: Yes sound eng: Yes
stage: 18' wide
Intimate 21+ Acoustic bar attracts wide array of original talent. Area bands gig nitely; Touring acts monthly. 3 acts play 1hr for 100% of door, sometimes a flat fee. Multi-track recording avail. Also books Threadgill's, Antone's, Momo's & Lorraine's in Marble Falls. Email or snail mail kit to 12824 Council Bluff Dr., Austin, TX 78727.

Shady Grove
1624 Barton Springs Rd.
Austin, TX 78704
p: 512-474-9991
e: shadygrove@chuys.com
www.theshadygrove.com
contact: Marsha Milam
p: 512-472-3444
e: marsha@milamandcompany.com
genres: S/S, Americana
advance: 3+ months
capacity: 1500
pa: Yes sound eng: Yes
stage: 20 x 15
Eatery presents mostly top original Local-Reg'l acts & few Nat'ls for free Thu outdoor shows Apr-Oct w/ AAA radio stn. KGSR. 1 act play 2hrs from 8-10pm for flat fee to all ages crowd. Email or mail press kit: Marsha Milam Music, 1506 W 13th St., #17, Austin, TX 78703.

Stubb's Bar-BQ
801 Red River Rd.
Austin, TX 78701
p: 512-480-8341
e: info@c3presents.com
www.stubbsaustin.com
contact: Brooke Wirth
p: 512-478-7211
call: M-F 11am-4pm
genres: Rock, Alt. Country, Americana, S/S, Roots, Alt.
advance: 2-3 months
capacity: 2500
pa: Yes sound eng: Yes
stage: 40 x 32; 21 x 11
Popular original music spot serves up great Local-Int'l talent & world famous BBQ sauce. TX talent plays on indoor stage & Touring acts perform outside. Each show features 1 act w/ opener. Some all ages, 18+ & 21+ shows. Gospel Brunch on Sun. Prefers calls, but may mail promos: 98 San Jacinto Blvd., Ste. 430, Austin, TX 78701.

Threadgill's World Headquarters
301 W Riverside Dr.
Austin, TX 78704
p: 512-472-9304
e: geninfo@threadgills.com
www.threadgills.com
contact: David Cotton
p: 512-835-5997
e: cottonaustin@aol.com
genres: Roots Rock, S/S, Alt. Country, Rock
advance: 3+ months
capacity: 450
pa: Yes sound eng: Yes
stage: large (outdoor)
Landmark venue books 2 original Local-Nat'l acts Thu-Sat on outdoor stage. Also books North Austin location, Saxon Pub, Antone's, Momo's & Lorraine's. Promos: David Cotton, 12824 Council Bluff, Austin, TX 787047.

Triple Crown
206 N Edward Gary St.
San Marcos, TX 78666
p: 512-396-2236
www.triplecrownlive.com
contact: Eric Shaw
p: 512-396-2874
e: booking@triplecrownlive.com
call: Mon 1-6pm
genres: Rock, Blues, Country, Punk, Alt., Reggae, Hip-Hop, Bluegrass
advance: 4-8 weeks
capacity: 150
pa: Yes sound eng: Yes
stage: 22 x 12
open mics: Sun sign in: 8pm
One of area's top live music rooms 30mi from Austin, books original TX & Touring bands nitely for the door. 2-4 acts play 45min-3hrs; 18+ after 8pm. Email or mail press kit to venue w/ ATTN: Eric Shaw.

Trophy's
2008 S Congress Ave.
Austin, TX 78704
p: 512-447-0969
www.myspace.com/trophystx
contact: Dave Sprauer
e: davebooking@yahoo.com
genres: Rock, Punk, Space Rock, Honky-Tonk
advance: 45-60 days
capacity: 400
pa: Yes sound eng: Yes
stage: 12 x 15
open mics: Tue S/S 9:15pm
Dive bar w/ character, books mostly Reg'ls & some Nat'ls nitely for tips or door after $90 for costs; bigger names play during SXSW. 2-4 mostly original bands play 45-60min to 21+ crowd. Mark kits w/ ATTN: Dave.

The White Rabbit
2410 N St. Mary's St.
San Antonio, TX 78212
p: 210-737-2221
www.sawhiterabbit.com
contact: Jennifer
e: booktherabbit@hotmail.com
genres: Hard Rock, Emo, Pop, Rock, Acoustic, Metal
advance: 6-12 weeks
capacity: 850
pa: Yes sound eng: Yes
stage: 2 stages
Premier all ages Rock club w/ crystal clear sound system 60+mi from Austin, hosts original estab. & rising talent 6 nites & Touring DJs wkly. 4 acts play 40min; merch splits 80/20. Email, contact via MySpace booking page or mail press kit to venue w/ 'Promo Package' written on outside; Nat'ls acts call.

Dallas/Ft. Worth

The Aardvark
2905 W Berry St.
Ft. Worth, TX 76109
p: 817-926-7814
e: theaardvarkrocks@yahoo.com
www.the-aardvark.com
contact: Danny Weaver
p: 817-926-1512
e: music@the-aardvark.com
call: Tue-Thu noon-5pm
genres: All Styles
advance: 1 month
capacity: 400
pa: Yes sound eng: Yes
stage: 20 x 13
Popular original music room near Texas Christian U, showcases up to 4 Reg'l-Int'l Touring bands Thu-Sat for 17+ crowd. Openers play 40min, headliners 90min. Email w/ links to music or snail mail kit.

Adair's Saloon
2624 Commerce St.
Dallas, TX 75226
p: 214-939-9900
e: contact@adairssaloon.com
www.adairssaloon.com
contact: Joel
e: joel@adairssaloon.com; bookings@adairssaloon.com
genres: Country, TX Music
advance: 2 months
capacity: 150
pa: Yes sound eng: Yes
stage: medium
Beloved 21+ burger & music joint near several colleges, draws rising Country & TX artists 6 nites. Email for booking. No unsolicited mail.

AllGood Cafe
2934 Main St.
Dallas, TX 75226
p: 214-742-5362
www.allgoodcafe.com
contact: Mike Snider
p: 214-348-9426
e: txmuzik@swbell.net
genres: Rock, Alt. Country, Jazz, Jam, S/S, Zydeco, Folk, Alt. Country
capacity: 100
pa: Yes
A bit of laid-back Austin in Deep Ellum, draws estab. & rising original bands Thu-Sat to 21+. Use email for booking.

Barley House
5612 Yale Blvd.
Dallas, TX 75206
p: 214-824-0306
www.barleyhouse.com
contact: Richard Winfield
e: richard@barleyhouse.com
call: M-F 9am-5pm
genres: Americana, Alt., Rock, Surf
advance: 1-2 months
capacity: 258
pa: Yes sound eng: Yes
stage: 8 x 6
Prime music club w/ love of twangy Rock, books Local-Int'l popular & emerging artists 4 nites. Up to 4 original acts play 45+min for % of door. Major acts often play incognito.

Club Dada
2720 Elm St.
Dallas, TX 75226
p: 214-742-3400
e: info@clubdada.com
www.clubdada.com
contact: Ben Tapia
p: 214-586-3358
e: bensurfs69@yahoo.com
genres: Jam, Jazz, R&B, Punk, Alt.
advance: 1-2 months
capacity: 450
pa: Yes sound eng: Yes
stage: 18 x 20; 30 x 30
open mics: Sun 8pm
Legendary music club features polished Reg'ls 4 nites, Nat'ls & Int'ls wkly. 3-4 mostly original acts play 60-90min sets for % of door; 21+ w/ some all ages shows. Call or email.

The Curtain Club & Liquid Lounge
2800 Main St.
Dallas, TX 75226
p: 214-742-6207
www.curtainclub.com
p: 214-342-2030
genres: Rock, Alt.
advance: 3 months
capacity: 600
pa: Yes sound eng: Yes
stage: 25 x 15
Prime club w/ 2 stages & top sound showcases original Local & Nat'l talent 3 nites for 17+; some cover bands. 4-5 acts play 30-45min for % of door. Promos: Elite Ent., PMB 132, 6780 Abrams Rd., Ste. 103, Dallas, TX 75231.

Dan's Silverleaf
103 Industrial St.
Denton, TX 76201
p: 940-320-2000
www.danssilverleaf.com
contact: Dan Mojica
e: dan@charterinternet.com
genres: Alt. Country, Bluegrass, Acoustic, Rock, Metal, Pop, Punk
advance: 2-3 months
capacity: 190
pa: Yes sound eng: Yes
stage: 12 x 15
Crowded 18+ venue 30+mi from Dallas/Ft. Worth, hosts Local legends & Nat'l recording stars for original music 3-5 nites. Featured act plays 45min for % of door. Use online form.

The Door (Dallas)
2513 Main St.
Dallas, TX 75226
p: 214-742-3667
e: thedoor@thedoordallas.com
www.thedoorclubs.com
contact: Russell David Hobbs

p: 214-742-3667 x3
genres: Rock, Punk, Emo, Metal, Acoustic
advance: 1-2 months
capacity: 1250
pa: Yes **sound eng:** Yes
stage: 32 x 20 (main stage); side stage; bar stage
All ages venue w/ 3 stages books 4-8 original bands up to 5 nites for% of door. Unknowns paired w/ known acts; 35-60min sets. Also books the Ft. Worth & Canton locations as well as The Prophet Bar in Dallas. Prefers EPKs, or snail mail kit to: 2546 Elm St., Ste. 200, Dallas, TX 75226. See site for FAQs.

Double Wide
3510 Commerce St.
Dallas, TX 75226
p: 214-887-6510
www.double-wide.com
contact: Chelsea Callahan
p: 214-448-1371
e: bookings@thedoublewidebar.com
call: M-F evenings
genres: Rock, Country, Indie, Metal, Punk, Hip-Hop, Folk
advance: 2+ months
capacity: 150
pa: Yes **sound eng:** Yes
Trailer trash themed dive, offers premier location for live music. 3-4 Local-Int'l acts play 40-60min for door split minus $80. Email or snail mail kit.

Kirby's
3305 E Hwy. 114
Southlake, TX 76092
p: 817-410-2221
www.kirbyssteakhouse.com
contact: Art Riddles
p: 214-327-6168
e: artriddles@sbcglobal.net
call: M-F afternoons
genres: Jazz, R&B, Acoustic, Pop, S/S, Blues
advance: 2 months
capacity: 75 (lounge)
pa: Yes
stage: 10 x 12 **in-house:** Piano
21+ steak chain books Local-Reg'l performers in piano lounge 4 nites; all ages w/ guardian. Featured act plays 3-4hrs for flat fee. Email or mail press kit to: Art Riddles, Art Music, 8643 San Benito Way, Dallas, TX 75218.

Poor David's Pub
1313 S Lamar St.
Dallas, TX 75215
p: 214-565-1295
www.poordavidspub.com
contact: David Card
e: david@poordavidspub.com
genres: Blues, Americana, Country, Bluegrass, Eclectic
advance: 2-3 months
capacity: 425
pa: Yes **sound eng:** Yes
stage: 14 x 24
open mics: 1st Wed of mo
Lauded, low-key 21+ listening room w/ emphasis on original songwriting, showcases top-notch veterans & rising stars Thu-Sat. 1-2 Local-Nat'l acts perform 45-90min sets.

The Prophet Bar
2548 Elm St
Dallas, TX 75226
p: 214-939-4321
e: prophet@theprophetbar.com
www.theprophetbar.com
e: prophet@theprophetbar.com
genres: Indie, Alt., Roots, Dub, Alt. Country, Post Punk, Hip-Hop, Jazz, Soul, Metal
Lauded room books polished & top acts up to 5 nites, many all ages shows. Booking by email.

Rubber Gloves Rehearsal Studios
411 E Sycamore St.
Denton, TX 76205
p: 940-387-7781
e: info@rubberglovesdentontx.com
www.rubberglovesdentontx.com
contact: Josh Baish
e: joshbaish@hotmail.com
call: M-F 1-5pm
genres: Indie Rock, Country, Hip-Hop, Hardcore
advance: 2 months
capacity: 200
pa: Yes **sound eng:** Yes
stage: 20 x 8
open mics: Tue **sign in:** 10pm
Nestled b/w Dallas & Ft. Worth, quirky former cement factory has good sound & stage for the Local-Int'l bands & DJs booked 5 nites for all ages. 3-4 acts play original 45min sets. Mail press kit to venue or contact via MySpace. No unsolicited emails, or calls.

Sambuca Jazz Cafe
2120 McKinney Ave.
Dallas, TX 75201
p: 214-744-0820
e: marketing@sambucarestaurant.com
www.sambucarestaurant.com
contact: James Gee
p: 972-685-8455
genres: Jazz, Blues, World, R&B, Rock, S/S, Dance
advance: 2 months
capacity: 299
pa: Yes **sound eng:** Yes
stage: 12 x 12
Award-winning upscale niteclub w/ Atlanta, Houston & Denver stages, presents polished Local-Int'l talent nitely for 21+. Featured act performs 4-5hrs for flat fee. Try calling for booking.

Sons of Hermann Hall
3414 Elm St.
Dallas, TX 75226
p: 214-747-4422
www.sonsofhermann.com
contact: Jo Nicodemus
call: M-F 9am-5pm
genres: Americana, Rockabilly, Roots, Folk, Western Swing, Country, Blues, Reggae, Celtic, Zydeco, Cajun, Rock, Acoustic
advance: 6 months
capacity: 350-400
pa: Yes **sound eng:** Yes
stage: 20 x 15
Authentic all ages Honky Tonk draws exceptional TX & name Touring acts Fri-Sat. 2-3 acts play 1hr for% of door. Mail promos w/ ATTN: Band Booking, PO Box 710277, Dallas, TX 75371. Call to follow up.

Uncle Calvin's Concert Coffeehouse
9555 N Central Expy.
Dallas, TX 75231
p: 214-363-0044
e: info@unclecalvins.org
www.unclecalvins.org
contact: Booking Committee
p: 214-363-0044 x4
e: booking@unclecalvins.org
genres: Americana, Celtic, Country, Blues, Bluegrass, Folk
advance: 10-12 months
capacity: 200
pa: Yes **sound eng:** Yes
stage: 15 x 30
Premier all-ages listening room showcases top-notch known & emerging Acoustic artists Fri. Up to 3 original Local-Int'l acts perform 45min for% of door. Returning acts can email or phone avail. dates; new acts mail bio & music w/ ATTN: Booking Committee. Will contact if interested.

Houston

19th Hole Grill & Bar
202 Sawdust Rd.
Spring, TX 77381
p: 281-363-2574
e: band19thhole@charter.net
www.19th.cc
contact: Mike Pruneda
p: 832-289-3677
call: M-F 6-9pm
genres: Rock, Metal, Alt.
advance: 6 weeks
capacity: 300
pa: Yes **sound eng:** Yes
stage: 20 x 12
open mics: Thu **sign in:** 9pm
18+ hang 30+mi from Houston, books 3 original bands 2x/wk. Openers play 45-60min, headliners 90; acts get% of door. New bands audition at open mic. Snail mail press kit w/ song list, pics & tour history ATTN: Mike P.

Anderson Fair
2007 Grant St.
Houston, TX 77006
p: 713-528-8576
www.andersonfair.com
contact: Tim Leatherwood
e: admin@andersonfair.com
call: Fri & Sat 8-11pm
genres: Folk, S/S, Acoustic, Honky-Tonk
advance: 1-2 months
capacity: 99
pa: Yes **sound eng:** Yes
stage: 20' wide
All ages original music venue presents 1-2 top Local & Touring acts Thu-Sat for% of door. Opener plays 45min; headliner 1hr.

The Big Easy
5731 Kirby Dr.
Houston, TX 77005
p: 713-523-9999
www.myspace.com/thebigeasyblues
contact: Tom McLendon
genres: Blues, Zydeco
advance: 2-3 months
capacity: 175
pa: Upon Request
stage: 10 x 10
Popular 21+ Blues room showcases Local-Int'l talent 7 nites. Featured act plays 4hrs w/ break, for flat fee. Mail press kit to venue.

Continental Club
3700 Main St.
Houston, TX 77002
p: 713-529-9899
www.continentalclub.com
contact: Pete Gray
e: pete@continentalclub.com
call: M-F 10am-3pm
genres: Blues, Roots, Rock, Country, Rockabilly, Folk, Americana
advance: 3 months
capacity: 300
pa: Yes **sound eng:** Yes
stage: 16 x 10
Sister club to notable Austin venue, presents 2-5 top Local-Int'l artists nitely for 21+. Mostly originals, some covers. EPKs or promos: PO Box 66408, Houston, TX 77266.

Fitzgerald's
2706 White Oak Dr.
Houston, TX 77007
p: 713-862-3838
www.fitzlive.com
contact: Frances Tofte
e: fitzbooking@aol.com
call: M-F 10am-5pm
genres: Rock, Pop, Emo, Blues, Folk, Jazz, Country, Metal, Punk, Hip-Hop, R&B
advance: 3-6 months
capacity: 300; 700 (upstairs)
pa: Yes **sound eng:** Yes
stage: 10 x 20; 14 x 25
Prime music room books Local-Int'l talent on 2 stages 3-5 nites Wed-Sun for all ages. Up to 5 acts play 30-90min & Touring acts keep 80% merch sales. Mail press kit to venue; allow 2-4 wks for response..

FitzWilly's
303 University Dr.
College Station, TX 77840
p: 979-846-8806
e: manager@fitzwillysbar.com
www.fitzwillysbar.com
contact: Earl Stone
e: booking@fitzwillysbar.com
call: prefers email
genres: All Styles
advance: 2-3 months
capacity: 200
pa: Yes **sound eng:** To hire
stage: indoor & outdoor
open mics: Wed 11pm
Venue b/w Houston & Austin & near Texas A&M campus, attracts Local & Reg'l bands Thu-Sat; 18+ after 8pm. 1-2 acts play 10pm-2am for 90% of door or flat fee. Use email or mail kit to venue.

Hickory Hollow
101 Heights Blvd.
Houston, TX 77007
p: 713-869-6300
www.hickoryhollowrestaurant.com
contact: Joseph Boehm
e: joseph@hickoryhollowrestaurant.com
call: M-F after 2pm
genres: Bluegrass, Country, Western Swing, Acoustic Folk, Classic Rock, Pop
advance: 3 months
capacity: 75 **stage:** floor space
All ages eatery hosts Local & Reg'l bands on Fri & Sat. Featured band plays 3hrs w/ breaks for flat fee. Call or mail press kit to venue & incl fee.

Last Concert Cafe
1403 Nance St.
Houston, TX 77002
p: 713-226-8563
e: lastconcertcafe@sbcglobal.net
www.lastconcert.com
contact: Dawn Fudge

genres: Jam, Funk, Roots, Rock, Acoustic, Blues
advance: 2-3 months
capacity: 400
pa: Yes sound eng: To hire
stage: indoor & outdoor
open mics: Mon 6:30pm
Low key Tex-Mex eatery brings Reg'l-Touring bands to patio stage nitely for 21+; 18+ Wed shows. 2-3 acts play 90-120min from 10:30pm-2am for 90% of door. Nat'l bands eat free, Locals 1/2 price. Mail press kit to venue.

McGonigel's Mucky Duck
2425 Norfolk St.
Houston, TX 77098
p: 713-528-5999
e: theduck@mcgonigels.com
www.mcgonigels.com
contact: Rusty Andrews
call: M-F noon-4pm
genres: Most Styles
advance: 3-4 months
capacity: 140
pa: Yes sound eng: Yes
stage: 15 x 15 (wedge)
open mics: Mon sign in: 7pm
21+ Irish pub spotlights 1 original Acoustic act 5 nites for serious music fans. Local-Int'l artists take % of door for two 1hr sets. No Hip-Hop or Blues. Mail press kit to venue.

Meridian
1503 Chartres St.
Houston, TX 77003
p: 713-225-1717
www.meridianhouston.com
contact: D'neta Cavazos
e: booking@meridianhouston.com
call: M-F daytime
genres: All Styles
advance: 2+ weeks
capacity: 1000
pa: Yes sound eng: Yes
stage: 2 stages
Recent star on the all ages scene, books Nat'l & developing bands on 2 stages w/ stellar sound & lights. 2-6 play til 1am. Only accepts EPKs; No unsolicited mail.

Rudyard's British Pub
2010 Waugh Dr.
Houston, TX 77006
p: 713-521-0521
e: rudyards@hotmail.com
www.rudyards.com
contact: Mike Sims
call: Fri 1-4pm
genres: All Styles
advance: Up to 3 months
capacity: 260
pa: Yes sound eng: Yes
stage: 30 x 30
Popular 21+ pub hosts eclectic, loud Local-Int'l bands Thu-Sat & some other nites on upstairs stage. 2-3 original bands play 45-60min for % of the door. Email or mail press kit to venue.

Walter's on Washington
4215 Washington Ave.
Houston, TX 77007
p: 713-862-2513
e: walters@4215washington.com
www.4215washington.com
contact: Pam Robinson
e: booking@4215washington.com
call: afternoons
genres: Roots, Rockabilly, Blues, Rock, Indie Rock, Punk
advance: 2-6 months
capacity: 250
pa: Yes sound eng: Yes
stage: 32 x 16
Unassuming all ages club features music nitely. Up to 6 original acts play 45-60min for % of door; some cover acts. Prefers email link but can mail kit or call.

Greater TX

Bash Riprock's
2419 Main St.
Lubbock, TX 79401
p: 806-762-2274
e: bashs@bashriprocks.com
www.bashriprocks.com
contact: Mike Fuqua
e: mikefuqua@hotmail.com
call: M-F 2-5pm
genres: Rock, Alt., Country
advance: 2-3 months
capacity: 381
pa: Yes sound eng: Yes
stage: 20 x 15
Wood-paneling gives this in NW TX bar great acoustics for its Local-Int'l acts. Up to 4 bands fill 3hrs any nite of wk. Send EPK or snail mail kit.

Blue Light
1806 Buddy Holly Ave.
Lubbock, TX 79401
p: 806-762-1185
www.thebluelightlive.com
contact: David Stroot
e: dstroot@thebluelightlive.com
genres: TX Country, TX Rock
advance: 1-2 months
capacity: 260
pa: Yes sound eng: Yes
stage: 12 x 30
Located near NM border, 21+ music venue welcomes Locals & Reg'ls Tue-Sat. 1-2 acts play 90-120 sets for % of door; Locals play til closing. Mail press kit w/ ATTN: David Stroot, 1808 Buddy Holly Ave., Lubbock, TX 79401.

Doctor Rockits Blues Bar
709 N Chaparral St.
Corpus Christi, TX 78401
p: 361-884-7634
e: rockits@stx.rr.com
www.drrockits.com
contact: Jennifer Williams
p: 361-884-7634 x1
genres: Blues, Rock
advance: 1 month
capacity: 300
pa: Yes sound eng: Yes
open mics: Sun 3-7pm
Local & Touring talent gig Wed & Fri-Sun at swinging Blues bar located on southern coast. 1-2 original acts play 2hrs w/ breaks for 21+. Try email for booking.

Utah

Salt Lake City

ABG's Libation Emporium
190 W Center St.
Provo, UT 84601
p: 801-373-1200
www.abgsbar.com
contact: Darrin Whittaker
e: booking@abgsbar.com
call: Tue, Wed & Fri after 3pm
genres: Rock, Reggae, Ska, Jazz, Americana
advance: 1-2 months
capacity: 149
pa: Yes sound eng: Yes
stage: medium
Popular dive bar/pvt. club, books Local/Reg'l & some Nat'ls Fri & Sat. Featured act plays three 45min sets for door after prod. costs. No Punk or Hardcore. Prefers hard copy kit sent to venue.

Avalon Theatre
3605 S State St.
Salt Lake City, UT 84115
p: 801-266-0258
e: info@thekollective.com
www.theavalontheater.com
contact: Jimmy Parks
p: 801-414-3320
call: afternoons
genres: Emo, Pop, Punk, Rock, Alt. Country, Metal, Christian Hardcore
advance: 6-12 months
capacity: 500
pa: Yes sound eng: Yes
stage: 30 x 16
Concert venue/church has up to 6 Local-Int'l bands playing 30min Mon-Sat. VIP dressing room w/ shower, bathroom & wi-fi avail. Prefers contact thru MySpace, but may email links or snail mail kit.

Burt's Tiki Lounge
726 S State St.
Salt Lake City, UT 84111
p: 801-521-0572
www.myspace.com/burtstikilounge
contact: Jeremy Sundeaus
call: Wed & Thu 3-6pm; prefers MySpace
genres: Punk, Rockabilly, Metal, Alt.
advance: 1 month
capacity: 250
pa: Yes sound eng: Yes
stage: 12 x 8
Prime hole-in-the-wall books Local-Int'l acts 6 nites. 2-5 acts play 1hr for flat fee vs door. Ska/Jazz on Mon; all other genres from Tue-Sat. Most booking done via MySpace, but may email or snail mail kit.

In The Venue
219 S 600 W
Salt Lake City, UT 84101
p: 801-359-3219
www.myspace.com/inthevenue
contact: Will Sartain
p: 801-554-6195
e: willsartain@yahoo.com
genres: Rock, Punk, Techno, Hardcore, Metal, Trance, Indie
advance: 4 months
capacity: 500; 1500-1800
pa: Yes sound eng: Yes
stage: large
All ages dance club w/ 2 rooms, showcases top indie Touring talent up to 5 nites. Up to 3 original acts play for mostly 18+; all ages w/ guardian; some 21+ shows. All booking done by outside promoters that call or contact via MySpace.

Kilby Court
741 S Kilby Ct.
Salt Lake City, UT 84101
p: 801-364-3538
e: kilby.court@yahoo.com
www.kilbycourt.com
contact: Will Sartain
p: 801-554-6195
e: willsartain@yahoo.com
genres: Indie Rock, Experimental, Acoustic
advance: 2-5 months
capacity: 200
pa: Yes sound eng: Yes
stage: 12 x 12
All ages venue books original Local-Int'l bands 4-5 nites. 3 bands play 30-45min for % of door. Also books some shows at In the Venue & Urban Lounge. Email or mail promos: 748 S Kilby Ct., Salt Lake City, UT 84101.

Liquid Joe's
1249 E 3300 S
Salt Lake City, UT 84106
p: 801-467-JOES
e: info@liquidjoes.net
www.liquidjoes.net
contact: Kelly Petersen
p: 801-467-JOES (5637) x2
e: kelly@liquidjoes.net
call: Wed-Fri
genres: All Styles
advance: 1-2 months
capacity: 400
pa: Yes sound eng: Yes
stage: 50 x 40
Hard rockin' spot attracts Reg'ls, & some Touring bands up to 7 nites; 2 acts play 60-90min. Prefers EPKs or snail mail.

Mojos Caffe
2210 Washington Blvd.
Ogden, UT 84401
p: 801-603-6737
e: mojosogden@aol.com
www.myspace.com/mojoscaffe
contact: Ron Atencio
p: 801-399-1166
genres: All Styles
advance: 1-2 months
capacity: 200+
pa: Yes sound eng: Yes
stage: 10 x 24
All ages coffeehouse books mostly Local & some Reg'l-Int'l acts. 4 original acts play 45min for % of door after expenses. Mail press kit to venue.

Monk's House of Jazz
19 E 200 S
Salt Lake City, UT 84111
p: 801-350-0950
contact: Alex Woodruff
p: 801-637-4244
e: alex78@irishnation.com
genres: All Styles mainly Indie, Hip-Hop & Punk
advance: 1 month
capacity: 195
pa: Yes sound eng: Yes
Hipster basement lounge features Reg'l & some Touring talent Tue, Fri & Sun for 21+. 1-3 acts play for door minus $25. Contact by any means.

Mo's Bar & Grill
358 SW Temple
Salt Lake City, UT 84101
p: 801-359-0586
e: mokhodadad@aol.com
www.mosbarandgrill.com
contact: Terrance
call: Tue evenings
advance: 1 month
capacity: 160
pa: Yes
stage: small
open mics: Mon; Tue S/S
Busy tavern mixes house & Local-Reg'l acts Wed-Sat. 1-2 acts play from 9pm-1am w/ breaks for % of door. Mail press kit to venue.

Mountain Town Stages
PO Box 680896
Park City, UT 84068
p: 435-901-7664
www.mountaintownstages.com
contact: Brian Richards
e: brianrichards@gmail.com
genres: All Styles
advance: 3-4 months
capacity: 5000; 150; 150; 150
pa: Yes **sound eng:** Yes
Non-profit books 150, mostly all ages shows at multiple area stages. Up to 9 shows/wk in summer; some nites have multiple shows w/ Local-Int'l acts & DJs playing for flat fee. Prefers EPKs; Local-Touring bands use online form.

The Urban Lounge
241 S 500 E
Salt Lake City, UT 84101
p: 801-746-0558; 801-746-0557
www.myspace.com/theurbanlounge
contact: Will Sartain
e: willsartain@yahoo.com
call: email only
genres: All Styles
advance: 3 months
21+ venue books Local-Int'l acts nitely. Email from booking agents or promoters only. Also, contacting a Local band w/ a following & has worked w/ club is a possibility. No booking via mail, calls or MySpace.

Velour
135 N University Ave.
Provo, UT 84601
p: 801-818-BAND
www.velourlive.com
contact: Corey Fox
e: booking@velourlive.com
genres: Indie Rock, Alt. Country, Indie Folk, S/S, Mainstream Rock
advance: 1-3 months
capacity: 300
pa: Yes **sound eng:** Yes
stage: 14 x 17
open mics: Tue Acoustic 8pm
Prime all ages, original music room owned by local music veteran, hosts 3-4 Local-Touring bands Wed-Sat & some Mon. No Hardcore or Hip-Hop. No calls.

Greater UT

The Electric Theater
68 E Tabernacle St.
St. George, UT 84770
p: 435-688-7469
www.theelectrictheater.com
contact: Bucky, Craig or Beau
e: booking@theelectrictheater.com
genres: Rock, Emo, Punk, Ska, Electronica
capacity: 500+
pa: Yes **sound eng:** Yes
stage: 16 X 24
All ages venue 2hrs N of Vegas, & 5hrs S of Salt Lake City, draws young crowd for 2-4 original Local-Nat'l bands a few times/wk. Great stop on routes thru AZ, CA or Denver. Email link to music; will contact if interested.

Vermont

Burlington/ Montpelier

1/2 Lounge
136 1/2 Church St.
Burlington, VT 05401
p: 802-865-0012
e: booking@onehalflounge.net
www.myspace.com/onehalflounge
contact: Jessica Bridge
p: 802-233-9817
genres: All Styles
advance: 6 weeks
capacity: 60
pa: Yes
stage: 10 x 6
Intimate cocktail lounge in college town w/ tourists, books original Local-Reg'l bands 2 nites for 21+. Featured act plays 3hrs for% of sales. Prefers email w/ music links or snail mail; but promos to venue ok. Booker can be hard to reach.

242 Main
250 Main St.
Burlington, VT 05401
p: 802-862-2244
www.myspace.com/242main
contact: Frankie
e: booking242main@hotmail.com
genres: Punk, Hardcore, Metal
advance: 1-2 months
capacity: 126
pa: Yes **sound eng:** Yes
stage: 10 x 15
All ages teen ctr. hosts Reg'ls & Nat'ls Fri & Sat. 5 acts play 20min sets for the door. Email for booking; No unsolicited mail.

After Dark Music Series
The United Methodist Church, Rte. 7 & Seminary St.
Middlebury, VT 05753
p: 802-388-0216
www.afterdarkmusicseries.com
contact: Carol Green
e: aftdark@sover.net
genres: Folk, Blues, Celtic, S/S, Americana, Western Swing, Acoustic, Bluegrass
advance: 8-12 months
capacity: 200
pa: Yes **sound eng:** Yes
stage: 15 x 7
Estab. original music series presents 6 monthly all ages Acoustic shows in fall & winter in village church. A top-notch Touring Nat'l act plays two 45+min sets for flat fee & % of door. Promos: PO Box 684, Middlebury, VT. 05753.

The Bee's Knees
82 Lower Main St.
Morrisville, VT 05661
p: 802-888-7889
www.thebeesknees-vt.com
contact: Sharon Dietz
p: 802-888-9954
e: sharondeitz@pshift.com
genres: S/S, Folk, Jazz, Blues, Celtic, Bluegrass
advance: 1+ months
capacity: 50+
pa: Limited
open mics: Last Sat of mo
All ages cafe 30mi from Montpelier, books original, acoustic Locals-Touring Tue-Sun for tips & meals. Mailing: PO Box 461, Morrisville, VT 05661. See FAQs at website.

Club Metronome
188 Main St.
Burlington, VT 05401
p: 802-865-4563
e: info@clubmetronome.com
www.clubmetronome.com
contact: Alex Budney
e: booking@clubmetronome.com
call: M-F 11am-5pm
genres: Funk, Blues, Reggae, Hip-Hop, Drum n Bass, Rock
advance: 1-2 months
capacity: 218
pa: Yes **sound eng:** Yes
stage: 15 x 12
Notable launching pad books Local-Int'l acts & DJs 5 nites for mostly door deals; some all ages shows. Also books Nectar's. Email first for booking; must draw 50+.

Higher Ground
1214 Williston Rd.
South Burlington, VT 05403
p: 802-652-0777
e: info@highergroundmusic.com
www.highergroundmusic.com
contact: Alex Crothers
e: alex@highergroundmusic.com
genres: Indie Rock, S/S, Americana, Jam, Reggae
advance: 3-6+ months
capacity: 300; 600
pa: Yes **sound eng:** Yes
Busy music hall w/ 2 spaces, books top Touring acts, Local-Reg'ls w/ following & DJs up to 7 nites. Up to 4 original acts perform mostly all ages gigs. Merch splits 85/15. No unsolicited mail.

The Matterhorn
4969 Mountain Rd.
Stowe, VT 05672
p: 802-253-8198
e: horn@stowevt.net
www.matterhornbar.com
contact: Charlie Schaffer
call: prefers email
genres: Blues, Rock, Reggae, Bluegrass, Jazz
advance: 3-4 months
capacity: 300
pa: Yes **sound eng:** Yes
stage: 15 x 12
Popular 18+ hang 30mi from Burlington, books top Local-Reg'l & some Touring acts 2 nites in summer & 4 nites in winter for tourists & locals. Featured act plays 3hrs w/ breaks. Use email only for booking. No unsolicited mail.

Nectar's
188 Main St.
Burlington, VT 05401
p: 802-658-4771
e: info@liveatnectars.com
www.liveatnectars.com
contact: Alex Budney
p: 802-865-4563
e: booking@liveatnectars.com
call: prefers email
genres: Blues, Jazz, Rock, Folk, Jam, Soul, Hip-Hop, Reggae
advance: 1-2 months
capacity: 240
pa: Yes **sound eng:** Yes
stage: 6 x 15
Popular college town stage & birthplace of Phish, showcases polished Local-Reg'l talent & some Touring acts up to 7 nites. Up to 3 acts play 1-3hrs. Also books Club Metronome. Prefers EPKs; see website FAQs before emailing. No unsolicited mail or calls.

Radio Bean
8 N Winooski Ave.
Burlington, VT 05401
p: 802-660-9346
www.radiobean.com
contact: Lee Anderson
e: booking@radiobean.com
genres: Experimental, Blues, S/S, Bluegrass, Polka, Indie Rock, Klezmer, Eclectic
advance: 1-2 months
capacity: 50
pa: Yes
stage: 7 x 8
open mics: Mon **sign in:** 7pm
Coffeehouse & launching pad for original artists features Local-Int'ls nitely. 4-8 acts play 1hr sets for tips to all ages. Prefers email or snail mail. No calls or booking via MySpace.

Rusty Nail Bar & Grille
1190 Mountain Rd.
Stowe, VT 05672
p: 802-253-6245
www.rustynailbar.com
contact: Rob Cocker
e: robert@rustynailbar.com
genres: Rock, Reggae, S/S, Jam, Jazz, Blues
advance: 3-6 months
capacity: 500
pa: Yes **sound eng:** Yes
stage: 35 x 20
Niteclub books 1-2 original Local & Touring bands Fri & Sat for 21+; busier in ski season. Locals play for flat fee, Touring acts get % vs flat fee & lodging. Promos: PO Box 1433, Stowe, VT 05672.

Rutland/Manchester

The Arkell Pavilion at Southern Vermont Arts Center
930 SVAC Dr., West Rd.
Manchester, VT 05254
p: 802-362-1405
e: info@svac.org
www.svac.org
contact: Christopher Madkour
genres: Jazz
advance: 6+ months
capacity: 400
pa: Yes **sound eng:** Yes
Non-profit, all ages arts ctr. books Reg'l-Int'l acts 1-3 nites/mo in summer. Promos: PO Box 617, West Rd., Manchester, VT 05254.

Hooker-Dunham Theater & Gallery
139 Main St.
Brattleboro, VT 05301
p: 802-254-9276
e: hdtandg@sover.net
www.hookerdunham.org
contact: Barry Stockwell
p: 802-254-9276 x2
genres: Acoustic, Jazz, Blues, Americana, Folk, S/S
capacity: 99
pa: Yes **sound eng:** Yes
stage: 13 x 19
All ages theater in hip town 40+mi from Manchester, presents diverse original Local-Int'l Acoustic acts several times/mo. Call or email.

Paramount Theatre
30 Center St.
Rutland, VT 05701
p: 802-775-0570
e: alice@paramountvt.org

www.paramountvt.org
contact: Tim Marceau
p: 802-775-0570 x203
e: tim@paramountvt.org
genres: Pop, Rock, Oldies, Jazz, World
advance: 6-12 months
capacity: 846
pa: Yes **sound eng:** Yes
stage: 31 x 31
Restored cinema palace books original Touring talent w/ draw a 20 times/yr for all ages crowd.

Virginia

Charlottesville

Baja Bean Co.
9 W Beverley St.
Staunton, VA 24401
p: 540-885-9988
www.bajabean.com
contact: Sarah Lynch
e: slynch1111@comcast.net
genres: Alt. Country, Folk, S/S, Rock, Blues, Jazz, Bluegrass
advance: 1-2 months
capacity: 50-120
pa: Request **sound eng:** Request
stage: floor space
21+ cantina w/ a SoCal vibe, hosts mostly Local acts on Sun. Featured act plays two 1hr sets for flat fee & tips.

Gravity Lounge
103 S 1st St.
Charlottesville, VA 22902
p: 434-977-5590
e: booking@gravity-lounge.com
www.gravity-lounge.com
contact: Bill Baldwin
e: bill@gravity-lounge.com
call: no calls
genres: Americana, Rock, Folk, Jazz, S/S, Country
advance: 2-6 months
capacity: 120-170
pa: Yes **sound eng:** Yes
Funky all ages listening room spotlights mostly original Reg'l & Touring bands nitely. Up to 4 bands play for % of gross. Email info for booking; will contact if interested. No Calls.

Miller's
109 W Main St.
Charlottesville, VA 22902
p: 434-971-8511
contact: Jeyon Falsini
e: jeyon11@mindspring.com
call: email only
genres: Folk, Blues, Jazz, Bluegrass, Rock
advance: 3 months
capacity: 75-100
pa: Yes **sound eng:** Yes
stage: 10 x 10 **in-house:** Piano
Popular spot & home of Dave Matthews, books original Local & Nat'l bands nitely for 18+ crowd. 1-2 acts play 45+min for flat fee & % of door. Email or mail press kit to venue; or at myspace.com/magnusmusicllc.

The Outback Lodge
917 Preston Ave.
Charlottesville, VA 22901
p: 434-979-7211
www.myspace.com/theoutbacklodge
contact: Terry Martin
genres: Rock, Blues, Jazz, Reggae, Punk, Hippie
advance: 6-8 weeks
capacity: 350
pa: Yes **sound eng:** Yes
stage: 10 x 14
18+ dive strip mall bar books original Local & Reg'l bands & some Nat'ls 4 nites. 2-3 acts play 30+min for 80% of door. Call 1 wk after submitting.

Wild Wing Cafe
820 W Main St.
Charlottesville, VA 22903
p: 434-979-9464
e: contactus@wildwingcafe.com
www.wildwingcafe.com
contact: Rob Lamble
e: roblamble@aol.com
genres: Rock, Blues, Reggae, Pop, Country
advance: 2 months
capacity: 400 **stage:** 30 x 12
Restaurant chain books Reg'l acts 2-3 nites for 18+ crowd; 21+ on Fri. 2 acts play 45-60min for flat fee & 80% merch sales. Prefers calls or snail mail kit.

Fairfax/Alexandria

Birchmere
3701 Mt. Vernon Ave.
Alexandria, VA 22305
p: 703-549-7500
e: booking@birchmere.com
www.birchmere.com
contact: Michael Jaworek
p: 703-549-7500 x14
e: michael@birchmere.com
call: M-F 10am-6pm
genres: Americana, S/S, Jazz, Rock, World, Bluegrass, R&B, Country
advance: 2-12 months
capacity: 500
pa: Yes **sound eng:** Yes
stage: 28 x 16; 32 x 16
Legendary all ages music hall just outside of DC, books 1-2 original & polished Reg'l-Int'l acts nitely. Merch split is 75/25. Snail mail kit w/ ATTN: Booking.

Fast Eddie's
9687 Lee Hwy.
Fairfax, VA 22032
p: 703-266-1888
www.fasteddies.com
contact: Brian J. Anderson
p: 703-469-2222
e: brian_anderson@lastcallent.com
call: M-F 10am-6pm
genres: Rock, Alt., Funk, Punk
advance: 2-3 months
capacity: 400
pa: Yes **sound eng:** Yes
stage: 16 x 20
Niteclub & billiards hall books up to 3 original Local-Reg'l acts & DJs Fri from 9:30pm-1:30am. Use email or mail promos to: 2325 Dulles Corner Blvd., Ste. 500, Herndon, VA 20171.

Fat Tuesday's
10673 Braddock Rd.
Fairfax, VA 22032
p: 703-385-5717
e: fatsfairfax@aol.com
www.fatsfairfax.com
contact: Kelly Butler
e: fatsbooking@yahoo.com
call: M-F 10am-5pm
genres: Rock, R&B, Alt., Reggae
advance: 2 months
capacity: 200
pa: Yes **sound eng:** Yes
stage: medium
open mics: Sun 8pm-1am
New Orleans-style eatery books Reg'l acts Wed-Sat for 21+. 3 acts play 1+hrs for % of door. Prefers MySpace for booking, but accepts email & snail mail.

Fatty J's
106 George St.
Fredericksburg, VA 22401
p: 540-368-9500
contact: Bryan Hoskins
e: schizodj@yahoo.com
call: M-F after 2pm
genres: Reggae, Funk
advance: 3 months
capacity: 250 **stage:** 10 x 15
21+ bar & grill books Local-Nat'l's Fri & some Sat nites. 1-2 acts play three 45min sets. Also books sister club Wings.

Firehouse Grill
3988 University Dr.
Fairfax, VA 22030
p: 703-383-1030
e: thefirehousegrillfx@yahoo.com
www.thefirehousegrill.com
contact: Joanna Miller
call: M-F 11am-noon; 6-7pm
genres: Most Styles
advance: 1 month
capacity: 100
pa: Yes
Casual eatery is home to Local acts on Fri & Sat. No booking agent; the staff chooses Local bands they enjoy. No Hard Rock, Metal or Rap.

Galaxy Hut
2711 Wilson Blvd.
Arlington, VA 22201
p: 703-525-8646
e: galaxyhut@hotmail.com
www.myspace.com/galaxyhut
contact: Lary Hoffman
call: email only
genres: Indie Rock, Pop, Experimental, Alt. Country, Electronica
advance: 2-4 months
capacity: 48
pa: Yes **sound eng:** Yes
stage: small
Area's coolest 21+ spot to hear & hang w/ DC area talent. Original Local/Reg'l's gig Sun-Mon; 2 acts play 45min sets for % of door. Touring acts should pair w/ Locals. Email MP3 links & est. draw. No unsolicited pkgs.

Iota Club & Cafe
2832 Wilson Blvd.
Arlington, VA 22201
p: 703-522-8340
www.iotaclubandcafe.com
contact: Steven Negrey
call: M-F 1-6pm
genres: Pop, Rock, Alt., Country, Jam, Americana
advance: 6-8 weeks
capacity: 200
pa: Yes **sound eng:** Yes
stage: 15 x 25
open mics: Wed **sign in:** 7pm
Original music room books polished Local-Reg'l bands up to 6 nites & Nat'l acts 2 nites; some Touring DJs. 2-3 acts play 45-60min for 21+ & keep 90% merch sales; 85% if house sells. Mail press kit to venue.

Jammin' Java
227 Maple Ave. E
Vienna, VA 22180
p: 703-255-1566
www.jamminjava.com
contact: Daniel Brindley
p: 703-255-3747
e: daniel@jamminjava.com
genres: All Styles
advance: 1-2 months
capacity: 200
pa: Yes **sound eng:** Yes
stage: 15 x 25
open mics: Most Mon 7pm
Top DC area coffee & music joint, books mostly Nat'l acts w/ some Local-Reg'ls for all ages nitely & has 'DC's Best Open Mic.' Books Touring DJs & has kids music too. Prefers EPKs. No unsolicited mail.

Jaxx
6355 Rolling Rd.
West Springfield, VA 22152
p: 703-569-5940
e: jaxxwebmaster@cox.net
www.jaxxroxx.com
contact: Jay Nedry
call: M-F 11am-5pm
genres: Metal, Rock, Alt., Folk, Funk, Christian, Jazz
advance: 6 wks - 6 mo
capacity: 500
pa: Yes **sound eng:** Yes
stage: 30 x 18
Popular all ages music club features mostly Touring acts but many Local-Reg'ls as well. 2-7 original, hi-energy bands perform 30+min 2-7 nites for flat fee; some cover bands & 21+ shows. Merch split 90/10. 'Battle of the Bands' from Jun-Sep used to discover new talent. Email or mail press kit to: PO Box 404, Aldie, VA 20105.

KC's Music Alley At Central Station
1917 Princess Anne St.
Fredericksburg, VA 22401
p: 540-371-0300
e: info@centralstationva.com
www.centralstationva.com
contact: Timmy Martini
e: tourmanagertimmy@aol.com
genres: Rock, Metal, Punk, Pop, Country
advance: 4-6 months
capacity: 1500
pa: Yes **sound eng:** Yes
stage: 3 stages; main: 19 x 24 w/ drum riser
Located in VA's largest ent. complex & hosts Local-Reg'l acts Fri & Sat; Nat'ls booked 1-2 nites/mo. Up to 5 bands play 20-60min; some all ages shows. Prefers email, but may mail kit to: 614 Kenmore Ave., Fredericksburg, VA 22401.

St. Elmo's Coffee Pub
2300 Mt. Vernon Ave.
Alexandria, VA 22301
p: 703-739-9268
www.stelmoscoffeepub.com
contact: Nora Partlow
e: norastelmos@hotmail.com
call: M-F noon-3pm
genres: Folk, Jazz, Acoustic, Blues, Pop
advance: 6 months
capacity: 75
open mics: 3rd Wed of mo
All ages coffeehouse books original Local bands Wed-Sat; Reg'ls & Nat'ls 3/mo. Featured act plays two 1hr sets & receives flat fee, % of door & tips.

Wolf Trap: The Barns & The Filene Center
1645 Trap Rd.
Vienna, VA 22182
p: 703-255-1900
e: wolftrap@wolftrap.org
www.wolftrap.org
contact: Peter Zimmerman
p: 703-255-1902
call: M-F 9am-5pm
genres: All Styles
advance: 2-6 months
capacity: 382; 7028
pa: Yes **sound eng:** Yes
stage: 50' wide; 70' wide
All ages PAC w/ indoor & outdoor stages hosts known original Reg'l & Touring artists up to 7 nites Oct-May at The Barns & Jun-Sep at the larger Filene Ctr. Up to 5 acts play 90-120min sets & keep 65% merch sales if house sells. Send EPK, call or mail kit to: 1645 Trap Rd., Vienna, VA 22182. No booking via MySpace.

Norfolk/ Virginia Beach

Club Relevant
929 Level Green Blvd.
Virginia Beach, VA
23464
p: 757-714-9874
www.relevant-ministries.org
contact: Pastor Mike Osborn
e: austin5@harvestva.org
genres: Christian, Hardcore, Metal, Rap, Folk, Indie, Punk, Acoustic, Alt., Rock
capacity: 500
Formerly the Warehouse now w/ upgraded sound, lights & mgmt., ministry-run venue hosts Local-Touring bands for teens-20+. Also books Acoustic indie acts for wknd gigs at adjacent coffeehouse, Jolt 180. Promos: 1028 Austin Dr., Chesapeake, VA 23320.

Goodfellas
13 E Queens Way
Hampton, VA 23669
p: 757-723-4979
e: diane@goodfellas.hrcoxmail.com
www.goodfellasbluesbar.com
contact: Kenny Lupton
e: kenny@goodfellas.hrcoxmail.com
genres: Blues, Rock, Alt.
advance: 2-4 months
capacity: 200
sound eng: Yes
open mics: Tue 8:30pm
Crowded all ages eatery books Local-Touring bands w/ local draw Fri-Sat for 21+. Mail press kit to venue w/ ATTN: Diane.

J.M. Randall's Classic American Grill & Bar
4854-16 Long Hill Rd.
Williamsburg, VA 23188
p: 757-259-0406
www.jmrandalls.com
contact: Randall
e: randall@jmrandalls.com; jmrandall@aol.com
call: M-F 9am-7pm
genres: Blues, Jazz, Classic Rock, Neo Soul, Acoustic
advance: 4-6 months
capacity: 300
pa: For Nat'l acts
stage: 10 x 27
Blues room 40mi from Norfolk, books Local-Nat'l groups for all ages 3-7 nites. 1-2 acts play 60-90min w/ shows starting at 9:30 or 10pm. Send EPKs.

The NorVa
317 Monticello Ave.
Norfolk, VA 23510
p: 757-627-4547
e: questions@thenorva.com
www.thenorva.com
contact: Rick Mersel
p: 757-622-9877 x15
call: M-F 10am-6pm
genres: Rock, Reggae, Country, Funk
advance: 2-4 months
capacity: 1450
pa: Yes **sound eng:** Yes
stage: 32 x 24
Top all ages venue w/ state-of-the art sound & lights, features estab. Touring acts, buzz bands or polished Reg'l acts nitely; 3 acts/bill. Also books The Nat'l in Richmond. Prefers calls, but may email or snail mail kit.

Richmond

Alley Katz
10 Walnut Alley
Richmond, VA
23223
p: 804-643-2816
www.alleykatzrva.com
contact: Heidi Paul-Gonzales
p: 804-643-2816 x6
e: booking@alleykatzrva.com
call: M-F noon-6pm
genres: Metal, Alt., Reggae, Rock, Punk, Ska, Hip-Hop, Rockabilly, Jazz
advance: 1-3 months
capacity: 400
pa: Yes **sound eng:** Yes
stage: 20 x 24
Top-notch bi-level original music venue w/ full sound & lights, books Reg'l & Touring acts 4-7 nites. 3 acts play 45-55min for % of door. Call, snail mail or use online form.

Ashland Coffee & Tea
100 N Railroad Ave.
Ashland, VA 23005
p: 804-798-1702
e: mary@ashlandcoffeeandtea.com
www.ashlandcoffeeandtea.com
contact: Kay Landry
genres: S/S
advance: 3 months
capacity: 150
pa: Yes **sound eng:** Yes
stage: Fits 7 piece act
All ages listening room w/ great rep & sound just outside of Richmond, hosts polished original Reg'l talent & some Nat'l-Int'l acts Thu-Sat; few Locals booked. 1 act plays two 45-60min sets for flat fee vs % of gross. Mail press kit to venue.

Bogart's Back Room
203 N Lombardy St.
Richmond, VA 23220
p: 804-353-9280
e: bogartsbackroom@aol.com
www.richmond.com
contact: Georgia Thornburg
call: M-F after 4:30pm
genres: Jazz, Bluegrass, Funk, Rock, Folk, Big Band, Indie
advance: 3 months
capacity: 150
pa: Yes
stage: 20 x 20
Jazz speakeasy features Local-Touring artists Mon-Sat for % of door; some Nat'l acts. Featured act plays 45-60min to 21+. Mail press kit to venue w/ ATTN: Georgia. No EPKs.

The Canal Club
1545 E Cary St.
Richmond, VA 23219
p: 804-643-2582
www.thecanalclub.com
contact: Bobby Walsh
e: booking@thecanalclub.com
call: Wed-Sun
genres: Rock, Blues, Jazz, Hip-Hop, Reggae, Folk, Pop, Punk, Hardcore, Metal
advance: 2-4 months
capacity: 720; 450
pa: Yes **sound eng:** Yes
stage: 28 x 24
All ages music venue books known & emerging Local-Nat'l acts up to 7 nites/wk. Also books mostly Local acts at Downstairs Lounge. Up to 4 acts play 45min sets; merch splits 85/15. Email or contact via MySpace; No unsolicited mail.

Cary St. Café
2631 W Cary St.
Richmond, VA
23220
p: 804-353-7445
e: cscafe@carystreetcafe.com
www.carystreetcafe.com
contact: Robyn Chandler
call: Tue-Thu 9am-1pm
genres: Jam, Bluegrass, Jazz, Rock, Funk, Country
advance: 3-4 months
capacity: 70
pa: Yes
stage: 20 x 15
Hippy-themed music room showcases mostly original Local acts & some Reg'l-Nat'l talent nitely. 1-2 acts fill 4hrs w/ breaks for % of door to 21+. Daytime shows & jams are all ages. Mail press kit to venue w/ ATTN: Robyn Chandler; No Calls.

Poe's Pub
2706 E Main St.
Richmond, VA
23223
p: 804-648-2120
e: music@poespub.com
www.poespub.com
contact: Mike Britt
e: poespub@aol.com
genres: All Styles
advance: 3-4 months
capacity: 99
pa: Yes
stage: 8 x 12
open mics: Tue 9pm
Biker-friendly roadhouse books polished Local bands & some Reg'l-Int'l acts Thu-Sat & some other nites for 100% of door. 1-2 mostly original acts play 45-60min sets to 21+ crowd. Mail press kit to venue.

Rocks
1814 E Main St.
Shockoe Bottom
Richmond, VA
23223
p: 804-648-ROCK
www.rocksbooking.com
contact: William Jennings
e: booking@noom.com
call: M-F noon-4pm
genres: Rock
advance: 2 months
capacity: 300-500
pa: Yes **sound eng:** Yes
stage: 16 x 20
Does not book bands separately, just shows. Touring bands or a Local acts should match up w/ venue's promoters found in the Top 12 friends on MySpace or one of the Local Richmond bands. 4 acts play 30-45min nitely to all ages for % of door. Read policy on MySpace first. No Reggae, Country, Rap, R&B, Hardcore or Straight Edge. Email, send EPK, call or contact via MySpace.

Roanoke

Cattle Annie's
4009 Murray Pl.
Lynchburg, VA
24502
p: 434-846-3206; 434-846-1977 (office)
www.cattleannies.com
contact: Gary Shotwell
e: gshotwell@cattleannies.com
call: M-F 10am-6pm
genres: Country, Rock
advance: 3 months
capacity: 1000
pa: Yes **sound eng:** To hire
stage: 40 x 20
Central VA's premier music venue ideally situated b/w DC, Atlanta & Nashville, presents Local-Nat'l acts 15-20 nites/yr to 21+; some 18+ shows. 1-2 bands play three 40min sets for flat fee & bonuses. Mail press kit to venue.

The Coffee Pot
2902 Brambleton Ave. SW
Roanoke, VA 24015
p: 540-774-8256
www.myspace.com/coffeepotroadhouseinc
contact: Lisa Cosnotti
e: lccosnotti@yahoo.com
call: M-F 9am-6pm
genres: Blues, Rock, Bluegrass, Jazz, Acoustic, Country, Alt.
advance: 3 months
capacity: 150 **stage:** 20 x 8
Cool & quirky roadhouse showcases Reg'l & Nat'l artists 2 nites. Featured act performs 3hrs w/ breaks for 21+. Mail press kit to venue.

Theater at Lime Kiln
699 Lime Kiln Rd.
Lexington, VA
24450
p: 540-463-7088
e: info@theateratlimekiln.com
www.theateratlimekiln.com
contact: Kim Edward Renz
call: M-F 9am-5pm
genres: Mainly Rock, Bluegrass, Country, Americana, Blues, Jazz
advance: 6-12 months
capacity: 350-500
pa: Yes **sound eng:** Yes
stage: 30 x 15
All ages venue presents outdoor concerts Sat-Sun from May-Oct at The Bowl & The Kiln. 1-2 acts play 45min for flat fee & % of door. Merch split 85/15. Send EPKs or mail to: PO Box 1244, Lexington, VA 24450.

Washington

Seattle

Blue Moon Tavern
712 NE 45th St.
Seattle, WA 98105
p: 206-675-9116
www.myspace.com/bluemoonseattle
pa: Yes
Iconic dive bar in the University District, has large stage, ok sound & loyal 21+ crowd. Books original Local-Touring acts via MySpace; must have web presence to be considered

The Central Saloon
207 1st Ave. S
Seattle, WA 98104
p: 206-622-0209
www.centralsaloon.com
contact: Charlie Mann
p: 206-660-0250
e: booking@centralsaloon.com
genres: Rock, Pop, Funk, Ska
advance: 8-12 weeks
capacity: 200
pa: Yes **sound eng:** Yes
stage: 20 x 13
Music bar features original Reg'l & Touring bands nitely. 3 acts play 1hr sets for 21+.

Chop Suey
1325 E Madison St.
Seattle, WA 98122
p: 206-324-8000
e: info@chopsuey.com
www.chopsuey.com
contact: Pete Greenberg
e: pete@chopsuey.com
genres: Electronic, Rock, Hip-Hop, Alt. Country
advance: 3 months
capacity: 550
pa: Yes **sound eng:** Yes
stage: 22 x 11 (pentagon)
Hip club showcases Touring acts & Reg'ls w/ buzz nitely. 3 acts play 45-60min original sets. Some all ages shows. Mail press kit to venue or use email.

Conor Byrne's
5140 Ballard Ave. NW
Seattle, WA 98107
p: 206-784-3640
www.conorbyrnepub.com
contact: Alana King
e: music@conorbyrnepub.com
genres: Celtic, Folk, Acoustic, S/S, Rockabilly, Bluegrass, Pop, Alt. Country, Blues, Country
advance: 1-6 months
capacity: 100
pa: Yes **sound eng:** Yes
stage: 8 x 8
open mics: Sun
Pub books 2-3 Reg'l & Touring performers 3 nites for % of door. Frequent open jams & women in music series. Email or use online booking form.

Crossroads Bellevue Shopping Center
15600 NE 8th St.
Bellevue, WA 98008
p: 425-644-1111
www.crossroadsbellevue.com
contact: Lynn Terpstra
e: le.terpstra@comcast.net; lterpstra@crossroadsbellevue.com
call: email only
genres: Americana, World, S/S, Jazz, Blues, Acoustic, Bluegrass, Big Band, Celtic, Reggae, Latin
advance: 3 months
capacity: 1000
pa: Yes **sound eng:** Yes
stage: 16 x 16
open mics: 1st Thu of mo
Shopping ctr. complex w/ stage & good sound, books family-friendly, low volume original acts for all ages. A featured Reg'l or Touring band plays two 1hr sets for flat fee Thu & Fri-Sat. Email w/ subject: Crossroads Music Booking.

El Corazón
109 Eastlake Ave. E
Seattle, WA 98109
p: 206-262-0482
www.elcorazonseattle.com
contact: Dana Sims
e: booking@elcorazonseattle.com
call: afternoons
genres: Alt., Rock, Punk, Metal, Electronic, Pop, Indie
advance: 2-3 months
capacity: 750
pa: Yes **sound eng:** Yes
stage: 21 x 16 x 3h
Formerly Graceland, this stage packs mostly all ages shows & has great sound. 3-4 Local-Touring bands play 35+min nitely. See 'Booking' on website for detailed policy. Prefers CD mailed, but accepts EPKs.

The Funhouse
206 5th Ave. N
Seattle, WA 98109
p: 206-374-8400
www.thefunhouseseattle.com
contact: Brian Foss
e: myfatassproductions@yahoo.com
genres: Pop, Rock, Punk, Garage, Rockabilly
capacity: 199
pa: Yes **sound eng:** Yes
stage: 12 x 16
City's oldest surviving Punk club, books 3-5 original Local & Touring bands nitely. Prefers EPKs.

Hayley's Bar & Grill
1716 Hewitt Ave.
Everett, WA 98201
p: 425-339-2424
e: schuyler.mieyr@gmail.com
contact: Hayley
e: hayley.mieyr@gmail.com
call: M-F 9am-closing
genres: Rock, Metal, Punk
advance: 2+ months
capacity: 300
pa: Yes **sound eng:** Yes
stage: 16 x 20
21+ Rock showcase 30mi from Seattle & now under new ownership, presents Local-Nat'l bands 3 mites - original acts 1 nite. Up to 4 acts play 45min sets for % of door. Contact by any means.

Heavens
172 S Washington St.
Seattle, WA 98104
p: 206-622-1863
e: paul@heavenseattle.com
www.heavenseattle.com
contact: Bob Tomazic
e: bob@heavenseattle.com
genres: Rock, Pop, Gothic, Electronic, Funk
advance: 1 month
capacity: 750-1000
pa: Yes **sound eng:** Yes
stage: 30 x 20
Formerly Catwalk Club, now remodeled w/ lights, sound & dressing rooms. Original Reg'l & Nat'l bands Wed & Fri. 2-3 acts play 30-50min for 21+ crowd. Email or mail kit to: PO Box 4058, Seattle, WA 98194.

The Highliner Pub
3909 18th Ave. W
Seattle, WA 98119
p: 206-283-2233
e: thehighlinerpub@hotmail.com
www.highlinerpub.com
contact: Stan Kopf
call: M-F 8-10am
genres: 60s, 70s, 80s, R&B
advance: 3-4 months
capacity: 122
pa: Yes
stage: 10 x 20 wedge
Landmark pub books Local-Touring bands Fri or Sat. 1 act plays 3hrs w/ break from 9:30pm-1am for door plus 10% of sales w/ negotiable min. guarantee. Snail mail kit.

Jazz Alley
2033 6th Ave.
Seattle, WA 98121
p: 206-441-9729
e: jazzalley@jazzalley.com
www.jazzalley.com
contact: Gary Bannister
p: 206-441-9729 x229
e: gary@jazzalley.com
call: M-F 10am-3pm
genres: Blues, Jazz, Latin, Fusion, World
advance: 6 months
capacity: 350
pa: Yes **sound eng:** Yes
stage: 16 x 24
Industry & audiences praise this all ages dinner club that hosts original Nat'l & Int'l recording artists 6 nites. 1 act plays 70-90min. Email for booking.

The Old Fire House
16510 NE 79th St.
Redmond, WA 98052
p: 425-556-2370
www.theoldfirehouse.org
contact: Meli Darby
p: 425-556-2389
e: oldfirehousebooking@gmail.com
call: Wed-Fri
genres: Hardcore, Punk, Pop, Hip-Hop, Ska, Emo, Electronic
advance: 2 months
capacity: 469
pa: Yes **sound eng:** Yes
Teen ctr. books 3-4 up & coming young bands & popular Reg'l recording acts & DJs Fri & some Sat. Bands receive flat fee after %. Also produces a comp CD. No racist, sexist, homophobic or violent acts booked. Prefers EPK; No unsolicited mail, MySpace contact or calls.

Paragon Bar & Grill
2125 Queen Anne Ave. N
Seattle, WA 98109
p: 206-283-4548
e: webmaster@paragonseattle.com
www.paragonseattle.com
contact: Todd Ivester
e: toddivester@paragonseattle.com
genres: R&B, Jazz, Soul
capacity: 140 **stage:** small
Eatery transforms into music club after dinner. Original Local-Reg'l bands gig Tue-Sun. Featured act plays 3 sets from 9:30pm-12:30am for flat fee. All ages up to 11pm.

Q Cafe
3223 15th Ave. W
Seattle, WA 98119
p: 206-352-2525
www.qcafe.org
contact: Melissa
e: melissa@qcafe.org
advance: 3 months
capacity: 238
pa: Yes **sound eng:** Yes
All ages cafe hosts original Local-Nat'l acts Fri w/ profits to help Seattle homeless. 3 acts play 40-90min sets for % of door. Send EPK.

Sirens
823 Water St.
Port Townsend, WA 98368
p: 360-379-1100
e: sirenspt@gmail.com
www.myspace.com/sirenspt
contact: Oceanna Van Lelyveld
genres: All Styles
advance: 1-2 months
capacity: 150
pa: Yes
stage: 2 stages
open mics: Wed 9pm
Local & Touring bands gig Fri & Sat at 21+ pub; great opp. for Local bands. Mail press kit to venue, email or message thru MySpace. No unsolicited calls.

Sunset Tavern
5433 Ballard Ave. NW
Seattle, WA 98107
p: 206-784-4880
www.sunsettavern.com
contact: Michael Jaworski
e: mike@sunsettavern.com
genres: Rock, Jazz, Country, Hip-Hop, Punk, Electronic, Klezmer
advance: 2-3 months
capacity: 200
pa: Yes **sound eng:** Yes
stage: 14 x 16
3-4 Local & Touring bands gig up to 7 nites for 21+ crowd at popular dive-bar w/ Chinese decor. Prefers emails w/ short bio & contact info; put band name in subject!

Trabant Coffee & Chai
1309 NE 45th St.
Seattle, WA 98105
p: 206-675-0668
www.trabantcoffee.com
contact: Jeff
e: events@trabantchailounge.com
call: email only
genres: Acoustic, Folk, Rock, Indie, Alt.
advance: Up to 2 months
capacity: 50
pa: Yes
stage: 10 x 10
open mics: Mon 7:50pm
Popular all ages spot hosts 2 quality original Local-Int'l bands Fri & Sat. Sets run 8pm-11pm w/ breaks & acts are paid a flat fee. Use email only.

Tractor Tavern
5213 Ballard Ave. NW
Seattle, WA 98107

p: 206-789-3599
www.tractortavern.com
e: booking@tractortavern.com
call: M-F noon-4pm
genres: Rock, Alt. Country, Celtic, Rockabilly, Folk, Groove, Psychedelic, Blues, Jazz
advance: 2 months
capacity: 350
pa: Yes **sound eng:** Yes
Popular down-home 21+ venue books Reg'l & Touring bands w/ draw. 2 acts play 5-7 nites for % of door. Prefers email w/ links, MP3s, dates & contact info. May also mail press kit to venue; will contact if interested. No contact via MySpace.

Traditions Cafe & World Folk Art
300 5th Ave. SW
Olympia, WA 98501
p: 360-705-2819
www.traditionsfairtrade.com
contact: Dick Meyer
e: dick@traditionsfairtrade.com
call: M-F midday
genres: Acoustic, World, Jazz, Swing, Folk
advance: 6 months
capacity: 90
pa: Yes **sound eng:** Yes
stage: 6 x 10 **in-house:** Piano
Socially-conscious arts venue features 1 original Local-Touring act Sat from Sep-May for all ages. Shows are 2 sets from 8-10:15pm; other nites avail. for estab. talent. Pay is % of door & sometimes flat fee.

Tula's
2214 2nd Ave.
Seattle, WA
98121
p: 206-443-4221
e: tulas1@msn.com
www.tulas.com
contact: Mack Waldron
call: M-F 1-5pm
genres: Jazz
advance: 3 months
capacity: 96
pa: Yes **sound eng:** Yes
stage: large **in-house:** Piano
open mics: Mon 8pm
Polished Local or a Touring act plays 3 sets nitely; 21+ after 10pm. Snail mail kit.

The Vera Project
Republican & Warren Ave. N
Seattle, WA 98109
p: 206-956-8372
www.theveraproject.org
contact: Tristan Pelton
e: booking@theveraproject.org
call: M-F 2-6pm
genres: DIY Hip-Hop, Punk, Indie, Loud
advance: 1-3 months
capacity: 300
pa: Yes **sound eng:** Yes
All ages, non-profit venue features original Local-Int'l bands Fri & Sat. 3 acts play 45min for % of door. Developing bands can open for headliners; see website for guidelines. Promos: 305 Harrison St., Seattle, WA 98109.

Spokane

Blue Spark
15 S Howard St.
Spokane, WA 99201
p: 509-838-5787
www.bluesparkspokane.com
contact: Steve
e: dildy51@yahoo.com
genres: Alt.
sound eng: Yes
open mics: Mon
Original Local-Touring bands gig Sat for the door at this popular 21+ venue. Email or use myspace.com/steveo51.

Caterina Winery
905 N Washington St.
Spokane, WA
99201
p: 509-328-5069
www.caterinawinery.com
contact: Patrick Kendrick
e: patrickrockcoffee@gmail.com
call: M-F
genres: Most Styles
advance: 2 months
capacity: 100+
pa: Yes **sound eng:** Yes
stage: 8 x 16
All ages venue has large outdoor stage & indoor space w/ amazing acoustics. 2-4 acts play 40min sets for % of door after prod. costs. No Metal or Harcore. Use MySpace email or snail mail kit.

Empyrean Coffee House
154 S Madison St.
Spokane, WA
99201
p: 509-838-9819
e: empyreancoffeehouse@gmail.com
www.empyreancoffee.com
contact: Michelle
genres: All Styles
advance: 6 months
capacity: 100
pa: Yes **sound eng:** Yes
open mics: Mon **sign in:** 7pm
Has a small Acoustic stage in the front & larger stage in back that serves as the 'main venue.' 3-4 Local-Int'l acts play 30min to all ages.
Use MySpace or snail mail kit.

The Zombie Room
230 W Riverside Ave.
Spokane, WA 99201
p: 509-747-5826
e: thespreadclub@gmail.com
www.myspace.com/thespreadclub
genres: All Styles
advance: 2 weeks
capacity: 162
pa: Yes **sound eng:** Yes
stage: 12 x 12
Formerly the B-Side & later The Spread, now, this unique venue books original Reg'l & Touring acts & DJs up to 7 nites for 21+ crowd. Up to 3 bands play 45-55min sets for % of door.
Use MySpace or snail mail kit.

Bellingham

Green Frog Acoustic Tavern
902 N State St., #104
Bellingham, WA
98225
p: 360-756-1213
e: wb.wildbuffalo@gmail.com
www.acoustictavern.com
myspace.com/acoustictavern
contact: James Hardesty
genres: S/S, Americana, Nu-Grass, Alt. Country
open mics: Sun
Original music club & micro brewery features polished Local-Touring talent Wed-Sat; popular open mic on Sun. Use online form for booking or snail mail kit.

Wild Buffalo House of Music
208 W Holly St.
Bellingham, WA
98225
p: 360-312-3684
e: wb.wildbuffalo@gmail.com
www.wildbuffalo.net
contact: John Goodman
p: 360-752-0720
e: wb@nas.com
call: M-F noon-4pm
genres: Blues, Rock, Funk, R&B, Country, Americana, Folk, Jazz, Groove, Rockabilly, Jam, World
advance: 8 weeks
capacity: 311
pa: Yes **sound eng:** Yes
stage: 15 x 20
open mics: Wed Acoustic 7pm
Popular music club 53mi S of Vancouver w/ good sound, lights & views, books Local & Touring bands w/ draw Tue, Thu-Sun for 21+. Up to 3 bands play 9pm-1am w/ breaks. Prefers online booking form, but call & email OK; will call if interested.

West Virginia

Charleston/ Huntington

Empty Glass
410 Elizabeth St.
Charleston, WV 25311
p: 304-345-9893
e: theemptyglass@gmail.com
www.emptyglass.com
contact: Roadblock
call: M-F after 5pm
genres: Rock, Rockabilly, Ska, Reggae, Blues, Jazz, Funk, Metal, Electronica
advance: 1-3 months
capacity: 125
pa: Yes **sound eng:** Yes
stage: 20 x 15
open mics: Mon **sign in:** 9pm
Scene stronghold books Locals & Nat'ls nitely. Up to 4 original acts play two 45min sets. Prefers email but may mail promos to: Roadblock, c/o Empty Glass, 909 S Ruffner Rd., Charleston, WV 25314.

Monkeybar
611 4th Ave.
Huntington, WV 25701
p: 304-522-6570
e: booking@monkeybarlive.com
www.myspace.com/monkeybar
contact: Herman Beaver
e: herman@monkeybarlive.com
genres: Mostly Rock
advance: 6 weeks
capacity: 600-1000
pa: Yes **sound eng:** Yes
stage: 32 x 24
Area's biggest Rock club hosts 5 Local-Touring acts up to 5 nites. Bands play 45-60min to 18+ for flat fee. Mail press kit to venue.

Morgantown

123 Pleasant St.
123 Pleasant St.
Morgantown, WV 26505
p: 304-292-0800
www.123pleasantstreet.com
contact: LJ Giuliani
e: peastreet@cs.com
call: M-F 10am-6pm
genres: Rock, Reggae, Country, Blues, Hip-Hop, World, Metal, Punk, Jam
advance: 2-3 months
capacity: 350
pa: Yes **sound eng:** Yes
stage: 18 x 13
open mics: Wed
Prime club presents original Reg'l & Touring bands Thu-Sat. Sun all ages Punk shows. 2-3 acts play 60-90min for % of door. Mail press kit to venue w/ ATTN: LJ; incl. 8x10 glossy.

All Star Sports Garden
9685 Mall Loop
Fairmont, WV 26554
p: 304-368-0055
contact: Dave
call: M-F evenings
genres: Country, Rock, Alt
capacity: 300
pa: Yes
stage: 16 x 24
New 18+ sports bar w/ original Local-Reg'l acts; some all ages shows; No Metal or Rap. Call first.

Gibbie's Pub
368 High St.
Morgantown, WV 26505
p: 304-296-4427
contact: Mike Gainer
e: gib@mountain.net
call: Mon 10am-4pm
genres: Classic Rock, Alt., Reggae, Jazz, Latin
advance: 1-2 months
capacity: 250
stage: floor space
Monthly Reg'l & occasional Touring bands play 3-4hrs on Fri or Sat at neighborhood watering hole. Mail press kit to venue or use email for booking.

Greater WV

Blue Moon Cafe
200 E High St.
Shepherdstown, WV 25443
p: 304-876-1920
e: bluemooncafe@citilink.net
www.bluemoonshepherdstown.com
contact: Cheryl Mansley
p: 304-702-0554
e: bluemoonsundays@earthlink.net
genres: Folk, Acoustic
advance: 1 month
capacity: 75
pa: Yes
stage: floor space
p: 301-992-5469
Small cafe 72mi W of Baltimore in the heart of small college town, books 1 Local-Nat'l Acoustic artist for all ages. Mail press kit to venue or email links to mp3s.

Fort Savannah Inn
204 N Jefferson St.
Lewisburg, WV 24901
p: 304-645-9050
contact: David Walton
e: david_walton69@hotmail.com
call: M-F after 2pm
genres: Most Styles
advance: 2 months
capacity: 125
stage: 10 x 15
open mics: Tue **sign in:** 9pm
21+ bar books Local-Nat'l acts Fri from 10pm-1am. 1-2 acts

play mostly original tunes. No Country. Promos to: 12 Honeysuckle Ln., Lewisburg, WV 24901.

The Purple Fiddle
21 East Ave.
Thomas, WV 26292
p: 304-463-4040
e: purplefiddle@citlink.net
www.purplefiddle.com
contact: John Bright
call: email only
genres: Bluegrass, Jazz, Folk, S/S, Blues, Acoustic, Rock, Americana, Newgrass
advance: 2-8 months
capacity: 200
pa: Yes **sound eng:** Yes
stage: 17 x 14
Great stop on the Pittsburgh, Charleston & DC/Baltimore circuit, showcases Local-Int'l acts nitely for all ages shows. Lone original act plays 2.5hrs or two 50+min sets for flat fee vs % of door. Wknd dates usu. book up to 8 mos in advance. Prefers email w/ link to music but may mail promo to: PO Box 87, Thomas, WV 26292. No Calls.

Wisconsin

Green Bay

Copper Rock Coffee Co.
210 W College Ave., Ste. B
Appleton, WI 54911
p: 920-882-9462
e: info.copperrock@gmail.com
www.copperrockcoffee.com
contact: Ben
e: booking.copperrock@gmail.com
call: email only
genres: S/S, Folk, Rock, Jazz
advance: 1 month
capacity: 100+
stage: small floor space
Books 1-2 low volume Local-Touring acts for 1+hr sets Wed/Thu for tips & Fri/Sat for small fee plus % of door. Use online booking form.

Cup O' Joy Coffee House
232 S Broadway St.
Green Bay, WI 54303
p: 920-435-3269
www.cupojoy.com
contact: Jan
p: 920-437-6694
e: jano@cupojoy.com
genres: Pop, Punk, Folk, S/S, Country
advance: 3-6 months
capacity: 300+
pa: Yes **sound eng:** Yes
stage: 25 x 16
Non-profit Christian listening room books family-friendly Reg'l & Nat'l acts most wknd nites. 1-2 acts play for split of donations. Accepts EPKs.

Door Community Aud.
3924 Hwy. 42
Fish Creek, WI 54212
p: 920-868-2728
e: boxoffice@dcauditorium.org
www.dcauditorium.org
contact: Pete Evans
e: pete@dcauditorium.org
genres: Jazz, Celtic, Folk, Country, Rock, Big Band, Cajun, Blues, Bluegrass
advance: 6 months
capacity: 750
pa: Yes **sound eng:** Yes
stage: large
PAC w/ top sound & stage 60mi from Green Bay, presents original Touring talent 25/yr & books Local/Reg'ls for winter coffeehouse series.

IQ's
2105 University Ave.
Green Bay, WI 54302
p: 920-437-2950
e: bill@iqsbar.com
www.iqsbar.com
contact: Sandra Hickey
e: sandy@iqsbar.com
genres: Rock, Jazz
advance: 3-4 months
capacity: 150
pa: Yes **sound eng:** Yes
stage: 20 x 10 **in-house:** Piano
open mics: Wed 9pm
No cover bar books Local-Nat'l bands Fri-Sat for 21+. 1-2 acts play 45+min sets for flat fee + % of till. Mail press kit to venue.

New Moon Café
401 N Main St.
Oshkosh, WI 54901
p: 920-232-0976
www.newmooncafe.com
contact: Aaron Baer
e: aaron@newmooncafe.com
call: email only
genres: All Styles
advance: 1-2 months
capacity: 60
pa: Yes
stage: 10 x 15
open mics: Tue **sign in:** 6:30pm
Eatery 50mi from Green Bay, hosts mostly Acoustic talent for all ages shows. Up to 3 original Local-Touring acts fill 3hrs for % of door. Email or snail mail. No Calls.

La Crosse

House of Rock
422 Water St.
Eau Claire, WI 54703
p: 715-838-0158
www.house-of-rock.com
contact: Joey G.
e: joeyg@house-of-rock.com
genres: Hard Rock, Rock, Blues, Alt., Folk, Hip-Hop
advance: 2 months
capacity: 350
pa: Yes **sound eng:** Yes
Loud bar books 2-3 original Local-Reg'l bands up to 4 nites. Email for booking.

The Joint
324 Jay St.
La Crosse, WI 54601
p: 608-785-6468
www.inthejoint.com
contact: Jeff Ritcherts
e: jeff@inthejoint.com
genres: Blues, Jam, Rock, Reggae
advance: 4 months
capacity: 150
pa: Yes **sound eng:** Yes
stage: 17 x 11
Formerly 324 Live now under new mgmt., books original Reg'l & Touring acts 1-3 nites for 1hr sets; must be 18+. Use email for booking.

The Stones Throw
304 Eau Claire St.
Eau Claire, WI 54701
p: 715-552-5882
e: info@pernsteiner.com
www.thestonesthrow.com
contact: Andrew Pernsteiner
e: stbooking@gmail.com
call: afternoons
genres: All Styles
advance: 3 months
capacity: 375
pa: Yes **sound eng:** Yes
stage: 15 x 12
open mics: Wed & Sun 9pm
Historic multi-level music spot books Local-Nat'l bands up to 7 nites for 21+. 2-3 bands play 90min for the door. Snail mail or use email w/ bio, description w/ influences, info on stage show/set length, venues played, photo, press, & CD demo. No booking via MySpace.

Warehouse
328 Pearl St.
La Crosse, WI 54601
p: 608-784-1422
www.warehouserocks.com
contact: Steve D.
e: booking@warehouserocks.com
call: email only
genres: Punk, Rock, Ska, Industrial, Goth, Emo, Screamo, Metal, Acoustic, S/S, Hip-Hop, Hardcore, Christian
capacity: 200
pa: Yes **sound eng:** Yes
stage: 24 x 16
Long-running all ages, alcohol-free Rock club b/w Madison & St. Paul, draws Touring acts & buzz bands 1-5 nites. 3-5 acts play 30-40min of original tunes. Email w/ links preferred; reluctantly accepts press kits w/ ATTN: MA, PO Box 2044, La Crosse, WI 54602. No EPKs, calls or contact via MySpace.

Madison

Angelic Brewing Co.
322 W Johnson St.
Madison, WI 53703
p: 608-257-2707
www.angelicbrewing.com
contact: Tom
genres: Rock, Jazz, Blues, Reggae, R&B
advance: 3-6 months
capacity: 232
Pub w/ college crowd books hi-energy original Local/Reg'l bands Tue, Wed & Fri w/ some Nat'l act. 1-2 acts play 45min for flat fee. Snail mail kit; allow 1 wk for review.

The Annex
1206 Regent St.
Madison, WI 53715
p: 608-256-7750
e: intheannex@intheannex.com
www.intheannex.com
contact: Darwin Sampson
e: booktheannex@hotmail.com
call: M-F noon-6pm
genres: Rock, Funk, Jazz, Blues, Reggae
advance: 2 months
capacity: 400
pa: Yes **sound eng:** Yes
stage: 30 x 14
Prime mid-sized venue w/ pro sound presents Reg'l & Touring acts nitely; 18+ shows wkly. Prefers email, but may snail mail or use MySpace.

The Bar At Madison Concourse Hotel
1 W Dayton St.
Madison, WI 53703
p: 608-257-6000
www.concoursehotel.com
contact: Dan Tommet
e: dtommet@concoursehotel.com
genres: Jazz
advance: 4 months
capacity: 80
pa: Yes
Lounge presents live Local-Reg'l acts nitely. Featured act plays 3hrs for fee vs door or guarantee. Only books bands that can draw. Mostly works w/ previously booked bands. No unsolicited mail or calls!

Cafe Carpe
18 S Water St. W
Fort Atkinson, WI 53538
p: 920-563-9391
e: cafecarpe@sbcglobal.net
www.cafecarpe.com
contact: Bill Camplin
call: email only
genres: Varies
advance: 3-4 months
capacity: 65
pa: Yes **sound eng:** Yes
stage: 6 x 7
Intimate listening room presents low-volume Local-Int'l solos & duos up to 3 nites. Artists play to all ages for 70-75% of door & food/lodging. Read FAQs on web first. No Calls; No unsolicited materials.

Café Montmartre
127 W Mifflin St.
Madison, WI 53703
p: 608-255-5900
e: cafe@themomo.com
www.themomo.com
contact: Justin Bricco
e: booking@themomo.com; momobooking@gmail.com
genres: Rock, Alt., Country, Jazz, Trip-Hop, S/S, Folk, Blues, Bluegrass, Funk
advance: 2 months
capacity: 150
pa: Yes **sound eng:** Yes
stage: 6 x 10
Music room presents original Local-Nat'l artists Sat-Sun & Tue-Thu. 1-3 bands play for % of door.

Capital Brewery
7734 Terrace Ave.
Middleton, WI 53562
p: 608-836-7100
e: capbrew@capital-brewery.com
www.capital-brewery.com
contact: Monica Greenheck
genres: Blues, Rock, Jazz
advance: 6+ months
capacity: 1500
pa: Upon Request
stage: 15 x 10
Brewpub hosts shows every Fri b/w Memorial & Labor Day in outdoor beer garden. Mostly Local-Reg'ls & some Touring act plays 6-9pm for flat fee & drink comps. Snail mail kit.

Club Tavern
1915 Branch St.
Middleton, WI 53562
p: 608-836-3773
e: moose@clubtavern.com
www.clubtavern.com
contact: Michael Alexander
e: malexander@clubtavern.com

genres: Blues, Rock, Country, R&B
advance: 2 months
capacity: 350
pa: Yes sound eng: Yes
stage: 12 x 10
Local-Touring acts & DJs play Fri-Sat for 21+ crowd. 1-3 acts play either two 50min sets or 1+hrs for fee &/or door. Mail press kit to venue.

Crystal Corner Bar
1302 Williamson St.
Madison, WI
53703
p: 608-256-2953
www.thecrystalcornerbar.com
contact: Joel Lambert
p: 608-358-2027
e: crystalbooking@yahoo.com
genres: Rock, Reggae, Zydeco, Pop, Acoustic, Americana, Alt.
capacity: 99
pa: Yes sound eng: Yes
stage: 20 x 16
Storied neighborhood watering hole books up to 3 original Local-Nat'l acts 3-4 nites. Email for booking.

Harmony Bar & Grill
2201 Atwood Ave.
Madison, WI
53704
p: 608-249-4333
www.myspace.com/theharmonybar
contact: Keith Daniels
call: M-F 9-11am
genres: Blues, Roots, R&B
advance: 2-5 months
capacity: 200
pa: Yes sound eng: Yes
stage: 10 x 20
Blues hang books mostly original Reg'l acts for three 45min sets every Sat; some Fri & Sun shows & some Nat'l bands. Snail mail kit.

High Noon Saloon
701A E Washington Ave.
Madison, WI
53703
p: 608-268-1122
e: info@high-noon.com
www.high-noon.com
contact: Cathy Dethmers
e: booking@high-noon.com
call: Mon & Thu 2-5pm
genres: Rock, Alt., Metal, Alt. Country, Pop, Punk, Bluegrass, Folk, Blues
advance: 6-12 weeks
capacity: 400
pa: Yes sound eng: Yes
stage: 21 x 15
Top area venue presents Local-Int'l talent nitely. Up to 4 original acts play 46-60min; rarely cover acts. Send EPKs or snail mail kit.

Mother Fool's Coffeehouse
1101 Williamson St.
Madison, WI 53703
p: 608-259-1030
e: fools@uvulittle.com
www.motherfools.com
contact: Jon Hain
call: Tue-Thu 1-5pm
genres: Folk, S/S, Experimental, Roots
advance: 2-3 months
capacity: 65
pa: Yes
stage: 10 x 16
Popular all ages college town hang, books original Local-Int'l acts Fri & Sat for % of door. 1-2 acts play 45-50min for % of door. Call or email first.

Restaurant Magnus
120 E Wilson St.
Madison, WI 53703
p: 608-258-8787
e: magnus@chorus.net
www.restaurantmagnus.com
contact: Prentice Berge
call: M-F 10:30am-3pm
genres: Jazz, Swing, Jump, Blues, Latin
advance: 3-6 months: Oct for Jan-Jun; in Mar for Jul-Dec
capacity: 120; 50-60
pa: Yes
stage: 18 x 15
Solo acts play upscale eatery's bar room nitely for 21+. Touring bands gig Fri-Sat. Prefers email or mailed kits w/ ATTN: Prentice. No booking thru MySpace or calls.

Wild Hog in the Woods
953 Jenifer St.
Madison, WI 53703
p: 608-233-5687
e: tglh@tds.net
http://personalpages.tds.net/~rpmccabe/wildhoghomepage.htm
contact: Ramona Johannes
p: 608-246-0436
genres: Folk, Acoustic, Bluegrass, Jazz
advance: 2-4 months
pa: Yes sound eng: Yes
Long-running volunteer Acoustic showcase presents Reg'l & some Touring artists most Fri nites. Featured acts plays 45-60min for tips. Prefers mailed press kit to venue or calls, but may also email.

Milwaukee

BBC Upper Level
2022 E North Ave.
Milwaukee, WI 53202
p: 414-272-7263
www.myspace.com/upperlevel
contact: Susan Manske
p: 414-272-9857
e: bbcbooking@aol.com
call: M-F 10am-6pm
genres: Rock, Pop, Funk, New Jazz, R&B
advance: 2-3 months
capacity: 300 (upstairs)
pa: Yes sound eng: Yes
stage: 25 x 12
Rockin' bar books up to 5 original Reg'l & some Nat'l acts Fri & Sat for flat fee &/or door. Mail or drop off press kit. Contact before sending EPKs.

Brat Stop
12304 75th St.
Kenosha, WI 53142
p: 262-857-2011
e: info@bratstop.com
www.bratstop.com
contact: Tracy Hill
e: trcyhill@yahoo.com; bands@bratstop.com
genres: Rock, Metal, Blues, Alt. Country, Folk
advance: 2 months
capacity: 2000
pa: Yes sound eng: Yes
Sports bar features polished acts Fri & Sat nites for 21+ crowd.

Bremen Cafe
901 E Clarke St.
Milwaukee, WI 53212
p: 414-431-1932
e: info@bremencafe.com
www.bremencafe.com
contact: David Kopp
e: booking@bremencafe.com
call: M-F noon-5pm
genres: S/S, Indie, Acoustic, Folk, Roots
advance: 2-4 months
capacity: 70
pa: Yes sound eng: Yes
stage: 10 x 8
open mics: Thu sign in: 9pm
Original Reg'l's & some Nat'l's play 2-3 nites in intimate listening room. All booking done via email w/ EPK & music attached. No calls or packages.

Cactus Club
2496 S Wentworth Ave.
Milwaukee, WI 53207
p: 414-897-0663
e: cactusclubwebsite@gmail.com
www.cactusclubmilwaukee.com
contact: Eric Uecke
p: 414-704-2582
e: cactuscl@execpc.com
call: Mon-Thu 4-6pm
genres: Alt., Underground, Rock, Punk
advance: 2-3 months
capacity: 150
pa: Yes sound eng: Yes
Newly remodeled 21+ Rock room books mostly Local acts 2-4 nites; Touring-Nat'l acts must be able to draw. Up to 4 original acts play 30-60min sets. Email for booking.

Caroline's
401 S 2nd St.
Milwaukee, WI 53204
p: 414-221-9444
e: info@carolinesjazz.com
contact: Caroline Rubitsky
genres: Jazz, Blues
advance: 3 months
capacity: 100
pa: Yes sound eng: Yes
stage: 7 x 12
open mics: Thu 8:30pm Jazz
Elegant listening room hosts veterans & rising stars; Local-Reg'l & rare Nat'l acts perform up to 5 nites for 21+. 1-2 acts fill 3.5hrs w/ break for % of door or flat fee. Mail press kit to venue.

Cedarburg Cultural Center
W62 N546 Washington Ave., PO Box 84
Cedarburg, WI 53012
p: 262-375-3676
www.cedarburgcultural center.org
contact: Matthew Brockmeier
e: cccenter_matthew@ameritech.net
call: Tue-Fri 10am-5pm
genres: Blues, Jazz, Folk, Celtic, S/S, World, Classical
capacity: 300
pa: Yes sound eng: Yes
stage: 15 x 20
Non-profit arts ctr. 17mi from Milwaukee, books original Reg'l-Int'l acts for all ages. 1 act play 2hrs for flat fee.

The Jazz Estate
2423 N Murray Ave.
Milwaukee, WI 53211
p: 414-467-9886
www.jazzestate.com
contact: Brian Sanders
e: bsanders8@wi.rr.com
call: M-F 9am-5pm
genres: Jazz, Blues
advance: 2 months
capacity: 65
pa: Yes sound eng: Yes
stage: 10 x 6 in-house: Piano
Hip, 50's-styled listening room, spotlights polished original Local-Reg'l talent & Jazz greats 4 nites. Featured act plays for fee.

Linneman's Riverwest Inn
1001 E Locust St.
Milwaukee, WI 53212
p: 414-263-9844
e: info@linnemans.com
www.linnemans.com
contact: Jim Linneman
e: jim@linnemans.com
genres: Rock, S/S, Jazz
pa: Yes sound eng: Yes
open mics: Wed Acoustic 9pm
Uniquely intimate tavern books 1-2 original Local-Reg'l & some Touring acts up to 5 nites for 21+.

The Mad Planet
533 E Center St.
Milwaukee, WI 53212
p: 414-263-4555
www.mad-planet.net
contact: Alex Hall
e: madplanetbooking@hotmail.com
genres: All Styles
advance: 6+ weeks
capacity: 299
pa: Yes sound eng: Yes
stage: 20 x 20
21+ music club packs in Alt. crowd for original Local & Touring acts Sat; some Nat'l acts on other nites. Up to 4 acts play 30-45min sets for flat fee &/or % of door & 90% merch. Snail mail kit.

Milwaukee Ale House
233 N Water St.
Milwaukee, WI 53202
p: 414-226-BEER
e: jim@ale-house.com
www.ale-house.com
contact: John McCabe
p: 414-226-2336 x102
e: john@ale-house.com
genres: Blues, Swing, Acoustic, Jazz
advance: 2 months
capacity: 400
pa: Yes sound eng: Yes
stage: 20 x 15
All ages brewpub hosts mostly Local-Reg'l acts Wed-Sat; Tue is Swing nite. 1 act plays two 1hr sets for flat fee &/or % of door. For booking, mail press kit to venue w/ ATTN: John.

Paradigm [the coffee house]
1022 Michigan Ave.
Sheboygan, WI 53081
p: 920-457-5277
www.myspace.com/paradigm_thecoffeehouse
contact: Kate Krause
e: paradigmbooking@gmail.com
call: M-F 1-6pm; prefers email
genres: Most Styles
advance: 1 month
capacity: 84
pa: Yes sound eng: Yes
stage: 15 x 10 in-house: Piano

All ages coffeehouse 50mi from Milwaukee, boasts good stage & sound. Up to 3 original Local-Touring acts play 45min 3 nites. No Metal. Prefers EPK. No unsolicited mail or calls.

Points East Pub
1501 N Jackson St.
Milwaukee, WI 53202
p: 414-277-0122
e: mark@pointseastpub.com
www.pointseastpub.com
contact: Mark Rasmussen
e: booking@pointseastpub.com
genres: Alt., Rock, Pop, Acoustic
advance: 4-6 weeks
capacity: 160
pa: Yes **sound eng:** Yes
stage: 12 x 10
Venue w/ upgraded sound & stage, books original Local & Nat'l bands up to 4 nites for flat fee & % of door after expenses. 2 acts play 1hr sets. Prefers EPKs or email, but may mail promos to venue.

The Rave/Eagles Club
2401 W Wisconsin Ave.
Milwaukee, WI 53233
p: 414-342-RAVE
www.therave.com
contact: Justin Moralez
e: justin@therave.com
call: M-F
genres: Rock, Punk, Hardcore, Metal, Trance, Techno, Indie, Alt., Hip-Hop, Electronica
capacity: 125; 245; 1429
pa: Yes **sound eng:** Yes
Prime niteclub complex w/ 5 venues. presents nitely music ranging from brand new Local acts up to top Nat'l acts. Email, call, mail press kit to venue, or contact via www.myspace.com/performattherave.

Stonefly Brewery
735 E Center St.
Milwaukee, WI 53212
p: 414-264-3630
www.myspace.com/stoneflybrewery
contact: Julia LaLoggia
e: stoneflybooking@gmail.com
genres: Indie Rock, Electronic, Hip-Hop, Punk, Electro, AfroBeat, Downtempo, Jazz, Soul, Dub
capacity: 250
pa: Yes **sound eng:** Yes
Formerly Onopa Brewing Co., attracts diverse crowds w/ indie Touring acts & DJs. Original Local-Reg'ls can open for estab. headliners 2-3 nites, mostly Thu-Sat. 2-4 acts perform 35-50min for 21+. Prefers email.

Up & Under Pub
1216 E Brady St.
Milwaukee, WI 53202
p: 414-276-2677
www.myspace.com/upandunderpub
contact: Brody
p: 773-562-4670
e: tbrodersen02@hotmail.com
call: M-F after noon
genres: Blues, Rock, Reggae, Alt., Zydeco
advance: 3-4 months
capacity: 150
pa: Yes **sound eng:** Yes
stage: 12 x 10
open mics: Mon **sign in:** 9pm
Prime all ages club w/ dance floor attracts top tier Local-Reg'ls & some Nat'ls Thu-Sat. Single original act plays 2-3 sets for the door. Prefers email or mailed press kit, but may contact via MySpace. Incl. gig history & estimated draw.

Vnuk's Lounge
5036 S Packard Ave.
Cudahy, WI 53110
p: 414-481-1655
www.vnuks.com
contact: Dave Vnuk
e: bigdave@vnuks.com
call: M-F after 5pm
genres: Rock, Alt., Punk, Metal, Americana, Country, Rockabilly
advance: Call for availability
capacity: 300
pa: Yes **sound eng:** Yes
One of area's largest & preferred live music rooms just outside of Milwaukee, presents original Local-Nat'l bands on the rise or past their prime. 3 acts play 5 nites for 21+. Email or mail kit.

Greater WI

Big Top Chautauqua
Mount Ashwabay, Ski Hill Rd.
Bayfield, WI 54891
p: 715-373-5552
e: info@bigtop.org
www.bigtop.org
contact: Terry Meyer
e: terry@bigtop.org
call: M-F 9am-5pm
genres: Folk, Americana, S/S, Roots, Bluegrass
capacity: 900
pa: Yes **sound eng:** Yes
State-of-the-art tent-theater hosts 1-3 Reg'l-Int'l acts up to 5 nites Jun-Sept. All ages shows are recorded for WI Public Radio. Send promos: PO Box 455, Washburn, WI 54891.

Mabel Tainter Theater
205 Main St.
Menomonie, WI 54751
p: 715-235-9726
e: mtainter@mabeltainter.com
www.mabeltainter.com
contact: Gary Schuster
p: 715-235-9726 x105
e: schuster@mabeltainter.com
genres: All Styles
advance: 3 months
capacity: 313
pa: Yes **sound eng:** Yes
stage: 24 x 20 (proscenium)
Non-profit utilizes this intimate Victorian Theater for concerts. 1 Local-Int'l act plays two 45min sets for flat fee &/or % of door; merch split is 85/15. Some wknds have matinee & evening shows. Snail mail kit.

Wyoming

Casper/Laramie

Coal Creek Coffee Co.
110 Grand Ave.
Laramie, WY 82070
p: 307-745-7737
e: contact@coalcreekcoffee.com
www.coalcreekcoffee.com
contact: Kyle Chitty
e: kylechitty@gmail.com
genres: S/S, Folk, Americana, Jazz, Blues, Bluegrass
advance: 1 month
capacity: 60
pa: Yes
stage: floor space
open mics: 1st Wed of mo
All ages room books family-friendly Touring acts w/ some Reg'l openers 3 nites. 1-2 original acts play 8-10pm. Mail press kit to venue.

Wyoming Blues & Jazz Society
PO Box 1643
Evansville, WY 82636
p: 307-267-7852
e: webmaster@wyobluesandjazz.org
www.wyobluesandjazz.org
contact: Lou Morris
e: events@wyobluesandjazz.org
genres: Blues, Jazz
advance: 2-3 months
capacity: 112; 300
pa: Yes **sound eng:** Yes
stage: 15 x 30
open mics: 3rd Sun of mo
Presents Reg'l-Int'l acts for 4-8 ages shows/yr at area venues. Two acts play 75min for flat fee. Email or snail mail kit.

Jackson

Mangy Moose Saloon
3295 W Village Dr.
Teton Village, WY 83025
p: 307-733-4913
www.mangymoose.net
contact: Dom Gagliardi
p: 307-733-9779
e: booking@mangymoose.net; dom@mangymoose.net
genres: All Styles
advance: 5 months
capacity: 425
pa: Yes **sound eng:** Yes
stage: 20 x 20
Saloon books 1-2 Local-Reg'l acts w/ buzz & Nat'ls for 70+min up to 3 nites for 21+. Busier in summer & winter. Promos: PO Box 590, Teton Village, WY 83025.

Million Dollar Cowboy Bar
25 N Cache St.
Jackson, WY 83001
p: 307-733-2207
e: cowboybar@bresnan.net
www.milliondollarcowboybar.com
contact: Art Andersen
genres: Country Western
advance: 6+ months
capacity: 472
pa: Yes **sound eng:** Yes
Landmark bar has Local-Int'l acts Mon-Sat; busiest in summer & ski season. Featured act plays several sets for 21+ mix of locals & tourists. Mail press kit to venue.

Pinedale Auditorium
147 E Hennick St.
Pinedale, WY 82941
p: 307-367-7322
e: pfac@wyoming.com
www.pinedalefinearts.com
contact: Dana Tully
call: M-F 9am-5pm
genres: All Styles
capacity: 517
pa: Yes **sound eng:** Yes
stage: 78 x 41 **in-house:** Pianos
Non-profit, hosts 8 all ages shows during school yr. Shows feature mostly original Touring acts for flat fee. Also holds smaller performances in Sublette County Library.

Greater WY

Lander Bar
126 Main St.
Lander, WY 82520
p: 307-332-7009 x4
e: landerbar@wyom.net
www.landerbar.com
contact: Jim Mitchell
p: 307-332-7009
genres: Blues, Bluegrass, Classic Rock, Funk, Jazz
advance: 1-2 months
capacity: 250+
stage: floor space
Classic saloon books some live bands. Featured act plays 9pm-1:30am to 21+ for flat fee.

WYO Theater
42 N Main St.
Sheridan, WY 82801
p: 307-672-9083
www.wyotheater.com
contact: Nick Johnson
p: 307-672-9083 x23
e: execdir@wyotheater.com
genres: Country, Folk, Jazz, Ethnic, Blues, Bluegrass
advance: 1 year
capacity: 483
pa: Yes **sound eng:** Yes
stage: 33 x 16
Non-profit Art Deco theater 130mi from Billings, MT, hosts 1 Local-Int'l band a few nites/mo for all ages. Email, call or mail press kit: PO Box 528, Sheridan, WY 82801.

FROM THE PAGES OF THE atlas plugged eNEWSLETTER

FANS, FUN AND FORTUNE: WILL PSYCHOSTICK BE LAUGHING ALL THE WAY TO THE BANK?

Known for onstage antics that involve rubber chickens and kick a** metal riffs, the satirical Metalcore/Humorcore act, Psychostick, (Rob "Rawrb" Kersey, vocals; Josh "Guitar Ninja" Key, guitar; Jake "Jakermeister" Reynolds, guitar; Jimmy Grant, bass; and Alex Preiss, drums) maintain a grueling touring schedule. Gigging covers the costs for life on the road but leaves little time or money to satisfy fans demand for a new release.

Solution? Give the fans what they want and reap the rewards.

Psychostick fans are paying $50 to have their names included as a lyric in Psychostick's soon to be recorded song – working title "400 Thank Yous" on its upcoming release, "Sandwich."

Formed in 2001 and assembled from several states across the country, Psychostick found Tempe, Arizona to be the place they call home. After releasing several demos (2002's "Don't Bitch It's Free" and 2003's "Die.... A Lot") the band was signed to Rock Ridge Music and released its debut album "We Couldn't Think of a Title" in September, 2006. By this time their homemade flash video for "Beer!!!" had become a hit on Ebaumsworld.com.

Soon the song found its way into the hands of Evil J, bassist for Otep, who in turn introduced it to XM Radio where it eventually became a #1 single for seven weeks.

Becoming virtual road-dogs, the members of Psychostick found themselves in a touring cycle that didn't allow enough time to properly record a new album. It was decided that when their Terrible Shirt Tour ended, they would hit the studio.

Guitarist Josh Key explains - "The problem we kept running in to was that we could make enough money to survive on the road, but not enough to survive while we record. We could get day jobs while we're home for those four to eight weeks, but who'll hire us for that short a time? Besides, this is our livelihood and we need to focus on our band if we want it to succeed – which we do."

Going into the six-week May-June tour, the members of Psychostick felt confident that this was the tour that would earn some actual money. The game plan was to put all of the profits towards the recording of "Sandwich."

Ultimately the financial strain of day-to-day survival would leave little for the piggy bank. With few options available, the band turned to their fans for help in raising the needed $23,000. The idea, described as "genius" by Rock Ridge Music President, Tom Derr, had never been done before. In fact, it seemed so ridiculous that if anyone was going to try it, Psychostick was the band to give it a shot.

The idea, borne from the musings of manager Anthony Caroto of Elepractic Entertainment, was simple: Any fan who donates $50 will have their name – first and last – used as a lyric in the song "400 Thank Yous". To sweeten the deal, each person will also get a signed copy of the CD and a poster. One lucky winner will get a pair of tickets to the CD release party with airfare and accommodations included.

To strengthen this fan-fueled endeavor, the band uploaded a video of their pitch onto YouTube. It has since been viewed over 12,000 times.

On July 14th the fundraiser was launched and Psychostick turned to MySpace for its promotion. By responding to each Friend Request with a fundraiser message, posting specifically timed Bulletins and "mentions" tagged onto outgoing fan mail, the band had the social site covered.

Also Rock Ridge Music got involved by providing Skye Media & Design for additional publicity. Their press release was now showing up on music websites all over the country. The word was getting out – which in turn was exposing the band to new audiences.

"There was definitely a difference in mail once the fundraiser started. There was mail from new fans, fans who had donated, and also mail from the fans who couldn't afford it, but who wanted to wish us luck and encouragement," says vocalist Rob "Rawrb" Kersey. "That in itself is very rewarding."

Once a fan has donated, Psychostick provides a fancy .jpg for their MySpace page that reads "My name is going to be in a Psychostick Song. Click here to be awesome like me."

As with many fundraisers, some people give the hairy eyeball regarding where exactly these funds are going. Psychostick was prepared for the scrutiny and a special page on their website was made available: www.psychostick.com/newalbum which details the money trail. (Editor's note: at press time this page reports that no more names are being accepted, however funds are still being solicited.)

Psychostick has also introduced the "audience participation" drunken webcast. In what has now become a fan-favorite, the members of Psychostick will chat via webcast while doing shots of Jagermeister – all paid for by the fans via PayPal. Fans are buying shots for the member of their choice, while chatting it up about whatever comes to mind.

"What I think a lot of bands don't remember, and what a lot of bigger bands forget, is that the time you spend with fans can be a lifelong highlight - especially the younger fans that will tell the story in school the next day and add your songs to their MySpace profile," says Caroto. "It's amazing to see how many fans will use a photo they took at a recent show of them with the band as their MySpace (or social network of choice) default picture."

When asked for advice on successful fundraising, Rawrb had this to say: "Get to know your fans and appreciate each one. They didn't have to buy your album or come to your show – but they did. Show them the respect and attention they deserve; and they'll be there when you need them most. Also with fundraising, it's important to be practical and reasonable. Don't insult the fans."

Adds Caroto – "Doing this fundraiser and all of the other things we do to raise money has been an incredible learning experience on marketing. It's one aspect of the industry that many bands don't consider enough. Proper marketing is how any good business will survive and excel - we're in the business of music."

Over the years Psychostick has created a solid bond with its fans. On its most recent tour, The Terrible Shirt Tour, they asked their fans to wear the most terrible shirt they could find. The response was impressive to say the least.

After spending September and October in the studio, Psychostick will hit the road in November to headline The Holiday Hate Tour: Season Two with Screaming Mechanical Brain and Retard-O-Bot. Going into 2009, the band will launch a massive national tour to promote the new album – ready to face the next round of touring challenges. And while the experience of this fundraiser has provided numerous rewards, Psychostick hopes that with the release of Sandwich, financial success is just around the corner.

"Sandwich" is expected to be released in March 2009.

Psychostick website: www.psychostick.com
Psychostick MySpace: www.myspace.com/psychostick
Elepractic Entertainment: www.elepractic.com

college radio & venues

College Radio

Alabama

Auburn U
WEGL 91.1 FM
116 Foy Union Bldg.
Auburn, AL 36849
watts: 3000
main: 334-844-4114
request: 334-844-9345
f: 334-844-4118
e: wegl@auburn.edu
http://wegl.auburn.edu
genres: Alt., Underground, Jazz, Blues, World, CCM
reports to: CMJ
pd: Kaitlin Knapp
e: programdirector@auburn.edu
md: Nick McElhany
ext: 334-844-4113
e: mcelhnc@auburn.edu
Holds on-air performances.

Jacksonville State U
WLJS 91.9 FM
700 Pelham Rd. N, Self Hall Rm. 120
Jacksonville, AL 36265
watts: 610
main: 256-782-5572
request: 256-782-5571
f: 256-782-5645
www.jsu.edu/92j
webcast: Yes
genres: Rock, Latin, Metal, Christian Rock, New Age, Hip-Hop
reports to: CMJ
pd: John Nickelson
md: Matt Reece
ext: 256-782-5509
e: music92j@gmail.com
Holds benefit concerts throughout the year.

U of Alabama/ Tuscaloosa
WVUA 90.7 FM
PO Box 870152
Tuscaloosa, AL 35487
watts: 120
main: 205-348-6461
request: 205-348-9070
f: 205-348-0375
e: wvua@sa.ua.edu
www.thecapstone.ua.edu
webcast: Yes
genres: Rock, Metal, Alt., Pop, Punk, Reggae, Country, Urban, Underground, Hardcore
reports to: CMJ
pd: Joe Pritchard
md: Troy Davenport
e: wvuamusic@sa.ua.edu
Sponsors 2 benefits/semester w/ Locals only.

Arizona

Arizona State U
KASC 1260 AM
123 E University Dr.
Tempe, AZ 85281
watts: 10
main: 480-965-4163
request: 480-965-1260
f: 480-727-6413
e: sam.eshelman@theblaze1260.com
www.theblaze1260.com
webcast: Yes
genres: Alt., Hip-Hop, Metal, Local, Electronica
reports to: CMJ
pd: Becky Bartkowski
ext: 480-965-4235
e: becky@theblaze1260.com
md: Owen Marshall
ext: 480-965-4160
e: md@theblaze1260.com
Sponsors events. Promos to: KASC 555 N Central Ave., Ste. 302, Phoenix, AZ 85004.

Northern Arizona U
KJACK 1680 AM
PO Box 5619,
School of Communications
Flagstaff, AZ 86011
watts: 30
main: 928-523-3036
request: 928-523-4554
f: 928-523-1505
e: kjackattack@gmail.com
www.kjack.org
webcast: Yes
genres: Alt, Loud Rock, Urban, World, RPM, Jazz
reports to: CMJ
pd: Veronica Figueroa
e: vmf3@nau.edu
md: Jason Weichert
Sponsors on-campus gigs, in-studio sets & releases annual live in-studio CD. For booking, email Kino: padilla@yahoo.com.

U of Arizona
KAMP 1570 AM/ Ch. 20
615 N Park Ave., #101
Tucson, AZ 85721
main: 520-621-8173
request: 520-621-5806
f: 520-626-5986
e: gm@kamp.arizona.edu
http://kamp.arizona.edu
webcast: Yes
genres: Alt., RPM, Metal, World, Jazz, Hip-Hop, Punk, Electronica
reports to: CMJ
pd: Greg Goodrum
ext: 520-621-8173 x1
e: pd@kamp.arizona.edu
md: Neema Neshrati
ext: 520-626-4460
e: kampheadmusic@gmail.com
Send promos, w/ genre on the package to: PO Box 3605, Tucson, AZ 85722.

Arkansas

Henderson State U
KSWH 99.9 FM
HSU Box 7872,
1100 Henderson St.
Arkadelphia, AR 71999
watts: 100
main: 870-230-5185
request: 870-230-5218
f: 870-230-5144
e: kswh@hsu.edu
www.kswh.org
webcast: Yes
genres: Alt., Rock, Urban
reports to: CMJ
pd: Jaris Johnson
Some fundraisers w/ Local bands.

Hendrix College
KHDX 93.1 FM
1600 Washington Ave.
Conway, AR 72032
watts: 10
main: 501-450-1339
request: 501-450-1312
f: 501-450-1399
e: khdx@hendrix.edu
www.hendrix.edu/khdx
webcast: Yes
genres: Rock, Punk, Country, Hip-Hop, Electronic, Folk
reports to: CMJ
pd: Alexander Jones
e: jonesat@hendrix.edu
md: Elizabeth Jones
Books Local acts 3-4 times/yr.

U of Arkansas/ Fayetteville
KXUA 88.3 FM
A665 Arkansas Union
Fayetteville, AR 72701
watts: 468
main: 479-575-4273
request: 479-575-5883
e: kxua@uark.edu
www.kxua883.blogspot.com
webcast: Yes
genres: All Styles
reports to: CMJ
pd: Chrustay Davies
e: onair@uark.edu
md: Nathan Rowe/ Beth Ibrahim
ext: 479-283-5299
e: charts@uark.edu
Sponsors gigs w/ mostly Local & Reg'l acts; contact Jordan Bennett at promo@uark.edu. Also does phone & in-studio interviews & performances.

California

Cal State U/ Long Beach
KBEACH Ch. 65
1212 Bellflower Blvd., Ste. 110, USU Rm. 100
Long Beach, CA 90803
main: 562-985-1624; 562-985-2484
request: 562-985-2282
e: info@kbeach.org
www.kbeach.org
webcast: Yes
genres: Rock, Hip-Hop, Punk, RPM, Eletronic, Alt.
reports to: CMJ
pd: Reeny Wang
e: pdkbeach@yahoo.com
md: Stephanie Funk
e: kbeachmd@yahoo.com
Sponsors Thu campus concerts; shows are archived & available for download.

Cal State U/ Sacramento
KSSU 1580 AM
6000 J St., c/o ASI
Sacramento, CA 95819
watts: 10
main: 916-278-3343
request: 916-278-3666
f: 916-278-6278
e: manager@kssu.com
www.kssu.com
webcast: Yes
genres: Rock, Electronica, World, Hip-Hop, Alt., Top 200
reports to: CMJ
pd: Robert Young
md: Susie Kuo
ext: 916-278-5882
e: music@kssu.com
Sponsors concerts on campus.

California Polytechnic State U
KCPR 91.3 FM
Graphic Arts Bldg. 26, 3rd Fl.
San Luis Obispo, CA 93407
watts: 2000
main: 805-756-5277
e: kcpr@calpoly.edu
www.kcpr.org
webcast: Yes
genres: All Styles
reports to: CMJ
pd: Eric Jorgensen/ Katie Boyer
e: kcprprogramdirectors@gmail.com
md: Jack LaPorte/Matt Zenick
ext: 805-756-2965
e: kcprmd@kcpr.org
Non-profit volunteer station sponsors shows for indie artists at venues in & around town.

Cuesta College
KGUR 105.3 FM
Hwy. 1, PO Box 8106
San Luis Obispo, CA 93403
watts: 10
main: 805-546-3191
request: 805-544-0838
f: 805-546-3904

e: kgur@cuesta.edu
www.cuesta.cc.ca.us/deptinfo/kgur
genres: College Rock, Classic Rock, AAA, Hip-Hop
reports to: CMJ
pd: Jason McFarland
md: Will Pompe
All indie submissions added to daily rotation.

Humboldt State U
KRFH 610 AM
1 Harpst St.
Arcata, CA 95521
watts: 30
main: 707-826-3257
request: 707-826-6077
f: 707-826-4770
e: krfh@humboldt.edu
www.krfh.net
webcast: Yes
genres: All Styles
reports to: CMJ
pd: Daniel Gannotta
md: Alana Chenevert
Sponsors wkly shows in the Quad.

Loyola Marymount U
KXLU 88.9 FM
1 LMU Dr., Malone 402
Los Angeles, CA 90045
main: 310-338-2866
request: 310-338-5958
f: 310-338-5959
e: laurenkxlu@gmail.com
www.kxlu.com
webcast: Yes
genres: Indie, Rock, Pop, Punk, Folk, Metal, Electronic
reports to: CMJ
pd: Megan Dembkowski
e: megankxlu@gmail.com
md: Matt Strasser
ext: 310-338-2866 x1
e: mattkxlu@gmail.com
Acclaimed non-commercial station sponsors in-studio performances & LA club shows. Airs popular "Demolisten" program on Fri evenings.

Pomona College
KSPC 88.7 FM
Thatcher Music Bldg.
340 N College Ave.
Claremont, CA 91711
watts: 3000
main: 909-621-8157
request: 909-626-5772
f: 909-621-8769
www.kspc.org
webcast: Yes
genres: All Styles
reports to: CMJ
pd: Zach Lester
e: pd@kspc.org
md: Sam Zipper
e: md@kspc.org
Airs Indie artists exclusively, promotes area concerts on site & on-air calendar. Sponsors "Blow-Out Concert Series" each semester.

Saddleback College
KSBR 88.5 FM/Ch. 967
28000 Marguerite Pkwy.
Mission Viejo, CA 92692
watts: 600
main: 949-582-5727
f: 949-347-9693
www.ksbr.net
webcast: Yes
genres: Jazz, Indie, Rock
reports to: RPM, R&R, CMJ, AirplayAddBoard
pd: Terry Wedel
ext: 949-582-4714
e: twedel@saddleback.edu
md: Vienna Yip
ext: 949-582-4228
e: jazziegirl.ksbr@gmail.com
Contact Vienna for Jazz & JJ for Rock: rockradio@gmail.com. Sponsors events on campus. Prefers CDs, but email submissions accepted.

San Diego State U
KCR 1620 AM/Ch. 957
5200 Campanille Dr.
San Diego, CA 92182
main: 619-594-7014
request: 619-594-6982
f: 619-594-6092
e: gm@kcrlive.com
www.kcrlive.com
webcast: Yes
genres: Rock, Jazz, Blues, Country, Hip-Hop, World, Electronica, Latin, Talk
reports to: CMJ, Dusted
pd: Tommy Garry
e: kcrprogramdirector@gmail.com
md: Andrew Lockard
e: kcrmusicdirector@gmail.com
Snail mail copies of full-length vinyl w/ short bio & description.

San Jose State U
KSJS 90.5 FM
HGH Rm. 132
San Jose, CA 95192
watts: 1500
main: 408-924-4548
request: 408-924-5757
e: ksjs@ksjs.org
www.ksjs.org
webcast: Yes
genres: Rock, Alt., Electronic, World, Jazz, Blues, Urban, Spanish Rock
reports to: CMJ, Hits
pd: Rob Soul
ext: 408-924-4596
e: programdirector@ksjs.org
md: Andrea Garcia
ext: 408-924-4547
e: rock@ksjs.org; melodramatic@ksjs.org
Indies in rotation; in-studio opps. & ticket giveaways. Also books campus gigs.

San Rafael H.S.
KSRH 88.1 FM
185 Mission Ave.
San Rafael, CA 94901
watts: 10
main: 415-457-5314
request: 415-457-5774
e: ksrh@hotmail.com
genres: Rock, Alt., Hip-Hop, Pop, Punk, World, Latino
reports to: CMJ
pd: Marianne Melnik
md: Nelson Cruz
Sponsors 3-4 Reg'l gigs/yr. Phone contact preferred.

Santa Clara U
KSCU 103.3 FM
500 El Camino Real, #3207
Santa Clara, CA 95053
watts: 30
main: 408-554-4414
request: 408-554-5728
f: 408-985-5728
e: info@kscu.org
www.kscu.org
genres: Indie, Punk, Ska, Jazz, Blues, Reggae, Rock
reports to: CMJ
pd: Tyler Kogura
e: programming@kscu.org
md: Eidelyn Gonzales
ext: 408-554-4907
e: music@kscu.org

Stanford U
KZSU 90.1 FM
PO Box 20190
Stanford, CA 94309
watts: 500
main: 650-725-4868
request: 650-723-9010
f: 650-725-5865
e: info@kzsu.stanford.edu
http://kzsu.stanford.edu
webcast: Yes
genres: All Styles
reports to: CMJ
pd: Andrea Leonard
e: pd@kzsu.stanford.edu
md: Mike Howes
e: music@kzsu.stanford.edu
Sponsors events. Promos to: Memorial Hall, 540 Memorial Way, Stanford, CA 94305.

U of Cal/Berkeley
KALX 90.7 FM
26 Barrows Hall, #5650
Berkeley, CA 94720
watts: 500
main: 510-642-1111
request: 510-642-5259
e: mail@kalx.berkeley.edu
http://kalx.berkeley.edu
webcast: Yes
genres: All Styles
reports to: CMJ
pd: Erin Ruiz
md: James Croft/Casey Koon
e: music@kalx.berkeley.edu
Sponsors concerts on-campus.

U of Cal/Davis
KDVS 90.3 FM
14 Lower Freeborn Hall
Davis, CA 95616
watts: 9200
main: 530-752-0728
request: 530-752-2777; 530-754-5387
f: 530-752-8548
e: gm@kdvs.org
www.kdvs.org
webcast: Yes
genres: Alt.
reports to: CMJ
pd: Daniel Harkin/Alicia Edelman
ext: 530-757-7239
e: programming@kdvs.org
md: AJ/Roxanne
e: music@kdvs.org
Freeform station sponsors events.

U of Cal/Irvine
KUCI 88.9 FM
PO Box 4362
Irvine, CA 92616
watts: 200
main: 949-824-6868
request: 949-824-5824
e: kuci@kuci.org
www.kuci.org
webcast: Yes
genres: All Styles
reports to: CMJ
pd: Beth Hughes
e: pd@kuci.org
md: Sam Farzin
e: music@kuci.org
Sponsors concerts on-campus.

U of Cal/Riverside
KUCR 88.3 FM
691 Linden St.
Riverside, CA 92521
watts: 175
main: 951-827-3737;
request: 951-827-5827
e: kcurinfo@kucr.org
www.kucr.org
webcast: Yes
genres: Indie, Rock, Electronic, Alt., Jazz, World, Classical, Experimental, Hip-Hop, Folk
reports to: CMJ
pd: Walter Douglas
e: walter@kucr.org
Sponsors lunchtime concerts w/ Student Activities. On-air opps. & ticket giveaways.

U of Cal/Santa Barbara
KCSB 91.9 FM
1025 Storke Comm Bldg.
Santa Barbara, CA 93106
watts: 620
main: 805-893-3757
request: 805-893-2424
f: 805-893-7832
e: info@kcsb.org
www.kcsb.org
webcast: Yes
genres: Eclectic, Rock, World, Hip-Hop, Jazz, Blues
reports to: CMJ
pd: Rebecca Redman
e: program.director@kcsb.org
md: Devon Blunden/Avalon Jeffrey
e: external.music@kcsb.org; internal.music@kcsb.org
Sponsors 50 gigs/yr. Send CDs for airplay to: PO Box 13401, UCSB, Santa Barbara, CA 93107.

U of San Francisco
KUSF 90.3 FM
2130 Fulton St.
San Francisco, CA 94117
watts: 3000
main: 415-386-5873
e: kusf@usfca.edu
www.kusf.org
webcast: Yes
genres: All Styles
reports to: CMJ
pd: Trista Bernasconi
e: bernasconi@usfca.edu
md: Irwin/Miguel/Howard/Lenode
e: kusfmusic@yahoo.com
Sponsors events.

U of Southern Cal
KSCR 1560 AM
Student Union 404
Los Angeles, CA 90089
watts: 10
main: 213-740-1483
request: 213-740-5727
e: gm@kscr.org
www.kscr.org
webcast: Yes
genres: Rock, Indie, Punk, World, Latin, Jazz, Electronica, Hip-Hop
reports to: CMJ
pd: Sara Schlievert
e: pd@kscr.org
md: Maura Klosterman
ext: 213-740-1486
e: music@kscr.org
Sponsors many concerts at 500 capacity clubs & lunchtime stage. Snail mail only; no MP3s.

Colorado

Colorado State U
KCSU 90.5 FM
Lory Student Ctr., Box 13
Ft. Collins, CO 80523
watts: 10,000
main: 970-491-7611

request: 970-491-5278
f: 970-491-7612
www.kcsufm.com
webcast: Yes
genres: Hip-Hop, Alt., Punk, Rock, AAA
reports to: CMJ, Hits, Urban Network
pd: James Lopez
e: program@colostate.edu
md: Trent Milligan/ Steve Hendrikson
ext: 970-491-1695
e: kcsumusic@gmail.com

Mesa State College
KMSA 91.3 FM
1175 Texas Ave.
Grand Junction, CO 81501
watts: 3000
main: 970-248-1718
request: 970-248-1240
www.mesastate.edu/kmsa
webcast: Yes
genres: Alt., Hip-Hop, Electronic, Metal, World, Reggae, Blues, Jazz, Bluegrass, Alt. Country, Punk
reports to: CMJ
pd: Dustin Coren
ext: 970-248-1402
e: d_coren@yahoo.com
md: Jesse Rose
ext: 970-248-1718 x1
Broadcast covers a 150mi radius.

U of Colorado/ Boulder
KVCU 1190 AM
Campus Box 207
Boulder, CO 80309
watts: 6800/110
main: 303-492-5031
request: 303-492-1190
f: 303-492-1369
e: dj@radio1190.org
www.radio1190.org
webcast: Yes
genres: Hip-Hop, Electronic, Pop, Indie, Punk, Rap
reports to: CMJ
pd: Tyler Broeren
e: tbroeren@radio1190.org
md: Katerine Peterson
ext: 303-492-7405
e: kpeterson@radio1190.org
Highlights indie releases & sponsors gigs.
No electronic submissions.

Western State College
KWSB 91.1 FM
Taylor Hall 112
Gunnison, CO 81230
watts: 100
main: 970-943-3033
request: 970-943-3222
e: kwsbmanagement@ western.edu
www.kwsb.org
webcast: Yes
genres: Hip-Hop, Punk, Indie, Top 200, Metal, Country
reports to: CMJ
pd: Frank Venturo
e: fventuro@western.edu
md: Walter
ext: 970-943-2117

Connecticut

Central Connecticut State U
WFCS 107.7 FM
1615 Stanley St.
New Britain, CT 06050
watts: 36
main: 860-832-1883
request: 860-832-1077
f: 860-832-3757
e: wfcs1077@yahoo.com
http://clubs.ccsu.edu/wfcs/
genres: Alt., Metal, Urban, Folk, Jazz, Blues
reports to: CMJ
e: wfcsalternative@yahoo.com

Connecticut College
WCNI 90.9 FM
270 Mohegan Ave.
New London, CT 06320
watts: 2000
main: 860-439-2853
request: 860-439-2850
f: 860-439-2805
e: wcni@conncoll.edu
www.wcniradio.org
webcast: Yes
genres: Rock, Alt., Jazz, Blues
reports to: CMJ
pd: Conor Walsh
e: cwlsh2@conncoll.edu
md: Alison Christian
Also sponsors events.

Eastern Connecticut State U
WECS 90.1 FM
83 Windham St.
Willimantic, CT 06226
watts: 440
main: 860-465-5354
request: 860-465-2164
f: 860-465-5073
e: wecs@hotmail.com
www.easternct.edu/ depts/wecs
webcast: Yes
genres: Alt., Urban, Electronic, Jazz, Rock
reports to: CMJ
pd: John Zatowski
e: zatowski@easternct.edu
Write genre on outside of promos.

Fairfield U
WVOF 88.5 FM
PO Box R
Fairfield, CT 06824
watts: 100
main: 203-254-4144
request: 203-254-4111
f: 203-254-4224
e: wvofstationmanager@ gmail.com
www.wvof.org
webcast: Yes
genres: Rock, Urban, Reggae, Alt.
reports to: CMJ
pd: James Maresca
e: wvofprogram@gmail.com
md: Meredith Moses
e: wvofmusic2@gmail.com
Sponsors campus gigs & hosts live sets & on-air interviews.

Quinnipiac U
WQAQ 98.1 FM
275 Mt. Carmel Ave.
Hamden, CT 06518
watts: 16
main: 203-582-5278
request: 203-582-5555
f: 203-582-5203
e: wqaq@quinnipiac.edu
www.wqaq.com
webcast: Yes
genres: Alt., Emo, Metal, Classic Rock, Hip-Hop
reports to: CMJ
pd: Steph Pensa
e: stephanie.pensa@ quinnipiac.edu
md: Fred Hoxsi
Sponsors concert in Mar.

Southern Connecticut State U
WSIN 1590 AM
501 Crescent St., Student Ctr. Rm. 210
New Haven, CT 06456
watts: 11
main: 203-392-6930
request: 203-392-5353
f: 203-392-5507
e: mcgraths2@southernct.edu
www.wsinradio.org
webcast: Yes
genres: Rock, Hip-Hop, Country, Top 40, Punk
reports to: CMJ
pd: Katie Zold
e: zoldk1@southernct.edu
md: Doug Liggins
e: ligginsd1@southernct.edu

Trinity College
WRTC 89.3 FM
300 Summit St.
Hartford, CT 06106
watts: 300
main: 860-297-2439
request: 860-297-2450
f: 860-297-5201
e: bobparzych@hotmail.com
www.wrtcfm.com
webcast: Yes
genres: Alt., Jazz, Rock, Rap, Reggae, Latin, Polka, World
reports to: CMJ
pd: Matt Milner

e: matt.milner@trincoll.edu
md: Bob Zizzamia
e: christopher.zizzamia@trincoll.edu
Sponsors & books some shows on campus including Jazz Fest.

U of Connecticut
WHUS 91.7 FM
Student Union Bldg., Rm. 412
2110 Hillside Rd., Unit 3008R
Storrs, CT 06269
watts: 4200
main: 860-486-4007
request: 860-486-9487
f: 860-486-2955
e: info@whus.org
www.whus.org
webcast: Yes
genres: Indie, Hip-Hop, Punk, Jazz, Folk, Blues, World, Metal, Polka
reports to: CMJ
pd: Chris Sampson
e: programdirector@whus.org
md: Brendan Sudol
ext: 860-486-8607
e: whus.musicdirector@gmail.com
Sponsors 4-5 on-campus concerts/yr. Some on-air interviews.

U of Hartford
WSAM 105.3 FM
200 Bloomfield Ave.
West Hartford, CT 06117
watts: 300
main: 860-768-4238
request: 860-768-4769
f: 860-768-5184
e: manager@wsam.hartford.edu
http://wsam.hartford.edu
webcast: Yes
genres: Metal, Punk, Prog, Hip-Hop, Jazz
reports to: CMJ
pd: Sam Favata
ext: 860-768-4768 x103
md: Billy Wang
e: music@wsam.hartford.edu

U of New Haven
WNHU 88.7 FM
300 Boston Post Rd.
West Haven, CT 06516
watts: 1700
main: 203-479-8800
request: 203-934-9296
f: 203-306-3073
e: info@wnhu.net; roarequest@wnhu.net
www.wnhu.net
webcast: Yes
genres: Rock, Alt., Metal, Punk, World, Jazz, Urban, Electronic, Reggae, Oldies
reports to: CMJ, RapAttackLives, Mixrevolution
pd: Michael Valente
e: programdirector@wnhu.net
md: Elyse Bongiovanni
ext: 203-934-8888
e: newmusic@wnhu.net
Sponsors some on-campus gigs.

Yale U
WYBC 1340 AM
142 Temple St., Ste. 203
New Haven, CT 06510
watts: 1000
main: 203-776-4118
request: 203-562-1340
f: 203-776-2446
e: sean@wybc.com
www.wybc.com
webcast: Yes
reports to: R&R, Billboard
pd: Jesse Bradford
e: jesse.bradford@yale.edu
Eclectic playlist features indie & mainstream music. Sister station 94.3FM spins R&B hits and oldies. PD: Juan Castillo, jc@yalebroadcasting.com

Wesleyan U
WESU 88.1 FM
45 Broad St.
Middletown, CT 06459
watts: 1500
main: 860-685-7703
request: 860-685-7700
f: 860-704-0608
e: wesu@wesufm.org
www.wesufm.org
webcast: Yes
genres: Rock, Electronic, Reggae, World
reports to: CMJ, AAAradio.com
pd: Max Lavine
e: pad@wesufm.org
md: Ben Castanon/Josh Sharp
e: wesumd@wesufm.org
Many specialty shows & sponsors some campus gigs. Promos to: 222 Church St., Middletown, CT 06459.

Western Connecticut State U
WXCI 91.7 FM
181 White St.
Danbury, CT 06810
watts: 3000
main: 203-837-8387
request: 203-837-9924
f: 203-837-8599
e: wxcisuggestions@yahoo.com
www.wxci.org
webcast: Yes
genres: Hip-Hop, Indie, Americana, Metal, Jazz
reports to: CMJ
pd: Chris Kiley
e: wxcipd@yahoo.com
md: Matt Gray
2nd largest college station in CT. Snail mail promos.

Delaware

Delaware Tech. Community College
WDTS 620 AM
PO Box 610, Seashore Hwy.
Georgetown, DE 19947
watts: 30
main: 302-856-5400 x2110
f: 302-858-5461
www.dtcc.edu
genres: Rock, Alt., Loud Rock
reports to: CMJ
pd: Tamera Postles
e: tpostles@dtcc.edu
Snail mail submissions.

U of Delaware
WVUD 91.3 FM/Ch. 2
Perkins Student Ctr., Academy St.
Newark, DE 19716
watts: 1000
main: 302-831-2701
f: 302-831-1399
e: ud-wvud@udel.edu
www.wvud.org
webcast: Yes
genres: All Styles
reports to: CMJ
pd: Michael Nigro
e: wvudprogramming@gmail.com
md: Mary Hutchins
e: wvudmusic@gmail.com
Sponsors events.

District of Columbia

Catholic U of America
WCUA Web only
129 Pryzbyla Ctr.
Washington, DC 20064
main: 202-319-6106
request: 202-319-5106
f: 202-299-2807
e: cua-radio@cua.edu
http://wcua.cua.edu
webcast: Yes
genres: Rock, Hip-Hop, Alt., Dance, Punk, Jazz
reports to: BMI
pd: Christopher Pierno
e: 25pierno@cua.edu
md: Justin Cartagena
Promotes area gigs & sponsors various events. Promos to: 129 Pryz., 620 Michigan Ave. NE, Washington, DC 20064.

George Washington U
WRGW Web & cable only
800 21st St. NW, Ste. G-02
Washington, DC 20052
main: 202-994-7554
request: 202-944-9749
f: 202-994-4551
e: wrgw@gwu.edu
www.gwradio.com
webcast: Yes
genres: Indie, Hard Rock, Electronic, Urban, Punk, Classical, World, Jazz
reports to: CMJ
pd: Hannah Byam
e: generalmanager@gwradio.com
md: Ben Doak
e: music@gwradio.com
Sponsors 2-6 concerts/yr; on-campus events & in-studios.

Georgetown U
WGTB Web only
432 Leavey Ctr.
Washington, DC 20057
main: 202-687-3702
request: 202-687-9482
f: 202-687-8940
e: wgtb.gm@gmail.com
www.georgetownradio.com
webcast: Yes
genres: Hip-Hop, Rock, World
reports to: CMJ
pd: Talia Sandwick
e: wgtb.programming@gmail.com
md: Leah Nestico
e: wgtb.music@gmail.com
DJs required to play a quota of new music. In-studio opps. & on-campus concerts.

Florida

Eckerd College
WECX 99.9 FM
4200 54th Ave. S
St. Petersburg, FL 33711
watts: 5
main: 727-864-8419
request: 727-864-8414
e: wecx@eckerd.edu
www.eckerd.edu/wecx
genres: Hip-Hop, Rock, R&B, Jazz, World, Electronica
reports to: CMJ
pd: Charlotte Quandt
md: Jake Woerner
e: musicwecx@eckerd.edu
Sponsors monthly concerts on campus feat. mostly Local acts. Email contact preferred.

Embry Riddle Aeronautical U
WIKD 104.7/99.1 FM
600 S Clyde Morris Blvd.
c/o SGA Office
Daytona Beach, FL 32114
watts: 100
main: 386-226-7056
request: 386-226-6272
f: 386-226-6083
e: general@eaglesfm.com
www.eaglesfm.com
webcast: Yes
genres: Metal, House, R&B, Hip-Hop, Alt., Country
reports to: CMJ
pd: Tom Flannery
e: studiodirector@eaglesfm.com
md: Mayank Kumar
e: media.manager@eaglesfm.com
Freeform station covers a 12mi radius & sponsors 2 annual concerts w/ Touch & Go Productions.

Flagler College
WFCF 88.5 FM
74 King St.
St. Augustine, FL 32084
watts: 10,000
main: 904-819-6449
f: 904-826-3471
e: wfcf@flagler.edu
www.flagler.edu/wfcf
genres: All Styles
reports to: CMJ
pd: Carmen Richter
ext: 904-819-6313
md: Jesse Jarvis/Amber Jain
Sponsors events. Send promos to: PO Box 1027, St. Augustine, FL 32085.

Florida Atlantic U
OWL Radio Web & cable only
777 Glades Rd.,
Student Union, Ste. 207-D
Boca Raton, FL 33431
main: 561-297-3759
request: 561-297-2842
f: 561-297-3771
e: owlradio@wowl.fau.edu
http://owlradio.fau.edu
webcast: Yes
genres: Punk, Rock, Urban, Jazz, World, Breakbeat
reports to: CMJ
pd: Louis Blas
e: owlradioprogramdirector@gmail.com
md: Nathan Lyons
ext: 561-271-6054
e: nlyonsowlradiomd@gmail.com
Sponsors campus Rap & Rock shows.

Florida State U/Tallahassee
WVFS 89.7 FM
420 Diffenbaugh Bldg.
Tallahassee, FL 32306
watts: 2700
main: 850-644-1879
request: 850-644-1837
f: 850-644-8753
e: wvfs@wvfs.fsu.edu
www.wvfs.fsu.edu
webcast: Yes
genres: All Styles
reports to: CMJ, Dusted Magazine
pd: Anna Lisa Bradshaw
e: alb07@fsu.edu
md: Stone Hanson
e: music@wvfs.fsu.edu

Nova Southeastern U
WNSU 88.5 FM
3301 College Ave.
Ft. Lauderdale, FL 33314
watts: 3000
main: 954-262-8457
request: 954-262-8460
e: wnsu@nova.edu
www.nova.edu/radiox
webcast: Yes
genres: Hip-Hop, Rock, Alt., R&B, Electronic, Soca, Reggae, Jazz, Blues, Local
reports to: CMJ
pd: Ashley Schwartz
e: aschwart@nova.edu
md: Michelle Manley
e: wnsu@nova.edu
Airs on WKPX from 7pm-1am. Sponsors 3-4 concerts/yr.

Rollins College
WPRK 91.5 FM
1000 Holt Ave., PO Box 2745
Winter Park, FL 32789
watts: 1300
main: 407-646-2241
request: 407-646-2915
e: wprkfm@rollins.edu
www.wprkdj.org
webcast: Yes
genres: Rock, Hip-Hop, Punk, Classical, Indie, Breakbeat
reports to: CMJ
pd: Matt Tonner
md: John Milford
e: wprkmusic@hotmail.com
Sponsors concerts at The Social.

U of Miami
WVUM 90.5 FM
1306 Standford Dr., Rm. 110
Coral Gables, FL 33124
watts: 1500
main: 305-284-3131
request: 305-284-5786
e: info@wvum.org
www.wvum.org
webcast: Yes
genres: Alt., Hip-Hop, Metal, Classical
reports to: CMJ
pd: Chris Bennett
ext: 305-284-3131 x2
e: pd@wvum.org
md: Bensen
ext: 305-284-3131 x3
e: music@wvum.org
Send promos: PO Box 248191, Coral Gables, FL 33124.

U of N Florida
WOSP Cable & podcasts only
4567 St. John's Bluff Rd. S
Jacksonville, FL 32224
main: 904-620-2908
f: 904-620-1560
e: wosp@unf.edu
www.ospreyradio.com
genres: Alt., Urban, Jazz, Rock
reports to: CMJ
pd: Benson Huges
e: sudramaboy@aol.com
md: Chris Lloyd
e: chrisel@gmail.com
Sponsors concerts on campus.

Georgia

Abraham Baldwin
WPLH 103.1 FM
2802 Moore Hwy.
Tifton, GA 31794
watts: 30
main: 229-391-4977
request: 229-386-7158
e: wplh@stallions.abac.edu
www.abac.edu/wplh
webcast: Yes
genres: Rock, Alt., Punk, CCM, Hip-Hop,
reports to: CMJ
pd: Keith Lee
DJs spin promos every hour.

Georgia Institute of Technology
WREK 91.1 FM
350 Ferst Dr. NW, Ste. 2224
Atlanta, GA 30332
watts: 40,000
main: 404-894-2468
e: general.manager@wrek.org
www.wrek.org
webcast: Yes
genres: Jazz, Classic Rock, Folk, Alt., Rock, Avant Garde, Urban, Folk, Electronic, World
reports to: CMJ
pd: Chris Pool
e: program.director@wrek.org
md: Curtis Stephens
e: music.director@wrek.org
"Live at WREK" on Tue nite features Local-Nat'ls.

Georgia State U
WRAS 88.5 FM
33 Gilmer St. SE, Ste. 280
Atlanta, GA 30303
watts: 100,000
main: 404-413-1630
request: 404-413-9727
f: 404-413-1636
e: wras88@gmail.com
www.wras.org
webcast: Yes
genres: Jazz, Hip-Hop, Rock, Alt., Funk, Metal, Electronic
reports to: CMJ
pd: Chelsea Taylor
md: Thomas Niles
ext: 404-413-1631
e: musicdir88@gmail.com
Send promos to: PO Box 4048, Atlanta, GA 30302.

U of Georgia
WUOG 90.5 FM
153 Tate Ctr.
Athens, GA 30602
watts: 26,000
main: 706-542-4567
f: 706-542-0070
e: info@wuog.org
www.wuog.org
webcast: Yes
genres: All Styles
reports to: CMJ
pd: Amanda Perofsky
ext: 706-542-8466
e: programming@wuog.org
md: Max Martin/ Claire Paffenhofer
e: md@wuog.org
Promotes gigs on campus, releases Local & genre-specific CDs, reviews albums on "Liner Notes" & sponsors AthFest. Local MD: Erika Frank, lmd@wuog.org. Send promos to: PO Box 2065, Tate Student Ctr., Athens, GA 30612.

Idaho

Idaho State U
KISU 91.1 FM
921 S 8th Ave., Mail Stop 8014
Pocatello, ID 83209
watts: 4500
main: 208-282-3691
request: 208-282-5939
e: kisufm91@gmail.com
www.kisu.org
webcast: Yes
genres: Rock, Folk, Alt., Jazz, Bluegrass
reports to: CMJ
pd: Jamon Anderson
e: kisu91@gmail.com
md: Levi Keller
Indie & Jazz acts contact Jerry Miller, milljerr@isu.edu for station gigs.

U of Idaho
KUOI 89.3 FM
3rd Fl., Student Union Bldg.
Box 444272
Moscow, ID 83844
watts: 400
main: 208-885-2218
request: 208-885-6392
f: 208-885-2222
e: kuoi@uidaho.edu
www.kuoi.com
webcast: Yes
genres: Rock, Pop, Punk, Experimental, S/S, Electronic
reports to: CMJ
pd: Andrew Siemens
e: msiemens@kuoi.org
md: Marcus Kellis
ext: 208-885-6433
e: marcus@kuoi.org

Illinois

Augustana College
WAUG 97.9 FM
639 38th St.
Rock Island, IL 61201
watts: 500
main: 309-794-7513
f: 309-794-7511
e: waug@augustana.edu
http://waug.augustana.edu
webcast: Yes
genres: Punk, Alt., Metal, Techno, Rock, Hip-Hop, World
reports to: CMJ
pd: Jenna Svatos
e: jenna-svatos@augustana.edu
md: Alicia Matuszewski
e: alicia-matuszewski@augustana.edu

De Paul U
Radio DePaul Web only
2250 N Sheffield Ave.
Ste. 317, Box #640
Chicago, IL 60614
main: 773-325-7308
request: 773-325-7341
f: 773-325-7399
www.radio.depaul.edu
webcast: Yes
genres: Ska, Punk, Pop, Rock, Hip-Hop, Jazz
reports to: CMJ
pd: Kevin
e: programmingradiodepaul@gmail.com
md: Prash
ext: 773-325-7342
e: radiodepaulmusicdirector@gmail.com
Sponsors gigs on & off campus.

Eastern Illinois U
WEIU 88.9 FM
600 Lincoln Ave.
1521 Buzzard Hall
Charleston, IL 61920
watts: 4000
main: 217-581-6954
request: 217-581-6116
f: 217-581-6650
e: hitmix@weiu.net
www.weiufm.org
webcast: Yes
genres: Rock, Jazz, Soul, Urban, Classical
reports to: CMJ
pd: Jeff Owens
e: jeff@weiu.net
md: Bryant Fritz
Sponsors on-campus concerts.

Illinois State U
WZND Web only
07 Fell Hall
Normal, IL 61790
main: 309-438-5491
request: 309-438-2171
f: 309-438-2652
e: requests@wznd.com
www.wznd.com
webcast: Yes
genres: Rock, Alt., Hip-Hop
reports to: CMJ
pd:
ext:
md: N
ext: 30

Illinois
WESN 8
PO Box 290
Bloomingtor
watts: 120
main: 309-55
request: 309-5
f: 309-556-2949
e: wesn@iwu.edu
www.wesn.org/88
genres: Rock, Hip-
Electronic, Metal, Pun
reports to: CMJ
pd: Jason Prechtel
e: jprechtel@iwu.edu
md: Tony Farruggia
e: afarrugg@iwu.edu
Sponsors Far Left Fest.

Lyons Township H.S.
WLTL 88.1 FM
100 S Brainard Ave.
LaGrange, IL 60525
watts: 180
main: 708-482-9585
f: 708-482-7051
e: cthomas@lths.net
www.wltl.net
webcast: Yes
genres: All Styles of Rock
reports to: CMJ
pd: Kaitlin Roelofs
md: Brian Griffin
Indie music in the mix & also on 2 hr weekly show.

Northwestern U
WNUR 89.3 FM
1877 Campus Dr.
Evanston, IL 60208
watts: 7200
main: 847-491-7101
request: 847-866-9687
f: 847-467-2058
e: wnur@wnur.org
www.wnur.org
webcast: Yes
genres: Jazz, Indie, Dance, World, Urban
reports to: CMJ
pd: Taylor Dearr
e: gm@wnur.org
md: Chris Wade
ext: 847-491-7102
e: rock-md@wnur.org
Many Indie & underground artists in rotation. Other MDs: Fritz Schenker, jazz-md@wnur.org; John Pappas, streetbeat-md@wnur.org; DJ Delug, hiphop@wnur.org.

Olivet Nazarene U
WONU 89.7 FM
1 University Ave.
Bourbonnais, IL 60914

...8424

...org

...org

...: Yes

...s: Rock, Jazz, Hip-Hop, ...e, Metal, World, Alt., Folk, ...assical, Blues, Experimental
reports to: CMJ
pd: Rick McWilliams
e: pd@whpk.org
md: Dave McQuown/JJ Mack
e: md-rock@whpk.org
Sponsors semi-frequent concerts & annual "Summer Breeze."

Indiana

DePauw U
WGRE 91.5 FM
609 S Locust St.
Greencastle, IN 46135
watts: 1000
main: 765-658-4643
request: 765-658-4641
f: 765-658-4693
e: wgre@depauw.edu
www.wgre.org
webcast: Yes
genres: Alt.
reports to: CMJ
pd: Tiffany Camhi
e: tiffanycamhi_2010@depauw.edu
md: Hannah Harp
ext: 765-658-4637
e: hannahharp_2010@depauw.edu
Sponsors concerts featuring mostly Local & Reg'l bands.

Indiana State U
WISU 89.7 FM
217 N 6th St., Dreiser Hall Rm. 217
Terre Haute, IN 47809
watts: 13,500
main: 812-237-3252
request: 812-237-3690
f: 812-237-3241

...rg

...Rock, Urban

...FM

...gton, IN 47408

...22

...n: 812-855-7862
request: 812-855-9489
f: 812-855-1073
e: manager@wiux.org
www.wiux.org/new
webcast: Yes
genres: Rock, Alt., Hip-Hop, Jazz, Techno
reports to: CMJ
pd: Kevin Small
e: ksmall@wiux.org
md: George Drake, Jr.
e: gdrake@wiux.org
Holds free all-ages show every other Fri w/ Touring & Reg'l bands.

Manchester College
WBKE 89.5 FM
604 College Ave., Box 19
North Manchester, IN 46962
watts: 3000
main: 260-982-5424
request: 260-982-5272
f: 260-982-5043
e: wbke@manchester.edu
http://wbke.manchester.edu
webcast: Yes
genres: Alt., Punk, Top 40, Classic Rock, Alt. Country
reports to: CMJ
pd: Alicia Smith
e: wbkestation management@manchester.edu
md: Chris Greenwood
e: wbkerequests@manchester.edu
Sponsors events.

Rose-Hulman Institute of Tech.
WMHD 90.7 FM
5500 Wabash Ave.
Terre Haute, IN 47803
watts: 1400
main: 812-872-6923
request: 812-877-6924
f: 812-872-6926
e: manager@wmhdradio.org
http://wmhd.rose-hulman.edu
webcast: Yes
genres: Electronic, Rock, Metal, Punk, Ska, Hip-Hop, Reggae
reports to: CMJ
pd: Kevin Hengehold
e: program@wmhdradio.org
md: Tim Hasler
e: indie@wmhdradio.org
Sponsors events & accepts vinyl. Loud Rock programming contact: Jimmy Magargee, loudrock@wmhdradio.org.

U of Evansville
WUEV 91.5 FM
1800 Lincoln Ave.
Evansville, IN 47722
watts: 6100
main: 812-479-2022
request: 812-479-2020
e: wuevfm@evansville.edu
http://wuev.evansville.edu
webcast: Yes
genres: Jazz, Blues, Hip-Hop, Christian, Metal, Children's
reports to: CMJ, R&R
pd: Kayleigh Weisman
ext: 812-479-2689
e: kf65@evansville.edu

U of Notre Dame
WSND 88.9 FM
315 LaFortune Student Ctr.
Notre Dame, IN 46556
watts: 3430
main: 574-631-4069
request: 574-631-7342
f: 574-631-3653
e: wsnd@nd.edu
www.nd.edu/~wsnd
genres: Classical, Jazz, Celtic, Blues, Rock, Indie
reports to: CMJ
pd: Ed Jaroszewski
e: ejarosze@nd.edu
md: Ben Vincent
ext: 574-631-4068
Broadcasts to a 35mi area.

Valparaiso U
WVUR 95.1 FM
32 Schnabel Hall
1809 Campus Dr.
Valparaiso, IN 46383
watts: 36
main: 219-464-5383
request: 219-464-6673
f: 219-464-6742
e: thesource95.1@valpo.edu
www.valpo.edu/wvur
webcast: Yes
genres: Indie, Rock
reports to: CMJ
pd: Adam Amin
e: adam.amin@valpo.edu
md: Patrick Lay
e: patrick.lay@valpo.edu
Hosts specialty shows in a variety of genres. Also sponsors annual "Sourcestock."

Iowa

Cornell College
KRNL 89.7 FM
600 First Ave. SW
Mt. Vernon, IA 52314
watts: 45
main: 319-895-4431
request: 319-895-5765
e: krnl@cornellcollege.edu
http://orgs.cornellcollege.edu/krnl
webcast: Yes
genres: Alt., Electronic, RPM, Hip-Hop, Rock
reports to: CMJ
pd: Ashley Murray
e: a-murray@cornellcollege.edu
md: Chris Scholtens/Amanda Abbott
e: c-scholtens@cornellcollege.edu
Contact Mike Mulholland: m-mulholland@cornellcollege.edu for station-sponsored concerts.

Iowa State U
KURE 88.5 FM
1199 Friley Hall
Ames, IA 50012
watts: 250
main: 515-294-4332
request: 515-294-9292
e: kure@kure885.org
www.kure885.org
webcast: Yes
genres: Alt., Rock, Jazz, Hip-Hop
reports to: CMJ
pd: Alden Turner
e: programming@kure885.org
md: Justin Milligan
e: music@kure885.org
Sponsors campus concerts & "Battle of the Bands."

Morningside College
KMSC 92.9 FM
1501 Morningside Ave.
Sioux City, IA 51106
watts: 10
main: 712-274-5241
request: 712-274-5665
e: kmsc@morningside.edu
http://webs.morningside.edu/kmsc
webcast: Yes
genres: College Alt.
reports to: CMJ
pd: Matt Wilmes
e: kmscmanager@morningside.edu
md: Andy Cunningham
e: kmscmusic@morningside.edu
Evening & wknd specialty shows & sponsors some events.

St. Ambrose U
KALA 88.5/105.5 FM
518 W Locust St.
Davenport, IA 52803
watts: 10,000
main: 563-333-6219
request: 563-333-6216
f: 563-333-6218
e: kala@sau.edu
www.sau.edu/kala
genres: Blues, Jazz, Gospel, Urban, Rock, World
reports to: CMJ, Living Blues
pd: David Baker
e: bakerdavidw@sau.edu
Sponsors Local Gospel & Blues festivals. Some in-studio opps.

U of Iowa
KRUI 89.7 FM
379 Iowa Memorial Union
Iowa City, IA 52242
watts: 100
main: 319-335-9525
request: 319-335-8970
f: 319-335-9526
e: krui@uiowa.edu
www.kruiradio.org
webcast: Yes
genres: All Styles
reports to: CMJ
pd: Erica Barnes
md: Josh Hoffman
ext: 319-335-7215
Specializes in Indie & local music & sponsors events. Prefers CD & vinyl submissions.

Wartburg College
KWAR 89.1 FM
100 Wartburg Blvd.
Waverly, IA 50677
watts: 40
main: 319-352-8209
request: 319-352-8306
f: 319-352-8610
e: yoursound.kwar@gmail.com
www.kwar.org
webcast: Yes
genres: Alt.
reports to: CMJ
pd: Andrew Nostvick
md: Vince Abrahamson
Students spin during the day & community members present specialty shows in the evenings.

Kansas

Bethel College
KBCU 88.1 FM
300 E 27th St.
North Newton, KS 67117
watts: 150
main: 316-284-5273
request: 316-284-5228
f: 316-284-5286
e: kbcu@bethelks.edu
www.bethelks.edu/kbcu
webcast: Yes
genres: Freeform
pd: Tim Buller
e: tbuller@bethelks.edu
Sponsors events.

Kansas State U
KSDB 91.9 FM
105 Kedzie Hall

Manhattan, KS 66506
watts: 1400
main: 785-532-2769
request: 785-532-0919
f: 785-532-5484
e: radio@k-state.edu
www.wildcat919.com
webcast: Yes
genres: Alt., Rock, Urban, Gospel, Bluegrass, Jam, Blues
reports to: CMJ, Hits
pd: Chuck Armstrong
md: Scott Smith
ext: 785-532-2330
e: scsm@k-state.edu
Sponsors events. Write genre on outside of promos.

Kentucky

U of Kentucky
WRFL 88.1 FM
PO Box 777, University Stn.
Lexington, KY 40506
watts: 250
main: 859-257-4636
request: 859-257-9735
f: 859-323-1039
e: gm@wrfl881.org
www.wrfl.fm
webcast: Yes
genres: Indie, Metal, Reggae, Hip-Hop, World, Soul
reports to: CMJ, Dusted
pd: Carley Bryant
e: programming@wrfl881.org
md: Ainsley Waggoner
ext: 859-257-1557
e: music@wrfl881.org
Student-run station w/ some Local volunteer DJs boasts 24hr/day programming w/ no automation. Hosts on-air opps. & sponsors "FreeKY Fest."

Western Kentucky U
WWHR 91.7 FM
1906 College Heights Blvd.
Bowling Green, KY 42101
watts: 3000
main: 270-745-5439
request: 270-745-5350
e: info@revolution.fm
www.revolution.fm
webcast: Yes
genres: Prog, Soul, Punk, Goth, Club, Metal, Hip-Hop
reports to: CMJ
pd: Justin Pitt
e: pd@revolution.fm
md: Laura Haggard
e: music@revolution.fm
Sponsors 1 concert/semester.

Louisiana

Louisiana State U
KLSU 91.1 FM
B39 Hodges Hall, LSU
Baton Rouge, LA 70803
watts: 5000
main: 225-578-8688
request: 225-578-5578
f: 225-578-0579
e: klsufm@yahoo.com
http://appl003.lsu.edu/slas/osm/klsu.nsf/index
webcast: Yes
genres: Alt., Hip-Hop, Metal, Jazz, Rock
reports to: CMJ
pd: Jen Pearce
e: program.director@klsu.fm
md: Randy Faucheux
ext: 225-578-4620
e: music.director@klsu.fm
Broadcast covers 60mi. Sponsors some campus gigs.

Louisiana Tech. U
KLPI 89.1 FM
100 Wysteria St.
Ruston, LA 71272
watts: 250
main: 318-257-4851
request: 318-257-3689
http://klpi.latech.edu/
webcast: Yes
genres: Rock, Metal, Urban, World, Electronic
reports to: CMJ
md: Gerard Rau
ext: 318-257-4852
e: music@891klpi.org
Sponsors 2-3 on-campus concerts/year. Send promos to: PO Box 8638, Ruston, LA, 71272.

Nicholls State U
KNSU 91.5 FM
PO Box 2664, Nicholls State U
Thibodaux, LA 70310
watts: 250
main: 985-448-4447
request: 985-448-5678
e: knsu@its.nicholls.edu; knsustaff@gmail.com
www.nicholls.edu
webcast: Yes
genres: Alt., Metal, Punk
reports to: CMJ
pd: Josh Crosby
e: crosj615@nicholls.edu
md: Chris Poole
Sponsors events.

Northwestern State U
KNWD 91.7 FM
NSU Box 3038
Natchitoches, LA 71497
watts: 255
main: 318-357-4523
request: 318-357-5693
f: 318-357-4398
www.nsula.edu/thedemon
genres: Alt., Hip-Hop, Rock, Techno, Jazz, Blues, Metal
reports to: CMJ
pd: Kevin Clark
e: kclarkst01@student.nsula.edu
Sponsors events.

Southeastern Louisiana U
KSLU 90.9 FM
D Vickers, Rm. 112, SLU 10783
Hammond, LA 70402
watts: 3000
main: 985-549-2330
request: 985-549-5758
f: 985-549-3960
e: kslu@selu.edu
www.kslu.org
webcast: Yes
genres: AAA, College Rock, Blues, Jazz, World
reports to: CMJ, FMQB
pd: Terry Havel
e: thavel@selu.edu
Broadcast blankets Baton Rouge & New Orleans.

U of Louisiana/Monroe
KXUL 91.1 FM
130 Stubbs Hall
Monroe, LA 71209
watts: 8500
main: 318-342-5986
request: 318-342-5985
e: tunes@kxul.com
www.kxul.com
webcast: Yes
genres: Alt., Rock
reports to: CMJ
pd: Joel Willer
ext: 318-342-1426
md: Eric Hosak
ext: 318-342-5662
Broadcasts thru northeastern LA & southern AR.

U of Southwestern Louisiana/Lafayette
KRVS 88.7 FM
Rm. 126, Burke Hall
Hebrard Blvd.
Lafayette, LA 70503
watts: 100,000
main: 337-482-5787
f: 337-482-6101
e: krvs@louisiana.edu
www.krvs.org
webcast: Yes
genres: Cajun, Zydeco, Blues, Jazz
reports to: CMJ
pd: Dave Spizale
e: dspizale@krvs.org
md: Cecil Doyle
ext: 337-482-6991
e: doylececil@hotmail.com
Send promos to: PO Box 42171, Lafayette, LA 70504.

Maine

Bowdoin College
WBOR 91.1 FM
Smith Union
Brunswick, ME 04011
watts: 300
main: 207-725-3210
request: 207-725-3250
e: wbor@bowdoin.edu
www.wbor.org
webcast: Yes
genres: Indie Rock, Hip-Hop, Electronic, Folk, Jazz
reports to: CMJ
pd: Andrew Sudano
ext: 631 974-8283
e: asudano@bowdoin.edu
md: Audrey Chee
e: achee@bowdoin.edu
Books 3-4 campus gigs/yr; contact Micah McKay: mmckay@bowdoin.edu.

Colby College
WMHB 89.7 FM
4000 Mayflower Hill Dr.
Waterville, ME 04901
watts: 110
main: 207-859-5454
request: 207-859-5450
e: info@wmhb.org
www.wmhb.org
webcast: Yes
genres: Rock, Punk, Ska, Blues, Folk, World, Jazz, Metal, Techno, Gospel, Urban
reports to: CMJ, Crossroads, Album Network, Hits
ext: 207-859-5451
md: Fiona Sheridan McIver
e: radio200@wmhb.org
Follow up via specific genre directors: Alt., AAA, Indie & Rock (radio200@wmhb.org); Americana, Bluegrass, Country, Folk, Gospel (americana@wmhb.org); Blues (blues@wmhb.org); Hip-Hop (hiphop@wmhb.org); Jazz (jazz@wmhb.org); Loud Rock, Punk (loudrock@wmhb.org

U of Maine/Farmington
WUMF 101.1 FM
111 South St.
Farmington, ME 04938
watts: 13.8
main: 207-778-7352
request: 207-778-7353
e: onehundredpointone@yahoo.com
http://wumf.umf.maine.edu
webcast: Yes
genres: Alt., Hip-Hop, Metal, Ska, World, Jazz
reports to: CMJ
pd: Bill Moss
md: Shawn Rogers
Sponsors open mics at campus coffeehouse & 2 large concerts/semester.

U of Maine/Orono
WMEB 91.9 FM
5748 Memorial Union
Orono, ME 04469
watts: 640
m
req
e: w
un
www.
webca
genres:
Jazz, Hip-
reports to
pd: James M
e: james.mac
umit.maine
md: Tim Grucz
ext: 207-581-43
e: timothy.grucza
umit.maine.edu
jmgrant11@gmai
For station-sponsored contact: Tyler Brown: william.t.brown@umit.maine.edu.

Maryland

Johns Hopkins U
WJHU Web only
3400 N Charles St.
c/o Martin Ctr.
Baltimore, MD 21218
main: 410-516-3884
request: 410-516-3835
f: 410-516-4495
e: wjhu@jhu.edu
www.wjhuradio.com
webcast: Yes
genres: Rock, Classical, Dance, Folk, Jazz, Rap
reports to: CMJ
pd: Sam Messing
e: samuel.messing+wjhu@gmail.com
md: Mike Normyle
e: mnormyle@jhu.edu
Airs some specialty shows. Contact Nick Evoy: evoy@jhu.edu for campus gigs.

Salisbury U
WXSU 96.3 FM
PO Box 3151
Salisbury, MD 21801
watts: 100
main: 410-543-6195
request: 410-548-4760
e: wxsu963fm@gmail.com
http://orgs.salisbury.edu/wxsu
webcast: Yes
genres: All Styles
reports to: CMJ
pd: Taneisha McCannon
e: lilneisha@aol.com
md: Kiya Amajioyi
Books "Happy Birthday WXSU Concert" along w/ smaller monthly shows.

U of Maryland/Baltimore County
WMBC 560 AM
UC Rm. 101, UMBC

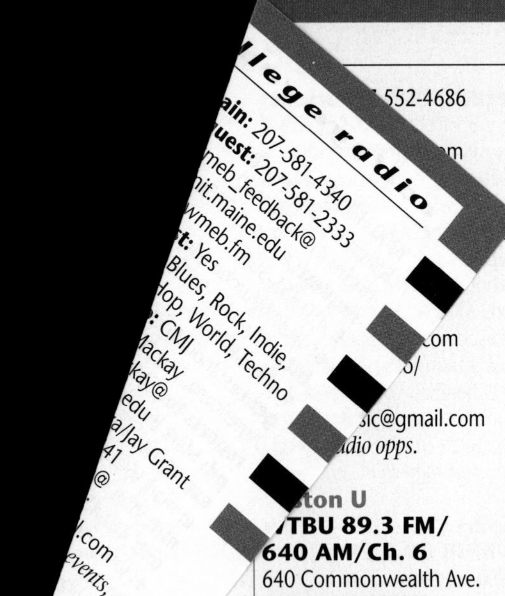

...ll
...all
...MD 20742
...1-314-7868
...st: 301-314-8800
...1-314-7879
...scotty@wmucradio.com
www.wmucradio.com
webcast: Yes
genres: Alt., Hip-Hop, Rock, Jazz, World, Punk
reports to: CMJ, Hits
pd: Alexandra Douglas-Barrera
e: adb@wmucradio.com
md: Ebbie Bonczek
e: musicdirector@wmucradio.com
Freeform station, heard in DC & MD. Contact Chris Berry: thirdrail@wmucradio.com for campus gigs.

Massachusetts

Amherst College
WAMH 89.3 FM
AC #1907, Campus Ctr.
Amherst, MA 01002
watts: 150
main: 413-542-2224
request: 413-542-2288
e: wamh@amherst.edu
www.amherst.edu/~wamh
webcast: Yes
genres: Indie, Rock, Jazz, Hip-Hop, Folk, World, Classical
reports to: CMJ, Radio 200, Radio 200 Adds
md: Claire Kiechel
Live show every Sun w/ on-air performances; recordings avail.

Boston College
WZBC 90.3 FM
McElroy Commons, Rm. 107
Chestnut Hill, MA 02467
watts: 1000
main: 617-552-3511
...552-4686
...m
...,
...com
.../
...sic@gmail.com
...adio opps.

...ston U
...TBU 89.3 FM/ 640 AM/Ch. 6
640 Commonwealth Ave.
Boston, MA 02215
main: 617-353-6401
request: 617-353-6400
f: 617-353-6403
www.wtburadio.org
webcast: Yes
genres: Indie, Hip-Hop, Electronic, Blues, Folk, Pop, Rock, Metal
reports to: CMJ
pd: John Schwartz
e: programming@wtburadio.org
md: Keith Simpson/Jen Brown
e: music@wtburadio.org
Sponsors monthly campus gigs.

Brandeis U
WBRS 100.1 FM
415 South St.
Waltham, MA 02454
watts: 25
main: 781-736-5277
e: gm@wbrs.org
www.wbrs.org
webcast: Yes
genres: Rock, Folk, Jazz, World, Electronic, Hip-Hop, Country
reports to: CMJ
pd: Sarah Costrell
ext: 781-736-4754
e: pd@wbrs.org
md: Jeremy Karp/Max Price
ext: 781-736-4785
e: music@wbrs.org
On-air performances; mark envelope w/ music genre.

College of the Holy Cross
WCHC 88.1 FM
1 College St., Box G
Worcester, MA 01610
watts: 100
main: 508-793-2475
request: 508-793-2474
e: wchc@holycross.edu
http://college.holycross.edu/wchc
webcast: Yes
genres: Rock, Indie, Rap, Metal, Jazz, World
reports to: CMJ
pd: Robert Valenti
e: rlvale11@holycross.edu
md: Caitlin Rhoades/Tom Steinert
e: carhoa10@holycross.edu; tmstei09@holycross.edu
New music in rotation.

Emerson College
WERS 88.9 FM
120 Boylston St.
Boston, MA 02116
watts: 4000
main: 617-824-8891
request: 617-482-8890
e: info@wers.org
www.wers.org
webcast: Yes
genres: Folk, Jazz, Urban, World, Electronic, Children's
reports to: CMJ, FMQB
pd: Sam Citron
ext: 617-824-8084
e: pd@wers.org
md: John Parsons
e: music@wers.org
Many specialty shows & sponsors campus events.

Fitchburg State College
WXPL 91.3 FM
160 Pearl St.
Fitchburg, MA 01420
watts: 110
main: 978-665-3692
request: 978-665-4848
f: 978-665-3694
e: wxpl@fsc.edu
www.myspace.com/wxpl
genres: Alt., Punk, Metal, Hip-Hop, Acoustic
reports to: CMJ
pd: Ben Hassey
e: bhassey@student.fsc.edu
md: Lee Martin
e: lmarti25@student.fsc.edu
Sponsors events.

Harvard U
WHRB 95.3 FM
389 Harvard St.
Cambridge, MA 02138
watts: 3000
main: 617-495-4818
request: 617-495-9472
f: 617-384-7887
e: mail@whrb.org
www.whrb.org
webcast: Yes
genres: Classical, Jazz, Rock, Hip-Hop, Blues
reports to: CMJ
pd: Alasdair Wilkins
e: pd@whrb.org
Sponsors some campus gigs.

Massachusetts Institute of Tech.
WMBR 88.1 FM
3 Ames St.
Cambridge, MA 02142
watts: 720
main: 617-253-4000
request: 617-253-8810
f: 617-232-1384
e: station-manager@wmbr.org
www.wmbr.org
webcast: Yes
genres: Rock, Electronic, Jazz, World, Alt.
reports to: CMJ
pd: Jack Murphy
e: program-director@wmbr.org
md: Patrick Bryant
ext: 617-253-7777
e: music-director@wmbr.org

Mount Holyoke
WMHC 91.5 FM
Blanchard Student Ctr.
South Hadley, MA 01075
watts: 100
main: 413-538-2019
request: 413-538-2044
e: general.manager@wmhcradio.org
www.wmhcradio.org
webcast: Yes
genres: Rock, World, Urban, Folk, Electronic, Americana, Jazz
reports to: CMJ
pd: Alex Krensky
e: program.director@wmhcradio.org
md: Sarah Schaefer/Julie Phreaner
e: music.directors@wmhcradio.org
Sponsors annual "Radio Week" w/ live bands.

Northeastern U
WRBB 104.9 FM
360 Huntington Ave., #174
Curry Student Ctr.
Boston, MA 02115
watts: 10
main: 617-373-4338
request: 617-373-2658
f: 617-373-5095
e: manager@wrbbradio.org
www.wrbbradio.org
webcast: Yes
genres: Alt., Rock, Hip-Hop, Jazz, World
reports to: CMJ
pd: Marybeth Miller
ext: 617-373-8400
e: program@wrbbradio.org
md: Sam Coren
ext: 617-373-4339
e: music@wrbbradio.org
New PD every 6 mos.

Smith College
WOZQ 91.9 FM
100 Elm St., Campus Ctr. 106
Northampton, MA 01063
watts: 130
main: 413-585-4956
request: 413-585-4977
f: 413-585-2075
e: wozq@email.smith.edu
www.smith.edu/wozq
webcast: Yes
genres: Alt., Urban, Rock, Folk, Pop, Punk, Electro, Jazz, Ska, Country, World, Oldies
reports to: CMJ
pd: Dana Feldesman
e: dfeldesm@email.smith.edu
md: Carolyn Cunha
ext: 413-585-6755; 413-585-7730
e: ccunha@email.smith.edu
Publishes a music mag w/ CD & live reviews; contact Kayden Moore, kmoore3@email.smith.edu. Contact Dana for gigs on campus.

Tufts U
WMFO 91.5 FM
474 Boston Ave., Curtis Hall
Medford, MA 02155
watts: 125
main: 617-625-0800
request: 617-627-3800
e: wmfo@wmfo.org
www.wmfo.org
webcast: Yes
genres: Rock, Electronic, Jazz, Experimental, Metal, Urban, Gospel, World, Folk, Blues
reports to: CMJ
pd: Mose Berkowitz
e: pd@wmfo.org
md: Alex Gomez
ext: 617-625-0800 x2
e: md@wmfo.org
Promos to: PO Box 65, Medford, MA 02155. Local acts email: localmusic@wmfo.org.

U of Mass/Amherst
WMUA 91.1 FM
105 Campus Ctr.
Amherst, MA 01003
watts: 450
main: 413-545-2876
request: 413-545-3691
f: 413-545-0682
e: claudio@wmua.org
www.wmua.org
webcast: Yes
genres: Rock, Jazz, World, Blues, Hip-Hop
reports to: CMJ
pd: Corey Charron
ext: 413-545-2876 x9
e: programmer@wmua.org
md: Alex Hornbeck
ext: 413-545-2876 x1
e: music@wmua.org
Many specialty shows in diverse genres & sponsors gigs in this packed college town.

U of Mass/Dartmouth
WUMD 89.3 FM
285 Old Westport Rd.

North Dartmouth, MA 02747
watts: 9600
main: 508-999-8149
request: 508-999-8150
e: wumd@umassd.edu
www.893wumd.org
webcast: Yes
genres: Alt., Jazz, Reggae, Folk, Blues
reports to: CMJ
pd: Geary Kaczorowski
ext: 508-999-8149 x8
e: mesh5@mesh5.com
Sponsors events.

U of Mass/Lowell
WUML 91.5 FM
1 University Ave.
Lowell, MA 01854
watts: 1400
main: 978-934-4975
request: 978-934-4969
www.wuml.org
genres: Rock, Jazz, Electronic, Urban, World, Folk, Blues, Metal, Reggae, Punk, Hardcore
reports to: CMJ, Living Blues, Crossroads
pd: Zach Trethaway
e: pd@wuml.org
md: Amy Sifferlen
ext: 978-934-4970
e: md@wuml.org
Contact fallout@gatehouseanchor.com for weekly live performances. Sponsors some school concerts.

Williams College
WCFM 91.9 FM
Baxter Hall
Williamstown, MA 01267
watts: 440
main: 413-597-3265
request: 413-597-2197
e: wcfmbd@gmail.com
http://wcfm.williams.edu
webcast: Yes
genres: Hip-Hop, Jazz, Blues, Rock
reports to: CMJ
pd: Nick Colella
e: 09nsc@williams.edu
md: Jessica Chung
ext: 413-597-2373
e: wcfmbd@wso.williams.edu
Sponsors on-campus concerts.

Michigan

Andover High School
WBFH 88.1 FM
4200 Andover Rd.
Bloomfield Hills, MI 48302
watts: 360
main: 248-341-5690
request: 248-341-9234
f: 248-341-5679
e: wbfh@bloomfield.org
www.wbfh.fm
webcast: Yes
genres: Alt., Hip-Hop, Rock, Jazz, Eclectic
reports to: CMJ
pd: Ron Witteboles
e: rwitteboles@bloomfield.org
md: Billy Whiting
e: wbfhmusic@yahoo.com
Broadcasts to 40mi area.

Lake Superior State U
WLSO 90.1 FM
680 W Easterday Ave.
Sault Ste. Marie, MI 49783
watts: 100
main: 906-635-7504; 906-635-2107
request: 906-635-2863
f: 906-635-2111
http://wlso.lssu.edu
genres: Alt., Urban, Metal, CCM, Electronic, Country, Ska, Punk, Jazz
reports to: CMJ
pd: Lam Nguyen
e: altdir@lssu.edu
md: Mitchell Potratz
e: oneeyedmitch@yahoo.com
Books some area gigs.

Michigan State U
WDBM 88.9 FM
G-4 Holden Hall
East Lansing, MI 48825
watts: 2000
main: 517-353-4414
request: 517-355-4237
f: 517-355-6552
e: wdbm89fm@msu.edu
www.impact89fm.org
webcast: Yes
genres: Alt., AAA, Urban, Alt. Country, Metal
reports to: CMJ
pd: Shannon Awrylo
e: pd@impact89fm.org
md: Branden Jaksim
e: md@impact89fm.org
Sponsors events on campus.

Paul Cousino H.S.
WPHS 89.1 FM
30333 Hoover Rd.
Warren, MI 48093
watts: 100
main: 586-698-4501
request: 586-751-3689
f: 586-751-3755
e: wphs@wphs.com
www.wphs.com
genres: Electronic, World, Top 40, Punk, Metal
reports to: CMJ
pd: Carlita Kranz
md: Joelle Harder
e: joelle.wphs@gmail.com
Sponsors events.

U of Michigan/ Ann Arbor
WCBN 88.3 FM
530 Student Activities Bldg.
Ann Arbor, MI 48109
watts: 200
main: 734-763-3535
request: 734-763-3500
f: 734-647-4127
e: fm@wcbn.org
www.wcbn.org
webcast: Yes
genres: All Styles
reports to: CMJ
pd: Kristen Sumrall
e: programming@wcbn.org
md: Brad Detjen/Bill Corrigan
ext: 734-763-3501
e: music@wcbn.org
Student-run/community freeform station airs on campus & to community.

U of Michigan/ Dearborn
WUMD Web & cable only
4901 Evergreen Rd.
Dearborn, MI 48128
main: 313-593-5439
request: 313-593-5515
f: 313-593-0943
e: wumdgm@gmail.com
www.wumd.org
webcast: Yes
genres: Punk, Rock, Alt., Metal, Techno, Hip-Hop
reports to: CMJ
pd: Mike Morland
ext: 313-593-5167
e: wumdprogamdirector@gmail.com
md: Chelsey Knapp
e: wumd_music_director@hotmail.com
Features a variety of specialty shows & sponsors many events.

Western Michigan U
WIDR 89.1 FM
1501 Faunce Student Services Bldg.
Kalamazoo, MI 49008
watts: 100
main: 269-387-6301
request: 269-387-6303
f: 269-387-2839
www.widr.org
webcast: Yes
genres: Freeform
reports to: CMJ
pd: Mallory Dowd
e: widr.gm@gmail.com
md: Jessica Kizer
ext: 269-387-6306
e: widr.music@gmail.com
Sponsors some live events & actively supports area scene.

Minnesota

Carleton College
KRLX 88.1 FM
300 N College St.
Northfield, MN 55057
watts: 100
main: 507-222-4102
request: 507-646-4127
www.krlx.org
webcast: Yes
genres: All Styles
reports to: CMJ
pd: Ben Blink
e: programming@krlx.org
md: Michael Mintz/ Nicole Feldman
e: music@krlx.org
Freeform station has several indie specialty shows.

Macalester College
WMCN 91.7 FM
1600 Grand Ave.
St. Paul, MN 55105
watts: 10
main: 651-696-6082
request: 651-696-6312
f: 651-696-6685
e: wmcn@macalester.edu
www.macalester.edu/wmcn
webcast: Yes
genres: Rock, World, Hip-Hop, Electronic, Roots, Jazz, Classical
reports to: CMJ
pd: Aaron Mendelson
ext: 651-696-7364
e: amendelson@macalester.edu
md: Abby Tofte
e: atofte@macalester.edu
Sponsors concerts & benefits. Genre MDs listed on site.

St. Cloud State U
KVSC 88.1 FM
SCSU, 27 Stewart Hall
720 4th Ave. S
St. Cloud, MN 56301
watts: 16,500
main: 320-308-3126
request: 320-308-5872
e: info@kvsc.org
www.kvsc.org
webcast: Yes
genres: Alt., Rock, Techno, Jazz, Hip-Hop, Blues, Folk, World, Bluegrass, Fusion, R&B, Native American
reports to: CMJ
pd: Michael Jamnick
e: programming@kvsc.org
md: Max Brown
e: brma0605@stcloudstate.edu

U of Minnesota/ Minneapolis
KUOM 770 AM/ 106.5/100.7 FM
610 Rarig Ctr., 330 21st Ave. S
Minneapolis, MN 55455
watts: 5000/8
main: 612-625-3500
request: 612-626-4770
f: 612-625-2112
http://radiok.cce.umn.edu
webcast: Yes
gen[...]
Elect[...]
Punk,[...]
repor[...]
pd: Mat[...]
ext: 612-[...]
e: progra[...]
md: Dana [...]
ext: 612-62[...]
e: music@rad[...]
Broadcast cover[...]
Sponsors over 10[...]

U of Minneso[...]
KUMM 89.7 F[...]
600 E 4th St.
Morris, MN 56267
watts: 500
main: 320-589-6076
request: 320-589-6355
e: kumm@kumm.org
www.kumm.org
webcast: Yes
genres: Alt., Hip-Hop
reports to: CMJ
pd: KT Engdahl
ext: 320-589-6076 x1
e: program@kumm.org
md: Martin Powers
e: music@kumm.org
Sponsors 2-3 events/yr.

Winona State U
KQAL 89.5 FM
PO Box 5838
Winona, MN 55987
watts: 1800
main: 507-453-2222
f: 507-457-5226
e: mmartin@winona.edu
www.kqal.org
webcast: Yes
genres: Alt., Jazz, World, Electronic
reports to: CMJ
pd: Lindsey Verbeten
e: lkverbert0726@winona.edu
md: Alyssa Frankin
ext: 507-457-5229
e: hafrankl5681@winona.edu

Mississippi

Alcorn State U
WPRL 91.7 FM
1000 ASU Dr., PO Box 269
Alcorn State, MS 39096
watts: 3000
main: 601-877-6290
request: 601-877-6595
f: 601-877-2360
e: mnorman@alcorn.edu
www.alcorn.edu
genres: R&B, Jazz, Gospel, Blues
reports to: CMJ
pd: Charles Edmond
NPR outlet airs specialty shows.

Mississippi State U
WMSV 91.1 FM
PO Box 6210, Student Media Ctr.

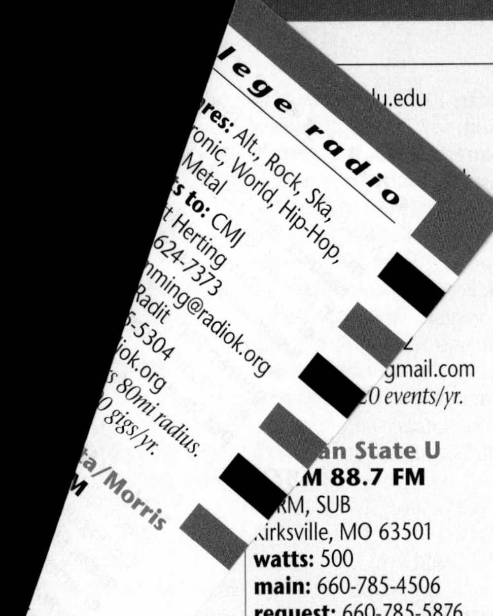

, Alt.,
, World

261
...s wide variety of
...ng and many wknd
shows.

...st College
WURC 88.1 FM
150 Rust Ave.
Holly Springs, MS 38635
watts: 3000
main: 662-252-5881
f: 662-252-8869
e: wfiddis@rustcollege.edu
www.wurc.org
webcast: Yes
genres: Jazz, Gospel, Blues, Reggae, R&B, Talk, News
pd: Pat Boga
e: pboga@hotmail.com
md: Sharron Goodman-Hill
e: sgoodman-hill@rustcollege.edu
NPR affiliate w/ student-involvement & many specialty shows broadcasts 18hrs/day.

Missouri

Lindenwood U
KCLC 89.1 FM
209 S Kings Hwy.
St. Charles, MO 63301
watts: 35,000
main: 636-949-4891
e: fm891@lindenwood.edu
www.891thewood.com
genres: AAA
reports to: CMJ
pd: Richard Reighard

St. Louis U
KSLU Web & cable only
20 N Grand Blvd.
St. Louis, MO 63108
main: 314-977-1578
request: 314-977-1581
f: 314-977-1579
e: kslu@slu.edu

...u.edu

...2
...gmail.com
...0 events/yr.

...an State U
...M 88.7 FM
...RM, SUB
Kirksville, MO 63501
watts: 500
main: 660-785-4506
request: 660-785-5876
f: 660-785-7261
e: ktrm.theedge@gmail.com
http://ktrm.truman.edu
webcast: Yes
genres: Alt., Techno, Emo, Hip-Hop, Country, Folk, World, Blues, Jazz, Punk, Ska, Metal
reports to: CMJ
pd: Jessica Wright
md: Ben Sells
e: ktrm_music@hotmail.com

U of Missouri/Rolla
KMNR 89.7 FM
113 E UCW, 1870 Miner Cir.
Rolla, MO 65409
watts: 450
main: 573-341-4272
e: kmnr-m@lists.mst.edu
www.kmnr.org
genres: All Styles
reports to: CMJ, Hits
pd: Danni Corrier
md: Josh Bohde
ext: 573-341-4273
e: music@kmnr.org
Sponsors Halloween concert, spring concert & gigs every 2/mos.

Washington U/St. Louis
KWUR 90.3 FM
Campus Box 1205,
1 Brookings Dr.
St. Louis, MO 63130
watts: 100
main: 314-935-5952
request: 314-935-5987
f: 314-935-8833
e: gm@kwur.com
www.kwur.com
webcast: Yes
genres: All Styles
reports to: CMJ, Urban Network
pd: Hunter Richards
e: station@kwur.com
md: Daniel Burton/Kenny Hofmeister
ext: 314-935-5952 x1
e: music1@kwur.com; music2@kwur.com

Sponsors week long Spring music showcase & 1-2 Fall shows. New release show plays 3 new releases/hr.

Montana

Montana State U/Bozeman
KGLT 91.9 FM
330 Strand Union Bldg.
Bozeman, MT 59717
watts: 11,000
main: 406-994-6484
request: 406-994-3001 x1
e: wwwkglt@montana.edu
www.kglt.net
genres: Alt., Americana, Rock, Urban, Jazz
reports to: CMJ, Crossroads, Living Blues
pd: Philip Charles
md: Jim Kehoe
ext: 406-994-6483
e: kgltmus@montana.edu
Send promos: MSU Box 174240, Bozeman, MT 59717.

Montana Tech.
KMSM 107.1 FM
1300 W Park St.
Butte, MT 59701
watts: 440
main: 406-496-4601
request: 406-496-1071
f: 406-496-4389
www.mtech.edu
genres: Alt., Rock, Hip-Hop, R&B, Techno
reports to: CMJ
Contact via MySpace.

U of Montana
KBGA 89.9 FM
University Ctr., Rm. 208
Missoula, MT 59812
watts: 1000
main: 406-243-6758
request: 406-243-6226
f: 406-243-6427
e: kbgaradio@kbga.org
www.kbga.org
genres: Alt., Techno, Bluegrass, Punk, Reggae, Jazz, Hip-Hop, World, Classical
reports to: CMJ, Dusted, Living Blues
pd: Ashley Barber
ext: 406-243-6427
e: programming@kbga.org
md: Travis Morss/Lina Miller
ext: 406-243-5715
e: md@kbga.org
Sponsors some on-campus concerts/fund raisers.

Nebraska

Doane College
KDNE 91.9 FM
1014 Boswell Ave.
Crete, NE 68333
watts: 100
main: 402-826-8677
request: 402-826-8611
f: 402-826-8634
e: kdne@doane.edu
http://webcast.doane.edu
webcast: Yes
genres: Punk, Indie Rock
reports to: CMJ
pd: Corey Rotschafer
md: Jason Sitzman

Hastings College
KFKX 90.1 FM
710N Turner Ave., Gray Ctr.
Hastings, NE 68901
watts: 1000
main: 402-461-7342
f: 402-461-7442
e: kfkx@hastings.edu
www.hastings.edu
genres: Alt., Blues, Hip-Hop
reports to: CMJ
pd: Logan Dobbs
md: James Hanseling
Books mainly Local bands.

U of Nebraska/Lincoln
KRNU 90.3 FM
147 Andersen Hall
PO Box 880466
Lincoln, NE 68588
watts: 100
main: 402-472-6856
request: 402-472-5768
f: 402-472-8403
e: krnu@unl.edu
http://krnu.unl.edu
webcast: Yes
genres: Alt., Urban, Rock, Electronic, Jazz, Blues, Alt. Country, Christian Rock
reports to: CMJ
pd: Rick Alloway
ext: 402-472-8277
e: krnu-music@unl.edu
Hosts on-air performances.

Nevada

U of Nevada/Reno
KUNR 88.7 FM
1664 N Virgina
Mail Stop 0294
Reno, NV 89557
main: 775-327-5867
request: 775-784-1867
f: 775-327-5386
e: feedback@kunr.org
www.kunr.org
webcast: Yes
genres: News, Classical, Jazz, Reggae, Blues, Folk, World
pd: David Stipech
e: dstipech@kunr.org
md: Terry Joy
ext: 775-682-6053
e: tjoy@kunr.org
Plays lots of Indies on "Notes From the Underground."

Sponsors movie promotions, special events & a Jazz brunch.

U of Nevada/Reno
NVWR 1700 AM
Joe Crowley Student Union,
Mail Stop 058
Reno, NV 89557
main: 775-784-7073
request: 775-784-7074
f: 775-329-0653
e: wolfpackradio@asun.unr.edu
www.wolfpackradio.org
webcast: Yes
genres: Alt., Punk, Hip-Hop, Electronic, Folk, Jazz
reports to: CMJ, Top 200, CMJ Loud Rock
pd: Steve Owens
e: programs@wolfpackradio.org
md: Troy Micheau
e: radiowolfpack@gmail.com
Plays Indie & Local releases, posts reviews of some albums received & Local concerts. Sponsors shows w/ small touring acts & Locals.

New Hampshire

Colby Sawyer College
WSCS 90.9 FM
541 Main St.
New London, NH 03257
watts: 250
main: 603-526-3493
request: 603-526-3494
e: wscs@colby-sawyer.edu
www.colby-sawyer.edu/wscs
webcast: Yes
genres: Rock, Jazz, Hip-Hop, Alt., Country, World
reports to: CMJ
md: Sean Ahern
ext: 603-526-3443

Dartmouth College
WDCR 1340 AM
Robinson Hall, 3rd Fl.
Hanover, NH 03755
watts: 1000
main: 603-646-3313
e: pavel.sotskov@dartmouth.edu
www.webdcr.com
genres: Alt., Jazz, Hip-Hop, World, Electronic, Latin, Blues, Metal
reports to: CMJ
pd: Zachary Mason
e: zachary.mason@webdcr.com
md: Lauren Dowling
e: lauren.dowling@dartmouth.edu
Send promos: 6176 Robinson Hall, Hanover, NH 03755.

Keene State College
WKNH 91.3 FM
229 Main St.

Keene, NH 03435
watts: 275
main: 603-358-2421
request: 603-358-8863
e: gm@wknh.org
www.wknh.org
genres: Alt., Rock, Americana, Hip-Hop
reports to: CMJ
pd: Aimee Athnos
e: program@wknh.org
md: Sam Sudhalter
ext: 603-358-2420
e: music@wknh.org

Southern New Hampshire U
SNHU 1620 AM/Ch. 22
2500 N River Rd.
Manchester, NH 03106
main: 603-629-4695
f: 603-629-4634
e: radiosnhu@snhu.edu
http://radio.snhu.edu
webcast: Yes
genres: Rock, Hip-Hop, Country, Pop, Jazz, Classic Rock, R&B, Funk
reports to: CMJ
pd: Nick Tasso
e: nicholas.tasso@snhu.edu
md: Martha Johnson
e: martha.johnson@snhu.edu
Sponsors events; contact daniel.smith1@snhu.edu.

U of New Hampshire
WUNH 91.3 FM
Memorial Union Bldg.
Durham, NH 03824
watts: 6000
main: 603-862-2541
request: 603-862-2222
f: 603-862-2543
e: gm@wunh.org
www.wunh.org
webcast: Yes
genres: Hip-Hop, Folk, Alt., Jazz, Electronic
reports to: CMJ
pd: Mallory Adamcyk
e: program@wunh.org
md: Brandon MacNeil
ext: 603-862-2087
e: music@wunh.org
Strives to bring Indie music to a wider audience.

New Jersey

Burlington County College
WBZC 88.9/95.1/100.7 FM
601 Pemberton Browns Mill Rd.
Pemberton, NJ 08068
watts: 10,000/470
main: 609-894-9311
request: 609-894-8900
f: 609-894-9440
www.z889.org
webcast: Yes
genres: Dance, Rock, Metal, Bluegrass, Urban, Reggae
reports to: CMJ, FMQB
pd: Brett Holcomb
ext: 609-894-9311 x1189
e: bholcomb@bcc.edu
md: Glenn Kalina
ext: 609-894-9311 x1592
e: gkalina@bcc.edu
Specialty shows & sponsors gigs.

College of New Jersey
WTSR 91.3 FM
Kendall Hall, PO Box 7718
Ewing, NJ 08628
watts: 1500
main: 609-771-3200
request: 609-771-2554
f: 609-637-5113
e: wtsr@wtsr.org
www.wtsr.org
webcast: Yes
genres: Alt., Indie Rock, Punk
reports to: CMJ
pd: Jeff Rupert
e: program@wtsr.org
md: Rob Viviano
ext: 609-771-2420
e: tsrmusic@tcnj.edu
Sponsors concerts on campus.

Drew U
WMNJ 88.9 FM
36 Madison Ave., CM353
Madison, NJ 07940
watts: 10
main: 973-408-4753
request: 973-408-5678
e: wmnj@drew.edu
www.drew.edu/wmnj
webcast: Yes
genres: Alt., Rap, Blues, Classical, Pop, Jazz, Rock
reports to: CMJ
pd: Alexandria Braboy
e: abraboy@drew.edu
md: Sinclair Sharp
e: ssharp@drew.edu
Plays submitted material. Remote broadcasts from campus events.

Monmouth U
WMCX 88.9 FM
400 Cedar Ave.
West Long Branch, NJ 07764
watts: 1000
main: 732-571-3482
request: 732-571-3493
f: 732-263-5145
e: wmcxradio@monmouth.edu
www.wmcx.com
webcast: Yes
genres: Urban, Rock, Punk, Goth, Americana, Metal, Reggae
reports to: CMJ
pd: Steve Paravati
ext: 732-263-5807
e: wmcxpd@monmouth.edu
md: Ryan Reber
ext: 732-263-5229
e: wmcxmusic@monmouth.edu
Station books & promotes area gigs.

Montclair State U
WMSC 90.3 FM
1 Normal Ave.
Upper Montclair, NJ 07043
watts: 10
main: 973-655-4257
request: 973-655-4256
f: 973-655-7433
e: sandersd@mail.montclair.edu
www.wmscradio.com
webcast: Yes
genres: Hardcore, Punk, Rock, Metal, Indie, Pop, Folk, Hip-Hop, Electronica
reports to: CMJ
pd: Matt Kersetter
ext: 973-655-4387
e: programming@wmscradio.com
md: Ashley Dorian
e: music@wmscradio.com
Also sponsors events.

Rutgers U/Livingston
RLC/WVPH 90.3 FM
Livingston Student Ctr., Ste. 117, 84 Joyce Kilmer Ave.
Piscataway, NJ 08854
watts: 132
main: 732-445-4105
request: 732-445-9300
f: 732-445-0753
www.thecore.fm
webcast: Yes
genres: Freeform
reports to: CMJ
pd: Jonathon LaCarrubba
ext: 732-445-4100 x3
e: programdirector@thecore.fm
md: Erin Nelson
ext: 732-445-4100 x91
e: headmusicdirector@thecore.fm
Lots of on-air opps. & new/indie releases added to the mix.

Rutgers U/New Brunswick
WRSU 88.7 FM
126 College Ave.
New Brunswick, NJ 08901
watts: 1360
main: 732-932-7800
request: 732-932-8800
f: 732-932-1768
www.rutgers.edu
webcast: Yes
genres: Freeform
reports to: CMJ
pd: Katie Hughes
ext: 732-932-7800 x18
e: pd@wrsu.org
md: Lisa Uber
ext: 732-932-7800 x23
e: music@wrsu.org
For station-sponsored concerts, email: promotions@wrsu.org.

Seton Hall U
WSOU 89.5 FM
400 S Orange Ave.
South Orange, NJ 07079
watts: 2400
main: 973-275-2000
request: 973-761-9768
f: 973-761-7593
e: wsou@shu.edu
www.wsou.net
webcast: Yes
genres: Eclectic, Rock, Punk, Hardcore, Metal
reports to: CMJ
pd: Annie Wilson
ext: 973-761-6461
e: wsoupd@hotmail.com
md: Greg Ahrens
ext: 973-761-7546
e: thatwsoumdguy@gmail.com
Prime outlet plays underground music & promotes NY/NJ gigs.

William Paterson U
WPSC 88.7 FM
Hobart Hall, 300 Pompton Rd.
Wayne, NJ 07470
watts: 260
main: 973-720-3319
request: 973-720-2738
f: 973-720-2454
e: quicker@wpunj.edu
www.wpradio887.org
webcast: Yes
genres: Rock, Alt., Metal, World, Punk, Jazz, Hip-Hop, Blues, R&B
reports to: CMJ
pd: Risa Pappas
ext: 973-720-3333
e: programming@wpradio887.org
md: Stefania Orrù
ext: 973-720-2005
e: music@wpradio887.org
Airs Reg'l & indie releases hrly & sponsors events. Mark promos: WPSC, 88.7FM ATTN: MD.

New Mexico

New Mexico Institute Mining & Technology
KTEK College Radio 1670 AM
Socorro, NM 87801
main: 575-835-6013
e: ktek@nmt.edu
www.nmt.edu/~ktek
webcast: Yes
genres: World, Jazz, Rock, Hip-Hop, Metal, Classical, Noise, Anime, J-Pop, Synthpop
reports to: CMJ
pd: Brad Smith
e: ktek-manager@nmt.edu
md: Patrick Leahy
Located 77mi from Albuquerque. Sponsors campus performances, including Pandafest. Prefers "Geek/Internet" culture submissions over "Pop Boy Band" or "Angsty Teenage Rock".

New Mexico State U
KRUX 91.5 FM
Corbett Ctr., Box 30004, New Mexico State U
Las Cruces, NM 88003
watts: 1000
main: 575-646-5951
request: 575-646-5667
f: 575-646-5219
e: krux@nmsu.edu
www.kruxradio.com
webcast: Yes
genres: Indie Rock, Urban, Electronic
reports to: CMJ
pd: Mark Gouldsmith
ext: 575-646-3505
e: programming@kruxradio.com
md: Oscar Zubia
ext: 575-646-4640
e: krux_music@hotmail.com

New York

Alfred U
WALF 89.7 FM
1 Saxon Dr., Powell Campus Ctr.
Alfred, NY 14802
watts: 200
main: 607-871-2287
request: 607-871-2200
e: walf@alfred.edu
www.walfradio.org
webcast: Yes
genres: Prog, Punk, Emo, 80s, Classic Rock, Rap, Indie
reports to: CMJ
pd: Luke Murphy
e: lcm41@alfred.edu
md: Margaret Storms
e: mjs6@alfred.edu
Sponsors small theme parties.

Clarkson U
WTSC 91.1 FM
CU Box 8743
Potsdam, NY 13699
watts: 700
main: 315-268-7658
request: 315-268-7657
e: radio@clarkson.edu
http://radio.clarkson.edu
webcast: Yes
genres: Alt., Urban, Electronic, Roots, Reggae
reports to: CMJ
pd: Chris Talbot
e: sm@radio.clarkson.edu
md: Gerlinde Wolf
e: music@radio.clarkson.edu
Sponsors campus events.

Hamilton College
WHCL 88.7 FM
198 College Hill Rd.

Clinton, NY 13323
watts: 270
main: 315-859-4200
request: 315-859-4561
f: 315-859-4570
e: mngrwhcl@hamilton.edu
www.whcl.org
webcast: Yes
genres: Indie Electronic, Metal, Folk, Jazz, World
reports to: CMJ
pd: Winston Cook-Hill
e: wcookwil@hamilton.edu
md: Chris Rand
e: crand@hamilton.edu
Sponsors events on campus.

Hobart & William Smith
WEOS 89.7/90.3/ 88.1 FM
300 Pulteney St.
Geneva, NY 14456
watts: 4000
main: 315-781-3456
request: 315-781-3897
e: weos@hws.edu
www.weos.org
webcast: Yes
genres: Hip-Hop, Jazz, Blues, Punk, Folk, Metal, World, Pop, Rock
reports to: CMJ
pd: Genoa Boswell
ext: 315-781-3897
md: Anessa Amer/ Mike Monteiro/Emily Sheehan
ext: 315-781-3812
e: weosmusic@hws.edu

Hofstra U
WRHU 88.7 FM
111 Hofstra U, Rm. 127
Dempster Hall
Hempstead, NY 11549
watts: 470
main: 516-463-9748
e: stationmanager@wrhu.org
www.wrhu.org
webcast: Yes
genres: Jazz, Indie Metal, Jam, Hip-Hop, Reggae, Blues, Punk, Electronic, Top 40, Spanish
reports to: CMJ, FMQB, Album Network
pd: Alicia Alford
ext: 516-463-6773
e: programming@wrhu.org
md: Kris Ortiz
ext: 516-463-3674
e: wrhumusic@wrhu.org

Ithaca College
WICB 91.7 FM
953 Danby Rd., 118 Park Hall
Ithaca, NY 14850
watts: 5500
main: 607-274-1040
request: 607-274-3217
e: wicb@ithaca.edu
www.wicb.org
webcast: Yes
genres: Rock, Jazz, Urban
reports to: CMJ
pd: Nate Hodge
e: programming@wicb.org
md: Reece Lazarus
e: wicbmusic@yahoo.com
Spins & interviews Indies & has ticket & album giveaways. Sponsors events.

Long Island U/ C.W. Post
WCWP 88.1 FM
C.W. Post Campus,
720 Northern Blvd.
Brookville, NY 11548
watts: 265
main: 516-299-2683
f: 516-299-2038
e: wcwp@cwpost.liu.edu
www.mywcwp.com
webcast: Yes
genres: Rock, Jazz, Alt., Urban, Latin, Funk, Top 40
reports to: CMJ, Hits, Album Network, FMQB
pd: Milan Nevidomsky
e: wcwpprogram@yahoo.com
md: Nick Sekela
ext: 516-299-2627
e: wcwpmusicdirector@yahoo.com
Broadcasts into NYC, parts of Long Island & southern CT & sponsors campus concerts.

Niagara U
WNIA Ch. 20
PO Box 1920
Niagara University, NY 14109
main: 716-286-8478
request: 716-286-8479
f: 716-286-8469
http://cis.niagara.edu/silverstripe
webcast: Yes
genres: Rock, Urban, Pop, Jazz
reports to: CMJ
pd: Jessica Garfinkel
ext: 716-286-8655
md: Fred Heuer
e: fjh@niagara.edu
Extremely indie-friendly station sponsors live music series. Promos: Upper Level, Gallagher Ctr., Niagara University, NY 14109.

Nyack College
WNYK 88.7 FM
1 South Blvd.
Nyack, NY 10960
watts: 10
main: 845-358-1710 x7149
request: 845-358-1828
e: wnyk@nyack.edu
www.wnykradio.com
genres: Mellow Rock, Pop, Alt., Punk
reports to: CMJ
pd: Orlando Suazo
e: suazoo@nyack.edu
Rockland county's only non-comm FM station.

Rensselaer Polytechnic Institute
WRPI 91.5 FM
1 WRPI Plaza
Troy, NY 12180
watts: 10,000
main: 518-276-2648
request: 518-276-6248
f: 518-276-2360
e: wrpi-sm@rpi.edu
www.wrpi.org
webcast: Yes
genres: All Styles
reports to: CMJ
pd: Justus Waldron
e: wrpi-pd@rpi.edu
md: Blair Neal
e: wrpi-md@rpi.edu
Sponsors events.

Rochester Institute of Technology
WITR 89.7 FM
32 Lomb Memorial Dr.
Rochester, NY 14623
watts: 910
main: 585-475-2000
request: 585-475-2271
www.modernmusicandmore.com
webcast: Yes
genres: Alt., Indie
reports to: CMJ
pd: Adara Wilczak
e: pd@witr.rit.edu
md: Luke Auburn
ext: 585-475-5643
e: music@witr.rit.edu; witrmusic@gmail.com
Sponsors events.

Siena College
WVCR 88.3 FM
515 Loudon Rd.
Loudonville, NY 12211
watts: 35,000
main: 518-782-6751; 518-783-6750
request: 518-783-2400
e: dkibbey@siena.edu
www.wvcr.com
webcast: Yes
genres: Freeform
reports to: Indie Labels
pd: Cassandra Salonich
md: Rachel Walker
Sponsors events.

Skidmore College
WSPN 91.1 FM
815 N Broadway
Saratoga Springs, NY 12866
watts: 310
main: 518-580-5787
request: 518-580-5783
e: wspn@skidmore.edu
www.skidmore.edu/~wspn
webcast: Yes
genres: Freeform
reports to: CMJ
pd: Shannon Hassett
e: shassett@skidmore.edu
md: Garrett Cook
ext: 415-694-3555
e: gcook@skidmore.edu
Sponsors events.

St. Bonaventure U
WSBU 88.3 FM
Drawer O
St. Bonaventure, NY 14778
watts: 165
main: 716-375-2307
request: 716-375-2332
f: 716-375-2583
e: wsbufm@sbu.edu
www.wsbufm.net
webcast: Yes
genres: Rock, Alt., Hip-Hop
reports to: CMJ
pd: Bobby Gohn
md: Zack Witzel/Peter Couvel
Sponsors monthly events. Send CDs, bio & description for airplay.

Stony Brook U
WUSB 90.1 FM
Stony Brook Union 266
Stony Brook, NY 11794
watts: 3600
main: 631-632-6498
request: 631-632-6901
f: 631-632-7182
e: info@wusb.fm
www.wusb.fm
webcast: Yes
genres: Freeform
reports to: CMJ
pd: Christine Massi/ Evan Johnson
ext: 631-632-6501
md: Keri Fico
ext: 631-632-6500
e: qtsangel05@hotmail.com
New music & broadcasts all over Long Island, Westchester & CT. Sponsors community & local events & on-air marathons.

SUNY Institute of Tech
Wildcat Radio Ch. 10
PO Box 3050
Utica, NY 13504
main: 315-792-7363
f: 315-792-7824
e: wildcatmedia@gmail.com
http://clubs.sunyit.edu/wm
genres: Rock, Hip-Hop, Electronic, Pop, Alt., Country, Classical, Vocal, World, Dance, Hardcore, Old-Time
reports to: CMJ
pd: Craig Helfer
ext: 315-351-3676
md: Matthew Paulini
e: paulinm@sunyit.edu
Airs wkly "Local CD Listening Party" & hosts many campus gigs.

SUNY/Albany
WCDB 90.9 FM
1400 Washington Ave.,
Campus Ctr., Rm. 316
Albany, NY 12222
watts: 100
main: 518-442-5234
request: 518-442-4242
f: 518-442-4366
e: generalmanager@wcdbfm.com
www.wcdbfm.com
webcast: Yes
genres: Rock, Jazz, Hardcore, Techno, Salsa, Alt., Urban, Metal
reports to: CMJ
pd: Seth Tillinghast
e: wcdbpd@gmail.com
md: Peter Mollica
ext: 518-442-5262
e: wcdb.music@gmail.com
Sponsors school & area gigs

SUNY/Binghamton U
WHRW 90.5 FM
PO Box 2000
Binghamton, NY 13902
watts: 1500
main: 607-777-2139
request: 607-777-2137
f: 607-777-6501
e: gm@whrwfm.org
www.whrwfm.org
webcast: Yes
reports to: CMJ, RPM, Hits
pd: Kate Menton
e: pd@whrwfm.org
md: Geri Rosenblum
e: pop@whrwfm.org
Sponsors events.

SUNY/Brockport
WBSU 89.1 FM
Seymour College Union
Brockport, NY 14420
watts: 7338
main: 585-395-2580
request: 585-395-5632
f: 585-395-5334
www.891thepoint.com
webcast: Yes
genres: Rock, Alt., Top 40
reports to: CMJ
pd: Daniella Viavattine
e: dviav1@brockport.edu
md: Josh Stellworth
Sponsors events.

SUNY/ Buffalo State College
WBNY 91.3 FM
1300 Elmwood Ave.,
Campbell Student Union 220
Buffalo, NY 14222
watts: 100
main: 716-878-3080
request: 716-878-5104
f: 716-878-6600
e: wbny@buffalostate.edu; wbny@hotmail.com
www.wbny.org

webcast: Yes
genres: Punk, Metal, Emo
reports to: CMJ
pd: Dave Vogan
md: Johanna Berlin
e: wbnymd@gmail.com
Broadcasts covers western NY.

SUNY/Fredonia
WCVF 88.9 FM
115 McEwen Hall
Fredonia, NY 14063
watts: 150
main: 716-673-3420
request: 716-673-3428
f: 716-673-3427
e: fredoniaradio@gmail.com
www.fredoniaradio.com
genres: Rock, Hard Rock
reports to: CMJ
pd: Jeremy Steinkamp
ext: 716-673-3420 x109
md: Bill Mulligan
ext: 716-673-3420 x110
Sponsors remote broadcasts from area gigs. Send hard copy promos ATTN: Bill Mulligan.

SUNY/New Paltz
WFNP 88.7 FM/ 640 AM/Ch. 3, 6 & 8
1 Hawk Dr., SUB 413
New Paltz, NY 12561
watts: 230
main: 845-257-3094
request: 845-257-3090
f: 845-257-3099
e: wfnp@newpaltz.edu
www.wfnp.org
webcast: Yes
genres: Alt., Punk, Electronic, Metal, Hip-Hop, Classic Rock, Reggae, Jazz, Rock, Pop, Latin
reports to: CMJ, BMI
pd: Emily Canty
e: canty74@newpaltz.edu
md: Jeff Canino
ext: 845-257-3041
e: wfnpmusic@newpaltz.edu
Broadcast covers the Hudson Valley & streams 24/7. Plays only new music, mostly from Top 200 Indie Rock.

SUNY/Oswego
WNYO 88.9 FM
101 Campus Ctr.
Oswego, NY 13126
watts: 100
main: 315-312-2907
f: 315-312-5410
e: wnyo@oswego.edu
www.wnyo.org
webcast: Yes
genres: Indie, Metal, Urban, Punk, Jazz, World
reports to: CMJ
pd: Kelli Ariel
ext: 518-527-0843
e: kelliariel@gmail.com
md: Justin Laird
e: justindlaird@gmail.com
New releases in weekly rotation & sponsors gigs.

Syracuse U
WERW 1570 AM
303 University Pl.
126G Schine Student Ctr.
Syracuse, NY 13244
watts: 20
main: 315-443-2021
request: 315-443-1278
e: werwgm@gmail.com
www.werw.org
webcast: Yes
genres: Freeform
reports to: CMJ, BMI
pd: Dana Beierle
e: werwpd@gmail.com
md: Kathryn Wakeman/ Conor Orr
e: werwmusic@gmail.com

North Carolina

Appalachian State U
WASU 90.5 FM
Ste. 332, Wey Hall - ASU
Boone, NC 28608
watts: 220
main: 828-262-3170
request: 828-264-4905
f: 828-262-2543
e: stationmanager@ wasurocks.com
www.wasurocks.com
webcast: Yes
genres: Alt., Rock, Hip-Hop, Jazz
reports to: CMJ
pd: Jesse Davis
e: programming@ wasurocks.com
md: Daniel Earney
e: music@wasurocks.com
Co-sponsors yrly on & off-campus gigs. Hosts 1hr features w/ artists, including interviews & on-air performances.

East Carolina U
WZMB 91.3 FM
Mendenhall Student Ctr.
Greenville, NC 27858
watts: 282
main: 252-328-4751
request: 252-328-6913
f: 252-328-4773
e: wzmb@ecu.edu
www.ecu.edu/wzmb
genres: Jazz, Hip-Hop, Metal, Rock, Indie, Reggae
reports to: CMJ
pd: Matthew McKnight
md: Michael Harrington

Elon U
WSOE 89.3 FM
Campus Box 6000
Elon, NC 27244
watts: 500
main: 336-278-7211
request: 336-278-9763
f: 336-278-7298
e: nwasikowski@elon.edu
www.wsoe893.com
webcast: Yes
genres: Alt., Rock, Hip-Hop, Punk
reports to: CMJ
pd: Greg Peel
md: Kelson
Sponsors events.

Guilford College
WQFS 90.9 FM
17714 Founders Hall
5800 W Friendly Ave.
Greensboro, NC 27410
watts: 1900
main: 336-316-2352
request: 336-316-2444
f: 336-316-2949
e: wqfsgreensboro@gmail.com
www.guilford.edu/wqfs
genres: Freeform
reports to: CMJ
pd: Kip Reynolds
e: kreynold@guilford.edu
md: Andy Freedman
e: andywqfs@gmail.com
Some gigs on & off campus.

NC State U
WKNC 88.1 FM
343 Witherspoon Student Ctr., Box 8607
Raleigh, NC 27695
watts: 25,000
main: 919-515-2401
request: 919-860-0881
f: 919-513-2693
e: gm@wknc.org
www.wknc.org
webcast: Yes
genres: Indie, Rock, Electronica, Hip-Hop, Metal
reports to: CMJ, FMQB
pd: Adam Kincaid
e: pd@wknc.org
md: Kelly Reid
e: music@wknc.org
Voted area's best station. Also hosts campus gigs. Use web submission form; include genre & FCC approp. tracks.

U of NC/Greensboro
WUAG 103.1 FM
Taylor Bldg. - UNCG
Greensboro, NC 27412
watts: 18
main: 336-334-4308
request: 336-334-5450
e: wuag@uncg.edu
www.wuag.net
webcast: Yes
genres: Prog, Rock, Hip-Hop, Jazz
reports to: CMJ, Dusted Magazine
pd: Nathan Foster
e: nathan.fostermail@gmail.com
md: Lane Sowinski
ext: 336-334-5688
e: wuagmd@gmail.com
Lots of indie music & in-studio opps. Sponsors 8 campus gigs/yr feat. mostly Touring acts.

U of NC/Chapel Hill
WXYC 89.3 FM
Carolina Union, Box 5210
Chapel Hill, NC 27599
watts: 400
main: 919-962-7768
request: 919-962-8989
e: wxyc@unc.edu; info@wxyc.org
www.wxyc.org
webcast: Yes
genres: All Styles
reports to: CMJ
pd: Kellen Carpenter
md: John Page
e: md@wxyc.org

North Dakota

Minot State U
KMSU Ch. 19
500 University Ave. W
Minot, ND 58703
main: 701-858-3829
www.minotstateu.edu/ brdcstng/kmsu.shtml
genres: Hip-Hop, Rock, Alt.
reports to: CMJ
pd: Neil Roberts
e: neil.roberts@minotstateu.edu
md: Audra Myerchin
e: audra.myerchin@ minotstateu.edu

North Dakota State U
KNDS 96.3 FM
1233 N University Dr.
Fargo, ND 58102
watts: 54
main: 701-231-6702
request: 701-231-6703
e: generalmanager@ kndsradio.com
www.kndsradio.com
webcast: Yes
genres: All Styles
reports to: CMJ
pd: Randy Schwartz
e: knds.program@gmail.com
md: Katie Hughes
e: musicdirector@ kndsradio.com
Sponsors local events; contact Randy. Promos: PO Box 5694, Fargo, ND 58105.

Ohio

Baldwin-Wallace
WBWC 88.3 FM
275 Eastland Rd.
Berea, OH 44017
watts: 4000
main: 440-826-2145
request: 440-826-7846
f: 440-826-3426
e: comments@wbwc.com
www.wbwc.com
webcast: Yes
genres: Rock, Hip-Hop, Alt., AAA
reports to: CMJ
pd: Emerson Emser
e: programming@wbwc.com
md: Cynthia Luna
e: music@wbwc.com
Hosts campus gigs w/ Local & Touring bands.

Bowling Green State U
WBGU 88.1 FM
120 West Hall
Bowling Green, OH 43403
watts: 1000
main: 419-372-8657
request: 419-372-8810
f: 419-372-0202
e: wbgufm@wbgufm.com
www.wbgufm.com
webcast: Yes
genres: World, Folk, Latin, Jazz, Indie, Punk, Urban, Goth, Experimental, Metal, Hardcore
reports to: CMJ
pd: Mike Hertz
e: mhertz@wbgufm.com
md: Tim Friedman
ext: 419-372-2826
e: music@wbgufm.com
See site for 12 addt'l genre MDs. Station brings bands to Local clubs & works w/ Shakin Promotions for concerts at Howard's Club H.

Case Western Reserve
WRUW 91.1 FM
11220 Bellflower Rd.
Cleveland, OH 44106
watts: 15,000
main: 216-368-2207
request: 216-368-2208
e: gm@wruw.org
www.wruw.org
webcast: Yes
genres: All Styles
reports to: CMJ
pd: Andy Krajewski
e: pd@wruw.org
md: Roger Weist
e: md@wruw.org
Sponsors summer concert & shows at local clubs.

Cleveland State U
WCSB 89.3 FM
Rhodes Tower 956
2121 Euclid Ave.
Cleveland, OH 44115
watts: 1000
main: 216-687-3523
request: 216-687-3515
e: gm@wcsb.org
www.wcsb.org

webcast: Yes
genres: Indie, Electronic, Folk, Latin, Reggae, Jazz, Hip-Hop, Country, Blues, Noise, Garage
reports to: CMJ
pd: Adam Reynolds
ext: 216-523-7543
e: program@wcsb.org
md: Matt Itomlenskis
ext: 216-687-3721
e: musicdirector@wcsb.org
Prefers email contact.

Denison U
WDUB 91.1 FM
Slayter Union
Granville, OH 43023
watts: 100
main: 740-587-5775
request: 740-587-6367
e: thedoobie@wdub.org
www.wdub.org
webcast: Yes
genres: All Styles
reports to: CMJ
pd: Kat Lenhart
md: Michael Warshauer
ext: 740-587-3008
e: music@wdub.org
Sponsors several concerts/yr.

Mt. Union College
WRMU 91.1 FM
1972 Clark Ave.
Alliance, OH 44601
watts: 2800
main: 330-823-3777
e: wrmu@muc.edu
www.muc.edu/wrmu
webcast: Yes
genres: Jazz, Oldies, Rock, Latin
reports to: CMJ
pd: Kate Schell
e: schellke@muc.edu
md: Dani Rizzo/Christina Best/ Alex Ulbricht
e: rizzobd@muc.edu; bestce@muc.edu; ulbricak@muc.edu
Sponsors various concerts around campus. Also podcasts.

Muskingum College
WMCO 90.7 FM
163 Stormont St.
New Concord, OH 43762
watts: 1320
main: 740-826-8380
request: 740-826-8907
f: 740-826-6122
e: wmco@muskingum.edu
www.muskingum.edu/ ~wmco
genres: Alt., Rock, Hip-Hop
reports to: CMJ
pd: Matt Hott
e: mhott@muskingum.edu
md: Josh Doerschuk
ext: 740-826-8377
Specializes in new music.

Oberlin College
WOBC 91.5 FM
135 W Lorain St.
Wilder Hall, Rm. 319
Oberlin, OH 44074
watts: 1000
main: 440-775-8107
request: 440-775-8139
f: 440-775-6678
e: wobc@oberlin.edu
www.wobc.org
webcast: Yes
genres: Pop, Rock, Jazz, Blues, Hip-Hop, Americana, Folk, Metal, World, Classical
reports to: CMJ
pd: Ian Page
e: pd.wobc@oberlin.edu
md: Gavin Baker
e: music.wobc@oberlin.edu

Ohio State U
KBUX 91.1 FM
Drake Performance & Events Ctr., 1849 Cannon Dr.
Columbus, OH 43210
main: 614-292-0436
request: 614-688-4287
f: 614-688-5788
e: newmusic@ohio.fm
www.ohio.fm
webcast: Yes
genres: Rock, Electronic, Metal, World, Latin, Hip-Hop, Jazz, Blues
reports to: CMJ
pd: Rachael Crichton
e: crichton@ohio.fm
md: Dorian Slaybod
ext: 614-688-3780
e: marley@ohio.fm
Sponsors events.

Ohio U
ACRN Web only
1 Park Pl., Ste. 329
Athens, OH 45701
main: 740-593-4905
request: 740-593-2276
f: 740-593-4908
e: acrn@ohio.edu
www.acrn.com
webcast: Yes
genres: Indie, Hip-Hop, Electronic, Experimental
reports to: CMJ
pd: Erin Schroettinger
ext: 740-593-4911
e: programming@acrn.com
md: Ty Owen
ext: 740-593-4910
e: music@acrn.com
Sponsors 5 concerts/quarter in campus coffeehouse w/ Reg'l bands; Fall "Welcome Back" concert w/ 3-4 bands & Spring festival w/ 8-10 bands.

Otterbein College
WOBN 97.5 FM
Westerville, OH 43081
watts: 28
main: 614-823-1557
request: 614-823-1015
www.wobn.net
webcast: Yes
genres: Alt.
reports to: CMJ
pd: Andrew DePaul
e: music@wobn.net
Airs indie "Fresh Tracks" & live in-studios w/ Touring bands.

Streetsboro H.S.
WSTB 88.9 FM
1900 Annalane Dr.
Streetsboro, OH 44241
watts: 1000
main: 330-626-4906
request: 330-626-4906
f: 330-626-4906
e: mail@rock889.com
www.rock889.com
webcast: Yes
genres: Alt., Modern Rock
pd: Bob Long
md: Arlin Bradford
ext: 330-626-4906 x104
e: abradford@rock889.com
Call before sending material.

U of Dayton
WUDR 99.5/98.1 FM
300 College Park
Dayton, OH 45469
watts: 50
main: 937-229-2774
request: 937-229-3058
e: flyerradio@gmail.com
http://flyer-radio.udayton.edu
webcast: Yes
genres: All Styles
reports to: CMJ
pd: Michael Kane
e: kanemicw@ notes.udayton.edu
md: Katie Sunday
e: sundayke@ notes.udayton.edu
Sponsors local Battle of the Bands.

U of Toledo
WXUT 88.3 FM
MS118
2801 W Bancroft, SU2515
Toledo, OH 43606
watts: 1000
main: 419-530-4172
request: 419-530-4455
f: 419-530-2210
http://wxut.utoledo.edu
webcast: Yes
genres: Freeform
reports to: CMJ
pd: Jesse Spildener
e: wxutprogramming@ utoledo.edu
md: Theo Cross
e: wxutmusicdept@ utoledo.edu
Sponsors few campus concerts.

Wright State U
WWSU 106.9 FM
W018 Student Union
Dayton, OH 45435
watts: 10
main: 937-775-5554
request: 937-775-5555
f: 937-775-5553
http://listen.to/wwsu
webcast: Yes
genres: Alt., Hip-Hop, R&B, Classic Rock, Electronic
reports to: CMJ
pd: Ashley Baumgarten
e: wwsuprogramming@ yahoo.com
md: Katybeth Mannix
e: mannix.4@wright.edu
Sponsors events.

Oklahoma

Oklahoma State U
KXZY Ch. 75
206 Paul Miller Bldg., #317C
Stillwater, OK 74078
main: 405-744-7435
request: 405-744-8274
http://kxzy.okstate.edu
webcast: Yes
genres: Alt., Rock, Hip-Hop, Pop, Electronic
reports to: CMJ
pd: Kevin Sears
e: kxzy_radio@hotmail.com
Hosts 2 campus concerts.

Rogers State U
KRSC 91.3 FM
1701 W Will Rogers Blvd.
Claremore, OK 74017
watts: 3000
main: 918-343-7669
request: 918-343-7913
f: 918-343-7952
e: rsuradio@hotmail.com
www.rsu.edu/rsuradio/ index.asp
webcast: Yes
genres: AAA, Alt., Rock, Jazz, Alt. Country, Punk, Electronica, Bluegrass, Metal
reports to: CMJ
pd: Steve Doyle
ext: 918-343-7670
e: sdoyle@rsu.edu
md: Tip Crowley
Hip station sponsors Jam band benefits & Local Acoustic acts.

U of Tulsa
KWGS 89.5 FM
Kendall Hall 150, 600 S College Ave.
Tulsa, OK 74104
watts: 50,000
main: 918-631-2577
f: 918-631-3695
e: answers@ publicradiotulsa.org
www.kwgs.org; www.folksalad.com
webcast: Yes
genres: Folk, Western Swing, Americana, S/S, Bluegrass, Country
pd: Rich Fisher
e: fm89@kwgs.org
NPR outlet produces 2hrs/wk of specialty music shows & on-air opps. Signal covers northeastern OK.

Oregon

Eastern Oregon U
KEOL 91.7 FM
1 University Blvd.
La Grande, OR 97850
watts: 310
main: 541-962-3698
request: 541-962-3333
e: 91.7keol@gmail.com
www.eou.edu/keol
webcast: Yes
genres: All Styles
reports to: CMJ
pd: Brian Hempel
e: hempelb@eou.edu
md: Jenifre Tarkus
ext: 541-962-3466
e: keol@eou.edu

Linfield College
KSLC 90.3 FM
900 S Baker St., #A498
McMinnville, OR 97128
watts: 265
main: 503-883-2550
request: 503-883-2666
f: 503-883-2665
e: kslc@linfield.edu
www.linfield.edu/kslc
webcast: Yes
genres: Alt., Punk, Hip-Hop, Jazz, Reggae, Electronic, Emo
reports to: CMJ
pd: Paul Anderson
e: panderson@linfield.edu
md: Matt Jonathon
e: mjonathon@linfield.edu
Contact Alex Maxson: 503-883-2550; amaxson@linfield.edu for station-sponsored gigs.

Oregon State U
KBVR 88.7 FM/Ch. 26
210 Memorial Union E
Corvallis, OR 97331
watts: 350
main: 541-737-6323
request: 541-737-4962
f: 541-737-4545
e: kbvrfmpromo@ oregonstate.edu
www.kbvr.com
webcast: Yes
genres: Rock, Hip-Hop, Jazz, Blues, World, Techno, Folk
reports to: CMJ
ext: 541-737-2008

e: kbvrfmprogdir@oregonstate.edu
md: Katie
ext: 541-737-3640
e: kbvrfmrock@oregonstate.edu
Sponsors annual campus concert.

Pacific U
KPUR 94.3 FM
2043 College Way
Forest Grove, OR 97116
watts: 100
main: 503-352-2822
request: 503-352-2255
f: 503-352-2936
www.boxerradio.com
genres: Alt., World, AAA
reports to: CMJ
pd: Starlit
md: Steve Klein
e: kleinsk@pacificu.edu
Sponsors events.

Portland State U
KPSU 1450 AM/ 98.1 FM
1825 SW Broadway, Rm. S18
Portland, OR 97201
watts: 1000
main: 503-725-5669
request: 503-725-5945
f: 503-725-4534
e: kpsu@pdx.edu
www.kpsu.org
webcast: Yes
genres: Indie, Electronic, Urban, Jazz, Rock, Local
reports to: CMJ
pd: Tony Prato
e: programming@kpsu.org
md: Shannon Williams
ext: 503-725-4071
e: music@kpsu.org
Sponsors campus gigs & "PDX Pop Now Music Festival." Touring & Local bands featured live every Fri. Send promos: PO Box 751, KPSU/VG, Portland, OR 97207.

U of Oregon
KWVA 88.1 FM
EMU, Ste. M-112
Eugene, OR 97403
watts: 515
main: 541-346-4091
request: 541-346-0645
f: 541-346-0648
e: kwva@uoregon.edu
www.kwvaradio.org
webcast: Yes
genres: All Styles
reports to: CMJ
pd: Charlotte Nisser
e: cnisser@uoregon.edu
md: Sheila
e: music@kwvaradio.org
Co-sponsors many live events around Eugene. Send promos: PO Box 3157, Eugene, OR 97403.

Pennsylvania

Allegheny College
WARC 90.3 FM
520 N Main St.
Campus Box C
Meadville, PA 16335
watts: 400
main: 814-332-3376
request: 814-332-5275
e: warc@allegheny.edu
http://warc.allegheny.edu
webcast: Yes
genres: Alt., Jazz, World, Hip-Hop, Metal, Rock, Reggae
reports to: CMJ
pd: Richard Shafranek
md: Tim Good
See site for genre MDs & booking campus gigs.

Bloomsburg U
WBUQ 91.1 FM
400 E 2nd St.,
1250 McCormick Bldg.
Bloomsburg, PA 17815
watts: 600
main: 570-389-4686
request: 570-389-2891
f: 570-389-5071
e: wbuq@bloomu.edu
http://orgs.bloomu.edu/wbuq
webcast: Yes
genres: Alt., Urban, Punk, Metal, Country, World
reports to: CMJ
pd: Kelly Barnett
e: dmsecoul@bloomu.edu
md: Cachete Hird
e: cchird@bloomu.edu
Indicate genre on outside of promos.

Cabrini College
WYBF 89.1 FM
610 King of Prussia Rd.
Radnor, PA 19087
watts: 700
main: 610-902-8363
request: 610-902-8453
e: wybf891@gmail.com
www.wybf.com
webcast: Yes
genres: Alt., Variety
reports to: CMJ, Sound Exchange
pd: Heather Shanley
md: Greg Matarazzo
ext: 610-902-8457
Airs genre specialty shows.

Carnegie Mellon U
WRCT 88.3 FM
1 WRCT Plaza
5000 Forbes Ave.
Pittsburgh, PA 15213
watts: 1760
main: 412-621-0728
request: 412-268-9728
e: info@wrct.org
www.wrct.org
webcast: Yes
genres: Techno, Jazz, Punk, World, Blues, Metal, Rock, Experimental, IDM
reports to: CMJ
pd: Hyun-Soo Lee
e: program@wrct.org
md: Pete Landwehr
e: extmusic@wrct.org

Dickinson College
WDCV 88.3 FM
WDCV HUB
PO Box 448 College & Louger Sts.
Carlisle, PA 17013
watts: 450
main: 717-245-1661
request: 717-245-1444
e: wdcvfm@gmail.com
www.wdcvfm.com
webcast: Yes
genres: Alt., World, Rock, Urban, Pop, Electronic
reports to: CMJ
pd: Joel Usher
e: usherh@dickinson.edu
md: Alex Brown
Sponsors events.

Drexel U
WKDU 91.7 FM
3210 Chestnut St.
Philadelphia, PA 19104
watts: 800
main: 215-895-2082
request: 215-895-5917
e: wkdu-gm@wkdu.org
www.wkdu.org
webcast: Yes
genres: Rock, Hip-Hop
reports to: CMJ
pd: Evan Bernard
ext: 215-895-5920
e: programming@wkdu.org
md: Fred Knittel
e: musicdirector@wkdu.org
Sponsors events.

East Stroudsburg U
WESS 90.3 FM
200 Prospect St.,
McGarry Communication Ctr.
East Stroudsburg, PA 18301
watts: 1000
main: 570-422-3512
request: 570-422-3133; 570-422-3134
f: 570-422-3615
e: wess@po-box.esu.edu
www.esu.edu/wess
webcast: Yes
genres: All Styles
reports to: CMJ
pd: Amber Olsen
ext: 570-422-3512 x2
md: Anthony Garbarino
ext: 570-422-3512 x3
Sponsors events.

Franklin & Marshall
WFNM 89.1 FM
c/o WFNM, PO Box 3220
Lancaster, PA 17604
watts: 1000
main: 610-715-2140
request: 717-291-4096
http://wfnm.freeflux.net
webcast: Yes
genres: Rock, Rap, Alt., Blues, Jazz, Reggae
reports to: CMJ, Hits, Urban Network
pd: Brian Hughes
e: brian.hughes@fandm.edu
md: Aamer Bajwa
e: aamer.bajwa@fandm.edu
Contact CJ Arayata: charles.arayata@fandm.edu for campus gigs.

Gannon U
WERG 90.5 FM
University Sq.
Erie, PA 16541
watts: 3000
main: 814-871-5841
request: 814-459-9374
e: werg@gannon.edu
www.wergfm.com
webcast: Yes
genres: Urban, Jazz, Alt., AAA, Latin, Italian, Polka, Gospel
reports to: CMJ
pd: Abby Badach
md: Kristin Babjak
e: babjak001@gannon.edu
Covers a 50mi radius including metro Erie & southern ON. Sponsors several campus events.

Juniata College
WKVR 92.3 FM
1700 Moore St.
Huntingdon, PA 16652
watts: 13
main: 814-641-5871
request: 814-641-9587
e: wkvr@juniata.edu
http://clubs.juniata.edu/wkvr
webcast: Yes
genres: Rock, Urban, Punk, Electronic, World, Metal
reports to: CMJ
pd: Jigar Patel
ext: 814-641-3341
md: Patrick Haskins
Send promos: JC Box 1005, Huntingdon, PA 16652. Also sponsors some campus gigs.

Lehigh Carbon Community College
WXLV 90.3 FM
4525 Education Park Dr.
Schnecksville, PA 18078
watts: 400
main: 610-799-1145
request: 610-799-4141
www.wxlv.org
webcast: Yes
genres: Americana
reports to: CMJ, AMA
pd: Burr Beard
e: bbeard@lccc.edu
md: Josh Hock
Community/student-run station sponsors campus gigs.

Lehigh U
WLVR 91.3 FM
Ulrich Student Ctr.
39 University Dr.
Bethlehem, PA 18015
watts: 26
main: 610-758-4187
request: 610-758-3913
f: 610-758-6313
e: inwlvr@lehigh.edu
www.wlvr.org
webcast: Yes
genres: Rock, Hip-Hop, Blues, Alt.
reports to: CMJ
pd: AJ Fritz
e: fritzrocks@hotmail.com
md: Mike Moll
e: mam7@lehigh.edu
Sponsors few campus concerts.

Lycoming College
WRLC 91.7 FM
700 College Pl.
Williamsport, PA 17701
watts: 768
main: 570-321-4060
request: 570-321-4054
www.lycoming.edu/orgs/wrlc
webcast: Yes
genres: Alt., Rock, R&B, Punk, Country, Pop
pd: Trisha Hanssler
e: hantris@lycoming.edu
md: April Mandell
e: manapri@lycoming.edu
Sponsors "Battle of the Bands."

Mansfield U of PA
WNTE 89.5 FM
Hemlock Manor
Mansfield, PA 16933
watts: 150
main: 570-662-4653
request: 570-662-4650
f: 570-662-4652
e: management@wnte.com
www.wnte.com
webcast: Yes
genres: Alt., Loud Rock, Hip-Hop, Country
reports to: CMJ
pd: Sarah Raub
md: Wes Cromley
ext: 570-662-4652
e: mdwnte@gmail.com
See site for other MDs. Contact Connie Jordan for station-sponsored events.

Marywood U
WVMW 91.7 FM
2300 Adams Ave.

Scranton, PA 18509
watts: 2000
main: 570-348-6202
f: 570-961-4768
genres: Alt., Metal, Techno, Rock, Hip-Hop
reports to: CMJ
Broadcasts to a 50mi area & sponsors concerts.

Millersville U of PA
WIXQ 91.7 FM
Student Memorial Ctr.
Millersville, PA 17551
watts: 5493
main: 717-872-3518
request: 717-872-3519
e: comments@wixq.com
www.wixq.com
webcast: Yes
genres: Rock, Hip-Hop, Techno, Indie, Emo, Punk, Hardcore, Metal, Ska
reports to: CMJ
pd: Lauren Brown
ext: 717-872-3520
e: program.director@wixq.com
md: Jeff Baum
ext: 717-871-3333
e: music.director@wixq.com

Muhlenberg College
WMUH 91.7 FM
Walson Hall, 2400 W Chew St.
Allentown, PA 18104
watts: 440
main: 484-664-3239
request: 484-664-3456
f: 484-664-3539
e: wmuh@muhlenberg.edu
www.muhlenberg.edu/wmuh
webcast: Yes
genres: Prog, Rock, Indie, Native American, Electronic, Jazz, World, Latin
reports to: CMJ
pd: Sean Surdoval
md: Carolyn Shadood
Considers everything received for airplay & sponsors events.

Pennsylvania College of Technology
WPTC 88.1 FM
1 College Ave.
Williamsport, PA 17701
watts: 494
main: 570-326-3761 x7214
request: 570-327-4778
f: 570-320-2423
e: wptc@pct.edu
www.pct.edu/wptc
webcast: Yes
genres: Rock, Hip-Hop, Jazz
reports to: CMJ
pd: Brad Nason
md: Renee Alexander
ext: 570-326-3761 x7548
Snail mail materials. Reg'l contact Ian Killian for Fall concert bookings.

Shippensburg U
WSYC 88.7 FM
1871 Old Main Dr.
3rd Fl. CUB
Shippensburg, PA 17257
watts: 135
main: 717-532-6006
request: 717-477-1480
f: 717-477-4024
e: wsyc@wsyc.org
www.wsyc.org
webcast: Yes
genres: Rock, Blues, New Age, Gospel, Americana
reports to: CMJ, Crossroads, Album Network, Jazz Weekly
pd: Matt Malone
e: pd@wsyc.org
md: Jen Keith
e: md@wsyc.org

Slippery Rock U
WSRU 88.1 FM
C-211 University Union
Slippery Rock, PA 16057
watts: 100
main: 724-738-2931
request: 724-738-2947
f: 724-738-2754
e: radiowrsk@hotmail.com
webcast: Yes
genres: Top 30, Loud Rock, Hip-Hop, Alt., Folk
reports to: CMJ
pd: Paul Joseph
e: pcj2560@sru.edu
md: Jami Loalbo
e: wsru.music.director@gmail.com
Promotes Indie bands/labels & sponsors small shows on campus.

Susquehanna U
WQSU 88.9 FM
514 University Ave.
Selinsgrove, PA 17870
watts: 12,000
main: 570-372-4030
request: 570-372-4100; 570-286-8400
f: 570-372-2745
e: wqsufm@susqu.edu; wendtp@susqu.edu
www.wqsu.com
webcast: Yes
genres: Rock, Alt., Bluegrass, Country, Blues, AAA
reports to: CMJ, FMQB, Album Network
pd: Justin Chambers
e: chambers@susqu.edu
md: Jordan Young
e: youngje@susqu.edu
Broadcasts to a 70mi radius & hosts in-studio performances & 2 Bluegrass concerts.

Swarthmore College
WSRN 91.5 FM
500 College Ave.
Swarthmore, PA 19081
watts: 110
main: 610-328-8335; 610-328-8340
www.wsrnfm.org
webcast: Yes
genres: Blues, Electronica, Folk, Hip-Hop, Jazz, Rock, World, Soul, Funk
reports to: CMJ
pd: Sofia Pinedo-Padoch
e: spinedo1@swarthmore.edu
md: Sam Phong
ext: 610-328-8337 x5534
e: sphong1@swarthmore.edu
Fiercely indie station books annual "WorthStock." Does not broadcast during winter break.

U of Pittsburgh
WPTS 92.1 FM
411 William Pitt Union
Pittsburgh, PA 15260
watts: 17
main: 412-648-7990
request: 412-383-9787
f: 412-648-7988
e: wpts@pitt.edu
www.wpts.org
webcast: Yes
genres: Alt., Metal, Urban, Electronic, Jazz, Folk
reports to: CMJ
pd: Emily Tantillo
e: wptsprogramdirector@gmail.com
md: Jeff Pentuk
ext: 412-648-7992
e: wptsmusicdirector@gmail.com
Send promos: 3959 5th Ave., Pittsburgh, PA 15260. Also sponsors events.

U of Scranton
WUSR 99.5 FM
800 Linden St.
Scranton, PA 18510
watts: 300
main: 570-941-7648
request: 570-941-9877
f: 570-941-4628
e: wusrfm@scranton.edu
http://playlist.wusr.scranton.edu
webcast: Yes
genres: Alt., Urban, Jazz, Ska, Blues, Rock, World, Classical, Punk, Latin, Polka, Soundtracks
reports to: CMJ
pd: Jon Buryk
e: program.director@wusrfm.com
md: AJ Manderichio
e: manderichia2@scranton.edu

Widener U
WDNR 89.5 FM
Box 1000, 1 University Pl.
Chester, PA 19013
watts: 10
main: 610-499-4439
request: 610-499-4440
f: 610-499-4387
e: wdnr895@mail.widener.edu
webcast: Yes
genres: All Styles
reports to: CMJ
pd: Dwight DeWerth-Pallmeyer
e: dwdewerth-pallmeyer@widener.edu
md: Kris Gill
e: krgill@mail.widener.edu

York College of Pennsylvania
WVYC 99.7 FM/640 AM
399 Country Club Rd.
York, PA 17405
watts: 100
main: 717-815-1932
request: 717-815-1311 (FM); 717-815-1453 (AM)
f: 717-849-1602
www.ycp.edu/wvyc; www.wvyc.org
webcast: Yes
genres: Alt., Hip-Hop, Rock, Techno, Reggae, Punk
reports to: CMJ
e: fm@wvyc.org
e: music@wvyc.org
Indies in rotation, lots of on-air opps. & heavily promotes bands.

Rhode Island

Brown U
WELH 88.1 FM
PO Box 1930
Providence, RI 02912
watts: 150
main: 401-863-9600
request: 401-863-9277
e: info@bsrlive.com
www.bsrlive.com
webcast: Yes
genres: Indie, Hip-Hop, Jazz, Electronic, Country, World, Rock, Folk, Blues
reports to: CMJ
pd: Lisa Qing
e: pd@bsrlive.com
md: Crow Norlander
e: md@bsrlive.com
Eclectic station w/ some community involvement sponsors annual Halloween show. Note genre on envelope & follow up to appropriate email: rock@bsrlive.com; hiphop@bsrlive.com; rpm@bsrlive.com; world@bsrlive.com; loudrock@bsrlive.com; countryfolk@bsrlive.com.

Bryant U
WJMF 88.7 FM
1150 Douglas Pike, Box 6
Smithfield, RI 02917
watts: 225
main: 401-232-6044
request: 401-232-6150
f: 401-232-6748
e: msage@bryant.edu
www.wjmf887.com
webcast: Yes
genres: Alt., Rock, Hip-Hop, Emo, Classic Rock, Electronic
reports to: CMJ
pd: Kevin Douglas
e: kdouglas@bryant.edu
md: Mark Benisatto
ext: 802-338-0980
e: mbenisat@bryant.edu
Welcomes new music.

Providence College
WDOM 91.3 FM
549 River Ave.
Providence, RI 02918
watts: 125
main: 401-865-2460
request: 401-865-2091
f: 401-865-2822
e: wdomdj@yahoo.com
http://studentweb.providence.edu/~wdom
webcast: Yes
genres: Indie, Punk, Post-Hardcore, Hip-Hop, Jam, Reggae, Electronic
reports to: CMJ
pd: Helena Qvicklund
e: hqvick06@providence.edu
md: Karen Bileski
e: kbiles06@providence.edu

Roger Williams U
WQRI 88.3 FM
1 Old Ferry Rd.
Bristol, RI 02809
watts: 800
main: 401-254-3282
request: 401-253-9774
f: 401-254-3355
e: generalmanager_wqri@hawks.rwu.edu
http://wqri.rwu.edu
webcast: Yes
genres: Rock, Jazz, Hip-Hop, Punk, Classic Rock, Alt.
reports to: CMJ
pd: Tucker Silva
e: programdirector_wqri@hawks.rwu.edu
md: Tim Hollan
ext: 401-254-3283
e: musicdirector_wqri@hawks.rwu.edu
In-studio opps., inclusion into automation rotation & plugs on daily shows.

U of Rhode Island
WRIU 90.3 FM
326 Memorial Union
Kingston, RI 02881
watts: 3440
main: 401-874-4949
request: 401-792-9030
f: 401-874-4349

e: comments@wriu.org
www.wriu.org
webcast: Yes
genres: Rock, Jazz, Hip-Hop, Children's, World, Reggae, Folk, Roots, Classical
reports to: CMJ
pd: Pat Murphy
e: fmpd@wriu.org
md: Leslie Flagg
e: rock@wriu.org
Sponsors some campus events & airs many specialty shows. See site for genre MDs.

South Carolina

Clemson U
WSBF 88.1 FM
315 Hendrix Ctr.
Clemson, SC 29634
watts: 3000
main: 864-656-4009
request: 864-656-9723
f: 864-656-4011
www.wsbf.net
webcast: Yes
genres: Rock, Hip-Hop, Folk, Blues, Punk, Jazz, Pop, World
reports to: CMJ
pd: Graham Fowler
ext: 864-630-1176
e: program@wsbf.net
md: Nichole Bennett
ext: 864-656-4010
e: music@wsbf.net
Sponsors gigs on campus.

South Carolina State U
WSSB 90.3 FM
300 College St.
Orangeburg, SC 29117
watts: 80,000
main: 803-536-8196
request: 800-344-8563
e: wssb@scsu.edu
www.scsu.edu
genres: Oldies, Smooth Jazz, Caribbean, Hip-Hop, R&B
reports to: Radio Network
pd: James White
e: jwhite@scsu.edu

U of SC/Columbia
WUSC 90.5 FM
Rm. 343, Russell House, University Union
Columbia, SC 29208
watts: 2500
main: 803-777-5468
request: 803-576-9872
f: 803-777-6482
e: wuscsm@gwm.sc.edu
http://wusc.sc.edu
webcast: Yes
genres: Rock, Americana, Hip-Hop, Electronic, World
reports to: CMJ
pd: Josh Smith/Eric Saa
ext: 803-777-0653
e: wuscpd@gwm.sc.edu
md: Ryan Kitchens/Kyle Petersen
ext: 803-777-5124
e: wuscmd@gwm.sc.edu
New artists in rotation wkly & opps. for Local-Reg'l unsigned acts. Sponsors fundraisers, concerts & dance parties.

South Dakota

Augustana College
KAUR 89.1 FM
2001 S Summit Ave.
Sioux Falls, SD 57197
watts: 680
main: 605-274-4388
request: 605-274-5287
e: kaurfm@gmail.com
http://kaur.augie.edu
genres: All Styles
reports to: CMJ
pd: Abby Berger
md: Justine Lueth
ext: 605-274-4386
Also contact Dan Nguyen, GM: 605-274-4385; kaurfm@gmail.com.

Black Hills State U
KBHU 89.1 FM
1200 University St., Unit 9003
Spearfish, SD 57799
watts: 100
main: 605-642-6265
request: 605-642-6737
e: kbhufm@gmail.com
www.bhsu.edu/bh/studentlife/organizations/kbhu
webcast: Yes
genres: Alt., Rock, AAA
reports to: CMJ
pd: David Martin
md: Steph Bechen

U of Sioux Falls
KCFS 94.5 FM
1101 W 22nd St.
Sioux Falls, SD 57105
watts: 2500
main: 605-331-6691
request: 605-331-6696
e: kcfs@usiouxfalls.edu
www.last.fm/user/kcfs
genres: Indie, Experimental, Underground Hip-Hop
pd: Ryan Gage
Mail CDs or email MP3s.

U of South Dakota
KAOR 91.1 FM
414 E Clark St.
Vermillion, SD 57069
watts: 150
main: 605-677-6477
f: 605-677-4250
www.usd.edu/kaor
webcast: Yes
genres: Alt., Rock, Urban
reports to: CMJ
pd: Kenny Bass
e: kenny.bass@usd.edu
md: Candace Walton
e: candace.walton@usd.edu

Tennessee

Austin Peay State U
WAPX 91.9 FM
PO Box 4627
Clarksville, TN 37044
watts: 6000
main: 931-221-6364
request: 931-221-7205
f: 931-221-7265
www.apsu.edu
genres: Blues, Jazz, Metal, Bluegrass, Alt., 60s, R&B, Soul, Folk
pd: David Von Palko
e: vonpalkod@apsu.edu
No Rap or Hip-Hop.

Freed-Hardeman U
WFHU 91.5 FM
158 E Main St., Rm. 303
Henderson, TN 38340
watts: 10,500
main: 731-989-6949
request: 731-989-6691
e: wfhu@fhu.edu
www.fhu.edu/radio
webcast: Yes
genres: Rock, Classic Rock, Jazz, Classical
reports to: CMJ
pd: Chad Landman
ext: 731-989-6751
e: chad.landman@students.fhu.edu
md: Jesse Smith
e: jesse.smith@students.fhu.edu
Reg'ls get spins on "LocalRock."

Memphis City Schools
WQOX 88.5 FM
2485 Union Ave.
Memphis, TN 38104
watts: 30,000
main: 901-324-6954
www.jukenjamm.com
genres: Urban, Bluegrass, Blues, Southern Rock, Rockabilly, Memphis Music
pd: Rick Wagner
md: Sherman Austin
High schoolers share the air w/ staff & volunteers. Broadcasts to an 80mi radius around Memphis. Non-Urban acts contact Bob: bhold2u@yahoo.com.

Middle Tennessee State U
WMTS 88.3 FM
MTSU Box 58, 1301 E Main St.
Murfreesboro, TN 37132
watts: 680
main: 615-898-2636
request: 615-898-5051
f: 615-898-5682
e: manager@wmts.org
www.wmts.org
webcast: Yes
genres: Indie, Metal, Rock, Country, Hip-Hop, Bluegrass
reports to: CMJ
pd: Malcolm Lockridge
ext: 615-898-2636 x2
e: program@wmts.org
md: Brad Wilson
ext: 615-898-2636 x3
e: music@wmts.org
Sponsors events.

U of Tennessee/Knoxville
WUTK 90.3 FM
P103 Andy Holt Tower
Knoxville, TN 37996
watts: 1000
main: 865-974-2228
request: 865-974-2535
f: 865-974-2814
e: wutk@utk.edu
www.wutkradio.com
webcast: Yes
genres: Rock, Alt., Hip-Hop, Jazz, Americana, Funk, Metal, Electronic, World, Punk, Experimental
reports to: CMJ
pd: Benny Smith
ext: 865-974-2229
e: bsmith60@utk.edu
md: Zak Losher/Katie Cauthen
e: slosher@utk.edu; kcauthen@utk.edu
Lots of indies & on-air opps. in the mix. Local music stores stock & display CDs that get spins. Also sponsors gigs at venues in town & on campus.

Vanderbilt U
WRVU 91.1 FM
PO Box 9100, Stn. B
Nashville, TN 37235
watts: 10,000
main: 615-322-3691
request: 615-322-7625; 615-421-7625
f: 615-343-2582
www.wrvu.org
webcast: Yes
genres: Americana, Indie, Hip-Hop, Soul, Funk, Blues, Jazz, World, Bluegrass, R&B, Electronica, Classical
reports to: CMJ
pd: Alyson
e: wrvupd@gmail.com
md: Becky Lou
e: wrvumd@gmail.com

Texas

Amarillo College
KACV 89.9 FM
PO Box 447
Amarillo, TX 79178
watts: 100,000
main: 806-371-5222
request: 806-371-5228
f: 806-371-5258
e: kacvfm90@actx.edu
www.kacvfm.org
webcast: Yes
genres: Alt., Metal, 80s, AAA, Urban, Blues, Tejano, Jazz, New Age
reports to: FMQB, Hits
pd: Lacey
ext: 806-371-5227
md: Cheryl Marshall
Promos to: 2408 S Jackson, Amarillo, TX 79109. Also sponsors some campus gigs.

Rice U
KTRU 91.7 FM
6100 Main St.
Houston, TX 77005
watts: 50,000
main: 713-348-4098
request: 713-348-5878
e: ktru@ktru.org
www.ktru.org
webcast: Yes
genres: Freeform
reports to: CMJ
pd: Rachel O.
e: rno1@ktru.org
md: Miguel O./Tyler M.
e: noise@ktru.org
Sponsors several gigs & an underground music festival.

San Antonio College
KSYM 90.1 FM
1300 San Pedro Ave.
San Antonio, TX 78212
watts: 6000
main: 210-733-2787
request: 210-733-2800
f: 210-733-2801
e: ksym@accd.edu
www.ksym.org
webcast: Yes
genres: Alt., Rock, Pop, Latin, Blues, World, Jazz, Reggae, AAA
reports to: CMJ
pd: Leora Uribe
e: sac-ksym@mail.accd.edu
md: Brian Zavala
e: ksymmd@yahoo.com
Sponsors events.

Stephen F. Austin State U
KSAU 90.1 FM
PO Box 13048 SFA Stn.
Nacogdoches, TX 75962
watts: 3500
main: 936-468-4000
f: 936-468-1042
e: ksau@sfasu.edu
www.sfasu.edu/ksau
webcast: Yes
genres: Alt., Rock, Jazz, Blues, World, AC

reports to: CMJ
pd: Sherry Williford
ext: 936-468-1278
e: swilliford@sfasu.edu
ext: 936-468-1124
e: ksaumusic@gmail.com

Texas Christian U
KTCU 88.7 FM/Ch. 3
TCU Box 298020
Fort Worth, TX 76129
watts: 10,000
main: 817-257-7631
e: ktcu@tcu.edu
www.ktcu.net
webcast: Yes
genres: Rock, Oldies, Alt., Classical, Bluegrass
reports to: CMJ
pd: Ross Murray/Brian Fox
e: ross.murray@tcu.edu; b.fox@tcu.edu
md: Leslie Ward/ Sam Wunderl
e: l.a.ward@tcu.edu; s.j.wunderl@tcu.edu
Sponsors events.

Texas State U/ San Marcos
KTSW 89.9 FM
601 University Dr.
Old Main 106
San Marcos, TX 78666
watts: 10,500
main: 512-245-3485
request: 512-245-3473
f: 512-245-3732
e: ktsw@txstate.edu
www.ktsw.net
webcast: Yes
genres: Alt., Electronic, Hip-Hop, World, Country, Punk, Hardcore, Folk
reports to: CMJ
pd: Sarah White
ext: 512-245-8248
e: ktswprogram@txstate.edu
md: Jenn Kelly
ext: 512-245-8089
e: ktswmusic@txstate.edu
Sponsors "Southwest Music Fest" & frequent campus events, contact Nick Kukowski, 512-245-7808.

Texas Tech. U
KTXT 88.1 FM
PO Box 43081
Lubbock, TX 79409
watts: 35,000
main: 806-742-3914
request: 806-742-5898
e: ktxtfm@yahoo.com
www.ktxt.net
webcast: Yes
genres: All Styles
reports to: CMJ
pd: Jorge Penso
e: ktxtprogramming@ gmail.com
md: Ben Williams
ext: 806-742-3916
e: ktxtmusic@gmail.com
Sponsors events.

U of Texas/Austin
KVRX 91.7 FM
PO Box D
Austin, TX 78713
watts: 3000
main: 512-471-5106
request: 512-495-5879
www.kvrx.org
webcast: Yes
genres: Indie, World, Reggae, Hip-Hop, Jazz
reports to: CMJ
pd: Andrew Thompson
e: pm@kvrx.org
md: Daren Carter/ Tim Hodgin
ext: 512-232-5431
e: music@kvrx.org
Sponsors concerts in Austin.

U of Texas/Dallas
Radio UTD Web only
PO Box 830688
SU 21 - Radio UTD
Richardson, TX 75083
main: 972-883-6304
request: 972-883-6305
http://radio.utdallas.edu
webcast: Yes
genres: Indie, Punk, Ska, Emo, Rock, Hip-Hop, Eclectic
reports to: CMJ
pd: Stu McAfee
ext: 214-354-7422
e: ssm051000@utd.edu
md: Kaitlin Butler
e: radioutd.musicaq@ gmail.com
Sponsors campus Rock concerts.

West Texas A&M
KWTS 91.1 FM
WT Box 60754
Canyon, TX 79016
watts: 6000
main: 806-651-2911
f: 806-651-2818
e: dtroach1@go.wtamu.edu
www.wtamu.edu/kwts
webcast: Yes
genres: Freeform
reports to: CMJ
pd: Niki Bryan
e: nikibryan@gmail.com
md: Ryan Renick
e: kwtsmusic@gmail.com
Also podcasts.

Utah

Snow College
KAGJ 89.5 FM
150 College Ave.
Ephraim, UT 84627
watts: 300
main: 435-283-7007
e: dance_duke81@yahoo.com
www.snow.edu/~kage
genres: Top 40, Classic Rock, Pop, Hip-Hop, R&B, Alt.
reports to: CMJ
pd: Kendra Neu
md: Jason Moffat
On-air performances & some station-sponsored events.

Southern Utah U
KSUU 91.1 FM
351 W Center St.
Cedar City, UT 84720
watts: 10,000
main: 435-865-8224
request: 435-586-7975
f: 435-865-8352
e: ksuu@suu.edu
www.suu.edu/ksuu
webcast: Yes
genres: Alt., Rock
reports to: CMJ
md: Jordan Sharp
ext: 435-865-8691

Vermont

Castleton State College
WIUV 91.3 FM
Campus Ctr.
Castleton, VT 05735
watts: 230
main: 802-468-1264
request: 802-468-1377
e: wiuv@castleton.edu
www.castleton.edu/campus/ media.htm
genres: Alt., Jazz, Electronic, Urban, Punk, Country, Folk, Hardcore, Pop, Rock
reports to: CMJ
pd: Roy Mercon
md: Sarah Parker
Sponsors events.

Lyndon State College
WWLR 91.5 FM
1001 College Rd., Box F
Lyndonville, VT 05851
watts: 2725
main: 802-626-6214
request: 802-626-6213
f: 802-626-4806
e: wwlr@lyndonstate.edu
www.lyndonstate.edu
webcast: Yes
genres: Alt., Rock, Hip-Hop, R&B, Jazz, World
reports to: CMJ
pd: Stevie Allen
e: stevie.allen@lyndonstate.edu
md: Nick Phelan
e: ngp08110@lyndonstate.edu

Middlebury College
WRMC 91.1 FM
Middlebury, VT 05753
watts: 2900
main: 802-443-2471
request: 802-443-6323
f: 802-443-5108
e: wrmc911@gmail.com
http://wrmc.middlebury.edu
webcast: Yes
genres: Rock, Folk, Blues, Hip-Hop, Electronic, World
reports to: CMJ, Dusted
pd: Sam Libby
ext: 802-355-5312
e: slibby@middlebury.edu
md: Andrew Ward/ Rachael Carrasquillo
ext: 802-443-6324
e: atward@middlebury.edu; rcarrasq@middlebury.edu
Sponsors annual Indie Rock fest.

St. Michael's College
WWPV 88.7 FM
SMC Box 274, Winooski Park
Colchester, VT 05439
watts: 103
main: 802-654-2334
request: 802-654-2887
f: 802-654-2336
e: wwpv@smcvt.edu
www.wwpv.org
webcast: Yes
genres: Rock, Bluegrass, Folk, Classical, Jazz, World, Hip-Hop, Electronica
reports to: CMJ
pd: Andrew Parise
ext: 617-763-3887
e: aparise@smcvt.edu
md: Tyler Machado
e: tmachado@smcvt.edu
Sponsors some concerts. Jazz inquiries email: wwpvjazz@hotmail.com.

U of Vermont
WRUV 90.1 FM
Davis Student Ctr.
Burlington, VT 05405
watts: 460
main: 802-656-0796
request: 802-656-4399
f: 802-656-2281
e: wruv@wruv.org
www.wruv.org
webcast: Yes
genres: Indie, Hip-Hop, Punk, Reggae, Industrial, Folk, Metal, Avant-Garde, Americana
reports to: CMJ
pd: MaCrae Hathaway
ext: 802-656-8700
md: Brooke Morrison/ Ben Crockett
Eclectic station airs live sets from Reg'l acts featured on "Exposure" w/ Jeremy Ayers: ayersjeremy@hotmail.com. Also sponsors events.

Virginia

College of William & Mary
WCWM 90.9 FM
PO Box 8793
Williamsburg, VA 23185
watts: 1800
main: 757-221-3287
request: 757-221-3288
f: 757-221-2118
e: wcwmxx@wm.edu
www.wcwm.org
webcast: Yes
genres: Indie, Rock, Jazz, Hip-Hop, Blues, Dance, Folk, Classical, Metal
reports to: CMJ
pd: Michael W.
e: mxwill@wm.edu
md: Michelle Kelley
e: wcwmmd@wm.edu
Books 3-4 gigs/yr & sponsors "Band Nights" on campus.

George Mason U
WGMU Ch. 22
4400 University Dr., MS 4B7
Fairfax, VA 22030
main: 703-993-2940
request: 703-993-9468
f: 703-993-2941
e: wgmu@gmu.edu
www.wgmuradio.com
webcast: Yes
genres: Alt., Rock, Blues, Hip-Hop, Jazz, Local
reports to: CMJ
pd: Allison Bodsford
e: abosdsfor@gmu.edu
md: Lars Laing-Peterson
ext: 703-993-2935
e: llaingpe@gmu.edu
Sponsors on-campus concerts.

Hampton U
WHOV 88.1 FM
Scripps Howard Bldg., Rm. 119 - Hampton U
Hampton, VA 23668
watts: 10,000
main: 757-727-5408
request: 757-727-5407
f: 757-727-5427
e: conductor5@go.com
genres: Gospel, Contemporary Jazz, Blues, R&B, Hip-Hop, Reggae, Latin
reports to: BMI, BRE, CMJ, Smooth Jazz, R&R Radio, Rapnetworks
pd: Robert J. Dixon II
ext: 757-727-5670
e: robert.dixon@hamptonu.edu
md: Kevin Anderson
e: kanderson881@hotmail.com
Part of the Norfolk Jazz Fest & the Hampton Jazz Fest. Books "Fridays at Sunset" in Richmond during the summer.

James Madison U
WXJM 88.7 FM
983 Resevoir St.
Harrisonburg, VA 22801
watts: 390
main: 540-568-3425

request: 540-568-7907
f: 540-568-7156
e: general@wxjmradio.com
http://wxjmlive.com
webcast: Yes
genres: Prog, Urban, World, Americana, Jazz, Rock
reports to: CMJ
pd: Sarah Delia
ext: 540-568-6878
e: programming@wxjmradio.com
md: Rick Ponfart
e: wxjmradio@hotmail.com
Airs many specialty shows & sponsors annual "MacRock Festival" & "Cool-Aid."

Old Dominion U
WODU Ch. 51
2102 Webb Ctr.
Norfolk, VA 23529
main: 757-683-3441
request: 757-683-4405
e: manager@woduradio.com
www.woduradio.com
webcast: Yes
genres: Rock, Alt., Hip-Hop, Local, Electronic
reports to: CMJ
pd: Reuben Carrington
e: cuban_reuben@hotmail.com
md: James Duval
e: jduva001@odu.edu

Radford U
WVRU 89.9 FM
Radford U, PO Box 6973
Radford, VA 24142
watts: 500
main: 540-831-6059
request: 540-831-5171
e: wvru@radford.edu
www.wvru.org
webcast: Yes
genres: Rock, Jazz, Blues, Hip-Hop, AAA
reports to: CMJ
pd: Ashlee Claud
e: aclaud@radford.edu
md: Zachary Carrol
Specialty shows reach southwestern VA.

Roanoke College
WRKE/LPFM 100.3 FM
c/o Colket Ctr.
221 College Ln.
Salem, VA 24153
watts: 100
main: 540-375-2277
e: radio@roanoke.edu
www.wrke.org
webcast: Yes
genres: Rock, Rap, Reggae, Country, Bluegrass, Children's
pd: Sheree Mullen
e: scmullen@roanoke.edu
md: Jeremy Stroup
Also sponsors events.

U of Richmond
WDCE 90.1 FM
PO Box 85
28 Westhampton Way
Richmond, VA 23173
watts: 100
main: 804-289-8698
request: 804-289-8790
f: 804-289-8996
e: wdce@richmond.edu
www.student.richmond.edu/~wdce
www.wdcefm.org
webcast: Yes
genres: Indie, Hip-Hop, Jazz, Electronic, World, Punk, Jam, Metal
reports to: CMJ
pd: Carly Vendegna
e: carly.vendegnaramirez@richmond.edu
md: Herb King
e: herb.king@aol.com
Sponsors gigs on & off campus.

Virginia Tech
WUVT 90.7 FM/ 1150 AM
350 Squires Student Ctr.
Blacksburg, VA 24061
watts: 3000
main: 540-231-9880
request: 540-231-9888
e: wuvtamfm@vt.edu
www.wuvt.vt.edu
webcast: Yes
genres: All Styles
reports to: CMJ
pd: Paul Cornett
md: Chris Myers
e: wuvtmusic@vt.edu
Sponsors gigs on campus & at local bars plus a "Battle of the Bands" every semester.

Washington

Central Washington U
KCWU 88.1 FM
400 E University Way
SURC 120
Ellensburg, WA 98926
watts: 500
main: 509-963-2283
request: 509-963-2311
e: kcwu@cwu.edu
www.881theburg.com
webcast: Yes
genres: Alt., Urban, Reggae, World, Blues, Jazz
reports to: CMJ
pd: Randy Beckstead
ext: 509-963-2414
e: beckster@cwu.edu
md: Kelly Larsen
ext: 509-963-2284
e: md@cwu.edu
Sponsors campus gigs including "The Gorge" concerts.

Eastern Washington U
KEWU 89.5 FM
104 Radio-Television Bldg.
Cheney, WA 99004
watts: 10,000
main: 509-359-2850
request: 509-359-4226
e: jazz@mail.ewu.edu
www.kewu.ewu.edu
webcast: Yes
genres: Jazz, Blues, World, Ambient, Chill
reports to: JazzWeek
pd: Elizabeth Farriss
e: elizabeth.farriss@mail.ewu.edu
Broadcasts to inland Pacific NW, parts of ID & Canada.

Green River Community College
KGRG 89.9 FM
12401 SE 320th St.
Auburn, WA 98092
watts: 250
main: 253-833-5004
www.kgrg.com
webcast: Yes
genres: Punk, Hardcore, Indie, Ska, Psychobilly
reports to: CMJ
pd: Brittany
e: kgrgpd@hotmail.com
Sponsors local concerts.

The Evergreen State College
KAOS 89.3 FM
CAB 301
2700 Evergreen Pkwy. NW
Olympia, WA 98505
watts: 1100
main: 360-867-6888
request: 360-867-5267
f: 360-867-6697
e: kaos@evergreen.edu
www.kaosradio.org
webcast: Yes
genres: Freeform, Indie
reports to: CMJ
pd: Jerry Drummond
ext: 360-867-6895
e: drummonj@evergreen.edu
md: Nicki Thompson/ Jesse Callahan
ext: 360-867-6896
e: kaos_music@evergreen.edu
Blankets 30mi radius w/ ecclectic music. Contact John Ford at 360-867-6894 for station-sponsored gigs.

U of Puget Sound
KUPS 90.1 FM
1500 N Warner
Tacoma, WA 98416
watts: 100
main: 253-879-3288
request: 253-879-3267
e: thesound@ups.edu
www.kups.net
webcast: Yes
genres: Alt., Rock, Hip-Hop, Electronic, Metal, Punk
reports to: CMJ
pd: Aaron Lynch
ext: 253-879-3144
e: kupsprogramming@ups.edu
md: Kayla Morrison
ext: 253-879-2974
e: kupsalternative@ups.edu
Sponsors 3-4 campus gigs/yr.

Washington State U
KZUU 90.7 FM
Smith Gym, 126B
Pullman, WA 99163
watts: 800
main: 509-335-2208
request: 509-335-2207
e: kzuu@wsu.edu
www.kzuu.wsu.edu/kzuu.aspx
webcast: Yes
genres: Indie, Hip-Hop, World, Electronic, Jazz, Blues, Reggae
reports to: CMJ
pd: Chelan Lippincott
e: program.kzuu@wsu.edu
md: Javier Suarez
e: md.kzuu@wsu.edu
Sponsors concerts on campus.

Whitworth College
KWRS 90.3 FM
300 W Hawthorne Rd.
Spokane, WA 99251
watts: 10
main: 509-777-4560
request: 509-777-3278
e: kwrsgm@whitworth.edu
www.kwrs.fm
webcast: Yes
genres: All Styles
reports to: CMJ
pd: Bud Bareither
md: Nic Vargus
ext: 509-777-4575
e: kwrsmd@whitworth.edu
Spokane's only source of Indie music, airs up & coming bands.

West Virginia

Bethany College
WVBC 88.1 FM
Bethany House, Main St.
PO Box 368
Bethany, WV 26032
watts: 1100
main: 304-829-7564
request: 304-829-7881
e: wvbc@bethanywv.edu
www.myspace.com/wvbc
genres: Rock, AC, Punk, Ska, Hip-Hop, Alt.
reports to: CMJ
pd: Gordon Everett
e: geverett@bethanywv.edu
Located 53mi from Pittsburgh, PA. Sponsors annual event.

Marshall U
WMUL 88.1 FM
1 John Marshall Dr.
Huntington, WV 25755
watts: 1150
main: 304-696-2295
request: 304-696-6651
e: wmul@marshall.edu
www.marshall.edu/wmul
webcast: Yes
genres: Hip-Hop, Rock, Jazz, Blues, World, Gospel, Latin, Reggae, Oldies, Classic Rock
reports to: CMJ
pd: Stephanie Bartram
ext: 304-696-6640
md: Jesi Kirk
e: wmulmd@yahoo.com
Sponsors 2 annual campus gigs.

West Virginia State U
WVSU 106.7 FM
Campus 1000,
Wilson Student Union #202
Institute, WV 25112
main: 304-766-5124
request: 304-766-4170
e: cobbkim@wvstateu.edu
www.wvstateu.edu/general/radio
webcast: Yes
genres: Jazz, World, Alt., Urban, Reggae
pd: Justin Litten
e: vxgafattack@gmail.com
Sponsors "May Day" fest, Homecoming & special Feb events during Black History Month.

West Virginia U
WWVU 91.7 FM
Mountainlair, West Virginia U
Morgantown, WV 26506
watts: 2600
main: 304-293-3329
request: 304-293-3692
f: 304-293-7363
e: u92@mail.wvu.edu
http://u92.wvu.edu
webcast: Yes
genres: Alt., Jazz, Reggae, Metal, Classic Rock, World, Electronica, Urban
reports to: CMJ
pd: Kodi McKinney
ext: 304-293-2128
e: u92programdirector@gmail.com
md: Rupam Sofsky
ext: 304-293-4045
e: wwvumd@gmail.com
Sponsors 4 concerts/yr.

Wisconsin

Beloit College
WBCR 90.3 FM
700 College St., Box 39
Beloit, WI 53511
watts: 130
main: 608-363-2402

request: 608-363-2409
f: 608-363-2718
e: wbcfm@gmail.com
www.beloit.edu/wbcr
webcast: Yes
genres: Indie, Folk, Rock, Metal, Electronic, Jazz, Hip-Hop, World
reports to: CMJ
pd: Bebe Santa-Wood
e: wbcrprogramdirector@gmail.com
md: Jeff Gage
e: wbcrtop200@gmail.com
Sponsors events.

Burlington H.S.
WBSD 89.1 FM
400 McCanna Pkwy.
Burlington, WI 53105
watts: 300
main: 262-763-0195
e: arlo@wbsdfm.com
www.wbsdfm.com
webcast: Yes
genres: Blues, Jazz, AAA
reports to: CMJ, FMQB, Living Blues
pd: Dylan Epping
e: epping@wbsdfm.com
md: Nick Strong
e: nick@wbsdfm.com
Features Indies in rotation. Send CDs & bios.

Lawrence U
WLFM Web only
420 E College Ave.
Appleton, WI 54911
main: 920-832-6567
request: 920-832-6566
www.wlfm.net
webcast: Yes
genres: Top 30, RPM, Jazz, Hip-Hop, Loud Rock, World, Blues, Folk, Country, Classical
reports to: CMJ
pd: Drew Baumgardner
e: wlfm.top200@gmail.com
md: Willy Bauer
e: wlfm.loudrock@gmail.com
Books Local & Reg'ls for spring benefit.

U of Wisconsin/ Madison
WSUM 91.7 FM
602 State St., Ste. 200
Madison, WI 53703
watts: 6000
main: 608-262-1864
request: 608-265-9786
f: 608-265-3549
e: wsum@wsum.wisc.edu
www.wsum.org
webcast: Yes
genres: Rock, Punk, Classical, Hip-Hop, Jam, Techno, Jazz, Ska, World, Experimental, Noise
reports to: CMJ
pd: Eric Moody
e: prog@wsum.wisc.edu
md: Amanda Bruno
ext: 608-262-1206
e: music@wsum.wisc.edu

U of Wisconsin/ Oshkosh
WRST 90.3 FM
926 Woodland Ave., Arts & Communications 418
Oshkosh, WI 54901
watts: 960
main: 920-424-0444
request: 920-424-3113
e: wrstfm@uwosh.edu
www.wrst.org
webcast: Yes
genres: Rock, Urban, Punk, Ska, Electronic, Jazz, Metal, Blues, Bluegrass, Country, Oldies
reports to: CMJ
pd: James Mutter
ext: 920-424-1095
e: wrstprogramming@uwosh.edu
md: Kiesha Dauer/Max Grill
ext: 920-424-0455
e: wrstmusic@uwosh.edu
Send promos: WRST FM, AC 418, 800 Algoma Blvd., Oshkosh, WI 54901. Also books bands for in-studios.

U of Wisconsin/ Platteville
WSUP 90.5 FM
42 Pioneer Tower
1 University Plaza
Platteville, WI 53818
watts: 1000
main: 608-342-1165
request: 608-342-1291
e: management@wsup.org
www.wsup.org
webcast: Yes
genres: Rock, Alt., Metal, Ska, Hip-Hop, Punk, Classic Rock
reports to: CMJ, FMQB
pd: Sean Rogan
e: programming@wsup.org
md: Robert Berres
e: music@wsup.org

U of Wisconsin/ River Falls
WRFW 88.7 FM
306 N Hall
River Falls, WI 54022
watts: 3000
main: 715-425-3886
request: 715-425-3887
f: 715-425-3532
e: wrfw@uwrf.edu
www.pureradio887.com
webcast: Yes
genres: Rock, Hip-Hop, Country
reports to: CMJ
pd: Adam Lee/ Rick Burgsteiner
e: adam.lee@uwrf.edu; richard.bursteiner@uwrf.edu
md: Jerry Clark
e: gerald.clark@uwrf.edu

U of Wisconsin/ Stevens Pt.
WWSP 89.9 FM
1101 Reserve St., Ste. 105
Stevens Point, WI 54481
watts: 30,000
main: 715-346-3755
request: 715-346-2696
f: 715-346-4012
e: wwsp@uwsp.edu
www.uwsp.edu/stuorg/wwsp
webcast: Yes
genres: Indie, Metal, Electronic, Acoustic, New Age, Jazz, World
reports to: CMJ
pd: Jim Priniski
ext: 715-346-2194
e: jprin643@uwsp.edu
md: Chad Walhood
ext: 715-346-4722
e: cwalh373@uwsp.edu
Send promos: 1101 Reserve St., Ste. 105, Stevens Point, WI 54481. Also books "Jazzfest."

U of Wisconsin/ Whitewater
WSUW 91.7 FM
800 W Main St.
Whitewater, WI 53190
watts: 1500
main: 262-472-1323
request: 262-472-1312
e: wsuw@uww.edu
www.wsuw.org
webcast: Yes
genres: Alt., Metal, Hip-Hop, Classic Rock, Acoustic, 80s
reports to: CMJ
pd: John Prast
e: john@wsuw.org
md: Matt Alba
e: md@wsuw.org
Feat. Indie Rock specialty show.

Wyoming

Central Wyoming College
KCWC 88.1 FM
2660 Peck Ave.
Riverton, WY 82501
watts: 3000
main: 307-855-2268
genres: Lite Jazz, New Age, Folk, Acoustic
reports to: CMJ, New Age Reporter
pd: Dale Smith
ext: 307-855-2121
e: dsmith@cwc.edu
Broadcast covers 90mi radius.

U of Wyoming
KUWR/WPR 91.9 FM
Dept. 3984
1000 E University Ave.
Laramie, WY 82071
main: 307-766-4240
request: 800-729-5897
f: 307-766-6184
http://uwadmnweb.uwyo.edu/wpr
webcast: Yes
genres: Classical, Jazz, Folk, Bluegrass
pd: Roger Adams
ext: 307-766-3587
e: radams@uwyo.edu
md: Grady Kirkpatrick
ext: 307-766-6624
e: wkirkpa1@uwyo.edu
Request music by email: onair@uwyo.edu. Sponsors live music. NPR affiliate with some student input that airs wknd specialty shows.

Canada

Alberta

U of Alberta
CJSR 88.5 FM
SUB Rm. 0-09, U of Alberta
Edmonton, AB T6G 2J7
Canada
watts: 900
main: 780-492-2577
request: 780-492-2577 x1
f: 780-492-3121
www.cjsr.ualberta.ca
webcast: Yes
genres: Freeform
reports to: CMJ, !earshot
pd: Jay Hannley
ext: 780-492-2577 x2
e: prog@cjsr.com
md: Aaron Levin
ext: 780-492-2577 x5
e: music@cjsr.com
Campus/community station features specialty shows, on-air performances & sponsors events.

U of Calgary
CJSW 90.9 FM
Rm. 127, Mac Ewan Hall
U of Calgary
Calgary, AB T2N 1N4
Canada
watts: 4000
main: 403-220-3902
request: 403-220-3991
f: 403-289-8212
e: office@cjsw.com
www.cjsw.com
webcast: Yes
genres: All Styles - Mainly Multi-cultural, Spoken Word
reports to: CMJ, !earshot
pd: Sonja Bloomer
ext: 403-220-3903
e: cjswpd@ucalgary.ca
md: Myke Atkinson
ext: 403-220-3085
e: cjswfm@ucalgary.ca
Sponsors events. No electronic submissions.

U of Lethbridge
CKXU 88.3 FM
SU 164, 4401 University Dr. W
Lethbridge, AB T1K 3M4
Canada
watts: 125
main: 403-329-2335
request: 403-329-5189
f: 403-329-2224
e: ckxu@ckxu.com
www.ckxu.com
webcast: Yes
genres: Rock, Pop, Folk, Hip-Hop, Electronica, Punk, Jazz, Metal
reports to: Vice, !earshot, Chart Attack
pd: Alan Gillespie
e: program@ckxu.com
md: John Pantherbone
e: music@ckxu.com

British Columbia

U of Victoria
CFUV 101.9 FM
PO Box 3035
Victoria, BC V8W 3P3
Canada
watts: 2290
main: 250-721-8704
request: 250-721-8700
http://cfuv.uvic.ca
webcast: Yes
genres: All Styles
reports to: CMJ, !earshot, Chart Magazine
pd: David Boffa
e: director@uvic.ca
md: Justin Lanoue
e: cfuvmd@uvic.ca
Freeform station w/ strong community involvement has varied playlists & sponsors events. CDs & vinyl only. No MP3s.

Malaspina College
CHLY 101.7 FM
34 Victoria Cres. 2
Nanaimo, BC V9R 5B8
Canada
watts: 1300
main: 250-716-3410
request: 250-740-1017
f: 250-716-1082
e: stationmanager@chly.ca
www.chly.ca
webcast: Yes
genres: Alt., Rock, Blues, Folk, Jazz, Alt. Country, Electronic, Hip-Hop
reports to: CMJ, !earshot, Chart Attack, Roots Music
pd: Dylan Perry
e: programdirector@chly.ca
md: George Millar
e: music@chly.ca
Campus/community station airs wide variety of music & sponsors street fair & concerts.

U of British Columbia
CITR 101.9 FM
6138 SUB Blvd., Rm. 233
Vancouver, BC V6T 1Z1
Canada
watts: 100
main: 604-822-1242
request: 604-822-2487
f: 604-822-9364
e: citrmgr@ams.ubc.ca
www.citr.ca
webcast: Yes
genres: Indie, World Beat, Noise, Underground Hip-Hop, Punk
reports to: !earshot
pd: Bryce Dunn
ext: 604-822-3017
e: citrprogramming@club.ams.ubc.ca
md: Luke Meat
ext: 604-822-3017
e: citrmusic@club.ams.ubc.ca
Eclectic station w/ community involvement features wkly, in-studio live music programs & hosts annual "Battle of the Bands."

British Columbia Institute of Tech.
CFML 107.9 FM
3700 Willingdon Ave.
Burnaby, BC V5G 3H2
Canada
watts: 5
main: 604-432-8510
request: 604-432-8511
e: allofus@evolution1079.com
www.evolution1079.com
webcast: Yes
genres: AAA, Underground, Eclectic
pd: John Oliver
e: john_oliver@bcit.ca
md: Kristina Mameli
e: music@evolution1079.com
Plays lots of Indie/new artists & sponsors events.

Thompson Rivers U
CFBX 92.5 FM
900 McGill Rd., House 8
Kamloops, BC V2C 5N3
Canada
watts: 420
main: 250-377-3988
f: 250-852-6350
e: radio@tru.ca
www.thex.ca
webcast: Yes
genres: Eclectic
reports to: Chart Magazine, Exclaim!
pd: Brant Zwicker
md: Steve Marlow
e: radio8music@yahoo.com
Sponsors events.

Camosun College
CKMO 900 AM
3100 Foul Bay Rd.
Victoria, BC V8P 5J2
Canada
watts: 10,000
main: 250-370-3658
request: 250-370-3450
f: 250-370-3679
e: feedback@village900.ca
www.village900.ca
webcast: Yes
genres: Folk, Roots, World Beat
pd: Doug Ozeroff
e: doug@village900.ca
Sponsors events. Email first. No MP3s.

Manitoba

U of Manitoba
CJUM 101.5 FM
University Ctr., Rm. 308
Winnipeg, MB R3T 2N2
Canada
watts: 1200
main: 204-474-7027
request: 204-269-8636
e: cjumpromo@gmail.com
www.cjum.com
webcast: Yes
genres: All Styles
reports to: CMJ, !earshot
pd: Michael Elves
e: michael@umfm.com
Freeform campus/community station airs live performances, 110 shows in a variety of genres & sponsors events. No electronic submissions.

U of Winnipeg/ Manitoba
CKUW 95.9 FM
4CM11 - 515 Portage Ave.
Winnipeg, MB R3B 2E9
Canada
watts: 450
main: 204-786-9782
request: 204-774-6877
f: 204-783-7080
e: ckuw@uwinnipeg.ca
www.ckuw.ca
webcast: Yes
genres: All Styles
reports to: Exclaim!, Chart Magazine
pd: Robin Eriksson
e: r.eriksson@uwinnipeg.ca
md: Don Bailey
e: donb@uwinnipeg.ca
Volunteer-run freeform station supports new & non-mainstream music.

New Brunswick

U of New Brunswick/ Saint John
CFMH 107.3 FM
100 Tucker Park Rd.
Saint John, NB E2L 4L5
Canada
watts: 250
main: 506-648-5667
request: 506-648-5925
e: cfmh@unbsj.ca
www.cfmh.ca
webcast: Yes
genres: All Styles
reports to: CMJ, !earshot
pd: Jud Crandall
e: cfmhprogramming@gmail.com
md: Peter McDonald
e: cfmhmd@hotmail.com
Promos: PO Box 5050, St. John, NB E2L 4L5. Also sponsors events.

Mount Allison U
CHMA 106.9 FM
152-A Main St., Ste. 303
Sackville, NB E4L 1B3
Canada
watts: 50
main: 506-364-2221
request: 506-364-2222
e: chma@mta.ca
www.mta.ca/chma
webcast: Yes
genres: Canadian Indie Rock
reports to: Dusted, Chart Attack, !earshot
pd: Ilse Kramer
e: chma_pro@mta.ca
md: James Goddard
e: chma_music@mta.ca
Campus/community station airs lots of Indie releases & sponsors events. Prefers CDs in full-size jewel cases labeled w/ artist, album name & track listing. Vinyl LPs & 45s are also accepted. No MP3s or CDs w/ less than 4 tracks.

U of New Brunswick/ Fredericton & St. Thomas U
CHSR 97.9 FM
21 Pacey Dr., Rm. 223
Fredericton, NB E3B 5A3
Canada
watts: 250
main: 506-453-4985
request: 506-453-4979
e: chsr@unb.ca
www.unb.ca/chsr
webcast: Yes
genres: All Styles
reports to: !earshot
ext: 506-452-6173
e: chsrpd@unb.ca
md: Sarah Robinson
e: chsrmd@unb.ca
Mark packages "Promo" & send: PO Box 4400, Fredericton, NB E3B 5A3 Canada. No Top 40.

Newfoundland

Memorial U of Newfoundland
CHMR 93.5 FM
Memorial Univ. Box A119
St. John's, NL A1C 5S7
Canada
watts: 50
main: 709-737-4777
request: 709-737-7935
f: 709-737-7688
e: chmr@mun.ca
www.chmr.ca
webcast: Yes
genres: Alt., Bluegrass, Folk, Blues, Classical, Hip-Hop, Jazz, World, Country
reports to: CMJ
pd: Ernst Rollman
Freeform station sponsors events. Send CDs or cassette. No MP3s.

Nova Scotia

Dalhousie U
CKDU 88.1 FM
6136 University Ave.
Halifax, NS B3H 4J2
Canada
watts: 3200
main: 902-494-6479
request: 902-494-2487
f: 902-494-1110
e: info@ckdu.ca
www.ckdu.ca
webcast: Yes
genres: All Styles
reports to: !earshot
pd: Pierre Loiselle
e: pierre@ckdu.ca
md: Reed Jones
e: reed@ckdu.ca
Indie-friendly campus/ community station. No Top 40.

St. Francis Xavier U
CFXU 93.3 FM
PO Box 948
Antigonish, NS B2G 2X1
Canada
watts: 50
main: 902-867-2410
request: 902-867-2321
f: 902-867-5138
e: thefox@stfx.ca
www.radiocfxu.ca
webcast: Yes
genres: Rock, Alt. Country, Indie, Folk, Bluegrass, Jazz, Pop
reports to: !earshot
pd: Joanna Barker
e: cfxuprog@stfx.ca
md: Joshua Downey/ Madeline Driscoll
e: cfxumd@stfx.ca
Many in-studio performances.

Ontario

McMaster U
CFMU 93.3 FM
Student Ctr. B119, MUSC
Hamilton, ON L8S 4S4
Canada
watts: 160
main: 905-525-9140 x27631
request: 905-528-9888
f: 905-529-3208
http://cfmu.mcmaster.ca
webcast: Yes
genres: All Styles
reports to: CMJ
pd: James Tennant
ext: 905-525-9140 x27208
e: jtennant@msu.mcmaster.ca
md: Rachel Palmieri
ext: 905-525-9140 x22053
e: cfmumusic@msu.mcmaster.ca
Freeform & sponsors some events.

Loyalist College
CJLX 91.3 FM
PO Box 4200
Belleville, ON K8N 5B9
Canada
watts: 3000
main: 613-966-0923
request: 613-966-2559
f: 613-966-1993
e: contact@91x.fm
www.91x.fm
webcast: Yes
genres: Alt., Folk, Jazz, Roots, Blues, Reggae, Classical
pd: Greg Schatzmann
md: Meghan Ashley
e: music@91x.fm
Sponsors events.

Brock U
CFBU 103.7 FM
c/o 500 Glenridge Ave.
St. Catharines, ON L2S 3A1
Canada
watts: 250
main: 905-346-2644
request: 905-346-2645
www.cfbu.ca
webcast: Yes
genres: All Styles
reports to: !earshot, Chart Magazine
pd: Deborah Cartmer
e: pd@cfbu.ca
md: Jordy Yack/Julie Demery
e: md@cfbu.ca
Freeform station w/ student & volunteer DJs plays many Indie releases & sponsors area shows. Snail mail CDs for airplay.

Queen's U
CFRC 101.9 FM
Carruthers Hall
Kingston, ON K7L 3N6
Canada
watts: 3000
main: 613-533-2121
request: 613-533-2372
f: 613-533-6049
e: cfrc@ams.queensu.ca
www.cfrc.ca
webcast: Yes
genres: Rock, Jazz, Folk, Blues, Dance, Indie, Spoken Word

reports to: !earshot
pd: Christopher Currie
md: Scott Stevens
ext: 613-533-6000 x74849
Spins tons of indies & sponsors gigs.

U of Toronto/ Mississauga
CFRE 91.9 FM
3359 Mississauga Rd. N,
Student Ctr., Rm. 131
Mississauga, ON L5L 1C6
Canada
main: 905-369-0503
request: 905-828 3447
e: info@cfreradio.com
www.cfreradio.com
webcast: Yes
genres: All Styles
reports to: CMJ, Chart, !earshot
pd: Peter Holm
e: peter@cfreradio.com
md: Tenni Gharakhanian
e: tenni@cfreradio.com
Airs live sessions, produces podcasts & sponsors events.

U of Guelph
CFRU 93.3 FM
UC Level 2, U of Guelph
Guelph, ON N1G 2W1
Canada
watts: 250
main: 519-824-4120 x53502
request: 519-837-2378
f: 519-763-9603
e: info@cfru.ca
www.cfru.ca
webcast: Yes
genres: Hip-Hop, Punk, Salsa, Reggae, Metal, Drum n Bass
reports to: CMJ, !earshot
ext: 519-824-4120 x56920
e: musicprogramming@gmail.com
md: Peter Bradley
ext: 519-824-4120 x56919
e: cfru.records@gmail.com
Sponsors monthly live music events on campus. Broadcasts in 8 different languages.

U of Western Ontario
CHRW 94.9 FM
1151 Richmond St.
UCC Rm. 250
London, ON N6A 3K7
Canada
watts: 5300
main: 519-661-3601
request: 519-661-3600
f: 519-661-3372
e: chrwmp@uwo.ca
www.chrwradio.com
webcast: Yes
genres: All Styles
reports to: CMJ, Chart Attack, Exclaim!, !earshot, Dusted
pd: Michael Brown
ext: 519-661-3601 x2
e: chrwpd@uwo.ca
md: Alicks Girowski
ext: 519-661-3601 x5
Spins lots of indies, on-air opps.

York U
CHRY 105.5 FM
4700 Keele St.
Student Ctr., Rm. 413
Toronto, ON M3J 1P3
Canada
watts: 158
main: 416-736-5293
request: 416-736-5656
f: 416-650-8052
e: chry@yorku.ca
www.chry.fm
webcast: Yes
genres: Punk, Experimental, Jazz, Hip-Hop, Rock, Blues, Contemporary Classical, Electronica, Gospel
reports to: !earshot
e: chryprog@yorku.ca
md: Matthew Fava
ext: 416-736-2100 x20185
e: chrymd@yorku.ca
Indies featured on station's eclectic playlists. Acoustic-based acts hosted live in-studio. Also sponsors events.

U of Ottawa
CHUO 89.1 FM
65 University Pvt., Ste. 0038
Ottawa, ON K1N 9A5
Canada
watts: 18,200
main: 613-562-5965
request: 613-562-5967
e: info@chuo.fm
www.chuo.fm
webcast: Yes
genres: All Styles - Mainly African-Caribbean
reports to: CMJ, !earshot
pd: Dave Aardvark
ext: 613-562-5800 x2724
e: programming@chuo.fm
md: Joni Sadler
ext: 613-562-5965 x2720
e: music@chuo.fm
Freeform English & French station spins lots of Indies & reaches into upstate NY. Sponsors some events.

U of Toronto
CIUT 89.5 FM
91 St. George St.
Toronto, ON M5S 2E8
Canada
watts: 15,000
main: 416-978-0909
request: 416-946-7000
f: 416-946-7004
e: r_burd@ciut.fm
www.ciut.fm
webcast: Yes
genres: Roots, World, Electronic, Urban, Jazz, Blues, Rock, Reggae, Dub, Rockabilly, Garage, Punk, Instrumental
reports to: !earshot, Dusted, Chart Magazine, Exclaim!, No Depression
pd: Ken Stowar
ext: 416-978-0909 x201
e: ken.stowar@ciut.fm
md: Ron Burd
ext: 416-978-0909 x214
e: r_burd@ciut.fm
Innovative station w/ powerful signal & community involvement reaches part of upstate NY. Also sponsors concerts.

U of Windsor
CJAM 91.5 FM
401 Sunset Ave.
Windsor, ON N9B 3P4
Canada
watts: 50
main: 519-971-3606; 519-253-3000 x2525
request: 519-971-3630
f: 519-971-3605
e: statcjam@uwindsor.ca
www.cjam.ca
webcast: Yes
genres: All Styles
reports to: CMJ, !earshot
pd: Cassandra Caverhill
ext: 519-253-3000 x2526
e: progcjam@uwindsor.ca
md: Chris White
ext: 519-253-3000 x2527
e: cjammd@uwindsor.ca
Mark packages "For Promotional Use" & send to: 14300 Henn St., Dearborn, MI, 48126.

Carleton U
CKCU 93.1 FM
Rm. 517, University Ctr.
1125 Colonel By Dr.
Ottawa, ON K1S 5B6
Canada
watts: 12,000
main: 613-520-2898
request: 613-520-2528
e: info@ckcufm.com
www.ckcufm.com
webcast: Yes
genres: All Styles - Mainly Indie
reports to: CMJ, Chart
pd: Dave Sarazin
ext: 613-520-3533
e: dsarazin@ckcufm.com
md: Christian Rosplesch
e: music@ckcufm.com
Sponsors events.

Ryerson U
CKLN 88.1 FM
55 Gould St., 2nd Fl.
Ryerson Student Campus Ctr.
Toronto, ON M5B 1E9
Canada
watts: 250
main: 416-979-5251
request: 416-595-1655
f: 416-595-0226
www.ckln.fm
webcast: Yes
genres: All Styles
reports to: CMJ
pd: Tony Barnes
ext: 416-979-5251 x2374
e: programdirector@ckln.fm
e: music@ckln.fm
Sponsors concerts.

Laurentian U
CKLU 96.7 FM
935 Ramsey Lake Rd.
Sudbury, ON P3E 2C6
Canada
watts: 1300
main: 705-673-6538
e: info@cklu.ca
www.cklu.ca
genres: All Styles
reports to: !earshot
pd: Carrie Graham
e: pd@cklu.ca
md: Mark Brohning
e: music@cklu.ca
Sponsors events.

Mohawk College
CIOI 101.5 FM
135 Fennell Ave. W
Hamilton, ON L8N 3T2
Canada
watts: 240
main: 905-575-2175
request: 905-575-2101
f: 905-575-2385
www.mohawkcollege.ca/msa/cioi/index.htm
webcast: Yes
genres: All Styles
reports to: !earshot
pd: Jamie Smith
ext: 905-575-2175 x2
e: program.director@mohawkcollege.ca; jamie.smith@mohawkcollege.ca
Station w/ community volunteers plays lots of Locals & some indies.

Trent U
CFFF 92.7 FM
715 George St. N
Peterborough, ON K9H 3T2
Canada
watts: 2000
main: 705-741-4011
request: 705-748-4761
e: info@trentradio.ca
www.trentradio.ca
webcast: Yes
genres: Freeform
pd: James Kerr
e: jkerr@trentradio.ca
md: Jean Reno
e: jreno@trentradio.ca
Gives Locals priority & features on-air. If playing in the area, write "Touring" on the envelope.

Quebec

U of Quebec/ Trois-Rivieres
CFOU 89.1 FM
3351 Boul. des Forges,
1013 Pavillion Neree-Beauchemin
Trois-Rivieres, QC G9A 5H7
Canada
watts: 3000
main: 819-376-5184
request: 819-376-5183
f: 819-376-5239
www.cfou.ca
webcast: Yes
genres: Alt., Metal, Hip-Hop, Punk, Electronic
reports to: Chart Attack, !earshot
pd: Alain Lefebvre
ext: 819-376-5184 x4
e: progcfou@uqtr.ca
Mostly French-language station.

U of Montreal
CISM 89.3 FM
2332 Edouard-Montpetit,
Bureau C-1509, CP 6128
Montreal, QC H3C 3J7
Canada
watts: 10,000
main: 514-343-7511
request: 514-343-2476
f: 514-343-2418
e: jhebert@cism893.ca
www.cism.umontreal.ca
webcast: Yes
genres: Alt., World, Jazz, Rock
reports to: !earshot
pd: Guillaume Vincenot
e: gvincenot@cism893.ca
md: Martin Roussy
e: mroussy@cism893.ca
World's biggest French college radio station. Music tracking by email only.

Concordia U
CJLO 1690 AM
7141 Sherbrooke St. W
Ste. CC-430
Montreal, QC H4B 1R6
Canada
watts: 1000
main: 514-848-8663
request: 514-848-7471
f: 514-848-7470
e: manager@cjlo.com
www.cjlo.com
webcast: Yes
genres: All Styles
reports to: CMJ
pd: Brian Joseph
ext: 514-848-7472
e: program@cjlo.com
md: Omar Husain
ext: 514-848-7401
e: md-alt@cjlo.com
Sponsors events.

McGill U
CKUT 90.3 FM
3674 University St.
Montreal, QC H3A 2B3
Canada
watts: 5700
main: 514-448-4041
request: 514-448-4103
f: 514-398-8261
www.ckut.ca
webcast: Yes
genres: Jazz, World, Indie, Reggae, Electronic, Metal, Folk, Noise, Blues, Bluegrass, Urban
reports to: !earshot
e: programming@ckut.ca
md: Kristiana Clemens
ext: 514-448-4041 x0842
e: music@ckut.ca
Freeform station broadcasts to reach the surrounding area. Sponsors events w/ Indie Touring acts. Email contact preferred.

Venues

Alabama

Auburn U- UPC
316 Foy Student Union
Auburn, AL 36849
p: 334-844-5292
f: 334-844-5365
e: upc@auburn.edu
www.auburn.edu/upc
advisor: Michelle Murphy
e: murphmi@auburn.edu
student: Chris Hornbuckle
p: 334-844-5362
e: hornbcr@auburn.edu
venue1: Coliseum
capacity: 8500
gigs: 5-7/year
advance: 3-6 months
genres: Rock, Pop, Alt.
venue2: Student Activities Ctr.
capacity: 2400
gigs: 5-7/year
advance: 3-6 months
genres: Rock, Pop, Alt.

Jacksonville State U
SAC
700 Pelham Rd. N
Jacksonville, AL 36265
p: 256-782-5491
f: 256-782-5087
www.jsu.edu
advisor: Debbie Taylor
e: dbtaylor@jsu.edu
student: Jacolby Parks
venue1: Pete Matthews Coliseum
capacity: 4000
gigs: 1/year
advance: 1 semester
genres: Alt., Country, Pop, Rock, Hip-Hop
venue2: Jack Hopper Dining Hall
capacity: 400
gigs: 1-3/month
advance: 1-2 months
genres: S/S, Acoustic

U of Alabama/ Tuscaloosa - UP
PO Box 870292
Tuscaloosa, AL 35487
p: 205-348-7525
f: 205-348-8251
e: upmusiccoffeehouse@sa.ua.edu
www.up.ua.edu
advisor: M. Kendrick Durham
e: mkdurham@sa.ua.edu
student: William Morris
venue1: The Ferguson Center
capacity: 250
gigs: 10/year
advance: 2-4 months
genres: Funk, World, Alt., R&B
venue2: The Quad
capacity: 500+
gigs: 10/year
advance: 2-4 months
genres: Funk, World, Alt., R&B
venue3: Moody Music Hall
capacity: 100+
gigs: 10/year
advance: 2-4 months
genres: Funk, World, Alt., R&B
Also has a "Front Row Coffee House Series" located in the Starbucks. Shows are well-promoted & mostly free for students; some are GA.

Arizona

Arizona State U
6110 N Scottsdale Rd.
Scottsdale, AZ 85253
p: 480-596-2660
e: jsamson@asu.edu
www.asukerr.com
venue1: Kerr Cultural Center
booker: Jane Samson
e: jsamson@asu.edu
capacity: 250
gigs: 100+/year
pa: Yes
genres: Jazz, Classical, World, Blues, Folk

Mesa Comm. College
Student Life & Ldrshp.
1833 W Southern Ave.
Mesa, AZ 85202
p: 480-461-7285
f: 480-461-7953
e: aloha@mail.mc.maricopa.edu; asmcc@mcmail.maricopa.edu
www.mc.maricopa.edu/services/student_activities
advisor: Greg Reents
e: gar2@mail.mc.maricopa.edu
venue1: Kirk Ctr. - Outside
capacity: 500
gigs: 3-4/year
advance: 1 semester
genres: Acoustic, S/S, Jazz, World
venue2: Kirk Center - Inside
capacity: 100
gigs: 3-4/year
advance: 1 semester
genres: Acoustic, S/S, Jazz, World
Some shows open to public.

Northern Arizona U
Sun Entertainment
PO Box 5670, Bldg. 30, Rm. 152
Flagstaff, AZ 86011
p: 928-523-5638
f: 928-523-9219
e: info@sunentertainment.org
www.sunentertainment.org
advisor: Rachel Cole
p: 928-523-1801
e: rachel.cole@nau.edu
student: Matt White
e: matt.white@nau.edu
venue1: University Union
gigs: 1/month
advance: 1 semester
genres: Acoustic, Alt., Jazz, Bluegrass
venue2: Ardrey Auditorium
capacity: 1500
gigs: 1/year
advance: 1 semester
genres: All Styles
venue3: Prochnow
capacity: 950
gigs: 2-3/year
advance: 1 semester
genres: Acoustic, Alt., Jazz, Bluegrass
Most shows open to public; tix sold at Ticketmaster.

U of Arizona
UAB Concerts
1303 E University Blvd.
SUMC 404
Tucson, AZ 85721
p: 520-621-5779
f: 520-621-6930
e: uabcrts@u.arizona.edu
www.union.arizona.edu/concerts
advisor: Chrissy Lieberman
p: 520-621-8046
e: ceagan@u.arizona.edu
student: UAB Concerts
venue1: UA Mall Stage
gigs: 40/year
advance: 1 year
genres: All Styles
venue2: Cellar Restaurant Stage
capacity: 200
gigs: 1/week
advance: 1 semester
genres: Acoustic
venue3: Plaza Stage
capacity: 1000+
gigs: 3-4/year
advance: 6 months - 1 year
genres: All Styles
Some shows open to public.

Arkansas

Arkansas State U
SAB
479 State University
State University, AR 72467
p: 870-972-2055
f: 870-972-3017
www.astate.edu
advisor: Martha Spack
e: mspack@astate.edu
venue1: ASU Convention Ctr.
capacity: 1000+
gigs: 8-10/year
advance: 6 months
pa: Yes
genres: All Styles
venue2: Fowler Center
capacity: 1000+
gigs: 25-30/year
advance: 6 months
pa: Yes
genres: Rock, Reggae, Jazz
venue3: Student Union
capacity: 500+
gigs: 25-30/year
advance: 6 months
pa: Yes
genres: All Styles

Henderson State U
SAB
1100 Henderson St.
HSU Box 7553
Arkadelphia, AR 71999
p: 870-230-5228
f: 870-230-5046
www.hsu.edu
advisor: Jordan O'Roark
p: 870-230-5228
e: oroarkj@hsu.edu
venue1: Arkansas Hall
booker: Douglas Gilpin
p: 870-230-5338
e: gilpin@hsu.edu
capacity: 920
gigs: 4/year
advance: 6 months - 1 year
pa: Yes **sound eng:** Yes
genres: Rock, Alt.
venue2: Garrison Center
booker: Ernie Higgs
p: 870-230-5252
e: higgse@hsu.edu
capacity: 400; 300
gigs: 10/year
advance: 6 months - 1 year
pa: Yes **sound eng:** Yes
genres: All Styles
venue3: The Quad
capacity: 4000-5000
gigs: 24-30/year
advance: 10-11 months
pa: Yes **sound eng:** Yes
genres: All Styles
Also books several outdoor venues. Send promos or emails w/ MySpace or web links.

Hendrix College
Social Committee
1600 Washington Ave.
Conway, AR 72032
p: 501-450-1291
f: 501-450-1477
e: activities@hendrix.edu
www.hendrix.edu/studentactivities
advisor: Tonya Hale
student: Social Committee
e: soco@hendrix.edu
venue1: Staples Auditorium
capacity: 850
gigs: 2/year
advance: 6 months
pa: Yes **sound eng:** Yes
genres: Acoustic, Jazz, Rock, Alt.
venue2: The Burrow
capacity: 147
gigs: 4-7/year
advance: 10-12 weeks
pa: Yes **sound eng:** Yes
genres: S/S, Acoustic
Co-books gigs w/ campus station KHDX. Shows are well-promoted, free & for students only.

Lyon College - SAC
2300 Highland Rd.
Batesville, AR 72501
p: 870-307-7000; 870-307-7314
f: 870-307-7369
e: sac@lyon.edu
http://www.lyon.edu
advisor: Matt Tolson
p: 870-307-7369
e: mtolson@lyon.edu
student: Sheena Highsmith
venue1: Lower Union
capacity: 100
gigs: 4-6/year
advance: 3 months
pa: Yes **sound eng:** Yes
genres: All Styles
venue2: Outdoors
advance: 1 semester
pa: Yes **sound eng:** Yes
genres: All Styles
venue3: Brown Chapel
capacity: 500
advance: 1 semester
pa: Yes **sound eng:** Yes
genres: All Styles
Nat'l indie acts booked thru NACA; Locals booked by students. Tix sold on campus for ltd. GA shows. Hard copies preferred.

Southern Arkansas U
SAB
100 E University St.
SAU Box 9146
Magnolia, AR 71753
p: 870-235-4925
f: 870-235-5265
www.saumag.edu
advisor: Sandra Smith

p: 870-235-4928
venue1: Student Center
capacity: 100
gigs: 2/year
advance: 3-6 months
genres: All Styles

U of Arkansas/ Fayetteville - UP
A665 Campus Life Ctr.
Arkansas Union
Fayetteville, AR 72701
p: 479-575-5255
f: 479-575-4844
e: upconcrt@uark.edu
www.uark.edu/up
advisor: Mary Coonley
e: mcoonley@uark.edu
student: Liz Huges
venue1: Greek Theater
booker: Grant Spencer
e: upconcrt@uark.edu
capacity: 2800
gigs: 2/year
advance: 4-6 months
genres: Rock, Alt.
venue2: Barn Hill Arena
capacity: 8000
advance: 4-6 months
genres: All Styles
All shows are free.

U of Central Arkansas SAB
201 Donaghey Ave.
UCA Box 5101
Conway, AR 72035
p: 501-450-3235
f: 501-450-5874
www.uca.edu/divisions/student/activities
advisor: Kendra Regehr
e: kendrap@uca.edu
venue1: Reynolds Performance Hall
capacity: 1200
gigs: 2/year
advance: 6 months - 1 year
pa: Yes
genres: Jazz, R&B
venue2: Farris Center
capacity: 4500
gigs: 1/year
advance: 6 months - 1 year
genres: Rock, Country, R&B
venue3: Ballroom
capacity: 450+
gigs: 1/year
advance: 6 months - 1 year
pa: Yes
genres: All Styles
Also books the Student Center Courtyard. All shows are GA.

California

Cal State U/Chico AS Presents
BMU 209
Chico, CA 95929
p: 530-898-6005
f: 530-898-4198
e: aspresents6@csuchico.edu
www.aschico.com/presents
advisor: Dwight Frey
e: dfrey@csuchico.edu; aspresentssubmission@csuchico.edu
student: Marina Maroste
e: aspresents3@csuchico.edu
venue1: The BMU
capacity: 999
gigs: 8-10/semester
advance: 6 months
pa: Yes
genres: All Styles
venue2: The Rosegarden
capacity: 1500
gigs: 1/year
advance: 6 months
pa: Yes
genres: Rock, Gospel, Pop, Funk, Reggae
venue3: The Coffeeshop
capacity: 75
advance: 6 months
genres: Acoustic, S/S, Jazz
Also hosts some outdoor shows. All shows are GA & 18+.

Cal State U/Fresno USU Productions
5280 N Jackson Ave., SU 36
Fresno, CA 93740
p: 559-278-2741
f: 559-278-7786
e: usuproductions@cvip.net
www.auxiliary.com/usu/productions.shtml
advisor: Shawna Blair
e: shblair@csufresno.edu
student: Kathy Paez
venue1: Satellite Student Union/Whitfield Union
capacity: 800
gigs: 2/semester
advance: 1 month
pa: Yes
genres: All Styles
venue2: The Pit
capacity: 300
gigs: 2/week
advance: 1 month
pa: Yes
genres: Rock, Indie, Jazz, Blues
Shows are well-promoted & most open to public. Email contact preferred.

Cal State U/ Long Beach - PC
1212 Bellflower Blvd., Rm. 116
Long Beach, CA 90815
p: 562-985-4023
f: 562-985-5245
e: pcinfo@programcouncil.org
www.programcouncil.org
advisor: Keya Allen
e: krallen@csulb.edu
student: Alex Silva
e: asilva71988@yahoo.com
venue1: Univ. Student Union
capacity: Outdoors
gigs: Weekly (Wed)
advance: 3 weeks
pa: Yes
genres: Hip-Hop, R&B, Alt., Rock, Pop
venue2: The Nugget
booker: KBEACH
p: 562-985-1624
e: showsatthebeach@gmail.com
capacity: 299
gigs: 52/year
pa: Yes
Hosts indoor & outdoor concerts. Free concerts on Wed. Tix sold at PC Office or Info Booth.

Cal State U/Northridge UPC
Univ. Student Union
18111 Nordhoff St.
Northridge, CA 91330
p: 818-677-2640
f: 818-677-3615
http://usu.csun.edu
advisor: Shannon Krajewski
p: 818-677-6494
e: shannon.krajewski@csun.edu
student: Lindsey San Miguel
e: lindsey.sanmiguel@csun.edu
venue1: Plaza del Sol (outdoor)
capacity: 500+
gigs: every 2 weeks
advance: 1 month
pa: Yes
genres: All Styles - No Rap
venue2: Pub
capacity: 70
gigs: 1/month
advance: 1 semester
genres: Acoustic, S/S, Rock, Jazz
venue3: Northridge Center
capacity: 300
gigs: 3/semester
advance: 1 semester
genres: Acoustic, S/S, Rock, Reggae, Hip-Hop
Shows booked by UPC are for Students only. Some other campus shows are GA. Associated Students also does booking: 818-677-2477.

Cal State U/Sacramento Unique Programs
University Union, Unique Programs 6000 J St.
Sacramento, CA 95819
p: 916-278-3928
f: 916-278-4850
e: csusunique@yahoo.com
www.csus.edu/union
advisor: Zenia Diokno
student: Karen Chu
venue1: University Ballroom
capacity: 1500
gigs: 20+/year
advance: 2+ months
genres: Rock, Jazz, S/S, World, Blues, Hip-Hop
venue2: Hinde Auditorium
capacity: 100+
gigs: 20+/year
advance: 2+ months
genres: Rock, Jazz, S/S, World, Blues, Hip-Hop
venue3: Redwood Room
capacity: 500+
gigs: 20+/year
advance: 2+ months
genres: Rock, Jazz, S/S, World, Blues, Hip-Hop
Some shows open to public.

Pepperdine U - SPB
24255 Pacific Coast Hwy. #4201
Malibu, CA 90263
p: 310-506-4201
f: 310-506-4827
e: spconcerts@pepperdine.edu
advisor: Jarrett Fisher
e: jarett.fisher@pepperdine.edu
venue1: Howard A. White Ctr.
booker: Anthony Kennada
p: 310-506-7153
capacity: 50-100
gigs: 4/year
advance: 1 semester
pa: Yes
genres: S/S, Acoustic
venue2: The Sandbar
capacity: 50-100
gigs: 4/year
advance: 1 semester
pa: Yes
genres: S/S, Acoustic
venue3: Smothers Theater
capacity: 500
gigs: 2/year
advance: 1 semester
pa: Yes
genres: Rock, Alt., Christian
Also books 1-2 shows/yr for Alumni Park (cap. 2000). Shows are GA; tix thru Ticketmaster.

San Diego State U Associated Students
5500 Campanile Dr.
San Diego, CA 92182
p: 619-594-6487
f: 619-594-8932
e: case@sdsu.edu
http://as.sdsu.edu
advisor: Jamie Lynn Cochran
p: 619-594-6453
e: jamie.cochran@sdsu.edu
venue1: Cox Arena
capacity: 12,000
gigs: 20/year
advance: 2 months
genres: Rock, Pop, Country, World, Reggae, Latin
venue2: Open Air Theater
capacity: 4600
gigs: 12/year
advance: 2 months
genres: Rock, Pop, Country, World, Reggae, Latin, Alt.
venue3: Starbucks/Aztec Ctr.
capacity: 100
gigs: 5/week
advance: 1 semester
pa: Yes
genres: S/S, Acoustic
Live Nation books Cox Arena & Open Air Theater. CASE books weekly gigs at The Aztec Ctr. Outdoor Patio & Montezuma Hall. Starbucks hosts Acoustic open mics.

San Jose State U Associated Students
1 Washington Sq.
San Jose, CA 95192
p: 408-924-6240
f: 408-924-6258
www.as.sjsu.edu
advisor: Duncan Lange
p: 408-924-6226
e: dclange@as.sjsu.edu
student: Tobi Richards
p: 408-924-6416
e: trichards@as.sjsu.edu
venue1: AS Barbecue Pits
capacity: 200
advance: 2-4 months
genres: Rock, Pop, Hip-Hop, Blues, Jazz, World, Folk
venue2: Amphitheater
capacity: 300
gigs: 12/year
advance: 2-4 months
genres: Rock, Pop, Hip-Hop, Blues, Jazz, World, Folk
Please add "-1028" to postal code when mailing promos.

Santa Clara U - APB
500 El Camino Real
Benson Ctr., #1
Santa Clara, CA 95053
p: 408-554-6939
f: 408-554-5544
e: cajordan@scu.edu
www.scu.edu/apb
advisor: Erica Bratton
p: 408-554-5423
e: ebratton@scu.edu
student: Leslie Henry
venue1: Leavey Center
capacity: 3000
gigs: 2/year
advance: 1 month
genres: Big Acts
venue2: The Bronco
capacity: 300
gigs: 15-20/year
advance: 10 days
genres: Indie Acts

U of Cal/Berkeley ASUC Superb Productions
4 Eshleman Hall, #4500
Berkeley, CA 94720
p: 510-642-7477
f: 510-642-7947

e: superb@ocf.berkeley.edu
http://superb.berkeley.edu
advisor: Jan Crowder
p: 510-642-8294
e: janicec@berkeley.edu
student: Kevin Huynh
venue1: Bear's Lair
capacity: 200
gigs: 12-15/semester
advance: 3-5 months
pa: Yes
genres: Rock, Hip-Hop, Alt.
venue2: Lower Sproul
capacity: Outdoors
gigs: 2-3/semester
advance: 1-3 months
pa: Yes
genres: Rock, Hip-Hop, Alt.
venue3: Pauley Ballroom
capacity: 1000
gigs: 2-3/semester
pa: Yes
genres: Rock, Hip-Hop
All shows are GA.

U of Cal/Irvine
ASUCI
G-244 Student Ctr.
Irvine, CA 92697
p: 949-824-5547
f: 949-824-2010
e: servicesvp@asuci.uci.edu
www.asuci.uci.edu
advisor: Alex Kushner
e: kushnera@asuci.uci.edu
venue1: Student Ctr. Terrace
capacity: 200
gigs: 15/year
advance: 2 months
genres: All Styles
venue2: Phoenix Grill
capacity: 100
gigs: Weekly
genres: Acoustic
venue3: Bren Events Center
capacity: 5600
genres: All Styles
Hosts a variety of shows for Local-Nat'l acts. Shows open to public & tix available thru Ticketmaster. Prefers email.

U of Cal/Los Angeles
CEC
319 Kerckhoff Hall, 308
Westwood Plaza
Los Angeles, CA 90024
p: 310-825-1958;
310-825-8989
f: 310-825-1070
e: info@uclacampusevents.com; cec.onlinemarketing@gmail.com; cec.concerts@gmail.com
www.campusevents.ucla.edu
advisor: Ken Heller
p: 310-206-8817
e: kheller@saonet.ucla.edu
venue1: Westwood Plaza
capacity: Outdoors
gigs: 5/semester
advance: 1 month
pa: Yes
genres: Pop, Hip-Hop, Punk, Alt., Rock
venue2: The Cooperage
capacity: 192
gigs: 8-10/semester
advance: 1 month
pa: Yes
genres: Pop, Hip-Hop, Punk, Alt., Rock
venue3: Kerckhoff Coffeehouse
capacity: 156
gigs: 1/semester
advance: 1 month
pa: Yes
genres: Acoustic, S/S
Also does shows at The Ackerman Ballroom. Shows are free & open to public. Cultural Affairs Commission also books events on campus. Prefers EPKs.

U of Cal/Riverside
ASPB/Concert
Commons 111
Riverside, CA 92507
p: 951-827-2772
f: 909-787-2144
e: aspb@ucr.edu
www.aspb.ucr.edu
advisor: Toannetzin Oseguera
e: toannetzin.oseguera@ucr.edu
student: Amanda Schwartz
venue1: Student Wreck Ctr.
capacity: 3000
gigs: 1-2/semester
advance: 6 months
pa: Yes
genres: Rock, Hip-Hop, Alt., Indie Rock, Latin
venue2: Outdoors
gigs: 1-2/week
advance: 1-6 months
pa: Yes
genres: Rock, Hip-Hop, Alt., Indie Rock, Latin
venue3: The Lecture Hall
capacity: 500-600
gigs: 2/week
advance: 2-3 months
Some shows open to public.

U of Cal/San Diego
AS Programming
9500 Gilman Dr.
Dept. #0077
La Jolla, CA 92093
p: 858-534-5259
f: 858-534-7665
e: asprogramming@ucsd.edu; asvpstudentlife@ucsd.edu
http://as.ucsd.edu
advisor: Lauren Weiner
p: 858-534-1611
e: lsweiner@ucsd.edu
student: Garrett Berg
p: 858-534-0791
e: gberg@csd.edu
venue1: Price Center Ballroom
capacity: 1500
gigs: 50+/year
advance: 2-5 months
genres: Rock, Hip-Hop, Pop, Alt.
venue2: Stage at Porter's Pub
capacity: 400
gigs: 50/year
advance: 2-5 months
genres: Rock, Hip-Hop, Electronic, Alt.
venue3: Cafe Roma
capacity: 50-75
gigs: 1/week
advance: 1 semester
genres: Acoustic, S/S
Books 200+ GA shows/year. Also hosts performances at the RIMAC Arena (cap. 4741) & the Mandeville Auditorium (cap. 800). Email contact preferred.

U of Cal/ Santa Barbara - ASPB
1519 University Ctr.
Santa Barbara, CA 93106
p: 805-893-3536
f: 805-893-8436
e: aspb@as.ucsb.edu
www.as.ucsb.edu
advisor: Marilyn Dukes
e: marilynd@as.ucsb.edu
student: Kayleigh Barnes
e: aspbconcerts@as.ucsb.edu
venue1: Storke Plaza
booker: Sina Sadighi
e: booking@as.ucsb.edu
capacity: Outdoors
gigs: Weekly
advance: 1 month
pa: Yes **sound eng:** Yes
genres: All Styles
venue2: UCSB Hub
capacity: 850
gigs: 3-4/month
advance: 3-4 weeks
pa: Yes **sound eng:** Yes
genres: Alt. Rock, Hip-Hop, Jam
venue3: Events Center
capacity: 3000-5000
pa: Yes **sound eng:** Yes
genres: Nat'l Acts
Offers GA shows w/ discounts for students. Also books on the Lagoon Lawn weekly.

U of Southern California - UPB
3601 Trousdale Pkwy., STU B7
Los Angeles, CA 90089
p: 213-740-5656
f: 213-740-2524
e: prgbrd@usc.edu
advisor: Enrique Trujillo
e: etrujill@usc.edu
student: Jessica Ducey
e: sconcerts@usc.edu
venue1: McCarthy Quad
capacity: Outdoors
gigs: 4/year
pa: Yes
sound eng: Yes
genres: Rock, Hip-Hop, R&B, Pop
venue2: Ground Zero Coffeehouse
capacity: 200-300
gigs: 10/year
advance: 2 months
pa: Yes
sound eng: Yes
genres: Acoustic, S/S, Rock
venue3: Bovard Auditorium
capacity: 1200
gigs: 2/year
advance: 2 months
pa: Yes
sound eng: Yes
genres: Rock, Hip-Hop, Classical
Sponsors several campus events. Shows open to students only.

U of the Pacific
ASUOP Arts & Entertainment
3601 Pacific Ave.
Stockton, CA 95211
p: 209-946-2233
f: 209-946-2744
e: asuopfyi@pacific.edu
http://asuop.pacific.edu
advisor: Jen Mazzotta
e: jmazzotta@pacific.edu
student: Elisa Asato
e: e_asato@pacific.edu
venue1: Alex G. Spanos Stadium
capacity: 3200
gigs: 5/year
pa: Yes
genres: Alt., Rock, Hip-Hop, Classical, Jazz
venue2: Faye Spanos Hall
capacity: 950
gigs: 10/year
pa: Yes
genres: Alt., Rock, Hip-Hop, Classical, Jazz
venue3: The Lair
capacity: 200
gigs: 6-10/month
pa: Yes
genres: Acoustic, S/S
Most shows are GA & free except for big concert at yr end.

Colorado

Colorado College
Live Sounds
14 E Cache La Poudre St.
Colorado Springs, CO 80903
p: 719-389-6680
f: 719-389-6609
e: livesounds@coloradocollege.edu; campusactivities@coloradocollege.edu
www.coloradocollege.edu/campusactivities
advisor: Keri Shiplet
p: 719-389-6027
e: keri.shiplet@coloradocollege.edu
student: Dan Foldes
e: d_foldes@coloradocollege.edu
venue1: Various campus areas
gigs: 6/year
advance: 1-3 months
pa: Yes
genres: Funk, Hip-Hop, Rock, Folk, World
Sponsors "Llamapaloosa" for Reg'l bands recommended by students & books Reg'l & Nat'l acts. Shows are open to students only. Greater Performers & Ideas also does some booking.

Colorado State U
ASAP
Lory Student Ctr., # 8033
Ft. Collins, CO 80523
p: 970-491-2727
f: 970-491-0972
e: asap_concerts@mail.colostate.edu
www.asap.colostate.edu
advisor: Mary Branton-Housely
p: 970-491-7476
e: mary.branton-housely@colostate.edu
student: Nathan Kogut
venue1: Lory Student Center Theater
capacity: 650
gigs: 1/year
advance: 3 months
genres: Punk, Hip-Hop, Alt.
venue2: Ramskeller
capacity: 200
gigs: 5/year
advance: 1 month
genres: Punk, Hip-Hop, Alt.
venue3: Ballroom
capacity: 1500-2000
gigs: 1/year
advance: 3 months+
genres: Punk, Hip-Hop, Alt.
Accepts EPKs from indies. Some shows at the Commons in the basement of the Lory Student Ctr. & books the Plaza (outdoors) in the Spring. Most shows are free to students.

U of Colorado/Boulder
PC
UMC Ste. 401
Boulder, CO 80309
p: 303-492-7704
f: 303-492-7706
e: director@programcouncil.com
www.programcouncil.com
advisor: Megan Bell
p: 303-735-0656
student: Christine Cao
venue1: Club 156
capacity: 157

gigs: 2-4/year
advance: 2+ weeks
genres: All Styles
venue2: Macky Auditorium
capacity: 2000
gigs: 1-2/month
advance: 2+ weeks
genres: All Styles
venue3: Balch Fieldhouse
capacity: 3000
gigs: 1-2/month
advance: 2+ weeks
genres: All Styles
Also books concerts at 4 other campus venues. Some shows are GA; tix sold thru Ticketswest.com & UMC Connection.

U of Northern Colorado - UPC
SA Office - UC
2045 10th Ave., Box 78
Greeley, CO 80639
p: 970-351-3205
f: 970-351-1055
www.unco.edu
advisor: Sherri Moser
p: 970-351-2871
e: sherri.moser@unco.edu
student: Kelly Vasta
e: kelly.vasta@unco.edu
venue1: Ballroom
venue2: Garden Theater
venue3: Panorama

Connecticut

Connecticut College SAC
270 Mohegan Ave.
PO Box 5256
New London, CT 06320
p: 860-439-2834
f: 860-439-2897
e: sac@conncoll.edu
www.conncoll.edu/campuslife/cl_student_activities_orgs.htm
advisor: Scott McEver
p: 860-439-2842
e: scott.mcever@conncoll.edu
student: SAC
venue1: 1941 Room
capacity: 50
gigs: 50+/year
advance: 4 months
genres: Acoustic, Blues, Alt., Jazz
venue2: Crow's Nest
capacity: 200
gigs: 2/week
advance: 4 months
genres: Alt., Blues, Rock, Jazz, Acoustic
Shows are free & for students only.

Fairfield U Activities Office
1073 N Benson Rd.
Fairfield, CT 06824
p: 203-254-4000 x2346
f: 203-254-4267
e: jbuswell@mail.fairfield.edu
www.fairfield.edu
advisor: Robyn Kaplan
p: 203-254-4000 x3281
e: rkaplan@mail.fairfield.edu
student: Meghan Doyle
e: mdoyle@mail.fairfield.edu
venue1: Alumni Hall
capacity: 2000
gigs: 2/year
advance: 2 months
genres: Rock, Jazz, Alt., Hip-Hop
venue2: Oak Room
capacity: 500
gigs: 6/year
advance: 2 months
genres: Rock, Jazz, Alt. Hip-Hop
venue3: Barone Campus Ctr.
capacity: 200
gigs: 6/year
advance: 2 months
genres: Rock, Jazz, Alt. Hip-Hop
Few shows are open to public. Email contact only.

Quinnipiac College SPB
275 Mt. Carmel Ave.
Hamden, CT 06518
p: 203-582-8477
f: 203-582-5203
e: spb@quinnipiac.edu
www.quinnipiac.edu/x404.xml
advisor: Carrie Robbins-O'Connell
e: carrie.robbins-o'connell@quinnipiac.edu
student: Alysse Rossner
e: alysse.rossner@quinnipiac.edu
venue1: Alumni Hall
capacity: 600
gigs: 2-3/year
genres: All Styles
venue2: Cafeteria
capacity: 1000
gigs: 1-2/year
genres: All Styles
Some shows open to public.

Sacred Heart U SE Team
5151 Park Ave.
Fairfield, CT 06825
p: 203-371-7846
f: 203-365-4780
www.sacredheart.edu
advisor: Amy Ricci
p: 203-371-7954
e: riccia@sacredheart.edu
student: Kelly Linskey
e: linskeyk@sacredheart.edu
venue1: University Commons
capacity: 300
advance: 1 week
genres: World, Rock, Alt.
venue2: The Outpost
capacity: 100
gigs: 2-3/week
genres: All Styles
Shows are for students only.

U of Connecticut SUBOG
2110 Hillside Rd., Unit 3008
Storrs, CT 06269
p: 860-486-3904
f: 860-486-4484
e: subogconcert@gmail.com
www.subog.uconn.edu
advisor: Kevin Fahey
p: 860-486-3423
e: kevin.fahey@uconn.edu
student: Beth Cheney
venue1: S Campus Bllrm.
capacity: 600
gigs: 5-6/year
advance: 1 semester
genres: Rock, Alt., S/S
venue2: Jorgenson Center
capacity: 2500
gigs: 5/year
genres: Rock, Urban, Alt., Punk
Some GA shows.

U of Hartford - PC
200 Bloomfield Ave.
West Hartford, CT 06117
p: 860-768-4283
f: 860-768-4229
http://uhaweb.hartford.edu/sca
advisor: Irwin Nussbaum
p: 860-768-7905
e: nussbaum@hartford.edu
student: Christian Lyhus
e: catmusic@hartford.edu
venue1: Lincoln Theater
capacity: 1022
gigs: 6/year
advance: 6 months - 1 year
genres: Classical, Rock, Jazz, Alt.
venue2: Millard Auditorium
capacity: 428
gigs: 12/year
advance: 6 months - 1 year
genres: All Styles
Some shows open to public.

U of New Haven SCOPE
300 Boston Post Rd.
West Haven, CT 06516
p: 203-932-7465
f: 203-931-6014
e: scope@newhaven.edu
www.newhaven.edu/student-life/CampusLife_StudentAffairs/student_activities
advisor: Greg Overend
p: 203-932-7430
e: studentactivities@newhaven.edu
student: Amanda Zeruth
venue1: Batel's Lobby
capacity: 250
gigs: 9/year
advance: 2 weeks
venue2: Dodd's Theater
capacity: 300
gigs: 1-2/year
advance: 1 month
genres: All Styles
venue3: The German Club
capacity: 200-300
gigs: 3/month
advance: 1 month
genres: All Styles
Shows are for students only.

Western Connecticut State U - PAC
181 White St.
Danbury, CT 06810
p: 203-837-8414
f: 203-837-8213
e: studentcenter@wcsu.edu
www.wcsu.edu/studentcenter
advisor: Dennis Leszko
p: 203-837-8214
e: leszkod@wcsu.edu
student: PAC
p: 203-837-8421
venue1: Student Ctr. Theater
capacity: 120
gigs: 3-5/year
advance: 2-3 weeks
genres: Rock, Urban, Alt.
venue2: Student Ctr. Lounge
capacity: 120
gigs: Weekly
advance: 2-3 weeks
genres: Rock, Hip-Hop
venue3: Ives Concert Park
capacity: Outdoor
gigs: 1-2/year
advance: 2-3 weeks
genres: Rock, Urban, Alt.
Midtown Coffeehouse (cap. 60) hosts live acts on Thu; Email cramerw@wcsu.edu. Shows are for students only. Prefers on-line press kits.

Delaware

Delaware State U SLA
1200 N Dupont Hwy.
Dover, DE 19901
p: 302-857-6398
f: 302-857-6333
www.desu.edu
advisor: Mr. Lalande
p: 302-857-6392
e: elalande@desu.edu
venue1: Student Center
gigs: 1/month
advance: 1 month
genres: All Styles
venue2: EH Theater
booker: John Samardza
p: 302-857-6665
gigs: 1/month
advance: 1 month
genres: Rock, Reggae, Caribbean, Hip-Hop, R&B
venue3: The Auditorium
capacity: 980; 500 seated
gigs: 3/month
advance: 1 month
genres: Rock, Reggae, Caribbean, Hip-Hop, R&B
Holds about 30 shows/year w/ Local-Nat'l acts.

U of Delaware SCPAB
226 Trabant University Ctr.
Newark, DE 19716
p: 302-831-8192
f: 302-831-6336
e: scpab@udel.edu
www.scpab.com
advisor: Alex Keen
p: 302-831-1403
e: advisor@scpab.com
student: Mike Fraatz
e: majorevents@scpapb.com
venue1: The Bob Carpenter Convocation Center
capacity: 300+
gigs: 1/semester
advance: 1 semester
genres: Rock, Funk, Urban, Reggae, Acoustic
venue2: Bacchus Theater
capacity: 5000+
gigs: 1/semester
advance: 2 months
pa: Yes
genres: Rock, Funk, Urban, Reggae, Acoustic
Uses any space on campus for shows. Usually 1 Nat'l act & 1 Local show booked/semester.

District of Columbia

American U SUB
4400 Massachusettes Ave. NW,
Mary Graydon Ctr., Rm. 271
Washington, DC 20016
p: 202-885-3390
f: 202-885-3396
e: activities@american.edu
www:american.edu/ocl/activities
advisor: Andrew Toczydlowski
e: toczydlo@american.edu
venue1: The Tavern
capacity: 700
gigs: 8-10/year
advance: 1 semester
genres: All Styles
Sometimes guests are allowed at shows.

George Washington U PB
800 21st St. NW, Ste. 429
Washington, DC 20052
p: 202-994-5956
f: 202-994-1347
e: gwpb@gwu.edu
http://pb.gwu.edu
advisor: Tiffany Meehan
p: 202-994-8214

e: chair@gwupb.org
student: Tom Caruso
e: concerts@gwpb.org
venue1: The Marvin Center Grand Ballroom
capacity: 700+
gigs: 3/semester
advance: 6 weeks
genres: Rock, Rap, Pop
venue2: Lisner Auditorium
capacity: 1400
gigs: 3/month
advance: 1-2 months
genres: S/S, Indie, Acoustic
venue3: Charles E. Smith Ctr.
capacity: 4000
gigs: 3/semester
advance: 6 weeks
genres: Rock, Rap, Pop

Georgetown U - GPB
316 Leavey Ctr.
Washington, DC 20057
p: 202-687-3704
e: gpb@georgetown.edu; gpbconcerts@georgetown.edu
http://gpb.georgetown.edu
advisor: Tanesha S. Stewart/Christine Mikulski
e: tss33@georgetown.edu; kj29@georgetown.edu
venue1: McDonough Arena
capacity: 3000
gigs: 2/Year
advance: 3-6 months
genres: Rock, Pop, Rap
Campus station also books events.

Florida

Flagler College - CAB
PO Box 1027
St. Augustine, FL 32085
p: 904-819-6238
f: 904-810-2253
www.flagler.edu
advisor: Kristen Nelson
p: 904-819-6238 x459
e: knelson@flagler.edu
venue1: Flagler Gym
capacity: 1200
gigs: 1/year
advance: 6 months
genres: All Styles
venue2: Flagler Auditorium
capacity: 750
gigs: 1-4/year
advance: 6 months
genres: All Styles
Local-Touring acts paid up to $1000; shows for students only.

Florida International U SP Council
University Park, GC 2304
Miami, FL 33199
p: 305-348-3068
f: 305-348-3823
e: spc@fiu.edu
www.fiu.edu
advisor: Josh Brandfon
venue1: Gracie's Grill
capacity: 300
gigs: 2/year
advance: 1 semester
genres: Hip-Hop, Reggae, Latin, Rock
venue2: US Century Bank Arena
capacity: 2000+
gigs: 1-2/year
Live music every Tue. Shows are for students only; free tix at Campus Life Office.

Florida State U - UP
A303 Oglesby Union
Tallahassee, FL 32306
p: 850-644-6673
f: 850-644-8349
e: cdubooking@admin.fsu.edu
www.union.fsu.edu/cdu/
advisor: Lori Vaughn
e: lvaughn@fsu.edu
student: Rachel Pestik
p: 850-644-4239
venue1: Club Downunder
capacity: 350
gigs: 80-100/year
pa: Yes **sound eng:** Yes
genres: Indie Rock
venue2: The Moon
capacity: 1500
gigs: 4-6/year
pa: Yes **sound eng:** Yes
genres: All Styles
venue3: Union Green
capacity: 4000
gigs: 20/year
advance: 1 semester
genres: All Styles
Occasionally sponsors "Battle of the Bands." Also books 3-5 shows at Union Ballroom, cap. 1000. Shows are GA, well-promoted & free for students. Prefers email.

Stetson U - CSA
421 N Woodland Blvd.
Unit 8334
Deland, FL 32720
p: 386-822-7225
f: 386-822-7096
e: csa@stetson.edu
www.stetson.edu/csa
advisor: Jeannie Dellutro
p: 386-822-7200
e: jdellutr@stetson.edu
venue1: Nightlights
capacity: 150
gigs: 12/year
advance: 1 month
genres: Blues, Acoustic, Rock
venue2: Hat Rack
capacity: 150
gigs: 5-10/year
advance: 1 month
genres: Acoustic
venue3: Rinker Field House
capacity: 2000
gigs: 3-4/year
advance: 7 months
genres: Rock, Alt., Hip-Hop
Shows are GA.

U of FL/Gainesville Reitz Union Board
PO Box 118505
Gainesville, FL 32611
p: 352-392-1655
f: 352-392-6450
e: rub@union.ufl.edu
www.union.ufl.edu/rub; www.union.ufl.edu/involvement
advisor: Nancy Chrystal-Green
e: nancycg@union.ufl.edu
student: Nick Lamberth/Adam D'Augelli
e: heynick@ufl.edu; adamd911@ufl.edu
venue1: Rion Ballroom
capacity: 800
gigs: 10/year
advance: 2 months
genres: Rock, Alt., Jazz, Hip-Hop
venue2: Orange & Brew
capacity: 185
gigs: 5/year
advance: 2 months
genres: Rock, Alt.
Email contact preferred.

U of Miami Hurricane Prod.
1306 Stanford Dr., Ste. #206
Coral Gables, FL 33124
p: 305-284-4606
f: 305-284-5987
e: info@um-hp.com
www.miami.edu/student-activities
advisor: Laura Stott
e: lrstott@miami.edu
student: Elena Smukler
e: e.smukler@u.miami.edu
venue1: UC Patio
booker: Parker Smith
e: concerts@um-hp.com; parkersmithatl@gmail.com
capacity: 3000
gigs: 2-4/year
advance: 2 months
genres: Rock, Alt., Jazz, Hip-Hop
venue2: UC Green
booker: Andrew Hunter
e: a.hunter@u.miami.edu
capacity: 5000
gigs: 2/year
advance: 3-6 months
genres: All Styles
venue3: The Rat
booker: Molly Matthieson
e: concerts@um-hp.com
capacity: 350
gigs: 6/year
advance: 3-6 months
genres: Nat'l Acts
Email contact preferred.

U of North Florida Osprey Productions
1 UNF Dr., Bldg. 14
Rm. 12540
Jacksonville, FL 32224
p: 904-620-2460
f: 904-620-2433
e: ospprod@unf.edu
www.unf.edu/groups/osprod
advisor: Randall Robinson
p: 904-620-1760
e: r.robinson98747@unf.edu
student: Ben Tollin
venue1: UNF Arena
booker: Lauren McAllister
e: ospprod@unf.edu
capacity: 5000
gigs: 2/year
advance: 2 months
genres: All Styles
venue2: Various
capacity: 300+
gigs: 1+/month
advance: 1 month
pa: Yes **sound eng:** Yes
genres: All Styles
"Come Out & Play" series hosts weekly gigs. Arena shows are GA & sold at Ticketmaster.

U of South Florida/ Tampa - CAB
4202 E Fowler Ave., Ctr. 246
Tampa, FL 33620
p: 813-974-5306
f: 813-974-5466
e: cab@admin.usf.edu
www.ctr.usf.edu/cab
advisor: Cindy Greenwood
p: 813-974-9837
e: cgreenwood@admin.usf.edu
student: Lindsey Dominguez
e: usfcabmusic@yahoo.com
venue1: Special Events Ctr.
capacity: 2200
gigs: 5/year
advance: 3 months
genres: Rock, Alt., Hip-Hop, Jazz
venue2: The Games Room
capacity: 150
gigs: 28/year
advance: 2 months
genres: Rock, Alt.
Mostly Reg'l Rock, Pop & S/S acts play for students at weekly "Basement Band" series. Annual Rock fest, "Bullstock" books buzz bands & Nat'l recording acts; shows are GA; all Events Ctr. gigs are also GA..

U of Tampa - SP
401 W Kennedy Blvd., Box P
Tampa, FL 33606
p: 813-253-6233
e: studentproductions@ut.edu
advisor: Rachel Rollo
e: rrollo@ut.edu
venue1: Outdoor Shows
gigs: 1-2/semester
advance: 1 semester
genres: Rock, Hip-Hop, Alt.
venue2: Reeves Theater
capacity: 180
gigs: 2/year
advance: 1 semester
genres: Rock, Hip-Hop, Alt.

U of W Florida University Commons
11000 University Pkwy.
Pensacola, FL 32514
p: 850-474-2406
www.uwf.edu/ucommons
advisor: Joy Tompkins
e: jtompkin@uwf.edu
venue1: The Commons
capacity: 425
gigs: 10-11/semester
advance: 1 month
genres: Rock, Hip-Hop, Acoustic, Country
Shows are GA; prefers electronic submissions.

Georgia

Georgia Southern U
Eagle Entertainment
PO Box 7990
Statesboro, GA 30460
p: 912-486-7270
f: 912-486-7359
e: eagleent@georgiasouthern.edu
www.eagleentertainmentonline.com
advisor: Bill Pickett
e: wpickett@georgiasouthern.edu
student: Sriravong Sriratanakoul
e: ssriratanakoul@georgiasouthern.edu
venue1: Russell Union Ballroom
capacity: 700
gigs: 10/year
advance: 1 month
genres: Rock, Alt., Blues
venue2: The Rac
capacity: 2000
gigs: 3/year
advance: 1.5 months
genres: Rock, Alt., Blues
venue3: Hanner Field House
capacity: 2500
gigs: 1-2/year
advance: 2 months
genres: Rock, Alt., Blues
Does most booking at APCA in spring. Some shows are GA.

Georgia State U - SPB
Student Ctr., Ste. 380
Atlanta, GA 30303
p: 404-413-1610
f: 404-413-1608
e: spotlight@gsu.edu
www.gsu.edu/spotlight
advisor: Tari Wimbley
e: twimbley@gsu.edu
student: Brandon Jackson
e: spotlightconcerts@gsu.edu
venue1: Student Ctr. Bllrm.
capacity: 900
gigs: 6/year
advance: 2 months
genres: Rock, Hip-Hop, Alt., Funk, Blues
venue2: Speakers Auditorium
capacity: 400
gigs: 10/year
advance: 2 months
genres: Acoustic, S/S
Some shows open to public. Tix sold at the Rialto, the venue's door or Ticketmaster.

Southern Polytechnic State U - CAB
1100 S Marietta Pkwy.
Marietta, GA 30060
p: 678-915-7374
f: 678-915-7409
e: cab@spsu.edu
http://cab.spsu.edu
advisor: Ron Lunk
p: 678-915-4101
e: rlunk@spsu.edu
venue1: Student Ctr. Bllrm.
capacity: 200
advance: 4 months
genres: Rock, Blues, Alt., Country, Hip-Hop
venue2: Amphitheatre
capacity: 2000
advance: 4 months
genres: Rock, Blues, Alt., Country, Hip-Hop
venue3: Community Ctr.
capacity: 60-75
genres: S/S, Folk

U of Georgia
Ent. Committee
153 Tate Student Ctr.
Athens, GA 30602
p: 706-542-6396
f: 706-542-5584
e: union@uga.edu
www.uga.edu/union
advisor: Marc LaMotte
e: mlamotte@uga.edu
student: Lauren Mullins
e: unionent@uga.edu
venue1: Legion Field
gigs: 1-2/year
advance: 1 semester
genres: Rock, Punk, Alt., Country
Sponsors "Day of Soul" at Legion Field.

Idaho

Boise State U - SPB
1910 University Dr.
Boise, ID 83725
p: 208-426-3835
f: 208-426-2160
e: spbconcerts@boisestate.edu
http://spb.boisestate.edu
student: Michelle Nieves
venue1: Student Union/SUB
capacity: 50-1500
gigs: 12+/year
advance: 3 months
pa: Yes
genres: All Styles
Hosts GA shows. Prefers EPKs.

Idaho State U
SAB
921 S 8th, Stop 8118
Pocatello, ID 83209
p: 208-282-3451
f: 208-282-4327
www.isu.edu/sab
advisor: Val Davis
e: davival@isu.edu
student: Sara Archibald
e: archsara@isu.edu
venue1: PAC
capacity: 1200
gigs: 1-2/year
advance: 3-6 months
genres: S/S, Acoustic, Int'l
venue2: Student Union Bllrm.
capacity: 800
gigs: 3-4/year
advance: 3-6 months
genres: All Styles (Nat'l)
Some shows are open to public.

North Idaho College
SEB
Student Union
1000 W Garden Ave.
Coeur D'Alene, ID 83814
p: 208-769-5933
f: 208-769-5942
e: asnic_events@nic.edu
www.nic.edu/asnic
advisor: Heather Erikson
venue1: Schuler PAC
capacity: 1200
gigs: 1-2/year
advance: 2-6 months
genres: All Styles
venue2: Student Union
capacity: 200-300
gigs: 14/year
advance: 2-6 months
genres: All Styles
Most shows are GA; lots of booking at NACA. Prefers emails.

U of Idaho
Vandal Ent.
Idaho Commons
PO Box 442535
Moscow, ID 83844
p: 208-885-6485
f: 208-885-6944
e: concerts@sub.uidaho.edu
www.asui.uidaho.edu
advisor: Christina Kerns
p: 208-885-5471
e: ckerns@sub.uidaho.edu
venue1: SU Ballroom
booker: Mandolyn Duclose
e: mandolyn@sub.uidaho.edu
capacity: 900
gigs: 15-20/year
advance: 1 semester
genres: All Styles
venue2: Food Court
gigs: 2/month
genres: Acoustic, S/S, Folk
Some shows open to public.

Illinois

DePaul U/ Lincoln Park - DAB
2250 N Sheffield Ave.
Chicago, IL 60614
p: 773-325-7446
f: 773-325-7359
e: dab@depaul.edu
www.depaul.edu; http://dab.depaul.edu/
advisor: Adam Heney
p: 773-325-7361
e: ahaney2@depaul.edu
student: Chris/Jackie
e: cfree1@student.depaul.edu
venue1: The MPR
capacity: 500
gigs: 3-6/year
advance: 2-3 months
genres: Rock, Alt., Hip-Hop
venue2: Brownstone's
capacity: 100
gigs: 9-12/year
advance: 1 month
genres: Acoustic, S/S, Small Jazz Groups
Music Committee is a division of the Activities Board.

Eastern Illinois U - UB
600 Lincoln Ave.
Charleston, IL 61920
p: 217-581-5117; 217-581-5522
f: 217-581-3837
www.eiu.edu/~uboard
advisor: Ceci Brinker
p: 217-581-3829
e: cbrinker@eiu.edu
student: Lauren Phillips
e: lcphillips@eiu.edu
venue1: University Ballroom
capacity: 500
gigs: 27-30/year
advance: 2-3 months
pa: Yes
genres: Hip-Hop, Rock, Alt., R&B
venue2: Lantz Gym
capacity: 3000
gigs: 2/year
advance: 2-3 months
pa: Yes
genres: Hip-Hop, Rock, Alt., R&B
Shows are GA; free for students.

Illinois Wesleyan U
SA
300 Beecher St.
Bloomington, IL 61702
p: 309-556-3850
advisor: Kevin Clark
e: kclark@iwu.edu
venue1: Hansen Student Center - Tommy's Pub
capacity: 200
gigs: 9-10/year
advance: 2 months
pa: Yes **sound eng:** Yes
genres: Acoustic, S/S
Send promos to: PO Box 2900, Bloomington, IL 61702.

Northern Illinois U
CAB
Campus Life Bldg., Rm. 160
Dekalb, IL 60115
p: 815-753-1580
f: 815-753-1557
e: cabniu@niu.edu
www.niu.edu/cab
advisor: Karla Neal
e: kneal@niu.edu
student: Marlon Haywood
e: hay132775@wpo.cso.niu.edu
venue1: HSC Diversions Show Lounge
capacity: 100+
gigs: 5/year
advance: 1 semester
genres: Alt., Folk, S/S
venue2: MLK Commons
Some shows open to public.

Quincy U - SPB
1800 College Ave.
Quincy, IL 62301
p: 217-228-5432
f: 217-228-5638
www.quincy.edu
advisor: Crystal Sutter
p: 217-228-5432 x3788
e: suttecr@quincy.edu
venue1: The Student Center
capacity: 550-600
gigs: 1-2/year
advance: 1-2 years
genres: Rock, Alt., Hip-Hop, Country, Christian
Shows are free for students; few are GA.

U of Chicago
MAB & COUP
1212 E 59th St.
Chicago, IL 60637
p: 773-834-4182
http://mab1.uchicago.edu; http://coup.uchicago.edu
advisor: Stacy Ann Ergang
e: sergang@uchicago.edu
student: Soraya Lambote
e: slambott@uchicago.edu
venue1: Mandell Hall
capacity: 980
gigs: 2-3/year
advance: 6 months
genres: Alt., Rock, Hip-Hop
venue2: Hutchinson Commons & Courtyard
capacity: 350 (Commons); 2500 (Courtyard)
gigs: 1/year
advance: 6 months
genres: Alt., Rock, Hip-Hop
venue3: Ida Noves Hall
gigs: 1/year
genres: Alt., Rock, Hip-Hop
Tix must be purchased w/ U Chicago student ID, but all shows are GA.

Western Illinois U
UB
University Union
Office of Student Activities
1 University Cir.
Macomb, IL 61455
p: 309-298-3286
f: 309-298-2879
e: AT-Comerford@wiu.edu
www.osa.wiu.edu
advisor: Diane Cumbie
p: 309-298-3232
e: dm-cumbie@wiu.edu
venue1: Grand Ballroom
capacity: 1000

pa: Yes **sound eng:** Yes
genres: Rock, Alt., Country, Jazz
venue2: Heritage Room
capacity: 800
advance: 3+ months
pa: Yes **sound eng:** Yes
genres: Rock, Alt., Country, Jazz
venue3: Western Hall
capacity: 2600
advance: 3+ months
pa: Yes **sound eng:** Yes
genres: All Styles
Some shows open to public & promoted on campus.

Indiana

Ball State U - UPB
2000 W University Ave.,
Student Ctr., Rm. L-20
Muncie, IN 47306
p: 765-285-1031
e: upb@bsu.edu
www.bsu.edu/upb
advisor: Matt Marshall
e: mmmarshall@bsu.edu
student: Dillon Kimmel
p: 765-285-1946
e: dekimmel@bsu.edu
venue1: Emens Auditorium
capacity: 3500
gigs: 1-2/year
advance: 1 month
genres: All Styles
venue2: Pruiss Hall
capacity: 650
gigs: 16/year
advance: 1 month
genres: All Styles

DePauw U
Union Board
408 S Locust St., MSU
Greencastle, IN 46135
p: 765-658-4850
www.depauw.edu/student/campusactivities
advisor: Vincent Greer
e: vgreer@depauw.edu
student: Raymond Marra
venue1: The Duck
capacity: 100+
gigs: 10-15/year
advance: 3-6 months
genres: Acoustic, Jazz, Folk, S/S
venue2: Kresge Auditorium
capacity: 750
gigs: 2-5/year
advance: 6 months
genres: Rock, Alt.
venue3: The Gym
capacity: 1000+
gigs: 1-2/year
advance: 6 months
genres: Rock, Alt., Hip-Hop, Pop

Earlham College
SAB
801 National Rd. W
Drawer 35
Richmond, IN 47374
p: 765-983-1581
f: 765-983-1641
www.earlham.edu/studentcenter/sab
advisor: Richard Dornberger
e: dornbri@earlham.edu
student: Samantha Bossman
venue1: Comstock Room
capacity: 300-350
gigs: 15/year
advance: 1 semester
genres: Jazz, Folk, S/S, Rock, Alt.
venue2: Goddard Auditorium
capacity: 615
gigs: 15/year
advance: 1 semester
genres: All Styles w/ emphasis on Jazz, Folk, S/S, Rock, Alt.
venue3: Wilkinson Theatre
capacity: 350
gigs: 2/year
advance: 1 semester
genres: Jazz, Folk, S/S, Rock, Alt.
Also has outdoor venue, cap. 2500.

Indiana U - UB
Indiana Memorial Union
900 E 7th St., Rm. 270
Bloomington, IN 47405
p: 812-855-4682
f: 812-855-8697
e: concerts@indiana.edu
www.ub.indiana.edu
advisor: Rob Meyer
e: robemeye@indiana.edu
student: Kathy Cook
e: concerts@indiana.edu
venue1: Alumni Hall
capacity: 1200 (standing)
gigs: 2-6/year
advance: 2-3 months
genres: Pop
venue2: IU Auditorium
capacity: 3200
gigs: 2-6/year
advance: 1-3 months
genres: Pop
Mostly Locals booked for weekly Wed noon & Thu nite gigs. Nat'l play Apr "Little 500" Fest. All shows are GA.

Manchester College
SA/MAC
604 E College Ave.
North Manchester, IN 46962
p: 260-982-5029
f: 260-982-4147
www.manchester.edu/osd/activity
advisor: Shannon Green
e: slgreen@manchester.edu
student: Amanda Hayward
e: ahayward@manchester.edu
venue1: Cordier Auditorium
capacity: 1300
gigs: 1-3/year
advance: 1 semester
genres: Hip-Hop, Latin
venue2: Wampler Auditorium
capacity: 200
gigs: 1-3/year
advance: 1 semester
genres: Hip-Hop, Latin
Also books bands for parties, etc.

Rose-Hulman Institute of Tech. - SAB
5500 Wabash Ave.
Terre Haute, IN 47803
p: 812-877-8448
f: 812-877-8746
www.rose-hulman.edu/sab
advisor: Donna Gustafson
p: 812-877-8275
e: gustafdj@rose-hulman.edu
student: Keldon Reller
e: rellerkj@rose-hulman.edu
venue1: Hatfield Hall
capacity: 500
genres: Rock, Acoustic
venue2: Student Union
capacity: 200
genres: All Styles

St. Joseph's College
SUB
PO Box 910
Rensselaer, IN 47978
p: 219-866-6404
f: 219-866-6355
e: sub@saintjoe.edu
www.saintjoe.edu
advisor: John May
student: Mike Koscielny
p: 219-866-6116
venue1: The Halleck Center Ballroom
capacity: 400+
gigs: 5/year
advance: 1 semester
genres: Rock
No tix for shows.

U of Evansville - SAB
1800 Lincoln Ave.
Union Bldg., Rm. 102
Evansville, IN 47722
p: 812-479-2041
f: 812-479-2156
e: sab@evansville.edu
http://sab.evansville.edu
advisor: Britney Gentry
p: 812-479-2371
e: bg67@evansville.edu
venue1: Underground
capacity: 100-200
gigs: 6/year
genres: Solo/Duo Acoustic
Annual gig w/ Nat'l acts.

U of Notre Dame -SUB
201 LaFortune
Notre Dame, IN 46556
p: 574-631-7308
f: 574-631-8139
e: sub@nd.edu
www.nd.edu/~sub/
advisor: Amy Geist
e: ageist@nd.edu
student: Clint Simkins
e: csimkins@nd.edu
venue1: Joyce Center Arena
capacity: 12,000
advance: 6 months
genres: Rock, Hip-Hop, Jazz, Alt.
venue2: Legends
capacity: 600
gigs: 30+/year
advance: 3 months
genres: Rock, Hip-Hop, Jazz, Alt., Acoustic
venue3: Stepan Center
capacity: 1500-2000
gigs: 2-5/year
advance: 6 months
Tix sold thru campus box office. Dennise Bayona & Brian Hagerty are the programmers for the Acousticafe. Chris Francica is the progammer for the Collegiate Jazz Festival.

Valparaiso U - SUB
Union Bldg., Rm. 405
Valparaiso, IN 46383
p: 219-464-5194
f: 219-464-6748
www.valpo.edu/student/ub
advisor: Angie Zemke
p: 219-464-6710
e: angela.zemke@valpo.edu
student: Jenny Halbert
e: jennifer.halbert@valpo.edu
venue1: Athletic Rec. Center
capacity: 5,500
gigs: 1/year
advance: 1 semester
genres: Rock, Alt.
venue2: Union Great Hall
capacity: 400
gigs: 3-4/year
advance: 1 semester
genres: All Styles
venue3: The Round Table
capacity: 300
gigs: 10/year
advance: 3-4 months
genres: Acoustic, Soft Rock, Jazz
Sponsors "Spring Week." Usually books bands at NACA. Some shows open to public.

Wabash College
SSAC
301 W Wabash Ave.
Crawfordsville, IN 47933
p: 765-361-6299
f: 765-361-6126
www.wabash.edu
advisor: Steve House
e: houses@wabash.edu
venue1: Chadwick Court
capacity: 2000
gigs: 2/year
genres: Nat'l Acts
venue2: Fine Arts Center
gigs: 0-2/year
Fine Art Theater produces Visiting Artist Series; contact: Jerry Bowie, bowiej@wabash.edu.

Iowa

Central College
CAB
812 University Ave.
Pella, IA 50219
p: 641-628-7610
f: 641-628-5338
e: cab@central.edu
www.central.edu
advisor: Bonnie Dahlke
p: 641-628-5243
e: dahlkeb@central.edu
student: Kati
venue1: Douwstra Aud.
capacity: 600
gigs: 1/year
advance: 1 semester
genres: Acoustic, Alt., Rock
venue2: Kuyper Gym
capacity: 2000
gigs: 1/year
advance: 1 semester
genres: Acoustic, Alt., Rock, Jam
venue3: Grand Central Stn.
capacity: 100
gigs: 4-5/year
advance: 1 semester
genres: Acoustic, S/S
Books mostly thru NACA.

Iowa State U - SUB
2229 Lincoln Way
Memorial Union, Rm. 1615
Ames, IA 50011
p: 515-294-8081
f: 515-294-0215
www.sub.iastate.edu; www.m-shop.com
venue1: Maintenance Shop
booker: Ben Day/Andy Schramm
p: 515-294-2772
e: ben@m-shop.com; andy@m-shop.com
capacity: 195; 175 (seated)
gigs: 2-7/week
advance: 1-4 months
pa: Yes
genres: Folk, Blues, Jazz, Rock, Alt.
Hosts original Reg'l & Nat'l acts; up to 3 acts play 45-90min sets. Venue takes 5% merch, if they provide seller.

Luther College - SAC
700 College Dr.
1st Fl. Union
Decorah, IA 52101
p: 563-387-1023
f: 563-387-2195
e: sac@luther.edu
http://activity.luther.edu
advisor: Trish Neubauer
p: 563-387-1567
e: neubautr@luther.edu
student: Josh Bruflodt
e: brufjo01@luther.edu
venue1: Regent Center
capacity: 2600
gigs: 1/year

advance: 3 months
genres: Rock, Hip-Hop, Alt., Folk
venue2: Ctr. For Faith & Life
capacity: 1500
gigs: 2/year
advance: 6-12 months
pa: Yes
genres: Acoustic, Alt. Rock, Softer Volume Shows
venue3: Marty's Cyber Cafe
booker: David Lester
e: lesterda@luther.edu
capacity: 450
gigs: 2-3/month
pa: Yes
genres: Rock, Alt., Rap, Hip-Hop, Indie Rock
Shows are GA & free for students.

Simpson College CAB
701 N C St.
Indianola, IA 50125
p: 515-961-1536
f: 515-961-1672
e: cab@simpson.edu
www.simpson.edu/activities
advisor: Rich Ramos
e: ramos@simpson.edu
student: CAB
venue1: Brenton St. Center
capacity: 250
gigs: 48/year
advance: 3 months
genres: Alt., Rock, Pop, Country
venue2: Coles Field House
capacity: 3000
gigs: 1/year
advance: 6-8 weeks
genres: Alt., Rock, Pop, Country
venue3: Pote Theater
capacity: 600
gigs: 1/year
advance: 3 months
genres: Alt., Rock, Pop, Country
Some shows open to public.

U of Iowa SCOPE Productions
154 Iowa Memorial Union
Iowa City, IA 52242
p: 319-335-3395
f: 319-335-3893
e: scope@uiowa.edu
www.scopeproductions.org
advisor: Cindy Thrapp
p: 319-335-3041
e: cynthia-thrapp@uiowa.edu
student: Chris Kapolas
e: ckapolas@gmail.com
venue1: IMU Main Lounge
capacity: 1600
gigs: 6-10/year
genres: Alt., Rock, Hip-Hop, CCM, Acoustic
venue2: IMU 2nd Fl. Bllrm.
capacity: 1000
gigs: 6-10/year
genres: Alt., Rock, Hip-Hop, CCM, Acoustic
venue3: Hancher Auditorium
capacity: 2500
gigs: 1-5/year
Some GA shows; tix sold thru Ticketmaster. Hard copies preferred.

Wartburg College ETK
100 Wartburg Blvd.
Waverly, IA 50677
p: 319-352-8305
f: 319-352-8305
e: etk@wartburg.edu
www.wartburg.edu/etk
advisor: Sarah Glascock
p: 319-352-8536
e: sarah.glascock@wartburg.edu; studentorgs@wartburg.edu
venue1: Neumann Aud.
capacity: 1200
gigs: 6/year
advance: 1 year
genres: Alt., World, Folk, Jazz
venue2: Ballroom
booker: Bryan McCarty
capacity: 30-100
gigs: 4/year
advance: 1 year
genres: Alt., World, Folk, Jazz
venue3: McCaskey Lyceum
capacity: 300
advance: 1 year
genres: All Styles
Shows are for students only.

Kansas

Kansas State U - UPC
Student Union, Rm. 301
Manhattan, KS 66506
p: 785-532-6571
f: 785-532-7325
e: upc@ksu.edu
www.ksu.edu/upc
advisor: Beth Bailey
e: lebailey@ksu.edu
student: Erica Boatman/Courtney Hauser
e: ericab@ksu.edu; hauser2@ksu.edu
venue1: Grand Ballroom
capacity: 1000+
gigs: 10/year
advance: 3-6 months
pa: Yes
genres: All Styles
venue2: Forum Hall
capacity: 600
gigs: 1-2/year
advance: 6-8 months
pa: Yes
genres: All Styles
venue3: Union Courtyard
capacity: 500
gigs: 1/week
advance: 3-6 months
pa: Yes
genres: Acoustic
Also books Bosco Plaza 3+/year. Send CDs.

Wichita State U - SNL
1845 N Fairmount
Rhatigan Student Ctr., Box 56
Wichita, KS 67260
p: 316-978-3495
f: 316-978-7208
e: sac@wichita.edu
www.wichita.edu
advisor: Mike Madecky
e: mike.madecky@wichita.edu
student: Philip Smith
e: philip.smith@wichita.edu
venue1: The RSC Patio
capacity: 200
gigs: 15-20/year
advance: 6-12 months
genres: Rock, Cultural, Acoustic, Jazz
venue2: The RSC Theater
capacity: 300
gigs: 7-8/year
advance: 6-12 months
genres: Rock, Jazz
venue3: SU Lounge
capacity: 75
gigs: 2-3/year
advance: 6-12 months
genres: Rock, Jazz, Acoustic, Electronic

Kentucky

U of Kentucky Concert Committee
UC Student Activities Bd.
203 Student Ctr.
Lexington, KY 40508
p: 859-257-8867
f: 859-323-1024
e: sabconcerts@yahoo.com
www.uksab.org
advisor: Heather Yattaw
e: hayatt2@email.uky.edu
student: Josh Rupp
e: joshuarupp@uky.edu
venue1: Memorial Hall
capacity: 700
gigs: 4-6/year
advance: 3-6 months
pa: Yes **sound eng:** Yes
genres: Alt., Jazz, Rock, R&B
venue2: Grand Ballroom
capacity: 1000
gigs: 5-10/year
advance: 3-6 months
pa: Yes **sound eng:** Yes
genres: Acoustic, Blues
venue3: Memorial Coliseum
capacity: 5400
gigs: 1/year
advance: 3-6 months
pa: Yes **sound eng:** Yes
genres: Alt., Jazz, R&B
Shows open to students & guests; tix sold thru Ticketmaster. Singletary Center also books gigs.

U of Louisville - SAC
SAC W301, 2100 S Floyd St.
Louisville, KY 40292
p: 502-852-6691
f: 502-852-7332
e: sabtalk@louisville.edu
www.louisville.edu
advisor: Stuart Neff
p: 502-852-0320
venue1: The Red Barn
capacity: 350
gigs: 4/year
advance: 3-6 months
pa: Yes
genres: All Styles
venue2: The Half-Time Grill
capacity: 100-125
gigs: 1/week
pa: Yes
genres: Acoustic, Blues

Western Kentucky U CAB
328 Downing U Ctr.
Bowling Green, KY 42101
p: 270-745-2459
f: 270-745-5795
e: wkucab@wku.edu
www.wku.edu/cab
advisor: Kenneth Johnson
p: 270-745-5809
e: kenneth.johnson@wku.edu
venue1: Downing U Center
capacity: 700
gigs: 25-30/year
advance: 3-6 months
genres: All Styles
venue2: Garett Ballroom
capacity: 1200
gigs: 15-20/year
advance: 3-6 months
genres: All Styles
venue3: Diddle Arena
capacity: 4500+
gigs: 1/year
advance: 6 months - 1 year
genres: All Styles

Louisiana

Louisiana State U SAB
PO Box 25123
Baton Rouge, LA 70894
p: 225-578-5118
f: 225-578-9311
e: sab@lsu.edu
www.lsu.edu/sab
advisor: Avery Smith
e: avery@lsu.edu
student: Cherie Teamer
venue1: The Ballroom
capacity: 800
advance: 6 months
genres: Hip-Hop, Rock, Alt.
Sponsors various concerts w/ Local-Nat'l acts on campus.

Louisiana Tech U UB
Rm. 214-215, S Tolliver Hall
Ruston, LA 71272
p: 318-257-4237
f: 318-257-4292
e: ub@latech.edu
www.latech.edu/tech/org/ub
advisor: Barry Morales
p: 318-257-2115
e: bmorales@latech.edu
student: Daniel Flowers
e: dwf011@latech.edu
venue1: Student Center
capacity: 800
gigs: 10/year
advance: 1 month
genres: Acoustic, Alt., Rock
venue2: Tolliver Staging Area
capacity: 1000
gigs: 4-6/year
advance: 3 weeks
genres: Acoustic, Alt., Rock, Christian Rock
Sponsors campus events. Some shows are GA; tix sold at Tolliver Hall. Send promos to: PO Box 8566, Ruston, LA 71270.

Nicholls State U - SPA
PO Box 2975
Thibodaux, LA 70310
p: 985-448-4528
f: 985-448-4554
www.nicholls.edu/spa
advisor: Francisco Chacon
p: 985-448-4452
e: francisco.chacon@nicholls.edu
student: Ketura Kemp
e: kempk407@its.nicholls.edu
venue1: Student Ballroom
capacity: 800
gigs: 1/year
advance: 1 semester
pa: Yes **sound eng:** Yes
genres: Rock, Alt., Hip-Hop, Country
Local-Touring shows for students only. Nat'l acts are GA. Tix sold at box office.

Southeastern Louisiana U - CAB
SLU 12840
Hammond, LA 70402
p: 985-549-3805
f: 985-549-3804
e: cab@selu.edu
www.selu.edu
advisor: Jason Leader
e: jleader@selu.edu
venue1: The Student Union
capacity: 300
gigs: 1-2/year
advance: 1-2 months
genres: Rock, Alt.
venue2: University Center
capacity: 2000
gigs: 1/year
genres: Rock, Alt.

Tulane U - TUCP
6823 St. Charles Ave.

Lavin Bernick Ctr., G-11
New Orleans, LA 70118
p: 504-865-5143
f: 504-865-5144
e: tucp@tulane.edu
www.tucp.net
advisor: Josh Long
p: 781-201-9631
e: jlong1@tulane.edu
student: Liza Mandelup
e: jlmandelu@tulane.edu
venue1: McAllister Aud.
capacity: 1800
gigs: 6/year
advance: 2 months
pa: Yes **sound eng:** Yes
genres: Rock, Alt., Hip-Hop, Country
Shows are GA; tix sold at door, online at Musictoday.com or at the Lavin-Bernick Center. Promos: 835 Broadway St., New Orleans, LA 70118.

Maine

Bowdoin College CAB

6200 College Stn.
Brunswick, ME 04011
p: 207-725-3917
e: cab@bowdoin.edu
www.bowdoin.edu/campuslife/activities.shtml
advisor: Megan Brunmier
p: 207-798-4244
e: mbrunmie@bowdoin.edu
venue1: Morrell Lounge
capacity: 100
gigs: 12/year
advance: 2-8 weeks
genres: Hip-Hop, Rock
venue2: Jack McGee
capacity: 50+
gigs: 12/year
advance: 2-8 weeks
genres: Rock, Pop, S/S, Folk, World
venue3: Pickard Theater
capacity: 600
gigs: 20/year
advance: 8-12 weeks
genres: Rock, Pop, Jazz, Reggae, World
Mostly estab. acts gig in theater. 2nd faculty contact: Christine Drasba: 207-725-4338; cdrasba@bowdoin.edu.

Colby College - SPB

Student Activities Office
5900 Mayflower Hill Dr.
Waterville, ME 04901
p: 207-872-4098
e: spb@colby.edu
www.colby.edu/spb/
advisor: Jessica Dash
p: 207-859-4283
e: jadash@colby.edu
student: Ben Green
venue1: Cutter Union
capacity: 1000
gigs: 1-2/year
advance: 1 semester
genres: Rock, Alt.
venue2: Mary Low Coffeehouse
capacity: 100+
gigs: 10/year
advance: 1 semester
genres: S/S, Folk, Jazz, Rock
venue3: Marchese Blue Light Pub
capacity: 200
gigs: 2/year
advance: 1 semester
genres: Rock, Jazz
Some shows open to public.

U of Maine/ Farmington - WUMF

111 South St.
Farmington, ME 04938
p: 207-778-7339
e: onehundredpointone@yahoo.com
http://wumf.umf.maine.edu
advisor: Melvin Adams
p: 207-778-7346
e: melvin.adams@maine.edu
student: Tyler Littlefield
p: 207-778-7353
venue1: Student Center South Dining Hall
capacity: 975
gigs: 1-2/year
advance: 1 semester
genres: Rock, Techno, Hardcore, Alt
venue2: Latte Landing
capacity: 135
gigs: 4/year
advance: 1 semester
genres: Acoustic
Some shows are GA.

U of Maine/Machias Concert Committee

9 O'Brien Ave.
Machias, ME 04654
p: 207-255-1245
www.umm.maine.edu
advisor: Peder Moe
e: pedermoe@maine.edu
venue1: Portside/ Kimball Hall
capacity: 150
gigs: Weekly (Fri)
advance: 4-6 months
pa: Yes **sound eng:** Yes
genres: Alt., Acoustic, Rock, Blues, Jam, Folk, Reggae, Funk, Hip-Hop
venue2: PAC
capacity: 350
gigs: 1/year
advance: 4-6 months
genres: Alt., Acoustic, Rock, Blues, Jam, Folk, Reggae, Funk, Hip-Hop
Most shows are for students & their guests. Prefers hard copies.

U of Maine/ Presque Isle - SAB

181 Main St.
Presque Isle, ME 04769
p: 207-768-9582
f: 207-768-9583
www.umpi.maine.edu
advisor: Alyson Gibbs
e: alyson.gibbs@maine.edu
venue1: Wieden Auditorium
capacity: 410
gigs: 1-2/year
advance: 1 semester
genres: Rock, Country, Blues, Acoustic
venue2: Campus Center
capacity: 225
gigs: 1-2/month
advance: 1 semester
genres: Acoustic
Prefers hard copies.

Maryland

Anne Arundel Community College CAB

101 College Pkwy.
Arnold, MD 21012
p: 410-777-2218
www.aacc.edu/studentlife
advisor: Chris Storck
p: 410-777-2219
e: cmstorck@aacc.edu
venue1: Dinning Hall
capacity: 400
advance: Previous Oct & Mar
pa: Yes
genres: All Styles
venue2: Pascal Center
capacity: 400
genres: All Styles
Holds 4 concerts/year. Tix sold on campus & open to public.

Frostburg State U UPC

Lane Ctr., Loop Rd.
Frostburg, MD 21532
p: 301-687-4411
e: upc@frostburg.edu
www.frostburg.edu
advisor: Robert Cooper
p: 301-687-4049
e: rncooper@frostburg.edu
venue1: Assembly Hall
capacity: 700
gigs: 6-8/year
advance: 4 weeks
genres: All Styles
venue2: The Loft
capacity: 200
gigs: 6-8/year
advance: 4 weeks
genres: Acoustic, S/S
Some GA shows.

Johns Hopkins U Student Development & Programming

3400 N Charles St.
Mattin Ctr., 2nd Fl.
Baltimore, MD 21218
p: 410-516-4873
f: 410-516-2227
e: studentactivities@jhu.edu
www.jhu.edu
advisor: Rachel Navarre
p: 410-516-2224
e: rnavarr4@jhu.edu
venue1: Dining Hall
capacity: 100+
gigs: 1/month
advance: 3 months+
pa: Yes **sound eng:** Yes
genres: Acoustic
Also books 1 touring act/year for "Spring Fest." No GA shows.

McDaniel College CAPB

2 College Hill
College Activities
Westminster, MD 21157
p: 410-857-2267
f: 410-857-2773
www.mcdaniel.edu
advisor: Mitchell Alexander
e: malexand@mcdaniel.edu
venue1: Pub/Terrace Room
capacity: 100
gigs: 15/year
advance: 3-6 months
pa: Yes **sound eng:** Yes
genres: Acoustic, Folk, Rock, World, Jazz
venue2: Forum
capacity: 250
gigs: 1-2/year
advance: 3-6 months
genres: All Styles
Books about 25% indies. Prefers electronic submissions.

Salisbury State U SOAP

GUC, Rm. 125-G, 1101 Camden Ave.
Salisbury, MD 21801
p: 410-543-6197
f: 410-677-5359
e: soap@salisbury.edu
http://orgs.salisbury.edu/soap
advisor: Todd Ostrom
student: Brad Deise
venue1: MAGGS
capacity: 2300
gigs: 1-2/year
advance: 2 months
pa: Yes **sound eng:** Yes
genres: Acoustic, Hip-Hop, Punk, Alt.
venue2: Halloway Hall Aud.
capacity: 700
gigs: 4+/year
pa: Yes **sound eng:** Yes
genres: Classical, Local Bands
venue3: Del Marva Shore Birds Stadium (Off Campus)
capacity: 7000
gigs: 1/year
advance: 2 months
pa: Yes **sound eng:** Yes
genres: Acoustic, Hip-Hop, Punk, Alt.
Most shows are free & GA.

St. Mary's College PB

18952 E Fisher Rd.
St. Mary's City, MD 20686
p: 240-895-4209
f: 240-895-4445
e: sgaprogramsboard@smcm.edu
www.smcm.edu/sga/pb
advisor: Kelly Schroder
e: kjschroder@smcm.edu
student: Nora Onley
e: neonley@smcm.edu
venue1: Admissions Field
capacity: Outdoors
gigs: 1-2/semester
pa: Yes
genres: All Styles
venue2: Campus Center Patio
capacity: Outdoors
gigs: 1-2/semester
pa: Yes
genres: All Styles
Hosts annual multi-band concert "World Carnival." Shows are free & for students only.

Towson U - CAB

8000 York Rd.
Towson, MD 21252
p: 410-704-2070
f: 410-704-2219
e: cab@towson.edu
www.towson.edu/cab
advisor: Bridget Chase
e: bchase@towson.edu
student: Tiffany Sutherland
e: tsuthe2@towson.edu
venue1: Towson Ctr. Arena
capacity: 3600
gigs: 1-4/year
advance: 3-6 months
pa: Yes **sound eng:** Yes
genres: All Styles
venue2: PAWS Lounge
capacity: 400
gigs: 6/year
pa: Yes **sound eng:** Yes
genres: All Styles
venue3: Burdick Field
gigs: 1/year
advance: 3-6 months
pa: Yes **sound eng:** Yes
genres: All Styles
Most shows are general admission. Tix available thru Ticketmaster.

U of Maryland/ Baltimore County SEB

Commons 336
1000 Hilltop Cir.
Baltimore, MD 21250
p: 410-455-3618

f: 410-455-3642
e: studentevents@umbc.edu
www.umbc.edu/seb
advisor: Jennifer Dress
p: 410-455-2868
e: dress@umbc.edu
student: Cat Falduto/ Kathryn Peria
e: cath4@umbc.edu; aperia1@umbc.edu
venue1: The UMBC Quad
capacity: 3500+
gigs: 3-4/year
advance: 6 months
genres: All Styles
venue2: UMBC Ballroom
capacity: 600+
gigs: 5-6/year
advance: 6 months
genres: All Styles
venue3: Coffee House
capacity: 100
gigs: 1/week
advance: 6 months
genres: Acoustic, S/S
Most shows are GA. Submit via Sonicbids only.

U of Maryland/ College Park SEE
0221 Stamp Student Union
College Park, MD 20742
p: 301-314-8498
f: 301-314-9634
e: seeconcerts@umd.edu
www.see.umd.edu
advisor: Laura Barrantes
p: 301-314-7315
e: laura@umd.edu
student: Jessica Thompson
venue1: Grand Ballroom
capacity: 1000
gigs: 2-5/year
advance: 2 months
genres: All Styles
venue2: Colony Ballroom
capacity: 600
gigs: 2-5/year
advance: 2 months
genres: All Styles
venue3: Ritchie Coliseum
capacity: 1200
gigs: 3-5/year
advance: 3-6 months
genres: All Styles
Most shows open to public.

Massachusetts

Amherst College PB
Keefe Campus Ctr., #1908
Box 5000, Amherst, MA 01002
p: 413-542-5773
f: 413-542-5845
e: kking08@amherst.edu
www.amherst.edu/ ~campuscenter
advisor: Hannah Fatemi
e: hfatemi@amherst.edu
venue1: The Front Room
capacity: 250
gigs: 3-7/year
advance: 1 semester
pa: Yes
genres: All Styles
venue2: The Gym
capacity: 1000+
gigs: 2/year
pa: Yes
genres: All Styles
Books some music on other campus locations. Most shows are GA. Tix sold at Campus Center.

Bentley College CAB
310 C Student Ctr.
175 Forest St.
Waltham, MA 02452
p: 781-891-2197
f: 781-891-3142
e: ga_cab@bentley.edu
http://student-organizations .bentley.edu/cab
advisor: Jess Kenerson
p: 781-891-2700
venue1: The 1917 Tavern
capacity: 125+
gigs: 20/year
advance: 1-2 months
genres: All Styles
venue2: Back Bay
capacity: 400
gigs: 1/year
advance: 1-2 months
genres: Rock, Punk, Alt.
No general admission.

Boston College UGBC
21 Campanella Wy., Rm. 242
Chestnut Hill, MA 02467
p: 617-552-4650
f: 617-552-3473
www.ugbc.org
advisor: Mark Miceli
p: 617-552-3480
e: mark.miceli.1@bc.edu
student: Julian Kiani
e: julian.kiani.1@bc.edu
venue1: Gym/The Forum
capacity: 3000+
gigs: 2/year
advance: 3-6 months
genres: Touring Bands - All Styles
venue2: The Perch
capacity: 150
genres: S/S, Rock
venue3: The Rat
capacity: 300+
gigs: 12/year
advance: 2-3 months
genres: Rock
Shows for students only.

Boston U - PC
1 University Rd.
Boston, MA 02215
p: 617-353-5052
f: 617-353-5257
e: bupc@bu.edu
www.bu.edu/sao/pc
advisor: Gina Regonini
p: 617-353-4474
e: gina@bu.edu
venue1: BU Central
capacity: 350
gigs: 3/week
advance: 2-3 weeks
genres: Underground, S/S, Rock
venue2: Sargent
capacity: 1200
gigs: 2-3/year
advance: 6 months
genres: Touring Bands - All Styles
venue3: Metcalfe Hall
capacity: 1000+
gigs: 1-2/year
advance: 6 months
genres: Touring Bands - All Styles
Some GA shows. Email contact preferred.

Brandeis U - SE
Shapiro Campus Ctr., 2nd Fl.,
415 South St.
Waltham, MA 02454
p: 781-736-4750
f: 781-736-4754
e: studentevents@ brandeis.edu
http://people.brandeis.edu/ ~studentevents
advisor: Sarah Richardson
p: 781-736-5065
e: slrichardson@brandeis.edu
student: Ilyssa Adler
e: studentevents@brandeis.edu
venue1: Atrium / Great Lawn
capacity: 200
gigs: 1-4/year
advance: 3-5 months
genres: Acoustic, Solo
venue2: Shapiro Gym
capacity: 2200
gigs: 2/year
advance: 6 months
genres: Rock
venue3: Levin Ballroom
capacity: 700
Larger shows open to public; tix sold at Ticketmaster & Ticket Leap.

Bridgewater State College - PC
BSC Campus Ctr., #103C
Bridgewater, MA 02325
p: 508-531-2292
f: 508-531-1786
e: pc@bridgew.edu
www.bridgew.edu/pc
advisor: Matthew Miller
p: 508-531-1273
e: m5miller@bridgew.edu
venue1: Campus Center Ballroom
capacity: 200
gigs: 2-4/year
advance: 2-6 months
genres: Rock, Alt., Covers
venue2: Swenson Field
capacity: 1000+
gigs: 1/year
advance: 3-6 months
genres: Rock, Alt., Cover Bands
Books "Spring Fest" w/ Local & Reg'ls. Email contact preferred.

College of the Holy Cross - CAB
1 College St., PO Box 4A
Worcester, MA 01610
p: 508-793-3370
f: 508-793-3643
e: cab@holycross.edu
http://college.holycross.edu /studentorgs/cab.html
advisor: Benjamin Correia
p: 508-793-3487
e: bcorreia@holycross.edu
venue1: Crossroads
capacity: 200
gigs: 10/year
advance: 1 week - 2 months
pa: Yes
genres: Acoustic
venue2: Hogan Ballroom
gigs: 10/year
advance: 2 months+
Accepts Sonicbids EPKs.

Curry College - CAB
1071 Blue Hill Ave.
Milton, MA 02186
p: 617-333-2256
f: 617-333-2910
e: activities@curry.edu
www.curry.edu
advisor: Joe DiMaria
p: 617-333-2939
venue1: The Drapkin
capacity: 75-100
gigs: 5/year
advance: Up to 1 month
pa: Yes **sound eng:** Yes
genres: All Styles
venue2: Keith Auditorium
capacity: 200
gigs: 1-2/year
advance: 3-4 months
pa: Yes **sound eng:** Yes
genres: All Styles

Salem State College PC
352 Lafayette St.
Salem, MA 01970
p: 978-542-6445
f: 978-542-8307
www.salemstate.edu
advisor: Allison Stinson
p: 978-542-7701
e: allison.stinson@ salenstate.edu
venue1: Campus Center
capacity: 200+
gigs: 4/year
advance: 1-6 months
pa: Yes **sound eng:** Yes
genres: All Styles
venue2: O'Keefe Complex
capacity: 1000+
gigs: 1/year
advance: 3-6 months
pa: Yes **sound eng:** Yes
genres: All Styles
Uses various campus venues. Tix sold at Strawberries & FYE. Some shows are GA. Email contact preferred.

Smith College - SA
Campus Ctr. 106
Northampton, MA 01063
p: 413-585-2639
f: 413-585-4166
e: campuscenter@ email.smith.edu
www.smith.edu/ campuscenter
advisor: Patrick Connelly
e: pconnell@smith.edu
venue1: The Campus Center
capacity: 250
gigs: 20/year
advance: 3-6 months
genres: Acoustic, Dance, Rock, Latin
Email contact preferred.

Stonehill College SGA Programming
320 Washington St.
Easton, MA 02357
p: 508-565-1308
f: 508-565-1416
www.stonehill.edu/x10529 .xml
advisor: Kristie Gerber
e: kgerber@stonehill.edu
venue1: The Hill
capacity: 300
gigs: 30-40/year
advance: 1 semester
pa: Yes **sound eng:** Yes
genres: All Styles
venue2: Sports Complex
gigs: 1/year
genres: Nat'l acts
Books 30-40 shows/yr for various campus parties.

Tufts U Campus Life
44 Professors Row
Medford, MA 02155
p: 617-627-3212
f: 617-627-6043
e: ocl@tufts.edu
http://ocl.tufts.edu
advisor: Jamie Engle
e: jamie.engle@tufts.edu
venue1: Duwick-MacPhie Hall
capacity: 400
gigs: 2-3/year
advance: 2-4 months
genres: All Styles
venue2: Cohen Auditorium
capacity: 600
gigs: 6/year
advance: 3-6 months
pa: Yes **sound eng:** Yes

genres: All Styles
venue3: Club Hotung
capacity: 110
gigs: 20/year
advance: 3-6 months
genres: Folk, Acoustic
Also books Brown & Brew Coffee House for 20 Acoustic shows/year. Concert Board & AppleJam also books events. Few GA shows.

U of Mass/Amherst
UPC
416 Student Union
41 Campus Ctr. Way
Amherst, MA 01003
p: 413-545-1278
f: 413-545-4751
e: umass.upc@gmail.com
www.umass.edu/csd
advisor: Lloyd Henley
e: lhenley@stuaf.umass.edu
venue1: Campus Center
capacity: 600
gigs: 4/year
advance: 6 weeks
genres: All Styles
venue2: Fine Arts Center
capacity: 1900
advance: 6 weeks
genres: All Styles
venue3: Mullins Center
booker: Global Spectrum
Some GA shows open to public. Electronic submissions preferred.

U of Mass/Dartmouth
CAB
285 Old Westport Rd., Campus Ctr., 2nd Fl., Rm. 207
North Dartmouth, MA 02747
p: 508-999-8134
f: 508-910-6597
e: cab@umassd.edu
www.umassd.edu/cab
advisor: Chris Laib
p: 508-999-8777
e: claib@umassd.edu
venue1: Main Auditorium
capacity: 800
gigs: Weekly
advance: 1 semester
genres: All Styles
venue2: Woodland Commons
capacity: 500
gigs: 4/year
pa: Yes **sound eng:** Yes
genres: Local Acts
Shows are for students only. Tix are sold at door. SAIL also books some gigs.

U of Mass/Lowell
CAPA
71 Wilder St., Ste. 1
Lowell, MA 01854
p: 978-934-5001
f: 978-934-3072
e: student_activities@uml.edu
www.uml.edu/student-services/student_activities
advisor: Amy Liss
p: 978-934-5019
e: amy_liss@uml.edu
student: Tammy Nguyen
p: 978-934-5026
e: capa@student.uml.edu
venue1: VPAC
capacity: 200-300
gigs: 10+/year
advance: 2 months
pa: Yes **sound eng:** Yes
genres: All Styles
venue2: The Rec Center
capacity: 2000
gigs: 1-2/year
advance: 1 semester
genres: Rock, Alt.
Few shows open to public.

Western New England College
CAB
1215 Wilbraham Rd.
Springfield, MA 01119
p: 413-782-1203
f: 413-796-2008
advisor: Ian Martin
e: imartin@wnec.edu
student: Erin Twomey
e: etwomey@wnec.edu
venue1: Rock Cafe
capacity: 150
gigs: 1-5/year
genres: All Styles
venue2: Coffeehouse
capacity: 150
gigs: 1-5/year
genres: All Styles

Williams College
All Campus Entertainment
Paresky Student Ctr.
PO Box 455
Williamstown, MA 01267
p: 413-597-5012
f: 413-597-3619
www.williams.edu/dean/campus_life
advisor: Jessica Gulley
p: 413-597-4749
e: jessica.a.gulley@williams.edu
venue1: Goodrich Hall
capacity: 300
gigs: 1/month
genres: All Styles
venue2: Lasell Auditorium
capacity: 700-800
gigs: 2/year
genres: All Styles
Books many GA events. Email contact preferred.

Michigan

Albion College - UB
4680 Kellogg Ctr.
Albion, MI 49224
p: 517-629-0433
f: 517-629-0930
www.albion.edu/ub/
advisor: Jennifer Schreer
e: jschreer@albion.edu
student: Josh Rontal
p: 517-629-0837
e: jrr10@albion.edu
venue1: The Stick
capacity: 350
gigs: 40/year
genres: Acoustic & Small Bands, Reg'l Acts
venue2: Chapel
capacity: 1200
genres: Nat'l Acts - All Styles
venue3: Field House
capacity: 2500
gigs: 1/year
genres: All Styles

Central Michigan U
PB
111 Bovee UC, PO Box 003
Mt. Pleasant, MI 48858
p: 989-774-3174
f: 989-774-7456
e: cmu_pb@cmich.edu
www.rso.cmich.edu/prgmbd
advisor: Damon Brown
student: David Breed
e: breed1dj@cmich.edu
venue1: Rose Arena
capacity: 4600
gigs: 1/year
advance: 3-9 months
genres: Alt., Urban, Country
venue2: Coffee House
booker: On The Fly Prod.
p: 989-774-1189
capacity: 100+
gigs: 4/year
advance: 1-3 months
genres: S/S, Jazz, Folk, Rock
venue3: Plachta Auditorium
capacity: 1350
gigs: 1/year
advance: 3-9 months
genres: Alt., Urban, Country
Hosts "Mainstage Show" & Homecoming. Also books at Finch Field House. Nat'l acts headline. Most shows are GA w/ discounted tix for students, sold at Box Office on campus.

Hope College - SACA
PO Box 9000, 141 E 12th St.
Holland, MI 49422
p: 616-395-7942
f: 616-395-7183
e: sac@hope.edu
www.hope.edu
advisor: Wilma Hart
p: 616-395-7800
e: hart@hope.edu
student: Andy Kadzban
p: 616-395-7145
e: andrew.kadzban@hope.edu
venue1: The Kletz
capacity: 150
gigs: 30/year
advance: 2-6 months
genres: Jazz, Folk, S/S
Books campus events.

Northwestern Michigan College
SGA
1701 E Front St.
Traverse City, MI 49686
p: 231-995-1400
f: 231-995-1399
e: nmc.sga@gmail.com
www.nmc.edu/sga
advisor: Lisa Blackford
p: 231-995-1043
e: lblackford@nmc.edu
venue1: Miliken Auditorium
capacity: 367
gigs: 4-5/year
advance: 6-12 months
genres: Rock
Also books smaller bands in the lower level of West Hall.

U of Detroit/Mercy
Student Life/SPB
4001 W McNichols Rd.
Detroit, MI 48221
p: 313-993-1000
f: 313-993-3275
e: programboard@students.udmercy.edu
www.udmercy.edu/student_life
advisor: Dorothy Stewart
p: 313-993-1033
e: stewardm@udmercy.edu
venue1: Grounds Coffeehouse
capacity: 100
gigs: 10/year
advance: 1-3 months
genres: Rock, Folk, S/S, Jazz, World
venue2: Ballroom
capacity: 400
gigs: 3-4/year
advance: 2-3 months
genres: Reg'l Acts

U of Michigan/Ann Arbor - UUAP
Michigan Union, Rm. #4303
530 S State St.
Ann Arbor, MI 48109
p: 734-763-3202
f: 734-763-1388
e: uuap@umich.edu
www.umich.edu/~uuap
advisor: Angela Esquivel
e: angelace@umich.edu
venue1: The Union
capacity: 200-500 SRO
gigs: 1-2/month
advance: 1-5 months
pa: Yes
genres: All Styles
venue2: The League
capacity: 200-500 SRO
gigs: 1-2/month
advance: 1-5 months
pa: Yes
genres: All Styles
venue3: Pierpont Commons
capacity: 200-500 SRO
gigs: 1-2/month
advance: 1-5 months
pa: Yes
genres: All Styles
Prime college town campus books all styles of Local thru Touring bands. All shows are GA & sold at Ticketmaster or at www.umich.edu/~muto; discount tixs for students. Pay range $100-4000.

U of Michigan/Dearborn - SAB
4901 Evergreen Rd., 2116 UC
Dearborn, MI 48128
p: 313-593-5419
f: 313-593-0943
e: sab@umd.umich.edu
www.umd.umich.edu/student/sab
advisor: Amy Karaban
p: 313-593-5390
e: akaraban@umd.umich.edu
venue1: University Center
capacity: 375
gigs: 25-30/year
advance: 1 semester
genres: All Styles - No Country

Western Michigan U
CAB & SET
1114 Faunce Student Services
WMU
Kalamazoo, MI 49008
p: 269-387-2112
e: cab-president@groupwise.wmich.edu
http://cab.wmich.edu
advisor: Jordan Hochstetler
p: 269-387-2547
e: salp-cabga@groupwise.wmich.edu
student: Lindsey Smith
e: cab-concerts@groupwise.wmich.edu
venue1: Center Stage
capacity: 200
gigs: 12/year
advance: 1 semester
genres: Jazz, Folk, Rock, S/S
venue2: Dalton Center
capacity: 450
advance: 1 semester
genres: Rock, Alt., Jazz, World, S/S

Minnesota

Bemidji State U
Hobson UPB
1500 Birchmont Dr. NE, #31
Bemidji, MN 56601
p: 218-755-3760
f: 218-775-3757
e: hupb@bemidjistate.edu
www.bemidjistate.edu/stude

nts/hobson_union
advisor: Chinwuba Okafor
e: cokafor@bemidjistate.edu
venue1: Coffee House
capacity: 75
gigs: 4-6/year
advance: 3 months
pa: Yes
genres: Acoustic, Rock, Folk
venue2: John Glass Fieldhouse
capacity: 1500
gigs: 1/year
advance: 3-6 months
pa: Yes
genres: Rock, Pop, Alt.
Some shows open to public.

Carleton College - CA
1 N College Ave.
Northfield, MN 55057
p: 507-222-4462
e: thecaveatcarleton@gmail.com
http://orgs.carleton.edu/cave
advisor: Becca Campbell
e: bcampbel@carleton.edu
venue1: The Cave
booker: Charlie Gokey
e: thecaveatcarleton@gmail.com
capacity: 150
gigs: 1-2/week
advance: 1 semester
Indies open for Nat'l acts at Spring concert. Shows are free & all ages. Promos to: The Cave, c/o Booking, 300 N College St., Northfield, MN 55057.

College of St. Benedict/St. John's JEC
37 College Ave. S
Mary Commons 209
St. Joseph, MN 56374
p: 320-363-5755
f: 320-363-5006
e: jointevents@csbsju.edu
www.csbsju.edu/jec
advisor: Gwen Schimek
e: gschimek@csbsju.edu
venue1: Brother Willie's Pub
capacity: 200
gigs: 2/month
genres: Acoustic, Rock, World
venue2: O'Connell's Coffee House
capacity: 200
gigs: 1/month
genres: Acoustic, Rock, World
Over 20 gigs/yr in 3 venues & annual "Pinestock" w/ Nat'l headliners. Email contact only.

Gustavus Adolphus College - CAB
800 W College Ave.
St. Peter, MN 56082
p: 507-933-7583
f: 507-933-7298
www.gustavus.edu/oncampus/sao
advisor: Andrea Junso
p: 507-933-7590
e: ajunso@gac.edu
student: Kevin Clevette
e: kclevett@gac.edu
venue1: Courtyard Cafe
capacity: 100
gigs: 9-10/year
advance: 2-3 months
pa: Yes
genres: Acoustic, S/S
venue2: Alumni Hall
capacity: 1500
gigs: 3-4/year
advance: 2-3 months
pa: Yes
genres: All Styles
venue3: The Dive
capacity: 200-300
gigs: 3-4/year
advance: 2-3 months
pa: Yes
genres: All Styles

Macalester College PB
1600 Grand Ave.
Campus Ctr., Rm. 232
St. Paul, MN 55105
p: 651-696-6132
f: 651-696-6447
e: pb@macalester.edu
www.macalester.edu/pb
advisor: Allison Greenlee
p: 651-696-6202
e: greenlee@macalester.edu
student: Jenny Chon/Corbin Cavallero
e: jchon@macalester.edu; ccavalle@macalester.edu
venue1: Mary Gwen Owen Performing Arts Stage/Campus Center
capacity: 400
gigs: 10-15/year
advance: 1 semester
genres: All Styles
venue2: Outdoors
capacity: 1000
gigs: 2/year
advance: 1 semester
genres: All Styles
Also helps other campus orgs book music. Most shows open to public.

Mankato State U Impact Team
173 Centennial Student Union
Mankato, MN 56001
p: 507-389-6076
f: 507-389-5632
www.mnsu.edu
advisor: Jackie Dittrich
p: 507-389-5135
e: jacqueline.dittrich@mnu.edu
venue1: Chet's Place
capacity: 100+
gigs: 5/year
advance: 1 semester
genres: Rock, Pop, Acoustic
8-10 gigs/yr in 2 venues.

Minnesota State U/Moorhead - Dragon Entertainment Group
1104 7th Ave. S
Moorhead, MN 56563
p: 218-477-2264
e: msucab@mnstate.edu
www.mnstate.edu/cab
advisor: Becky Boyle-Jones
p: 218-477-2524
e: boyle@mnstate.edu
student: Dustin DeTar
e: detardu@mnstate.edu
venue1: CMU Ballroom
capacity: 600
gigs: 4/year
advance: 1 semester
pa: Yes
venue2: CMU Underground
capacity: 300
gigs: 30/year
advance: 1 semester
venue3: Weld Auditorium
capacity: 450
gigs: 1-2/year
advance: 1 semester
pa: Yes
Most shows are GA; tix sold at door. Also contact the Executive Director, Emma Dillinger at rapunzeleed@aol.com. For Acoustic/Coffeehouse, low-budget acts in the CMU Underground, contact: Amy Griese at grieseam@mnstate.edu. Accepts EPKs. No faxes.

St. Cloud State U UPB
118 Atwood Memorial Ctr.
720 4th Ave. S
St. Cloud, MN 56301
p: 320-308-2205
f: 320-308-1669
e: upb@stcloudstate.edu
www.stcloudstate.edu/upb/
advisor: Jessica Ostman
p: 320-308-4079
e: jostman@stcloudstate.edu
student: Laura Hoffman
e: hola0301@stcloudstate.edu
venue1: Ritsche Auditorium
capacity: 900
gigs: 4/year
advance: 2 months
genres: All Styles
venue2: Atwood Quarry
capacity: 150
gigs: 4/year
advance: 1 semester
genres: All Styles
venue3: Halenback Hall
capacity: 5700
gigs: 1-3/year
advance: 3 months+
genres: All Styles

St. Olaf College - SAC
1520 St. Olaf Ave.
Northfield, MN 55057
p: 507-786-3046
f: 507-646-3548
www.stolaf.edu/orgs/sga/sac/index.htm
advisor: Chris Vatter
e: vatter@stolaf.edu
student: Morgan Harden
e: harden@stolaf.edu
venue1: Lion's Pause
capacity: 1000
gigs: 25/year
advance: 1-3 months
genres: Folk, Rock, Jazz, S/S
venue2: The Lair
capacity: 30
genres: Acoustic, S/S

U of Minnesota/Morris Office of SA
600 E 4th St.
Morris, MN 56267
p: 320-589-6080
f: 320-589-6084
e: ummstact@morris.umn.edu
www.mrs.umn.edu/services/stac
advisor: Dave Swenson
p: 320-589-6353
e: dswenson@morris.umn.edu
student: Ashley Gaschk
venue1: Edson Hall
capacity: 500
gigs: 2/year
advance: 1 semester
genres: Rock
venue2: Oyate Hall
capacity: 450
advance: 1 semester
venue3: Louie's Lower Level
capacity: 50
gigs: 50/year
Assists student groups in booking music. Some shows are GA.

U of Minnesota/Twin Cities - MPAC
Coffman Memorial Union
Rm. 500
300 Washington Ave. SE
Minneapolis, MN 55455
p: 612-624-6224
e: concerts@umn.edu
www.coffman.umn.edu/whole
advisor: Ed Kim
p: 612-626-6534
e: edkim@umn.edu
student: Eli/Heather
venue1: Whole Music Club
capacity: 238
gigs: Weekly (Fri)
advance: 2 months
genres: Punk, Indie, Hip-Hop
venue2: The Great Hall
capacity: 700
gigs: 4/year
advance: 3 months
pa: Yes **sound eng:** Yes
genres: Rock, Alt., Pop

Winona State U UPC
Kryzsko Commons, Rm. 6
Winona, MN 55987
p: 507-457-5315
e: upac@winona.edu
www.winona.edu/upac
advisor: Joe Reed
p: 507-457-5312
e: jreed@winona.edu
student: Paul Johnson
e: psjohnso0333@winona.edu
venue1: Student Commons
capacity: 100
gigs: 10/year
genres: Rock, Folk, S/S, Jazz
venue2: Memorial Gym
capacity: 3500
gigs: 1/year
advance: 1 semester
genres: Rock, Pop
Some shows open to public.

Mississippi

Alcorn State U - SAB
1000 ASU Dr., Box 180
Alcorn, MS 39096
p: 601-877-6328
f: 601-877-6329
e: misszelda@yahoo.com
www.alcorn.edu
advisor: Joshua Knox
e: jknox@alcorn.edu
student: Eddie Davenport
e: jarell20@excite.com
venue1: JL Bolden Ballroom
capacity: 400
gigs: 1/year
advance: 1 month
pa: Yes
genres: R&B, Hip-Hop
venue2: Davey Whitney Complex
capacity: 1500
gigs: 1/year
advance: 1 month
pa: Yes
genres: R&B, Hip-Hop

Mississippi State U Music Maker Prod.
PO Box 5368
Mississippi State, MS 39762
p: 662-325-2930
www.msstate.edu/org/mmp
advisor: Samantha Musil
e: smusil@saffaris.msstate.edu
venue1: Humphrey Coliseum
capacity: 10,000
gigs: 2/year
advance: 1 month
venue2: The Amphitheater
gigs: 2/year
advance: 1 month

U of Mississippi - SPB
419 Student Union, Box 1848
University, MS 38677
p: 662-915-1044
f: 662-915-6719
www.olemiss.edu/orgs/spb
advisor: Jennifer Taylor
p: 662-915-7992
e: jtaylor@olemiss.edu
venue1: The Grove
capacity: Outdoors
gigs: 1-3/year
advance: 6 months
genres: Rap, Alt., Bluegrass, Country
venue2: Ford Center
capacity: 1200
gigs: 1/year
advance: 6 months
genres: Rap, Alt., Bluegrass, Country
venue3: Stotler Lounge
capacity: 300-400
gigs: 1-3/year
advance: 1.5 months
pa: Yes
genres: Acoustic, Jazz, Blues
Looks for Nat'l acts for "The Missouri Derby." Also hosts "Battle of the Bands" outside for indies. Shows are GA; tix sold thru Ticketmaster.

Missouri

Truman State U - SAB
Lower Level Student Union
100 E Normal
Kirksville, MO 63501
p: 660-785-4722
f: 660-785-7436
e: sab@truman.edu
http://sab.truman.edu
advisor: Winston Vanderhoof
e: ad96@truman.edu
student: Haley Ray
venue1: Pershing Arena
capacity: 2500+
gigs: 2/year
advance: 2 months
pa: Yes
genres: All Styles
venue2: SUB Down Under
capacity: 150+
gigs: 3-5/year
advance: 2 months
pa: Yes
genres: All Styles
Shows are GA; discounted student tix.

U of Missouri/ Columbia - SA
A022 Brady Commons
Columbia, MO 65211
p: 573-882-3780
f: 573-884-7348
http://stufftodo.missouri.edu
advisor: Kathy Murray
e: murrayk@missouri.edu
venue1: The Hearnes Center
capacity: 5000-6000
gigs: 2/year
advance: 2-3 months
pa: Yes
genres: All Styles
venue2: Jesse Auditorium
capacity: 1756
gigs: 3-4/semester
advance: 2-3 months
pa: Yes
genres: All Styles

Washington U
Gargoyle Booking
Campus Box 1068
1 Brookings Dr.
St. Louis, MO 63130
p: 314-935-5917
f: 314-935-8488
e: gargoylebooking@hotmail.com
www.thegargoylestl.com
student: Alex Esche
venue1: The Gargoyle Club
capacity: 500
gigs: 4-5/month
advance: 6-8 weeks
genres: Rock
Student-run club books 4-5 prominent indies/mo & hosts a "Battle of the Bands."

Webster U
Campus Activities
470 E Lockwood Ave.
St. Louis, MO 63119
p: 314-961-2660 x7708
f: 314-968-7121
e: campusactivities@webster.edu
www.webster.edu/campusactivities
advisor: Elizabeth Eisley
p: 314-961-2660 x7837
venue1: Grant Gymnasium
capacity: 1000
gigs: 1/year
advance: 2-3 months
pa: Yes
genres: All Styles
venue2: The Sunner Lounge
capacity: 100-150
gigs: 1-2/year
advance: 2-3 months
pa: Yes
genres: Folk, Acoustic
venue3: The Quad
capacity: Outdoor
gigs: 1-2/year
advance: 2-3 months
pa: Yes
genres: All Styles
Shows open to public. Multicultural Ctr. also books events.

Montana

Montana State U/ Bozeman
ASMSU Concerts
221 Strand Union Bldg.
Bozeman, MT 59717
p: 406-994-2933
f: 406-994-6911
e: concerts@montana.edu
www.montana.edu
advisor: Colleen Lindner
p: 406-994-3591
e: asmsu@montana.edu
student: Josh Walker/ Johnathan Rios
p: 406-994-5821
venue1: North West Lounge
capacity: 100
gigs: 20/year
advance: 1 semester
genres: Alt., Jam
venue2: Fieldhouse
gigs: 1/year
advance: 1 semester
genres: Alt., Jam
venue3: The Gym
capacity: 1000
gigs: 1/year
advance: 1 semester
genres: Alt., Jam
Shows open to public.

Montana Tech. - SAC
1300 W Park St.
Butte, MT 59701
p: 406-496-4458
f: 406-496-4702
e: sac@mtech.edu
www.mtech.edu
advisor: Chris Van Nuland
p: 406-496-4211
e: cvannuland@mtech.edu
student: SAC
venue1: The Copper Lounge
capacity: 100+
gigs: 1-5/year
advance: 1 semester
genres: Rock, Jazz, World, Hip-Hop, Alt.
Also does 1-2 outdoor shows/ year. Some GA shows.

U of Montana
UM Productions
University Ctr., Rm. 104
Missoula, MT 59812
p: 406-243-6661
f: 406-243-4905
e: director@umproductions.org
www.umproductions.org
advisor: Marlene Hendrickson
p: 406-243-5448
e: marlene.hendrickson@mso.umt.edu
student: Ryan Hamilton
p: 406-243-4981
venue1: Adams Center
booker: Mary Muse
p: 406-243-5355
capacity: 7200
gigs: 12/year
advance: 2 weeks - 1 year
genres: Alt., Roots, Country, Jam, Funk, Loud Rock, Hip-Hop, World
venue2: UC Ballroom
capacity: 1000
gigs: 1-2/year
advance: 6-12 months
genres: Alt., Roots, Country, Jam, Funk, Loud Rock, Hip-Hop, World
venue3: University Theater
capacity: 1100
gigs: 12/year
advance: 2 weeks - 1 year
genres: Alt., Roots, Country, Jam, Funk, Loud Rock, Hip-Hop, World
Some general admission shows.

Nebraska

Doane College - SAC
1014 Boswell Ave.
Crete, NE 68333
p: 402-826-8400
e: sac@doane.edu
www.doane.edu
advisor: Talu Kayode
p: 402-826-8111
e: talu.kayode@doane.edu
venue1: The Coffee House & The Tiger Inn
capacity: 100
gigs: 15/year
advance: 3 weeks
pa: No **sound eng:** No
genres: All Styles
venue2: Heckman Auditorium
capacity: 450
gigs: 1-2/year
advance: 3+ weeks
pa: No **sound eng:** No
genres: All Styles
Shows are for students only. Tix are sold at gym facility.

U of Nebraska/Kearney
Mainstage Committee
1013 W 27th St.
Kearney, NE 68849
p: 308-865-8396
e: schaffnittjn@unk.edu
www.unk.edu/studentlife/student_org/LPAC/index.php?id=509
advisor: Tim Danube
p: 308-865-8523
e: danubet@unk.edu
venue1: Health & Sports Ctr.
capacity: 5000
gigs: 1-2/year
advance: 6-12 months
genres: Nat'l Touring Acts
venue2: The Ponderosa
capacity: 500
Also books bands for the "Blue & Gold Welcome Week." Shows are GA & free to students.

U of Nebraska/Omaha SP
6001 Dodge St., MBSC, 1st Fl.
Omaha, NE 68182
p: 402-554-2711
f: 402-554-3179
http://spo.unomaha.edu
advisor: Erin Cron
e: ecron@mail.uomaha.edu
student: Hope Vavra
p: 402-554-2623
venue1: Nebraska Room
pa: Yes
genres: S/S, Country
Books bands for GA outdoor parties, festivals & events.

Nevada

U of Nevada/Las Vegas SA
4505 Maryland Pkwy.
PO Box 452009
Las Vegas, NV 89154
p: 702-895-3221
f: 702-895-4103
e: csun@unlv.edu
www.unlvcsun.com
advisor: Savannah Baltera
p: 702-895-3645
e: savannah.baltera@unlv.edu
student: Josh Ouzer
p: 702-895-2316
e: csunep@unlv.edu
venue1: Intramural Field
capacity: Outdoors
gigs: 2/year
genres: Rock
venue2: Amphitheater
gigs: Monthly
genres: Reg'l Rock, Jam, Acoustic
All shows are open to public.

U of Nevada/Reno
FLiPSiDE PB
Student Union, MS 058
Reno, NV 89557
p: 775-784-6589
e: concerts@asun.unr.edu
advisor: Jason Entsminger
e: directorco@asun.unr.edu
student: Heather Turk
p: 775-784-6025
e: hturk@unr.edu
venue1: Pine Lounge
capacity: 150+
gigs: 12/year
advance: 3-6 months
genres: Alt., Hip-Hop, Jazz
venue2: The Tailgate Area
capacity: Outdoors
gigs: 5/year
advance: 3-6 months
genres: Alt., Hip-Hop, Jazz
venue3: Lawler Events Ctr.
booker: Lauren O'Brien
p: 775-784-6025
e: vpprogramming@asun.unr.edu
capacity: 11,000
gigs: 1-2/year
advance: 6 months
genres: Alt., Hip-Hop, Jazz
Most shows open to public.

New Hampshire

Colby Sawyer College
CAB
541 Main St.
New London, NH 03257
p: 603-526-3759
f: 603-526-2135
e: cab@colby-sawyer.edu
www.colby-sawyer.edu/campus-life/campus_activities
advisor: Tim Fenton
p: 603-526-3490
e: tfenton@colby-sawyer.edu
student: Liz O'Donnell
e: lodonnell@colby-sawyer.edu
venue1: Wheeler Hall
capacity: 300
gigs: 4/year
advance: 6-12 months
genres: Rock, Punk, Pop, Jazz, Classical, Blues, Folk
venue2: Sawyer Center
capacity: 60
gigs: 6/year
advance: 1 year
genres: Jazz, Blues, Folk
Some shows open to public. Most booking via Sonicbids.

Daniel Webster College - SAB
20 University Dr.
Nashua, NH 03063
p: 603-577-6589
f: 603-577-6177
e: sab@dwc.edu
www.dwc.edu/studentlife
advisor: Jay Gargas
student: Nicholas Candelier
venue1: Common Thread
capacity: 80
gigs: 1/month
advance: 3-12 months
genres: Alt., Jazz, World, Acoustic, Country
venue2: Collings Auditorium
capacity: 250
gigs: 2-3/year
advance: 3-12 months
genres: Alt., Jazz, World, Acoustic, Country, Cover
venue3: Dining Hall
capacity: 150
gigs: 2-3/year
advance: 3-12 months
genres: Alt., Jazz, World, Acoustic, Country, Cover

Dartmouth College
PB
6181 Collis Ctr., Ste. 303
Hanover, NH 03755
p: 603-646-3399
f: 603-646-1386
e: programming.board@dartmouth.edu
www.dartmouth.edu/~sao
advisor: Elizabeth Agosto
e: elizabethagosto@dartmouth.edu
venue1: Common Ground
advance: 3-6 months
genres: Urban, Alt., Rock, Blues
venue2: Spaulding Aud.
advance: 3-6 months
genres: Urban, Alt., Rock, Blues
venue3: Hopkins Center
advance: 3-6 months
genres: Urban, Alt., Rock, Blues
Most shows are GA.

Franklin Pierce College
CAB
PO Box 60
Rindge, NH 03461
p: 603-899-4309
f: 603-899-4339
e: pac@franklinpierce.edu
www.myspace.com/campusactivities
advisor: Leah Robichaud
p: 603-899-4152
student: CAB
venue1: Pierce Hall
capacity: 200
gigs: 1-5/year
advance: 1 semester
genres: Acoustic
venue2: Field House
capacity: 100
gigs: 1-5/year
advance: 1 semester
genres: Acoustic
Also books some coffeehouse gigs.

Keene State College
SAC
229 Main St., Student Ctr.
Keene, NH 03435
p: 603-358-2664
f: 603-358-2604
e: kscsac@yahoo.com
www.keene.edu/young/stuact.cfm
advisor: Jennifer Ferrell
e: jferrell1@keene.edu
student: SAC
Over 10 shows/year at various venues; some open to the public.

New England College
CAB
Box #99, 24 Bridge St.
Henniker, NH 03242
p: 603-428-2248
f: 603-428-2515
www.nec.edu
advisor: Megan Hotaling
e: mhotaling@nec.edu
student: Ashlee Rowley
e: arowley06@nec.edu
venue1: West Lawn
capacity: 400
gigs: 1-2/year
advance: 3-6 months
genres: Rock, Pop
venue2: Great Room
capacity: 300
gigs: 30/year
advance: 3-6 months
genres: Acoustic, S/S
venue3: Coffeehouse
capacity: 1000
gigs: 10/year
advance: 3-6 months
genres: Rock, Pop

Plymouth State U
PACE
19 Highland Ave., Ste. A25
Plymouth, NH 03264
p: 603-535-2248
f: 603-535-2795
e: pace@mail.plymouth.edu
www.paceevents.org
advisor: Rodney Ekstrom
e: advisor@paceevents.org
student: Sarah Noyes/Dan Fornash
e: djfornash@plymouth.edu
venue1: Fireplace Lounge
capacity: 30-75
gigs: 2/month
genres: Acoustic
venue2: Court Room
capacity: 500
gigs: 1-2/year
genres: Jam, Hip-Hop, Rock
venue3: Multi Purpose Room
capacity: 200
gigs: 1/year
genres: Jam, Hip-Hop, Rock
Most shows free for students; GA for select shows. Snail mail kits or use Sonicbids.

U of New Hampshire
MUSO Board
Memorial Student Bldg., Rm. 139, Main St.
Durham, NH 03824
p: 603-862-1485
f: 603-862-3952
e: muso1485@yahoo.com
www.unh.edu/muso
advisor: David Zamansky
p: 603-862-1586
e: david.zamansky@unh.edu
student: Anthony
venue1: Stratford Room
capacity: 300
gigs: 1-2/year
advance: 1-6 months
venue2: Wild Cat Den
capacity: 100
gigs: 1-2/month
advance: 1-6 months
venue3: Stateroom
capacity: 800+
gigs: 1/year
advance: 1-6 months
Some shows open to public.

New Jersey

The College of NJ
College Union Board
PO Box 7718
Ewing, NJ 08628
p: 609-771-2467
f: 609-637-5122
e: cub@tcnj.edu
http://cgi.tcnj.edu/~cub
advisor: Jessica Claar
student: Katerina Gkionis
venue1: The Rat
booker: Michael Lawrence
e: cubrat@tcnj.edu
capacity: 200+
gigs: Weekly
advance: 3-4 months
pa: Yes **sound eng:** Yes
genres: All Styles
Also books various campus venues.

Monmouth U - SAB
400 Cedar Ave.
West Long Branch, NJ 07764
p: 732-923-4704
f: 732-263-5100
e: sab@monmouth.edu
www.monmouth.edu/campus_life/activities
advisor: Amy
p: 732-571-3586
student: Holly Cannon
venue1: Anacon Hall
capacity: 500
gigs: 12/year
advance: 1 semester
pa: Yes
genres: All Styles
venue2: Pollak Theatre
capacity: 714
gigs: 2/year
advance: 1 semester
pa: Yes
genres: All Styles
venue3: Java City Cafe
capacity: 60
gigs: 20/year
advance: 1 semester
pa: Yes
genres: All Styles
Most shows are free; larger shows open to public. Also books 50 shows/year at The Underground.

Montclair State U
Class One Concerts
1 Normal Ave., Student Ctr. Annex, Rm. 117
Upper Montclair, NJ 07043
p: 973-655-4478
f: 973-655-4098
e: sga@mail.montclair.edu
www.myspace.com/classoneconcerts
advisor: Julie Fleming
p: 973-655-7819
e: flemingj@mail.montclair.edu
student: Class One Concerts
e: classoneconcerts@gmail.com
venue1: The Ratt
capacity: 150
gigs: 10/year
advance: 1-3 months
genres: All Styles
venue2: The Bar Room
capacity: 400+
gigs: 6/year
genres: All Styles

Ramapo College
SA/Ramashows
505 Ramapo Valley Rd., Student Ctr., 2nd Fl.
Mahwah, NJ 07430
p: 201-684-7593
f: 201-825-0276
e: student_activities@ramapo.edu
www.ramapo.edu/studentlife/studentactivities/studentact
venue1: Friends Hall
capacity: 275
gigs: 8/year
advance: 2-3 months
pa: Yes **sound eng:** Yes
genres: All Styles
venue2: J. Lee's
capacity: 75
gigs: 12-15/year
advance: 2-3 months
pa: Yes **sound eng:** Yes
genres: S/S, Acoustic
Books monthly shows featuring indies. Concert Core books the larger events. Shows are well-promoted & open to public.

Rider U - SEC
2083 Lawrenceville Rd.
Lawrenceville, NJ 08648
p: 609-896-5332
f: 609-895-5479
e: sec@rider.edu
www.rider.edu/~sec
advisor: Nicholas Barbati/Dave Keenan
e: barbati@rider.edu; keenand@rider.edu
student: Jenny Benack
e: benack@rider.edu
venue1: The Gym
booker: Jason Miller/Dianna Clauss
e: jamiller@rider.edu; dclauss@rider.edu
capacity: 1100+
gigs: 1-2/year
advance: 1-3 months
genres: Nat'l Acts
venue2: Cavalla Room
booker: Danielle Marasco
e: dmarasco@rider.edu
capacity: 1100+
gigs: 1-2/year
advance: 1-3 months
genres: Nat'l acts
Books only Nat'l Touring acts, no coffee shop or Local performers.

Rutgers U
RUPA
84 Joyce Kilmer Ave.
Piscataway, NJ 08854
p: 732-445-3561

f: 732-445-2752
e: music.rupa@gmail.com
http://rupa.rutgers.edu
advisor: Matt Ferguson
e: ruferg@rci.rutgers.edu
student: Jasmine Wang
venue1: College Hall
capacity: 500+
gigs: 3/year
advance: 2-4 months
pa: Yes
genres: Hip-Hop, Jazz, Rock, Ska, Punk, Reggae
venue2: Livingston Recreation Center
capacity: 3000+
gigs: 1/year
advance: 2-4 months
pa: Yes
genres: Rock, Pop, Hip-Hop, Reggae, Jazz
venue3: Yorba Lounge
capacity: 150
gigs: 1/year
advance: 2-4 months
pa: Yes
genres: Rock, Pop, S/S, Reggae
RUPA books events on all University campuses: Livingston, Newark, Camden & New Brunswick. Shows are GA.

Seton Hall U - SAB
400 S Orange Ave.
South Orange, NJ 07079
p: 973-761-9084
f: 973-275-2805
e: sab@shu.edu
http://studentaffairs.shu.edu/SAB
advisor: Kyle Warren
p: 973-275-2566
e: warrenky@shu.edu
venue1: The Main Lounge
booker: Kyle Warren
e: warrenky@shu.edu
capacity: 700
gigs: 1-5/year
advance: 3-6 months
pa: Yes **sound eng:** Yes
genres: World, DJs, Rock, Acoustic
venue2: The Pirate's Cove
capacity: 100+
gigs: 10/year
genres: World, DJs, Rock, Acoustic
Mostly free concerts. Tix sold at University Center.

New Mexico

College of Sante Fe SAB
1600 St. Michael's Dr.
Sante Fe, NM 87505
p: 505-473-6217
www.csf.edu/campus_life/student_activities
advisor: Yorgun Marcel
e: ymarcel@csf.edu
venue1: The Sub
capacity: 250-300
gigs: 20/year
advance: 1 month
pa: Yes
genres: All Styles
venue2: The Garage
capacity: 87; 200 (SRO)
gigs: 6/year
advance: 2-3 months
pa: Yes
genres: All Styles
venue3: The Forum
capacity: 200
gigs: 4-5/year
advance: 1 month
pa: Yes
genres: Acoustic
Most shows are Local/Reg'ls. Also books outdoor yr-end event for 2000+. Some shows are GA & well-promoted on & off campus.

Eastern New Mexico U/Portales Associated SAB
Student Activities, Stn. 39
1500 S Ave. K
Portales, NM 88130
p: 575-562-2631
www.enmu.edu/studentlife/organizations/index.shtml
advisor: Tracy Henderson
e: tracy.henderson@enmu.edu
venue1: Ground Zero Coffeehouse
capacity: 200
gigs: 2/month
advance: 4 weeks
pa: Yes
genres: Country, Alt. Rock
venue2: Union Ballroom
capacity: 1200
gigs: 1/semester
advance: 1 semester
pa: Yes
genres: Country, Alt. Rock
venue3: Greyhound Arena
capacity: 5000
gigs: 1/year
advance: 1 year
pa: Yes
genres: Country, Alt., Rock
Focus on emerging talent. Reg'ls & open mics in coffeehouse; Nat'ls in larger rooms.

U of New Mexico SSE
Student Union Bldg.
Rm. 1018
Albuquerque, NM 87131
p: 505-277-5602
f: 505-277-7345
e: sse@unm.edu
www.unm.edu/~sse
advisor: Ryan Lindquist
p: 505-277-4706
e: depar@unm.edu
student: Lesley McKinney
e: llmcknny@unm.edu
venue1: SUB Ballroom
capacity: 1200
gigs: 5/year
pa: Yes **sound eng:** Yes
genres: All Styles
venue2: SUB Atrium
capacity: 250
gigs: 50/year
advance: 1 week
pa: Yes **sound eng:** Yes
genres: All Styles
venue3: SUB Mall
capacity: 500
gigs: 25/year
advance: 1 week
pa: Yes **sound eng:** Yes
genres: All Styles
Mostly indie acts, esp. at Wed noon time gigs. "Spring Fiesta" has Nat'l headliner & 5+ smaller acts. Shows are GA & well-promoted. Snail mail promos or use Sonicbids.

New York

Alfred U - SAB
1 Saxon Dr.
Alfred, NY 14802
p: 607-871-2175
f: 607-871-2088
e: csi@alfred.edu
www.alfred.edu
advisor: Dan Napolitano
e: napolitano@alfred.edu
venue1: The Knight Club
capacity: 350
gigs: 50/year
advance: 3-4 months
pa: Yes **sound eng:** Yes
genres: Hip-Hop, Rock, S/S, World
venue2: Holmes Auditorium
capacity: 450
gigs: 8/year
advance: 3-4 months
pa: Yes **sound eng:** Yes
genres: Hip-Hop, Rock, World
venue3: McLane Gym
capacity: 2000
gigs: 1/year
advance: 1-3 months
genres: Ska, Punk, Alt.
Most concerts are free & GA.

Cornell U Concert Commission
518D Willard Straight Hall
Ithaca, NY 14853
p: 607-255-7231
e: concert@cornell.edu
www.cornell-concert.com
advisor: Joseph Scaffido
p: 607-255-4169
e: jss44@cornell.edu
student: Justin Fields
e: jlf77@cornell.edu
venue1: Barton Hall
capacity: 5000
gigs: 3-4/year
advance: 2-3 months
genres: Hip-Hop, Rap, Rock, Alt.; No Country (mainly Nat'l acts w/ a Reg'l opener)
venue2: Bailey Hall
capacity: 1300
gigs: 1-2/year
advance: 2-3 months
genres: Hip-Hop, Rap, Rock, Alt.; No Country (mainly Nat'l acts w/ a Reg'l opener)
Most shows GA. Books about 20% indie shows. Fanclub Collective also books indie shows; contact: fanclubcollective@yahoo.com. Bailey Hall was recently renovated. Tix on pre-sale to students first at www.cornellconcerts.com.

Hofstra U Hofstra Concerts
200 Hofstra U
260 Student Ctr.
Hempstead, NY 11549
p: 516-463-6967
f: 516-463-6030
e: hofstraconcerts@yahoo.com
www.hofstra.edu
advisor: Anita Ellis
p: 516-463-6914
e: anita.ellis@hofstra.edu
student: Veronica
venue1: Hofstra USA
capacity: 500
gigs: 2/year
advance: 2-3 months
genres: Nat'l Acts
venue2: The Rat
capacity: 150
gigs: 6/year
advance: 1-2 months
genres: Acoustic, Hip-Hop, Punk, Folk, Rock
venue3: The Playhouse
capacity: 1176
gigs: 1-2/year
advance: 3 months
genres: All Styles

Ithaca College - SAB
319 Egbert Hall
Ithaca, NY 14850
p: 607-274-3383
f: 607-274-1725
e: icsab@googlegroups.com
www.ithaca.edu/sab
advisor: Russell Martin
p: 607-274-3222
e: rjmartin@ithaca.edu
venue1: The IC Square
capacity: 300
gigs: 6/year
advance: 1+ month
pa: Yes
genres: Acoustic, S/S, Rock
venue2: Ben Light Gym
capacity: 200
gigs: 2/year
advance: 3-6 months
genres: Nat'l Acts
venue3: Emerson Suites
capacity: 700
gigs: 3/year
advance: 2 months
genres: Nat'l Acts
Mark submission - ATTN: SAB.

Long Island U/ C.W. Post - ACP
Hillwood Commons
Office of Student Activities
Rm. 102
Brookville, NY 11548
p: 516-299-2828
f: 516-299-4041
e: acp_cwpost@yahoo.com
www.liu.edu
advisor: Angela Layne
p: 516-299-3909
e: angela.layne@liu.edu
student: Eric Zirlinger
p: 516-299-2800
e: eric.zirlinger@liu.edu
venue1: Hillwood Commons Lecture Hall
capacity: 500
gigs: 3-4/year
advance: 1 semester
genres: Hip-Hop, Rock, R&B
venue2: Tilles Center
capacity: 2500
gigs: 1-2/year
advance: 1 year
genres: Nat'l acts
venue3: The Pioneer Room
All shows are GA.

New York U - UPB
60 Washington Sq. S
Kimmel Ctr., 7th Fl., Rm. 707
New York, NY 10012
p: 212-998-4987
e: program.board@nyu.edu
www.osa.nyu.edu/pb
advisor: Michelle Luff
e: michelle.luff@nyu.edu
student: Brenda Malvini
e: blm267@nyu.edu
venue1: The Eisner & Lubin Auditorium
capacity: 600
gigs: 2+/year
advance: 2-4 months
genres: Hip-Hop, Electronic, Alt., World, Rock
venue2: Skirball Auditorium
capacity: 850
gigs: 2/year
advance: 2-4 months
pa: Yes **sound eng:** Yes
genres: Hip-Hop, Electronic, Alt., World, Rock
venue3: Shorin Music Performance Center
capacity: 200
gigs: 2-3/year
advance: 2-4 months
genres: Folk, Acoustic
Some shows are GA. Tix sold at Ticket Central.

Niagara U
Live Music & Broadcast Committee
Upper Level Gallagher Ctr.
Niagara University, NY 14109
p: 716-286-8655
f: 716-286-8422
www.niagara.edu
advisor: Fred Heuer
e: fjh@niagara.edu
venue1: Under The Taps
capacity: 250
gigs: 10-14/year
advance: 2-6 months
pa: Yes
genres: All Styles
Mostly Reg'l acts gig; shows are GA.

Rochester Institute of Technology - CAB
34 Lomb Memorial Dr.
Rochester, NY 14623
p: 585-475-2509
f: 585-475-5630
e: cab@rit.edu
http://cab.rit.edu
advisor: Ryan Giglia
p: 585-475-7685
e: rjgccl@rit.edu
student: Brian Linquist
e: bdlcab@rit.edu
venue1: The Clark Gym
booker: Danielle Akins
e: dmacab@rit.edu
capacity: 1700
gigs: 2-3/year
advance: 3 months
pa: Yes **sound eng:** Yes
genres: Nat'l Acts
venue2: Gordon Field House
capacity: 4800
gigs: 3-4/year
advance: 3 months
pa: Yes **sound eng:** Yes
genres: Touring Acts
venue3: The Ritz
booker: Tim Hong & Luz Rameriz
e: thhcab@rit.edu; lercab@rit.edu
capacity: 250
gigs: 30/year
advance: 3 months
pa: Yes **sound eng:** Yes
genres: Punk, Indie Rock, Emo, S/S, World, Hip-Hop
Shows are GA & well-promoted on & off campus.

Siena College - SEB
Sarazen Student Union
Rm. 203, 515 Louden Rd.
Loudonville, NY 12211
p: 518-783-2524
e: seb@siena.edu
advisor: Jen Fraley
p: 518-782-6581
e: jfraley@siena.edu
student: Amy McCartney
venue1: The Coffee House
capacity: 250
gigs: 8/year
advance: 2-3 months
pa: Yes **sound eng:** Yes
genres: Metal, Acoustic, Punk, Jazz
venue2: The ARC
capacity: 2000+
gigs: 1/year
advance: 1 semester
pa: Yes **sound eng:** Yes
genres: Touring Nat'ls
Music booked for many events & themed wknds. Snail mail kits.

St. Bonaventure U
CAB
3261 W State Rd., PO Box V
Reilly Ctr., Rm. 208
St. Bonaventure, NY 14778
p: 716-375-2506
f: 716-375-2583
www.sbu.edu
advisor: Rob DeFazio
student: Steve Kuchera
e: skuchera@sbu.edu
venue1: The Rathskeller
capacity: 200
gigs: 10/year
advance: 1-3 months
pa: Yes **sound eng:** Yes
genres: Rock, Cover Bands, Blues, S/S, Pop, Indie
venue2: Riley Center Arena
capacity: 3500-4000
gigs: 1-2/year
advance: 2-3 months
genres: All Styles
Local & Nat'l Indie Rock acts play "The Rathskeller" Fri nites. Larger Nat'l acts play Riley Center Arena; few shows are GA. Prefers email w/ link to music.

SUNY/Buffalo - SA
363 Student Union
Amherst, NY 14260
p: 716-645-2957
f: 716-645-2236
www.sa.buffalo.edu
advisor: Marc Rosenblitt
e: mpr@buffalo.edu
student: Rebecca Powell
e: rapowell@buffalo.edu
venue1: Alumni Arena
capacity: 6500
gigs: 6/year
advance: 1-3 months
genres: Rock, Hip-Hop, Jazz, World, S/S
venue2: Triple Gym
capacity: 3000
gigs: 6/year
advance: 1-3 months
genres: All Styles
venue3: CFA Main Stage
capacity: 600
gigs: 6/year
advance: 1-3 months
genres: All Styles
Also books parties, festivals & other venues on campus. About 15-20% of tix are held for GA. Tix sold at www.tickets.com or at the Alumni Arena Box Office.

SUNY/Oneonta
CUAC
Office of Campus Activities,
Hunt College Union Bldg.
Oneonta, NY 13820
p: 607-436-3012
f: 607-436-2415
e: cuac@oneonta.edu
www.organizations.oneonta.edu/cuac
advisor: Bill Harcleroad
p: 607-436-2550
e: harclewg@oneonta.edu
venue1: The Water Front
capacity: 160
gigs: 20/year
advance: 1 semester
pa: Yes **sound eng:** Yes
genres: All Styles
venue2: Hunt Union Ballroom
capacity: 1000
gigs: 2-5/year
advance: 1 semester
pa: Yes **sound eng:** Yes
genres: Rock
venue3: The Dewar Arena
capacity: 3000
gigs: 4/year
advance: 1 semester
pa: Yes **sound eng:** Yes
genres: Pop, Alt., Rock
Most shows are GA. Tix sold thru Box Office. Books thru NACA & by student recommendation. Other orgs also books gigs.

SUNY/Potsdam - SES
9013 Barrington Dr.
Potsdam, NY 13676
p: 315-267-2583
f: 315-267-2798
e: sga@potsdam.edu
www.potsdam.edu/student_life
advisor: Maureen Taylor
p: 315-267-2579
e: taylorme@potsdam.edu
student: Rob Carita
e: carita51@potsdam.edu
venue1: Hurley's Niteclub
booker: Ben O'Brien Smith
e: smithbo190@potsdam.edu
capacity: 125
gigs: 1-2/week
advance: 2 weeks
pa: Yes **sound eng:** Yes
genres: All Styles

Syracuse U
303 University Ave.
Syracuse, NY 13244
p: 315-443-2718
f: 315-443-4617
http://students.syr.edu
advisor: J.R. McGrat
p: 315-443-9826
e: jrmcgrat@syr.edu
student: Dennis Jacobs
e: dejacobs@syr.edu
venue1: Schine Underground
capacity: 350
advance: 1 semester
pa: Yes
venue2: Jabberwocky Café
venue3: Goldstein Auditorium
Hosts original Local-Int'l music for flat fee. Bandersnatch & The University Union also book shows.

U of Rochester
Wilson Commons SA
201 Wilson Commons
Rochester, NY 14627
p: 585-275-9390
f: 585-273-5306
e: sao@rochester.edu
www.sa.rochester.edu/sao
advisor: Melissa Schmidt
venue1: The Palestra
capacity: 1600
gigs: 1/year
advance: 6 months
pa: Yes **sound eng:** Yes
genres: Rock, Pop, Jazz, Folk, Emo
venue2: Strong Auditorium
capacity: 975
gigs: 3-4/year
advance: 2-6 months
pa: Yes **sound eng:** Yes
genres: All Styles
venue3: Starbucks
capacity: 80
gigs: 1/week
advance: 2 months
pa: Yes **sound eng:** Yes
genres: Acoustic, S/S (3-pieces & under)
Also books other campus venues. Shows are GA & promoted on & off campus.

North Carolina

Appalachian State U
APPS
231 Plemmons Student Union
Boone, NC 28608
p: 828-262-3032
f: 828-262-2937
e: apps@appstate.edu
www.apps.appstate.edu
advisor: Randy Kelly
e: kellyrm@appstate.edu
student: Patrick Leitner
e: stageshows@appstate.edu
venue1: The Coffeehouse
capacity: 120
gigs: 30/year
advance: 3 months
pa: Yes **sound eng:** Yes
genres: Acoustic, S/S
venue2: Legends
capacity: 1000
gigs: 50/year
advance: 3 months
pa: Yes **sound eng:** Yes
genres: Rock, Alt.
venue3: Farthing Auditorium
booker: Courtney Cooper
e: cc60164@appstate.edu
capacity: 1600
gigs: 1-2/year
pa: Yes **sound eng:** Yes
MEISA also books events.

Duke U
DUU
PO Box 90834
Durham, NC 27708
p: 919-684-2911
f: 919-684-8395
e: union@duke.edu
www.union.duke.edu
advisor: Janicanne Shane
e: janicanne.shane@duke.edu
p: 919-684-4741
student: Amelia Fernandez
e: amelia.fernandez@duke.edu
venue1: The Blue Devil at The Armadillo Grill
booker: Hillary Waugh
e: hillary.waugh@duke.edu
capacity: 100
gigs: 1/week
advance: 3 months
genres: Alt., Hip-Hop, Jazz, Jam
venue2: The Coffeehouse on East Campus
booker: Jennifer Fuh
e: jcf16@duke.edu
capacity: 200
advance: 1 month
genres: Rock, Alt., Hip-Hop, Acoustic
venue3: Page Auditorium
booker: Heather Jernigan
e: heather.jernigan@duke.edu
Books Locals-Int'ls & heavily promotes shows. Sponsors "Oktoberfest" & "Springternational." Some GA shows. FedX: 101 Bryan Ctr., Duke U, Durham, NC 27708.

East Carolina U - PEC
236 Mendenhall, Student Ctr.
Greenville, NC 27858
p: 252-328-4715
f: 252-328-2305
e: studentunion@ecu.edu
www.ecu.edu/student_union
advisor: Levy Brown, Jr.
p: 252-328-5733
e: brownl@mail.ecu.edu
student: Erin Edwards
p: 252-328-4715
e: supopent@mail.ecu.edu
venue1: Pirate Underground
capacity: 500
gigs: 1/week
advance: 1 semester
genres: Rock, Hip-Hop, Ska, Alt., Country, Jazz
venue2: Hendrix Theatre
capacity: 7660
gigs: 3-4/year

advance: 1 semester
genres: Rock, Hip-Hop, Ska, Alt., Country, Jazz
venue3: Performing Arts Hall
capacity: 1500
gigs: 1/year
advance: 1 semester
genres: Rock, Hip-Hop, Alt., Country, Jazz

Elon U
SUB
Campus Box 2975
Elon, NC 27244
p: 336-278-7208
f: 336-278-7299
e: sub@elon.edu
www.elon.edu/sub
advisor: Janis Baughman
e: jbaughman@elon.edu
student: Katie Gettier
e: kgettier@elon.edu
venue1: Lighthouse Tavern
booker: Anna Davis
e: adavis21@elon.edu
capacity: 300
gigs: 1/week
advance: 1 semester
pa: Yes
genres: Rock, Acoustic, Alt., Hip-Hop, World
venue2: McKinnon Hall
capacity: 500
gigs: 8-10/year
advance: 1 semester
pa: Yes
genres: Rock, Alt.
venue3: Gym & Outdoors
pa: Yes
Books mostly indies. Some shows open to public.

Guilford College
SUPB
5800 W Friendly Ave.
Greensboro, NC 27410
p: 336-316-2303
f: 336-316-2943
e: cablive@guilford.edu
www.guilford.edu
advisor: Erica Constentino
p: 336-316-2388
e: constentino@guilford.edu
student: Lauren Manley
p: 336-316-2618
venue1: The Grill
capacity: 1000
gigs: 1-3/month
advance: 1 week - 3 months
pa: Yes **sound eng:** Yes
genres: Indie, Acoustic, S/S
venue2: Sternburger
capacity: 1000
gigs: 1/year
advance: 3 weeks - 3 months
pa: Yes **sound eng:** Yes
genres: Rock, Alt.
venue3: Dana Auditorium
capacity: Outdoor
gigs: 1/year
advance: 3 weeks - 3 months
pa: Yes **sound eng:** Yes
genres: Rock, Alt.
Radio station also books some GA events. Good gig btwn DC & Atlanta.

North Carolina State U
Union AB
1200 Talley Student Ctr.
NCSU Box 7306
Raleigh, NC 27695
p: 919-515-5918
f: 919-513-4204
e: uab_entertain@ncsu.edu
http://uab.ncsu.edu
advisor: Rick Gardner
p: 919-515-5161
e: rick_gardner@ncsu.edu
student: Scott Richardson
venue1: The Ballroom
capacity: 200-300
gigs: 1-2/year
advance: 1.5 months
genres: Rock, Jazz, Alt., Blues
venue2: Witherspoon
capacity: 460
gigs: 1-2/year
advance: 1-2 months
genres: Rock, Alt., Blues, Jazz
venue3: The B.A.R.
capacity: 80-100
gigs: 1-2/year
advance: 1-2 months
genres: Acoustic, S/S
IRC, Greek Life, Alumni Assoc. & Student Gov. also book events. No EPKs.

U of NC/Greensboro
CAB
221 Elliott University Ctr.
PO Box 26170
Greensboro, NC 27402
p: 336-334-3552
f: 336-334-3008
e: cab@uncg.edu
http://cab.uncg.edu
advisor: Curtis Tarver
p: 336-334-3033
e: cwtarver@uncg.edu
student: Joe Cashman
e: jgcashma@uncg.edu
venue1: Cone Ballroom
capacity: 700
gigs: 2/year
advance: 6-12 months
venue2: EUC West Lawn
gigs: 2/year
advance: 6-12 months
venue3: Auditorium
capacity: 500
gigs: 2/year
advance: 6-12 months
genres: CCM, Hip-Hop, Bluegrass
Sponsors "Spring Fling" & "Fall Concert." Shows are GA.

U of NC/ Wilmington - ACE
601 S College Rd., CAIC
Fisher Student Ctr.
Rm. 2029K
Wilmington, NC 28403
p: 910-962-3842
f: 910-962-7438
e: ace@uncw.edu
www.uncw.edu/ace
advisor: Krista Harrell
p: 910-962-7722
e: harrellk@uncw.edu
student: Meredith Kelly
e: mkk5634@uncw.edu
venue1: Hawk's Nest
capacity: 150-200
gigs: 15/year
advance: 2-3 months
genres: Acoustic, S/S
venue2: The Commons Amphitheatre
capacity: 300
gigs: 8-10/year
advance: 2-3 months
genres: Rock, Alt., Hip-Hop
venue3: Warwick
capacity: 600
gigs: 3-4/year
advance: 2-3 months
genres: Rock, Alt., Hip-Hop
Books indie artists for "Battle of the Bands" & frequent shows.

North Dakota

Minot State U - SA
500 University Ave. W
Minot, ND 58707
p: 701-858-3090
e: msusac@minotstateu.edu
www.minotstateu.edu/sga
advisor: Ann Rivera/ Leon Perzinski
p: 701-858-3987
e: ann.rivera@my.minotstateu.edu; leon.perzinski@my.minotstateu.edu
student: Sarah Perry
p: 701-858-3412
e: sarah.perry@my.minotstateu.edu
venue1: Beaver Dam
capacity: 300
gigs: 1-2/year
advance: 1 semester
pa: Yes
genres: All Styles
venue2: The Dome
capacity: 5000+
gigs: 1/year
advance: 1 semester
pa: Yes
genres: All Styles
venue3: The Aleshire Theater
capacity: 250
gigs: 10/year
advance: 3-4 months
pa: Yes
genres: Acoustic, Jazz
Books Nat'ls thru NACA. Shows are free for students. Locals send hard copies.

North Dakota State U
Campus Attractions
124 A Memorial Union
Fargo, ND 58105
p: 701-231-7221
e: ndsu.campus.attractions@ndsu.edu
www.ndsu.edu/campusattractions
advisor: Kim Bruemmer
e: kimberly.bruemmer@ndsu.edu
student: Kaylie Young
e: kaylie.young@ndsu.edu
venue1: Ballroom
booker: Concerts Coordinator
e: ndsu.campus.attractions@ndsu.edu
capacity: 500-600
gigs: 2/semester
advance: 1 semester
Uses several venues - depends on size of band; all shows are GA.

Ohio

Bowling Green State U - UAO
408 Bowen-Thompson SU
Bowling Green, OH 43403
p: 419-372-2486
e: myuao@bgsu.edu
www.bgsu.edu/studentlife/organizations/uao
advisor: Denny Bubrig
p: 419-372-2343
e: dbubrig@bgsu.edu
student: Scott Loehrke
venue1: Anderson Arena
capacity: 4000
gigs: 1-2/year
advance: 6-12 months
genres: All Styles
venue2: The Ballroom
capacity: 1000
gigs: 12/year
advance: 6-12 months
genres: All Styles
venue3: Black Swamp Pub
capacity: 250+
gigs: 24/year
advance: 3-6 months
genres: All Styles
Shows are GA. Most shows are free except large events. Tix sold at Union Info Center. Also books festivals & various other campus events.

Heidelberg College
Berg EC
310 E Market, Office of Student Activities
Tiffin, OH 44883
p: 419-448-2261
f: 419-448-2707
www.heidelberg.edu
advisor: Reetha Perananamgam
e: rperanan@heidelberg.edu
venue1: Rickley Chapel
capacity: 500
gigs: 5-10/year
advance: 1 semester
pa: Yes
genres: 4-piece bands, Acoustic
venue2: Campus Ctr. Great Hall
capacity: 300
gigs: 8-12/year
advance: 1 semester
pa: Yes
genres: 4-piece bands, Acoustic
venue3: Campus Ctr. Lobby
capacity: 70
gigs: 8/year
advance: 1 semester
pa: Yes
genres: 4-piece bands, Acoustic
Most shows open to public. Prefers if artists bring their own sound equipment.

Miami U
CAC
372 Shriver Ctr.
Oxford, OH 45056
p: 513-529-7129
f: 513-529-1504
e: miamicac@gmail.com
www.mucac.org
advisor: Vanessa Braun
p: 513-529-7127
e: braunvr@muohio.edu
student: Julie Camp/ Andrew DeRoberts
venue1: The Schriver Center
capacity: 1500+
genres: Cover Bands, Rock
Some GA shows.

Mt. Union College
Raider PB
1972 Clark Ave.
Alliance, OH 44601
p: 330-823-7288
f: 330-829-8737
www.muc.edu
advisor: Kate Carnell
p: 330-823-2885
e: carnelke@muc.edu
venue1: Campus Grounds
booker: SAC
p: 330-823-2878
e: sac@muc.edu
capacity: 180
gigs: 2-3/semester
advance: 1 semester
genres: All Styles
venue2: Mt. Union Theater
capacity: 680
gigs: 1/semester
advance: 1 semester
genres: All Styles
Some GA shows.

Oberlin College
Concert Board
Wilder Hall, Rm. 111

Oberlin, OH 44074
p: 440-775-8106
f: 440-775-8480
www.oberlin.edu/stuorg/cncrtbrd
advisor: Tina Zwegat
student: Benjamin Neufeld
e: benjamin.neufeld@oberlin.edu
venue1: Cat in the Cream Coffeehouse
capacity: 250
pa: Yes **sound eng:** Yes
genres: Folk, S/S
venue2: Dionysus Nightclub
capacity: 500
pa: Yes **sound eng:** Yes
genres: Indie Rock, Hip-Hop
venue3: Finney Chapel
capacity: 1200
pa: Yes **sound eng:** Yes
genres: All Styles
Books about 225 gigs/yr. Email MySpace link.

Ohio Northern U
SPC
McIntosh Ctr.
402 W College Ave.
Ada, OH 45810
p: 419-772-2403
f: 419-772-2708
e: spc@onu.edu
www.onu.edu/org/spc
advisor: Lee Anne Sipe
e: l-sipe@onu.edu
student: Levi Good
e: lgood@onu.edu
venue1: Sports Center
capacity: 2500+
gigs: 1-2/year
advance: 6 months
pa: No **sound eng:** Yes
genres: Pop, Rock
venue2: Ballroom
capacity: 750
gigs: 2/year
advance: 6 months
pa: Yes **sound eng:** Yes
genres: Rock, Jazz, CCM, R&B
All shows are GA & free.

Ohio U - UPC
363 Baker University Ctr.
1 Park Pl.
Athens, OH 45701
p: 740-593-4060
f: 740-593-0223
e: upcevent@ohiou.edu
www.ohiou.edu/~upc
advisor: Chad Barnhardt
p: 740-593-9935
e: barnhard@ohio.edu
student: Molly Hoyt/ John Fouser
e: mhoyt14@gmail.com; jf692905@ohio.edu
venue1: The Front Room
capacity: 100+
gigs: 40/year
advance: 1-3 months
genres: Acoustic, Blues, Bluegrass, Rock
venue2: The Donkey
capacity: 100+
gigs: 1/year
genres: All Styles
venue3: Templeton Blackburn Memorial Auditorium
capacity: 1500
gigs: 15/year
advance: 3-6 months
pa: Yes **sound eng:** Yes
genres: All Styles
Shows are well-promoted & GA.

U of Toledo - CAP
2801 W Bancroft
Mail Stop 105
Toledo, OH 43606
f: 419-530-2509
e: capactivities@utoledo.edu
www.utcap.org
advisor: Ricardo Reddick/ Anthony Kapp
p: 419-530-4431; 419-530-5324
e: ricardo.reddick@utoledo.edu; anthony.kapp@utoledo.edu
venue1: Rocky's Attic
capacity: 150
gigs: 2/semester
advance: 1 semester
genres: All Styles
venue2: The Auditorium
capacity: 1000
gigs: 1/semester
advance: 1 semester
genres: All Styles
venue3: Savage Hall
capacity: 4000-5000
gigs: 1/year
advance: 1 semester
Some GA shows; discount tix for students.

Wittenberg U
Union Board
PO Box 720
Springfield, OH 45501
p: 937-327-7815
f: 937-327-7442
e: unionboard-contact@wittenberg.edu
www4.wittenberg.edu/student_organizations/union_board/index.htm
advisor: Mark DeVilbiss
e: mdevilbiss@wittenberg.edu
student: Mae Jackson
p: 937-327-7816
venue1: Gymnasium
capacity: 2000
gigs: 2/year
advance: 1-6 months
genres: Rock, Alt., Hip-Hop
venue2: Coffee House
booker: Mike Griest
e: mgriest@wittenberg.edu
capacity: 150
gigs: 12/year
advance: 1-6 months
genres: S/S, Rock
All shows are GA. Books outdoor "Spring Fest" in May w/ a major Touring band. Uses NACA for most acts, but will also focus on Local bands.

Wright State U - UAB
029G Student Union
Dayton, OH 45435
p: 937-775-5500
f: 937-775-5573
e: sa_uab@wright.edu
www.wright.edu/students/union/activities
advisor: Tonya Mathis
p: 937-775-5570
e: tonya.mathis@wright.edu
student: Shana Cunningham
e: cunningham.62@wright.edu
venue1: Student Union
capacity: 100
gigs: 15/year
advance: 3 months
genres: Alt., Rock, Hip-Hop, Folk
venue2: The Nutter Center
capacity: 9000-10,000
gigs: 1/year
advance: 6 months
genres: Nat'l Acts: Alt., Rock
Books several outdoor concerts. Concert series runs every 2 weeks. Events usually GA w/ tix sold at door or at the Student Union Box Office. There are over 200 student orgs. on campus & any # of them can & do book music occasionally.

Oklahoma

Northeastern State U
Concert Committee
University Ctr.
612 N Grand Ave.
Tahlequah, OK 74464
p: 918-456-5511 x2526
f: 918-458-2308
www.nsuok.edu
advisor: Kate Abad
student: Wes Lester/ Patrick Vaughn
e: lester@nsuok.edu; vaughapm@nsuok.edu
venue1: Center For Performing Arts
booker: Dave McCaslin
e: mccaslid@nsuok.edu
capacity: 800
gigs: 1-2/year
advance: 1 semester
pa: Yes
genres: All Styles
venue2: Jazz Lab
capacity: 200
gigs: 3-4/semester
pa: Yes
genres: Jazz
Presents mostly Reg'ls; most shows are GA. Also books outdoor fall & spring events.

Oklahoma State U
SUAB
030 Student Union
Stillwater, OK 74078
p: 405-744-8977; 405-744-5232
f: 405-744-2680
e: suab@orgs.okstate.edu
http://union.okstate.edu/suab
advisor: Kathleen Kennedy
p: 405-744-5213
e: kathleen.kennedy@okstate.edu
venue1: Starlight Terrace
capacity: 130
gigs: 40/year
advance: 1 semester
pa: Yes
genres: Acoustic, Rock, Alt.
venue2: 2nd Fl. Balcony
gigs: 5-7/year
advance: 1 semester
pa: Yes
genres: Acoustic, Jazz, S/S
Some shows open to public.

Oregon

Eastern Oregon U
SU
1 University Blvd.
La Grande, OR 97850
p: 541-962-3704
f: 541-962-3706
e: ese@eou.edu
www.eou.edu
advisor: Robin Weinman
e: rweinman@eou.edu
student: Liz Orwick
p: 541-962-3625
venue1: McKenzie Theater
capacity: 455
gigs: 3-5/year
advance: 1 year
pa: Yes
genres: All Styles
venue2: Hoke Main Lounge
capacity: 120
gigs: 3/year
advance: 6 months
genres: S/S
Most shows open to public.

Oregon State U
MUPC
103 Memorial Union
Corvallis, OR 97331
p: 541-737-6872
f: 541-737-1565
e: mupc.admin@oregonstate.edu
http://osumu.org/events.html
advisor: Machelle Kennedy
e: machelle.kennedy@oregonstate.edu
student: Deb Mott
p: 541-737-6688
e: deb.mott@oregonstate.edu
venue1: MU Ballroom
capacity: 600
gigs: 3/year
advance: 6 months - 1 year
pa: Yes **sound eng:** Yes
genres: All Styles
venue2: Club Escape/ International Forum
capacity: 150
gigs: 1-2/year
advance: 2 weeks
pa: Yes **sound eng:** Yes
genres: Local Touring Acts
venue3: LaSelles Stewart Ctr.
booker: Tina Green-Price
capacity: 1208
Books indies for "Battle of the Bands" & sponsors many outdoor concerts. Some GA shows. Visit www.tixrus.us for tix.

Pacific U - ACE
2043 College Way
Forest Grove, OR 97116
p: 503-352-2822
f: 503-352-2936
www.pacificu.edu
advisor: Steve Klein
e: kleinsk@pacificu.edu
venue1: Milky Way
capacity: 200
gigs: 5+/year
advance: 4-8 months
pa: Yes **sound eng:** Yes
genres: All Styles - No Classical
Prefers acts airing on college radio.

U of Oregon
EMU/Cultural Forum
1228 University St.
EMU Ste. 2
Eugene, OR 97403
p: 541-346-4373
f: 541-346-4400
e: cultural@uoregon.edu
http://culturalforum.uoregon.edu/music
advisor: Darrel Kau
Books tons of Reg'ls & some Nat'l acts; gigs are GA & on & off campus. Reg'l contact: Patrick Mackenzie: musicr@uoregon.edu. Bryson Hansen books Nat'ls. Snail mail or use Sonicbids.

Pennsylvania

Bloomsburg U
CGA Concert Committee & PB
400 E 2nd St., Kehr Union
Bloomsburg, PA 17815
p: 570-389-4344; 570-389-4402
f: 570-389-2615
e: progbd@bloomu.edu
www.bloomu.edu
advisor: Jimmy Gilliand

e: jgillila@bloomu.edu
venue1: Nelson Fieldhouse
capacity: 2500
gigs: 2/year
advance: 6-12 weeks
genres: All Styles (Nat'l)
venue2: Kehr Union
capacity: 500
gigs: 8/year
advance: 8 weeks
sound eng: Yes
genres: Acoustic & smaller acts
venue3: Hass Center
capacity: 1800
gigs: 1/year
advance: 6-12 weeks
sound eng: Yes
genres: All Styles (Nat'l)
Most shows are GA & well-promoted on & off campus. Also books outdoor events & Celebrity Artist Series. Locals contact: progbd@bloomu.edu; Nat'l acts: jgillila@bloomu.edu.

Bucknell U - ACE
701 Moore Ave., Box C-3954
Lewisburg, PA 17837
p: 570-577-1217
f: 570-577-3268
e: ace@bucknell.edu
www.bucknell.edu/ace.xml
advisor: Carrie Ingoldsby
e: cfi001@bucknell.edu
student: Doan Huynh
e: dthuynh@bucknell.edu
venue1: Uptown Nightclub
capacity: 300
gigs: 18/year
advance: 1 semester
genres: Rock, Punk
venue2: 7th Street Cafe
capacity: 100
gigs: 12/semester
advance: 1 semester
genres: S/S
Shows open to students only. Books primarily thru NACA but also accepts Sonicbids.

Carnegie Mellon U AB
University Ctr., Box 97
5032 Forbes Ave.
Pittsburgh, PA 15213
p: 412-268-8704
f: 412-268-7900
e: ab@andrew.cmu.edu
www.activitiesboard.org
student: Zach Murray
e: zmm@andrew.cmu.edu
venue1: The Underground
capacity: 200
advance: 2+ weeks
genres: All Styles
venue2: Skibo Coffeehouse
capacity: 200
advance: 2+ weeks
genres: S/S
Books various campus venues. Shows are GA.

Drexel U - CAB
3210 Chestnut St.
Creese Student Ctr., Rm. 215
Philadelphia, PA 19104
p: 215-895-2575
f: 215-895-2205
e: cab@drexel.edu
www.drexel.edu/cab
advisor: Rebecca Dzara
p: 215-895-6076
e: rad49@drexel.edu
student: Anu Singh
venue1: The Armory
capacity: 3000
gigs: 1/year
advance: 2 months
pa: Yes **sound eng:** Yes
genres: Alt., Indie, Rock
venue2: Mandell Theater
venue3: The Dac
gigs: 5-7/year
advance: 2 months
pa: Yes **sound eng:** Yes
genres: Alt., Indie, Rock, Rap
Books venues around campus.

Duquesne U - DPC
600 Forbes Ave.
Pittsburgh, PA 15282
p: 412-396-5853
f: 412-396-6696
e: dpc@duq.edu
www.duq.edu
advisor: Marc Grandillo
e: grandillom@duq.edu
venue1: Union Nite Spot
capacity: 150
gigs: 2-3/semester
genres: S/S
venue2: Union Ballroom
capacity: 1000
gigs: 2/year
advance: 1 semester
genres: Rock, Alt.
Indies booked in Mar-Apr for fall gigs & Sep-Oct for spring. Also hosts outdoor concerts; shows are for students & their guests.

Edinboro U - UPB
University Ctr., Ste. 233
Edinboro, PA 16444
p: 814-732-2768
f: 814-732-2665
e: upb@edinboro.edu
www.edinboro.edu
advisor: Michelle Barbich
p: 814-732-1457
e: mbarbich@edinboro.edu
venue1: McComb Fieldhouse
capacity: 3000
gigs: 2/year
advance: 1 semester
pa: Yes **sound eng:** Yes
genres: All Styles
venue2: Memorial Aud.
capacity: 800
gigs: 1-2/year
advance: 1 semester
pa: Yes **sound eng:** Yes
genres: All Styles
venue3: Multi-Purpose Room
capacity: 600
gigs: 12/semester
pa: Yes **sound eng:** Yes
genres: All Styles

Franklin & Marshall CEC
Student Activities Office
PO Box 3003
Lancaster, PA 17604
p: 717-291-4397
f: 717-358-4437
e: cec@fandm.edu
www.fandm.edu/cec.xml
advisor: Cindy Galgon
e: cgalgon@fandm.edu
venue1: Mayser Gym
capacity: 1000
gigs: 1/year
advance: 2-3 months
pa: Yes **sound eng:** Yes
genres: All Styles
venue2: Sports & Fitness Ctr.
capacity: 3000
gigs: 1/year
advance: 2-3 months
pa: Yes **sound eng:** Yes
genres: All Styles
venue3: Ben's Underground
capacity: 200
gigs: 5-10/year
advance: 1-2 months
pa: Yes **sound eng:** Yes
genres: All Styles

Gettysburg College CAB
Campus Box 2999
College Union Bldg.
Gettysburg, PA 17325
p: 717-337-6304
f: 717-337-8573
e: cab@gettysburg.edu
www.gettysburg.edu
advisor: Brian Stephenson
p: 717-337-6301
e: bstephen@gettysburg.edu
student: Toni Truscott
venue1: College Union Bllrm.
capacity: 300
gigs: 1/semester
advance: 1 semester
genres: All Styles
venue2: The Attic
capacity: 500
gigs: 3/semester
advance: 1 semester
genres: All Styles
venue3: The Junction
capacity: 75
gigs: 2-3/year
advance: 1 semester
genres: S/S
Some shows open to public.

Kings College - CAO
133 N River St.
Wilkes-Barre, PA 18711
p: 570-208-5966
f: 570-208-6013
e: campusactivities@kings.edu
www.kings.edu
advisor: Sean Cryan
p: 570-208-5802
e: seancryan@kings.edu
venue1: Campus Center
capacity: 100-150
gigs: 2/semester
advance: 5+ months
pa: Yes **sound eng:** Yes
genres: Rock
Some GA shows.

La Salle U University Life
1900 W Olney Ave., #412
Philadelphia, PA 19141
p: 215-951-3558
f: 215-951-1942
www.lasalle.edu
advisor: Chris Kazmierczak
p: 215-951-5044
e: kazmierc@lasalle.edu
venue1: Late Night La Salle
booker: Julie Pompizzi
e: pompizzi@lasalle.edu
gigs: Fri & Sat nites
Some GA shows.

Lafayette College LAF PB
115 Farinon College Ctr.
Easton, PA 18042
p: 610-330-5554
f: 610-330-5560
e: laf@lafayette.edu
www.lafayette.edu
advisor: Lauren Ibbotson
e: ibbotsol@lafayette.edu
student: Steve Melnic/Brian Thomson
p: 610-330-5031
venue1: Farinon Center
gigs: 2/year
genres: All Styles
venue2: Kirby Sports Center
genres: All Styles
Hosts 2-3 Local shows/year for students; Annual show at Kirby Sport Center is open to public & features a Nat'l headliner.

Lycoming College CAB
Campus Box 145
700 College Pl.
Williamsport, PA 17701
p: 570-321-4118
f: 570-321-4236
e: cab@lycoming.edu
www.lycoming.edu/stuprograms; www.lycoming.edu/orgs/cab
advisor: Larry Mannolini
e: mannolin@lycoming.edu
venue1: Recreation Center
capacity: 4000
gigs: 1/year
genres: All Styles
venue2: Jack's Corner
capacity: 150
gigs: 2-3/semester
pa: Yes **sound eng:** Yes
genres: All Styles
venue3: East Hall Coffeehouse
capacity: 150
gigs: 2-3/semester
pa: Yes **sound eng:** Yes
genres: All Styles
Most shows are GA. Accepts snail mail or Sonicbids.

Mansfield U of PA SAO/MAC
Student Activites Office
Rm. 324, Alumni Hall
Mansfield, PA 16933
p: 570-662-4982
www.mansfield.edu
advisor: Steve Plesac
e: splesac@mansfield.edu
student: Meredith Bennett
venue1: Decker Gym
capacity: 3000
gigs: 4/year
genres: All Styles
venue2: Straughn Aud.
capacity: 1100
gigs: 30/year
pa: Yes **sound eng:** Yes
genres: All Styles
venue3: The Hut
capacity: 300
gigs: 30/year
pa: Yes **sound eng:** Yes
genres: All Styles
Shows are well-promoted & GA.

Millersville U of PA - SP
128 Student Memorial Ctr.
Millersville, PA 17551
p: 717-872-3508
f: 717-871-4942
e: spstudent@millersville.edu
www.millersville.edu/~sprogram
advisor: Marsha McQuate
e: marsha.mcquate@millersville.edu
venue1: Student Memorial Ctr.
capacity: 100
gigs: 30/year
advance: 1 semester
pa: Yes
genres: Rock, Alt., Hip-Hop, Country
Bands every Thu. Promos to: PO Box 1002, Millersville, PA 17551.

Penn State / Berks CAB
PO Box 7009
Tulpehocken Rd.
Reading, PA 19610
p: 610-396-6068
www.psu.edu
advisor: John Gallagher
e: jag38@psu.edu
venue1: Jitters

capacity: 150
gigs: 15/year
advance: 1 semester
sound eng: No
genres: Acoustic
Books mostly via NACA, but seeks more Local & Reg'l acts. Shows are free for students & promoted on campus.

Penn State U/Altoona
Student Life
3000 Ivyside Park
205 Slep Student Ctr.
Altoona, PA 16601
p: 814-949-5064
www.aa.psu.edu
advisor: Dr. Jay Burlingame
e: ljb2@psu.edu
student: Jessica Bayer
e: jub32@psu.edu
venue1: Wolf Cuhn Theatre
capacity: 394
gigs: 4/year
advance: 1 month
pa: Yes **sound eng:** Yes
genres: Rock, Hip-Hop
venue2: Student Union
capacity: 200
gigs: 3/year
advance: 1 month
pa: Yes **sound eng:** Yes
genres: S/S, Acoustic
venue3: Adler Athletic Complex
capacity: 1200
gigs: 1-2/year
advance: 1 month
genres: All Styles
CAB also books campus events.

Penn State U/Behrend
LEB
4701 College Dr.
Erie, PA 16563
p: 814-898-6221
www.behrendleb.com
advisor: Jill Caldwell
e: jmp30@psu.edu
student: Brad Kovalcik
e: bck5013@psu.edu
venue1: Brunos Cafe
capacity: 400
gigs: 32-64/year
advance: 1 semester
pa: Yes **sound eng:** Yes
genres: All Styles
venue2: McGarvey Commons
capacity: 400
gigs: 3/semester
advance: 1 semester
genres: All Styles
venue3: Erie Hall
capacity: 1000
gigs: 1/year
advance: 90 Days
pa: Yes
genres: Nat'l Acts
Mostly books thru NACA & APCA, but looking for new talent. Email thru site.

Penn State U/University Park
SPA
230 Hub
University Park, PA 16802
p: 814-865-9273
f: 814-863-9576
e: spaevents@sa.psu.edu
www.spa.psu.edu; www.latenight.psu.edu
advisor: John Harlow
p: 814-863-4659
e: jrh201@sa.psu.edu
venue1: Various Venues
Books 8 gigs/yr around campus; "Late Night Series" bookings are more staff-driven. Some GA shows; tix sold at Ticketmaster.

U of Pennsylvania
SPEC
200 Houston Hall, 3417 Spruce St.
Philadelphia, PA 19104
p: 215-898-4444
www.specevents.net
advisor: Katie Hanlon
p: 215-898-2753
e: hanlonkj@upenn.edu
student: Preston Hershorn/ Allison Rapoport/Scott Iles
e: concerts@specevents.net
venue1: Irvine Auditorium
capacity: 1260
gigs: 2/year
advance: 1 semester
pa: Yes **sound eng:** Yes
genres: All Styles
venue2: Franklin Field
capacity: 8000
gigs: 1/year
advance: 1 semester
pa: Yes **sound eng:** Yes
genres: All Styles
Books all styles of music for various events on & off campus. Some shows open to public.

U of Scranton - SA
Student Activities & Orientation
205 DeNaples Ctr.
Scranton, PA 18510
p: 570-941-6233
e: uspb@scranton.edu; student-programming@scranton.edu
www.scranton.edu
advisor: Lisa Bealla
e: beallal2@scranton.edu
venue1: Theater
capacity: 100
gigs: 10/year
advance: 4-5 months
genres: S/S, Acoustic
Books primarily Indie Rock acts.

York College of PA
CAB
Country Club Rd.
Student Union, Rm. 124
York, PA 17405
p: 717-815-1473
f: 717-849-1617
e: ycpcabbuddy@hotmail.com
www.ycp.edu
advisor: Terri Cooke
e: tcooke@ycp.edu
student: Alex Crouse
e: ycpcabbuddy@hotmail.com
venue1: Sparts Den
capacity: 300
gigs: 1-2/month
advance: 1-2 months
genres: All Styles
venue2: The Grumbaker
gigs: 1/year
advance: 4-5 months
genres: All Styles
The Grumbaker hosts Spring concert w/ Nat'l acts. Most shows are free. New buildings w/ venue space will be complete in 2009.

Rhode Island

Brown U - BCA
PO Box 1930
Providence, RI 02912
p: 401-863-2341
f: 401-863-1090
e: bca@brown.edu
www.brown.edu/students/Brown_Concert_Agency
advisor: Shelley Adriance
p: 401-863-1912
e: shelley_adriance@brown.edu
venue1: Meehan Auditorium
genres: Alt. Rock, Jam, World
Limited public tix for some shows.

Bryant U - SPB
1150 Douglas Pike, Box 10
Smithfield, RI 02917
p: 401-232-6118
f: 401-232-6368
e: spb@bryant.edu
www.bryantspb.org
advisor: Meredith Morris
p: 401-232-6160
e: mmorris@bryant.edu
student: Dave Georgantas
e: dgeorgan@bryant.edu
venue1: Dining Hall
capacity: 200
gigs: 5-10/year
genres: All Styles
venue2: Gym
capacity: 1000+
gigs: 1/year
genres: All Styles
Books 10 Reg'l bands/year & 1 Touring band for "Spring Wknd."

Providence College
BOP
549 River Ave., Slavin Ctr.
Providence, RI 02918
p: 401-865-2493
f: 401-865-1250
e: bop@studentweb.providence.edu
www.providencebop.org
advisor: Sharon Hay
p: 401-865-2079
e: sharhay@providence.edu
venue1: Slavin Lawn
capacity: 3000
gigs: 2/year
advance: 1 semester
genres: Rock, Pop
venue2: Peterson Gym
capacity: 3000
gigs: 1-2/year
advance: 1 semester
genres: Rock, Pop
venue3: McPhail's
capacity: 200
gigs: 20/year
advance: 1 semester
genres: Acoustic
Some shows open to public.

Roger Williams U
CEN
1 Old Ferry Rd.
Bristol, RI 02809
p: 401-254-3248
f: 401-254-3355
www.rwu.edu/studentlife
advisor: Adrienne Henderson
p: 401-254-3076
e: ahenderson@rwu.edu
venue1: Common Ground
capacity: 150
gigs: 10/year
genres: Acoustic, World, S/S
venue2: The Gym
capacity: 1600
gigs: 1/year
genres: Major Touring Artists
venue3: Hawks Hangout
capacity: 400
gigs: 12/year
genres: Acoustic

U of Rhode Island
SEC
50 Lower College Rd., Memorial Union, Rm. 208
Kingston, RI 02881
p: 401-874-5298
f: 401-874-5317
e: urisecconcerts@gmail.com
http://urisec.onlyhere.net
advisor: Michael Nolfe
p: 401-874-2726
e: mnolfe@uri.edu
student: Sara Biancuzzo
venue1: Edwards Auditorium
capacity: 1000
gigs: 6-7/year
advance: 1 semester
genres: Rock, Hip-Hop, Alt.
venue2: The Ryan Center
capacity: 6000
gigs: 1-2/year
advance: 1 semester
genres: Rock, Hip-Hop, Alt.
Shows are GA w/ tix for sale at Ticketmaster. Hard copies preferred.

South Carolina

Anderson U - SA
316 Anderson Blvd.
Anderson, SC 29621
p: 864-231-2064
www.ac.edu
advisor: Jon Gropp
e: jgropp@andersonuniversity.edu
venue1: Daniel Recital Hall
capacity: 225
gigs: 4/year
advance: 1 year
genres: CCM
venue2: Merritt Theater
capacity: 175
gigs: 10/year
advance: 1 year
pa: Yes
genres: CCM
venue3: Hunt Chapel
capacity: 100
gigs: 2-3/year
advance: 1 year
genres: CCM, Gospel
Sponsors events on campus. Shows are GA.

Clemson U
Clemson Live
602 University Union
Clemson, SC 29634
p: 864-656-8722
e: live@clemson.edu
www.clemsonlive.com
advisor: Brian Stuart
p: 864-656-1221
e: stuart2@clemson.edu
venue1: Edgars
capacity: 250
gigs: 3-5/year
advance: 3 months
genres: Ska, Punk, Rock, Alt., Hip-Hop
venue2: The Loggia
capacity: 250
gigs: 4-6/year
advance: 3 months
genres: Acoustic, S/S
venue3: Clemson Aud.
pa: Yes
genres: Nat'l Acts

Lander College - UPC
CPO Box 6053
Greenwood, SC 29649
p: 864-388-8244
www.lander.edu
advisor: Jeff Constant
e: jconstant@lander.edu
venue1: Student Activities
capacity: 120
gigs: 1-2/year
advance: 3 weeks
pa: Yes **sound eng:** Yes
genres: All Styles
venue2: Sproles Rec Center
capacity: 250
gigs: 2-3/year
advance: 3 weeks

pa: Yes **sound eng:** Yes
genres: All Styles
venue3: Horne Arena
capacity: 2500
gigs: 2-3/year
advance: 3 months
pa: Yes **sound eng:** Yes

South Carolina State U
CAB & SLL
300 College St. NE
Orangeburg, SC 29117
p: 803-536-7057
e: ccalloway@scsu.edu
www.scsu.edu
advisor: Lillian Adderson
e: ladderson@scsu.edu
venue1: SHM Auditorium
booker: Ariel Singleton
p: 803-536-8488
capacity: 3800+
gigs: 3+/year
advance: 3 months
pa: Yes
genres: Hip Hop, R&B, Neo Soul
venue2: MLK, Jr. Aud.
booker: Ariel Singleton
capacity: 800+
gigs: 4+/year
advance: 3 months
pa: Yes
genres: Hip-Hop, R&B, Neo Soul
Books Local-Touring acts; indies usually open. Hosts other indoor & outdoor events w/ some Jazz & Gospel in the mix; shows are GA. Prefers hard copies & phone contact; call first.

U of South Carolina/ Columbia
Carolina Productions
1400 Greene St., Ste. 227, Russell House
Columbia, SC 29208
p: 803-777-7130
f: 803-777-7132
http://cp.sc.edu
advisor: Sarah Morgan
venue1: Russell House Bllrm.
capacity: 650
gigs: 9-10/year
advance: 6 months
genres: Rock, Alt., Hip-Hop, Punk, S/S
venue2: Koger's Center
capacity: 2200
gigs: 1-2/year
advance: 1 year
pa: Yes
genres: Rock, Alt.
Also books indies for patio series.

South Dakota

Augustana College
UBG
2001 S Summit Ave.
Sioux Falls, SD 57197
p: 605-274-4429
f: 605-274-5828
www.augie.edu/student_serv/sa/index.html
advisor: Jeff Venekamp
p: 605-274-4412
e: jeff_venekamp@augie.edu
student: Clarissa Thompson
e: cmthompson@ole.augie.edu
venue1: Back Alley
capacity: 400
gigs: 10-15/year
advance: Months
pa: Yes **sound eng:** Yes
genres: S/S, Acoustic, World Beat, Alt. Country, Blues, Jazz, Pop/Rock
venue2: Elmen Center
capacity: 4000
gigs: 3/year
advance: 1-3 months
genres: S/S, Acoustic, World Beat, Alt. Country, Blues, Jazz, Pop/Rock
Books Local-Touring acts; 50% thru NACA. Open to all styles except Hard & Loud; shows are GA. Last minute gigs avail. for acts passing thru. Promos to: 2001 S Summit Ave., Box 773, Sioux Falls, SD 57197.

Black Hills State U
The UP Team
1200 University Ave.
Unit 9000
Spearfish, SD 57799
p: 605-642-6418
f: 605-642-6119
e: theupteam@bhsu.edu
www.bhsu.edu/bh/studentlife/organizations/UP%20Team/index.htm
advisor: Shelley Stoltenberg
p: 605-642-6370
e: shelleystoltenbergo@bhsu.edu
venue1: S.U. Marketplace
capacity: 200+
gigs: 2-5/year
advance: 2-6 months
genres: S/S, Jazz, Folk
venue2: The Jacket Legacy Room
capacity: 500
gigs: 1-2/year
advance: 2-6 months
genres: Alt., Rock
Hosts 2 shows/year on campus.

South Dakota State U
UPC
Box 2815, U Student Union
Brookings, SD 57007
p: 605-688-5524
f: 605-688-6174
e: upcconcerts@hotmail.com
http://sdsupc.com
advisor: Lindsie Bartley
p: 605-688-6129
e: lindsie.bartley@sdstate.edu
student: Carly Zebell
e: crzebell@jacks.sdstate.edu
venue1: Jack's Place
capacity: 200
gigs: 5/year
advance: 2-4 months
pa: Yes
genres: Folk, Jazz, S/S
venue2: Sullivan Green
capacity: Outdoors
gigs: 1/year
advance: 3-6 months
pa: Yes
genres: Rock, Jazz, Blues
venue3: Volstorfs Ballroom
capacity: 800
gigs: 1/year
advance: 3-6 months
pa: Yes
genres: Rock, Jazz, Blues
Also books the PAC.

U of South Dakota
PC
414 E Clark St., TSC
Vermillion, SD 57069
p: 605-677-5334
f: 605-677-6039
e: pc@usd.edu
http://orgs.usd.edu/pc/
advisor: Kristin Hoesing
e: kristin.hoesing@usd.edu
venue1: Dakota Dome
capacity: 8000
gigs: 1/year
advance: 6 weeks
genres: All Styles
venue2: Slagle Auditorium
capacity: 2000
gigs: 3/year
advance: 5 weeks+
genres: All Styles
Shows open to public.

Tennessee

Austin Peay State U
SLL
APSU Campus Box 4695
Clarksville, TN 37044
p: 931-221-7431
f: 931-221-1044
e: gpcspecialevents@apmail.apsu.edu
www.apsu.edu/sll
advisor: Melissa Davis
e: davisma@apsu.edu
student: Stephanie Woods
venue1: Java City
capacity: 75
gigs: 10/year
advance: 2-6 months
pa: Yes
genres: Jazz, S/S, Folk, Rock, CCM
venue2: Clement Auditorium
capacity: 550
gigs: 3/year
advance: 1 semester
pa: Yes
genres: Rock, Alt., R&B, Jazz, CCM, World
venue3: Recreation Center
gigs: 2/year
genres: Rock, Alt., R&B, Jazz, CCM, World
Some shows open to public.

Middle Tennessee State U
SP & Events
1301 E Main St., MTSU Box 11
Murfreesboro, TN 37132
p: 615-898-2551
f: 615-898-2873
e: events@mtsu.edu
www.mtsu.edu/~specevnt
advisor: Greg Feiling
p: 615-898-5608
e: gfeiling@mtsu.edu
student: Ryan Hug
e: mtsuconcerts@gmail.com
venue1: Tucker Theatre
capacity: 985
gigs: 5/year
advance: 6+ months
genres: Rock, Country, Jazz, Urban
venue2: Union Bldg. Theatre
capacity: 300+
gigs: 5/year
advance: 6+ months
genres: S/S, Folk, Rock, Jazz
venue3: KUC Courtyard
capacity: Outdoor
gigs: 5-8/year
advance: 6 months
genres: Rock, Country, Jazz, Urban
Most shows open to public; tix sold at campus BO & Ticketmaster.

U of Tennessee/Knoxville
CEB
305 University Ctr., 1501 W Cumberland Ave.
Knoxville, TN 37996
p: 865-974-5455
f: 865-974-9252
e: ticket@utk.edu
http://cpc.utk.edu
advisor: Tyger Lynn Glauser
e: tglauser@utk.edu
student: Cory Blackledge
e: cory@utk.edu
venue1: University Ctr. Aud.
capacity: 550
gigs: 2/year
advance: 1 semester
pa: Yes
genres: Rock, Alt., Country, Hip-Hop
venue2: Alumni Memorial Gym
booker: Sherry Satterfield
p: 865-974-2200
e: ssatterf@utk.edu
capacity: 900
advance: 1 semester
pa: Yes
genres: Rock, Alt., Country, Hip-Hop
venue3: Fuji Island
p: 865-974-3179
e: dos@utk.edu
capacity: 10,000
gigs: 1/year
advance: 1 semester
genres: Rock, Alt., Country, Hip-Hop
Also books some off-campus gigs. Most shows are GA & well-promoted.

Texas

Richland College
SPAR
12800 Abrams Rd.
Dallas, TX 75243
p: 972-238-6132
www.richlandcollege.edu/spar
student: Bobbie Harrison/ Wilfred Manyango
p: 972-238-6915; 972-238-6130
e: bjharrison@dcccd.edu; wmanyango@dcccd.edu
venue1: Performance Hall
capacity: 500
gigs: 6+/year
advance: 3 months
pa: Yes
genres: Rock, Jazz, World, Country, R&B, Hip-Hop, Rap
venue2: Student Cafeteria
capacity: 700
gigs: 6/year
advance: 3 months
pa: Yes
genres: Rock, World, Country, Blues, Alt., Urban
venue3: Outdoor Area
capacity: 1000
gigs: 4-5/year
advance: 1 month
pa: Yes
genres: Rock, Jazz, World, Country, R&B, Rap, Hip-Hop

Sam Houston State U
PC
PO Box 2507
Huntsville, TX 77341
p: 936-294-1763
f: 936-294-3477
e: pc@shsu.edu; studentactivities@shsu.edu
www.shsu.edu/studentactivities
advisor: Leah Mulligan
p: 936-294-3861
e: leahw@shsu.edu
venue1: Johnson Coliseum
capacity: 7094
gigs: 4-5/year
advance: 3 months
pa: Yes
genres: Rock, Alt., Gospel, Country, World, Reggae
venue2: LSC Ballroom
capacity: 500

gigs: 3-4/year
advance: 1 semester - 1 year
pa: Yes
genres: Rock, Alt., Jazz, Blues, World, Reggae
venue3: Old Main Pit
capacity: Outdoor
gigs: 1/month
genres: Alt., Rock, Country
Accepts EPKs. Shows are for students only. Also contact Brandon Cooper, Events Manager at Brandon Cooper, Event Manager, 936-294-3861 or brandon@shsu.edu. FedX: 1802 Ave. I, LSC 328, Huntsville, TX, 77341.

San Antonio College
Office of Student Life
1300 San Pedro Ave.
San Antonio, TX 78212
p: 210-733-2641
f: 210-785-6366
www.accd.edu/sac/stulife/
advisor: Carrie Hernandez
e: chernandez@mail.accd.edu
venue1: Lofton Student Ctr.
capacity: 250-300
gigs: 8-12/year
advance: 1-2 months
genres: Rock, Country, Jazz, Tejano, Reggae, Folk
venue2: McAllister Hall
capacity: 1000-1500
gigs: 4/year
advance: 1-3 months
genres: Rock, Country, R&B, Reggae, Jazz, Rap, Tejano
venue3: The Mall
capacity: Outdoor
gigs: 1-2/month
advance: Ongoing
genres: All Styles

Stephen F. Austin State U - SA
1936 North St.
Nacogdoches, TX 75962
p: 936-468-3723
f: 936-468-7278
www.sfasu.edu
advisor: Carol Lombardo
p: 936-468-3703
e: clombardo@sfasu.edu
venue1: UC Grand Ballroom
capacity: 900
gigs: 6-8/year
advance: 6 months
genres: Rock, Country, Alt., Blues, Bluegrass, Folk
venue2: UC Twilight Ballroom
capacity: 400
gigs: 4-5/year
advance: 6 months
genres: All Styles
venue3: WR Johnson
capacity: 7000
gigs: 2-3/year
advance: 3 months
genres: Acoustic, Rock, Alt., Blues, Country
Shows are GA & tix sold at door. Send promos to: Birdwell Bldg., Rm. 203, Nacogdoches, TX 75962.

Texas A&M U
MSC Town Hall
Box J-1
College Station, TX 77844
p: 979-845-1515
f: 979-845-5117
e: townhall@msc.tamu.edu
http://townhall.tamu.edu
advisor: Dave Salmon
e: salmon@msc.tamu.edu
student: Marcus Handy
p: 979-575-4259
e: marcus.handy09@gmail.com
venue1: Rudder Auditorium
capacity: 2500
gigs: 1-2/year
advance: 3 weeks
pa: Yes
genres: All Styles
venue2: The Coffeehouse @ Rumours
capacity: 50-100
gigs: 10-20/year
advance: 3 weeks
pa: No
genres: All Styles
venue3: Rudder Plaza
capacity: 750-1000
gigs: 25-30/year
advance: 3 weeks
pa: No
genres: All Styles
Big school in big music state books Local-Touring acts for several campus stages & events; shows are GA. Most shows are free.

Texas Christian U
PC
TCU Box 297320
Fort Worth, TX 76129
p: 817-257-5233
f: 817-257-5788
e: sga@tcu.edu
www.pc.tcu.edu
advisor: Natale Boone
p: 817-257-7927
e: n.boone@tcu.edu
student: Kristen Chapman
e: kristen.chapman@tcu.edu
venue1: Student Ctr. Lounge
capacity: 300
gigs: 15-20/year
advance: 3 weeks
genres: Rock, Alt., Hip-Hop, Reggae
venue2: The Rec Center
capacity: 500
gigs: 6/year
advance: 3 weeks
genres: DJs
venue3: Frog Fountain
capacity: 1500-2000
gigs: 20/year
advance: 1-2 months
genres: Rock, Alt.

Texas State U/ San Marcos
SACA
601 University Dr.
LBJ Student Ctr. 4-4.1
San Marcos, TX 78666
p: 512-245-8263
f: 512-245-8245
e: saca@txstate.edu
www.lbjsc.txstate.edu/saca
advisor: Earl Moseley, Jr.
e: em05@txstate.edu
student: Nelly Chavez
e: nc1119@txstate.edu
venue1: Georges
capacity: 300
gigs: Biweekly
advance: 1-1.5 months
genres: Rock, Alt., Hip-Hop, DJ's, Indie Rock, Punk
venue2: Stadium Parking Lot
capacity: 2000+
gigs: 2/year
advance: 1-1.5 months
pa: Yes
genres: Tailgates: TX Country
venue3: Sewell Park
capacity: 7000 (outdoors)
gigs: 2/year
advance: 1-1.5 months
genres: Rock, Alt., Hip-Hop, Country
Hosts several big events; all shows are GA & free.

U of Dallas - SGP
1845 E Northgate
Irving, TX 75062
p: 972-721-5101
f: 972-721-5291
www.udallas.edu
advisor: Brittany Cameron
p: 972-721-6273
e: bcamero@udallas.edu
student: Lauren Hartkin/ Joe Barvick
e: lhartkin@udallas.edu; jbarvick@udallas.edu
venue1: The Rath Skeller
capacity: 200
gigs: 1/week
advance: 3 weeks - 3 months
genres: Acoustic, S/S
venue2: The Mall
capacity: 500
gigs: 2-3/year
advance: 1 semester
genres: Rock, Alt.
Also hosts large events, "Battle of the Bands" & Thu music series; some shows GA.

U of Texas/Austin
SE Center
24th St. @ Guadalupe
Austin, TX 78705
p: 512-475-6645
f: 512-475-6414
e: studentevents@union.utexas.edu
http://sec.union.utexas.edu
advisor: Crystal King
p: 512-475-6630
e: cking@union.utexas.edu
student: Ameer Mobarak
venue1: The Texas Union Theatre
capacity: 374
gigs: 6-8/year
advance: 6 months
genres: Rock, Alt., Blues, Country
venue2: The Texas Union Ballroom
capacity: 1100
gigs: 6-8/year
advance: 6 months
genres: Rock, Alt., Blues, Country
Sponsors various events. Shows are mostly students-only w/ tix sold at the Student Events Ctr. Send promos to: PO Box 7338, Austin, TX 78713.

U of Texas/Dallas
SUAAB
800 W Campbell Rd., SU 21, SU 2.506
Richardson, TX 75083
p: 972-883-6438
f: 972-883-6442
e: suaab@utdallas.edu
www.utdallas.edu/suaab
advisor: Gno White
p: 972-883-6449
e: jcw017600@utdallas.edu; g.n.o@utdalls.edu
student: Nick Hinojosa
e: nicky_h@msn.com
venue1: The Pub
capacity: 199
gigs: 7-10/year
advance: 1 month
pa: Yes
genres: Rock, Alt., Urban
venue2: SU Mall
capacity: Outdoors
gigs: 5/year
pa: Yes
genres: Rock, Alt., Urban
venue3: The Galaxy Room
capacity: 300
gigs: 10-20/year
advance: 1 month
pa: Yes
genres: Rock, Alt., Urban
Shows open to students & their guests w/ tix sold at the Info Depot. Send promos to: PO Box 830688, SU 21, Richardson, TX 75080.

U of Texas/ San Antonio - CAB
1 University Cir.
Rm. UC 1.02.08
San Antonio, TX 78249
p: 210-458-4160
f: 210-458-4772
e: getinvolved@utsa.edu
www.utsa.edu/sa
advisor: Michelle Montanio
p: 210-458-2817
e: michelle.montanio@utsa.edu
venue1: The Coffeehouse
capacity: 50
gigs: 1/month
advance: 2 months
pa: Yes
genres: Acoustic, Alt., Rock, World
venue2: The Sombrilla
capacity: 300
gigs: 7-8/year
advance: 2-3 months
pa: Yes
genres: Rock, Alt., World, Country
venue3: UC Ski Lodge
capacity: 60
gigs: 6-8/year
advance: 2 months
pa: Yes
genres: S/S, Acoustic
Also books big shows at Convocation Ctr. & hosts large campus events. Tix for students & their guests.

West Texas A&M - SA
2301 4th Ave.
Canyon, TX 79016
p: 806-651-2392
f: 806-651-2391
www.wtamu.edu
advisor: Matt Maples
e: mmaples@wtamu.edu
venue1: The Legends Club
capacity: 200
gigs: 12-14/year
advance: 1-2 months
pa: Yes
genres: Rock, Alt., Country
venue2: Ballroom
capacity: 500
gigs: 4-6/year
advance: 1-2 months
pa: Yes
genres: Rock, Alt., Country
venue3: 1st United Bank Ctr.
capacity: 5500
gigs: 3-4/year
advance: 5-6 months
pa: Yes
genres: Rock, Alt., Country, Christian
Also hosts campus events; all shows are GA.

Utah

Southern Utah U
STAB
351 W University Blvd., #205
Cedar City, UT 84720
p: 435-586-7762
www.suu.edu/ss/stuact

advisor: Dir. of Student Life
p: 435-589-7763
student: Tyson Pulsipher
e: tyspuls@gmail.com
venue1: Centrum Arena
capacity: 4000
gigs: 4/year
venue2: SUU Ballroom
capacity: 1500
gigs: 1-2/year
venue3: Lightning Lounge
capacity: 150
gigs: 1-2/month
Some shows open to public.

U of Utah
ASUU Presenter's Office
200 S Central Campus Dr.
Rm. 234
Salt Lake City, UT 84112
p: 801-581-2788
www.asuu.utah.edu
advisor: Brian Burton
e: bburton@asuu.utah.edu
student: Concert Chair
venue1: Free Speech Area
capacity: 8000
gigs: 3-4/year
advance: 1 semester
genres: All Styles
venue2: Kingsbury Hall
capacity: 1913
gigs: 10/year
advance: 1 semester
pa: Yes
genres: All Styles
venue3: The Union Ballroom
capacity: 1500
gigs: 10/year
advance: 1 semester
genres: Rock, Folk
Shows are general admission.

Utah State U - STAB
USU 0105, Old Main Hill Rd.
Logan, UT 84322
p: 435-797-1721
f: 435-797-2919
e: stab@cc.usu.edu
http://a-station.usu.edu
advisor: Keri Mecham
p: 435-797-1740
e: kerim@cc.usu.edu
student: STAB
venue1: Spectrum
capacity: 10,000+
gigs: 1/year
advance: 3 months
genres: All Styles
venue2: Camp Concert Hall
capacity: 2100
gigs: 1-2/year
advance: 3 months
genres: All Styles
venue3: Student Center Bllrm.
capacity: 1000
gigs: 10-12/year
advance: 2 months
genres: Acoustic, Rock, Alt.
Usually books bands at NACA.

Vermont

Bennington College
Student Life
Rte. 67-A
Bennington, VT 05201
p: 802-440-4330
e: cab@bennington.edu
www.bennington.edu
advisor: Sarah Walcott
e: swalcott@bennington.edu
student: Sam Clement
e: sclement@bennington.edu
venue1: Student Center
capacity: 200+
gigs: 20/year
advance: 1 semester
pa: Yes
genres: Acoustic, Alt., Rock, Ska
venue2: Downstairs Cafe
capacity: 100
gigs: 20/year
advance: 1 semester
pa: Yes
genres: Acoustic, Alt., Rock, Ska
Some general admission shows.

Castleton State College - SAAB
49 College Dr.
Castleton, VT 05735
p: 802-468-1231
f: 802-468-1357
www.castleton.edu/campus
advisor: Melissa Paradee
p: 802-468-6085
e: melissa.paradee@castleton.edu
venue1: Fireside Cafe
capacity: 80
gigs: 1/week
advance: 3 months+
genres: Acoustic, S/S, Rock
venue2: The Gym
capacity: 500+
gigs: 1/year
advance: 1 semester
genres: Rock, Alt., Jam
Also books bands for theme wknds.

Middlebury College
Campus Activities
McCullough Student Ctr.
Middlebury, VT 05753
p: 802-443-3103
f: 802-443-3012
e: mcab@middlebury.edu
www.middlebury.edu/~mcab
advisor: Douglas Adams
e: dadams@middlebury.edu
student: MAB
p: 802-443-3944
venue1: Kenyon Arena
capacity: 2500
gigs: 1-2/year
advance: 1 semester
genres: Acoustic, Jazz, Blues, World, Rock, Hip-Hop, Pop
venue2: Student Center
capacity: 500
gigs: 10/year
advance: 1 semester
pa: Yes
genres: Acoustic, Jazz, Blues, World, Rock
venue3: The Grille
capacity: 100
gigs: 30/year
advance: 1 semester
pa: Yes
genres: Acoustic
Well-promoted shows open to the public. Promos to: 14 Old Chapel Rd., Middlebury, VT 05753.

U of Vermont
Campus Activities
590 Main St.
Davis Student Ctr., Rm. 310
Burlington, VT 05405
p: 802-656-2076
f: 802-656-7731
e: upb@uvm.edu
www.uvm.edu
advisor: Tamara Plummer
p: 802-656-2060
e: tamara.plummer@uvm.edu
student: Program Board
p: 802-656-3090
venue1: Ira Allen Chapel
booker: Shelly Peitzmeier
p: 802-656-2060
e: shelly.peitzmeier@uvm.edu
capacity: 200
gigs: 10/year
advance: 2 months
pa: Yes
genres: Rock, S/S, World
venue2: North Lounge
capacity: 100
gigs: 5/year
advance: 2 months
pa: Yes
genres: Rock, S/S, World
venue3: Davis Center Pub
capacity: 250
advance: 2 months
pa: Yes
genres: Rock, S/S, World
Some shows open to public.

Virginia

College of William & Mary
UCAB/Homebrew
203 Campus Ctr.
PO Box 8795
Williamsburg, VA 23187
p: 757-221-2132
f: 757-221-3451
e: ucabxx@wm.edu
http://web.wm.edu/ucab/
advisor: Joe Lowder
p: 757-221-3254
e: jclowd@wm.edu
student: Sean O'Mealia
e: sromea@wm.edu
venue1: Lodge 1
capacity: 300
advance: 1 semester
genres: Rock, Acoustic, Eclectic
venue2: Chesapeake Room
capacity: 700
gigs: 5/year
advance: 1 semester
genres: Rock, Acoustic, Eclectic
venue3: Lake Matoaka Amphitheater
capacity: 2300
gigs: 20-25/year
pa: Yes
sound eng: Yes
genres: All Styles
Features Reg'l, Nat'l & student acts.

Ferrum College
SLE
PO Box 1000
Ferrum, VA 24088
p: 540-365-4441
f: 540-365-4440
www.ferrum.edu/studentactivities
advisor: Justin Muse
p: 540-365-4463
e: jmuse@ferrum.edu
student: Anthony Adams
e: aadams@ferrum.edu
venue1: The Panthers' Den
capacity: 250
gigs: 3-6/year
advance: 3-6 months
pa: Yes **sound eng:** Yes
genres: Country, Rock, Rap, Hip-Hop, Alt.
venue2: Fitness Center
capacity: 1500
gigs: 1-2/year
advance: 6 months
pa: Yes **sound eng:** Yes
genres: Rock, Alt., Pop, Hip-Hop
venue3: Sale Theatre
capacity: 500
gigs: 3/year
advance: 2 months
pa: Yes **sound eng:** Yes
genres: Rock, Pop, Hip-Hop, Reggae
Shows for students only & promoted on campus. Tix sold at website. FedX: 445 Ferrum Mountain Rd.,Franklin Hall, Ferrum, VA 24088.

George Mason U - PB
4400 University Dr., SUB # 1
Rm. 101
Fairfax, VA 22030
p: 703-993-2909
f: 703-993-4566
e: pbmusic@gmu.edu
www.gmu.edu/student/soap
advisor: Michelle Davis
p: 703-993-2925
e: mdavih@gmu.edu
venue1: Bistro
gigs: 2-5/year
advance: 1 month
genres: Acoustic, Rock, Blues, Folk
venue2: Dewberry Hall
capacity: 800
gigs: 1-2/year
advance: 3-4 months
genres: Rock, Alt., Dance, Hip-Hop, R&B, Jazz
venue3: JC Auditorium
gigs: 1/month
pa: Yes
genres: Local-Nat'l

Hampton U - SA
135 Marshall Ave.
Hampton, VA
23668
p: 757-727-5691
www.hamptonu.edu
advisor: Sharon Trabbold
p: 757-727-5495
e: sharon.trabbold@hamptonu.edu
student: Devin Jones
e: devin.jones@pipeline.hamptonu.edu
venue1: Holland Hall
capacity: 4000
gigs: 4-5/year
advance: 2 months
pa: Yes **sound eng:** Yes
genres: Hip-Hop, R&B
venue2: Ogden Hall
capacity: 1500
gigs: 20+/year
advance: 2 months
pa: Yes **sound eng:** Yes
genres: All Styles
venue3: Convocation Center
capacity: 4500
gigs: 15/year
advance: 2 months
pa: Yes **sound eng:** Yes
genres: All Styles
Convocation Ctr. booked independently. Some shows open to public.

James Madison U
UPB
800 S Main St.
MSC 3505
Harrisonburg, VA 22807
p: 540-568-6217
f: 540-568-3424
http://upb.jmu.edu
advisor: Sarah Sunde
p: 540-568-7892
e: sundesa@jmu.edu
student: Patrick White
e: whitepk@jmu.edu
venue1: Wilson Hall Aud.
capacity: 1300
gigs: 1-2/year
advance: 3-4 weeks
genres: Rock, Alt., Blues, Jazz
venue2: Convocation Ctr.
capacity: 3200

gigs: 2/year
genres: Rock, Alt., Blues, Jazz
Great music campus also hosts indie fest, MACROCK. All shows are GA; discount tix for sutdents.

Roanoke College
CAB
221 College Ln.
Salem, VA 24153
p: 540-378-5125
www.roanoke.edu/colket
advisor: Mark Petersen
p: 540-375-5298
e: petersen@roanoke.edu
venue1: Colket Center
capacity: 80
gigs: 12/year
advance: 1-2 months
pa: Yes
genres: Rock, Alt., S/S, Acoustic
venue2: Bast Center
capacity: 1800
advance: 45 days
pa: Yes
genres: Nat'l Acts
venue3: Alumni Gym
capacity: 800
advance: 45 days
pa: Yes
genres: Nat'l Acts
Accepts last minute booking & all shows are GA.

U of Richmond - CAB
28 Westhampton Way
Richmond, VA 23173
p: 804-289-8505
www.richmond.edu
advisor: John O'Donnell
venue1: The Cellar
capacity: 120
gigs: 30/year
advance: 1 semester
genres: Alt., Jazz, S/S
venue2: Greek Theatre
capacity: 2000
gigs: 2-3/semester
advance: 1 semester
genres: All Styles

U of Virginia - UPC
Newcomb Hall, Programs Office, PO Box 400701
Charlottesville, VA 22904
p: 434-924-3286
f: 434-243-2007
www.uvaupc.com
advisor: Lisa Thompson
e: lpt2s@virginia.edu
venue1: Tuttle Lounge
capacity: 130
gigs: 1/week
advance: 1 semester
genres: Acoustic, Punk, Rock, S/S
venue2: Martin Luther King PAC
capacity: 1275
gigs: 1/year
advance: 1 semester
genres: Hip-Hop, Rock, Alt., Jazz, Pop, Country
venue3: Old Cabell Hall
capacity: 847
advance: 1 semester
genres: Hip-Hop, Rock, Alt., Jazz, Pop, Country

VA Commonwealth U
APB
907 Floyd Ave.
PO Box 842032
Richmond, VA 23284
p: 804-828-7550
f: 804-828-4581
www.vcu.edu
advisor: Krista Carson
p: 804-828-4554
e: fawilker@vcu.edu; carsonkn@vcu.edu
student: Tiffany Nason
venue1: University Student Commons Ballroom
booker: Whitney Brown
e: brownws@vcu.edu
capacity: 600
gigs: 10/year
advance: 2 months
genres: Rock, Alt.
venue2: Siegel Center
capacity: 2000-3000
gigs: 10/year
advance: 6 months
genres: Rock, Alt.

Virginia Polytechnic Institute & State U
SA
327 Squires Student Ctr.
Blacksburg, VA 24061
p: 540-231-7117
f: 540-231-7028
e: vturocks@vtu.org
www.vtu.org
advisor: Laura Bedenbaugh
p: 540-231-4059
e: lbedenba@vt.edu
student: Dave
venue1: Commonwealth Bllrm.
capacity: 2000
gigs: 1/year
advance: 1 month
genres: Hip-Hop, Rock, Alt.
venue2: Old Dominion Bllrm.
capacity: 550
gigs: 1/year
advance: 1 month
genres: Hip-Hop, Rock, Alt., Country
venue3: Deet's Place
capacity: 100-125
gigs: 3/year
advance: 1 month
genres: Acoustic, S/S
Also books other campus venues.

Washington

Central Washington U
Campus Life
400 E University Way
Ellensburg, WA 98926
p: 509-963-1691
e: gallaghl@cwu.edu
www.cwu.edu/~camplife/activities.html
advisor: Scott Drummond
p: 509-963-1684
e: drummond@cwu.edu
student: Sara Grant
venue1: Student Union
gigs: 20/year
advance: 1-3 months
pa: Yes
genres: All Styles
venue2: Music Dept.
genres: Smaller Local Acts
venue3: McConnel Aud.
pa: Yes
genres: Nat'l Acts
Civil Engagement Ctr. & Diversity Ctr. also book gigs.

Evergreen State College
S&A Productions/ Musician's Club
2700 Evergreen Pkwy. NW
CAB 320
Olympia, WA 98505
p: 360-867-6220; 206-351-7934
f: 360-867-6412
e: cutmar11@evergreen.edu
www.evergreen.edu; www.evergreen.edu/conference
advisor: Greg Porter
p: 360-867-6222
e: porterg@evergreen.edu
venue1: The Long House
capacity: 300
gigs: 10/year
advance: 3-6 months
genres: All Styles
venue2: The CRC
capacity: 2000
gigs: 1/year
advance: 3-6 months
genres: All Styles
venue3: Red Square
capacity: Outdoor
gigs: 1/year
advance: 3-6 months
genres: All Styles
Phone contact preferred.

U of Puget Sound
ASUPS/Popular Entertainment
1500 N Warner
Tacoma, WA 98416
p: 253-879-3600
http://asups.ups.edu
advisor: Serni Solidarios
p: 253-879-3366
e: ssolidarios@ups.edu
venue1: UPS Fieldhouse
capacity: 3400
gigs: 6/year
advance: 2-4 months
pa: Yes **sound eng:** Yes
genres: Alt., R&B, Jazz, Rock
venue2: The Concert Hall
capacity: 500
gigs: 6/year
advance: 2-4 months
pa: Yes **sound eng:** Yes
genres: Jazz, World, Classical
venue3: Kilworth Chapel
capacity: 325
gigs: 7/year
advance: 2-4 months
pa: Yes **sound eng:** Yes
genres: Jazz, Classical
Some shows open to public.

Western Washington U
ASP
Viking Union 422
516 High St.
Bellingham, WA 98225
p: 360-650-2846
f: 360-650-6507
e: asp.pop.music@wwu.edu
http://popmusic.as.wwu.edu
advisor: Lisa Rosenberg
p: 360-650-6123
student: Hunter Motto
venue1: Viking Union
capacity: 800
gigs: 20/year
advance: 1-4 months
pa: Yes **sound eng:** Yes
genres: Rock, Alt., Hip-Hop, Punk, Indie
venue2: P.A.C. Concert Hall
capacity: 600
gigs: 2-5/year
advance: 2-6 months
pa: Yes **sound eng:** Yes
genres: Acoustic, Alt., Urban
venue3: P.A.C. Mainstage
capacity: 1076
gigs: 2-5/year
advance: 2-6 months
pa: Yes **sound eng:** Yes
genres: Rock, Alt., Hip-Hop, R&B, Acoustic
Books mostly indies. Most shows open to public.

West Virginia

Bethany College
SAC
PO Box 368
Bethany, WV 26032
p: 304-829-7901
f: 304-829-7788
www.bethanywv.edu
advisor: Brian Fernandes
e: bfernandes@bethanywv.edu
student: Chase Butler
e: chasebutler@bethanywv.edu
venue1: Wailes Theater
capacity: 200
gigs: 1-2/year
advance: 3-6 months
genres: Rock, Alt., Jazz, Acoustic, R&B
venue2: Renner Too
capacity: 400
gigs: 2-3/year
advance: 3-6 months
genres: All Styles
venue3: Rec Center
capacity: 1000
gigs: 2-3/year
advance: 3-6 months
genres: Alt., Rock

Marshall U
SAPB
1 John Marshall Dr.
2W31 MSC
Huntington, WV 25755
p: 304-696-2290
f: 304-696-4347
e: student-activities@marshall.edu
www.marshall.edu/student-activities/sapb/main.html
advisor: Andy Hermansdorfer
e: hermansd@marshall.edu
student: Kenny Cox
e: cox95@marshall.edu
venue1: Marco's
capacity: 190
gigs: 15/year
advance: 1 semester
genres: All Styles w/ emphasis on Rock
venue2: The Patio Extension
capacity: 500
gigs: 10/year
advance: 1 semester
genres: All Styles w/ emphasis on Rock
venue3: Don Morris Room
capacity: 850
gigs: 6/year
advance: 1 semester
pa: Yes
genres: All Styles w/ emphasis on Rock
Books thru NACA.

Shepherd U - PB
210 N King St., PO Box 3210
Shepherdstown, WV 25443
p: 304-876-5326
f: 304-876-5137
e: pbweb@shepherd.edu
www.shepherd.edu/pbweb
advisor: Rachel Meads
p: 304-876-5113
e: rmeads@shepherd.edu
venue1: Reynolds Hall
capacity: 200
gigs: 1-2/year
advance: 1-2 months
pa: Yes
genres: All Styles
venue2: Fireside Bistro
capacity: 20-30
advance: 1 month
genres: S/S, Acoustic
venue3: Frank Arts Center
capacity: 400

advance: 1-2 months
pa: Yes
genres: All Styles
GA shows are rare.

West Virginia State U
Concert Committee
Campus Box 1000
201 Davis Fine Arts Bldg.
Institute, WV 25112
p: 304-766-3196
www.wvstateu.edu
advisor: Richard Wolfe
p: 304-766-3188
e: rwolfe@wvstateu.edu
venue1: Fine Arts Theatre
capacity: 340
gigs: 1/month
advance: 1 year
pa: Yes
genres: Jazz, World, Blues, Hip-Hop
venue2: PA Williams Aud.
capacity: 711
gigs: 3/year
pa: Yes
genres: Jazz, World, Blues, Hip-Hop

West Virginia U
Arts & Entertainment
PO Box 6017
Morgantown, WV 26506
p: 304-293-4406
f: 304-293-7574
advisor: Eric Andrews
e: andrews@events.wvu.edu
venue1: The Mountainlair
capacity: 1200
gigs: 2-4/year
pa: Yes
genres: All Styles
venue2: Creative Arts Center
capacity: 1500
pa: Yes
genres: All Styles
venue3: The Colosseum
capacity: 8500-8800
pa: Yes
genres: All Styles
Books lots of family-friendly indie & estab. acts; all shows are GA.

WV Wesleyan College
CAB
59 College Ave.
Buckhannon, WV 26201
p: 304-473-8104
f: 304-473-8705
e: cab@wvwc.edu
www.wvwc.edu/cab
advisor: Alisa Lively
e: lively_a@wvwc.edu
student: Jess Starcher
e: starcher_jw@wvwc.edu
venue1: The Cat's Claw
capacity: 150+
gigs: 6-8/year
advance: 1 semester
genres: Acoustic, Jazz
venue2: WVWC Gymnasium
capacity: 3000
gigs: 1/year
advance: 1 semester
genres: Alt., Rock, R&B, Jazz
venue3: WVWC Chapel
capacity: 1800
gigs: 4-6/year
advance: 1 year
genres: All Styles

Wisconsin

Beloit College - SA
700 College St.
Beloit, WI 53511
p: 608-363-2301
f: 608-363-2670
www.beloit.edu/studentactivities
advisor: Jenny Hartzheim
p: 608-363-2379
e: hartzhei@beloit.edu
student: SPB
p: 608-363-2866
e: pboard@belcon.beloit.edu
venue1: C-Haus
gigs: 1/week
genres: Grunge, Alt., Rock
venue2: The Java Joint
genres: Folk, S/S, Rock
Holds annual "Folk & Blues Fest" w/ 10 touring acts & "Spring Days" & "Vortex" weekends w/ Reg'l & Local acts.

Carroll College - SA
100 N East Ave.
Waukesha, WI 53186
p: 262-524-7350
f: 262-524-7101
http://depts.cc.edu/studentlife
advisor: Elizabeth Brzeski
e: ebrzeski@cc.edu
venue1: The Ballroom
capacity: 500
gigs: 10-12/year
advance: 2-6 months
pa: Yes **sound eng:** Yes
genres: Pop, Rock, Reggae, Blues
venue2: The Pits
capacity: 100
gigs: 2-5/year
advance: 2-6 months
pa: Yes **sound eng:** Yes
genres: Pop, Rock, Reggae, Blues
Some GA shows.

Lawrence U - Soup
115 S Drew St.
Appleton, WI 54911
p: 920-832-6600
f: 920-832-7695
www.lawrence.edu
advisor: Amy Uecke
e: amy.uecke@lawrence.edu
student: Chris McGeorge
e: christopher.j.mcgeorge@lawrence.edu
venue1: Underground Coffee House
booker: Claire Gannon
e: claire.e.gannon@lawrence.edu
capacity: 100
gigs: 20/year
advance: 3-9 months
genres: Folk, S/S, Jazz
venue2: Lawrence Memorial Chapel
capacity: 1248
gigs: 2/year
advance: 12+ months
genres: Jazz, Classical
venue3: Riverview Lounge
capacity: 300
gigs: 8/year
advance: 3-9 months
genres: All Styles
Promos to: PO Box 599, Appleton, WI, 54912.

U of Wisconsin/Eau Claire - UAC
132 W.R. Davies Ctr.
Eau Claire, WI 54701
p: 715-836-2970
f: 715-836-2521
e: uac@uwec.edu
www.uwec.edu/studentsenate/uac
advisor: Jim Brockpahler
p: 715-836-4805
e: brockpja@uwec.edu
venue1: The Cabin
capacity: 100
gigs: 10+/year
advance: 3-6 months
pa: Yes **sound eng:** Yes
genres: Acoustic, Folk, Jazz
venue2: Council Fire Room
capacity: 700+
gigs: 8+/year
advance: 3-6 months
genres: Dance, Rock & Roll, Ska, Punk, Hip-Hop
venue3: Higherground
booker: HPC
capacity: 300
gigs: 20+/year
advance: 1-2 months
genres: All Styles

U of Wisconsin/Madison - WUD Music
800 Langdon St., Memorial Union, Rm. 514
Madison, WI 53703
p: 608-262-2215
f: 608-263-5593
e: music@union.wisc.edu; asawyers@wisc.edu
www.union.wisc.edu/music
advisor: Patrick Tilley
e: ptilley@wisc.edu
venue2: Der Rathskeller/Union Terrace
capacity: 2500/650
gigs: 2+/week
advance: 2 months
pa: Yes
genres: All Styles
Most shows open to public. Prefers online press kits.

U of Wisconsin/Parkside
SA/PAB/WIPZ Radio
900 Wood Rd.
Kenosha, WI 53141
p: SA 262-595-3339; PAB 262-595-2650
f: 262-595-2776
www.uwp.edu
advisor: Stephanie Sirovatka-Marshall
e: sirovatk@uwp.edu
student: Aaron Taliaferro
e: psidepub@yahoo.com
venue1: The Den
capacity: 375
advance: 1 year
pa: Yes
genres: Acoustic, Rock, Jazz, Blues, R&B
venue2: Communication Arts Theater
booker: Keith Harris
p: 262-595-2564
e: keith.harris@uwp.edu
capacity: 810
gigs: 2-3/semester
advance: 1 year
genres: All Styles
venue3: Student Ctr. Cinema
capacity: 370
pa: Yes
genres: All Styles
Some shows open to public.

U of Wisconsin/Platteville
CPR
1 University Plaza
Pioneer Involvement Ctr.
Platteville, WI 53818
p: 608-342-1497
f: 608-342-1084
e: cpr@uwplatt.edu
http://reslife.saf.uwplatt.edu/cpr
advisor: Val Wetzel
p: 608-342-1448
e: wetzelv@uwplatt.edu
student: Chelsea A Sutcliffe
e: sutcliffec@uwplatt.edu
venue1: The Patio
booker: Ali Wetzel
e: karbassia@uwplatt.edu
capacity: Outdoors
gigs: 2/year
advance: 6-12 months
pa: Yes
genres: Alt., Urban, Jazz, Folk
venue2: The Pioneer Haus
capacity: 50
gigs: 10-15/year
advance: 6-12 months
pa: Yes
genres: S/S, Folk, Jazz
venue3: Pioneer Crossing
capacity: 200
gigs: weekly
advance: 6-12 months
pa: Yes
genres: Acoustic
Books mainly thru NACA.

U of Wisconsin/River Falls - E.C.
Leadership Ctr., 410 S 3rd St.
River Falls, WI 54022
p: 715-425-4911
www.uwrf.edu
advisor: Karyn Kling
e: karyn.kling@uwrf.edu
venue1: Brandy's Coffee House
capacity: 200+
gigs: 5/year
genres: Acoustic, Rock
venue2: Wall Amphitheater
capacity: 500+
gigs: 15/year
genres: Blues, Covers, Rock, World
Also books 2 auditoriums.

U of Wisconsin/Stevens Pt.
Centertainment Productions
2100 Main St.
Stevens Pt., WI 54481
p: 715-346-2412
f: 715-346-4365
e: cntrtain@uwsp.edu
www.uwsp.edu/centers/centertainment
advisor: Greg Diekroeger
e: gdiekroe@uwsp.edu
student: Sam Matteson
e: smatt314@uwsp.edu
venue1: The Encore
capacity: 500
gigs: 15/year
advance: 3-5 months
pa: Yes
genres: R&B, Urban, World
venue2: Alternative Sounds @ The Encore
capacity: 50
gigs: 10/year
advance: 3-5 months
pa: Yes
genres: Rock, Urban, S/S, World
Shows are GA; discount tix for students.

U of Wisconsin/Stout
Blue Devil Prod.
140 Memorial Student Ctr., 302 10th Ave. E
Menomonie, WI 54751
p: 715-232-2432
f: 715-232-2504
e: bdp@uwstout.edu
http://bdp.uwstout.edu
advisor: Emily Ascher
p: 715-232-4051
e: aschere@uwstout.edu
student: Bethany Barberg

e: bdpbdl@uwstout.edu
venue1: Underground
capacity: 120
gigs: 20/year
advance: 3-6 months
pa: Yes **sound eng:** Yes
genres: All Styles
venue2: Great Hall
capacity: 922
gigs: 2/year
advance: 3-6 months
pa: Yes **sound eng:** Yes
genres: Rock, Alt., Jazz, S/S
Mostly Local & NACA acts. Latinos Unidos, Black Student Union & Student Union also book gigs. Shows are GA & well-promoted; tix sold for large events.

U of Wisconsin/ Waukesha - ACT
1500 N University Dr.
Waukesha, WI 53188
p: 262-521-5043
f: 262-521-5530
e: wakact@uwc.edu
www.waukesha.uwc.edu
advisor: Sue Kalinka
e: sue.kalinka@uwc.edu
venue1: The Courtyard
capacity: 250+
gigs: 5/year
advance: 3-6 months
genres: S/S, Folk, Jazz, Rock, Alt., Urban
venue2: The Cafeteria
capacity: 250+
gigs: 5/year
advance: 3-6 months
genres: S/S, Folk, Jazz, Rock, Alt., Urban
Also books events on campus. Member of NACA. Shows are GA & free.

Wyoming

Central Wyoming College - SA
2660 Peck Ave.
Riverton, WY 82501
p: 307-855-2260
f: 307-855-2090
www.cwc.edu
advisor: Britt Ready
e: bready@cwc.edu
venue1: Arts Center Theater
capacity: 940
gigs: 2/year
advance: 1 year
genres: Rock, Pop, Jazz, Classical, Folk, Country
Some shows open to public.

Northwest College SAB
231 W 6th St.
Powell, WY 82435
p: 307-754-6205
f: 307-754-6700
www.northwestcollege.edu/sactivities/
advisor: Mike Taylor
e: mike.taylor@northwestcollege.edu
venue1: Nelson Performing Arts
capacity: 500
gigs: 1/year
advance: 1 year
genres: Country, Pop, Jazz
venue2: Dwight Student Ctr.
capacity: 250
gigs: 1/year
advance: 1 month
genres: Country, Rock, Pop, DJs
venue3: Residence Halls
gigs: 1/month
genres: Country, Western
Books mostly Locals & Reg'ls. All shows open to public. Prefers hard copies.

U of Wyoming - SAC
1000 E Univ. Ave.
PO Box 3625
Wyoming Union, Rm. 012
Laramie, WY 82071
p: 307-766-6343
f: 307-766-3762
e: sac@uwyo.edu
www.uwyo.edu/cac
advisor: Michael Lange
p: 307-766-6340
student: Jason Joyce
venue1: Union Gardens
capacity: 100
gigs: 3-4/year
advance: 1-2 months
genres: Rock, Pop, Hip-Hop, Folk, Alt.
venue2: Union Ballroom
capacity: 400
gigs: 3-4/year
advance: 2 months
genres: Rock, Pop, Hip-Hop, Folk, Alt.
venue3: Arts & Sciences Aud.
capacity: 1700
gigs: 1/year
advance: 3 months
genres: Rock, Pop, Jazz, World, Blues
Some shows open to public.

Canada

Alberta

Grande Prairie Reg'l College - SA
10726 106th Ave.
Grande Prairie, AB T8V 4C4
Canada
p: 780-539-2962
f: 780-539-2776
www.gprc.ab.ca
advisor: Ninette Laliberte
p: 780-539-2821
e: nlaliberte@gprc.ab.ca
student: Jules Laprairie
e: vploungeprogrammer@gprc.ab.ca
venue1: Howlers Lounge
capacity: 450
gigs: 6/year
advance: 3 weeks
genres: All Styles
venue2: Black Box
booker: Amy Johnson
p: 780-539-2858
e: bookings@gprc.ab.ca
capacity: 70
genres: All Styles
venue3: The Gym
booker: Dwayne Head
p: 780-539-1221
e: dhead@gprc.ab.ca
capacity: 1000
genres: All Styles
Shows are GA. For Douglas Cardinal Theatre gigs, contact Robert Cole at 780-539-2012.

Medicine Hat College SA
299 College Dr. SE
Medicine Hat, AB T1A 3Y6
Canada
p: 403-529-3924
f: 403-504-3522
e: mhc_sa@mhc.ab.ca; sa_events@mhc.ab.ca
www.medhatsa.ca
student: Amber Herman
venue1: Rattler's Den
capacity: 250
gigs: 4/year
advance: 2 months
pa: Yes **sound eng:** Yes
genres: All Styles
venue2: College Theatre
capacity: 549
gigs: 2/year
advance: 6 months
pa: Yes **sound eng:** Yes
genres: Rock
venue3: Cafeteria
capacity: 350
pa: Yes **sound eng:** Yes
genres: All Styles
Hosts Local-Touring acts in Rattler's Den & Touring acts in the College Theatre. Some all ages shows in cafeteria. Email contact preferred.

Mount Royal College SA
4825 Mount Royal Gate SW
Calgary, AB T3E 6K6
Canada
p: 403-440-6401
f: 403-240-8909
www.samrc.com
advisor: Josh Boser
p: 403-440-7708
e: j.boser@samrc.com
student: Kourtney Smith
p: 403-440-6993
e: vpstudentlife@samrc.com
venue1: The Liberty Lounge
capacity: 300
gigs: 75/year
advance: 3 months
pa: Yes **sound eng:** Yes
genres: All Styles
venue2: Wyckham House
capacity: 600
gigs: 5/year
advance: 3 months
pa: Yes **sound eng:** Yes
genres: All Styles
venue3: Leacock Theatre
capacity: 330
gigs: 2/year
advance: 4 months
pa: Yes **sound eng:** Yes
genres: S/S
Presents 80+ shows/year at various venues.

Southern Alberta Institute of Tech. - SA
1301 16th Ave. NW, V204
Calgary, AB T2M 0L4
Canada
p: 403-284-8036
f: 403-284-8037
e: the.gateway@edu.sait.ca
www.saitsa.com
advisor: Mark Thususka
p: 403-210-4378
e: marc.thususka@edu.sait.ca
student: Rebecca Kiss
p: 403-284-8040
e: rebecca.kiss@sait.ca
venue1: The Gateway
capacity: 450-1200
gigs: 40+/year
advance: 3-4 months
pa: Yes
genres: Rock, Alt., Hip-Hop, Folk
venue2: Orpheus Theatre
capacity: 390
gigs: 5-10/year
pa: Yes
genres: All Styles
venue3: Symposium Hall
capacity: 1200
gigs: 1-2/year
pa: Yes
genres: All Styles
Shows are GA & tix sold at Ticketmaster.

U of Alberta - SU
2-900 SUB, 8900 114 St.
Edmonton, AB T6G 2J7
Canada
p: 780-492-2048
f: 780-492-4643
www.su.ualberta.ca
advisor: Christine Rogerson
e: christine.rogerson@su.ualberta.ca
student: Kristen Flath
e: vp.studentlife@su.ualberta.ca
venue1: Horowitz Theatre
capacity: 720
gigs: 20+/year
advance: 2-3 months
genres: Rock, Pop, Indie, Country, Hip-Hop, Jazz
venue2: Dinwoodie Lounge
capacity: 680
gigs: 2/year
advance: 2-3 months
genres: Rock, Pop, Indie, Country, Hip-Hop, Jazz
Some shows booked by outside promoters & open to public.

U of Calgary - SU
251 MacEwan Student Ctr.,
2500 Univ. Dr. NW
Calgary, AB T2N 1N4
Canada
p: 403-220-6551
f: 403-284-1653
www.su.ucalgary.ca
advisor: Greg Curtis
p: 403-313-5456
e: gtcurtis@ucalgary.ca
student: Luke Valentine
p: 403-220-3912
e: suvpeve@ucalgary.ca
venue1: MacEwan Hall
capacity: 2000
pa: Yes **sound eng:** Yes
genres: All Styles
venue2: The Den
capacity: 450
pa: Yes **sound eng:** Yes
genres: All Styles
venue3: Rozsa Centre
capacity: 380
pa: Yes **sound eng:** Yes
genres: All Styles
Over 50 gigs booked at 6 on-campus venues. All shows open to public w/ tix @ Ticketmaster.

U of Lethbridge - SU
4401 University Dr.
Lethbridge, AB T1K 3M4
Canada
p: 403-329-2222
f: 403-329-2224
e: su.internal@uleth.ca
www.ulsu.ca
advisor: Cheri Polarney
p: 403-329-2769
e: su.manager@uleth.ca
student: Eric Hawthorne
venue1: The Zoo
capacity: 564
gigs: 1/month
advance: 2-6 months
pa: Yes **sound eng:** Yes
genres: All Styles
Books monthly Touring acts & 2 major acts/year. Radio station also books events. Tix are for students & their guests. Electronic submissions preferred.

British Columbia

U of British Columbia AMS Events
6138 SUB Blvd., Rm. 210

Vancouver, BC V6T 1Z1
Canada
p: 604-822-5336
f: 604-822-9019
e: programs@ams.ubc.ca
www.ams.ubc.ca/events
advisor: Shea Dahl
venue1: The Pit Pub
capacity: 400
advance: 2 months
pa: Yes
genres: Indie, Alt., Rock, Hip-Hop
venue2: SUB Theatre
capacity: 422
pa: Yes
genres: All Styles
Books 30+ gigs/year for 6 venues & various events. Most shows open to public. Tix sold thru Ticketweb.

Manitoba

Brandon U - BUSU
270 18th St.
Brandon, MB R7A 6A9
Canada
p: 204-727-9682
f: 204-727-3498
e: busu@brandonu.ca
www.busu.ca
advisor: Kyle Lougheed
p: 204-727-7478
e: lougheedk@brandonu.ca
student: Riley McIntyre
p: 204-727-9660
e: music@busu.ca
venue1: Suds
capacity: 150-230
gigs: Weekly (Locals); Monthly (Touring)
pa: Yes **sound eng:** Yes
genres: All Styles
Books Touring indies monthly.

U of Manitoba - SU
101 University Ctr.
Winnipeg, MB R3T 2N2
Canada
p: 204-474-6822
f: 204-269-1299
e: umsu@umsu.ca
www.umsu.ca
advisor: Melanie Myers
p: 204-480-1457
e: events@umsu.ca
student: Sid Rashid
p: 204-474-6521
e: vpss@umsu.ca
venue1: Fireside Lounge
capacity: 40
advance: 6 weeks
pa: Yes
genres: All Styles
venue2: Manitoba Room/Multipurpose Room
capacity: 1000
advance: 3 months+
pa: Yes
genres: All Styles
venue3: Campo
capacity: 50
advance: 6 weeks
pa: Yes
genres: All Styles
Also books unplugged acts for small venue & bands that can fill 3500 cap. arena. Shows are GA & well-promoted.

New Brunswick

U of New Brunswick/ Fredericton - SU
21 Pacey Dr., Rm. 126
PO Box 4400
Fredericton, NB E3B 5A3
Canada
p: 506-453-4955
f: 506-453-4958
e: cellar@unb.ca; cellarpub@gmail.com
www.unbsu.ca
advisor: Patrick Hanson
p: 506-451-1184
venue1: Cellar Pub
capacity: 225
gigs: 60/year
advance: 2-4 months
pa: Yes
genres: Jam, Jazz, Funk, Alt. Country, Reggae, Rock, Punk, Ska, Blues, Hip-Hop
venue2: The Ballroom
capacity: 1500
gigs: 6-8/year
advance: 2-4 months
genres: All Styles
venue3: Cafeteria
capacity: 1000
gigs: 1/year
advance: 2-4 months
genres: All Styles
Shares campus w/ St. Thomas U. Shows for students & guests. Prefers electronic submissions.

U of New Brunswick/ Saint John - SRC
Thomas Condon Centre
PO Box 5050
Saint John, NB E2L 4L5
Canada
p: 506-648-5684
f: 506-648-5541
e: src-social@unbsj.ca
www.unbsjrocks.com
advisor: Jane MacKaye
e: mackayj@unbsj.ca
student: Paul Gallagher
p: 506-648-5981
venue1: Colonel Tuckers
booker: Odeen Whitter
e: src-social@unbsj.ca
capacity: 200
gigs: 2-6/year
pa: Yes
genres: Alt., Rock, Folk
venue2: Baird Dining Room
capacity: 350
gigs: 1/year
pa: Yes
genres: Alt., Rock, Folk
venue3: The Gym
capacity: 3000
gigs: 1/year
pa: Yes
genres: Alt., Rock
Shows for students & their guests.

Nova Scotia

Acadia U - SU
ASU Box 6002
Wolfville, NS B4P 2R5
Canada
p: 902-585-2146
f: 902-542-3901
e: asuvpcampuslife@acadiau.ca
www.theasu.com
advisor: Shelley MacNeill
e: shelley.macneill@acadiau.ca
student: Jon Cottreau
p: 902-585-2126
venue1: The Axe Lounge
capacity: 300
gigs: 1/month
advance: 1 semester
genres: All Styles
Electronic submissions preferred.

Cape Breton U - SU
PO Box 5300
1250 Grand Lake Rd.
Sydney, NS B1P 6L2
Canada
p: 902-563-1192
f: 902-539-2886
e: info@cbusu.com
www.cbusu.com
advisor: Marco Amati
p: 902-563-1191
e: marco@cbusu.com
student: Mike MacKenzie
p: 902-563-1483
e: mike@cbusu.com
venue1: The Pit Lounge
capacity: 350
gigs: 10-15/year
advance: 2-8 weeks
pa: Yes
genres: All Styles
Books a variety of Local-Touring acts. Email submissions preferred.

Dalhousie U - SU
6136 University Ave., Rm. 222
Halifax, NS B3H 4J2
Canada
p: 902-494-1106
f: 902-494-6647
www.dsu.ca
advisor: Greg Wright
p: 902-494-6891
e: greg.wright@dal.ca
student: Ken Osmond
p: 902-494-1281
e: dsuvpsl@dal.ca
venue1: McInnes Room
capacity: 1100
gigs: 2/year
venue2: Grawood Lounge
capacity: 360
gigs: 10/year
venue3: T-Room
capacity: 150
gigs: 10/year

St. Francis Xavier U SU
PO Box 271
Antigonish, NS B2G 2X1
Canada
p: 902-867-2220
f: 902-867-5138
e: su_activ@stfx.ca
www.theu.ca
advisor: Kris MacSween
p: 902-867-2477
e: kmacswee@stfx.ca
student: Jeff Paddon
venue1: MacKay Room
capacity: 500
gigs: 3/year
advance: 1 semester
pa: Yes
genres: Rock, S/S, Punk, Dance
venue2: Golden X Inn
capacity: 250
gigs: 6/year
advance: 4 weeks
pa: Yes
genres: Folk, Rock
venue3: Millennium Centre
capacity: 200
gigs: 3/year
advance: 1 semester
pa: Yes
genres: Rock, S/S
Up to 12 acts/year appear at 3 venues & special events. Tix are free & shows open to students & their guests. Send EPKs.

St. Mary's U - SMUSA
Student Ctr., 5th Fl.
Halifax, NS B3H 3C3
Canada
p: 902-496-8700
f: 902-425-4636
e: vpinternal@smusa.ca
www.smusa.ca
advisor: Rob Finn
p: 902-496-8702
e: rob.finn@smu.ca
student: Fadi Al Qassar
p: 902-496-8709
venue1: Grosebrook Lounge
booker: Lorne Caborn
p: 902-496-8712
e: lorne.caborn@smu.ca
capacity: 350
gigs: Weekly
advance: 1 month
pa: Yes
genres: Acoustic, Local, Top 40, Punk
venue2: The Fieldhouse
capacity: 1300
gigs: 3/year
advance: 1 month
pa: Yes
genres: All Styles
venue3: The Conference Hall
capacity: 800
gigs: 2/year
advance: 1 month+
pa: Yes
genres: All Styles
Books a wide variety of Local-Int'l acts.

Ontario

Algoma U - SA
1520 Queens St. E
Sault Ste. Marie, ON P6A 2G4
Canada
p: 705-949-2301 x4725
f: 705-949-6583
e: ausu@auc.ca; ausu@algomau.ca
www.auc.ca
advisor: Erin Lemke
e: elemke@algomau.ca
venue1: The Speak Easy
capacity: 245 (+70 outside)
gigs: 10/year
advance: 2-3 months
pa: Yes
genres: Acoustic, Alt., Rock, Pop, DJ's
Email contact preferred.

Algonquin College SA
1385 Woodroffe Ave.
Rm. C-151
Ottawa, ON K2G 1V8
Canada
p: 613-727-4723
f: 613-727-7712
www.algonquinsa.com
advisor: Paul Norman
p: 613-727-4723 x5327
e: normanp1@algonquincollege.com
venue1: Observatory Lounge
booker: Ken Macleod
p: 613-727-4723 x5240
e: macleok@algonquincollege.com
capacity: 300
gigs: 1/week
advance: 3-6 months
genres: All Styles
All shows are GA; email contact for booking.

Brock U - SU
Student Centre, 1st Fl.
500 Glenridge Ave.
St. Catherines, ON L2S 3A1
Canada
p: 905-688-5550 x4202
f: 905-641-7581
e: info@busu.net
www.busu.net
advisor: Rob Morosin
e: rmorosin@busu.net
student: Mark Wrzosek

p: 905-688-5550 x3750
e: vpss@busu.net
venue1: Isaac's Pub
capacity: 700
venue2: O'Sullivan Theatre
capacity: 884
venue3: The Playhouse
capacity: 565
Holds 30-40 gigs/year.

Carleton U - CUSA
1125 Colonel By Dr.
401 Unicentre
Ottawa, ON K1S 5B6
Canada
p: 613-520-6688
f: 613-520-3704
e: vpx@cusaonline.com
www.cusaonline.com
student: James Witherspoon
venue1: Oliver's Pub
capacity: 410
gigs: 15/year
advance: 1-2 months
pa: Yes
genres: Rock, Hip-Hop
venue2: Rooster's Coffeehouse
gigs: 5/year
pa: Yes
genres: Acoustic
Between 15-30 gigs/year at various venues; some GA shows.

Durham College, UOIT & Trent - SA
2000 Simcoe St. N
Oshawa, ON L1H 7L7
Canada
p: 905-721-0457
www.your-sa.ca
advisor: Scott Toole
p: 905-721-0457 x227
e: scott.toole@dc-uoit.ca
student: Chris Nelan
p: 905-721-0457 x225
e: savpcampuslife@dc-uoit.ca
venue1: E.P. Taylor's
capacity: 400
gigs: 100+/year
genres: All Styles
Some GA shows.

Fanshawe College SU
1460 Oxford St. E
London, ON N5Y 5R6
Canada
p: 519-453-3720
e: fsuentertain@fanshawec.ca
www.fsu.ca
advisor: Pat Maloney
p: 519-453-3720 x244
e: pmaloney@fanshawec.on.ca
student: Jeff Burling
p: 519-453-3720 x227
venue1: Forwell Hall
capacity: 500
gigs: 100/year
pa: Yes
genres: All Styles
venue2: Outback Shack
capacity: 180
gigs: 50/year
pa: Yes
genres: All Styles
venue3: J Gym
booker: Mark Rawson
capacity: 1000
gigs: 1/year
pa: Yes
genres: All Styles
Also books parties & events; 60% of acts are Touring. Shows are GA. Prefers electronic submissions.

Humber College HSF
205 Humber College Blvd.
Toronto, ON M9W 5L7
Canada
p: 416-675-5051
e: info@hsfweb.com
www.hsfweb.com; www.humberlife.com
advisor: Aaron Miller
p: 416-675-6622 x4411
e: amiller@hsfweb.com
student: Aynur Duzgeren
p: 416-675-5051 x4155
e: vpcl.north@hsfweb.com
venue1: Caps
capacity: 480
advance: 1-3 months
pa: Yes
genres: Rock, Alt., Urban
venue2: The Amphitheater
capacity: 1000
gigs: 4-5/year
advance: 1-3 months
pa: Yes
genres: All Styles
Email contact preferred.

Lakehead U - LUSU
955 Oliver Rd.
Thunder Bay, ON P7B 5E1
Canada
p: 807-343-8551
www.lusu.ca
advisor: Dave Lible
e: outpost@lusu.ca
venue1: The Outpost
capacity: 650
advance: 1 month
pa: Yes sound eng: Yes
genres: Rock
venue2: The Study
capacity: 150
gigs: 15/year
advance: 1 month
pa: Yes sound eng: Yes
genres: Acoustic
Hosts Local-Touring acts; shows are GA. Electronic submissions preferred.

Queen's U - AMS
162 Barrie St.
Kingston, ON K7L 3N6
Canada
p: 613-546-3427
e: gradclub@post.queensu.ca
www.queensu.ca/gradclub
advisor: Virginia Clark
venue1: The Grad Club
capacity: 170
gigs: 100+/year
advance: 1 month
pa: No
genres: All Styles w/ focus on Indie Rock, Soul, Jazz
Shows for students only.

Ryerson U - SU
55 Gould St., Rm. SCC 311
Toronto, ON M5B 1E9
Canada
p: 416-979-5255 x1-2312
e: vp.life@rsuonline.ca
www.rsuonline.ca
advisor: De Silva Zinzi
p: 416-979-5255 x1-2313
e: events@rsuonline.ca
student: Sid Naidu
p: 416-597-0723 x272
venue1: Ram in the Rye
capacity: 250
gigs: 1/week
advance: 1-2 months
pa: Yes
genres: Acoustic, S/S
venue2: Ryerson Theater
gigs: 1/year
pa: Yes
Hard copies preferred.

Seneca College Student Federation
1750 Finch Ave. E
Toronto, ON M2J 2X5
Canada
p: 416-491-5050 x2980
e: nate.howell@senecac.on.ca
www.ssfinc.ca
advisor: Stephanie Skelton
p: 416-491-5050 x6780
e: stephanie.skelton@senecac.on.ca
student: David Russo
p: 416-491-5050 x2985
e: ssfpres.king@senecac.on.ca
venue1: Missing Link Pub
capacity: 274
gigs: 3-4/year
advance: 1 semester
pa: Yes
genres: All Styles
Mostly Reg'l & Touring acts at the Pub.

Sheridan College SU
1430 Trafalgar Rd.
Oakville, ON L6H 2L1
Canada
p: 905-845-9430 x2302
www.sheridansu.net
advisor: Chuck Erman
e: chuck.erman@sheridanc.on.ca
student: Andre Guindi
p: 905-845-9430 x2304
e: studentlife.ssuitrc@sheridanc.on.ca
venue1: Connexion
capacity: 640
gigs: 5-6/year
advance: 1-3 months
pa: Yes
genres: Rock, S/S
venue2: The Rec Room
capacity: 350
gigs: 2/year
advance: 1-3 months
pa: Yes
genres: All Styles
About 8 events/year at various venues.

U of Guelph UC Programming
50 Stone Rd. E, University Ctr., Rm. 266
Guelph, ON N1G 2W1
Canada
p: 519-824-4120 x52896
www.studentlife.uoguelph.ca
advisor: Sam Baijal
e: sbaijal@uoguelph.ca
venue1: Brass Taps
capacity: 500
gigs: 25/year
pa: Yes
genres: All Styles
venue2: Peter Clark Hall
capacity: 600-1000
gigs: 5-10/year
pa: Yes
genres: All Styles
venue3: Mitchell Athletic Ctr.
capacity: 2500
gigs: 1/year
pa: Yes
genres: All Styles
Also books for other on & off campus venues. CSA also books. Electronic submissions preferred.

York U Student Centre
Ste. 335, Student Ctr.
4700 Keele St.
Toronto, ON M3J 1P3
Canada
p: 416-736-5658
f: 416-736-5884
e: events@yorkstudentcentre.com
www.yorkstudentcentre.com; www.myunderground.ca/events.php
advisor: Saqueeb Rajan
e: srajan@yorku.ca
venue1: The Underground
capacity: 500-800
gigs: 1/month
advance: 1-3 months
pa: Yes
genres: Acoustic, Solo, Indie, Rock
Monthly indie nites at The Underground.

Quebec

Champlain College CSA
900 Riverside Dr.
St. Lambert, QC J4P 3P2
Canada
p: 450-672-7360
f: 450-672-9299
www.champlainonline.com
advisor: Ray Corbeil
p: 450-672-7360 x249
e: corbeil@champlaincollege.qc.ca
venue1: The Auditorium
booker: Enzo Abrico
capacity: 400
gigs: 1/year
advance: 2-6 months
pa: Yes
Tix sold at Students' Assoc. Books occasional bands for "Welcome Week" & outdoor BBQs.

John Abbott College SA
21, 275 Lakeshore Rd.
PO Box 2000
Ste. Anne-de-Bellevue
QC H9X 3L9 Canada
p: 514-457-6610
www.johnabbott.qc.ca
advisor: Bill Mahon
p: 514-457-6610 x5317
e: billmahon@johnabbott.qc.ca
venue1: Agora
capacity: 350
gigs: 6/year
pa: Yes
genres: All Styles
venue2: Oval Coffee House
capacity: 75
gigs: 2/year
pa: Yes
genres: All Styles

Saskatchewan

U of Saskatchewan SU
1 Campus Dr. S
Saskatoon, SK S7N 0W0
Canada
p: 306-966-6960
e: contactus@ussu.ca
http://ussu.usask.ca
advisor: Jason Kovitch
p: 306-966-6963
e: jason.kovitch@ussu.ca
venue1: Louis'
capacity: 400
gigs: 8/year
genres: Folk, Rock
venue2: Upper MVB Hall
capacity: 250
gigs: 1/year
venue3: Prairieland Hall
capacity: 2500
gigs: 1/year
genres: Rock, Dance

conferences & festivals

☺ = *Accepts Sonicbids EPK (Electronic Press Kits)*

Conferences

AMC (Atlantis Music Conference & Festival)

50 Barrett Pkwy., Ste. 1200
PMB 342
Marietta, GA 30066
p: 770-499-8600
f: 770-499-8650
e: atlantis@atlantismusic.com
www.atlantismusic.com
contact: Kathy Gates
ext: 404-763-2445
e: kathy@atlantismusic.com
genres: Rock, Pop, Alt., Latin, Americana, Jazz, Gospel, Country, Christian, Urban
2009 dates: Fall
submit: Jan 15 - Jun 15
location: Atlanta, GA
accepts epk: Yes ☺
Presents 250+ nat'l & int'l acts on 18 city stages to 72,000 press, industry & fans. 3000 registrants network & attend panels, trade show & showcases. Download application from site.

Americana Music Conference

411 E Iris Dr., Ste. D
Nashville, TN 37204
p: 615-386-6936
f: 615-386-6937
e: info@americanamusic.org
www.americanamusic.org
contact: Danna Strong
e: danna@americanamusic.org
genres: Americana, Roots, Alt. Country, Folk, Blues
2009 dates: Sept 16-19
submit: Jan 15 - May 30
location: Nashville, TN
accepts epk: Yes ☺
Trade org. unites 1000+ radio & label execs, artists, media, managers, retailers & distributors for conference, tradeshow & showcases. More than 70 estab. & emerging acts play on 5 stages. Free for AMA members & $25 for non-members. Download application & mail w/ CD, bio, fact sheet & photos to: PO Box 128077, Nashville, TN 37212. No MP3s.
See Ad On Page 19

Asbury Park Music Expo

1775 Hwy. 34, Unit D-13
Wall Township, NJ 07727
p: 732-449-0300
f: 732-449-0044
e: contact@themusicexpo.com
www.themusicexpo.com
contact: Greg Race Pirillo
e: race@lincstarrecords.com
genres: All Styles
location: Asbury Park, NJ
Over 3000 industry execs, press, radio & artists gather for panels, workshops & networking. Over 30 Local artists showcase at 6 area venues, including the Stone Pony & Paramount Theater.

ASCAP Expo 2009

1 Lincoln Plaza
New York, NY 10023
p: 212-621-6000
f: 212-724-9064
e: expo@ascap.com
www.ascap.com/expo
contact: Jonathan Bahr
genres: All Styles
2009 dates: Apr 23-25
location: Los Angeles, CA
Three-day music conference includes celebrity Q&As, master classes, songwriting and technology workshops, and one-on-one sessions.
See Ad On Page 14

AthFest

PO Box 327
Athens, GA 30603
p: 706-548-1973
f: 706-316-0752
e: info@athfest.com
www.athfest.com
contact: Jared Bailey
e: director@athfest.com
genres: All Styles
2009 dates: Jun 25-28
submit: Jan 1 - Apr 1
location: Athens, GA
accepts epk: Yes ☺
Non-profit event showcases 150+ mostly reg'l artists on 2 outdoor stages & 15 Athens venues for 35,000 fans & media. Outdoor stages are uncovered. Event also includes local music awards. Accepts mailed submissions only.

Baltimore Music Conference

PO Box 6066
Baltimore, MD 21231
p: 443-850-7389
www.bmcon.org
contact: Lisa Chaplin Suit
e: lsuit@bmcon.org
genres: All Styles
2009 dates: Fall
submit: Jan 28 - May 1
location: Baltimore, MD
accepts epk: Yes ☺
More than 100 US & Int'l buzz bands, DJs & developing talent attend workshops & perform at 8-10 city venues for 3000 fans, press, artists, label execs & industry pros. Submit via Sonicbids or snail mail downloaded form.

Billboard

770 Broadway, 6th Fl.
New York, NY 10003
p: 646-654-4660
f: 646-654-4674
e: bbevents@billboard.com
www.billboardevents.com
contact: Michele Jacangelo
genres: Urban
Industry trade pub. holds many annual events w/ performances, panels, workshops & awards. Check site for dates & locations.

Canadian Music Week

5355 Vail Ct.
Mississauga, ON L5M 6G9
Canada
p: 905-858-4747
f: 905-858-4848
e: info@cmw.net
www.cmw.net
contact: Neill Dixon
ext: 905-858-4747 x225
e: neill@cmw.net
genres: All Styles
2009 dates: Mar 11-14
submit: Apr 1 - Oct 31
location: Toronto, ON
accepts epk: Yes ☺
Combines 2 conferences, a trade show, several competitions & 5 awards shows. Over 500 mainly Indie acts play on 40 stages for 2000+ industry execs & fans. Also contact Bessie Bullard, bessie@cmw.net.

CMJ Music Marathon, Music Fest & Film Fest

151 W 25th St., 12th Fl.
New York, NY 10001
p: 917-606-1908
f: 917-606-1914
e: marketing@cmj.com
www.cmj.com/marathon
contact: Matt McDonald
e: showcase@cmj.com
genres: Alt., Rock, Pop, Electronica, Hip-Hop, Metal, Americana, World, Jazz
2009 dates: Oct
submit: Dec 10 - Jul 14
location: New York, NY
accepts epk: Yes ☺
Influential music conference dedicated to new music brings 1000+ acts & rising stars on 65 city stages for over 100,000 fans, industry pros, artists, filmmakers & press. $45 submission fee.
See Ad On Page 179

Cutting Edge Music Business Conference & Roots Music Gathering

1524 N Claiborne Ave.
New Orleans, LA 70116
p: 504-945-1800
f: 504-945-1873
e: conference@cuttingedgemusicbusiness.com
www.cuttingedgemusicbusiness.com
contact: Eric Cager
e: cut_edge@bellsouth.net
genres: Roots, Rock, Pop, Alt., Urban, New Age, Jazz, Country, Gospel
2009 dates: Aug
submit: Apr 1 - Jul 15
location: New Orleans, LA
accepts epk: Yes ☺
Up to 2500 descend upon the steamy Big Easy for music biz forums, legal seminars, showcases, panels workshops & exhibits. Nearly 100 nat'l & int'l acts perform at area venues for crowds exceeding 2500. Sponsored by New Orleans Music Business Instit. & LA Economic Development.

Dewey Beach Music Conference & Festival

113 Dickinson St.
Dewey Beach, DE 19971
p: 302-703-2929
f: 302-226-2406
www.deweybeachfest.com
contact: Vikki Walls
ext: 302-448-5650 (cell)
e: vwalls@deweybeachfest.com; showcases@deweybeachfest.com
genres: Alt., Rock, Country, Power Pop, S/S
2009 dates: Oct 1-3
submit: Jan 1 - Jul 15
location: Dewey Beach, DE
accepts epk: Yes ☺
Cool little showcase offers panels, mentoring & tradeshow & 3 nites of showcases at 17 area venues for 10,000+ artists, labels, agents, producers, lawyers, Internet companies & press. Up to 175 reg'l-int'l acts play & attend conference & related events for free. Bands get free food/beverages at 3 different VIP parties. Send promos to: PO Box 507, Rehoboth Beach, DE 19971.

DIY Convention: Do It Yourself In Film, Music & Books

7095 Hollywood Blvd.
Ste. 864
Hollywood, CA 90028

p: 323-665-8080
f: 323-372-3883
e: diyconvention@aol.com
www.diyconvention.com
contact: Bruce Haring
e: bruce@diyconvention.com
genres: All Styles of Indie
2009 dates: Feb
submit: Jan 25
location: Los Angeles, CA
accepts epk: Yes
Attracts 6000+ DIY music & arts entrepreneurs for panels & workshops on creating, promoting & distributing Indie music, film & books. Showcases with mostly developing acts run concurrently to conference. Must register online.

Future of Music Policy Summit
1615 L St. NW, Ste. 520
Washington, DC 20036
p: 202-822-2051
f: 202-429-8857
e: summit@futureofmusic.org
www.futureofmusic.org
contact: Chhaya Kapadia
Int'l forum for 400+ musicians, lawyers, policymakers & music industry execs to discuss & debate digital technology issues, artists rights & the current state of the music industry.

Great Escape
59-65 Worship St.
London, EC2A 2DU UK
p: 44-207-688-9000
f: 44-207-688-8999
e: info@escapegreat.com
www.escapegreat.com
contact: Lucy Bannatyne
ext: 44-207-688-8978
e: lucy.bannatyne@mamagroup.co.uk
genres: Rock, Pop
2009 dates: May 14-16
location: Brighton, UK
accepts epk: Yes
A series of daytime interviews w/ 5000 leading industry execs & a nighttime festival of 150 Int'l artists playing at 20 area venues.

Holy Hip-Hop Artist Showcase & Music Awards
1375 W Peachtree St. NW
Atlanta, GA 30309
p: 404-893-5752
e: holyhiphopweek@holyhiphop.com
www.holyhiphopweek.com
contact: Eddie Velez
e: press@holyhiphop.com
genres: Holy Hip-Hop
2009 dates: Jan 16-17
submit: May 21 - Jul 21
location: Atlanta, GA
accepts epk: Yes
Faith-based event promotes the Gospel thru Holy Hip-Hop. 2000+ press, industry execs & 100 artists gather for showcases. Must include ministerial statement, complete bio & mp3 file.

In The City
8 Brewery Yard, Deva Centre
Trinity Way
Salford, Manchester M3 7BB
UK
p: 44-161-839-3930
f: 44-161-839-3940
e: register@inthecity.co.uk
www.inthecity.co.uk
contact: Jon Paul
e: jonpaul@inthecity.co.uk
genres: Rock, Alt., Urban, Pop, Punk, Electronic, Grime, Garage, Indie
2009 dates: Oct 18-20
location: Manchester, England
accepts epk: Yes
Over 500 artists showcase on 50 stages for 2000 attendees. Panels, seminars, showcases & master classes draw musicians, fans, & industry pros from all over Europe.

International DJ Expo
25 Willowdale Ave.
Port Washington, NY 11050
p: 516-767-2500
f: 516-767-9335
e: djtimes@testa.com
www.djtimes.com
contact: Robin Hazan
ext: 516-767-2500 x503
e: rhazan@testa.com
genres: House, Hip-Hop, Dance
2009 dates: Aug
Industry trade mag DJ Times event draws 5000+ int'l DJs, artists, press & sound/light contractors to network, party & attend workshops & competitions. Up to 20 performances. Email before sending material.

International Folk Alliance Conference
510 S Main St.
Memphis, TN 38103
p: 901-522-1170
f: 901-522-1172
e: fa@folk.org
www.folk.org
contact: Louis Meyers
e: louis@folk.org
genres: Folk, World, S/S, Acoustic, Americana, Blues, Bluegrass, Celtic, Spoken-Word
2009 dates: Feb 18-22
submit: Jul - Nov 20
location: Memphis, TN
accepts epk: Yes
Premier event for the new Folk industry unites the sprawling community w/ focus on supporting both trad. & the broader hybrid genres. Workshops, panels, tradeshow plus official & DIY showcases. Over 200 developing & estab acts play on 10 stages for 2250 attendees. Also holds Reg'l conferences: FARWest contact: Steve Dulson, 949-646-1964; tinkersown@ca.rr.com & SERFA contact: Kari Estrin, 615-262-0883; kari@kariestrin.com. Submit via Sonicbids or on site.
See Ad On Page 177

Invasion of the GoGirls
PO Box 16940
Sugar Land, TX 77496
e: info@gogirlsmusic.com
www.gogirlsmusic.com/sxsw
contact: Madalyn Sklar
e: madalyn@gogirlsmusic.com
genres: All Styles
2009 dates: Mar 18-22
submit: Dec - Jan 30
location: Austin, TX
accepts epk: Yes
Unofficial SXSW showcase draws 1500+ for 60 developing acts at 4 venues. Must be GoGirls Elite Member to submit. Sonicbids only.

LAMC (Latin Alternative Music Conference)
10627 Burbank Blvd.
North Hollywood, CA 91601
p: 818-763-1397
f: 818-763-1398
e: info@latinalternative.com
www.latinalternative.com
contact: Jennifer Sarkissian
e: jennifer.sarkissian@cookman.com
genres: Latin Alt., Latin Rock, Latin Hip-Hop
2009 dates: Jul
location: New York, NY
Over 1200 artists, label pros, talent brokers & press flock to this premiere summit showcasing the edgier side of Latin music. Up to 50 nat'l & int'l acts perform on 10 city stages & compete in the Battle of the Unsigned Bands.

MACROCK (Mid-Atlantic College Radio Conference)
Anthony Seeger Hall
MSC 6801
Harrisonburg, VA 22807
p: 540-568-6346
f: 540-568-7156
www.macrock.org
contact: Jenn Disse
e: jennmacrock@hotmail.com
genres: Indie, Rock, Hip-Hop, Electronic, Americana, Jazz, Pop, Metal
2009 dates: Apr 3-4
submit: Nov
location: James Madison U
Student-run fest puts emerging talent & buzz bands in front of 6000 music fans & industry. 100+ US & int'l acts perform on & off campus. Send material to: MACROCK, c/o WXJM, 983 Reservoir St., Harrisonburg, VA 22801.

Midatlantic Music Conference
5588 Chamblee Dunwoody Rd., #110
Dunwoody, GA 30338
p: 888-755-0036
f: 770-300-0175
e: info@wholeteam.com
www.midatlanticmusic.com
contact: Kysii Ingram
genres: Rock, Alt., Gospel, Dance, World, R&B, Urban, Pop, Soul, Jazz, Blues, Folk
2009 dates: Nov 14-16
submit: By Oct 13
location: Charlotte, NC
accepts epk: Yes
Up to 100 area bands showcase on 6 stages & network w/ 1500 industry execs. Submit at site.

MIDEM
360 Park Ave. S, 14th Fl.
New York, NY 10010
p: 212-284-5142
f: 212-284-5148
e: midemusa@reedmidem.com
www.midem.com
contact: John Jenkinson
e: john.jenkinson@reedmidem.com
genres: Electronic, Urban, Rock, Pop, Americana, World, Jazz, New Age
2009 dates: Jan 18-21
submit: Jan - Oct 31
location: Cannes, France
accepts epk: Yes
Top int'l networking event for creating licensing, publishing & distrib. alliances. 13,000+ industry pros attend - 250 acts perform on 10 stages. Only registered artists are considered for showcases.

MOBfest
1658 N Milwaukee Ave.
Ste. 292
Chicago, IL 60647
p: 773-227-8777
f: 773-227-2509
www.chicagomobfest.com
contact: Roger Jansen
e: roger@kmamanagement.com
genres: Rock, Metal, Alt., Punk, Hip-Hop
submit: Jan 15 - May 15
accepts epk: Yes
Brings artists w/ reg'l following to the next level. About 150 acts, strut their stuff industry for pros & attend panels, mentoring & showcases at 15 city stages. 500 attend panels; 4000 attend club shows. Showcasing artists are included on CD compilation. Must submit according to guidelines on site.

MUSEXPO
8383 Wilshire Blvd., #100
Beverly Hills, CA 90211
p: 323-782-0770
f: 323-782-9835
www.musexpo.net
contact: Sat Bisla
e: sat@anrworldwide.com
genres: Alt., New Rock, S/S
submit: Nov - Feb 8
accepts epk: Yes
High-profile event presented by artist development firm, A&R Worldwide, exposes new & unsigned artists to 750 members of the global music industry. About 30-35 Nat'l/Int'l acts perform on 3 stages. Snail mail material.

NACA (National Association for Campus Activities)
13 Harbison Way
Columbia, SC 29212
p: 803-732-6222
e: info@naca.org
www.naca.org
contact: Gordon Schell
e: gordons@naca.org
genres: All Styles
2009 dates: Feb
submit: Sept 19
accepts epk: Yes
Prime showcase for college bookings presents up to 80 polished acts & buzz bands on 2 stages for 3000 college ent. buyers & exhibitors. Artists must join NACA to perform. Also holds 7 Reg'l conferences.

NXNE (North By Northeast Music & Film Festival & Conference)
189 Church St., Lower Level
Toronto, ON M5B 1Y7
Canada
p: 416-863-6963
f: 416-863-0828

e: info@nxne.com
www.nxne.com
contact: Andy McLean
genres: All Styles
2009 dates: Jun 18-21
submit: Nov 1 - Jan 31
location: Toronto, ON
accepts epk: Yes
Nearly as popular as its sister SXSW event, this event draws 60,000+ artists, media & industry. More than 450 North American & int'l acts showcase at 40+ city venues for pros & music fans. Accepts material thru SonicBids & online. Also contact Gillian Zulauf, 416-863-6963; gillz@nxne.com.
See Ad On Page 183

OCFF (Ontario Council of Folk Festivals)
410 Bank St., Ste. 225
Ottawa, ON K2P 1Y8
Canada
p: 866-292-6233; 613-560-5997
f: 613-560-2001
e: info@ocff.ca
www.ocff.ca
contact: Jennifer Fornelli
genres: Folk, Roots, Blues, Traditional, World
2009 dates: Oct
submit: Jan 31 - May 9
location: Ottawa, ON
accepts epk: Yes
Up to 700 festival organizers, presenters, artists, directors & press attend seminars, showcases & jam sessions. Snail mail or submit via Sonicbids, include CD, bio, photo, stage plot, band member list, a short description of your live show & a check or money order for $30 for non-members; $20 for members. No cassettes, D.A.T.S., Vinyl Video or MP3s.

Popkomm
Messedamm 22
Berlin, D-14055
Germany
p: 49-303-038-3009
f: 49-303-038-2149
e: info@popkomm.de
www.popkomm.de
contact: Klaus Gropper
ext: 49-303-038-2155
e: gropper@messe-berlin.de
genres: All Styles
2009 dates: Sept 16-18
submit: Jan - Mar
location: Berlin, Germany
accepts epk: Yes
Int'l meeting place where 15,000+ artists, press, agents, labels, managers, publishers & distributors from 55 countries, attend panels, tradeshow & showcases. Over 400 acts play on 30+ city stages; up to 50% are emerging artists.

Remix Hotel (Los Angeles)
6400 Hollis St.
Ste. 12
Emeryville, CA 94608
p: 510-985-3272
www.remixmag.com
contact: Joanne Zola
e: joanne.zola@penton.com
genres: Electronic, Urban, Dance
Reg'l events, produced by Remix mag, for producers, engineers, musicians & DJs, provides hands-on access to technology & equip. Hosts similar events in: Atlanta, Las Vegas, Miami & NYC. Possible showcase opps. No unsolicited material.

Singer/Songwriter of Cape May
35 Fieldview Dr.
North Cape May, NJ 08204
p: 717-221-1124
e: sscapemay@yahoo.com
www.sscapemay.com
contact: John Harris
e: johnharris@johnharris.com
genres: All Styles
2009 dates: Mar 27-28
submit: Jul - Jan
location: Cape May, NJ
accepts epk: Yes
Features panels, workshops, mentoring & exhibitors. Over 125 emerging & estab. talent perform on 12 stages over 300 industry attendees. Selected artists will receive free registration for the event. No unsolicited material.

SXSW (South by Southwest Music & Media Conference & Festival)
PO Box 4999
Austin, TX 78765
p: 512-467-7979
f: 512-451-0754
e: sxsw@sxsw.com
http://sxsw.com
contact: Luann Williams
e: sales@sxsw.com
genres: Alt., Rock, S/S, Pop, Jazz, Americana, Country, Blues, Reggae, Hip-Hop, Electronica
2009 dates: Mar 18-22
submit: Aug-Oct 24 (Int'l); Aug-Nov 7 (USA)
location: Austin, TX
accepts epk: Yes
Premiere, hi-profile industry event places 1500 rising & estab. acts on 70 city stages, plus tons of unofficial showcases running non-stop. Nearly 12,000 of the global music industry attend panels, tradeshow & performances. Submit online at www.sxsw.com/showcase or at Sonicbids.
See Ad On Page 175

Texas Summer Music Conference
c/o The Movement Entertainment Group
PO Box 494555
Garland, TX 75043
p: 214-336-4313
f: 214-336-4313
e: txsmc@yahoo.com
www.texassummermusicconference.com
contact: Mike Senters/ Mic Moodswing
ext: 214-403-9918
genres: Hip-Hop, R&B, Soul, Spoken Word
2009 dates: Summer
Features panels, showcases, networking opps. & off-site performances for over 3000 developing Hip-Hop & R&B artists & labels. Between 22-30 perform on 1 stage.

Winter Music Conference
3450 NE 12th Terr.
Ft. Lauderdale, FL 33334
p: 954-563-4444
f: 954-563-1599
e: info@wintermusicconference.com
www.wintermusicconference.com
contact: Bill Kelly
e: bill@wintermusicconference.com
genres: Alt., Pop, Electronic, Dance, R&B, Prog, Dancehall
2009 dates: Mar 24-28
location: Miami, FL
Premiere genre event w/ int'l draw attracts A-list talent & industry for networking, panels, workshops, exhibits, showcases & the Int'l Dance Music Awards. Up to 3500 attend, 500+ artists & DJs perform.

World of Bluegrass
2 Music Cir. S, Ste. 100
Nashville, TN 37203
p: 615-256-3222
f: 615-256-0450
e: info@ibma.org
www.ibma.org
contact: Dan Hays
genres: Bluegrass
2009 dates: Sept 28-Oct 4
location: Nashville, TN
Prime event sponsored by Int'l Bluegrass Music Assoc. helps propel the genre beyond obscure niche w/ biz seminars, workshops, showcases & fanfest. Attracts 20,000 fans & industry from 30 countries; 40+ acts, some developing, perform on 4 stages.

Festivals

10,000 Lakes Festival
FACE
PO Box 1227
Detroit Lakes, MN 56502
p: 218-847-1681
f: 218-847-0533
e: info@10klf.com
www.10klf.com
contact: Gene Hollister
e: bands@10klf.com
genres: Jam
2009 dates: Jul
submit: ongoing
location: Detroit Lakes, MN
Over 20,000 fans are treated to a beautiful setting & 60+ Reg'l & Nat'l acts on 4 stages. Fees vary. Submit online. No calls.

A Call To Peace
World Peace Sanctuary
26 Benton Rd.
Wassaic, NY 12592
p: 845-877-6093
f: 845-877-6862
e: info@worldpeace.org
www.worldpeace.org
contact: Jim Dugan
e: jim@worldpeace.org
genres: All Styles
2009 dates: TBD
submit: Nov 15 - Jun 15
location: Wassaic, NY
Free, day-long event welcomes up to 15,000 fans & 3-6 Local-Nat'l bands on 2 stages to promote peace.

Affiliated Foods Midwest Country Stampede
Country Stampede
3003 Anderson
Ste. 949
Manhattan, KS 66503
p: 785-539-2222
f: 785-539-3787
e: stampede@countrystampede.com
www.countrystampede.com
contact: Wayne Rouse
genres: Country
2009 dates: Jun 25-28
location: Manhattan, KS
One of the largest festivals in the region features 30 Country acts on 3 stages to over 150,000. Food supplied to artists.

Agape Music Festival
Greenville College
315 E College Ave.
Greenville, IL 62246
p: 618-664-1806
f: 618-664-1868
e: director@agapefest.com
www.agapefest.com
contact: Ivan Filby
e: info@agapefest.com
genres: CCM
2009 dates: May 1-2
submit: Until Mar 12
location: Greenville, IL
accepts epk: Yes
College student ministry event celebrates Christ w/ 2-day secular music fest for up to 7000 on 2 fairground stages. 25 top acts & 10 emerging bands perform for all ages. Bands paid, but fees vary. Developing acts compete in Battle of Bands on 2nd stage for main stage bid. Only unsolicited kits for 2nd stage accepted - send ATTN: Ivan.

All Good Summer Music Festival & Campout
Walther Productions
2801 Chevy Chase Cir.
Jefferson, MD 21755
p: 301-834-4100
f: 301-834-3373
e: info@walther-productions.com
www.allgoodfestival.com
contact: Tim Walther
genres: Rock, Jam, Jazz, Funk, S/S, Americana, Folk, Bluegrass, Hip-Hop Fusion
2009 dates: Jul
submit: Jul - May 17
location: Masontown, WV
accepts epk: Yes
Celebration of music & good vibes attracts 18,000 trad. neo-hippies of all ages. Up to 40 touring & emerging acts perform on 2 outdoor stages. Bands are compensated. All booking is done thru Sonicbids.

Amsterdam Roots Festival
Stichting Amsterdam Roots
Lijnbaansgracht 234a
Amsterdam, 1017 PH
The Netherlands
p: 31-20-531-8181
e: info@amsterdamroots.nl
www.amsterdamroots.nl
contact: Frans Goossens
e: frans@amsterdamroots.nl
genres: World
2009 dates: Jun
location: Amsterdam

Any fears that folk music will die out with the current generation of gray- ponytailed performers were allayed at the annual Folk Alliance conference, where the young outnumbered the old.

– *Cleveland Plain Dealer*

www.folk.org

www.myspace.com/thefolkalliance

Art by A Man Called Wrycraft

Presents 62 World music acts on 10 indoor & outdoor stages for an int'l crowd of 65,000.

Arkansas Blues & Heritage Festival
Sonny Boy Blues Society
233 Cherry St.
Helena, AR 72342
p: 870-338-8798
f: 870-338-8110
e: rayne49@yahoo.com
www.bluesandheritage.com
contact: Jerry Pillow
ext: 870-338-7042
genres: Blues & Gospel
2009 dates: Oct 8-10
submit: ongoing
location: Helena, AR
accepts epk: Yes
Formerly the King Biscuit Blues Fest features 100+ Local-Nat'l bands on 4 stages for 80,000+ all ages fans. "Emerging Artist Program" exposes developing talent to reps from 45 int'l Blues societies. Also books "busqueing space" on Helena street corners. Festival budget: $100,000-$150,000; bands receive stipend. Hard copy submissions preferred.

Artscape
Baltimore Office of The Arts
7 E Redwood St., Ste. 500
Baltimore, MD 21202
p: 410-752-8632
f: 410-385-0361
www.artscape.org
contact: Sheila Goodwin
e: sgoodwin@promotionandarts.com
genres: R&B, Rock, Blues, Jazz, Alt., Folk, Pop
2009 dates: Jul 17-19
submit: Jan - Mar 31
location: Baltimore, MD
accepts epk: Yes
America's largest free municipally-sponsored all ages arts show hosts 60+ top Local-Nat'l acts on 4 outdoor stages for 500,000+ fans. Festival budget is: $1,000,000, bands are compensated. Submissions via Sonicbids.

AthFest
PO Box 327
Athens, GA 30603
p: 706-548-1973
f: 706-316-0752
e: info@athfest.com
www.athfest.com
contact: Troy Aubrey
e: music@athfest.com
genres: All Styles
2009 dates: Jun 25-28
submit: Jan - Mar 1
location: Athens, GA
accepts epk: Yes
More than 125 polished & developing acts & 15,000 fans descend on 2 outdoor stages & nitely club crawls thru 12 area venues in the house that REM built. Bands are compensated.

Atlanta Dogwood Festival
Pure Entertainment
887 W Marietta St. NW, #S-105
Atlanta, GA 30318
p: 404-817-6642
f: 404-817-9508
e: coordinator@dogwood.org
www.dogwood.org
contact: Laura Valente
ext: 678-309-0031
e: laura@pureentertainmentinc.com
genres: Blues, Jazz, Rock, Americana, Acoustic, World
2009 dates: Apr 17-19
submit: Sep - Jan
location: Atlanta, GA
Free all ages event for 100,000+ places nearly 20 paid Reg'l & Nat'l Indie acts on 2 stages. Mail promos to: 4355 Cobb Pkwy., Ste. J329, Atlanta, GA 30339. Prefers Sonicbids submissions.

Austin City Limits Music Festival
98 San Jacinto Blvd., Ste. 400
Austin, TX 78701
p: 877-FEST-ACL
f: 512-476-0611
e: info@aclfest.com
www.austincitylimits.com
contact: Amy Corbin
genres: Rock, Pop, Jam, Alt., Blues, S/S, Alt. Country, Hip-Hop, Gospel, Reggae
2009 dates: Oct 2-4
submit: Nov - Jan 15
location: Austin, TX
Prestigious event showcases 130 recording acts, rising stars & developing bands on 8 stages for sold out crowds of 75,000+ music fans. Bands are paid. No unsolicited material.

Babbfest
419 Productions
Hwy. 89, Mile Marker 32
Babb, MT 59411
p: 406-249-2903
www.myspace.com/babb_fest
contact: Ryan Braswell
e: rcbmon@hotmail.com
genres: All Styles
2009 dates: Jul
submit: Jan - Apr
location: Babb, MT
Over 10 acts play on 1 stage for 2000 all ages music fans. Also features a DJ Tent & free beer! Festival budget is: $40,000; bands are paid $200-$6000. Email before sending material to: 162 Harvard Ave., Salt Lake City, UT 84111.

The Bamboozle
Live Nation
1775 Hwy. 34
Unit D13
Wall, NJ 07727
p: 732-449-0300
f: 732-714-0191
e: contact@linkstarrecords.com
www.thebamboozle.com
contact: Bill O'Brien
genres: Rock
2009 dates: May 2-3
submit: Nov - Feb
location: The Meadowlands, East Rutherford, NJ
accepts epk: Yes
"MTV Best Festival" winner pays 100+ Nat'l recording acts & buzz bands to perform on 9-10 indoor & outdoor stages for 30,000+ all ages fans. Also hosts 'The Break Contest' for unsigned acts. Enter contest to perform at the festival: www.thebreakcontest.com.

Bayfest Music Festival
205 Government St.
Mobile, AL 36644
p: 251-208-7835
f: 251-208-7624
e: info@bayfest.com
www.bayfest.com
contact: Robert Bostwick, Jr.
genres: Blues, Rock, Soul, Rap, Hip-Hop
2009 dates: Oct 2-4
submit: Apr - Jun (Local & Reg'l) & ongoing (Nat'l)
location: Mobile, AL
accepts epk: Yes
Annual all ages celebration gathers 125+ Local-Nat'l acts on 9 stages for a crowd of 200,000; offers excellent exposure for developing talent. Local & Reg'l acts send promos to: Red Mountain Entertainment, 2107 Fifth Ave. N, Ste. 50, Birmingham, AL 35203; Nat'l acts send promos to: Robert O. Bostwick, Jr., PO Box 1827, Mobile, AL 36633.

Bean Blossom Gospel Jubilee
Bean Blossom Bluegrass
5163 State Rd., 135 N
Morgantown, IN 46160
p: 800-414-4677
f: 812-988-1203
e: beanblossombg@hotmail.com
www.beanblossom.com
contact: Margie Sullivan
ext: 251-246-4553
e: dwight@beanblossom.com
genres: Gospel, Bluegrass Gospel, Southern Gospel
2009 dates: Jun 13-20
location: Bill Monroe Park & Campground, Bean Blossom, IL
Oldest continuing faith-based Bluegrass festival in the world features up to 25 acts on 2 stages to 7000 attendees of all ages. Bands are compensated.

Beloit Riverfest
1003 Pleasant St.
Beloit, WI 53511
p: 608-365-4838
f: 608-365-6850
e: beloitriverfest@aol.com; info@beloitriverfest
www.beloitriverfest.com
contact: Rod Beaudoin
genres: Rock, Pop
2009 dates: Jul 9-12
location: Riverside Park
Outdoor city-sponsored all ages event features 1-2 major label headliners plus 30-60 indies on 4 stages for 60,000 music fans. Email submissions & put "Entertainment Package for RF" in the subject field.

Birmingham Int'l Jazz Festival
Big Bear Music
PO Box 944
Edgbaston, West Midlands B16 8UT UK
p: 44-121-454-7020
f: 44-121-454-9996
e: admin@bigbearmusic.com; festival@bigbearmusic.com
www.birminghamjazzfestival.com
contact: Tim Jennings
e: tim@bigbearmusic.com
genres: Jazz, Blues, Swing
2009 dates: Jul 4-13
location: Birmingham, UK
Over 70 Local-Int'l developing & polished acts perform for 160,000 all ages fans at 60+ area venues. Bands are paid.

Black Potatoe Music Festival
Black Potatoe Entertainment
PO Box 414
Stanhope, NJ 07834
p: 908-391-0769
e: festival@blackpotatoe.com
www.blackpotatoe.com
contact: Matt Angus
ext: 908-735-6429
genres: Roots, Folk, Blues, Funk, Rock, Jazz, Pop, Country
2009 dates: Jul 9-12
submit: Jul 1 - Apr 1
location: Clinton, NJ
accepts epk: Yes
Indie fest features 30+ developing & estab. acts on 2 stages for all ages - up to 5000 attend. Some bands are compensated. Submissions thru Sonicbids only.

Blistered Fingers Family Bluegrass Festival
263 Trafton Rd.
Waterville, ME 04901
p: 207-873-6539
e: blist-f@blisteredfingers.com
www.blisteredfingers.com
contact: Sandy Cormier
genres: Acoustic Bluegrass
2009 dates: Jun 18-21 & Aug 27-30
submit: Jul - Dec
location: Sidney, ME
Bi-annual event presents 13-15 Local-Int'l acts to 4000+ mostly "mature" Bluegrass fans. Up & comers share "open stage" w/ estab. talent for great exposure. Festival budget is: $40,000; bands paid $3000.

Block Island Music Festival
On-Island Ent. & Media
PO Box 1253
Block Island, RI 02807
p: 401-466-5670
e: blockislandmusic@hotmail.com
www.blockislandmusic.com
contact: Marc Scortino
genres: All Styles
2009 dates: Jun
submit: Until Mar 1
location: Block Island, RI
accepts epk: Yes
Free 21+ grassroots festival features 48 buzz bands & up & coming acts from Northeast USA playing on indoor & outdoor stages to over 2000 fans. Bands get lodging, food & drink in lieu of pay. Submit via Sonicbids.

Blue Balls Festival
Weinbergstrasse 31, Postfach
Zurich, CH-8021 Switzerland
p: 41-43-243-7323
f: 41-43-243-7324
e: info@blueballs.ch
www.blueballs.ch
contact: Urs Leierer
genres: Jazz, Blues, Soul, Funk, Pop, Rock, World
2009 dates: Jul 17-25
location: Lucerne, Switzerland
Largest music festival in the German-speaking region of Switzerland presents 90 top & polished USA & Int'l acts on 4 indoor & 4 outdoor stages. Area clubs also benefit from the 100,000+ attendees.

Blues by the Bay
Redwood Coast Music Festivals

PO Box 314
Eureka, CA 95502
p: 707-445-3378
f: 707-445-1240
e: info@bluesbythebay.org; info@redwoodjazz.org
www.bluesbythebay.org
contact: Glenn Maxon
genres: Blues, Roots
2009 dates: Sep 5-6
submit: Sep - Mar
location: Eureka, CA
Outdoor all ages event presents 12+ top USA & Int'l developing Blues acts for 5000+. Bands are compensated.

Bluesfest Int'l Windsor
Bluesfest International
1185 Argyle Rd.
Windsor, ON N8Y 3K2 Canada
p: 519-977-9631
f: 519-977-9519
e: info@thebluesfest.ca
www.thebluesfest.com
contact: Ted Boomer
e: ted@thebluesfest.ca
genres: Blues
2009 dates: Jul 16-19
submit: Nov - Mar 1
location: Windsor, ON
accepts epk: Yes
Top Canadian Blues event presents 20+ N American & Int'l bands on 2 stages for 30,000+ 19+ fans; at least 4 slots secured for emerging talent for viable exposure. Books sister event in London, ON. Bands are paid $500-$30,000. Include pay requirements along w/ kit.

Bonnaroo
e: info@bonnaroo.com
www.bonnaroo.com
genres: Rock, Alt., Hip-Hop, Jazz, Americana, Electronica
2009 dates: Jun
location: Manchester, TN
Top grossing event mixes 80,000 fans, 100+ top tier & buzz acts on 10 stages, camping & assorted activities, to create a pop culture phenom. No unsolicited material.

Bumbershoot, Seattle's Music & Arts Festival
One Reel
100 S King St., Ste. 100
Seattle, WA 98104
p: 206-281-7788
e: info@onereel.org
www.bumbershoot.org
contact: Chris Porter
e: programming@onereel.org
genres: Alt., Rock, Hip-Hop, Pop, Blues, World, Electronic
2009 dates: Aug 30 - Sep 1
location: Seattle, WA
accepts epk: Yes
All ages music, art & drinking extravaganza presents potent mix of 200 estab. artists & rising stars on 7 stages to 150,000+ music fans in dramatic outdoor setting. About 50 slots for developing acts reserved for Pacific NW talent, w/ room for buzz bands. Bands are paid.

California World Fest
Maple Creek Presents
PO Box 3339
Chico, CA 95927
p: 530-891-4098
f: 530-891-4098
www.worldfest.net
contact: Dan DeWayne
e: dan@worldfest.net
genres: Country, Americana, Folk, Rock, World, Reggae, Blues
2009 dates: Jul 16-19
submit: ongoing
location: Grass Valley Fairgrounds
Family-themed event features diverse lineup of 40-50 polished & notable USA & Int'l acts on 8 stages for 3000-4000/day. Bands paid. No calls.

Centerfest
Bedford Main Street
PO Box 405
Bedford, VA 24523
p: 540-586-2148
f: 540-586-5775
e: mainst@bedfordva.gov
www.centertownbedford.com
contact: Linda Exley
genres: Rock, Bluegrass, Gospel, Country, Christian
2009 dates: Sep 25-26
submit: Jan - May
location: Bedford, VA
Free, street festival features up to 25 bands on 4 stages for 25,000 fans; headliners change every year. Kickoff concert held at Farmer's Market. Only Fri nite bands get paid.

Central Park Summer Stage
City Parks Foundation
830 5th Ave.
New York, NY 10021
p: 212-360-2756
f: 212-360-2754
e: info@summerstage.org
www.summerstage.org
contact: Erika Elliott
e: talent@summerstage.org
genres: World, Americana, Spoken Word, Electronic, Pop, Rock, Hip-Hop
2009 dates: Jun - Aug
location: Central Park - NYC
Premier free music festival features 90 USA & Int'l artists. A-list & polished acts perform for 220,000 on outdoor stage. Bands are compensated. No unsolicited material.

Chicago Blues Festival
Mayor's Office / Special Events
121 N LaSalle St., Rm. 806
Chicago, IL 60602
p: 312-744-3315
f: 312-744-8523
www.cityofchicago.org/specialevents
contact: Barry Dolins
e: bdolins@cityofchicago.org
genres: Blues
2009 dates: Jun 12-14
submit: Until Oct 1
location: Grant Park
City's largest music festival draws 750,000 fans. Up to 100 USA & Int'l artists perform on 6 outdoor stages. Send CD, bio & photo.

Chicago Jazz Festival
Mayor's Office / Special Events
121 N LaSalle St., Rm. 806
Chicago, IL 60602
p: 312-744-3315
f: 312-744-8523
www.cityofchicago.org/specialevents
contact: Jennifer Johnson Washington
e: jjwashington@cityofchicago.org
genres: Jazz
2009 dates: Sep 4-6
submit: Oct 1 - Dec 31
location: Chicago, IL
Notable free celebration run by the Jazz Inst. of Chicago, pairs 35-40 world famous & rising stars on 4 stages for 300,000+. Bands paid; send hard copies only. Also sponsors Country & Gospel events.

Chico World Music Festival
CSU Chico/Chico Performances
University Public Events @ CSU Chico, 400 W 1st St.
Chico, CA 95929
p: 530-898-5917
f: 530-898-4797
www.chicoperformances.com
contact: Dan DeWayne
e: ddewayne@csuchico.edu
genres: All Styles
2009 dates: Sep
submit: ongoing
location: Chico, CA
All ages cultural celebration welcomes 20+ USA & Int'l acts from a variety of styles & genres on 3 stages for 3000/day. No unsolicited material.

Chippewa Valley Rock Fest
24447 County Hwy. S
Cadott, WI 54727
p: 715-289-4401
f: 715-289-3910
www.rock-fest.com
contact: Mike Asher
e: mikea@countryfest.com
genres: Rock, Pop, Hard Rock
2009 dates: Jul 16-19
location: Cadott, WI
Family-oriented outdoor event showcases 18 Nat'l acts & 8 Reg'ls on 5 stages for 25,000 fans/day. Bands are paid. Also books a Country event.

Cisco Ottawa Bluesfest
265 Catherine St., 2nd Fl.
Ottawa, ON K1R 7S5 Canada
p: 613-247-1188; 866-258-3748
f: 613-247-2220
e: info@ottawabluesfest.ca
www.ottawabluesfest.ca
contact: Mark Monahan
e: programming@ottawabluesfest.ca
genres: Blues, R&B, Gospel, Soul, World, Pop, Alt. Country
2009 dates: Jul 9-19
submit: Nov 1 - Mar 31
location: Ottawa, ON
accepts epk: Yes
Canada's premier all ages music fest mixes 170+ N American superstars & rising stars on 5 stages for 300,000 fans. Pay varies.

Clearwater Festival: Great Hudson River Revival
Hudson River Sloop Clearwater
112 Little Market St.
Poughkeepsie, NY 12601
p: 845-454-7673
f: 845-454-7953
e: office@clearwater.org
www.clearwaterfestival.org
contact: Ron Aja
ext: 845-454-7673 x102
e: raja@clearwater.org
genres: Blues, Folk, Rock, Gospel, Bluegrass, World, S/S, Zydeco, Salsa, Reggae, Roots
2009 dates: Jun 20-21
submit: Dec - Feb
location: Croton-on-Hudson, NY
Non-profit all ages event attracts 11,000 music fans & environmentalists to see Pete Seeger, along w/ 60 estab. & developing acts on 5 outdoor stages. Event broadcast live on WBAI, 99.5 FM. Bands are paid.

CMA Music Festival
Country Music Association
1 Music Cir. S
Nashville, TN 37203
p: 615-244-2840; 800-CMA-FEST
f: 615-726-0314
www.cmafest.com; **www.**fanfair.com
contact: Jeff Walker
e: communications@cmaworld.com
genres: Country
2009 dates: Jun 11-14
location: Nashville, TN
Gathers 200+ acts on 5 stages for 200,000 fans & 600 media reps from around the world. Polished developing acts booked on "Riverfront Stages". Also aired on ABC. Bands aren't paid. No unsolicited material.

Columbus Jazz & Rib Fest
Music in the Air
111 E Broad St., Ste. 101
Columbus, OH 43205
p: 614-645-7995
f: 614-645-6278
e: mita@columbus.gov
www.musicintheair.org; www.hotribscooljazz.org
contact: Ed Myers
ext: 614-645-6144
e: eamyers@columbus.gov
genres: All Styles of Jazz
2009 dates: Jul 24-26
submit: ongoing
location: Columbus, OH
City-sponsored outdoor festival featuring 25 paid Local-Int'l bands on 2 stages for 400,000 Jazz & rib lovers. Submit online application first, then send bio & full length recording.

Comstock Country
PO Box 74
Ord, NE 68828
p: 308-370-1023; 866-939-7798
e: service@comstockmusic.net
www.comstockmusic.net
contact: Don & Jim
genres: Country
2009 dates: Jun 4-7
submit: ongoing
location: Comstock, NE
Up to 30 Local-Nat'l artists perform for 20,000+ on 3 stages at this all ages event. Bands are compensated. Reg'l talent send promos to: Christy Oestreich, 540 Bolson Dr., Apt. B, Oconomowoc, WI 53066; Nat'l talent send promos to: Harry Nuxoll, PO Box 49, Comstock, NE 68828.

Cornerstone Festival
Cornerstone Communications
920 W Wilson Ave.
Chicago, IL 60640
p: 773-989-2087
f: 773-913-2216
e: info1@cornerstonefestival.com

www.cornerstonefestival.com
contact: John Herrin
e: john@cornerstonefestival.com
genres: Christian, Jazz, Blues, World, Punk, Metal, Alt., Gospel, Rap, Gothic
2009 dates: Jun 29 - Jul 4
submit: Sep - Jan
location: Bushnell, IL
accepts epk: Yes
20,000 of the faithful flock to hear up to 250 major & developing Christian artists perform on 10 stages at this notable all ages camping fest. Also hosts "New Band Showcase", which places 15 finalists on a sidestage & 1 grand prize winner on the main stage. Festival budget is: $300,000. Bands paid $500-$1000. For label showcases, email: erin@gyroscopearts.com. Sonicbids entries only.

Creation Festival
Come Alive Ministries
PO Box 86
Medford, NJ 08055
p: 800-327-6921
f: 609-654-8466
www.creationfest.com
contact: Bill Darpino
ext: 609-654-8440
e: bill@comealive.com
genres: CCM
2009 dates: Jun 24-27; Jul 22-25
location: Gorge, WA; Union, PA
accepts epk: Yes
Trad. & cutting edge USA & Canadian Christian talent is presented on 2 coasts - PA & WA. Up to 65,000 faithful of all ages enjoy 75 acts - estab. on main stage, emerging talent on "fringe" stage. Bands are paid.

Cully Jazz Festival
Place de l'Hotel de Ville 2,
Case Postale 138
Cully, Suisse CH-1096
Switzerland
p: 41-21-799-4040
f: 41-21-799-4550
e: info@cullyjazz.ch; presse@cullyjazz.ch
www.cullyjazz.ch
contact: Carine Zuber
genres: Blues, Funk, Jazz, Latin Jazz
2009 dates: Mar 27 - Apr 4
submit: Aug 1 - Nov 30
location: Cully, Switzerland
Up to 40 Local-Int'l polished acts play at this 9 day Jazz fest located in Cully, Switzerland.

Das Fest
Stadtjugendausschuss e.V.
Karlsruhe
Durlacher Allee 64
Karlsruhe, 76131 Germany
p: 49-721-781-7212
f: 49-721-6648
www.dasfest-karlsruhe.de
contact: Rolf Fluhrer
e: r.fluhrer@stja.karlsruhe.de
genres: Rock, Alt., Funk, Jazz, Acoustic, Pop, Hip-Hop, Techno, Classical
2009 dates: Jul
location: Karlsruhe
Free, youth-sponsored event hosts 40 top USA & Int'l artists, including 20 developing acts on 5 outdoor stages for 200,000+.

Dewey Beach Music Conference & Festival
113 Dickinson St.
Dewey Beach, DE 19971
p: 302-703-2929
f: 303-226-2406
www.deweybeachfest.com
contact: Vikki Walls
ext: 302-448-5650 (cell)
e: showcases@deweybeachfest.com; vwalls@deweybeachfest.com
genres: Alt., Rock, Country, Power Pop, S/S
2009 dates: Sep
submit: Jan 1 - Jul 15
location: Dewey Beach, DE
accepts epk: Yes
Free conference & festival w/ industry buzz presents up & coming acts to industry panels & fans. Up to 175, mostly Reg'l acts w/ some touring & Int'l talent, play at 17 venues along the DE beachfront to 10,000. Each venue has it's own policy. Bands are not paid. Apply to showcase online thru Sonicbids or complete online application & send to: PO Box 507, Rehoboth Beach, DE 19971.

Dewey Beach Popfest
113 Dickinson St.
Dewey Beach, DE 19971
p: 302-703-2929
f: 302-226-2402
e: popfest@deweybeachfest.com
www.deweybeachfest.com/popfest
contact: Vikki Walls
ext: 302-448-5650; 302-448-5650
e: vwalls@deweybeachfest.com
genres: Pop, Power Pop, BritPop, Punk Pop
2009 dates: Apr 17-18
submit: Nov - Feb 15
location: Dewey Beach, DE
accepts epk: Yes
Free 21+ Pop celebration presents 60 developing & polished USA & Int'l acts at 7 beachfront clubs for up to 2500. Bands receive $50-$100. Download application from site or submit via Sonicbids.

Diversafest (Dfest)
Raincrow Media
PO Box 33141
Tulsa, OK 74153
p: 918-640-9519
f: 918-742-0767
www.dfest.com
contact: Tom Green
e: tgreen@dfest.com
genres: All Styles
2009 dates: Jul
submit: Dec - Apr 3
location: Tulsa, OK
accepts epk: Yes
Conference & festival combo places 130 estab. indie & developing acts on 3 outdoor stages & 8 area clubs for 40,000+ fans & industry moguls. Outdoor stages & 2 clubs are all ages. Send 3 songs, press kit & $15 submission fee.

DuPont Clifford Brown Jazz Festival
City of Wilmington
800 N French St.
Wilmington, DE 19801
p: 302-576-3095
f: 302-571-4089
www.cliffordbrownjazzfest.com
contact: Tina Betz
ext: 302-576-2136
e: tbetz@ci.wilmington.de.us; festivalartists@ci.wilmington.de.us
genres: Jazz, Latin, Funk, Fusion
2009 dates: Jun
submit: Dec - Jan
location: Wilmington, DE
Annual free city-sponsored all ages outdoor event celebrates it's prodigal son w/ showcases & a diverse line-up of 20+ USA & Int'l acts for 35,000 Jazz buffs. Festival budget is $175,000; Bands paid $3500-$12,500. Also produces Riverfront Blues Festival. Send music sample, performance fee, photographs, tech & hospitality rider.

Earshot Jazz Festival
3429 Fremont Pl. N
#309
Seattle, WA 98103
p: 206-547-6763; 206-547-9787
e: jazz@earshot.org
www.earshot.org
contact: John Gilbreath
e: john@earshot.org
genres: Jazz
2009 dates: Oct 23 - Nov 8
submit: ongoing
location: Seattle, WA

Notable non-profit Jazz org. showcases 50 estab. & emerging artists on 15 stages for 15,000 Jazzbos. Event is well-covered by press. Age policy varies by stage. Bands are compensated.

Edmonton Folk Music Festival
Terry Wickham
10115 97-A Ave.
Edmonton, AB T6E 4T2 Canada
p: 780-429-1899
e: access@efmf.ab.ca
www.edmontonfolkfest.org
contact: Terry Wickham
e: twickham@efmf.ab.ca
genres: Folk, World, Blues
2009 dates: Aug
location: Edmonton, AB
World-class all ages event showcases estab. artists & makes room for polished emerging talent. Up to 70 acts play on 7 stages for 85,000. Bands paid $200-$150,000. Submit bio & CDs to: PO Box 4130, Edmonton, AB T6E 4T2, Canada.

Essence Music Festival
135 W 50th St.
New York, NY 10020
p: 212-522-1662
e: festival@essence.com
www.essence.com/essence/emf
contact: Sheila Harris
e: sharris@essence.com
genres: R&B, Classic Soul, NeoSoul, World Beat, Jazz
2009 dates: Jul 4th wknd
location: New Orleans, LA
Afro-American lifestyle mag presents 25 top acts on 3 stages to 250,000 fans of all ages. Artists reps call: 504-410-4100 before sending material. Bands are compensated.

EXIT Festival
Novi Sad
Trg Mladeneca 5
Novi Sad, Serbia
e: answerme@exitfest.org; play@exitfest.org
www.exitfest.org
genres: Rock, Indie, Hip-Hop, Rap, Electronic, Dance, Techno, House, Drum n Bass, Breaks, Electro, Prog
2009 dates: Jul 9-12
location: Petrovaradin Fortress
Takes place in the 17th century fortress overlooking the Danube. Over 600 acts play on 25 stages for 50,000 attendees. Festival is promoted internationally & popular w/ the UK audience.

Falcon Ridge Folk Festival
PO Box 144
Sharon, CT 06069
p: 860-364-0366
e: falcridge@aol.com
www.falconridgefolk.com
contact: Anne Saunders
ext: 860-364-2138
e: anne@falconridgefolk.com
genres: Folk, World, Celtic, S/S, Bluegrass, Blues, Swing, Polka, Americana, Reggae
2009 dates: Jul
submit: Until Feb 1 (Features) & May 1 (Emerging Artist)
location: Hillsdale, NY
accepts epk: Yes
Annual all ages Berkshire community-sponsored music & camping event presents 50 top & polished acts on 4 outdoor & tented stages for crowds of 10,000-12,000/day. Budget is $100,000 & pay range is $1000-$10,000. Also has an emerging artist showcase hosting Indie acts. Sonicbids entries only.

Festival Internacional de Benicassim
Maraworld S.A.
Preciados 27-2
Madrid, 28013 Spain
p: 34-91-523-4114
e: info@fiberfib.com
www.fiberfib.com
contact: Ana Sanabia
e: ana@fiberfib.com
genres: Pop, Indie, Electronic
2009 dates: Jul 16-19
location: Benicassim (Castellon), Spain
Diverse arts & music event showcases 100 USA & Int'l acts on 4 stages; recording stars & buzz bands play for 40,000.

Festivals at Nelson Ledges Quarry Park
Nelson Ledges Quarry Park
PO Box 116
Nelson, OH 44231
p: 440-548-2716
e: nlqp@modex.com
www.nlqp.com
contact: Evan Kelley
genres: Jam, Acoustic, Roots, Reggae, Bluegrass, Jazz
2009 dates: summer
location: Garretsville, OH
Campground hosts a series of eclectic outdoor family music events presenting 18+ top Reg'l & Nat'l talent on 2 stages for up to 8000 attendees. Festival budget is: $200,000; bands paid from $300-$70,000. 18+ unless w/ guardian.

Finger Lakes GrassRoots Festival of Music & Dance
PO Box 941
Trumansburg, NY 14886
p: 607-387-5098
f: 607-387-5630
e: info@grassrootsfest.org
www.grassrootsfest.org
genres: World, Zydeco, Cajun, Americana, Celtic, Rock, Reggae, Bluegrass, Folk, Hip-Hop, Country, Blues, Jazz
2009 dates: Jul 16-19
location: Trumansburg, NY
AIDS awareness benefit showcases Local-Int'l talent for 15,000 attendees & campers. Up to 60 acts perform on 4 outdoor stages.

Florida Music Festival & Conference
Axis Talent & Promotions
116 S Orange Ave.
Orlando, FL 32801
p: 407-839-0039
f: 407-839-0040
e: artistrelations@floridamusicfestival.com
www.floridamusicfestival.com
contact: Rick Wheeler
genres: Rock, Urban, Acoustic
2009 dates: May
submit: Dec - Mar 10
location: Orlando, FL
accepts epk: Yes
Presents 250+ acts on 15 downtown Orlando stages for 25,000+ industry insiders & fans; showcases 15 developing Reg'l acts. Venue age restrictions apply.

Floydfest
Across The Way Productions
PO Box 243
Floyd, VA 24091
p: 540-745-FEST
f: 540-745-3256
e: info@floydfest.com
www.floydfest.com; www.atwproductions.com
contact: Kris Hodges
e: kris@floydfest.com
genres: World, Jam, Funk, Bluegrass, Folk, Americana, Jam, Afrobeat, Reggae
2009 dates: Jul
submit: Oct 8 - Jan 9
location: Floyd, VA
Attracts quirky all ages music fans plus top & polished performers. Up to 60 acts on 7 stages play for crowds of 10,000. Festival budget is $120,000, developing acts paid $200.

Folkfestival Dranouter
VZW Folkfestival Dranouter
Dikkebusstraat 234
Heuvelland, Dranouter 8950
Belgium
p: 32-5-744-6933; 32-5-744-6424
f: 32-5-744-6243
e: info@folkdranouter.be
www.folkdranouter.be
contact: Geert Gombeir
e: geert@folkdranouter.be
genres: Folk, World, Rock Roots, Pop, Fusion
2009 dates: Aug
location: Dranouter, Belgium
Eclectic array of 100 top & emerging USA & Int'l artists on 8 stages play for 90,000 all ages fans. Festival budget: 750,000 Euros.

Food Lion Speed Street
600 Festival Association
6427 Saddle Creek Ct.
Harrisburg, NC 28075
p: 704-455-6814; 704-455-5555
www.600festival.com
contact: Jacqueline Gafrarar
e: jacq@gojne.com
genres: Country, Rock n Roll
2009 dates: Memorial wknd
location: Charlotte, NC
Family-oriented NASCAR event pays top Local-Nat'l talent to festivities. Up to 400,000 check out 40 acts on 3+ outdoor stages. For Local/Reg'l bookings contact: Doug Daniel at 704-333-2122 or doug@danielentertainment.com.

Four Corners Folk Festival
Folk West
PO Box 3665
Pagosa Springs, CO 81147
p: 970-731-5582
e: folkwest@folkwest.com
www.folkwest.com
contact: Dan Appenzeller
e: dan@folkwest.com
genres: Folk, Rock, Celtic, Bluegrass, Newgrass, Blues
2009 dates: Sep 4-6
location: Pagosa Springs, CO
accepts epk: Yes
Non-profit org celebrates Folk & related styles & pays 17 estab. & polished acts to perform on 3 stages for 3500 fans. Lively campground w/ 24/7 Jam sessions & workshops. Also produces IndieFest. Festival budget is: $500,000; bands are paid $35,000-$500,000. No snail mail.

Fuji Rock Festival
SMASH Corp.
202 Mikuni, Yuzawa-machi
Minami-Uonuma-gun
Niigata, Japan
p: 025-789-3973; 035-720-9999
www.smash-uk.com/frf09
genres: Indie Rock, Pop, Dance
2009 dates: Jul 24-26
location: Naeba Ski Resort
Annual festival features 200+ Japanese & Int'l musicians on 10 stages for crowds exceeding 50,000 making it the largest outdoor music event in Japan. Opening party is free & features bon-odori (traditional Japanese folk dance).

Gathering of the Vibes
Terrapin Presents
PO Box 3377
Bridgeport, CT 06605
p: 203-908-3030
e: info@gatheringofthevibes.com
www.gatheringofthevibes.com
contact: Ken Hayes
genres: Rock, Jam, Acoustic, Blues, World, Americana
2009 dates: Jul 23-26
location: Bridgeport, CT
accepts epk: Yes
Celebrating the Grateful Dead ethos, annual family music & camping event hosts 30+ polished Reg'l-Nat'l acts on 3 stages for thousands of fans. Features Master of Ceremonies Wavy Gravy. Bands are paid & keep % of merch sales.

Georgia Mountain Fair
PO Box 444
Hiawassee, GA 30546
p: 706-896-4191
f: 706-896-4209
e: gamtfair@alltel.net
www.georgiamountainfairgrounds.com
contact: Hilda Thomason
genres: Country Rock, Bluegrass, Gospel
2009 dates: Jul 15-25
location: Fairgrounds
19 acts play to nearly 60,000 attendees from TN, NC, SC & GA. Bands are compensated.

Glastonbury Festival
28 Northload St.
Glastonbury, Somerset
BA6 9JJ UK
p: 44-145-883-4596
e: office@glastonburyfestivals.co.uk
www.glastonburyfestivals.co.uk
genres: Pop, World, Dance, Acoustic, Cabaret, Jazz
2009 dates: Jun 26-28
location: Worthy Farm
Largest outdoor festival hosts 2000+ USA & Int'l chart toppers & rising stars on 35+ stages for 180,000+ fans. Also hosts "Emerging Talent" series for great exposure. No unsolicited material.

Graspop Metal Meeting
Graspop VZW

Kerkhofweg 3
Dessel, B-2480 Belgium
p: 32-14-37-5981
f: 32-14-37-5982
e: graspop@graspop.com
www.graspop.com
contact: Bob Schoenmaekers
e: biebob@pandora.be
genres: Metal, Hard Rock
2009 dates: Jun 26-28
location: Dessel, Belgium
Belgian's largest Metal & camping fest lures 100,000 music fans to bang heads w/ 70+ top & emerging USA & Int'l acts on 3 stages.

Great Escape
Barfly - The Great Escape
59-65 Worship St.
London, EC2A 2DU UK
p: 44-207-688-9000
e: info@escapegreat.com
www.escapegreat.com
contact: Jon Mcildowie
e: jon.mac@barflyclub.com
genres: All Styles
2009 dates: May 14-16
submit: Jun - Apr
location: Brighton, UK
accepts epk: Yes
European 18+ fest showcases 250 rising bands from around the world in 30 Brighton venues for 25,000 attendees.

Grey Fox Bluegrass Festival
TMD
PO Box 535
Utica, NY 13503
p: 888-946-8495; 315-724-4473
e: office@greyfoxbluesgras.com
www.greyfoxbluegrass.com
contact: Chuck Wentworth
ext: 401-783-3926
e: chukwent@cox.net
genres: Bluegrass, Acoustic, Zydeco, Swing, Old-Time
2009 dates: Jul 16-19
location: Walsh Farm, Oak Hill, NY
accepts epk: Yes
All ages family event presents 40 of the genres' heroes & new stars on 5 stages to 28,000. Bands are compensated. Also hosts artist showcases, workshops & jams. Promos to: 255 Holly Rd., Wakefield, RI 02879 or thru Sonicbids.

Guinness Cork Jazz Festival
Quest Jazz
80 Haddington Rd., Ballsbridge
Dublin, 4 Ireland
p: 353-1-637-5219
www.corkjazzfestival.com
contact: Jack McGouran
e: jack@questcom.iol.ie
genres: Jazz, Blues, Funk
2009 dates: Oct 23-36
submit: Dec 1 - Jan 31
location: Cork City, Ireland
Showcases 50 USA & Int'l acts at 15 area venues including Cork Opera House. Headliners & emerging talent play for 40,000 fans & press. Festival budget is: $200,000; bands are paid 500 Euro. Send CD & bio.

Harborfest
Oswego Harbor Festivals
41 Lake St.
Oswego, NY 13126
p: 315-343-6858
e: info@oswegoharborfest.com
www.oswegoharborfest.com
contact: Barbara Manwaring
ext: 315-343-6858 x1229
e: entertainment@oswegoharborfest.com
genres: All Styles
2009 dates: Jul 23-26
submit: Until Jan 7
location: Oswego, NY
Community-sponsored free outdoor event hosts 60+ popular Reg'l-Int'l acts for pay on 5 stages for 300,000 fans. All bands must submit online application form, along w/ press kit & CD.

Harmony Festival
PO Box 2001
Sebastopol, CA 95476
p: 707-861-2035
e: info08@harmonyfestival.com; info@harmonyfestival.com
www.harmonyfestival.com
contact: Sean Ahearn
ext: 415-721-7515
e: programming@harmonyfestival.com; sean@harmonyfestival.com
genres: Pop, Rock, R&B, Hip-Hop, Electronica, Techno
2009 dates: Jun 12-14
submit: Oct 7 - Apr 1
location: Sonoma County Fairgrounds - Santa Rosa, CA
All ages music, arts & ecology event hosts 70+ Local-Int'l acts 13 stages to promote all things green. Up to 25,000 attend. 90% of bands are paid. Send CDs or audio links w/ website, bio & booking/mgmt. contacts to Sean Ahearn.

The Heavy Rebel Weekender
127 Hudson Hills Rd.
Pittsboro, NC 27312
p: 919-444-4904
www.heavyrebel.net
contact: David Quick
e: dquick@nc.rr.com
genres: Punk, Rock, Bizarro, Honky-Tonk, Rockabilly, Garage, Psychobilly, Ska, Surf, Lounge
2009 dates: Jul 3-5
submit: Jul - Dec 31
location: Winston-Salem, NC
More than 2000 retro auto, music & mud-wrestling fans watch 75+ USA & Int'l small label & unsigned acts shake it up on 3 stages. Bands are paid; must be 18+ to attend. Also publishes The Heavy Rebel Weekender mag.

Heitere Open Air
Henzmannstrasse 39
Zofingen, CH-4800 Switzerland
p: 41-62-745-9060
f: 41-62-745-9065
e: info@heitere.ch
www.heitere.ch
contact: Andy Locher
ext: 41-33-222-1313
e: andy.locher@heitere.ch
genres: Pop, Rock, Hip-Hop, Funk, World
2009 dates: Aug 7-9
location: Heitere-Platz Zofingen
Hosts an array of top & cutting-edge USA & Int'l artists. Up to 12,000 music fans per day

enjoy 25 acts on 3 stages. Send all material to: Pleasure Prod., Militärstrasse 6, CH-3600 Thun, Switzerland.

High Sierra Music Festival
PO Box 99529
Emeryville, CA 94662
p: 510-420-1529; 510-420-1115
f: 510-420-1589
e: highsierramusic@highsierramusic.com
www.highsierramusic.com
contact: Roy Carter
genres: Roots, Jam, Rock, Bluegrass, Folk, Americana, Pop, Electronica
2009 dates: Jul 4th weekend
location: Plumas Fairgrounds - Quincy, CA
All ages music & camping event showcases eclectic line-up of estab. & emerging acts. USA & Int'l talent perform on 5 outdoor stages & tented stages; 75 acts play for up to 10,000 attendees. Some bands are compensated. Contact via email only!

Hip Hop Mile
BOTS Entertainment
18313 John R. St.
Detroit, MI 48203
p: 877-819-5974; 313-743-3870
e: karinda@bots-ent.com
www.hiphopmile.com
contact: Johnny Greasy
ext: 313-926-1273
e: johnny@hiphopmile.com
genres: Hip-Hop, Gospel, Holy Hip-Hop, Neo-Soul, Singing, Poetry, Spoken Word
2009 dates: Jun 13
submit: Until May 30
location: Detroit, MI
All ages family event presents 100+ Indie musicians on 14 stages for crowds of up to 10,000 at this free talent showcase for notable, unsigned Hip-Hop artists. Bands are not paid. All material must be radio edited & no cursing allowed; no exceptions!

Hultsfred Festival
Rockparty
PO Box 170
Hultsfred, 577 24 Sweden
p: 46-4-956-9500
f: 46-4-956-9550
e: info@rockparty.se
www.rockparty.se
contact: Janne Kleman
e: jk@rockparty.se
genres: Pop, Rock, Metal, Hip-Hop, Soul, Reggae, Dance, Techno, S/S
2009 dates: Jun
location: Hultsfred Folkets Park
Sweden's largest youth-oriented event pays 100 top USA & Int'l artists & buzz bands to perform on 5 tented stages for hordes of 30,000/day.

Hyperactive Conference & Music Festival
Hyperfestival
11024 Montgomery, PMB #253
Albuquerque, NM 87111
p: 505-856-7602
e: allie@hyperfestival.com
www.myspace.com/hyperactivefestival
contact: Jenny Gamble
ext: 505-903-2046
e: jenny@hyperfestival.com
genres: All Styles
2009 dates: May 14-16
location: Albuquerque, NM
accepts epk: Yes
Over 120 Local-Int'l Indie acts perform on 10+ Albuquerque stages for crowds exceeding 10,000. Festival also features 50+ panel speakers from all facets of the music biz & daily band showcases for emerging talent. 30+ artists will be selected for inclusion on festival compilation CD. Certain clubs are all ages. Bands are not paid; Sonicbids submissions only.

Iceland Airwaves
Reykjavik, Iceland
p: 35-4-552-0380
f: 35-4-552-0390
e: info@destiny.is
www.icelandairwaves.com
contact: Eldar Astthorsson
ext: 35-4-869-8179
e: eldar@destiny.is
genres: Rock, Pop, Alt., Electronica, Hip-Hop, Indie
2009 dates: Oct 21-25
submit: Jan 1 - Jun 15
location: Reykjavik, Iceland
accepts epk: Yes
Uber-hip new music showcase presents 140+ US/Int'l cutting-edge bands & DJs on 8 city stages to press & 5000 20+ hipster music fans. Some bands are compensated. Send promos CD, bio & tour dates to: Mr. Destiny, PO Box 326, 121 Reykjavik, Iceland.

Ilosaarirock
Joensuun Popmuusikot ry
PO Box 240
Joensuu, 80101 Finland
p: 35-81-312-5030
f: 35-81-322-5224
e: popoffice@ilosaarirock.fi
www.ilosaarirock.fi
contact: Panu Hattunen
ext: 35-850-506-7405
e: panu.hattunen@ilosaarirock.fi
genres: Rock, Metal, Reggae, Hip-Hop, Pop, Punk
2009 dates: Jul 17-19
location: Laulurinne - Joensu, Finland
Popular all ages event on the Finnish Rock calendar presents 90+ polished Int'l acts on 6 stages for 21,000/day. Many opps. to play at area clubs & incentives for up-&-comers.

Indie Week Toronto
Gen-Sub Records
705 King St. W, Ste. 1714
Toronto, ON M5V 2W8 Canada
p: 647-893-9468
e: info@indieweek.com
www.indieweek.com
contact: Darryl Hurs
genres: Acoustic, Alt., World, Americana, Bluegrass, Blues, Country, Electronic, Dance, DJ, Folk, Funk, Goth, Jam, Metal, Pop, Punk, Reggae, Rock, S/S
2009 dates: Oct
submit: Feb 12 - Jul 23
location: Toronto, ON
accepts epk: Yes
Acts are chosen thru submissions, performances are judged by industry pros & prizes are awarded to top acts, along w/ media & networking opps. Over 80 indie acts play on 10 stages for a crowd exceeding 1200. Submit thru Sonicbids or download a mail-in application from site.

International Pop Overthrow (IPO)
David Bash
14641 Magnolia Blvd., #2
Sherman Oaks, CA 91403
e: intlpop@earthlink.net
www.internationalpopoverthrow.com
contact: David Bash
genres: Pop, Rock
2009 dates: Nov
location: USA, Canada & Liverpool, UK
accepts epk: Yes
Traveling festival bounces across USA w/ stops in Canada & UK. Each event showcases hundreds of indie acts to thousands of fans & music biz reps. Bands are not paid to perform. Mostly 21+, some all ages shows.

Italia Wave Love Festival
Arezzo Wave Foundation-Fondazione Arezzo Wave Italia
Corso Italia 236
Arezzo, 52100 Italy
p: 39-57-540-1722
f: 39-57-529-6270
e: fondazione@arezzowave.com; info@arezzowave.com
www.italiawave.com
contact: Giusi Nibbi
e: giusy.nibbi@arezzowave.com; info@elettrowave.eu
genres: Rock, Hip-Hop, Pop, World, Techno, Dance, Electronic
2009 dates: Jul
submit: Oct - Mar
location: Livorno, Italy
accepts epk: Yes
Free Rock festival showcases 200+ cutting-edge USA & Int'l polished bands & DJ's on 10 stages for a crowd of 250,000 world fans of all ages. Bands are compensated. Send DVD, CD, press release, latest album description, availability & verify past visits to Italy.

Jazz Fest Wien-Vienna
Live Performance Service
Lammgasse 12/8
Vienna, A-1080 Austria
p: 43-1-712-4224
f: 43-1-712-3434
e: office@viennajazz.org
www.viennajazz.org
contact: Heinz Krassnitzer
genres: Jazz, Blues, R&B, World, Electronic, Rock
2009 dates: summer
location: Vienna, Austria
A top all ages European event draws 72,000+ to hear 122 estab. & polished USA & Int'l talent perform on 14 indoor & outdoor city stages including the Vienna Opera House.

Joshua Tree Music Festival
JavaGoGo
PO Box 2205
Joshua Tree, CA 92252
p: 877-327-6265
f: 877-327-6265
e: jtmusicfest@gmail.com
www.joshuatreemusicfestival.com
contact: Barnett English
genres: Folk, Pop, Rock, Jazz, World, Soul, S/S, Groove, Funk, Jam, Bluegrass
2009 dates: May 15-17
submit: ongoing
location: Joshua Tree Lake Campground - Joshua Tree, CA
Nearly 25 polished USA & Int'l acts play on 2 outdoor stages for thousands of original music fans. Also organizes the Joshua Tree Roots Music Festival. Pay Range: $500-$10,000. Snail mail submissions.

JVC Jazz Festival
Festival Network
30 Irving Pl., 6th Fl.
New York, NY 10003
p: 212-533-7292
f: 212-877-9916
e: info@festivalnetwork.com
www.festivalnetwork.com
contact: John Phillips
ext: 212-533-7293
e: jphillips@festivalnetwork.com
genres: Jazz
2009 dates: summer
location: New York, NY
Notable Jazz showcases presents 30 prime USA & Int'l artists play at 8 stages at various events held in NYC, CA, Miami, Newport, Chicago, Paris & Warsaw for 30,000+. Email links.

Kerrville Folk Festival
PO Box 291466
Kerrville, TX 78029
p: 830-257-3600
f: 830-257-8680
e: info@kerrville-music.com
www.kerrvillefolkfestival.com
contact: Dalis Allen
genres: Folk, S/S, Americana, Blues, Reggae, Bluegrass, Acoustic Rock
2009 dates: May 21 - Jun 7
location: Quiet Valley Ranch
accepts epk: Yes
Premier Acoustic showcase presents 100+ top performers & rising stars on 2 stages for 30,000. Bands are paid. Only original music considered. Submit via Sonicbids.

Langerado Music Festival
290 SW 12th Ave., Ste. 11
Pompano Beach, FL 33309
p: 954-782-7500
e: langinfo@langerado.com
www.langerado.com
genres: Indie, Jam, Hip-Hop, Electronica
2009 dates: Mar 6-8
location: Miami, FL
accepts epk: Yes
Popular all ages event features 80 bands on 5 stages for 30,000 fans. Late nite shows will take place at multiple venues.

Larmer Tree Festival
J & J Events
PO Box 1790
Salisbury, Wiltshire SP5 5WA UK
p: 44-172-555-2300
f: 44-172-555-3090
e: info@larmertreefestival.co.uk
www.larmertreefestival.co.uk
contact: James Shepard
e: james@larmertreefestival.co.uk
genres: World, Roots, Blues, Folk, Americana, Reggae
2009 dates: Jul 15-19
submit: Oct - May
location: Larmer Tree Gardens
Popular all ages independent event presents 70 recording acts

& rising stars on 5 outdoor stages to sold out crowds of 5000.

Legendary Rhythm & Blues Cruise
313 Lawrence Ave.
Kansas City, MO 64111
p: 816-753-7979
e: bluesin@bluescruise.com
www.bluescruise.com
contact: Roger Naber
genres: Blues, Rock
2009 dates: Oct 17-24; Jan 23-30
location: Pacific Coast; Eastern Caribbean
All ages cruise presents 20 bands on 5 stages w/ over 2000 vacationers in attendance. Bands are compensated.

Limestone City Blues Festival
Downtown Kingston! B.I.A.
177 Wellington St., Ste. 202
Kingston, ON K7L 3E3 Canada
p: 613-542-8677
f: 613-542-0274
e: info@downtownkingston.ca
www.kingstonblues.com
contact: Michele Langlois
genres: Blues
2009 dates: Aug 27-30
submit: Sep 1 - Jul 31
location: Kingston, ON
Features 30 Reg'l-Int'l Blues acts on 3 outdoor & 15+ area venues to 10,000 music fans. All ages for outdoor; 19+ for clubs. Bands are compensated. Send press package & CD.

Live Oak Music Festival
KCBX
4100 Vachell Ln.
San Luis Obispo, CA 93401
p: 805-781-3030
www.liveoakfest.org
contact: Marisa Waddell
ext: 805-549-8855
e: mwaddell@kcbx.org
genres: Folk, Bluegrass, Jazz, Blues, World, Gospel, Reggae, Classical Crossover, Roots
2009 dates: Jun 19-21
submit: Jul 1 - Oct 31
location: Santa Barbara, CA
All ages fundraiser for public radio station, KCBX places 20+ developing & estab. acts on 3 outdoor stages. More than 3000 fans/day; musicians are paid to perform. Send email w/ link or submit via Sonicbids.

Locobazooka!
3-D Entertainment
75 Webster St., Ste. 16
Worcester, MA 01603
p: 508-831-7399
f: 508-831-7308
www.locobazooka.com
contact: Dan Hartwell
ext: 508-797-3305
e: locobooking@aol.com
genres: Rock
2009 dates: summer
submit: Starting Aug 15
location: Boston, MA
accepts epk: Yes
Covered by MTV & SPIN, New England's largest all ages Rock showcase provides 5 stages for 40 unsigned Reg'l bands & 10 Nat'l/Int'l Rock gods. 20,000 attend. Unsigned acts paid per ticket they sell up to $10,000.

Lollapalooza
C3 Presents
98 San Jacinto Blvd., Ste. 430
Austin, TX 78701
e: info@lollapalooza.com
www.lollapalooza.com
contact: Huston Powell
e: hpowell@c3presents.com
genres: Rock, Indie, Alt., S/S, Hip-Hop
2009 dates: Aug 7-9
location: Grant Park - Chicago
accepts epk: Yes
Brain child of rocker Perry Farrell, the all ages event now calls the windy city home & pays 120+ top acts & developing bands to perform on 7 stages to 40,000/day.

The Los Angeles Women's Music Festival
Gaia Rocks & Warrior Girl Music
2461 Santa Monica Blvd., #207
Santa Monica, CA 90404
p: 310-919-3548
f: 310-919-3548
e: info@lawmf.com; bookings@lawmf.com
www.lawmf.com
genres: All Styles
2009 dates: Aug
submit: Jan 1 - Jul 15
location: Encino, CA
Over 50 female acts play on several stages for music fans & animal lovers. Proceeds benefit animal rights. Only female-fronted acts considered. Submit via Sonicbids.

Lowell Folk Festival
Lowell Festival Foundation
67 Kirk St.
Lowell, MA 01852
p: 978-275-1706
f: 978-275-1762
e: duey_kol@nps.gov
www.lowellfolkfestival.org
contact: Joshua Kohn
ext: 301-565-0654 x15
genres: Traditional Folk, Bluegrass, Celtic, Blues, Ethnic
2009 dates: Jul 24-26
submit: Sep - Mar
location: Lowell, MA
Prime free all ages event presents 27 top acts on 6 stages to 200,000+ fans. Bands are paid. Traditional & ethnic acts send material to: Program Manager National Council for the Traditional Arts, 1320 Fenwick Ln., Ste. 200, Silver Spring, MD 20910. No fee to apply.

Lowell Summer Music Series
Lowell Festival Foundation
67 Kirk St.
Lowell, MA 01852
p: 978-275-1722
f: 978-275-1762
www.lowellsummermusic.org
contact: Peter Aucella
e: peter_aucella@nps.gov
genres: Folk, Blues, Pop, Ethnic, Zydeco, Celtic
2009 dates: summer
submit: Dec - Mar
location: Lowell, MA
Family-oriented program presents 25 top Nat'l headliners & Local/Reg'l buzz acts to an all ages crowd of 2500 fans. Local/Reg'ls receive $100 fee & 100% merch sales.

M.E.A.N.Y. FEST
344 W 46th St., Ste. 2F
New York, NY 10036
p: 212-592-9090
f: 212-246-0705
e: gnyctv@aol.com
www.meanyfest.com
contact: Denise Gerardi
e: denise@meanyfest.com
genres: All Styles
2009 dates: Fall
submit: Feb - Jul
location: NYC, NY
accepts epk: Yes
Over 260 emerging & estab. bands network & perform for free on 15+ city stages for 15,000 attendees. Most shows are 21+. Submit via Sonicbids only.

Merritt Mountain Music Festival
Active Mountain Ent.
613 5th Ave., 2nd Fl.
New Westminster, BC
V3M 1X3 Canada
p: 604-525-3330
e: info@mountainfest.com
www.mountainfest.com
contact: Don Adams
e: don@mountainfest.com
genres: Country, Rock
2009 dates: Jul 9-12
submit: Oct 15 - Feb 15
location: Merritt, BC
All ages music & camping event has 80+ N American acts gig on 3 stages for 100,000. Bands are paid. Send CD, 8x10 photo & bio.

Michigan Womyn's Music Festival
WWTMC
PO Box 22
Walhalla, MI 49458
p: 510-652-5441
www.michfest.com
genres: Dance, Hip-Hop, Classical, Rock, Pop, R&B, Folk
2009 dates: Aug 4-9
submit: Sep - Nov 1
location: Near Hart, MI
Utopian camping & music gathering for up to 5000 womyn, many w/ kids in tow. Offers 36-40 female-centric acts on 3 stages. Bands are compensated. Female artists only. Send press kits to: PO Box 7430, Berkeley, CA 94707.

MidPoint Music Festival
CityBeat
811 Race St.
Cincinnati, OH 45202
p: 513-665-4700
f: 513-665-4368
e: info@mpmf.com
www.myspace.com/mpmf
contact: Dan McCabe
e: musicstarts@mpmf.com
genres: All Styles
2009 dates: Sep
submit: Feb 1 - May 15
location: Cincinnati, OH
accepts epk: Yes
Region's largest showcase for emerging talent offers 300+ USA & Int'l acts at 18 area clubs & tented stages. More than 50,000 fans & industry attend. Each performer paid $20 or gets full delegate badge; must be 21+ to perform.

Mississippi Delta Blues & Heritage Festival
MACE
119 S Theobald St.
Greenville, MS 38701
p: 662-335-3523
f: 662-334-2939
e: maceblues@bellsouth.net
www.deltablues.org
contact: Robert Terrell
genres: Blues
2009 dates: Sep 19
submit: Until Jan
location: Greenville, MS
Event set in the "home of the Blues" attracts over 5000 fans from around the world; 7+ top tier & polished artists gig on 2 stages. Bands are not paid.

Monolith Festival at Red Rocks
Monolith Festival
550 E 12th Ave., Ste. 901
Denver, CO 80203
p: 317-843-8008
www.monolithfestival.com
contact: Josh Baker
e: jb@monolithfestival.com
genres: Alt., Hip-Hop, Indie, Pop, Punk, S/S, Roots, Bluegrass, Metal, Experimental
2009 dates: Oct
submit: Until Jun 15
location: Morrison/Denver, CO
accepts epk: Yes
The producers of the popular South Park Music Festival & Midwest Music Summit bring 60 of the world's top emerging artists on 5 stages to 10,000+/day. Bands paid $250. Submit at site or via Sonicbids.

Monterey Bay Blues Festival
PO Box 1400
Seaside, CA 93955
p: 831-394-2652
f: 831-393-8273
e: mbbf@montereyblues.com
www.montereyblues.com
contact: Vivian Patterson
ext: 831-394-2652 x102
e: vivian@montereyblues.com
genres: Blues, R&B, Gospel, Soul
2009 dates: Jun 26-28
submit: Aug - Feb
location: Monterey Fairgrounds - Monterey, CA
Non-profit, all ages premier event showcases 56 renowned & budding artists from USA & abroad on 3 outdoor stages for 30,000+ fans & press. Also produces 'Battle of the Blues Bands' - winner opens the main stage at festival. Bands are paid. Send CD, photo & bio.

Monterey Jazz Festival
PO Box JAZZ
Monterey, CA 93942
p: 831-373-3366
f: 831-373-0244
e: jazzinfo@montereyjazzfestival.org
www.montereyjazzfestival.org
contact: Tim Jackson
ext: 831-373-3366 x306
genres: Jazz, Blues
2009 dates: Sep 18-20
submit: Nov 1 - Feb 15
location: Monterey Fairgrounds in Monterey CA
Prestigious all ages music event presents 500+ polished USA & Int'l acts on 9 outdoor & tented stages for 45,000+. Send promos to: 9699 Larkspur Ln., Ste. 204, Monterey, CA 93940.

Moogfest
In Touch Live
445 Park Ave., 9th Fl.

New York, NY 10022
p: 212-714-7722
f: 212-202-7579
e: info@intouchhome.com
www.moogfest.net
contact: Charles Carlini
genres: Synth-driven Music
2009 dates: Oct
submit: Aug 4 - Sep 15
location: New York, NY
accepts epk: Yes
Aligns top performing acts w/ up & coming bands. 5-10 acts play for 1500 attendees. Lodging is provided & bands paid $500+. Submit via Sonicbids only.

Motongator Joe's Country Music Festival
Motongator Productions
N6629 County Rd. 571
Wallace, MI 49893
p: 866-245-2702
f: 615-469-1390
e: motongator@motongator.com
www.motongator.com; www.bigtimecountry.com
contact: Joe Grinsteiner
genres: Country, Bluegrass, Alt. Country, Classic Country
2009 dates: Jun
submit: Until Feb 15
location: Wallace, MI
Largest annual Country music fest in the Upper Peninsula of MI features 25+ Local & Reg'l acts on 2 stages to 6000 all ages music fans. Local & Reg'ls receive $200 for 1.5 hours. Send audio demo, picture, bio, price & dates available.

MusicfestNW
Willamette Week
2220 NW Quimby St.
Portland, OR 97210
p: 503-243-2122
f: 503-243-1115
www.musicfestnw.com
contact: Trevor Solomon
e: tsolomon@wweek.com
genres: All Styles
2009 dates: Sep
submit: Mar 30 - Jun 15
location: Portland, OR
accepts epk: Yes
More subdued, but just as cool as Bumbershoot, conference & festival event co-sponsored by the area's alt. weekly pub showcases top Pacific NW & Nat'l acts for fans & industry. More than 200 bands play at nearly 17 city venues; 20,000+ attend. Bands paid $100+. Submit via Sonicbids only.

Musikfest
ArtsQuest
25 W 3rd St., Ste. 300
Bethlehem, PA 18015
p: 610-861-0678 x1; 610-332-1300
f: 610-861-2644
e: info@fest.org
www.musikfest.org; **www.**fest.org
contact: Patrick Brogan
ext: 610-332-1300 x334
e: pbrogan@fest.org
genres: All Styles
2009 dates: Aug 7-16
submit: Nov 1 - Mar 1
location: Bethlehem, PA
Showcases 200+ USA & Int'l performers at 3 ticketed & 7 free venues - over 1 million attendees of all ages. Bands are compensated. Download form from site or submit via Sonicbids.

National Folk Festival
NCTA & Venture Richmond Org.
200 S 3rd St.
Richmond, VA 23219
p: 804-788-6466
e: info@nationalfolkfestival.com
www.nationalfolkfestival.com
contact: Stephen Lecky
e: slecky@venturerichmond.com
genres: Folk, Jazz, Blues, Bluegrass, World Trad.
2009 dates: Jul 10-12
submit: Jan 31 - Oct
location: Butte, MT
Prestigious celebration of America's diverse cultural roots & musical influences presents 35 acts on 7 stages. 135,000+ all ages fans attend; bands paid. Email kits only.

National Harvest Festival
Silver Dollar City
399 Indian Point Rd.
Branson, MO 65616
p: 417-338-2611; 800-831-4386
f: 417-338-8095
www.bransonsilverdollarcity.com/festivals
contact: D.A. Callaway
e: dacallaway@silverdollarcity.com
genres: Bluegrass, Cowboy, Southern Gospel, Western Swing
2009 dates: Sep 11 - Oct 31
submit: ongoing
location: Greater Branson, MO
Family-friendly event presents 55 estab. & polished acts on 8 stages for 8000 daily fans. Pay varies. Also produces Southern Gospel, Bluegrass, Kids & World festivals. Submit w/ video or DVD.

National Women's Music Festival
Women In the Arts
PO Box 1427
Indianapolis, IN 46206
p: 317-713-1144
e: wia@wiaonline.org
www.wiaonline.org
contact: Jane Weldon
e: nwmfpro@yahoo.com
genres: All Styles
2009 dates: Jul 2-5
location: Middleton, WI
Unique event showcases 25+ Indie female only & female fronted acts - on 5 stages for 1000, mostly women, fans of all ages. Festival budget is $120,000; headliners receive $1500 w/ union pay for side support; emerging artists paid $250. Submit via Sonicbids or mail promos to: PO Box 8024, Madison, WI 53708.

Nattjazz
Georgernes Verft 12, 5011
Bergen, 5817 Norway
p: 47-5-530-7250
f: 47-5-530-7260
e: nattjazz@nattjazz.no
www.nattjazz.no
contact: Tom Svendsgaard
ext: 47-5-530-7252
e: tom@nattjazz.no
genres: Modern Jazz, World, Electronica, Rock
2009 dates: Late May
location: Bergen, Norway
Innovative program on 5 stages in a converted sardine factory & area venues attracts an int'l crowd of 20,000. Up to 100 cutting-edge USA & Int'l artists seek intersection btwn. Jazz & other modern music.

Nederland Music & Arts Festival
Michigan Mike Presents
PO Box 830
Nederland, CO 80466
www.nedfest.com
contact: Michigan Mike Torpie
e: mike@michiganmike.com
genres: Bluegrass, Jazz, World, Jam, Funk, Acid Jazz
2009 dates: Last wknd in Aug
submit: ongoing
location: Nederland, CO
Outdoor all ages music festival located 17mi west of Boulder features up to 6 bands/day on 1 stage to a crowd of 2000. Also has Acoustic 'tweeners sets btwn. each band. Budget: $30,000-60,000; some bands are paid.

New Music West
29 Productions
301-062 Homer St.
Vancouver, BC V6B 2W9
Canada
p: 604-689-2910
f: 604-689-2912
e: info@29productions.ca
www.newmusicwest.com
contact: Jory Groberman
genres: All Styles
2009 dates: May
location: Vancouver, BC
Gathers 30,000+ industry & music fans to hear 250 emerging acts play on 20 downtown stages. Also has workshops, panels & showcases. 2nd contact: Micah Groberman, 604-689-2910; michah@29productions.ca.

New Orleans Jazz & Heritage Festival Presented by Shell
Festival Productions of New Orleans
336 Camp St., Ste. 250
New Orleans, LA 70130
p: 504-410-4100
f: 504-410-4122
www.nojazzfest.com
contact: Liz Schoenberg
e: musicprod@nojazzfest.com
genres: Jazz, Zydeco, Rock, Hip-Hop, Funk, R&B, Blues
2009 dates: Apr 24-26; Apr 30 - May 3
location: New Orleans, LA
Acclaimed all ages event creates magic w/ 500+ top Reg'l- Int'l performers on 11 stages for 375,000+ avid fans. Send promos ATTN: Music Production.

New Orleans Voodoo Music Experience
Rehage Entertainment
179 Franklin St., Ste. 4R
New York, NY 10013
p: 212-379-3190
f: 212-208-3025
www.voodoomusicfest.com
contact: Stephen Rehage
e: booking@voodoomusicfest.com
genres: Alt., Loud Rock, Urban, Indie, Latin, New Orleans, Funk, Jam
2009 dates: Oct
location: New Orleans, LA
accepts epk: Yes
Prime all ages event presents up to 100 top Reg'l & Nat'l acts on several indoor & outdoor stages for 120,000+ fans. Bands paid. Email before sending material.

New York State Blues Festival
224 Harrison St.
Syracuse, NY 13202
p: 315-461-0068
www.nysbluesfest.com
contact: Kevin Samlois
ext: 315-422-9400
e: kevin@theeventscompany.com
genres: Blues
2009 dates: Jul
submit: Until Dec 31
location: Syracuse, NY
All ages free event showcases Reg'l & Nat'l acts on 3 main stages & area clubs for 25,000 fans. Budget is $200,000; bands are paid. Submit online.

Newport Folk Festival
Festival Network
30 Irving Pl., 6th Fl.
New York, NY 10003
p: 212-533-7292
f: 212-253-2921
e: info@festivalnetwork.com
www.newportfolk.com
contact: John Phillips
ext: 212-533-7293
e: jphillips@festivalnetwork.com
genres: Folk, World
2009 dates: Jul 31 - Aug 2
location: Newport, RI
Legendary all ages festival showcases A-list talent & acts w/ buzz; 33 acts play on 3 stages for 6000+/day. New artists play 2nd & 3rd stage & at area venues. Bands paid. No unsolicited material.

Noise Pop
2180 Bryant St., Ste. 105
San Francisco, CA 94110
p: 415-375-3370
f: 415-341-1135
e: heyheyhey@noisepop.com
www.noisepop.com
contact: Stacy Horne
ext: 415-375-3373
e: stacy@noisepop.com
genres: Pop, Rock
2009 dates: Feb 24 - Mar 1
submit: Oct - Jan 7
location: San Francisco, CA
Premier underground event held at 15 top area venues pays 150+ cutting-edge acts to perform for 15,000-20,000 music lovers & industry pros per day. Tickets are $10-$25/show; festival badge is $150. Bands are compensated. Submissions thru Ourstage, Sonicbids or www.noisepop.com/bandemail.

Northeast Kingdom Music Festival
Edified Presents
PO Box 1370
Montpelier, VT 05602
p: 802-229-9942
e: info@nekmf.com
www.nekmf.com
contact: Ed DuFresne
genres: Funk, Reggae, Rock, Bluegrass, Americana, S/S, Hip-Hop, Roots, Rhythm

2009 dates: Aug
location: Albany, VT
accepts epk: Yes
Non-corporate, all ages music & camping event places 21 acts on 2 stages for up to 2000 attendees. Festival budget: $20,000 to $50,000 (total). No unsolicited material.

NYC Popfest
Collective Pop
51 Main St.
Hastings-on-Hudson, NY 10706
p: 914-231-5996
f: 646-349-5598
e: nycpopfest@gmail.com
www.nycpopfest.org
contact: Courtney Bennett
ext: 347-276-0035
genres: Pop, Dance-Pop, Twee, S/S, Folk, Indie Rock
2009 dates: Jun
location: New York, NY
Int'l all ages event bringing together nearly 40 fun-loving indie bands to NYC from all over the world to play at multi-staged event. Bands paid. Send CD & bio or submit thru MySpace.

Old Settler's Music Festival
PO Box 151947
Austin, TX 78715
e: info@oldsettlersmusicfest.org
www.oldsettlersmusicfest.org
contact: Jean Spivey
genres: Americana, Blues, Bluegrass, Roots, Latin Jazz
2009 dates: Apr 16-19
submit: ongoing
location: Salt Lick Pavilion & Camp Ben McCulloch - Austin, TX
accepts epk: Yes
Premier TX live music & camping event combines over 25 Grammy winners & rising stars on 4 outdoor stages. Well attended by 11,000 fans & industry. Also features performance workshops & a youth talent competition. Bands are paid.

Old Songs Festival Of Trad. Music & Dance
Old Songs
37 S Main St., PO Box 466
Voorheesville, NY 12186
p: 518-765-2815
e: oldsongs@oldsongs.org
www.oldsongs.org
contact: Andy Spence
genres: Acoustic Folk, Trad., Celtic, World, Blues, Gospel
2009 dates: Jun 26-28
submit: Jul - Nov
location: Altamont Fairgrounds - Altamont, NY
Family friendly event features 30 mostly Indie bands playing on 7 stages for 4000 music fans. Includes 120 daytime workshops given by performers. Bands are compensated.

Ollesummer Festival
Oll Meediaeskpess
Narva MNT 95
Tallinn, Harjumaa 10127
Estonia
p: 37-2-611-2112
e: info@ollesummer.ee
www.ollesummer.ee
contact: Andrius Videnski
ext: 37-26-11-2113
e: andrius@ollesummer.ee
genres: Rock, Pop
2009 dates: Jul 8-12
submit: Sep - Apr
location: Tallinn, Estonia
Biggest outdoor fest in Baltic states presents 100+ Int'l acts on 10 stages for 80,000+.

Oregon Jamboree in Sweet Home
CenturyTel
PO Box 430
Sweet Home, OR 97386
p: 541-367-8800; 888-613-6812
f: 541-367-8400
e: info@oregonjamboree.com
www.oregonjamboree.com
contact: Peter LaPonte
ext: 541-367-8909
e: jamman@oregonjamboree.com
genres: All Styles of Country
2009 dates: Jul 31 - Aug 2
submit: Until Jan 31
location: Sweet Home, OR
Non-profit all ages Country music & camping, family-style event features 14 Nat'l recording acts & rising stars for 30,000+ fans. Bands are paid.

The Oyafestival
Oya Booking AS
Olav VS GT 1
Oslo, 161 Norway
p: 47-9-008-4252
f: 47-2-287-7501
e: jonas@oyafestivalen.com
www.oyafestivalen.com
contact: Claes Olsen
e: booking@oyafestivalen.com; claes@oyafestivalen.com
genres: Rock, Alt., Pop, Electronica, Hip-Hop, Metal, Punk, World, Jazz, S/S
2009 dates: Aug 6-8
location: Oslo, Norway
Cool event in medieval ruins presents 120+ paid USA & Int'l acts on 4 outdoor stages & at 26 city clubs. More than 70 are developing acts, 65,000 attend. Must be 18+ for clubs.

Park City Jazz Festival
PO Box 680720
Park City, UT 84068
p: 435-940-1362
f: 435-940-1464
e: info@parkcityjazz.org
www.parkcityjazz.org
contact: Kris Severson
genres: Jazz, Jazz Rock, Blues, Latin Jazz, Swing
2009 dates: Aug 21-23
location: Park City, UT
Up to 12 Reg'l openers paired w/ Nat'l & Int'l headliners play on 2 stages in outdoor amphitheater for 15,000. Bands are compensated. No unsolicited material.

Philadelphia Folk Festival
Philadelphia Folksong Society
7113 Emlen St.
Philadelphia, PA 19119
p: 800-556-FOLK; 215-247-1300
f: 215-247-0293
e: info@folkfest.org
www.folkfest.org; **www.**pff.org
contact: Pat Gourley
genres: Folk, Bluegrass, Celtic, S/S, Blues, World, Folk, Gospel, Pysch Folk, Folk Rock, Country
2009 dates: Aug 14-16
submit: Fall - Spring
location: Old Pool Farm - Schwenksville, PA
Non-profit all ages Folk & camping fest presents over 50 Grammy winners & rising stars on 6 outdoor stages - 30,000 attend. Bands are compensated.

Playboy Jazz Festival
The Festival Network
2601 Ocean Park Blvd., Ste. 207
Santa Monica, CA 90405
p: 310-314-4484
f: 310-314-4488
www.playboyjazz.com
contact: Darlene Chan
e: mail@festivalnetwork.com
genres: Jazz, Latin, Blues, World Beat
2009 dates: Jun 13-14
submit: Sep - Nov
location: TBD
High-profile all ages event presents diverse USA & Int'l acts. Up to 24 estab. artists & rising stars play on a revolving stage for 18,000. Bands are paid. Email submissions.

Pop Montreal
5445 De Gaspé, #213
Montreal, QC H2T 3B2
Canada
p: 514-842-1919
www.popmontreal.com
contact: Dan Seligman
e: danseligman@popmontreal.com
genres: All Styles
2009 dates: Sep 30 - Oct 4
submit: Until Jun 2
location: Montreal, QC
accepts epk: Yes
Cool newcomer selects unknown & forgotten artists to showcase to int'l audience - 20,000 fans, journalists & industry reps are exposed to 300 cutting-edge bands on 35 city stages. Pay range from $100-$10,000. Snail mail or Sonicbids submissions; kit must include 3 songs & fave religious parable or zen koan.

Potomac Celtic Festival
The Potomac Celtic Alliance
525-K E. Market St., #295
Leesburg, VA 20176
p: 703-938-9779
e: information@pcfest.org; publicity@pcfest.org
www.potomaccelticfest.org
contact: Kent Murray
ext: 703-304-6157
e: kentmurray@sunspotpro.com
genres: Irish, Scottish, Welsh, Breton, Manx, Galician, Asturian
2009 dates: Jun 13-14
submit: Oct - Mar
location: Morven Park
Family fun fest features continual Celtic music & dance by 15 acts on 3 stages for up to 5000 fans. Festival Budget: $15,000-$20,000; bands paid between $300-$3000. Send CD or links to online music, band info, venues/festivals performed at to: Kent Murray, Sunspot Production, 2414 Andorra Pl., Reston, VA 20191.

Provinssirock
Seinäjoki Live Music Assoc.
PO Box 180
Seinäjoki, 60101 Finland
p: 35-86-421-2700
f: 35-86-414-8622
e: info@provinssi.fi
www.provinssi.fi
contact: Juha Koivisto
ext: 35-86-421-2714
e: juha.koivisto@provinssi.fi
genres: Rock, Pop
2009 dates: Jun 12-14
location: Seinajoki, Finland
"The party of the people" showcases 60 cutting-edge USA & Int'l acts on 5 outdoor stages for 60,000+ all ages fans. Send promos to: Kalevankatu 6-9 C 2, Seinajoki, Finland 60100.

Quart Festival
Postboks 260, N-4663
Kristiansand, 4600 Norway
p: 47-3-814-6969
f: 47-3-814-6968
www.quart.no
contact: Andy Inglis
ext: 47-4-528-6604
e: andy@quart.no
genres: Rock, Pop, Hip-Hop, R&B, Electronica, Metal, Indie
2009 dates: Jun 30 - Jul 4
location: Kristiansand, Norway
An orgy of music & partying w/ 60+ USA & Int'l bands on 4 outdoor stages & in area clubs for crowds over 40,000. Promos to: Stiftelsen Quarfestivalen, Odderoya Bygg 29, 4664 Kristiansand, Norway.

Rhythm & Roots
255 Holly Rd.
Wakefield, RI 02879
p: 888-855-6940
e: office@rhythmandroots.com
www.rhythmandroots.com
contact: Chuck Wentworth
ext: 401-783-3926
e: chukwent@cox.net
genres: Blues, Cajun, Roots, Zydeco, Swing, Bluegrass, Americana, Honky-Tonk
2009 dates: Sep 4-6
submit: Oct 1 - Jan 15
location: Ninigret Park - Charlestown, RI
accepts epk: Yes
All ages music & camping event draws over 5000/day. Over 30 top & polished Reg'l & Nat'l artists on 4 outdoor stages. Bands are compensated.

Rhythm & Soul Music Festival
MixCraft Media
244 5th Ave.
Ste. 2141
New York, NY 10001
p: 212-252-2528; 917-405-4423
f: 347-702-9636
e: info@soulmusicfestival.net
www.myspace.com/rsmf
contact: Freedom Justice
e: freedom@spinradiofm.net
genres: R&B, Soul, Acid Jazz, House
2009 dates: Jan 18 (Richmond); Feb 24 (New Orleans); May 22-24 (Miami)
submit: open (will consider up to 2 months from the date of each festival)
location: Richmond, VA; New Orleans, LA; Miami, FL
Up to 36 acts on 3 stages gain exposure to 21+ crowd of 5000 urban professionals. Festival budget: $2500-$20,000; bands paid $250-$1000 & must sell at least 25 tickets. Send 3+ songs & a link to video footage.

The Riverbend Festival
Friends of the Festival Event
180 Hamm Rd.
Chattanooga, TN 37405
p: 423-756-2211
f: 423-756-2719
e: info@riverbendfestival.com
www.riverbendfestival.com
contact: Joe Fuller
e: dixie@riverbendfestival.com
genres: Jazz, Country, Folk, R&B, Classic Rock, CCM, Gospel, Bluegrass, Pop
2009 dates: Jun 5-13
submit: Aug - Dec 31
location: Chattanooga, TN
The city's top family event presents 100+ Nat'l recording stars & polished Reg'l talent on 6 stages - attended by 80,000/day. Some bands are compensated.

Riverboat Jazz Festival
Aahavevej 2 A
Silkeborg, D-8600 Denmark
p: 45-8-680-1617
f: 45-8-681-6180
e: info@riverboat.dk
www.riverboat.dk/uk/index.asp
contact: Steffen Juul Hansen
e: booking@riverboat.dk
genres: Jazz
2009 dates: Jun 24-28
submit: Until Nov 1
location: Silkeborg, Denmark
Top Scandinavian Jazz event takes over the town & river. More than 30,000 flock to the Jazz boats & 9 area clubs to hear 70 known & polished performers from USA & abroad.

Riverfront Blues Festival
City of Wilmington
800 N French St.
Wilmington, DE 19801
p: 302-576-2136
f: 302-571-4089
www.riverfrontbluesfest.com
contact: Tina Betz
e: tbetz@ci.wilmington.de.us
genres: Blues
2009 dates: Aug 7-9
submit: Jan - Mar
location: Wilmington, DE
About 10,000 fans gather for the all ages city-sponsored event featuring up to 20 polished Reg'l & touring acts on 2 stages. Also sponsors DuPont Clifford Brown Jazz Festival. Bands are paid.

Rochester Int'l Jazz Festival
14 Franklin St., Ste. 808
Rochester, NY 14604
p: 585-454-2060
f: 585-454-2061
e: info@rochesterjazz.com
www.rochesterjazz.com
contact: John Nugent
genres: Jazz, Southern Rock, Funk, Improv
2009 dates: Jun 12-20
submit: Oct 1 - Dec 15
location: Rochester, NY
Gathers 150+ acts from 15 countries on 15 stages; 125,000+ fans from all over the world attend. Presented in 4 series: Eastman Theater (Headliners), Club Series, Outdoor Stages, & Museum & Gallery Series. Clubs 19+. Bands are compensated. No unsolicited material.

Rock for People
Ameba Production
Prokopa Velikého 105
Cesky Brod, 282 01
Czech Republic
p: 42-031-400-0913
f: 42-031-400-0916
e: ameba@ameba.cz
www.rockforpeople.cz
contact: Stepan Suchochleb
ext: 42-031-400-0915
e: stepan@ameba.cz
genres: Rock, World
2009 dates: Jul
location: Hradec Králové's Airport
Just beyond Prague, this fest features 150 USA & Int'l acts on 6 stages; 45,000 attend.

Rockin' the Rivers
201 N Main St.
PO Box 699
Three Forks, MT 59752
p: 866-285-0097; 406-285-0099
f: 406-285-0088
e: info@rockintherivers.net
www.rockintherivers.net
contact: Mark Vandolah
genres: Rock
2009 dates: Aug
location: Three Forks, MT
Region's largest all ages Rockfest, held in dramatic outdoor arena boasts awesome natural acoustics. Artists on their way up & down are booked - 20+ bands paid to perform for up to 8000 on 2 stages. Bands are compensated.

Roger's Spring Music Festival
BLR Entertainment
730 Upper James, Unit 4
Hamilton, ON L9C 2Z9 Canada
p: 905-730-6874
e: promotions@blrentertainment.com
www.springmusicfestival.com
contact: Rob Rapity
e: rob@blrentertainment.com
genres: Modern Rock
2009 dates: May
submit: Nov 30 - Feb 20
location: Hamilton, ON
All ages celebration showcasing 100 of the hottest "buzz acts" from Canada & the USA at 10+ live music venues in Hamilton & Burlington, ON to 5000 fans. Festival Budget is: $50,000 & bands are paid. At least 3 slots reserved for Sonicbids members.

Roskilde Festival
Roskilde Kulturservice
Havsteensvej 11
Roskilde, 4000 Denmark
p: 45-4-636-6613
f: 45-4-632-1499
e: info@roskilde-festival.dk
www.roskilde-festival.dk
contact: Rikke Oexner
genres: Electronic, Rock, Hip-Hop, Rap, World Beat
2009 dates: Jul 2-5
location: Roskilde, Denmark
N Europe's largest, environmentally friendly, non-profit music & camping event showcases top-tier talent & rising stars - 160 cutting-edge acts play on 6 stages to 75,000.

Salt Lake City Int'l Jazz Festival
Four Floors Productions
3617 Astro Cir.
Salt Lake City, UT 84109
p: 801-277-2056
f: 801-277-0941
www.slcjazzfestival.org
contact: Jerry Floor
e: jerry.floor@comcast.net
genres: Jazz
2009 dates: Early Jul
submit: Dec 1 - Mar 1
location: Salt Lake City, UT
Prime area all ages event presents 15+ top & polished acts on 2 stages for 60,000+ jazzbos. Free event; festival budget is $500,000; bands get $10-30,000 plus 5-star lodgings. Snail mail w/ CD, photo & backline needs.

San Francisco Blues Festival
PO Box 460608
San Francisco, CA 94146
p: 415-979-5588
e: info@sfblues.com
www.sfblues.com
contact: Tom Mazzolini
e: sfblues@earthlink.net
genres: Blues, Zydeco, R&B, Roots
2009 dates: Sep
location: San Francisco, CA
Long-running all ages event showcases 20 top & polished acts on beautiful outdoor stage for 18,000+ fans. Pay starts at $1000. No unsolicited material.

Sasquatch! Music Festival
Live Nation & House of Zacks
40 Lake Bellevue Dr., Ste. 340
Bellevue, WA 98005
p: 425-990-0222
f: 425-990-0221
e: info@sasquatchfestival.com
www.sasquatchfestival.com
contact: Adam Zacks
ext: 206-467-5510
e: adamzacks@theparamount.com
genres: All Styles
2009 dates: May 23-24
submit: Until Jan/Feb
location: The Gorge Amphitheatre - Bellevue, WA
Prestigious event mixes 52 top-tier recording acts, buzz bands & polished Indies on 3 stages for 20,000 fans/day; shows are all ages. Bands are paid. Promos to: Talent Buyer, Seattle Theatre Group, 901 Pine St., Seattle, WA 98101.

Seaside Music Fest
Motor Marketing
41 Washington St.
Ste. 4C
New York, NY 10013
p: 212-965-8036
e: rhyan@seasidemusicfest.com
www.seasidemusicfest.com
contact: Indian
ext: 732-241-8997
e: indian@seasidemusicfest.com
genres: All Styles except Hard Rock or Metal
2009 dates: May 14-17
submit: Dec - Apr 7
location: Seaside, NJ
accepts epk: Yes
21+ event features 50-200 mostly indie acts playing at 15 area stages for an expected crowd of 10,000. Material via Sonicbids or mail CDs w/ online submission form & $25. Festival budget is: $70,000; some bands are paid.

Sfinks Festival
Sfinks Animation
Ja Frans Willemsstraat 10a
Boechout, Antwerp 2530
Belgium
p: 32-3-455-6944
f: 32-3-454-1162
e: info@sfinks.be
www.sfinks.be
contact: Patrick De Groote
e: pdegroote@sfinks.be
genres: World
2009 dates: Jul 24-26
submit: Until Apr
location: Molenveld, Belgium
Premier Belgian music event celebrates diversity as it hosts 60 top USA & Int'l acts on 5 stages for 40,000 fans. Bands are compensated. CDs/DVDs preferred.

Shoreline Arts Festival
Lake Forest Park Arts Council
18560 First Ave. SE
Shoreline, WA 98155
p: 206-417-4645
e: info@shorelinearts.net
www.shorelinearts.net
contact: Nancy Frey
genres: World, Folk, Country, Bluegrass, Rock, Blues, Jazz
2009 dates: summer
submit: Nov 15 - Jan 15
location: Shoreline, WA
4-16 acts play on 2 stages to 10,000 music fans of all ages. Also books a concert series in the park. Bands paid $300-$400.

Sierra Nevada World Music Festival
Epiphany Artists
PO Box 208
Ryde, CA 95680
p: 916-777-5550
f: 916-777-5551
e: info@snwmf.com
www.snwmf.com
contact: Warren Smith
e: epiphanya@aol.com
genres: Reggae, World, Latin
2009 dates: Summer
submit: Sep - Mar 30
location: Boonville, CA
Utopian all ages music & camping event promotes a positive force via music & community. 33 world class Indie bands perform at 3 venues for 6,000+. Bands paid $750+.

Sioux Falls Jazz & Blues Festival
123 S Main Ave., Ste. 204
Sioux Falls, SD 57104
p: 605-335-5101; 605-367-1764
f: 605-367-1764
e: info@sfjb.org
www.jazzfestsiouxfalls.com
contact: Robert Joyce
ext: 605-335-6101
genres: Jazz, Blues, Zydeco, World, Reggae, Rock, Funk, Jam, Big Band, Swing
2009 dates: Jul 17-18
submit: Oct - Jan
location: Yankton Trail Park
Free all ages festival features 20 acts on 2 stages. Up to 95,000 fans. Festival budget is: $105,000; performers paid $350 & plus food & lodging.

Soul Festival
New Sound Int'l

PO Box 197
Merrimac, MA 01860
p: 978-346-4577
e: info@thesoulfest.com
www.thesoulfest.com
contact: Dan Russell
genres: All Styles
2009 dates: Jul 29 - Aug 1
submit: Sep - Dec 31
location: Gunstock Mountain - Gilford, NH
accepts epk: Yes
New England's premiere all ages Christian music event, formerly known as The Inside Out Soul Festival, presents 100 bands, 1/2 are developing acts, on 5 stages. Up to 12,000/day faithfully attend. Bands paid $250-$1500.

Spirit West Coast
Celebration Concerts
1952 Camden Ave., #206
San Jose, CA 95124
p: 408-377-9232
e: questions@spiritwestcoast.org
www.spiritwestcoast.org
contact: Jon Robberson
genres: Christian, CCM
2009 dates: May 22-24 (Del Mar); Jul 30 - Aug 1 (Monterey)
submit: Until Jun 19
location: San Diego, CA & Monterey, CA
accepts epk: Yes
All ages fest presents up to 50 acts on 9 stages for 15,000 music fans/day. Pay range $200-$45,000. Submit via Sonicbids only.

Sterling Stage Folkfest
Astronomical Productions
4239 Lexington Ave.
Los Angeles, CA 90029
p: 323-644-0429
e: sterlingstage@gmail.com
www.sterlingstage.com
contact: Eric McElveen
genres: Folk, Roots, New Grass, Jam
2009 dates: May 22-24
submit: Oct - Mar 15
location: Sterling, NY
Former Xmas tree farm hosts 30 Local-Nat'l developing acts & legendary performers on 3 stages for 1500 music & camping fans. Festival budget is: $15,000; bands paid $100-$5000. Material must be emailed & include all links & contact info.

Stern Grove Festival
44 Page St., Ste. 600
San Francisco, CA 94102
p: 415-252-6253
e: info@sterngrove.org
www.sterngrove.org
contact: Judy Tsang Henderson
e: program@sterngrove.org
genres: Jazz, World, Folk, Electronic, Classical
2009 dates: summer
location: San Francisco, CA
Long-running all ages summer series presents 10 free Sun concerts in an outdoor amphitheatre. Presents 18+ eclectic acts - 8000/day attend. Email submission requests.

Street Scene
Rob Hagey Productions
PO Box 2671
La Jolla, CA 92038
p: 619-557-8490
e: press08@street-scene.com
www.street-scene.com
contact: Rob Hagey
genres: Rock, Alt., Hip-Hop, Punk, Ska, Latin, Blues, Alt.
2009 dates: Sep
location: San Diego, CA
Four stages filled w/ over 40 top acts, buzz bands & rising stars for 50,000+. Bands are paid. No unsolicited material.

Summerfest
Milwaukee World Festival
200 N Harbor Dr.
Milwaukee, WI 53202
p: 414-273-2680
e: summerfestinfo@summerfest.com
www.summerfest.com
contact: Vic Thomas
e: mwfproduction@summerfest.com
genres: Rock, Pop, Blues, Country, Alt., Latin, Jazz, R&B, Reggae, Zydeco
2009 dates: Jun 25 - Jul 5
submit: Oct - Mar 1
location: Maier Festival Park
accepts epk: Yes
Notable all-ages event places 700 chart-toppers, buzz bands & Nat'l acts on 11 stages; 900,000 attend. Includes "Emerging Artist" series contest. Bands are paid.

SunFest
525 Clematis St.
West Palm Beach, FL 33401
p: 800-SUN-FEST
e: info@sunfest.com
www.sunfest.com
contact: Stewart Auville
genres: Rock, Pop, R&B, Jazz, Gospel, World, Reggae, Latin
2009 dates: Apr 29 - May 3
location: West Palm Beach
FL's largest music & arts festival draws up to 300,000 tourists & fans. More than 60 Nat'l & Int'l recording artists & some Reg'l acts perform on 3 main stages.

Sweden Rock Festival
Sweden Rock Productions
Norjebokevägen 2
Sölvesborg, SE 29476 Sweden
p: 46-4-563-1795
f: 46-4-563-1794
e: info@swedenrock.com; festival@swedenrock.com
www.swedenrock.com
contact: Ingolf Persson
e: ingolf@swedenrock.com
genres: All Styles of Rock
2009 dates: Jun 3-6
submit: Sep - Mar
location: Sölvesborg, Sweden
Premier European music & camping event presents 95 top/emerging USA & Int'l bands on 5 stages to a crowd of 30,000.

Syracuse Jazz Fest
314 North Ave., Ste. 2
Syracuse, NY 13206
p: 315-437-5627
e: info@syracusejazzfest.com
www.syracusejazzfest.com
contact: Frank Malfitano
e: fmalfitano@syracusejazzfest.com
genres: Jazz
2009 dates: Jun
submit: Dec - Mar
location: Onondaga Community College Campus
Free all ages Jazz event presents 25 top recording artists & acts w/ a buzz on 2 stages for 25,000/day. Festival budget: $200,000; pay range: $5000-$50,000. Send bios, reviews, photos & CD.

Tabfest
Harmony for Ohio Foundation
PO Box 14492
Columbus, OH 43214
p: 614-268-7600
www.tabfest.com
contact: Mike Wilson
e: wilson@tabfest.com
genres: All Styles
2009 dates: Summer
submit: Jan - Apr
location: Mendon, OH
accepts epk: Yes
All ages fundraising event for the Ronald McDonald House, presents 20 Reg'l acts on 2 stages for 1600. Bands paid small fee.

TD Canada Trust Ottawa Int'l Jazz Festival
61A York St.
Ottawa, ON K1N 5T2 Canada
p: 613-241-2633; 888-226-4495
f: 613-241-5774
e: info@ottawajazzfestival.com
www.ottawajazzfestival.com
contact: Catherine O'Grady
e: director@ottawajazzfestival.com
genres: Jazz, World, Blues, Funk, Dixieland, Swing, Gospel, Electronic
2009 dates: Jun 25 - Jul 5
submit: Until Jan 30
location: Ottawa, ON
Prime all ages showcase for top tier & emerging artists - 125 acts gig on 11 stages for 150,000. Contact Jacques Emond: 613-255-8196 before submitting.

TD Canada Trust Toronto Jazz Festival
Toronto Downtown Jazz
82 Bleecker St.
Toronto, ON M4X 1L8 Canada
p: 416-928-2033
e: tdjs@tojazz.com
www.torontojazz.com
contact: Jim Galloway
genres: Jazz
2009 dates: Jun 26 - Jul 5
submit: Aug 1 - Jan 1
location: Toronto, ON
Annual all ages showcase takes over 40 downtown venues - 1500 estab. & emerging artists gig, 400,000+ attend. Pay varies. Send CD & short bio.

TD Canada Trust Vancouver Int'l Jazz Festival
Coastal Jazz & Blues Society
316 W 6th Ave.
Vancouver, BC V5Y 1K9 Canada
p: 604-872-5200
e: cjbs@coastaljazz.ca
www.coastaljazz.ca
contact: Ken Pickering
ext: 604-872-5200 x32
e: ken@coastaljazz.ca
genres: Jazz, Blues, World Beat, Electronic
2009 dates: Jun 26 - Jul 5
submit: Jul 17 - Nov 30
location: Vancouver, Canada
Notable event presents 400 top & polished Canadian & imported talent for appearances at 40 area venues for 510,000 jazzbos.

Telluride Bluegrass Festival
Planet Bluegrass
PO Box 769
Lyons, CO 80540
p: 800-624-2422
f: 303-823-0849
e: planet@bluegrass.com
www.bluegrass.com
contact: Craig Ferguson
ext: 800-624-2422 x101; 303-823-0848
genres: Bluegrass, S/S, Acoustic, Folk, Rock, Celtic
2009 dates: Jun 18-21
submit: ongoing
location: Telluride, CO
accepts epk: Yes
All ages fest features 30 Reg'l-Int'l virtuosos performing for 10,000. Bands are paid.

Telluride Blues & Brews Festival
SBG Productions
PO Box 2966, 101 E Colorado Ave., Unit 203
Telluride, CO 81435
p: 970-728-8037
f: 970-728-1350
e: info@tellurideblues.com
www.tellurideblues.com
contact: Steve Gumble
ext: 866-515-6166
genres: Blues, New Orleans, Funk, Rock n Roll
2009 dates: Sep 18-20
location: Telluride, CO
All ages festival features 20 world-renowned musicians performing on 1 stage to over 9000/day. Late nite jams in Local juke joints. Bands are compensated. Snail mail preferred.

Telluride Jazz Celebration
PO Box 2132
Telluride, CO 81435
p: 970-728-7009
e: info@telluridejazz.org
www.telluridejazz.org
contact: Paul Machado
e: paul@telluridejazz.org
genres: Jazz, Latin, Cuban, Funk, Jam
2009 dates: Jun 4-7
submit: Oct - Dec
location: Telluride, CO
Unique event where headliners perform on 7 indoor & tented stages. More than 20 top & polished acts play for 3000 daily. All ages show but some are 21+. Bands are paid.

Temecula Valley Int'l Film & Music Festival
27740 Jefferson Ave.
Ste. 100
Temecula, CA 92591
p: 951-699-5514
e: festival@tviff.com
www.tviff.com
contact: Dana Archer
e: jmoulton@tviff.com
genres: All Styles
2009 dates: Sep
submit: Until Jun 30
location: Temecula, CA
accepts epk: Yes
All ages original music & film event showcases emerging acts & rising stars. Submit via Sonicbids or download form at site & mark ATTN: Music Entry.

Temecula Valley Int'l Jazz Festival
Musicians Workshop
27315 Jefferson Ave., J-231
Temecula, CA 92590
p: 951-678-2517
e: email@jonlaskin.com
www.temeculajazzfest.com
contact: Jon Laskin
genres: Jazz, Blues, Bebop, Latin, Swing
2009 dates: TBD
submit: ongoing
location: Temecula, CA
accepts epk: Yes
Over 12,000 all ages fans gather to listen to 25 bands playing at 5 area venues. Also features clinics, workshops & The Chuck Niles Jazz Music Award Competition. Finalists of competition get $500. Send bio, photo & audio sample. Submit via Sonicbids.

Tønder Festival
Vestergade 80
Tønder, 06270 Denmark
p: 45-7-472-4610
www.tf.dk
contact: Carsten Panduro
ext: 45-7-472-5400
e: carsten@tf.dk
genres: Folk, Roots, Celtic, Scottish
2009 dates: Aug 27-30
location: Tønder, Denmark
Europe's leading Folk & Roots festival presents a stellar line-up of N American & Int'l talent. More than 40 acts perform for 15,000+ on 9 city stages.

Tree Frog Music Festival
Fette Productions
205 Central Ave.
Faribault, MN 55021
p: 507-333-1631
www.treefrogmusic.org
contact: Dick Kettering
e: rkettering@s-sm.org
genres: Blues, Country, World, Roots Rock, Folk, Jazz, Bluegrass
2009 dates: Sep 19-20
location: Teepee Tonka Park
All ages events hosts 20 acts for 3000 fans on 2 stages. Budget is $12,000; band members paid $50 min. Promos to: PO Box 218, Fairbault, MN 55021.

Verizon Wireless American Music Festival
Beach Events/Clear Channel Entertainment
302 22nd St., 2nd Fl.
Virginia Beach, VA 23451
p: 757-425-3111
www.beachstreetusa.com
contact: Brandy Rausch
e: brandyrausch@livenation.com
genres: All Styles
2009 dates: Aug
location: TBD
Over 30 Reg'l & Nat'l recording acts perform for 50,000+ attendees of all ages on 7 stages. Bands are compensated.

Viaero Wireless Comstock Rock Festival
Comstock Music Series
PO Box 74
Ord, NE 68862
p: 866-939-7798
e: service@comstockmusic.net
www.comstockmusic.net
contact: Don Proskocil
genres: Rock
2009 dates: Jul 30 - Aug 2
submit: ongoing
location: Comstock, NE
Outdoor venue w/ natural amphitheatre & camping presents 20-30 acts on 3 stages for 20,000+ all ages fans. Bands are compensated. Reg'l acts send promos to: Christy Oestreich, 540 Bolson Dr., Apt. B, Oconomowoc, WI 53066; Nat'l talent send promos to: Harry Nuxoll, PO Box 49, Comstock, NE 68828.

Viva! Chicago Latin Music Festival
Mayor's Office / Special Events
121 N LaSalle St., Rm. 806
Chicago, IL 60602
p: 312-744-3315
www.cityofchicago.org/specialevents
contact: Enrique Munoz
e: moseinquiry@cityofchicago.org
genres: Latin
2009 dates: Aug 29-30
location: Chicago, IL
Free city-sponsored event celebrates all things Latin & draws 150,000. More than 20 Nat'l & Int'l acts perform on 2 stages.

W.C. Handy Blues & Barbecue Festival
Henderson Music Preservation Society
PO Box 1456
Henderson, KY 42419
p: 270-826-4474; 270-827-1852 x217
e: handyblues@gmail.com
www.handyblues.org
contact: Dorin Luck
e: luck@insightbb.com
genres: Blues, Zydeco
2009 dates: Jun 13-20
submit: Until Dec 15
location: Henderson, KY
accepts epk: Yes
Notable all ages free event gathers 30,000 & features stellar performances by 22 top Nat'l & Reg'l acts on 2 outdoor stages. Festival budget is: $50,000; bands are compensated. Send CDs & DVDs.

Walnut Valley Festival
PO Box 245
Winfield, KS 67156
p: 620-221-3250
e: hq@wvfest.com
www.wvfest.com
contact: Bob Redford
genres: Bluegrass, Country, Acoustic, Folk, Jazz, Celtic
2009 dates: Sep 16-20
submit: ongoing
location: Cowley County Fairgrounds - Winfield, KS
Family camping/music event presents 35 USA & Int'l talent & up & comers on 4 outdoor stages to 15,000+. New song showcases & Nat'l Championship competitions for fiddle, banjo, fingerstyle, etc. Bands are compensated.

Winterfolk
A Better World
182-4936 Young St.
Toronto, ON M2N 6S3 Canada
p: 416-224-2192
e: admin@winterfolk.com; brian@winterfolk.com
www.abetterworld.ca
genres: Roots, Blues, Folk, Ethnic, First Nations, S/S
2009 dates: Feb 13-16
submit: Until Dec 15
location: Toronto, ON
accepts epk: Yes
Annual indoor music festival featuring 120+ artists playing at 10 area venues for 5000 all ages fans. Bands are paid. Submit via Sonicbids.

Wintergrass
Acoustic Sound
PO Box 2356
Tacoma, WA 98401
p: 253-428-8056
e: patriceo@comcast.net
www.wintergrass.com;
contact: Stephen Ruffo
ext: 360-385-6836
e: ruffo@cablespeed.com
genres: Bluegrass, Celtic, Blues, Americana, Jazz, Gospel
2009 dates: Feb 19-22
submit: May - Aug 1
location: Tacoma, WA
Up to 4000 fans of all ages enjoy 40 polished USA & Canadian bands on 5 indoor stages. Festival budget is: $300,000; bands are compensated. For workshop info contact Anita Graham: anitag57@hotmail.com. Send CD, 1 page bio, complete contact info, current photo & list of current band members.

Winterthurer Musikfestwochen
PO Box 2562
Winterthur, CH-8401 Switzerland
p: 41-52-212-6116
e: info@musikfestwochen.ch
www.musikfestwochen.ch
contact: Pascal Mettler
genres: Rock, Pop, Hip-Hop, Reggae, Electro, Jazz, Blues
2009 dates: Aug 19-30
location: Winterthur, Switzerland
Popular event hosts 50+ USA & Int'l recording artists & buzz bands on 4 stages for crowds over 45,000.

Winthrop Rhythm & Blues Festival
Winthrop Music Association
PO Box 1092
Twisp, WA 98856
p: 509-997-0022
e: wstolberg@aol.com
www.winthropbluesfestival.com
contact: Jim Smith
ext: 509-264-3611
e: jimmytheblues2003@yahoo.com
genres: R&B
2009 dates: Jul 17-19
submit: Until Jan
location: Winthrop, WA
accepts epk: Yes
Longest running NW outdoor & all ages camping festival features 10+ bands for 3000 R&B fans. Festival budget is: $140,000; bands paid $1000 plus food & lodging. Submit via Sonicbids.

Womex
Bergmannstr. 102
Berlin, 10961 Germany
p: 49-303-186-1430
e: womex@womex.com; showcase@womex.com
www.womex.com
genres: World, Roots, Folk, Ethnic, Electronic, Alt.
2009 dates: Oct 28 - Nov 1
submit: Until Apr 18
location: Copenhagen, Denmark
accepts epk: Yes
Annual trade fair, conference & showcase festival welcomes over 40 acts on 3 stages for crowds up to 2000 fans.

Woody Guthrie Folk Festival
PO Box 661
Okemah, OK 74859
f: 918-825-8203
e: djones@ecewb.com
www.woodyguthrie.com
contact: Bill McCloud
ext: 918-623-2440
e: mccloudb@sbcglobal.net
genres: Folk, S/S
2009 dates: Jul
submit: Oct 1 - Apr 1
location: Okemah, OK
accepts epk: Yes
Homage to Woody Guthrie & Folk music, features 50+ USA & Int'l performers at 4 area venues & outdoor stage for 10,000+. Send promos to: Concert Committee, PO Box 45, Pryor, OK 74362 or via Sonicbids.

X Fest
Chris Ricci Presents
930 11th St.
Modesto, CA 95354
p: 209-312-3463
www.xfestmodesto.com
contact: Chris Ricci
e: chris@chrisriccipresents.com
genres: Rock, Alt., Pop, Classic Rock, Old School, R&B
2009 dates: Jul 18
location: Modesto, CA
accepts epk: Yes
Celebration of summer features 40 acts on 8 stages for 15,000 21+ fans. Bands are paid.

contests, compilations & tours

(icon) = **Accepts Sonicbids EPK (Electronic Press Kits)**

Contests

The Artists Forum Juried Music Competition
The Artists Forum
PO Box 1645
New York, NY 10026
p: 212-865-6836
e: info@theartistsforum.org
www.theartistsforum.org
contact: Amos White V
Entrants judged by industry pros for a chance to win thousands of dollars in prizes.

Best Song of the Month
SongwriterUniverse
11684 Ventura Blvd.
#975
Studio City, CA 91604
e: info@songwriteruniverse.com
www.songwriteruniverse.com
contact: Dale Kawashima
e: dale@songwriteruniverse.com
genres: Acoustic, Alt., Blues, CCM, Americana, Electronic, Contemporary Classical, World, Dance, Folk, Funk, Gospel, Goth, Jam, Jazz, Latin, Metal, New Age, Pop, Punk, Rock, S/S, Urban
freq: Monthly
submit: Last day of month
Honors & publicizes top songwriting talent. Winning songwriter receives cash & other prizes, as well as an online feature article. Enter online.

Best Vocalist of the Month
SingerUniverse
11684 Ventura Blvd., #975
Studio City, CA 91604
e: info@singeruniverse.com
www.singeruniverse.com/bestvocal.htm
contact: Dale Kawashima
e: dale@singeruniverse.com
genres: Acoustic, Alt., World, Americana, Blues, CCM, Contemporary Classical, Electronic, Dance, Folk, Funk, Gospel, Goth, Jam, Jazz, Latin, Metal, New Age, Pop, Punk, Reggae, Rock, S/S, Urban
freq: Monthly
submit: Last day of month
Honors & publicizes top singing & artist talent. Winner, as well as 4 finalists announced on the home page of SingerUniverse site & will be spotlighted in a lead article on the site.
No unsolicited material.

Billboard Song Contest
PO Box 1000
Mounds, OK 74047
p: 918-624-2100
f: 918-827-7498
www.billboardsongcontest.com
contact: Mark Furnas
e: mark@jimhalsey.com
genres: Rock, Acoustic, AC, Alt., Americana, R&B, Blues, Jazz, Latin, World, Electronic, Hip Hop, Pop, Punk, Country, Folk, Celtic, S/S, Gospel, Metal, CCM, Funk, Goth, Jam
freq: Annual
submit: Mar - Nov 15
accepts epk: Yes
Gives entrants opp. to be heard by big names in the industry. Over $30,000 in prizes, including musical equipment, song placement on the winners CD, a subscription to Billboard mag. All entries receive a personal song evaluation.

The Canary Islands Int'l Song Contest
Tabaiba Records
Drago, 28 Tabaiba Alta,
Tenerife The Canary Islands
38190 Spain
p: 34-92-268-0426
f: 34-92-268-0426
e: tabaibamusic@tabaibarecords.e.telefonica.net
www.festivalinternacional.com; www.tenerifesongcontest.com
contact: Guillermo Albelo
e: tabaiba@tabaibarecords.com
genres: Acoustic, AC, Alt., Americana, Country, Electronica, Folk, Latin, Pop, Rock, S/S, World, Jazz
submit: Mar 15 - Sep 15
Int'l event in the Canary Islands, where composers & singers/vocalists compete w/ other World artists. Winners are promoted to tons of industry contacts & are included on a CD compilation.

Chris Austin Songwriting Competition
MerleFest
PO Box 121855
Nashville, TN 37212
p: 800-799-3838
f: 336-838-6277
www.merlefest.org/songwritingcontest.htm
contact: Art Menius
e: art.menius@wilkescc.edu
genres: Country, Gospel, Bluegrass
freq: Annual
submit: Jul 27 - Mar 4
accepts epk: Yes
3 finalist songs picked in each category by music industry pros & winners perform songs live at MerleFest. Finalists receive: lodging for 4 nites @ MerleFest; 3 all-access passes; Guitar Strings & 1-year subscription to Acoustic Guitar Mag. 1st Place Winners receive: slot @ Cabin Stage of MerleFest; Epiphone Guitar; Guitar Strings & $300. 2nd Place Winners receive: slot @ MerleFest & $250. 3rd Place Winners receive: slot @ MerleFest & $50. Send in tape, CD or EPK; $35 by mail & $25 via Sonicbids.

CMT/NSAI Song Contest
1710 Roy Acuff Pl.
Nashville, TN 37203
p: 615-256-3354; 800-321-6008
f: 615-256-0034
e: nsai@nashvillesongwriters.com
www.nashvillesongwriters.com
contact: Dave Petrelli
ext: 615-256-3354 x248
e: davidpetrelli@nashvillesongwriters.com
genres: Mainly Country
freq: Annual
submit: Aug 1 - Nov 30
Non-profit contest where 6 winners receive 1-song contracts w/ a major publisher. Grand Prize includes mentoring sessions from top songwriters. Send 1 song/CD, lyric sheet & entry form. Members pay $30/song & non-members pay $40/song.

Durango Songwriters Expo "Write With The Hitmakers" Contest
300 Waters Way
Durango, CO
81301
p: 970-259-9747
f: 970-259-9747
www.durango-songwriters-expo.com
contact: Jim Attebery
e: jattebery@frontier.net; jim@durangosong.com
genres: Acoustic, AC, Americana, Blues, CCM, Country, Folk, Pop, Rock, R&B, S/S
freq: 2/year
submit: Oct 26 - Jan 19
Winners compete to collaborate w/ top songwriters & get a 1-song publishing deal. Send a tape or CD w/ up to 2 original copywritten songs, 2 copies of typewritten lyric sheets & a check for $15/category. Mark CD clearly specifying your selected track.

Grassy Hill Kerrville New Folk Competition
Kerrville Folk Festival
PO Box 291466
Kerrville, TX 78029
p: 830-257-3600
f: 830-257-8680
e: info@kerrville-music.com
www.kerrvillefolkfestival.com/newfolk.htm
contact: Dalis Allen
e: dalis@kerrvillefolkfestival.com
genres: S/S, Folk, Blues, Bluegrass, Rock, Country
freq: Annual
submit: Dec - Mar 15
accepts epk: Yes
Features 32 finalist performers & 6 winners to perform at the Kerrville Folk Festival in May. Prizes include cash & a subscription to Performing Songwriter Magazine.

Great American Song Contest
Songwriters Resource Network
PMB 135
6327-C SW Capitol Hill Hwy.
Portland, OR
97239
e: info@greatamericansong.com
www.greatamericansong.com
genres: All Styles
freq: Annual
submit: Mar 28 - Nov 21
accepts epk: Yes
Awards for 45 winners in 9 categories & provides up to $10,000 in cash & prizes.

Great Waters Songwriting Contest
PO Box 488
Wolfeboro, NH 03894
p: 603-569-7710
f: 603-569-7715
e: info@greatwaters.org
www.greatwaters.org
contact: Michael Harrison
e: michael@greatwaters.org
genres: Folk
freq: Annual
submit: Feb - May 15
accepts epk: Yes
5 finalists will be chosen to perform their songs for the festival audience & a panel of music industry pros during the Great Waters Folk Festival in Jul. $500 cash prize & opp. for the 1st place winner to perform on the main stage, before the headliner's set. Finalists receive: performer lodging, 1 performer & 1 guest festival pass. Send 1 song per cassette, CD or MP3

file w/ 1 completed entry form per song, 3 copies of typed lyrics.

Independent Music Awards (IMAs)
Music Resource Group
32 Ann St.
Clifton, NJ 07013
p: 973-767-1800
f: 973-767-1844
www.independentmusicawards.com
contact: Lauren Veteri
e: lauren@independentmusicawards.com
genres: Pop, Rock, Metal, Hard Rock, , Rap, Hip-Hop, Blues, R&B, Children's, Folk, S/S, Country, Americana, Dance, Electronica, Jazz, Latin, CCM, Gospel, World Traditional & Fusion, New Age, Live Performance, Social Action, Music Video, College Record Label, Cover Songs, Love Songs, Contemporary Classical, Alt. Country, Punk, Design, Music Video, Cabaret
freq: Annual
submit: Dec-Aug 21
accepts epk: Yes
Unique int'l program helps indie artists & releases overcome mainstream obstacles to reach wider audiences via print, online, broadcast & distribution promotions & programs. It's yearlong marketing campaigns, partnerships & distribution alliances put winners & finalists in front of millions of music fans & industry decision makers around the world. The IMA Winners CD compilation is distributed to 10,000 music fans & industry at SXSW, Ozzfest, Warped Tour, Spring Break, etc. throughout the year and promoted to 650 US & Canadian college & public radio stations. Winners determined by influential artist & industry judging panel; music fans also vote for their favorite Finalists online. The multi-genre program honors 50+ music categories including Song For Social Action; Music For Children & College Label Release & design categories including Album Packaging, Album Photography, Poster Art, Band Website, Indie Record Label Website and Swag. Winners receive 12 months of promotion & announced in Dec. Mail in CD, entry form & $30 fee/song via Credit Card, Check or Money Order or Sonicbids.

Independent Music World Series (IMWS)
Disc Makers
7905 N Rte. 130
Pennsauken, NJ 08110
p: 888-800-5796
f: 856-661-3450
e: imws@discmakers.com
www.discmakers.com/imws
contact: Angelino Vasquez
ext: 800-468-9353 x5027
e: avasquez@discmakers.com
genres: All Styles
freq: 4 events/year
submit: Oct 1 - May 14
Awards 4 Reg'l grand prize winners w/ a $50,000 prize package, including cash, CD replication & gear. Live events held in Los Angeles, New York, Atlanta & Chicago. Only independent artists are eligible.

Int'l Acoustic Music Awards (IAMA)
2881 E Oakland Park Blvd. #414
Ft. Lauderdale, FL 33306
e: info@inacoustic.com
www.inacoustic.com
contact: Jessica Brandon
genres: Folk, Americana, Roots, Alt., Pop, World, Country, Bluegrass
freq: Annual
submit: Nov 10
accepts epk: Yes
Promotes excellence in Acoustic music performance & artistry. Winners & finalists are featured on a CD compilation & gain radio/web exposure.

Int'l Narrative Song Competition
Narrative Music Canada
PO Box 446
Sioux Lookout, ON P8T 1A5
Canada
e: insc@narrativemusic.ca
www.narrativemusic.ca/insc.html
contact: Edward Campbell
genres: All Styles
freq: Annual
submit: Mar 15 - Aug 15 (early) or Dec 15 (final)
accepts epk: Yes
Advances narrative storytelling in music w/overall Grand Prize & individual prizes; more than $5,000 in cash & prizes. Entries must be original compositions w/o copyright infringements. Fees begin at $10; accepts snail mail or Sonicbids submissions.

Int'l Songwriting Competition (ISC)
1307 Eastland Ave.
Nashville, TN 37206
p: 615-251-4441
f: 615-251-4442
e: info@songwritingcompetition.com
www.songwritingcompetition.com
contact: Candace Avery
genres: Pop, Rock, Country, AAA, Folk, S/S, Urban, Jazz, World, Dance/Electronic, Roots, Americana, Blues, Gospel, Christian, Music Video, Instrumental, Children's, Latin, Teen, Performance, Comedy/Novelty, Lyrics Only
freq: Annual
submit: Feb - Dec 1
accepts epk: Yes
Entrants judged by top recording artists, songwriters & industry execs. Over $150,000 in cash & prizes awarded to 56 winners, including a $25,000 cash Grand Prize.

JAM OFF!
Relix Magazine
104 W 29th St.
11th Fl.
New York, NY 10001
p: 646-230-0100
f: 646-230-0200
www.relix.com/jamoff
contact: John Schwartz
e: schwartz@relix.com
genres: All Styles
freq: 8/year
submit: 8 deadlines/year
accepts epk: Yes
One artist will be selected by industry pros & featured on a Relix CD sampler included w/ over 100,000 issues of Relix distributed internationally. All artists must be unsigned. Label the CD (up to 3 songs), enclose entry form, fee, bio & picture. $35 for 1st entry fee & $25 for each addt'l entry.

The John Lennon Songwriting Contest
83 Riverside Dr.
New York, NY 10024
p: 212-873-9300
f: 212-579-4320
e: info@jlsc.com
www.jlsc.com
contact: Leon Lyazidi
e: leon@jlsc.com
genres: Rock, Country, Jazz, Pop, World, Hip-Hop, Gospel, Inspirational, Latin, R&B, Electronic, Folk, Children's
freq: 2 sessions/year
submit: Jun 15th (1st Session); Dec 15th (2nd Session)
accepts epk: Yes
Int'l songwriting contest open to amateurs & pros awards over $30,000 cash & prizes for 72 finalists. 24 Grand Prize winners & 1 Maxell Song of The Year. Snail mail submissions to: 180 Brighton Rd., Ste. 801, Clifton, NJ 07012.

Low Budget Love Music Competition
Innovation Entertainment
PO Box 5354
Santa Monica, CA 90409
p: 310-396-0710
f: 310-496-3157
e: info@innovationentertainment.com
www.innovationentertainment.com
contact: Mohit Sherchan
e: mohit@innovationentertainment.com
genres: All Styles
freq: Monthly
submit: May 31; Aug 31; Nov 31; Feb 31
accepts epk: Yes
Music entertainment outfit runs ongoing int'l competition for unsigned talent. Prizes include cash, licensing opportunity & chance to be on professional release. Submissions juried by industry pros & chart-topping artists.

Mid-Atlantic Song Contest
Songwriters Association of Washington
PMB 106-137
4200 Wisconsin Ave., NW
Washington, DC 20016
p: 301-654-8434
e: masc@saw.org
www.saw.org/masc.asp
contact: Siobhan Quinn
ext: 703-489-9448
genres: Contemporary Folk, Acoustic, Dance, Urban, Go-Go, Rock, Alt., AC, Soft Rock, Country, Bluegrass, Gospel, Inspirational, Christian, Jazz, Blues, Pop, Children's
freq: Annual
submit: May 1 - Sep 15
accepts epk: Yes
Long-running program awards cash & prizes to winners in 10+ categories. Awards ceremony held in Washington DC. Only artists that have not earned more than $5,000 in publishing royalties or publishing co. staff writers are eligible; material must be wholly original & w/o copyright infringement. Submit by snail mail or Sonicbids.

Mountain Stage NewSong Contest
NewSong
PO Box 93
New York, NY 10159
e: contest@newsong-music.com
www.newsong-music.com/contest
contact: Gar Ragland
ext: 347-410-7311
e: gar@newsong-music.com
genres: Rock, Blues, Americana, Folk, World, Christian, Country, Hip-Hop, Jazz, Pop, Alt., Children's
freq: Annual
submit: Jun 4 - Dec 1
accepts epk: Yes
Premier int'l showcase, presented by Folk Alliance, features 12 finalists vying for cash prizes, packages from Oasis CD Manufacturing & the Musician's AtlasOnline, as well as the chance to perform live on the internationally broadcasted "Mountain Stage" show. All 5 co-winners will be invited to participate in future NewSong productions at various venues in the USA, possible film & TV placement opps. & a showcase slot at Folk Alliance in Memphis, TN. Enter via Sonicbids or snail mail: 1st 2 songs are $30; songs 3&4 are $20.

OriginalSessions National Band Search
17 John St.
New York, NY 10038
p: 201-795-1878
e: osarthouse@aol.com
www.originalsessions.com
genres: Most Styles
freq: Quarterly
submit: Every 3 months
Selected bands in 12 US cities will compete in showcases for a $50,000 produced music video, placement in an indie film, a SXSW showcase, gig swaps, 1000 CDs, merch, spot on CD compilation, photo spread in FMFB & more. Winner crowned at the end of the 4th quarter. No Death Metal, Hardcore Rap, Polka

Peacedriven Songwriting Awards
The Peacedriven Organization
PO Box 609
New York, NY 10014
p: 910-322-6335
e: info@peacedriven.com
www.peacedriven.com
contact: Anthony Stokes
genres: All Styles
freq: Annual
submit: Dec 22
accepts epk: Yes
Int'l program sponsored by non-profit, non-partisan org

dedicated to inspiring a new generation of social activists, promotes songs w/message of peace. Music judged by strength of message & melody. Winners promoted & win $200. Submit via Sonicbids.

QuickLaunch Song Contest
FlightSafe Music
PO Box 1112
Tiburon, CA
94920
p: 415-381-1409
f: 415-381-1429
e: info@flightsafemusic.com
www.flightsafemusic.com/contest
contact: Oliver Meissner
genres: Rock, Pop, Jazz, Country, Alt., Gospel, Children's, Urban, Reggae, Metal, Punk, AC, Instrumental, Dance, Electronica
freq: Notifications - Oct 15; Payout - Nov 15
submit: Jun 1 - Sep 8
accepts epk: Yes
Music publishing & licensing firm seeks original tunes. Cash prize up to $1,500, a featured position on flightsafemusic.com & exposure to film/TV biz. Fee range $20 /$30/song. Submit via Sonicbids.

The Singer/ Songwriter Awards
We Are Listening
London, SW11 3WG UK
p: 44-779-375-2982
e: info@wearelistening.org
www.wearelistening.org
contact: Lior Shamir
e: l.shamir@wearelistening.org
genres: All Styles except Instrumental
freq: 6/year
submit: Jan 2
accepts epk: Yes
In association w/ Berklee College of Music, contest provides artists w/ opportunity to get original music evaluated by music industry elite. Winners enjoy an all expense paid trip to London to record their winning entry in a state-of-the-art studio, as well as other prizes. Submit via Sonicbids only.

Songwriting & Lyric Contest & Music Competition
Goodnight Kiss Music
10153 1/2 Riverside Dr., #239
Toluca Lake, CA 91602
p: 831-479-9993
www.goodnightkiss.com/contest.html
contact: Janet Fisher
e: prosongwriter1@aol.com
genres: All Styles
freq: Yearly
submit: Depends on project
Music publishing company runs varied contests w/several prize options including gear & possible licensing opp. Songs must be commitment-free, radio friendly, hi-quality CD & be under 5 min. Pay $25/song.

Unisong Int'l Songwriting Contest
Unisong
6250 Platt Ave., #729
West Hills, CA 91307
p: 213-673-4067
e: info@unisong.com; entries@unisong.com
www.unisong.com
contact: Alan Scott
genres: Pop Ballad, Country, Pop Uptempo/Dance, Rock, Acoustic/Folk, Urban, Americana, Instrumental, Gospel/Christian, Jazz, Blues, Social, Children's, World, Seasonal/Specialty, Lyrics Only, Performance
freq: Annual
submit: Jun 1 - Nov 5
accepts epk: Yes
Int'l songwriting contest w/16 diverse categories has prize pkg. of more than $60,000 & all expenses paid writing/performing retreat in either Ireland, Crete, Denmark, Sweden, Spain or Big Sur. "Winners Of The Month" contest awards $250 cash & prizes & spotlight position on their site. Fees vary w/early bird discounts. Submit via Sonibids or snail mail.

West Coast Songwriters Int'l Song Contest
West Coast Songwriters
1724 Laurel St., Ste. 120
San Carlos, CA 94070
p: 800-FOR-SONG; 650-654-3966
e: info@westcoastsongwriters.org
www.westcoastsongwriters.org/contest.htm
contact: Ian Crombie
e: ian@westcoastsongwriters.org
genres: All Styles
freq: Annual
submit: Aug 1 - Jan 31
accepts epk: Yes
Noted singer-songwriters judge entrants for a chance play at the Sunset Concert & win numerous prizes.

Williamsburg Live Songwriter Competition
Jezebel Music
PO Box 220234
Greenpoint Stn.
Brooklyn, NY 11222
p: 718-874-6484
e: info@jezebelmusic.com
www.wlsc2008.com
contact: Gabriel Levitt
e: gabriel@jezebelmusic.com
genres: All Styles
freq: Annual
submit: Oct 10
accepts epk: Yes
Entrants are selected to perform at 8 NYC venues w/ $4000 cash & studio time for the winners.

CD Compilations

BandRadio Airwaves Compilation CD
BandRadio
PO Box 6927
Folsom, CA 95763
p: 916-521-2050
f: 866-869-0581
www.bandradio.com/comp
contact: Mike Stahl
e: mike@bandradio.com
genres: All Styles
submit: Ongoing
14 bands selected to have their music distributed to industry execs, A&R, labels, radio, attorneys, agents, film & TV execs, managers, producers, programmers & retail outlets. Over 1000 CDs pressed & promoted to retail, music conferences & online. Send CD or EPK w/ 3 songs. Check site for rules, cost & addt'l info.

Best New Bands
Apache Rose Publishing
5019 Peachtree St.
Valdosta, GA 31605
p: 229-560-6423
e: info@apacherose.net
www.apacherose.net
contact: Mark Swift
genres: Mostly Alt, Hard Rock, Americana
street date: Jan
submit: Sept - Oct
1600 promo CDs distributed. to 1000+ USA college & public stations, frats & sororities. Bands get 30 copies for themselves. No Country!

Carnelian Agency CD Compilation
Carnelian Agency
2328 Iron St.
Bellingham, WA 98225
p: 360-752-9829
f: 360-752-3282
www.carnelianagency.com
contact: Teri Cruzan
e: tericruzan@

carnelianagency.com
genres: Rock, Alt., Reggae, Tribute, Hip-Hop
accepts epk: Yes
Booking/artist development agency sometimes produces CD compilations for festivals. Seeking new distrib. Also provides CD duplication, PA rental, graphic design & photography services. Unsigned acts submit thru Sonicbids.

Creative American Music Compilation
Paved Earth Music
New York, NY
p: 212-459-4900
e: info@pavedearthmusic.com
http://pem.cadoaartsand science.com
genres: Jazz, Rock, Country, Blues, Hip-Hop, Americana, S/S
submit: Aug-Dec
accepts epk: Yes
Compilation released int'lly to press & radio seeks submissions. Submit via Sonicbids; fee is $5.

Digital Bliss
Digital Bliss Productions
1255 26th St., #203
Oakland, CA 94607
www.digitalblissproductions .com
contact: Lynda Arnold
ext: 510-469-6295
e: divasonic@gmail.com
genres: Electronic, Instrumental, Pop
accepts epk: Yes
Series focuses on women producers & vocalists in Electronic music. Check web & blog for more info. No entry fee.

Dream On!
The Dream Continued
e: info@ thedreamcontinued.org
www.thedreamcontinued.org
genres: All Styles
submit: May - Jun
accepts epk: Yes
Two-disc Martin Luther King tribute CDs. Royalties distrib. from the sale of the 5000 CDs but most will be free MP3 downloads. Artists participating are filmed for documentary. Songs should be inspired by Dr. King or be in alignment w/ his message of peaceful empowerment.

Faith Rocks
Celebrate Radio
e: celebrateradio@ yahoo.com
www.celebrateradio.com/ cds.htm
contact: Don Fass
e: info@celebrateradio.com
genres: Faith-based Rock
accepts epk: Yes
Faith-based Rock compilation series, presses 600 CDs & benefits social justice orgs. & promoted thru Satellite & Web Radio; artists granted 12.5 cents royalty/song, per CD after the 1st 50 each year ($.10 per download).

Females On Fire
Warrior Girl Music
12115 Magnolia Blvd.
Ste. 219
North Hollywood, CA 91607
p: 800-871-9021 x73615
f: 801-838-5411
e: info@warriorgirlmusic.com
www.femalesonfire.com
contact: Gilli Moon
genres: Female Artists
street date: Ongoing
Celebrates talented female artists in all genres of music from around the world. Distribution/Promotion includes conferences, festivals, online, media, Film & TV, publishers, labels, press, producers & industry execs. Over 6000 CDs pressed. All applications must go thru online form on site.

Free Lap Dances
Save Our Strays
2017 Freeland Ave., #2
Cincinnati, OH 45208
p: 513-871-2308
e: soscinti@yahoo.com
www.soscats.org
contact: Jacob Heintz
e: buckra@buckra.com
genres: All Styles
submit: Nov - Feb
accepts epk: Yes
Ongoing CD comp. series raises money to house, feed & find homes for stray animals. Distributed to greater Cincinnati local retailers, Borders Bookstores (in Tri-County area) & Everybody's Records & for sale at CDBaby.com. Promoted thru benefit shows & via press. All proceeds go to Save Our Strays of the Tri-State (www.soscinci.org). Receives nat'l press & has sold thousands of copies.

Fresh Produce
mvyradio.com
PO Box 1148
Tisbury, MA 02568
p: 859-215-2728
f: 508-693-8211
e: freshproduce@ mvyradio.com
www.mvyradio.com
contact: Gary Guthrie
e: gary@mvyradio.com
genres: Adult Alt., Folk, S/S, Americana
street date: Quarterly
submit: Mar-May
accepts epk: Yes
Produced by mvyradio.com, a Heritage Adult Alternative Station & one of the most listened to online stations, 11,000 copies of this CD are scheduled for quarterly delivery to all CIMS Stores. Promoted online, in CIMS stores, thru Vineyard Vines & email blasts. Fee is $5.95 per song.

GoGirlsMusicFest Compilation CD
GoGirlsMusic.com
PO Box 16940
Sugar Land, TX 77496
p: 281-541-0981
e: info@gogirlsmusic.com
www.gogirlsmusic.com
contact: Madalyn Sklar
genres: All Styles
street date: Oct
submit: Jun - Jul
accepts epk: Yes
2000 CDs pressed & promoted online & at shows. Free at all GoGirls MusicFest Showcases & at www.gogirlsmusicfest.com. Must be a GoGirls Elite member to submit.

I'm Too Young For This!
Cancer Foundation, Inc.
34-71st St.
Brooklyn, NY 11209
p: 877-735-4673
f: 718-745-1928
e: stupidcancer@ imtooyoungforthis.org
www.imtooyoungforthis.org
contact: Matthew Zachary
ext: 877-735-4674 x701
e: mzachary@ imtooyoungforthis.org
genres: All Styles
street date: Jan 2010
accepts epk: Yes
Only nat'l music advocacy project for young adults affected by cancer. 50,000+ CDs promoted worldwide to audience 21-39 through arts projects, concerts, tours, social media, grassroots & medical education. Accepts digital submissions or mail promos to: 40 Worth St., New York, NY, 10013. No entry fee.

Indie Country Gold
Colt Records
108 Maplewood Dr.
PO Box 105
Ashley, OH 43003
p: 740-747-0360
f: 740-747-0360
www.coltrecords.com
contact: J.K. Coltrain
e: ken@coltrecords.com
genres: Country, Americana, Bluegrass, Gospel, Folk, S/S
street date: Jul 15
submit: Apr 11 - Jun 22
accepts epk: Yes
Ongoing series selects polished tracks to sell & promote to worldwide audience of mostly trad. country fans 35+. Promoted to over 680 terrestrial & digital stations & sold for $11.99. Artists get 10 copies & approx. 30% of sales. Accepts Sonicbids but prefers snail mailed hi-quality CD/DVD w/ $15 fee, bio, photo, musical influences & band contact info - mark Attn: New Artists.

Indie Music For Life
Indie Music For Life
PO Box 4021
Martinsville, VA 24112
p: 276-224-0485
e: indiemusicforlife@ yahoo.com
www.indiemusicforlife.org
contact: Vicki Blankenship
e: vicki@indiegrrl.com
genres: Children's, AC, CCM, Folk, Americana, R&B, Country, Acoustic, Rock, Pop, Jazz, Reggae
street date: Mar
submit: Jul - Oct
Non-profit org. produces 5 annual compilations distrib. online to raise money for cancer research & educational music therapy programs for pediatric cancer patients, promoted online and thru events, fundraisers & SonicBids. Initial run of 1000 CDs. Also runs Laughs for Life & Indie Grrl. Send submissions to PO Box address w/ demo & $5.00 fee; no press kit necessary.

Java With Javelyn Indie Music
X-It Rite Records
PO Box 641351
Los Angeles, CA 90064
p: 310-281-7454
e: info@javawithjavelyn.com
www.javawithjavelyn.com
contact: Linda Fair
e: submissions@ javawithjavelyn.com
genres: Rock, Alt., Acoustic, Pop, Jazz, Blues, Folk, Alt. Country, Classical, World, Reggae, Hip-Hop
street date: Jan
submit: Sept - Feb
Distrib. to industry execs, publishing companies, heavy emphasis on Film/TV, as well as attorneys, radio programmers & producers. Promoted thru various events in LA & online. All songs must be original & at least 2.5 minutes & no longer than 4.10 minutes. Selected artists will receive 50 free copies of CD to distribute. Must be 18+ to submit.

Let Me Be Heard Independent Artists Compilation CD Series
Music Independence Summit Connection
86 S Main St.
Freeport, NY 11520
p: 516-378-3301
f: 516-868-0485
e: info@ musicindependence.net
www.musicindependence.net
contact: Jimmy Newson
genres: All Styles
submit: Ongoing
accepts epk: Yes
DIY org. known by acronym MISC, showcases all styles w/ ongoing compilation series. 1,000+ CDs distrib. at MISC & partner events. Songs must be original & sample free. NO lyrics w/ profanity, violence or disrespect to women considered. Fee is $10/song. Submit via Sonicbids.

The Lost Art of Tape Trading
Lost Tape Traders
e: info@losttapetraders.com
www.losttapetraders.com
genres: Acoustic, Alt., AC, Pop, Rock, S/S
submit: Aug-Oct
accepts epk: Yes
5-6 bands/CD & each artist gets 3 songs on compilation. Bands can sell & set their own fee or freely distribute. First 25 CDs are free w/ $20 shipping fee, then $2.50 + shipping per CD. Accepts EPKs thru Sonicbids.

Master Plan Compilation Project
Roo Records
www.roorecords.net
genres: All Styles of Christian
accepts epk: Yes
Digital compilation series

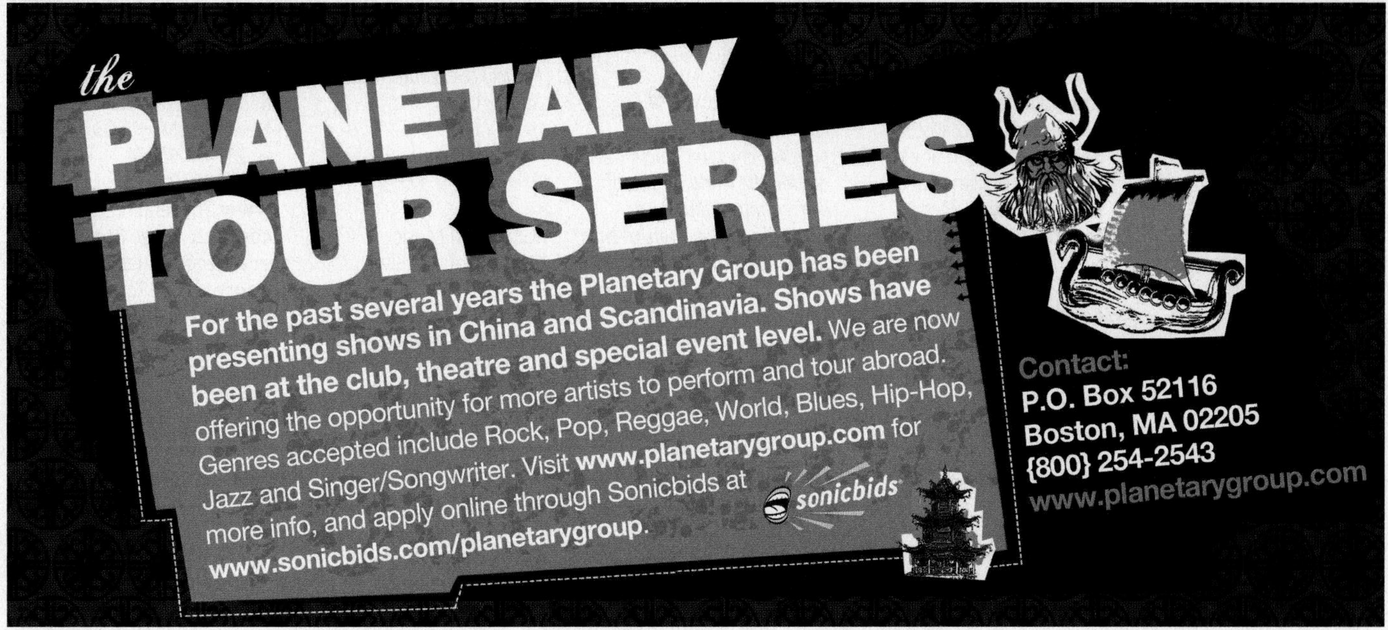
the PLANETARY TOUR SERIES
For the past several years the Planetary Group has been presenting shows in China and Scandinavia. Shows have been at the club, theatre and special event level. We are now offering the opportunity for more artists to perform and tour abroad. Genres accepted include Rock, Pop, Reggae, World, Blues, Hip-Hop, Jazz and Singer/Songwriter. Visit www.planetarygroup.com for more info, and apply online through Sonicbids at www.sonicbids.com/planetarygroup.
sonicbids
Contact:
P.O. Box 52116
Boston, MA 02205
{800} 254-2543
www.planetarygroup.com

from Christian label is distrib. digitally thru iTunes, Rhapsody, Napster & Amazon.com. $25 fee waived for 5 artists & royalties received from digital downloads.

Metal for Troops Various Compilations
Music For Troops
PO Box 295
Lyon Station, PA 19536
p: 617-850-5967
f: 866-211-2294
www.musicfortroops.com
contact: Tom Hughes
e: thughes@musicfortroops.com
genres: All Styles
submit: Ongoing
accepts epk: Yes
Non-profit org. creates 6 CD compilations to entertain US troops stationed at home & abroad. 1,000 CDs pressed - 50% distrib. to troops; 50% sold on Ebay to cover prod. & shipping costs. Upload tracks or mail CDs to: PO Box 295, Lyon Station, PA 19536.

MPress Records New Arrivals: CD Compilation Vol. 2
MPress Records
118 E 28th St., Ste. 1010
New York, NY 10016
p: 212-481-7243
f: 212-481-1073
www.mpressrecords.com; www.newarrivalscd.com
contact: Jojo Gentry
e: jojo@mpressrecords.com
genres: S/S, Folk, Rock, Pop
street date: Jun 6
Over 5000 CDs distrib. at major industry conferences, such as SXSW & CMJ, as well as on CDBaby.com. All benefits go to Artist for Eating Disorder Awareness/NEDA. Radio promotion provided by Planetary Group to AAA & College stations; ads in mags such as Performing Songwriter & CMJ. Publicity provided by Think Press. Check website for submission dates. Sonicbids submissions only.

Music For Coffee Beings
Magic Puddle Productions
24254 100 B Ave.
Maple Ridge, BC
V2W 1X6 Canada
p: 604-463-8339
f: 604-476-1089
www.rpwrecords.com
contact: Pam Southwell
e: pam@rpwrecords.com
genres: Acoustic, Pop, Jazz
submit: every 6-8 weeks
accepts epk: Yes
Series promotes Canadian & some int'l artists. Promotional CDs & color brochures are distrib. to coffee shops in the USA & Canada. New CDs released every 6-10 wks. Submit via Sonicbids; $700/track.

Musician's Atlas ARTIST SPOTLIGHT
Music Resource Group
32 Ann St.
Clifton, NJ 07013
p: 973-767-1800
f: 973-767-1844
www.musiciansatlas.com
contact: Martin Folkman
e: martin@musiciansatlas.com
genres: All Styles
street date: May
submit: Yearlong
Effective marketing program for active, radio-friendly recording artists. Program highlights include a 6 week targeted radio campaign to 650+ USA & Canadian college, public & commercial stations; direct distribution to press & film, TV & gaming music supervisors; online promotion & a spread in the annual best-selling print edition of The Musician's Atlas. Contact before sending material.

No Lip
Mohawk Bomb Records
www.mohawkbomb.com
contact: Ivan Pena
e: ar@mohawkbomb.com
genres: Punk, Hardcore, Rock, Metal, Indie, Pop
street date: Every5-6 months
accepts epk: Yes
Record label's promo series produces 1000 CDs that are distrib. for free at eMusic, iTunes, Amazon & Rhapsody. Bands are promoted & get CDs, posters & stickers for their own use.

Now Hear This: Independent Music Awards Winners CD
Music Resource Group
32 Ann St.
Clifton, NJ 07013
p: 973-767-1800
f: 973-767-1844
www.independentmusicawards.com
contact: Lauren Veteri
ext: 973-509-3140
e: lauren@independentmusicawards.com
genres: All Styles
street date: Feb
submit: Dec - Jul
accepts epk: Yes
Prime compilation series promotes IMA winners to thousands of industry gatekeepers & music fans. Benefits include yearlong promotion to print, online & broadcast media, a targeted radio campaign by The Planetary Group to 650+ US & Canadian college, public & commercial stations; direct distribution to film, TV & gaming music supervisors & ad agencies plus distrib. at industry trade events & consumer music festivals. 5,000 CDs; $30 entry fee.

On That Note College Compilation
On That Note Entertainment
141 New Rd.
Ste. 1J
Parsippany, NJ 07054
p: 973-486-0867
f: 866-486-0875
e: jeff@onthatnote.net; jay@onthatnote.net
www.onthatnote.net
contact: Dan Balassone
e: dan@onthatnote.net
genres: All Styles
street date: Aug
submit: Jun/Jul - Sep/Oct
accepts epk: Yes
Free CDs distributed at NACA conferences & the national APCA college conference. 2500 CDs are pressed & promoted.

OPERATION: Music Storm!
Bare Metal Records
PO Box 42
Canal Winchester, OH 43110
f: 614-837-7016
www.baremetalrecords.com
contact: Bill & Jaymz Enyart
e: staff@baremetalrecords.com
genres: Rock, Metal, Country, Pop, Latin, Alt.
Over 5000 CDs sent to US troops stationed in Iraq & Afghanistan, college & FM stations, as well as music industry personnel. Each selected artist will receive 10 copies. Promoted online, thru press & college & FM stations. No digital submissions.

OUTLOUD Music Series
Tomasian Ent!
497 W Side Ave.
Jersey City, NJ 07304
p: 201-633-5748
f: 201-633-5750
e: info@tomasianent.com
www.tomasianent.com
contact: Kevin Fitzpatrick
ext: 888-465-3560 x500
e: kfitzpatrick@tomasianent.com
genres: All Styles
street date: 5 dates/year
submit: Ongoing
accepts epk: Yes
Five CD series: Sing OUTLOUD (S/S), Dance OUTLOUD, Jam OUTLOUD (Instrumental), Rock OUTLOUD & Rap OUTLOUD, all distrib. online & goes to promote & provide exposure to the music of Lesbian, Gay, Bi, Transgender, Queer, and Intersex artists. Sonicbids submissions only.

Planetary Group Presents: Stranded In Stereo
Planetary Group
63A Wareham St.
Boston, MA 02118
p: 617-226-1036
f: 617-350-3134
e: submissions@strandedinstereo.com
www.strandedinstereo.com
contact: Adam Lewis
ext: 617-275-7660
e: adam@planetarygroup.com
genres: All Styles
street date: Quarterly
submit: Ongoing
accepts epk: yes
Dual-disc CD/DVD compilation provides great nat'l exposure & is distrib. & promoted to nearly 15,000 fans & industry, college radio stations & at CMJ.

Rhythm Latino
Melody Ent.
www.rhythmlatino.com
contact: Leonard Woshczyn
genres: Latin, Samba, Cha Cha, Rumba, Jive
Latin Ballroom music compilation distrib. thru Amazon.com, iTunes, CDBaby, www.groupietunes.com, www.digistation.com, www.payplay.fm & www.tradebit.com.

Rock Against Parkinson's
MAP Music
Montreal, QC Canada
e: info@mapmusic.org
www.mapmusic.org
contact: Robbie Tucker
genres: All Styles
accepts epk: Yes
Series promoted thru Confront Magazine & concerts to raise $1,000,000 to help those living w/ Parkinson's Disease.

Sin City Social Club
Sin City Social Club
Los Angeles, Austin & Nashville, CA, TX & TN
http://sincitysocialclub.com
genres: Country, Punk, Roots, Rock, Americana, S/S
accepts epk: yes
Promoted thru concerts & audio programming on Continental Airlines.

Songs of Canada
The Association of Artists for a Better World
1406-28 Hollywood Ave.
Toronto, ON M2N 6S4
Canada
p: 416-224-2192
e: mastermail@abetterworld.ca
www.abetterworld.ca
contact: Brian Gladstone
genres: Songs on any topic w/ themes of Canadiana
submit: May 1 - Dec 1
accepts epk: Yes
Submitted to 200 radio stations throughout N America, Europe, Australia & web radio. Songs on any topic w/ themes of Canadiana. Benefits Doctors Without Borders program. Entry fee is $19.95/1st song & $5 for addt'l songs. Sonicbids submissions only.

Songs With Vision
Songs With Vision
www.songswithvision.com
contact: Danny
accepts epk: Yes
Licensing company produces various compilations including Winery & Women's Shelter comps. Charges for song evaluation. No unsolicited material.

Songwriters and Storytellers
Indie Artists Alliance
855 Kifer Rd., Ste A
Sunnyvale, CA 94806
p: 866-945-6800; 408-735-6800
f: 408-735-6805
www.indieartistsalliance.com
contact: Phil Peretz
e: phil@indieartistsalliance.com
genres: Americana, Roots, Blues, Southern Rock, S/S, Country
accepts epk: Yes
Roots music compilation series/contest incl. the production of 1000 retail-ready CDs, several short run CD production packages, cash prizes & promo on Create411.com, Indie Artists Alliance site & www.iMuzic.com through Dropcards to 14-60 demo. Free to Indie radio stations, music licensing supervisors, event planners & venue promoters.

Sounds Like Cafe
Sounds Like Cafe
230 Crown St.
Sydney, NSW 2010
Australia
p: 61-29-331-0666
e: info@soundslikecafe.com
www.soundslikecafe.com
contact: Marshall Cullen
e: marshall@damiengerard.net
genres: All Styles
street date: Sept
submit: Jun - Aug
accepts epk: Yes
Over 1200 CDs featuring polished emerging talent from around the world are distrib. to coffee shops throughout Australia. Unique opp. to enter the Australian music market. Promo address: PO Box 3262, Umina Beach, NSW, 2257 Australia.

Stomp Out Cancer: Indie Musicians Fight Ewing's Sarcoma
Indie Music Unified
8018 3rd St. Rd., #3
Louisville, KY 40214
p: 502-489-1501
f: 866-533-2023
e: info@stompoutcancer.com
www.stompoutcancer.com
contact: Jake Wheat
e: jake@streetblast.com
genres: All Styles
street date: Oct
submit: Jul - Aug
accepts epk: Yes
All proceeds go to researching less toxic treatment methods & early detection methods for Ewing's Sarcoma. Over 2500 copies printed & promoted online & thru Streetblast.

Underground Rising
Dark Sky Records
e: song_submissions@darkskyrecordsonline.com; underground@darkskyrecordsonline.com
contact: Rich Macke
e: rich_macke@darkskyrecordsonline.com
genres: Hardcore, Metal, Punk, Thrash, Death Metal
street date: Jan 26, 2009
submit: Nov - Dec
accepts epk: Yes
Gains exposure for unsigned acts thru web & radio. Presses 1,000 CDs for nat'l distrib. Accepts unsolicited material, but no unsolicited audio files.

United Against Poverty
United Against Poverty
e: youthagainstpovertyeurope@hotmail.com
www.myspace.com/youthagainstpovertyeurope
genres: All Styles
accepts epk: Yes
Non-governmental org. benefits poverty stricken children. 10,000 CDs are distrib. to Europe, Africa, China, India & Russia thru labels Divolprod (France) & Lezarder (France, Canada).

Warrior Girl Music Film & TV Music Sampler
Warrior Girl Music
12115 Magnolia Blvd.
Ste. 219
North Hollywood, CA 91607
p: 800-871-9021 x73615
f: 801-838-5411
e: warriorgirlmusic@gmail.com
www.warriorgirlmusic.com
contact: Gilli Moon
genres: All Styles of Music for Film & TV
street date: Ongoing
submit: Ongoing
Various samplers & compilations produced throughout the year for different projects. Over 1000 samplers are distrib. worldwide to Film & TV Programs. Promoted thru music conferences, industry lists & prod. houses.

Tours

Bama Hip-Hop
Bama Hip-Hop
1628 Christine Dr.
Anniston, AL 36207
p: 256-282-0799
f: 925-475-7458
e: bamahiphop@yahoo.com
www.bamahiphop.homestead.com
contact: Ali Shabazz
genres: Hip-Hop, Crunk, R&B
where: Cities in AL, MS & FL
Organizes open mics & tours for Urban acts - female only. Prefers Sonicbids but accepts all submission formats except MP3s.

Blowout Lounge Circuit
Renee Sebastian Creation
30 Vesey St.
Rm. 901
New York, NY 10007
e: hello@blowoutlounge.com
http://net.blowoutlounge.com/
contact: Renee Sebastian
ext: 925-858-7051
e: bookings@blowoutlounge.com
genres: Pop, Urban, Spoken Word
where: USA
accepts epk: Yes
Tours major cities from March-May. Artists get 50% of door after 10th paying fan. No backline or equip. provided.

Camplified
Alternative Venue Entertainment
853 Broadway, Ste. 1711
New York, NY 10003
p: 212-842-8478
f: 212-254-4800
www.2generations.com
contact: Aimee Berger
e: aimee@2generations.com
genres: Pop, Rock, Emo, Alt.
where: From ME to MD
accepts epk: Yes
Developing artists play at summer camps. Also contact: Carl Freed, 212-358-0100, carl@trevanna.com. Acts pay $600-$750 for each tour date. Email before sending material.

Cirque Du Singe Brise
Shattered Monkey
PO Box 1382
North Massapequa, NY 11758
www.theshatteredmonkey.com
contact: Rich Van Vleet
e: rich@theshatteredmonkey.com
genres: Alt., Experimental, Acoustic, Jam, Americana, Jazz, Instrumental, World
where: northeast USA
Circus-like event presents a collection of nat'l & int'l acts; Locals join tour at each stop. $1 of every CD sale donated to the Interstitial Cystitis Assoc. Sonicbids submissions only.

CME Presents: Tour the UK!
CME Artist Services
3 Kensington House
Greaves Rd.
Lancaster, Lancashire LA1 4UY
UK
p: 44-152-438-0990
e: contact@cmeas.com
www.cmeas.com
contact: Ben Ruth
ext: 44-798-049-5549
e: ben@cmeas.com
genres: All Secular - No Tribute or Cover
where: England, Wales, Scotland
accepts epk: Yes
Tours top music pubs & venues in England, Wales & Scotland in spring & fall. All travel, costs, evening meals, promotion & work permits provided. Only original, non-secular acts considered. Check Sonicbids.com for details.

FODfest
FODfest, Inc.
PO Box 1190
Sheffield, MA 01257
p: 413-229-9939;

e: info@fodfest.org
www.fodfest.org
contact: Todd Mack
genres: All Styles
where: MA, CT, NY, VA, NC, SC, TN, GA, WA, OR, CA
accepts epk: Yes
Non-profit corp. celebrates life & ideals of the late Daniel Pearl. Feats. 100's of artists from all genres & countries. Artists agree to play in a jam/song swap format. Promos: Attn: Michelle Roche Media Relations.

Girls Rock & Girls Rule
Revolutionary Records
200 W 15th St., 7G
New York, NY 10011
p: 646-336-0041
e: info@revolutionaryrecords.com
www.revolutionaryrecords.com
contact: Gail Silverman
genres: Women Rock Bands
where: DC, VA, NC, SC, GA, TN, OH, PA & MD
accepts epk: Yes
Showcases female Rock bands & donates portion of proceeds to Voices of Women Organizing Project, Battered Women's Resource Center, Habitat for Humanity & Women & Girl Build Programs. Also contact: Michele at tourgrrl@revolutionaryrecords.com.

Harvest Tour
Digitone Records
PO Box 3834
Chester, VA
23831
p: 800-595-4937
www.digitonerecords.com
contact: Gary Gaskin
e: g@digitonerecords.com
genres: All Styles
where: VT, RI, MA, NY, VA, DC, NC, OH & TN
Hosts 10 showcases in clubs, theatres & event spaces during 2wk period. Bands must be 18+.

TheMusicReps: Tour The Netherlands
TheMusicReps
Lisdoddelaan 19
Leerdam, VG 4143
The Netherlands
p: 31-34-584-8405
www.themusicreps.com
contact: Chris Fraikin
e: chris@themusicreps.com
genres: All Styles
where: Netherlands
Dutch agency seeks int'l acts to tour Netherlands. Artists paired w/ similar Dutch band for 6 shows in 2wk period. Band pays travel costs but get free food, lodging & payment up to 150 euros minus 15%. Materials to: Akeleibaan 60, 2098 KA Capelle, A/D Ijssel, The Netherlands.

Planetary Tour Series
The Planetary Group
PO Box 52116
Boston, MA 02205
p: 617-275-7660
f: 617-275-7661
e: info@planetarygroup.com
www.planetarygroup.com
contact: Adam Lewis
genres: Rock, Pop, Reggae, World, Hip-Hop, Jazz, Blues, Punk, S/S
where: China & Scandinavia
Cool opportunity arranged by radio promotion gurus to gig in China & Scandinavia. Must be 18+. Check site for details. Submit thru Sonicbids only.
See Ad On Page 195

Rhythm Road: American Music Abroad
Jazz at Lincoln Center
33 W 60th St., 11th Fl.
New York, NY
10023
p: 212-258-9899
e: amap@jalc.org
www.jalc.org/theroad
contact: Van Monak Chhun
ext: 212-258-9825
e: vchhun@jalc.org
genres: Jazz, Urban, Roots, Country, Blues, Gospel
where: Int'l
accepts epk: Yes
Month long tour produced by Jazz at Lincoln Center & US State Dept. to bring indigenous American music abroad. Only polished acts of the above genres considered. Must be 21+ & have valid US passport. Check Sonicbids for details.

Van's Warped Tour
e: askme@warconent.com
www.warpedtour.com
contact: Kate Truscott
ext: 617-502-1399
e: sarahsaturday@aol.com
genres: Punk, Rock, Alt., Emo, Metal
where: USA
accepts epk: Yes
Celebrates music & extreme sports w/ 100+ bands on several stages. Produces yearly CD compilation.

W.O.A. The India Tour
W.O.A International
B7, Shangri La Apts.
St. Marys Colony
Miramar, Panaji, Goa 403001
India
p: 91-832-651-2569
e: info@woarecords.com
www.woarecords.com
contact: Alan Alvarez
e: manager@woarecords.com
genres: All Styles
where: Major metros in India
India Tour Booking agency produces annual tour featuring indie acts to play 15 major venues from April 15-30th.

Zig Zag Live Club Tour
Zig Zag
151 W 25th St.
New York, NY 10001
p: 917-606-1908
e: zigzaglive@cmj.com
www.zigzaglive.com
genres: Indie, Rock, Metal, Hip-Hop, Afrobeat, Jam
where: US Cities
Tour brings great new music to US cities & supports local artists. Offers a spring tour, as well as a slot to play the CMJ Music Marathon in NYC.

FROM THE PAGES OF THE atlas plugged eNEWSLETTER

CHANGING YOUR LIVE SET MINDSET IN 6 STEPS

Live performance - performing under the lights in front of cheering fans - is often the most intense and rewarding aspect of being a musician. This is why many of you first joined a band, and maybe why you pursue a career that has been mostly just expensive up to this point.

Your live performance is key to your band's success – it will create a lasting impression with fans & press. Too many bands overlook the fact that live performance and songwriting are different skill sets – and often leave their live show to the vagaries of chance. A killer live set, like a song, must be carefully planned and perfected.

Typically, a band preparing for a gig runs through their set list a few times, then think they are good-to-go. The problem with this "roll the dice" approach is that the pacing and audience impact of the set list is unknown until it is performed in front of an audience.

Often, the band has no idea why the crowd's reaction is substantially different from night to night. Typically, they blame a bad show on a dead crowd, while attributing a great audience reaction to the fact that they "rocked."

I suggest taking an entirely different philosophical approach to live performance: from now on, don't play any more shows. Play a "Show" (note the capital "S"). The goal is to put together a solid and repeatable Show that has maximum audience impact, and leaves no room for error in regards to logistical considerations such as lighting and sound.

I suggest that you strategically design your Show for maximum audience impact, and rehearse exactly as you will perform it. Here are the basic 6 Steps to making every show your best:

1. EXPLOSIVE BOOK ENDS

Immediately after you take the stage, own it. Your Show must explode and hit fans like a sledgehammer–at the beginning and at the end. Opening with strength is critical, as potential fans will form an unchanging opinion of your band in the first forty-five seconds. Furthermore, if you don't end strong, you're dead in the water.

2. THE VALLEY

With the exception of Metallica, few bands can keep a relentless set going with no let-up and keep the audience interested. Imagine going to a movie, and watching an unending shoot-out for 90 minutes. No matter how great the action is, you will eventually become desensitized and bored. The same principle applies to live performance. The solution is to carefully plan the pacing and intensity level of the Show, and depending on its length, include one or two "energy valleys."

There are several ways to do this, but it is typically done by changing the instrumentation or intensity level of the music. This gives the audience time to breath, and makes the end of the set much more effective.

3. THE COVER TUNE

Yeah, I know. You never play covers. Well, unless you are famous and relentlessly heckled on TMZ.com already, I suggest you rethink that philosophy.

By incorporating a strategic cover tune into the Show, you'll see many of these previously "unengaged" audience members drop their arms and move closer to the stage, where they will stay. Yeah, it's like some weird psychological experiment–but it works. The basic principle is that the presence of one tune they are familiar with draws them into your world, so to speak, and they will be more open to your original music.

The one caveat is never pick a tune where the original recording sounds similar to your band. For example, if you're in a band that sounds like the Smashing Pumpkins, don't pick a Smashing Pumpkins tune. Instead, play a Goth version of a Duran Duran tune or whatever. By making a well-known cover your own, you will break the ice with new fans.

4. THE SCRIPT

So now you have a brilliant set list, aka the Show. The next thing to consider is the "space" between the songs. Simply put, rehearse the Show as it will be performed–including what is said between the tunes.

Instead of launching from song to song without ever saying anything to the audience, have your singer say a few words about a tune before it is played. This will make the song memorable, and will make a huge difference in how the audience relates to your music. Your singer should also mention the merchandise table and your website's URL once or twice (only) during the Show, without sounding desperate.

5. ACCESSIBILITY

The music industry is a strange and wicked animal, where its denizens are drawn towards successful and inaccessible figures, and repelled from everybody else. Without overdoing it so you cross into the realm of arrogance, your band should come across as if it already is successful and famous.

After the Show, don't hang around trying to hawk albums. A little accessibility is cool, but being desperate and asking everyone what they thought of your band is counterproductive, and will only destroy your marketing image. After a great show, create an "aura of indifference" which will be seen as cool by the fans. This is not intuitive–but it is how the music industry works at a world-class level.

6. SOUND AND LIGHTING

This is your career–do not leave sound and lighting to chance. Since few bands have the financial resources to afford a sound and lighting crew during the initial phases of their career, sound and lighting should be dealt with in two stages.

First create a sound and light cue sheet to add new dimensions to your Show and keep the sound and lighting person engaged during your set. This sheet should list the order of the tunes, featured instrumentation and lighting effects.

Think about amazing lighting effects for certain songs which can become a "visual hook" to support that tune. For example, every time you play the chorus of your killer ballad, the club is bathed in red lights. Cool, no? It's certainly better than hoping that the lighting guy knows when to stop talking to the chick in the leather pants long enough to push a button or two.

Second, and the most obvious but expensive solution, is to bring your own sound and lighting crew to each show. Once your band starts to generate substantial revenue, this is a must. The good news is that if you followed this advice, you already have a detailed and refined sound and lighting cue sheet ready to go. Thus, your sound and lighting team will have an excellent resource, and they'll get up to speed quickly.

Finally, with the minor exception of test-market shows, your band must come to the philosophical agreement that there will be no more small shows. Period. From here on out, you will treat every show as if you were headlining Madison Square Garden – whether you are in front of five fans or five thousand fans. If a show is not worth giving 110%, it is not worth doing. You never know who will be at a show, and you will only have one shot to make a great first impression on potential new fans.

Rock-n-Roll.

Lee Rudnicki is an entertainment lawyer, producer, and artist manager in Los Angeles. He stays out of out trouble by sitting on the board of the San Francisco Renegades drum corps and the New York music licensing company Sir Groovy, and running Broken Ocean Entertainment, which manages Hollywood Kill.

YOU CAN ALSO FIND LEE AT:
Website: **http://www.drumlaw80.com** • Blog 7: **http://drumlaw80.blogspot.com**

disc replicators

Crystal Clear Disc Promo & Apparel
10486 Brockwood Rd.
Dallas, TX 75238
p: 800-880-0073
f: 214-349-3819
e: cds@crystalclearcds.com
www.crystalclearcds.com
contact: Jim Cocke
ext: 800-880-0073 x114
e: jim@crystalclearcds.com
formats: CD, CD-ROM, DVD, Cassette,
services: Replication, Printing, Packaging, Mastering, Graphic Design, Fulfillment, Promo Items
See Ad On This Page

DigiMasterFaster.com
350 Park Ave.
New York, NY 10022
p: 888-DIGI-NOW
e: digimasterfaster@gmail.com
www.digimasterfaster.com
contact: Dave Dambreville
services: Online audio mastering service for musicians and bands allows them to upload individual songs or albums for complete, one-stop mastering.
See Ad On Page 200

Disc Makers
7905 N Rte. 130
Pennsauken, NJ 08110
p: 800-468-9353; 856-663-9030
f: 856-661-3458
e: info@discmakers.com
www.discmakers.com
contact: John Borkowski
e: jborkowski@discmakers.com
formats: CD, CD-ROM, DVD
services: CD/DVD Manufacturing, Graphic Design, Printing, Download Cards, Distribution, Mastering Packaging, Authoring, Manual & Automated CD & DVD Printers, Blank Media, Distribution, Marketing Services
See Ad On Page 32

Disc Makers
3112 Roswell Rd.
Atlanta, GA 30305
p: 404-842-0221
f: 404-842-0211
e: info@discmakers.com
www.discmakers.com
contact: Noel Plaugher
e: nplaugher@discmakers.com
formats: CD, CD-ROM, DVD
services: Authoring, Blank Media, CD/DVD Manufacturing, Graphic Design, Manual & Automated CD/DVD Printers, Mastering, Packaging, Printing

Disc Makers
562 W Washington Blvd.
Chicago, IL 60661
p: 800-468-9353; 312-441-9622
f: 312-441-9626
www.discmakers.com
contact: Bob Pirri
ext: 800-731-8009; 323-876-1411
e: bpirri@discmakers.com
formats: CD, CD-ROM, DVD
services: CD/DVD Manufacturing, Graphic Design, Printing, Packaging, Authoring, Mastering, Manual & Automated CD & DVD Printers, Blank Media

Disc Makers
1305 16th Ave. S
1st Fl.
Nashville, TN 37212
p: 866-409-7201; 615-321-6275
f: 615-321-6277
www.discmakers.com
contact: Richard Furtner
ext: 800-731-8009; 323-876-1411
e: rfurtner@discmakers.com
formats: CD, CD-ROM, DVD
services: CD/DVD Manufacturing, Graphic Design, Printing, Packaging, Authoring, Mastering, Manual & Automated CD & DVD Printers, Blank Media

Disc Makers
701 Richmond Ave.
Ste. 150
Houston, TX 77006
p: 800-468-9353; 713-523-0202
f: 713-533-9630
www.discmakers.com
contact: Ryan Harris
e: rharris@discmakers.com
formats: CD, CD-ROM, DVD
services: CD/DVD Manufacturing, Graphic Design, Printing, Packaging, Authoring, Mastering, Manual & Automated CD & DVD Printers, Blank Media

Disc Makers
3445 Cahuenga Blvd. W
Los Angeles, CA 90068
p: 800-731-8009; 323-876-1411
f: 323-876-6724
www.discmakers.com
contact: Syd Alston
ext: 800-468-9353; 510-845-1440
e: salston@discmakers.com
formats: CD, CD-ROM, DVD
services: CD/DVD Manufacturing, Graphic Design, Printing, Packaging, Authoring, Mastering, Manual & Automated CD & DVD Printers, Blank Media

Disc Makers
36 Prospect St.
Cambridge, MA 02139
p: 800-468-9353; 617-354-0099
f: 617-354-1176
www.discmakers.com
contact: Ted Deacon
e: tdeacon@discmakers.com
formats: CD, CD-ROM, DVD
services: CD/DVD Manufacturing, Graphic Design, Printing, Packaging, Authoring, Mastering, Manual & Automated CD & DVD Printers, Blank Media

Disc Makers
16 W 18th St.
New York, NY 10011
p: 800-446-3470; 212-645-0312
f: 212-352-0573
www.discmakers.com
contact: John Borkowski
e: jborkowski@discmakers.com
formats: CD, CD-ROM, DVD
services: Replication, Graphic Design, On-Disc Printing, Packaging, Authoring, Recordable Media, Mastering, Master Transfers Multimedia Authoring, Manual & Automated CD & DVD Printers, Blank Media

Furnace Manufacturing
2719-C Dorr Ave.
Fairfax, VA 22031
p: 703-205-0007
f: 703-205-2951
e: sales@furnacecd.com
www.furnacecd.com
contact: Eric Astor
ext: 703-205-0007 x107
formats: CD, DVD, Blu-Ray, CDR, DVD-R, Audiophile Quality Vinyl: 12', 10', 7', Picture Disc, Shaped Disc, Color Vinyl, Heavyweight Vinyl
services: Replication, Duplication, Vinyl Pressing, Graphic Design, Printing, Mastering, Authoring
See Ad On Page 7

Groove House Records
20501 Ventura Blvd.
Ste. 324
Woodland Hills, CA 91364
p: 888-GROOVE-8
f: 818-883-8386
e: cdrep@groovehouse.com
www.groovehouse.com
contact: Bryan Kelley
formats: CD-Audio, CD-Rom, DVD
services: Short-Run Duplication, Replication, CD/DVD Manufacturing, Packaging, Printing including Digipaks, Graphic Design
All CD-Audio projects include real-time direct to glass mastering. Eco-friendly, 100% recycled cardboard & soy based ink options.

Imperial Media Services
3202 Pennsylvania Ave.
Santa Monica, CA 90404
p: 800-736-8273; 310-396-2008
f: 310-396-8894
e: info@imperialmedia.com
www.imperialmedia.com
formats: CD, CD-ROM, DVD
services: Duplication, Replication, Printing, Packaging, Graphic Design, Mastering, Authoring

Klarity Multimedia
PO Box 160
North Vassalboro, ME 04962
p: 888-387-8273
207-873-3911
f: 207-873-3924
www.klarity.com
formats: CD, CD-ROM, DVD, DVD-ROM
services: Printing, Packaging, Graphic Design, Inventory Management, Fulfillment

Lightscribe
1000 NE Circle Blvd.
Corvallis, OR 97330
www.lightscribe.com/go/now
formats: All Disc Formats
services: Direct Disc Labeling, Software Application, Hardware, Media
LightScribe is an innovative technology that uses a special disc drive, special media & label-making software to burn labels directly onto CDs & DVDs. Because the labels are laser-etched, not printed, there's no ink, no smudging, & no peeling. Your labels can be whatever you want them to be. Create one-of-a-kind designs w/ your own photos, text & artwork using your label-making software.
See Ad On Back Cover

MAM-A
10045 Federal Dr.
Colorado Springs, CO 80908
p: 888-626-3472
f: 888-923-7203
e: info@mam-a.com
www.mam-a.com
formats: CD, DVD, CD-R, DVD-R, DVD+R, DVD+/-RW, CD-RW, Mini CDR, Mini DVD-R
services: Printing, Packaging, Silk Screening
See Ad On This Page

Mixonic
140 2nd St.
5th Fl.
San Francisco, CA 94105
p: 888-464-9664; 415-375-8258
f: 415-495-9201
www.mixonic.com
formats: CD, CD-ROM, DVD, USB, Flashdrives
services: CD/DVD Duplication & Replication, Printing, Packaging, Fulfillment, Design Services
Fast turnaround for high quality production.

MusicToday CD Replication
5391 Three Notched Rd.
Croozet, VA 22932
p: 877-DISCREP
f: 434-984-6798
e: cds@musictoday.com
www.mtcdrep.com
contact: Sales Dept.
formats: CD, DVD, CD-ROM, Enhanced CD
services: Mastering, DVD Authoring, Printing, Packaging, Fulfillment

Oasis CD Manufacturing
7905 N Crescent Blvd.
Delair, NJ 08110
p: 888-296-2747; 540-987-8810
f: 866-229-1465
e: info@oasiscd.com
www.oasiscd.com
formats: CD, CD-ROM, Enhanced CD, DVD, SACD
services: CD/DVD Manufacturing, Graphic Design, Printing, Eco-Packaging, Direct Glass Cutting (Audiophile)
See Ad On Cover 3

Odds On Recording
14 Sunset Way
Henderson, NV 89014
p: 702-697-5351
f: 702-697-5341
e: info@oddsonrecording.com
www.oddsonrecording.com
contact: Sales Dept.
formats: CD, DVD
services: Mastering, DVD Authoring, Graphic & Web Design

Precision Disc Manufacturing
#116-19292 60th Ave.
Surrey, BC V3S 3M2
Canada
p: 866-530-0770
f: 604-530-2909
e: contact@predisc.com
www.predisc.com
contact: A.T.
ext: 866-530-0770 x237
e: andrewt@predisc.com
formats: CD, DVD, CD Business Cards
services: Replication, Manufacturing, Printing, Graphic Design, Packaging
See Ad On Page 3

Vegas Disc
5320 Styers St.
N. Las Vegas, NV 89031
p: 800-246-5667; 702-735-4283
f: 702-207-4964
e: sales@vegasdisc.com
www.vegasdisc.com
contact: Tom Parham
formats: CD, DVD
services: CD Duplication, Mastering
See Ad On Page 5

film & tv

Clearance & Licensing

A.S.A.P. Music & Clip Clearances
1768 S Wooster St.
Los Angeles, CA 90035
p: 310-815-1996
f: 310-815-1888
www.asapmusic.com
contact: Meryl Ginsberg
e: meryl@asapclearances.com
genres: All Styles
territories: Film, TV, Ads, Radio, Video Games
No unsolicited material.

All Clear
315 Meigs Rd., Ste. A, Box 196
Santa Barbara, CA 93109
p: 805-569-2538
f: 805-569-7128
contact: Chad Jensen
e: cjallclear@earthlink.net
genres: All Styles
territories: Film, TV, Ads, Radio
No unsolicited material.

Bates Meyer
714 Brookside Ln.
Sierra Madre, CA 91024
p: 626-355-9201
f: 626-355-5807
www.batesmeyer.com
contact: Nancy Meyer
e: nancy@batesmeyer.com
genres: Blues, Folk, Jazz, Gospel
territories: Film, TV, Ads, Radio, Video Games
No unsolicited material.

BZ/Rights & Permissions
2350 Broadway, Ste. 224
New York, NY 10024
p: 212-924-3000
f: 212-924-2525
e: info@bzrights.com
www.bzrights.com
contact: Barbara Zimmerman
genres: All Styles
territories: Film, TV, Plays, Corporate
No unsolicited material.

Clear Music One
425 Prospect Pl., Ste 4I
Brooklyn, NY 11238
p: 646-232-0167
e: info@clearmusic1.com
www.clearmusic1.com
contact: Fran Mady
e: fmady@clearmusic1.com
genres: Urban
territories: Film, TV, Ads, Radio, Video Games
No unsolicited material.

Clearance Quest
2112 Sunset Pl.
Nashville, TN 37212
p: 615-298-2463
f: 615-298-2327
e: clearancequest@comcast.net
contact: Cheryl Smith
genres: All Styles
territories: Film, TV, Ads, Radio, Video Games

Collective Communications
350 N 9th St., Ste. 500
Boise, ID 83712
p: 208-908-5317
www.collective.mu
contact: Phil Hardy
ext: 208-340-8232 (cell)
e: phil@collective.mu
genres: Rock, Jazz, Dance, Pop
territories: Film, TV, Ads, Radio
Also does mgmt, mktg & label representation.
No unsolicited material.

Creative Clearance
4570 Van Nuys Blvd., #594
Sherman Oaks, CA 91403
p: 818-728-4622
f: 818-332-7070
e: contact@creativeclearance.com
www.creativeclearance.com
contact: Llyswen Franks
genres: All Styles
territories: Film, TV
No unsolicited material.

CUESYNC
221 S Fuller Ave.
Los Angeles, CA 90036
p: 323-842-7039
e: info@cuesync.com
www.cuesync.com
contact: Ben Nachman
e: ben@cuesync.com
genres: All Styles
territories: Film, TV, Ads, Radio, Internet
Mainly works w/ Indie artists.
See site before sending material.

Diamond Time
630 9th Ave., Ste. 1012
New York, NY 10036
p: 212-274-1006
f: 212-274-1938
e: info@diamondtime.net
www.diamondtime.net
contact: Chris Robertson
e: chris@diamondtime.net
genres: All Styles
territories: Film, TV, Ads, Radio, Video Games

Diane Prentice Music Clearance
9010 Corbin Ave., Ste. 14A
Northridge, CA 91324
p: 818-678-0471
f: 818-678-0475
contact: Diane Prentice
e: diane.p@dpmci.com
genres: All Styles
territories: Film, TV, Ads, Radio, Video Games
Also does supervision, music research & publishing admin.
No unsolicited material.

DMG Clearances
13 Robin Dr.
Hockessin, DE 19707
p: 302-239-6337
f: 302-239-6875
e: info@dmgclearances.com
www.dmgclearances.com
contact: Deborah Mannis-Gardner
ext: 302-239-6337 x2
e: deborah@dmgclearances.com
genres: All Styles mainly Rap & R&B
territories: Film, TV, Ads, Video Games
Also contact Madeleine Smith, VP, 302-239-6337 x4, madeleine@dmgclearances.com.

Freeplay Music
1650 Broadway, Ste. 1108
New York, NY 10019
p: 212-974-0548
f: 212-664-7737
www.freeplaymusic.com
contact: Scott Schreer
e: scott@freeplaymusic.com
genres: All Styles
territories: Film, TV, Ads, Radio, Video Games
Send original material & online submission form.

Fricon Entertainment
134 Bluegrass Cir.
Hendersonville, TN 37075
p: 615-826-2288
f: 615-826-0500
contact: Terry Fricon
e: fricon@comcast.com
genres: All Styles
territories: Film, TV, Ads, Radio, Video Games
No unsolicited material.

Goff Law
250 N Harbor Dr., Ste. 319
Redondo Beach, CA 90277
p: 310-376-3300
f: 310-376-3318
www.gofflaw.com
contact: Roger Goff
genres: All Styles
territories: Film, TV
No unsolicited material.

Helene Blue Musique
421 7th Ave., Ste. 901
New York, NY 10001
p: 212-724-5900
f: 212-564-3113
www.helenebluemusic.com
contact: Helene Blue
e: helene@helenebluemusic.com
genres: Pop, Rock, Urban, Jazz, Broadway, Country, Reggae, Classical, Indie, Rock, Socca
territories: Film, TV, Ads, Radio, Video Games, Ringtones
Clear promo w/ Brian Kaplan first.

Jeff Wayne Music Group
97 Mortimer St.
London, W1W 7SU UK
p: 44-207-724-2471
f: 44-207-927-8364
e: info@jeffwaynemusic.com
www.jeffwaynemusic.com
contact: Jane Jones
e: jane@jeffwaynemusic.com
genres: All Styles
territories: Film, TV, Ads, Radio, Video Games
Also runs a music library.
No unsolicited material.

Jill Meyers Music Consultants
1460 4th St.
Santa Monica, CA 90401
p: 310-576-1387
f: 310-576-6989
e: jill@jillmeyersmusic.com
contact: Mike Mallen
e: mike@jillmeyersmusic.com
genres: All Styles
territories: Film, TV, Ads, Radio, Video Games
No unsolicited material.

Music Gorilla
12407 Mopac Expressway N Suite 100-#312
p: 512-918-8978
f: 512-258-6394
e: info@musicgorilla.com
www.musicgorilla.com
contact: Alexia Erlichman
e: alexia@musicgorilla.com
genres: All Styles
territories: Film, TV, Ads, Web-Video Games
Guarantees music will be heard by industry reps. No submission fee. No % of licensing taken.
See Ad On Page 39

Music Resources
6671 Sunset Blvd., #1574 A
Los Angeles, CA 90028
p: 323-993-9915

f: 323-993-9921
e: mr@musicresources.com
www.musicresources.com
contact: Nancie Stern
genres: All Styles
territories: Film, TV, Ads, Video Games
No unsolicited material.

The Parker Music Group
1354 East Ave., Ste. R, #382
Chico, CA 95926
p: 530-343-0300
f: 530-230-2725
www.musicclearance.com
contact: Kathleen Merrill
e: kathleen@musicclearance.com
genres: All Styles
territories: Film, TV, Ads, Radio, Video Games, Cell Phones, Corporate Videos, Trade Show Videos, Educational Material
Emails or links - no CDs.

The Permissions Place
2315 Fox Meadow Dr.
Allentown, PA 18104
p: 610-439-3410
f: 610-439-3412
e: thepermissionsplace@mac.com
www.thepermissionsplace.com
contact: Lisa Merlo
e: lisa@thepermissionsplace.com
genres: Rock, Pop, Folk
territories: Film, TV, Ads, Licensed Merchandise

Position Music
PO Box 25907
Los Angeles, CA 90025
p: 310-442-8170
f: 310-442-8180
www.positionmusic.com
contact: Tyler Bacon
e: tyler@positionmusic.com
genres: Rock, Electronic, Hip-Hop
territories: Film, TV, Ads, Video Games
Also does mgt. No calls.

Ruckert Music
119 W 71st St., Ste. 3A
New York, NY 10023
p: 212-724-6309
f: 212-873-8807
e: ruckmusic@aol.com
www.ruckertmusic.com
contact: Ann Ruckert
genres: All Styles
territories: Film, TV, Ads, Ringtones, Internet
Music rights & consultations.

Runs the label 13 Stories & hires out musicians for Film/TV scores. Mainly does commercials & works in-house.

Sessing Music Services
1125 E Broadway, #38
Glendale, CA 91205
p: 818-790-7269
f: 818-688-8119
www.sessingmusicservices.com
contact: Julie Sessing-Turner
e: julie@sessingmusicservices.com
genres: All Styles
territories: Film, TV, Ads, Radio, Video Games
Also does music supervision. No unsolicited material.

Songfinder
765 St. Charles Ave., Ste. 8
Atlanta, GA 30306
p: 404-876-2967
f: 404-876-5644
www.musicsongfinder.com
contact: Chris Bailey
e: chrisbailey@musicsongfinder.com
genres: All Styles
territories: Film, TV, Ads

Soundtrax Music Services
622 Front St.
Ste. 802
Nelson, BC V1L 4B7
Canada
p: 250-825-4400
f: 250-825-4449
www.soundtraxservices.com
contact: Androo Mitchell
ext: 250-825-4400 x1
e: androo@soundtraxservices.com
genres: All Styles
territories: Film, TV, Ads, Video Games, Internet, CD Compilations
Also does music placement & supervision. Send mastered material, contact info, bio & publishing/masters ownership.

Steve Gordon Law & Clearance Services
41 River Terr., Ste. 1203
New York, NY 10282
p: 212-924-1166
f: 212-924-4150
www.stevegordonlaw.com
contact: Steve Gordon
e: stevegordonlaw1@aol.com
genres: All Styles
territories: Film, TV, Ads, Radio, Video Games, Podcasts
No unsolicited material.

Sugaroo
3650 Helms Ave.
Culver City, CA 90232
p: 310-842-9151
f: 310-842-7393
e: info@sugaroo.com
www.sugaroo.com
contact: Michael Nieves
genres: All Styles
territories: Film, TV, Ads, Video Games, Trailers
No unsolicited material.

Westwood Music Group
2740 Kalsted St., Ste. 200
North Port, FL 34288
p: 941-429-9000
f: 941-429-6855
e: filmmusic@westwoodmusicgroup.com
www.westwoodmusicgroup.com
contact: Kevin McCabe
e: music@westwoodmusicgroup.com
genres: Rock, R&B, Soul, Pop, Folk, Jazz, Americana
territories: Film, TV, Ads, Radio, Video Games
Also does music publishing. Contact before sending material.

The Winogradsky Company
11240 Magnolia Blvd., Ste. 104
North Hollywood, CA 91601
p: 818-761-6906
f: 818-761-5719
www.winogradsky.com
contact: Steven Winogradsky
e: steve@winogradsky.com
territories: Film, TV, Ads, Video Games, Digital Media
Only deals w/ composers who have contracts.

Game Developers

2K Games
10 Hamilton Landing
Novato, CA 94949
p: 415-479-3634
e: inquiries@2kgames.com
www.2kgames.com
contact: Greg Gobbi
ext: 415-479-3634 x7521
e: greg.gobbi@2kgames.com
genres: Game Music
territories: Video Games
Int'l Office: 2-4 Victoria St., SL4 1EN Windsor, UK; PH: 44-175-349-6600. No unsolicited material.

3D Realms
PO Box 496389
Garland, TX 75049
p: 972-278-5655
f: 972-278-4670
www.3drealms.com
contact: George Broussard
e: georgeb@3drealms.com
genres: All Styles
territories: Video Games
No unsolicited material.

Activision
3100 Ocean Park Blvd.
Santa Monica, CA 90405
p: 310-255-2000
f: 310-255-2100
www.activision.com
contact: Tim Riley
e: timriley@activision.com
genres: All Styles
territories: Video Games
No unsolicited material.

Alpine Studios
599 S 500 E
American Fork, UT 84003
p: 801-772-0313
f: 801-756-8047
e: info@alpine-studios.com
www.alpine-studios.com
contact: Les Pardew
e: les@alpine-studios.com
genres: All Styles
territories: Video Games

Amaze Entertainment
12421 Willows Rd. NE, #200
Kirkland, WA 98034
p: 425-825-6800
f: 425-825-6700
e: info@amazeent.com
www.amazeent.com
contact: Brent Latta
e: blatta@amazeent.com
territories: Film, Video Games

Babaroga
1400 N La Salle Blvd.
Chicago, IL 60610
p: 312-375-1946
e: contact@babaroga.com
www.babaroga.com
contact: Andreja Djokovic
e: andreja@babaroga.com
territories: Video Games

Backbone Entertainment
1375 55th St.
Emeryville, CA 94608
p: 510-547-6101
f: 510-547-6104
e: pr@f9e.com
www.backboneentertainment.com; www.f9e.com
genres: All Styles
territories: Video Games

Blue Fang Games
1601 Trapelo Rd., Ste. 105
Waltham, MA 02451
p: 781-547-5475
f: 781-547-5480
e: press@bluefang.com
www.bluefang.com
contact: Hank Howie
territories: Video Games
No unsolicited material.

Capcom
800 Concar Dr., Ste. 300
San Mateo, CA 94402
p: 650-350-6500
f: 650-350-6655
www.capcom.com
territories: Video Games
No unsolicited material.

Critical Mass Interactive
7427 N Lamar Blvd., Ste. 200
Austin, TX 78752
p: 512-219-1600
f: 512-219-1976
e: jobs@criticalmassinteractive.com
www.criticalmassinteractive.com
contact: Billy Cain
genres: All Styles
territories: Video Games
Send CD or DVDs to: PO Box 203924, Austin, TX 78729. No calls.

Delta Tao Software
8032 Twin Oaks
Citrus Heights, CA 95610
p: 408-730-9336
www.deltatao.com
contact: Nancy Williams
e: nancy@deltatao.com
genres: All Styles
territories: Video Games
No unsolicited material.

Electronic Arts
5510 Lincoln Blvd.
Playa Vista, CA 90094
p: 310-754-7000
f: 310-754-7099
www.ea.com
contact: Raphi Lima
ext: 310-754-7204
e: rlima@ea.com
genres: All Styles
territories: Video Games
No unsolicited material.

Empire Interactive
9442 Capital of Texas Hwy. N, Plaza 1, Ste. 500
Austin, TX 78759
p: 512-343-4585
f: 866-473-6091
www.empireinteractive.com
contact: Simon Jeffrey
ext: 415-439-4854

e: simon.jeffrey@empireinteractive.com
territories: Video Games
No unsolicited material.

Epic Games
620 Crossroads Blvd.
Cary, NC 27511
p: 919-854-0070
f: 919-854-0055
e: licensing@epicgames.com
www.epicgames.com
contact: Michael Larson
e: mike.larson@epicgames.com
genres: All Styles
territories: Video Games
No unsolicited material.

Genuine Games
6303 Owensmouth Ave., 10th Fl.
Woodland Hills, CA 91376
p: 818-936-3452 x2445
f: 818-936-2964
e: info@genuinegames.com
www.genuinegames.com
genres: All Styles
territories: Video Games
No unsolicited material.

High Voltage Software
2345 Pembroke Ave.
Hoffman Estates, IL 60169
p: 847-490-9567
f: 847-490-9951
e: info@high-voltage.com
www.high-voltage.com
contact: John Kopecky
e: john.kopecky@high-voltage.com
territories: Video Games

Music Departments

ABC Television
4151 Prospect Ave.
Los Angeles, CA 90027
p: 323-671-5211
f: 323-671-3311
www.abc.com
contact: Gregory Yantek
e: gregory.e.yantek@abc.com
territories: TV
No unsolicited material.

Bunim Murray Productions
6007 Sepulveda Blvd.
Van Nuys, CA 91411
p: 818-756-5118
f: 818-756-5140
www.bunim-murray.com
contact: Dave Stone
e: dstone@bunim-murray.com
territories: TV
Promos: Music Dept., PO Box 10421, Van Nuys, CA 91410. No calls.

CBS Television
1675 Broadway, 17th Fl.
New York, NY 10019
p: 646-557-4321
f: 212-265-9371
www.cbs.com
contact: Donald Steever
ext: 646-557-4322
e: dsteever@cbs.com
territories: TV
CA office: Karen Takata, 323-634-3415; karen.takata@cbs.com.

Dino de Laurentiis
100 Universal City Plaza, Bungalow 5195
Universal City, CA 91608
p: 818-777-2111
f: 818-866-5566
www.unistudios.com
contact: Stuart Boros
e: stuart.boros@univfilms.com
territories: Film, TV
No unsolicited material.

DreamWorks
100 Universal City Plaza, Bldg. 4115
Universal City, CA 91608
p: 818-695-5000
f: 818-695-6570
www.dreamworks.com
contact: Julie Butchko
ext: 818-695-6484
territories: Film
No unsolicited material.

ESPN
545 Middle St.
Bristol, CT 06010
p: 860-766-2000
f: 860-766-2428
www.espn.com
contact: Claude Mitchell
e: claude.mitchell@espn.com
genres: Upbeat Sports Music
territories: TV
No unsolicited material.

Faulconer Productions
17817 Davenport Rd., #110
Dallas, TX 75252
p: 972-818-2427
f: 972-818-2686
e: info@cakemixrecording.com
www.faulconer.com; www.cakemixrecording.com
contact: Lisa Faulconer
e: lisa@faulconer.com
genres: All Styles
territories: Film, TV, Ads, Radio, Video Games
No unsolicited material.

Fox Music
10201 W Pico Blvd.
Los Angeles, CA 90064
p: 310-369-1000
f: 310-369-3102
www.foxmusic.com
contact: Jerry Davis
ext: 310-369-6616
e: jerry.davis@fox.com
territories: Film, TV
No unsolicited material.

Fox Sports
10201 W Pico Blvd.
Bldg. 101, Rm. 3500
Los Angeles, CA 90035
p: 310-369-1000
f: 310-969-6319
www.foxsports.com
contact: Jerry Davis
ext: 310-369-6616
e: jerry.davis@fox.com
genres: All Styles
territories: TV

Lawrence Bender Productions
8530 Wilshire Blvd., Ste. 500

Los Angeles, CA 90211
p: 323-951-4600
f: 323-951-4401
contact: Lawrence Bender
e: lbasst2@abandapart.com
genres: All Styles
territories: Film, TV
No unsolicited material.

Millennium Films/ Nu Image
6423 Wilshire Blvd.
Los Angeles, CA 90048
p: 310-388-6900
f: 323-939-2924
contact: Ashley Miller
e: ashm@earthlink.net
genres: All Styles
territories: Film
Send CDs in a labeled jewel case w/ title of project on outside of the package & include your contact info. Material not returned. No calls.

MTV
770 Broadway, 10th Fl.
New York, NY 10003
p: 212-258-8000
f: 212-654-7034
www.mtv.com
contact: Allison Thiel
ext: 212-654-5997
e: allison.thiel@mtvstaff.com
territories: Film, TV
For MTV Music, contact: Wills Glasspiegel, 212-654-7210; william.glasspiegel@mtvnmix.com. For MTV Specials contact: Caprice Crane, 212-758-1524; cinnamongrrrl1@aol.com. No unsolicited material.

NBC Universal
30 Rockefeller Plaza, 16th Fl.
New York, NY 10112
p: 212-664-4444
f: 212-664-6644
www.nbc.com
contact: Cira Limoli Nisco
ext: 212-664-3564
e: cira.limolinisco@nbcuni.com
territories: TV
For CA shows contact: Alicen Catron Schneider, 818-777-0192; alicen.schneider@nbcuni.com. No unsolicited material.

New Line Cinema
116 N Robertson Blvd., Ste. 700
Los Angeles, CA 90048
p: 310-854-5811
f: 310-854-0422
www.newline.com
contact: Paul Broucek
ext: 310-967-6930
e: paul.broucek@newline.com
territories: Film, TV
No unsolicited material.

Oxygen Media
75 9th Ave., 7th Fl.
New York, NY 10011
p: 212-651-2000
f: 212-651-2038
e: feedback@oxygen.com
www.oxygen.com
contact: John
genres: All Styles
territories: TV
Call before sending material.

Paramount Pictures Film Music
5555 Melrose Ave., Roddenberry Bldg., Rm. 4035
Hollywood, CA 90038
p: 323-956-5000
f: 323-862-3736
www.paramount.com
contact: Denise Carver
ext: 323-956-4121
e: denise_carver@paramount.com
territories: Film, TV
No unsolicited material.

Remote Control Productions
1547 14th St.
Santa Monica, CA 90404
p: 310-260-3171
f: 310-260-3172
territories: Film, TV
No unsolicited material.

Saban Music Group
10100 Santa Monica Blvd., Ste. 2600
Los Angeles, CA 90067
p: 310-557-5177
f: 310-235-5172
www.saban.com
contact: Teri Nelson-Carpenter
e: teri@saban.com
genres: All Styles
territories: Film, TV
No unsolicited material.

Sesame Workshop
1 Lincoln Plaza, 3rd Fl.
New York, NY 10023
p: 212-875-6625
www.sesameworkshop.org
contact: Sharon Lyew
ext: 212-875-6910
e: sharon.lyew@sesameworkshop.org
genres: Children's
territories: TV
All music produced in-house. No unsolicited material.

Sony Pictures
10202 W Washington Blvd., Thalberg Annex 2008
Culver City, CA 90232
p: 310-244-4000
f: 310-244-2258
www.sonypictures.com
contact: Lia Vollack
ext: 310-244-8681
e: lia_vollack@spe.sony.com
genres: All Styles
territories: Film
No unsolicited material.

Universal Pictures
100 Universal City Plaza, Bldg. 1320 W
Universal City, CA 91608
p: 818-777-1000
f: 818-866-1513
www.nbcuni.com
contact: Kathy Nelson
ext: 818-777-3800
e: kathy.nelson@nbcuni.com
territories: Film
No unsolicited material.

Walt Disney Music
500 S Buena Vista St.
Burbank, CA 91521
p: 818-560-1000
f: 818-560-9080
www.disney.com
contact: Chris Montan
ext: 818-560-7495
e: chris.montan@disney.com
territories: Film
Mail must use 4-digit mail code after the zip code. Chris Montan: 1877. No unsolicited material.

Warner Brothers Pictures Music
4000 Warner Blvd.
Burbank, CA 91522

p: 818-954-1606
f: 818-954-3418
www.warnerbros.com
contact: Niki Sherrod
e: niki.sherrod@warnerbros.com
territories: Film, Video Games, Internet
Provides music for WB & New Line Cinema films. TV contact, Gay DiFusco, 818-954-3104; gay.difusco@warnerbros.com. Only submissions by an authorized agent or attorney.

Music Libraries

5 Alarm Music
35 W Dayton St.
Pasadena, CA 91105
p: 626-304-1698
f: 626-795-2058
e: info@5alarmmusic.com
www.5alarmmusic.com
contact: E. Tyler Harp
e: tyler@5alarmmusic.com
genres: All Styles
territories: Film, TV, Ads, Radio, Video Games
Also does placement, supervision & editing & has over 39 Music Libraries. No unsolicited material.

5.1 FX
1232 17th Ave. S
Nashville, TN 37212
p: 615-320-5050
f: 615-340-9559
e: info@jamsync.com
www.5point1fx.com
contact: KK Proffitt
e: kk@jamsync.com
genres: Mainly Sound Effects
territories: Film, TV, Ads, Radio, Video Games
Also has full service post production facility specializing in surround sound.

615 Music Productions
1030 16th Ave. S
Nashville, TN 37212
p: 615-244-6515
f: 615-242-2455
e: info@615music.com
www.615music.com
contact: Randy Wachtler
ext: 615-244-6515 x102
territories: Film, TV, Ads, Radio, Video Games
No unsolicited material.

ACM Records
PO Box 195
Fair Lawn, NJ 07410
p: 201-796-0848
f: 201-796-0848
www.acmrecords.com
contact: Eve Adams
ext: 201-637-0977
e: eve@acmrecords.com
genres: Action, Ambient, Jazz, Blues, Country, Electronica, Jazz, Rock, Metal, Hardcore, Classical, Goth, Urban, World
territories: Film, TV, Radio, Video Games
Also does large Classical orchestrations on a project by project basis. See site before sending material.

AirCraft Production Music Library
162 Columbus Ave.
Boston, MA 02116
p: 617-303-7600; 800-343-2514
e: info@aircraftmusiclibrary.com
www.aircraftmusiclibrary.com
contact: Josh Hoekwater
e: jhoekwater@aircraftmusiclibrary.com
genres: Blues, Ethnic, Jazz, Latin, New Age, Rock, Urban, Classical, Broadcast Specialty
territories: Film, TV, Ads, Radio, Video Games
No unsolicited material.

Archive Of Contemporary Music
54 White St.
New York, NY 10013
p: 212-226-6967
e: arcmusic@inch.com
www.arcmusic.org
contact: B. George
genres: All Styles
territories: Film, TV, Ads, Radio, Video Games, Educational Videos
Largest archive of popular music in the world. Send 2 copies of everything.

Associated Production Music
381 Park Ave. S, Ste. 1101
New York, NY 10016
p: 800-276-6874; 212-856-9800
f: 212-856-9807
e: accountservices@apmmusic.com
www.apmmusic.com
contact: Richard Judice
e: rjudice@apmmusic.com
genres: All Styles
territories: Film, TV, Ads, Radio, Video Games
CA office: 323-461-3211. No unsolicited material.

Audio Recording Unlimited
400 N Michigan Ave., #1900
Chicago, IL 60611
p: 312-527-7000
f: 312-527-3360
e: brake@aruchicago.com
www.aruchicago.com
contact: Jessie LaBelle
e: jlabelle@aruchicago.com
territories: Film, TV, Ads, Radio
No unsolicited material.

Brassheart Music
256 S Robertson Blvd., #2288
Beverly Hills, CA 90211
p: 323-932-0534
f: 323-937-6884
e: brassheartmusic@aol.com
www.brassheartmusic.com
www.dreamaworld.com
contact: Bunny Hull
genres: Pop, Children's, Alt., Gospel, Latin, R&B, Jazz
territories: Film, TV, Ads
No unsolicited material.

Chris Stone Audio Productions
45 Charles St. E, 3rd Fl.
Toronto, ON M4Y 1S2
Canada
p: 877-920-6700; 416-923-6700
f: 416-923-3351
www.stockmusicconsultants.com
contact: Chris Stone
e: csap@interlog.com
genres: Rock, Techno, Blues, Folk, Jazz, Classical
territories: Film, TV

Creative Musical Services
13547 Ventura Blvd., Ste. 358
Sherman Oaks, CA 91423
p: 818-426-7727
e: info@creativemusicalsvcs.com
www.creativemusicalsvcs.com
contact: Dana Ferandelli
territories: Film, TV, Ads, Radio, Video Games
No unsolicited material.

CSS Music/D.A.W.N.
1948 Riverside Dr.
Los Angeles, CA 90039
p: 800-468-6874
e: info@css.com
www.cssmusic.com
contact: Michael Fuller
genres: All Styles
territories: Film, TV, Ads, Radio, Video Games
Material on a case-by-case basis.

Dewolfe/Corelli Jacobs Music Library
25 W 45th St., Ste. 401
New York, NY 10036
p: 212-382-0220
f: 212-382-0278
e: info@dewolfemusic.com
www.dewolfemusic.com
contact: Andrew Jacobs
e: ajacobs@dewolfemusic.com
genres: Contemporary, Pop, Rock, Jazz, Classical, Hip-Hop, Ethnic, Dance, Electronica
territories: Film, TV, Ads, Radio, Video Games
Call before sending material.

DL Music
3575 Cahuenga Blvd. W, Ste. 400
Los Angeles, CA 90068
p: 323-878-0400
www.dl-music.com
contact: David Zumsteg
e: davez@dl-music.com
genres: All Styles
territories: Film, TV, Ads, Radio, Video Games, Internet
Call before sending material.

DSM Producers
PO Box 1160
Marco Island, FL 34146
p: 212-245-0006
f: 239-393-1754
contact: Suzan Bader
genres: Rock, Jazz, Latin, Hip-Hop, Country, CCM
territories: Film, TV
Seeks master recordings from artists w/ legal representation.

E-MU Systems
1500 Green Hills Rd., Ste. 101
Scotts Valley, CA 95066
p: 888-372-1372
f: 831-439-0363
www.emu.com
genres: Electronic
territories: Film, TV, Ads, Radio, Video Games
No unsolicited material.

Extreme Music
1547 14th St.
Santa Monica, CA 90404
p: 800-542-9494
f: 310-395-0409
e: info@extrememusic.com
www.extrememusic.com
contact: Joe Mazzone
e: joe@extrememusic.com
genres: All Styles
territories: Film, TV, Ads, Radio, Video Games
No unsolicited material.

Fresh Music
34 S Main St.
Hanover, NH 03755
p: 800-545-0688
f: 603-643-1388
e: freshmusic@mac.com
www.freshmusic.com
contact: Tom Cote
ext: 888-211-8576
genres: Alt., Rock, Blues, New Age, Jazz, Ska
territories: Film, TV, Ads, Radio, Video Games
CDs, MP3s & links.

Gene Michael Productions
306 E Main St., Ste. 110
Niles, MI 49120
p: 800-955-0619
e: info@gmpmusic.com
www.gmpmusic.com
contact: Gene Ort
genres: All Styles
territories: Film, TV, Ads, Radio
No unsolicited material.

G-Man Music & Radical Radio
5000 Beckley Ave.
Woodland Hills, CA 91364
p: 818-223-8486
f: 818-224-3439
e: immedia@pacbell.net
www.gmanmusic.com
contact: Scott G.
e: scott@gmanmusic.com
genres: Electronic, Pop, Rock, Alt., Easy Listening, Country, Trance, Dance
territories: Film, TV, Ads, Radio, Video Games, Internet, CD-ROM, Viral Videos
No unsolicited material.

Groove Addicts Production Music Catalogue
12211 W Washington Blvd.
Los Angeles, CA 90066
p: 800-400-6767
f: 310-572-4654
e: info@grooveaddicts.com
www.grooveaddicts.com
contact: Bill Stolier
e: bill@grooveaddicts.com
genres: Alt., Dance, Rock, New Age, World, Hip-Hop, Jazz, Blues
territories: Film, TV, Ads, Radio
CDs only.

Intricate Unit
47 Hull St.
Ansonia, CT 06401
p: 203-668-7162
f: 203-723-9546
e: intricateunit@gmail.com
www.intricateunit.com
contact: Ben Kopec

e: benkopec@gmail.com
genres: Dark Acoustic Guitar, Hard Industrial Rock, Dark Dance, Diverse Electronic, Jazz, Blues, Edgy Orchestral, Rock, Metal
territories: Film, TV, Video Games

JRT Music
143 28th St.
Brooklyn, NY 11232
p: 718-499-4635
f: 718-499-0470
e: info@jrtmusic.com
www.jrtmusic.com
contact: Catherine Bogin
e: cat@jrtmusic.com
genres: All Styles
territories: Film, TV, Ads, Radio, Video Games
No unsolicited material.

Killer Tracks/ Network Music
8750 Wilshire Blvd., Ste.200
Beverly Hills, CA 90211
p: 310-358-4455; 800-454-5537
f: 310-358-4470
e: sales@killertracks.com; production@killertracks.com
www.networkmusic.com
contact: Kat Green
e: kgreen@killertracks.com
genres: Rock, Hip-Hop, Electronica, Jazz, Orchestral, World
territories: Film, TV, Ads, Radio, Video Games

Manhattan Production Music
355 W 52nd St., 6th Fl.
New York, NY 10019
p: 800-227-1954; 212-333-5766
f: 212-262-0814
e: info@mpmmusic.com
www.mpmmusic.com
contact: Ron Goldberg
genres: All Styles
territories: Film, TV, Ads, Radio, Video Games
No unsolicited material.

Master Source
28030 Dorothy Dr., Ste. 201
Agoura Hills, CA 91301
p: 818-706-9000
f: 818-706-1900
e: info@mastersource.com
www.mastersource.com
contact: Marc Ferrari
ext: 818-994-3400
genres: All Styles
territories: Film, TV, Ads, Radio, Video Games, Corporate
No unsolicited material.

Megatrax
7629 Fulton Ave.
North Hollywood, CA 91605
p: 818-255-7100
f: 818-255-7199
e: info@megatrax.com
www.megatrax.com
contact: Belinda Robles
genres: All Styles
territories: Film, TV
Now distributing Amusicom.

Metro Music Productions
37 W 20th St.
New York, NY 10011
p: 212-229-1700
f: 212-229-9063
contact: Mitch Coodley
e: mcoodley@metromusicinc.com
genres: All Styles
territories: Film, TV, Ads, Radio
Send link to your MP3s/site or send CDs.

Music Bakery
7522 Campbell Rd., #113
Dallas, TX 75248
p: 800-229-0313; 972-578-7863
f: 972-424-3680
e: helpnow@musicbakery.com
www.musicbakery.com
contact: Jack Waldenmaier
e: jackw@musicbakery.com
genres: All Styles
territories: Film, TV, Radio, Video Games

The Music Group
16161 Ventura Blvd., Ste. 714
Encino, CA 91436
p: 818-342-1385
f: 818-342-FAXX
e: mscgrp@aol.com.com
contact: Danny Sheridan
ext: 818-342-1385 x1
genres: Rock, AC Rock, House, Blues, Outlaw Country, Alt. Country, Country, Hip-Hop, Electronica, Trance, Ambient,
territories: Film, TV, Radio, Advertising, Video Games
Email before sending material.

NOMA Music
2219 E Thousand Oaks Blvd., #295
Thousand Oaks, CA 91362
p: 805-498-4900
f: 805-498-5241
e: licensing@nomamusic.com
www.nomamusic.com
contact: Jim Justice
e: jimjustice@nomamusic.com

genres: All Styles
territories: Film, TV, Ads, Video Games, Animation, Video, Multimedia
Contact before sending kits.

Non Stop Music
915 W 100 S
Salt Lake City, UT 84104
p: 801-531-0060
f: 801-531-0346
e: info@nonstopmusic.com
www.nonstopmusic.com
contact: Randy Thornton
e: randy@nonstopmusic.com
genres: All Styles
territories: Film, TV
Also does music supervision, contact: Tim Arnold, 818-752-1898; tim@nonstopmusic.com. No unsolicited material.

OGM Production
6464 Sunset Blvd., #790
Hollywood, CA 90028
p: 800-421-4163
f: 323-461-1543
e: info@ogmmusic.com
www.ogmmusic.com
contact: Ole George
genres: Classical, Soft Rock, Pop, Jazz, Contemporary
territories: Film, TV
No unsolicited material.

Omnimusic
52 Main St.
Port Washington, NY 11050
p: 800-828-6664
f: 516-883-0271
e: omni@omnimusic.com
www.omnimusic.com
contact: Barbara Ring
e: bring@omnimusic.com
genres: All Styles
territories: Film, TV, Ads, Radio, Video Games
Submissions: Dave Hab, dave@omnimusic.com. Also runs Omni BlueDot, Flash Point Music, CDM Library & Omni SFX Music Libraries.

Pat Appleson Studios
2359 Hwy. 70 SE, Ste. 102
Hickory, NC 28602
p: 828-465-5500
f: 828-465-0440
www.appleson.com
contact: Pat Appleson
e: appleson@gate.net
genres: All Styles
territories: Film, TV, Radio, Web
No unsolicited material.

Private Wavs
907 Foursome Dr.
Castle Rock, CO 80104
p: 720-733-6830
f: 303-814-1317
e: info@privatewavs.com
www.privatewavs.com
contact: Brett Walker
ext: 714-536-8032
genres: Mainstream Rock
territories: Film, TV
No unsolicited material.

Production Garden
510 E Ramsey, Ste. 4
San Antonio, TX 78216
p: 800-247-5317
f: 210-530-5230
e: info@productiongarden.com
www.productiongarden.com
contact: Mel Taylor
e: mel@productiongarden.com
genres: All Styles
territories: Film, TV, Radio, Ads, Educational Training, Corporate Video Promos
Call before sending material.

Public Domain Research
PO Box 3102
Margate City, NJ 08402
p: 800-827-9401
f: 609-822-1638
e: info@pubdomain.com
www.pubdomain.com
contact: Sharon Walter
genres: All Styles
territories: Film, TV, Ads, Radio
No unsolicited material.

Radio Mall
2412 Unity Ave., N, Dept. WEB
Minneapolis, MN 55422
p: 763-522-6256
f: 763-522-6256
e: info@radio-mall.com
www.radiomall.com
contact: Dave Dworkin
genres: All Styles
territories: Film, TV, Radio
Submit complete & ready-to-sell products only.

Reliable Source Music
67 Upper Berkeley St.
London, W1H 7QX UK
p: 44-207-563-7028
f: 44-207-563-7029
e: library@reliable-source.co.uk
www.reliable-source.co.uk
contact: Wayne Bickerton
genres: Dance, R&B, Rock, Hip-Hop, Classical, Jazz, Funk
territories: Film, TV, Ads, Radio, Video Games
Production music & non-commercial demos only.

Ren Music Library
1544 Irving St., Ste. 210
Rahway, NJ 07065
p: 732-382-6815
f: 732-382-5329
e: renmedia@aol.com
www.renmusiclibrary.com
contact: Joe Kurasz
genres: Underscore, Composition
territories: Film, TV
Composer material only.

River City Sound
PO Box 750786
Memphis, TN 38175
p: 800-755-8729
f: 901-274-8494
e: info@rivercitysound.com
www.rivercitysound.com
contact: Bob Pierce
genres: Instrumental
territories: Film, TV, Radio
No unsolicited material.

Serafine
PO Box 1798

Simi Valley, CA 93065
p: 310-399-9279
www.frankserafine.com
contact: Frank Serafine
e: fserafine@earthlink.net
genres: Film, World
territories: Film, TV, Ads, Radio, Video Games, Interactive
CDs only.

Sounddogs.com
2633 Lincoln Blvd., #148
Santa Monica, CA 90405
p: 877-315-3647
f: 310-496-3135
e: support@sounddogs.com
www.sounddogs.com
genres: All Styles of Production Music
territories: Film, TV, Ads, Radio, Video Games
Must be professionally mastered production music. Email link & catalog.

Taxi
5010 N Pkwy. Calabasas, Ste. 200
Calabasas, CA 91302
p: 800-458-2111
f: 818-888-8811
e: memberservices@taxi.com
www.taxi.com
contact: Clint McBay
e: clint@taxi.com
genres: All Styles
territories: Film, TV
Must become a Taxi member to submit.

Timeless Entertainment
15 Alicante Aisle
Irvine, CA 92614
p: 949-756-1600
f: 949-756-1661
e: info@timelessentertainment.com
www.timelessentertainment.com
contact: Fred Bailin
e: fbailin@goldisc.com
genres: Pop, Rock, R&B, Jazz, Hip-Hop, Vocal, Big Band, Easy Listening
territories: Film, TV
Send CD w/ return address info.

Transition Music
PO Box 2586
Toluca Lake, CA 91610
p: 323-860-7074
f: 323-860-7986
e: onestopmus@aol.com
www.transitionmusic.com
contact: Mike Dobson
e: onestopmusic@sbcglobal.net
genres: All Styles
territories: Film, TV, Ads, Radio, Video Games
Send CDs, emails or links. No tapes & no calls.

Trax Connection
PO Box 618
Stratford, NJ 08084
p: 856-783-2245
f: 856-783-2247
e: info@traxconnection.com
www.traxconnection.com
contact: Tom Adams
e: tomadams@traxconnection.com
genres: All Styles
territories: Film, TV, Ads, Radio, Video Games
No unsolicited material.

Unique Tracks
PO Box 150414,
Van Brunt Stn.
Brooklyn, NY 11215
p: 718-965-2318
f: 718-965-1215
e: info@uniquetracks.com
www.uniquetracks.com
contact: John Bickerton
genres: Contemporary, Dance, Electronica, Soundtrack, Jazz, Classical
territories: Film, TV, Ads, Radio, Video Games, Web, Corporate
CDs only. No emails or links.

VideoHelper
18 W 21st St.,
7th Fl.
New York, NY 10010
p: 212-633-7009
f: 212-633-9014
e: info@videohelper.com
www.videohelper.com
contact: Brian Randazzo
e: brian@videohelper.com
genres: All Styles
territories: Film, TV, Ads, Radio, Video Games

Music Placement

Evolution Music Partners
9100 Wilshire Blvd.,
Ste. 201
Beverly Hills, CA 90212
p: 310-623-3388
f: 310-623-1897
e: info@evolutionmusicpartners.com
www.evolutionmusicpartners.com
contact: Seth Kaplan
genres: All Styles
territories: Film, TV
Submit material online.

Feature Sounds
2249 Duane St.,
Ste. 4
Los Angeles, CA 90039
p: 323-698-9615
f: 323-698-9619
e: info@featuresounds.com; submission@featuresounds.com
www.featuresounds.com
contact: Irene Tuomainen
e: irene@featuresounds.com
genres: All Styles
territories: Film, TV, Ads, Radio, Video Games, Ringtones, Multimedia
Sonicbids EPKS only.

Indie911
8949 Sunset Blvd.,
Ste. 201
West Hollywood, CA 90069
p: 310-943-7164
f: 310-919-3091
e: info@indie911.com
www.indie911.com
contact: Gregg Allen
e: gregg@indie911.com
genres: All Styles
territories: Film, TV, Ads, Radio, Video Games, Ringtones
Works specifically w/ Indie artists. CDs must be labeled & include contact name, artist name, phone number & email.

Kaufman Agency
12007 Laurel Terrace Dr.
Studio City, CA 91604
p: 818-506-6013
f: 818-506-7270
www.kaufmanagency.net
contact: Jeff H. Kaufman
e: jhk@pacbell.net
genres: Music Soundtracks
territories: Film, TV, Radio, Advertising, Video Games
Represents composers, lyricists & S/S. Must have quality & previous experience in Film & TV.

Natural Energy Lab
7424 1/2 Sunset Blvd.,
Ste. 5
Los Angeles, CA 90046
p: 323-876-2408
f: 323-874-0442
www.naturalenergylab.com
contact: Danny Benair
e: danny@naturalenergylab.com
genres: All Styles
territories: Film, TV, Ads, Radio, Video Games, Internet
Specializes in the creative placement of songs. Email before submitting material.

Shelly Bay Music
49 Irving Pl., Ste. 1F
New York, NY 10003
p: 212-529-3945
www.shellybay.com
contact: Michelle Bayer
e: michelle@shellybay.com
genres: All Styles
territories: Film, TV, Ads, Video Games, Ringtones
No unsolicited material.

Shop For Songs
1223 Wilshire Blvd.,
Ste. 1610
Santa Monica, CA 90403
p: 888-OF-SONGS
f: 310-578-2304
e: services@circleofsongs.com
www.circleofsongs.com
genres: All Styles
territories: Film, TV, Ads, Radio, Video Games
Must be a member to submit.

True Talent Management
9663 Santa Monica Blvd.,
#320, Dept. MA
Beverly Hills, CA 90210
p: 310-560-1290
f: 310-441-2005
e: webinfo@truetalentmgmt.com
www.truetalentmgmt.com
contact: Jennifer Yeko
e: musiciansatlas@truetalentmgmt.com
genres: All Styles, mainly Rock, Pop, S/S/, Hip-Hop
territories: Film, TV, Radio, Advertising, Video Games
Boutique firm also does management.
Email before sending material.

VersusMedia
556 S Fair Oaks Ave.,
#245
Pasadena, CA 91105
p: 877-633-8764
e: info@versusmedia.com
www.versusmedia.com
contact: Ryan Vinson
e: ryanv@versusmedia.com
genres: All Styles
territories: Film, TV, Video Games
No unsolicited material.

Music Supervision

35 Sound
PO Box 217
Pacific Palisades, CA 90272
p: 310-454-1280
e: info@35sound.com
www.35sound.com
contact: G. Marq Roswell
genres: All Styles
territories: Film, TV, Ads
No unsolicited material.

The Agency Group
1880 Century Park E,
#711
Los Angeles, CA
90067
p: 310-385-2800
f: 310-385-1220
www.theagencygroup.com
contact: Linda Kordek
e: lindakordek@theagencygroup.com
genres: All Styles
territories: Film, TV, Ads, Video Games
No unsolicited material.

Air-Edel Associates
18 Rodmarton St.
London, W1U 8BJ UK
p: 44-207-486-6466
f: 44-207-224-0344
e: air-edel@air-edel.co.uk
www.air-edel.co.uk
contact: Matt Biffa
e: mbiffa@air-edel.co.uk
genres: All Styles
territories: Film, TV, Ads, Video Games
CA office: Mark Thomas, 310-205-5079; mark.thomas@air-edel.co.uk. Contact Mike Biffa before sending CDs.

Antonelli Music
1014 4th St., #11
Santa Monica, CA 90403
p: 818-655-5922
f: 818-655-8342
contact: Paul Antonelli
e: hawk111972@aol.com
genres: All Styles
territories: TV
Email before sending material.

Arlene Fishbach Enterprises
1223 Wilshire Blvd,
#304
Santa Monica, CA 90403
p: 310-451-5916
f: 310-393-5313
e: afent@att.net
contact: Arlene Fishbach
territories: Film, TV, Feature Trailers, Promos
No unsolicited material.

Arpix Media
670 Richmond St. W,
Ste. 201
Toronto, ON M6J 1C3
Canada
p: 416-203-3547
f: 416-203-5207
e: studio@arpix.com
www.arpix.com
contact: Chris Robinson
ext: 416-203-3547 x207
e: chris@arpix.com
genres: All Styles
territories: Film, TV, Ads, Video Games
No unsolicited material.

Avatar Records
2029 Hyperion Ave.
Los Angeles, CA 90027
p: 323-878-1100
e: info@avatarrecords.com
www.avatarrecords.com
contact: Lynnette Jenkins
e: lynnette@avatarrecords.com
genres: Hip-Hop, R&B, Soundtracks, Latin, Reggaeton
territories: Film, TV, Ads, Radio
Also has music library. CDs only.

Bass/Treble Staff Productions
PO Box 382
Pacifica, CA 94044
p: 415-863-9021
e: hsl@sprintmail.com
contact: Hank London
genres: All Styles
territories: Film, TV, Ads, Radio, Video Games
Contact before sending kits.

Brewman Music Entertainment
1337 Talmadge St.
Los Angeles, CA 90027
p: 310-318-4104
f: 310-356-3557
e: infowest@bmemusic.com
www.bmemusic.com
contact: Alan Brewer
genres: All Styles
territories: Film, TV, Ads, Radio
No unsolicited material.

Chris Douridas
1900 Pico Blvd.
Santa Monica, CA 90405
p: 310-420-7766
f: 310-202-6981
www.chrisdouridas.com
contact: Chris Douridas
e: chrisdouridas@gmail.com
genres: All Styles
territories: Film, TV, iTunes
CDs only.

Cinecall Soundtracks
PO Box 854
Red Bank, NJ 07701
p: 732-450-8882
e: mail@cinecall.com
www.cinecall.com
contact: George McMorrow
genres: All Styles
territories: Film, TV
No unsolicited material.

Clearance Dept.com
c/o Michael Welsh Productions,
2215 Lambert Dr.
Pasadena, CA 91107
p: 626-796-7821
f: 626-796-0847
www.clearancedept.com
contact: Michael Welsh
ext: 818-766-2106
e: michael@clearancedept.com
genres: All Styles
territories: Film, TV, Digital Media, Internet
No unsolicited material.

Clearsongs
601 W 26th,
Ste. 1765
New York, NY 10001
p: 212-627-8767
f: 646-349-1110
e: info@clearsongs.com
www.clearsongs.com
contact: Jim Black
e: jim@clearsongs.com
genres: All Styles
territories: Film, TV, Ads, Video Games
No unsolicited material.

Collins Music
333 Washington Blvd.,
#343
Marina Del Rey, CA 90292
p: 310-283-4864
contact: Steve Collins
e: collinsmusic2002@yahoo.com
genres: All Styles
territories: Film, TV, Ads, Video Games
No unsolicited material.

Compact Collections
8-12 Camden High St.,
3rd Fl.
London, NW1 0JH UK
p: 44-207-874-7480
f: 44-207-383-7868
e: info@compactcollections.com
www.compactcollections.com
contact: James Sellar
e: jsellar@compactcollections.com
genres: All Styles
territories: Film, TV, Video Games

Creative Control
3427 Overland Ave.
Los Angeles, CA 90034
p: 310-845-7146
f: 310-237-5311
e: info@creativecontrolent.com
www.creativecontrolent.com
contact: Joel C. High
genres: All Styles
territories: Film, TV
Contact before sending material.

David Franco Int'l Music Productions
4342 Redwood Ave.,
Ste. 310
Marina Del Rey, CA 90292
p: 310-823-5547
f: 310-821-0707
e: dfintlprod@aol.com
contact: David Franco
genres: All Styles
territories: Film, TV, Soundtrack Album Production
Also offers music production, supervision, clearance & licensing. Call before sending kits.

De Roche Music
17153 Rayen St.
Northridge, CA 91325
p: 818-886-5262
f: 818-886-2090
e: derochemusic@aol.com
www.derochemusic.com
contact: Ross De Roche
e: ross@derochemusic.com
genres: Original Scores
territories: Film, TV, Video Games
No unsolicited material.

Demon Music Group
33 Foley St.
London, W1W 7TL UK
p: 44-207-612-3303
f: 44-207-612-3366
e: info@tracklicensing.com
www.tracklicensing.com
contact: Glen D. D'Souza
e: glen.d'souza@demonmusicgroup.co.uk
genres: Pop, Rock, Electronic, Rap, Hip-Hop
territories: Film, TV, Ads, Video Games
Submit CDs only.

Dilbeck Entertainment
5855 Greenvalley Cir.,
#310
Culver City, CA 90230
p: 310-670-0704
contact: Michael Dilbeck
e: md90230@aol.com
genres: Pop
territories: Film, TV
No unsolicited material.

Don Grierson
7651 Woodrow Wilson Dr.
Los Angeles, CA 90046
p: 323-874-6992
f: 323-874-7655
www.dongrierson.com
contact: Don Grierson
e: donunda@earthlink.net
genres: All Styles
territories: Film, TV
Contact before sending kits.

Ears To The Drum
e: earstothedrum@mindspring.com
contact: Dan Lieberstein
genres: All Styles
territories: Film, TV, Ads
No unsolicited material.

Firstcom Music
1325 Capital Pkwy.,
Ste. 109
Carrollton, TX 75006
p: 800-858-8880
f: 972-242-6526
e: info@firstcom.com
www.firstcom.com
contact: Karen Helm
e: karenh@firstcom.com
genres: All Styles
territories: Film, TV, Ads, Radio, Video Games
No unsolicited material.

Gerry Gershman
322 S Topanga Canyon Blvd.
Topanga, CA 90290
p: 310-455-1700
f: 310-455-1121
contact: Gerry Gershman
e: invisiblefilms@earthlink.net
genres: All Styles
territories: Film, TV
CDs only.

Harvey Shield Music Supervision
1411 Carroll Ave.
Los Angeles, CA 90026
p: 213-250-1977
f: 213-482-4813
contact: Harvey Shield
e: harveyshield@earthlink.net
territories: Film, TV
Contact before sending kits.

Holloway House
PO Box 48645
Los Angeles, CA 90048
p: 213-384-0269
f: 213-384-0272
e: hollowayhouse@aol.com
contact: Danny Holloway
genres: All Styles
territories: Film, TV

HotHouse Music
,172a Arlington Rd.
1st Fl.
London, NW1 7HL UK
p: 44-207-446-7446
e: info@hot-house-music.com
www.hot-house-music.com
contact: Nyree Pinder
e: nyree@hot-house-music.com
genres: All Styles
territories: Film, TV, Ads
No unsolicited material.

IDM Music & Associates
111 E 14th St., #140
New York, NY 10003
p: 212-695-3911
f: 212-967-6284
e: info@idmmusic.com
www.idmmusic.com
contact: Miriam Westercappel
genres: Specializing in Italian Indies & Sample Clearance
territories: Film, TV, Ads, Radio, Video Games
No unsolicited material.

Indy Hits Music Publishing
PO Box 4102
Los Angeles, CA 90078
p: 323-276-1000
f: 323-276-1001
e: info@indyhits.com
www.indyhits.com; www.bandpromote.com
contact: Mike Galaxy
e: mike@indyhits.com
genres: All Styles mainly Rock
territories: Film, TV, Ads, Radio, Video Games, Ringtones
CDs only.

License It
9903 Santa Monica Blvd.,
#1103
Beverly Hills, CA 90212
p: 310-289-7232
f: 310-772-0985
e: licenseit@aol.com
contact: Lauren Brown
genres: All Styles
territories: Film, TV, Ads, Video Games
No unsolicited material.

Luke Hits
137 N Larchmont Blvd.,
#555
Los Angeles, CA 90004
p: 310-236-5853
e: writelukehits@yahoo.com
contact: Luke Hits
genres: All Styles
territories: Film, TV, Radio, Advertising, Video Games
Mail submissions.

Machine Head
1641 20th St.
Santa Monica, CA 90404
p: 310-392-8393
e: info@machinehead.com
www.machinehead.com
contact: Vicki Ordershook
e: vicki@machinehead.com
genres: Classical, Orchestral, Electronic, Jazz, Alt., Pop
territories: Film, TV, Ads, Radio, Video Games
Also does music & sound design.
No unsolicited material.

MCS Music
10 Heathfield Terr., Chiswick
London, W4 4JE UK
p: 44-208-987-4150
f: 44-208-987-4160
e: info@mcsmusic.com
www.mcsmusic.com
contact: Guy Fletcher
ext: 44-208-987-4151
e: guy@mcsmusic.com
genres: All Styles
territories: Film, TV, Ads

Media Creature Music
4470 W Sunset Blvd.,
Ste. 107-500
Los Angeles, CA 90027
p: 323-468-8888
e: info@mediacreature.com
www.mediacreature.com
contact: Sharal Churchill
e: sc@mediacreature.com
genres: All Styles
territories: Film, TV, Ads, Video Games, Special Markets
Also does music publishing & has a record label.

Mike Flicker Music Services
Burbank, CA
p: 626-793-0379
f: 562-684-0374
www.mikeflicker.com
contact: Mike Flicker
e: mxflick@mikeflicker.com
genres: All Styles
territories: Film, TV
No unsolicited material.

The Music Bridge
PO Box 661918
Los Angeles, CA 90066
p: 310-398-9650
f: 310-398-4850
e: inquiry@themusicbridge.com
www.themusicbridge.com
contact: David G. Powell
genres: All Styles
territories: Film, TV, Ads, Video Games
Also does clearance & licensing. No unsolicited material.

Music For Picture
5 E 19th St.
3rd Fl.
New York, NY
10003
p: 212-420-7730
f: 212-420-7732
e: info@musicforpicture.com
www.musicforpicture.com
contact: Ben Davis
e: ben@musicforpicture.com
genres: All Styles
territories: Film, TV, Ads, Radio
No unsolicited material.

Music Sales West/ Rudolph Productions
1321 7th St., Ste. 300
Santa Monica, CA 90401
p: 310-458-9861
f: 310-458-9862
e: media@musicsales.com
www.musicsales.com
contact: Richard Rudolph
e: richard.rudolph@musicsales.com
genres: All Styles
territories: Film, TV, Ads
No unsolicited material.

Musicalities Limited
Snows Ride Farm
Snows Ride
Windlesham, Surrey
GU20 6LA UK
p: 44-127-647-4181
e: info@musicalities.co.uk
www.musicalities.co.uk
contact: Ivan Chandler
e: ivan@musicalities.co.uk
genres: All Styles
territories: Film, TV, Ads, Radio, Video Games, Mobile Phone Content
No unsolicited material.

Mutato Muzika
8760 Sunset Blvd.
West Hollywood, CA 90069
p: 310-360-0561
f: 310-360-0837
e: media@mutato.com
www.mutato.com
contact: Danping Wong
e: info@mutato.com
genres: All Styles
territories: Film, TV, Ads, Video Games
CDs only.

Naxos of America
416 Mary Lindsay Polk Dr.,
Ste. 509
Franklin, TN 37067
p: 615-771-9393
f: 615-771-6747
www.naxos.com
contact: Justyn Baker
ext: 615-465-3809
e: jbaker@naxosusa.com
genres: Classical
territories: Film, TV, Ads, Radio
No unsolicited material.

Neophonic
9320 Wilshire Blvd.,
#200
Beverly Hills, CA 90212
p: 310-550-0124
e: soundtracks@neophonic.com
www.neophonic.com
contact: Evyen Klean
ext: 310-550-0124 x287
genres: All Styles
territories: Film, TV
Email submission request.

Peace Bisquit
936 Kent Ave., Bldg. E,
#3
Brooklyn, NY 11205
p: 718-789-1689
www.peacebisquit.com
contact: Bill Coleman
e: bill@peacebisquit.com
genres: All Styles
territories: Film, TV, Radio
No unsolicited material.

Playback Music Supervision
1041 N Fermosa Ave.,
Santa Monica East Bldg., Rm. 110
West Hollywood, CA 90046
p: 323-852-1838
e: info@playbackmusic.net
www.playbackmusic.net
contact: Billy Gottlieb
e: billyg@playbackmusic.net
genres: All Styles
territories: Film, TV, Ads, Video Games
Email submission request.

Red Hots Entertainment
67885 Foothill Rd.,
Cathedral Canyon Cove
Cathedral City, CA 92234
p: 760-992-7047; 818-795-4235
f: 760-324-9424
e: pogmothon@dc.rr.com
contact: Chip Miller
e: chipdaniel2@excite.com
genres: Alt., Rock, Blues, Americana, Pop, Hip-Hop, Jazz, Reggae, World
territories: Film, TV, Ads
No unsolicited material.

Reel Entertainment
11684 Ventura Blvd.,
Ste. 134
Studio City, CA 91604
p: 818-386-9135
f: 818-386-9135
www.reelent.com
contact: Mark Wolfson
ext: 818-501-1811
e: mark@reelent.com
genres: Radio Friendly
territories: Film, TV, Radio
Also does artist development, licensing & training for on-camera. Email submission request.

Reflection Music
1754 15th St., Ste. 6
Santa Monica, CA 90404
p: 818-219-0180
www.reflectionmusic.com
contact: Carrie Hughes
e: carrie.hughes@reflectionmusic.com
genres: All Styles
territories: Film, TV

The Rights Workshop
39 Mesa St., Ste. 112
San Fransisco, CA 94129
p: 415-561-3333
e: info@rightsworkshop.com
www.rightsworkshop.com
contact: Brooke Wentz
e: bmw@rightsworkshop.com
genres: All Styles
territories: Film, TV
Also does Music Publishing Administration. Email before sending material.

S.L. Feldman & Associates
1505 W 2nd Ave.,
#200
Vancouver, BC V6H 3Y4
Canada
p: 604-734-5945
e: feldman@slfa.com
www.slfa.com
contact: Sarah Webster
e: webster@slfa.com
territories: Film, TV
No unsolicited material.

Screenmusic Int'l
18034 Ventura Blvd.,
Ste. 450
Encino, CA 91316
p: 818-789-2954
f: 818-789-5801
e: screenmusic@aol.com
www.screenmusic.com
contact: Nick Castelli
e: bigmoviemusic@aol.com
genres: All Styles
territories: Film, TV, Ads, Radio, Video Games
Call before sending CDs.

Selak Entertainment
PO Box 1475
Burbank, CA 91507
p: 818-842-5800
www.selakentertainment.com
contact: Steve Selak
e: steve@selakentertainment.com
genres: All Styles
territories: Film, TV, Ads, Radio, Video Games
No unsolicited material.

SMC Artists
4400 Coldwater Canyon,
Ste. 127
Studio City, CA 91604
p: 818-505-9600
f: 818-505-0909
www.smcartists.com
contact: Otto Vavrin II
e: ovavrin@smcartists.com
genres: All Styles
territories: Film, TV
Call before sending material.

Soundtrack Music Associates
2229 Cloverfield Blvd.
Santa Monica, CA
90405
p: 310-392-1401
e: info@soundtrk.com
www.soundtrk.com
contact: John Tempereau
territories: Film, TV, Ads, Video Games
No unsolicited material.

Supervision
165 Hudson St.,
Rear Entrance
New York, NY
10013
p: 212-219-9170
e: supervision@mindspring.com
contact: Susan Jacobs
e: jonathan.supervision@mindspring.com
genres: All Styles
territories: Film, TV
No unsolicited material.

Sweet & Doggett
Boston, MA
p: 617-872-0455
f: 508-384-8507
e: info@sweetdoggett.com
www.sweetdoggett.com
contact: Jay Sweet
genres: All Styles
territories: Film, TV, Ads, Video Games, Internet
No unsolicited material.

TLS Music Services
423 Cornell Dr.
Burbank, CA 91504
p: 818-848-2330
f: 818-848-4006
www.tlsms.com
contact: Tracy Lynch-Sanchez
e: tracy@tlsms.com
genres: All Styles
territories: Film, TV, Ads, Radio, Video Games
No unsolicited material.

TRF Music
1 International Blvd.,
Ste. 212
Mahwah, NJ
07495
p: 800-899-6874; 201-335-0005
f: 201-335-0004
e: info@trfmusic.com
www.trfmusic.com
contact: Anne Marie Russo
ext: 201-335-0005 x14
e: annmarie@trfmusic.com
genres: Acoustic & Instrumental
territories: Film, TV, Ads, Radio, Video Games
Also has a music library.

gear

Allparts
13027 Brittmoore Park Dr.
Houston, TX
77041
p: 713-466-6414
f: 713-466-5803
e: allparts@allparts.com
www.allparts.com
products: Guitars & Bass Parts

Audio-Technica US, Inc.
1221 Commerce Dr.
Stow, OH 44224
p: 330-686-2600
f: 330-686-0719
e: pro@atus.com
www.audio-technica.com
contact: Gary Boss
e: gboss@atus.com
products: Microphones, Wireless Systems, Cables, Headphones, Mixers
Manufacturers of award-winning audio equipment for live performances, broadcast & recording. Product line includes high performance microphones, studio headphones, wireless microphone systems, mixers, noise-canceling headphones, wireless in-ear monitor systems, turntables & DJ gear.
See Ad On Page 35

Bias
140 Keller St.
Petaluma, CA
94952
p: 707-782-1866
f: 707-782-1874
e: sales@bias-inc.com
www.bias-inc.com
contact: Christine Berkeley
e: christine@bias-inc.com
products: Digital Recorder Software, VST Plug-ins
Mainly Mac-based, but also has some PC software.

Bose Corp.
The Mountain
Framingham, MA 01701
p: 877-335-2673
f: 508-766-4066
e: musicians@bose.com
www.bose.com/musicians
products: Bass Modules, Headphones, Amplification
Also sponsors events.

Crate/ Crate Pro Audio
1400 Ferguson Ave.
St. Louis, MO 63133
p: 800-727-4512; 314-727-4512
f: 314-727-8929
www.crateamps.com; www.stlouismusic.com
contact: Annie Taylor
ext: 425-402-6214
e: annie.taylor@loudtechinc.com
products: Guitars, Basses, Amps
Sponsors events.

George L's Cables
PO Box 238
Madison, TN 37116
p: 615-868-6976
f: 615-868-4637
e: georgels@bellsouth.net
www.georgels.com
contact: Kimberly Lewis
products: George L's Cables, Plugs, Acoustic Pickups, Steel Guitar Pickups & Strings
Sponsors events.

John Pearse Strings
PO Box 295
Center Valley, PA 18034
p: 800-235-3302; 610-691-3302
f: 610-691-3304
www.jpstrings.com
contact: Mary Faith Rhoads
e: jpinfo@aol.com
products: Musical Instrument Strings, Thumb Picks, Accessories, Capos
Endorsed by string artists the world over, John Pearse Strings are known for their extra stiffness resulting in exceptional sound for all styles of stringed instruments. Specially formulated & designed to be long-lasting w/ more accurate vibration & nodal pattern.
See Ad On This Page

Kyser Musical Products
28141 State Hwy. 64
Canton, TX 75103
p: 866-500-2799
f: 903-567-2704
www.kysermusical.com
contact: Nick Palmer
e: nick@kysermusical.com
products: Capos, Finger Picks, Guitar Care Products

Martin Guitar
510 Sycamore St.
Nazareth, PA 18064
p: 800-633-2060; 610-759-2837
f: 610-759-5757
e: info@martinguitar.com
www.martinguitar.com
contact: Dick Boak
e: dboak@martinguitar.com
products: Acoustic Guitars, Ukuleles, Strings, Accessories

M-Audio
5795 Martin Rd.
Irwindale, CA 91706
p: 800-969-6434; 626-633-9050
f: 626-633-9078
e: info@m-audio.com
www.m-audio.com
contact: Kevin Walt
e: kevin@m-audio.com
products: MIDI Interfaces, Synchronizers, Mixers, Preamps

Mesa/Boogie
1317 Ross St.
Petaluma, CA 94954
p: 707-778-6565
f: 707-765-1503
e: info@mesaboogie.com
www.mesaboogie.com
contact: Tim McKee
e: artist@mesaboogie.com
products: Guitar & Bass Amps, Preamps
Known for high-end amp equipment used & endorsed by all styles of superstars & pros. Artist endorsers are not paid & not given free product. US-based musician's/bands on a major label or prominent Indie label w/ a Nat'l tour booked for 2009 can send electronic press kits & current touring itineraries to: artist@mesaboogie.com. Also sponsors events.
See Ad On Page 210

Minnetonka Audio
17113 Minnetonka Blvd.
Ste. 300
Minnetonka, MN
55345
p: 952-449-6481
f: 952-449-0318
e: info@minnetonkaaudio.com
www.minnetonkaaudio.com
contact: Steve Clarke
e: steve.clarke@minnetonkaaudio.com
products: DVD-Audio Authoring Software, Surround Audio Encoding,

MusicPro Insurance Agency
135 Crossways Park Dr., Ste. 300, PO Box 9017
Woodbury, NY 11797
p: 1-800-MUSICPRO
f: 516-622-1098
e: insurance@musicproinsurance.com
www.musicproinsurance.com
products: All forms of insurance for the music industry including: Studio, Touring, Health & Instrument Policies
Specializing in affordable insurance for working musicians, studios & other music pros. By aggregating their pro subscribers of 4,000+, they're able to deliver low rates & flexible options. Coverage includes instruments & equipment, studios, tours, events, health & liability.
See Ad On Page 37

Paul Reed Smith Guitars
380 Log Canoe Cir.
Stevensville, MD 21666
p: 410-643-9970
f: 410-643-9980
e: custserv@prsguitars.com
www.prsguitars.com
contact: Winn Krozack
e: wkrozack@prsguitars.com
products: Guitars, Pickups, Strings, Accessories
Sponsors events.

Yamaha Corp. of America
6600 Orangethorpe Ave.
Buena Park, CA
90620
p: 714-522-9011
www.yamaha.com
contact: Ben James
ext: 714-522-9011 x3327
products: Keyboards, Drums, Percussion, Mixers, Speakers, Guitars, Basses, Pianos, Woodwinds

lawyers

Law Office of Mark A. Abbattista
1125 Lindero Canyon Rd.
#A8, Ste. 321
Westlake Village, CA
91362
p: 818-991-7399
f: 818-735-0543
contact: Mark Abbattista
e: kingabba@aol.com
focus: Entertainment Law, Int'l Law
Also does personal mgmt.

Richard Alvoid
356 W 9 Mile Rd.
Pensacola, FL 32534
p: 850-857-1960
f: 850-857-4311
e: visa@alvoid.com
www.alvoid.com
contact: Richard Alvoid
focus: Entertainment Law, Immigration Law

Law Offices of Douglas C. Anton
3 University Plaza Dr., Ste. 207
Hackensack, NJ 07601
p: 201-487-2055
f: 201-487-9698
contact: Douglas C. Anton
e: douganton@aol.com
focus: Entertainment Law

Baker & Kelley
1227 17th Ave S.
Nashville, TN 37212
p: 615-329-0900
f: 615-329-2148
e: info@rowlawyers.com
www.rowlawyers.com
contact: Page Kelley
e: pkelley@rowlawyers.com
focus: Entertainment Law, Intellectual Property

Bannerot Law Firm
1114 Lost Creek Blvd.
Ste. 420
Austin, TX 78746
p: 512-327-8930
e: ruth@bannerot.com
www.bannerot.com
contact: Kenneth W. Pajak
e: ken@bannerot.com
focus: Entertainment Law

Barnes, Morris, Klein, Mark, Yorn, Barnes & Levine
2000 Ave. of the Stars
3rd Fl., North Tower
Los Angeles, CA 90067
p: 310-319-3900
f: 310-319-3999
e: deklein@bmkylaw.com
www.bmkylaw.com
contact: P. Kevin Morris
e: km@bmkylaw.com
focus: Entertainment Law

Bartley F. Day & Associates
4635 SW Hillside
Ste. 3100
Portland, OR 97221
p: 503-291-9300
f: 503-292-8462
contact: Bart Day
e: bart@entertainmentlawwest.com
focus: Entertainment Law, Intellectual Property

The Bayne Law Group
116 Village Blvd.
Ste. 200
Princeton, NJ 08543
p: 609-924-4295
f: 609-924-4298
e: lawfirm@baynelaw.com
www.baynelaw.com
contact: Andrew Bayne
focus: Contracts, Immigration, Entertainment Law, Litigation, Intellectual Property
Offices in NYC: 212-679-2205 & Philadelphia: 215-561-1707.

Beldock, Levine & Hoffman
99 Park Ave.
Ste. 1600
New York, NY 10016
p: 212-490-0400
f: 212-557-0565
www.blhny.com
contact: Peter Matorin
e: pmatorin@blhny.com
focus: Entertainment Law, Intellectual Property
For Intellectual Property, contact Jeff Greenberg at jgreenberg@blhny.com.

Berliner, Corcoran & Rowe
1101 17th St. NW, Ste. 1100
Washington, DC 20036
p: (DC): 202-293-5555; (MD): 301-570-1761
f: (DC): 202-293-9035; (MD): 301-570-4183
e: bcr@bcr.us
www.bcr.us
contact: Jay Rosenthal
e: jrose13@aol.com
focus: Entertainment Law, IP, Internet Law, Int'l Law

Bienstock & Michael
411 Hackensack Ave., 7th Fl.
Hackensack, NJ 07601
p: 201-525-0300
f: 212-399-1278
e: info@musicesq.com
www.musicesq.com
contact: Ronald Bienstock
e: ronald.bienstock@musicesq.com
focus: Entertainment Law, Intellectual Property
Office in NYC: 212-247-0848.

Blackwell, Sanders
4801 Maine St., Ste. 1000
Kansas City, MO 64112
p: 816-983-8000
f: 816-983-8080
e: aebright@blackwellsanders.com
www.blackwellsanders.com
contact: Wade Kerrigan
ext: 816-983-8248
e: wkerrigan@blackwellsanders.com
focus: Entertainment Law, Immigration Law
Offices in MO, NE, KS, IL, DC, & London. For Immigration Law, contact: Toni Blackwood at tblackwood@blackwellsanders.com.

Branfman & Assoc.
12750 High Bluff Dr., #100
San Diego, CA 92130
p: 858-481-5800
f: 858-481-3709
e: info@branfman.com
www.branfman.com
contact: April Jernigan
focus: Entertainment Law, Intellectual Property
For Intellectual Property, contact: David Branfman.

Bricker & Eckler
100 S 3rd St.
Columbus, OH 43215
p: 614-227-2300
f: 614-227-2390
e: info@bricker.com
www.bricker.com
contact: T. Earl LeVere
e: elevere@bricker.com
focus: Entertainment Law, Intellectual Property
Cleveland: 216-523-5405 & Cincinnati: 513-870-6700.

Law Office of Suzanne G. Brummett
8 Corporate Park, Ste. 300
Irvine, CA 92606
p: 949-705-6575
f: 866-305-7227
www.americavisalaw.com
contact: Suzanne G. Brummett
e: suzanne@americavisalaw.com
focus: Immigration Law

Eric D. Bull
126 N 3rd St., Ste 150
Minneapolis, MN 55401
p: 612-354-3644
f: 612-354-3645
www.ebull-law.com
contact: Eric Bull
e: ebull@ebull-law.com
focus: Entertainment Law
Specializes in Indie artists.

Burns & Levinson
125 Summer St.
Boston, MA 02110
p: 617-345-3000
f: 617-345-3299
e: gtobia@burnslev.com
www.burnslev.com
contact: Susan E. Stenger
e: sstenger@burnslev.com
focus: Entertainment Law, Intellectual Property, Immigration Law
Intellectual Property, contact: Jerry Cohen, 617-345-3276; jcohen@burnslev.com. Immigration Law, contact: Evelyn Haralampu, eharalampu@burnslev.com.

California Lawyers for the Arts
Fort Mason Ctr., Bldg. C
Rm. 255
San Francisco, CA 94123
p: 415-775-7200
f: 415-775-1143
e: cla@calawyersforthearts.org
www.calawyersforthearts.org
contact: Josie Porter
ext: 415-775-7200 x767
focus: Entertainment Law
Non-profit lawyer referral service w/ 3 other CA locations.

Law Offices of Randall Caudle
350 Townsend St.
Ste. 305
San Francisco, CA 94107
p: 415-541-9290
f: 415-358-4104
www.caudleimmigration.com
contact: Randall Caudle
e: randall@caudleimmigration.com
focus: Immigration Law

Law Office of James I. Charne
425 Idaho Ave., Unit 9
Santa Monica, CA 90403
p: 310-458-9345
www.charnelaw.com
contact: James Charne
e: charne@usa.net
focus: Entertainment Law, Intellectual Property
No deal shopping. Also does artist management.

Chouest & Associates
4732 Utica St., #100
Metairie, LA 70006
p: 504-455-7300
f: 504-455-1252
e: law@metairie.com
www.metairie.com
contact: Stephen Chouest
focus: Entertainment Law, IP, Immigration Law

Bobby C. Chung
10505 Valley Blvd.
Ste. 633
El Monte, CA 91731
p: 626-279-5341
f: 626-279-5613
e: info@bccvisalaw.com
www.bccvisalaw.com
contact: Bobby C. Chung
e: bchung@bccvisalaw.com
focus: Entertainment Law, IP, Immigration Law

Clarke Law Firm
4606 FM 1960 W, #400
Houston, TX 77069
p: 713-568-8904
f: 713-456-2585
e: law@clarkelegal.com
www.clarkelegal.com
contact: Yemane Clarke
focus: Entertainment Law

Law Office of Alan S. Clarke
3355 Lenox Rd., Ste. 750
Atlanta, GA 30326
p: 404-816-9800
f: 404-816-0555
contact: Alan Clarke
e: alansclarke@bellsouth.net
focus: Entertainment Law, IP

Cohen & Gordon
8050 Melrose Ave.
2nd Fl.
Los Angeles, CA 90046
p: 323-951-9500
f: 323-651-3726
e: peter@lawnet1.com
www.lawnet1.com
contact: Peter Gordon
e: gordon@cohen-gordon.com
focus: Entertainment Law, IP, Contracts, Litigation

Cowan, DeBaets, Abrahams & Sheppard
41 Madison Ave., 34th Fl.
New York, NY 10010
p: 212-974-7474
f: 212-974-8474
e: cdas@cdas.com
www.cdas.com
contact: Robert Siegel
e: rlsentlaw@aol.com
focus: Entertainment Law, IP

Cumberland Law Group
1222 16th Ave. S
Nashville, TN 37212
p: 615-383-8335
f: 615-383-8134
e: info@cumberlandlawgroup.com
www.cumberlandlawgroup.com
contact: Kevin Norwood
focus: Entertainment Law

Randall M. Cutler
2198 Hwy. 48 W
McComb, MS 39648
p: 601-783-6616
f: 601-783-9884
contact: Randall M. Cutler
e: randall.cutler@verizon.net
focus: Entertainment Law

Law Office of Kevin L. Dixler
28 E Jackson Blvd., Ste. 1905
Chicago, IL 60604
p: 312-588-0500
www.dixler.com
contact: Kevin L. Dixler
e: kd@dixler.com
focus: Immigration Law

Dollinger, Gonski & Grossman
1 Old Country Rd., Ste. 102
PO Box 9010
Carle Place, NY 11514
p: 516-747-1010
f: 516-747-2494
www.dggny.com
contact: Joyce Dollinger
e: jdollinger@dgglawoffices.com
focus: Entertainment Law, IP

Driebe & Driebe
6 Courthouse Way
Jonesboro, GA 30236
p: 770-478-8894
f: 770-478-9606
contact: Charles Driebe, Jr.
ext: 770-478-8894 x2
e: cdriebe@springmail.com
focus: Entertainment, IP
Also provides mgmt. w/ Blind Ambition Mgmt. in New Orleans.

Entertainment Law Chicago
PO Box 558023
Chicago, IL 60655
p: 773-882-4912
f: 708-206-1663
e: info@entertainmentlawchicago.com
www.entertainmentlawchicago.com
contact: Donald R. Simon
e: dsimon@entertainmentlawchicago.com
focus: Entertainment Law
Does deal shopping.

The Entertainment Law Office
208 S LaSalle St., Ste. 1400
Chicago, IL 60604
p: 312-641-5300
f: 312-641-5301
www.ent-law.net
contact: Hillel Frankel
e: hf@ent-law.net
focus: Entertainment Law, IP, Contracts, Litigation

Music oriented firm w/ satellite office in NY: 646-641-7012.

Eskridge & Eskridge
100 N Main Bldg., Ste. 1036
Memphis, TN 38103
p: 901-522-9600
f: 901-276-3800
e: info@eskridgelaw.com
www.eskridgelaw.com
contact: Janelle R. Eskridge
e: janelle@eskridgelaw.com
focus: Entertainment Law, IP

Eveline, Davis & Phillips
7735 Maple St.
New Orleans, LA 70118
p: 504-861-6404
f: 504-861-6405
e: akeaton@edp.nocoxmail.com
http://nolaentertainmentlaw.com/
contact: Gregory Eveline
e: geveline@edp.nocoxmail.com
focus: Entertainment Law, IP
New Orleans music specialists.

Law Office of Monica Ewing
6323 Roosevelt Hwy.
Union City, GA 30291
p: 678-325-5402
f: 678-325-5401
contact: Monica Ewing
e: monicaewingesq@mindspring.com
focus: Entertainment Law, IP
No deal shopping.

Fishbach, Perlstein, Lieberman & Almond
1875 Century Park E
Ste. 1450
Los Angeles, CA 90067
p: 310-556-1956
f: 310-556-4617
www.fpllaw.com
contact: Michael Perlstein
e: mperlstein@fpllaw.com
focus: Entertainment Law, IP

Fritz, Byrne, Head & Harrison
98 San Jacinto Blvd., Ste. 2000
Austin, TX 78701
p: 512-476-2020
f: 512-477-5267
e: firm@fbhh.com
www.fbhh.com
contact: Bruce Perkins
e: bperkins@fbhh.com
focus: Entertainment Law, IP
Corpus Christi: 361-883-1500.

FTM Arts Law
10509 Judicial Dr., Ste. 300
Fairfax, VA 22030
p: 703-385-9500
f: 703-385-9893
e: arts@ftm-pc.com
www.ftmartslaw-pc.com
contact: Brian Taylor Goldstein
e: bgoldstein@ftm-pc.com
focus: Entertainment Law, Immigration Law, IP

Law Office of Jeffrey Gandel
160 E 88th St., Ste. 16B
New York, NY 10128
p: 212-289-0709
f: 212-289-0686
contact: Jeffrey Gandel
e: jeffgandelesq@nyc.rr.com
focus: Entertainment Law, Intellectual Property, Litigation
Also recovers royalties for writers & artists: info@royaltyrecovery.org; www.royaltyrecovery.org.

Garvey, Schubert & Barer
1191 2nd Ave.
#1800
Seattle, WA 98101
p: 206-464-3939
f: 206-464-0125
www.gsblaw.com
contact: Scott Warner
ext: 206-816-1319
e: sgwarner@gsblaw.com
focus: Entertainment Law, Immigration, IP
Offices in Beijing, NYC, DC & Portland. Immigration contact: Greg Rogers, 206-816-1404, grogers@gsblaw.com.

Gerber Law Firm
105 W 4th St., Ste. 800
Winston-Salem, NC 27101
p: 336-773-1324
f: 336-722-0804
contact: Andrew Gerber
e: gerbs@prodigy.net
focus: Entertainment Law

Graves, Dougherty, Hearon & Moody
401 Congress, Ste. 2200
Austin, TX 78701
p: 512-480-5600
f: 512-478-1976
e: gdhm@gdhm.com
www.gdhm.com
contact: Rick Triplett
ext: 512-480-5764
e: rtriplett@gdhm.com
focus: Entertainment Law, IP

Green & Green
1 Embarcadero Ctr., Ste 500
San Francisco, CA 94111
p: 415-835-1250
f: 415-457-8757
www.musiclawyer.com
contact: Beverly Robin Green
e: bev@musiclawyer.com
focus: Entertainment Law, IP

Greenberg Traurig
Met Life Bldg., 200 Park Ave.
New York, NY 10166
p: 212-801-9334
f: 212-801-6400
www.gtlaw.com
contact: Andy Tavel
e: tavela@gtlaw.com
focus: Entertainment Law
Offices in NY, LA, DC, Miami & Zurich.

Law Offices of Habib & Jadallah
6530 Chase Rd.
Dearborn, MI 48126
p: 313-582-1996
f: 313-582-1958
e: chadih10@yahoo.com
contact: Samer N. Jadallah
e: attysamer@yahoo.com
focus: Entertainment Law, Intellectual Property, Immigration
Specializes in USA & Canadian Immigration, contact: Donna Habib.

Hanrahan Trapp
522 E Capitol Ave.
PO Box 362
Jefferson City, MO 65102
p: 573-634-8964
f: 573-556-6340
www.hanrahantrapp.com
contact: Samuel E. Trapp
e: sam.trapp@hanrahantrapp.com; samtrapp@earthlink.net
focus: Immigration Law

Hart Law Group
224 W 30th St., Ste. 1205
New York, NY 10001
p: 212-629-9377
f: 212-629-9395
e: info@hartlawonline.com
www.hartlawonline.com
contact: Rose Meade Hart
focus: Entertainment Law, IP
London: 44-20-7583-2222; Mexico City: 52-55-5148-3244.

Jim Tom Haynes
1666 Connecticut Ave. NW
Ste. 5000
Washington, DC 20009
p: 202-293-3123
f: 202-293-6230
www.jthaynes.com
contact: Jim Tom Haynes
e: jth@jthaynes.com
focus: Immigration Law

Law Office of David Herlihy
14 Staniford St.
Newton, MA 02466
p: 617-964-4006

f: 617-964-4016
e: contact@herlihylaw.com
www.herlihylaw.com
contact: David Herlihy
e: david@herlihylaw.com
focus: Entertainment Law

Hertz Schram
1760 S Telegraph Rd., #300
Bloomfield Hills, MI 48302
p: 248-335-5000
f: 248-335-3346
www.hertzschram.com
contact: Howard Hertz
ext: 248-335-5000 x319
e: hhertz@hertzschram.com
focus: Entertainment Law, Contracts, Litigation

Heyman Law
26 Perry St., Ste. 4-A
New York, NY 10014
p: 212-414-9522
www.heylaw.com
contact: Barry J. Heyman
e: barry@heylaw.com
focus: Entertainment Law

Holland & Knight
131 S Dearborn St., 30th Fl.
Chicago, IL 60603
p: 312-715-5756
f: 312-578-6666
www.hklaw.com
contact: Peter Strand
e: peter.strand@hklaw.com
focus: Entertainment Law, Intellectual Property, Immigration
Offices worldwide.

Law Office of Christopher W. Hoyt
350 Fifth Ave., Ste. 7315
New York, NY 10118
p: 212-268-3414
e: info@cwhesq.com
www.cwhesq.com
contact: Christopher Hoyt
focus: Entertainment Law, Intellectual Property

Jeffer, Mangels, Butler & Marmaro
1900 Ave. of the Stars, 7th Fl.
Los Angeles, CA 90067
p: 310-203-8080
f: 310-203-0567
e: oa1@jmbm.com
www.jmbm.com
contact: Michael Sherman
ext: 310-201-3576
e: msherman@jmbm.com
focus: Entertainment Law, IP
San Francisco: 415-398-8080. Intellectual Property, contact: Rod Berman, 310-201-3517; rberman@jmbm.com.

Johnston, Barton, Proctor & Rose
569 Brookwood Village St.
901
Birmingham, AL 35209
p: 205-458-9400
f: 205-458-9500
www.johnstonbarton.com
contact: John P. Strohm
ext: 205-458-9440
e: jps@jbpp.com
focus: Entertainment Law, IP

Katten, Muchin & Rosenman
575 Madison Ave.
New York, NY 10022
p: 212-940-8800
f: 212-894-5597
www.kattenlaw.com
contact: Marc Reisler
e: marc.reisler@kattenlaw.com
focus: Entertainment Law
Offices in NY, Chicago, DC, Charlotte, Newark & Palo Alto.

Keniley Law Firm
4610 Peachtree Industrial Blvd.
Norcross, GA 30071
p: 770-263-0000
f: 404-420-2260
www.k5law.com
contact: Scott Keniley
e: scott@k5law.com
focus: Entertainment Law

Kia Law Firm
234 5th Ave., Ste. 405
New York, NY 10001
p: 212-679-4200
f: 212-679-4155
e: info@kialawfirm.com
www.kialawfirm.com
contact: Atossa Kia
ext: 212-684-1001 x619
e: atossakia@kialawfirm.com
focus: Entertainment Law

King & Ballow
1100 Union St. Plaza
315 Union St.
Nashville, TN 37201
p: 615-259-3456
f: 615-726-5419
e: comment@kingballow.com
www.kingballow.com
contact: Richard Busch
ext: 615-726-5422
e: rbusch@kingballow.com
focus: Entertainment Law, Immigration, Intellectual Property
Office in San Diego: 858-597-6000. For Immigration Law, contact: Max Nuyen at kmnuyen@kingballow.com or immigration@kingballow.com.

Law Office of Matthew L. Kletter
27 N Broadway
Tarrytown, NY 10591
p: 914-332-1008
f: 914-206-3561
www.myspace.com/mlk
contact: Matthew Kletter
e: mkletter@msn.com
focus: Entertainment Law

Lampert & O'Connor
1776 K St. NW
Ste. 700
Washington, DC 20006
p: 202-887-6230
f: 202-887-6231
e: info@l-olaw.com
www.l-olaw.com
contact: Donna Lampert
e: lampert@lojlaw.com
focus: Entertainment Law, IP

LaPolt Law
9000 Sunset Blvd., Ste. 800
West Hollywood, CA 90069
p: 310-858-0922
f: 310-858-0933
www.lapoltlaw.com
contact: Dina LaPolt
e: dina@lapoltlaw.com
focus: Entertainment Law

Lathrop & Gage
10 S Broadway, Ste. 1300
St. Louis, MO 63102
p: 314-613-2500
f: 314-613-2550
www.lathropgage.com
contact: David Barnard
ext: 816-460-5430
e: dbarnard@lathropgage.com
focus: Entertainment Law, Immigration, Intellectual Property
Locations in NYC, MO, CO & DC. Immigration contact: Alfred Hupp, 816-460-5833; ahupp@lathropgage.com.

Lee & Lawless
11 Embarcadero W
Ste. 140
Oakland, CA 94607
p: 510-272-0200
e: franck.info@leelawless.com
www.leelawless.com; www.culturelaw.com
contact: Peter Franck
ext: 510-272-0200 x305
e: pfranck@leelawless.com
focus: Entertainment Law, IP

Lewis, Brisbois, Bisgaard & Smith
1 Sansome St., Ste. 1400
San Francisco, CA 94107
p: 415-362-2580
f: 415-434-0882
www.lbbslaw.com
contact: Glen Umeda
e: umeda@lbbslaw.com
focus: Entertainment Law
*Offices in **LA**: 213-250-1800; **San Diego**: 619-233-1006; **NYC**: 212-232-1300 & **Las Vegas**: 702-893-3383.*

Loeb & Loeb
10100 Santa Monica Blvd.
Ste. 2200
Los Angeles, CA 90067
p: 310-282-2000
f: 310-282-2200
www.loeb.com
contact: John T. Frankenheimer
ext: 310-282-2135
e: jfrankenheimer@loeb.com
focus: Entertainment Law
*Offices in **NYC**: 212-407-4000; **Chicago**: 312-464-3100; **Nashville**: 615-749-8300.*

Lommen, Abdo, Cole, King & Stageberg
2000 IDS Ctr., 80 S 8th St.
Minneapolis, MN 55402
p: 612-339-8131
f: 612-339-8064
www.lommen.com
contact: Ken Abdo
e: ken@lommen.com
focus: Entertainment Law
Offices in NYC: 212-683-8775.

McLane & Wong
11135 Weddington St.
Ste. 424
North Hollywood, CA 91601
p: 818-587-6801
f: 818-587-6802
www.benmclane.com
contact: Ben McLane
e: bcmclane@aol.com
focus: Entertainment Law

Susan L. Mende
39 Jaffe Terr.
Colchester, CT 06415
p: 860-537-1176; 860-917-4020 (cell)
e: mendemgmt@aol.com
contact: Susan L. Mende
focus: Entertainment Law
Actively seeking new clients to manage; No Hip-Hop.

Law Office of Linda S. Mensch
200 S Michigan Ave.
Ste. 1240
Chicago, IL 60604
p: 312-922-2910
f: 312-922-1865
e: menschlaw@yahoo.com
www.menschlaw.com
contact: Linda Mensch
e: lmensch@menschlaw.com
focus: Entertainment Law, Contracts
Also does licensing & distribution deals.

Mike Tolleson & Associates
2106 E Martin Luther King Blvd.
Austin, TX 78702
p: 512-480-8822
f: 512-479-6212
www.miketolleson.com
contact: Mike Tolleson
e: mike@miketolleson.com
focus: Entertainment Law

Milom, Joyce, Horsnell, Crow
3310 W End Ave., Ste. 610
Nashville, TN 37203
p: 615-255-6161
f: 615-254-4490
www.mjhclaw.com
contact: David S. Crow
e: dcrow@mjhclaw.com
focus: Entertainment Law

Law Office of Sheela Murthy
10451 Mill Run Cir., Ste. 100
Owings Mills, MD 21117
p: 410-356-5440
f: 410-356-5669
e: law@murthy.com
www.murthy.com
contact: Sheela Murthy
focus: Immigration Law

National Immigration Services
18760 E Amar Rd., #150
Walnut, CA 91789
p: 626-810-1357
e: immigr8@yahoo.com
www.myvisa.com
contact: Theodore Huang
focus: Immigration Law
Visa assistance for musicians to play in the USA.

Eric Norwitz
3333 W 2nd St., Ste. 52-214
Los Angeles, CA 90004
p: 213-389-3477
f: 213-388-3737
contact: Eric Norwitz
e: enorwitz@pacbell.net
focus: Entertainment Law, IP
Works w/ Indie musicians & labels.

Law Office of Marty O'Toole
1999 Ave. of the Stars
Ste. 1100
Century City, CA 90067
p: 310-888-4000
f: 310-356-4688
e: mx@lawofficesofmartyotoole.com
www.lawofficesofmartyotoole.com
contact: Marty O'Toole
e: marty@martyotoole.com
focus: Entertainment Law, Contracts, Intellectual Property

Pelosi, Wolf, Effron & Spates
233 Broadway, 22nd Fl.
New York, NY 10279

p: 212-334-4801
f: 212-571-9149
www.pwes.com
contact: John Pelosi
ext: 212-334-3599
e: jpelosi@pwes.com
focus: Entertainment Law, IP

Law Office of Janis Peterson-Lord
3454 E Anaheim St.
Long Beach, CA
90804
p: 562-494-1010
f: 562-494-4545
e: immigration.law@verizon.net
www.janispetersonlord.com
contact: Janis Peterson-Lord
focus: Immigration Law

Proskauer Rose
2049 Century Park E
Ste. 3200
Los Angeles, CA
90067
p: 310-557-2900
f: 310-557-2193
e: webmaster@proskauer.com
www.proskauer.com
contact: Bert H. Deixler
ext: 310-284-5663
e: bdeixler@proskauer.com
focus: Entertainment Law, IP
*Offices in **NYC:** 212-969-3000; **Washington, DC:** 202-416-6800; **NJ:** 973-274-3200; **FL:** 561-241-7400; **Boston:** 617-526-9600; **New Orleans:** 504-310-4088.*

Vesna N. Rafaty
15851 Dallas Pkwy., Ste. 600
Addison, TX 75001
p: 214-561-8621; 214-995-8371
f: 214-561-8622; 972-818-7284
www.lawyers.com/rafaty
contact: Vesna N. Rafaty
e: vesnarafaty@msn.com
focus: Entertainment Law, IP

Law Office of Tod Ratfield
1233 Alpine Rd.
Walnut Creek, CA 94596
p: 925-934-3300
f: 925-934-9775
contact: Tod M. Ratfield
e: todratfield@yahoo.com
focus: Entertainment Law
No deal shopping.

Bernard Max Resnick
2 Bala Plaza, Ste. 300
Bala Cynwyd, PA 19004
p: 610-660-7774
f: 610-668-0574
www.bernardresnick.com
contact: Bernard Resnick
e: bmresnick@aol.com
focus: Entertainment Law, Immigration, Intellectual Property

Ricks Rainey
Howard Hughes Ctr., 6100 Center Dr., Ste. 630
Los Angeles, CA 90045
p: 310-670-4868
f: 310-670-4789
contact: Georgetta Ricks Rainey
e: raineyatty@aol.com
focus: Entertainment Law

Roberts, Ritholz, Levy, Sanders, Chidekel & Fields
183 Madison Ave.
19th Fl.
Penthouse
New York, NY 10016
p: 212-448-1800
f: 212-448-0020
e: info@robritlaw.com
www.robritlaw.com
contact: Jaimison Roberts
e: jroberts@robritlaw.com
focus: Entertainment Law

Robinson, Brog, Leinwand, Greene, Genovese & Gluck
1345 Ave. of the Americas
31st Fl.
New York, NY 10105
p: 212-603-6300
f: 212-956-2164
www.ipmegroup.com
contact: Gary Adelman
ext: 212-603-0481
e: gpa@robinsonbrog.com
focus: Entertainment Law, IP, Contracts, Litigation, Internet Law
Also does Indie label consulting.

Romanello Professional Assoc.
1560 Sawgrass Corporate Pkwy., 4th Fl.
Sunrise, FL 33323
p: 954-331-8020
f: 954-827-0472
http://romanellopa.com/contact.html
contact: Steven Romanello
e: sromanello@romanellopa.com
focus: Entertainment Law, IP, Contracts, Int'l Law

Richard D. Rose
9 Music Sq. S, #3700
Nashville, TN 37203
p: 615-330-7673
e: info@copyrightcafe.com
www.copyrightcafe.com
contact: Richard D. Rose
e: richard@copyrightcafe.com
focus: Entertainment Law, IP

Law Office of Chris J. Roy, Sr.
2006 Gus Kaplan Dr.
Ste. 2B
Alexandria, LA 71301
p: 318-767-1114
f: 318-767-1404
www.lawyers.com/croy
contact: Chris Roy
e: croy929@cox-internet.com
focus: Entertainment Law

Law Offices of Michael Norman Saleman
100 Congress Ave.
11th Fl.
Austin, TX 78701
p: 512-263-5932
f: 512-263-5929
www.salemanlaw.com
contact: Michael Saleman
e: saleman@aol.com; saleman@movielaw.net
focus: Entertainment Law
*Offices in **LA:** 310-553-1600 **Dallas:** 888-222-8959.*

Scott D. Sanders
21 8th St. NE
Atlanta, GA 30309
p: 404-873-4422
f: 404-873-4480
contact: Scott Sanders
e: scott@entlaw.com
focus: Entertainment Law, IP

Sedgwick, Detert, Moran & Arnold
3 Park Plaza
17th Fl.
Irvine, CA 92614
p: 949-852-8200 x7828
f: 949-852-8282
www.sdma.com
contact: Michael E. Fox
e: michael.e.fox@sdma.com
focus: Entertainment Law, IP
Does demo shopping. Offices in San Francisco, Los Angeles, Chicago, Dallas, Houston, Austin, NYC Metro, London, Paris & Zurich.

Shukat, Arrow, Hafer, Weber & Herbsman
111 W 57th St., #1120
New York, NY 10019
p: 212-245-4580
f: 212-956-6471
e: info@musiclaw.com
www.musiclaw.com
contact: Jonas Herbsman
e: jonas@musiclaw.com
focus: Entertainment Law, Intellectual Property, Contracts
No deal shopping.

David Carlson Smith
125 Lincoln Ave.
Ste. 400
Santa Fe, NM
87501
p: 505-988-8868
f: 505-988-2746
e: attydcs@earthlink.net
www.lawyers.com/davidcarlsonsmith
contact: David Carlson Smith
focus: Entertainment Law, IP

SmithAmundsen
150 N Michigan Ave.,
Ste. 3300
Chicago, IL 60601
p: 312-894-3358
f: 312-894-3210
www.salawus.com
contact: Brian Rosenblatt
e: brosenblatt@salawus.com
focus: Entertainment Law, IP

Stairs, Dillenbeck, Finley & Rendon
330 Madison Ave.
29th Fl.
New York, NY 10017
p: 212-697-2700
f: 212-687-3525
e: stairs@stairsdillenbeck.com
www.stairsdillenbeck.com
contact: David Glinert
focus: Entertainment Law

Stephens & Rueda
2926 Maple Ave.
Ste. 200
Dallas, TX 75201
p: 214-528-5353
f: 214-528-5354
e: stephenslaw@hotmail.com
contact: Michael Stephens
ext: 214-528-5353 x2
focus: Entertainment Law
Does deal shopping.

Stewart, Estes & Donnell
Sun Trust Ctr.
424 Church St.
Ste. 1401
Nashville, TN
37219
p: 615-244-6538
f: 615-256-8386
e: info@sedlaw.com
www.sedlaw.com
contact: R. Horton Frank, III
e: hfrank@sedlaw.com
focus: Entertainment Law, IP

Tabor Law Firm
1608 Hartford Rd.
Ste. 100
Austin, TX 78703
p: 512-708-8584
f: 512-708-8766
www.lawyers.com/taborlaw
contact: Catherine Tabor
e: ctabor@bga.com
focus: Entertainment Law, IP

Texas Accountants & Lawyers for the Arts
1540 Sul Ross
Houston, TX 77006
p: 800-526-8252; 713-526-4876 x201
f: 713-526-1299
e: info@talarts.org
www.talarts.org
contact: Darby Mair
ext: 713-526-4876 x205
e: darby@talarts.org
focus: Entertainment Law
Non-profit org provides legal services for artists.

Julius L. Thompson
5080 Spectrum Dr.
Ste. 114W
Addison, TX
75001
p: 972-385-3700
f: 972-385-1271
www.jltlawoffice.com
contact: Julius L. Thompson
e: julius@jltlawfirm.com
focus: Entertainment Law

Underwood, Perkins & Ralston
5420 LBJ Frwy.,
Ste. 1900
Bldg. 2
Dallas, TX 75240
p: 972-661-5114
f: 972-661-5691
www.uprlaw.com
contact: Evan Fogelman
e: efogelman@suplaw.com
focus: Entertainment Law, IP

Peter Vaughan Shaver/ Sound Advice
3939 NE Hancock St.
Ste. 308
Portland, OR 97212
p: 503-473-8252
f: 503-288-5219
contact: Peter Vaughan Shaver
ext: 503-295-2787
e: pvshaver@hotmail.com
focus: Entertainment Law, IP, Contracts, Internet Law

Weston, Garrou, Walters, Mooney
50 W Broadway
10th Fl.
Salt Lake City, UT
84101
p: 801-364-5635
f: 310-442-0899
www.mooneylaw.com
contact: Jerome H. Mooney
ext: 801-364-6500
e: jerrym@mooneylaw.com
focus: Entertainment Law
Los Angeles: 310-442-0072.

managers

10th St. Entertainment
700 San Vincente Blvd.
Ste. G410
West Hollywood, CA 90069
p: 310-385-4700
f: 310-385-4742
e: info@10thst.com
www.10thst.com
contact: Allen Kovac
ext: 212-334-3160
genres: Rock, Pop, Country
clients: Motley Crue, Buckcherry, Sixx AM, Drowning Pool, Papa Roach
NY office: 212-334-3160. Send music, bio, press & photos.

2 Generations SPA Music Management
225 E 34th St.
Ste. 8J
New York, NY 10016
p: 212-842-8478
f: 212-735-6862
www.2generations.com
contact: Aimee Berger
e: aimee@2generations.com
genres: Rock, Pop, S/S
clients: Matt Stamm, Natascha Sohl, Jeff Stephens, Nicolette Hart
Not seeking new clients.

21st Century Management
3302 W Wrightwood Ave.
Chicago, IL 60647
p: 773-235-0030
f: 773-235-0030
e: 21centurymngt@earthlink.net
contact: Michael Ryan
genres: Industrial, Rock, Pop, S/S, Alt., Punk
clients: Sister Machine Gun, Judybats, The Moment, Micronaut

2Deep Entertainment
PO Box 20097
New York, NY 10001
p: 240-882-2202
e: info@2deepentertainment.com
www.2deepentertainment.com
contact: Frankie Davis
e: frankie@2deepentertainment.com
genres: Urban, Gospel, Pop
clients: Amerie, Sunshine Anderson, Nataly, Lil Bink

5B Artist Management
581 6th Ave.
4th Fl.
New York, NY 10011
p: 212-445-3500
f: 212-445-3543
e: livanos@5bam.com
contact: Cory Brennan
ext: 212-445-3533
genres: Metal, Rock, Alt.
clients: Slipknot, Stone Sour, State Of Shock, Madina Lake, Black Tide, Dirty Little Rabbits
No unsolicited material.

Access Talent Consultant Services
6265 Bellinger Dr.
Galloway, OH 43119
p: 614-878-7292
f: 614-878-7292
e: spotlight3records@yahoo.com
www.myspace.com/spotlight3records
contact: James Bruce
genres: Country, Rock, Pop
clients: Category IV, Debbie Collins, Brandi Howard
Send demos & photos.

Adina Management
New York, NY 10019
p: 248-310-5648
contact: Adina Friedman
e: adinaf@gmail.com
genres: Pop, Rock, Alt.
clients: April Smith
Not seeking new clients.

AIC Entertainment
321 High School Rd. NE
Ste. D3, PMB210
Bainbridge Island, WA 98110
p: 206-781-3956
f: 206-842-5337
e: info@aicentertainment.com
www.aicentertainment.com
contact: Amanda Case
genres: S/S, Folk, Pop, Rock, Americana, Jazz, World
clients: Ian Moore, Two Loons For Tea, Spottiswoode & His Enemies, Bronwen Exter, Don DiLego
No unsolicited material & not seeking new clients.

AIF Music Productions
PO Box 691
Mamaroneck, NY 10543
p: 914-381-3559
e: aifrecords@verizon.net
www.robertjackson.net/aif%20records.htm
contact: Robert Jackson
genres: All Styles mainly Rock & Alt.
clients: Young Spank, Connecticut Drums, Liquor Daddies
Payment is a combo of fee & %.

Alert Music
51 Hillsview Ave.
Toronto, ON M6P 1J4
Canada
p: 416-364-4200
f: 416-364-8632
e: contact@alertmusic.com
www.alertmusic.com
contact: W. Tom Berry
genres: Jazz, Folk, Blues, Roots
clients: Holly Cole, Kim Mitchell, Roxanne Potvin, Michael Kaeshammer
No unsolicited material & not seeking new clients.

Allure Media Entertainment
PO Box 648
Conshohocken, PA 19428
p: 215-601-1499
www.allureartists.com
contact: Casey Alrich
genres: Rock, Alt. Rock, Pop, Adult Rock, R&B, Hip-Hop
clients: Stealing Love Jones, Greg Howe, Gallucio, Tom Taylor, The Wonder Years
Submission guidelines on site.

American Artists Entertainment Group
2106 79th Ct.
Vero Beach, FL 32966
p: 772-569-1040
f: 772-569-1051
e: online@aaegec.com
www.aaeg.com
contact: Anthony Messina
genres: Pop, Rock, R&B, Country, S/S
clients: Anagoes, We Are Only Fiction, Jenny Galiardi, Juda, Sterling
Offices located in NYC, Los Angeles & Philadelphia. Not seeking new clients.

American Management
19948 Mayall St.
Chatsworth, CA 91311
p: 818-993-9943
f: 818-993-6459
www.muzbiz2000.com
contact: Jim Wagner
e: jrwagner@earthlink.net
genres: Rock, Country
clients: Tommy Roe, Bobby Vee, The Original Tymes, Cathy Young, Merle Haggard
No unsolicited material.

Angelica Arts & Entertainment/ Tuscan Sun
Nashville, TN
p: 615-794-0485
f: 615-591-1463
e: mgmt@angelica.org
www.angelica.org
contact: Jules Delgado
genres: Ambient, Lounge, New Age, Pop, World
clients: Seay, Pat Thomi
No unsolicited material & not seeking new clients.

Anglo Management
Fulham Palace, Bishops Ave.
London, England SW6 6EA
UK
p: 44-207-384-7373
f: 44-207-384-7375
www.angloplugging.co.uk
contact: Garry Blackburn
genres: Hip-Hop, Rock, R&B
clients: Fatboy Slim, Stereo MCs, Richard Scanty, Scratch Perverts,Spacemonkeyz
Not seeking new clients.

Apple Core Productions
1204 NE 71st Ave.
Portland, OR 97213
p: 503-939-6155
www.applecoreproductions.com
contact: Mike Tucker
e: mike@applecoreproductions.com
genres: Pop, Rock
clients: Climber
No unsolicited material & not seeking new clients.

Area 67 Entertainment
2216 W 103rd St.
Cleveland, OH 44102
p: 216-235-4549
f: 216-939-8715
e: mvillegas@area67entertainment.com
www.area67entertainment.com
contact: Jill Bandella
e: info@area67entertainment.com
genres: Rock, Metal, Urban, Pop, Punk, Reggae, Jam, Rock, Prog, Jazz, AC
clients: Doc Mav, The M-Collective, Falling Over Failure
Prefers online EPKs, but accepts snail mail.

Arkiteks Music Group
10061 Riverside Dr.
North Hollywood, CA 91602
p: 505-280-8394
f: 818-506-6276
e: info@thearkiteks.com
www.thearkiteks.com
contact: Marco Nunez
e: thearkiteks@aol.com
genres: Urban, Gospel, Rock, Electronic, Remixes
clients: The James Douglas Show, David Wade, AB, Melanie Heinz, Honore
Material to: 401 Espejo NE, Albuquerque, NM 87123. No calls!

Artist In Mind
14625 Dickens St., Ste. 207
Sherman Oaks, CA 91403
p: 818-752-8020
f: 818-752-8026
e: info@artistinmind.com
contact: Doug Buttleman
genres: Rock, Alt., Pop, AAA
clients: The Verve Pipe, Remy Zero, Will Hoge, Sanders Bohlke, Brian Vander Ark
No unsolicited material & not seeking new clients.

Artist Management Group
1131 LaMonte
Houston, TX 77018
p: 713-263-7115
www.amgtexas.com
contact: Richard Cagle
e: recagle@montroserecords.net
genres: Rock, Blues, Country, Pop
clients: Carolyn Wonderland, Crash Comfort, Grey Eyed Athena, Simpleton
Focuses on TX artists. Send CD, pics & press.

ASquared Management
624 Davis St.
2nd Fl.
Evanston, IL 60201
p: 847-424-2000
f: 847-424-2001
e: awareinfo@awaremusic.com
www.asquaredmgmt.com
contact: Jason Rio
ext: 773-248-4210
e: jason@awaremusic.com
genres: S/S, Acoustic, Rock
clients: Liz Phair, Motion City Soundtrack, The Fray, Jackopierce, Mat Kearney
No unsolicited material & not seeking new clients.

Asti Management
66 Irving Pl.
Ste. 1
New York, NY 10003
p: 212-529-6400
f: 212-529-9315
contact: Kristi Clifford
ext: 212-529-6400 x4
e: kristi@astientertainment.com
genres: Urban, Pop, Rock
clients: Kid Capri, Styles P, The Lo, Mike Epps, Uninvited Guests
No unsolicited material & not seeking new clients.

Avenue Management Group
1801 Ave. of the Stars
Ste. 421
Los Angeles, CA 90067
p: 310-312-0300
f: 310-479-1356
e: info@avenuemanagementgroup.com
www.avenuemanagementgroup.com
contact: Peter Durando
e: peter@avenuemusicgroup.com
genres: All Styles
clients: War, Sly Stone
No unsolicited material & not seeking new clients. No calls.

Azoffmusic Management
1100 Glendon Ave.
Ste. 2000
Los Angeles, CA 90024
p: 310-209-3100
f: 310-209-3101
contact: Susan Markheim
e: susan.markheim@azoffmusic.com
genres: Pop, Rock
No unsolicited material & not seeking new clients.

B.A.M. Management
2409 21st Ave. S, #100
Nashville, TN 37212
p: 615-320-7041
f: 615-320-0856
e: entartnash@aol.com
contact: Bobby Bessone
genres: Rap, Hip-Hop, Rock
clients: Coolio, Digital Underground, Tone Loc, Shock G, Young MC
No unsolicited material & not seeking new clients.

Backstage Artist Management
18352 N Dallas Pkwy.
Ste. 545
Dallas, TX 75287
p: 214-407-7992
f: 214-387-0785
e: bamrecords@msn.com
www.bamrecordsmusic.com
contact: Jerry Roy
genres: Rock, Pop, Country, R&B, Christian
clients: Mia Kulba
Also runs B-A-M Records.

Backstage Entertainment
26239 Senator Ave.
Harbor City, CA 90710
p: 310-325-9997
f: 310-427-7333
e: staff@backstageentertainment.net
www.backstageentertainment.net
contact: Paul Loggins
ext: 310-325-2800
genres: Rock, Pop, Urban, S/S, Smooth Jazz, Alt., Country
Also does web development, publicity & charts radio airplay. Not seeking new clients.

B.A.M. Management
2409 21st Ave. S
#100
Nashville, TN 37212
p: 615-320-7041
f: 615-320-0856
e: entartnash@aol.com
contact: Bobby Bessone
genres: Rap, Hip-Hop, Rock
clients: Coolio, Digital Underground, Tone Loc, Shock G, Young MC
No unsolicited material & not seeking new clients.

BandGuru Management
PO Box 11192
Denver, CO 80211
p: 303-477-6987
f: 303-561-1496
www.bandguru.com
contact: Mark Bliesner
e: mark@bandguru.com
genres: All Styles
clients: Alan Parsons, George Inai
No unsolicited material & not seeking new clients.

Barbra Baker Management
1346 Masselin Ave.
Los Angeles, CA 90019
p: 323-939-9964
f: 323-931-3273
contact: Barbra Baker
e: barbra.baker@ca.rr.com
genres: All Styles
clients: When In Rome, Streetside
Send CD, bio, pics & reviews.

Bear Creek Producer Management
6313 Maltby Rd.
Woodinville, WA 98072
p: 425-481-4100
f: 425-486-2718
www.bearcreekstudio.com
contact: Manny Hadlock
e: mannyhadlock@hotmail.com
genres: Rock, Indie, Folk, Jazz
clients: Anne Hadlock, Vertigo, Gordon Raphael, Ryan Hadlock, Holy Ghost Revival, Transgressive
Manages artists, producers & engineers. Also a studio. Looking for new clients; contact first. No unsolicited material.

Benchmark Entertainment
8721 Sunset Blvd.
Penthouse 1, 3rd Fl.
Los Angeles, CA 90069
p: 310-289-3530
f: 310-289-3531
e: benchmarkla@earthlink.net
contact: John Dee
ext: 310-289-3531 x106
genres: R&B, S/S, Blues, Rock
clients: Maxwell, Megadeth, eels, Mark Lanegan, Chris Stills
No unsolicited material & not seeking new clients.

Berkeley Agency
2608 9th St.
#301
Berkeley, CA 94710
p: 510-843-4902
f: 510-843-7271
e: mail@berkeleyagency.com
www.berkeleyagency.com
contact: Jim Cassell
e: jim@berkeleyagency.com
genres: Latin, Jazz, Blues
clients: Marlena Shaw, Tania Maria, Claudia Villela, Lavay Smith, Eddie Palmieri
No unsolicited material & not seeking new clients.

Big Hassle Management
44 Wall St., 22nd Fl.
New York, NY 10005
p: 212-619-1360
f: 212-619-1669
www.bighassle.com
contact: Mike Maska
ext: 215-247-8523
e: maska@bighassle.com
genres: Alt., Indie, Rock, Pop
clients: Eric Hutchinson, Joe Jackson, The National, Nicole Atkins, Clogs
Not seeking new clients.

Big Noise
11 S Angell St.
Ste. 336
Providence, RI 02906
p: 401-274-4770
www.bignoisenow.com
contact: Al Gomes
e: al@bignoisenow.com
genres: Pop, Rock, R&B, Metal, Jazz, Acoustic, Blues, Punk, Techno, Christian
clients: Christina Aguilera, Katharine McPhee, Chicago, Little Anthony & The Imperials, Jay Geils, Paul Doucette (Matchbox 20)
Currently seeking new clients. Does artist development, A&R, music marketing, and Film & TV licensing. Also runs Big Noise Records. Please call or email first.
See Ad On Next Page

Bitchin Entertainment
PO Box 413
Lindale, GA 30147
p: 706-235-3475
www.bitchinentertainment.com
contact: Theresa Yarbrough
e: ty@bitchinentertainment.com
genres: Rock, Pop, Urban, Americana, Country, Jazz, Punk, Metal, Folk, S/S
clients: Karma, State Of Man, Blasternaut, Baby Strange, Donal Hinely
Seeking unsigned "Label Ready Artists" to showcase & market. Must have copyrighted original music & composition.

Black Rose
409 Rte. 112
Pt. Jefferson Station, NY 11776
p: 631-928-0660
f: 631-928-5705
www.blackroseproductions.com
contact: Tito Batista
e: titobatista@blackroseproductions.com
genres: Jazz, Rock, R&B, Gospel, Hip-Hop, Country, Blues, Pop
clients: Bulldog Evans Records, Layaway, Nitrogen Enterprises, Warren Kelson, Chris Rose
Must be copyrighted to Library of Congress. Send up to 3 songs.

Blanton, Harrell, Cooke & Corzine
5250 Virginia Way
Ste. 110
Brentwood, TN 37027
p: 615-627-0444
f: 615-627-0449
www.bhccmgt.com
contact: Chaz Corzine
ext: 615-627-0453
e: cherry@bhccmgt.com
genres: Christian
clients: Michael W. Smith, Amy Grant, Frank Peretti, Aaron Shust, Bebo Norman
No unsolicited material.

Bliss Artist Management
PO Box 5011
Laurel, MD 20726
p: 301-938-0838
f: 888-608-5936
e: bliss51@onebox.com
www.blissartistmgt.com
contact: Linda Sharpless
genres: Urban, Gospel, Rock, Blues, Jazz
clients: Nexxzit, DJ Sir, Jamm, Fox Burner, Tabbo
Send bio, photo & CD.

Blue Moon Music
37 West St., Wigton
Cumbria, CA7 9NX UK
f: 44-797-346-3767
www.bluemoonmusic.co.uk
contact: Jil Barke
ext: 44-167-934-2779
e: jil@bluemoonmusic.co.uk
genres: Folk, Acoustic
clients: While & Matthews Band, Helen Watson, St. Agnes Fountain
Not seeking new clients.

Bob Benjamin Management
201 S 2nd Ave., #22
Highland Park, NJ 08904
p: 732-249-3911
f: 732-249-3715
contact: Bob Benjamin
e: njbob113@aol.com
genres: Rock
clients: Joe Grushecky, Boccigalupe, Joe D'Urso, Dawne Alynne
No unsolicited material.

Borman Entertainment
1250 6th St., Ste. 401
Santa Monica, CA 90401
p: 310-656-3150
f: 310-656-3160
e: bormanent@bormanla.com
contact: Gary Borman
genres: Rock, Country, Folk
clients: Faith Hill, Keith Urban, Natalie Cole, Kenny Loggins
Nashville office: 615-320-3000. No unsolicited material.

Brick Wall Management
39 W 32nd St., Ste. 1403
New York, NY 10001
p: 212-501-0748
f: 212-268-3544
e: bwmgmt@brickwallmgmt.com
www.brickwallmgmt.com
contact: Michael Solomon
e: michael@brickwallmgmt.com
genres: Pop, Rock, Country, R&B
clients: Marc Broussard, The Clarks, Slow Runner, Alternate Routes
Contact before sending material.

Bridge Entertainment Group
1404 3rd St. Promenade
Ste. 202
Santa Monica, CA 90401
p: 310-451-4400
e: info@tbentgroup.com
www.tbentgroup.com
contact: Chelsea Laird
genres: Pop, Alt.
clients: Tori Amos, Leslie Mendelson

Agency founded by Tori Amos to help artists manage everything from creating marketing campaigns to tours. No unsolicited material & not seeking new clients.

Brilliant Productions
Decatur, GA 30030
p: 404-373-2299
www.brilliant-productions.com
contact: Nancy Lewis-Pegel
e: npegel@mindspring.com
genres: Roots, Rock, Jam, Americana, Blues
clients: Col. Bruce Hampton, Webb Wilder, David Gans, Delta Moon, Geoff Achison
No unsolicited material & not seeking new clients.

Bruce Allen Talent
500-425 Carrall St.
Vancouver, BC V6B 6E3
Canada
p: 604-688-7274
f: 604-688-7118
e: info@bruceallen.com
www.bruceallen.com
contact: Bruce Allen
genres: Pop, Rock, Country
clients: Bryan Adams, Martina McBride, Bob Rock, Michael Buble, Anne Murray
No unsolicited material & not seeking new clients.

Bumstead Productions
PO Box 158, Stn. E
Toronto, ON M6H 4E2
Canada
p: 416-656-2600
f: 416-656-9822
e: info@bumstead.com
www.bumstead.com
contact: Larry Wanagas
genres: Rock, Pop
clients: The Trews, Boy, Peter Elkas, Two Hours Traffic
No unsolicited material & not seeking new clients.

Burgess Worldco
PO Box 646
Mayo, MD 21106
p: 410-798-7798
f: 410-798-0099
e: info@burgessworldco.com
www.burgessworldco.com
contact: Richard James Burgess
e: rjb@burgessworldco.com
genres: Rock, Alt., Blues
clients: Jimmie's Chicken Shack, Jarflys, The Electrofied Blues Band, DZK

BusyBoy Productions
1721 Minnehaha Ave., Ste. 1
St. Paul, MN 55104
p: 651-230-4362
www.busyboyproductions.com
contact: Jack Paar
e: jack@busyboyproductions.com
genres: Rock, Metal, Pop, Country, Alt.
clients: Core, Ella Reid, Roxi Rae, Lizzy Borden, White Lion
Send music, photo & bio.

Capitol Artist Management
PO Box 221266
Sacramento, CA 95822
p: 916-422-7262
f: 916-422-3670
contact: Catherine Walden
e: cathiwalden@prodigy.net
genres: Jazz, Urban, Gospel, Blues, Funk, Spoken Word
clients: LynAnn King, Symposium, Brown Suga, Costie Payne

Capitol Management Group
1214 16th Ave. S
Nashville, TN 37212
p: 615-321-0600; 800-767-4984
f: 615-321-0182
e: info@capitolmanagement.com
www.capitolmanagement.com
contact: Robert Metzgar
e: robertmetzgar@aol.com
genres: Pop, Country, Bluegrass, Gospel, CCM, Americana, Rock, Traditional
clients: Smokey River Boys, Stampede, Bone Creek, Ali Shumate, Heartland
Write Attn: Requested Material on package.

Carlson Entertainment
PO Box 692081
Orlando, FL 32869
p: 407-362-7782
www.carlsonentertainment.com
contact: John K. Carlson
e: john@carlsonentertainment.com
genres: Alt., Country, Latin, Pop, Rock, S/S, Pop, Soul
clients: Detlef Zoo, Stars Go Dim, Winter Moods, The Morning After
Submit material via Sonicbids.

CEC Management
520 Eighth Ave.
Ste. 2001
New York, NY 10018
p: 212-206-6765
f: 212-563-5099
www.myspace.com/cecmanagementmusic
contact: Alan Wolmark
e: alan@cecmgmt.com
genres: Pop, Rock, Alt., Jazz
clients: David Berkeley, Hotel Lights, Eldar, Switches, Small Mercies
London office: 44-207-837-2517. No unsolicited material & not seeking new clients.

Chris Smith Management
21 Camden St.
5th Fl.
Toronto, ON M5V 1V2
Canada
p: 416-362-7771
f: 416-362-6648
e: info@chrissmithmanagement.com
www.chrissmithmanagement.com
contact: Cheryl Murphy
ext: 416-362-7771 x24
genres: Rock, Pop, Alt., Urban, Reggae
clients: James Bryan, Jarvis Church, Nelly Furtado, Jon Levine, Reamonn
No unsolicited material & not seeking new clients.

CMO Management
Studio 2.6, Sheperds East, Richmond Way
London, W14 0DQ UK
p: 44-207-316-6969
f: 44-207-316-6970
e: reception@cmomanagement.co.uk
www.cmomanagement.co.uk
contact: Chris Morrison
genres: Rock, Pop
clients: Blur, Turin Brakes, Capricorn 2, Graham Coxon, Gorillaz
No unsolicited material & not seeking new clients.

Coalition Entertainment
10271 Yonge St., Ste. 302
Richmond Hill, ON L4C 3B5
Canada
p: 905-508-0025
f: 905-508-0403
e: info@coalitionent.com
www.coalitionent.com
contact: Derek Camastra
e: derek.camastra@coalitionent.com
genres: Rock, Pop
clients: Our Lady Peace, Simple Plan, Finger 11, Neverending White Lights, The Waking Eyes
Not seeking new clients.

Cookman Int'l
10627 Burbank Blvd.
North Hollywood, CA 91601
p: 818-763-1397
f: 818-763-1398
e: mail@cookman.com
www.cookman.com
contact: Tomas Cookman
genres: Latin Alt., Rock, Pop
clients: Fabulosos Cadillacs, Manu Chao, Aterciopelados, Plastilina Mosh, Bostich & Fussible
Also sponsors LAMC & runs Nacional Records. No unsolicited material & not seeking new clients.

Countdown Entertainment
110 W 26th St., 3rd Fl.
New York, NY 10001
p: 212-645-3068
e: info@countdownentertainment.com
www.countdownentertainment.com
contact: James Citkovic
e: james@countdownentertainment.com
genres: Urban, Pop, Rock, Country, Alt., Dance, Club
clients: Steve Ronsen, Ken Tamplin
Also does record & publishing deals, int'l licensing, soundtrack placement & consulting. Seeking new clients. Check site for submission details.

Courtright Management
201 E 87th St.
Ste. 21C
New York, NY 10128
p: 212-410-9055
f: 212-831-0823
www.courtrightmgmt.com
contact: Hernando Courtright
e: courtrightmgmt@aol.com
genres: Indie Female Artists/Female Fronted Groups
clients: Deena Miller, Colporter, Stutter, Sasha Sokel, Constant Wonder
See site for submission policy. Will deal shop.

Creamer Management
32 Oak Sq. Ave.
Brighton, MA 02135
p: 617-783-6308
f: 617-787-5992
contact: Michael Creamer
e: creamermgt@aol.com
genres: Rock, Alt., Pop, S/S
clients: Superdrag, Kim Taylor, Todd Thibaud, Kay Hanley, Oteil Burbridge & The Peacemakers

Crush Management
60-62 E 11th St.
7th Fl.
New York, NY 10003
p: 212-334-4446
www.crushmm.com
contact: Jonathan Daniel
genres: Rock, Pop, Indie, Hip-Hop, S/S, Punk
clients: Butch Walker, The Academy Is..., Fall Out Boy, Panic At the Disco, Gym Class Heroes
No unsolicited material.

Cuervo Management
4924 Balboa Blvd.
#485
Encino, CA 91316
p: 818-788-2578
f: 818-788-2546
e: cuervomgt@yahoo.com
www.cuervomusic.com
contact: Javier Willis
genres: Reg'l Mexican Music, Spanish Rock, Alt., Reggaeton, Hip-Hop
clients: Pepe Aguilar, Sergio Arau, Cristian Castro, Ricardo Caballero, Carmen Jara

Dan Gillis Management
202 Scott Ave.
Nashville, TN 37206
p: 615-320-8730
f: 615-320-8766
e: info@dgmanagement.com
contact: Dan Gillis
e: dan@dgmanagement.com
genres: Alt. Country, Rock, Country, Cross-over Classical
clients: Steve Earle, Jessi Colter, Mark McGuinn, Nicholas Tremulis
No unsolicited material & not seeking new clients.

Danny Kahn/Cross Road Management
45 W 11th St., Ste. 7B
New York, NY 10011
p: 212-807-1509
f: 718-504-7899
contact: Danny Kahn
e: dkahn@crossroadmanagement.com
genres: Americana, Pop, Jazz, World
clients: Rosanne Cash, Ben Vaughn, The Jazz Passengers
No unsolicited material & not seeking new clients.

DAS Communications
83 Riverside Dr.
New York, NY 10024

p: 212-877-0400
f: 212-595-0176
contact: Rachel Cox
e: rachel@dasgroup.com
genres: Rock, Pop, Urban
clients: John Legend, Wyclef Jean, Black Eyed Peas, The Veronicas, Pixies
No unsolicited material.

Dave Kaplan Management
1126 S Coast Hwy. 101
Encinitas, CA 92024
p: 760-944-8800
f: 760-944-7808
e: anita@surfdog.com
www.surfdog.com
contact: Dave Kaplan
genres: Rock
clients: Brian Setzer, Stray Cats, Dave Stewart, Wylde Bunch, Dylan Donkin
Also runs Surfdog Records. No unsolicited material & not seeking new clients.

DCA Productions
676A 9th Ave.
#252
New York, NY 10036
p: 212-245-2063
f: 609-259-8260
e: info@dcaproductions.com
www.dcaproductions.com
contact: Daniel C. Abrahamsen
genres: Pop, Folk, Rock
clients: Total Soul Party, Andjam, Backbeat A Tribute, Alison Fraser, Lorna Bracewell
East Coast artists only send DVD, CD & presskit to: New Talent Submissions DCA Productions.

Deep South Entertainment
PO Box 17737
Raleigh, NC
27619
p: 919-844-1515
f: 919-847-5922
e: info@deepsouth entertainment.com
www.deepsouth entertainment.com
contact: Steve Williams
genres: Pop, Rock, Alt., Country, Americana, Christian
clients: Stryper, Vienna Teng, Lee Roy Parnell, The Subdudes, Kyler England
Other location in Nashville. Not seeking new clients. No calls.

Def Ro
60 Myrtle St., Ste. 1
Bloomfield, NJ 07003
p: 973-748-1970
f: 973-535-6569
e: defroinc@juno.com
www.myurl.in/defroinc
contact: Ro Smith
genres: R&B, Hip-Hop, Pop
clients: Mary J. Blige, Joe & Jaheim
Mail demo packages w/ photos & contact info.

Degy Management Services
PO Box 3036
West End, NJ 07740
p: 732-263-1000
f: 732-263-1500
e: info@degy.com
www.degy.com
contact: Ari Nisman
e: ari@degy.com
genres: All Styles
clients: Flickerstick, Nadine Zahr, Spiraling, Hero Pattern, The Finals
Also does booking. Office in Norcross, GA: 770-300-9655.

Direct Management Group
947 N La Cienega Blvd.
Ste. G
Los Angeles, CA 90069
p: 310-854-3535
f: 310-854-0810
www.directmanagement.com
contact: Dana Collins
genres: All Styles
clients: Jamie Cullum, The Gabe Dixon Band, Go-Go's, Boney James, k.d. lang
No unsolicited material & not seeking new clients.

Dream Street Management
4346 Redwood Ave.
Marina del Rey, CA 90292
p: 310-305-2699
f: 310-821-5448
e: dsmsm@aol.com
contact: Daniel Markus
genres: Blues, Jazz, R&B, World
clients: Hiroshima, Teddy Pendergrass
No unsolicited material & not seeking new clients.

DreaMakers
PO Box 5359
Crestline, CA 92325
p: 818-292-3090
f: 909-338-8560
contact: Richard Burkhart
e: rabdreamaker@aol.com
clients: Chuck Mangione, David Hooten, M-Pact, Mona Golabeck, The Red Letters Project
Contact before sending material. Not seeking new clients.

DS Management
PO Box 121499
Nashville, TN 37212
p: 615-385-3191
f: 615-385-3192
e: info@dsmanages.com
contact: Denise Stiff
e: denise@dsmanages.com
genres: Country, Bluegrass
clients: Alison Krauss, Jedd Hughes, Dan Tyminski
No unsolicited material & not seeking new clients.

East End Management
13721 Ventura Blvd., 2nd Fl.
Sherman Oaks, CA 91423
p: 818-784-9002
f: 818-784-9027
contact: Tony Dimitriades
ext: 818-985-5060
genres: Rock, Pop, Funk, Jazz
clients: Billy Idol, Tom Petty
No unsolicited material & not seeking new clients.

EGM
1040 Mariposa St., #200
San Francisco, CA 94107
p: 415-522-5292
f: 415-522-5293
e: hatemail@egminc.com
contact: Eric Godtland
genres: All Styles Of Rock
clients: Denny Porter
No unsolicited material.

Eichner Entertainment
381 Broadway
Westwood, NJ 07675
p: 201-664-6666
f: 201-664-6799
e: eichent@aol.com
www.eichnerentertainment .com
contact: Mark Eichner
genres: Pop, Rock, Urban
clients: Amy Atchley, Dirt Bike Annie, Steve Walsh
Material must be copyrighted.

Elevation Group
1408-A Encinal Ave.
Alameda, CA 94501
p: 510-864-2600
f: 510-864-2615
e: info@elevationgroup.net
www.elevationgroup.net
contact: Kent Sorrell
genres: All Styles
clients: Aaron Neville, Funky Meters, The New Mastersounds
No unsolicited material & not seeking new clients.

Elliot Cahn Management/Law Offices of Elliot Cahn
1035 7th St.
Oakland, CA 94607
p: 510-652-1615
f: 510-550-2770
www.elliotcahn.com
contact: Elliot Cahn
e: cahnman@aol.com
genres: Rock, Pop, Punk, S/S, R&B
clients: Goapele, Justin King
Email for permission to send material. Not seeking new clients.

Elysian Artist Management/EAM
37321 Cypress Ave.
Burney, CA 96013
p: 303-832-7679
f: 303-284-7871
e: info@elysianartists.com
www.myspace.com/ elysianartists
contact: Jeremy S. Walker
genres: Hip-Hop, Funk, Rock
clients: Yo, Flaco!, On The One, Free Sol
Seeking new clients. Accepts EPKs only - email first.

Emcee Artist Management
189 Franklin St.
Ste. 294
New York, NY 10013
p: 212-925-6458
f: 212-925-6482
e: info@mmw.net
contact: Liz Penta
e: liz@emceeartist.com
genres: Jazz, Rock, Blues
clients: Medeski, Martin & Wood, Marc Ribot
No unsolicited material & not seeking new clients.

Emerging Music
Sarah's Cottage, Horns Cross
Bideford, Devon EX39 5DW
UK
p: 44-123-745-1933
f: 44-123-745-1931
e: sue@ emerging.demon.co.uk
www.emergingmusic.co.uk
contact: Ken Bradburn
e: ken@ emerging.demon.co.uk
genres: Folk
clients: Bella Hardy, Annabelle Chvostek, Cathie Ryan, Nancy Kerr & James Fagan, Niamh Parsons
Not seeking new clients.

Entertainment Management Group
PO Box 91766
Elk Grove Village, IL 60009
p: 847-364-6400
f: 847-364-6409
e: emgtalent@aol.com
contact: Murray Weiner
ext: 847-364-6400 x1
genres: All Styles except Country & Rap
clients: O.vad.ya
Email for permission to submit No Country or Rap.

Eye for Talent
PO Box 280786
San Francisco, CA 94128
p: 650-595-2274
f: 650-595-2258
e: staff@eyefortalent.com
www.eyefortalent.com
contact: Bill Smith
e: bill@eyefortalent.com
genres: World, Jazz
clients: Amazones - Women Drummers Of Guinea, Andy Narell, Claudia Calderon, Culture Musical Club, Feufollet
No unsolicited material & not seeking new clients.

Finkelstein Management Co.
137 Berkeley St.
Toronto, ON M5A 2X1
Canada
p: 416-596-8696
f: 416-596-6861
e: info@finkelstein management.com
www.finkelstein management.com
contact: Bernie Finkelstein
e: bernie@finkelstein management.com
genres: Rock, S/S, Jazz
clients: Bruce Cockburn, Grand Analog, The Golden Dogs, Hunter Valentine
Seeking new clients.

The Firm
9465 Wilshire Blvd.
Ste. 600
Beverly Hills, CA
90212
p: 310-860-8000
f: 310-860-8100
e: info@firmmusic.net
www.firmmusic.com
contact: Pete Katsis
genres: Rock, Pop, Hip-Hop
clients: 30 Seconds To Mars, A Perfect Circle, Weezer, Jermaine Dupri, Michelle Branch
No unsolicited material & not seeking new clients.

The Fitzgerald Hartley Co.
34 N Palm St.
Ste. 100
Ventura, CA 93001
p: 805-641-6441
f: 805-641-6444
e: fitzhart34@aol.com
www.fitzhart.com
contact: Mark Hartley
genres: Country, Pop, Rock
clients: Colbie Caillat, Big Bad Voodoo Daddy, Brad Paisley, Crosby Loggins & The Namedroppers, Dwight Yoakam
No unsolicited material & not seeking new clients.

Fleming Artists
543 N Main St.
Ann Arbor, MI 48104
p: 734-995-9066
f: 734-662-6502
e: contact@ flemingartists.com
www.flemingartists.com
contact: Karla Rice
e: karla@flemingartists.com
genres: Rock, Pop, S/S, Contemporary Roots Rock, Folk, Bluegrass
clients: Ani Difranco, Dan Bern, Ellis Paul, Hamell On Trial, Melissa Ferrick
No unsolicited material & not seeking new clients.

Fontaine Music Agency
11669 Santa Monica Blvd.
Ste. 202
Los Angeles, CA
90025
e: fontainetalent@aol.com
www.fontainetalent.com
contact: Judith Fontaine
genres: Pop, Rock, Urban
clients: Devon, Fallon, Lynsey, Princess Adana
Focused on record deals for

youth-oriented acts.
No calls & not seeking new clients.

Freeze Artist Management
32941 Calle Perfecto, #C
San Juan Capistrano, CA
92653
p: 949-429-0929
f: 949-429-5760
www.freezemanagement.com
contact: John Reese
ext: 949-305-5570 x3002
e: jreese3067@aol.com
genres: Rock, Alt.
clients: Adair, Evaline, Head Automatica, Richard Kaplan, Steve Evetts
Other office in LA.

Fun Palace Entertainment
PO Box 20806
New York, NY
10023
p: 212-489-2425
f: 212-333-7226
e: funpalace@walrus.com
www.funpalaceentertainment.com
contact: Jack Bookbinder
genres: Alt., Rock
clients: The A.M., Ours, Crazy James, Jeff Buckley Music Inc.
No unsolicited material & not seeking new clients.

Fuzed Music
PO Box 19436
Seattle, WA 98109
p: 206-352-6892
f: 206-374-2429
e: info@fuzedmusic.com
www.fuzedmusic.com
contact: Grady Chapman
genres: Alt., Folk, Rock, Hip-Hop
clients: Blue Scholars, Common Market, The Presidents Of The United States Of America
SonicBids submissions only. Not seeking new clients.

Gailforce
55 Fulham High St.
London, SW6 3JJ UK
p: 44-207-384-8989
f: 44-207-384-8988
contact: Gail Colson
e: gail@gailforcemanagement.co.uk
genres: Rock
clients: Chrisse Hynde, The Pretenders, Peter Hammill, The Subways, Stephen Street
No unsolicited material & not seeking new clients.

Garvan Media, Management & Marketing
PO Box 737
Sandpoint, ID
83864
p: 208-265-1718
f: 208-265-7296
contact: Steve Garvan
e: steve@garvanmanagement.com
genres: Rock, S/S, Roots, Country, Americana
clients: Big Wide Grin, Cari Cole, Chris Daniels & the Kings, Cliff Eberhardt, Ezio
Mainly works w/ estab Nat'l acts.

Gold Mountain Entertainment
11 Music Sq. E
Ste. 103
Nashville, TN 37203
p: 615-255-9000
f: 615-255-9001
e: gmenash@bellsouth.net
www.gmemusic.com
contact: Burt Stein
genres: Country, Rock, Folk
clients: Ronnie Milsap, Nanci Griffith, The Crickets, Vince Neil, Todd Snider
CA office: 818-508-2210.
No unsolicited material & not seeking new clients.

Gorfaine-Schwartz Agency
4111 W Alameda Ave.
Ste. 509
Burbank, CA 91505
p: 818-260-8500
f: 818-260-8522
e: reception@gsamusic.com
www.gsamusic.com
clients: Todd Rundgren, Will Jennings, Barry Mann, Cynthia Weil, Glen Ballard
No unsolicited material & not seeking new clients.

Halfpipe Entertainment
PO Box 10534
Hollywood, CA
90213
p: 310-651-6233
e: mail@halfpipemusic.net
www.halfpipe-entertainment.com
contact: Lee Scheinbaum
e: halfpipe_ent@sbcglobal.net
genres: Alt., Rock, Indie, S/S, Surf Pop, Electronic, Lounge
clients: Andy Sturmer, Jeff Martin, Jeff Russo, Stefano Tomaselli, Scott Thomas
Not seeking new clients. Prefers streaming audio submissions.

Hard Head Management
PO Box 651
New York, NY 10014
p: 212-337-0760
f: 212-337-0708
e: info@hardhead.com
www.hardhead.com
contact: Stefani Scamardo
genres: Rock, Americana, S/S, Electronica
clients: Gov't Mule, Warren Haynes, DJ Logic, John Popper Project, Dumpstaphunk
Seeks new clients.

Hoffman Entertainment
362 5th Ave., Ste. 804
New York, NY 10001
p: 212-765-2525
f: 212-765-2888
e: info@hoffmanentertainment.com
www.hoffmanentertainment.com
contact: Randy Hoffman
genres: R&B, Rock, Pop, Country
clients: John Mellencamp, Gran Bel Fisher, Your Vegas, Jessie Baylin
No unsolicited material.

Horizon Management
PO Box 8770
Endwell, NY 13762
p: 607-785-9120
f: 607-785-4516
e: hmi67@aol.com
www.horizonmanagementinc.net
genres: All Styles
clients: The Pete Best Band, Queen Makedak, Frankie Kelly, Wawa Sylvestre, The Vognes
Call for permission to sumbit. Seeks new clients.

Hornblow Group USA
38 High Ave., 4th Fl.
Nyack, NY 10960
p: 845-358-7270
f: 845-358-8041
e: hbgusa@aol.com
www.hornblowgroup.com
contact: Jamie Kitman
genres: Alt., Rock
clients: They Might Be Giants, OK Go, Oppenheimer, Knife & Fork
Send promos to: PO Box 176, Palisades, NY 10964.

Impact Artist Management
356 W 123rd St.
New York, NY 10027
p: 212-280-0800
f: 212-280-0808
e: info@impactartist.com
www.impactartist.com
contact: Peter Himberger
ext: 212-280-0800 x1
e: peter@impactartist.com
genres: Jazz, World, Rock, Pop, R&B, Folk, Alt. Country
clients: Dr. John, Tom Wopat, Gipsy Kings, Shannon McNally, The New Standards
2nd contact: Aki Oduola; aki@impactartist.com.
No unsolicited material & not seeking new clients.

In De Goot Entertainment
119 W 23rd St., Ste. 609
New York, NY 10011
p: 212-924-7775
f: 212-691-8303
www.indegoot.com
contact: Tony Couch
e: tcouch@indegoot.com
genres: Rock, Pop
clients: Bo Bice, Puddle Of Mudd, The Parlor Mob, Saliva, Sevendust
Also runs McGathy Promotions.

In Touch Entertainment
445 Park Ave., 9th Fl.
New York, NY 10022
p: 212-714-7722
f: 212-202-7579
e: info@intouchhome.com
www.intouchhome.com
contact: Charles Carlini
genres: All Styles
clients: Dessy, Shayna Steele, Lisa Tingle, Jon Regen, Kashif
Submit material via SonicBids only. Not seeking new clients.

Invasion Group
133 W 25th St., 5th Fl.
New York, NY 10001
p: 212-414-0505
f: 212-414-0525
e: invasion@invasiongroup.com
www.invasiongroup.com
contact: Peter Casperson
ext: 212-414-0505 x106
genres: Rock, World, Folk, S/S
clients: Hamell On Trial, Marc Copely, Mary Fahl, Sara Lee, Guggenheim Grotto
Seeking new clients.

Jacobson & Colfin
60 Madison Ave., Ste. 1026
New York, NY 10010
p: 212-691-5630
f: 212-645-5038
e: thefirm@thefirm.com
www.thefirm.com
contact: Jeffrey Jacobson
e: jejesq@thefirm.com
genres: Rock, Blues, World
clients: Mick Taylor, Sly & Robbie, Masters At Work, Marty Balin, Shabba Ranks
Other location in Hewlett, NY: 212-691-5630. Submit material w/ a S.A.S.E. & proper postage for return.

Jealous Dogs Management
418 Jessie St., #701
San Francisco, CA 90027
p: 415-974-1755
contact: Sheila Scott
e: scottsheila@mac.com
genres: Rock, Pop, Alt.
clients: Ivy, Brookville
No unsolicited material & not seeking new clients.

Jerry Lembo Entertainment Group
742 Bergen Blvd.
Ridgefield, NJ 07657
p: 201-840-9980
f: 201-840-9921
www.lemboentertainment.com
contact: Jerry Lembo
e: jerry@lemboentertainment.com
genres: Pop, Rock, AAA
clients: Ben Green, Lucinda, No More Kings, Aranda, Dirt Poor Robins
Send CD, bio, touring history & photo. Seeking new clients mainly in S/S, Pop & Rock.

Joe Priesnitz Artist Management
PO Box 5249
Austin, TX 78763
p: 512-472-5435
f: 512-472-5717
contact: Joe Priesnitz
e: jpamaustin@aol.com
genres: Country, Rock, Americana
clients: Eric Johnson, The Gourds
No unsolicited material & not seeking new clients.

Joseph V. Hartlaub
52 Westerville Sq.
PMB #284
Westerville, OH 43081
p: 614-804-7579
f: 614-898-0120
www.myspace.com/joehartlaub
contact: Joseph Hartlaub
e: josephhartlaub@aol.com
genres: Alt., Rock, Country, Urban
clients: Fall of Man, FD, Volume Dealer, Odious,

Tu Rann
No unsolicited material.

Kari Estrin Management & Consulting
PO Box 60232
Nashville, TN
37206
p: 615-262-0883
www.kariestrin.com
contact: Kari Estrin
e: kari@kariestrin.com
genres: Americana, AAA, Roots
clients: David Llewellyn, Si Kahn, Helene & Michael Kates, Judith-Kate Friedman, Ben Bedford
See site before sending material.

Kragen & Co.
14039 Aubrey Rd.
Beverly Hills, CA 90210
p: 310-854-4400
f: 310-854-0238
e: info@kragenandcompany.com
www.kenkragen.com
contact: Ken Kragen
e: kenkragen@aol.com
genres: Country, Pop
clients: Suzanne Whang, Ronn Lucas, The Smothers Brothers, 12 Dogs of Christmas, Alisha Mullally
No unsolicited material & not seeking new clients.

Kuper Personal Management
PO Box 66274
Houston, TX 77266
p: 713-520-5791
e: info@recoveryrecordings.com
www.recoveryrecordings.com
contact: Koop Kuper
genres: Folk, Roots Rock, Americana
clients: The Very Girls, The Watchman, David Rodriguez, Los Vertigos, Def Squad Texas
Seeks new clients. Send press kit, CD-R, tear sheet & photo to:: 1119 Waugh Dr., #1, Houston, TX 77266.

Kurfirst-Blackwell Management
76 9th Ave.
Ste. 1110
New York, NY 10011
p: 212-320-3680
f: 212-320-3639
e: info@kurfirst-blackwellentertainment.com
www.kurfirst-blackwellentertainment.com
contact: Gary Kurfirst
genres: Rock, Alt., Pop
clients: Live, Tom Tom Club, Indigenous, Los Amigos Invisibles, Yerba Buena
LA office: 310-659-6958. No unsolicited material & not seeking new clients.

Latin Music Artists
10335 Juniper Creek Ln.
Las Vegas, NV 89145
p: 702-363-7273
f: 323-206-4116
e: info@latinmusicartists.com
www.latinmusicartists.com
contact: Issa Wilson
genres: Latin

Len Weisman Personal Management
357 S Fairfax Ave.
#430
Los Angeles, CA 90036
p: 818-362-9853
f: 323-653-7670
e: parlirec@aol.com
www.parliamentrecords.com
contact: Len Weisman
ext: 323-653-0693
e: persmanmnt@aol.com
genres: R&B, Blues, Gospel, Rap, Soul, Pop
clients: E'Morey, Jusvon, Jewel With Love, Chosen Gospel Recovery Singers, Big 'D'
Send CDs & self-addressed CD-sized envelope.

Lippman Entertainment
23586 Calabasas Rd.
#208
Calabasas, CA
91302
p: 818-225-7480
f: 818-225-7483
e: info@lippman-ent.com
www.lippman-ent.com
contact: Michael Lippman
ext: 818-225-7480 x101
e: lynnek@lippman-ent.com
genres: Rock, Pop, Urban, Alt.
clients: George Michael, Anna Nalick, Bernie Taupin, Rob Thomas, Matchbox 20
No unsolicited material & not seeking new clients.

Lo-Down Entertainment
1244 Pelican Pl.
New Braunfels, TX
78130
p: 626-219-6728
f: 830-632-6899
www.lodownent.net
contact: Francisco Logan
e: kidd20@hotmail.com
genres: Pop, R&B, Hip-Hop
clients: Gigi Harville, NeCee Wilson, Mahli, Boku, Valet, The New Era
Send press kit, photos, bio, 3 songs, gig listings & reviews.

Lorito Management
PO Box 729
Holbrook, NY 11741
p: 631-737-3743
f: 631-648-0543
e: info@loritomgt.com
www.loritomgt.com
contact: Philip Lorito
genres: Rock, Pop, Roots, Alt. Country, Americana
clients: Frank Carillo & The Bandoleros, Audioviolet
CDs only.

Luckie Pierre Recordings & Management
100 N Sycamore Ave., Ste. 11
Los Angeles, CA 90036
p: 323-571-3868
f: 877-572-0985
e: info@luckiepierre.com
www.luckiepierre.com
contact: Graham Kurzner
e: gkurzner@luckiepierre.com
genres: Alt., Rock, Folk, Bluegrass, Country, Pop, Ambient, Jazz
clients: Arnold, Voyager One, Buddy, Sirhan Duran
Snail mail material ATTN: Panda. Use S.A.S.E. if you want material returned - allow 4-6 wks. Not seeking new clients. No Calls!

Lupo Entertainment
725 River Rd., Ste. 32-388
Edgewater, NJ 07020
p: 201-736-3311
www.lupoentertainment.com
contact: Steve Corbin
e: steve@lupomusic.com
genres: Rock, Pop, R&B, Country
clients: Megan McCallon, PTM, Jim Wilson, Widescreen Mode
Send CD or DVDs.

Luther Wolf Agency
PO Box 685138
Austin, TX 78768
p: 512-448-3065
f: 512-448-3067
e: info@lutherwolf.com
www.lutherwolf.com
contact: Cory Moore
e: como@lutherwolf.com
genres: Rock, Blues
clients: Jimmie Vaughn, Lou Ann Barton, Greyhounds, Charlie Sexton, DeGuello
No unsolicited material.

M. Hitchcock Management
5101 Overton Rd.
Nashville, TN 37220
p: 615-333-0015
f: 615-333-0577
e: info@mhmgmt.com
www.mhmgmt.com
contact: Monty Hitchcock
e: mhitchcock@mhmgmt.com
genres: Alt. Country, Rock, Contemporary Folk, Country
clients: Jon Randall, John Starling & Carolina Star, Monte Montgomery, Ben Cyllus, Danny Flowers
No unsolicited material & not seeking new clients.

Macklam/Feldman Management
1505 W 2nd Ave., Ste. 200
Vancouver, BC V6H 3Y4
Canada
p: 604-734-5945
f: 604-732-0922
e: management@mfmgt.com
www.slfa.com
contact: Sam Feldman
e: feldman@slfa.com
genres: Pop, Jazz, World, Folk, Hip-Hop, Rock
clients: Joni Mitchell, Diana Krall, Norah Jones, Elvis Costello, Ry Cooder
No unsolicited material.

MAD Management
5355 Cartwright Ave., Ste. 115
North Hollywood, CA 91601
p: 323-908-1970
f: 425-977-1970
e: demo@madmanage.com
www.madmanage.com
contact: Michael Dutcher
e: michael@madmanage.com
genres: Rock, Alt, Hip-Hop, Country, Punk, Jazz, Blues
clients: The Bellrays, The Deadly Syndrome, Lisa Kekaula, Laura Turner, The Greater Good
Email for permission to submit.

Maine Road Management
195 Chrystie, Ste. 901F
New York, NY 10002
p: 212-979-9004
f: 212-979-0985
e: mailbox@maineroadmanagement.com
www.maineroadmanagement.com
contact: David Whitehead
ext: 212-226-0384
genres: Rock, S/S, Pop
clients: David Byrne, David Bowie, Joe Henry, Laura Cantrell, The Flatlanders
No unsolicited material & not seeking new clients.

Major Bob Music
1111 17th Ave S.
Nashville, TN 37212
p: 615-329-4150
f: 615-329-1021
www.majorbob.com
contact: Bob Doyle
genres: Country, Pop
clients: Garth Brooks, Mike Daly, Larry Bastian, Casey Kessel, Brent Anderson
No unsolicited material & not seeking new clients.

Manage This!
PO Box 256
New York, NY 10113
p: 212-229-3800
f: 212-229-9482
contact: David Newgarden
e: david.newgarden@managethis.net
genres: Alt.
clients: Guided By Voices, Robert Pollard, Tift Merritt, Turbo Fruits
No unsolicited material & not seeking new clients.

Management Ark
116 Village Blvd., Ste. 200
Princeton, NJ 08540
p: 609-734-7403
f: 609-799-6566
e: managearkeast@comcast.net
www.managementark.com
contact: Vernon Hammond III
e: vernon@managementark.com
genres: Jazz
clients: Wynton Marsalis, Kenny Garrett, Stanley Jordan
Also has an office in Bethesda, MD. No unsolicited material

Management By Jaffe
68 Ridgewood Ave.
Glen Ridge, NJ 07028
p: 973-743-1075
f: 973-743-1075
contact: Jerry Jaffe
e: jerjaf@aol.com
genres: Rock, Pop, S/S
Material by referral only. No Calls.

Management Trust
411 Queen St. W, 3rd Fl.
Toronto, ON M5V 2A5
Canada
p: 416-979-7070
f: 416-979-0505
e: mail@mgmtrust.ca
www.mgmtrust.ca
contact: Jake Gold
genres: Rock, Pop
clients: Chris Koster, Dearly Beloved, David Martel, Public, The Cliks
No unsolicited material & not seeking new clients.

Mark Spector Co.
100 Fifth Ave., 11th Fl.
New York, NY 10011
p: 212-277-7175
f: 212-840-3256
contact: Mark Spector
e: ms44post@aol.com
genres: Folk, Rock
clients: Sinead Lohan, Joan Baez, Michael Penn, Mary Gauthier, Cowboy Junkies
Only works w/ estab artists. No unsolicited material.

Mauldin Brand Agency
1280 W Peachtree St., Ste. 300
Atlanta, GA 30309
p: 404-733-5511
f: 404-733-5512
e: info@artisticcontrol.com
www.mauldinbrand.com
contact: Lucy Raoof
e: juice@artisticcontrol.com
genres: Urban, Pop
clients: Da Brat, Maleek Kenny Lattimore, Common
No unsolicited material & not seeking new clients.

Mazur Entertainment
PO Box 2425
Trenton, NJ 08607
p: 609-448-7886
e: mazurent@yahoo.com
www.mazurent.com
contact: Michael Mazur
ext: 609-462-9905
genres: All Styles
clients: Jeanie Bryson,

Mortiis
Also does publicity.
Call before sending material.

MCT Management
520 8th Ave., Ste. 2001
New York, NY 10018
p: 212-563-0630
f: 212-563-5099
e: mailbox@mctbold.com
contact: Barry Taylor
genres: All Styles
clients: A Girl Called Eddy, Guillemots, Rufus Wainwright, Laura Veirs, Let's Go Sailing
Email before sending material.

Metropolitan Hybrid
100 5th Ave.
11th Fl.
New York, NY 10011
p: 212-277-7171
f: 212-719-9396
e: info@metrohybrid.com
www.metro-talent.com
contact: John Scher
ext: 212-277-7155
genres: Pop, Rock
clients: Art Garfunkel, Bob Weir, Bruce Hornsby, Little Feat
No unsolicited material & not seeking new clients.

Michael Hausman Artist Management
511 Ave. of the Americas
Ste. 197
New York, NY 10011
p: 212-505-1943
f: 212-505-1127
e: info@michaelhausman.com
www.michaelhausman.com
contact: Michael Hausman
ext: 212-505-1943 x201
e: michael@michaelhausman.com
genres: Rock, Pop, S/S
clients: Aimee Mann, Suzanne Vega, Marc Cohn, Angie Mattson, Kristina Train
Also runs record label United Musicians & Superego Records. Email site or MySpace links. No CDs.

Mike's Artist Management
PO Box 35880
Tucson, AZ 85740
p: 520-628-8655
f: 520-628-9072
e: info@mikesmanagement.com
www.mikesmanagement.com
contact: Mike Lembo
genres: Rock, Pop, Americana
clients: Tony Furtado, Jules Mark Shear, Mostly Bears, The Mother Truckers, Luca
No unsolicited material.

Miller Entertainment Group Management
15303 Ventura Blvd., Ste. 960
Sherman Oaks, CA 91403
p: 323-932-6500
e: gmacher@gmail.com
contact: Larry Miller
genres: Rap, R&B, Rock, Alt.
New clients must have referral.

Million Dollar Artists
13001 Dieterle Ln.
St. Louis, MO 63127
p: 888-521-8146; 314-965-5648
f: 314-984-0828
www.milliondollarartists.net
contact: Dr. Charles "Max" E. Million
e: maxmillion@milliondollarartists.net
genres: All Styles
clients: Well Hungarians, Sable, J. Nueman Edwards
See site for submission policy.

Mitchell Fox Management
PO Box 190515
Nashville, TN 37219
p: 615-202-2177
f: 615-354-5555
contact: Mitchell Fox
e: nashvillediner@bellsouth.net
genres: Country, Rock N Roll

Mood Indigo Entertainment
227 W 29th St., 6th Fl.
New York, NY 10001
p: 212-766-8040
www.moodindigoentertainment.com
contact: John Porter
ext: 212-239-3449
e: johnporter@moodindigoentertainment.com
clients: Carrie Rodriguez, Javier Vercher, KaiserCartel, Patty Hurst Shifter, Tai Burnette
Div. of bluhammock music. No unsolicited material & not seeking new clients.

NEM Productions
PO Box 123
South Shields, Tyne & Wear, NE33 2ZR UK
p: 44-191-427-6207
f: 44-191-427-6323
www.nemproductions.com
contact: Dave Smith
e: dave@nemproductions.com
genres: Acoustic, Folk
clients: Tommy Emmanuel, John Renbourn, Adrian Legg, Stefan Grossman, Bob Brozman
No unsolicited material & not seeking new clients.

Nettwerk Management
1650 W 2nd Ave.
Vancouver, BC V6J 4R3
Canada
p: 604-654-2929
f: 604-654-1993
e: info@nettwerk.com
www.nettwerk.com
contact: Dan Fraser
genres: Rock, Pop, Alt.
clients: Avril Lavigne, Barenaked Ladies, Melissa McClelland, Sarah McLachlan, Stereophonics
Offices in NY, LA, London, Boston, Nashville & Hamburg. No unsolicited material & not seeking new clients.

New Heights Entertainment
PO Box 8489
Calabasas, CA 91372
p: 818-992-7910
f: 818-992-5724
www.newheightsent.com
contact: Alan Melina
e: alanmelina@newheightsent.com
genres: All Styles
clients: Ayanna Howard, Jimmy Barret, Room For Two, Adam Anders, Nikki Anders
No unsolicited material & not seeking new clients.

Nocturnal Movements Music Resources
PO Box 5583
Vancouver, WA 98668
p: 360-513-9121
e: info@nocturnalmovements.net
www.nocturnalmovements.net
contact: Jett Black
e: jett@nocturnalmovements.net
genres: All Styles
clients: Dope Stars Inc., Collide, Minefield, Julian Tulip's Licorice, Jennifer Maione
See site for submission policy.

On The Moon Music
190 Bedford Ave., Ste. 136
Brooklyn, NY 11211
e: info@onthemoonmusic.com
www.onthemoonmusic.com
contact: Jin Moon
ext: 646-267-2902
e: jinners@onthemoonmusic.com
genres: Rock
clients: Cheeseburger, Dirty on Purpose, Gabby Glaser, Neckbeard Telecaster, Purse Snatchers
Also does consulting. Submit via YouSendIt, MySpace, Imeem. No mp3 attachments; will respond if interested.

Open Door Management
865 Via De La Paz
Pacific Palisades, CA 90272
p: 310-459-2559
f: 310-454-7803
www.opendoormanagement.com
contact: Bill Traut
e: bill@opendoormanagement.com
genres: Jazz, World
clients: Jon Hendricks, L, H&R Redux
No unsolicited material & not seeking new clients.

OTB Productions
5 Oldridge View
Tedburn St. Mary Devon
EX6 6AB UK
p: 44-164-761-237
www.otbproductions.co.uk
contact: Dave McCrory
e: dave@otbproductions.co.uk
genres: Roots, World, Folk, Celtic
clients: Huckleberries, FOS Brothers
Not seeking new clients.

Pathfinder Management
1009 16th Ave. S
Nashville, TN 37212
p: 615-750-5938
f: 615-810-9492
e: thepathfinder@mindspring.com
contact: Jim Della Croce
ext: 615-269-3670
genres: Country, Rock, Folk
clients: Robert Hazard, Thompson Ward, Justin Gaston
Seeking new clients.

Patrick Rains & Associates
1255 5th Ave., #7K
New York, NY 10029
p: 212-860-3233
f: 212-860-5556
www.prarecords.com
contact: Patrick Rains
e: pra@prarecords.com
genres: Jazz, Pop, Rock
clients: Jonatha Brooke, Joe Sample, The Crusaders, Randy Crawford, David Sanborn
No unsolicited material & not seeking new clients.

Pat's Management Co.
5900 Wilshire Blvd., Ste. 1720
Los Angeles, CA 90036
p: 323-965-8502
f: 323-965-8553
www.patsrecordcompany.com
contact: Tyler Willingham
e: tyler@pmmla.com
genres: Rock
clients: Green Day, Goo Goo Dolls, All American Rejects, Plain White T's, Ryan Bingham
No unsolicited material.

Periwinkle Productions
340 Water St.
St. Andrews, NB E5B 2R3
Canada
p: 506-529-4585
f: 506-529-4160
www.periwinkleproductions.ca
contact: Jamie Steel
e: steeljm@nbnet.nb.ca
genres: Folk, Roots, Jazz
clients: Debbie Ashdale, Hot Toddy, Isaac & Blewett, Jamie Junger, Alan Gerber
Also tour support & promotion.

Powerblast Worldwide
15663 SW 41st St.
Miami, FL 33027
p: 305-335-2529
f: 305-335-2529
www.powerblastworldwide.com
contact: Ernest W. Coleman
e: ewc@powerblastworldwide.com
genres: Hip-Hop, Reggae, R&B, Soul, Alt. Rock, Metal
clients: Gino Black, Bombthreat, Cutty B. Spooky
Contact before sending material.

Prodigal Son Entertainment
115 Penn Warren Dr.
Ste. 300 - Box 380
Brentwood, TN 37027
p: 615-377-0057
f: 866-899-7536
www.prodigalson-entertainment.com
contact: Scott Williams
e: scott@prodigalsonent.com
genres: Rock, Alt., Country, Christian, Instrumental
clients: Jill Paar, Salient, Evensong Rising, The Vow
No unsolicited material & not seeking new clients.

Q Prime Management
729 7th Ave., 16th Fl.
New York, NY 10019
p: 212-302-9790
f: 212-302-9589
e: admin@qprime.com
www.qprime.com
contact: Randi Seplow
e: randi@qprime.com
genres: Rock, Pop
clients: Fountains of Wayne, Garbage, Gillian Welch, The Black Keys, Silversun Pickups
Offices in Nashville & Los Angeles. No unsolicited material & not seeking new clients.

R.L.M./ Mission Management
24 Middleton St.
Nashville, TN 37210
p: 615-340-9500
f: 615-340-9505
www.missionmgmt.net
contact: Shelley Rose Richardson
ext: 615-340-9500 x25
e: shelley@missionmgmt.net
genres: Christian, Country, Rock
clients: Little Big Town, Floord, Levi Rose, Heaven Hill, Darryl Worley
No unsolicited material & not seeking new clients.

Rainmaker Artists
3300 Bee Caves Rd., Ste. 650
Box 1314
Austin, TX 78746
p: 888-540-2112
f: 888-540-2112
e: management@

rainmakerartists.com
www.rainmakerartists.com
contact: Paul Nugent
e: paul@rainmakerartists.com
genres: Rock, Pop
clients: Blue October, Bowling For Soup, Bob Schneider, The Black & White Years, Pretty Baby
Other contact: Randy Miller: randy@rainmakerartists.com & Ernie Diaz at ernie@ rainmakersartists.com.

Rare Artists
794 44th Ave.
San Francisco, CA 94121
p: 415-386-1046
f: 415-386-1049
contact: Chris Powers
e: chris@rareartists.com
genres: Rock, Pop, Folk
clients: Jolie Holland, Sean Hayes, The Entrance Band
Email w/ link to music. No calls or mail.

Raspberry Jam Music
4 Berachah Ave.
South Nyack, NY 10960
p: 845-353-4001
f: 845-353-4332
e: muzik@verizon.net
www.musicandamerica.com
contact: Fred Porter
genres: Reggae, Pop, Rock, R&B, Jazz
clients: Anya, Jason Wilson & Tabarruk
Contact for permission to submit materials.

Raspler Management
946 N Croft Ave.
West Hollywood, CA 90069
p: 323-654-4094
f: 323-654-4096
contact: Adam Raspler
genres: Indie Rock, Pop, Punk
clients: 311, Sugarcult

Rebel Waltz Management
31652 2nd Ave.
Laguna Beach, CA 92651
p: 949-499-4497
f: 949-499-4496
e: info@rebelwaltz.com
www.rebelwaltz.com
contact: Jim Guerinot
genres: Punk, Rock
clients: No Doubt, The Offspring, Hot Hot Heat, Mike Ness, Social Distortion
No unsolicited material & not seeking new clients.

Red Light Management
44 Wall St.
22nd Fl.
New York, NY 10007
p: 646-292-7400
f: 646-292-7450
www.redlightmanagement.com
contact: Randy Nichols
ext: 646-825-7612
e: randyn@musictoday.com
genres: Rock, Pop, Hip-Hop
clients: The Starting Line, Underoath, The Almost, Say Anything
HQ in VA: 434-245-4900. No unsolicited material & is not seeking new clients.

Right Side Management
PO Box 250806
New York, NY 10025
p: 212-586-1223
f: 646-390-6360
e: info@rightsidemgt.com
www.rightsidemgt.com
contact: Marc Silag
genres: World, Instrumental Pop, Electronic, Alt.
clients: Tony Levin, Diane Schuur, Jonathan Brielle, Nadia Ackerman, Jordan Carp
No unsolicited material & not seeking new clients.

Riot Squad
3384 Robertson Pl., Ste. 200
Los Angeles, CA 90034
p: 310-202-0434
f: 310-202-0435
www.riotsquadrecords.com
contact: Brian Schechter
e: brian@riotsqadmanagement.com
genres: Rock, Indie
clients: My Chemical Romance, Circa Survive, Drive By, Fever Club, Lost Alone
Also contact: Jeff Pereira, jeff@riotsquadmanagement.com. No unsolicited material & not seeking new clients.

RJ Entertainment & Sports Management
148 Cadrow Castle Ct.
Las Vegas, NV 89148
p: 702-617-3533
f: 909-861-0741
contact: Reginald Jackson
e: regjack16@aol.com
genres: Alt., R&B, Rap, Hip-Hop, Jazz, Pop
clients: Kirk Joseph Backyard Groove, Town Kingz, D'Hante Jackson, T. Houseman De CLouet, Dramatics
Send CD or DVDs.

Ron Rainey Management
315 S Beverly Dr., Ste. 407
Beverly Hills, CA 90212
p: 310-277-4050
f: 310-557-8421
e: rrmgmt@aol.com
www.ronrainey.com
contact: Ron Rainey
ext: 310-557-0661 x101
e: rrainey425@aol.com
genres: Rock, Pop
clients: The Blasters, August Darnell, Kid Creole & The Coconuts, Marshall Tucker Band, Alvin Lee
No unsolicited material & not seeking new clients.

Rosebud Agency
PO Box 170429
San Francisco, CA 94117
p: 415-386-3456
f: 415-386-0599
e: info@rosebudus.com
www.rosebudus.com
contact: Mike Kappus
genres: Blues, S/S, Jazz, Folk, Rock, Gospel, R&B, Latin
clients: J.J. Cale, Sierra Leone's Refugee All Stars
Primarily a booking agency that represents a few artists. No unsolicited material & not seeking new clients.

Rosen Music
717 El Medio Ave.
Pacific Palisades, CA 90272
p: 310-230-6040
f: 310-230-4074
e: dorina@rosenmusiccorp.com
www.rosenmusiccorp.com
contact: Steven Rosen
e: steven@rosenmusiccorp.com
genres: All Styles
clients: Three Graces, Orianthi, Bret Ryan, Justin Gray, Mark Portmann
No unsolicited material & not seeking new clients.

Russell Carter Artist Management
567 Ralph McGill Blvd.
Atlanta, GA 30312
p: 404-377-9900
f: 404-377-5131
www.myspace.com/rcam
contact: Russell Carter
e: russell.rcam@gmail.com
genres: S/S, Alt., Americana, Pop, Rock
clients: Indigo Girls, Jayhawks, Matthew Sweet & Susanna Hoffs, Sarah Lee Guthrie & Johnny Irion, Dar Williams

Scott Evans Productions
PO Box 814028
Hollywood, FL 33081
p: 954-963-4449
e: evansprod@aol.com
www.theentertainmentmall.com
contact: Scott Evans
genres: Rock, Pop, Jazz, Dance

Sharpe Entertainment Services
683 Palmera Ave.
Pacific Palisades, CA 90272
p: 310-230-2100
f: 310-230-2109
e: frances@ses-la.com
www.ses-la.com
contact: Wil Sharpe
genres: Alt., Pop, S/S, Rock
clients: PJ Olsson, Sarah Bettens, Edison Glass, K's Choice, John O'Brien
No unsolicited material & not seeking new clients.

Shotclock Management
PO Box 45
Olympia, WA 98507
p: 360-259-7696
f: 443-337-2267
www.shotclockmanagement.com
contact: Portia Sabin
e: portia@shotclockmanagement.com
genres: Rock, Punk, Folk, Blues, Pop
clients: Dragons of Zynth, Thao Nguyen, Anais Mitchell, The Callen Sisters
No unsolicited material & not seeking new clients.

Silent Partner Management
536 Pantops Ctr., #343
Charlottesville, VA 22911
p: 434-245-4951
f: 434-245-4933
e: contact@silentpartnermanagement.com
www.silentpartnermanagement.com
contact: David Frey
genres: Rock
clients: The Ramones, Cheap Trick, Brazilian Girls, Local H
No unsolicited material & not seeking new clients.

Silva Artist Management
722 Seward St.
Los Angeles, CA 90038
p: 323-856-8222
f: 323-856-8256
e: info@sammusicbiz.com
www.sammusicbiz.com
contact: John Silva
ext: 323-856-8240
genres: Rock
clients: Foo Fighters, Band of Horses, Ryan Adams, Jimmy Eat World, Tenacious D
No unsolicited material & not seeking new clients.

Siren Music
PO Box 12110
Portland, OR 97212
p: 503-238-4771
www.sirenmusiccompany.com
contact: December Carson
e: december@sirenmusiccompany.com
genres: Roots, Americana, Pop, Rock, S/S, Alt. Country, Irish
clients: Caleb Klauder, The Foghorn Stringband, The Flat Mountain Girls, Johnny B. Connolly
Not seeking new clients.

Skyline Exposure
9144 Burnet Ave
#35
North Hills, CA 91343
e: info@skylineexposure.com
www.skylineexposure.com
contact: Justin Sena
e: justin@skylineexposure.com
genres: Rock, Pop, Alt., Urban
clients: Doug Cameron, Jamey Tate, Leland Grant
Also does web design, distribution deals & A&R. No unsolicited material.

SLK Entertainment
PO Box 480589
Los Angeles, CA 90048
p: 323-807-8711
www.slkent.com
contact: Shauna Krikorian
e: shauna@slkent.com
genres: Rock, Alt., Hip-Hop
clients: Bad Fathers, Chris Parish, Saturday's Child, Lee Newman, Lauren Wild
Email before sending material. No calls.

So What Media & Management
890 W End Ave.
Ste. 1-A
New York, NY 10025
p: 212-877-9631
f: 212-877-9735
contact: Lisa Barbaris
e: sowhatinfo@aol.com
genres: Rock, Pop
clients: Simply Red, Cyndi Lauper, Vivian Green
No unsolicited material & not seeking new clients.

Sonic Management
3112 Washington Blvd.
Marina del Rey, CA 90292
p: 310-578-1617
f: 310-578-1657
e: info@sonicmanagement.com
www.sonicmanagement.com
contact: Ben Laski
genres: All Styles
clients: The Yards, AM Radio Show, Slow Train Soul, Last Days of April, Vincent Van GoGo
Email w/ site & MySpace info. Not seeking new clients.

Soundtrack Music Associates
2229 Cloverfield Blvd.
Santa Monica, CA 90405
p: 310-392-1401
f: 310-392-1407
e: info@soundtrk.com
www.soundtrk.com
contact: John Tempereau
e: johnt@soundtrk.com
genres: All Styles
clients: Pray For Rain, Phil Collins, Tom Scott, Francis Lai, Tyler Bates
No unsolicited material & not seeking new clients.

Spy Girl Entertainment
PO Box 40031
Studio City, CA 91614
p: 310-702-1600
e: spygirlent@yahoo.com
www.spygirlentertainment.com
contact: Lili Barnes
genres: Rock, Pop, Alt.

clients: Simon Stinger, Suffocate, Tre Props, Logan's Heroes, Alestar Digby
Contact before sending material.

SRO Management
189 Carlton St.
Toronto, ON M5A 2K7
Canada
p: 416-923-5855
f: 416-923-1041
e: sro-anthem@sro-anthem.com
www.anthementertainmentgroup.com
contact: Ray Danniels
genres: Rock, Alt.
clients: Rush, Thornley, Stabilo

Starlista Music Group
Boston, MA
p: 888-691-4876
e: management@starlista.com
www.starlista.com
contact: John Cappucci
genres: Rock, Hard Rock, Indie Pop, Punk
clients: Myopic, Raleigh, Store at the Sun, While Rome Burns
Seeking new clients.
Send email w/ info & link to management@starlista.com.
No Country or Hip-Hop.

Steve Stewart Management
10 Universal City Plaza 20th Fl., Universal City, CA 91608
p: 818-753-2380
f: 818-753-2303
www.stevestewart.com
contact: Steve Stewart
e: stevestewart@stevestewart.com
genres: Alt., Rock, Pop
clients: Screaming Trees, Paige Lewis, Stone Temple Pilots, Home Town Hero
Seeks new clients.

Steven Scharf Entertainment
126 E 38th St.
New York, NY
10016
p: 212-779-7977 x3905
f: 212-725-9681
www.stevenscharf.com
contact: Steven Scharf
e: sscharf@carlinamerica.com
genres: Rock, Alt., S/S, Hip-Hop, World
clients: Ali Eskandarian, Intercooler, Julius 'Juice' Butty, Rob Friedman, Michael Vail Blum
Licenses for Film & TV & oversees the Film & TV division for Carlin America.
Email before submitting.
Not seeking new clients.

Strictly Heavy Management
10928 Coverstone Dr., #C3
Manassas, VA 20109
e: stricthvy@aol.com
www.strictlyheavymanagement.com
contact: Theresa C. Mulins-Aldao
genres: Metal, Grindcore, Rock
clients: Georgian Skull, Dead Jesus, Krisiun
Send presskit w/ CD.

Survival Management
30765 PCH, #325
Malibu, CA 90265
p: 310-317-9223
f: 310-317-9225
e: survivalmgmt1@aol.com
contact: Bob Ringe
genres: Rock, Hard Rock, Alt.
clients: Zakk Wylde, Black Label Society, Dope, Mountain Feat. Leslie West & Corky Laing
Not seeking new clients.

Ted Kurland Associates
173 Brighton Ave.
Boston, MA
02134
p: 617-254-0007
f: 617-782-3577
e: agents@tedkurland.com
www.tedkurland.com
contact: Ted Kurland
ext: 617-254-0007 x131
e: ted@tedkurland.com
genres: Jazz, Blues, Vocals
clients: Pat Metheny, Pat Martino, Chick Corea, Taylor Eigsti & Julian Lage, Ellis Marsalis
No unsolicited material & not seeking new clients.

TenEntertainment
1449 Alteras Cir.
Nashville, TN 37211
p: 615-289-2822
e: info@tenentertainment.com
www.tenentertainment.com
contact: Shannon Brown
e: shannon@tenentertainment.com
genres: All Styles
clients: Our Heart's Hero, Philmont, Shay Watson, Eric Mizelle
No MP3s unless requested.

Three Artist Management (3 A.M.)
14260 Ventura Blvd., Ste. 201
Sherman Oaks, CA 91423
p: 818-380-0303
f: 818-380-0484
e: info@threeam.net
www.threeam.net
contact: Richard Bishop
genres: Rock, Electronic, Composer
clients: The Crystal Method, Tobias Enhus, Grandaddy, Paul Oakenfold, Henry Rollins
Not seeking new clients.

Three E
17 W 20th St., 5E
New York, NY 10011
p: 212-684-9242
f: 212-488-2054
e: info@erikegerentertainment.com
www.threee.biz
contact: Erik Eger
e: erik@threee.biz
genres: All Styles
clients: Michael H. Brauer, Dan Carey, Sly & Robbie, Stuart Matthewman, Athlete
Not seeking new clients.

Thunderbird Management Group
11840 Hwy. 308
Larose, LA 70373
p: 985-798-5665; 985-798-5109
f: 985-798-7244
e: info@thunderbirdmanagementgroup.com
contact: Rueben Williams
e: thunderbird@cajunnet.com
genres: All Styles
clients: Tab Benoit, Cyril Neville & the Uptown Allstars, Jimmy Thackery & the Drivers, John Sinclair & the Blues Scholars, Big Chief Monk Boudreaux & the Golden Eagles
Promos to: PO Box 1686, Larose, LA 70373.

TKO Artist Management
2303 21st Ave. S, 3rd Fl.
Nashville, TN 37212
p: 615-383-5017
f: 615-292-3328
www.tkoartistmanagement.com
contact: T.K. Kimbrell
genres: Country
clients: Mac McAnally, Toby Keith, Carter's Chord, Flynnville Train, Western Underground
No unsolicited material & not seeking new clients.

Tony Margherita Management
1140 Broadway
Ste. 1603
New York, NY
10001
e: info@tmmchi.com
www.tmmchi.com
contact: Emily Rosenblum
e: emily@tmmchi.com
genres: Rock, Jazz
clients: Wilco, Glenn Kotche, Jeff Tweedy, Dave Douglas
No unsolicited material.

Tower Management
30 Music Sq. W
Ste. 103
Nashville, TN 37203
p: 615-401-7111
f: 615-401-7119
e: castlerecords@castlerecords.com
www.castlerecords.com
contact: Ed Russell
e: edrussell@castlerecords.com
genres: Country, Rock, AC, Bluegrass, Blues
clients: Kebo Irus, Bridgette Elise, Abby, Shane Keane, Carl Butler
Affiliated w/ Castle Records.
See site for policy.

Trace Management
20 Berkeley Rd.
Ste. A
Avondale Estates, GA
30002
p: 404-822-5327
f: 404-299-1781
e: gertrace@mindspring.com
contact: Jerry Finley
genres: Alt., Pop, Rock, College, Cover/Tribute Bands
clients: The Breakfast Club
Contact before submitting.

True Talent Management
9663 Santa Monica Blvd., #320, Dept. MA
Beverly Hills, CA 90210
p: 310-560-1290
f: 310-441-2005
e: musiciansatlas@truetalentmgmt.com
www.truetalentmgmt.com
contact: Jennifer Yeko
genres: Rock, S/S, Pop
clients: Split Habit, Elysia, The Michael Miller Crusade
Specializes in Film/TV.
Email before submitting.

Union Entertainment Group
31225 La Baya Dr.
Ste. 213
Westlake Village, CA 91362
www.ueginc.com
contact: John Greenberg
e: greenberg@ueginc.com
genres: Rock
clients: Candlebox, Nickelback, Default, Cinderella, Lynam
No unsolicited material & not seeking new clients.

Vector Management
1607 17th Ave. S
Nashville, TN
37212
p: 615-269-6600
f: 615-269-6002
e: info@vectormgmt.com
contact: Ken Levitan
e: ken@vectormgmt.com
genres: Country, Pop, S/S
clients: Emmylou Harris, Lyle Lovett, Angelique Kidjo, Kings of Leon, Trace Adkins
NY office: 212-317-2323.
No unsolicited material & not seeking new clients.

Velvet Hammer Music & Management Group
9911 W Pico Blvd.
Ste. 350W
Los Angeles, CA 90035
p: 310-657-6161
f: 310-657-0310
www.velvethammer.net
contact: Jennifer Rauch
e: jennifer@streetwise.com
genres: Rock, Alt., Hip-Hop
clients: System of a Down, Deftones, Taproot, Achozen, As Cities Burn

W Management
266 Elizabeth St.
Rm. 1A
New York, NY
10012
p: 212-274-8952
f: 212-925-2937
e: wmgmt@aol.com
contact: Stephen Weintraub
genres: Pop, Rock
clients: Sheryl Crow, Doyle Bramhall II, Matt White, Todd Wolfe, Antigone Rising
No unsolicited material & not seeking new clients.

Wilkins Management
323 Broadway
Cambridge, MA
02139
p: 617-354-2736
f: 617-354-2396
e: info@wilkinsmanagement.com
contact: Ann Marie Wilkins
genres: Jazz
clients: Branford Marsalis, Joshua Redman, Harry Connick, Jr.
No unsolicited material & not seeking new clients.

William Morris Agency
1 William Morris Pl.
Beverly Hills, CA 90212
p: 310-859-4000
f: 310-859-4462
www.wma.com
contact: James A. Wiatt
genres: Rock, Pop, Urban, Country, Latin, Christian
clients: Herbie Hancock, A Tribe Called Quest, David Byrne, The Killers, Thievery Corporation
Other locations in NY, Nashville, London & Shanghai.
No unsolicited material & not seeking new clients.

Zenmaster Presents
2096 E Streetsboro Rd.
Hudson, OH
44236
p: 330-289-0589
f: 330-650-1430
www.myspace.com/zennymray
contact: Marky Ray
e: fuzzunit@aol.com
genres: Rock, Experimental, Avant Garde
clients: Iguanadonho, Death On a Stick
Bands use email/MySpace before sending material.
Not seeking new clients.

THE 9th ANNUAL INDEPENDENT MUSIC AWARDS

THE IMAs DELIVER MAJOR RESULTS FOR INDIE RELEASES

The Independent Music Awards is a unique, international program that helps indie artitsts, record labels and their releases overcome mainstream obstacles and reach millions of music fans and industry decision-makers.

The IMAs accepts submissions from all independent artists and labels. Submissions that are self-released or distributed by an indie and major distributor are all eligible to participate in the IMA program.

Presented by Music Resource Group, publisher of The Musician's Atlas and the AtlasOnline, the Independent Music Awards honors Winners & Finalists in a wide variety of Music, Design and Music Video categories.

The IMAs deliver year-long print, online, broadcast & distribution support for artists whose songs, albums, music videos, marketing & merchandising creativity deserve greater recognition from industry professionals and fans — the world over!

Panels of influential artist and industry judges review IMA submissions and make their determinations based solely on artistic merit. Whether an artist or band has sold 10 records or 10,000, or recorded in a commercial or home studio, has absolutely no impact on the judging.

Additionally, music fans from around the world have their say by voting for their favorite songs on the IMA Vox Populi Jukebox. While this "people's choice" vote does not affect the Judges' final decisions, Winners of both the "general" and vox populi polls are promoted.

The IMAs is not a contest or a battle of the bands. We do not award cash or prize packages. This program was built to support top-notch talent with marketing campaigns and sales opportunities that reach millions via strategic partnerships and active promotions.

Additionally, an IMA Winners CD compilation *Now Hear This!*, is distributed to 5,000 music fans and industry insiders at high-profile events including SXSW, Folk Alliance, CMJ, The Warped Tour and others throughout the year. The CD is also promoted to more than 650 US and Canadian college and public radio stations courtesy of The Planetary Group.

Many past IMA Winners & Finalists credit the program for boosting their profile with festival and club talent buyers, distributors, publishers, press, radio programmers, record label A&R executives and fans.

Previous Winners include Joan As Police Woman, Sugarcult, Mary Gauthier, Lionel Loueke, Koko Taylor, Miguel Migs, Girl In A Coma, Apples In Stereo, Lacuna Coil, Bitter:Sweet, Richard Julian, Speech, Eleni Mandell, The Mooney Suzuki, Dan Bern, God Forbid, Melissa McClelland and many others.

The submission deadline for the 9th Annual Independent Music Awards is **FRIDAY, AUGUST 21, 2009.** An entry form follows the Winners gatefold.

Additional entry forms, judges, program updates and additional IMA benefits will be posted at: **IndependentMusicAwards.com** as details are finalized.

PAST JUDGES INCLUDE:

Peter Gabriel
Buddy Guy
Keith Urban
Snoop Dogg
Roger Daltrey
Les Claypool
George Jones
Wynonna
Frank Iero (My Chemical Romance)
Ozzy Osbourne
Norah Jones
Chad Smith
Tom Waits
Suzanne Vega
Clint Black
James "Blood" Ulmer
Lee Ritenour
MickDeth
Mobb Deep
Ray Davies
Charlie Musselwhite
Zakk Wylde
Susan Tedeschi
Ice-T
McCoy Tyner
Rob Wasserman
Paul Oakenfold
Bill Frisell
Duncan Sheik
Joe Perry
Judy Collins
Bill Wyman
Jonatha Brooke
Terence Blanchard
Amy Ray
Lou Reed
Bebel Gilberto
Chuck Comeau (Simple Plan)
George Clinton
Tim Pagnotta (Sugarcult)
Melissa Etheridge
Chris Thile
Erykah Badu
Arturo Sandoval
Patty Loveless
William Ackerman
Delbert McClinton
Hubert Sumlin
Aimee Mann
Howard Tate
Steve Vai
Martin Atkins (P.I.L./Nine Inch Nails)
DJ Spooky
Paquito D'Rivera
Yolanda Adams
Ben Folds
Loudon Wainwright III
Me'shell Ndegeocello
Ricky Skaggs
Don Byron
Mickey Hart
Rosanne Cash
Mavis Staples
Jose Feliciano
Jimmy Cliff
Tina Weymouth
John Medeski
Kelly Willis
Wilson Pickett
Charlie Hunter
Joshua Redman
Robbie Fulks
Joe Henry
Mitchell Froom
and others

THE INDEPENDENT MUSIC AWARDS ARE SPONSORED BY COMPANIES THAT SUPPORT INDEPENDENT MUSIC.

SESAC

myxer Go with it

press

National

20th Century Guitar
135 Oser Ave.
Hauppauge, NY 11788
p: 800-291-9687; 631-273-1674
f: 631-434-9057
e: tcguitar@tcguitar.com
www.tcguitar.com
frequency: Monthly
circulation: 18,000
contact: Larry Acunto
emphasis: Guitar Based Music & Collectible Guitars
Reviews mostly major releases w/ a handful of Indies. Sold at bookstores & by subscription to 25-50-yr-old males.

The Absolute Sound
Absolute Media, 4544 S Lamar Blvd., G300
Austin, TX 78745
p: 512-892-8682
www.theabsolutesound.com
frequency: 11/year
circulation: 48,000
contact: Bob Gendron
e: bgendron@nextscreen.com
emphasis: High End Audio
Nat'l specialty mag covers hi-end audio equipment & reviews all styles of uniquely recorded music. Reviews online at www.avguide.com.

ABYSSJazz Magazine
8947 Washington Ave.
Jacksonville, FL 32208
p: 904-264-4642
f: 904-264-4667
e: mailbox@abyssjazz.com
www.abyssjazz.com
frequency: Bimonthly
circulation: 60,000
contact: Lyndah Glover
e: lyndah@abyssjazz.com
emphasis: Contemporary
Free print/online mag for Jazzbos includes "Developing Artists Program". Distrib. at major Jazz festivals & retail.

Access Magazine
1317 Davenport Rd.
Toronto, ON M6H 2H4
Canada
p: 416-335-0747
f: 416-335-0748
e: crossfire@accessmag.com
www.accessmag.com
frequency: 6/year
circulation: 125,000
contact: Sean Plummer
ext: 416-964-7198
e: sean@accessmag.com
emphasis: Music & Lifestyle
Available at lifestyle retailers & targets 18-24-yr-old pros & college kids. Reviews high profile indies & nat'l acts. Contact before sending links.

Acoustic Guitar
PO Box 767
San Anselmo, CA 94979
p: 415-485-6946
f: 415-485-0831
e: editors.ag@stringletter.com
www.acousticguitar.com
frequency: Monthly
circulation: 63,000
contact: Dan Gabel
Reviews products & estab. acts & runs release dates. Promos to: 255 W End Ave., San Rafael, CA 94901.

Alarm
53 W Jackson Blvd., Ste. 1005
Chicago, IL 60604
p: 312-341-1290
f: 312-341-1318
e: info@alarmpress.com
www.alarmpress.com
frequency: Bimonthly
circulation: 45,000
contact: Chris Force
e: music@alarmpress.com; chris@alarmpress.com
emphasis: Indie Music & Art
Indie-focused mag profiles emerging & estab. artists. Show previews & news updated daily. Int'l distrib. at record & book stores. Discounted ad rates.

Altercation Magazine
PO Box 1509
Austin, TX 78767
e: altercation@altercation.net
www.altercation.net
frequency: Quarterly
circulation: 10,000
contact: Justin T. Habersaat
e: editor@altercation.net
emphasis: Punk, Alt.
Underground music & culture mag, reviews & profiles estab. & obscure talent. Sold at indie music shops worldwide.

Alternative Press Magazine
1305 W 80th St., Ste. 2F
Cleveland, OH 44102
p: 216-631-1510
f: 216-631-1016
e: editorial@altpress.com
www.altpress.com
frequency: Monthly
circulation: 293,000
contact: Scott Heisel
ext: 216-631-1510 x113
e: heisel@altpress.com
emphasis: Alt., Punk Rock, Metal, Indie
Top dog of DIY Punk mags reviews 100+ releases & features estab. & rising talent. Sold int'lly & by subscription to Warped Tour crowd.

American Songwriter
1303 16th Ave., 2nd Fl.
Nashville, TN 37212
p: 615-321-6096
f: 615-321-6097
e: info@americansongwriter.com
www.americansongwriter.com
frequency: Bimonthly
circulation: 35,000
contact: Doug Waterman
e: dwaterman@americansongwriter.com
emphasis: Songwriters
Covers all styles for pros & music fans. Profiles estab., rising talent & industry issues. Nat'l distrib. Submit CDs only.

Amp Magazine
PO Box 1070
Martinez, CA 94553
p: 925-228-1423
f: 925-228-1423
e: info@ampmagazine.com
www.ampmagazine.com
frequency: Bimonthly
circulation: 75,000-80,000
contact: Scooter McGavin
e: scoot@ampmagazine.com
emphasis: Punk, Rock, Metal, Alt., Hardcore
Covers Alt. music scene & produces CD comp. Sold nationwide at record, book & lifestyle shops.

Arthur
339 S 5th St., 3rd Fl.
Brooklyn, NY 11211
www.arthurmag.com
frequency: Bimonthly
circulation: 70,000
contact: Jay Babcock
e: editor@arthurmag.com
emphasis: Alt.
Hip DIY music/culture mag reviews releases & profiles artists. Nat'l distrib. at 800+ locations.

Bass Player
1111 Bayhill Dr.
Ste. 125
San Bruno, CA 94066
p: 650-238-0300
f: 650-238-0261
e: bassplayer@musicplayer.com
www.bassplayer.com
frequency: Monthly
contact: Bill Leigh
e: bleigh@musicplayer.com
emphasis: Bass Players
Follows equipment trends & players for hobbyists & pros. Reviews up to 30 new releases. Part of Music Player Network, sold on mag racks, bookstores & music stores. Send digital kits.

Bassics
PO Box 1178
Lewiston, NY 14092
p: 716-754-4462
f: 716-754-4465
e: bassicsrg@aol.com
www.bassics.com
frequency: Bimonthly
circulation: 10,000
contact: Ron Garant
emphasis: Bass Driven Music
Product & artist profiles w/up to 10 Indie reviews per issue. Sold in music & book stores.

The Beat
PO Box 65856
Los Angeles, CA 90065
p: 818-500-9299
f: 818-500-9454
e: getthebeat@sbcglobal.net
www.getthebeat.com
frequency: Bimonthly
circulation: 48,000
contact: C.C. Smith
emphasis: Reggae, African, Caribbean, World
Top int'l pub for this varied genre covers artists, releases & gigs.

Big Cheese
Unit 7, Clarendon Bldgs
25 Horsell Rd.
Highbury, London N5 1XL
UK
p: 44-207-607-0303
e: info@bigcheesemagazine.com
www.bigcheesemagazine.com
frequency: Monthly
circulation: 18,000
contact: Eugene Butcher
e: eugene@bigcheesemagazine.com
emphasis: Alt., Rock, Punk, Metal
Popular UK Rock mag includes reviews, news, gigs & features. Available in the UK & select USA newsstands.

The Big Issue
1-5 Wandsworth Rd.
London, SW8 2LN UK
p: 44-207-526-3200
e: contact@bigissue.com
www.bigissue.co.uk
frequency: Weekly
circulation: 79,000
contact: A. John Bird
e: editorialinfo@bigissue.com
emphasis: Issues & Arts
The Body Shop's socially concious mag has reg'l editions throughout the UK, Australia, Japan, S Africa, Namibia & Kenya. Proceeds support homeless & other marginalized people.

Big Shot Magazine
93 Montague St., #240

Brooklyn, NY 11201
p: 718-643-4701
f: 718-802-0902
e: info@bigshotmag.com; incoming@bigshotmag.com
www.bigshotmag.com
frequency: Bimonthly
circulation: 80,000
contact: Darren Ressler
e: darren@bigshotmag.com
emphasis: Clubbing, Art, Fashion & Recording
Profiles indie lifestyle & music w/focus on DJs. Sold in the US.

Billboard Magazine
770 Broadway, 6th Fl.
New York, NY 10003
p: 323-525-2300
e: info@billboard.com
www.billboard.com
frequency: Weekly
circulation: 23,036
contact: Jonathan Cohen
ext: 646-654-5582
e: jacohen@billboard.com
emphasis: Issues & Arts
Music trade pub. covers industry issues, charts & releases. Reviews majors & polished indies. Sold in 110+ countries.

Bitch Magazine
4930 NE 29th Ave.
Portland, OR 97211
p: 503-282-5699
f: 503-282-5661
e: bitch@bitchmagazine.org
www.bitchmagazine.org
frequency: Quarterly
circulation: 47,000
contact: Andi Zeisler
e: andi@bitchmagazine.org
emphasis: Music & Lifestyle
Int'l non-profit mag focuses on Pop culture, feminism & media.

Black Radio Exclusive (BRE)
15030 Ventura Blvd., Ste. 864
Sherman Oaks, CA 91403
p: 818-907-9959
f: 818-907-9958
e: bremagazin@aol.com
www.bremagazine.com
frequency: Monthly
circulation: 32,000
contact: Sidney Miller
emphasis: Urban Entertainment Industry
Nat'l pub. covers black music industry w/emphasis on radio. Sponsors industry trade events. Also publishes consumer mag, Black Renaissance Exclusive, covering Urban entertainment.

Blender
1040 6th Ave.
New York, NY 10018
p: 212-302-2626
f: 212-719-9310
www.blender.com
frequency: 11/year
circulation: 925,000
contact: Rob Tannenbaum
e: rtannenbaum@alphamediagroup.com
emphasis: All Styles
Nat'l racy music mag offspring of Maxim, spotlights estab. & emerging acts w/ coverage of the rich & tuneful for consumers. Only finished releases considered.

Blue Suede News
PO Box 25 E
Duvall, WA 98019
p: 425-788-2776
www.bluesuedenews.com
frequency: Quarterly
circulation: 3700
contact: Marc Bristol
e: shakinboss@aol.com
emphasis: Roots, Rockabilly, R&B, Americana, Cajun, Blues, Honky Tonk, Country
Int'l pub. devoted to American Roots music & its devotees. Includes up to 100 CD reviews/issue. Email before sending material.

Bluegrass Unlimited
PO Box 771
Warrenton, VA 20188
p: 800-258-4727
f: 540-341-0011
www.bluegrassmusic.com
frequency: Monthly
circulation: 20,000
contact: Sharon McGraw
e: editor@bluegrassmusic.com
emphasis: Bluegrass
Available in music & bookstores worldwide.

Blues Revue
Rte. 1, Box 75
Salem, WV 26426
p: 304-782-1971
f: 304-782-1993
e: info@bluesrevue.com
www.bluesrevue.com
frequency: Bimonthly
circulation: 25,000
contact: Ken Bays
e: editor2@bluesrevue.com
emphasis: Blues
Issues include up to 100 reviews & CD sampler. Also publishes Blueswax zine. Submit 2 copies for consideration.

Boom!
PO Box 398752
Miami Beach, FL 33239
p: 305-718-3612
f: 305-468-1983
www.boomonline.com
frequency: Bimonthly
circulation: 25,000
contact: Kike Posada
e: enrique.posada@boomonline.com
emphasis: Hispanic Music & Culture
Spanish language music mag for Latin Alt. fans includes features, interviews, tour & release info. Send digital kits.

BPM Magazine
6725 Sunset Blvd., Ste.320
Hollywood, CA 90028
p: 323-655-9600 x6
f: 310-360-7171
www.bpmmagazine.net
frequency: 10/year
circulation: 80,000
contact: Dean DeCosta
e: dean@overamerica
emphasis: DJ Music & Culture
Music & lifestyle mag for males 25+, reviews up to 100, mostly indie releases. Widely avail. in USA; ltd. distrib. in Canada & London.

Bust
78 5th Ave., Ste. 5
New York, NY 10011
p: 212-675-1707
e: submissions@bust.com
www.bust.com
frequency: 6/year
circulation: 93,500
contact: Laurie Henzel
ext: 212-675-1707 x102
e: laurie@bust.com
emphasis: Women
Int'l hip Alt. mag for ladies 18-34 reviews indie releases & publishes annual music issue. Send promos & full contact info to: PO Box 1016, Cooper Station, New York, NY 10276.

Cadence
Cadence Bldg.
Redwood, NY 13679
p: 315-287-2852
f: 315-287-2860
e: cadence@cadencebuilding.com
www.cadencebuilding.com
frequency: Quarterly
contact: Dave Bernstein
e: dave@cadencebuilding.com
emphasis: Improv, Jazz, Blues
Comprehensive coverage & reviews. Sold worldwide in music & book stores. Submit 2 copies of release.

Carib News
7 W 36th St., 8th Fl.
New York, NY 10018
p: 212-944-1991
f: 212-944-2089
e: news@nycaribnews.com
www.nycaribnews.com
frequency: Weekly
circulation: 70,000
contact: Walter Greene
emphasis: Caribbean, Gospel, Urban, Afro-Beat
Int'l mag for Caribbean music fans, includes reviews & features.

CCM
104 Woodmont Blvd., Ste. 300
Nashville, TN 37205
p: 615-386-3011
f: 615-312-4266
e: feedback@ccmmagazine.com
www.ccmmagazine.com
frequency: Monthly
circulation: 65,000
contact: Jay Swartzendruber
ext: 615-312-4230
e: jays@salempublishing.com
emphasis: CCM
Nat'l faith-based music mag includes reviews & features.

Chart Attack
34 Britain St., 2nd Fl.
Toronto, ON M5A 1R7
Canada
p: 416-363-3101
f: 416-363-3109
e: chart@chartattack.com
www.chartattack.com
frequency: 10/year
circulation: 40,000-100,000
contact: Aaron Brophy
e: aaron@chartattack.com
emphasis: Rock, Hip-Hop, Electronic, College
Features Canadian & int'l music scenes & buzz bands. Covers Canadian college radio charts & provides music news & reviews for the Canadian Press.

Clubworld Magazine
25 Willowdale Ave.
Port Washington, NY 11050
p: 516-767-2500
f: 516-767-9335
e: clubworld@testa.com
www.clubworld.us
frequency: Monthly
circulation: 20,000
contact: Vinny Testa
e: vtesta@testa.com
emphasis: Niteclub Culture
Trade mag formerly Club Systems Int'l covers sound & lighting issue for music venues. Subscription only.

CMJ New Music Monthly
151 W 25th St., 12th Fl.
New York, NY 10001
p: 917-606-1908
f: 917-606-1914
e: newmusicmonthly@cmj.com
www.cmj.com/newmm
frequency: Monthly
circulation: 16,000
contact: Rev. Moose Raber
ext: 917-606-1908 x236
e: moose@cmj.com
emphasis: New Music
Satiates new music fans w/reviews, features & interviews w/ buzz bands, obscure acts & name talent. CD compilation w/ each issue.

CMJ New Music Report
151 W 25th St., 12th Fl.
New York, NY 10001
p: 917-606-1908
f: 917-606-1914
e: customersupport@cmj.com
www.cmj.com/nmrsite/nmr.php
frequency: Weekly
circulation: 2000
contact: Rev. Moose Raber
ext: 917-606-1908 x236
e: moose@cmj.com
emphasis: New Music, College Radio News, Indie Retail & College Charts
College-centric trade pub. reports college & Alt. commercial radio & cutting-edge retail activity. CD reviews, artist features & industry trends.

Dazed & Confused
112-116 Old St.
London, EC1 9BG UK
p: 44-207-336-0766
f: 44-207-336-0966
e: editorialexperience@dazedgroup.com
www.dazeddigital.com; www.dazedgroup.com
frequency: Monthly
circulation: 350,000
contact: Nicki Bidder
e: nicki@dazedgroup.com
Hip fashion, music & lifestyle mag available in over 40 countries includes coverage of new & estab. acts.

Death & Taxes
200 E 10th St., #125
New York, NY 10003
p: 212-966-8770
f: 212-966-8770
e: info@deathandtaxesmagazine.com
www.deathandtaxesmagazine.com; www.dt-mag.com
frequency: Bimonthly
circulation: 54,000
contact: Stephen Blackwell
e: stephen@deathandtaxesmagazine.com

emphasis: Indie Rock
Fairly new on the indie Rock block from Liquid Pub., attracts mostly females 18-37. Distrib. on newsstands & by subscription in USA, UK, France, Canada & S America.

Decibel
1032 Arch St., 3rd Fl.
Philadelphia, PA 19107
p: 215-625-9850 x1
f: 215-625-9967
www.decibelmagazine.com
frequency: Monthly
circulation: 50,000
contact: Albert Mudrian
e: albert@redflagmedia.com
emphasis: Metal
Published by Red Flag Media, covers entire spectrum of extreme Metal, from platinum acts & genre pioneers to the best of the underground.

Dirty Linen
PO Box 66600
Baltimore, MD 21239
p: 410-583-7973
f: 410-337-6735
e: office@dirtylinen.com
www.dirtylinen.com
frequency: Bimonthly
circulation: 13,000
contact: D.D. Nelson
emphasis: Roots, Traditional, Folk, World Music
Runs CD & gig reviews, articles & features. Available at book & music stores in USA, Canada & Europe. Only new releases avail. for sale are considered for review; accepts CDs only.

DJ Times
25 Willowdale Ave.
Port Washington, NY 11050
p: 516-767-2500
f: 516-944-8372
e: djtimes@testa.com
www.djtimes.com
frequency: Monthly
circulation: 30,000
contact: Jim Tremayne
ext: 516-767-2500 x702
e: jtremayne@testa.com
emphasis: Dance, Urban, DJs
Trade for pro mobile & club DJs. Includes indie reviews, artist features, chart info & gear reviews. Sold at nat'l book & record shops.

Down Beat Magazine
102 N Haven Rd.
Elmhurst, IL 60126
p: 630-941-2030;
800-554-7470
f: 630-941-3210
e: editor@downbeat.com
www.downbeat.com
frequency: Monthly
circulation: 67,000
contact: Frank Alkyer
ext: 630-941-2030 x108
e: franka@downbeat.com
emphasis: Jazz
Top mag for players & fans 49+ runs reviews, features & interviews. Sold at nat'l book & record retail. No EPKs.

Drum!
95 S Market St.
San Jose, CA 95113
p: 408-971-9794
f: 408-971-0382
www.drummagazine.com
frequency: 12/year
circulation: 36,500
contact: Andy Doerschuk
e: andy@drumlink.com
emphasis: Drum & Percussion
Niche pub., sold worldwide at newsstands & equipment stores, runs some reviews & interviews.

Electronic Musician
6400 Hollis St., #12
Emeryville, CA 94608
p: 510-653-3307
f: 510-653-5142
e: emeditorial@penton.com
www.emusician.com
frequency: Monthly
circulation: 80,000
contact: Tracy Katz
ext: 510-985-3218
e: tkatz@emusician.com
emphasis: Recording
Resourceful Penton Media pub. for the home recording musician covers gear, software & tips for recording & live performances. Sold nationwide & via subscription.

Exclaim!
849A Bloor St. W
Toronto, ON M6G 1M3
Canada
p: 416-535-9735
f: 416-535-0566
e: exclaim@exclaim.ca
www.exclaim.ca
frequency: Monthly
circulation: 105,000
contact: James Keast
ext: 416-535-9735 x21
e: james@exclaim.ca
emphasis: Cutting-edge Music
Free mag w/ distrib. at Canadian bars & cafes provides in-depth coverage of new music, emphasis on Canadian talent.

Fiddler Magazine
PO Box 101
North Sydney, NS B2A 3M1
Canada
p: 902-794-2558
e: info@fiddle.com
www.fiddle.com
frequency: Quarterly
circulation: 2500
contact: Paul Anastasio
e: panastasio@w-link.net
emphasis: Fiddle Music
Quarterly resource for fiddlers & their fans available via subscription & at some music stores. Promos to: PO Box 30153, Seattle, WA 98113.

Filter
5908 Barton Ave.
Los Angeles, CA
90038
p: 323-464-4775
f: 323-464-4294
e: info@filtermmm.com
www.filter-mag.com
frequency: 5/year
circulation: 85,000
contact: Pat McGuire
ext: 323-464-4170
e: pat@filter-mag.com
emphasis: Alt., Indie Pop, Brit Pop, Jazz, Punk
Hip int'l music mag for serious fans of new, undiscovered talent provides reviews, top picks, artists to watch & interviews.

Fingerstyle Guitar Magazine
PO Box 1178
Lewiston, NY 14092
p: 716-754-4462
f: 716-754-4465
e: fingerguitar@aol.com
www.fingerstyleguitar.com
frequency: Bimonthly
circulation: 20,000+
contact: Bill Piburn
e: fgeditor@comcast.net
emphasis: Fingerstyle Technique
Includes CD w/ tracks from featured artists & complete tabs. Avail. bimonthly by subscription & select music & book stores. Send review copies to: Bill, PO Box 8120, Gallatin, TN 37066.

The Fly
59-65 Worship St.,
London, EC2A 2DU
UK
p: 44-207-688-9000
f: 44-207-691-4666
e: info@channelfly.net
www.the-fly.co.uk
frequency: Monthly
circulation: 200,000
contact: Adrienne Coultis-Pittman
e: press@channelfly.net
emphasis: New Music
Free mag covers new music & UK artists; distrib. at HMV, venues, student unions & bars.

Friday Morning Quarterback
Executive Mews, F-36, 1930 E Marlton Pike
Cherry Hill, NJ 08003
p: 856-424-9114
f: 856-424-6943
e: fmqb@fmqb.com
www.fmqb.com
frequency: Monthly
circulation: 10,000
contact: Fred Deane
e: fdeane@fmqb.com
emphasis: Radio Industry
Covers programming, mgmt., promo, marketing, imaging & music for CHR, Rhythm Crossover, Rock, Modern Rock, Alt., AAA & AC radio formats. By subscription only.

fROOTS Magazine
PO Box 337
London, N4 1TW UK
p: 44-208-340-9651
f: 44-208-348-5626
e: froots@frootsmag.com
www.frootsmag.com
frequency: Monthly
circulation: 12,000
contact: Ian Anderson
emphasis: Roots, Folk, World
Includes news, features & reviews & sold at UK retail.

Giant Magazine
50 E 42nd St., 14th Fl.
New York, NY 10017
p: 646-837-0200;
646-837-0210
f: 212-661-7292
e: info@giantmag.com;
gntcustserv@cdsfulfillment.com
www.giantmag.com
frequency: Bimonthly
circulation: 313,000
contact: Smokey D. Fontaine
ext: 646-837-0205
emphasis: Urban Music & Culture
Hip culture mag targets African-American readers 22+. Covers Urban genres w/ reviews & interviews.

Global Rhythm Magazine
104 W 29th St., 11th Fl.
New York, NY 10011
p: 646-674-1746
f: 212-868-4356
www.globalrhythm.net
frequency: 8/year
circulation: 120,000
contact: Tad Hendrickson
e: thendrickson@globalrhythm.net
emphasis: World Beat
Catering to the global-minded, well-heeled music fan & covers all styles of World music, travel & lifestyle. Sold at major music chains.

Grooves Magazine
18 Eastwood Dr.
Voorhees, NJ 08043
p: 866-717-3804;
866-717-3804
www.groovesmag.com
frequency: Quarterly
circulation: 15,000
contact: Sean Portnoy
emphasis: Experimental Electronic
Nat'l pub. features news, reviews, interviews & podcasts for DJs & fans. No House or Trance.

Guitar Player
1111 Bayhill Dr.
San Bruno, CA 94066
p: 650-238-0300
f: 650-238-0261
e: guitplyr@musicplayer.com
www.guitarplayer.com
frequency: Monthly
circulation: 150,000
contact: Michael Molenda
e: mmolenda@musicplayer.com
emphasis: Guitar
Subscription-driven mag. published by New Bay Media, geared toward pros & serious hobbyists. Artist interviews, guitar tabs, product, CD & demo reviews. Int'l distrib.

Guitar World
149 Fifth Ave., 9th Fl.
New York, NY 10010
p: 212-768-2966
f: 212-944-9279
e: soundingboard@guitarworld.com
www.guitarworld.com
frequency: Monthly
circulation: 200,000
contact: Jeff Kitts
ext: 646-723-5420
e: jeffkitts@aol.com
emphasis: Rock Guitar
Int'l pub. contains lessons, tabs, interviews, CD & product reviews for wannabe Rock stars.

Hear/Say
11012 Aurora Hudson Rd.
Streetsboro, OH 44241
p: 330-528-0410
f: 330-528-0423
www.hearsay.cc
frequency: 10/year
circulation: 50,000
contact: Jeff Niesel
ext: 216-479-2033 x263
e: jniesel@freetimes.com
emphasis: Alt., Hip-Hop, Rock, Pop
Free music pub. distrib. to 700

USA college campuses & 150 Indie music stores.

Hits Magazine
6255 Sunset Blvd., Ste. 910
Hollywood, CA 90028
p: 323-461-6100
f: 323-860-0858
www.hitsdailydouble.com
frequency: Biweekly
circulation: 10,000
contact: Roy Trakin
e: roy.trakin@hitsmagazine.com
emphasis: Urban, Rock, Pop, Top 40, AC, AAA
Read primarily by radio stations & labels, tracks radio hits, charts & industry.

Hittin' the Note
8343 Roswell Rd., Ste. 345
Atlanta, GA 30350
p: 770-640-1124
f: 770-643-8657
www.hittinthenote.com
frequency: Quarterly
circulation: 25,000
contact: John Lynskey
e: jplhtn@aol.com
emphasis: Southern Roots, Americana, Blues, Jazz, Country, Jam, Rock
Celebrates all things Allman Brothers & new Indies that follow in their footsteps w/profiles, interviews & 6 pgs of CD reviews. Distrib. to nat'l & indie bookstores.

HM (The Hard Music Magazine)
PO Box 367
Hutto, TX 78634
p: 512-989-7309
f: 512-535-1827
www.hmmag.com
frequency: Bimonthly
circulation: 13,000
contact: Doug Van Pelt
e: dvanpelt@hmmag.com
emphasis: Christian Hard Music
Sleekly designed niche pub. skews 16-24+ & spotlights indies w/ interviews & CD reviews. Avail. at newsstands & by subscription. Accepts EPKs, but prefers hard copy.

Hollywood Reporter
5055 Wilshire Blvd., 6th Fl.
Los Angeles, CA 90036
p: 323-525-2000
f: 323-525-2377
www.hollywoodreporter.com
frequency: Daily
circulation: 26,000/day
contact: Erik Pedersen
e: epedersen@hollywoodreporter.com
emphasis: Entertainment
Int'l trade pub. reviews buzz bands, estab. artists & industry trends & issues. Worldwide distrib.

Hot Press Music Magazine
13 Trinity St.
Dublin, 2 Ireland
p: 35-31-241-1500
f: 35-31-241-1538
e: info@hotpress.ie
www.hotpress.com
frequency: Bimonthly
circulation: 25,000
contact: Niall Stokes
emphasis: Alt., Top 40, Traditional, Electronic, Dance
Stylish coverage of UK music makers & the scene runs interviews, profiles, features & reviews of top tier talent & rising stars. Targets male readers 18-35.

Jazz Improv Magazine
PO Box 26770
Elkins Park, PA 19027
p: 215-887-8808
e: info@jazzimprov.com; jazz@jazzimprov.com
www.jazzimprov.com
frequency: Quarterly
circulation: 15,000-20,000
contact: Eric Nemeyer
e: eric@jazzimprov.com
emphasis: Jazz
For serious jazzbos & artists. Chock-full of features, reviews, interviews & charts. Int'l distrib. in bookstores. Also publishes downloadable "Jazz Improv NY Jazz Guide".

Jazziz Magazine
2650 N Military Tr., Ste. 140
Boca Raton, FL 33431
p: 561-893-6868 x303
f: 561-893-6867
www.jazziz.com
frequency: Monthly
circulation: 192,000
contact: Michael Koretzky
ext: 561-893-6868 x306; 561-901-0651 (cell)
e: reviews@jazziz.com
emphasis: Jazz
Contains charts, features & products, hundreds of reviews & a CD sampler. Available on newsstands & by subscription.

JazzTimes
8737 Colesville Rd., 9th Fl.
Silver Spring, MD 20910
p: 301-588-4114
f: 301-588-5531
e: info@jazztimes.com
www.jazztimes.com
frequency: 10/year
circulation: 90,000
contact: Lee Mergner
ext: 301-588-4114 x513
e: lmergner@jazztimes.com
emphasis: Jazz
Leading int'l Jazz pub. for fans & pros offers hundreds of reviews, studio news, interviews, profiles & events per issue. Covers some Blues & World.

Juice Magazine
2058 N Sycamore Ave.
Hollywood, CA 90068
p: 310-399-5336
e: juicemag@aol.com
www.juicemagazine.com
frequency: Quarterly
circulation: 25,000
contact: Terri Craft
e: juicesss@aol.com
emphasis: Music, Surfing, & Skateboarding
Caters to 18-48 skate & Punk crowd. Int'l distro in 1300+ skate, surf & music stores. No EPKs.

Kerrang!
Mappin House, 4 Winsley St.
London, W1W 8HF UK
p: 44-207-436-1515

e: editor@kerrang.com
www.kerrang.com
frequency: Weekly
circulation: 76,937
contact: Nick Ruskell
e: nick.ruskell@kerrang.com
emphasis: Hard Rock, Metal, Punk
Leading UK pub. includes news, reviews & in-depth features. Available on newsstands & subscriptions, some int'l distrib. Site is gathering spot for Hard Rock community & hosts Kerrang!Radio, Kerrang!TV, forums & store. Send press pack w/CD, bio & press photo.

Latin Beat Magazine
15900 Crenshaw Blvd.
Ste. 1-223
Gardena, CA 90249
p: 310-516-6767
f: 310-516-9916
e: info@latinbeatmagazine.com; editor@lbmo.com
www.latinbeatmagazine.com
frequency: 10/year
circulation: 50,000
contact: Rudy Mangual
e: rudy@latinbeatmagazine.com
emphasis: Latin Jazz, Salsa Afro-Caribbean, Latin Pop
Covers estab. & emerging talent in the Latin music scene w/features & reviews. Available in N America, Europe & Puerto Rico.

Living Blues
PO Box 1848, 301 Hill Hall
University, MS 38677
p: 800-390-3527; 662-915-5742
f: 662-915-7842
e: lblues@olemiss.edu
www.livingblues.com
frequency: Bimonthly
circulation: 20,000
contact: Brett Bonner
e: brett@livingblues.com
emphasis: Blues
Authoritative mag for true Blues fans, published by U Miss, includes features & CD reviews. Email submissions only.

Magnet
1218 Chestnut St., Ste. 508
Philadelphia, PA 19107
p: 215-413-8570
f: 215-413-8569
e: magnet@magnetmagazine.com
www.magnetmagazine.com
frequency: Quarterly
circulation: 35,000
contact: Eric T. Miller
e: eric@magnetmagazine.com
emphasis: Alt.
Int'l mag reviews below the radar artists & releases. Includes music news, features & product reviews. Send full releases only.

Mass Appeal
261 Vandervoort Ave.
Brooklyn, NY 11211
p: 718-858-0979
e: support@massappealmag.com
www.massappealmag.com
frequency: Bimonthly
circulation: 140,000
contact: Felipe Delerme
e: felipe@massappealmag.com
emphasis: Urban Music & Lifestyle
Off beat mag for Rap fans & beyond. Covers innovative artists, producers & releases.

Metal Edge
104 W 29th St., 11th Fl.
New York, NY 10001
p: 646-230-0100
e: metaledgemag@gmail.com
www.metaledgemag.com
frequency: 10/year
circulation: 155,000
contact: Phil Freeman
e: pfreeman@zenbumedia.com
emphasis: Metal
Covering the harder side of Rock w/features, reviews & interviews - past legends & new label darlings. Sold in N America at book & music stores.

Metal Hammer
2 Balcombe St.
London, NW1 6NA UK
e: james.gill@futurenet.co.uk
www.metalhammer.co.uk
frequency: Monthly
contact: Jonathan Selzer
e: jselzer@futurenet.co.uk
emphasis: Metal
Must-have mag for fans in UK & abroad spotlights major acts. Mini mag inserts focus on indies.

Metal Maniacs
104 W 29th St., 11th Fl.
New York, NY 10001
p: 646-230-0100
f: 646-230-0200
www.metalmaniacs.com
frequency: Monthly
circulation: 55,000
contact: Liz Ciavarella
ext: 646-674-2394
e: nuclearliz@aol.com
emphasis: Metal
Reviews & features underground & buzz Metal acts. Free ads: send band photo & description to Attn: Band Shorts.

Modern Drummer Publications
12 Old Bridge Rd.
Cedar Grove, NJ 07009
p: 973-239-4140
f: 973-239-7139
e: mdinfo@moderndrummer.com
www.moderndrummer.com
frequency: Monthly
circulation: 103,000
contact: Adam Budofsky
ext: 973-239-4140 x110
e: adamb@moderndrummer.com
emphasis: Drum-Related
Specialty pub. covers drum-related topics & releases. Sold in book & music shops worldwide to mostly male readers. Submit digital kits only.

Mojo
Mappin House, 4 Winsley St.
London, W1W 8HF UK
p: 44-207-436-1515
f: 44-207-312-8296
e: mojo@bauerconsumer.co.uk
www.mojo4music.com
frequency: Monthly
contact: Phil Alexander
emphasis: Rock
Sister pub of "Q", reviews a wide selection of major & Indie releases monthly for int'l readership of Rock fans. Promos w/ ATTN: Jenny Bulley.

Music Connection
14654 Victory Blvd.
Van Nuys, CA 91411
p: 818-995-0101
f: 818-995-9235
e: contactmc@musicconnection.com
www.musicconnection.com
frequency: Monthly
circulation: 75,000
contact: Mark Nardone
e: markn@musicconnection.com
emphasis: Rock, Pop, S/S, Hip-Hop, Country, Jazz
Respected music mag for musicians & industry covers issues & trends & evaluates performances of emerging artists. Send EPKs: musicconnection.com/amp/reviews.
See Ad On Page 228

Music Row
1231 17th Ave. S
Nashville, TN 37212
p: 615-321-3617
f: 615-329-0852
e: news@musicrow.com
www.musicrow.com
frequency: 6/year
circulation: 3000-4000
contact: David Ross
ext: 615-321-3617 x202
e: ross@musicrow.com
emphasis: Country Music
Trade pub. only covers the Nashville Country music scene & its stars, some polished indie releases may slip in.

Musico Pro
5408 Idylwild Tr., Ste. 100
Boulder, CO 80301
p: 303-516-9118
f: 303-516-9119
e: info@musicopro.com
www.musicopro.com
frequency: Monthly
circulation: 50,000
contact: Rodrigo Sanchez
e: rodrigo@musicopro.com
emphasis: Rock, Jazz, Latin, Urban, Blues, World, Metal, Country
Spanish language trade covers indie releases & industry topics. Runs indie artist spotlight.

New Music Weekly
2530 Atlantic Ave., Ste. C
Long Beach, CA 90806
p: 310-325-9997
f: 310-427-7333
e: staff@newmusicweekly.com
www.newmusicweekly.com
frequency: Weekly
contact: Paul Loggins
e: ploggins@newmusicweekly.com
Int'l trade pub. covers the Radio & Music industry by tracking nat'l playlists & radio related issues. No EPKs.

No Cover Magazine
7770 Telegraph Rd., Ste.E #207
Ventura, CA 93004
p: 619-276-0247
www.nocover.com
frequency: Bimonthly
circulation: 20,000
contact: Jonathan Cholewa
e: jonekat@juno.com
emphasis: New Music
New music mag has broken many artists in all genres. Publishes 3 free event guides for Santa Barbara/Ventura counties in CA.

Northeast Performer Magazine
24 Dane St.
Somerville, MA 02143
p: 617-627-9200
f: 617-627-9930
e: nepeditorial@performermag.com
www.performermag.com
frequency: Monthly
circulation: 35,000
contact: Adam Arrigo
e: adam@performermag.com
emphasis: Indie Musicians
Covers USA indie scene w/ northeast, southeast & west coast editions. Free distib. to studios, gear & music retail.

NYLON
110 Greene St., Ste. 607
New York, NY 10012
p: 212-226-6454
f: 212-226-7738
www.nylonmag.com
frequency: 10/year
circulation: 225,000
contact: Samantha Gilewicz
e: samantha@nylonmag.com
emphasis: Fashion & Music
Covers items that appeal to gals 18-34 in USA, Japan, Korea & Mexico. Has similar pub., NYLON GUYS.

Outburn
PO Box 3187
Thousand Oaks, CA 91359
p: 805-493-5861
e: outburn@outburn.com
www.outburn.com
frequency: 5/year
circulation: 65,000
contact: Octavia Laird
emphasis: Rock, Metal, Punk, Hardcore, Alt.
Consumer mag profiles buzz bands w/profiles, gig reviews & 100+ new music reviews. Sold in music & bookstores in US & Canada. Mail submissions.

Paper
15 E 32nd St., 11th Fl.
New York, NY 10016
p: 212-226-4405
f: 212-226-5929
e: edit@papermag.com
www.papermag.com
frequency: Monthly
circulation: 135,000
contact: David Hershkovits
e: davidh@papermag.com
emphasis: Hip-Hop, Rock, Punk
Pop culture mag profiles artists & reviews major & indie releases for 21-34-yr-olds. Available in 500 metro-area newsstands, bars & boutiques.

Paste
619 E College Ave., Ste. E
Decatur, GA 30030

p: 404-207-1200
f: 404-378-8872
e: editor@pastemagazine.com
www.pastemagazine.com
frequency: Monthly
circulation: 180,000+
contact: Josh Jackson
e: josh@pastemagazine.com
emphasis: Rock, Pop, Hip-Hop, Americana
Stuffed w/ reviews, features & includes CD/DVD sampler for subscribers, mostly males 18-54. Sold nationwide at book/record shops. Promos to: PO Box 1606, Decatur, GA 30031; or send digital kits.

Penguin Eggs Magazine
10942 80th Ave.
Edmonton, AB T6G 0R1
Canada
p: 780-433-8287
f: 780-437-4603
e: penguineggs@shaw.ca
www.penguineggs.ab.ca
frequency: Quarterly
circulation: 5000
contact: Roddy Campbell
emphasis: Folk, Roots, World
Sole Canadian Folk mag includes artist profiles, reviews & features.

Performing Songwriter Magazine
2805 Azaela Pl.
Nashville, TN 37204
p: 800-883-7664 x32
f: 615-385-5637
www.performingsongwriter.com
frequency: 8/year
circulation: 55,000
contact: Jesse Thompson
ext: 615-385-7796 x34
e: jesse@performingsongwriter.com
emphasis: S/S
Premier coverage of artists that write, perform & record their own music for pros & fans. Reviews, profiles & industry issues Distrib. at book & music stores.

Pit Magazine
PO Box 9545
Colorado Springs, CO 80932
p: 719-633-5752
f: 719-633-8081
e: pitmag@aol.com
www.pitmagazine.com
frequency: Quarterly
circulation: 30,000
contact: Wendy Perelstein
e: wendy@pitmagazine.com
emphasis: Extreme Metal
Demo reviews & release news in the underground, extreme music scene. Sold at newsstands & book stores nationwide.

Profane Existence
PO Box 18051
Minneapolis, MN 55418
p: 612-722-1134
f: 612-605-1216
www.profaneexistence.com
frequency: Quarterly
circulation: 5000
contact: Daniel Siskind
e: blackened@visi.com
emphasis: Punk, Hardcore
Anti-capitalist, anarchy zine profiles & reviews only true indie Punk acts & releases. Available in 35 countries. CD comp. in every issue.

Progression Magazine
PO Box 7164
Lowell, MA 01852
p: 978-970-2728; 800-545-7371
f: 978-970-2728
e: progmagazine@aol.com
www.progressionmagazine.com
frequency: Quarterly
circulation: 11,000
contact: John Collinge
emphasis: Prog Rock
Features legends & newbies w/ album/gig reviews, music & video previews. Hits 20-60-yr-olds in 42 countries. Send full kit w/ 2 review copies & contact info.

Q
Mappin House, 4 Winsley St.
London, W1W 8HF UK
p: 44-207-182-8482
f: 44-207-182-8547
e: qmail@qthemusic.com
www.q4music.com
frequency: Monthly
circulation: 200,000
contact: Paul Rees
emphasis: Rock, Pop, Hip-Hop
Serves as buyers guide for music fans worldwide. Over 200 reviews, profiles & interviews w/ buzz acts & estab. artists. Sold at music & bookstores & newsstands worldwide. Also publishes "MOJO".

Radio & Records
5055 Wilshire Blvd., 6th Fl.
Los Angeles, CA 90036
p: 323-954-3400
f: 323-954-3411
e: newsroom@radioandrecords.com
www.radioandrecords.com
frequency: Weekly
circulation: 10,000
contact: Cyndee Maxwell
e: cmaxwell@radioandrecords.com
emphasis: Commercial Radio
Subscription only trade pub. part of the Nielsen family, tracks airplay, industry news & charts for radio & record biz.

Rap-Up
23679 Calabasas Rd.
Calabasas, CA 91302
p: 818-591-5837
f: 818-591-8645
e: info@rap-up.com
www.rap-up.com
frequency: Bimonthly
circulation: 90,000
contact: Devin Lazerine
e: editor@rap-up.com
emphasis: Hip-Hop, R&B
Covers the major stars of the Urban scene for 14-28-yr-olds. Sold at retail & newsstands nationwide.

Real Blues Magazine
PO Box 1201
Victoria, BC V8W 2T6
Canada
p: 250-537-2505
f: 250-537-2505
e: realblues@uniserve.com
www.realbluesmagazine.com
frequency: Bimonthly
circulation: 15,000
contact: Andy Grigg
e: andy@realbluesmagazine.com
emphasis: Authentic Blues, Soul, Gospel, Zydeco
Indie-laden music guide for Blues & related styles, sold & 33 counties & reviews 100 new releases & has artist profiles & festival info.

Relix Magazine
104 W 29th St.
11th Fl.
New York, NY 10001
p: 646-230-0100
f: 646-230-0200
e: editors@relix.com
www.relix.com
frequency: 8/year
circulation: 85,000
contact: Josh Baron
e: josh@relix.com
emphasis: Jam, Live Improv, S/S, Rock, Bluegrass
Oriented towards Grateful Dead, Zappa & related styles, runs in-depth interviews w/high-profile acts & covers genre-related events. Co-sponsors the "Jammy's."

Remix
6400 Hollis St., #12
Emeryville, CA 94608
p: 510-653-3307
f: 510-653-5142
e: remixeditorial@remixmag.com
www.remixmag.com
frequency: Monthly
circulation: 50,000
contact: Kylee Swenson
e: kswenson@remixmag.com
emphasis: Electronic, Urban
Music mag covers underground music production, performance & gear.

Revolver
149 Fifth Ave.
9th Fl.
New York, NY 10010
p: 212-768-2966; 800-266-3312
f: 212-944-9279
e: revolvermag@aol.com
www.revolvermag.com
frequency: Monthly
circulation: 150,000
contact: Tom Beaujour
ext: 212-768-5467
e: tom@revolvermag.com
emphasis: Alt., Hard Rock, Metal, Punk
Genre mag for 18-34 crowd, read by artists & fans runs features & reviews of new & name acts, studio & release news & includes mp3 compilations.

Rolling Stone
1290 Ave. of the Americas
2nd Fl.
New York, NY 10104
p: 212-484-1616
f: 212-484-1621
www.rollingstone.com
frequency: Biweekly
circulation: 1,445,900
contact: Melissa Maerz
ext: 212-484-3471
e: melissa.maerz@rollingstone.com
emphasis: All Styles
Career-making int'l music & lifestyle mag covers everything & everyone w/a buzz. CD reviews, interviews & profiles.

Sing Out!
PO Box 5460
Bethlehem, PA 18015
p: 610-865-5366
f: 215-895-3052
e: info@singout.org
www.singout.org
frequency: Quarterly
circulation: 13,500
contact: Mark D. Moss
ext: 610-865-5366 x203
e: mark@singout.org
emphasis: Folk
Coves a broad spectrum of Folk & related styles w/release schedules, festival guide, sampler & 200+ reviews. Nat'l distrib. at music & bookstores.

Singer & Musician/L2P
PO Box 10
Naples, NY 14512
p: 585-303-3006
f: 585-303-1793
www.l2pnet.com; www.iradio.ws
frequency: Quarterly
circulation: 55,000
contact: Robert Lindquist
e: ral@l2pnet.com
emphasis: Vocalists
Features artist profiles, performance & biz tips for aspiring pros. Sold at newsstands, industry events & by subscription.
See Ad On Page 235

Skyscraper Magazine
PO Box 486
Mamaroneck, NY 10543
p: 303-544-9858
f: 801-912-7291
e: skyscraperzine@hotmail.com
www.skyscrapermagazine.com
frequency: 4/year
circulation: 10,000
contact: Peter Bottomley
emphasis: Indie Rock, Underground
Profiles & reviews gigs & finished product w/artwork for adventurous music fans in N America, Europe & Japan.

Slap Magazine
1303 Underwood Ave.
San Francisco, CA 94124
p: 415-822-3083
f: 415-822-8359
e: info@slapmagazine.com
www.slapmagazine.com
frequency: Monthly
circulation: 60,000
contact: Mark Whiteley
ext: 415-822-3083 x431
e: mark@slapmagazine.com
emphasis: Skate Music & Lifestyle
Runs interviews, features & reviews of Rock, Punk, Alt., Jazz & Hip-Hop releases for fans in the Americas, Europe & Japan. Sold at skate shops, bookstores & by subscription.

Songlines World Music Magazine
Unit F, Shepherds Studios
Rockley Rd.
London, Windsor W14 ODA
UK
p: 44-207-371-2777
f: 44-207-371-2220
e: info@songlines.co.uk
www.songlines.co.uk
frequency: 7/year
contact: Simon Broughton
e: editor@songlines.co.uk

emphasis: World Music
Companion to "The Rough Guide to World Music" & packed w/CD reviews, concert listings, interviews & a CD sampler. Highlights of each issue podcast on iTunes.

Spin Magazine
205 Lexington Ave., 3rd Fl.
New York, NY 10016
p: 212-231-7400
f: 212-231-7312
www.spin.com
frequency: Monthly
circulation: 450,000
contact: Charles Aaron
e: caaron@spin.com
emphasis: Rock
Prime int'l music & lifestyle pub. focuses on music fans ages 18-32. Reviews buzz bands & top tier talent.

Swindle
PO Box 291458
Los Angeles, CA 90029
e: info@swindlemagazine.com; submissions@swindlemagazine.com
http://swindlemagazine.com
frequency: 6/year
contact: Shepard Fairey
emphasis: Pop Culture
Photo & illustration heavy mag targets artsy/intellectual crowd. Available in LA & NYC book & music stores.

Tape Op Magazine
PO Box 14517
Portland, OR 97293
p: 916-444-5241
f: 916-444-8972
www.tapeop.com
frequency: Bimonthly
circulation: 55,000
contact: John Baccigaluppi
e: john@tapeop.com
emphasis: Creative Music
Free int'l specialty mag covers issues pertaining to recording music & reviews up to 6 releases. Send promos to: John Baccigaluppi, PO Box 160995, Sacramento, CA 95816. No follow up calls or EPKs.

Thrasher
1303 Underwood Ave.
San Francisco, CA 94124
p: 415-822-3083
f: 415-822-8359
e: info@thrashermagazine.com
www.thrashermagazine.com
frequency: Monthly
circulation: 965,614
contact: Stanislous Clemens
e: stanislous@thrashermagazine.com
emphasis: Punk, Hardcore, Metal, Hip-Hop
Indie-heavy skater music & lifestyle mag pleases headbangers in the Americas, Europe & Japan.

Trace Magazine
41 Great Jones St., 3rd Fl.
New York, NY 10012
p: 212-625-1192
f: 212-625-1195
e: info@trace212.com
www.trace212.com
frequency: 8/year
circulation: 1000
contact: Yolanda Sangweni
e: yolanda@trace212.com
emphasis: Hip-Hop, Soul, World, Rock
Transcultural music & lifestyle mag focuses on multi-ethnic youth culture. Reviews mostly non-mainstream releases.

Under the Radar
238 S Tower Dr., #204
Beverly Hills, CA 90211
p: 323-653-8705
f: 323-658-5738
e: info@undertheradarmag.com; submissions@undertheradarmag.com
www.undertheradarmag.com
frequency: Quarterly
circulation: 55,000
contact: Mark Redfern
e: mark@undertheradarmag.com
emphasis: Indie Rock
Runs 25 interviews & 140+ CD reviews. Sold at book shops & record stores nationwide.

URB
8484 Wilshire Blvd., Ste. 560
Beverly Hills, CA 90211
p: 323-315-1700
f: 323-315-1799
e: office@urb.com
www.urb.com
frequency: Bimonthly
contact: Josh Glazer
ext: 323-315-1700 x108
e: jglazer@urb.com
emphasis: Urban, Rock, Electronic, Jazz
Slick music & culture mag covers artists, releases & events w/articles, charts & reviews. Sold in North America at bookstores & newsstands.

Utne Reader
12 N 12th St., Ste. 400
Minneapolis, MN 55403
f: 612-338-6043
e: editor@utne.com
www.utne.com
frequency: 6/year
circulation: 125,000
contact: David Schimke
emphasis: AAA, Electronic, Pop, Americana, Jazz, Folk, Bluegrass, World
Culture & politics mag appeals to 25+ demographic. Includes features & CD reviews & a CD sampler in Nov issue.

Vapors
6725 Sunset Blvd., Ste.320
Hollywood, CA 90028
p: 323-655-9600
http://vaporsmagazine.com
frequency: 6/year
circulation: 75,000
contact: PJ Canale
e: pj@overamerica.com
emphasis: Skate Culture
Sister pub of DJ mag, "BPM", skews toward 26-yr-old males. Sold nationwide at record & mag retailers & skate & lifestyle shops.

Venus Zine
2000 N Racine, Ste. 3400
Chicago, IL 60614
p: 773-327-9790
f: 773-296-6103

e: feedback@venuszine.com
www.venuszine.com
frequency: Quarterly
circulation: 60,000
contact: K. Tighe
e: tighe@venuszine.com
emphasis: Music, Fashion, Film & DIY Culture
Glossy int'l mag celebrates sleeker side of DIY fashion & arts & geared towards gals. Int'l distrib. at newsstands, bookstores & music fests.
See Ad On Page 231

Vibe
215 Lexington Ave.
New York, NY 10016
p: 212-448-7300
www.vibe.com
frequency: Monthly
circulation: 850,000
contact: Danyel Smith
ext: 212-448-7416 x7393
e: dsmith@vibe.com
emphasis: Urban, Dance-Hall, Reggae
Nat'l music & culture mag chronicles Urban stars.

Wax Poetics Magazine
45 Main St.
#224
Brooklyn, NY 11201
p: 718-624-5696
f: 718-624-5695
e: editorial@waxpoetics.com
www.waxpoetics.com
frequency: Bimonthly
circulation: 70,000+
contact: Jon Kirby
ext: 718-624-5696 x207
e: jon@waxpoetics.com
emphasis: Vinyl
Int'l streetwise & tech laden niche journal for DJs, producers, beatmakers & enthusiasts. Includes interviews w/the stars of the art & its overall legacy.

West Coast Performer Magazine
1278 20th Ave., Ste. C-1
San Francisco, CA 94122
p: 415-742-0775
f: 415-593-8342
e: wcpeditorial@performermag.com
www.performermag.com
frequency: Monthly
circulation: 30,000
contact: Katherine Hoffert
emphasis: Rock, Pop, Alt., Americana, Urban, Indie, Punk, Experimental, Electronica, Jazz, World
Free mag covers the USA music scene via 3 Reg'l pubs. Features interviews & reviews w/ indie musicians only.

Wire
23 Jack's Pl., 6 Corbert Pl.
London, E1 6NN UK
p: 44-207-422-5010
f: 44-207-422-5011
www.thewire.co.uk
frequency: Monthly
contact: Anne Hilde Neset
ext: 44-207-422-5014
e: anne@thewire.co.uk
emphasis: Modern Rock, Pop, Jazz, World Beat, Electronic
Sleek British mag covers int'l cutting-edge music from indies & majors. No demos or MP3s.

Worship Musician
4227 S Meridian, Ste. 275
Puyallup, WA 98373
p: 253-445-1973
f: 253-770-0659
www.worshipmusicianmagazine.com
frequency: Bimonthly
circulation: 10,000
contact: Bruce Adolph
e: bruce@christianmusician.com
emphasis: Church Musicians & Worship Teams
Provides practical help for worship teams & church musicians. Sold at retail shops, conferences & by mail. Send digital kits.

XLR8R
1388 Haight St., #105
San Francisco, CA 94117
p: 415-861-7583
f: 415-861-7584
www.xlr8r.com
frequency: 10/year
contact: Vivian Host
e: vivian.host@xlr8r.com
emphasis: Electronic, Dance, Underground
For young trendsetters in N America, Europe & Japan. Available in newsstands, book & music stores. For features: Vivian Host, 442-D Lorimer St. #143 Brooklyn, NY 11206.

XXL
1115 Broadway
New York, NY 10010
p: 212-807-7100
f: 212-807-0216
e: xxl@harris-pub.com
www.xxlmag.com
frequency: Monthly
circulation: 285,000
contact: Vanessa Satten
ext: 212-807-7100 x630
emphasis: Urban
Promoting top-tier & buzz Hip-Hop acts w/ coverage of music & lifestyles. Submit 2 reviews w/ press kit.

Regional

Alabama

Auburn/Montgomery

The Corner News
117 N College
Auburn, AL 36831
p: 334-821-7150
f: 334-887-0037
e: news@thecornernews.com
www.thecornernews.com
frequency: Weekly
circulation: 10,000
contact: Carla Merrill
e: cmerrill@mindspring.com; cmerrill@thecornernews.com
music lead: 1 Week
calendar lead: 1 Week
New pub. geared toward college audiences covers Metal, Alt., Punk, Rap, Bluegrass & Jazz.

Birmingham/Anniston

Birmingham News
2201 4th Ave. N
Birmingham, AL 35202
p: 205-325-4444
f: 205-325-2494
www.bhamnews.com/newsroom
frequency: Daily
circulation: 175,000 (Daily); 193,000 (Sun)
contact: Alec Harvey
ext: 205-325-2100
e:aharvey@bhamnews.com
music lead: 2 Weeks
calendar lead: 2 Weeks
Major metro pub. runs most music coverage in Fri ent. & calendar section; Sun 'Pop & Culture' section. Send promos to: PO Box 2553, Birmingham, AL 35202.

Birmingham Weekly
2014 Sixth Ave. N
Birmingham, AL 35203
p: 205-939-4030
f: 205-212-1005
www.bhamweekly.com
frequency: Weekly
circulation: 76,000
contact: Glenny Brock
ext: 205-939-4030 x338
e: editor@bhamweekly.com; glenny@bhamweekly.com
e: events@bhamweekly.com
Free alt. weekly previews nat'l releases & area gigs, runs profiles & interviews.

Black & White
2210 2nd Ave. N, 2nd Fl.
Birmingham, AL 35203
p: 205-933-0460
e: music@readbw.com
www.bwcitypaper.com
frequency: Biweekly
circulation: 30,000
contact: Kerry Echols
ext: 205-933-0460 x102
music lead: 2 Weeks
calendar lead: 2 Weeks
Free alt. coverage incl. features, reviews of reg'l-nat'l releases & previews metro area gigs.

Tuscaloosa

The Tuscaloosa News
315 28th Ave.
Tuscaloosa, AL 35401
p: 205-345-0505
f: 205-349-0802
www.tuscaloosanews.com
frequency: Daily
circulation: 39,000
contact: Doug Ray
e: doug.ray@tuscaloosanews.com
music lead: 4 Days
calendar: Peggy Skelton
e: peggy.skelton@tuscaloosanews.com
calendar lead: 1 Week
New York Times daily covers 10 counties w/ previews, reviews & interviews.

Arizona

Phoenix/Tempe

Arizona Republic
200 E Van Buren St.
Phoenix, AZ 85004
p: 602-444-8000
f: 602-444-8933
e: newstips@arizonarepublic.com
www.azcentral.com
frequency: Daily
circulation: 438,723
contact: Stacy Sullivan
ext: 602-444-8749
e: stacy.sullivan@arizonarepublic.com
music lead: 10 Days
calendar: Jana Aguirre
ext: 602-444-8689
e: jana.aguirre@arizonarepublic.com
calendar lead: 10 Days
Gannett pub. & AZ's largest daily runs Local CD reviews & features in Thu ent. section & Sun A&E section.

East Valley Tribune
120 W 1st Ave.
Mesa, AZ 85210
p: 480-898-6500
f: 480-898-6360
e: newstips@aztrib.com
www.eastvalleytribune.com
frequency: Daily
circulation: 150,000
contact: Jim Ripley
ext: 480-898-6546
e: jripley@evtrib.com
music lead: 2 Weeks
calendar: Francis Marlow
ext: 480-898-6427
e: fmarlow@evtrib.com
calendar lead: 1 Week
Freedom Communications pub. showcases reg'l talent & nat'l touring acts for metro Phoenix, Mesa & Scottsdale.

Phoenix New Times
PO Box 2510
Phoenix, AZ 85002
p: 602-271-0040
f: 602-340-8806
www.phoenixnewtimes.com
frequency: Weekly/Thu
circulation: 140,000
contact: Martin Cizmar
e: martin.cizmar@newtimes.com
music lead: 3-4 Weeks
calendar: Clay McNear
ext: 602-229-8438
e: clay.mcnear@newtimes.com
calendar lead: 3-4 Weeks
Metro region's only alt. weekly previews & features acts entertaining area & reviews reg'l & nat'l CDs. Part of Village Voice Media & widely read by readers 18-34.Mail press kits.

Tucson

Arizona Daily Star
4850 S Park Ave.
Tucson, AZ 85714
p: 520-573-4131
f: 520-573-4140
e: abrown@azstarnet.com
www.azstarnet.com
frequency: Daily
circulation: 110,000
contact: Inger Sandal
e: isandal@azstarnet.com
music lead: 3 Weeks
calendar lead: 3 Weeks
Daily pub. covers southern AZ venues. CD reviews & interviews in Fri. ent. section. Promos: PO Box 26807, Tucson, AZ 85726.

The Tucson Weekly
3280 E Hemisphere
Loop #180
Tucson, AZ 85706
p: 520-294-1200
f: 520-792-2096
e: mailbag@tucsonweekly.com
www.tucsonweekly.com
frequency: Weekly
circulation: 50,000
contact: Stephen Seigel
e: musiced@tucsonweekly.com
music lead: 2+ Weeks
calendar: Irene Messina
ext: 520-295-4221

e: listings@tucsonweekly.com
calendar lead: 2 Weeks
Free alt. previews, profiles & features reg'l & touring artists & releases. Sold in 900 area locations. Send promos to: PO Box 27087, Tucson, AZ 85726.

Arkansas

Fayetteville

The Morning News
PO Box 7
Springdale, AR 72765
p: 479-751-6200
www.nwaonline.net
frequency: Daily
circulation: 39,000 (Daily); 43,000 (Sun)
contact: Becca Bacon Martin
ext: 479-872-5054
e: bmartin@nwaonline.net
music lead: 2+ Weeks
calendar lead: 2+ Weeks
Previews releases & music events in northwest AR, St. Louis & Kansas City, MO, Oklahoma City, OK & Dallas, TX on Fri. Daily blog.

Northwest Arkansas Times
PO Box 1607
Fayetteville, AR 72702
p: 479-442-1700
e: living@nwarktimes.com
www.nwanews.com
frequency: Daily
circulation: 22,000
contact: Sandra Cox
ext: 479-571-6481
music lead: 2 Weeks
calendar: Kevin Kinder
This Wehco Media's music coverage favors college radio releases. Gig calendar runs in Fri 'What's Up' section; acts touring northwest AR covered in daily blog.

Little Rock

Arkansas Democrat Gazette
121 E Capitol Ave.
Little Rock, AR 72201
p: 501-378-3400
f: 501-372-4765
www.arkansasonline.com
frequency: Daily
circulation: 175,000 (Daily); 295,000 (Sun)
contact: Werner Trieschmann
ext: 501-378-3514
e: wtrieschmann@arkansasonline.com
music lead: 2 Weeks
calendar: Jennifer Nixon
ext: 501-399-3632
e: jnixon@arkansasonline.com
calendar lead: 2 Weeks
Gannett pub. w/ statewide distro incl. calendar, previews & reviews. Contact Jennifer Christman for wknd pull-out Arts section: jchristman@arkansasonline.com. Promos to: PO Box 2221, Little Rock, AR 72203.

Arkansas Times
201 E Markham St., Ste. 200
Little Rock, AR 72201
p: 501-375-2985
f: 501-375-3623
www.arktimes.com
frequency: Weekly
circulation: 30,000
contact: Lindsey Miller
ext: 501-375-2985 x368
e: lindsey@arktimes.com
music lead: 1 Week
calendar lead: 1 Week
Area's liberal A&E pub. w/ central AR distro runs events & features in 'Local Music Guide.' Promos: PO Box 34010, Little Rock, AR 72203.

Little Rock Free Press
PO Box 165117
Little Rock, AR 72216
p: 501-372-4719
e: freep@aristotle.net
frequency: Monthly
circulation: 25,000
contact: Dotty Oliver
music lead: 2 Months
calendar lead: 2 Months
Only free alt. monthly in central AR w/ distro in 600 locations, leans twds Modern Rock & Alt. Country but reviews all styles. Runs Heavy Metal column & calendar includes Fayetteville, Hot Springs & Pine Bluffs gigs.

Nightflying
PO Box 250276
Little Rock, AR 72225
p: 501-354-8577
f: 501-354-1994
www.nightflying.com
frequency: Monthly
circulation: 40,000
contact: Peter Read
e: pr@nightflying.com
music lead: 1 Month
calendar lead: 1 Month
Free A&E distrib. into neighboring states covers indie scene. Gig guide w/ calendar previews AR, TN, MS, MO, OK & TX shows for fans 18-60.

California

Los Angeles

All Access Magazine
15981 Yarnell St., Ste. 122
Rancho Cascades, CA 91342
p: 818-833-8852
e: allaccessmgzn@aol.com
www.allaccessmagazine.com; www.allaccessrocks.com
frequency: Monthly
circulation: 55,000
contact: Debra Stocker
music lead: 1 Month
calendar lead: 1 Month
Music lovin' pub. tracks worldwide new music scene for fans & industry. CD & live reviews, interviews & photos favor Rock, Pop, Punk, Metal, Glam & Rockabilly. Also hosts 'All Access Music Awards' & CD comp. Webzine gets 2.4 mill hits/mo. Snail mail 2 copies of CDs/DVDs; No digital kits.

Easy Reader
PO Box 427
Hermosa Beach, CA 90254
p: 310-372-4611
f: 310-318-6292
www.easyreader.info
frequency: Weekly/Thu
circulation: 57,000
contact: Bondo Wyszpolski
ext: 310-372-4611 x124
e: entertainment@easyreader.info
music lead: 2 Weeks
calendar: Beverly Morse
ext: 310-372-4611 x100
e: calendar@easyreader.info
calendar lead: 2 Weeks
Serves affluent south bay LA & runs extensive ent. coverage for bands hitting SoCal stages.

L.A. Weekly
3861 Sepulveda Blvd.
Culver City, CA 90230
p: 310-574-7100
f: 310-574-7492
www.laweekly.com
frequency: Weekly
circulation: 201,000
contact: Randall Roberts
e: rroberts@laweekly.com
music lead: 10 Days
calendar: James Moreland
e: listhappens@laweekly.com
calendar lead: 2 Weeks
Part of Village Voice Media, this A&E covers all styles, w/ an emphasis on indies.

Los Angeles Times
202 W 1st St.
Los Angeles, CA 90012
p: 213-237-5000
f: 213-237-7679
e: letters@latimes.com
www.latimes.com
frequency: Daily
circulation: 850,000+
contact: Richard Cromelin
ext: 213-237-7866
e: richard.cromelin@latimes.com
music lead: 2 Weeks
calendar lead: 1 Week
Influential Tribune metro paper runs features, columns, reviews & gigs. Submit gig listings online at www.latimes.com/submit.

Mean Street Magazine
6747-A Greenleaf Ave.
Whittier, CA 90601
p: 714-952-1124
e: hello@meanstreet.com
www.meanstreet.com
frequency: Monthly
circulation: 70,000
contact: Roberto Hernandez
e: roberto@meanstreet.com
music lead: 2 Months
Prime alt. music mag covers Electronic, Alt., Hardcore, Punk & Hip-Hop music & services. Free distro to southern CA clubs, lifestyle & music shops.

OC Weekly
1666 N Main St.
#500
Santa Ana, CA 92701
p: 714-550-5900
f: 714-550-5904
e: submissions@ocweekly.com
www.ocweekly.com
frequency: Weekly/Thu
circulation: 70,000+
contact: Dave Segal
e: dsegal@ocweekly.com
music lead: 2 Weeks
calendar: Tom Child
e: calendar@ocweekly.com
calendar lead: 3 Weeks
Hip alt. pub. part of Village Voice Media runs deep calendar for the vibrant Orange County & Long Beach music scenes.

Pasadena Weekly
50 S DeLacey Ave., Ste. 200
Pasadena, CA 91105
p: 626-584-1500
f: 626-795-0149
www.pasadenaweekly.com
frequency: Weekly/Thu
circulation: 42,000
contact: Julie Rissott
ext: 626-584-1500 x117
e: julier@pasadenaweekly.com
music lead: 2 Weeks
calendar: John Sollenberger
e: johns@pasadenaweekly.com
calendar lead: 2 Weeks
Prime free alt. part of Southland Publishing covers acts playing southern CA. Sister pubs. in San Diego & San Bernadino.

Rock City News
5552 Hollywood Blvd.
Hollywood, CA 90028
p: 323-461-6600
f: 323-461-6622
e: webmaster@rockcitynews.com
www.rockcitynews.com
frequency: Monthly
circulation: 25,000
contact: Ruben MacBlue
music lead: 2 Weeks
calendar lead: 2 Weeks
Entertainment Today pub. for Rock fans 16-35, gives broad support to area music scene. Free distro to music shops, studios, clubs & boxes.

Skinnie Entertainment
10184 6th St., Ste. A
Rancho Cucamonga, CA 91730
p: 909-476-0270
f: 909-476-5931
e: editorial@skinniemagazine.com
www.skinniemagazine.com
frequency: Monthly
circulation: 40,000
contact: Hans Fink
e: hans@skinniemagazine.com
music lead: 2 Months
calendar: Paige Stone
e: paige@skinniemagazine.com
calendar lead: 2 Months
Full color lifestyle & music mag for readers 18-34 is free at shops, clubs & eateries. Sister pub. in Las Vegas.

Ventura County Reporter
700 E Main St.
Ventura, CA 93001
p: 805-648-2244
f: 805-648-7801
e: editor@vcreporter.com
www.vcreporter.com
frequency: Weekly/Thu
circulation: 35,000
contact: Matt Singer
ext: 805-648-2244 x212
e: matt@vcreporter.com
music lead: 2 Weeks
calendar: Sandra Sorenson
e: happenings@vcreporter.com; sandra@vcreporter.com
calendar lead: 2 Weeks
Area's largest free weekly part of Southland Publishing, profiles acts, covers area gigs & reviews releases. Prints music edition in April - distro covers 60miles. Sister pubs. include San Diego CityBeat & Los Angeles CityBeat/ValleyBeat.

Sacramento/Chico

Chico News & Review
353 E 2nd St.
Chico, CA 95928
p: 530-894-2300
www.newsreview.com/chico/Home

frequency: Weekly/Thu
circulation: 40,000+
contact: Mark Lore
ext: 530-894-2300 x2242
e: markl@newsreview.com
music lead: 1 Month
calendar: Jason Cassidy
ext: 530-894-2300 x2243
e: jasonc@newsreview.com
calendar lead: 1 Week
Free alt. w/ distro to Sacramento & N Valley boxes, previews CDs & reg'l & touring acts. Also hosts "Cammies Award Show" for area talent.

The Sacramento Bee
PO Box 15779
Sacramento, CA 95826
p: 916-321-1000
f: 916-556-5625
www.sacbee.com
frequency: Daily
circulation: 250,000 (Daily); 300,000 (Sun)
contact: Rita Blomster
ext: 916-321-1126
e: rblomster@sacbee.com
music lead: 2 Weeks
calendar: Listings
ext: 916-321-1154
e: featcal@sacbee.com
calendar lead: 2 Weeks
McClatchy pub., biggest in Sacramento & 4th largest in the state runs extensive coverage of acts playing the region which stretches east to OR border & west to NV. May cover notable San Francisco gigs.

Sacramento News & Review (SNR)
1015 20th St.
Sacramento, CA 95811
p: 916-498-1234
f: 916-498-7920
www.newsreview.com
frequency: Weekly
circulation: 87,000
contact: Nick Miller
ext: 916-498-1234 x1360
e: nickam@newsreview.com
music lead: 3 Weeks
calendar: Jenn Kistler
ext: 916-498-1234 x1361
e: sactocalendar@newsreview.com; jenn@newsreview.com
calendar lead: 2 Weeks
Free weekly from Chico Community Publishing previews area gigs, profiles local acts & reviews a few CDs.

Synthesis
210 W 6th St.
Chico, CA 95928
p: 530-899-7708
www.synthesis.net; www.synthesisradio.net
frequency: Weekly
contact: Spencer Teilman
ext: 530-899-7708 x28
e: spencer@synthesis.net
music lead: Wed prior
calendar: Dani Kay
e: dani@synthesis.net
calendar lead: Wed prior
Popular culture mag & website covers all styles w/ features, CD & live reviews, podcasts & video interviews.

San Diego

San Diego City Beat
3550 Camino Del Rio N
Ste. 207
San Diego, CA 92108
p: 619-281-7526
f: 619-281-5273
e: editor@sdcitybeat.com
www.sdcitybeat.com
frequency: Weekly/Wed
circulation: 50,000+
contact: Nathan Dinsdale
e: nathand@sdcitybeat.com
music lead: 2 Weeks
calendar: Todd Kroviak
e: listings@sdcitybeat.com; toddk@sdcitybeat.com
calendar lead: 2 Weeks
Formerly SLAMM now a prime alt. w/ deep calendar & respected reviews. Free distro stretches to Mexico & the coast. Sister pubs.: LA City Beat, LA Valley Beat, Pasadena Weekly, Ventura County Reporter.

San Diego Reader
PO Box 85803
San Diego, CA 92186
p: 619-235-3000
f: 619-231-0489
www.sandiegoreader.com
frequency: Weekly/Thu
circulation: 160,000+
contact: Robert Mizrachi
e: blurt@sdreader.com
music lead: 1 Month
calendar: Leslie Venolia
calendar lead: 3 Weeks
Free alt. runs previews, reviews, interviews, show & band listings.

San Diego Union Tribune
350 Camino De La Reina
San Diego, CA 92108
p: 619-299-3131
f: 619-260-5082
www.signonsandiego.com
frequency: Daily
circulation: 300,000+
contact: George Varga
ext: 619-293-2253
e: george.varga@uniontrib.com
music lead: 6 Weeks
calendar: Gwen Jackson
ext: 619-293-2228
e: night&day@uniontrib.com
calendar lead: 3+ Weeks
Part of Creators News Syndicate, runs gig reviews & features daily; more in Thu edition & music & lifestyle insert 'Street,' which skews 18-34. George's reviews posted on wire svc. which goes out to 1500 US & int'l papers. Prefers snail mail.

San Francisco

East Bay Express
1335 Stanford Ave., Ste. 100
Emeryville, CA 94608
p: 510-879-3700
f: 510-879-3794
e: clubs@eastbayexpress.com
www.eastbayexpress.com
frequency: Weekly/Wed
circulation: 80,000
contact: Nate Seltenrich
ext: 510-879-3776
e: music@eastbayexpress.com
music lead: 4 Weeks
Owned by Village Voice Media, free alt. serves affluent & ideologically diverse area & covers E Bay, San Francisco & Berkeley/Oakland music scenes.

San Francisco Bay Guardian
135 Mississippi St.
San Francisco, CA 94107
p: 415-255-3100
f: 415-487-2506
www.sfbg.com
frequency: Weekly/Wed
circulation: 250,000
contact: Kimberly Chun
ext: 415-487-4613
e: kimberly@sfbg.com
music lead: 2 Weeks
calendar: Duncan Davidson
e: listings@sfbg.com
calendar lead: 10 Days
Free alt. digs deep into area's vibrant scene & reviews all styles, runs profiles & features of acts playing the bay.

San Francisco Weekly
185 Berry St., Lobby 5
Ste. 3800
San Francisco, CA 94107
p: 415-536-8100
f: 415-777-1839
e: feedback@sfweekly.com
www.sfweekly.com
frequency: Weekly/Wed
circulation: 100,000
contact: Jennifer Maerz
e: jennifer.maerz@sfweekly.com
music lead: 2+ Weeks
calendar: Michael Leaverton
e: michael.leaverton@sfweekly.com
calendar lead: 2 Weeks
Free alt. for young & affluent, previews, reviews & interviews local-touring acts. Email preferred.

West Coast Performer Magazine
1278 20th Ave.
Ste. C-1
San Francisco, CA 94122
p: 415-742-0775
f: 415-742-0776
e: wcpeditorial@performermag.com
www.performermag.com
frequency: Monthly
circulation: 30,000
contact: Katherine Hoffert
music lead: 10 Weeks
Performer Publication's pacific coast trade pub. supports indie artists & services. Covers all styles of area talent w/ live gig & CD reviews plus music biz articles & gear reviews. Free distro to music shops, studios & clubs. Sister pubs. cover northeast & southeast USA.

Santa Cruz/San Jose

Good Times
PO Box 1885
Santa Cruz, CA 95061
p: 831-458-1100
f: 831-458-1295
www.gtweekly.com
frequency: Weekly
circulation: 45,000
contact: Amanda Martinez
ext: 831-458-1100 x223
e: amartinez@gtweekly.com
music lead: 3 Weeks
calendar: Chris Magyar
ext: 831-458-1100 x216
e: calendar@gtweekly.com
calendar lead: 3 Weeks
Free A&E distro countywide, covers local & touring acts; weekly gig previews & CD reviews monthly.

The Mercury News
750 Ridder Park Dr.
San Jose, CA 95190
p: 408-920-5000
f: 408-271-3786
www.mercurynews.com
frequency: Daily
circulation: 230,000 (Daily); 260,000+ (Sun)
contact: Charlie McCollum
e: cmccollum@mercurynews.com
music lead: 3 Weeks
Major Silicon Valley pub., owned by MediaNews Group, previews & lists area gigs & reviews major indie releases. Distro to San Jose & Greater Bay area. Submit calendar listings: www.mercurynews.com/submitanevent.

Zero Magazine
12 S 1st St., Ste. 300
San Jose, CA 95113
p: 408-971-8511
www.zeromag.com
frequency: Monthly
circulation: 50,000
contact: Rob Trisler
ext: 408-998-1630 x15
e: rob@zeromag.com
music lead: 3 Weeks
calendar lead: 3 Weeks
Widely read music mag extensively covers northern CA scene w/ emphasis on indie & underground. Submit 2 copies & full contact info.

Colorado

Colorado Springs

Colorado Springs Independent
235 S Nevada Ave.
Colorado Springs, CO 80903
p: 719-577-4545
e: newsroom@csindy.com
www.csindy.com
frequency: Weekly
circulation: 38,000
contact: Kirk Woundy
e: kirk@csindy.com
music lead: 2-4 Weeks
calendar: Jill Thomas
ext: 719-577-4545 x2838
e: listings@csindy.com
calendar lead: 2 Weeks
Free, liberal alt. widely read in southern CO covers area gigs & touring bands emphasis on Pop/Rock acts that appeal to upscale readership. Calendar includes notable Denver shows.

Denver/Boulder

5280 Magazine
1514 Curtis St., Ste. 300
Denver, CO 80202
p: 303-832-5280
f: 303-832-0470
e: news@5280.com
www.5280.com
frequency: Monthly
circulation: 80,000
contact: Lindsey Koehler
ext: 303-832-5280 x221
e: lindsey@5280.com
music lead: 4-6 Weeks
calendar: Julie Dugdale
ext: 303-832-5280 x220
e: julie@5280.com
calendar lead: 8 weeks
CO's most widely read A&E by readers 18-54 covers reg'l & some major & indie releases Extensive Denver-area calendar.

Boulder Weekly
690 S Lashley Ln.

Boulder, CO 80305
p: 303-494-5511
f: 303-494-2585
e: editorial@boulderweekly.com
www.boulderweekly.com
frequency: Weekly
circulation: 25,000 +
contact: Vince Darcangelo
ext: 303-494-5511 x108
e: buzz@boulderweekly.com
music lead: 2 Weeks
calendar lead: 2 Weeks
Leading alt. read by affluent Gen-Xr's & entrepreneurs, reviews Boulder/Denver scene & nat'l releases.

Colorado Daily
2610 Pearl St.
Boulder, CO 80302
p: 303-443-6272
f: 303-443-9357
www.coloradodaily.com
frequency: Daily
circulation: 20,000
contact: Wendy Kale
ext: 303-443-6272 x128
e: kale@coloradodaily.com
music lead: 1 Week
calendar lead: 1 Week
Free alt. pub. serves Boulder & U Colorado readers, 18-34. Gigs covered daily, music articles on Fri, w/ some picks of the day. No digital kits.

Colorado Music Buzz
PO Box 2739
Littleton, CO 80161
p: 303-797-1800
e: editor@coloradomusicbuzz.com
www.coloradomusicbuzz.com
frequency: Monthly
circulation: 60,000+
contact: Keith Schneider
ext: 303-870-7376
music lead: 1 Month
Oversized free music mag promotes CO artists & music biz; some ink spilt on unique acts touring the state. Distro statewide; classifieds & calendar online only.

Daily Camera
1048 Pearl St.
Boulder, CO 80302
p: 303-442-1202
f: 303-473-1131
www.dailycamera.com; boulderdirt.com
frequency: Daily
circulation: 35,000
contact: Greg Glasgow
ext: 303-473-1342
e: glasgowg@dailycamera.com
music lead: 2+ Weeks
calendar: Elizabeth Clark
ext: 303-473-1351
e: clarke@dailycamera.com
calendar lead: 1 Week
Scripps pub. covers reg'l & touring acts daily; calendar & local coverage on Fri. Submit gig listings online. Promos: PO Box 591, Boulder, CO 80306.

Denver Post
101 W Colfax Ave.
Denver, CO 80202
p: 800-336-7678; 303-820-1010
f: 303-954-1679
e: arts@denverpost.com
www.denverpost.com
frequency: Daily
circulation: 255,000 (Daily); 700,000 (Sun)
contact: Rick Bacha
ext: 303-820-1394
e: rbacha@denverpost.com
music lead: 2 Weeks
calendar: Calendar Editor
e: weekend@denverpost.com
calendar lead: 2 Weeks
Area's major daily, owned by MediaNews Group, previews CO, UT, NM, WY & KS gigs & reviews nat'l releases.

Rocky Mountain News
101 W Colfax Ave., Ste. 500
Denver, CO 80202
p: 303-954-5000
e: editor@rockymountainnews.com
www.rockymountainnews.com
frequency: Daily
circulation: 300,000 (Daily); 625,000 (Sat & Sun)
contact: Joe Rassenfoss
ext: 303-954-5410
e: rassenfossj@rockymountainnews.com
music lead: 2 Weeks
calendar: Alex Neth
ext: 303-954-1434
e: spotlight@rockymountainnews.com
calendar lead: 2 Weeks
Daily runs CO calendar plus previews, reviews & profiles of reg'l & touring acts. Also reviews nat'l releases.

Westword
PO Box 5970
Denver, CO 80217
p: 303-296-7744
www.westword.com
frequency: Weekly/Thu
circulation: 106,000
contact: Dave Herrera
e: dave.herrera@westword.com
music lead: 3 Weeks
calendar: Susan Froyd
e: susan.froyd@westword.com
calendar lead: 3 Weeks
Free alt., widely read by area's college crowd includes reg'l calendar, show previews & CD reviews.

Fort Collins

Scene Magazine
PO Box 489
Ft. Collins, CO 80522
p: 970-490-1009
e: editor@scenemagazine.info
www.scenemagazine.info
frequency: Monthly
circulation: 20,000
contact: Greta Cornett
music lead: 4-6 Weeks
e: calendarinfo@scenemagazine.info
calendar lead: 21st of/ mo
Free nitelife pub. runs comprehensive calendar that includes Denver, Boulder, Ft. Collins & Greeley gigs.

Connecticut

Bridgeport/ New Haven

New Haven Advocate
900 Chapel St., Ste. 1100
New Haven, CT 06510
p: 203-789-0010
www.newhavenadvocate.com
frequency: Weekly/Thu
circulation: 48,000+
contact: Jim Motavalli
ext: 203-789-0010 x219
e: tmotavalli@newhavenadvocate.com
music lead: 3 Weeks
calendar: Alison Geisler
ext: 203-789-0010 x218
e: listings@newhavenadvocate.com
calendar lead: 3 Weeks
Free alt. devotes ink to local-touring talent, previewing eastern CT gigs & nat'l releases. Sponsors local music fests. Part of New Mass Media.

New Haven Register
40 Sargent Dr.
New Haven, CT 06511
p: 203-789-5678
www.nhregister.com
frequency: Daily
circulation: 100,000
contact: Patrick Ferrucci
e: pferrucci@nhregister.com
music lead: 2 Weeks
calendar lead: 2 Weeks
State's 2nd largest paper serves several colleges & wealthy suburbs & runs columns, previews, reviews & statewide calendar. Other Journal Register pubs. in Philadelphia, NY, MI & OH.

Hartford

Hartford Advocate
121 Wawarme Ave., 1st Fl.
Hartford, CT 06114
p: 860-548-9300
f: 860-548-9335
www.hartfordadvocate.com; www.newmassmedia.com
frequency: Weekly
circulation: 55,000
contact: John Adamian
e: jadamian@hartfordadvocate.com
music lead: 3 Weeks
calendar: Brianna Snyder
e: listings@hartfordadvocate.com; bsnyder@hartfordadvocate.com
calendar lead: 3 Weeks
Tribune Corp. free alt. skews young & covers reg'l & touring acts, nat'l releases & area gigs. Sister pubs are Valley Advocate, Fairfield County Weekly & New Haven Advocate.

The Hartford Courant
285 Broad St.
Hartford, CT 06115
p: 860-241-6200
f: 860-520-6927
www.courant.com
frequency: Daily
circulation: 185,000 (Daily); 280,000 (Sun)
contact: Eric R. Danton
ext: 860-241-6467
e: edanton@courant.com
music lead: 2 Weeks
calendar: Amy Ellis
ext: 860-241-6463
e: aellis@courant.com
calendar lead: 2 Weeks
Part of Tribune empire, music covered in Thu ent. & Sun A&E sections. Calendar may include gigs in western MA. Touring acts & nat'l releases reviewed.

Sound Waves Magazine
PO Box 710
Old Mystic, CT 06372
p: 860-572-5738
f: 860-572-5738
e: editor@swaves.com
www.swaves.com
frequency: Monthly
circulation: 8000-10,000
contact: David Pottie
music lead: 3+ Weeks
Free music mag serves southern New England w/ profiles, previews & reviews of acts touring or connected to the region.

Delaware

Wilmington

Spark
950 W Basin Rd.
New Castle, DE 19720
p: 302-324-7728
f: 302-324-7774
www.sparkweekly.com
frequency: Weekly/Wed
circulation: 30,000
contact: Matt Sullivan
e: msullivan@sparkweekly.com
music lead: 2+ Weeks
calendar: Melissa Duko
ext: 302-324-2851
e: events@sparkweekly.com; mduko@delawareonline.com
calendar lead: 2+ Weeks
A&E spinoff of Wilmington News Journal, both part of Gannett, broadly covers area music for hipsters 18-28+. Calendar stretches for 25mi & may include notable gigs at major Philly venues - listings shared w/ News Journal (see listing below).

Wilmington News Journal
950 W Basin Rd.
New Castle, DE 19720
p: 302-324-2500
f: 302-324-5509
www.delawareonline.com
frequency: Daily
circulation: 100,000+
contact: Betsy Price
ext: 302-324-2884
e: bprice@delawareonline.com
music lead: 2+ Weeks
e: events@delawareonline.com
Gannett paper distrib. statewide & to parts of NJ & PA runs daily coverage of area scene; Fri calendar lists notable Philly gigs. Email before sending material to: PO Box 15505, Wilmington, DE 19850.

District of Columbia

Washington City Paper
2390 Champlain St. NW,
Washington, DC 20009
p: 202-332-2100
f: 202-332-8500
e: mail@washingtoncitypaper.com
www.washingtoncitypaper.com
frequency: Weekly/Thu
circulation: 82,000
contact: Mark Athitakis
ext: 202-332-2100 x452
e: mathitakis@washingtoncitypaper.com
music lead: 3 Weeks
calendar: Jacqueline Law
ext: 202-332-2100 x472
e: marketing@washingtoncitypaper.com; jlaw@washingtoncitypaper.com
calendar lead: 2 weeks
Though parent company Creative Loafing recently filed chapter 11, this prime alt. pub w/extensive coverage of area music scene is still

the A&E of choice throughout Beltway & VA/MD triangle.

The Washington Post
1150 15th St. NW
Washington, DC 20071
p: 202-334-6000
f: 202-334-5587
e: styleonthego@washpost.com; style@washpost.com
www.washingtonpost.com
frequency: Daily
circulation: 1,000,000
contact: Josh du Lac
ext: 202-334-5268
e: dulacj@washpost.com
music lead: 2+ Weeks
calendar: Amy Orndorff
e: orndorffa@washpost.com
calendar lead: 10 Days
Influential paper read worldwide covers acts playing the DC/MD/VA triangle. CD previews Tue & Sun; gig reviews, features & calendar in Fri ed. Prefers EPKs.

Florida

Gainesville

The Gainesville Sun
2700 SW 13th St.
Gainesville, FL 32608
p: 352-378-1411
f: 352-338-3128
e: scene@gvillesun.com
www.gainesville.com
frequency: Daily
circulation: 50,000
contact: Bill Dean
ext: 352-374-5039
music lead: 1 Week
calendar: Joe Gordon
e: calendar@gvillesun.com
calendar lead: 1 Week
NY Times published college-town daily runs most music coverage Thu. Previews & reviews area gigs, reviews nat'l releases & rising talent. Also publishes a 10,000-circ. 'Scene Campus Edition' w/ expanded reviews & distro to U of FL & Santa Fe Community College.

INsite Magazine
PO Box 15192
Gainesville, FL 32604
p: 352-377-1402
f: 352-377-6602
e: editor@insitegainesville.com
www.insitegainesville.com
frequency: Monthly
circulation: 15,000+
contact: Maghan McDowell
ext: 352-377-1402 x14
music lead: 1.5 Months
Free A&E part of Assoc. of Alt. & Collegiate Pubs. reaches readers 18-34 citywide & at area colleges. Music coverage includes month long calendar, interviews & previews - reg'l acts must be in 2/hr radius to be considered.

Jacksonville

Florida Times-Union
1 Riverside Ave.
Jacksonville, FL 32202
p: 904-359-4111
f: 904-359-4260
e: lifestyle@jacksonville.com
www.jacksonville.com
frequency: Daily
circulation: 250,000
contact: Dave Bauer
e: dave.bauer@jacksonville.com
music lead: 1 Week
calendar: Melinda Kurtzo
ext: 904-359-4511
e: melinda.kurtzo@jacksonville.com
calendar lead: 1+ Week
Influential area paper runs most music coverage on Fri w/ gig & CD reviews & interviews - mostly known acts but seeking buzz bands. Calendar includes St. Augustine & Clay County & some Gainsesville shows. Part of Morris Communications.

Folio Weekly
9456 Philips Hwy., Ste. 11
Jacksonville, FL 32256
p: 904-260-9770; 800-940-9770
f: 904-260-9773
e: themail@folioweekly.com
www.folioweekly.com
frequency: Weekly/Tue
circulation: 51,000
contact: John E. Citrone
ext: 904-260-9770 x120
e: jcitrone@folioweekly.com
music lead: 3 Weeks
calendar lead: 3 Weeks
Regions largest free alt. widely read in northeast FL & southeast GA. Runs gig previews & reviews; mostly estab. releases reviewed. Distro at campuses, bars & retail.

Miami/ Ft. Lauderdale

944- Miami
1691 Michigan Ave., Ste. 340
Miami Beach, FL 33139
p: 305-695-9990
f: 305-695-9998
e: editorial@944.com
www.944.com
frequency: Monthly
circulation: 55,000
contact: Hadley Henriette
ext: 305-695-9990 x2520
e: hadley@944.com
Lifestyle media conglomerate w/ glossy reg'l pubs in Las Vegas, Phoenix & Los Angeles/San Diego covers the arts for trendy readers 18-30+. Free distro to clubs, hotels & retail.

City Link
4611 Johnson Rd., Ste. 4
Coconut Creek, FL 33073
p: 954-356-4943
f: 954-356-4949
e: metromix-southflorida@metromix.com
www.metromix.com
frequency: Weekly
circulation: 52,000
contact: Jay Smith
ext: 954-596-5675
e: jaysmith@citylinkmagazine.com
music lead: 2 Weeks
calendar: Listings
e: listings@citylinkmagazine.com
calendar lead: 2 Weeks
Tribune's weekly youth culture mag w/ club listings, music columns, CD reviews & features of touring acts in Miami/ W Palm area interests older crowd, too. Dec music edition & weekly podcasts.

Miami Herald
1 Herald Plaza
Miami, FL 33132
p: 800-437-2535
f: 305-376-5287
e: dadenews@miamiherald.com
www.herald.com
frequency: Daily
circulation: 261,476 (Daily); 335,038 (Sun)
contact: Sara Frederick
ext: 305-376-3646
e: sfrederick@miamiherald.com
music lead: 2 Weeks
calendar: Michael Hamersly
ext: 305-350-2111
e: newscalendar@herald.com
calendar lead: 2 Weeks
McClatchy paper covers area's vibrant music scene w/ extensive listings, features, CD & show previews & reviews. Distro reaches Broward, & Palm Beach counties: Latin reviews by Jordan Levin, 305-376-3639, jlevin@herald.com.

Miami New Times
PO Box 011591
Miami, FL 33101
p: 305-576-8000
f: 305-571-7677
e: editorial@miaminewtimes.com
www.miaminewtimes.com
frequency: Weekly/Thu
circulation: 100,000
contact: Arielle Castillo
ext: 305-576-7579
e: arielle.castillo@miaminewtimes.com
music lead: 2+ Weeks
calendar: Patrice Yursik
ext: 305-571-7591
e: calendar@miaminewtimes.com; patrice.yursik@miaminewtimes.com
calendar lead: 3+ Weeks
Widely read free alt. part of Village Voice Media, covers area's vibrant scene for tourists & resident hipsters 21-49. Extensive calendar has Ft. Lauderdale gigs, previews, reviews & features.

New Times Broward-Palm Beach
PO Box 14128
Ft. Lauderdale, FL 33302
p: 954-233-1600
f: 954-233-1521
www.browardpalmbeach.com
frequency: Weekly/Thu
circulation: 69,000+
contact: Jonathan Cunningham
ext: 954-233-1582
e: jonathan.cunningham@browardpalmbeach.com
music lead: 2-3 Weeks
calendar: Calendar Editor
ext: 954-233-1584
e: calendar@browardpalmbeach.com
calendar lead: 2-3 Weeks
Alt. part of Village Voice Media, covers the south FL music scene w/ reviews, previews, profiles & gig calendar.

Orlando

aXis Magazine
116 S Orange Ave.
Orlando, FL 32801
p: 407-839-0039
f: 407-839-0040
e: editorial@axismag.com
www.axismag.com
frequency: Monthly
circulation: 28,000
contact: Sean Perry
ext: 407-839-1499
e: sperry@axismag.com
music lead: 1 Month
calendar: Colleen Pitrone
calendar lead: 1 Month
Free A&E skews twds. readers 17-35 yrs is distrib. to college campuses, bars, & in shops.

Florida Today
1 Gannett Plaza
Melbourne, FL 32940
p: 321-242-3500
f: 321-242-6620
www.floridatoday.com
frequency: Daily
circulation: 125,000
contact: Bruce Hickman
ext: 321-242-3789
e: bhickman@floridatoday.com
music lead: 2 Weeks
calendar lead: 2 Weeks
Gannett pub. runs features, previews & CD reviews & extensive coverage of indie touring acts on Fri.

Orlando Weekly
100 W Livingston St., 2nd Fl.
Orlando, FL 32801
p: 407-377-0400
f: 407-377-0420
e: music@orlandoweekly.com
www.orlandoweekly.com
frequency: Weekly
circulation: 50,000
contact: Justin Strout
ext: 407-377-0400 x223
e: jstrout@orlandoweekly.com
music lead: 4-6 Weeks
calendar: Trevor Fraser
ext: 407-377-0400 x262
e: listings@orlandoweekly.com; tfraser@orlandoweekly.com
calendar lead: 2 Weeks
Area's liberal-leaning free alt. covers local - nat'l music scene for central FL w/ previews, reviews & gig calendar.

Tallahassee

Tallahassee Democrat
PO Box 990
Tallahassee, FL 32302
p: 850-599-2170
www.tallahassee.com
frequency: Daily
circulation: 50,000+
contact: Kati Schardl
ext: 850-599-2149
e: kschardl@tallahassee.com
music lead: 2+ Weeks
calendar: Lyssa Oberkreser
ext: 850-671-6595
e: loberkreser@tallahassee.com
calendar lead: 2 Weeks
Gannett paper covers nat'l music items & the areas vibrant Hip-Hop, Rock, Folk, Alt. & World music scenes for broad segment of readers incl. several colleges. Post gigs & sound clips online - 1wk advance.

Tampa/ St. Petersburg

Accent on Tampa Bay
PO Box 20044
St. Petersburg, FL 33742
p: 727-577-5500
e: accentmagazine@aol.com
www.accentontampabay.com
frequency: Bimonthly
circulation: 40,000

contact: Melissa Wolcott
music lead: 10th of prior mo
calendar lead: 10th of prior mo
Area's largest A&E free at clubs, hotels, & retail covers nat'l reviews & area gigs for readers 18-65+. Only releases w/ distrib. reviewed. Part of AM Media Group.

Reax Music Magazine
PO Box 5809
Tampa, FL 33605
p: 813-247-6975
f: 813-247-4792
www.reaxmusic.com
frequency: Monthly
circulation: 40,000
contact: Scott Harrell
e: scott@reaxmusic.com
music lead: 2 Months
calendar: Events
e: reax@reaxmusic.com
calendar lead: 1 Month
Free A&E mag targets readers 18-45 & covers cutting edge sounds & culture. Distro in every FYE store in FL & nat'l at 160 indie music retailers.
See Ad On Page 233

St. Petersburg Times
490 First Ave. S
St. Petersburg, FL 33701
p: 727-893-8111
f: 727-892-2327
www.sptimes.com
frequency: Daily
circulation: 323,031 (Daily); 422,410 (Sun)
contact: Sean Daly
ext: 727-893-8467
e: sdaly@sptimes.com
music lead: 2+ Weeks
calendar: Wilma Norton
ext: 727-893-8855
e: wilma@sptimes.com
calendar lead: 10 Days
SE region's largest daily previews & reviews shows plus reg'l & nat'l releases in Thu 'Weekend' mag. Distro all over the Tampa Bay area.

Georgia

Athens

Athens Banner Herald
1 Press Pl.
Athens, GA 30601
p: 706-208-2212
f: 706-208-2246
e: news@onlineathens.com
www.onlineathens.com
frequency: Daily
circulation: 30,000
contact: Julie Phillips
ext: 706-208-2221
e: julie.phillips@onlineathens.com
music lead: 2 Weeks
calendar: April Burkhart
e: april.burkhart@onlineathens.com
calendar lead: 2 Weeks
Morris Comm. general interest pub. features native talent & acts playing the area. Weekly ent. section runs gig calendar.

Flagpole Magazine
PO Box 1027
Athens, GA 30603
p: 706-549-9523
f: 706-548-8981
e: editor@flagpole.com
www.flagpole.com
frequency: Weekly
circulation: 16,000
contact: Michelle Gilzenrat
ext: 706-549-9523 x203
e: music@flagpole.com
music lead: 3 Weeks
calendar: Jennifer Bryant
e: calendar@flagpole.com
calendar lead: 1 Week
Free alt. serving hip college town covers area's vibrant music scene. Gig & CD previews & reviews; calendar includes Atlanta shows.

Atlanta

Creative Loafing
384 Northyards Blvd.
Ste. 600
Atlanta, GA 30313
p: 404-688-5623
f: 404-420-1402
www.creativeloafing.com
frequency: Weekly
circulation: 151,000
contact: Rodney Carmichael
e: rodney.carmichael@creativeloafing.com
music lead: 6 Weeks
calendar: Debbie Mischad
e: debbie.mischad@creativeloafing.com
calendar lead: 1 Week
Though parent company has filed Chapter 11, this free alt. w/extensive music coverage continues w/ gig & CD previews, reviews & extensive calendar. Special College editions. Sister pubs. in Sarasota, FL; Charlotte, NC; IL (Chicago Reader) & DC (Washington City Paper).

Rolling Out Urban Style Weekly
1269 Pryor Rd. SW
Atlanta, GA 30315
p: 404-635-1313
f: 404-635-9989
e: editorial@rollingout.com
www.rollingout.com
frequency: Weekly
circulation: 2,100,000
contact: Jacinta Howard
ext: 404-681-2001
e: jacinta@rollingout.com
music lead: 10 Days
calendar: Yvette Caslin
e: yvette@rollingout.com
calendar lead: 10 Days
Steed Media's free A&E covers African American interests & accomplishments. Reviews & features Urban & Jazz artists & releases for readers 21-45+. Sister pubs. in 19 USA major urban markets.

Southeast Performer Magazine
4491/2 Morelands Ave.
Ste. 206
Atlanta, GA 30307
p: 404-582-0088
f: 404-582-0089
www.performermag.com
frequency: Monthly
circulation: 30,000
contact: Leila Regan-Porter
e: leila@performermag.com
music lead: 3 Months
calendar lead: 5 Weeks
Largest trade mag for all genres of indies also publishes northeast & west coast editions. Articles cover gear, promotion & recording issues. Gig & CD coverage has reg'l bias. Free distro to studios, shops & clubs.

Stomp and Stammer
PO Box 5440
Atlanta, GA 31107
p: 404-880-0733
e: mailroom@stompandstammer.com
www.stompandstammer.com
frequency: Monthly
circulation: 20,000
contact: Jeff Clark
e: jeff@stompandstammer.com
music lead: 1 Month
calendar lead: 1 Month
Hip, free music & opinion mag infiltrates Athens & southeastern USA w/ reviews, profiles & features. Snail mail material only.

The Sunday Paper
763 Trabert Ave., Ste. D
Atlanta, GA 30318
p: 404-351-5797
f: 404-351-2350
www.sundaypaper.com
frequency: Weekly
circulation: 75,000
contact: Kevin Forest Moreau
e: kevinmoreau@sundaypaper.com
music lead: 1 Month
calendar lead: 3 Weeks
Music section showcases reg'l & nat'l acts, CD reviews & calendar w/ blurbs & photos.

Greater GA

Columbus Ledger-Enquirer
17 W 12th St.
Columbus, GA 31901
p: 706-571-8565
f: 706-576-6290
www.ledger-enquirer.com
frequency: Daily
circulation: 50,000
contact: Dawn Minty
ext: 706-571-8524
e: dminty@ledger-enquirer.com
music lead: 3 Weeks
calendar: Sandra Okamoto
e: sokamoto@ledger-enquirer.com
calendar lead: 2 Weeks
McClatchey pub. covers local-reg'l acts & gigs, w/ some weekday spotlights of touring acts. Distro into AL. Prefers digital kits. Brad also runs music blog: bradbarnes.blogspot.com. Send promos to: PO Box 711, Columbus, GA 31902.

Idaho

Boise

The Boise Weekly
523 Broad St.
Boise, ID 83702
p: 208-344-2055
f: 208-342-4733
www.boiseweekly.com
frequency: Weekly
circulation: 35,000
contact: Amy Atkins
ext: 208-344-2055 x3006
e: amy@boiseweekly.com
music lead: 2 Weeks
calendar: Elaine Lacaillade
e: elaine@boiseweekly.com
calendar lead: 6 Days
Free alt. caters to thriving Boise/Sun Valley scene. Runs extensive gig calendar, previews & profiles, spotlights touring & local acts & Gig of the Week showcases.

The Idaho Statesman
1200 N Curtis Rd.
Boise, ID 83706
p: 800-635-8934; 208-377-6200
f: 208-377-6449
e: scene@idahostatesman.com
www.idahostatesman.com
frequency: Daily
circulation: 66,000 (Daily); 88,000 (Sun)
contact: Michael Deeds
ext: 208-377-6407
e: mdeeds@idahostatesman.com
music lead: 2 Weeks
calendar: Michelle Sugai
ext: 208-377-6451
e: calendar@idahostatesman.com
calendar lead: 2 Weeks
McClatchey Co. pub. runs most music coverage Fri w/ gig previews, reviews & CD reviews. Calendar includes eastern OR gigs. Promos: PO Box 40, Boise, ID 83707.

Illinois

Chicago

Chicago Innerview Magazine
1849 S Blue Island Ave.
Chicago, IL 60608
p: 312-850-3635
f: 312-850-3676
e: info@chicagoinnerview.com
www.chicagoinnerview.com
frequency: Monthly
circulation: 20,000
contact: Jay Gentile
e: editor@chicagoinnerview.com
music lead: 6 Weeks
calendar lead: 6 Weeks
Free music mag reaches music fans 16-35+ at 300 area lifestyle & music outlets. Extensive gig calendar & 40+ band interviews in ea. issue. Daily Web blog & podcast.

Chicago Reader
11 E Illinois St.
Chicago, IL 60611
p: 312-828-0350
f: 312-828-9926
e: music@chicagoreader.com
www.chicagoreader.com
frequency: Weekly/Thu
circulation: 135,000
contact: Philip Montoro
ext: 312-828-0350 x333
e: pmontoro@chicagoreader.com
music lead: 3 Weeks
calendar: Areif Sless-Kitain
calendar lead: 2 Weeks
Free alt. is prime source for music coverage - distro to 1400 metro & suburban outlets including music venues. Previews, reviews & features all styles. Pub. by Creative Loafing.

Chicago Sun-Times
350 N Orleans
Chicago, IL 60654
p: 312-321-3000
f: 312-321-2566
e: metro@suntimes.com
www.suntimes.com

frequency: Daily
circulation: 382,000
contact: Jim Derogatis
ext: 312-321-2170
e: jimdero@jimdero.com
music lead: 2 Weeks
calendar: Kyle Koster
ext: 312-321-2152
e: kksoter@suntimes.com
calendar lead: 2 Weeks
One of the country's largest dailies, reviews releases & covers shows in IL, WI, MI, IN & MO. City nite-life guide & bios of area talent on Web. Blues writer: Jeff Johnson: jjohnson@suntimes.com; 312-321-2419. For coverage in their daily ent. spin-off pub., Centerstage, contact Ben Rubenstein: brubenstein@centerstagechicago.com

Chicago Tribune
435 N Michigan Ave.
Chicago, IL 60611
p: 312-222-4440
f: 312-222-0236
www.chicagotribune.com
frequency: Daily
circulation: 700,000 (Daily); 1,200,000 (Sun)
contact: Scott Powers
ext: 312-222-4985
e: slpowers@tribune.com
music lead: 2 Weeks
The midwest's largest daily has worldwide distro & exclusive coverage of local-touring acts. Stories shared w/ other Tribune print & broadcast outlets. Jazz submissions: Howard Reich, hreich@tribune.com.

Illinois Entertainer
657 W Lake St., Ste. A
Chicago, IL 60661
p: 312-930-9333
f: 312-930-9341
www.illinoisentertainer.com
frequency: Monthly
circulation: 165,000
contact: Steve Forstneger
ext: 312-922-9333 x105
e: ed@illinoisentertainer.com
music lead: 60 Days
calendar lead: 15th prior/mo
Free mag broadly covers indie artists & releases w/ print & web calendars, previews, reviews & reg'l band directory.

Newcity
770 N Halsted, Ste. 303
Chicago, IL 60642
p: 312-243-8786
f: 312-243-8802
e: newcity@newcity.com
www.newcitychicago.com
frequency: Weekly/Thu
circulation: 50,000
contact: Tom Lynch
ext: 312-243-8786 x16
e: tom@newcity.com
music lead: 3 Weeks
e: calendar@newcity.com
calendar lead: 1-2 Weeks
Free alt. w/ distro to 1500 metro & suburban spots skews young & covers local scene & nat'l releases.

Red Eye
435 N Michigan Ave.
Chicago, IL 60611
p: 312-222-4970
f: 312-222-2407
http://redeye.chicagotribune.com
frequency: Daily
contact: Curt Wagner
e: cwwagner@tribune.com
music lead: 1 Week
calendar lead: 1 Week
Hip, niche Tribune pub. is a free read for 20-30 yr old urban pros. Mostly local news & pop culture - covers Rock & Hip-Hop only. Distro all over Chicago.

Time Out Chicago
247 S State St., 17th Fl.
Chicago, IL 60604
p: 312-924-9555
f: 312-924-9560
e: music@timeoutchicago.com
www.timeout.com/chicago
frequency: Weekly
contact: Brent Dicrescenzo
e: bdicrescenzo@timeoutchicago.com
music lead: 1 Month
calendar lead: 2 Weeks
Glossy A&E covers metro ent. scene for residents & tourists. Classical/Jazz info to: classical@timeoutchicago.com. Sister pubs. in NYC & int'l markets.

Springfield

Illinois Times
PO Box 5256
Springfield, IL 62705
p: 217-753-2226
f: 217-753-3958
e: editor@illinoistimes.com
www.illinoistimes.com
frequency: Weekly/Thu
circulation: 30,000
contact: Roland Klose
ext: 217-753-2226 x140
e: rklose@illinoistimes.com
music lead: 10 Days
calendar: Patrice Worthy
ext: 217-753-2226 x143
e: calendar@illinoistimes.com
calendar lead: 1 Week
Family-friendly free alt. in St. Louis/Chicago touring hub widely covers indie music- esp. Blues. Calendar may cover gigs in Champagne, Decatur, Peoria & St. Louis.

Indiana

Indianapolis/ Bloomington

The Herald Times/ The Scene
Box 909, 1900 S Walnut St.
Bloomington, IN 47401
p: 812-332-4401
f: 812-331-4383
e: getout@heraldt.com
www.bloomingtonscene.com
frequency: Daily
circulation: 28,000 (Daily); 49,000 (Sun)
contact: Kristina Wood
ext: 812-331-4357
e: kwood@heraldt.com
music lead: 1 Month
calendar lead: 2-3 Weeks
Coverage of local & touring acts for the county & Indiana U campus. Material w/ hi-res photos to: Dan Coleman, audibles@heraldt.com; submit tour schedules online.

NUVO Newsweekly
3951 N Meridian St., Ste. 200
Indianapolis, IN 46208
p: 317-254-2400
www.nuvo.net
frequency: Weekly
circulation: 47,000
contact: Leslie Benson
ext: 317-254-2400 x5232
e: lbenson@nuvo.net
music lead: 2 Weeks
calendar: Lisa Gauthier
e: lgauthier@nuvo.net; soundcheck@nuvo.net
Metro area's top free alt. covers local-touring acts & runs gig calendar. Email submissions to soundcheck@nuvo.net. Include the venue, performer/band's name, type of music, time & cover charge, if applicable.

Greater IN

Midwest Beat Magazine
PO Box 9069
Highland, IN 46322
www.midwestbeat.com
frequency: Monthly
contact: Tom Lounges
e: tom@midwestbeat.com
Free 40pg music mag features touring acts & bands from NW Indiana & Chicago; calendar covers Chicagoland gigs. Mag sponsors several Local artist showcases & hosts annual 'Region Rumble' talent showcase in Merrillville, IN.

Iowa

Des Moines

City View
414 61st St.
Des Moines, IA 50312
p: 515-953-4822
f: 515-953-1394
www.dmcityview.com
frequency: Weekly
circulation: 37,000
contact: Michael Swanger
ext: 515-953-4822 x308
e: michaelswanger@dmcityview.com; editor@bpcdm.com
music lead: 3 Weeks
calendar: Laci Strubble
ext: 515-953-4822 x301
e: calendar@dmcityview.com
calendar lead: 3 Weeks
Alt. pub. covers local & touring acts; distro in metro area & 4 surrounding counties.

Des Moines Register
PO Box 957
Des Moines, IA 50306
p: 515-284-8000
f: 515-286-2504
e: letters@dmreg.com
www.desmoinesregister.com
frequency: Daily
circulation: 150,000 (Daily); 239,000+ (Sun)
contact: Doug Peterson
ext: 515-284-8029
e: dopeterson@dmreg.com
music lead: 1 Week
calendar: Listings
ext: 800-247-5346
e: concertcall@dmreg.com
calendar lead: 1 Week
Gannett pub. is IA's major daily & covers metro area gigs & nat'l releases. Also prints free A&E weekly "Juice," targetting 25-34/demographic; Web version - dmJuice.com.

Iowa City

Iowa City Press Citizen
PO Box 2480
Iowa City, IA 52244
p: 319-337-3181
f: 319-339-7342
e: newsroom@press-citizen.com
www.press-citizen.com
frequency: Daily
circulation: 15,000
contact: Teresa Thorpe
ext: 319-337-3181 x620
e: tthorpe@press-citizen.com
music lead: 1 Week
calendar lead: 1 Week
Covers area's music scene in Thu A&E section - show previews, CD reviews & extensive calendar for reg'l & touring acts.

Quad Cities

Quad-City Times
500 E 3rd St.
Davenport, IA 52801
p: 563-383-2200
f: 563-383-2370
e: newsroom@qctimes.com
www.qctimes.com
frequency: Daily
circulation: 53,000 (Daily); 70,000 (Sun)
contact: David Burke
ext: 563-383-2400
e: dburke@qctimes.com
music lead: 2 Weeks
calendar: Heidi Engel
e: hengel@qctimes.com
calendar lead: Fri prior
A&E reviews artists playing IA/IL region. Calendar & most music covered on Thu. Distro in 10 counties in eastern IA & western IL.

Kansas

Lawrence

Journal World
609 New Hampshire
PO Box 888
Lawrence, KS 66044
p: 800-578-8748; 785-843-1000
f: 785-843-4512
www.ljworld.com
frequency: Daily
circulation: 19,500
contact: Jon Niccum
ext: 785-832-7178
e: jniccum@ljworld.com
music lead: 1 Week
calendar: Terry Rombeck
ext: 785-832-7145
e: calendar@ljworld.com
calendar lead: 1 Week
Liberal-leaning World Co. pub. covers acts playing the Topeka-Kansas City route. Show previews & reviews in Thu & Fri editions.

Wichita

Liberty Press
PO Box 16315
Wichita, KS 67216
p: 316-652-7737
f: 316-685-1999
www.libertypress.net
frequency: Monthly
circulation: 5000
contact: Kristi Parker
e: editor@libertypress.net
music lead: 2 Weeks
calendar: Vinnie Levin

calendar lead: 20th/mo
Free statewide Gay & Lesbian culture monthly reviews nat'l releases & previews area shows.

Wichita Eagle
825 E Douglas, PO Box 820
Wichita, KS 67201
p: 316-268-6351
f: 316-268-6627
www.kansas.com
frequency: Daily
circulation: 90,000 (Daily); 140,000 (Sun)
contact: Lori Linenberger
ext: 316-268-6321
e: llinenberger@wichitaeagle.com
music lead: 2+ Weeks
calendar: Deb Phillips
e: dphillips@wichitaeagle.com
calendar lead: 8 Days
Metro daily with statewide distro features music coverage & reviews mostly estab. acts. Gig guide & reg'l concerts run Fri.

Kentucky

Lexington

Ace Weekly
185 Jefferson St.
Lexington, KY 40508
p: 859-225-4889
e: editor@aceweekly.com
www.aceweekly.com
frequency: Weekly
circulation: 50,000
contact: Karen Smither
ext: 859-225-4889 x237
music lead: Fri prior
calendar lead: Fri prior
Free A&E w/ statewide distro, part of Standard Weekly Media, covers reg'l-touring bands. Gig & release previews & area calendar every Thu.

Lexington Herald Leader
100 Midland Ave.
Lexington, KY
40508
p: 800-950-6397
e: hlfeatures@herald-leader.com
www.lexgo.com
frequency: Daily
circulation: 120,000
contact: Scott Shive
ext: 859-231-1412
e: sshive@herald-leader.com
music lead: 3 Weeks
Weekly coverage of Lexington, Louisville & Cincinnati music scenes w/ columns, show previews & reviews distrib to central & eastern KY. Items may be included in wire service of parent co. McClatchy-Tribune

Louisville

Louisville Eccentric Observer
640 S 4th St., Ste. 100
Louisville, KY 40202
p: 502-895-9770
f: 502-895-9779
e: leo@leoweekly.com
www.leoweekly.com
frequency: Weekly
circulation: 153,000
contact: Mat Herron
ext: 502-895-9770 x224
e: mherron@leoweekly.com
music lead: 2 Weeks
calendar: Sara Havens
ext: 502-895-9770 x225
e: listings@leoweekly.com
calendar lead: 2 Weeks
Alt. paper runs previews, features & reviews of up to 7 releases/wk. Also distro in IN & OH. Calendar incl. Lexington, KY; Indianapolis, IN; Columbus, OH & major Nashville shows.

Louisville Music News
3705 Fairway Ln.
Louisville, KY 40207
p: 502-893-9933
f: 502-212-2097
e: editor@louisvillemusicnews.net
www.louisvillemusicnews.net
frequency: Monthly
circulation: 18,000
contact: Paul Moffett
music lead: 18th of mo
Free music mag supplies comprehensive coverage of Louisville & southern IN scenes.

Louisiana

Baton Rouge/ Lafayette

The Advocate
7290 Bluebonnet Blvd.
Baton Rouge, LA 70810
p: 225-383-1111
f: 225-388-0351
www.2theadvocate.com
frequency: Daily
circulation: 100,000 (Daily); 120,000 (Sun)
contact: John Wirt
ext: 225-388-0665
e: jwirt@theadvocate.com
music lead: 1-2 Weeks
calendar lead: 1-2 Weeks
Capitol City Press pub. previews & lists area shows & profiles local-nat'l artists & releases. Distro to southeastern LA.

The Independent
551 Jefferson St.
Lafayette, LA 70501
p: 337-988-4607
f: 337-983-0150
www.theind.com
frequency: Weekly
circulation: 20,000
contact: Dege Legg
ext: 337-988-4607 x110
e: degel@theind.com
calendar: Dege Legg
e: calendar@theind.com
Only indie weekly in region is avail. for free at area music venues & lifestyle stores.

New Orleans

Gambit Weekly
3923 Bienville St.
New Orleans, LA 70119
p: 504-486-5900
f: 504-483-3116
e: response@gambitweekly.com
www.bestofneworleans.com
frequency: Weekly/Tue
circulation: 40,000+
contact: William Coviello
e: willc@gambitweekly.com
music lead: 2 Weeks
calendar: Noah Bonaparte Pais
ext: 504-483-1120
e: listingsedit@gambitweekly.com
calendar lead: 10 Days
LA's largest alt. weekly runs comprehensive coverage of vibrant scene w/ previews & reviews of local & touring acts. Focus on local talent but reviews Indie Rock, Alt. Country & Jazz CDs.

OffBeat Magazine
421 Frenchmen St., Ste. 200
New Orleans, LA 70116
p: 504-944-4300
f: 504-944-4306
e: offbeat@offbeat.com
www.offbeatnola.mobi.
frequency: Monthly
circulation: 40,000
contact: Alex Rawls
ext: 504-944-4300 x14
e: alexrawls@offbeat.com
music lead: 1 Month
calendar: Craig Guillot
e: craigguillot@offbeat.com
calendar lead: 1 Month
Premier free A&E mag for music-centric city. Extensive calendar, previews, profiles & interviews.

Times Picayune
3800 Howard Ave.
New Orleans, LA 70125
p: 504-826-3300
f: 504-826-3186
www.nola.com
frequency: Daily
circulation: 200,000
contact: Keith Spera
ext: 504-826-3470
e: kspera@timespicayune.com
music lead: 2+ Weeks
calendar: Maryann Cook
ext: 504-826-3465
e: lagniappe@timespicayune.com
calendar lead: 2+ Weeks
Part of Newhouse empire, widely covers the city's venues & artists on Fri. Touring acts playing notable clubs may be interviewed & previewed. Widely read in southeastern LA, Baton Rouge & into coastal MS.

Maine

Portland

Portland Phoenix
16 York St., Ste. 102
Portland, ME 04101
p: 207-773-8900
f: 207-773-8905
e: submit@phx.com
www.thephoenix.com/Portland/
frequency: Weekly/Wed
circulation: 45,000
contact: Jeff Inglis
ext: 207-773-8900 x108
e: jinglis@phx.com
music lead: 2+ Weeks
calendar: Chris Gray
ext: 207-773-8900 x104
calendar lead: 2+ Weeks
Influential free alt. part of Phoenix Media Group runs features, extensive calendar, show previews & CD reviews for acts playing the ME, Portsmouth & Dover, NH region. Affiliated w/ local radio station, FNX. Prefers digital kits.

Portland Press Herald/ Maine Sunday Telegram
390 Congress St.
Portland, ME 04101
p: 207-791-6650
f: 207-791-6920
e: go@pressherald.com
www.pressherald.com
frequency: Daily
circulation: 75,000
contact: Stephanie Bouchard
ext: 207-791-6450
music lead: 3 Weeks
calendar lead: 3 Weeks
Daily pub. covers gigs statewide in Thu & Sun editions & reviews reg'l releases.

Maryland

Baltimore

Baltimore City Paper
812 Park Ave.
Baltimore, MD 21201
p: 410-523-2300
f: 410-523-0138
e: editorial@citypaper.com
www.citypaper.com
frequency: Weekly
circulation: 91,000
contact: Michael Byrne
ext: 410-523-2300 x238
e: mbyrne@citypaper.com
music lead: Fri prior to pub.
calendar: Wendy Ward
ext: 410-523-2300 x210
e: wward@citypaper.com
calendar lead: 3 Weeks
Free alt. pub., known for extensive coverage of Locals showcases talent in calendar, features, interviews & reviews. Bands upload bio & gig calendar on Web. Available in the surrounding counties & DC.

The Baltimore Sun
501 N Calvert St.
Baltimore, MD 21278
p: 410-332-6000
f: 410-783-2519
www.baltimoresun.com
frequency: Daily
circulation: 200,000 (Daily); 400,000 (Sun)
contact: Rashod Ollison
ext: 410-332-6605
e: rashod.ollison@baltsun.com
music lead: 2 Weeks
calendar: Nathan Pitts
ext: 410-332-6690
e: nathan.pitts@baltsun.com
calendar lead: 10-14 Days
Previews gigs & interviews touring acts in Thu A&E section. Calendar covers DC area & Baltimore shows. Music articles serviced thru Tribune newswire. Distro statewide.

Massachusetts

Boston

Boston Globe
PO Box 55819
Boston, MA 02205
p: 617-929-2000
f: 617-929-8329
www.boston.com
frequency: Daily
circulation: 400,000 (Daily); 587,000 (Sun)
contact: Joan Anderman
ext: 617-929-3053
e: anderman@globe.com
calendar: Anne Trout
e: atrout@globe.com
calendar lead: 10 Days
Metro area's largest paper covers New England w/ daily previews, reviews & profiles; calendar runs on Thu. Arts editor Scott Heller, heller@globe.com; Classical

Music Writer Jeremy Eichler, eichler@globe.com.

Boston Magazine
300 Massachusetts Ave.
Boston, MA 02115
p: 617-262-9700
e: editor@bostonmagazine.com
www.bostonmagazine.com
frequency: Monthly
circulation: 150,000
contact: Geoffrey Gagnon
e: ggagnon@bostonmagazine.com
music lead: 2 Months
calendar: Jason Schwartz
e: jschwartz@bostonmagazine.com
calendar lead: 2 Months
Monthly for mature readers has local talent focus thru CD previews, interviews & profiles of reg'l acts.

Boston Phoenix
126 Brookline Ave.
Boston, MA 02215
p: 617-536-5390
f: 617-536-1463
e: letters@phx.com
www.bostonphoenix.com
frequency: Weekly
circulation: 220,000
contact: Michael Brodeur
ext: 617-536-5390 x3270
e: mbrodeur@phx.com
music lead: Fri prior to pub.
calendar: Meghan Bell
ext: 617-536-5390 x2632
e: musiclistings@phx.com
calendar lead: 2 Weeks
Influential alt. paper widely read by the region's college students & hipsters includes extensive weekly coverage of gig & CD reviews & features.

Boston's Weekly Dig
242 E Berkeley St., 5th Fl.
Boston, MA 02118
p: 617-426-8942
f: 617-426-8944
e: editorial@weeklydig.com
www.weeklydig.com
frequency: Weekly
circulation: 70,000+
contact: David Day
ext: 617-426-8942 x238
e: david@weeklydig.com
music lead: 4 Weeks
calendar: Laura Dargus
e: listings@weeklydig.com
calendar lead: 4 Weeks
Free metro area pub. covers local-int'l music, mostly up-and-coming acts of all stripes. Distro in street kiosks, clubs & retail outlets.

Northeast Performer
24 Dane St., Ste. 3
Somerville, MA 02143
p: 617-627-9200
f: 617-627-9919
e: nepeditorial@performermag.com
www.performermag.com
frequency: Monthly
circulation: 35,000
contact: Brian King
music lead: 2 Months
calendar lead: 1 Month
For serious Indie musicians of all genres who buy recording gear, tour the northeast USA, & record albums. Distro at studios, rehearsal spaces, instrument retailers & repair, music venues & record retailers.

Western MA

Daily Hampshire Gazette
PO Box 299
Northampton, MA 01061
p: 413-584-5000
f: 413-585-5299
www.gazettenet.com
frequency: Daily
circulation: 20,000
contact: Phoebe Mitchell
ext: 413-585-5249
e: pmitchell@gazettenet.com
music lead: 2 Weeks
calendar: Dan DeNicola
e: calendar@gazettenet.com
calendar lead: Tue
Gannett pub. w/ distro in western MA covers touring acts.

North Adams Transcript
124 American Legion Dr.
North Adams, MA 01247
p: 413-663-3741
f: 413-662-2792
e: news@thetranscript.com
www.thetranscript.com
frequency: Daily
circulation: 15,000
contact: John Mitchell
ext: 413-663-3741 x229
e: jmitchell@thetranscript.com
music lead: 1-3 Weeks
calendar lead: 1 Week
Thu's arts section includes show previews, CD reviews & features. Promos: PO Box 1840, North Adams, MA 01247 or via email.

Valley Advocate
115 Conz St.
Easthampton, MA 01061
p: 413-529-2840
f: 413-529-2844
e: editor@valleyadvocate.com
www.valleyadvocate.com
frequency: Weekly/Wed
circulation: 50,000+
contact: James Heflin
ext: 413-529-2840 x298
e: jheflin@valleyadvocate.com
music lead: 2+ Weeks
calendar lead: 2+ Weeks
Free alt. covers reg'l shows plus reviews of major & indie releases. Distro in western MA & sneaks over the VT & CT borders. Promos: PO Box 477, Northampton, MA 01601. Must incl. phone & email. Submit calendar listings through www.valleyadvocate.com/calendar.

Michigan

Detroit/Ann Arbor

Detroit Free Press
615 W Lafayette Blvd.
Detroit, MI 48226
p: 313-222-6400
f: 313-223-4726
www.freep.com
frequency: Daily
circulation: 300,000 (Daily); 750,000 (Sun)
contact: Brian McCollum
ext: 313-223-4450
e: bmccollum@freepress.com
music lead: 2 Weeks
calendar: Rachel May
ext: 313-222-5990
e: events@freepress.com; rmay@freepress.com
calendar lead: 1 Week
Gannett-owned 'Freep' is linked w/ Detroit News & runs reviews & features acts w/ a buzz. Classical/Jazz, contact Mark Stryker: 313-222-6459; mstrykr@freepress.com. Local acts, contact Rachel May: rmay@freepress.com.

The Detroit News
615 W Lafayette Blvd.
Detroit, MI 48226
p: 313-222-2292
f: 313-222-2451
e: letters@detnews.com
www.detnews.com
frequency: Daily
circulation: 300,000
contact: Leslie Green
ext: 313-222-2486
e: lgreen@detnews.com
music lead: 2 Weeks
calendar lead: 1 Week
Gannett daily linked w/ Detroit Free Press, runs features, previews & reviews of metro area.

Metro Times
733 St. Antoine
Detroit, MI 48226
p: 313-961-4060
f: 313-961-6598
e: wkheron@metrotimes.com
www.metrotimes.com
frequency: Weekly
circulation: 100,000
contact: Bill Holdship
ext: 313-202-8068
e: bholdship@metrotimes.com
music lead: 2-4 Weeks
calendar: Megan O'Neil
ext: 313-202-8067
e: moneil@metrotimes.com
calendar lead: 2-4 Weeks
Influential free alt., w/ liberal leanings, distro in Detroit/Ann Arbor, previews & features local & touring talent.

Oakland Press
48 W Huron St.
Pontiac, MI 48342
p: 248-745-4786
f: 248-253-9948
www.theoaklandpress.com
frequency: Daily
circulation: 80,000
contact: Megan Frye
ext: 248-745-4786 x4617
e: megan.frye@oakpress.com
music lead: 2 Weeks
calendar lead: 2 Weeks
Covers artists playing southeastern MI w/ profiles, gig previews & reviews. Distro in selected spots in metro Detroit. Call before sending materials.

Real Detroit Weekly
359 Livernois Ave.
Ferndale, MI 48220
p: 248-591-7325
f: 248-544-9893
www.realdetroitweekly.com
frequency: Weekly/Wed
circulation: 65,000
contact: Travis Wright
ext: 248-591-7325 x202
e: travis@realdetroitweekly.com
music lead: 3+ Weeks
calendar: Eric Allen
ext: 248-591-7325 x212
e: listings@getrealdetroit.com
calendar lead: 3+ Weeks
Free pop culture & ent. guide digs deep into the greater Detroit & Ann Arbor scenes & beyond for readers 18-35. Issues filled w/ gig & CD previews, reviews & profiles; distro at 1,500 locations. Calendar covers greater Detroit, Ann Arbor, Ypsilanti & Canadian gigs, plus big shows in Flint & Lansing.

Grand Rapids/Lansing

Grand Rapids Press
155 Michigan St. NW
Grand Rapids, MI 49503
p: 616-222-5400
f: 616-222-5831
www.grpress.com
frequency: Daily
circulation: 309,590 (Daily); 503,080 (Sun)
contact: John Sinkevics
ext: 616-222-5594
e: jsinkevics@grpress.com
music lead: 10 Days
calendar: Mary Hefferan
ext: 616-222-5491
e: mhefferan@grpress.com
calendar lead: 10 Days
Largest of the Booth pubs. runs daily previews & reviews of reg'l-touring acts for Grand Rapids & Lakeshore residents.

Kalamazoo Gazette
401 S Burdick St.
Kalamazoo, MI 49007
p: 269-345-3511
f: 269-388-8447
e: news@kalamazoogazette.com
www.mlive.com/kzgazette/
frequency: Daily
circulation: 75,000
contact: Rebecca Pierce
ext: 269-388-8421
e: rpierce@kalamazoogazette.com
music lead: 2 Weeks
calendar: Maria McCreary
ext: 269-388-8553
e: mmccreary@kalamazoogazette.com
calendar lead: 2 Weeks
Newhouse pub. incl. Detroit & Grand Rapids gigs in calendar; previews & reviews may run in one of 8 affiliated papers. Distro throughout western MI.

Lansing State Journal
120 E Lenawee St.
Lansing, MI 48919
p: 517-267-1302
f: 517-377-1298
e: events@lsj.com
www.lsj.com
frequency: Daily
circulation: 79,000
contact: Robin Swartz
ext: 517-267-1302 x108
music lead: 1 Month
calendar lead: 1 Month
Gannett pub. spotlights reg'l & touring acts in weekly music insert for surrounding counties.

Revue Magazine
2422 Burton SE
Grand Rapids, MI 49546
p: 616-301-9200
f: 616-719-5940
e: editor@revuewm.com
www.revuewm.com
frequency: Monthly
circulation: 30,000+
contact: Jen Pider
e: jenpider@revuewm.com
music lead: 2 Weeks

Free music guide for readers 21-49, covers artists touring the region. Calendar extends to Lakeshore, Holland, Lansing & Kalamazoo; notable Detroit gigs may be included.

Minnesota

Minneapolis/St. Paul

City Pages
401 N 3rd St., Ste. 550
Minneapolis, MN 55401
p: 612-375-1015
f: 612-372-3737
e: news@citypages.com
www.citypages.com
frequency: Weekly
circulation: 150,000
contact: Sarah Askari
ext: 612-375-1015 x792
e: saskari@citypages.com
music lead: Thu prior
calendar: Jessica Armbruster
ext: 612-372-3788
e: jarmbruster@citypages.com
calendar lead: 1 Week
Free weekly arts pub. also prints annual Minneapolis Music Directory in March.

Mpls./St.Paul Magazine
220 S 6th St., Ste. 500
Minneapolis, MN 55402
p: 612-339-7571
f: 612-339-5806
e: arts@mspmag.com; edit@mspmag.com
www.mspmag.com
frequency: Monthly
circulation: 67,423
contact: Tad Simons
e: tsimons@mspmag.com
music lead: 3 Months
calendar lead: 3 Months
Twin Cities monthly runs extensive club listings, features & reviews.

Star Tribune
425 Portland Ave.
Minneapolis, MN 55488
p: 612-673-4000
f: 612-673-7872
www.startribune.com
frequency: Daily
circulation: 400,000 (Daily); 600,000 (Sun)
contact: Tim Campbell
ext: 612-673-4865
e: tcampbell@startribune.com
music lead: 1-3 Weeks
calendar: Mary Ellen Smith
e: culturecal@startribune.com
calendar lead: 2 Weeks
Avista pub. sold statewide & into parts of ND, SD, WI, & IA, runs most of its music coverage Tue, Fri & Sun.

Mississippi

Jackson

The Clarion-Ledger
201 S Congress St.
Jackson, MS 39201
p: 601-961-7000
f: 601-961-7325
e: style@jackson.ganett.com
www.clarionledger.com
frequency: Daily
contact: Carey Miller
ext: 601-961-7268
e: carey.miller@jackson.gannet.com
music lead: 1 Week
calendar lead: 1 Week
Pub. w/ statewide distro reviews area gigs & runs calendar, previews & interviews in Thu section. Promos: PO Box 40, Jackson, MS 39205.

Tupelo

Daily Journal
PO Box 909
Tupelo, MS 38802
p: 662-842-2611
f: 662-842-2233
e: planner@djournal.com
www.djournal.com
frequency: Daily
circulation: 36,000
contact: M. Scott Morris
ext: 662-678-1589
e: scott.morris@djournal.com
music lead: 1 Week
calendar lead: Tue
Independent & conservative pub. serving 16 counties in northeast MS, previews, reviews, interviews & runs ltd. CD reviews in Fri ent. section.

Missouri

Kansas City

The Pitch
1701 Main St.
Kansas City, MO 64108
p: 816-561-6061
f: 816-756-0502
www.pitch.com; music.pitch.com
frequency: Weekly
circulation: 90,000+
contact: Jason Harper
ext: 816-218-6774
e: jason.harper@pitch.com
music lead: 3+ Weeks
calendar: Crystal K. Wiebe
ext: 816-218-6780
e: crystal.wiebe@pitch.com
calendar lead: 3+ Weeks
Village Voice Media free alt. w/ distro at area clubs reviews & features local-touring acts & nat'l releases.

St. Louis

The Riverfront Times
6358 Delmar Blvd., Ste. 200
St. Louis, MO 63130
p: 314-754-5966
f: 314-754-5955
www.riverfronttimes.com
frequency: Weekly/Wed
circulation: 100,000+
contact: Annie Zaleski
e: annie.zaleski@riverfronttimes.com
music lead: 21 Days
calendar lead: 21 Days
Free alt. part of Village Voice Media previews & reviews area gigs & covers nat'l releases.

St. Louis Post Dispatch
900 N Tucker Blvd.
St. Louis, MO 63101
p: 314-340-8000
f: 314-721-1305
www.stltoday.com
frequency: Daily
contact: Kevin C. Johnson
ext: 314-340-8191
e: kjohnson@post-dispatch.com
music lead: 2+ Weeks
calendar: Patrick Derfler
ext: 314-340-8112
e: getout@post-dispatch.com
calendar lead: 10 Days
Metro daily runs most music coverage on Thu. Targets 35-55 affluent crowd. Web gets 50 million pg views/mo.

Montana

Bozeman

Bozeman Daily Chronicle
PO Box 1190
Bozeman, MT 59771
p: 406-587-4491
www.dailychronicle.com
frequency: Daily
circulation: 17,000
contact: Lu Ann Rod
ext: 406-587-4491 x232
e: thisweek@dailychronicle.com
music lead: 2 Weeks
calendar lead: 1 Week
Owned by Seattle's Pioneer Newspapers & one of largest in MT runs press blurbs to promote shows & calendar listings.

Missoula

Missoula Independent
317 S Orange St.
Missoula, MT 59801
p: 406-543-6609
f: 406-543-4367
www.missoulanews.com
frequency: Weekly/Thu
circulation: 23,000
contact: Erika Fredrickson
e: efredrickson@missoulanews.com
music lead: 2 Weeks
calendar: Jonas Ehudin
e: calendar@missoulanews.com
calendar lead: 2 Weeks
MT's largest alt. weekly covers western MT shows & runs extensive calendar listings; free distro. Promos: PO Box 8275, Missoula, MT 59807.

The Missoulian Daily
PO Box 8029
Missoula, MT 59807
p: 406-523-5200
f: 406-523-5294
e: entertainer@missoulian.com
www.missoulian.com
frequency: Daily
circulation: 33,000 (Daily); 38,000 (Sun)
contact: Joe Nickell
ext: 406-523-5258
e: jnickell@missoulian.com
music lead: 2 Weeks
calendar: Calendar Editor
ext: 406-523-5246
e: entertainment@missoulian.com
calendar lead: 2 Weeks
Part of Lee Enterprises, covers reg'l-nat'l acts touring western Montana. Calendar also includes ID & WA gigs.

Nebraska

Omaha/Lincoln

Lincoln Journal Star
926 P St.
Lincoln, NE 68508
p: 402-475-4200
e: features@journalstar.com
www.journalstar.com
frequency: Daily
circulation: 79,000 (Daily); 88,000 (Sun)
contact: L. Kent Wolgamott
ext: 402-473-7244
e: kwolgamott@journalstar.com
music lead: 10 Days
calendar: Linda Olig
e: lolig@journalstar.com
calendar lead: 1 Week
NE's largest daily runs calendar & most music blurbs, incl. touring band profiles Fri. Covers southeast NE w/ show previews, reviews & new releases. For monthly insert upscale lifestyle & arts mag w/ 15,000 distro, 'L Magazine,' contact Pam Thompson, 402-473-7113, pam.thompson@lee.net.

Omaha World Herald
1314 Douglas St., Ste. 700
Omaha, NE 68102
p: 402-444-1000
f: 402-345-0183
e: news@owh.com
www.omaha.com
frequency: Daily
circulation: 220,000
contact: Niz Proskocil
ext: 402-444-1089
e: niz.proskocil@owh.com
music lead: 2 Weeks
calendar: Calendar Editor
e: calendar@owh.com
calendar lead: 10 Days
Metro region's largest paper read statewide & into southwestern IA, runs calendar, interviews, show previews & reviews.

The Reader
2312 M St., Box 7360
Omaha, NE 68107
p: 402-341-7323
f: 402-341-6967
www.thereader.com
frequency: Weekly
circulation: 20,000
contact: Music Editor
ext: 402-341-7323 x120
e: backbeat@thereader.com
music lead: 2 Weeks
calendar: Alma Guttierez
e: listings@thereader.com
calendar lead: 1 Week
Provocative alt. runs in-depth previews, reviews & interviews w/ acts playing Omaha & Lincoln. Distro reaches Council Bluffs, IA.

Nevada

Las Vegas

Las Vegas City Life
1385 Pama Ln., Ste. 111
Las Vegas, NV 89119
f: 702-871-3298
e: letters@lvcitylife.com
www.lvcitylife.com
frequency: Weekly
circulation: 85,000
contact: Mike Prevatt
ext: 702-871-6780 x395
e: mprevatt@lvcitylife.com
music lead: 1 Month
calendar: Ivy Hover
ext: 702-871-6780 x309
e: ihover@lvcitylife.com
calendar lead: 1 Month
Free pub. covers mostly left-of-center Indie Punk bands & area tours & industry news, CD reviews & gig previews. Distro at 2,000 city venues. Also publishes annual local music guide. Owned by Stevens Media Group.

Las Vegas Weekly
2360 Corporate Circle Dr.

4th Fl.
Henderson, NV 89074
p: 702-990-2400
e: lvweekly@gmgvegas.com
www.lasvegasweekly.com
frequency: Weekly
circulation: 60,000
contact: Spencer Patterson
ext: 702-990-8188
e: spencer.patterson@gmgvegas.com
music lead: 2 Weeks
ext: 702-990-8995
e: listings@gmgvegas.com
calendar lead: Fri by 5pm
Indie-friendly free alt., part of Greenspun Media Group, covers metro region nitelife. Extensive calendar in print & web.

Smash Magazine
8665 W Flamingo Rd.
#131-201
Las Vegas, NV 89147
p: 702-401-3311
e: editor@smashmagazine.com; features@smashmagazine.com
www.smashmagazine.com
frequency: Bimonthly
circulation: 20,000
contact: Holmes Pooser
e: reviews@smashmagazine.com; homie@smashmagazine.com
music lead: 3 Months
Free local mag targets Warped Tour crowd & also produces events in St. George, UT. See web for details & contact booking@smashmagazine.com.

Reno

Reno Gazette-Journal
955 Kuenzli St.
Reno, NV 89502
p: 775-788-6200
e: entertainment@rgj.com
www.rgj.com
frequency: Daily
circulation: 60,000+
contact: Jason Kellner
ext: 775-327-6726
e: jkellner@rgj.com
music lead: 3 Weeks
calendar lead: 3 Weeks
Gannett paper's Fri edition previews, reviews & interviews acts hitting Reno/Tahoe stages. Email before sending materials to: PO Box 22000, Reno, NV 89520. Distro in northern NV coffee houses.

Reno News & Review
708 N Center St.
Reno, NV 89501
p: 775-324-4440
f: 775-324-4572
www.newsreview.com
frequency: Weekly
circulation: 27,000
contact: Brad Bynum
ext: 702-324-4440 x3520
e: bradb@newsreview.com
music lead: 1 Month
calendar: Kelley Lang
ext: 702-324-4440 x3526
e: renocalendar@newsreview.com; kelleyl@newsreview.com
Alt. paper serves readers 18-34+ in Tahoe, Carson City & Sparks w/ area's most complete gig calendar, reviews, previews & interviews. Sister pubs. in Sacramento & Chico, CA.

New Hampshire

Manchester/ Portsmouth

The New Hampshire Union Leader
100 William Loeb Dr.
PO Box 9555
Manchester, NH 03108
p: 800-562-8218
f: 603-668-0382
e: writeus@unionleader.com
www.unionleader.com
frequency: Daily
circulation: 57,753 (Daily); 71,298 (Sun)
contact: Julia Anne Weekes
ext: 603-668-4321 x315
e: jweekes@unionleader.com
music lead: 1 Week
calendar: Calendar Editor
ext: 603-668-4321
e: calendar@theunionleader.com
calendar lead: 1 Week
Avail. statewide & previews NH, ME, VT & MA shows & some nat'l CD reviews in Thu & Sun ed.

The Wire
10 Vaughan Mall, Ste. 1
Portsmouth, NH 03801
p: 603-427-0403
e: news@wirenh.com
www.wirenh.com
frequency: Weekly/Wed
circulation: 9000
contact: Matt Kanner
music lead: 2 Weeks
calendar: Liberty Hardy
calendar lead: 2 Weeks
Indie pub. w/ statewide distro only covers bands from, or touring coastal NH.

New Jersey

North

The Aquarian Weekly
52 Sindle Ave., PO Box 1140
Little Falls, NJ 07424
p: 973-812-6766
f: 973-812-5420
e: editor@theaquarian.com
www.theaquarian.com
frequency: Weekly
circulation: 40,000
contact: Chris Farinas
e: chrisf@theaquarian.com
music lead: 2+ Weeks
Covers underground arts & political scene & NJ tri-state gigs. Free distro at clubs & select indie music shops.

Current
1400 Washington St.
Hoboken, NJ 07030
p: 201-798-7800
f: 201-798-0018
www.hudsoncurrent.com
frequency: Weekly
circulation: 11,000
contact: Diana Schwaeble
ext: 201-798-7800 x405
e: current@hudsonreporter.com
music lead: 3-4 Weeks
calendar: Calendar Editor
calendar lead: 2 Weeks
Free alt. part of Hudson Reporter Group, covers the county's lively music scene. Features native talent & acts playing NYC/north NJ area. Distro in bars & retail spots in Hoboken, Jersey City & most of Hudson county.

The Star Ledger
1 Star Ledger Plaza
Newark, NJ 07102
p: 973-392-4040
f: 973-392-5845
www.nj.com
frequency: Daily
circulation: 350,000 (Daily); 500,000 (Sun)
contact: Jay Lustig
ext: 973-392-5850
e: jlustig@starledger.com
music lead: 2+ Weeks
calendar: Pamela Whitehurst
ext: 973-392-1500
e: event@starledger.com; pwhitehurst@starledger.com
calendar lead: 2+ Weeks
Major metro runs CD reviews, show previews & interviews w/ emphasis on reg'l talent & gigs.

Steppin' Out
21-07 Maple Ave.
Fair Lawn, NJ 07410
p: 201-703-0911
f: 201-703-0211
e: stepoutmag@aol.com
www.steppinoutmagazine.com
frequency: Weekly
circulation: 80,000
contact: Chaunce Hayden
ext: 201-358-2929
e: chaunce100@aol.com
music lead: 1 Month
calendar: Pam Sylsbury
calendar lead: 1 Week
Free alt. lists reg'l & nat'l acts playing the NJ/NYC area but caters to cover bands & bar scene.

South

Asbury Park Press
3601 Hwy. 66
Neptune, NJ 07754
p: 732-922-6000
f: 732-643-3612
www.app.com
frequency: Daily
circulation: 159,390 (Daily); 213,513 (Sun)
contact: Kathy Dzielak
ext: 732-643-4265
e: katydz@app.com
music lead: 3 Weeks
calendar: Ronna Weinberg
ext: 732-643-4263
e: calendar@app.com; ronnas@app.com
calendar lead: 3 Weeks
Friend of Local artists previews, reviews & runs features. Music writer, Stephen Bove: sbove@app.com, 732-643-4085.

Night & Day
2022 Hwy. 71, Ste. 204
Spring Lake, NJ 07762
p: 732-974-0047
f: 732-974-0163
e: info@ndmag.com
www.ndmag.com
frequency: Monthly
circulation: 37,000
contact: Bill Bodkin
e: bodkin@ndmag.com
Free ent. guide reviews local & touring acts playing Monmouth & Ocean counties. Distro to 1,500 locations. Publishes bi-weekly May-Aug.

New Mexico

Albuquerque

Albuquerque Journal
7777 Jefferson NE
PO Drawer J
Albuquerque, NM 87103
p: 505-823-3800
f: 505-823-3998
e: newsroom@abqjournal.com
www.abqjournal.com
frequency: Daily
circulation: 115,000 (Daily); 140,000 (Sun)
contact: Rene Kimball
ext: 505-823-3939
e: rkimball@abqjournal.com
music lead: 1 Month
calendar: Brianna Stallings
ext: 505-823-3920
e: venue@abqjournal.com
calendar lead: 10 Days
Statewide paper covers all styles of indie releases & area gigs in Fri & Sun sections.

Weekly Alibi
2118 Central Ave. SE, Ste. 151
Albuquerque, NM 87106
p: 505-346-0660
f: 505-256-9651
e: editorial@alibi.com
www.alibi.com
frequency: Weekly
circulation: 50,000
contact: Laura Marrich
ext: 505-346-0660 x260
e: lauram@alibi.com
music lead: 2 Weeks
calendar: Amy Dalness
ext: 505-346-0660 x255
e: calendar@alibi.com; amy@alibi.com
calendar lead: 2 Weeks
Free alt. also read in Santa Fe covers acts playing the area's clubs. Gigs previewed, CDs reviewed plus profiles & features. Prefers snail mail, but email 1st.

Santa Fe

Santa Fe Reporter
132 E Marcy St.
Santa Fe, NM 87501
p: 505-988-5541
f: 505-988-5348
e: editor@sfreporter.com
www.sfreporter.com
frequency: Weekly/Wed
circulation: 23,000
contact: Patricia Sauthoff
ext: 505-988-5541 x217
e: culture@sfreporter.com
music lead: 2 Weeks
calendar lead: 1 Week
Free alt. covers acts playing the metro region, Albuquerque & northern NM. Extra 2,000-10,000 copies of select special issues.

New York

Albany

Albany Times Union
645 Albany Shaker Rd.
Albany, NY 12212
p: 518-454-5494
f: 518-454-5514
www.timesunion.com
frequency: Daily
circulation: 100,000
contact: Greg Haymes
ext: 518-454-5742
e: ghaymes@timesunion.com
music lead: 2 Weeks
calendar: Shannon Fromma
ext: 518-454-5479
e: sfromma@timesunion.com; livemusic@timesunion.com
calendar lead: 2 Weeks

Hearst pub. covers the NY Capital district, western MA & parts of Hudson Valley. Reviews & interviews local-nat'l acts of all genres in print & web blogs.

Metroland
419 Madison Ave.
Albany, NY 12210
p: 518-463-2500
f: 518-463-3712
e: metroland@metroland.net
www.metroland.net
frequency: Weekly/Thu
circulation: 45,000
contact: John Brodeur
ext: 518-463-2500 x145
e: tigerpop1@aol.com
music lead: Fri prior to pub.
calendar: Kathryn Lange
ext: 518-463-2500 x143
e: calendar@metroland.net
calendar lead: Thu prior*Free Capital region alt. serving Albany, Troy & Saratoga Springs reviews & previews gigs & CDs.*

Buffalo/Rochester/ Syracuse

Artvoice
810 Main St.
Buffalo, NY 14202
p: 716-881-6604
f: 716-881-6682
e: editorial@artvoice.com
www.artvoice.com
frequency: Weekly
circulation: 65,000
contact: Donny Kutzbach
e: donnykutzbach@gmail.com
music lead: 2-3 Weeks
calendar: Katherine O'Day
e: calendar@artvoice.com
Free alt. weekly w/ western NY distro, previews acts playing the Rochester circuit & reviews local-nat'l releases of all genres.

Freetime Magazine
850 University Ave.
Rochester, NY 14607
p: 585-473-2266
f: 585-473-5214
e: freetime@frontiernet.net
www.freetime.com
frequency: Biweekly
circulation: 35,000
contact: Michelle Picardo
music lead: 3 Weeks
calendar lead: 3 Weeks
Free A&E profiles & reviews reg'l & nat'l talent & releases. Distro in 600+ area locations.

Ithaca Journal
123-127 W State St.
Ithaca, NY 14850
p: 607-274-9262
f: 607-272-4248
e: ijticket@ithaca.gannett.com
www.theithacajournal.com
frequency: Daily
circulation: 20,000
contact: Jim Catalano
e: jcatalano@ithacajournal.com
music lead: 2 Weeks
calendar: Kathie Williams
ext: 607-274-9248
e: kwilliams@ithacajournal.com
calendar lead: 10 Days
Gannett pub. runs reg'l calendar & CD reviews in Thu A&E section. Free supplement, 'Buzz,' skews to younger demo incl. in sister pubs: Binghamton Press, Sun-Bulletin & Elmira Star-Gazette every other Wed.

Ithaca Times
109 N Cayuga St.
Ithaca, NY 14850
p: 607-277-7000
f: 607-277-1012
www.ithacatimes.com; www.ithacatimesartsblog.com
frequency: Weekly
circulation: 35,000
contact: Natasha Li Pickowicz
ext: 607-277-7000 x221
e: arts@ithacatimes.com
music lead: 2 Weeks
calendar lead: 2 Weeks
Free alt. runs reviews, previews & interviews. Also publishes blog, Popcorn Youth, at www.ithacatimesartsblog.com.

Night & Day
435 River Rd.
N Tonawanda, NY 14120
p: 716-693-1000 x116
f: 716-693-0124
e: nightandday@gnnewspaper.com
www.niagara-gazette.com
frequency: Weekly/Thu
circulation: 50,000
contact: Phil Dzikiy
ext: 716-693-1000 x308
A&E insert for 3 area pubs.: Tonawanda News, Lockport Union-Sun & Journal & Niagara-Gazette, reviews CDs & previews gigs in Niagara Falls & southern Ontario region w/ some notable Buffalo gigs.

The Post-Standard
101 N Salina St.
Syracuse, NY 13202
p: 315-470-0011
f: 315-470-3081
www.post-standard.com
frequency: Daily
circulation: 125,000 (Daily); 165,000 (Sun)
contact: Mark Bialczak
ext: 315-470-2175
e: mbialczak@syracuse.com
music lead: 1 Week
calendar: Calendar Editor
ext: 315-470-2141
e: calendar@syracuse.com
Runs extensive weekend calendar in Thu & Sun A&E 'Stars' magazine. Distro covers central NY. Promos: PO Box 4915, Syracuse, NY 13221.

Syracuse New Times
1415 W Genesee St.
Syracuse, NY 13204
p: 315-422-7011
f: 315-422-1721
e: snt@syracusenewtimes.com
www.syracusenewtimes.com
frequency: Weekly/Wed
circulation: 42,000
contact: Matt Mumau
ext: 315-422-7011 x128
e: mmumau@syracusenewtimes.com
music lead: 2 Weeks
calendar lead: 2 Weeks
Free alt. voice previews & reviews acts playing central NY & Syracuse; web features expanded reviews. Sponsors SAMMYS - Syracuse Area Music Awards - annually.

Long Island

Good Times Magazine
PO Box 33
Westbury, NY 11590
p: 516-280-2100
f: 516-280-2103
e: gtmag@optonline.net
www.goodtimesmag.com
frequency: Biweekly
circulation: 12,000
contact: Bob Smith
music lead: 3 Weeks
Music mag covers Long Island suburbs & NYC gigs, area recordings & happenings. Distro at 400 retailers & 20 campuses.

Long Island Press
1103 Stewart Ave.
Garden City, NY 11530
p: 516-284-3300
f: 631-648-2504
e: editor@longislandpress.com
www.longislandpress.com
frequency: Weekly/Thu
contact: Mike Nelson
e: mnelson@longislandpress.com
music lead: 2 Weeks
calendar lead: 2 Weeks
Weekly A&E distro to college campuses, record & book shops in Long Island previews & reviews LI & NYC gigs & nat'l releases.

Under The Volcano
PO Box 236
Nesconset, NY 11767
e: boss@underthevolcano.net
www.underthevolcano.net
frequency: Bimonthly
circulation: 7000
contact: Rich Black
ext: 631-585-7471
music lead: 2 Months
Covers Punk/Rock/Hardcore reviews, interviews & follows the scene - calendar lists only LI area gigs. Free at area bars, campuses, etc. & sold nat'lly.

New York City

The Deli Magazine
37 W 20th St., Ste 1006
New York, NY 10011
e: thedelinyc@gmail.com
www.thedelimagazine.com
frequency: Quarterly
circulation: 7500
contact: Paolo De Gregorio
e: paolo@thedelimagazine.com
music lead: 3 Months
Only reviews music from indie NYC-based artists; incl. industry tips. Web blog & separate editons for LA (www.thedelimagazine.com/la) & San Francisco (www.thedelimagazine.com/sf). Site gets 20k unique visitors/mo; feat. daily news, free MP3s & "buy it now" links. Read by musicians & fans. Distro all over NYC & most of Brooklyn. Do not send CD-Rs w/ hand-written titles.

New York Daily News
450 W 33rd St.
New York, NY 10001
p: 212-210-2100
f: 212-643-7831
e: news@edit.nydailynews.com
www.nydailynews.com
frequency: Daily
circulation: 729,124 (Daily); 805,350 (Sun)
contact: Jim Farber
e: jfarber@nydailynews.com
music lead: 2 Weeks
calendar: Nicole Carter
e: ncarter@nydailynews.com
calendar lead: 1 Week
Photo-centric pub. w/ metro region distro features & reviews nat'l acts & polished reg'l talent w/ a buzz in Sun, Tue & Fri.

New York Post
1211 Ave. of the Americas
New York, NY 10036
p: 212-930-8000
f: 212-930-8540
www.nypost.com
frequency: Daily
circulation: 652,426
contact: Dan Aquilante
ext: 212-930-8019
e: aquilanted@aol.com
music lead: 2 Weeks
calendar: Christina Tam
ext: 212-930-8600
e: ctam@nypost.com
calendar lead: 2 Weeks
Murdoch's News Corp.'s large metro runs columns, listings & blurbs for acts playing city. Sold in Long Island, northern NJ, southern CT & Philadelphia.

New York Press
79 Madison Ave., 16th Fl.
New York, NY 10031
p: 212-268-8600
f: 212-268-2935
e: editorial@nypress.com
www.nypress.com
frequency: Weekly/Wed
circulation: 116,000
contact: Adam Rathe
ext: 212-268-8600 x9730
e: arathe@nypress.com
music lead: 2+ Weeks
calendar: Listings
e: listings@nypress.com
calendar lead: 2+ Weeks
Free Manhattan Media weekly A&E, distro in NYC & northern NJ, covers releases & gigs. Focuses on emerging & indie artists. Show reviews & music news on web daily.

New York Times
620 8th Ave.
New York, NY 10018
p: 212-556-1234
f: 212-556-7617
e: music@nytimes.com
www.nytimes.com
frequency: Daily
circulation: 1,118,565 (Daily); 1,676,885 (Sun)
contact: Sia Michel
e: michel@nytimes.com
music lead: 3+ Weeks
calendar: Ben Sisario
ext: 212-556-1342
calendar lead: 3+ Weeks
Influential paper read around the world, incl. columns, features & reviews of local-int'l musicians. Extended listings & features on wknds. Call 212-556-4005 before submitting.

New York Waste
PO Box 20005, W Village Stn.
New York, NY 10014
p: 212-726-2337
e: info@newyorkwaste.com; letterbox@newyorkwaste.com
www.newyorkwaste.com
frequency: 6/year
circulation: 10,000
contact: Lucky Lawler
e: theluckster@newyorkwaste.com
Mainstay w/ free distro. in NYC, Brookyn & some NJ venues gives only unsigned Rock, Punk & Metal music attention.

Time Out New York
475 Tenth Ave., 12th Fl.
New York, NY 10018
p: 646-432-3000
f: 646-432-3010
e: music@timeoutny.com
www.timeoutny.com
frequency: Weekly
circulation: 139,108
contact: Steve Smith
e: steves@timeoutny.com
music lead: 10 Days
calendar: Bruce Tantum
e: brucet@timeoutny.com
calendar lead: 2 Weeks
A&E covers area artists & nat'l releases. Calendar spotlights all NYC neighborhoods & Hoboken, NJ gigs.

Village Voice
36 Cooper Sq.
New York, NY 10003
p: 212-475-3300
f: 212-475-8944
www.villagevoice.com
frequency: Weekly
circulation: 250,000
contact: Rob Harvilla
e: rharvilla@villagevoice.com
music lead: 2+ Weeks
calendar: Zach Baron
e: zbaron@villagevoice.com
calendar lead: 2 Weeks
NYC-centric pub. is influential alternative for urban adults across USA. Reviews worldwide releases & NYC area gigs. Free locally. Part of Village Voice Media.

North Carolina

Asheville

Asheville Citizen Times
PO Box 2090
Asheville, NC 28802
p: 800-800-4204
f: 828-251-0585
www.citizen-times.com
frequency: Daily
circulation: 70,000
contact: Tony Kiss
ext: 828-232-5855
e: tkiss@citizen-times.com
music lead: 3-4 Weeks
calendar lead: 10 Days
Gannett daily, sold in western NC, covers music on Fri. Calendar includes Knoxville, TN & Spartanburg, SC. Promos: 14 O'Henry Ave., Asheville, NC 28801.

Mountain Xpress
2 Wall St., Ste. 212
Asheville, NC 28801
p: 828-251-1333
f: 828-251-1311
www.mountainx.com
frequency: Weekly/Wed
circulation: 30,000
contact: Rebecca Sulock
ext: 828-251-1333 x113
e: rsulock@mountainx.com
music lead: 2 Weeks
calendar: Alli Marshall
ext: 828-251-1333 x124
e: clubland@mountainx.com
calendar lead: 1 Week
Free alt. penetrates Hendersonville, NC thru Spartanburg & Greenville, SC w/ comprehensive calendar, blurbs & reviews of acts touring area. Prefers email submissions & follow-up.

Charlotte

Creative Loafing
1000 Seaboard St.
Ste. C2
Charlotte, NC 28206
p: 704-522-8334
f: 704-944-3605
www.creativeloafing.com
frequency: Weekly
circulation: 60,000
contact: Jeff Hahne
ext: 704-944-3608
e: jeff.hahne@creativeloafing.com
music lead: 2 Weeks
calendar lead: 2 Weeks
Free alt. enjoyed by high school kids-40 year olds. Provides wide coverage of area music scene; reviews, previews & interviews touring acts. Atlanta, Tampa & Sarasota editions.

Greensboro/Winston-Salem

Go Triad
200 E Market St.
Greensboro, NC
27401
p: 336-373-7319
f: 336-373-7382
www.gotriad.com
frequency: Weekly/Thu
circulation: 225,000
contact: Carla Kucinski Seward
e: carla@gotriad.com
music lead: 2+ Weeks
calendar: Carl Wilson
ext: 336-373-7145
e: carl.wilson@gotriad.com
calendar lead: 2 Weeks
Free A&E pub., supplement to News & Record, covers Triad area & features show previews & reg'l & touring acts. Submit calendar listings at www.gotriad.com/scene. Nat'l reviews run in the larger News & Record Fri ed., contact Carla Kucinski Seward: 336-373-7319; carla@news-record.com.

Winston-Salem Journal
PO Box 3159
Winston-Salem, NC 27102
p: 336-727-7211
f: 336-727-4071
www.journalnow.com
frequency: Daily
circulation: 90,000
contact: Susan Gilmor
ext: 336-727-7298
e: sgilmor@wsjournal.com
music lead: 2+ Weeks
calendar: Heidi Freeman
ext: 336-727-7284
e: hfreeman@wsjournal.com
calendar lead: 2 Weeks
Metro daily runs most music coverage incl. reviews, interviews, previews & calendar on Thu.

High Country

Mountain Times
474 Industrial Park Dr.
PO Box 1815
Boone, NC 28607
p: 828-264-6397
f: 828-262-0282
e: letters@mountaintimes.com
www.mountaintimes.com
frequency: Weekly/Thu
circulation: 35,000
contact: Jeff Eason
e: eason@mountaintimes.com
music lead: Tue
calendar: Rob Moore
ext: 828-262-0282
e: notes@mountaintimes.com
calendar lead: Mon by 5pm
A&E in college & tourist town that hosts many live music fests, provides in-depth ent. section w/ features, CD reviews, interviews & gig guide in print & web. Distro to music venues & Appalachian State University. Part of High Country media.

Raleigh/Durham/Chapel Hill

Independent Weekly
302 E Pettigrew St., Ste. 3A
Durham, NC 27701
p: 919-286-1972
f: 919-286-4274
www.indyweek.com
frequency: Weekly/Wed
circulation: 50,000
contact: Grayson Currin
ext: 919-286-1972 x153
e: gcurrin@indyweek.com
music lead: 3 Weeks
calendar: Katherine
e: calendar@indyweek.com
calendar lead: 10+ Days
College-town's free alt. provides extensive coverage for native talent & acts performing in Raleigh, Chapel Hill & Durham. Features acts & previews area gigs & releases; some nat'l presence. Area boasts strong Indie Rock, Hip-Hop & Alt. Country scene, but all styles are covered. Grayson also writes for Pitchfork. Promos: PO Box 2690, Durham, NC 27715.

The News & Observer
PO Box 191
Raleigh, NC 27602
p: 919-829-4500
f: 919-829-4647
www.newsobserver.com
frequency: Daily
circulation: 169,382 (Daily); 210,035 (Sun)
contact: David Menconi
ext: 919-829-4759
e: dmenconi@newsobserver.com
calendar: Jennifer Bringle
e: jbringle@nando.com
Statewide pub. has daily reviews & features w/ emphasis on acts playing area; calendar runs Fri. Part of McClatchy Newspapers, w/ sister reg'l pubs. The Cary News & Chapel Hill News.

Wilmington

Encore
PO Box 12430
Wilmington, NC 28405
p: 910-791-0688
f: 910-762-9177
e: email@encorepub.com
www.encorepub.com
frequency: Weekly
circulation: 15,000+
contact: Shea Carver
ext: 910-791-0688 x1004
e: shea@encorepub.com
music lead: 2 Weeks
calendar: Emily Rae
ext: 910-791-0688 x1006
e: emily@encorepub.com
calendar lead: 14 Days
Free A&E blankets greater Wilmington area & covers worldwide talent. Musicians can post on web blog.

North Dakota

Bismarck

The Bismarck Tribune
PO Box 5516
Bismarck, ND 58506
p: 701-223-2500; 800-472-2273
f: 701-223-2063
www.bismarcktribune.com
frequency: Daily
circulation: 30,000
contact: Tony Spilde
ext: 701-250-8260
e: tony.spilde@bismarcktribune.com
music lead: 2 Weeks
calendar: Clarissa Goldsack
ext: 701-250-8241
e: clarissa.goldsack@bismarcktribune.com
calendar lead: 1 Week
Sold throughout ND notes Fargo, Minot, Dickinson & some Williston gigs; Fri section has Local interviews, previews & reviews.

Fargo

The Forum
PO Box 2020, 101 5th St. N
Fargo, ND 58102
p: 701-235-7311
f: 701-241-5487
www.in-forum.com
frequency: Daily
circulation: 55,000 (Daily); 70,000 (Sun)
contact: Robert Morast
ext: 701-241-5518
e: rmorast@forumcomm.com
music lead: 1 Week
calendar: Diana Baumann
ext: 701-241-5541
e: calendar@forumcomm.com
calendar lead: 1 Week
Covers acts playing eastern ND & northwestern MN. Statewide distro.

High Plains Reader
322 Broadway, Ste. C
Fargo, ND 58102
p: 701-235-1553
f: 701-297-6139
e: hpr@hpr1.com
www.hpr1.com
frequency: Weekly/Thu
circulation: 10,000
contact: Matt Beshear
e: mattb@hpr1.com
music lead: 2 Weeks
calendar: John Strand
e: events@hpr1.com
calendar lead: 10 Days
Free alt. blankets western MN & eastern ND w/ features, CD & show reviews & previews for 20-50+ demographic. Also contact 'Best Bets' editor, Mitch Mars: bestbets@hpr1.com; 701-235-1553.

Ohio

Cincinnati/Dayton

Cincinnati City Beat
811 Race St., 5th Fl.
Cincinnati, OH 45220
p: 513-665-4700
f: 513-665-4369
e: letters@citybeat.com
www.citybeat.com
frequency: Weekly/Wed
circulation: 61,000
contact: Mike Breen
ext: 513-665-4700 x140

e: mbreen@citybeat.com
music lead: 2 Weeks
calendar: Maija Zummo
ext: 513-665-4700 x145
e: calendar@citybeat.com
Free A&E previews gigs, reviews releases & has extensive concert/club listings. Covers Dayton OH, northern KY, & southeast IN music life.

Dayton City Paper
322 S Patterson Blvd.
Dayton, OH 45402
p: 937-222-8855
f: 937-222-6113
e: contactus@daytoncitypaper.com
www.daytoncitypaper.com
frequency: Weekly/Wed
circulation: 15,000
contact: Russell Florence
ext: 937-222-8855 x213
e: cultureeditor@daytoncitypaper.com
music lead: 2+ Weeks
calendar: Dennis Porter
ext: 937-222-8855 x216
e: calendar@daytoncitypaper.com
calendar lead: 2+ Weeks
Free alt. covers metro area w/ in-depth calendar & features & reviews touring acts.

Cleveland/Akron

Akron Beacon Journal
44 E Exchange St., Box 640
Akron, OH 44309
p: 330-996-3000
f: 330-996-3033
www.thebeaconjournal.com
frequency: Daily
circulation: 144,000 (Daily); 184,000 (Sun)
contact: Malcolm X. Abram
ext: 330-996-3758
e: mabram@thebeaconjournal.com
music lead: 2-4 Weeks
calendar: Yvonne Bruce
e: listings@thebeaconjournal.com
calendar lead: 8 Days
Top metro w/ statewide distro has expanded indie-friendly music coverage in Thu & Sun editions. Previews & reviews area gigs.

Cleveland Scene Magazine
1468 W 9th St., Ste. 805
Cleveland, OH 44113
p: 216-241-7550
f: 216-802-7212
www.clevescene.com
frequency: Weekly
circulation: 100,000
contact: Jeff Niesel
ext: 216-241-7550 x210
e: jniesel@clevescene.com
music lead: 1 Week
calendar: Cris Glaser
ext: 216-241-7550 x280
e: cglaser@clevescene.com
calendar lead: 1 Week
Fave resource for northeast OH's 25-59 yr olds runs features & reviews local & touring acts w/ a buzz. Merged with sister pub. Cleveland Free Times.

The Plain Dealer
1801 Superior Ave. E
Cleveland, OH 44114
p: 800-688-4802
f: 216-999-6269
www.plaindealer.com
frequency: Daily
circulation: 800,000 (Weekly); 1,000,000 (Sun)
contact: Laura Demarco
ext: 216-999-4577
e: ldemarco@plaind.com
music lead: 3+ Weeks
calendar: Mark Rapp
ext: 216-999-4317
e: friday@plaind.com; mrapp@plaind.com
calendar lead: 3+ Weeks
Largest circ. in OH reviews, previews & profiles acts playing the Cleveland market & reviews local-nat'l releases. Part of S.I. Newhouse chain.

Columbus

Columbus Alive
62 E Broad St.
Columbus, OH 43215
p: 614-221-2449
f: 614-461-8746
www.columbusalive.com
frequency: Weekly/Thu
circulation: 55,000
contact: Melissa Starker
e: mstarker@columbusalive.com
music lead: 3 Weeks
calendar: Nikki Davis
e: ndavis@columbusalive.com
calendar lead: 1 Week
Free Columbia Dispatch alt. w/ distro throughout central OH extensively covers reg'l scene.

Columbus Dispatch
34 S 3rd St.
Columbus, OH 43215
p: 614-461-8838
f: 614-469-6198
www.dispatch.com
frequency: Daily
circulation: 250,000 (Daily); 300,000 (Sun)
contact: Aaron Beck
e: abeck@dispatch.com
music lead: 2 Weeks
calendar: Nikki Davis
ext: 614-221-2449
e: ndavis@columbusalive.com; weekender@dispatch.com
calendar lead: 2 Weeks
Conservative-leaning pub. part of Dispatch Broadcast Group, previews & covers metro area scene in Thu 'Weekender' & Sun 'This Week in the Arts' sections. Sister weekly ent. pub., Columbus Alive. Boxes located at area clubs & large venues.

The Other Paper
5255 Sinclair Rd.
Columbus, OH 43229
p: 614-847-3800
f: 614-848-3838
e: letters@theotherpaper.com
www.theotherpaper.com
frequency: Weekly/Thu
circulation: 53,000
contact: Richard Ades
e: rades@acncolumbus.com
music lead: 1 Week
calendar: Catherine McConnell
e: agenda@theotherpaper.com
calendar lead: Fri prior
Free ACN alt. news & ent. paper previews & reviews area gigs & interviews acts touring region. Distro at 900 retail stores & nightlife locations. Sister pub., Columbus Monthly, skews older.

Oklahoma

Oklahoma City

Oklahoma Gazette
3701 N Shartel
Oklahoma City, OK 73118
p: 405-528-6000
f: 405-528-4600
www.okgazette.com
frequency: Weekly/Wed
contact: Joe Wertz
e: jwertz@okgazette.com
music lead: 2 Weeks
calendar: Brandi Guthery
e: bguthery@okgazette.com
calendar lead: 1 Week
Free A&E covers metro music scene w/ CD reviews, show previews & reviews & features.

The Oklahoman
9000 N Broadway
Oklahoma City, OK 73114
p: 405-475-3311
f: 405-475-3971
www.newsok.com
frequency: Daily
circulation: 300,000
contact: Gene Triplett
ext: 405-475-4105
e: etriplett@oklahoman.com
music lead: 2 Weeks
calendar: Carolyn Flowers
ext: 405-475-3381
e: cflowers@oklahoman.com
calendar lead: 1 Month
Statewide calendar runs interviews, reviews & previews in Fri ent. section. Features editor: Sonya Colberg, scolberg@oklahoman.com. Owned by Opubco.

Tulsa

Urban Tulsa Weekly
710 S Kenosha
Tulsa, OK 74120
p: 918-592-5550
f: 918-592-5970
e: urbantulsa@urbantulsa.com
www.urbantulsa.com
frequency: Weekly/Wed
circulation: 35,000
contact: Gerry Hizer
e: ghizer@urbantulsa.com
music lead: 1 Month
calendar: Listings
e: events@urbantulsa.com
calendar lead: 10 Days
Cutting edge pub. for metro music scene coverage w/ show previews, profiles & CD reviews. Distro free to 1,000+ locations in metro area. Special music issues run 3/yr. Promos: PO Box 50499, Tulsa, OK 74150.

Oregon

Portland/Salem

Music Specator
Portland, OR
p: 360-314-2914
e: spectatormail@aol.com
www.musicspectator.com
frequency: Monthly
circulation: 100,000
contact: Craig Marquardo
e: fathommpc@aol.com
music lead: 60 Days
calendar lead: 1 Week
Columbia River Media music pub. includes interviews, new artist spotlights, reviews, comprehensive listings & produces 'Portland Music Awards.' Distro to 400+ Portland/Vancouver spots. Promos: 14407 NE 6th Ave., Vancouver, WA 98685.

Portland Mercury
605 NE 21st Ave.
Portland, OR 97232
p: 503-294-0840
f: 503-294-0844
e: mercuryeditorial@portlandmercury.com
www.portlandmercury.com
contact: Amy J. Ruiz
e: amy@portlandmercury.com
e: events@portlandmercury.com
Free local arts guide provides music, DJ listings & club guide. Area musicians can create Band Page on site.

Willamette Week
2220 NW Quimby St.
Portland, OR 97210
p: 503-243-2122
f: 503-243-1115
www.wweek.com
frequency: Weekly/Wed
circulation: 90,000
contact: Casey Jarman
e: cjarmen@wweek.com
music lead: 2+ Weeks
e: headout@wweek.com
calendar lead: 2 Weeks
Free alt. reviews releases & area gigs.

Pennsylvania

Allentown/Bethlehem

The Morning Call
101 N 6th St.
Allentown, PA 18101
p: 610-820-6500
f: 610-820-6693
www.mcall.com
frequency: Daily
circulation: 120,000 (Daily); 159,000 (Sat & Sun)
contact: Jodi Duckett
ext: 610-820-6704
e: jodi.duckett@mcall.com
music lead: 1-2 Weeks
calendar lead: 1 Week
Part of the Tribune family & offering broad music coverage thru southeastern PA & Warren county, NJ in Thu-Sat editions. Also distro 20,000 copies of free sister pub., 'Merge,' on Wed, which skews 18-34. Calendars for both incl. Philly, Scranton, Wilkes-Barre & Reading gigs.

Pulse Weekly
930 N 4th St., Ste. 205
Allentown, PA 18102
p: 610-437-7867
f: 610-437-7869
www.pulseweekly.com
frequency: Weekly/Wed
circulation: 20,000
contact: Mike Fallace
ext: 610-437-7867 x6
e: michaelf@pulseweekly.com
music lead: 2 Weeks
Free pub. promotes reg'l talent & acts playing in Allentown, Bethlehem, Easton & Reading w/ previews, reviews & gig calendar.

Harrisburg/Lancaster/York

Fly Magazine
22 E McGovern Ave.
Lancaster, PA 17602
p: 717-293-9772
f: 717-295-7561
e: info@flymagazine.net

www.flymagazine.net
frequency: Monthly
circulation: 45,000
contact: Jeff Royer
e: jeff@flymagazine.net
music lead: 1 Month
calendar lead: 1 Month
Free A&E targets readers 18-45 at central PA clubs. Previews & reviews all reg'l shows & runs extensive calendar. Submissions must incl. full names of all band members, genre, tour schedule & when record was released.

Harrisburg Magazine
3400 N 6th St.
Harrisburg, PA 17110
f: 717-232-6010
e: editor@harrisburgmagazine.com
www.harrisburgmagazine.com
frequency: Monthly
circulation: 20,000
contact: Patti Boccassini
ext: 717-233-0109 x130
e: pattib@harrisburgmagazine.com
music lead: 2 Months
calendar lead: 2 Months
Coverage of acts playing the Capital District's clubs, concerts & festivals for readers 35-55. Published by Benchmark Media Group. Also publishes annual A&E special issue in Sep (deadline for entries - Jul) and quarterly '717' Magazine.

Philadelphia

The City Paper
123 Chestnut St., 3rd Fl.
Philadelphia, PA 19106
p: 215-735-8444
f: 215-599-0634
www.citypaper.net
frequency: Weekly/Thu
circulation: 245,000
contact: Pat Rapa
ext: 215-735-8444 x202
e: pat@citypaper.net
music lead: 2 Weeks
calendar: Monica Weymouth
e: monica@citypaper.net
calendar lead: 1 Week
Free alt. targets readers 18-44. Extensive music coverage of greater Philly, southern NJ & 8 area counties. Distro in boxes, retail, bars & clubs.

Origivation
249 Market St.
Philadelphia, PA 19106
p: 215-922-1798
f: 215-922-1799
www.origivation.com
frequency: Monthly
circulation: 10,000
contact: Dominic Nicosia
e: dominic@origivation.com
music lead: 3 Weeks
calendar lead: 3 Weeks
Primo original music mag now under new mgmt., has expanded coverage to include entire indie universe. Artists & fans 21-34 in Philly/ S Jersey/Delaware get release news, interviews & gig info. Submit w/ online form; only mastered albums reviewed.

Philadelphia Weekly
1500 Sansom St., 3rd Fl.
Philadelphia, PA 19102
p: 215-563-7400
f: 215-563-0620
www.philadelphiaweekly.com
frequency: Weekly/Wed
circulation: 107,234
contact: Brian McManus
ext: 215-563-7400 x124
e: bmcmanus@philadelphiaweekly.com
music lead: 2+ Weeks
calendar: Erica Palan
e: listings@philadelphiaweekly.com; epalan@philadelphiaweekly.com
calendar lead: 10 Days
All eyes in Philly, Delaware & S Jersey are on this free alt. that covers the tri-state music scene. Distro in 2,000 yellow boxes. Owned by Review Publishing.

Pittsburgh

Pittsburgh City Paper
650 Smithfield St., Ste. 2200
Pittsburgh, PA 15222
p: 412-316-3342
f: 412-316-3388
www.pghcitypaper.com
frequency: Weekly/Wed
circulation: 72,000
contact: Aaron Jentzen
ext: 412-316-3342 x165
e: ajentzen@steelcitymedia.com
music lead: 2+ Weeks
calendar: Andy Mulkerin
ext: 412-316-3342 x194
e: happenings@steelcitymedia.com
calendar lead: 10 Days
Free alt. w/ extensive calendar covers acts playing western PA. Coverage may be picked up by 2 area Rock stations - classic Rock WRRK 97 & WLTJ Lite Rock, also owned by Steel City Media.

Pittsburgh Post-Gazette
34 Blvd. of the Allies
Pittsburgh, PA 15222
p: 412-263-1100
f: 412-263-1313
www.post-gazette.com
frequency: Daily
circulation: 200,000
contact: Scott Mervis
ext: 412-263-2576
e: smervis@post-gazette.com
music lead: 2 Weeks
e: magazine@post-gazette.com
calendar lead: 1 Week
Most widely read daily paper in western PA covers gigs & reviews mostly in Thu wknd mag. Artists playing in area submit music for review. Web gets 43 million pg views/mo. Expecting staff changes in early 2009.

Pittsburgh Tribune-Review
D.L. Clark Bldg.,
503 Martindale St., 3rd Fl.
Pittsburgh, PA 15212
p: 412-321-6460
www.pittsburghlive.com/x/pittsburghtrib
frequency: Daily
circulation: 150,000+
contact: Rege Behe
ext: 412-320-7852
e: rbehe@tribweb.com
music lead: Several Weeks
Daily pub. runs music coverage on site & in-print with focus on CD reviews Sun. Submit & search event listings: http://calendar.triblive.com. Additional music contacts: Mark Kanny, Classical Music: mkanny@tribweb.com, 412-320-7877; Bob Karlovits, Features Reporter/Jazz: bkarlovits@tribweb.com, 412-320-7852; Kellie Gormly, Country/Features: kgormly@tribweb.com, 412-320-7824.

Rhode Island

Providence

Providence Journal
75 Fountain St.
Providence, RI 02902
p: 401-277-7000
f: 401-277-8175
e: pjfeat@projo.com
www.projo.com/music
frequency: Daily
circulation: 165,000 (Daily); 230,000 (Sun)
contact: Phil Kukielski
ext: 401-277-7274
e: philk@projo.com
music lead: 2+ Weeks
calendar: Steve Smith
ext: 401-277-7265
e: stevensm@projo.com
calendar lead: 10 Days prior
Profiles bands playing the area & previews gigs in RI & parts of MA & CT. Distro all over RI & Bristol County, MA.

Providence Phoenix
150 Chestnut St.
Providence, RI 02903
p: 401-273-6397
f: 401-351-1399
www.providencephoenix.com
frequency: Weekly/Thu
circulation: 66,000+
contact: Lou Papineau
ext: 401-273-6397 x203
e: lpapineau@phx.com
music lead: 10 Days
calendar lead: 10 Days
Influential alt. part of the Phoenix Media Group runs features, show previews & CD reviews for readers ages 18-40. Statewide calendar includes some southern New England gigs. Runs annual Best Music Poll.

South Carolina

Charleston

Charleston City Paper
1049 B Morrison Dr.
Charleston, SC 29403
p: 843-577-5304
f: 843-576-0380
e: editor@charlestoncitypaper.com
www.charlestoncitypaper.com
frequency: Weekly
circulation: 40,000+
contact: T. Ballard Lesemann
ext: 843-577-5304 x118
e: ballard@charlestoncitypaper.com
music lead: 1 Week
calendar: Erica Jackson
ext: 843-577-5304 x130
e: calendar@charlestoncitypaper.com
calendar lead: 1 Week
Area's only free, left-leaning alt. is widely read by students & tourists for arts coverage. Local band directory & gigs also online. Include hi-res press photo.

Charleston's Free Time
PO Box 51448
Summerville, SC 29485
p: 843-873-3044
f: 843-821-5246
e: chfreetime@aol.com
frequency: Monthly
circulation: 7000
contact: Eddie Hogan
music lead: 1st Week of/mo
calendar lead: 1st Week of/mo
Free music mag w/ distro to 160+ clubs & music shops; previews & reviews shows at select NC, SC, GA & FL venues.

Columbia

Columbia's Free Times
PO Box 8295
Columbia, SC 29202
p: 803-765-0707
f: 803-765-0727
e: music@free-times.com
www.free-times.com
frequency: Weekly/Wed
circulation: 40,000
contact: Patrick Wall
ext: 803-765-0707 x138
music lead: 2 Weeks
calendar lead: 2 Weeks
A&E w/ distro thru the greater metro area covers reg'l-nat'l CD reviews & show previews. A Portico publication.

The State
1401 Shop Rd.
Columbia, SC 29201
p: 800-888-5353
f: 803-771-8430
www.thestate.com
frequency: Daily
circulation: 107,153 (Daily); 139,521 (Sun)
contact: Otis Taylor
ext: 803-771-8362
e: otaylor@thestate.com
music lead: 2+ Weeks
calendar lead: 1 Week
Web gets 750,000 unique visitors & 7 million pg views/mo & is SC's most highly trafficked site. McClatchey Co print version w/ statewide distro skews 18-34 & incl. interviews, reviews & previews of gigs & touring artists. Promos to: PO Box 1333, Columbia, SC 29202.

South Dakota

Rapid City

Rapid City Journal
PO Box 450
Rapid City, SD 57709
p: 605-394-8300
f: 605-394-8463
e: features@rapidcityjournal.com
www.rapidcityjournal.com
frequency: Daily
circulation: 28,000+
contact: Crystal Hohenthaner
ext: 605-394-8329
e: crystal.hohenthaner@rapidcityjournal.com
music lead: 2+ Weeks
calendar: Laura Tonkyn
ext: 605-394-8405
e: bhj@rapidcityjournal.com; laura.tonkyn@rapidcityjournal.com
calendar lead: 1+ Week

Fri wknd. section covers western SD music scene w/ interviews, reviews, previews & gig calendar in Lee Enterprises pub. Music Blog, 'Feedback & Distortion,' on web.

Sioux Falls

The Argus Leader
200 S Minnesota Ave.
Sioux Falls, SD 57104
p: 800-530-6397
f: 605-331-2294
www.argusleader.com
frequency: Daily
circulation: 65,000 (Daily); 80,000 (Sun)
contact: Brenda Wade Schmidt
ext: 605-331-2321
e: bschmidt@argusleader.com
music lead: 2-3 Weeks
calendar lead: 2-3 Weeks
Largest SD daily profiles local musicians of all genres. Mostly wire editorials.

Tennessee

Knoxville

Metro Pulse
602 S Gay St.
Knoxville, TN 37902
p: 865-522-5399
f: 865-522-2955
e: editor@metropulse.com
www.metropulse.com
frequency: Weekly/Thu
circulation: 40,000
contact: Matthew Everett
ext: 865-522-5399 x23
e: everettm@metropulse.com
music lead: 3 Weeks
calendar lead: 8 Days
Free alt. writes blurbs & features acts playing the area; CD reviews bi-weekly, mostly majors. Also runs articles on web. Distro into Knox County, Blount County and some parts of Anderson County. Prefers snail mail materials.

Memphis

Commercial Appeal
495 Union Ave.
Memphis, TN 38103
p: 901-529-2345; 800-444-6397
f: 901-529-2787
www.commercialappeal.com
frequency: Daily
circulation: 150,000 (Daily); 200,000 (Sun)
contact: Peggy Burch
ext: 901-529-2392
e: burch@commercialappeal.com
music lead: 2-4 Weeks
calendar: William Fason
ext: 901-529-2739
e: fason@commercialappeal.com
calendar lead: 2-4 Weeks
Daily coverage of TN, AK & MS events. Also profiles touring acts Fri; CDs reviewed Sat. Distro into AK, MS & MO.

The Memphis Flyer
460 Tennessee St., Ste. 200
Memphis, TN 38103
p: 901-521-9000
f: 901-521-0129
e: letters@memphisflyer.com
www.memphisflyer.com
frequency: Weekly
circulation: 55,000
contact: Chris Herrington
ext: 501-575-9428
e: herrington@memphisflyer.com
music lead: 2 Weeks
calendar lead: 2 Weeks
City's largest liberal alt. voice, owned by Contemporary Media covers Memphis scene w/ show previews — no show reviews. Sister pub., Memphis Magazine, contact Chris Herrington: 501-575-9428; herrington@memphisflyer.com

Nashville

The Nashville Scene
210 12th Ave. S, Ste. 100
Nashville, TN 37203
p: 615-244-7989
f: 615-254-4743
www.nashvillescene.com
frequency: Weekly/Wed
circulation: 55,000
contact: Tracy Moore
ext: 615-244-7989 x362
e: tmoore@nashvillescene.com
music lead: 2 Weeks
calendar: Steve Haruch
e: listings@nashvillescene.com
calendar lead: 2 Weeks
Free alt., part of City Press Publishing, previews area gigs w/ emphasis on TN talent.

The Tennessean
1100 Broadway
Nashville, TN 37203
p: 615-259-8000
e: living@tennessean.com
www.tennessean.com
frequency: Daily
circulation: 180,000
contact: Linda Zettler
ext: 615-259-8232
e: lzettler@tennessean.com
music lead: 2 Weeks
calendar: Listings
ext: 615-259-8300
e: calendar@tennessean.com
calendar lead: 2 Weeks
Daily coverage of reg'l & touring acts includes previews, features & CD reviews.

Texas

Austin

Austin American-Statesman
PO Box 670
Austin, TX 78767
p: 512-445-3607
f: 512-445-3968
www.austin360.com
frequency: Daily
circulation: 19,000 (Daily); 260,000 (Sun)
contact: Kathy Blackwell
e: kblackwell@statesman.com
music lead: 2 Weeks
calendar: Courtney Sebesta
ext: 512-445-3965
e: csebesta@statesman.com
calendar lead: 2 Weeks
Covers the Capital District w/ previews, reviews & interviews.

Austin Chronicle
PO Box 49066
Austin, TX 78765
p: 512-454-5766
f: 512-458-6910
www.austinchronicle.com
frequency: Weekly
circulation: 90,000
contact: Raoul Hernandez
e: music@austinchronicle.com
music lead: 1 Month
calendar: Anne Harris
e: aharris@austinchronicle.com
calendar lead: 2 Weeks
Primo free alt. by co-founders of famed SXSW Fest covers area's incredible scene for music fans 18-49+. Avail. at all clubs, shops & retail; expanded online ed. has artist directory & features; accepts MP3s & epks.

Dallas/Ft. Worth

Dallas Morning News
508 Young St., 4th Fl.
Dallas, TX 75202
p: 214-977-8222
e: guide@dallasnews.com; music@dallasnews.com
www.dallasnews.com; www.guidelive.com
frequency: Daily
circulation: 500,000 (Daily); 800,000 (Sun)
contact: Dawn Burkes
ext: 214-977-7790
e: dawn.burkes@dallasnews.com
music lead: 2-4 Weeks
calendar: Mike Daniel
e: mdaniel@dallasnews.com
calendar lead: 3 Weeks
Major read for Dallas, Ft. Worth, N Texas, & Austin incl. previews, calendar & profiles. Also runs daily coverage at Guidelive.com. Promos: PO Box 655237, Dallas, TX 75265.

Dallas Observer
2501 Oak Lawn Ave., Ste. 700
Dallas, TX 75219
p: 214-757-9000
f: 214-757-8593
www.dallasobserver.com
frequency: Weekly/Thu
circulation: 110,000
contact: Pete Freedman
ext: 214-757-8463
e: pete.freedman@dallasobserver.com
music lead: 1 Month
calendar: Rich Lopez
e: rich.lopez@dallasobserver.com
calendar lead: 2 Weeks
Metro alt. w/ free distro to shops & nitelife spots runs gig listings, features, CD reviews & local 'Spotlight.' Parent co., Village Voice Media.

Fort Worth Weekly
3311 Hamilton Ave.
Fort Worth, TX 76107
p: 817-321-9700
f: 817-335-9575
www.fwweekly.com
frequency: Weekly/Wed
circulation: 75,000
contact: Anthony Mariani
ext: 817-321-9717
e: anthony.mariani@fwweekly.com
music lead: 1 Week
calendar: Kristian Lin
ext: 817-321-9715
e: kristian.lin@fwweekly.com
calendar lead: Wed prior
Free alt. pub. runs in-depth CD reviews, preview blurbs & features, news, columns & comprehensive listings. Distro reaches Arlington & Denton.

Houston

Best in Texas Music Magazine
2500 Tanglewilde, Ste. 106
Houston, TX 77063
p: 713-952-9221
f: 713-952-1207
www.bestintexasonline.com
frequency: Monthly
circulation: 30,000
contact: Ed Shane
e: eshane@shanemedia.com; ed@bestintexasonline.com
music lead: 6 Weeks
calendar: Amy Lacey
e: amy@shanemedia.com
calendar lead: 6 Weeks
Focuses on TX talent w/ music calendar, concert photos & reviews written by TX radio programmers & MDs. Updated news on site. Free distro statewide, targets 21-44 demo. Prefers hard copies.

Houston Press
1621 Milam St., Ste. 100
Houston, TX 77002
p: 713-280-2400
f: 713-280-2496
www.houstonpress.com
frequency: Weekly/Thu
circulation: 110,000
contact: John Nova Lomax
ext: 713-280-2473
e: john.lomax@houstonpress.com
music lead: 2-3 Weeks
calendar: Brett Koshkin
ext: 713-280-2440
e: brett.koshkin@houstonpress.com
calendar lead: 2-3 Weeks
Progressive, free alt. boasts 16+ music editors & supports indie releases w/ emphasis on Alt. Country, Hip-Hop, Rock, Zydeco & Blues. Gig calendar covers 50mi & incl. Galveston. Distro in stores & restaurants in Houston & the surrounding areas. Music blog, 'HouStoned Rocks' at www.houstonpress.com. Snail mail promos, follow up w/ email.

San Antonio

San Antonio Current
915 Dallas
San Antonio, TX 78215
p: 210-227-0044
f: 210-227-6611
e: mailbag@sacurrent.com
www.sacurrent.com
frequency: Weekly/Wed
circulation: 46,000
contact: Jeremy Martin
e: jmartin@sacurrent.com
music lead: 2 Weeks
calendar: Nicole Chavez
ext: 210-227-0044 x244
e: nchavez@sacurrent.com
calendar lead: 2 Weeks
Times Shamrock Comm. free alt. w/ distro to venues, campuses, lifestyle stores & hotels, spotlights reg'l & nat'l touring acts. Moving after Sep '09.

San Antonio Express
400 3rd St.
San Antonio, TX 78287
p: 210-250-3000
f: 210-250-3405
www.express-news.com
frequency: Daily
circulation: 250,000
contact: Jim Beal
ext: 210-250-3435

e: jbeal@express-news.net
music lead: 1 Week
calendar: Stefanie Arias
ext: 210-250-3416
e: weekender@express-news.net
calendar lead: 1 Week
Hearst daily prints interviews, CD & show reviews; calendar runs Fri.

Utah

Salt Lake City

Salt Lake City Weekly
248 S Main St.
Salt Lake City, UT 84101
p: 801-575-7003
f: 801-575-6106
www.slweekly.com
frequency: Weekly/Thu
circulation: 60,000+
contact: Jamie Gadette
e: jgadette@slweekly.com
music lead: 2+ Weeks
calendar lead: 2+ Weeks
Free alt. from Copperfield Pub. focuses on indies w/ gig previews & reviews, CD reviews & features. Calendar covers Provo, Ogden & Park City.

SLUG Magazine (Salt Lake Underground)
351 W Piermont Ave., Ste. 4B
Salt Lake City, UT 84101
p: 801-487-9221
f: 801-487-1359
e: info@slugmag.com
www.slugmag.com
frequency: Monthly
circulation: 30,000
contact: Angela Brown
e: angela@slugmag.com
music lead: 45 Days
calendar: Jeanette Moses
e: jeanette@slugmag.com
calendar lead: 45 Days
Celebrated free music pub. skews 16-34 & covers underground scenes in UT, WY, ID & NV. Filled w/ previews & reviews of gigs & releases plus Metal, Goth & Hardcore columns. Extras on web.

Vermont

Burlington/ Montpelier

Burlington Free Press
PO Box 10
Burlington, VT 05402
p: 802-863-3441
f: 802-660-1802
e: living@bfp .burlingtonfreepress.com
www.burlingtonfreepress.com
frequency: Daily
circulation: 50,000
contact: Brent Hallenbreck
ext: 802-660-1844
e: bhallenb@bfp .burlingtonfreepress.com
music lead: 2+ Weeks
calendar: Donna Myers
ext: 802-660-0940
e: calendar@bfp .burlingtonfreepress.com
calendar lead: 2 Weeks
Gannett pub. & region's influential voice runs profiles, reviews & previews & includes some NH, upstate NY & Montreal gigs.

Seven Days
PO Box 1164
Burlington, VT 05402
p: 802-864-5684
f: 802-865-1015
e: pamela@sevendaysvt.com
www.sevendaysvt.com
frequency: Weekly/Wed
circulation: 30,000+
contact: Daniel Bolles
e: dan@sevendaysvt.com
music lead: 2-3 Weeks
calendar: Meghan Dewald
e: calendar@sevendaysvt.com
calendar lead: 2-3 Weeks
VT-centric alt. paper focuses on homegrown talent & acts playing the area. Widely read by college kids.

Virginia

Charlottesville

C-Ville Weekly
308 E Main St.
Charlottesville, VA 22902
p: 434-817-2749
f: 434-817-2758
e: editor@c-ville.com
www.c-ville.com
frequency: Weekly
circulation: 24,000
contact: Brendan Fitzgerald
ext: 434-817-2749 x40
e: brendan@c-ville.com
music lead: 1 Week
calendar lead: 3 Weeks
Free metro Portico Pub. reviews local & nat'l CDs & area gigs. Calendar includes 'Pick of the Week' spotlight - send hi-res images only.

Norfolk/ Virginia Beach

Daily Press
7505 Warwick Blvd.
Newport News, VA 23607
p: 757-247-4600
f: 757-247-4848
www.dailypress.com
frequency: Daily
circulation: 95,000 (Daily); 100,000 (Sun)
contact: Sam McDonald
ext: 757-247-4732
e: smcdonald@dailypress.com
music lead: 10 Days
calendar: Nicole Stanley
ext: 757-247-4737
e: nstanley@dailypress.com
calendar lead: 10 Days
Runs music bites every other day, more in depth w/ show previews Fri.

Port Folio Weekly
258 Granby St.
Norfolk, VA 23510
p: 757-222-3939
f: 757-363-1767
www.portfolioweekly.com
frequency: Weekly/Tue
circulation: 40,000
contact: Jeff Maisey
ext: 757-222-3934
e: jmaisey@pilotonline.com
music lead: 2 Weeks
calendar lead: 2 Weeks
Free alt. from Targeted Pub. distro to southeastern VA, w/ previews & reviews area gigs & all styles of local-nat'l releases. Send press photo w/ review or listing request.

The Virginian-Pilot
150 W Brambleton Ave.
Norfolk, VA 23510
p: 757-446-2000
f: 757-446-2963
www.pilotonline.com
frequency: Daily
circulation: 175,000
contact: Dan Duke
ext: 757-446-2546
e: dan.duke@pilotonline.com
music lead: 2 Weeks
calendar: Listings
e: listings@pilotonline.com
calendar lead: 10 Days
Landmark Communications pub. previews, reviews & interviews acts playing in southeastern VA incl. VA Beach & Richmond thru northeastern NC.

Richmond

Richmond Times Dispatch
300 E Franklin St.
Richmond, VA 23219
p: 804-649-6000
f: 804-649-6836
www.inrich.com
frequency: Daily
circulation: 175,000 (Daily); 200,000 (Sun)
contact: Melissa Ruggieri
ext: 804-649-6120
e: mruggieri@ timesdispatch.com
music lead: 10 Days
calendar: Pat Row
ext: 804-649-6731
e: prow@timesdispatch.com
calendar lead: 10 Days
Previews & reviews nat'l CDs & covers acts playing northern VA. Owned by Gateway VA Network.

Style Weekly
1313 E Main St., Ste. 103
Richmond, VA 23219
p: 804-358-0825
f: 804-355-9089
e: info@styleweekly.com
www.styleweekly.com
frequency: Weekly
circulation: 45,000
contact: Brandon Reynolds
ext: 804-358-0825 x347
e: brandon.reynolds@ styleweekly.com
music lead: 2+ Weeks
calendar: Craig Belcher
ext: 804-358-0825 x358
e: calendar@styleweekly.com; craig.belcher@styleweekly.com
calendar lead: 2+ Weeks
Free Landmark Comm. alt. A&E covers the Richmond, Norfolk & DC triangle w/ numerous previews, reviews, interviews, calendar & columns. Editor Picks & CD reviews include touring acts.

Roanoke

The Roanoke Times
201 W Campbell Ave.
Roanoke, VA 24010
p: 800-346-1234; 540-981-3340
f: 540-981-3318
e: kathy.lu@roanoke.com
www.roanoke.com
frequency: Daily
circulation: 70,000 (Daily); 110,000 (Sun)
contact: Tad Dickens
ext: 540-777-6474
e: tad.dickens@roanoke.com
music lead: 2 Weeks
calendar: Jennie Tal
ext: 540-981-3269
e: jennie.tal@roanoke.com
calendar lead: 2 Weeks
Mostly concert previews & reviews w/ ltd. club & CD reviews - emphasis on mainstream. Features considered for Thu pop culture insert. Distro to 19 counties by Landmark Communications.

Washington

Olympia

The Sitting Duck
1919 Evergreen Park Dr. SW #10
Olympia, WA 98502
p: 360-753-3836
e: info@thesittingduck.net
www.thesittingduck.net
frequency: Bimonthly
circulation: 10,000
contact: Terrence Knight
e: terrysittingduck@ peoplepc.com
music lead: 3 Weeks
calendar: Jessica S. Dillon
calendar lead: 3 Weeks
Publishes 1st & 3rd Thu of each mo. & targets 25-50 yr old sophisticated, politically conscious Urbanites. For features: send event info & availability of band 1mo prior. For live reviews: mention comp. tickets for reporter.

Seattle

Seattle Post Intelligencer
101 Elliott Ave. W
Seattle, WA 98119
p: 206-448-8000
f: 206-448-8216
www.seattlepi.com
frequency: Daily
circulation: 128,000
contact: Gene Stout
ext: 206-448-8383
e: genestout@seattlepi.com
music lead: 2+ Weeks
calendar: Lino Fernandez
ext: 206-448-8074
e: wh@seattlepi.com
calendar lead: 2+ Weeks
Hearst paper runs daily coverage plus extensive calendar & features on Fri. Known artists, buzz bands & returning touring acts are top priority. Sold statewide & incl. Tacoma gigs. Email brief bio w/ link to site & music - no attachments.

Seattle Times
PO Box 70
Seattle, WA 98111
p: 206-464-2200
f: 206-464-2261
e: arts@seattletimes.com
www.seattletimes.com
frequency: Daily
circulation: 300,000 (Daily); 500,000 (Sun)
contact: Patrick MacDonald
ext: 206-464-2312
e: pmacdonald@ seattletimes.com
music lead: 3 Weeks
calendar lead: 3 Weeks
Prints most club & CD reviews in Fri section. Distro throughout WA. Submit calendar listing at www.seattletimes.com/ submitlistings.

Seattle Weekly
1008 Western Ave., Ste. 300
Seattle, WA 98104

p: 206-623-0500
f: 206-467-4377
e: music@seattleweekly.com
www.seattleweekly.com
frequency: Weekly/Wed
circulation: 110,000+
contact: Brian Barr
e: bbarr@seattleweekly.com
music lead: 2 Weeks
calendar: Sara Brickner
e: events@seattleweekly.com; sbrickner@seattleweekly.com
calendar lead: 2 Weeks
Free alt. part of Village Voice Media, serves up Seattle scene w/ previews, reviews & interviews of acts playing region. Distro statewide & into BC, Canada.

The Stranger
1535 11th Ave., 3rd Fl.
Seattle, WA 98122
p: 206-323-7101
f: 206-323-7203
e: editor@thestranger.com
www.thestranger.com
frequency: Weekly
circulation: 400,000
contact: Eric Grandy
e: egrandy@thestranger.com
music lead: 3+ Weeks
calendar: Megan Seling
e: megan@thestranger.com; music@thestranger.com
calendar lead: 3+ Weeks
Edgy alt. hits 20-30 yr olds w/ disposable income & appetite for adventure w/ CD & gigs coverage. Distro free on every campus, corner & store. Music blog: http://lineout.thestranger .com. Web gets 690,989 unique visitors. Part of Index Newspapers.

Spokane

Pacific Northwest Inlander
1020 W Riverside Ave.
Spokane, WA 99201
p: 509-325-0634
f: 509-325-0638
www.inlander.com
frequency: Weekly/Thu
circulation: 46,000
contact: Luke Baumgarten
ext: 509-325-0634 x234
e: luke@inlander.com
music lead: 2+ Weeks
calendar: Tammy Marshall
ext: 509-325-0634 x225
e: calendar@inlander.com
calendar lead: 2 Weeks
Free alt. previews & reviews shows, runs artist profiles & reviews CDs based on release date. Distro to lifestyle spots.

West Virginia

Charleston/ Huntington

Charleston Gazette
1001 Virginia St. E
Charleston, WV 25301
p: 800-982-6397
f: 304-348-1233
e: gazz@wvgazette.com
www.thegazz.com
frequency: Daily
circulation: 50,000 (Daily); 100,000 (Sun)
contact: Roselle Earle
ext: 304-348-5115
e: earle@wzgazette.com
music lead: 2-3 Weeks
calendar: Amy Robinson
ext: 304-348-4881
e: flipside@wvgazette.com
calendar lead: 2 Weeks
Liberal pub. boasts largest circ. in WV & runs gig & CD reviews of local-touring acts in print & on web.

Graffiti
519 Juliana St.
Parkersburg, WV 26101
p: 304-485-1891
f: 304-428-2934
e: news@graffitiwv.com
www.grafwv.com
frequency: Monthly
circulation: 30,000
contact: Justin McIntosh
e: jmcintosh@graffitiwv.com
music lead: 1 Month
calendar lead: 1 Month
WV's largest alt. voice also services readers 18-35 in parts of VA, OH & KY. Runs extensive gig listings & reviews all styles w/ emphasis on S/S, Metal & indie acts touring the area. An Ogden Media pub.

Wisconsin

Madison

Isthmus
101 King St.
Madison, WI 53703
p: 608-251-5627
f: 608-251-2165
www.thedailypage.com
frequency: Weekly
circulation: 64,000
contact: Kenneth Burns
ext: 608-251-5627 x143
e: kburns@isthmus.com
music lead: 3+ Weeks
calendar: Bob Koch
ext: 608-251-5627 x163
e: calendar@isthmus.com
calendar lead: 3+ Weeks
Top area alt. runs calendar, supports homegrown talent & reviews nat'l releases. Posts reviews & club guide on Web. Distro to clubs & music stores.

Maximum Ink Music Magazine
PO Box 3245
Madison, WI 53704
p: 608-245-0781
f: 608-245-0782
e: info@maximumink.com; publicity@maximumink.com
www.maximumink.com
frequency: Monthly
circulation: 25,000
contact: Rokker
e: rokker@maximumink.com
music lead: 1.5 Months
calendar: Staff
e: calendar3@maximumink.com
calendar lead: 2nd Fri of/mo
Rock/Pop-based mag features, reviews & interviews acts playing area - reviewers from across USA & abroad. Extensive calendar & web incl. gigs in Chicago, Minneapolis & Duluth. Distro statewide & the surrounding areas. Owned by Maximun Inc., LLC.

Wisconsin State Journal
1901 Fish Hatchery Rd.
Madison, WI 53713
p: 608-252-6200
f: 608-252-6194
www.madison.com
frequency: Daily
circulation: 90,000 (Daily); 140,000 (Sun)
contact: Tom Alesia
ext: 608-252-6122
e: talesia@madison.com
music lead: 2-3 Weeks
Major metro paper in college town runs most coverage on Thu & Sun w/ profiles, show & CD previews & reviews of acts playing the area. Owned by Lee Enterprises, items may also run in sister paper, Capital Times. Sold thru south central & southwestern WI. Accepts digital kits, but snail mail preferred. For Capital Times reviews contact Rob Thomas: 608-252-6464; rthomas@madison.com - Calendar contact: Mark Lundey: 77cal@madison.com.

Milwaukee

The Milwaukee Journal Sentinel
333 W State St.
Milwaukee, WI 53203
p: 414-224-2919; 414-223-5250
f: 414-224-2133
e: jsmetro@ournalsentinel.com
www.jsonline.com
frequency: Daily
circulation: 250,000 (Daily); 400,000 (Sun)
contact: Tina Maples
ext: 414-223-5500
e: tmaples@journalsentinel.com
music lead: 3 Weeks
calendar: Calendar Editor
e: wkndcue@ournalsentinel.com
calendar lead: 2 Weeks
WI's largest daily & Journal Communications pub. runs features, profiles, previews & reviews; calendar covers southeast WI. Submit calendar listings online. Promos: PO Box 371, Milwaukee, WI 53201.

Shepherd Express
207 E Buffalo St., Ste. 410
Milwaukee, WI 53202
p: 414-276-2222
f: 414-276-3312
e: postmaster@shepherd-express.com
www.shepherd-express.com
frequency: Weekly/Thu
circulation: 73,000+
contact: Evan Rytlewski
ext: 414-276-2222 x218
e: evanr@shepherd-express.com
music lead: 1 Month
calendar: Rip Tenor
ext: 414-276-2222 x210
e: rip@shepherd-express.com
calendar lead: 1 Week
Free weekly alt. reviews new CDs & gigs in metro area. Daily web coverage.

Wyoming

Casper/Laramie

Casper Star Tribune
PO Box 80
Casper, WY 82604
p: 307-266-0500
f: 307-266-0568
www.trib.com
frequency: Daily
circulation: 30,000
contact: Kristy Gray
ext: 307-266-0586
e: kristy.gray@trib.com
music lead: 2-3 Weeks
calendar: Joel Burgess
ext: 307-266-0532
e: joel.burgess@trib.com
calendar lead: 1 Week
The only statewide pub. covers area gigs & some features.

The Laramie Daily Boomerang
320 Grand Ave.
Laramie, WY 82070
p: 307-742-2176
f: 307-742-2973
www.laramieboomerang.com
frequency: Daily
circulation: 56,000 (Daily); 59,000 (Sun)
contact: Deb Thomsen
ext: 307-742-2176 x326
e: newsone@laramieboomerang.com
music lead: 3 Days
calendar lead: 3 Days
Runs expanded music coverage - mostly show previews- weekly for 18-29 demo.

Jackson

Jackson Hole News & Guide
PO Box 7445
Jackson, WY 83002
p: 307-733-2047
f: 307-733-2138
e: editor@jhnewsandguide.com
www.jhnewsandguide.com
frequency: Weekly
circulation: 10,500
contact: Johanna Love
ext: 307-733-2047 x118
e: features@

jhnewsandguide.com
music lead: 1 Week
Free pub. runs calendar & previews area shows in the 'Stepping Out' section.

Canada

Alberta

Calgary

Calgary Herald
215 16th St. SE
Calgary, AB T2E 7P5 Canada
p: 403-235-7100
f: 403-235-7379
e: submit@theherald.canwest.com
www.calgaryherald.com
frequency: Daily
circulation: 120,000
contact: Heath McCoy
ext: 403-235-7462
e: hmccoy@theherald.canwest.com
music lead: 2 Weeks
calendar: Shelly Youngblut
e: syoungblut@theherald.canwest.com
Div. of CanWest Global offers daily A&E coverage to wide swath of the region. Listings run in Fri insert. Promos: PO Box 2400, Stn. M, Calgary, AB Canada, T2P 0W8.

Swerve Magazine
215 16th St. SE
Calgary, AB T2E 7P5
Canada
p: 403-235-7281
f: 403-235-7197
e: swerve@theherald.com
www.calgaryherald.com
frequency: Weekly
circulation: 120,000
contact: Going Out Editor
ext: 403-235-7268
e: swervelistings@theherald.canwest.com
music lead: 2 Weeks
calendar: Meghan Jessiman
e: mjessiman@theherald.canwest.com
calendar lead: 2 Weeks
Alt. weekly insert in Fri edition of Calgary Herald w/ comprehensive music listings (gigs & releases), feature articles & industry stories. Hosts Juno Awards & sponsors festivals; skews 20-55.

Edmonton

Edmonton Journal
10006 101 St.
Edmonton, AB T5J 0S1
Canada
p: 780-429-5200
f: 780-498-5677
e: journalfeedback@reachcanada.com
www.edmontonjournal.com
frequency: Daily
contact: Sandra Sperounces
ext: 780-429-5348
e: ssperounces@thejournal.canwest.com
music lead: 1 Week
calendar: Linda Mah
ext: 780-498-5779
e: lmah@thejournal.canwest.com
calendar lead: 1 Week
Indie-friendly CanWest pub. runs CD reviews & spotlights shows throughout northern Alberta.

Vue Weekly
10303 108th St
Edmonton, AB T5J 1L7
Canada
p: 780-426-1996
f: 780-426-2889
e: music@vueweekly.com
www.vueweekly.com
frequency: Weekly/Thu
circulation: 26,000
contact: Eden Munro
ext: 780-426-1996 x33
e: eden@vueweekly.com
music lead: 2+ Weeks
calendar: Glenys Switzer
e: listings@vueweekly.com
calendar lead: Fri prior
Independent alt. arts weekly also films bands performing in its office studio & posts on web. Covers local-nat'l acts of all styles; skews 18-49.

British Columbia

Vancouver

Vancouver Province
200 Granville St., Ste. #1
Vancouver, BC V6C 3N3
Canada
p: 604-605-2000
f: 604-605-2308
e: provletters@png.canwest.com
www.vancouverprovince.com
frequency: Daily
circulation: 500,000
contact: Stuart Derdeyn
ext: 604-605-2052
e: sderdeyn@theprovince.com
music lead: 2 Weeks
calendar: Julia Piper
ext: 604-605-2039
e: jpiper@theprovince.com
calendar lead: 1 Week
Widely read sister pub. to Vancouver Sun, presents most music coverage Thu w/ previews, reviews, profiles & gig calendar.

Vancouver Sun
200 Granville St., Ste. #1
Vancouver, BC V6C 3N3
Canada
p: 604-605-2000
f: 604-605-2323
e: info@png.canwest.com
www.vancouversun.com
frequency: Daily
circulation: 400,000+
contact: Juanita Ng
ext: 604-605-2868
e: jng@vancouversun.com
music lead: 2+ Weeks
calendar: Nancy Lanthier
ext: 604-605-2128
e: listings@png.canwest.com
calendar lead: 1 Week
Major metro paper read throughout BC, has expanded its music coverage. Tue, Thu & Sat editions include color photos, extensive reviews, features & profiles. Web incl. review of entire show & photo gallery. Owned by CanWest; sister pub. is Vancouver Province. Snail mail kits.

Victoria

Monday Magazine
818 Broughton St.
Victoria, BC V8W 1E4
Canada
p: 250-382-6188
f: 250-381-2662
e: editorial@mondaymag.com
www.mondaymag.com
frequency: Weekly/Thu
circulation: 40,000+
contact: Amanda Farrell
ext: 250-382-6188 x132
e: artseditor@mondaymag.com
music lead: 1 Month
calendar: Bill Stuart
ext: 250-381-6188 x136
e: calendar@mondaymag.com
calendar lead: 10 Days
Region's only alt. weekly provides a liberal voice & extensive coverage of indie scene for readers 18-34. Distro reaches Vancouver. Features show previews, artist profiles & CD reviews. Part of Black Press.

Nova Scotia

Halifax

The Metro Halifax
3260 Barrington St., Unit 102
Halifax, NS B3K 0B5 Canada
p: 902-444-4444
f: 902-422-5667
e: metrohalifaxinfo@metronews.ca
www.hfxnews.ca
frequency: Daily
circulation: 40,000+
contact: Philip Croucher
ext: 902-421-5812
e: philip.croucher@metronews.ca
music lead: 1 Week
calendar lead: 1 Week
Formerly The Daily News/HFX now has daily music coverage w/ CD reviews for local & estab. acts & runs gig guide. Free distro thru region & skews 20+.

Ontario

Ottawa

Ottawa xPress
309 Cooper St., #401
Ottawa, ON K2P 0G5
Canada
p: 613-237-8226
f: 613-237-8220
www.ottawaxpress.ca
frequency: Weekly/Thu
circulation: 40,000
contact: Cormac Rea
ext: 613-237-8226 x229
e: crea@ottawaxpress.ca
music lead: 1 Week
e: listings@ottowaxpress.ca
calendar lead: 1 Week
Region-wide alt. paper spotlights touring acts. Attracts teens thru 40 yr olds in Ottawa.

Toronto

The Globe and Mail
444 Front St. W
Toronto, ON M5V 2S9
Canada
p: 416-585-5000
e: newsroom@globeandmail.com
www.theglobeandmail.com
frequency: Daily
circulation: 900,000 (Daily); 1,000,000 (Sat)
contact: Robert Everette-Green
ext: 416-585-5489
e: reverette-green@globeandmail.com
music lead: 2 Weeks
calendar: Brad Wheeler
ext: 416-585-5656
e: bwheeler@globeandmail.com
calendar lead: 1 Week
Nat'l paper focuses on Canadian artists. Best day for music ads: Sat.

Now Magazine
189 Church St.
Toronto, ON M5B 1Y7
Canada
p: 416-364-1300
f: 416-364-1166
e: entertainment@nowtoronto.com
www.nowtoronto.com
frequency: Weekly/Thu
circulation: 300,000
contact: Benjamin Boles
e: music@nowtoronto.com
music lead: Fri prior to pub.
calendar: Tim Perlich
e: timp@nowtoronto.com
calendar lead: Fri prior
Music-friendly free alt. provides reviews, interviews & previews for Toronto-area.

The Spill Magazine
3055 Harold Sheard Dr.
Mississauga, ON L4T 1V4
Canada
p: 905-677-8337
f: 905-677-9705
e: info@spillmagazine.com
www.spillmagazine.com
frequency: Quarterly
circulation: 5000
contact: Arvin Kashyap
music lead: 1 Month
Free music mag keeps readers abreast of Toronto underground scene w/ interviews & reviews of local-int'l emerging artists & releases for the 19-39 college/alt./indie crowd. Distro to clubs, pubs & shops.

Toronto Life
111 Queen St. E, Ste. 320
Toronto, ON M5C 1S2
Canada
p: 416-364-3333
f: 416-861-1169
e: letters@torontolife.com
www.torontolife.com
frequency: Monthly
circulation: 92,970
contact: Sarah Fulford
e: editorial@torontolife.com
music lead: 3 Months
ext: 416-364-3333 x3061
e: thismonth@torontolife.com
calendar lead: 3 Months
Canada's most widely read daily mostly covers estab. acts & buzz bands playing the area.

Quebec

Montreal

Hour Magazine
355 W St. Catherine, 7th Fl.
Montreal, QC H3B 1A5
Canada
p: 877-631-8647
f: 514-848-9004
e: letters@hour.ca
www.hour.ca
frequency: Weekly
circulation: 60,000
contact: Jamie O'Meara
ext: 514-848-0777
e: jomeara@hour.ca
music lead: 2 Weeks
calendar: Ann-Marie Rivard
e: listings@hour.ca
Free alt. showcases reg'l talent w/ CD reviews & features. Part of Communications Voir.

Montreal Gazette
1010 W St. Catherine, Ste. 200
Montreal, QC H3B 5L1
Canada
p: 514-987-2222
f: 514-987-2638
e: arts&life@thegazette.canwest.com
www.montrealgazette.com
frequency: Daily
circulation: 100,000+
contact: Mark Tramblay
ext: 514-987-2560
e: mtramblay@thegazette.canwest.com
music lead: 2 Weeks
calendar: Derrick Ramsey
ext: 514-987-2577
e: listings@hour.ca
calendar lead: 2 Weeks
Daily pub. owned by CanWest Global Communications is Montreal's only English-language paper.

Montreal Tribune
PO Box 91,Stn. B
Montreal, QC H3B 3J5
Canada
e: montrealtribune@yahoo.ca
www.montrealtribune.com
frequency: Weekly
circulation: 120,000
contact: Conrad David Brillantes
ext: 514-992-4261
music lead: 2 Weeks
calendar: Jessica Ruano
e: ruano.jessica@gmail.com
calendar lead: 2 Weeks
Free alt. is distro to newsstands, bookstores & cafes in Montreal area. Owned by The Tribune Group.

Zines

365MAG
e: info@365mag.com; reviews@365mag. com
www.365mag.com
Dutch-based eZine runs reviews & interviews about int'l music w/ Electronic twist.

Absolute Punk
e: linda@absolutepunk.net
www.absolutepunk.net
Reviews, downloads, interviews & artist profiles w/ unsigned & upcoming bands.

Addicted to Punk
e: admin@addictedtopunk.com
www.addictedtopunk.com
Meets all your Punk & Alt. needs. Reviews all material submitted.

All About Jazz
e: mricci@allaboutjazz.com
www.allaboutjazz.com
Covers all aspects of Jazz w/ downloads, label spotlights, bulletin board & classifieds.

AllHipHop.com
e: music@allhiphop.com
www.allhiphop.com
Up-to-the-minute news, reviews, community board & streaming audio.

Alternative Addiction
e: chad@alternativeaddiction.com
www.alternativeaddiction.com
Music charts, contests, downloads & streaming audio/video promote Local-Int'l bands. Allow 2-4-wk lead time for CD reviews & features. No gig reviews. Promos: Box 210369, Auburn Hills, MI 48326.

Amped
e: cherrypie_13@hotmail.com
www.ampedreviews.net
CD & gig reviews, interviews & Band of the Month feat. for those in the Rock, Emo, Punk, Alt. & Indie world.

Aversion.com
e: info@aversion.com
www.aversion.com
Interviews, reviews, message boards & news for the Rock, Punk & Indie music scene. Also contests & complete artist listing w/ discography.

Blabbermouth
e: bmouth@bellatlantic.net
www.blabbermouth.net
Heavy music go-to site run & operated independently of Roadrunner Records. Promos: Keith Bergman, Box 20143, Toledo, OH 43610 & Scott Alisoglu, 5837 SW 24th Ter., Topeka, KS 66614.

Brooklyn Vegan
e: brooklynvegan@hotmail.com
www.brooklynvegan.com
NYC-centric, mostly-music blog has live show reviews, tour dates, & videos.

Chaos Control Digizine
e: chaoszine@gmail.com
www.chaoscontrol.com
Covers bands ignored by commercial press. Send promos to: Bob Gourley, Box 1065, Hoboken, NJ, 07030.

Christian Music Daily
e: mark@christianmusicdaily.com
www.christianmusicdaily.com
News & views about CCM & Gospel music. Email before sending press kits w/ CD, bio & photos.

Crave Magazine
e: editor@cravemagazine.com
www.cravemagazine.com
Covers cutting-edge music, art & culture. Send bio, contact info & material to: 1013 NE 68th St., Vancouver, WA 98665. No EPKs or 4 song demos.

The Daily Chorus
e: thedailychorus@gmail.com
www.thedailychorus.com
Updated daily w/ Indie music news & interviews. Releases quarterly issue w/ top 40 unsigned bands. Send material w/ contact info to: Box 266, Waddell, AZ 85355.

The Deli
e: thedelinyc@gmail.com
www.thedelimagazine.com
NYC-centric free print pub. & online zine focuses on Indie Rock & Folk music. Reviews, profiles & follows all aspects of active NYC area. NYC acts only send promos (no CD-Rs or hand-written pkgs) to: 37 W 20th St., Ste. 1006, NY, NY 10011 or submit MP3s online. Separate submissions for The Deli Los Angeles (www.thedelimagazine.com/la) & San Francisco (www.thedelimagazine.com/sf).

Delusions of Adequacy (DOA)
e: doa@adequacy.net
www.adequacy.net
Chock full of Pop, Metal, Rock, Folk & Punk reviews plus contests, message board & interviews. Music writers welcome. Updated daily.

Enough Fanzine
e: info@enoughfanzine.com
www.enoughfanzine.com
Non-profit fanzine covering Punk, Hardcore, Emo & Ska. Does not review artists outside the above genres. Send promos to: Box 12 07 05, 68058, Manheim, Germany.

FEMMUSIC
e: alex@femmusic.com
www.femmusic.com
Int'l online mag focusing on women in music in all genres. Send kits to: 1550 Larimer St. #511, Denver, CO 80202.

Flavorpill
www.flavorpill.com
Focuses on New York, Los Angeles, Chicago, San Francisco, Miami & London scenes.

Igloomag.com
e: editor@igloomag.com
www.igloomag.com
Covers Electronic, Experimental, Ambient, Techno & all the digital debris in between. Site updated daily from int'l-based contributors. Promos to: Box 307, Corona, CA 92856.

In Music We Trust
e: alex@inmusicwetrust.com
www.inmusicwetrust.com
Geared toward young Indie community. Feat. articles, show reviews & interviews. Full MP3 downloads avail.

Jazzreview.com
e: info@jazzreview.com
www.jazzreview.com
Promotes all styles of Jazz. Send 2 copies of bio, press kit, CD & other promo material to: 10101 Hunt Club Cir., Mequon, WI 53097. State style of Jazz in cover letter.

Junk Media
www.junkmedia.org
News & reviews the Indie Rock scene. Reviews updated daily, interviews added wkly. Send promos to: Junkmedia, c/o Laura Sylvester, 102 Sand Hill Rd., Shutesbury, MA 01072.

Keenly Observed
e: info@keenlyobserved.com
www.keenlyobserved.com
Hip music & pop culture-obsessed site covers wide variety of thought-provoking acts. Promos to: Box 52382, Atlanta, GA 30355.

LA'Ritmo.com - Latin Music Magazine
e: info@laritmo.com
www.laritmo.com
Interviews estab. & up-and-coming artists, top Latin charts, music news, reviews, music resource links & charts the latest hits. Avail. in English & Spanish.

Music Dish
e: info@musicdish.com
www.musicdish.com
Weekly newsletter tracks trends, news & profiles Rock, Alt., Electronic, Jazz, Blues, Pop & Country artists.

Nude As The News
www.nudeasthenews.com
An extensive Alt. music review site by & for music fans. Material to: Troy Carpenter, 9006 Ginnylock Dr., Indianapolis, IN 46256.

Paste Punk
www.pastepunk.com
Punk zine w/ columns, feat. & live/show reviews. Email jordan@pastepunk.com for mailing address to send demos. Does not review music w/ DRM software.

Pitchfork
e: news@pitchforkmedia.com
www.pitchforkmedia.com
Updated daily w/ news, commentary & reviews. Site is a significant influence in the Indie music world. Also runs annual festival. Promos to: 1834 W North Ave., #2, Chicago, IL 60622.

Pop Matters
e: editor@popmatters.com
www.popmatters.com
Renowned site produces daily broadcast of all things pop culture. Promos to: 1555 Sherman Ave., #324, Evanston, IL 60201.

Prefix Magazine
www.prefixmag.com
Live & CD reviews & special 'Shameless Self-Promo' forum for unsigned bands. Promos to: 80 Cranberry St., #5A, Brooklyn, NY 11201.

Punkmusic.com
www.punkmusic.com
Jam packed w/ news, reviews, interviews & band links. Also runs Fastmusic label.

Punknews.org
www.punknews.org
Inclusive site for Punk, Ska, Hardcore, Emo, Metal & Indie musicians/fans. Feat. news, reviews, release schedules, video of the week & a vinyl file.

Revolt Media
www.revolt-media.com
Online Loud Rock & Punk music zine w/ news, reviews & interviews, operated by Revolt Clothing. Material to: Box 646, Forked River, NJ 08731.

promotion & publicity

Promotion & Marketing

American Campus
5416 Studeley Ave.
Norfolk, VA 23508
p: 757-624-8448
www.americancampus.com
contact: Brian Friedman
e: brianfacc@aol.com
genres: All Styles
markets: USA College
Nat'l campus postering campaigns & maintenance.

Atlas Artist Spotlight
32 Ann St.
Clifton, NJ 07013
p: 866-378-9356
f: 866-378-9358
www.musiciansatlas.com
contact: Martin Folkman
e: martin@musiciansatlas.com
genres: All Styles
markets: Radio, Film & TV
The Musician's Atlas' comprehensive program for radio-friendly artists. Includes CD compilation serviced at USA & Canadian radio, music press retailers, film, TV & gaming music supervisors. Artists also featured in Atlas print publication, online & at industry & music events.
See Spotlight On Pages 8-13

Bender Music Group
PMB 455, 835 W Warner Rd., Ste. 101
Gilbert, AZ 85233
p: 877-290-7536
e: info@bendermusicgroup.com
www.bendermusicgroup.com
contact: Jon Bergen
e: jbergen@bendermusicgroup.com
genres: Pop
Trad. & digital distrib. & web marketing & design.

Big Moon Marketing
702 W Joppa Rd.
Towson, MD 21204
p: 410-821-6861
e: contact@bigmoonmarketing.com
www.big-moon.com
contact: Marian Matthis
genres: All Styles
Emphasis on print & web design.

Ch'rewd Marketing & Promotion
200 N Michigan Ave.
Chicago, IL 60601
p: 312-255-1151; 888-450-1151
e: info@chrewd.com
www.chrewd.com
contact: Chris Watkins
genres: Urban, Rock, Indie
formats: College, Commercial
markets: Reg'l, USA
Specializes in youth-oriented street & lifestyle marketing.

Concrete Marketing
163 3rd Ave., Ste. 125
New York, NY 10003
p: 212-645-1360
www.concreteplanet.com
contact: Russ Gerroir
ext: 212-645-1360 x122
e: russgerroir@concreteplanet.com
genres: Hard Rock, Alt., Punk
markets: USA, Canada
Top agency specializes in under 30 demographic.

Crazy Pinoy
PO Box 46999
Seattle, WA 98146
p: 206-604-1276
e: hiphop206@aol.com
www.crazypinoy.com
contact: Gene Dexter
genres: Urban, Alt.
formats: College
markets: USA
Breaks new releases, street marketing & college radio.

D Music
New York, NY 11432
p: 917-941-2748
e: dmusic_entertainment@hotmail.com
www.myspace.com/damselmusic
contact: Joanne Meyers
genres: Rock, Urban, Alt.
markets: USA
Services include booking, radio airplay & film/TV song placement.

Downtown Marketing
2087 Union St., #2
San Francisco, CA 94123
p: 415-567-5652
f: 415-567-5990
www.downtownmarketing.com
contact: Celia Hirschman
e: celia@downtownmarketing.com
genres: Rock, Alt., S/S, Pop
markets: USA
Develops strategies for artists, labels & managers.

FanBridge
www. FanBridge.com
genres: All Styles
markets: Int'l
Free email & mobile fan list management.

Fizzkicks
7562 Penn Dr., Ste. 100
Allentown, PA 18106
p: 800-504-7132
e: inquires@fizzkicks.com
www.fizzkicks.com
contact: Aaron Burton
ext: 800-504-7132 x50
genres: All Styles
Offers custom designed download cards.

Hatchet Man Presents
55 Spalding Tr. NE
Atlanta, GA 30328
p: 404-423-3349
www.hatchetman.com
contact: John Sweep
e: john@hatchetman.com
genres: All Styles
markets: Local-USA
Nationwide network of paid street marketing pros.

IndiePower.com
11054 Ventura Blvd., #333
Studio City, CA 91604
p: 818-505-1836
e: info@indiepower.com
www.indiepower.com
contact: Jay Warsinske
genres: Rock, Hip-Hop, Alt., Country, Urban, Electronic
markets: USA, Int'l
Promotion, distribution & marketing for indie artists, producers & labels.
See Ad On Page 45

LiveWire Ent. Sales & Marketing
282 Thrasher St.
Norcross, GA 30071
p: 770-441-7844
f: 770-441-3216
www.livewireent.biz
contact: Alexis Kelley
e: alexis@livewireent.biz
genres: Rock, Pop, Hip-Hop, Alt., Country, Blues, World
markets: USA
Work w/ labels & managers to develop Internet & retail marketing campaigns.

The maniaTV Network
3863 Steele St.
Denver, CO 80205
p: 303-295-5000
f: 303-295-3363
e: submissions@maniatv.com
www.maniatv.com
contact: Stefan Goldby
ext: 310-876-2735
e: stefan@maniatv.com
genres: Rock, Alt., Electronic, Hip-Hop, Pop
markets: Worldwide
Internet TV w/ genre music shows plays videos, interviews & live footage. Mark ATTN: Music Video Submission.

Massive Music
1227 Perry St.
Denver, CO 80204
p: 720-221-8370
f: 877-571-4521
e: questions@massivemusicamerica.com
www.massivemusicamerica.com
contact: Randall Fraiser
e: randall@massivemusicamerica.com
genres: Rock, Pop, World, Jazz, Electronic, New Age, Alt., Hip-Hop, Experimental
markets: USA, Canada, Int'l
Pkgs. include press & tour support, press kit & web design, radio promo, & video prod. & editing.

Motor Marketing
520 Butler Ave.
Point Pleasant, NJ 08742
p: 732-701-1022
e: info@motormarketingusa.com
www.motormarketingusa.com
contact: Indian
e: indian@motormarketingusa.com
genres: All Styles
markets: USA, Europe
Offshoot of Gig Records provides street teams & custom outfits fleet of vehicles w/ state-of-the-art mobile listening stations.

Myxer
245 N Ocean Blvd., Ste. 306
Deerfield Beach, FL 33441
e: artist@myxer.com
www.myxertones.com
genres: All Styles
markets: USA & Int'l
Largest & fastest growing site for mobile content.
See Ad On Page 41

Noisy Planet
507 Casazza St., Ste. A
Reno, NV 89509
p: 775-825-3234
www.noisyplanet.net
contact: Kevin Petersen
e: kpetersen@noisyplanet.net
genres: All Styles
markets: USA & Int'l
Online music community helping artists connect with fans, industry contacts other musicians and production resources.
See Ad On Page 261

One Lucky Guitar
1301 Lafayette St., Ste. 201
Ft. Wayne, IN 46802
p: 260-602-6672
e: hello@oneluckyguitar.com
www.oneluckyguitar.com
contact: Matt Kelley
e: matt@oneluckyguitar.com
genres: Rock, Americana, Indie, Country
markets: USA
Designs memorable graphics & promo items for artists & releases. No unsolicited material.
See Ad On Opposite Page

OurStage
321 Billerica Rd.
Chelmsford, MA 01824
p: 978-244-1440
e: community@ourstage.com
www.ourstage.com
genres: All Styles
markets: USA, Int'l
Top ranked artists receive significant career-building promo & support from industry and assortment of event partners.
See Ad On Page 1

PureVolume.com
515 Victoria Ave.
Venice, CA 90291
p: 310-526-1488
www.purevolume.com
genres: All Styles
Artists can create profile pages, upload songs and establish a social-networking community of fans, friends and industry insiders.

Sneak Attack Media
109 S 5th St., Ste. 601
Brooklyn, NY 11211
p: 646-429-8425
e: info@sneakattackmedia.com
www.sneakattackmedia.com
contact: Marni Wandner
e: marni@sneakattackmedia.com
genres: Indie Rock, Alt., Folk, Pop, Hard Rock, Hip-Hop, S/S
markets: USA, Int'l
Web publicity & promo.

Social Networks For Musicians
PO Box 16940
Sugar Land, TX 77496
p: 281-541-0981
e: info@socialnetworksformusicians.com
www.socialnetworksformusicians.com
contact: Madalyn Sklar
genres: All Styles
markets: USA, Int'l
Offshoot of GoGirlsMusic helps indies boost their presence on MySpace, Facebook, etc. No unsolicited material.

Sonicbids
500 Harrison Ave.
4th Fl.
Ste. 404R
Boston, MA 02118
p: 617-502-1388
www.sonicbids.com
contact: Artist Relations
genres: All Styles
Online service helps members find promo & performance opps at industry events like Popkomm, MIDEM, SXSW, CMJ & the Independent Music Awards.
See Ads On Pages 43, 125, 181 & 193

Stomp & Burn Promotions
2733 W Pecan Rd.
Phoenix, AZ 85041
p: 602-469-2074
f: 602-795-3529
e: megad45@cox.net
www.stompandburn.com
contact: Steve Johnson
genres: Metal, Rock, Top 40, Indie, Hip-Hop
markets: AZ
Supports releases at music & lifestyle shops w/ street teams, postering & release parties. Include bio w/ promo packs.

takeoutMARKETING
185 Franklin St.
2nd Fl.
New York, NY 10013
p: 212-871-0714
f: 212-871-0833
e: info@takeoutmarketing.com
www.takeoutmarketing.com
contact: Mori Ninomiya
e: mori@takeoutmarketing.com
genres: Pop, Rock, Electronic, Urban
formats: College
markets: USA
clients: Virgin Records, Universal, Lava Records, Sony
PR, grassroots & event marketing.

Toolshed
45 Belcher Rd.
Warwick, NY 10990
p: 845-988-1799
f: 845-988-2009
e: info@toolshed.biz
www.toolshed.biz
contact: Dick Huey
genres: Indie Rock, Electronic, Acoustic
markets: USA
Also does publicity.

Two Sheps That Pass...
401 Broadway, Ste. 804
New York, NY 10013
p: 646-613-1101
f: 786-513-0692
e: info@twoshepsthatpass.com
www.twoshepsthatpass.com
contact: Vera Sheps
e: vera@twoshepsthatpass.com
genres: All Styles
markets: USA
Online & brick & mortar retail marketing, street teams & background music placement.

Radio Promotion

432miles
PO Box 21721
Lehigh Valley, PA 18002
p: 215-264-5612
e: four32miles@aol.com; musicnominations@aol.com
www.taylorinteractive.com/432miles
contact: Ian Bruce
genres: Alt., Americana, Blues, Hip-Hop, S/S, Christian
formats: College, Public, Commercial
markets: USA, Canada
clients: Melissa Gibson, Snacks, Bohagey Bowes
Non-profit org has affordable rates.

Advance Alternative Media
7 W 22nd St., 4th Fl.
New York, NY 10010
p: 212-924-3005
f: 212-929-6305
www.aampromo.com
contact: Justin Gressley
e: justin@aaminc.com
genres: Alt., S/S, Rock, Punk, Experimental
formats: College, Public, Commercial Specialty Shows
markets: USA, Canada
clients: Modest Mouse, Clap Your Hands Say Yeah, The Yeah Yeah Yeahs
Promotes hip bands for youth market. Contact Caroline Borolla: caroline@aaminc.com for publicity.

Airplay Access/ Backstage Entertainment
26239 Senator Ave.
Harbor City, CA 90710
p: 310-325-9997
f: 310-427-7333
e: staff@airplayaccess.com
www.backstageentertainment.net
contact: Paul Loggins
genres: Top 40, AC, Country, Urban, Christian, Rock, College
markets: Int'l

Airplay Specialists
1100 18th Ave. S
Nashville, TN 37212
p: 877-999-9975; 615-321-0033
f: 615-321-2244
e: airplay4u@aol.com
www.airplayspecialists.com
contact: Kelly Bolick
e: kelly@airplayspecialists.com
genres: Country, Americana
formats: Commercial, CHR, Top 40, Specialty Shows
markets: USA
clients: Rosanne Cash, Billy Gilman, Shelby Lynne

Al Moss Promotion
PO Box 150788
Nashville, TN 37215
p: 615-297-0258
e: almosspromo@aol.com
www.almosspromotion.com
contact: Al Moss
genres: Americana
markets: USA
clients: Dwight Yoakam, Steve Earle, Robert Plant & Alison Krauss, Ryan Bingham
Contact before sending kits.

Americana Media Group
117 S 6th St.
Emmaus, PA 18049
p: 800-469-3780; 484-239-3219
www.americanamediapro.com
contact: Fred Boenig
e: rrrootsr@ptd.net
genres: Alt. Country, Roots, Americana
formats: Comm. & Non-Comm., College, Americana, AAA
markets: USA, Europe
clients: Doug Spartz, Yarn, Kevin Deal, Girls, Guns & Glory
Prime outfit for indie releases in the above genres. Deeply involved in Americana & Roots scenes.

Anya Wilson Promotion & Publicity
401 Richmond St. W, Ste. 220
Toronto, ON M5V 1X3
Canada
p: 416-977-7704
f: 416-977-7719
www.anyawilson.com
contact: Anya Wilson
e: awilson@netsurf.net
genres: All Styles
formats: Country, CHR, AC, Alt., College, Commercial
markets: Canada
clients: Alison Krauss, Blackie & the Rodeo Kings
Top firm specializes in Canadian mainstream radio.

Arete Multimedia
64 Dupont St., #2L
Brooklyn, NY 11222
p: 718-349-1681
e: info@arete100.com
www.onestopindieshop.com
contact: John Whiteman
e: john@arete100.com
genres: Rock, Pop, Alt., Urban
formats: College
markets: USA
clients: The Imperial Orgy, Williamson, Mike Comfort

Ask Me PR
4b The Landmark,
21 Back Turner St.
Manchester, M4 1FR UK
p: 44-161-834-7434
e: info@askmepr.com
www.askmepr.com
contact: Liam Walsh
e: liam@askmepr.com
genres: Alt., Pop, Dance, Electronic, Rock
markets: UK
clients: The Killers, The Enemy, The Ting Tings
Also does press & mgmt.

Bryan Farrish Radio Promotion
1828 Broadway, 2nd Fl.
Santa Monica, CA 90404
p: 310-998-8305
e: airplay@radio-media.com
www.radio-media.com
contact: Bryan Farrish
genres: Alt., Rock, Pop, Dance, Urban, Christian, Americana, Blues, Jazz
formats: Rock, Alt., AC, AAA, Urban, Christian, College
markets: USA, Canada
Focuses on developing acts.

Charterhouse Music Group
12 E Butler Ave., Ste. 201
Ambler, PA 19002
p: 215-641-0459
f: 215-540-0555
e: info@biffco.com
www.biffco.com/home.html
contact: Biff Kennedy
e: kennedy@biffco.com
genres: S/S, Jam, Folk, Pop
formats: AAA, Americana
markets: USA
clients: Warner Bros., KOCH, Bar/None, Sci-Fidelity
Also does artist mgmt & label consultation.

Comstock Records
PO Box 19720
Fountain Hills, AZ 85269
p: 480-951-3115
www.comstockrecords.com
contact: Frank Fara
e: fara@comstockrecords.com
genres: Country, Americana, Alt. Country, Gospel
formats: Country, Top 40
markets: USA, Europe, Australia
clients: Kevin Atwater, KC Williams, Shake Russell
Snail mail submissions.

dB Promotions & Publicity
1365 Yonge St., Ste. 211
Toronto, ON M4T 2P7
Canada
p: 416-928-3550
f: 416-928-3401
e: info@dbpromotions.ca
www.dbpromotions.ca
contact: Dulce Barbosa
e: dulce@dbpromotions.ca
genres: All Styles
formats: AC, Top 40 Rock, College, Country, CBC, CHR
markets: Canada
clients: Tupelo Honey, Jim Brickman, Amy Sky, Pavlo
Also does publicity. Mail CDs.

Distinctive Promo
PO Box 95
Hewlett, NY 11557
p: 516-792-1498
e: distinctivepro@optonline.net
www.distinctivepromo.com
contact: Calvin Grant
genres: Dance, Electronica, Urban, Pop
formats: College, Mix Shows
markets: USA
clients: Speakerboxx, Nassiri, Matthew Wroda, Jacinta
Call before sending material.

Electric Light Entertainment Group
6977 Dover Ct.
Highland, CA 92346
p: 951-805-3767
www.myspace.com/johnnymusicmngr
contact: Johnny Uhrig
e: johnnymusicmngr@aol.com
genres: Rock, Indie, Metal, Pop, Ambient, Country
markets: USA
clients: Franky Dee, Nathan Bennett, Seduced by Suicide

Flanagan's Radio & Retail Promotions
Los Angeles, CA
p: 800-858-6650; 323-876-7027
e: submissions@radioandretail.com
www.radioandretail.com
contact: Cyndi S.
formats: Rock, AAA, College
markets: Reg'l, USA
clients: Cody Chesnutt, A Perfect Circle, Primus

FM Odyssey Radio
1425 Holiday Blvd.
Merritt Island, FL 32952
p: 321-452-6036
e: fmodyssey@aol.com
www.fmodyssey.com
contact: Fred Migliore
genres: Indie, Folk, Rock
formats: NPR, Commercial, Streaming, Podcasts
markets: USA, Int'l

Good Forks Promotion
20 NW 5th Ave., Ste. 305
Portland, OR 97209
p: 877-749-5738
f: 503-922-1966

www.goodforks.com/promo
contact: Peter Nochisaki
e: peter@goodforks.com
genres: Punk, Garage, Rock, Alt., Indie, Alt. Country
formats: College
markets: USA, Canada
clients: She-Mob, The Graves Brothers Deluxe, Hudson Bell
Also a record label.

Groov Marketing & Consulting South
1813 N Ave. 46
Los Angeles, CA 90041
p: 877-GROOV32
f: 866-750-8104
e: info@groovmarketing.com
www.groovmarketing.com
contact: Josh Ellman
e: josh@groovmarketing.com
genres: Jazz, World
formats: Non-Comm.
markets: USA
clients: Blue Note, Columbia, Mack Avenue, Decca
NW: 503-286-0006.

Heavy Lenny Promotions
2343 31st St.
Santa Monica, CA 90405
p: 310-450-6224
f: 310-450-8822
contact: Lenny Bronstein
e: heavylenny90405@yahoo.com
genres: Rock, Blues
formats: Active Rock, AAA
markets: USA
clients: V-12, Pyramid, Sanctuary, Funzalo, New West

Howard Rosen Promotion
5605 Woodman Ave., Ste. 206
Van Nuys, CA 91401
p: 818-901-1122
f: 818-901-6513
e: anthony@howiewood.com
www.howiewood.com
contact: Howard Rosen
e: howie@howiewood.com
genres: Rock, Pop, Country, Christian, Gospel
formats: CHR, Hot AC, College, Active Rock, Specialty
markets: USA, Int'l
clients: Fall Out Boy, The Killers, Fiona Apple, Coldplay
Submit via Sonicbids.

Insomniac
PO Box 568587
Orlando, FL 32856
e: insom@mindspring.com
www.insomniaconline.com
contact: Iz-Real Basquetelle
genres: Hip-Hop
formats: College, Satellite, Web
markets: USA
clients: Kool Keith, Poison Pen, Knotz

International Music Marketing & Promotions
20959 US Hwy. 160
Forsyth, MO 65653
p: 417-546-3965
e: worldwidemusic@yahoo.com
www.members.tripod.com/~cmusic
contact: Charlie Beth
genres: Rock, Pop, Alt., Jazz, Urban, Electronica, S/S, Country
formats: Comm. & Public
markets: Int'l
clients: Moe Bandy, Tim Holcomb, The Kendals

Jeff McClusky & Associates
1644 N Honore St., 2nd Fl.
Chicago, IL 60622
p: 773-938-1212
f: 773-486-7090
www.jmapromo.com
contact: Mel Floss
e: mel@jmapromo.com
genres: Rock, Alt., Hip-Hop
formats: Hot AC, CHR, Rhythmic, Crossover, Alt.
markets: USA
clients: Coldplay, Kanye West, Green Day, Madonna
Send material w/ ATTN: New Artist Development.

Jerome Promotions & Marketing
2535 Winthrope Way
Lawrenceville, GA 30044
p: 770-982-7055
f: 770-982-1882
e: hitcd@bellsouth.net
www.jeromepromotions.com
contact: Bill Jerome
genres: Rock, Pop, Alt., Dance
formats: Alt., CHR, Top 40 R&B Crossover, AC, Hot AC
markets: USA
clients: Gwen Stefani, Will Smith, 3 Doors Down
Mail CDs w/ bio, phone & email.

Jerry Duncan Promotions
2 Music Cir. S., Ste. 205
Nashville, TN 37203
p: 615-251-0905
f: 615-251-9848
www.duncanpromo.com
contact: Jerry Duncan
e: jduncanpro@aol.com
genres: Country
formats: Comm. Specialty
markets: USA
clients: Toby Keith, Faith Hill, Alan Jackson,Tim McGraw, Allison Krauss
Breaks new Country acts via secondary radio outlets. Contact before sending kits.

Jerry Lembo Entertainment Group
742 Bergen Blvd., 2nd Fl.
Ridgefield, NJ 07657
p: 201-840-9980
f: 201-840-9921
www.lemboentertainment.com
contact: Jerry Lembo
e: jerry@lemboentertainment.com
genres: Pop, Rock
formats: AC, Hot AC, CHR
markets: USA
clients: No More Kings, kd lang, Peter Gabriel, Red Hot Chili Peppers, Shelby Lynne

KDM Promotion
4058 Crystal Springs Dr. NE
Bainbridge Island, WA 98110
p: 206-842-1146
e: kdmpromo@mindspring.com
www.mc-kdm.com
contact: Kathleen Monahan
genres: World, New Age, Ambient, Acoustic
formats: Public, College, Comm., AAA
markets: USA
clients: Eric Tingstad, Ken Bonfield, R. Carlos Nakai

Lee Arnold Marketing
8340 N Links Way
Milwaukee, WI 53217
p: 414-351-9088
f: 414-351-6997
www.leearnold.com
contact: Lee Arnold
e: lee@leearnold.com
genres: Rock, Alt., AAA
formats: Rock, Active Rock, Classic Rock, AAA, Alt.
markets: USA
Works mostly w/ labels & mgmt but willing to work directly w/ artist.

Lift
474 Greenwich St., Ste. 4S
New York, NY 10013
p: 212-274-9800
f: 212-274-9899
e: lebeau@promotion-us.com
www.promotion-us.com
contact: Carmine Potenza
e: carmine@promotion-us.com
genres: Electronic, Dance, World, Hip-Hop, Latin
formats: College, Comm. Specialty
markets: USA, Canada, Int'l
clients: Ministry of Sound, Last Gang Records, Asphodel
Works secondary outlets for Indie labels.

Lisa Reedy Promotions
275 Bonnie Briar Pl.
Reno, NV 89509
p: 775-826-0755
www.jazzpromotion.com
contact: Lisa Reedy
e: lisa@jazzpromotion.com
genres: Jazz, Blues, World
formats: College, Public, Community, Cable & Satellite
markets: USA, Canada, Int'l
clients: Pearl Django, Connie Evingson, Laura Caviani

Loggins Promotion & Marketing
26239 Senator Ave.
Harbor City, CA 90710
p: 310-325-2800
f: 310-427-7333
www.logginspromotion.com
contact: Paul Loggins
e: ploggins@logginspromotion.com
genres: Rock, Pop, Urban, S/S, Jazz, Country
formats: AAA, Alt., Country, College, Rock
markets: USA, Int'l
clients: UXL, Brad Paisley, David Fagin, Fransisca London

M:M Music
6230 Wilshire Blvd., #14
Los Angeles, CA 90048
p: 323-939-8206
f: 323-934-4553
www.mmmusicsite.com
contact: Rene Magallon
e: a3rene@aol.com
genres: S/S, AAA, Rock, Adult Rock
formats: AAA, Comm., Public
markets: USA
clients: Brett Dennen, Travis, The Kooks, Ingrid Michaelson

Main Street Marketing & Promotion
4517 Minnetonka Blvd., Ste. 104
Minneapolis, MN 55416
p: 952-927-4487
f: 952-927-6427
www.main-st.net
contact: Tom Kay
e: tomk@main-st.net
genres: Rock, Pop, S/S
formats: Top 40, AAA, Modern Rock, AC
markets: USA
clients: Tim McGraw, Busted, Joss Stone, Mercy Me

McGathy Promotions
119 W 23 St., Ste. 609
New York, NY 10011
p: 212-924-7775
f: 212-691-8303
e: staff@indegoot.com
www.indegoot.com
contact: Adam Lebenfeld
genres: Rock, Alt.
formats: Active Rock, Alt., Rock, Top 40
markets: USA
clients: Chevelle, Shine Down, Saliva, Theory of a Dead Man, Puddle of Mudd
No unsolicited material.

Mindbenders Music
504-470 Dundas St.
London, ON N6B 1W3
Canada
p: 519-432-5317
www.mindbenders.ca
contact: Greg Simpson
e: gregsimpson@mindbenders.ca; gregsimpson2001@rogers.com
genres: Rock, Pop
formats: Commercial
markets: Canada
clients: Shelly Rastin, Kim Mitchell, Wild Strawberries
Call before sending material.

Music - East West
601 Van Ness, #927
San Francisco, CA 94102
p: 415-673-4620
contact: Linda Romano
e: musicew736@earthlink.net
genres: Jazz, Indie, Electronica
formats: College, Satellite
markets: USA, Canada
clients: Carl Saunders, Paul Hanson, Wayne Wallace

Music Media Network
503-639 Dupont St.
Toronto, ON M6G 1Z4
Canada
p: 888-746-7234
e: radio@musicmedianetwork.com
www.musicmedianetwork.com
contact: Rita Di Michele
genres: Jazz, World, Pop, Rock, Country, Latin, Electronica, Dance, Reggae
formats: College, CHR, Rock, AAA, Hot AC, AC, Urban, Country, CBC
markets: Canada, USA, Europe
clients: Brand New Heavies, Us3, Tortured Soul, The Duhks, Los Lonely Boys
Promos: PO Box 503, Toronto, ON Canada M6G 1Z4.

MVP Entertainment
1187 Coast Village Rd., Ste. 1-549
Santa Barbara, CA 93108
p: 805-969-7095
f: 805-456-4370

www.mvpent.com
contact: Sam Kaiser
e: sam@mvpent.com
genres: Pop, Rock, AC
formats: AC, Alt., Active Rock
markets: USA
Also promotes to video outlets & websites. Must be copyrighted material.

National Record Promotion
137 N Larchmont Blvd., Ste. 500
Los Angeles, CA 90004
p: 323-658-7449
f: 323-650-7122
www.larryweir.com
contact: Larry Weir
e: lweir@larryweir.com
genres: Country, Alt., R&B
formats: AC, Top 40, AAA
markets: USA
clients: Heartland, Taj Mahal, Sean King, Crystal Waters

New World 'N Jazz
PO Box 194
Fairfax, CA 94978
p: 415-453-1558
f: 415-453-1727
e: newworldjz@aol.com
www.newworldnjazz.com
contact: Neal Sapper
genres: Jazz, World
formats: Jazz, Smooth Jazz, World
markets: USA
clients: Telarc/HeadsUp, Warner Brothers, Concord
E Coast office: Matt Hughes, matt@newworldnjazz.com; 732-835-5050.

Nice PR
PO Box 352
Portland, OR 97207
p: 866-475-3820; 503-848-9976
f: 503-848-8448
e: info@nicepromo.com
www.nicepromo.com
contact: Daniel Aucken
ext: 866-475-3820 x201
e: daniel@nicepromo.com
genres: Experimental, Electronic, Hip-Hop
formats: College, Hip-Hop, RPM, Alt., World, AAA, Specialty
markets: USA, Int'l
clients: Women, Dot Tape Dot, The Cape May, Arms & Sleepers, Fessenden

Notorious Radio
31-15 30th St., #1R
Astoria, NY 11106
p: 718-545-9816
e: notorious@notoriousradio.com
www.notoriousradio.com
contact: Liz Cousins
genres: Alt., Indie, S/S
formats: Alt. Specialty, Web, AAA/Non-Commercial
markets: USA, Int'l
clients: Sponge, Arthur Yoria, Shade, Bang Sugar Bang

Pirate!
145 Columbia St.
Cambridge, MA 02139
p: 617-256-8709
f: 248-694-2949
e: radio@piratepirate.com
www.piratepirate.com
contact: Steve Theo
e: steve@piratepirate.com
genres: Indie, Punk, Rock
formats: College, Specialty, Non-Comm.
markets: USA, Canada
clients: Astralwerks, Blu Hammock, Drive Thru Records
NYC office: 617-571-8043 & Nashville: 615-631-2997.

Planetary Group
63A Wareham St.
Boston, MA 02118
p: 617-451-0444
f: 617-350-3134
www.planetarygroup.com
contact: Adam Lewis
ext: 617-226-1036
e: adam@planetarygroup.com
genres: Alt., Pop, S/S, Electronic, Urban
formats: College, AAA, Comm. & Non-Comm., Specialty
markets: USA, Canada, Europe
clients: Kings Of Leon, Portugal The Man, Isobel Campbell, Mark Lanegan, Bon Iver, Longwave
Targeted radio & PR campaigns include on-air, print & new media exposure. Also performance opps. in China & Scandinovia. NYC office: 212-595-9509; LA: 310-450-4949.
See Ad On Opposite Page

plug music
PO Box 6333
Picton, ON K0K 2T0 Canada
p: 613-476-3696
f: 613-476-4619
e: info@plugmusicinc.com
www.plugmusicinc.com
contact: Bobby Gale
e: bg@plugmusicinc.com
genres: Rock, Alt., Pop, Urban
formats: CHR, Hot AC, Rock, Urban, Alt.
markets: Canada
clients: 54.40, Alexisonfire, Sleddogs, Rides Again, Blush

Powderfinger Promotions
47 Mellen St.
Framingham, MA 01702
p: 800-356-1155
f: 508-820-7920
www.powderfingerpromo.com
contact: David Avery
e: david@powderfingerpromo.com
genres: Pop, Rock, Jam, S/S, Jazz, Americana
formats: College, Public, AAA
markets: USA
clients: String Cheese Incident, Medeski, Martin & Wood, Dresden Dolls, 311
Also does publicity.

Radiodirectx.com
503-639 Dupont St.
Toronto, ON M6G 1Z4
Canada
p: 888-746-7234; 416-588-3841
e: radio@radiodirectx.com
www.radiodirectx.com
contact: Jesse King
genres: All Styles
formats: NPR, College, Commercial, Digital, Internet
markets: Canada, Int'l
clients: US3, Sugar Minott/Morgan Heritage, Los Lonely Boys, Men Without Hats

Radiopromotions
PO Box 20
Banbury, Oxfordshire
OX17 3YT UK
p: 44-129-581-4995
f: 44-129-581-4995
e: music@radiopromotions.co.uk
www.radiopromotions.co.uk
contact: Steve Betts
e: steve@radiopromotions.co.uk
genres: Rock, Pop, Alt., Dance
formats: AC, AAA, Commercial & Student
markets: UK
clients: Tom Fuller Band, Billy Ocean, Mike & The Mechanics, Donna Lewis

Serina Promotions
8225 5th Ave., Ste. 833
Brooklyn, NY 11209
p: 347-866-1584
e: info@serinapromotions.com
www.serinapromotions.com
contact: Gene Serina
ext: 718-680-0873
e: serpro@serinapromotions.com
genres: Dance, Urban, Jazz, Pop
formats: Dance, Jazz, Urban, Top 40, R&B
markets: USA, Int'l

Serious Bob Promotion
250 W 85th St., Ste. 11-D
New York, NY 10024
p: 212-580-3314
f: 212-580-4179
e: seriousbob@nyc.rr.com
www.seriousbobpromotion.com
contact: Bob Laul
genres: Rock., Prog, Blues
formats: AAA, Commercial & Non-Comm.
markets: USA
clients: Astralwerks, Eddie Vedder, The Dears, Ben Harper

Shut Eye Records & Agency
1180 Vickers St., 2nd Fl.
Atlanta, GA 30316
p: 678-986-5110
f: 678-302-9810
e: hello@shuteyerecords.com
www.shuteyerecords.com
contact: Pete Knapp
e: knapp@shuteyerecords.com
genres: Alt. Country, Roots, Folk, Americana
formats: College, Americana
markets: USA, Canada, Europe
clients: Wrinkle Neck Mules, BR5-49, Brian Jonestown Massacre, Ambulance Ltd.

Skateboard Marketing Ltd.
1150 Agnes Ct.
Valley Stream, NY 11580
p: 516-328-1103
f: 516-328-1293
e: skatebmkt@aol.com
www.skateboard-marketing.com
contact: Munsey Ricci
e: excuseking@aol.com
genres: Hard Rock, Punk, Hardcore, Industrial
formats: Active Rock, College, Commercial Metal/Rock
markets: USA, Canada, Europe
clients: Atlantic, Warner Brothers, Universal, Virgin

Songlines
68 S Moger Ave.
Mount Kisco, NY 10549
p: 914-241-3669
f: 914-241-3601
www.songlinesmusic.com
contact: Sean Coakley
e: sean@songlinesmusic.com
genres: Americana, S/S
formats: AAA, Specialty
markets: USA
clients: Barsuk, Ato, New West, Sub Pop, Merge
Nashville office: 615-298-2262.

Sound Advice
PO Box 2144
Wakefield, MA 01880
p: 781-246-7944
f: 781-246-3661
www.soundadvicemanagement.com
contact: Kimball Packard
e: kp@soundadvicemanagement.com
genres: S/S, Blues, Funk
formats: College, AAA
markets: USA
clients: Henry Butler, Ernie & the Automatics, Paul Sanchez, John Boutte

South Beach Marketing & Promotion
7332 Erin Ct.
Longmont, CO 80503
p: 303-952-0249
f: 866-485-3362
e: info@musicpromotion.com
www.musicpromotion.com
contact: Amanda Alexandrakis
e: amanda@musicpromotion.com
genres: Pop, Alt.
formats: AC, Hot AC, AAA
markets: USA, Australia
clients: John Mellencamp, Natalie Grant, Rascal Flatts
Owns Dalin Promotions; PH: 303-652-0326. Call first before sending kits.

SPECTRE Entertainment Group
4836 SW Scholls Ferry Rd., #261
Portland, OR 97225
p: 503-790-9000
f: 503-790-9010
e: meredith@spectregroup.net
www.spectremusic.com
contact: Dave Sanford
e: dave@spectremusic.com
genres: Alt., Hip-Hop, RPM, World, Jazz
formats: AAA, Non-Commercial Specialty, College
markets: USA, Canada
clients: Domino, Rhymesayers, Luaka Bop, Island Def Jam, Dap Tone

Team Clermont
191 E Broad St., Ste. 310
Athens, GA 30601
p: 706-548-6008
f: 706-548-0094
e: prpeople@teamclermont.com
www.teamclermont.com
contact: Lucas Jensen
ext: 706-543-9455
e: lucas@teamclermont.com
genres: Alt., Rock, Pop, Prog, Indie, AAA, Jazz
formats: College, Public, Commercial Specialty
markets: USA, Canada
clients: Domino, Asthmatic Kitty, Pinback, Polyphonic Spree
Also does publicity:Jensen or Jon Polk, 706-543-9455.

Tim Sweeney & Associates
31805 Temecula Pkwy., #551
Temecula, CA 92592
p: 951-303-9506
www.tsamusic.com
contact: Tim Sweeney
e: sweeney@tsamusic.com
genres: Alt., Rock, Folk, Jazz, S/S
formats: AAA, Commercial & Non-Commercial Specialty
markets: USA

Tinderbox Music
3148 Bryant Ave. S
Minneapolis, MN 55408
p: 612-375-1113
www.tinderboxmusic.com
contact: Brandon Day
e: brandon@tinderboxmusic.com
genres: Indie, Alt., Pop, Punk Americana, , Acoustic, Hip-Hop, Loud Rock
formats: College, Non-Comm.
markets: USA, Canada, Int'l
clients: Halloween, Alaska, The Honeydogs, Josh Rouse

Twin Vision
261 5th Ave., #1F
Brooklyn, NY 11215
p: 718-369-1370
e: twinvision@aol.com
www.twinvision.net
contact: Peter Hay
genres: Folk, Blues, S/S,

Rock, Alt., World
formats: AAA, Americana, College
markets: USA, Canada
clients: Orba Squara, Bottle Rockats, Bow Thayer

Vigilante
138 Sinclair Rd.
London, W14 0NL UK
p: 44-207-371-6244
e: vigilante@peroxidemusic.com
contact: Rupert Withers
genres: Rock, Pop
formats: USA UK Radio, European Rock Press
markets: UK, Europe
clients: K.K. Downing, Vixen, W.A.S.P., Twisted Sister
Also does Rock press & mgmt.

Vitriol Promotion
3421 5th Ave. S
Minneapolis, MN 55408
p: 612-871-4916
www.vitriolpromotion.com
contact: Jerry Steller
ext: 651-698-3066
e: jerry@vitriolradio.com
genres: Indie, Pop, Rock, Alt. Country, Electronic
formats: College, AAA, Commercial Specialty
markets: USA, Canada
clients: Astralwerks Records, Last Gang Records
Include phone # & email w/ submissions.

Publicity

230 Publicity
304 Hudson St.7th Fl.
New York, NY 10013
p: 212-675-8959; 718-643-0517
www.230publicity.com
contact: Lisa Gottheil
e: lisag@230publicity.com
genres: Indie Rock
markets: Nat'l
clients: Joe Shithead Keithley, Dizzee Rascal, The Only Children, Minus the Bear, Of Montreal
W Coast Office: 503-226-4264.

360 Media
PO Box 725188
Atlanta, GA 31139
p: 404-577-8686
e: info@360media.net
www.360media.net
contact: Tara Murphy
genres: All Styles
markets: Nat'l
clients: Telluride Blues & Brews, The Rock Boat, Atlanta Jazz Festival, Croc's Next Step Campus Tour, Underground Atlanta Peach Drop

Alex Teitz Media
1550 Larimer St., #511
Denver, CO 80202
p: 720-341-8567
www.alexteitzmedia.com
contact: Alex Teitz
e: alexteitzmedia@yahoo.com
genres: Rock, S/S, Metal
markets: Reg'l, Nat'l
clients: femmusic.com, Phil Jensen, Love.45, Rockers for Kids, Sons of Armageddon

Another Reybee Production
518 Gregory Ave., Ste. A-313
Weehawken, NJ 07086
p: 201-223-9078
e: info@reybee.com
www.reybee.com
contact: Rey Roldan
e: rey@reybee.com
genres: Rock, Indie Rock, Dance, Punk, Metal
clients: Mindless Self Indulgence, Bayside, Chiodos, Less Than Jake, Meat Beat Manifesto

Ariel Publicity & Cyber PR
389 12th St.
Brooklyn, NY 11215
p: 212-239-8384
f: 212-239-8380
www.arielpublicity.com
contact: Ariel Hyatt
e: ariel@arielpublicity.com
genres: All Styles
markets: Nat'l
Works w/ Indie artists & specializes in cyber PR.
See Ad On Page 237

AristoMedia
PO Box 22765
Nashville, TN 37202
p: 615-269-7071
f: 615-269-0131
e: info@aristomedia.com
www.aristomedia.com
contact: Jeff Walker
genres: Country, Christian
clients: Sonny Burgess, Charlie Daniels Band, Digital Rodeo, CCMA, CRB/CRS
Radio, video & publishing promotions.

Ashworth Associates
192 Spadina Ave., Ste. 302
Toronto, ON M5T 2C2
Canada
p: 416-603-6005
f: 416-603-9272
e: ashworth.associates@sympatico.ca
www.ashworthassociates.com
contact: Peter Ashworth
genres: Folk, Country, Jazz, Instrumental
markets: Canada
clients: Luba, Penny Lang, Mo Koffman, Famous People Players

Audio Crush PR
15 Albert Terr.
Bloomfield, NJ
07003
e: audiocrushpr@gmail.com
www.audiocrushpr.com
contact: Joelle Batelli
genres: All Styles
markets: Worldwide
Specializes in magazine-style press kits. Contact first.

Australian Music Marketing Abroad
PO Box 319
Fitzroy, Victoria 3065
Australia
p: 61-39-419-2828
e: amma@netspace.net.au
contact: Norman McCourt
genres: All Styles
markets: Int'l
clients: Steve Morse, Kitaro, Elvis Costello, Leo Slayer, Thunderclap Newman
Affiliated w/ over 100 Int'l labels, publishers & producers. Distributes world-wide A&R catalogue.

Backstage Entertainment
26239 Senator Ave.
Harbor City, CA 90710
p: 310-325-9997
f: 310-427-7333
e: staff@backstageentertainment.net
www.backstageentertainment.net
genres: All Styles
markets: Int'l

Ballin' PR
214 1/2 S Hamilton Dr.
Beverly Hills, CA 90211
p: 323-651-1580
f: 415-480-1644
www.ballinpr.com
contact: Nicole Ballin
e: nik@ballinpr.com
genres: Hip-Hop, R&B
markets: Nat'l
clients: Zion-I, Aceyalone, Kool Keith, Katmasta Kurt, Raheem Jamal

Big Hassle
44 Wall St., 22nd Fl.
New York, NY 10005
p: 212-619-1360
f: 212-619-1669
e: info@bighassle.com
www.bighassle.com
contact: Ken Weinstein
ext: 917-853-3858
e: weinstein@bighassle.com
genres: Rock, Pop, Jam, Indie, Jazz
markets: Nat'l
Also does mgmt.
No unsolicited material.

Biz 3
1321 N Milwaukee, Ste. 452
Chicago, IL 60622
p: 773-645-1035
f: 773-645-1470
e: information@biz3.net
http://biz3.net
contact: Kathryn Frazier
e: kathryn@biz3.net
genres: Rock, Experimental, Electronic, Hip-Hop
clients: Definitive Jux, The Stills, Atmosphere, The Streets, Vice Records

Black & White PR
PO Box 15349
Boston, MA 02215
www.blackandwhitepr.net
contact: Jen Malone
e: jen@blackandwhitepr.net
genres: Rock
clients: The American Black Lung, Broken Teeth, Fairmont, Gearhead Records, The High Court
Reps hip Local-Int'l bands.

BlackCat Talent & Entertainment Group
PO Box 26174
El Paso, TX 79926
p: 915-252-3174
e: info@blackcattalent.com
www.blackcattalent.com
contact: David O. Samaniego
genres: Latin, R&B, Pop, Alt., Country, Rock, Punk, Mexican
markets: USA, Mexico, Canada
Check site before emailing.
AZ office: 602-332-9150.

Bobbi Marcus PR & Events
131 N Bundy Dr.
Los Angeles, CA 90049

p: 310-889-9200
f: 310-889-0019
www.bobbimarcuspr.com
contact: Bobbi Marcus
e: bobbi.marcus@bobbimarcuspr.com
genres: Pop, R&B, Soul, Jazz, Rock
markets: Nat'l
clients: ASCAP, BET, Flavor Unit, Leiber & Stoller

Braithwaite & Katz
248 S Great Rd.
Lincoln, MA 01773
p: 781-259-9600
f: 781-259-9606
e: info@bkmusicpr.com
contact: Ann Braithwaite
e: ann@bkmusicpr.com
genres: Jazz, World, Klezmer
clients: Maria Schneider, Satoko Fujii, Jonas Hellborg, Danilo Perez, Montreal Jazz Fest
Contact before sending material.

Capital Entertainment
217 Seaton Pl. NE
Washington, DC 20002
p: 202-506-5051
f: 202-636-4006
www.capitalentertainment.com
contact: Bill Carpenter
ext: 202-636-7028
e: billcarpenter@capitalentertainment.com
genres: Gospel, Soul, Pop, Americana
clients: Candi Stanton, Bryan Wilson, Smitty, Vickie Winans, TD Jakes
No unsolicited material.

conqueroo
11271 Ventura Blvd., #522
Studio City, CA 91604
p: 323-656-1600
www.conqueroo.com
contact: Cary Baker
e: cary@conqueroo.com
genres: Rock, Country, S/S, Experimental, Pop, Alt., Blues, Americana, Soul, Cajun, Jazz
markets: Nat'l
clients: John Cale, Marshall Crenshaw, Vernon Reid, Michelle Shocked, Jill Sobule

Costa Communications
8265 Sunset Blvd., #101
Los Angeles, CA 90046
p: 323-650-3588
f: 323-654-5207
e: info@costacomm.com
www.costacomm.com
contact: Ray Costa
genres: Soundtracks, Rock, Pop, Jazz, R&B, Country, Alt., S/S, Latin, Zydeco, Roots
clients: Alan Menken, Jon Brion, John Debney, Milan Records

Covers Media
138 W 25th St., 7th Fl.
New York, NY 10001
p: 212-582-5400
f: 212-582-6513
e: lindac@ksapublicity.com
www.pressherepublicity.com
contact: Christine McAndrews
e: christine@pressherepublicity.com
genres: Rock, Pop, Dance, Country, Hip-Hop, Jazz, S/S
markets: Nat'l

Crash Avenue Publicity
120 Webster St., Ste. 217C
Louisville, KY 40206
p: 502-583-4001
f: 502-583-4001
www.crash-avenue.com
contact: Jeffrey Smith
e: jeffrey@crash-avenue.com
genres: Indie, S/S, Rock, AAA
markets: USA, Western Europe
clients: Superdrag, Ben Sollee, The Details, Kim Taylor, The Old Ceremony
Tour support & press campaigns.

Creative Service Co.
4360 Emerald Dr.
Colorado Springs, CO 80918
p: 719-548-9872
f: 719-599-9607
e: creatserv9@aol.com
contact: Randall Davis
genres: Folk, Blues, World, New Age, Jazz, Alt., Country, Children's
markets: Nat'l, Int'l
clients: The Rippingtons, David Lanz, Michael Martin Murphey, Judy Collins, Paul Winter

Danger Village
1620 W 18th St., 3rd Fl.
Chicago, IL 60608
p: 212-721-3792
e: dangervillage@gmail.com
www.dangervillage.com
contact: Beth Martinez
e: beth@dangervillage.com
genres: Dance, Indie, Rock, Electronic, Alt. Country
markets: Nat'l
clients: Freezepop, Skybox, Walter Meego, Winston Jazz Routine, Shipwreck
Specializes in event sponsorship.

Dera, Roslan & Campion
132 Nassau St., Ste. 691
New York, NY 10038
p: 212-966-4600
f: 212-966-5763
www.drcpublicrelations.com
contact: Vicki
e: vicki@drcpublicrelations.com
genres: Rock, Pop, Christian, Bluegrass, Classical, Opera, Jazz, Hip-Hop
markets: Nat'l

DL Media
124 Highland Ave.
Bala Cynwyd, PA 19004
p: 610-667-0501
f: 610-667-0502
www.jazzpublicity.com
contact: Don Lucoff
e: dlmediapr@covad.net; don@jazzpublicity.com
genres: Jazz, World, Blues
clients: Marsalis Music, Blue Note Records, Marian McPartland

Double XXposure
1 W 34th St., Ste. 201
New York, NY 10001
p: 212-629-9404
f: 212-629-9410
e: info@dxxnyc.com
www.dxxnyc.com
contact: Desiree
e: desiree@dxxnyc.com
genres: Urban, Gospel
markets: Nat'l
clients: Bishop Jordan, Cassanova, Niyoka, Dion Davis, Justyn Matthew
Also does mgmt.

Earshot Media
2626 Manhattan Ave., PMB 301
Hermosa Beach, CA 90254
p: 310-318-8995
f: 310-318-5121
e: earshotmedia@earthlink.net
www.earshotmedia.com
contact: Mike Cubillos
genres: Indie, Punk, Hardcore
markets: Nat'l
clients: Greeley Estates, National Product, Plain White T's, Reel Big Fish, Sherwood
Primarily works w/acts signed to indie or major labels, but will consider unsigned artists.

Ellis Creative
1603 Horton Ave.
Nashville, TN 37212
p: 615-298-2009
e: info@ellis-creative.com
www.ellis-creative.com
contact: Tamara Saviano
e: tsaviano@comcast.net
genres: Americana, Alt. Country, Country, Roots Rock, Bluegrass, S/S
markets: Nat'l
clients: Kris Kristofferson, Beth Nielsen Chapman, Radney Foster, Guy Clark, Sweet Honey In The Rock
Formerly Saviano Media.

Explosive PR
PO Box 31227
Los Angeles, CA 90031
p: 323-223-2767
e: info@explosivepr.com
www.explosivepr.com
contact: Kim Cooper
genres: Rock, Folk, Pop, Psychedelic, Punk, Oldies
markets: Nat'l
clients: The Willowz, Old Hat Records, Planting Seeds Records, Don't Knock the Rock Film Festival, Save the 76 Ball
Targeted mailings for select musical genres.

Fanatic Promotion
135 W 29th St., Ste. 1101
New York, NY 10001
p: 212-616-5558
f: 212-202-4551
e: info@fanaticpromotion.com
www.fanaticpromotion.com
contact: Joshua Bloom
ext: 212-616-5556
e: josh@fanaticpromotion.com
genres: Rock, Hip-Hop, Electronic
markets: Reg'l, Nat'l

Fly On The Wall Media
10002 Kent Rd.
Bloomington, IN 47401
p: 812-336-7938
f: 812-336-7938
e: fly@flyonthewallmedia.com
www.flyonthewallmedia.com
contact: Anthony Scott Piatt
ext: 812-345-0342
e: anthony@flyonthewallmedia.com
genres: Reggae, Indie Rock, Jazz, Alt. Country, Rhythm, Bluegrass, World, Americana
markets: Nat'l, Int'l
clients: The Skatalites, David Grisman/Acoustic Disc, The Zydeco Experience, Cubanismo, Kingman & Jonah

Foley Entertainment
PO Box 358
Greendell, NJ 07839
p: 908-684-9400
www.foleyentertainment.com
contact: Eugene Foley
e: eugenefoleymusic@aol.com
genres: Rock, Pop, Rap, Jazz, Instrumental, Children's
markets: Nat'l

FrontPage Publicity
4505 Indiana Ave.
Nashville, TN 37209
p: 615-383-0412
f: 615-523-1347
www.frontpagepublicity.com
contact: Kathy Best
e: kathy@frontpagepublicity.com
genres: Country
clients: Martina McBride, George Strait, Rodney Atkins, Miranda Lambert, Little Big Town
No unsolicited material.

Girlie Action Media & Marketing
59 W 19th St., Ste. 4A
New York, NY 10011
p: 212-989-2222
f: 212-989-1499
e: info@girlie.com
www.girlieaction.com
contact: Vickie Starr
ext: 212-989-2222 x101
e: vickie@girlie.com
genres: Rock, Pop, Dance, S/S
markets: Reg'l, Nat'l
clients: Beth Orton, Morrissey, Martha Wainwright, Rye Coalition, Suzanne Vega
No unsolicited material.

Good Cop PR
111-25 75th Rd.
Forest Hills, NY 11375
p: 718-261-0174
f: 718-261-0174
www.goodcoppr.com
contact: Perry Serpa
e: perry@goodcoppr.com
genres: All Styles
markets: Nat'l
clients: CIMS, The Slackers, Red Robot, The Slip, Ursula Points

Gorgeous PR
7551 Melrose Ave., Ste. 7
Los Angeles, CA 90046
p: 323-658-9146; 323-782-9000
f: 323-658-6189
e: info@gorgeouspr.com
www.gorgeouspr.com
contact: Versa Manos
e: versa@gorgeouspr.com
genres: World, Rock, Rap, Hip-Hop, Latin, Pop, Country
markets: Nat'l
Works w/ limited indie budget.

Great Scott P.R.oductions
4750 Lincoln Blvd., Ste. 229
Marina Del Rey, CA 90292
p: 310-306-0375
f: 310-821-9414
e: greatscottproductions@earthlink.net
www.greatscottpr.com
contact: Rick Scott
genres: Urban, Jazz, Pop, AC
clients: Earth, Wind & Fire, Rick Braun, Howard Hewett, Joyce Coolings, Jeff Golub
Also events, mgmt. & marketing.

Green Light Go Entertainment
812 Flowerdale St.
Ferndale, MI 48220
p: 248-336-9696
e: info@greenlightgopublicity.com
www.greenlightgopublicity.com
contact: Janelle Rogers
ext: 248-761-9370
e: jrogers@greenlightgopublicity
genres: S/S, Indie Rock, Pop, Americana
markets: Reg'l, Nat'l
clients: Belle & Sebastian, Foo Fighters, The Kills, Kings of Leon, Tegan & Sara

Hard Pressed Publicity
PO Box 49001
Austin, TX 78765
p: 512-236-0969
www.hardpressedpublicity.com
contact: Jo Rae DiMenno
ext: 512-554-2799
e: jorae@hardpressedpublicity.com
genres: Eclectic, Americana, Alt., S/S, Jazz
markets: Nat'l, Int'l
clients: Trish Murphy, Ian McLagan, Aimee Bobruk, Future Clouds & Radar

Hype Music Publicity & Promotion
51 Robinson St.
Toronto, ON M6J 1L4

Canada
p: 416-360-3775
e: gr8pr@aol.com
contact: Paula Danylevich
genres: Rock, Pop, Punk, Emo, Metal, Jazz, Urban
markets: Canada
clients: Bif Naked, Boys Night Out, Suzie McNeil, Goldfinger, The Mission District
$1500-$2500/mo retainer fee depending on scope of project.

ISL PR
303 5th Ave., Ste. 702
New York, NY 10016
p: 917-338-6199
f: 917-338-6515
e: islpr@aol.com
www.islpr.com
contact: Ida S. Langsam
ext: 212-541-7595
genres: Rock, Heavy Metal, Pop, Hard Rock, Alt., Emo, AAA, Alt. Country, Folk, S/S
markets: Nat'l
clients: 1964...The Tribute, Loudlife, The Shake, Nona Hendrix, Dan Ferrari
Also does image consultancy.

Jane Ayer PR
3000 Olympic Blvd., #2408
Santa Monica, CA 90404
p: 310-315-4881
f: 310-581-1335
www.janeayerpr.com
contact: Jane Ayer
ext: 310-581-1330 x101
e: jane@janeayerpr.com
genres: All Styles
markets: Nat'l

Jazz Promo Services
269 S Rte. 94
Warwick, NY 10990
p: 845-986-1677
f: 845-986-1699
e: jazzpromo@earthlink.net
www.jazzpromoservices.com
contact: Jim Eigo
genres: Jazz, Blues, World
markets: USA, Canada, Europe, Asia
clients: The Jazz Museum In Harlem, 33rd Annual Jazz Record Bash, Merkin Hall, Cape May Jazz Festival
Advises artists on career development, self-producing & media campaigns.

Jensen Communications
709 E Colorado Blvd., Ste. 220
Pasadena, CA 91101
p: 626-585-9575
f: 626-564-8920
e: info@jensencom.com
www.jensencom.com
contact: Michael Jensen
genres: Rock, Blues
markets: Reg'l, Nat'l
clients: Santana, Jackson Browne, Crosby, Stills & Nash

JLM PR
580 Broadway, Ste. 1208
New York, NY 10012
p: 212-431-5227
f: 212-431-6818
www.jlmpr.com
contact: Jody Miller
e: jody@jlmpr.com
genres: Hip-Hop, Reggae, Electronic, Rock, Alt., World, Jazz, R&B
markets: Nat'l
clients: Kanye West, Billy Idol, Roc-A-Fella Records, VP Records, Russell Simmons/Hip-Hop Summit Action Network

Kayos Productions
928 Broadway, Ste. 405
New York, NY 10010
p: 212-366-9970
f: 212-366-9978
www.kayosproductions.com
contact: Carol Kaye
e: carol@kayosproductions.com
genres: All Styles
markets: Nat'l, Int'l
clients: Ace Frehley, Blackmore's Night, Cy Curnin, Geoff Emerick, NYC Hit Squad

Last Call Agency
26 Church St., Ste. 300
Cambridge, MA 02138
p: 781-922-1238
f: 617-649-0061
e: info@lastcallagency.com
www.lastcallagency.com
contact: Susan Scotti
e: susan@lastcallagency.com
genres: Indie, Pop, Rock, S/S, Folk, Americana
markets: Reg'l, Nat'l
clients: The Everyday Visuals, Vinyl Skyway, Session Americana, Club Passim, Ramona Silver
Strong focus on Boston scene. Also does show promotion.

Latin Industry Connection
21434 Audrey Ave.
Warren, MI 48091
p: 305-454-2711
e: latinindustryconnection@gmail.com
www.latinindustryconnection.com
contact: Angela Star
e: angela@latinindustryconnection.com
genres: Latin, Urban
markets: USA & Int'l
clients: Gueroloco, Tavito y Balin, La Sombra, Final 4our
Publicity, mgmt. & booking for hispanic community.

Lotos Nile Media Marketing Music
PO Box 90245
Nashville, TN 37209
p: 615-298-1144
f: 615-279-9535
www.lotosnile.com
contact: Kissy Black
e: kissyblack@lotosnile.com
genres: Rock, Pop, World, Folk, Blues, Country, Roots, Americana, S/S, AAA
clients: Trey Anastasio & Orchestra Nashville, John Prine, Jeff Black, Pam Tillis, Suzy Bogguss

Luck Media
NOHO Lofts #106,
5355 N Cartwright Ave.
North Hollywood, CA 91601
p: 818-760-8077
f: 818-760-7399
e: info@luckmedia.com
www.luckmedia.com
contact: Steve Levesque
ext: 702-221-5825
e: steve@luckmedia.com
genres: All Styles
markets: Reg'l, Nat'l
clients: Kottonmouth Kings, Air Supply, Josie Cotton, Bordello Nightclub

Madison House Publicity
4760 Walnut St., Ste. 106
Boulder, CO 80301
p: 303-413-8308
f: 303-413-8314
e: publicity@madisonhousepublicity.com
www.madisonhousepublicity.com
contact: Carrie Lombardi
genres: Rock, Pop, Jazz, Electronic
markets: Nat'l
clients: Los Lobos, Keller Williams, Richie Havens, Sound STS9, Umphrey's McGee

Maelstrom Music PR
PO Box 4680
Crestline, CA 92325
p: 562-627-9251
e: maelstrompr@gmail.com
www.maelstrompr.com
contact: Curtis Smith
genres: All Styles
markets: Nat'l, Int'l
clients: Alyssa Suede, Patrick Cornell, SiX, Roger Len Smith, Unit F
Also placement for film & TV.

Mark Pucci Media
5000 Oak Bluff Ct.
Atlanta, GA 30350
p: 770-804-9555
f: 770-804-0027
e: mpmedia@bellsouth.net
www.markpuccimedia.com
contact: Mark Pucci
e: mark@markpuccimedia.com
genres: Roots, Country, Blues, Jazz, Folk
markets: Reg'l, Nat'l
clients: Stony Plain Records, Johnny A, Landslide Records, Dave's True Story, Train Wreck Records

Mazur PR
PO Box 2425
Trenton, NJ 08607
p: 609-448-7886
f: 609-448-7886
www.mazurpr.com
contact: Michael Mazur
ext: 609-462-9905
e: michaelmazurpr@yahoo.com; michael@mazurpr.com
genres: Alt., Rock, Blues, Electronic, Goth, Jazz, Metal
markets: Nat'l, Int'l
clients: Hermano, Level-C, Mortiis, Sahg

McGuckin Entertainment PR
500 Riverside Dr., Ste. 160
Austin, TX 78704
p: 512-478-0578
f: 512-707-1439
www.mcguckinpr.com
contact: Jill McGuckin
e: jill@mcguckinpr.com
genres: Americana, S/S, Rock, Folk, Country
markets: Reg'l, Nat'l
clients: Reckless Kelly, Kevin Fowler, Paula Nelson, nelo, South Austin Jug Band
No unsolicited material.

MG Limited
15 W 26th St., 12th Fl.
New York, NY 10010
p: 212-532-3184
f: 212-689-0617
e: info@mglimited.com
www.mglimited.com
contact: Tracy Mann
ext: 212-956-3906
e: tmann@mglimited.com
genres: Alt., World, Electronica
markets: Nat'l, Int'l
clients: Ani DiFranco, Jorge Drexler, Maria Rita, Lenine, Bajofondo Tango Club

Motormouthmedia
2525 Hyperion Ave., Ste. 1
Los Angeles, CA 90027
p: 323-662-3865
f: 323-662-3844
www.motormouthmedia.com
contact: Judy Miller
e: judy@motormouthmedia.com
genres: Indie, Electronic, Hip-Hop, World, Rock
clients: Animal Collective, Rza, Black Mountain, Bon Iver, Jamie Lidell
Call before sending material.

MSO
14724 Ventura Blvd., Ste. 710
Sherman Oaks, CA 91403
p: 818-380-0400
e: msoorg@aol.com
www.msopr.com
contact: Mitch Schneider
ext: 818-380-0400 x235
e: mschneider@msopr.com
genres: Alt., Rock, Country, Pop
markets: Nat'l
clients: Depeche Mode, Aerosmith, Vans Warped Tour, Sex Pistols, David Bowie
Promotes estab. & developing acts w/ a buzz.

Music House
40 St. Peter's Rd.
Hammersmith, London
W6 9BD UK
p: 44-208-563-7788
f: 44-208-748-9431
www.music-house.co.uk
contact: Simon Walsh
e: simon.walsh@music-house.co.uk
genres: Metal, Dance
markets: UK
clients: Justin Timberlake, R Kelly, Mark Morrison, Britney Spears, Sir Bob Geldof
No unsolicited material.

My Rock Star Killed Yours
PO Box 532
Manalapan, NJ 07726
p: 917-548-0795
e: info@myrockstarkilledyours.com
www.myrockstarkilledyours.com
contact: Karin Graziadei
e: pressus@myrockstarkilledyours.com; karin@liveloveleglon.com
genres: Hardcore, Rock
markets: Nat'l, Int'l
clients: Biohazard, Suicide City, Ashes Are Nutritious, And This Army, Fake H
European press for nat'l & int'l artists. Offices in NY, San Paulo & Amsterdam.

Nasty Little Man Media
110 Greene St., #605
New York, NY 10012
p: 212-343-0740
f: 212-343-0630
e: info@nastylittleman.com
www.nastylittleman.com
contact: Steve Martin
e: steve@nastylittleman.com
genres: Pop, Alt., Rock, Dance, Electronic, Hip-Hop
markets: Nat'l
clients: Radiohead, Mars Volta, Foo Fighters, Beck, Nine Inch Nails

No Problem Productions
260 Harrison Ave., Ste. 407
Jersey City, NJ 07304
p: 201-433-3907
f: 201-433-8635
e: noprob@mindspring.com
contact: Andrew Seidenfeld
genres: Reggae, Latin, World
clients: Cherish The Ladies, Rokia Traore, Sepeto Nacional, Keola Beamer, Inner Circle

NorthStar Entertainment
501-I S Reino Rd., #380
Thousand Oaks, CA 91320
p: 805-498-5880
f: 805-498-5246
e: info@northstar-ent.com
www.northstar-ent.com
contact: Sheryl Northrop
e: sheryl@northstar-ent.com
genres: Pop, Rock, Blues, Roots, Country, Folk, Americana, S/S, Jam
markets: Nat'l
clients: Lisa Loeb, MyTunes, Ted Russell Kamp, Adam Levy

Organic Entertainment
114 W 137th St.

New York, NY 10030
p: 718-349-0241
f: 646-452-4503
e: info@organicentertainment.net
www.organicentertainment.net
contact: Reena Samaan
e: reena@organicentertainment.net
genres: All Styles
markets: Nat'l
clients: Billy Harvey, We Fest, Cindy Alexander, The Majestic Twelve

PAI Media
6 Greenwich St., 6th Fl.
New York, NY 10014
p: 212-206-1598
f: 212-989-7058
www.paimedia.com
contact: Paula Amato
e: paula@paimedia.com
genres: Rock, Indie, Pop, Alt. Country, Folk
markets: Local-Nat'l
clients: Rodrigo y Gabriela, Andy Summers, A.K.A.C.O.D., Blue Rodeo, Robert Gomez
No unsolicited material.

PLA Media
1303 16th Ave. S
Nashville, TN 37212
p: 615-327-0100
f: 615-320-1061
www.plamedia.com
contact: Pamela Lewis
e: pam.lewis@plamedia.com
genres: Country, Pop, Rock, Alt.
markets: Nat'l
clients: Deborah Allen, Orleans, William Lee Golden, Pat Waters

Planetary Group
63A Wareham St.
Boston, MA 02118
p: 617-451-0444
f: 617-350-3134
www.planetarygroup.com
contact: Adam Lewis
e: adam@planetarygroup.com
genres: Alt., Pop, S/S, Electronic, Urban
markets: USA, Canada, Europe
clients: Kings Of Leon, Portugal The Man, Isobel Campbell, Mark Lanegan, Bon Iver, Longwave
Offices in NYC: 212-595-9509 & LA: 310-657-0447.
See Ad On Page 263

Porkpie Publicity
126 Shrewsbury Ct.
Pennington, NJ 08534
p: 609-575-1263
f: 609-730-1791
e: info@porkpiepublicity.com
www.porkpiepublicity.com
contact: Lee Micai
genres: Rock
markets: Eastern USA
clients: Groove Pocket, The Cryptkeeper Five, Audiot, Split Decision, Bigg Romeo
Offers free press kit evaluation.

The Press House
302 Bedford Ave., #13
Brooklyn, NY 11211
p: 718-302-1522; 646-322-4903
f: 718-302-1522
www.thepresshouse.com
contact: Dawn Kamerling
e: dawn@thepresshouse.com
genres: All Styles
markets: Nat'l, Int'l
clients: Judy Collins, John Wesley Harding, Brazz Tree, Jupiter One

Press Network
PO Box 176
Pleasant Shade, TN 37145
p: 615-677-6645
f: 615-677-6644
www.pressnetwork.com
contact: Lisa Shively
e: lisa@pressnetwork.com
genres: Country, Rock, Folk, Blues, Bluegrass
markets: Nat'l
clients: Robbie Fulks, Chris Knight, Will Kimbrough, The Steeldrivers, Gandalf Murphy & The Slambovian Circus of Dreams

The Press Office
1009 16th Ave. S
Nashville, TN 37212
p: 615-750-5938
f: 615-810-9492
e: thepathfinder@mindspring.com
www.thepressoffice.com
contact: Jim Della Croce
genres: Country, Rock, Folk
markets: Nat'l, Int'l
clients: John Anderson, Karissa, Robert Hazard, Justin Gaston, Aaron Tippin
Specializes in legend acts.

Presto PR
1550 Sudden Valley
Bellingham, WA 98229
p: 360-734-8315
f: 360-733-2149
e: info@prestopublicrelations.com
www.prestopublicrelations.com
contact: Lydia Sherwood
e: presto.ls@gmail.com
genres: Alt., Rock, Folk, World
markets: USA, Canada
clients: ADA, Clickpop Records, Keali'i Reichel, Connie Talbot, Makana

Propaganda Media Group
1538 W Hopkins St.
San Marcos, TX 78667
p: 512-535-2286
e: prop2@austin.rr.com
www.propagandamediagroup.com
contact: Vickie Lucero
e: prop1@austin.rr.com
genres: Americana, S/S, Folk, Pop, Indie Rock
markets: Reg'l, Nat'l
clients: Old Settler's Music Festival, Slaid Cleaves, Todd Snider, Adam Carroll, Ruthie Foster

Public Emily
56 Main St., Ste. 206
Northampton, MA 01060
p: 413-585-5111
f: 413-585-5899
e: info@publicemily.com
www.publicemily.com
contact: Emily Lichter
e: emily@publicemily.com
genres: Rock, Pop, S/S
markets: Reg'l, Nat'l
clients: Erin McKeown, Eleni Mandell, Allison Miller, Patty Larkin

The Publicity Connection
3 Haversham Loge,
Melrose Ave.
London, NW2 4JS UK
p: 44-208-450-8882
f: 44-208-208-4219
www.thepublicityconnection.com
contact: Sharon Chevin
e: sharon@thepublicityconnection.com
genres: Rock, Soul, Pop
markets: UK, Europe
clients: Girlschool, Nashville Pussy, Billy Idol, Black Crowes, Chris de Burgh

Publicity House
PO Box 121551
Nashville, TN 37212
p: 615-297-7002
f: 760-437-4633; 615-825-0094
e: publicityhouse@comcast.net
www.wildfirepublicity.net
contact: Sharon Eaves
e: wildfirepublicity@comcast.net
genres: Country
markets: Nat'l, Int'l
clients: John Berry, Ann-Marita, Rustie Blue, Ryan Daniel, Jokers Wild Band
Call before sending material to: Laura Claffey, PO Box 558, Smyrna, TN 37167.

Rainmaker PR
398 Columbus Ave., PMB #183
Boston, MA 02116
p: 617-445-4383
e: rnmkrpr@aol.com
www.rainmakerpublicrelations.com
contact: Rhonda Kelley
e: rkelley283@aol.com
genres: Rock, Pop, Alt., Roots, Folk, Dance, New Age, Ambient, Country, Electronica
markets: Nat'l, Int'l
clients: Kingen, Rustic Fiona Joy, Overtones, Davina Robinson, This Holiday Life, Hawkins
Myspace & Twitter marketing. Offers flat rates. No Hip-Hop or Metal.

Red Rooster Publicity & Marketing
2507 Crestmoore Pl.
Los Angeles, CA 90065
p: 323-982-1400
f: 323-982-1500
e: roosterpub@aol.com
contact: Dave Budge
genres: Rock, Country, R&B, Rap, Blues, American, Pop, Jazz
markets: Reg'l, Nat'l
clients: Etta James, Fabulous Thunderbirds, Arthur Adams, Levon Helm, Sally Kellerman

rock paper scissors
PO Box 1788
Bloomington, IN 47402
p: 812-339-1195
f: 801-729-4911
e: music@rockpaperscissors.biz
www.rockpaperscissors.biz
contact: Dmitri Vietze
genres: World, Latin, Reggae, Celtic, Americana
markets: Nat'l
clients: Kiran Ahluwalia, Ladysmith Black Mambazo, Seu George, Globalfest Lura

Sable Soul Entertainment
3250 Dickerson Pike, Ste. 202
Nashville, TN 37207
p: 615-258-1990
f: 615-258-1992
www.sablesoul.com
contact: Wendy Collins Squirewell
e: wendy@sablesoul.com
genres: Gospel, Soul, Pop, Hip-Hop, Jazz, R&B
markets: Nat'l
clients: Bunny DeBarge, Deborah Smith, Pettidee, June Rochelle, Marci Mason

Sacks & Co.
427 W 14th St., 3rd Fl.
New York, NY 10014
p: 212-741-1000
f: 212-741-9777
e: sacks@sacksco.com
www.sacksco.com
contact: Carla Sacks
genres: All Styles
markets: Reg'l, Nat'l
clients: Herbie Hancock, David Byrne, Queen Latifah, John Mayer, Emmylou Harris

Serge Entertainment PR
PO Box 2760
Acworth, GA 30102
p: 678-445-0006
f: 678-494-9269
e: sergeent@aol.com
www.serge.org/sepr.htm
contact: Sandy Serge
genres: All Styles
markets: Nat'l, Int'l
clients: Asia Featuring John Payne, I-Am-Unlimited Records, Rocket Scientists, Lacey D., Erik Norlander
Email before sending material.

Shore Fire Media
32 Court St., Ste. 1600
Brooklyn, NY 11201
p: 718-522-7171
f: 718-522-7242
e: info@shorefire.com
www.shorefire.com
contact: Marilyn Laverty
e: mlaverty@shorefire.com
genres: Jazz, Rock, Latin, Pop, Country, Classical
markets: Nat'l
clients: Bruce Springsteen, Elvis Costello, The Hold Steady, First Act, Tunecore

Susan Blond Inc.
50 W 57th St.
New York, NY 10019
p: 212-333-7728
f: 212-262-1373
e: publicity@susanblondinc.com
www.susanblondinc.com
contact: Susan Blond
genres: Hip-Hop, Jazz, Rock
markets: Nat'l
clients: Akon, Sean Paul, CIAM, Guru, Candlebox
Call before sending material.

Tsunami Group
314 York St.
Ste. 3
Jersey City, NJ 07302
p: 856-269-9518
f: 201-435-1547
e: info@tsunamigroupinc.com
www.tsunamigroupinc.com
contact: CJ Robinson
genres: Urban, Pop
markets: Nat'l, Int'l
clients: Lil Wayne, TQ, Jody Breeze, Sqad Up, Kapone,
Specializes in exposure, branding & marketing.

Vermillion Media
2520 Vestal Pkwy.
Box 321
Vestal, NY 13850
p: 201-665-3942
www.vermillionmediagroup.com
contact: Ellyn Solis
e: ellyn@vermillionmediagroup.com
genres: Pop, Alt. Indie
markets: Reg'l, Nat'l

Warm Fuzzy Publicity
57 Grant St.
Sloatsburg, NY 10974
p: 845-753-5088
www.warmfuzzypublicity.com
contact: Jerry Graham
e: jerry@warmfuzzypublicity.com
genres: Hard Rock, Metal, Punk, Hip-Hop
markets: Int'l
clients: Alesana, The Devil Wears Prada, Poison The Well, John Joseph, Misery Signals

xo publicity
1707 NE Jarrett St.
Portland, OR 97211
p: 503-281-XOXO
e: info@xopublicity.com
www.xopublicity.com
contact: Kaytea McIntosh
e: kaytea@xopublicity.com
genres: All Styles
markets: Nat'l
Punk bands contact: Gianna at gianna@xopublicity.com.

radio

Alabama

Birmingham/ Tuscaloosa

WAPR/WUAL 88.3/91.5 FM
905 University Blvd.
166 Reese Phifer Hall
Tuscaloosa, AL 35487
watts: 100,000
main: 800-654-4262; 205-348-6644
e: apr@apr.org
www.apr.org
webcast: Yes **podcast:** Yes
genres: Classical, Jazz, Folk, Blues, S/S
format: Public
reports to: Roots Music Report
md: David Duff
e: dbduff@apr.org
Some opps. w/ indie Folk & S/S. Signal covers Tuscaloosa & is repeated on 5 stations statewide. Has various specialty shows.

WUHT 107.7 FM
244 Goodwin Crest Dr., Ste. 300
Birmingham, AL 35209
watts: 100,000
main: 205-945-4646
request: 205-741-1077
www.hot1077radio.com
webcast: Yes
genres: R&B
format: Commercial/Urban AC
pd: John Long
e: john.long@citcomm.com
Citadel Broadcasting station blankets the metro Birmingham area w/ indies & on-air interviews.

Huntsville/Normal

WJAB 90.9 FM
PO Box 1687
Normal, AL 35762
watts: 100,000
main: 256-372-4051
request: 256-372-5861
www.aamu.edu/wjab
webcast: Yes
genres: Jazz, Blues, Roots Rock, R&B, Gospel, World
format: Public
reports to: SmoothJazz.com, R&R
pd: Ellen Washington
e: ewashington@aamu.edu
Airs music calendar & on-air opps. to 11 counties in AL, 4 counties in TN & parts of GA & MS.

WRTT 95.1 FM
1555 The Boardwalk, Ste. 1
Huntsville, AL 35816
watts: 100,000
main: 256-536-1568
request: 256-534-9595
www.rocket951.fm
webcast: Yes
genres: Rock
format: Commercial/Rock
pd: Lee Reynolds
e: reynolds@rocket951.fm
md: Freak Daddy
e: freakdaddy@rocket951.fm
Airs syndicated indie specialty show "Reg's Coffeehouse" to northern AL.

Mobile

WHIL 91.3 FM
4000 Dauphin St.
Mobile, AL 36608
watts: 100,000
main: 251-380-4685
request: 251-380-4691
e: whil@whil.org
www.whil.org
webcast: Yes **podcast:** Yes
genres: Jazz, New Age, Classical
format: Public
reports to: SmoothJazz.com, New Age Reporter
pd: Kris Pierce
e: kris@whil.org
Indie-friendly station sponsors live events. Strong signal reaches parts of MS & FL. Promos to: PO Box 8509, Mobile, AL 36689.

Montgomery/ Greenville

WJWZ 97.9 FM
4101-A Wall St.
Montgomery, AL 36106
watts: 3000
main: 334-244-0961
request: 334-395-9797
www.979jamz.com
webcast: Yes
genres: Urban, Hip-Hop
format: Commercial/Urban
pd: Doughboy
e: doughboy@bluewater broadcasting.com
Promotes indie Hip-Hop releases to metro area. Contact Jay Swift for "Local Battle of the Beats."

WKXN/WKXK 107.1/95.9/96.7 FM
563 Manningham Rd.
Greenville, AL 36037
watts: 4000/41,000
main: 334-382-6555
request: 334-382-9596
e: wkxn@wkxn.com
www.wkxn.com
genres: Hip-Hop, R&B, Gospel, Blues
format: Commercial
reports to: Mediabase
pd: Nic Allen
ext: 334-613-1071
e: nicallenwkxn@gmail.com
md: Roscoe Miller
May air notable indies to 22 counties in southcentral AL. Send promos to: PO Box 369, Greenville, Alabama 36037.

WLBF 89.1 FM
381 Mendel Pkwy. E
Montgomery, AL 36117
watts: 100,000
main: 334-271-8900
e: mail@faithradio.org
www.faithradio.org
webcast: Yes
genres: Christian
format: Public/Christian AC
pd: Bob Crittenden
e: bob@faithradio.org
md: Andrew Luthold
e: andrew@faithradio.org
Faith Broadcasting's signal covers central & south AL & FL Panhandle. Airs interviews, indies & some specialty shows.

WOPP 1290 AM
1101 Cameron Rd.
Opp, AL 36467
watts: 2500 day/500 nite
main: 334-493-4545
request: 800-239-3323
e: wopp@wopp.com
www.wopp.com
webcast: Yes
genres: Country, Gospel
format: Public/Country
reports to: Inside Country
md: Kayla Burleson
e: md@wopp.com
Indie releases reach area's 19-59 demographic. 61mi from Greenville.

WXFX 95.1 FM
1 Commerce St., Ste. 300
Montgomery, AL 36104
watts: 50,000
main: 334-240-9274
request: 334-860-9500
www.wxfx.com
genres: Rock
format: Commercial/Rock
pd: Rick Hendrick
e: rick1.hendrick@cumulus.com
Cumulus Broadcasting station has on-air opps. for artists touring the area. "Consumer's Guide to Rock" highlights Locals alongside new Rock, on Sun nite. Covers a 50-mi radius.

Arizona

Phoenix/Scottsdale/ Tempe

KEDJ 103.9 FM
4745 N 7th St., Ste. 410
Phoenix, AZ 85014
watts: 100,000
main: 602-648-9800
request: 602-260-1039
www.theedge1039.com
webcast: Yes
genres: Alt., Punk, Rock
format: Commercial
pd: Bruce St. James
e: bruce@rbgphx.com
md: Tim Virgin
ext: 602-682-9368
e: virgin@theedge1039.com
Airs indies to Phoenix metro area.

KJZZ 91.5 FM
2323 W 14th St.
Tempe, AZ 85281
watts: 100,000
main: 480-834-5627
e: mail@kjzz.org
www.kjzz.org
webcast: Yes
genres: Jazz, Blues
format: Public
reports to: Jazziz
pd: Scott Williams
md: Blaise Lantana
e: music@kjzz.org
NPR affiliate w/ some Blues & Acoustic Jazz shows covers Phoenix metro area.

Tucson

KFMA 92.1/101.03 FM
3871 N Commerce Dr.
Tucson, AZ 85705
watts: 60,000
main: 520-407-4500
request: 520-880-KFMA
e: theego@kfma.com
www.kfma.com
webcast: Yes
genres: Modern Rock, Alt.
format: Commercial
reports to: R&R
pd: Matt Spry
ext: 520-407-4570
e: matt@kfma.com
md: Chris The Ego
ext: 520-407-4590
e: ego@kfma.com
Sun nite "Test Department" spins indies, imports, new & underground music.

KXCI 91.3 FM
220 S 4th Ave.
Tucson, AZ 85701
watts: 50,000
main: 520-623-1000
request: 520-622-5924
www.kxci.org
webcast: Yes **podcast:** Yes
genres: AAA, Jazz, Pop, Rock, Hip-Hop, World, Americana, S/S, Classical, Alt. Country
format: Public
pd: Ginger Doran
md: Duncan Hudson
ext: 520-623-1000 x16
e: duncan@kxci.org
Station for non-mainstream releases & citizens, blankets southern AZ w/ on-air acts & Reg'l & indie music.

Arkansas

Fayetteville

KUAF 91.3 FM
U of Arkansas
747 W Dickson St.
Fayetteville, AR 72701
watts: 100,000
main: 479-575-2556
request: 800-522-KUAF
e: kuafinfo@uark.edu
www.kuaf.com
webcast: Yes
genres: Blues, Jazz, Folk, Classical, Celtic
format: Public/Classical
reports to: Cinemedia
pd: Kyle Kellams
ext: 479-575-6574
e: kkellam@uark.edu
md: P.J. Robowski
ext: 479-575-6574
e: pjrobows@uark.edu
Mostly Classical w/ some wknd specialty shows. News mag reaches parts of OK, KS & MO.

Little Rock

KABF 88.3 FM
2101 S Main St.
Little Rock, AR 72206
watts: 100,000
main: 501-372-6119
e: kabf@acorn.org
www.kabf.org
webcast: Yes
genres: Gospel, Alt., Jazz, Blues, Alt. Country, Bluegrass, Tejano
format: Public
pd: John Cain
e: programs@kabf.org
md: Jay King
ext: 501-993-0012
e: jcking@sbcglobal.net
"Voice of the People" transmits diverse programs for 60 miles, reaching into central AR & parts of LA, MS, MO, TN, & TX.

KUAR 89.1 FM
U of Arkansas/Little Rock,
5820 Asher Ave., Ste. 400
Little Rock, AR 72204
watts: 100,000
main: 501-569-8485
e: kuar@ualr.edu
www.kuar.org
webcast: Yes
genres: Jazz, Classical
format: Public
pd: Ron Breeding
ext: 501-569-8491
md: Wayne Angerame
ext: 501-683-7389
Primarily news station w/ a few hours of Local Jazz; sister station KLRE plays Classical music w/ some Local hosts.

California

Los Angeles

KCLU 88.3/102.3 FM
California Lutheran U, 60 W Olsen Rd., #4400
Thousand Oaks, CA 91360
watts: 3200
main: 805-493-3900
request: 805-493-9200
e: kclu@clunet.edu
www.kclu.org
webcast: Yes
genres: Jazz, Latin, Blues
format: Public
pd: Jim Rondeau
e: jrondeau@callutheran.edu
Indie music in the mix & on specialty shows heard thru Santa Barbara & Ventura county. Sponsors area concerts.

KCRW 89.9 FM
Santa Monica College
1900 Pico Blvd.
Santa Monica, CA 90405
watts: 6900
main: 310-450-5183
e: music@kcrw.org
www.kcrw.org
webcast: Yes **podcast:** Yes
genres: All Styles
format: Public
pd: Ruth Seymour
e: ruth@kcrw.org
md: Nic Harcourt
ext: 310-450-4646
e: nic.harcourt@kcrw.org
Influential station heard round the world, airs eclectic & indie specialty shows to Los Angeles & Orange counties on 89.9 FM & provides service to southern CA on different frequencies.

KCSN 88.5 FM
18111 Nordhoff St.
Northridge, CA 91330
watts: 3000
main: 818-677-3090
request: 818-885-5276
e: web@kcsn.org
www.kcsn.org
webcast: Yes
genres: Americana, Roots, Classical
format: Public/AAA
pd: Martin Perlich
e: mperlich@kcsn.org
Airs indies on wknd specialty shows w/ some student input to Los Angeles, Santa Monica, San Fernando & Santa Clarita Valley areas. On-air opps. for Classical artists only.

KMRJ 99.5 FM
1061 S Palm Canyon Dr.
Palm Springs, CA 92264
watts: 50,000
main: 760-778-6995
request: 760-235-6995
e: info@955theheat.com
www.995theheat.com
genres: Alt., Classic Rock
format: Commercial
reports to: R&R
pd: Thomas Mitchell
ext: 760-778-6995 x2
e: tom@m995.com; thomas@995theheat.com
Indies & Acid Jazz, Reggae, Hip-Hop & Techno reach Coachella Valley.

KROQ 106.7 FM
5901 Venice Blvd.
Los Angeles, CA 90034
watts: 5500
main: 323-930-1067
request: 800-520-1067
www.kroq.com
webcast: Yes
genres: Alt., Rock
format: Commercial
reports to: FMQB, R&R, Hits
pd: Kevin Weatherly
e: kevin@kroq.com
md: Lisa Worden
Influential station airs music & on-air opps. throughout LA & Orange county.

KXLU 88.9 FM
One LMU Dr., Malone 402
Los Angeles, CA 90045
watts: 3000
main: 310-338-2866
e: laurenkxlu@gmail.com
www.kxlu.com
webcast: Yes
format: Public/Freeform
reports to: CMJ
pd: Megan Dembkowski
e: megankxlu@gmail.com
md: Matt
e: mattkxlu@gmail.com
Acclaimed station hosts LA club shows. Covers the west LA, San Fernando & San Gabriel Valley areas. Popular Fri PM "Demolisten" showcases indies. For Specialty Shows, contact: Eddie Becton, idojazz@aol.com; Lydia Ammossow, loungegirl@gmail.com or Michelle Krupkin, melodyfairkxlu@yahoo.com. No unsolicited material.

Sacramento

KMUD/KMUE/KLAI 91.1/88.3/90.3 FM
PO Box 135
Redway, CA 95560
watts: 5500
main: 707-923-2513
request: 707-923-3911
e: kmud@kmud.org
www.kmud.org
webcast: Yes **podcast:** Yes
genres: AAA, World, Jazz
format: Public
reports to: CMJ, Living Blues, New Age Reporter
md: Kate Klein
ext: 707-923-2513 x109
e: md@kmud.org
Community station airs music & on-air opps. to a 200-mile radius over 3 transmitters.

KOZT 95.3/95.9 FM
110 S Franklin St.
Fort Bragg, CA 95437
watts: 35,000
main: 707-964-7277
request: 707-964-0095
e: thecoast@kozt.com
www.kozt.com
genres: Rock, Folk, Jazz
format: Commercial
reports to: FMQB, R&R
pd: Tom Yates
md: Kate Hayes
e: kate@kozt.com
Mainly estab. acts but open to new artists. Books Local & Nat'l acts at annual "Whale Festival" & "Local Licks Live." Signal covers Mendocino County.

KRXQ 98.5 FM
5345 Madison Ave.
Sacramento, CA 95841
watts: 50,000
main: 916-334-7777
request: 916-766-5000
www.krxq.net
genres: Rock
format: Commercial/Active Rock
reports to: FMQB, Hits
pd: Jim Fox
ext: 916-339-4231
e: jfox@entercom.com
md: Pat Martin
e: pmartin@entercom.com
Airs Local & indie music to the metro area & sponsors area gigs. "Local Licks," w/ Mark airs Sun at 10pm.

KVMR 89.5 FM
401 Spring St.
Nevada City, CA 95959
watts: 2000
main: 530-265-9073
request: 530-265-1555
www.kvmr.org
webcast: Yes
genres: Americana, Blues, Folk, World, Jazz, Pop
format: Public/AAA
reports to: CMJ, AMA
pd: Steve Baker
ext: 530-265-9073 x211
e: programming@kvmr.org
md: Alice MacAllister
ext: 530-265-5531
e: music@kvmr.org
Indies in rotation & on specialty shows. On-air opps. broadcast into Sierra/Tahoe region.

KWOD 106.5 FM
5345 Madison Ave.
Sacramento, CA 95841
watts: 50,000
main: 916-334-7777
request: 916-766-1065
e: musicoffice@kwod.net
www.kwod.net
genres: Alt., New Rock
format: Commercial
reports to: R&R, FMQB, Mediabase
pd: Curtiss Johnson
e: cjohnson@entercom.com
md: Andy Hawk
e: ahawk@entercom.com
Also airs specialty shows & "New Music Pods" to the Valley. For specialty shows, contact: DJ David X at dfoster@entercom.com.

KXJZ 88.9 FM
7055 Folsom Blvd.
Sacramento, CA 95826
watts: 50,000
main: 916-278-8900
request: 916-278-JAZZ
e: info@capradio.org
www.capradio.org
webcast: Yes **podcast:** Yes
genres: Classical, Jazz, Blues, Alt., Rock, World, Latin Rhythm
format: Public/AAA
reports to: JazzWeek, CMJ
pd: Carl Watanabe
ext: 916-278-8905
e: programs@capradio.org
md: Gary Vercelli
ext: 916-278-8958
e: jazz@capradio.org
Blankets northern CA w/ indie releases & specialty shows.

San Diego

KIFM 98.1 FM
1615 Murray Canyon Rd., Ste. 710
San Diego, CA 92108
watts: 28,000
main: 619-297-3698
request: 619-570-3698
www.kifm.com
webcast: Yes
genres: Jazz
format: Commercial
reports to: R&R, SmoothJazz.com, Yellow Dog
pd: Mike Vasquez
e: mikev@jpc.com
md: Kelly Cole
e: kelly@kifm.net
Many specialty shows & on-air opps. reach all of southern CA.

KIOZ 105.3 FM
9660 Granite Ridge Dr., Ste. 100

San Diego, CA 92123
watts: 50,000
main: 858-292-2000
request: 619-570-1053
www.rock1053.com
webcast: Yes
genres: Alt., Rock, Metal
format: Commercial
reports to: CMJ, Hits, FMQB, Mediabase, R&R
pd: Shauna Moran
e: shaunamoran@clearchannel.com
md: Jim Richards
e: jimrichards@clearchannel.com
Wknd indie & Metal shows reach LA.

KSDS 88.3 FM
1313 Park Blvd.
San Diego, CA 92101
watts: 20,000
main: 619-388-3057
request: 619-234-1062
www.jazz88.org
webcast: Yes
genres: Jazz, Blues, Gospel, World, Rock, Hip-Hop
format: Public
reports to: JazzWeek
pd: Claudia Russell
ext: 619-388-3060
e: claudiar@jazz88.org
md: Joe Kocherhans
ext: 619-388-3068
e: joek@jazz88.org
Airs specialty shows & on-air opps. to the San Diego area.

XTRA 91.1 FM
9660 Granite Ridge Dr., Ste. 200
San Diego, CA 92123
watts: 100,000
main: 858-495-9100
request: 619-570-1919
www.91x.com
webcast: Yes
genres: Alt., Rock, Punk, Pop, Reggae, Electronic
format: Commercial/Alt.
reports to: R&R, Hits, Billboard, FMQB, CMJ
pd: Phil Manning
ext: 858-499-1899
e: pmanning@fcbroadcasting.com
md: Capone
ext: 858-499-1708
e: capone@91x.com
Transmits new releases & specialty shows throughout southern CA. Reg'ls featured on "Loudspeaker" Sun 1-3am.

San Francisco

KCSM 91.1 FM
1700 W Hillsdale Blvd., Bldg. 9
San Mateo, CA 94402
watts: 11,000
main: 650-524-6946
request: 650-547-9136
e: jesse_varela@kcsm.net
www.kcsm.org
webcast: Yes
genres: Jazz
format: Public
reports to: JazzWeek
md: Chuy Varela
e: chuyvarela@aol.com
Transmits indie, Latin Jazz & Blues shows to the Bay Area.

KFOG/KFFG 104.5/97.7 FM
55 Hawthorne St., #1000
San Francisco, CA 94105
watts: 9500
main: 415-817-5634
request: 800-300-KFOG
e: kfog@kfog.com
www.kfog.com
webcast: Yes
genres: Rock, Classic Rock, Alt., Blues, Reggae, Folk
format: Commercial
reports to: FMQB, R&R
pd: Dave Benson
ext: 415-543-1045
md: Kelly Ransford
Airs indies & Local releases to Silicon Valley & San Jose; sister stn. KFFG 97.7 FM.

KITS 105.3 FM
865 Battery St.
San Francisco, CA 94111
watts: 15,000
main: 415-402-6700
request: 415-478-LIVE
www.live105.com
webcast: Yes **podcast:** Yes
genres: Alt., Rock, Indie Rock, Punk, 80s, Electronic
format: Commercial
pd: Dave Numme
e: dave@live105.com
md: Aaron Axelsen
e: aaron@live105.com
Indie releases & specialty shows broadcast to 9 Bay Area counties.

KPFA 94.1 FM
1929 MLK Jr. Way
Berkeley, CA 94704
watts: 59,000
main: 510-848-6767
request: 510-848-4425
www.kpfa.org
webcast: Yes
genres: Americana, Urban, Jazz, Latin, Folk, World
format: Public
reports to: CMJ, AMA, Roots
pd: Sasha Lilley
ext: 510-848-6767 x209
md: Luis Medina
ext: 510-848-6767 x219
e: music@kpfa.org
Prime non-comm. w/ sister stns. WBAI, KPFT & WPFW airs eclectic mix & specialty shows to northern & central CA.

KPOO 89.5 FM
1329 Divisadero St.
San Francisco, CA 94115
watts: 270
main: 415-346-5373
request: 415-346-5376
e: info@kpoo.com
www.kpoo.com
webcast: Yes
genres: Blues, Jazz, Urban, Reggae, Gospel, Salsa
format: Public
Send promos to: PO Box 423030, San Francisco, CA 94142.

KWMR 90.5/89.7 FM
PO Box 1262
Point Reyes Station, CA 94956
watts: 235
main: 415-663-8068
www.kwmr.org
webcast: Yes
genres: Americana, Jazz, Latin, Folk, World, Reggae, Rock, Classical
format: Public
reports to: Living Blues, AMA
pd: Lyons Filmer
ext: 415-663-8068 x1
e: programming@kwmr.org
md: Kay Clements
ext: 415-663-8288
e: kay@kwmr.org
Area's only non-comm. plays indies & specialty shows. Repeater station 89.3 FM covers W Marin & parts of San Francisco & Sonoma.

San Jose/Santa Cruz

KCBX 90.1/89.5 FM
4100 Vachell Ln.
San Luis Obispo, CA 93401
watts: 5300
main: 805-549-8855
e: kcbx@kcbx.org
www.kcbx.org
webcast: Yes **podcast:** Yes
genres: World, Jazz, Folk, Blues, Classical, Funk
format: Public
pd: Guy Rathbun
e: grathbun@kcbx.org
md: Neal Losey
e: nlosey@kcbx.org
Indie-heavy station airs specialty shows to central CA from Santa Barbara to Paso Robles.

KPIG 107.5 FM
1110 Main St., Ste. 16
Watsonville, CA 95076
watts: 2850
main: 831-722-9000
request: 831-722-2299
www.kpig.com
webcast: Yes
genres: Rock, Blues, Folk, Country, Bluegrass
format: Commercial/AAA
reports to: R&R
pd: Laura Ellen Hopper
e: laura@kpig.com
Airs indie releases & produces notable syndicated shows; Sister stations in San Luis Obispo, Chico & San Francisco.

KUSP 88.9/91.7 FM
203 8th Ave.
Santa Cruz, CA 95062
watts: 50,000
main: 831-476-2800
request: 800-655-KUSP
e: kusp@kusp.org
www.kusp.org
webcast: Yes
genres: Jazz, Folk, World, R&B, Classical, Celtic, African, Pop
format: Public/Freeform
md: Rob Mullen
e: rmullen@kusp.org
Shows reach central coast including Monterey Bay & San Jose & down the coast on KBDN. Hosts live performances 3-4 times/wk.

KZSC 88.1 FM
1156 High St.
Santa Cruz, CA 95064
watts: 20,000
main: 831-459-2811
request: 831-459-4036
www.kzsc.org
webcast: Yes
genres: Rock, Folk, Hip-Hop, Reggae, World
format: Public
reports to: CMJ
pd: Program Review
ext: 831-459-4726
e: prc@kzsc.org
md: Scott Karoly
e: music@kzsc.org
Award-winning station, w/ mix of student & community DJs, airs 60+ diverse shows to Monterey Bay area.

Colorado

Boulder/Denver

KBCO 97.3 FM
2500 Pearl St., Ste. 315
Boulder, CO 80302
watts: 100,000
main: 303-444-5600; 303-713-8000
request: 303-631-2973
e: keefer@clearchannel.com
www.kbco.com
webcast: Yes **podcast:** Yes
genres: AAA, Rock
format: Commercial/AAA
reports to: R&R, Hits, FMQB
pd: Scott Arbough
e: scottarbough@clearchannel.com
md: Marcus Abuzzahab
e: marcus@kbco.com
Airs Local & Reg'l talent wkly plus a variety of specialty shows. Studio performances may be included on CD sampler. Broadcast covers Denver, Boulder, Colorado Springs & into WY. Snail mail CDs.

KSMT 102.1/102.7 FM
PO Box 7069
Breckenridge, CO 80424
watts: 6000
main: 970-453-2234
request: 970-453-5768
www.ksmtradio.com
genres: Alt., AAA
format: Commercial
pd: Steve Burrell
e: sburrell@nrcbroadcasting.com
md: Stacy Towar
e: stowar@nrcbroadcasting.com
Airs indies & specialty shows; Johnny Brokaw hosts "What's On Tap," feat. artists w/ upcoming area shows. 81mi from Denver.

KTCL 93.3 FM
4695 S Monaco St.
Denver, CO 80237
watts: 100,000
main: 303-713-8000
request: 303-631-2933
www.ktcl.com
webcast: Yes
genres: Modern Rock
format: Commercial
pd: Nerf
ext: 303-713-8256
e: nerf@area93.com
md: Eric 'Boney' Clouse
ext: 303-713-8295
e: boney@area93.com
A ClearChannel indie-friendly station has streaming audio of CO bands. For specialty shows, contact: Alf at alf@area93.com.

KUNC 91.5 FM
822 7th St., Ste. 530
Greeley, CO 80631
watts: 82,000
main: 970-378-2579
request: 800-443-5862
e: mailbag@kunc.org
www.kunc.org
genres: Jazz, New Age, Folk, S/S, Classical
format: Public/Classical
reports to: FMQB
pd: Kirk Mowers
ext: 970-350-0807
e: kirk.mowers@kunc.org
md: Kyle Dyas
ext: 970-350-0808
e: kyle.dyas@kunc.org
Broadcasts diverse music to northern CO. Studio performances limited to 2-3 band members.

KUVO 89.3 FM
2900 Welton St., #200
Denver, CO 80205
watts: 26,000
main: 303-480-9272
e: info@kuvo.org
www.kuvo.org
webcast: Yes
genres: Jazz, Latin, Blues, World, Avant-Garde
format: Public
reports to: JazzWeek
pd: Carlos Lando
ext: 303-480-9272 x25
e: carlos@kuvo.org
md: Arturo Gomez
ext: 303-480-9272 x17
e: arturo@kuvo.org
Transmits indies to most of CO & southern WY. Promos to: PO Box 2040, Denver, CO 80201.

KYSL 93.1/93.9 FM
701 E Anemone Trl.
Dillon, CO 80435
watts: 500
main: 970-513-9393
www.krystal93.com
webcast: Yes
format: Commercial/AAA
pd: Tom Fricke
e: production@krystal93.com
md: T.J. Sanders
e: feedback@krystal93.com
Indie-friendly w/ specialty shows for Eagle, Summit & western Clear Creek County. Promos to: PO Box 27, Frisco, CO 80435. 68mi from Denver.

Colorado Springs

KILO 94.3 FM
1805 E Cheyenne Rd.
Colorado Springs, CO 80906
watts: 83,000
main: 719-634-4896
request: 719-633-5456
e: kilostudio@kilo943.com
www.kilo943.com
genres: Rock
format: Commercial/Active Rock
pd: Ross Ford
e: ross@kilo943.com
Indies in the mix & feat. CO acts on Fri 'Locals Rule' w/ Sid Black; brent_h@kilo943.com.

KRCC 91.5 FM
Colorado College
912 N Weber St.
Colorado Springs, CO 80903
watts: 3600
main: 719-473-4801
request: 800-748-2727
e: info@krcc.org
www.krcc.org
genres: Blues, Celtic, Folk, Reggae, Jazz, Electronica
format: Public/AAA
reports to: CMJ, FMQB
pd: Jeff Bieri
e: jeff@krcc.org
md: Vicky Gregor
e: vicky@krcc.org
Mix of students & community air of indies & specialty shows for southern CO.

KRZA 88.7 FM
528 9th St.
Alamosa, CO 81101
watts: 9800
main: 719-589-8844
request: 800-290-0887
e: office@krza.org
www.krza.org
genres: Americana, Jazz, World, Rock, Classical, Spanish
format: Public
reports to: CMJ
pd: Deborah Nichols
e: programming@krza.org
md: Mike Sisneros
e: musicmankrza@yahoo.com
Transmits 100 miles north & south, 30 miles east & west.

KTLF 90.5 FM
1665 Briargate Blvd.
Ste. 100
Colorado Springs, CO 80920
watts: 20,000
main: 719-593-0600
request: 800-428-1201
e: lightpraise@ktlf.org
www.ktlf.org
webcast: Yes
genres: Christian, Instrumental
format: Public
pd: Lynn Carmichael
e: lcar@ktlf.org
Spins indies to an 80mi radius.

Western CO

KBUT 90.3 FM
508 Maroon Ave.
Crested Butte, CO 81224
watts: 250
main: 970-349-5225
request: 970-349-7444
e: kbut@kbut.org
www.kbut.org
webcast: Yes **podcast:** Yes
genres: Classic Rock, World, Jazz, Americana, Bluegrass, Jam, Country, Hip-Hop
format: Public
reports to: CMJ
pd: Erin Roberts
ext: 970-349-5225 x10
e: programs@kbut.org
md: Chad Reich
ext: 970-349-5225 x15
e: music@kbut.org
Send promos to: PO Box 308, Crested Butte, CO 81224.

KDNK 88.1/88.3/88.5 FM
76 S Second St.
Carbondale, CO 81623
watts: 1250
main: 970-963-0139
request: 970-963-2976
e: steve@kdnk.org
www.kdnk.org
webcast: Yes **podcast:** Yes
genres: Americana, Reggae, Rock, World, Blues, Latin, Electronica, Celtic
format: Public
reports to: CMJ, AMA, FMQB
pd: Luke Nestler
e: luke@kdnk.org
Area's most popular non-comm. w/ volunteer DJs, airs Reg'l & indie releases from Aspen to Rifle to Leadville. Promos to: PO Box 1388, Carbondale, CO 81623.

KDUR 91.9/93.9 FM
1000 Rim Dr.
Durango, CO 81301
watts: 6000
main: 970-247-7288
request: 970-247-7262
www.kdur.org
webcast: Yes
genres: All Styles
format: Public
reports to: CMJ
pd: Bryant Liggett
ext: 970-247-7628
e: kdur_pd@fortlewis.edu
md: Jon Lynch
e: kdur_st1@fortlewis.edu
Eclectic mix of indies & specialty shows for N LaPlata County.

KSPN 103.1 FM
Aspen Airport Business Ctr.
#402 D
Aspen, CO 81611
watts: 3000
main: 970-925-5776
request: 970-925-1997
e: kspn@kspnradio.com
www.kspnradio.com
format: Commercial/AAA
reports to: Hits, FMQB
pd: Sam Scholl
ext: 970-925-5776 x221
e: samiam@nrcbroadcasting.com
"Colorado Homegrown" features Reg'ls M-F.

KSUT/KUTE 90.1 FM
123 Capote Dr.
Ignacio, CO 81137
watts: 3000
main: 970-563-0255
www.ksut.org
webcast: Yes
genres: Jazz, Blues, World, Native American
format: Public/AAA
reports to: FMQB, AAAradio.com, Living Blues
pd: Ken Brott
e: ken@ksut.org
md: Stasia Laner
e: stasia@ksut.org
Spins 30+ hours of indies; signal reaches parts of CO, UT, NM & AZ. Send Jazz to: Ron, PO Box 737, Ignacio, CO 81137.

KVNF/KVMT 90.9/89.1 FM
233 Grand Ave.
Paonia, CO 81428
watts: 2800/3000
main: 970-527-4866
request: 970-527-4868
e: events@kvnf.org
www.kvnf.org
webcast: Yes
genres: All Styles
format: Public
reports to: FMQB, CMJ, AMA, New Age Reporter, Living Blues
pd: Daniel Costello
e: daniel@kvnf.org
md: Candy Pennetta
e: sugar@kvnf.org
Transmits indie releases & S/S performances to westcentral CO. Send promos to: PO Box 1350, Paonia, CO 81428.

Connecticut

Bridgeport/Fairfield/Stamford

WPKN/WPKM 89.5/88.7 FM
244 University Ave.
Bridgeport, CT 06604
watts: 10,000
main: 203-331-9756
request: 203-331-1328
e: wpkn@wpkn.org
www.wpkn.org
webcast: Yes
genres: All Styles
format: Public/Freeform
reports to: CMJ, STS
md: Phil Bowler
e: philcbowler@aol.com
Freeform pioneer airs indies to CT, RI, MA & northern Long Island. Send CD & J-card w/ title page, track titles, track timings, personnel & label/contact info. Everything submitted available for airplay.

WPLR 99.1 FM
440 Wheeler's Farm Rd., Ste. 302
Milford, CT 06460
watts: 50,000
main: 203-783-8200
request: 203-882-WPLR
www.wplr.com
webcast: Yes
genres: Rock
format: Commercial
reports to: R&R, FMQB
pd: Lee Davis
e: lee.davis@coxradio.com
Mostly mainstream w/ some specialty shows & indie releases. Reg'l promos to: Rick Allison, PO Box 6508, Whitneyville, CT 06517.

WSHU 91.1 FM
5151 Park Ave.
Fairfield, CT 06825
watts: 2600
main: 203-365-6604
request: 203-365-0425
e: lombardi@wshu.org
www.wshu.org
webcast: Yes
genres: Folk, Celtic, Acoustic, New Age, Classical
format: Public/Classical
pd: Tom Kuser
e: kuser@wshu.org
md: Kate Remington
e: remington@wshu.org
Specialty shows including "Acoustic Connections" & "Profiles In Folk" feature indies. Broadcasts to parts of Long Island, NY.

Hartford

WWUH 91.3/89.7/89.9/105.1 FM
U of Hartford
200 Bloomfield Ave.
West Hartford, CT 06117
watts: 1000
main: 860-768-4703
request: 860-768-4701
e: wwuh@hartford.edu
www.wwuh.org
webcast: Yes
genres: Ambient, Bluegrass, Blues, Classical, Folk, Jazz, Rock, Reggae, Polka, Opera, Native American, World
format: Public/Freeform
reports to: CMJ, New Age Voice
pd: Mark Helpern
e: helpern@hartford.edu
md: Andy Taylor
Freeform stn. considers all submissions for broadcast that reaches New Haven & Northampton. Genre MDs on site.

Delaware

Dover

WXHL 89.1 FM
179 Stanton-Christiana Rd.
Newark, DE 19702
watts: 1200
main: 302-731-0690
request: 800-220-8078
e: dan@thereachfm.com
www.thereachfm.com
genres: Christian AC
format: Public
reports to: CMJ

pd: Dave Kirby
e: dave@thereachfm.com
md: Sal April
e: sal@thereachfm.com
Some indies in the mix & specialty shows on Sat. No unsolicited material.

Wilmington

WSTW 93.7 FM
2727 Shipley Rd.
Wilmington, DE 19801
watts: 50,000
main: 302-478-2700
request: 302-478-1010
e: wstw@wstw.com
www.wstw.com
webcast: Yes
format: Commercial/ Hot AC, CHR, AC
reports to: R&R, FMQB, Hits, Hitmakers, Network 40
pd: Mike Yeager
e: myeager@wstw.com
md: Mike Rossi
e: mrossi@wstw.com
Airs to DE, southeast PA, southern NJ & northeast MD. Sun specialty show "Hometown Heroes" airs Local & Reg'l acts. Promo packs to: PO Box 7492, Wilmington, DE 19803.

District of Columbia

WHUR 96.3 FM
529 Bryant St. NW
Washington, DC 20059
watts: 16,500
main: 202-806-3500
request: 202-432-9487
www.whur.com
genres: R&B, Jazz, Reggae, Urban, Gospel
format: Commercial/Urban AC
reports to: R&R, Billboard, Urban Network
pd: David Dickinson
e: ddickinson@whur.com
md: Traci LaTrelle
e: tlatrelle@whur.com
Covers DE, VA & DC w/ few indies.

WPFW 89.3 FM
2390 Champlain St. NW
Washington, DC 20009
watts: 50,000
main: 202-588-0999
request: 202-588-0893
e: pinchback_ron@wpfw.org
www.wpfw.org
webcast: Yes
genres: Jazz, Blues, World, Latin, Hip-Hop
format: Public
pd: Bobby Hill
ext: 202-588-0999 x357
e: hill_bobby@wpfw.org
md: Katea Stitt
ext: 202-588-0999 x361
e: stitt_katea@wpfw.org
Indies & Locals in the mix reach MD, DC & northern VA.

Florida

Jacksonville/ Gainesville

WJCT 89.9 FM
100 Festival Park Ave.
Jacksonville, FL 32202
watts: 100,000
main: 904-353-7770
request: 904-353-9528
e: info@wjct.org
www.wjct.org
webcast: Yes **Podcast:** Yes
genres: Jazz, World, Classical, Club, Dub
format: Public
pd: Scott Kim
e: skim@wjct.org
md: David Luckin
e: dluckin@wjct.org
Specialty shows w/ some indies aired to northeast FL, northcentral FL & southeast GA.

WPLA 107.3 FM
11700 Central Pkwy.
Jacksonville, FL 32224
watts: 100,000
main: 904-636-0507
request: 904-737-0107
e: planet@planetradio1073.com
www.planetradio1073.com
webcast: Yes **podcast:** Yes
genres: New Rock
format: Commercial/Alt.
reports to: Mediabase
pd: Chumley
ext: 904-998-3052
e: chumley@clearchannel.com
ClearChannel station airs indies & specialty shows to males 18+ in Jacksonville, St. Augustine, Outer Orlando, Gainesville & southern GA. For specialty shows, contact: Malcolm Ryker.

WRUF 103.7 FM
3200 Weimer Hall, U of Fl.
Gainesville, FL 32611
watts: 100,000
main: 352-392-0771
request: 352-392-ROCK
www.rock104.com
webcast: Yes
genres: Classic Rock
format: Commercial
reports to: R&R, FMQB, Album Network
pd: Harry Guscott
ext: 352-392-0771 x2100
e: guscott@rock104.com
md: Jack Wich
e: md@rock104.com
Airs wkly new music & specialty shows; signal covers Gainesville to Jacksonville to Daytona Beach. Send promos to: PO Box 14444, Gainsville, FL 32604.

WUFT 89.1/90.1 FM
PO Box 118405
Gainesville, FL 32611
watts: 100,000
main: 352-392-5200
www.wuftfm.org
webcast: Yes
genres: Classical, Jazz, Blues, Folk, Eclectic
format: Public/Classical
reports to: Arbitron
pd: Bill Beckett
ext: 352-392-5200 x1119
e: bbeckett@wuft.org
md: Richard Drake
ext: 352-392-5200 x1117
e: rdrake@wuft.org
Specialty shows, indie releases & Reg'l Folk showcase heard throughout upper FL, central FL & into GA.

Miami/ Ft. Lauderdale

WDNA 88.9 FM
2921 Coral Way
Miami, FL 33245
watts: 8300
main: 305-662-8889
request: 866-688-9362; 305-497-WDNA
www.wdna.org
webcast: Yes
genres: Jazz, World, Latin, Reggae, Latin Jazz, Brazilian
format: Public
reports to: Jazziz, Latin Beat, Yellow Dog
pd: Joe Cassera
e: jcassera@wdna.org
md: Michael Valentine
e: michael@wdna.org
Indie releases & specialty shows transmitted 60 miles.

WLRN 91.3 FM
172 NE 15th St.
Miami, FL 33132
watts: 100,000
main: 305-995-1717
request: 305-995-2220
e: info@wlrn.org
www.wlrn.org
webcast: Yes **podcast:** Yes
genres: Jazz, Reggae
format: Public
pd: Peter Maerz
ext: 305-995-2228
e: peterj@wlrn.org
md: Ed Bell
ext: 305-995-2236
e: ebell@wlrn.com
Jazz & Reggae shows reach all of southeast Florida, the Keys & the Bahamas.

WMBM 1490 AM
13242 NW 7th Ave.
North Miami, FL 33168
watts: 1000
main: 305-769-1100
request: 305-953-9626
e: wmbm@wmbm.com
www.wmbm.com
webcast: Yes
genres: Gospel
format: Commercial
reports to: Gospel Today, BRE, R&R
pd: Greg Cooper
ext: 305-769-1100 x232
e: gcooper@wmbm.com
Features many indies & specialty shows. Sponsors "Annual Spirit Awards" & "Gospel in the Park."

WMKL 91.9 FM
PO Box 561832
Miami, FL 33256
watts: 50,000
main: 305-662-7736
e: callfm@callfm.com
www.callfm.com
webcast: Yes
genres: CCM, Rock, R&B
format: Public
reports to: R&R
pd: Kelly Downing
e: kelly@callfm.com
Airs some indie music & the word to 13-25 year olds throughout lower FL Keys, Miami & S Broward.

Orlando

WFIT 89.5 FM
150 W University Blvd.
Melbourne, FL 32901
watts: 8000
main: 321-674-8140
e: wfit@fit.edu
www.wfit.org
webcast: Yes **podcast:** Yes
genres: AAA, Rock, Americana, Alt., Blues, Folk, Jazz, New Age, Reggae, World, Classical
format: Public
reports to: FMQB, R&R, AAAaadio.com, JazzWeek, CMJ, Living Blues, New Age Voice
pd: Todd Kennedy
ext: 321-674-8949
e: tkennedy@fit.edu
Broadcasts new music & wknd specialty shows to eastern & central FL.

WUCF 89.9 FM
4000 Central Florida Blvd.
Communication Bldg. 75, Ste. 130
Orlando, FL 32816
watts: 5600
main: 407-823-0899
request: 407-823-3689
e: wucfhost@mail.ucf.edu
www.wucf.org
webcast: Yes
genres: Jazz, Blues, Reggae
format: Public
reports to: Jazz Times
pd: Kayonne Riley
e: kriley@mail.ucf.edu
Heard throughout central FL airs daily specialty shows. Promos: PO Box 162199, Orlando, FL 32816.

Pensacola

WUWF 88.1 FM
U of West Florida, 11000 University Pkwy.
Pensacola, FL 32514
watts: 100,000
main: 850-474-2787
e: wuwf@wuwf.org
www.wuwf.org
webcast: Yes
genres: World, Jazz, Celtic, Blues
format: Public
pd: Joe Vincenza
ext: 850-473-7451
e: joe@wuwf.org
md: Steve Tortoric
e: steve@wuwf.org
Some indies as well as a monthly Reg'l showcase reach Mobile, AL & into MS.

WZEP 1460 AM
449 N 12th St.
DeFuniak Springs, FL 32433
watts: 10,000
main: 850-892-3158
request: 800-881-1460
e: wzep@wzep1460.com
www.wzep1460.com
genres: Country, Gospel
format: Commercial/Country
pd: Marty Dees
Local artists & specialty shows reach south toAL. Send promos to: PO Box 627, De Funkian Springs, FL 33435. 74mi from Pensacola.

Tallahassee

WXSR 105.1 FM
325 John Knox Rd.
Bldg. G
Tallahassee, FL 32303
watts: 37,000
main: 850-422-3107
request: 850-386-3101
www.x1015.com
webcast: Yes **podcast:** Yes
genres: New Rock
format: Commercial
reports to: Mediabase
pd: Jeremy Menard
e: jeremymenard@clearchannel.com
Spins indies to metro area. Unsigned Rock, Alt., Urban & Country artists can upload their music to be rated online.

Tampa/Sarasota

WJIS/WLPJ/WHIJ 88.1/91.5 FM
6469 Parkland Dr.
Sarasota, FL 34243
watts: 100,000
main: 941-753-0401
request: 800-456-8910
e: thejoyfm@thejoyfm.com
www.thejoyfm.com
genres: CCM
format: Public/Christian AC
reports to: CRW, R&R
pd: Carmen Brown
e: carmen@thejoyfm.com
md: Jeff Macfarlane
e: jeff@thejoyfm.com
Covers most of the west coast of FL w/ specialty shows.

WMNF 88.5 FM
1210 E MLK Blvd.
Tampa, FL 33603
watts: 70,000
main: 813-238-8001
request: 813-239-9663
e: wmnf@wmnf.org
www.wmnf.org
genres: Rock, Americana, Jazz, R&B, Folk, Latin, Reggae, Hip-Hop, Blues
format: Public
reports to: CMJ
pd: Randy Wynne
ext: 813-238-8001 x104
e: randy@wmnf.org
md: Lee Courtney
e: flee@wmnf.org
Indies in the mix & on new music showcase heard from Tampa to Orlando to Venice Beach; 40% of programming is specialty shows.

WXTB 97.9 FM
4002 Gandy Blvd.
Tampa, FL 33611
watts: 100,000
main: 813-832-1000
request: 800-737-0098
www.98rock.com
format: Commercial/Active Rock
reports to: CMJ, FMQB, Album Network
pd: James 'Double Down' Howard
ext: 813-832-1464
e: doubledown@clearchannel.com
md: Mike Kilabrew
e: mikekilabrew@clearchannel.com

Georgia

Athens

WPUP 103.7 FM
1010 Tower Pl.
Bogart, GA 30622
watts: 25,000
main: 706-549-6222
request: 706-369-1037
www.thebulldogonline.com
genres: Active Rock
format: Commercial
reports to: Album Network, FMQB, CMJ
pd: Kevin Steele
e: kevin.steele@coxradio.com
Indie & Reg'l music blankets a 60-mile radius.

Atlanta

WCCV/WJCK 91.7/88.3 FM
779 S Erwin St.
Cartersville, GA 30120
watts: 7300
main: 770-387-0917
www.ibn.org; www.wccv.org; www.wjck.org
webcast: Yes
format: Public/Christian AC, Soft AC, Inspirational
pd: Jackson Edwards
e: jackson@ibn.org
md: Jimmy Hardee
e: jimmy@ibn.org
Heard on 11 frequencies throughout northwest GA, northeast AL, TN. Actively seeks new music & concert opps. for above styles; send promos to: PO Box 1000, Cartersville, GA 30120.

WHTA 107.9 FM
101 Marietta St., 12th Fl.
Atlanta, GA 30303
watts: 41,000
main: 404-765-9750
request: 404-688-7686
www.hot1079atl.com
genres: Urban, Hip-Hop, Jazz
format: Commercial
reports to: R&R, Urban Network, Hits, Billboard
pd: Steve Heggwood
md: Kevin Gogh
Some indie releases; submissions must be clean & radio ready.

WNNX 99.7 FM
780 Johnson Ferry Rd., 5th Fl.
Atlanta, GA 30342
watts: 100,000
main: 404-497-4700
request: 404-741-0997
www.99x.com
webcast: Yes
genres: Alt., New Rock, Acoustic
format: Commercial
reports to: R&R, Hits, FMQB
md: Steve Craig
ext: 404-497-4846
e: steve@99x.com; steve.craig@cumulus.com
Ample on-air opps. including "Locals Only Lounge" M-F 9pm; locals@99X.com & "Sunday School" w/ Elliot; sundayschool@99X.com; covers a 60-mile radius.

WRFG 89.3 FM
1083 Austin Ave. NE
Atlanta, GA 30307
watts: 100,000
main: 404-523-3471
request: 404-523-8989
e: info@wrfg.org
www.wrfg.org
webcast: Yes
genres: Dancehall, Calypso, Reggae, Blues, Bluegrass, Jazz, World, Latin, R&B, Gospel, Zydeco, Indian, African, Folk, Alt., Hip-Hop
format: Public
reports to: Billboard, Vibe, Source
pd: Wanique Shabazz
e: wanique@wrfg.org
Indies in rotation & many specialty shows for the metro area & beyond.

WVEE 103.3 FM
1201 Peachtree St., Ste. 800
Atlanta, GA 30361
watts: 100,000
main: 404-898-8900
request: 404-741-9833
www.v-103.com
webcast: Yes
genres: R&B, Rap
format: Commercial/Urban
reports to: Hits, R&R, Impact
pd: Reggie Rouse
ext: 404-898-8979
e: reggie.rouse@cbsradio.com
md: Amir Boyd
CBS Radio-owned station, w/ 18-34 market, reaches parts of AL.

WZGC 92.9 FM
1201 Peachtree St.
Ste. 800
Atlanta, GA 30361
watts: 64,000
main: 404-898-8900
request: 404-741-0929
www.929davefm.com
webcast: Yes **podcast:** Yes
genres: Alt., S/S
format: Commercial/AAA
pd: Mike Wheeler
ext: 404-898-8867
md: Margot Smith
ext: 404-741-9393
e: margot@929dave.fm
CBS Radio-owned station formerly Z93 FM, airs new music & variety of specialty shows for "Gen X" listeners.

Greater GA

WECC 89.3 FM
5465 Hwy. 40 E
Saint Mary's, GA 31558
watts: 16,000
main: 912-882-8930
request: 800-577-WECC
www.thelighthousefm.org
webcast: Yes
genres: CCM
format: Public/Christian AC
pd: Vickie Hafer
e: vickie@thelighthousefm.org
md: Mark McMillan
e: mark@thelighthousefm.org
Transmits some indies to southeast GA & northeast FL.

Idaho

Boise/Ketchum

KBSU 90.3/91.5 FM
Boise State Radio
1910 University Dr.
Boise, ID 83725
watts: 19,000/16,000
main: 208-426-3669
request: 888-859-5278
http://radio.boisestate.edu
webcast: Yes
genres: Jazz, Classical, Celtic, Blues, New Age, Rock, Folk, Alt.
format: Public
pd: Ele Ellis
ext: 208-947-5659
e: eleellis@boisestate.edu
md: Sean Buckallew
e: mlibrarian@boisestate.edu
Community/student-run station programs eclectic music heard throughout Boise/Twin Falls & into parts of NV & OR. AM sister station plays Jazz.

Greater ID

KECH 95.3 FM
PO Box 2750
Hailey, ID 83333
watts: 100
main: 208-726-5324
request: 208-726-9536
e: kech95@cox-internet.com
genres: Rock
format: Commercial
pd: Lenny Joseph
e: lennyjoseph@hotmail.com
md: Bob Thompson
ext: 208-947-5659
Plays touring acts passing thru & supports Local shows. Indie, Jazz, Folk & Blues specialty shows cover 50-mile radius.

KSKI 103.7 FM
201 S Main St.
Hailey, ID 83333
watts: 53,000
main: 208-788-7118
request: 800-611-KSKI
www.kski.com
genres: Alt.
format: Commercial/AAA, Alt.
reports to: CMJ
pd: Graham Rath
e: gdogkski@yahoo.com
KECH sister stn. targets listeners 12-65 & reaches into WY. Send promos to: PO Box 2750, Hailey, ID 83333.

Illinois

Champaign

WEFT 90.1 FM
113 N Market St.
Champaign, IL 61820
watts: 10,000
main: 217-359-9338
e: weft@weft.org
www.weft.org
webcast: Yes
genres: Jazz, World, Metal, Electronic, Americana, Blues, Folk, Hip-Hop, Soul, Indie
format: Public/Freeform
reports to: CMJ
pd: Mick Woolf
e: stationmanager@weft.org
md: Jay Eychaner
Eclectic playlist regularly airs indies to surrounding counties. Wkly "WEFT Session" features live Locals. Promos: PO Box 1223, Champaign, IL 61824.

WPGU 107.1 FM
512 E Green St.
Ste. 107
Champaign, IL 61820
watts: 3000
main: 217-337-3100
request: 217-337-1071
e: wpgu@wpgu.com
www.wpgu.com
webcast: Yes
genres: Alt., Rock, Punk
format: Commercial/Alt.
reports to: FMQB
pd: Joe Lamberson
ext: 217-337-3110
e: lamberson@wpgu.com
md: Matt Klomparens
ext: 217-244-3101
e: music@wpgu.com
Indies aired regularly on Hip-Hop, Jam, Electronic, Local & Hardcore specialty shows to all of central IL.

Chicago

WGCI 107.5 FM
233 N Michigan Ave., Ste. 2800
Chicago, IL 60601
watts: 50,000
main: 312-540-2000
request: 312-591-1075
www.wgci.com
webcast: Yes **podcast:** Yes
genres: Hip-Hop, R&B
format: Commercial/Urban
reports to: Mediabase
pd: Kris Kelley
ext: 312-540-2406
e: kriskelley@clearchannel.com
md: Kenard Karter
ext: 312-540-2802

e: kenardkarter@clearchannel.com
Specialty shows & indie releases cover a 60-mile radius.

WKQX 101.1 FM
230 Merchandise Mart Plaza
Chicago, IL 60654
watts: 8000
main: 312-527-8348
request: 312-591-8300
www.q101.com
webcast: Yes
genres: Alt., Rock
format: Commercial/Alt.
reports to: R&R, FMQB
pd: Marc Young
ext: 312-245-1231
Indies on specialty shows.

WLUW 88.7 FM
6525 N Sheridan Rd.
Chicago, IL 60626
watts: 100
main: 773-508-8080
request: 773-508-9589
e: wluw88.7@gmail.com
www.wluw.org
genres: Indie Rock, Hip-Hop, Electronic, Country, Latin, Alt., Ska, New Orleans
format: Public/Alt.
reports to: CMJ
pd: Christina Stevens
ext: 773-508-8071
md: Michael Radaiolo
ext: 773-508-8073
Station dedicated to indie releases airs in-studio opps.

WXRT 93.1 FM
455 North City Front Plaza
6th Fl.
Chicago, IL 60611
watts: 6700
main: 312-245-6000
request: 312-329-9978
e: comments@wxrt.com
www.wxrt.com
webcast: Yes **podcast:** Yes
genres: Rock
format: Commercial/AAA
reports to: FMQB, R&R
pd: Norm Winer
md: John Farneda
Indies & in-studio opps. cover a 60-mile radius. For specialty shows, contact: Marty Lennartz at marty@wxrt.com. See site for idiosyncratic submission info.

Peoria

WGLT 89.1 FM
Campus Box 8910
Illinois State U
Normal, IL 61790
watts: 25,000
main: 309-438-2255
request: 309-438-8910
e: wglt@ilstu.edu
www.wglt.org
webcast: Yes **podcast:** Yes
genres: Americana, Alt., Jazz, Blues, Folk, Bluegrass, Celtic
format: Public
reports to: CMJ, JazzWeek, Living Blues, Roots Music Report
pd: Mike McCurdy
ext: 309-438-2394
e: mjmccur@ilstu.edu
md: Jon Norton
ext: 309-438-7871
e: j.norton@ilstu.edu
Several indie-friendly specialty shows & artists interviews reach Bloomington & Peoria.

WIXO 105.7 FM
120 Eaton St.
Peoria, IL 61603
watts: 32,000
main: 309-676-5000
request: 877-495-9496
www.1057thexrocks.com
webcast: Yes
genres: Alt. Rock
format: Commercial/Active Rock
reports to: R&R
pd: Matt Bahan
e: matt.bahan@regentcomm.com
Broadcast reaches a 150-mile radius. No unsolicited material.

Greater IL

WXRX 104.9 FM
2830 Sandy Hollow Rd.
Rockford, IL 61109
watts: 6000
main: 815-874-7861
request: 815-874-2104
e: wxrx@maverick-media.ws
www.wxrx.com
genres: Rock
format: Commercial/Rock
pd: Jim Stone
e: jimstone@maverick-media.ws
Station has a reach of 35-40mi.

Indiana

Bloomington/Salem

WFIU 103.7 FM
Indiana U, 1229 E 7th St., Rm. 120
Bloomington, IN 47405
watts: 34,000
main: 812-855-1357
request: 812-856-5352
e: wfiu@indiana.edu
www.wfiu.org
webcast: Yes **podcast:** Yes
genres: Classical, Jazz
format: Public
pd: Kary Boyce
md: David Wood
Airs Jazz, World, Folk & Blues specialty shows & in-studio opps. to 50 miles in south-central IN. No unsolicited material.

WJAA 96.3 FM
1531 W Tipton St.
Seymour, IN 47274
watts: 3000
main: 812-523-3343
e: radio@wjaa.net
www.wjaa.net
genres: AAA, Classic Rock
format: Commercial/AAA
pd: Robert Becker
e: robert@wjaa.net
Spins some Local releases & a few specialty shows to a 45-mi radius. No unsolicited material.

WTTS 92.3 FM
400 One City Ctr.
Bloomington, IN 47404
watts: 37,000
main: 812-332-3366
e: comments@wttsfm.com
www.wttsfm.com
format: Commercial/AAA
reports to: R&R, Hits
pd: Brad Holtz
e: brad@wttsfm.com
md: Laura Duncan
e: laura@wttsfm.com
Blankets metro area & points south w/ on-air opps. & indie releases. Sponsors a "Battle of the Bands."

Fort Wayne

WBOI 89.1 FM
3204 Clairmont Ct.
Fort Wayne, IN 46808
watts: 50,000
main: 260-452-1189
www.nipr.fm
genres: Jazz
format: Public
reports to: JazzWeek
pd: Colleen Condron
e: ccondron@nipr.fm
md: Janice Furtner
e: jfurtner@nipr.fm
Airs some indies & about 30hrs of Jazz to a 60-mile radius. Send promos to: PO Box 8459, Fort Wayne, IN 46898.

WBYR 98.9 FM
1005 Production Rd.
Fort Wayne, IN 46808
watts: 50,000
main: 260-471-5100
request: 260-484-2327
www.989thebear.com
genres: Rock, Alt.
format: Commercial
reports to: FMQB, Hits, R&R
md: Marty 'Stiller' Oehlhof
e: stiller@989thebear.com
Airs in-studio opps. to a 100-mi radius. For "Local Licks" Mon at 11pm, send CD w/ bio & gig schedule ATTN: Jerrdog.

WVPE 88.1 FM
2424 California Rd.
Elkhart, IN 46514
watts: 10,500
main: 260-674-9873
www.wvpe.org
genres: Jazz, Blues, Folk
format: Public
pd: Lee Burdorf
ext: 574-262-5774
e: lburdorf@wvpe.org
Indie-friendly station, owned by Elkhart Community School System, airs in-studio opps. & specialty shows. Sponsors weekly concerts in summer & Local Festivals. Broadcasts over a 50-mile radius to northcentral IN & southwestern MI.

Indianapolis

WECI 91.5 FM
801 National Rd., Box E45
Richmond, IN 47374
watts: 400
main: 765-983-1246
request: 765-962-3541
e: stationmanager@weciradio.org
www.weciradio.org
genres: Indie Rock, Hip-Hop, Electronic, Country, Classical, Classic Rock, Jazz, Bluegrass, Folk, Gospel, Metal, Blues, World
format: Public
reports to: CMJ
pd: Brandon Budd
e: program@weciradio.org
md: Dan Whatley
e: wecimd@gmail.com
Student-run community station broadcasts from Earlham College & spins an indie-heavy mix w/ on-air opps.

WICR 88.7 FM
U of Indianapolis
1400 E Hanna Ave.
Indianapolis, IN 46227
watts: 5000
main: 317-788-3280
request: 317-788-3314
e: wicr@uindy.edu
www.wicr.uindy.edu
genres: Jazz, Classical
format: Public
reports to: CMJ
pd: Russ Maloney
e: rmaloney@uindy.edu
md: Crystal Mills
e: millscm@uindy.edu
Student & community station adds diverse indie, Folk, Blues & Bluegrass shows for metro area into Muncie & Marion, IN. For "Fields of Bluegrass," contact: Cary Allen, bluegrassindy@yahoo.com.

WRZX 103.3 FM
6161 Fall Creek Rd.
Indianapolis, IN 46220
watts: 18,500
main: 317-257-7565
request: 317-239-9103
www.x103.com
genres: Modern Rock
format: Commercial/Rock
pd: Lenny Diana
e: lenny@x103.com
ClearChannel station airs some indies on specialty shows heard 60 miles.

WZPL 99.5 FM
9245 N Meridian St., Ste. 300
Indianapolis, IN 46260
watts: 19,000
main: 317-816-4000
request: 317-228-1099
www.wzpl.com
format: Commercial/Hot AC
pd: Scott Sands
ext: 317-218-2224
e: ssands@entercom.com
md: Dave Decker
ext: 317-218-2234
e: ddecker@entercom.com
Locals & Reg'l in the spotlight M-F on "Homegrown Buzz."

Iowa

Cedar Falls

KBBG 88.1 FM
918 Newell St.
Waterloo, IA 50703
watts: 10,000
main: 319-234-1441
e: realmanagement@kbbg.org
www.kbbgfm.org
genres: Gospel, Blues, R&B, Jazz
format: Public
pd: Beverly Douglas
e: bev@kbbg.org
Freeform station broadcasts to 60-mile radius.

KUNI 90.9 FM
U of Northern Iowa, 3rd Fl., CAC
Cedar Falls, IA 50614
watts: 100,000
main: 319-273-6400
request: 800-772-2440
e: kuni@uni.edu
www.kuniradio.org
genres: Folk, Blues, World Beat, New Age, Alt., Rock
format: Public
reports to: CMJ
md: Al Schares
ext: 319-273-6489
e: allen.schares@uni.edu
Indies in rotation & on specialty shows reach 1/2 of eastern IA & parts of MN, IL & WI.

Des Moines

KCCQ 105.1 FM
415 Main St.
Ames, IA 50010

watts: 25,000
main: 515-232-1430
request: 515-232-0105
e: jamiem@clearchannel.com
www.kccq.com
genres: Alt.
format: Commercial
reports to: Mediabase
pd: Ryan Wild
e: ryanwild@clearchannel.com
Indies on specialty shows reach a 40-mile radius & Des Moines.

KGGO 94.9 FM
4143 109th St.
Urbandale, IA 50322
watts: 100,000
main: 515-331-9200
request: 515-312-3695
www.kggo.com
webcast: Yes **podcast:** Yes
genres: Classic Rock
format: Commercial
pd: Steve Brill
e: steve.brill@citcomm.com
md: Brian James
e: brian.kggo@citcomm.com
Andre Mosqueda plays indie Blues releases on "Roadhouse" Sun 7am-noon: andre.roadhouse@citcomm.com. Coverage is 60mi.

KNWI 107.1 FM
3737 Woodland Ave., Ste.111
West Des Moines, IA 50266
watts: 27,000
main: 515-327-1071
request: 515-327-1073
e: knwi@desmoines.fm
www.desmoines.fm
genres: CCM
format: Public/Christian AC, Christian CHR, Christian Rock
reports to: R&R, CRW
pd: Dave St. John
e: dave@desmoines.fm
Signal is repeated on 2500-watt KNWM 96.1 FM just north of Des Moines & into MO.

KPTL 106.3 FM
2141 Grand Ave.
Des Moines, IA 50312
watts: 18,000
main: 515-245-8900
e: feedback@capital1063.com
www.capital1063.com
webcast: Yes
format: Commercial/AAA
reports to: R&R
pd: Deeya McClurkin
e: deeya@clearchannel.com
ClearChannel station airs some indies & Reg'l releases & features weekly live "Studio C" session. Upload music online.

Iowa City

KSUI 91.7 FM
710 S Clinton St.
Iowa City, IA 52242
watts: 100,000/5000
main: 319-335-5730
e: ksui@uiowa.edu
www.ksui.uiowa.edu
webcast: Yes **podcast:** Yes
genres: Classical, Jazz, Folk
format: Public/Classical
pd: Barney Sherman
e: bernard-sherman@uiowa.edu
Mostly Classical station airs several specialty shows w/ indies. Repeated on 101.7 FM (Dubuque); KHKE 89.5 FM (Cedar Falls/Waterloo); KUNZ 919.1 FM (Ottumwa, IA) & WOI-FM (Ames) as part of a statewide classical network, Iowa Public Radio Classical.

WSUI 910 AM
710 S Clinton St.
Iowa City, IA
52242
watts: 5000
main: 319-335-5730
e: wsui@uiowa.edu
www.wsui.uiowa.edu
webcast: Yes
genres: Acoustic
format: Public
pd: Dennis Reese
ext: 319-335-5739
e: dennis-reese@uiowa.edu
md: Joan Kjaer
ext: 319-335-5746
e: joan-kjaer@uiowa.edu
"Java Blend" w/ Ben Kieffer airs live sets from indies & is heard on several stations across the state & shown on cable TV; ben-kieffer@uiowa.edu.

Sioux City

KWIT/KOJI 90.3/90.7 FM
4647 Stone Ave.
Sioux City, IA
51106
watts: 100,000
main: 712-274-6406
request: 800-251-3690
www.kwit-koji.org
webcast: Yes **podcast:** Yes
genres: Jazz, Blues, Classical, Film Scores, Latin, Salsa, Reggaeton, Regional Mexican
format: Public
reports to: Living Blues, JazzWeek
pd: Gretchen Gondek
e: gondekg@witcc.com
md: Steve Smith
e: smiths@witcc.com
Transmits new releases plus Blues & Jazz specialty shows to a 100-mile radius.
No Inspirational, Christian, Soft, Top 40 or Classic Rock.

Kansas

Kansas City/ Topeka/Lawrence

KANU 91.5 FM
U of Kansas, 1120 W 11th St.
Lawrence, KS 66044
watts: 100,000
main: 785-864-4530; 888-577-5268
e: jcampbell@ku.edu
www.kansaspublicradio.org
webcast: Yes
genres: Jazz, Classical
format: Public
pd: Darrell Brogdon
e: dbrogdon@ku.edu
md: Rachel Hunter
e: rhunter@ku.edu
NPR outlet squeezes in some trad. Folk & Bluegrass specialty shows; 90-mile coverage.

KDVV 100.3 FM
825 S Kansas Ave., Ste. 100
Topeka, KS 66612
watts: 100,000
main: 785-272-2122
request: 785-297-1003
www.v100rocks.com
webcast: Yes
genres: Mainstream Rock
format: Commercial
pd: Forrest Smithkors
e: forrest@v100rocks.com
Airs indies & in-studio performances to northeast KS. Sun nite "Download" features Local buzz bands & new Rock w/ host Forrest; forrest@v100rocks.com.

KMXN 92.9 FM
3125 W 6th St.
Lawrence, KS 66049
watts: 50,000
main: 785-843-1320
request: 785-830-9929
www.x929.com
webcast: Yes
genres: Rock
format: Commercial/Active Rock
pd: Jon Thomas
e: jon@lazer.com
md: Charles Newman
e: newman@lazer.com
Airs touring indie bands to Topeka & Kansas City area. "Local X," plays nitely & features 3 artists that are Local or touring the area.

Wichita

KDGS 93.9 FM
2120 N Woodlawn, Ste. 352
Wichita, KS 67208
watts: 25,000
request: 316-436-1093
www.power939.com
webcast: Yes
genres: R&B, Hip-Hop
format: Commercial/CHR/Urban
reports to: R&R, Mediabase, FMQB, Billboard
pd: Greg Williams
ext: 316-685-2121 x295
e: gwilliams@entercom.com
md: Dave 'Deuce' Jacobson
ext: 316-685-2121 x236
e: djacobson@entercom.com
Specialty shows & on-air opps.

KMUW 89.1 FM
Wichita State U
3317 E 17th St. N
Wichita, KS 67208
watts: 100,000
main: 316-978-6789
e: info@kmuw.org
www.kmuw.org
webcast: Yes
genres: Jazz, World, Classical, Gospel
format: Public
reports to: JazzWeek, CMJ, Jazziz
pd: LuAnne Stephens
e: stephens@kmuw.org
Airs some indies & specialty shows to 60 miles around south-central KS.

KTHR 107.3 FM
9323 E 37th St. N
Wichita, KS 67226
watts: 100,000
main: 316-832-9600
request: 316-436-1096
www.1073theroad.com
genres: Classic Rock, Blues
format: Commercial
reports to: R&R, FMQB, BDS
md: Lyman James
e: lymanjames@clearchannel.com
Indies on "Blues Brunch" w/ Robb Morrison Sun 9am-noon. Signal covers a 100-mile radius.

Greater KS

KANZ 89.5/90.5/ 91.1/90.7/91.5 FM
210 N 7th St.
Garden City, KS 67846
watts: 100,000
main: 620-275-7444 (KS); 806-367-9088 (TX)
e: hppr@hppr.org
www.hppr.org
webcast: Yes **podcast:** Yes
genres: Folk, Jazz, Bluegrass, Western Swing, Blues, S/S, World
format: Public
pd: Bob Kirby
e: programming@hppr.org
md: John Black
e: music@hppr.org; hpm@hppr.org
Broadcasting on 21 frequencies to western KS, southeast CO, TX & OK panhandles. Airs daily Acoustic & Jazz shows & sponsors living room concerts for Acoustic, Folk & Bluegrass acts. Send hard copies: 101 W 5th, Ste. 100, Amarillo, TX 79101.

Kentucky

Lexington

WLXX 92.9 FM
300 W Vine St., 3rd Fl.
Lexington, KY 40507
watts: 100,000
main: 859-253-5900
request: 859-280-2929; 877-777-9929
www.wlxxthebear.com
genres: Country
format: Commercial
pd: Robert John
e: robert.john@cumulus.com
md: Chris Slater
e: chris.slater@cumulus.com
No unsolicited material.

WMKY 90.3 FM
Morehead State U
132 Breckinridge Hall
Morehead, KY 40351
watts: 50,000
main: 606-783-2001
request: 606-783-2333
e: wmky@moreheadstate.edu
www.msuradio.com
webcast: Yes **podcast:** Yes
genres: Americana, S/S, Alt. Country, World, Jazz, Classical, Bluegrass, Blues
format: Public
reports to: FMQB, CMJ, Crossroads, AMA
pd: Jonese Franklin
e: j.franklin@moreheadstate.edu
Station w/ large student staff broadcasts indies in mix & on specialty shows for 150 miles throughout eastern KY, southern OH & western WV. Send promos to: Morehead State Univ., 150 University Blvd., Box 93, Morehead, KY 40351.

Louisville

WAMZ 97.5 FM
4000 Radio Dr., Ste. 1
Louisville, KY 40218
watts: 100,000
main: 502-479-2222
request: 502-571-97FM
www.wamz.com
webcast: Yes
genres: Country
format: Commercial
reports to: R&R, Mediabase
pd: Coyote Calhoun
e: coyote@wamz.com
ClearChannel station broadcasting to most of northern

KY & parts of IN, has indie interviews & performances.

WFPK 91.9 FM
619 S 4th St.
Louisville, KY 40202
watts: 6800
main: 502-814-6500
request: 502-814-9375
e: studio@wfpk.org
www.wfpk.org
webcast: Yes **podcast:** Yes
genres: Jazz, Alt., Rock
format: Public/AAA, Americana, Blues, World
reports to: R&R, FMQB
pd: Stacy Owen
ext: 502-814-6519
e: sowen@wfpk.org
Weekly indie show heard in northern KY & southern IN.

WLRS 104.3/105.1 FM
520 S 4th St., 2nd Fl.
Louisville, KY 40202
watts: 2200
main: 502-625-1220
request: 502-571-1051
www.wlrs.com
genres: Rock, Alt., Metal
format: Commercial
pd: Joe Stamm
Indie releases & interviews; Locals on "Louisville Underground" Sun 11pm-mid.

WTFX 93.1 FM
4000 Radio Dr., Ste. 1
Louisville, KY 40218
watts: 50,000
main: 502-479-2222
request: 502-571-0931
www.foxrocks.com
webcast: Yes **podcast:** Yes
format: Commercial/Active Rock
reports to: Hits, R&R, FMQB, CMJ, Billboard
pd: Charlie Steele
e: charliesteele@clearchannel.com
md: Frank Webb
e: frankwebb@clearchannel.com
Indie releases & a variety of specialty shows to KY.

Greater KY

WMMT 88.7 FM
91 Madison St.
Whitesburg, KY 41858
watts: 15,000
main: 606-633-1208
e: wmmtfm@appalshop.org
www.appalshop.org
webcast: Yes **podcast:** Yes
genres: Americana, Rock, Blues, Jazz, Gospel, Reggae, World, Bluegrass, Variety
format: Public/Classic Hits
reports to: AMA, Bluegrass Unlimited
md: Diana Champion
ext: 606-633-0108
Reg'l music & indies heard throughout KY, SW VA, & SW WV. For Specialty Shows, contact: Debbie Sutton at 606-633-0108 or wmmtfm@appalshop.org.

WNKU 89.7/94.5 FM
301 Landrum Academic Ctr.
Highland Heights, KY 41099
watts: 12,000
main: 859-572-6500
request: 859-572-7897
e: radio@nku.edu
www.wnku.org
webcast: Yes **podcast:** Yes
genres: Folk, Blues, Celtic, Bluegrass, Jazz, Acoustic
format: Public/AAA, Alt.
reports to: FMQB
pd: Michael Grayson
e: grayson@nku.edu
md: John McGue
e: mcguej@nku.edu
Indie releases & Sat specialty shows broadcasts to Cincinnati metro area, on YouTube & public TV stations.

Louisiana

Baton Rouge/ Lafayette

KAJN 102.9 FM
110 W Third St.
Crowley, LA 70527
watts: 100,000
main: 337-783-1560
www.kajn.com
webcast: Yes
genres: CCM
format: Commercial/ Christian AC, Christian CHR, Christian Rock
pd: Craig Thompson
e: craigt@kajn.com
Indies heard throughout Lake Charles, Alexandria, Lafayette & Baton Rouge. For specialty shows, contact: Tiffany Babineaux: tiffanyb@kajn.com. Sponsors concerts in association w/ churches. Promos to: PO Box 1469, Crowley, LA 70527.

KBON 101.1 FM
109 S 2nd St.
Eunice, LA 70535
watts: 25,000
main: 337-546-0007
request: 337-457-5266
www.kbon.com
webcast: Yes
genres: Cajun, Swamp Pop, Zydeco, Country, Blues
format: Commercial/Country
pd: Paul Marx
e: paul@kbon.com
Indies & specialty shows to all of Acadiana.

KBRH 1260 AM
2825 Government St.
Baton Rouge, LA 70806
watts: 5000
main: 225-388-9030
request: 225-387-1260
e: gkenyon@ebrpss.k12.la.us
genres: Blues, R&B
format: Commercial
pd: Larry Davis
md: Rob Payer
Playlist is 30% indies & Locals & covers a 40-mile radius.

KFTE 96.5 FM
1749 Bertrand Dr.
Lafayette, LA 70506
watts: 50,000
main: 337-233-6000
request: 337-235-9636
www.planet965.com
webcast: Yes
genres: Modern Rock
format: Commercial/Active Rock
reports to: R&R
pd: Scott Perrin
ext: 337-233-6000 x235
e: scott.perrin@regentcomm.com
md: Jude Vice
ext: 337-233-6000 x234
e: jude.vice@regentcomm.com
New releases & specialty shows covering up to 60 miles. Reg'ls featured on "New 4 Tuesday."

KQXL 106.5 FM
650 Wooddale Blvd.
Baton Rouge, LA 70806
watts: 50,000
main: 225-926-1106
request: 225-499-1065
e: kqxl.fm@citcomm.com
www.q106dot5.com
webcast: Yes **podcast:** Yes
format: Commercial/Urban AC
pd: Jay Michael
ext: 225-929-5129
e: jmichael.wxok@citcomm.com
Indies on "The Blues Cafe" w/ Ron Kelly; ron.kelly@citcomm.com; "Gospel Traxx" w/ Walt Love; "Sunday Morning Inspiration" w/ Gus Coleman & "Jazzentertainment w/ Jojo"; jo.jo@citcomm.com. Heard throughout Baton Rouge.

KRVS 88.7 FM
U of LA/Lafayette
Hubrard Blvd., Burke Hall
Rm. 126
Lafayette, LA 70504
watts: 100,000
main: 337-482-5787
request: 337-482-6991
www.krvs.org
webcast: Yes
genres: Zydeco, Cajun, Blues, World, Rock, Jazz
format: Public
reports to: CMJ, Living Blues
md: Cecil Doyle
e: cdoyle@krvs.org
Showcases indie & Reg'l music & airs in-studio/remote live sets to a 100-mile radius. Specialty shows feature Classical music. Send promos to: PO Box 42171, Lafayette, LA 70504.

WBRH 90.3 FM
2825 Government St.
Baton Rouge, LA 70806
watts: 21,000
main: 225-388-9030
e: gkenyon@ebrpss.k12.la.us
www.baton-rouge.com/wbrh
genres: Jazz, Smooth Jazz
format: Public
pd: Rob Payer
Airs 30% indies & Locals to a 40-mile radius.

New Orleans

KLRZ 100.3 FM
11603 Hwy. 308
PO Drawer 1350
Larose, LA 70373
watts: 89,000
main: 985-798-7792
request: 985-798-1003; 985-693-1600
e: klrz@mobiletel.com
www.klrzfm.com
webcast: Yes
genres: Cajun, Zydeco, Louisiana Music, Swamp Pop
format: Commercial
pd: Jerry Gisclair
e: truck@klrzfm.com
md: Buddy Miller
e: buddy@klrzfm.com
Happy to play indie acts to the greater New Orleans area.

WWOZ 90.7 FM
1008 N Peters St.
New Orleans, LA 70116
watts: 4000
main: 504-568-1239
request: 504-568-1234
e: wwoz@wwoz.org
www.wwoz.org
webcast: Yes
genres: Jazz, R&B, World, Blues, Zydeco, Cajun, Gospel
format: Public
pd: Dwayne Breashears
e: dwayne@wwoz.org
md: Scott Borne
e: scott@wwoz.org
Indies & all styles of Reg'l music; Gospel, Latin & Reggae shows on wknds. Promos: PO Box 51840, New Orleans, LA 70151.

Maine

Bangor

WERU 89.9/102.9 FM
1186 Acadia Hwy., Rte. 1
East Orland, ME 04431
watts: 15,000
main: 207-469-6600
request: 207-496-0500
e: info@weru.org
www.weru.org
webcast: Yes **podcast:** Yes
genres: Rock, Folk, Jazz, Blues, World, S/S
format: Public
reports to: CMJ, FMQB, AMA
pd: Joel Mann
e: radioboy@weru.org
md: Maggie Overton
ext: 207-469-3088
e: maggie@weru.org
Eclectic citizen-run station airs indie releases & specialty shows to over 60 miles.

Portland

WCYY 94.3 FM
1 City Ctr.
Portland, ME 04101
watts: 50,000
main: 207-774-6364
request: 207-792-WCYY
e: wcyy@wcyy.com
www.wcyy.com
webcast: Yes **podcast:** Yes
genres: Alt., Modern Rock
format: Commercial/Active Rock
reports to: Hits, FMQB
pd: Herb Ivy
e: herb.ivy@citcomm.com
md: Brian James
e: brian.james@citcomm.com
Indies in rotation & on "Spinout" Thu & Sun 7-10pm, spinout@wcyy.com. Reaches central & southern ME & eastern NH.

WMPG 90.9/104.1 FM
96 Falmouth St., Box 9300
Portland, ME 04104
watts: 1111
main: 207-780-4943
request: 207-780-4909
e: officemanager@wmpg.org
www.wmpg.org
webcast: Yes
genres: All Styles
format: Public
reports to: CMJ
pd: Dave Bunker
ext: 207-780-4598
e: programdirector@wmpg.org
md: Ron Raymond, Jr.
ext: 207-780-4976
e: musicdepartment@wmpg.org
Freeform station owned by U of Southern ME, has many

community/volunteer DJs & some student DJs spinning a wide variety of genres to Greater Gorham/Portland & mid-to-southern coastal ME. Snail mail submissions.

Maryland

Baltimore

WIYY 97.9 FM
3800 Hooper Ave.
Baltimore, MD 21211
watts: 50,000
main: 410-889-0098
request: 800-767-1098
www.98online.com
webcast: Yes **podcast:** Yes
genres: Rock
format: Commercial/Active Rock
reports to: R&R, Mediabase
pd: Dave Hill
ext: 410-388-6547
e: dshill@hearst.com
md: Rob Heckman
ext: 410-338-6631
e: rheckman@hearst.com
Showcases some indies & Reg'l talent for 60 miles. Reg'ls spin Sun 11pm-mid on "Noise In the Basement" w/ Matt Davis, mattdavis@hearst.com.

WRNR 103.1 FM
112 Main St., 3rd Fl.
Annapolis, MD 21401
watts: 8000
main: 410-626-0103
request: 410-269-1031
www.wrnr.com
webcast: Yes
genres: Alt., Prog
format: Commercial/AAA
reports to: Hits, FMQB, R&R
pd: Bob Waugh
ext: 410-626-0103 x14
e: bobw@wrnr.com
md: Alex Cortright
e: alex@wrnr.com
Reaches DC & MD w/ polished indies in the mix. Locals featured on "The Sunday Brunch" w/ Michael Buckley: voicesofthebay@aol.com; in-studio opps. on Thu.

WTMD 89.7 FM
8000 York Rd.
Towson, MD 21252
watts: 10,000
main: 410-704-8938
request: 410-704-8936
e: wtmd@towson.edu
www.wtmd.org
webcast: Yes
genres: S/S, Folk, Acoustic Rock, Blues, World, Alt. Country
format: Public/AAA
reports to: CMJ, R&R
pd: Mike Vasilikos
e: mvasilikos@towson.edu
Prime station for story-based music covers MD, DC & some VA. Specialty shows include: "Sounds Eclectic," "Putumayo World Music Hour," "Afro-pop Worldwide," "Reggae Rhythms," "Sunday Music," & "Afternoon Music." Send at least 1 copy of full album.

WWDC 101.1 FM
1801 Rockville Pike, Ste. 405
Rockville, MD 20852
watts: 50,000
main: 301-562-7157
request: 202-432-1101
www.dc101.com
webcast: Yes
genres: Rock, Alt.
format: Commercial/Alt.
reports to: BDS, Mediabase
pd: Dave Wellington
ext: 301-562-7128
e: davew@dc101.com
md: Greg Roche
e: roche@dc101.com
ClearChannel station airs indie releases & in-studio opps. "Local Lix" w/ Roche airs top VA, MD, DC metro area acts Sun 9pm - send FCC friendly CD w/ list of upcoming gigs & suggested track - No MP3s.

Greater MD

WOCM 98.1 FM
117 W 49th St.
Ocean City, MD 21842
watts: 3000
main: 410-723-3683
request: 877-723-9626
www.irieradio.com
webcast: Yes
genres: Rock
format: Commercial/AAA
pd: Skip Dixxon
ext: 410-723-3683 x202
e: skip.dixxon@irieradio.com
Indie-friendly station sponsors festivals. "Live Lixx" features in-studio performances by Local artists. Covers the Salisbury-Ocean City area.

Massachusetts

Boston

WBCN 104.1 FM
83 Leo M. Birmingham Pkwy.
Boston, MA 02135
watts: 50,000
main: 617-746-1400
request: 617-931-1041
www.wbcn.com
genres: Alt., Rock
format: Commercial
pd: Dan O'Brien
Some indies in mix & on-air opps. reach the metro area & into western MA. Local music show "Boston Emissions" Sun 10pm-midnite.

WBMX 98.5 FM
1200 Soldiers Field Rd.
Boston, MA 02134
watts: 9000
main: 617-779-2000
request: 617-931-1234
www.mix985.com
webcast: Yes
format: Commercial/Hot AC
pd: Jay Beau Jones
e: jaybeau@mix985.com
md: Mike Mullaney
e: mmullaney@mix985.com
CBS Radio station airs interviews & indies in the mix Sun 7-10am on "Acoustic Sunrise" w/ Dan O'Brien.

WCUW 91.3 FM
910 Main St.
Worcester, MA 01610
watts: 840
main: 508-753-1012
request: 508-753-2284
e: wcuw@wcuw.org
www.wcuw.com
genres: Folk, Jazz, Rock, Blues
format: Public
pd: Joe Cutroni
Features 80 very eclectic programs for central MA. Most music sent gets added to library.

WFNX 101.7 FM
25 Exchange St.
Lynn, MA 01901
watts: 3000
main: 781-595-6200
request: 781-595-WFNX
e: wfnx@wfnx.com
www.fnxradio.com
webcast: Yes **podcast:** Yes
genres: Alt., New Music, Jazz
format: Commercial/Alt., Rock
reports to: FMQB, R&R
pd: Keith Dakin
ext: 781-595-6200 x225
e: kdakin@fnxradio.com
md: Paul Driscoll
ext: 781-595-6200 x231
e: pdriscoll@fnxradio.com
Airs new music to MA, NH & southern ME. Reg'ls contact Dave Duncan host of "New England Product" at dduncan@fnxradio.com.

WGBH 89.7 FM
1 Guest St.
Boston, MA 02135
watts: 100,000
main: 617-300-2000
www.wgbh.org
webcast: Yes **podcast:** Yes
genres: Jazz, Folk, Blues, Classical
format: Public
pd: Jon Solins
e: jon_solins@wgbh.org
Indie-friendly NPR station w/ Jazz, Folk & Blues specialty shows broadcasts Reg'l releases & on-air opps. throughout parts of ME, NH, RI & MA.

WUMB 91.9 FM
U Mass/Boston
100 Morrissey Blvd.
Boston, MA 02125
watts: 660
main: 617-287-6900
request: 617-287-6919
e: wumb@umb.edu
www.wumb.org
webcast: Yes
genres: Folk, World, Blues, Acoustic
format: Public
md: John Laurenti
e: wumb.music@umb.org
Indie music & some on-air opps. on 5 transmitters reach MA, RI, NH, ME & CT.

Cape Cod

WPXC 102.9 FM
278 S Sea Ave.
West Yarmouth, MA 02673
watts: 6000
main: 508-775-5678
request: 800-445-7499
e: info@pixy103.com
www.pixy103.com
webcast: Yes
genres: Rock
format: Commercial
reports to: R&R, FMQB
pd: Suzanne Tonaire
ext: 508-775-5678 x6973
e: rockbabe@pixy103.com
Blankets Cape Cod & southeastern MA w/ Reg'ls featured on "Homegrown," Sun 8-10pm & indies on "Get Connected."

Springfield

WLZX 99.3 FM
45 Fisher Ave.
East Longmeadow, MA 01208
watts: 6000
main: 413-525-4141
request: 413-526-9932
e: comments@lazer993.com
www.lazer993.com
format: Commercial/Active Rock
pd: Courtney Quinn
e: courtney@lazer993.com
On-air opps. & indie releases broadcast to parts of CT, MA & VT. Sun nite "Big Bang" spotlights new Local releases.

WRNX 100.9 FM
1331 Main St., 4th Fl.
Springfield, MA 01103
watts: 5000
main: 413-536-1105
request: 413-536-1009
e: info@wrnx.com
www.wrnx.com
webcast: Yes **podcast:** Yes
format: Commercial/AAA
reports to: FMQB
pd: Pat McKay
e: patmckay@clearchannel.com
md: Kevin Johnson
e: kevinjohnson@clearchannel.com
Indies & specialty shows to MA & parts of CT, VT, & NH. Accepts MP3s via online uploader.

WRSI 93.9 FM
15 Hampton Ave.
Northampton, MA 01060
watts: 5000
main: 413-586-7400
request: 413-585-0927
www.wrsi.com
format: Commercial/AAA
reports to: FMQB
pd: Sean O'Mealy
e: sean@wrsi.com
md: Chris Belmonte
e: monte@wrsi.com
Some indie releases & Locals in rotation. Covers MA, NH, VT, & northern CT on 101.5, 104.3 & 97.1.

Michigan

Detroit/Ann Arbor

CIMX 88.7 FM
30100 Telegraph Rd., Ste. 460
Bingham Farms, MI 48025
watts: 100,000
main: 313-961-9811
request: 313-298-7999
www.89xradio.com
webcast: Yes **podcast:** Yes
genres: New Rock, Alt.
format: Commercial
reports to: R&R, Mediabase
pd: Vince Cannova
ext: 313-961-9811 x275
e: cannova@89xradio.com
md: Jay Hudson
ext: 313-961-9811 x262
e: jay@89xradio.com
Broadcasts from southeastern MI into Canada. Also has New Rock & Alt. specialty shows. Locals featured on "Homeboy Show."

WDET 101.9 FM
4600 Cass Ave.
Detroit, MI 48201
watts: 46,000
main: 313-577-4146
e: wdetfm@wdetfm.org
www.wdetfm.org
webcast: Yes **podcast:** Yes
genres: Jazz, Gospel, Folk, R&B, Bluegrass
format: Public

reports to: CMJ, R&R, FMQB, Hits
pd: Allen Mazurek
e: a.mazurek@wdetfm.org
Owned by Wayne State U & features various specialty shows heard in metro Detroit & Windsor, ON.

WEMU 89.1 FM
PO Box 980350
Ypsilanti, MI 48198
watts: 16,000
main: 734-487-2229
request: 734-487-8936; 888-299-8910
e: wemu@wemu.org
www.wemu.org
webcast: Yes
genres: Jazz, Blues, Afro-Cuban, Brazilian, Funk, Avant-Garde, Americana
format: Public
reports to: Living Blues, Roots Music Report, JazzWeek
pd: Clark Smith
e: csmith@emich.edu
md: Linda Yohn
e: lyohn@emich.edu
NPR station w/ 90+ hours of Jazz, varied specialty shows & indie releases covers southeast MI & northwest Ohio. On-air opps. from artists performing locally.

Grand Rapids/ Kalamazoo/Lansing

WBLV/WLBU 90.3/88.9 FM
300 E Crystal Lake Rd.
Twin Lake, MI 49457
watts: 100,000/650
main: 231-894-5656
e: radio@bluelake.org
www.bluelake.org/radio
webcast: Yes
genres: Classical, Jazz, Folk
format: Public
reports to: Groove Marketing, JazzWeek
pd: Steve Albert
md: Bonnie Bierma
Blue Lake Fine Arts Camp station airs indies at nite & wknds. Jazz & Folk shows, plus on-air opps. blanket 12 counties in western MI, repeater station, WBLV 90.3 FM covers the Muskegon region.

WGRD 97.9 FM
50 Monroe NW, Ste. 500
Grand Rapids, MI 49503
watts: 13,000
main: 616-459-4111
request: 616-770-9473
e: studio@wgrd.com
www.wgrd.com
webcast: Yes **podcast:** Yes
genres: Alt., Modern Rock, Latin, Pop
format: Commercial
reports to: R&R
pd: Jerry Tarrants
e: jtarrants@wgrd.com
Indies, in-studio opps. & "Ultra Sound," Sun 9-10pm featuring indie & Local acts. Reaches metro Grand Rapids. Posts Local music news on site.

WGVU 88.5 FM/ 850AM FM
301 W Fulton Ave.
Grand Rapids, MI 49504
watts: 3000
main: 616-331-6666
e: wgvunews@gvsu.edu
www.wgvu.org
webcast: Yes **podcast:** Yes
genres: Jazz, Blues, World, Reggae
format: Public/Jazz
pd: Scott Vander Werf
e: scott_vanderwerf@gvsu.edu
Owned by Grande Valley State U & features some indies & covers western MI. For specialty shows, contact: Shelley Irwin at irwinsh@gvsu.edu. Sponsors Thu nite Jazz concerts @ Z's Bar & Grill.

WLNZ 89.7 FM
400 N Capitol, Ste. 001
Lansing, MI 48933
watts: 1000
main: 517-483-1710
request: 517-483-1000
e: wlnzinfo@yahoo.com
www.wlnz.org
webcast: Yes
genres: Jazz, Blues, Reggae, Acoustic, Latin
format: Public/AAA
reports to: CMJ, Living Blues, Smooth Jazz, Yellow Dog
pd: Lyn Peraino
e: wlnzlyn@yahoo.com
md: Daedalian Lowry
e: wlnzdae@yahoo.com
Student/community station airs eclectic music to central MI.

WMUK 102.1 FM
Western Michigan U, 1903 W Michigan Ave.
Kalamazoo, MI 49008
watts: 50,000
main: 269-387-5715
e: webmaster@wmuk.org
www.wmuk.org
webcast: Yes **podcast:** Yes
genres: Jazz, Classical, Opera
format: Public
pd: Klayton Woodworth
ext: 269-387-5725
e: klayton.woodworth@wmich.edu
NPR station owned by Western Michigan U w/ 60-mile broadcast radius airs specialty shows: "Alma Latina" (Spanish language); "Grassroots" (Folk/Bluegrass); "The Teardrop" (Celtic) & "Rewind" (Eclectic Rock) + syndicates "Broadway Revisited."

WYCE 88.1 FM
711 Bridge St. NW
Grand Rapids, MI 49504
watts: 7000
main: 616-459-4788
www.wyce.org
webcast: Yes
genres: Folk, Blues, Jazz, Rock, World, Americana
format: Public/AAA
reports to: R&R, FMQB, Living Blues, JazzWeek
pd: Kevin Murphy
ext: 616-459-4788 x111
e: kevin@wyce.org
md: Peter Bruinsma
ext: 616-459-4788 x110
e: pete@wyce.org
Transmits over 40 miles.

Greater MI

WCMU 89.5 FM
1999 E Campus Dr.
Mount Pleasant, MI 48859
watts: 100,000
main: 989-774-3105
request: 989-774-3300
www.wcmu.org
webcast: Yes
genres: Classical, Jazz, Blues, Folk, Celtic, Bluegrass
format: Public/Classical
pd: Ray Ford
e: ford1r@cmich.edu
Station repeats signal to 6 stations throughout northern MI.

WNMC 90.7 FM
1701 E Front St.
Traverse City, MI 49686
watts: 600
main: 231-995-2562
request: 231-995-1090
e: wnmc@nmc.edu
www.wnmc.org
webcast: Yes
genres: Jazz, Folk, Rock, Country, Blues, Electronic
format: Public
reports to: CMJ
pd: Eric Hines
e: ehines@nmc.edu
Indie-friendly community station blankets northwest MI.

Minnesota

Duluth/Grand Rapids

KAXE 91.7 FM
260 NE 2nd St.
Grand Rapids, MN 55744
watts: 100,000
main: 218-326-1234
e: kaxe@kaxe.org
www.kaxe.org
webcast: Yes
genres: Folk, Rock, Blues, World, Jazz
format: Public
reports to: FMQB
pd: Mark Tarner
e: mtarner@kaxe.org
Volunteers spin eclectic mix to northcentral/northeast MN on repeater stations 89.9 FM & 105.3 FM.

KUMD 103.3 FM
U of Minnesota, 130 Humanities, 1201 Ordean Ct.
Duluth, MN 55812
watts: 100,000
main: 218-726-7181
request: 800-566-KUMD
e: kumd@d.umn.edu
www.kumd.org
webcast: Yes
genres: S/S, World, Americana, R&B, Jazz, Womyn's, Alt.
format: Public
reports to: CMJ
pd: John Ziegler
e: jziegler@d.umn.edu
Broadcasts indies in mix & specialty shows throughout northeast MN & northwest WI.

Minneapolis/ St. Paul/Mankato

KBEM 88.5 FM
1555 James Ave. N
Minneapolis, MN 55411
watts: 2900
main: 612-668-1745
request: 612-668-1735
e: studio@jazz88fm.com
www.jazz88fm.com
webcast: Yes
genres: Jazz
format: Public
reports to: Jazziz
pd: Michele Jansen
e: michele.jansen@mpls.k12.mn.us
md: Kevin O'Connor
ext: 612-668-1752
e: kevino@jazz88fm.com
Also airs interviews & wknd Blues & Bluegrass specialty shows to the Twin City metro area. For Bluegrass, contact: Phil Nusbaum at pnusbaum@bitstream.net.

KCMP 89.3/88.7 FM
480 Cedar St.
St. Paul, MN 55101
watts: 98,000
main: 651-290-1500
request: 651-989-4893
e: mail@mpr.org
www.thecurrent.org
webcast: Yes **podcast:** Yes
format: Public/AAA
reports to: FMQB, CMJ
pd: Steve Nelson
e: snelson@mpr.org
md: Melanie Walker
e: mwalker@mpr.org
Extremely indie-friendly station airs in-studio opps. & specialty shows to a 70-mile radius.

KDWB 101.3 FM
1600 Utica Ave. S, Ste. 400
Minneapolis, MN 55416
watts: 100,000
main: 952-417-3000
request: 651-989-KDWB
www.kdwb.com
webcast: Yes
genres: Top 40
format: Commercial/CHR
reports to: Soundscan
pd: Rob Morris
ext: 952-417-3268
e: robmorris@clearchannel.com
md: Lucas Phelan
ext: 952-417-3269
e: lucasphelan@clearchannel.com
Interviews/performances & on specialty shows for the Twin Cities.

KEEY 102.1 FM
1600 Utica Ave. S, Ste. 400
Minneapolis, MN 55416
watts: 100,000
main: 952-417-3220
request: 651-989-5102
e: k102studio@clearchannel.com
www.k102.com
webcast: Yes **podcast:** Yes
genres: Country
format: Commercial
pd: Gregg Swedberg
ext: 952-417-3247
e: greggswedberg@clearchannel.com
md: Mary Callas
e: marycallas@clearchannel.com
Mainstream Country w/ some indies; "The Roadhouse" plays 90% indie Rockabilly & Country, Sat 10pm-midnite, host Donna Valentine: donnavalentine@clearchannel.com.

KMOJ 89.9 FM
1422 W Lake St., Ste. #300
Minneapolis, MN 55408
watts: 1000
main: 612-377-0594
request: 612-377-3335
e: info@kmojfm.com
www.kmojfm.com
genres: R&B, Gospel, Jazz, Hip-Hop, Blues, Reggae
format: Public
pd: Kelvin Quarles

e: kquarles@kmojfm.com
md: LA Phillips
e: sonnyday@kmojfm.com
Features releases & specialty shows for metro listening area.

KMSU/KMSK 89.7/91.3 FM
1536 Warren St., #205
Mankato, MN 56001
watts: 20,000
main: 507-389-5678
www.kmsu.org
webcast: Yes
genres: Jazz, Blues, Hard Rock, Folk
format: Public
reports to: CMJ
pd: Jim Gullickson
e: james.gullickson@mnsu.edu
md: Shelley Pierce
e: shelley215@juno.com
Eclectic specialty shows heard throughout southern MN & northern IA. For specialty shows, contact: Nick "Jeffro" Iverson at badjeffro@gmail.com; send Blues, Jazz, Zydeco & R&B to Mark Havlerson.

KTCZ 97.1 FM
1600 Utica Ave. S
Minneapolis, MN 55416
watts: 100,000
main: 952-417-3222
request: 651-989-9797
www.cities97.com
webcast: Yes **podcast:** Yes
format: Commercial/AAA
reports to: Mediabase
pd: Lauren MacLeash
ext: 952-417-3291
e: laurenmacleash@clearchannel.com
md: Thorn
e: thorn@clearchannel.com
Covers the Twin Cities & parts of WI w/ Sun nite indies & imports played on "Freedom Rock" w/ Brian Oake: BrianOake@Cities97.com & Jason Nagel plays Reg'ls: Jason@Cities97.com.

KUOM 770 AM/ 106.5/100.7 FM
U of MN, 610 Rarig Ctr.
330 21st Ave. S
Minneapolis, MN 55455
watts: 5000/8
main: 612-625-3500
request: 612-626-4770
www.radiok.org
webcast: Yes **podcast:** Yes
genres: Rock, Punk, World, Ska, Goth, Metal, Americana, Jazz, Soul, Electronic, Hip-Hop
format: Public
reports to: CMJ
pd: Matt Herting
e: programming@radiok.org
md: Pushkar Ojha
ext: 612-625-5304
e: music@radiok.org
Indie beacon w/ mix of specialty shows covers a 60-mile radius.

WHMH 101.7 FM
1010 2nd St. N, PO Box 366
Sauk Rapids, MN 56379
watts: 50,000
main: 320-252-6200
request: 320-252-6201
e: mail@rockin101.com
www.rockin101.com
webcast: Yes
genres: Rock
format: Commercial
reports to: R&R, FMQB
pd: Gary Hoppe
md: Tim Dehn
e: tim.j.dehn@tricountybroadcasting.com
Showcases area artists throughout central MN. Sun nite's "MN Homegrown" features Locals w/ host Tim Ryan (www.myspace.com/101mnhomegrown).

Greater MN

WELY 94.5 FM
133 E Chapman St.
Ely, MN 55731
watts: 14,500
main: 218-365-4444
e: welydj@wely.com
www.wely.com
webcast: Yes
format: Commercial/AAA
reports to: Album Network, New Age Voice, Living Blues
pd: Brett Ross
e: production@wely.com
Eclectic programming reaches a 45-mile radius. Large front window & porch make on-air performances popular w/ artists.

Mississippi

Hattiesburg

WJZD 94.5 FM
PO Box 6216
Gulfport, MS 39506
watts: 6000
main: 228-896-5307
request: 866-945-9455; 228-367-1010
e: info@wjzd.com
www.wjzd.com
webcast: Yes
genres: Blues, Urban
format: Commercial/UC
pd: Rob Neal
ext: 228-896-5307 x115
e: robnealn@aol.com
md: Tabari Daniels
ext: 228-896-5307 x109
e: tabari@wjzd.com
One of the few Afro-American owned stations in the state broadcasts the syndicated "American Blues Network" aired throughout America.

WKNN 99.1 FM
286 DeBuys Rd.
Biloxi, MS 39531
watts: 99,000
main: 228-388-2323
request: 228-993-7529
www.k99fm.com
webcast: Yes
format: Commercial/Country
pd: Walter Brown
ext: 228-388-2323 x129
e: walterbrown@clearchannel.com
Broadcasts to a 90-mile radius; not much indie music.

WUSM 88.5 FM
U of Southern Miss.
118 College Dr., #10045
Hattiesburg, MS 39406
watts: 3000
main: 601-266-4287
e: wusm@usm.edu
www.usm.edu/wusm
webcast: Yes
genres: Alt., College Rock, Americana, Electronic, Jazz, Classical, Roots, Blues
format: Public
reports to: CMJ
Progressive station offers many specialty shows & indies in mix to southern MS.

Jackson

WJSU 88.5 FM
PO Box 18450
Jackson, MS 39217
watts: 24,500
main: 601-979-2140
request: 601-979-1291
e: wjsufm@jsums.edu
www.wjsu.org
webcast: Yes **podcast:** Yes
genres: Jazz
format: Public
reports to: BRE, JazzWeek
md: Jonas Adams
ext: 601-979-2877
e: jonas.r.adams@jsums.edu
Located on Jackson State U campus & reaches a 50-mile radius. Some indies & Reg'ls make the playlist, as well as on-air sets & specialty shows.

WMPR 90.1 FM
1018 Pecan Park Cir.
Jackson, MS 39209
watts: 100,000
main: 601-948-5835
request: 601-948-5950
e: frontoffice@wmpr901.com
www.wmpr901.com
webcast: Yes
genres: Blues, Gospel, R&B, Latin, Reggae, Hip-Hop, Jazz
format: Public/Blues, Gospel
pd: Wanda Johnson
Airs indie releases to an 80-mile range reaching into parts of AL & AR. Send promos to: PO Box 9782, Jackson, MS 39286.

Greater MS

WMSV 91.1 FM
Mississippi State U
Student Media Ctr.
PO Box 6210
Mississippi State, MS 39762
watts: 14,000
main: 662-325-8034
request: 662-325-8064
e: wmsv@msstate.edu
www.wmsv.msstate.edu
webcast: Yes
format: Public/AAA
reports to: AAAradio.com
pd: Steve Ellis
ext: 662-325-8434
Airs indie releases & on-air opps. to a 70-mile radius.

Missouri

Kansas City

KCUR 89.3 FM
4825 Troost Ave., Ste. 202
Kansas City, MO 64110
watts: 100,000
main: 816-235-1551
e: kcur@umkc.edu
www.kcur.org
webcast: Yes **podcast:** Yes
genres: Blues, Jazz, New Age, World, Gospel, Alt.
format: Public
reports to: CMJ, New Age Voice
pd: Bill Anderson
e: andersonw@umkc.edu
U of MO station covers a 90-mile radius w/ some indies & Local music shows: "The Fish Fry" (Blues, Jazz, Zydeco) & "Cypress Ave" (Eclectic).

KKFI 90.1 FM
PO Box 32250
Kansas City, MO 64171
watts: 100,000
main: 816-931-3122
request: 816-931-5534
e: billc@kkfi.org
www.kkfi.org
webcast: Yes
genres: Blues, Jazz, World, Americana, Alt., Folk, Reggae, Hip-Hop
format: Public
reports to: FMQB
pd: Linda Wilson
e: linda.kkfi@gmail.com
Lots of specialty shows & indie releases heard in Kansas City & beyond.

KMZU 100.7 FM
102 N Mason
Carrollton, MO 64633
watts: 100,000
main: 660-542-0404
request: 800-214-2173
www.kmzu.com
format: Commercial/Country
reports to: Bulls Eye
pd: Scott Powell
e: scottp@kmzu.com
md: Jim Woods
e: jimborama63@yahoo.com
Broadcasts reaches an 80-mile radius & 48 counties. Syndicates "The Rick Jackson Country Music Hall of Fame" shows.

KPRS/KPRT 103.3 FM/1590 AM
11131 Colorado Ave.
Kansas City, MO 64137
watts: 100,000/1000
main: 816-763-2040
request: 816-576-7103
www.kprs.com
webcast: Yes
genres: Hip-Hop, R&B
format: Commercial/Urban
pd: Myron D
e: myrond@kprs.com
Hip-Hop for Kansas City w/ indies & Locals in the mix.

KTBG 90.9/104.9 FM
Wood 11
Warrensburg, MO 64093
watts: 100,000
main: 866-909-2743
www.ktbg.fm
genres: Blues, Jazz, World
format: Public/AAA
reports to: R&R, FMQB, Hits, AAAradio.com
pd: Jon Hart
ext: 660-543-4491
e: jhart@ktbg.fm
Spins indies on "Eclectic Café" & "Blues Quest" to metro area. On-air opps. for bands w/ CDs in rotation.

Springfield

KADI 99.5 FM
5431 W Sunshine
Brookline Station, MO 65619
watts: 6000
main: 417-831-0995
request: 417-831-5234
www.99hitfm.com
genres: CCM, Christian Rock
format: Commercial
reports to: R&R, Billboard
pd: Rod Kittleman
ext: 417-831-0995 x17
e: rod@99hitfm.com

Signal covers a 50-mile radius. Indies send demos for a shot at air time.

KSMU 91.1 FM
901 S National Ave.
Springfield, MO 65897
watts: 40,000
main: 417-836-5878
e: ksmu@missouristate.edu
www.ksmu.org
podcast: Yes
genres: Jazz, Americana, World, Celtic, Classical, Blues
format: Public
pd: Missy Belote
ext: 417-836-4751
e: missyshelton@ksmu.org
md: Randy Stewart
ext: 417-836-6361
e: randystewart@missouristate.edu
Indies & Local on-air opps. reach 50 miles into northern AR. For Specialty Shows, contact: John Darkhorse at johndarkhorsetp@yahoo.com or Lee Worman.

St. Louis/Columbia

KDHX 88.1 FM
3504 Magnolia
St. Louis, MO 63118
watts: 43,000
main: 314-664-3955
request: 314-664-3688
www.kdhx.org
genres: Rock, Americana, Alt., World, Hip-Hop, Blues
format: Public
reports to: CMJ, AMA
pd: Larry Weir
ext: 314-664-3955 x303
e: ljweir@kdhx.org
md: Nico Leone
ext: 314-664-3955 x301
e: musicdepartment@kdhx.org
Over 75 non-mainstream programs transmitted for 80mi.

KOPN 89.5 FM
915 E Broadway
Columbia, MO
65201
watts: 40,000
main: 573-874-1139
request: 573-874-5676
e: mail@kopn.org
www.kopn.org
genres: Country, Classical, New Age, Jazz, Blues, World, Ethnic, Heavy Metal
format: Public
reports to: AMA, Freeform American Roots
pd: David Owens
e: kopngm@yahoo.com
md: Steve Jerrett
e: md@kopnmusic.org
Indies & Locals in rotation transmitted throughout central MO. Airs Locals on "Collective Hearts" from 3-5pmon Tue. Send packaged full-length CDs only.

Montana

Billings

KEMC 91.7 FM
1500 University Dr.
Billings, MT 59101
watts: 100,000
main: 406-657-2941; 800-441-2941
e: mail@ypradio.org
www.ypradio.org
genres: Classical, Jazz, Folk, Blues, Rock, Alt.
format: Public
pd: Lois Bent
e: lbent@ypradio.org
md: Brad Edwards
Indies & very few in-studio opps. to 2/3 of MT & northern WY & repeated on 30+ stations across the state. "Montana Muse" features Reg'l acts: scott@museco.org; "String n' Things" features Bluegrass, Folk & Celtic acts w/ Doug Ezell & Fred Buckley; "Blue Light Boogie" features Blues.

Bozeman

KGLT 91.9 FM
MSU SUB, Rm. 325
Bozeman, MT 59717
watts: 20,000
main: 406-994-3001
request: 406-994-4492
e: wwwkglt@montana.edu
www.kglt.net
genres: Rock, Americana, Blues, World, Hip-Hop
format: Public
reports to: CMJ
md: James Kehoe
ext: 406-994-6483
e: kgltmus@montana.edu
Freeform station has Bluegrass specialty show & live weekly performances w/ Local acts.

KMMS 95.1 FM
125 W Mendenhall St.
Bozeman, MT 59715
watts: 100,000
main: 406-586-2343
request: 406-587-0951
www.mooseradio.com
genres: Rock
format: Commercial/AAA
reports to: R&R, FMQB, AAAradio.com, Mediabase
pd: Michelle Wolfe
e: michellewolfe@gapbroadcasting.com
Some indie releases, specialty shows & to a 75-mile radius.

Great Falls

KGPR 89.9 FM
2100 16th Ave. S
Great Falls, MT 59406
watts: 9500
main: 406-268-3739
request: 406-268-3737
e: kgpr@msugf.edu
http://kgpr.msugf.edu
genres: Jazz, World, Urban, Blues, Alt., New Age, Americana
format: Public
reports to: CMJ
pd: Tom Halverson
Indie releases, specialty shows & Reg'l on-air performances transmitted over 80 miles.

Missoula

KUFM 89.1 FM
U of Montana
Missoula, MT 59812
watts: 17,400
main: 406-243-4931
request: 800-325-1565
www.mtpr.org
genres: Folk, Jazz, New Age, World
format: Public/Jazz
pd: Michael Marsolek
U of MT owned airs indie music & in-studio interviews to western & central MT via 11 repeater stations.

Nebraska

Lincoln/Omaha

KEZO 92.3 FM
5030 N 72nd St.
Omaha, NE 68134
watts: 100,000
main: 402-592-5300
request: 800-955-9230; 402-938-9200
www.z92.com
webcast: Yes **podcast:** Yes
genres: Rock
format: Commercial
reports to: R&R, FMQB, BDS
pd: Steve Brill
e: sbrill@journalbroadcastgroup.com
md: Jessica Dol
e: jessica@z92.com
Mostly mainstream station broadcasting on-air opps. for 120mi, slips some indies in the mix. Reg'ls send materials to: Scott Murphy; scott@z92.com for "Homegrown."

KIOS 91.5 FM
3230 Burt St.
Omaha, NE 68131
watts: 55,000
main: 402-557-2777
e: listener@kios.org
www.kios.org
webcast: Yes **podcast:** Yes
genres: Jazz, Blues, Folk, Bluegrass
format: Public
reports to: Living Blues, JazzWeek
pd: Bob Coate
ext: 402-557-2777 x2556
e: robert.coate@ops.org
md: Mike Jacobs
ext: 402-557-2557
e: mike.jacobs@ops.org
Omaha Public School station broadcasts to a 70-mile radius.

KQCH 94.1 FM
5030 N 72nd St.
Omaha, NE 68134
watts: 100,000
main: 402-592-5300
request: 402-962-9400
www.channel941.com
webcast: Yes **podcast:** Yes
genres: Pop, Hip-Hop, Dance, R&B, Rock, CHR
format: Commercial
reports to: R&R, BDS
pd: Mark Todd
ext: 402-592-5300 x5410
e: mtodd@journalbroadcastgroup.com
md: Corey Young
ext: 402-898-5322
e: corey@channel941.com
Spins on-air opps. & specialty shows to a 100-150-mile radius. Will consider indie releases that fit their format.

KUCV 91.1 FM
1800 N 33rd St.
Lincoln, NE 68503
watts: 100,000
main: 402-472-3611
e: radio@netnebraska.org
www.netnebraska.org/radio
webcast: Yes **podcast:** Yes
genres: Jazz, Blues, World, Classical
format: Public
pd: Nancy Finken
ext: 402-472-9333 x365
e: nfinken2@unl.edu
md: Bill Stibor
ext: 402-472-9333 x510
e: bstibor@netnebraska.org
Blankets the state w/ specialty shows & indie releases. Repeater stations hit Alliance, N Platte, Merriman, Bassett, Lexington, Hastings & Chadron. Send Jazz, Blues & World promos to: Dave Hughes at dhughes5@netnebraska.org.

KZUM 89.3 FM
941 O St., Ste. 1025
Lincoln, NE 68508
watts: 1500
main: 402-474-5086
e: webmaster@kzum.org
www.kzum.org
webcast: Yes
genres: Blues, Folk, Jazz, Urban, Americana, World, Gospel, New Age, Rock, Funk
format: Public
reports to: Jazziz
pd: Jesse Starita
e: programming@kzum.org
Specialty programs, & indies heard for 45-mile radius.

North Platte/Kearney

KELN 97.1 FM
1301 E 4th St., PO Box 248
North Platte, NE 69101
watts: 100,000
main: 308-532-1120
request: 308-532-1121
www.mix97one.com
genres: AC
format: Commercial
pd: David Fudge
e: david.fudge@eagleradio.net
Mostly mainstream station spins Local & new releases on "Outlaw Radio" Fri 8pm-midnite w/ host sean.condon@eagleradio.net. 70-mile radius.

KQKY 105.9 FM
2223 Central Ave.
Kearney, NE 68847
watts: 100,000
main: 308-698-2106
request: 308-698-2144
www.kqky.com
genres: Rock, Pop, Top 40
format: Commercial
reports to: New Music Weekly
pd: Mitch Cooley
ext: 308-236-6464
e: mcooley@nrgmedia.com
md: Mark Reid
Spins some indies for the entire state. Send promos to: PO Box 669, Tri-Cities, NE 68848.

Nevada

Las Vegas

KCEP 88.1 FM
330 W Washington Ave.
Las Vegas, NV 89106
watts: 10,000
main: 702-648-0104
request: 702-647-3688
e: power88@power88lv.com
www.power88lv.com
webcast: Yes
genres: Classic Soul, Jazz, Gospel
format: Public/UC
reports to: Spins
pd: Craig Knight
ext: 702-648-0104 x224
e: cknight@power88lv.com
md: DJ Benzo

ext: 702-648-0104 x226
e: djbenzo@power88lv.com
NPR & AAPRC outlet caters to the area's Black community w/ events & programming. Signal blankets metro region.

KOMP 92.3 FM
8755 W Flamingo
Las Vegas, NV 89147
watts: 100,000
main: 702-876-1460
request: 702-876-3692
www.komp.com
format: Commercial/Active Rock
reports to: R&R, FMQB
pd: John Griffin
e: johng@komp.com
md: Carlota Gonzalez
e: carlota@komp.com
"Homegrown Show," homegrown@komp.com, airs indies.

KSOS 90.5 FM
2201 S 6th St.
Las Vegas, NV 89104
watts: 100,000
main: 702-731-5452
e: info@sosradio.net
www.sosradio.net
webcast: Yes
genres: CCM
format: Public
reports to: CRW
pd: Scott Herrold
Flagship station of the SOS Network airs on 40+ stations in 9 states. Airs indies & hosts on-air interviews.

KUNV 91.5 FM
1515 E Tropicana Ave., Ste. 240
Las Vegas, NV 89119
watts: 15,000
main: 702-798-9169
request: 702-798-8797
e: david.reese@unlv.edu
www.kunv.org
genres: Jazz, Latin, Reggae, Blues, Folk, World, Hawaiian
format: Public
reports to: Media Guide
pd: Frank Mueller
ext: 702-798-9191
e: frank.mueller@unlv.edu
md: Kim Linzy
ext: 702-798-9161
e: kim.linzy@unlv.edu
Lots of indies in the mix & on specialty shows reach surrounding areas. Small acts perform in-studio.

KVGS 107.9 FM
2725 E Desert Inn Rd., Ste. 180
Las Vegas, NV 89121
watts: 98,000
main: 702-784-4000
request: 702-732-1079
www.area1079.com
webcast: Yes
genres: Alt., Punk
format: Commercial/Alt.
pd: Duncan
e: duncan@rbgvegas.com
md: Violet
e: violet@rbgvegas.com
Indies in the mix & on specialty shows heard throughout southern NV. 'Local Show Joe' spins Reg'ls Sun 10-11pm on "Local 107.9." Violet plays wide selection on "Indie 107.9" Sun 8-10pm; 702-784-4000, violet@rbgvegas.com.

KXTE 107.5 FM
6655 W Sahara Ave., Ste. #D110
Las Vegas, NV 89146
watts: 50,000
main: 702-257-1075
request: 702-791-1075
www.xtremeradio.com
genres: Rock
format: Commercial
reports to: R&R, FMQB
pd: Chris Ripley
e: chris@xtremeradio.fm
md: Homie
e: homie@xtremeradio.fm
Mainstream station features indies w/ Vegas gigs on "It Hurts When I Pee." Covers the greater Las Vegas area.

Reno/Carson City

KDOT 104.5 FM
2900 Sutro St.
Reno, NV 89512
watts: 45,000
main: 775-329-9261
request: 775-793-1045
www.kdot.com
webcast: Yes
genres: Rock, Alt.
format: Commercial
reports to: R&R, Mediabase
pd: Jave Patterson
e: javepatt@gmail.com
Indies in mix & on specialty shows & in-studio opps. for Reno & the surrounding areas. "Pure Rock Backyard" on Sun 9pm features Reg'l Rock, hosted by Chuck: justplainchuck@kdot.com.

KNIS 91.3 FM
6363 Hwy. 50 E
Carson City, NV 89701
watts: 67,000
main: 800-541-5647
e: info@pilgrimradio.com
www.pilgrimradio.com
webcast: Yes
genres: CCM
format: Public
pd: Bill Feltner
ext: 800-541-5647 x17
md: Patrick Herman
On-air interviews for Christian-oriented musicians is repeated on 50+ stations in MT, WY, NV & eastern CA. Send promos to: Pilgrim Radio, PO Box 21888, Carson City, NV 89721.

KRZQ 100.9 FM
300 E 2nd St., Ste. 1400
Reno, NV 89501
watts: 6000
main: 775-333-0123
request: 775-793-1009
e: contact@krzqfm.com
www.krzqfm.com
webcast: Yes
genres: Alt.
format: Commercial
reports to: R&R, Mediabase, FMQB
pd: Mel Flores
e: mel@krzqfm.com
md: Chris Payne
e: payne@krzqfm.com
Indie releases cover a 40-mile radius. Jason Sims hosts Sun nite "Wake The Neighbors" w/ spotlight on new & Reg'l releases: sims@krzqfm.com.

KTHX 100.1 FM
300 E 2nd St.
14th Fl.
Reno, NV 89501
watts: 824
main: 775-333-0123
request: 775-852-5849
e: contact@kthxfm.com
www.kthxfm.com
webcast: Yes
format: Commercial/AAA
reports to: R&R, FMQB, Mediabase
pd: Mark Keefe
ext: 775-333-7625
e: mark@kthxfm.com
md: David Herold
e: dave@kthxfm.com
A few Local & indie acts in the mix & on Blues, Alt. Country & Roots specialty shows.

KUNR 88.7 FM
U of Nevada/Reno
Mail Stop 0294
Reno, NV 89557
watts: 20,000
main: 775-327-5867
e: news@kunr.edu
www.kunr.org
webcast: Yes **podcast:** Yes
genres: Jazz, Reggae, Alt., Americana, Lounge, Blues
format: Public/Classical, Jazz
reports to: CMJ
pd: David Stipech
e: stipech@kunr.org
md: Danna Higley
ext: 775-682-6054
e: dannah@unr.edu
Jazz nitely, some indies & several specialty programs for Reno & Carson City areas.

New Hampshire

Dover/Manchester/Portsmouth

WGIR 101.1 FM
195 McGregor St., Ste. 810
Manchester, NH 03102
watts: 100,000
main: 603-625-6915
request: 603-668-0234
www.rock101fm.com
webcast: Yes **podcast:** Yes
genres: Mainstream Rock
format: Commercial
pd: Chris Garrett
ext: 603-625-6915 x1057
e: doc@wheb.com; chrisgarrett@clearchannel.com
md: Angela Anderson
Some indies slip in 50-mile radius.

WHEB 100.3 FM
815 Lafayette Rd.
Portsmouth, NH 03801
watts: 50,000
main: 603-436-7300
request: 603-431-7625
www.wheb.com
webcast: Yes **podcast:** Yes
genres: Active Rock
format: Commercial
reports to: Mediabase, R&R
pd: Doc
e: doc@wheb.com
md: J.R.
e: jr@wheb.com
ClearChannel station airs Nu Metal, Blues & Reg'l specialty shows to Manchester, south to Boston & north to Portland. Reg'ls every Mon-Fri @ 12:30am on "Local Licks" w/ J.R. & "Blues Power Hour" Sun 7:30am-9am.

WPHX 92.1 FM
1 Washington St.
Ste. 204
Dover, NH 03820
watts: 3000/1800
main: 603-749-5900
request: 877-369-7234
e: fnxradio@fnxradio.com
www.fnxradio.com
webcast: Yes
genres: Alt., Rock
format: Commercial
pd: Keith Dakin
ext: 781-595-6200 x225
e: kdakin@fnxradio.com
md: Paul Driscoll
ext: 781-595-6200 x231
e: pdriscoll@fnxradio.com
WFNX network member relays Boston station's programming including Dave Duncan's (dduncan@fnxradio.com) "New England Product" throughout NH & southern ME.

Hanover

WFRD 99.3 FM
6176 Robinson Hall,
Dartmouth College, 3rd Fl.
Hanover, NH 03755
watts: 6000
main: 603-646-3313
request: 603-643-ROCK
e: heath.cole@dartmouth.edu
www.wfrd.com
webcast: Yes
genres: Modern Rock
format: Commercial/Alt.
pd: Schuyler (Sketch) Evans
e: schuyler.s.evans@dartmouth.edu
md: Shirine Sajjadi
Unique commercial stn. w/ many student DJs, spins Local/Reg'l & indies in mix & on speciality shows. Coverage is 60mi. Promos: PO Box 957, Hanover, NH 03755.

New Jersey

Central

WBJB 90.5 FM
765 Newman Springs Rd.
Lincroft, NJ 07738
watts: 900
main: 732-224-2492
request: 732-224-2905; 732-224-2252 (studio)
e: comments@wbjb.org; info@wbjb.org
www.90.5thenight.org
webcast: Yes **podcast:** Yes
genres: Alt., S/S
format: Public/AAA
reports to: FMQB, AAAradio.com
pd: Rich Robinson
ext: 732-224-2432
e: rrobinson@wbjb.org
md: Jeff Raspe
ext: 732-224-2457
e: jraspe@wbjb.org
Brookdale Community College station has eclectic playlists & showcases area gigs throughout central NJ.

WDVR 89.7/91.9 FM
604 Rte. 604
Sergeantsville, NJ 08557
watts: 4800
main: 609-397-1620
e: host@wdvrfm.org
www.wdvrfm.org
webcast: Yes
genres: Americana, Country, Jazz, Blues, Bluegrass, Folk, World, Rock, New Age
format: Public/AAA
reports to: AMA
pd: Frank Napurano
e: napp2@comcast.net
md: Carla Ploghoft
e: carla@carlavandyk.com
Pen-Jersey Educational Radio

station sends indie releases to northeastern PA & western NJ. Check site for genre MD emails. Send promos to: PO Box 191, Sergeantsville, NJ, 08557.

WHTG/WBBO 106.3/106.5 FM
2355 W Bangs Ave.
Neptune, NJ 07753
watts: 4000
main: 732-774-4755
request: 866-76-G-ROCK
www.grockradio.com
webcast: Yes
genres: Rock, Alt.
format: Commercial/Alt.
reports to: R&R, Billboard, BDS, Album Network, Hits, FMQB
pd: Terrie Carr
e: terriec@grockradio.com
md: Matt Murray
e: mattm@grockradio.com
Variety of specialty shows reach northern NJ & into NYC.

WPRB 103.3 FM
30 Bloomberg Hall
Princeton, NJ 08544
watts: 14,000
main: 609-258-3655
request: 609-258-1033; 609-258-1233
www.wprb.com
webcast: Yes
genres: Classical, Freeform, Jazz, Rock, World
format: Commercial
reports to: CMJ, Dusted
pd: Ian Auzenne
e: program@wprb.com
md: Raymond Weitkamp
e: music@wprb.com
Princeton Broadcasting Service station w/ college sensibility blankets central & southern NJ & Philly w/ 95% indie music. Also has on-air opps., specialty shows & area gigs.

WRAT 95.9 FM
1731 Main St.
South Belmar, NJ 07719
watts: 4000
main: 732-681-3800
request: 732-681-3890
www.wrat.com
webcast: Yes **podcast:** Yes
genres: Active Rock
format: Commercial
reports to: CMJ, R&R, Album Network, FMQB
pd: Carl Craft
ext: 732-681-3800 x203
e: carlcraft@wrat.com
md: Robyn Lane
e: rocker@wrat.com
Broadcasts specialty shows & new/Reg'l music throughout Monmouth & Ocean counties; indies must fit format.

North

WBGO 88.3 FM
54 Park Pl.
Newark, NJ 07102
watts: 10,000
main: 973-624-8880
www.wbgo.org
webcast: Yes **podcast:** Yes
genres: Jazz, Blues, Latin
format: Public
reports to: JazzWeek
pd: Thurston Briscoe
e: tbriscoe@wbgo.org
md: Gary Walker
ext: 973-624-8880 x243
e: gwalker@wbgo.org
Prime station w/ signal that stretches to NYC metro area & southern PA also produces the syndicated "Jazz Set w/ Dee Dee Bridgewater." Submissions must fit format, will contact if interested.

WDHA 105.5 FM
55 Horsehill Rd.
Cedar Knolls, NJ 07927
watts: 3000
main: 973-455-1055
request: 973-480-1055
e: rock@wdhafm.com
www.wdhafm.com
webcast: Yes **podcast:** Yes
format: Commercial/Active Rock
reports to: FMQB, R&R
pd: Tony Paige
ext: 973-455-1055 x1345
e: tpaige@greatermedianj.com
md: Curtis Kay
ext: 973-455-1055 x1801
e: ckay@wmtr-wdha.com
Spins Reg'l releases M-F; signal stretches to NYC.

WFDU 89.1 FM
1000 River Rd.
Teaneck, NJ 07666
watts: 650
main: 201-692-2806
request: 201-692-2012
www.wfdu.fm
webcast: Yes **podcast:** Yes
genres: Americana, Urban, Alt. Rock, Celtic, Jazz, Blues, Salsa, World, Gospel
format: Public
reports to: CMJ
pd: Barry Sheffield
e: barrys@fdu.edu
md: Ghosty
e: ghostysshow@yahoo.com
FDU students & community volunteers offer diverse indie programming 50 miles to northern NJ/NYC metro area.

WFMU 91.1 FM
PO Box 2011
Jersey City, NJ 07303
watts: 1250
main: 201-521-1416
request: 201-200-9368
www.wfmu.org
webcast: Yes **podcast:** Yes
genres: Jazz, New World, Alt., Loud
format: Public
reports to: CMJ
pd: Brian Turner
ext: 201-521-1416 x223
e: bt@wfmu.org
Freeform haven for indie releases & specialty shows, hosts tons of live bands & sponsors area events. Covering the Hudson Valley, Lower Catskills, western NJ, NYC & eastern PA. Send promos to: PO Box 5101, Hoboken, NJ 07030.

South

WJSE 102.7 FM
1601 New Rd.
Linwood, NJ 08221
watts: 3300
main: 609-653-1400
request: 609-927-1027
e: info@wsje.net
www.wjse.net
webcast: Yes
genres: Alt., Modern Rock
format: Commercial/Active Rock
reports to: R&R, Mediabase
pd: Rich
e: msgsjr@yahoo.com
md: Shawn Castelluccio
Transmits to south NJ, PA & DE. Hosts weekly showcases at Atlantic City venues.

WSJQ 106.7 FM
3208 Pacific Ave., Fl. 2
Wildwood, NJ 08260
watts: 3300
main: 609-522-1987
request: 609-523-9700
www.1067coastcountry.com
webcast: Yes
genres: Country
format: Commercial
pd: Mark Hunter
e: mark@coastalbroadcasting.com
Signal covers Cape May, Cumberland & Atlantic Counties areas of NJ, & Dover, DE. Formerly WSJQ.

New Mexico

Albuquerque/ Santa Fe

KBAC 98.1 FM
2502 Camino Entrada, Ste. C
Santa Fe, NM 87507
watts: 100,000
main: 505-471-1067
request: 505-988-5222
www.kbac.com
genres: Alt., Acoustic, Reggae, Blues, Jazz, World, Groove, Swing
format: Commercial/AAA
pd: Ira Gordon
e: ira@huttonbroadcasting.com
Spins Local-Int'l indie releases; coverage is 80 miles. For specialty shows, contact: Lisa Clark at 505-471-1067 x107 or lisa@huttonbroadcasting.com.

KGLP 91.7 FM
200 College Rd.
Gallup, NM 87301
watts: 880
main: 505-863-7626
request: 505-863-7625
e: kglpradio@kglp.org
www.kglp.org
webcast: Yes
genres: Native American, Latin, World, Blues, Folk, Reggae, Jazz, Classical, Jam, Americana, S/S, Indie Rock
format: Public
reports to: CMJ
pd: Patrick Burnham
md: Tom Funk
Wide variety of specialty shows, indie & Reg'l releases have a 40-mi reach including parts of AZ. 138mi from Albuquerque.

KTAO 101.9 FM
9 State Rd. 150
Taos, NM 87571
watts: 50,000
main: 575-758-5826
request: 575-758-8882
e: ktao@newmex.com
www.ktao.com
webcast: Yes
genres: Acoustic, Blues, World
format: Commercial/AAA
reports to: FMQB, Hits, R&R
pd: Brad Hockmeyer
ext: 575-758-5826 x23
e: brad@ktao.com
Solar powered signal spans 150mi offering specialty shows, Reg'l spotlights & indie releases. Also operates KTAOS Solar Center music venue. For specialty shows, contact: Rick DeStefano at fivecorners@ktao.com. Promos to: PO Box 1844, Taos, NM 87571.

KTEG 104.1 FM
5411 Jefferson St. NE, Ste. 100
Albuquerque, NM 87109
watts: 100,000
main: 505-830-6400
request: 505-338-3343
www.1041theedge.com
webcast: Yes **podcast:** Yes
genres: Alt., Rock
format: Commercial
reports to: R&R
pd: Bill May
e: billmay@clearchannel.com
md: Aaron Burnett
e: buck@clearchannel.com
Indies featured on "Homegrown" to a 40-mi radius.

KUNM 89.9/ 91.1/91.9 FM
1 U of New Mexico
MSC06 3520, Onate Hall
Albuquerque, NM 87131
watts: 13,500
main: 505-277-4806
request: 505-277-5615
e: kunm@kunm.org
www.kunm.org
webcast: Yes
genres: Alt., Jazz, AAA, Blues, World, Folk, Techno
format: Public
reports to: CMJ
pd: Marcos Martinez
ext: 505-277-8014
e: programming@kunm.org
md: Matthew Finch
ext: 505-277-8369
e: mfinch@kunm.org; music@kunm.org
Indie-friendly station airs non-mainstream releases. Submissions accepted for "Freeform" Mon-Tue & Thu-Fri 1:30-4pm. Signal spans 70mi.

Greater NM

KENW/KMTH 89.5/98.7 FM
52 Broadcast Ctr., Eastern New Mexico U, 1500 S Ave. K
Portales, NM 88130
watts: 100,000
main: 575-562-2112
e: kenwfm@enmu.edu
www.kenw.org
genres: Jazz, New Age, Classical, Easy Listening
format: Public
pd: Duane Ryan
Mostly Classical station airs wknd Jazz shows & indies to most of eastern NM & western TX.

KRWG 90.7 FM
PO Box 3000
Las Cruces, NM 88003
watts: 100,000
main: 575-646-4525; 800-245-5794
request: 575-646-4623
e: krwgfm@nmsu.edu
www.krwgfm.org
genres: Jazz, Latin, Folk, Blues, World, Classical
format: Public
pd: Carrie Hamblen
e: chamblen@nmsu.edu
md: Chris Grisham
Classical station's signal repeats over 5 frequencies to southern NM & western TX. Airs indie evening & weekend specialty shows.

New York

Albany

WAMC 90.3 FM
318 Central Ave.
Albany, NY 12206
watts: 10,000
main: 800-323-9262; 518-465-5233
e: mail@wamc.org
www.wamc.org
genres: Americana, Jazz, Folk, Classical
format: Public
pd: David Galletly
ext: 518-465-5233 x151
e: david@wamc.org
Area's main NPR station w/ signal repeated to 14 stations throughout eastern NY & western New England airs indies. Produces "Performance Place" M-F 11:30am-noon featuring live set & CDs from Local musicians. Promos to: PO Box 66600, Albany, NY 12206.

WHRL 103.1 FM
1203 Troy-Schenectady Rd.
Latham, NY 12110
watts: 6000
main: 518-452-4800
e: feedback@channel1031.com
www.whrl.com
genres: Alt., Modern Rock
format: Commercial
reports to: R&R
pd: Tim Noble
e: timnoble@clearchannel.com
Many indie opps. including Reg'l showcase "Big Break" w/ Jason Keller, Sun 8-9pm. Heard throughout Hudson Valley & central NY to Pittsfield, MA & Bennington, VT.

WQBJ/WQBK 103.5/103.9 FM
Regent Communications, 1241 Kings Rd.
Schenectady, NY 12303
watts: 56,000
main: 518-881-1515
request: 518-476-1039
www.q103albany.com
format: Commercial/Rock
pd: Rob Dawes
e: rdawes@q103albany.com
md: Jeff Levack
ext: 518-785-9800
e: jlevack@q103albany.com
Specialty shows & on-air performances heard throughout the capital region of NY.

Buffalo/Rochester/Syracuse

WAER 88.3 FM
795 Ostrom Ave.
Syracuse, NY 13244
watts: 50,000
main: 315-443-9237
e: waer@syr.org
www.waer.org
webcast: Yes
genres: Jazz, New Age, Blues, Folk, World, Gospel
format: Public
reports to: JazzWeek
pd: Ron Ockert
ext: 315-443-4021
e: rgockert@syr.edu
md: Eric Cohen
ext: 315-443-5252
e: escohen@syr.edu
Area's top Jazz/NPR station, located on the campus of Syracuse U, airs wknd specialty shows & indie releases to central NY.

WAQX 95.7 FM
1064 James St.
Syracuse, NY 13203
watts: 25,000
main: 315-472-0200
request: 315-421-9595
www.95x.com
webcast: Yes **podcast:** Yes
genres: Rock
format: Commercial
reports to: R&R
pd: Alexis
ext: 315-472-0200 x230
e: alexis@95x.com
md: Don Kelley
ext: 315-472-0200 x224
e: stone@95x.com
Mostly mainstream stn. targets males 25-54 w/in 50-mi radius. Reg'l showcased on "Undiscovered" - send CDs w/ ATTN: Alexis.

WBFO 88.7 FM
205 Allen Hall, 3435 Main St.
Buffalo, NY 14214
watts: 50,000
main: 716-829-6000
e: mail@wbfo.org
www.wbfo.org
webcast: Yes **podcast:** Yes
genres: Jazz, Blues, World, Celtic, Indie
format: Public/AAA
reports to: JazzWeek
pd: David Benders
ext: 716-829-6000 x502
e: dbenders@wbfo.org
md: Bert Gambini
ext: 716-829-6000 x504
e: bgambini@wbfo.org
Top area station w/ repeater on HD1 & HD2, has specialty shows for upstate NY, western PA & southern ON.

WBUG/WBGK 101.1/99.7 FM
185 Genesee St., Ste. 1601
Utica, NY 13501
watts: 6000
main: 315-734-9245
request: 800-728-7126
www.bugcountry.com
webcast: Yes
genres: Country
format: Commercial
pd: Dave Silvers
ext: 315-734-9245 x3027
e: dave@bugcountry.com; dave@rosergroup.com
One of the few Country stations still willing to give indies a spin. Covers a 100-mile radius b/c of 2-station simulcast. 58mi from Syracuse.

WEDG 103.3 FM
50 James E. Casey Dr.
Buffalo, NY 14206
watts: 49,000
main: 716-881-4555
request: 716-644-9334
e: wedg@wedg.com
www.wedg.com
webcast: Yes **podcast:** Yes
format: Commercial/Active Rock
reports to: R&R, FMQB
pd: Jim Kurdziel
e: jim.kurdziel@citcomm.com
Targets listeners 18-49 & blankets western NY & southern ON w/ indie releases & specialty shows featuring new music.

WGMC 90.1 FM
1139 Maiden Ln.
Rochester, NY 14615
watts: 15,000
main: 585-966-2660
request: 800-790-0415; 585-966-5299
e: jazzinfo@jazz901.org
www.jazz901.org
webcast: Yes
genres: Jazz, Latin, Blues
format: Public
reports to: JazzWeek
pd: Rob Linton
e: rob@jazz901.org
md: Derrick Lucas
ext: 585-966-2404
e: derrick@jazz901.org
Area's beacon for Avant-Garde Jazz & non-mainstream programs heard for 50 miles.

WKRL 100.9 FM
235 Walton St.
Syracuse, NY 13202
watts: 50,000
main: 315-472-9111
request: 315-424-ROCK
www.krock.com
webcast: Yes
genres: Alt.
format: Commercial/Alt.
reports to: R&R, Monitor, FMQB
pd: Mimi Griswold
e: mgriswold@galaxy communications.com
Station w/ repeaters in Oswego, Utica & Rome spins some indies in regular rotation & on specialty shows: "Jam" on Sun 9pm-mid & Reg'l showcase, "KROCK-On Demand."

WLKK 107.7 FM
500 Corporate Pkwy., Ste. 200
Buffalo, NY 14226
watts: 20,000
main: 716-843-0600
request: 716-362-1077
www.1077thelake.com
webcast: Yes **podcast:** Yes
genres: Rock, Folk, Alt.
format: Commercial/Rock
pd: Hank Dole
e: hdole@entercom.com
Locals & indies in rotation & on "Lake Local Music Show" w/ Tina Peel & Robbie Takac (Goo Goo Dolls). Also releases Local music compilation CDs.

WSQX 91.5 FM
601 Gates Rd.
Vestal, NY 13850
watts: 3500
main: 607-729-0100
e: mail@wskg.org
www.wskg.com
genres: Jazz, Folk
format: Public/Jazz
pd: Gregory Keeler
ext: 607-729-0100 x311
e: gregory_keeler@wskg.pbs.org
md: Bill Snyder
ext: 607-729-0100 x380
e: wsnyder@wskg.org
Supports indie & Reg'l releases in the above genres & stretches into Susquehanna Valley, PA. Send promos to: PO Box 3000, Binghamton, NY 13902.

WVBR 93.5 FM
957 Mitchell St., Ste. B
Ithaca, NY 14850
watts: 3000
main: 607-273-4000
request: 607-273-2121
www.wvbr.com
webcast: Yes **podcast:** Yes
genres: Heritage Rock, Hardcore, Latin, Blues, Ska, Folk, World, Blues, Jazz
format: Commercial/Rock
pd: Dan Powers
e: dcp38@cornell.edu
md: Peter Knight
e: peterknight@wvbr.com
Indie releases, wknd specialty shows & on-air opps.

WVOA 95.3/101.5/103.9 FM
7095 Myers Rd.
East Syracuse, NY 13057
watts: 25,000
main: 315-656-2231
e: wvoaradio@cnymail.com
www.wvoaradio.com
webcast: Yes
genres: All Christian music
format: Commercial
pd: Sam
md: Allen L. Elson
Signal reaches parts of Canada.

Hudson Valley

WDST 100.1 FM
PO Box 367
Woodstock, NY 12498
watts: 6000
main: 845-679-7600
request: 845-679-WDST
e: live@wdst.com
www.wdst.com
webcast: Yes **podcast:** Yes
genres: Acoustic, Americana, Rock n Roll, Blues, Jazz, Roots, Reggae, Soul
format: Commercial/AAA
reports to: R&R, FMQB, Billboard
pd: Jimmy Buff
ext: 845-679-7600 x11
e: buff@wdst.com
md: Carmel Holt
ext: 845-679-7600 x20
e: carmelh@wdst.com
Area's last indie station reaches far into mid-Hudson Valley NY w/ specialty shows & indie releases.

WJFF 90.5/94.5 FM
4765 Rte. 52
Jeffersonville, NY 12748
watts: 3700
main: 845-482-4141
e: wjff@wjffradio.org
www.wjffradio.org
webcast: Yes **podcast:** Yes
genres: All Styles
format: Public
pd: Katie Armstrong
e: katie@wjffradio.org
md: John Bachman
e: jbachman@wjffradio.org
Award-winning station blankets the Catskills, northeast PA & upper DE w/ eclectic programs. Promos to: PO Box 546, Jeffersonville, NY 12748.

WKZE 98.1 FM
7392 S Broadway
Red Hook, NY 12571
watts: 5000
main: 845-758-9810
request: 866-393-9810
e: info@wkze.com
www.wkze.com
webcast: Yes
genres: Rock, Folk, Americana, Blues, World, Acoustic, Jazz, Womyn's, Eclectic, Alt. Country
format: Commercial
reports to: R&R
pd: Will Baylis

ext: 845-758-9810 x114
e: willb@wkze.com
Award-winning station airs eclectic weekday & specialty shows. "Off the Beat-n-Track" devoted to indie & Reg'l releases Sat 9-11pm w/ Todd Mack, info@offthebeat-n-track.com. Signal reaches parts of MA.

Long Island

WBAB 102.3 FM
555 Sunrise Hwy.
West Babylon, NY 11704
watts: 6000
main: 631-587-1023
request: 631-955-WBAB
e: wbab@wbab.com
www.wbab.com
webcast: Yes
genres: Rock, Metal
format: Commercial
pd: Chris Lloyd
e: chris.lloyd@coxradio.com
md: Matt Wolfe
e: matt.wolfe@coxradio.com
Covers Long Island & southern CT.

WLIR 107.1 FM
3075 Veterans Memorial Hwy.
Ste. 201
Ronkonkoma, NY 11779
watts: 6000
main: 631-648-2500
request: 631-648-1071
e: info@wlir.com
www.wlir.com
genres: Alt., Rock
format: Commercial/Alt.
pd: Harlan Friedman
e: harlan@tmoradio.com
World-famous station spins new music throughout LI, northern NJ, parts of CT & NYC.

WLVG 96.1 FM
32-41 Rte. 112, Bldg. 7, Ste. 2
Medford, NY 11763
watts: 3000
main: 631-451-1039
request: 631-955-0961
www.love961.com
webcast: Yes
format: Commercial/AC, Jazz
pd: Charlie Lombardo
ext: 631-451-1039 x209
e: clombardo@wrcn.com

WMJC 94.3 FM
234 Airport Plaza, Ste. 5
Farmingdale, NY 11735
watts: 3000
main: 631-770-4200
request: 631-955-0943
e: jon@wmjcfm.com
www.wmjcfm.com
webcast: Yes **podcast:** Yes
format: Commercial/Hot AC
reports to: BDS, Mediabase
pd: Jon Daniels
ext: 631-770-4343
e: jdaniels@liradiogroup.com
Indie releases & specialty shows.

New York City

Sirius XM Satellite
1221 6th Ave., Fl. 36 & 37
New York, NY 10020
e: genfeedback@sirius-radio.com
www.sirius.com; www.xmradio.com
podcast: Yes
genres: All Styles
format: Commercial
reports to: R&R, Mediabase
ext: 202-380-4000
In 2008, XM & Sirius merged. Check site for updated employee info. 120+ commercial free channels. Submit music to your genre's appropriate MD.

WBAI 99.5 FM
120 Wall St., 10th FL.
New York, NY 10005
watts: 50,000
main: 212-209-2800
request: 212-209-2900
e: editor@wbai.org
www.wbai.org
webcast: Yes **podcast:** Yes
genres: Jazz, World, Folk, Hip-Hop, R&B
format: Public/Jazz
reports to: CMJ
pd: Bernard White
ext: 212-209-2835
e: bwhite@wbai.org
md: Janet Coleman
ext: 212-209-2840
e: jcoleman@wbai.org
New music & specialty shows heard throughout tri-state region.

WFUV 90.7 FM
WFUV Radio
Fordham U
Keating Hall, Rm. B12
Bronx, NY 10458
watts: 50,000
main: 718-817-4550
e: thefolks@wfuv.org
www.wfuv.org
webcast: Yes **podcast:** Yes
genres: S/S, Americana, Rock, Folk, World
format: Public/AAA
reports to: Album Network, CMJ, Hits, Billboard
pd: Rich McLaughlin
e: rmclaughlin@wfuv.org
md: Rita Houston
e: rhouston@wfuv.org
Influential station & NPR affiliate airs indie & emerging talent. Eclectic programming & in-studio opps. heard throughout NYC, LI, southern CT & northern NJ. Check site to email genre MDs.

WKCR 89.9 FM
2920 Broadway
New York, NY 10027
watts: 2500
main: 212-854-9920
e: board@wkcr.org
www.wkcr.org
webcast: Yes
genres: Jazz, Experimental, Blues, Funk, Latin, World, Country, Bluegrass, Classical
format: Public
pd: Raphael Vagliano
md: Morgan Whitcomb
Airs indies & specialty shows transmitted throughout the tri-state region.

WNYC 93.9 FM
160 Varick St.
New York, NY 10013
watts: 5400
main: 646-829-4400
www.wnyc.org
webcast: Yes **podcast:** Yes
genres: All Styles
format: Public
pd: Chris Bannon
e: cbannon@wnyc.org
md: George Preston
e: gpreston@wnyc.org
Premiere NPR affiliate airs eclectic/Avant-Garde programs & on-air opps. 70 miles into the NYC, NJ & CT metro region & heard by millions online. Must be submitted to specific programs. Indies on "Soundcheck" & "New Sounds."

WQCD 101.9 FM
395 Hudson St.
New York, NY 10014
watts: 6200
main: 212-352-1019
request: 800-423-1019
e: cd1019@cd1019.com
www.cd1019.com
format: Commercial/Jazz
reports to: R&R
pd: Blake Lawrence
md: Caroline Bednorski
DJs spin some indies & interviews/performances to NYC, NJ & CT metro area.

WXRK 92.3 FM
40 West 57th St., 14th Fl.
New York, NY 10019
watts: 6000
main: 212-314-9230
request: 877-212-5762
www.923krock.com
webcast: Yes
format: Commerical/Alt./Active Rock
pd: Mike Tierney
ext: 212-314-9219
CBS station is back to its K-ROCK format. Indie opps. mostly for Local/Reg'ls. Only snail mailed unsolicited material accepted. NYC area acts send CDs w/ ATTN: "B Local" & include 1 pg bio, tracks - note strongest songs & which have cursing.

Greater NY

WSLU/WXLH 89.5/91.3 FM
North Country Public Radio
St. Lawrence U
Canton, NY 13617
watts: 40,000
main: 315-229-5356
request: 877-388-6277
e: radio@ncpr.org
www.ncpr.org
genres: World, Pop, Blues, Americana, R&B, Jazz, Bluegrass, Dance Groove
format: Public
pd: Jackie Sauter
e: jackie@ncpr.org
NPR outlets blankets northern NY, western/ southern VT & southern ON w/ freeform specialty shows.

North Carolina

Asheville

WKVS 103.3 FM
827 Fairview Dr.
Lenoir, NC 28645
watts: 6000
main: 828-758-1033
request: 828-754-1033
www.foothillsradio.com
genres: All Styles of Country
format: Commercial
pd: Davey Crockett
e: crockett@kicksradio.com
"American Christian Music Review" show & sponsors "Historic Morganton Festival." Send promos to: PO Box 1678, Lenoir, NC 28645.

WKYK 940 AM
749 Sawmill Hollow Rd.
Burnsville, NC 28714
watts: 5000
main: 828-682-3510
request: 800-949-3798
e: 940@wkyk.com
www.wkyk.com
genres: Country, Gospel
format: Commercial
pd: Holly Hall
ext: 828-682-3510 x227
e: holly@wkyk.com
md: Dennis Renfro
ext: 828-682-3510 x246
e: dennis@wkyk.com
Plays "Hot New Country" for northern NC. Promos: PO Box 744, Burnsville, NC 28714.

WNCW 88.7 FM
PO Box 804
Spindale, NC 28160
watts: 17,000
main: 828-287-8000
request: 828-287-8080
e: info@wncw.org
www.wncw.org
webcast: Yes **podcast:** Yes
genres: Americana, S/S, Alt., Reggae, Bluegrass, Blues, Celtic
format: Public/AAA
reports to: R&R, AMA
pd: Dave Kester
ext: 828-287-8000 x335
e: programming@wncw.org
md: Martin Anderson
ext: 828-287-8000 x349
e: martin@wncw.org
Diverse shows for Asheville, Charlotte, Boone, Knoxville, TN & Greenville, SC.

Charlotte

WEND 106.5 FM
801 Woodridge Ctr. Dr.
Charlotte, NC 28217
watts: 100,000
main: 704-714-9444
request: 704-570-1065; 800-934-1065
www.1065.com
webcast: Yes **podcast:** Yes
genres: New Rock, Alt.
format: Commercial/Active Rock
reports to: Mediabase
pd: Jack Daniel
ext: 704-339-3243
e: jackdaniel@1065.com
ClearChannel station airs some Indies to Piedmont & the SC foothills. Contact Divakar for specialty shows, at divakar@1065.com.

WGWG 88.3 FM
106 Emily Ln.
Boiling Springs, NC 28017
watts: 50,000
main: 704-406-3200
request: 704-406-3525
e: info@wgwg.org
www.wgwg.org
webcast: Yes **podcast:** Yes
genres: Americana
format: Public/AAA
reports to: FMQB, AMA
pd: Jeff Powell
ext: 704-406-3841
NC & SC tune in for eclectic daily programs & wknd specialty shows. Promos: PO Box 876, Boiling Springs, NC 28017. 52mi from Charlotte.

WPZS 100.9 FM
8809 Lenox Pointe Dr., Ste. A
Charlotte, NC 28273
watts: 3000
main: 704-548-7800
request: 704-570-1009
www.praise1009fm.com

webcast: Yes
genres: Gospel, R&B
format: Commercial
pd: AC Stowe
ext: 704-358-0211
e: astowe@praise1009fm.com
Radio One station airs some indies; sister station: WQNC 92.7 FM. No unsolicited material.

WSOC 103.7 FM
1520 South Blvd., Ste. 300
Charlotte, NC 28203
watts: 100,000
main: 704-522-1103
request: 800-522-WSOC
www.wsocfm.com
webcast: Yes
genres: Country
format: Commercial
reports to: Soundscan
pd: DJ Stout
e: djstout@cbs.com
md: Rick McCracken
e: rickm@wsocfm.com
Vital mainstream Country station welcomes indie submissions & airs specialty shows to the 7 county metro area in SC, NC & WV. Submit calendar listings at www.wsocfm.com/what-s-happening-in-your-hometown-/1430417.

Fayetteville/ Wilmington

WFSS 91.9 FM
1200 Murchison Rd.
Fayetteville, NC 28301
watts: 100,000
main: 910-672-1919
request: 910-672-2650
e: wfss@uncfsu.edu
www.wfss.org
webcast: Yes
genres: Jazz, Americana, Latin, World, Blues, Bluegrass, Classical, Alt., Urban, Jazz
format: Public
reports to: JazzWeek
pd: Janet Wright
ext: 910-672-2038
e: jwright@uncfsu.edu
md: Jimmy Miller
ext: 910-672-2032
e: jmiller@uncfsu.edu
Medley of specialty shows stretch 60-70mi. Send Jazz & Gospel promos to Jimmy Miller & all others to Janet Wright.

WHQR 91.3 FM
254 N Front St., Ste. 301
Wilmington, NC 28401
watts: 100,000
main: 910-343-1640
e: whqr@whqr.org
www.whqr.org
webcast: Yes
genres: Jazz, Folk, Blues, Bluegrass, Celtic, Classical, Alternative, Electronic
format: Public
md: Bob Workman
ext: 910-343-1640 x208
e: bob@whqr.org
Weekend specialty shows: "Smooth Landings" (Eclectic Local-Nat'l); "Soup To Nuts" (Eclectic monthly concert series) on Sat; "Midday Cafe" (Classical) & "Front Street Blues" Sat & Sun. Signal stretches along the Carolina coast & inland for 80 miles. Submit CDs or MP3s.

WRCQ 103.5 FM
1009 Drayton Rd.
Fayetteville, NC 28303
watts: 48,000
main: 910-864-5222
request: 910-860-3090
www.rock103rocks.com
genres: Rock
format: Commercial
pd: Al Fields
e: al.thevanman@cumulus.com
Indies on several weekday request shows; "Hard Drive" on Sun & Reg'l acts on "HomeGrown." Coverage sweeps 70 miles.

WSFM 98.3 FM
25 N Kerr Ave.
Wilmington, NC 28405
watts: 32,000
main: 910-791-3088
request: 910-332-0983
www.surf983.com
webcast: Yes
genres: Alt., New Rock
format: Commercial/Rock
reports to: R&R, FMQB
pd: Michael Kennedy
e: mud@surf983.com
Reg'l & indie buzz bands 6-7pm Sun on 'The Scene." Signal stretches to Nashville & targets mainly males 18-34.

WXNR 99.5 FM
207 Glenburnie Dr.
New Bern, NC 28560
watts: 50,000
main: 252-633-1500
request: 252-636-9967
www.wxnr.com
webcast: Yes
genres: Alt., New Rock
format: Commercial
reports to: R&R, FMQB, Hits, CMJ
pd: Jerry Wayne
e: jerry.wayne@bbgi.com
md: Blando
e: blando@995thex.com
Indie & Local specialty shows & in-studio opps. transmitted 90mi.

WXQR 105.5 FM
1361 Colony Dr.
New Bern, NC 28562
watts: 50,000
main: 252-639-7900
request: 800-501-1055
e: cbradioshow@yahoo.com
www.carolinaspurerock.com
webcast: Yes
genres: Rock
format: Commercial
pd: Wes Styles
ext: 252-639-7924
e: wes@carolinaspurerock.com
Indies on "Carolina Homegrown" reach the Greenville, Jacksonville, Wilmington, New Bern areas.

WZFX 99.1 FM
508 Person St.
Fayetteville, NC 28301
watts: 100,000
main: 910-486-4991
www.foxy99.com
webcast: Yes
genres: Hip-Hop, Rap, R&B
format: Commercial
pd: Mike Tech
ext: 910-486-2084
e: miketech@foxy99.com
md: DJ D-Rocc
ext: 910-486-2065
e: djdrocc@foxy99.com
Features "Independent Spotlight."

Greensboro/ Winston-Salem

WNAA 90.1 FM
Price Hall, Ste. 200, NC A&T U
Greensboro, NC 27411
watts: 10,000
main: 336-334-7936
request: 336-334-7952
e: wnaafm@ncat.edu
www.aggienewsonline.com
webcast: Yes **podcast:** Yes
genres: Gospel, R&B, Jazz, Blues, Rap, Reggae, House
format: Public
reports to: CMJ, Urban Network
pd: Cherie Lofton
e: loftond@ncat.edu
Underground Hip-Hop show & indie releases in the mix.

WSNC 90.5 FM
114 Hall-Patterson Bldg.
Winston-Salem, NC 27110
watts: 10,000
main: 336-750-2321
request: 336-750-2160
e: jenkinse@wssu.edu
www.wssu.edu/WSSU/UndergraduateStudies/College+of+Arts+and+Sciences/90.5+WSNC/
webcast: Yes
genres: Jazz, Blues, Gospel, World, Latin
format: Public/Jazz
pd: Monica Melton
ext: 336-750-2325
e: meltonm@wssu.edu
NPR station on Winston-Salem U campus airs specialty shows to 1 million in Piedmont Triad-area.

WTQR 104.1 FM
2B P.A.I. Park
Greensboro, NC 27409
watts: 100,000
main: 336-822-2000
request: 336-822-1041
e: wtqr@wtqr.com
www.wtqr.com
webcast: Yes **podcast:** Yes
genres: Country
format: Commercial
reports to: R&R, Billboard
pd: John Roberts
e: johnfroberts@clearchannel.com
Signal stretches 60-70 miles.

Raleigh/Durham

WIZS 1450 AM
535 Radio Ln.
Henderson, NC 27536
watts: 1000
main: 252-492-3001
e: wizs@wizs.com
www.wizs.com
genres: Country
format: Commercial
pd: Dan Simmons
e: djdan@wizs.com
Sporadically adds indies. Signal covers parts of VA. Send promos to: PO Box 1299, Henderson, NC 27536.

WNCU 90.7 FM
1801 Fayetteville St.
Durham, NC 27707
watts: 50,000
main: 919-530-7445
request: 919-560-9628
www.wncu.org
webcast: Yes **podcast:** Yes
genres: Jazz, Reggae, Afro-Pop, Latin, Gospel, Blues
format: Public
reports to: JazzWeek
pd: Edith Thorpe
e: ethorpe@nccu.edu
md: B.H. Hudson
e: bhhudson@nccu.edu
Central NC & southcentral VA tune in for mainstream Jazz, Local showcases, specialty shows & live broadcasts of area Blues events. Promos: PO Box 19875, Durham, NC 27707.

WZRU 90.1/90.5 FM
PO Box 1149
Roanoke Rapids, NC 27870
watts: 11,000
main: 252-308-0885
request: 888-308-0885
e: info@wzru.org
www.wzru.org
genres: Adult Mix Christian
format: Public
pd: Allen Garrett
e: garyh@schoollink.net; agarrett.wzru@charter.net
md: Mike Farley
ext: 252-747-8887
Airs releases & specialty shows to northeastern NC & southeastern VA. Promos: 232 Roanoke Ave., Roanoke Rapids, NC 27870.

Greater NC

WVOD 99.1 FM
637 Harbor Rd.
Wanchese, NC 27981
watts: 50,000
main: 252-475-1888
request: 252-473-9863
www.991thesound.com
genres: World, Blues, Reggae, S/S, New Grass, Alt.
format: Commercial/AAA
reports to: R&R
pd: Matt Cooper
e: matt@capsanmedia.com; matt@991thesound.com
md: Jeff White
e: jeff@capsanmedia.com
Local & indie music in the mix. Reggae, Americana, Blues & Jazz specialty shows.

North Dakota

Fargo/Grand Forks

KJKJ 107.5 FM
505 University Ave.
Grand Forks, ND 58203
watts: 100,000
main: 701-746-1417
request: 701-775-7625
e: barkforus@hotmail.com
www.kjkj.com
genres: Rock
format: Commercial
pd: Brian Lee Rivers
e: brianrivers@clearchannel.com; blrivers@hotmail.com
Indies in rotation & on specialty shows span 62-mile radius.

KQWB 98.7 FM
2720 7th Ave. S
Fargo, ND 58103
watts: 100,000
main: 701-237-4500
request: 701-234-9898
e: studio@q98.com
www.q98.com
genres: Rock, Active Rock
format: Commercial
pd: Novack
e: novack@q98.com
Daily "Rock Roots" show w/ Novak features Local acts & blankets 75 miles.

Ohio

Akron/Cleveland

WAPS 91.3 FM
65 Steiner Ave.
Akron, OH 44301
watts: 2000
main: 330-761-3099
www.913thesummit.com
webcast: Yes
genres: Rock, Folk, Acoustic, Blues, Pop, Reggae
format: Public/AAA
reports to: R&R, Album Network, FMQB, Hits
pd: Bill Gruber
ext: 330-761-3098
e: billgruber@913thesummit.com
Some indies in the mix. No unsolicited material.

WENZ 107.9 FM
2510 St. Clair Ave. NE
Cleveland, OH 44114
watts: 16,000
main: 216-579-1111
request: 216-578-1079
www.z1079fm.com
genres: Hip-Hop, R&B
format: Commercial/Urban
pd: Kim Johnson
md: Latin Assassin
Specialty shows w/ Local artists Sun-Thu at 10pm to the Cleveland area; also has some indies in the mix. Send promos ATTN: Cleveland Home Jamz.

WKSU 89.7 FM
1613 E Summit St.
Kent, OH 44242
watts: 50,000
main: 330-672-3114
e: letters@wksu.org
www.wksu.org
webcast: Yes **podcast:** Yes
genres: Classical, Americana, World, Celtic, Folk, Alt. Country, S/S, Bluegrass
format: Public
reports to: FolkRadio.org, Roots Music Report
pd: Mark Urycki
e: urycki@wksu.org
md: David Roden
e: roden@wksu.org
Kent State station mostly airs & sponsors Folk & Classical music events. Blankets northeast OH & reaches into part of NW OH & Western PA w/ indie releases & specialty shows. On-air opps. for Folk artists only. Send promos to: PO Box 5190, Kent, OH 44242.

WMMS 100.7 FM
6200 Oak Tree Blvd., 4th Fl.
Cleveland, OH 44131
watts: 28,500
main: 216-520-2600
request: 216-578-1007
e: buzzard@wmms.com
www.wmms.com
webcast: Yes **podcast:** Yes
genres: Rock
format: Commercial
reports to: Album Network
pd: Bo Matthews
e: bo@clearchannel.com
Spins some indies for northern OH. Submit calendar listings & music online.

Dayton/Cincinnati/Columbus

WAIF 88.3 FM
1434 E McMillan Ave.
Cincinnati, OH 45206
watts: 4000
main: 513-961-8900
request: 513-749-1444
www.waif883.org
webcast: Yes
genres: Indie, Alt., Rock, World, Reggae, Gospel, Urban, Jazz, New Age, Blues, Bluegrass, Surf, Christian Prog
format: Public
pd: Program Committee
ext: 513-375-3473
e: ladydar@fuse.net
Volunteer-run station offers 50+ eclectic programs & shares frequency w/ student-run WJVS 8am-3pm during the school year.

WBZX 99.7 FM
1458 Dublin Rd.
Columbus, OH 43215
watts: 50,000
main: 614-481-7800
request: 614-821-9970; 800-821-9970
www.wbzx.com
genres: Active Rock, Alt., New Rock
format: Commercial
reports to: FMQB, Hits, Album Network, Billboard
pd: Hal Fish
e: hfish@nabco-inc.com
md: Ronni Hunter
e: rhunter@wbzx.com
Interviews, live Acoustic sets & indies stretch 125 miles. "Local Stuff" w/ Hannibal & Aaron Benner on Sun 10-11pm; hannibal@wbzx.com.

WCBE 90.5 FM
540 Jack Gibbs Blvd.
Columbus, OH 43215
watts: 11,000
main: 614-365-5555
request: 614-821-9223
e: wcbe@wcbe.org
www.wcbe.org
webcast: Yes
genres: World, Americana, Eclectic
format: Public/AAA
reports to: CMJ, FMQB, R&R
pd: Dan Mushalko
e: dmushalko7108@columbus.k12.oh.us
md: Maggie Brennan
ext: 614-365-5555 x226
e: mbrennan@wcbe.org
Produces & broadcasts eclectic programs for metro area.

WWCD 101.1 FM
503 S Front St., Ste. 101
Columbus, OH 43215
watts: 6000
main: 614-221-9923
request: 614-221-1011
e: webmaster@cd101.com
www.cd101.com
webcast: Yes **podcast:** Yes
genres: Alt.
format: Commercial/Alt.
pd: Andy Davis
e: andyman@cd101.com
Indie releases on "Independent Playground" Thu/Sun. Send CDs or EPKs c/o Tom Butler.

WXEG 103.9 FM
101 Pine St.
Dayton, OH 45402
watts: 3000
main: 937-224-1137
request: 937-457-1039
www.wxeg.com
webcast: Yes
genres: Alt., Rock
format: Commercial
reports to: R&R, FMQB, Album Network, Hits
pd: Steve Kramer
ext: 937-224-1137 x183
e: kramer@wxeg.com
md: Jericho
ext: 937-224-1137 x184
e: jericho@wxeg.com
ClearChannel station spins indies in the mix & on "Spin Cycle." Reaches to central & western OH.

WYSO 91.3 FM
Antioch U
150 E South College St.
Yellow Springs, OH 45387
watts: 37,000
main: 937-767-6420
e: wyso@wyso.org
www.wyso.org
webcast: Yes **podcast:** Yes
genres: Eclectic, Bluegrass, Blues, Ambient, World, Jazz, Folk, Celtic
format: Public
reports to: FMQB, Bluegrass Unlimited
md: Niki Dakota
ext: 937-769-1383
e: ndakota@wyso.org
NPR outlet spins some indies M-F 10am-1pm & 8-11pm on "Excursions." Covers metro Dayton & beyond.

Toledo

WIOT 104.7 FM
125 S Superior
Toledo, OH 43604
watts: 50,000
main: 419-244-8321
request: 419-240-1047
e: wiot@wiot.com
www.wiot.com
webcast: Yes
genres: Rock
format: Commercial
reports to: R&R, Album Network, FMQB, BDS, Mediabase, Airplay Monitor
pd: Bill Michaels
e: billmichaels@clearchannel.com
Signal spans 65-mile radius. Locals spin on Sun 8-10pm on "New Rock Review," email: sledge@wiot.com; rarely airs out-of-state indies.

WJUC 107.3 FM
5902 Southwyck Blvd., Ste. 101
Toledo, OH 43614
watts: 3000
main: 419-861-9582
request: 419-826-1073
www.thejuice1073.com
webcast: Yes
genres: Hip-Hop, R&B
format: Commercial
reports to: R&R
pd: Charlie Mack
e: charliemack@thejuice1073.com
Transmits to western OH & eastern IN. No unsolicited material.

WRWK 106.5 FM
3225 Arlington Ave.
Toledo, OH 43614
watts: 3000
main: 419-725-5700
request: 419-861-1065
www.1065thezone.com
webcast: Yes
genres: Alt., New Rock
format: Commercial/Alt., Rock
reports to: FMQB, R&R, Album Network
pd: Dan McClintock
e: dan.mcclintock@cumulus.com
md: Carolyn Stone
e: carolyn.stone@cumulus.com
Surrounds 80 miles of Toledo w/ mostly mainstream Rock; indies on "Homegrown Zone" Sun 9-10pm; "All Request Lunch Zone" & "Independent Playground."

WXTS 88.3 FM
2400 Collingwood Blvd.
Toledo, OH 43620
watts: 1000
main: 419-244-6875
e: wxtsfm@gmail.com
genres: Jazz, Blues
format: Public
reports to: JazzWeek
pd: Jonathan Turner
md: John Kuschell
Indie releases & specialty shows for metro Toledo, & Detroit, MI.

Oklahoma

Oklahoma City

KATT 100.5 FM
4045 NW 64, Ste. 600
Oklahoma City, OK 73116
watts: 100,000
main: 405-848-0100
request: 405-460-KATT
www.katt.com
webcast: Yes **podcast:** Yes
genres: Hard Rock, Alt.
format: Commercial
reports to: R&R
pd: Chris Baker
e: chris.baker@citcomm.com
md: Jake Daniels
e: jakedaniels@katt.com
New releases spin on "Spy Radio" Thu at midnite; Local talent on "Big Metal" Fri at midnite; "Katt's 7th Day" Sun at 7pm. Signal stretches 90mi.

KGOU/KROU 106.3/105.7 FM
U of OK, Copeland Hall, Rm. 300
Norman, OK 73019
watts: 4000/6000
main: 405-325-3388
request: 405-325-3110
e: kholp@ou.edu
www.kgou.org
genres: World, Jazz, Blues
format: Public
reports to: CMJ, Crossroads, Living Blues, New Age Voice
pd: Jim Johnson
e: programming@kgou.org

KHBZ 94.7 FM
50 Penn Pl., 10th Fl., Ste. 1000
Oklahoma City, OK 73118
watts: 100,000
main: 405-840-5271
request: 405-460-9470
www.947thebuzz.com
webcast: Yes **podcast:** Yes
genres: Rock, Metal, Alt.
format: Commercial/Active Rock
reports to: FMQB, Mediabase
pd: Jeff Blackburn
e: jeffblackburn@clearchannel.com
For specialty shows, contact Jay Pitts: jaypitts@clearchannel.com. Send kit, CD, bio & contact info.

KVSP 103.5 FM
1528 NE 23rd St.
Oklahoma City, OK 73111
watts: 100,000
main: 405-427-5877
request: 405-460-5877
www.kvsp.com
webcast: Yes
genres: Hip-Hop, R&B
format: Commercial
reports to: R&R
pd: Terry Monday
e: largefathermonday@hotmail.com
md: Jo Corleone
e: jodaboss@gmail.com
Indies aired on "Unsigned Hype," heard for 80 miles. Reg'ls open for Nat'ls at station sponsored shows.

KZCD 94.3 FM
626 SW D Ave.
Lawton, OK 73501
watts: 100,000
main: 580-581-3600
request: 580-357-9494
e: z94@clearchannel.com
www.z94.com
webcast: Yes
genres: Rock, Blues
format: Commercial/Rock
pd: Don Brown
ext: 580-581-3600 x133
e: critter@gapbroadcasting.com
Airs indies on specialty shows to southwest OK & northern TX. "Crossroads" spins Blues Sun 7-9pm: crossroads@gapbroadcasting.com.

Tulsa

KJMM 105.3 FM
7030 S Yale, Ste. 302
Tulsa, OK 74136
watts: 50,000
main: 918-494-9886
request: 918-460-5105
www.kjmm.com
webcast: Yes
genres: Hip-Hop, R&B, Gospel
format: Commercial/UC
reports to: R&R
pd: Terry Monday
ext: 405-427-5877
md: Aaron Bernard
Top station throws a few indies in the mix & some in-studio interviews. Broadcast covers 80 miles. Locals open for Nat'ls at station-sponsored gigs.

KMOD 97.5 FM
2625 S Memorial
Tulsa, OK 74129
watts: 96,000
main: 918-664-2810
request: 918-460-5663
www.kmod.com
genres: Rock
format: Commercial
reports to: R&R, FMQB
pd: Don Cristi
ext: 918-664-2810 x5177
e: doncristi@clearchannel.com
Indies on "Local Bandwidth."

KMYZ 104.5 FM
5810 E Skelly Dr., Ste. 801
Tulsa, OK 74135
watts: 100,000
main: 918-665-3131
request: 918-460-1045
www.edgetulsa.com
webcast: Yes **podcast:** Yes
genres: Alt.
format: Commercial/Alt.
pd: Kenny Wall
e: kennywall@shamrocktulsa.com
Specialty shows aired throughout central OK, KS & parts of MO & AR. "Edge Homegroan" (OK artists only) w/ Matt Lipp & Ashlee; "UK in the OK" (UK Artists only) w/ Kenny Wall; "New From The Edge" (new indie & Nat'l releases) w/ Lunchbox. Sponsors "Edgefest."

Oregon

Eugene/Bend

KLCC 89.7 FM
136 W 8th Ave.
Eugene, OR 97401
watts: 81,000
main: 541-463-6000
request: 541-463-KLCC
e: music@klcc.org
www.klcc.org
webcast: Yes
genres: Americana, Latin, Electronic, World, R&B, Groove, Womyn's, Jazz
format: Public/AAA
reports to: FMQB, Yellow Dog
pd: Don Hein
ext: 541-463-6003
e: heind@lanecc.edu
md: Michael Canning
ext: 541-463-6004
e: canningm@lanecc.edu
Lane Community College station w/ affiliate's indie programs including "Fresh Tracks," M-F 9am-3pm, heard in Eugene, OR & the southern Willamette Valley.

KLRR 101.7 FM
63088 NE 18th St., Ste. 200
Bend, OR 97701
watts: 27,500
main: 541-382-5263
request: 541-389-1088
e: clear@clear1017.fm
www.clear1017.fm
format: Commercial/AAA
reports to: FMQB, R&R
pd: Doug Donoho
e: doug@clear1017.fm
"Homegrown Music Showcase" Sun 6pm w/ host Dori Donoho features Reg'ls: dori@clear1017.fm is heard throughout central OR. Send promos to: PO Box 5037, Bend, OR 37708.

KNRQ 97.9 FM
1200 Executive Pkwy., Ste. 440
Eugene, OR 97401
watts: 100,000
main: 541-284-8500
request: 541-684-0979; 800-905-0979
www.nrq.com
genres: Alt., Rock
format: Commercial
pd: Al Scott
e: al@nrq.com
Spins mostly mainstream; Reg'ls on "Native Noise" Sun 9-10pm.

KRVM 91.9 FM
1574 Coburg Rd., #237
Eugene, OR 97401
watts: 1100
main: 541-687-3370; 800-285-2895
request: 541-687-KRVM
www.krvm.org
genres: Blues, Electronica, Bluegrass, Indie Rock, Acoustic, Jam, Native American
format: Public/AAA
reports to: FMQB
pd: Ken Martin
e: ken@krvm.org
Indie-friendly station run by H.S. students/community & best known for its Blues shows offers tons of eclectic programs & in-studio opps. that travel north to Salem; south to Cottage Grove; west to Florence & east to Oakridge.

KSJJ 102.9 FM
705 SW Bonnett Way, Ste. 1100
Bend, OR 97702
watts: 100,000
main: 541-388-3300
request: 541-330-0103
e: sleavitt@bendradiogroup.com
www.ksjj.com
genres: Country
format: Commercial
pd: Ed Lambert
e: elambert@bendradiogroup.com
Mostly estab. artists, some indies aired to central & eastern OR.

Portland/Salem

KBOO 90.7 FM
20 SE 8th Ave.
Portland, OR 97214
watts: 26,500
main: 503-231-8032
request: 503-231-8187
www.kboo.fm
webcast: Yes
genres: Freeform
format: Public
reports to: CMJ, Media Monitor
pd: Chris Merrick
ext: 503-231-8032 x204
e: program@kboo.org
md: Brandon Lieberman
ext: 503-231-8032 x504
e: rockmd@kboo.org
Spins most styles except New Age & Classical. Send CDs only - no links or MP3s.

KINK 101.9 FM
1501 SW Jefferson
Portland, OR 97201
watts: 100,000
main: 503-517-6000
request: 503-228-KINK; 877-567-KINK
www.kink.fm
webcast: Yes **podcast:** Yes
format: Commercial/AAA
pd: Dennis Constantine
e: dennis@kink.fm
md: Dean Kattari
e: dean@kink.fm
Heard throughout metro area & into Vancouver. "Local Music Spotlight" M-F 9:20pm; produces special podcast program "New Music Channel."

KMHD 89.1 FM
26000 SE Stark St.
Gresham, OR 97030
watts: 8500
main: 503-491-7633
www.kmhd.fm
webcast: Yes
genres: Jazz, Blues
format: Public
reports to: JazzWeek, Media Guide
pd: Doug Sweet
e: station_manager@kmhd.fm
md: Greg Gomez
e: music_director@kmhd.fm
Produces specialty shows w/ indies in the mix to a 70-mile radius. "Homegrown Live" features Local musicians in-studio.

KMUN 91.9 FM
PO Box 269
Astoria, OR 97103
watts: 7500
main: 503-325-0010
e: kmun@kmun.org
www.kmun.org
webcast: Yes
genres: Alt., Americana, Womyn's, Electronic, World, Jazz, Classical, Folk, Blues
format: Public
pd: Elizabeth Grant
e: eliz@kmun.org
Eclectic mix cover north coastal OR & south coastal WA.

KNRK 94.7 FM
0700 SW Bancroft St.
Portland, OR 97239
watts: 25,000
main: 503-223-1441
request: 503-733-5470; 800-777-0947
www.947.fm
webcast: Yes
genres: Alt., Rock
format: Commercial
pd: Mark Hamilton
e: mhamilton@entercom.com
Indie-friendly station supports area's music scene & airs new releases & gig guide for greater Portland area.

KOAC 103.1 FM/ 550 AM
239 Covell Hall
Corvallis, OR 97331
watts: 5000
main: 541-737-4311
e: radiovp@opb.org
www.opbmusic.org
webcast: Yes
genres: Alt., Indie Rock, Pop
format: Public
pd: Lynne Clendenin
md: David Christensen
e: opbmusic@opb.org
Signal reaches into Portland.

KOPB 91.5 FM
7140 SW Macadam Ave.
Portland, OR 97219
watts: 70,000
main: 503-244-9900
e: radiovp@opb.org
www.opb.org
webcast: Yes
genres: Indie, Alt., Pop, S/S
format: Public
pd: Lynne Clendenin
ext: 541-737-5332
md: David Christensen
ext: 541-737-5333
e: dchristensen@opb.org
Airs indies on Sat & Sun specialty shows heard throughout OR & southwest WA. Some content is simulcast on KOAC & many repeaters/translators in OR. Some in-studio sessions, mostly w/ Local musicians.

Pennsylvania

Harrisburg/ Gettysburg/York

WCAT 102.3 FM
515 S 32nd St.
Camp Hill, PA 17011
watts: 50,000

main: 800-932-0505
request: 877-733-1023
www.red1023.com
webcast: Yes
genres: Country
format: Commercial
reports to: R&R
pd: Rich Kreeger
e: rich.kreeger@citcomm.com
Broadcasts to 8 major counties in central PA. Send promos to: PO Box 450, Hershey, PA 17033.

WGTY 107.7 FM
PO Box 3179
Gettysburg, PA 17325
watts: 16,000
main: 717-334-3101
request: 800-366-9489
e: info@wgty.com
www.wgty.com
webcast: Yes
genres: Country
format: Commercial/Country
reports to: R&R, Mediabase
pd: Scott Donato
ext: 717-334-3101 x415
e: scott@wgty.com
Weekly Bluegrass show reaches southeast PA & MD.

WQXA 105.7 FM
PO Box 500
Hershey, PA 17033
watts: 50,000
main: 717-635-7000; 800-932-0505
request: 717-635-7551
e: 1057thex.comments@citcomm.com
www.1057thex.com
webcast: Yes
genres: Active Rock
format: Commercial
reports to: R&R, FMQB, Mediabase
pd: Ken Carson
ext: 717-365-7030
e: ken.carson@citcomm.com
md: Nixon
e: x.nixon@citcomm.com
"X Under the Radar" spins Locals, Sun 9:30-10pm. Contact Maria for specialty shows: maria@1057thex.com; promos to: 515 S 32nd St., Camp Hill, PA 17011.

WWSM 1510 AM
621 Cumberland St., Ste. 4
Lebanon, PA 17042
watts: 5000
main: 717-272-1510
e: wwsm2@evenlink.com
www.wwsm.us
genres: Country
format: Commercial
reports to: Inside Country
pd: Pat Garrett
Mostly classic Country station adds some new hits; indies may slip in on wknd. Bluegrass & Gospel shows - mark pkgs. c/o Joann Thomas. Signal reaches 9 counties.

Philadelphia/ Allentown

WDAS 105.3 FM
111 Presidential Blvd., Ste. 100
Bala Cynwyd, PA 19004
watts: 16,500
main: 610-784-3333
request: 215-263-1053
www.wdasfm.com
webcast: Yes
genres: Classic Soul, R&B, Gospel
format: Commercial
reports to: R&R, Billboard, Hits, Mediabase
pd: Joe Tamburro
ext: 610-784-5259
e: joetamburro@clearchannel.com
md: Jo Gamble
ext: 610-784-5263
e: jogamble@clearchannel.com
Mostly mainstream releases except on weekly Gospel shows to a 90-mile radius.

WDIY 88.1 FM
301 Broadway
Bethlehem, PA 18015
watts: 100
main: 610-694-8100
request: 610-694-8100 x1
e: info@wdiy.org
www.wdiy.org
webcast: Yes
genres: Folk, Rock, Jazz, World, Alt., S/S, Classical
format: Public
reports to: FMQB
pd: Neil Hever
ext: 610-694-8100 x3
e: neil@wdiy.org
md: Kate Riess
NPR station covers Lehigh Valley w/ specialty shows; simulcast on 93.9 FM. No unsolicited material.

WRTI 90.1 FM
1509 Cecil B. Moore Ave., 3rd Fl.
Philadelphia, PA 19121
watts: 50,000
main: 215-204-8405
www.wrti.org
webcast: Yes
genres: Classical, Jazz
format: Public
reports to: JazzWeek
pd: Jack Moore
ext: 215-204-3393
e: jack@wrti.org
md: Maureen Malloy
e: maureen@wrti.org
Broadcasts from Temple U to Harrisburg, Scranton/Wilkes-Barre, Dover, DE & Atlantic City, NJ. Produces syndicated "Crossover" w/Jill Pasternak M-F 2-6pm & Sat 11:30-12:30pm; "The Bridge" Fri 10pm-2am spanning BeBop & Hip-Hop; Classical promos: c/o Jack Moore; Jazz c/o Maureen Malloy.

WUSL 98.9 FM
111 Presidential Blvd., Ste. 100
Bala Cynwyd, PA 19004
watts: 27,000
main: 610-784-3333
request: 215-263-6699
www.power99.com
webcast: Yes
genres: Hip-Hop, R&B
format: Commercial/Urban
pd: Thea Mitchem
e: theamitchem@clearchannel.com
md: Kashon Powell
e: kashonpowell@clearchannel.com
Features underground & upcoming Hip-Hop w/ artist interviews on "Da Come Up Show." Broadcasts to metro Philly & south NJ.

WXPN 88.5 FM
U of Pennsylvania
3025 Walnut St.
Philadelphia, PA 19104
watts: 5000
main: 215-898-6677
request: 215-573-WXPN
e: wxpndesk@xpn.org
www.xpn.org
webcast: Yes
genres: Folk, S/S, Rock, Alt. Country, World, Jazz, Blues
format: Public/AAA
reports to: R&R, FMQB
pd: Bruce Warren
md: Dan Reed
ext: 215-898-2570
Influential stn. blankets Philly & central PA w/ diverse programs & indie releases. Syndicated "World Cafe" heard on 180 public stations. Also broadcasts on 88.1 FM, 104.9 FM & 90.5 FM.

WZZO 95.1 FM
1541 Alta Dr., Ste. 400
Whitehall, PA 18052
watts: 30,000
main: 610-434-1742
request: 610-720-9595
e: studio@wzzo.com
www.wzzo.com
podcast: Yes
genres: Rock
format: Commercial
reports to: R&R, Mediabase
pd: Tori Thomas
ext: 610-841-7218
e: torithomas@clearchannel.com
md: Keith Moyer
ext: 610-841-7256
e: keithmoyer@clearchannel.com
Reaches parts of NJ, the Poconos & northern Philadelphia. "Backyard Bands" airs Locals Sun 9pm. Send band sites to: Kelly Travis: kellytravis@clearchannel.com or 610-841-7275. Contact Jain at jain@wzzo.com for specialty shows.

Pittsburgh

WDUQ 90.5 FM
Duquesne U
Pittsburgh, PA 15282
watts: 25,000
main: 412-396-6030
request: 412-396-6350
e: info@wduq.org
www.wduq.org
webcast: Yes
genres: Jazz
format: Public
reports to: JazzWeek
md: Shaunna Morrison Machovsky
e: music@wduq.org
Indie in the mix heard throughout metro area, southwestern PA & parts of OH, WV & MD. No attachments w/ emails.

WXDX 105.9 FM
200 Fleet St.
Pittsburgh, PA 15220
watts: 72,000
main: 412-937-1441
request: 412-333-9939
www.wxdx.com
webcast: Yes **podcast:** Yes
genres: Alt., Modern Rock
format: Commercial/Alt.
reports to: R&R
pd: John Mashida
md: Vinnie Ferguson
e: vinnie@wxdx.com
ClearChannel station airs "Edge Of The X" Sun 8pm-mid w/ indie/unsigned acts.

WYEP 91.3 FM
67 Bedford Sq.
Pittsburgh, PA 15203
watts: 18,500
main: 412-381-9131
request: 412-381-9900
e: info@wyep.org
www.wyep.org
webcast: Yes **podcast:** Yes
genres: Rock, World, Indie, Folk, Americana
format: Public/AAA
reports to: FMQB, R&R
pd: Kyle Smith
e: kyle@wyep.org
md: Mike Sauter
e: mike@wyep.org
Indies in the mix & on weekly RPM show heard throughout metro area, eastern OH & northern WV. Has performance space that fits 100 for live performances. Sponsors music-related events. Send CDs or MP3s.

Scranton/ Williamsport/ State College

WPSU 91.5 FM
100 Innovation Blvd.
Outreach Bldg., Rm. 174
University Park, PA 16802
watts: 1700
main: 814-865-1877
www.wpsu.org
webcast: Yes **podcast:** Yes
genres: Classical, Folk, World, S/S, Jazz, Blues
format: Public
pd: Kristine Allen
ext: 814-865-9778
e: kta1@outreach.psu.edu
NPR outlet on Penn State campus spins indies on specialty shows; north & central PA tune in.

WVIA/WVYA 89.9/89.7 FM
100 WVIA Way
Pittston, PA 18640
watts: 50,000/3000
main: 570-826-6144
request: 570-655-2808
e: wviafm@wvia.org
www.wvia.org
webcast: Yes
genres: Jazz, World, S/S, Blues, Fusion, Celtic, New Acoustic, Bluegrass, Cajun/Zydeco, Classical
format: Public/AAA, Classical
reports to: CMJ, FMQB
pd: Larry Vojtko
e: larryvojtko@wvia.org
md: George Graham
e: georgegraham@wvia.org
Mostly Classical NPR outlet plays lots of indies for northeast & central PA, Lehigh Valley, western NJ & southern NY. Produces & syndicates specialty shows including the eclectic "Mixed Bag" M-F 8pm & Reg'l showcase "Home Grown Music" Tue 9pm (both hosted by George Graham).

WZXR/WCXR 99.3/103.7 FM
1685 Four Mile Dr.
Williamsport, PA 17701
watts: 50,000
main: 570-323-8200
request: 570-323-9399
www.wzxr.com
genres: Classic Rock, Blues, Zydeco, Roots
format: Commercial
reports to: Living Blues
pd: Ted Minier

e: ted.minier@bybradio.com
Mainstream station transmits throughout Susquehanna Valley; may spin indies on specialty shows.

Rhode Island

Providence

WBRU 95.5 FM
88 Benevolent St.
Providence, RI 02906
watts: 20,000
main: 401-272-9550
request: 866-382-9555; 401-272-9555
e: wbru@wbru.com
www.wbru.com
webcast: Yes **podcast:** Yes
genres: Alt., Jazz, Urban
format: Commercial/Alt.
reports to: R&R, CMJ
pd: Chris Novello
ext: 401-272-9550 x124
e: chrisn@wbru.com
md: Alex Korzec
ext: 401-272-9550 x125
e: md@wbru.com
Alt. by day, Jazz at nite & Urban on Sun; Reg'ls showcased Mon & Wed on "Home BRU'd." Signal hits all of RI & touches MA & CT. For specialty shows, contact: Jonathan Weidman at 401-272-9550 x170 or 360md@wbru.com.

WHJY 94.1 FM
75 Oxford St.
Providence, RI 02905
watts: 50,000
main: 401-781-9979
request: 401-224-1994
www.whjy.com
genres: Rock
format: Commercial
reports to: FMQB, R&R, Hits
pd: Scott Laudani
e: scott@whjy.com
Mainly mainstream/Hard Rock Clear Channel stn. airs syndicated specialty shows from Providence to Boston. "Soundcheck" w/ Big Jim features New England bands, Sun mid-1am: bigjim@whjy.com.

South Carolina

Greenville

WROQ 101.1 FM
25 Garlington Rd.
Greenville, SC 29615
watts: 100,000
main: 864-271-9200
request: 800-763-0101
www.wroq.com
genres: Classic Rock
format: Commercial
reports to: FMQB
pd: Mark Hendrix
e: mhendrix@entercom.com
md: J.D. Stone
e: jdstone@entercom.com
Popular mainstream stn. w/ signal stretching 55mi, showcases Reg'l & indie releases on "Fresh Tracks," Sun 7-9pm & airs syndicated Rock shows.

WTPT 93.3 FM
25 Garlington Rd.
Greenville, SC 29615
watts: 100,000
main: 864-271-9200
request: 864-233-9393; 800-774-0093
www.newrock933.com
webcast: Yes
genres: Active Rock
format: Commercial
reports to: R&R, Billboard, FMQB, BDS
pd: Mark Hendrix
e: mhendrix@entercom.com
md: Twisted Todd
e: twistedtodd@entercom.com
Loud indies in the mix & on specialty shows; Locals spin on Sun nites. Mostly males 18-34 tune in, signal spans 55 miles.

South Dakota

Rapid City

KDDX 101.1/103.5 FM
2827 E Colorado Blvd.
Spearfish, SD 57783
watts: 100,000
main: 866-373-5339
request: 605-642-7800
www.xrock.fm
genres: Alt., Metal, Rock
format: Commercial/Active Rock
reports to: R&R
pd: Jim Kallas
ext: 605-642-5747
e: jim@xrock.fm; jfk@dberadio.com
Covers 80 miles w/ Reg'l-Nat'l releases & wkly new music show.

Sioux Falls

KUSD 89.7 FM
555 N Dakota St.
Vermillion, SD 57069
watts: 37,000
main: 605-677-5861
request: 800-456-0766
e: sdpr@sdpb.org
www.sdpb.org
webcast: Yes
genres: Jazz, New Age, Folk, Classical, Acoustic, Bluegrass
format: Public
pd: Susan Hanson
ext: 605-677-6448
e: susan.hanson@state.sd.us
Base of a 9 station network, heard statewide, spins new Jazz weeknites & on-air opps.

Tennessee

Chattanooga

WBDX/WLLJ 102.7/103.1 FM
5512 Ringgold Rd., Ste. 214
Chattanooga, TN 37412
watts: 6000/50,000
main: 423-892-1200; 877-262-J103
request: 423-642-9858
e: jocks@j103.com
www.j103.com
webcast: Yes
genres: CCM
format: Commercial
reports to: R&R, PD Advisor
pd: Jason McKay
e: jason@j103.com
md: Justin Wade
e: justin@j103.com
Spins estab. & emerging artists for devoted listeners in TN, GA, NC & AL.

WUTC 88.1 FM
615 McCallie Ave., Dept. 1151
Chattanooga, TN 37403
watts: 30,000
main: 423-425-4756
request: 423-265-9882
www.wutc.org
genres: Jazz, Blues, Prog., Alt., World, AAA
format: Public
reports to: AAAradio.com
pd: Mark Colbert
ext: 423-425-4790
e: mark-colbert@utc.edu
Airs diverse specialty shows to a 90-mile radius.

Knoxville/ Johnson City

WDVX 89.9 FM
PO Box 27568
Knoxville, TN 37927
watts: 200
main: 865-544-1029
e: mail@wdvx.com
www.wdvx.com
webcast: Yes
genres: Bluegrass, Americana, S/S, Blues, Celtic, Folk, Country
format: Public/Americana
pd: Tony Lawson
Indies in the mix & featured w/ live sets on daily "Blue Plate Special" blanket a 40-60-mile radius. Check site for DJ emails.

WETS 89.5 FM
89 Dr.
Johnson City, TN 37614
watts: 66,000
main: 423-439-6440
request: 888-895-WETS
e: wets@etsu.edu
www.wets.org
webcast: Yes
genres: Classical, Americana, Blues, Latino
format: Public
reports to: AMA, Living Blues
pd: Larry Mayer
ext: 423-439-6442
e: mayer@etsu.edu
md: Wayne Winkler
ext: 423-439-6441
e: winklerw@etsu.edu
NPR outlet, owned by E TN State U, is Classical by day & spins indies on PM specialty shows "Roots & Branches," Tue-Fri 12:30-4pm & Sat 3-5pm & "Studio One" to eastern TN, southwest VA, western NC & southeast KY. Email before sending material to: PO Box 70630, Johnson City, TN 37614.

WFIV 105.3 FM
517 Watt Rd.
Knoxville, TN 37934
watts: 6000
main: 865-675-4105
request: 865-777-4105
e: feedback@wfiv.com
www.wfiv.com
webcast: Yes
genres: AAA
format: Public
pd: Brian Tatum
e: briant@horneradio.com; brian@wfiv.com
Lots of specialty shows & indies in regular rotation & on Sun nites "Blues Deluxe."

WIVK 107.7 FM
4711 Old Kingston Pike
Knoxville, TN 37919
watts: 91,000
main: 865-588-6511
www.wivk.com
webcast: Yes
genres: Country
format: Commercial
pd: Mike Hammond
ext: 865-212-4516
e: mike.hammond@citcomm.com
md: Colleen Addair
ext: 865-212-4691
e: colleen.addair@citcomm.com; colleen@wivk.com
"Americana Highway" w/ Jack Ryan, Sun nites spins some indie Bluegrass, Country & Americana releases. Send CDs to: Eric Bohlen, show producer, PO Box 11167, Knoxville, TN 37939; or email eric.bohlen@citcomm.com. Signal spans 60 miles.

WYLV 89.1 FM
1621 E Magnolia Ave.
Knoxville, TN 37917
watts: 1600
main: 865-521-8910
request: 865-342-5089
e: jonathan@love89.org
www.love89.org
genres: Christian AC
format: Public/CHR
reports to: R&R
pd: Marshall Stewart
e: marshall@love89.org
md: Kris Love
e: kris@love89.org
Listener supported station airs some indies to the Knoxville area. Artists may submit to "Detour" Local & Reg'l artist program.

Memphis

WEGR 102.7 FM
2650 Thousand Oaks Blvd.
Memphis, TN 38118
watts: 87,000
main: 901-259-1300
request: 901-535-9103
www.rock103.com
webcast: Yes
genres: Classic Rock, Rock
format: Commercial
pd: Tim Spencer
e: spencer@rock103.com
ClearChannel station airs some indie releases & specialty shows to a 50-mile radius. Dennis & Rick play unsigned bands from Memphis & the mid-south on "The Great Unsigned." For Specialty Shows, contact: Dave Spain at spain@rock103.com or Melody Meadows, 901-259-6434, melodymeadows@clearchannel.com.

WEVL 89.9 FM
PO Box 40952
Memphis, TN 38174
watts: 4800
main: 901-528-0560
e: wevl@wevl.org
www.wevl.org
webcast: Yes
genres: Rock, Americana, S/S, Jazz, World, Rock, Blues, Country, Bluegrass, Reggae
format: Public
reports to: FMQB
pd: Brian Craig
e: prmmgr@wevl.org
Diverse programs heard throughout Memphis area, into MS & AK.

WHAL 95.7 FM
2650 Thousand Oaks Blvd., Ste. 4100
Memphis, TN 38118
watts: 6000
main: 901-259-1300
request: 901-535-9425

www.hallelujahfm.com
webcast: Yes **podcast:** Yes
genres: Gospel, Gospel Jazz
format: Commercial
reports to: R&R
pd: Eileen Collier
e: eileencollier@clearchannel.com
md: Tracy Bethea
e: tracybethea@clearchannel.com
Faith-based station adds indies to the mix & showcases Reg'l talent 9am every other Sat on "ND Radio Gospel."

WUMR 91.7 FM
U of Memphis, 143 T/C
Memphis, TN 38152
watts: 25,000
main: 901-678-2560
request: 901-678-4867
e: u92jazz@yahoo.com
http://wumr.memphis.edu
webcast: Yes
genres: Jazz
format: Public
reports to: Media Guide
pd: Mark Bialek
ext: 901-678-3176
md: Malvin Massey

Nashville

WANT/WCOR 98.9 FM/1490 AM
510 Trousdale Ferry Pike
PO Box 399
Lebanon, TN 37088
watts: 5000
main: 615-449-3699
request: 615-444-9899
e: info@wantfm.com
www.wantfm.com
genres: Country, Gospel, R&B, Bluegrass, Classics
format: Public/Soft AC
reports to: New Music Weekly
pd: Bill Goodman
md: MJ Lucas
e: mj@wantfm.com

WBOZ 104.9 FM
402 BNA Dr., Ste. 400
Nashville, TN 37217
watts: 6000
main: 615-367-2210
e: info@solidgospel.com
www.solidgospel105.com
webcast: Yes
genres: Gospel, Bluegrass, CCM
format: Commercial
reports to: Singing News
pd: Vance Dillard
e: vdillard@salemmusicnetwork.com

WBUZ 102.9 FM
1824 Murfreesboro Rd.
Nashville, TN 37217
watts: 100,000
main: 615-399-1029
request: 615-737-1029
e: programming@1029thebuzz.com
www.1029thebuzz.com
genres: Modern Rock
format: Commercial/Active Rock
pd: Troy Hanson
md: Zigz
Departs the mainstream w/ new Local Rock Sun 9pm on "Local Buzz" w/ Aljon: aljon@1029thebuzz.com.

WFFH 94.1 FM
402 BNA Dr., Ste. 400
Nashville, TN 37217
watts: 3200
main: 615-367-2210
request: 800-826-3637
e: mmiller@salemmusicnetwork.com
www.94fmthefish.net
webcast: Yes
genres: CCM
format: Commercial/CHR
pd: Vance Dillard
e: vdillard@salemmusicnetwork.com
Part of network of faith-based media "The Fish" airs indie releases. Simulcast on WFFI 93.7 the signal blankets central TN.

WFSK 88.1 FM
1000 17th Ave. N
Nashville, TN 37208
watts: 750
main: 615-329-8754
request: 615-329-8810
e: skay@fisk.edu
www.fisk.edu/wfsk
genres: Smooth Jazz, R&B
format: Public
pd: Xuam Lawson
e: xlawson@fisk.edu
Lots of indies in rotation & on Reggae, Gospel & African specialty shows. Sipho Dumasane plays Latin Jazz on:SuperSalsa Potente: siphod@aol.com. Signal covers 10-mile area.

WMOT 89.5 FM
MTSU, PO Box 3
Murfreesboro, TN 37132
watts: 100,000
main: 615-898-2800
www.wmot.org
webcast: Yes
genres: All Styles of Jazz
format: Public
pd: Greg Lee Hunt
e: ghunt@mtsu.edu
Community station on MTSU campus airs Reg'ls in rotation for Nashville area.

WQQK 92.1 FM
10 Music Cir. E
Nashville, TN 37203
watts: 3000
main: 615-321-1067
request: 615-737-9292
e: webmaster@92qnashville.com
www.92qnashville.com
webcast: Yes
genres: R&B, Hip-Hop, Gospel, Neo-Soul
format: Commercial/UAC
pd: Kenny Smoov
e: kenny.smoov@cumulus.com
Top rated area stn. targets more mature audience. Indies in mix & on "Gospel Inspirations," Sun 9am-1pm.

WRLT 100.1 FM
1310 Clinton St., Ste. 200
Nashville, TN 37203
watts: 3000
main: 615-242-5600
request: 615-777-5100
e: comments@wrlt.com
www.wrlt.com
webcast: Yes
format: Commercial/AAA
reports to: FMQB, Hits, R&R, Monitor
pd: David Hall
ext: 615-242-5600 x2300
e: dhall@wrlt.com
md: Keith Coes
e: kcoes@wrlt.com
Airs an unusually high amount of indie releases to Nashville. Specialty shows include "Indie Underground Hour" Sat 7pm hosted by Doyle of Grimey's Records fame; unsigned talent on "Local Lightning Spotlight" M-F; "Lightning Request Lunch Hour" M-F noon-1pm.

WVRY 105.1 FM
201 Hall Ln.
White Bluff, TN 37187
watts: 50,000
main: 615-797-9785
e: info@gracebroadcasting.com
www.gracebroadcasting.com
genres: Gospel, Christian Country, Southern Gospel
format: Commercial
pd: John Blankenship
ext: 731-664-9497

Texas

Abilene/Midland

KBCY 99.7 FM
2525 S Danville Dr.
Abilene, TX 79605
watts: 100,000
main: 325-793-9700
request: 325-673-4999
www.kbcy.com
webcast: Yes
genres: Country
format: Commercial
pd: Kelly Jay
e: kelly.jay@cumulus.com
md: JB Cloud
e: jb.cloud@cumulus.com
Spins Local talent along w/ Nat'ls & specialty shows to the Abilene/Sweetwater area. Bands traveling thru the area are encouraged to stop by. Indie music on Fri & Sat for 5 hrs/nite.

KFMX 94.5 FM
4413 82nd St., Ste. 300
Lubbock, TX 79424
watts: 100,000
main: 806-798-7078
request: 806-770-5369
e: voodoo@kfmx.com
www.kfmx.com
webcast: Yes
genres: Alt., Rock
format: Commercial
reports to: R&R
pd: Wes Nessman
Mainstream station airs some indie releases throughout west TX & parts on NM.

KHKX 99.1 FM
3303 N Midkiff, Ste. 115
Midland, TX 79705
watts: 100,000
main: 432-520-9912
request: 432-520-9910
www.kicks99.net
webcast: Yes
genres: Country
format: Commercial
pd: Mike Lawrence
e: morningkicks@aol.com
md: Kelley Peterson
e: kicks99kelley@hotmail.com
"TX Grill" w/ Kelley Peterson Mon-Sat 11:55am-1pm airs TX music.

Amarillo

KPAN 106.3 FM/860 AM
218 E 5th St.
Hereford, TX 79045
watts: 30,000/250
main: 806-364-1860
e: kpan@kpanradio.com
www.kpanradio.com
genres: Country, Spanish
format: Commercial/Country
pd: Chip Formby
e: chip@kpanradio.com
"TX Countdown" w/ Chuck Taylor airs some indies Tue 2pm. For specialty shows contact, Chuck Taylor. Signal stretches 40-90mi.

KQTY 106.7 FM/ 1490 AM
PO Box 165
Borger, TX 79007
watts: 6000/1000
main: 806-273-7533
request: 806-273-5889
e: kqtyradio@yahoo.com
www.kqtyradio.com
webcast: Yes
genres: Country
format: Commercial
reports to: Powersource, Best In Texas, Texas Reg'l Report
pd: George Grover
Spins indie Inspirational Country & TX Country releases. Coverage spans 60mi of the Panhandle. Promos to: 113 Union, Borger, TX 79007.

KXIT 96.3 FM
12421 US Hwy. 385
Dalhart, TX 79022
watts: 100,000
main: 806-249-4747
e: kxit@xit.net
www.kxit.com
webcast: Yes
format: Commercial/Classic Hits
pd: Jesse Torres
md: Jay Edwards
Located on the border of NM & OK, this station airs "Local Live" Fri 7-9pm highlights Reg'l & TX music. Contact George Chambers for specialty shows.

Austin

KAMX 94.7 FM
4301 Westbank Dr., Bldg. B, 3rd Fl.
Austin, TX 78746
watts: 100,000
main: 512-327-9595
request: 512-390-5947
www.mix947.com
webcast: Yes
genres: Alt., Pop, Rock
format: Commercial/Hot AC
reports to: Mediabase, Billboard, FMQB, Playlist, BDS
pd: Cat Thomas
e: catthomas@entercom.com
md: Carey Edwards
e: carey@mix947.com
New music daily span 90mi; Reg'l acts play at station-sponsored gigs.

KAZI 88.7 FM
8906 Wall St., Ste. 203
Austin, TX 78754
watts: 1620
main: 512-836-9544
request: 512-836-9545
e: mail@kazifm.org
www.kazifm.org
genres: R&B, Jazz, Blues, Rap, Gospel, Reggae, Zydeco, Soul
format: Public
reports to: BRE, Hits
pd: Marion Nickerson
ext: 512-836-9544 x14
e: marion@kazifm.org
md: Sharon J.
ext: 512-836-9544 x13
e: sharonjaye@kazifm.org

Indies in the mix & Local specialty shows heard 40 miles.

KGSR 107.1 FM
8309 N IH-35
Austin, TX 78753
watts: 46,000
main: 512-832-4000
request: 512-390-5477
www.kgsr.com
webcast: Yes
genres: S/S, Americana, Alt. Country, Blues
format: Commercial/AAA
reports to: R&R, FMQB
pd: Chris Edge
e: cedge@emmisaustin.com
md: Susan Castle
e: scastle@kgsr.com
Top station spins Reg'l-Int'l releases to 5 surrounding counties. Numerous specialty shows.

KOOP 91.7 FM
3823 Airport Blvd., Ste. B
Austin, TX 78722
watts: 3000
main: 512-472-1369
request: 512-472-5667
e: info@koop.org
www.koop.org
webcast: Yes
genres: Rock, Latin, Lounge, Americana, Celtic, World, Jazz, Womyn's, Alt., Roots, Country
format: Public
pd: Art Baker
e: programming@koop.org
md: George 'Rocky' White
e: music@koop.org
Music fans from 30mi tune in to this prime station. Promos to: PO Box 2116, Austin, TX 78768.

KROX 101.5 FM
8309 N IH-35
Austin, TX 78753
watts: 12,500
main: 512-832-4000
request: 800-561-KROX
www.krox.com
webcast: Yes
genres: Alt., Rock
format: Commercial
reports to: CMJ, FMQB
pd: Lynn Barstow
e: lbarstow@emmisaustin.com
md: Toby Ryan
e: toby@krox.com
Local/Reg'l acts showcased to a 60-mi radius. Sponsors area events.

KRXT 98.5 FM
1095 W Hwy. 79
Rockdale, TX 76567
watts: 6000
main: 512-446-6985
e: krxt1@tlabwireless.net
www.krxt.com
webcast: Yes
genres: Country
format: Commercial
reports to: Texas Music Chart
pd: Bill Gregory
e: billy@krxt.com
Covers central TX w/ a few indies in the mix & on "Texas Music Radio Show" w/ Bill Gregory, M-F 3-5pm: billy@krxt.com.

KUT 90.5 FM
U of TX, 1 University Stn., #A0704
Austin, TX 78712
watts: 100,000
main: 512-471-1631
request: 512-471-2345
e: music@kut.org
www.kut.org
webcast: Yes **podcast:** Yes
genres: World, Jazz
format: Public/AAA
reports to: FMQB, R&R, CMJ, AMA
pd: Hawk Mendenhall
e: hmendenhall@kut.org
md: Jeff McCord
e: jmccord@kut.org
Prime NPR outlet at U of TX airs eclectic specialty shows, along w/ sister station KUTX San Angelo signal blankets central TX.

KVET 98.1 FM
3601 S Congress Ave.
Bldg. F
Austin, TX 78704
watts: 50,000
main: 512-684-7300
request: 512-390-KVET
www.kvet.com
webcast: Yes
genres: Country, Texas
format: Commercial
pd: Mac Daniels
e: macdaniels@clearchannel.com
md: Eric Raines
e: ericraines@clearchannel.com
Blankets central TX w/ some indies in the mix, call-in show & the syndicated "Paul Harvey Music Commentary."

College Station

KAMU 90.9 FM
4244 TAMU
College Station, TX 77843
watts: 32,000
main: 979-845-5613
http://kamu.tamu.edu
webcast: Yes
genres: Jazz, Americana, Celtic, New Age, Acoustic
format: Public
reports to: CMJ
pd: Rick Howard
ext: 979-845-5684; 979-845-5611
e: rick@kamu.tamu.edu
PM & weekend specialty shows transmitted to 60 miles beyond this major college town.

KEOS 89.1 FM
202 E Carson
Bryan, TX 77801
watts: 1000
main: 979-779-5367
e: keos@keos.org
www.keos.org
genres: Folk, Texas, Country, Jazz, Blues, Rock, Reggae, Roots, Bluegrass, Hip-Hop
format: Public
pd: Mark Purcell
e: progdir@keos.org
md: John Roths
e: musdir@keos.org
Volunteer-run station transmits eclectic mix, specialty shows & interviews to entire Brazos Valley. Send promos to: PO Box 78, College Station, TX 77841.

Corpus Christi/ Brownsville

KBSO 94.7 FM
701 Benys Rd.
Corpus Christi, TX 78408
watts: 25,000
main: 361-289-0999
e: texasradio947@clearwire.net
www.texasradio947.com
webcast: Yes
genres: TX Music, Country
format: Commercial
pd: Rebecca Davila
e: rdavila@clearwire.net
Indies in the mix & on 1150 AM.

KEDT 90.3/90.7 FM
4455 S Padre Island Dr., #38
Corpus Christi, TX 78411
watts: 100,000
main: 361-855-2213
request: 800-307-KEDT
e: info@kedt.org
www.kedt.org
genres: Classical, Jazz, Blues, Cuban
format: Public/Classical
pd: Stewart Jacoby
e: stewartjacoby@kedt.org
NPR outlet covers south TX; indies mostly on "Local Spots."

KMBH 88.9 FM
1701 Tennessee Ave.
Harlingen, TX 78550
watts: 3000
main: 956-421-4111
request: 800-839-6771
e: rgveduca@aol.com
www.kmbh.org
genres: Jazz, Blues, World, Psych Rock, Classical
format: Public/Jazz
reports to: New Age Voice, Living Blues
pd: Chris Maley
e: kmbhkhid@aol.com
md: Mario Munoz
NPR outlet produces eclectic specialty shows for southern TX. Send promos to: PO Box 2147, Harlingen, TX 78551.

KVMV 96.9 FM
969 E Thomas Dr.
Pharr, TX 78577
watts: 100,000
main: 956-787-9700
www.kvmv.org
webcast: Yes
genres: CCM
format: Public/Christian AC
pd: James Gamblin
e: james@kvmv.org
md: Bob Malone
e: bob@kvmv.org
Airs some indie music to the southern tip of TX.

Dallas/Ft. Worth/ Jacksonville

KBFB 97.9 FM
13331 Preston Rd., Ste. 1180
Dallas, TX 75240
watts: 99,000
main: 972-331-5400
request: 214-787-1979
e: thebeat@979thebeat.com
www.979thebeat.com
genres: Hip-Hop
format: Commercial
pd: John Candelaria
e: jcandelaria@radio-one.com
md: DJ Bink
e: thturner@radio-one.com
Spins some indie tunes for the area. MD will chat w/ you Tue 3-4, while he reviews your music.

KBJS 90.3 FM
PO Box 193
Jacksonville, TX 75766
watts: 16,500
main: 903-586-5257
e: info@kbjs.org
www.kbjs.org
webcast: Yes
genres: Gospel, CCM
format: Public
pd: Eddie Baiseri
e: eddie@kbjs.org
"Southern Gospel Saturday" noon-6pm heard throughout northeast TX.

KCBI 90.9 FM
411 Ryan Plaza Dr.
Arlington, TX 76011
watts: 100,000
main: 817-792-3800
request: 214-787-1909
e: kcbi@kcbi.org
www.kcbi.org
webcast: Yes
genres: CCM, Inspirational
format: Public/AAA/Christian AC
reports to: CRW, R&R
pd: Mike Tirone
e: mtirone@kcbi.org
md: John Eddy
e: jeddy@kcbi.org
Chris Well College station covers a 100-mile radius. For specialty shows, contact: Rod Butler at 817-792-3800 x253.

KDGE 102.1 FM
14001 Dallas Pkwy., Ste. 300
Dallas, TX 75240
watts: 100,000
main: 214-866-8000
request: 214-787-1102
e: webguy@kdge.com
www.kdge.com
webcast: Yes
genres: Alt., Rock
format: Commercial/Alt.
reports to: R&R, FMQB
pd: Vince Richards
e: vincerichards@clearchannel.com
md: Alan Ayo
e: ayo@kdge.com
Showcases indie, British Punk & Rock on "The Adventure Club With Josh" (josh@kdge.com), Sun 7-10pm. Ayo hosts "The Local Show," Sun 11pm; send CD or MP3: ayoontheedge@yahoo.com

KERA 90.1 FM
3000 Harry Hines Blvd.
Dallas, TX 75201
watts: 100,000
main: 214-871-1390
www.kera.org
webcast: Yes
genres: Folk, Jazz, Blues, TX Music, Pop, Rock
format: Public
pd: Eric Bright
e: ebright@kera.org
"90.1 at Night" w/ Paul Slavens Sun 8-10pm features some indie & Local releases.

KFWR 95.9 FM
115 W 3rd St.
Ft. Worth, TX 76102
watts: 80,000
main: 817-332-0959
request: 817-787-1959
www.959theranch.com
webcast: Yes **podcast:** Yes
genres: TX Country
format: Commercial
reports to: Texas Music Chart, Texas Reg'l Music Chart
pd: Dingo
e: dingo@theranchradio.com
"TX Music Shootout" & "The Ranch Roadhouse" feature TX acts.

KHYI 95.3 FM
PO Box 940670
Plano, TX 75094
watts: 50,000
main: 972-633-0953
request: 972-767-5847

www.khyi.com
webcast: Yes
genres: Americana, Gospel, Hard Country, Alt. Country, Roots
format: Commercial/Americana
reports to: AMA
pd: Chance Cody
Popular station offers an alternative to packaged Country radio. Airs many indie releases & specialty shows.

KLTY 94.9 FM
6400 N Beltline Rd., Ste. 120
Irving, TX 75063
watts: 100,000
main: 972-870-9949
request: 214-797-1949
www.klty.com
webcast: Yes
genres: CCM
format: Commercial/Christian AC
reports to: R&R, CRW
pd: Chuck Finney
e: chuck.finney@klty.com
md: Mike Prendergast
e: mikep@klty.com
Produces "New Music Cafe," aired locally & on KFSH (CA), KKFS (CA), KBIQ (CO), KGBI (NE) & WFSH (GA). For specialty shows, contact: John Hudson at john.hudson@klty.com.

KNON 89.3 FM
PO Box 710909
Dallas, TX 75371
watts: 55,000
main: 214-828-9500
request: 972-647-1893
e: gm@knon.org
www.knon.org
webcast: Yes
genres: R&B, Jazz, World, Americana, Urban, Gospel, Rock, Latin, Blues, Hip-Hop, Country, Reggae
format: Public
reports to: CMJ
md: Christian Lee
ext: 214-828-9500 x234
e: md@knon.org
Diverse programs & specialty shows cover 60mi of northern TX.

KNTU 88.1 FM
1179 Union Cir., RTFP Bldg. Rm. 262
Denton, TX 76201
watts: 100,000
main: 940-565-3459
request: 940-565-3688
e: kntu@unt.edu
www.kntu.fm
webcast: Yes
genres: Jazz
format: Public
reports to: JazzWeek
pd: Mark Lambert
ext: 940-565-2435
md: Breanna Ukegbu
Send promos to: KNTU, U of North TX, PO Box 310881, Denton, TX 76203.

KPIR 1420 AM
1620 Weatherford Hwy.
Granbury, TX 76048
watts: 500
main: 817-736-0360
request: 817-736-0362
www.kpir.com
genres: Country
format: Commercial
reports to: Texas Music Chart
pd: Lee Riza
ext: 817-579-7850
e: lee@kpir.com
Airs specialty shows cover 30mi.

KPLX 99.5 FM
3500 Maple Ave., Ste. 1600
Dallas, TX 75219
watts: 100,000
main: 214-526-2400
request: 214-787-1995; 888-462-1995
www.995thewolf.com
webcast: Yes
genres: Country
format: Commercial
reports to: Billboard
pd: Jan Jeffries
e: jan.jeffries@cumulus.com
"Front Porch" airs Sun 7-9pm featuring TX S/S.

KSCH 95.9 FM
930 Gilmer St.
Sulphur Springs, TX 75482
watts: 6000
main: 903-885-1546
request: 903-885-1221
e: star959@easttexasradio.com
www.easttexasradio.com
genres: Country
format: Commercial
pd: Craig Morgan
e: craigmorgan@easttexasradio.com
"TX Music Hour" airs some Locals, M-F at 9pm. For specialty shows, contact: Jennifer Stinnet, jen@easttexasradio.com.

KSCS 96.3 FM
2221 E Lamar Blvd., Ste. 300
Arlington, TX 76006
watts: 100,000
main: 817-640-1963
request: 214-797-1963
e: hawkeye@kscs.com
www.kscs.com
webcast: Yes
genres: Country
format: Commercial
pd: Crash Poteet
ext: 817-695-0269
e: crash.poteet@citcomm.com
md: Chris Huff
ext: 817-695-0242
e: chris.huff@citcomm.com
Local TX S/S music featured Sun 8-10pm on "Honky Tonk TX." No unsolicited material.

KTFW 92.1 FM
115 W 3rd St.
Ft. Worth, TX 76102
watts: 27,000
main: 817-332-0959
request: 817-338-1921
www.countrylegends921.com
webcast: Yes
genres: Classic Country
format: Commercial
pd: Mike Crow
ext: 817-332-0959 x39
e: mikecrow@countrylegends921.com
For interviews, contact: marlee@theranchradio; performances: mikecrow@countrylegends921.com.

KVRK 89.7 FM
11061 Shady Tr.
Dallas, TX 75229
watts: 14,000
main: 214-353-8970
request: 214-787-1897; 866-787-1897
www.kvrk.com
webcast: Yes
genres: Christian Rock
format: Public
pd: Chris Goodwin
e: chris@kvrk.com; chris@897powerfm.com
md: Drue Mitchell
e: drue@kvrk.com
"Indie Spotlight" scattered throughout nitely programming.

Mandatory FM 98.5/107.9 FM
471 Harbin Dr., Ste. 102
Stephenville, TX 76401
watts: 12,000
main: 254-968-7459
request: 254-968-5282
e: pamela@mandatoryfm.com
www.mandatoryfm.com
webcast: Yes
genres: Americana, Blues, TX Music, Classic Rock
format: Commercial
reports to: AMA, TX Music Chart, Roots Radio Report, Texas Reg'l Radio Report
pd: Shayne Hollinger
e: shayne@mandatoryfm.com
Airs 80% indies plus on-air opps. to Abilene, Weatherford & Ft. Worth/Dallas areas. "Thu Night Live" features home-grown music w/ John Hollinger.

El Paso

KLAQ 95.5 FM
4180 N Mesa
El Paso, TX 79902
watts: 100,000
main: 915-544-9550
request: 915-880-4955
www.klaq.com
webcast: Yes
genres: Rock
format: Commercial
reports to: R&R, Mediabase
pd: Courtney Nelson
ext: 915-544-8864
e: cnelson@klaq.com
md: Glen Garza
ext: 915-544-8864
e: ggarza@klaq.com
Mainstream outlet airs indie releases, interviews/ performances & new music on "Q-Connected" 100 miles in every direction.

KTEP 88.5 FM
500 W University Ave.
Cotton Memorial, Ste. 203
El Paso, TX 79968
watts: 100,000
main: 915-747-5152
request: 915-747-5153
e: ktep@utep.edu
www.ktep.org
webcast: Yes
genres: Jazz, World, Gospel, New Age, Electronic, Classical, Folk
format: Public/Classical, Jazz
reports to: Crossroads
pd: Patrick Piotrowski
e: patrickp@utep.edu
md: Dennis Woo
e: dwoo@utep.edu
Some indies & Local Folk & Jazz artists to a 100-mile area.

Houston

KACC 89.7 FM
Alvin Comm. College
3110 Mustang Rd.
Alvin, TX 77511
watts: 6000
main: 281-756-3766
request: 281-756-3897
e: music@kacclive.com
www.kaccradio.com
webcast: Yes
genres: New Rock, Country, Classic Rock, Blues
format: Public
pd: Mark Moss
e: mmoss@alvincollege.edu
Locals, indies & specialty shows to the Houston area.

KBXX 97.9 FM
24 Greenway Plaza, Ste. 900
Houston, TX 77046
watts: 95,000
main: 713-623-2108
request: 713-390-5979
www.kbxx.com
webcast: Yes
genres: Hip-Hop, Rap
format: Commercial/Urban
pd: Terri Thomas
e: tthomas@radio-one.com
md: James Garrett
e: jgarrett@radio-one.com
"Walter D's MixTape" features Local Hip-Hop music & interviews. No demos, but artists can submit to New Music Days.

KILT 100.3 FM
24 Greenway Plaza, Ste. 1900
Houston, TX 77046
watts: 95,000
main: 713-881-5100
request: 713-390-KILT
www.kilt.com
webcast: Yes
genres: Country
format: Commercial
pd: Jeff Garrison
e: jlgarrison@cbs.com
md: Greg Frey
e: gfrey@cbs.com
"TX Roadhouse" airs on Sun from 7pm-mid & features TX Music.

KPFT 90.1 FM
419 Lovett Blvd.
Houston, TX 77006
watts: 100,000
main: 713-526-4000
request: 713-526-5738
www.kpft.org
webcast: Yes **podcast:** Yes
genres: Blues, Roots, World, Jazz, Hip-Hop, Americana, Cajun, Folk, Tejano
format: Public/AAA
reports to: CMJ
pd: F. Ernesto Aguilar
ext: 713-526-4000 x308
e: ernesto@kpft.org
Indie music in the mix, on live sets & on specialty shows transmitted over 75 miles.

KTBZ 94.5 FM
2000 W Loops S, Ste. 300
Houston, TX 77027
watts: 100,000
main: 713-212-8000
request: 713-212-5945
www.thebuzz.com
webcast: Yes
genres: Alt., Rock
format: Commercial/Alt.
reports to: FMQB, R&R
pd: Vince Richards
ext: 713-212-8044
e: vincerichards@clearchannel.com
md: Don Jantzen
e: donjantzen@clearchannel.com
Indies in the mix & spots native talent on "Texas Buzz." Signal blankets Houston metro area.

KTSU 90.9 FM
Texas Southern U

3100 Cleburne
Houston, TX 77004
watts: 18,500
main: 713-313-7591
request: 713-313-4354
e: ktsufm@tsu.edu
www.ktsufm.org
genres: Jazz, Gospel, Reggae, Roots, R&B
format: Public/Jazz
pd: Charles Hudson
ext: 713-313-7432
e: hudson_cl@tsu.edu
Top area station targets Urban audience w/ specialty shows.

KTTX 106.1 FM
PO Box 1280
Brenham, TX 77834
watts: 50,000
main: 979-836-3655
request: 800-259-1061
e: mail@ktex.com
www.ktex.com
webcast: Yes
genres: Texas Country Music
format: Commercial
reports to: Texas Music Chart, Texas Regional Radio Chart
pd: Ken Murray
e: ken@ktex.com
"Club Lonestar," Fri 8:50pm-midnite, plays all TX artists.

KVLU 91.3 FM
Lamar U, PO Box 10064
Beaumont, TX 77710
watts: 40,000
main: 409-880-8164
www.kvlu.org
webcast: Yes
genres: Jazz, Alt., Americana, New Age, Blues, Classical
format: Public
reports to: Jazziz, New Age Voice
pd: Byron Balentine
e: byron.balentine@lamar.edu
md: Joe Elwell
e: joe.elwell@lamar.edu
TX releases & specialty shows span 50 miles into southeast TX & southwest LA. Does phone interviews w/ selected Jazz musicians; for Jazz, contact: Jason Miller , jmiller@my.lamar.edu.

KYKR 95.1 FM
PO Box 5488
Beaumont, TX 77726
watts: 100,000
main: 409-896-5555; 800-329-9595
request: 409-896-5957
e: kykr@broadcast.com
www.kykr.com
webcast: Yes
genres: Country, Rock, Classic Hits
format: Commercial/Country/AC
pd: Trey Poston
ext: 409-896-5555 x129
e: treyposton@clearchannel.com
"HomeGrown Country" w/ Chrissie Roberts spins some Local/Reg'ls. Signal covers 60mi.

San Antonio

KBBT 98.5 FM
1777 NE Loop 410, Ste. 400
San Antonio, TX 78217
watts: 97,000
main: 210-829-1075
request: 210-470-5985
www.thebeatsa.com
webcast: Yes **podcast:** Yes
genres: Hip-Hop, R&B
format: Commercial
reports to: Mediabase
pd: Mark Arias
md: Jaime 'Hamm' Valenzuela
ext: 210-804-6992
e: jaimevalenzuela@univisionradio.com
"TX Beats" Sun 8-9pm features TX Hip-Hop.

KFAN/KEEP 107.9/103.1 FM
PO Box 311
Fredericksburg, TX 78624
watts: 50,000
main: 830-997-2197
request: 800-KFAN-107
e: txradio@ktc.com
www.texasrebelradio.com
webcast: Yes
genres: Americana, Blues, Jazz, Texas
format: Commercial/AAA
reports to: FMQB, AMA, R&R, New Music Weekly
pd: Rick Star
e: kfanrick@gmail.com
Playlist is 90% indie w/ an emphasis on TX acts. Weekly on-air opps. & specialty shows cover a 60-mile radius.

KNBT 92.1 FM
1540 Loop 337 N
New Braunfels, TX 78130
watts: 6000
main: 830-625-7311
request: 800-326-9292
www.knbtfm.com
webcast: Yes
genres: Americana
format: Commercial
reports to: AMA
pd: Mattson Rainer
ext: 830-625-7311 x218
e: mattson@knbtfm.com
Indies in rotation & on specialty shows.

KRTU 91.7 FM
Trinity U, 1 Trinity Pl.
San Antonio, TX 78212
watts: 8900
main: 210-999-8917
request: 210-999-8313
e: krtu@trinity.edu
www.krtu.org
webcast: Yes
genres: Jazz
format: Public
reports to: JazzWeek
pd: Aaron Prado
ext: 210-999-8159
e: aprado@trinity.edu
Contact Aaron for Brazilian, Latin, Soul Jazz, Blues & Swing specialty shows.

KRVL 94.3 FM
2125 Sidney Baker St.
Kerrville, TX 78028
watts: 35,000
main: 830-896-1230
request: 877-738-5785
www.revfmradio.com
webcast: Yes
genres: TX Music
format: Commercial/Americana
pd: Marti Ashcraft
e: marti@krvl.com
md: Roland J
e: rolandj@krvl.com
Just north of San Antonio & west of Austin, this station airs indies & in-studio opps. to a 50-mile radius.

KSTX 89.1 FM
8401 Davenport Dr., Ste. 800
San Antonio, TX 78229
watts: 100,000
main: 210-614-8977
www.tpr.org
webcast: Yes **podcast:** Yes
genres: World, TX Music, Classical
format: Public/Classical
pd: Nathan Cone
e: ncone@tpr.org
md: Randy Anderson
e: randy@tpr.org
Airs mostly news, w/ some on-air opps. to the San Antonio metro area. "Sunday Night Session" w/ David Furst (sns@tpr.org) features TX artists. Sister station to KPAC & KTXI.

KXTN 107.5 FM
1777 NE Loop 410
Ste. 400
San Antonio, TX 78217
watts: 100,000
main: 210-829-1075
request: 210-470-5107
e: sawebmaster@netmio.com
www.kxtn.com
webcast: Yes
genres: Tejano
format: Commercial
pd: Jonny Ramirez
e: jonnyramirez@kxtn.com; jonramirez@univisionradio.com
Bi-lingual station airs indie music & in-studio opps.for 30mi.

Utah

Salt Lake City

KHTB 94.9 FM
2835 E 3300 S
Salt Lake City, UT 84109
watts: 47,000
main: 801-412-6040
request: 801-470-9490
www.theblazeonline.com
webcast: Yes **podcast:** Yes
genres: Mainstream Rock
format: Commercial
reports to: R&R
pd: Kayvon Motiee
e: kayvon@millcreekslc.com
md: Roger Orton
e: rorton@millcreekslc.com
Specialty shows & a few new indies on "Out of the Box" w/ Big Rog, Sun 10-11pm; rorton@millcreekslc.com. Covers Salt Lake City, Provo & Ogden.

KRCL 90.9 FM
1971 W N Temple
Salt Lake City, UT 84116
watts: 25,000
main: 801-363-1818
request: 801-359-9191
e: donnal@krcl.org
www.krcl.org
webcast: Yes
genres: World, Jazz, R&B, Hip-Hop, Blues, Indie Rock, Americana, Roots
format: Public/AAA
reports to: CMJ
pd: Ryan Tronier
ext: 801-363-1818 x105
e: ryant@krcl.org
md: Ebay Hamilton
ext: 801-363-1818 x102
e: ebayh@krcl.org
Indie-centric volunteers transmits diverse playlist 90+ miles into northern UT, southern ID, & southwestern WY.

KUER 90.1 FM
101 S Wasatch Dr., Eccles Broadcast Ctr.
Salt Lake City, UT 84112
watts: 38,000
main: 801-581-6625
request: 801-581-6625 x8
e: fm90@kuer.org
www.kuer.org
webcast: Yes
genres: Jazz
format: Public
md: Steve Williams
ext: 801-581-4997
e: swilliams@kuer.org
U of Utah stn. has Jazz on nites & wknds w/ a few indies in the mix. Covers UT, parts of ID & WY.

KXRK 96.3 FM
515 South 700 E, #1C
Salt Lake City, UT 84102
watts: 25,000
main: 801-524-2600
e: feedback@x96.com
www.x96.com
webcast: Yes
genres: Rock, Punk, Alt.
format: Commercial
reports to: R&R
pd: Todd Nuke'em
e: todd@x96.com
md: Corey O'Brien
e: corey@x96.com
New music programs & weekly specialty shows stretch over 80 miles. Sun nite "Live & Local" spotlights Reg'ls w/ Portia: portia@X96.com.

Greater UT

KZMU 90.1/106.7 FM
PO Box 1076
Moab, UT 84532
watts: 500/100
main: 435-259-8824
request: 435-259-5968
e: kzmu@kzmu.org
www.kzmu.org
webcast: Yes
genres: Jazz, Latin, World, Reggae, Native American, Rock, Americana, R&B, Indie
format: Public
reports to: CMJ, Roots Music Report
pd: Christy Williams
e: program-director@kzmu.org
md: Glenn Peart
e: music-director@kzmu.org
Community DJs play eclectic, indie-friendly mix & specialty shows throughout southeast UT.

Vermont

North

WBTZ 99.9 FM
PO Box 4489
Burlington, VT 05406
watts: 100,000
main: 802-860-2465
request: 802-658-4999; 877-893-2899
e: mailbag@999thebuzz.com
www.999thebuzz.com
webcast: Yes
genres: Alt. Rock
format: Commercial
reports to: R&R, BDS
pd: Matt Grasso
e: mrgrasso@wizn.com
md: Kevin Mays
Programs buzz acts, on-air opps. & all request shows. Locals featured on Sun nites: "Buzz Homebrew" w/ Matt Gadouas & heard throughout western VT, eastern NY & southern Canada. Send clearly labeled CDs. No calls.

WGDR 91.1 FM
123 Pitkin Rd.
Plainfield, VT 05667
watts: 920
main: 802-454-7367
request: 802-454-7762
www.wgdr.org
genres: Hip-Hop, Loud Rock, Folk, Jazz, World
format: Public
reports to: CMJ, FolkRadio.org, Roots & Radio Report
pd: Jennifer Isaacs
ext: 802-454-7367 x3
e: jennifer.isaacs@goddard.edu
e: wgdrmusic@goddard.edu
Freeform community/campus station sponsors Local gigs & hosts numerous in-studio opps. & specialty shows to a 20-mi radius. Send promos to: PO Box 336, Plainfield, VT 05667.

WIZN 106.7 FM
PO Box 4489
Burlington, VT 05406
watts: 50,000
main: 802-860-2440
request: 802-862-1067; 888-873-WIZN
e: wizn@wizn.com
www.wizn.com
genres: Rock
format: Commercial
pd: Matt Grasso
e: mrgrasso@999thebuzz.com; mrgrasso@wizn.com
Indies in the mix on Sun "Blues For Breakfast" for Burlington & surrounding areas. For specialty shows, contact: Mitch Terri at mitch@wizn.com; Dave Marshall at davem@wizn.com or Mr. Charlie at mrcharlie@gmavt.net for "Blues for Breakfast." Send promos to: 255 S Champlain St., Burlington, VT 05401.

WNCS 104.7 FM
169 River St.
Montpelier, VT 05602
watts: 50,000
main: 802-223-2396
request: 877-367-6468
e: feedback@pointfm.com
www.pointfm.com
webcast: Yes
genres: Pop, Folk, Reggae, Blues
format: Commercial/AAA
reports to: FMQB, R&R, Billboard
pd: Zeb Norris
e: zeb@pointfm.com
md: Jamie Canfield
e: jamie@pointfm.com
Groundbreaking station spins indies regularly & airs specialty shows & on-air opps. Covers northern & central VT on 4 addt'l frequencies.

WVPR 88.5/88.7/94.3/89.5/107.9 FM
365 Troy Ave.
Colchester, VT 05446
watts: 1800+
main: 802-655-9451
e: news@vpr.net
www.vpr.net
webcast: Yes
genres: Jazz, Blues, Folk, Classical
format: Public/Jazz
pd: Cheryl Willoughby
ext: 802-654-4348
e: cwilloughby@vpr.net
md: Walter Parker
e: wparker@vpr.net
Airs indie releases & Reg'l Jazz acts on "Jazz In The Evening" w/ George Thomas: jazz@vpr.net. Signal reaches parts of NH, NY, MA & Canada.

South/Central

WEBK 105.3 FM
67 Merchants Row
Rutland, VT 05702
watts: 1250
main: 802-775-7500
e: thepeak@catamountradio.com
www.webk.com
genres: Rock
format: Commercial/AAA
reports to: R&R, FMQB, AAAradio.com
pd: Judy Anderson
ext: 802-776-7631
e: janderson@catamountradio.com
Indie releases aired to southcentral VT, western NH & parts of ME & NY. Send promos to: PO Box 30, Rutland, VT 05701.

WEQX 102.7 FM
161 Elm St.
Manchester, VT 05255
watts: 50,000
main: 802-362-4800
request: 802-362-1027
e: eqx@weqx.com
www.weqx.com
genres: Alt., Rock
format: Commercial
reports to: R&R, Billboard, Mediabase
pd: Willobee
e: willobee@weqx.com
md: Amber Miller
ext: 802-362-4875
e: amber@weqx.com
Eclectic programming & in-studio performances to southcentral VT, western MA & western NY w/ many specialty shows. Send Jam, indie, Folk & Acoustic releases to: "The Coffee House," nikki@weqx.com. Promos to: PO Box 1027, Manchester, VT 05254.

WTSA 96.7 FM
PO Box 819
Brattleboro, VT 05302
watts: 5000
main: 802-254-4577
request: 802-254-2979
e: info@wtsa.net
www.wtsa.net
format: Commercial/Hot AC
pd: Bill Corbeil
e: corbeil@wtsa.net
Bob Coffee plays indies on "Coffee & Jazz" Sun 6am-noon, coffeeandjazz@cheshire.net. Broadcast covers 30 miles

Virginia

Charlottesville

WUVA 92.7 FM
1928 Arlington Blvd., Ste. 312
Charlottesville, VA 22903
watts: 6000
main: 434-817-6880
request: 434-293-KISS
e: programming@92.7kissfm.com
www.92.7kissfm.com
genres: R&B, Urban, Soul
format: Commercial/Urban
reports to: Urban Network, R&R
pd: Tanisha Thompson
e: tanisha@92.7kissfm.com
Rarely plays indies.

Fairfax

WEBR Ch. 27 & 37
2929 Eskridge Rd., Ste. S
Fairfax, VA 22031
watts: Cable Station
main: 571-749-1100
request: 703-560-TALK
e: webr@fcac.org
www.fcac.org/webr
webcast: Yes
genres: Rock, Pop, Folk, Jazz, Prog, S/S, Dance, Electronica, R&B, Metal
format: Public/Freeform
reports to: SWCast.net
pd: Maryam Shah
ext: 571-749-1118
e: mshah@fcac.org
Features 60+ weekly shows & reaches 258,000 households in northern VA & DC metro area. Email before sending CDs.

Norfolk/Virginia Beach

WHRV 89.5 FM
5200 Hampton Blvd.
Norfolk, VA 23508
watts: 23,000
main: 757-889-9400
e: info@whro.org
www.whro.org
webcast: Yes **podcast:** Yes
genres: Jazz, Folk
format: Public/Alt., Americana, Blues, Jazz
reports to: CMJ
pd: Heather Mazzoni
e: heather.mazzoni@whro.org
md: Paul Shugrue
e: paul.shugrue@whro.org
Indie releases reach southeast VA & northeast NC. For "Shot at the Blues," contact: Paul Shugrue at paul.shugrue@whro.org.

WOWI 102.9 FM
1003 Norfolk Sq.
Norfolk, VA 23502
watts: 50,000
main: 757-466-0009
request: 757-466-0103
e: 103jamz@clearchannel.com
www.103jamz.com
webcast: Yes
format: Commercial/Urban AC
reports to: R&R, Mediabase, Album Network
pd: DJ Law
e: djlaw@clearchannel.com
md: DJ Fountz
e: djfountz@clearchannel.com
Local indie music on "Sunday Night Spotlight."

WROX 96.1/106.1 FM
500 Dominion Tower, 999 Waterside Dr.
Norfolk, VA 23510
watts: 23,000
main: 757-640-8500
request: 757-622-9696
e: info@96xwrox.com.fm
www.96x.fm
webcast: Yes
genres: Alt.
format: Commercial
reports to: Billboard, R&R
pd: Jay Michaels
e: jaymichaels@sinclairstations.com
Indies on Sat & Sun nites & on-air opps. for major artists only.

Richmond/Charlottesville

WMRA 89.9/90.7/94.5/103.5 FM
983 Reservoir St.
Harrisonburg, VA 22801
watts: 11,000
main: 540-568-6221
e: wmra@jmu.edu
www.wmra.org
genres: Folk, Blues, Celtic, S/S
format: Public/Blues
pd: Matt Bingay
e: bingaymc@jmu.edu
James Madison U owned station airs weekend specialty shows, Local music & live performances throughout Shenandoah Valley & Charlottesville. For specialty shows, contact: Tina Owens at wmra@jmu.edu. Do not send press releases.

WNRN 91.9/88.1/89.9 FM
2250 Old Ivy Rd.
Ste. #2
Charlottesville, VA 22903
watts: 350
main: 434-971-4096
request: 434-979-0919
e: wnrn@rlc.net
www.wnrn.org
webcast: Yes **podcast:** Yes
genres: Rock, Acoustic, Hip-Hop
format: Public/AAA
reports to: CMJ, FMQB, R&R, AMA
pd: Mike Friend
e: wnrnmike@hotmail.com
md: Ronda Chollock
e: rchollock@wnrn.org
Genre shows to central VA & beyond Charlottesville.

WRXL 102.1 FM
3245 Basie Rd.
Richmond, VA 23228
watts: 20,000
main: 804-474-0000
request: 804-345-1021
www.1021thex.com
genres: Rock, Alt.
format: Commercial/Alt.
reports to: Mediabase
pd: Casey Krukowski
ext: 804-474-1021
e: caseykrukowski@clearchannel.com
"Studio B" plays Locals Sun at 9pm; mail promos c/o host Jay Smack; smackstudiob@hotmail.com.

WTJU 91.1 FM
PO Box 400811
Charlottesville, VA 22904
watts: 600
main: 434-924-0885
e: wtju@virginia.edu
www.wtju.net
webcast: Yes **podcast:** Yes
genres: Jazz, Folk, Americana, Indie Rock, World
format: Public
reports to: CMJ, Various Folk, Jazz & Blues Publications
pd: Chuck Taylor
md: Roger Barker
ext: 434-924-8995
Indie releases & specialty shows stretch to 60 miles. For Jazz, contact: David Eisenman at 434-243-8833.

Roanoke

WROV 96.3 FM
3807 Brandon Ave. SW, Ste. 2350

Roanoke, VA 24018
watts: 14,000
main: 540-725-1220
request: 800-476-9603
www.rovrocks.com
genres: Rock
format: Commercial/Rock
reports to: Mediabase
pd: Jay Prater
e: jayprater@rovrocks.com
md: John 'JD' Sutphin
e: jd@rovrocks.com
ClearChannel station broadcasts Local, Blues & new music shows throughout central & southwestern VA.

Washington

Seattle

KBCS 91.3 FM
3000 Landerholm Cir. SE
Bellevue, WA 98007
watts: 8000
main: 425-564-2427
request: 425-564-2424
e: office@kbcs.fm
www.kbcs.fm
webcast: Yes **podcast:** Yes
genres: Electronica, Global, Jazz, Folk, Americana, Hip-Hop, Funk, Avant-Garde, Soul, Blues, R&B, Celtic, Gospel, Bluegrass, Country
format: Public
reports to: CMJ, AMA, R&R, Roots Music Report
pd: Peter Graff
ext: 425-564-6162
e: pgraff@kbcs.fm
md: Christine Linde
ext: 425-564-6171
e: clinde@kbcs.fm
Volunteer-run station on Bellevue Community College campus spins eclectic programs & specialty shows throughout Seattle region. Send full-length recordings only.

KCMS 105.3 FM
19303 Fremont Ave. N
Seattle, WA 98133
watts: 54,000
main: 206-546-7350
e: comments@spirit1053.com
www.spirit1053.com
genres: CCM
format: Commercial
reports to: R&R, CRW
pd: Scott Valentine
e: scott@spirit1053.com
md: Sarah Taylor
e: sarah@spirit1053.com
Part of faith-based Christa Broadcasting airs Locals M-F 5:30pm on "Local Music Project." Broadcast covers a 60-mile radius w/ some indies in the mix.

KEXP 90.3 FM
113 Dexter Ave. N
Seattle, WA 98109
watts: 4300
main: 206-520-5800
request: 206-903-KEXP
e: info@kexp.org
www.kexp.org
webcast: Yes **podcast:** Yes
genres: Rock, Alt., Urban, Electronic, World, Jazz, Blues, Country, Roots, Americana
format: Public
reports to: CMJ
pd: Kevin Cole
ext: 206-520-5237
e: kevin@kexp.org
md: Don Yates
ext: 206-520-5833
e: don@kexp.org
Blankets Seattle, Tacoma, Olympia & surrounding areas w/ indies, daily specialty shows & 400+ on-air opps./year.

KISW 99.9 FM
1100 Olive Way, Ste. 1650
Seattle, WA 98101
watts: 100,000
main: 206-285-7625
request: 206-421-7625
www.kisw.com
webcast: Yes **podcast:** Yes
genres: Classic Rock, Rock, Metal, Alt., Indie Rock
format: Commercial
reports to: R&R
pd: Dave Richards
e: drichards@entercom.com
md: Ryan Castle
e: rcastle@entercom.com
Spins indies on "Loud & Local" to the Seattle & Puget Sound areas. For specialty shows, contact: Jolene at jolene@entercom.com.

KKWF 100.7 FM
1100 Olive Way, Ste. 1650
Seattle, WA 98101
watts: 57,000
main: 206-285-7625
request: 800-328-WOLF; 206-421-WOLF
www.1007thewolf.com
webcast: Yes
genres: Country
format: Commercial
pd: Dave Richards
ext: 206-577-2465
e: drichards@entercom.com
Slips some indies in the otherwise mainstream playlist & has some on-air opps. Signal covers Seattle metro area.

KMPS 94.1 FM
1000 Dexter Ave. N, Ste. 100
Seattle, WA 98109
watts: 69,000
main: 206-805-0941
request: 206-421-9436
e: email@kmps.com
www.kmps.com
webcast: Yes **podcast:** Yes
genres: Country
format: Commercial
reports to: Mediabase, BDS
pd: Becky Brenner
e: becky@kmps.com
md: Tony Thomas
e: tony@kmps.com
Indie releases & "Music From Your Own Backyard" features Local acts. Signal reaches a 100-mile radius.

KMTT 103.7 FM
1100 Olive Way, Ste. 1650
Seattle, WA 98101
watts: 100,000
main: 206-233-1037
request: 206-233-8984
e: studio@kmtt.com
www.1037themountain.com
webcast: Yes
genres: Alt., S/S, R&B, World
format: Commercial/AC
reports to: FMQB
pd: Kevin Welch
e: kwelch@entercom.com
md: Shawn Stewart
e: sstewart@entercom.com
Blankets entire state of w/ new music & neglected tracks. Specialty shows include: "The Chill Side of the Mountain" (Ambient & Electronic) & "Sunday Brunch" (Acoustic & S/S).

KNDD 107.7 FM
1100 Olive Way, Ste. 1650
Seattle, WA 98101
watts: 57,000
main: 206-622-3251
request: 206-421-1077; 800-423-1077
www.1077theend.com
webcast: Yes
genres: Alt.
format: Commercial
reports to: R&R
pd: Lazlo
md: Andrew Harms
e: harms@1077theend.com
Indie releases in the mix & on specialty shows heard statewide.

KSER 90.7 FM
2623 Wetmore Ave.
Everett, WA 98201
watts: 5800
main: 425-303-9070
request: 425-303-9076
www.kser.org
webcast: Yes
genres: Alt. Rock, World, Americana, Folk
format: Public/AAA
pd: Bruce Wirth
e: bruce@kser.org
md: Tracy Myers
e: tracy@kser.org
Very eclectic mix, on-air opps. & 30% specialty shows throughout north Puget Sound.

KUOW 94.9 FM
4518 University Way NE
Ste. 310
Seattle, WA 98105
watts: 100,000
main: 206-221-4706
e: letters@kuow.org
www.kuow.org
webcast: Yes **podcast:** Yes
format: Public/AAA
pd: Jeff Hansen
ext: 206-221-2731
e: jwhansen@kuow.org
Local-Int'l releases Mon-Fri 2pm; soundfocus@kuow.org. For specialty shows, contact: Amanda Wilde at 206-616-3680 or awilde@kuow.org. Covers the Puget Sound & west WA.

Spokane/Bellingham

KEWU 89.5 FM
104 Radio-Television Bldg.
Cheney, WA 99004
watts: 10,000
main: 509-359-2850
request: 509-359-4226
e: jazz@mail.ewu.edu
www.kewu.ewu.edu
webcast: Yes
genres: Jazz, Blues, World, Ambient, Downbeat, Chill
format: Public
reports to: JazzWeek
pd: Elizabeth A. Farriss
e: elizabeth.farriss@mail.ewu.edu
Top small market Jazz station run by Eastern Washington U students & community DJs serves the entire Spokane market & reaches inland Pacific NW, parts of ID & Canada. Hosts interviews, studio performances & airs specialty shows & indie releases.

KPBX 91.1 FM
2319 N Monroe St.
Spokane, WA 99205
watts: 56,000
main: 509-328-5729; 800-328-5729
e: kpbx@kpbx.org
www.kpbx.org
webcast: Yes **podcast:** Yes
genres: Jazz, World, Americana, New Age, Celtic, Classical, Folk, Blues, Pop, Rock, Children's
format: Public/Classical
pd: Brian Flick
e: bflick@kpbx.org
md: Verne Windham
e: vwindham@kpbx.org
Airs genre specialty shows, in-studio opps. & produces "Nacho Celtic Hour" (Folk & Children's) on Sun 4-5pm w/ Carlos Alden. Repeater stations carry the broadcasts to eastern WA, northeast OR, western MT, northern ID & into Canada. Indies perform live.

KRFA 91.7 FM
Washington State U
PO Box 642530
Pullman, WA 99164
watts: 14,500
main: 509-335-6552
e: nwpr@wsu.edu
www.nwpr.org
webcast: Yes **podcast:** Yes
genres: Classical, Jazz, Folk, Celtic
format: Public
pd: Roger Johnson
ext: 509-335-6551
e: rogerj@wsu.edu
md: Robin Rilette
e: rilette@wsu.edu
Weekend Folk, Blues, Celtic & Jazz specialty shows to all of Moscow, ID. Covers the Bellingham area & The San Juan Islands. 74mi from Spokane.

KYRS 89.9/92.3 FM
35 W Main
Ste. 340E
Spokane, WA 99201
watts: 100
main: 509-747-3012
request: 509-747-3807
e: info@kyrs.org
www.kyrs.org
webcast: Yes
genres: All Styles
format: Public
pd: Angela Johnson
md: Theresa Sanderson
Eclectic programming/specialty shows & in-studio opps. to a 20-mile radius. Send CDs.

KZAZ 91.7 FM
Washington State U
PO Box 642530
Pullman, WA 99164
watts: 120
main: 509-335-6552
e: nwpr@wsu.edu
www.nwpr.org
webcast: Yes **podcast:** Yes
genres: Classical, Jazz, Folk, Celtic
format: Public
pd: Roger Johnson
ext: 509-335-6551
e: rogerj@wsu.edu
md: Robin Rilette
e: rilette@wsu.edu
NW Public Radio stn. airs wknd Folk, Blues, Celtic & Jazz specialty shows to all of Moscow, ID, Bellingham area & The San Juan Islands. Sponsors Classical concerts. 74mi from Spokane.

Tacoma/Olympia

KAOS 89.3 FM
The Evergreen State College,
2700 Evergreen Pkwy. NW
CAB 301
Olympia, WA 98505
watts: 1100
main: 360-867-6888
request: 360-867-KAOS
e: kaos@evergreen.edu
www.kaosradio.org
webcast: Yes
genres: Rock, Jazz, Americana, Gospel, Womyn's, Electronic, Blues, World, Experimental
format: Public
reports to: CMJ
md: Nicki Thompson
ext: 360-867-6896
e: kaos_music@evergreen.edu
Playlist is 80% indie & heard throughout Olympia, Lacey, & Tumwater. Hosts on-air opps. & tons of specialty shows.

KPLU 88.5 FM
12180 Park Ave. S
Tacoma, WA 98447
watts: 58,000
main: 253-535-7758
request: 800-NPR-KPLU
e: info@kplu.org
www.kplu.org
webcast: Yes
genres: Jazz, Blues
format: Public
reports to: Living Blues
pd: Joey Cohn
e: jcohn@kplu.org
md: Nick Francis
e: nfrancis@kplu.org
Indie releases & specialty shows daily to the Seattle area.

West Virginia

Charleston/ Huntington

WAMX 106.3 FM
134 4th Ave.
Huntington, WV 25701
watts: 1650
main: 304-525-7788
request: 888-933-WAMX; 304-529-WAMX
e: x1063@x1063.com
www.x1063.com
webcast: Yes **podcast:** Yes
format: Commercial/Active Rock
reports to: R&R, Mediabase
pd: Erik Raines
ext: 304-525-7788 x127
e: erikraines@clearchannel.com
"Loud & Local" Sun 7pm & syndicated show, "Undiscovered" on Sun 10pm. Broadcast reaches parts of OH, WV & KY. Reg'l Rock acts send promos for on-air consideration.

WVPN 88.5 FM
600 Capitol St.
Charleston, WV 25301
watts: 50,000
main: 304-556-4900
e: feedback@wvpubcast.org
www.wvpubcast.org
webcast: Yes
genres: Classical, World, Eclectic
format: Public
pd: James A. Muhammad
e: jmuhammad@wvpubcast.org
Classical station airs weekly new music shows. Signal stretches 60 miles.

Morgantown

WCLG 100.1 FM
343 High St.
Morgantown, WV 26505
watts: 6000
main: 304-292-2222
request: 304-284-7625
e: psa@wclg.com
www.wclg.com
podcast: Yes
genres: Rock, Oldies
format: Commercial/Active Rock
reports to: R&R, FMQB
pd: Jeff Miller
e: jeff@wclg.com
Area's top station rocks northcentral WV & southwest PA w/ Local specialty show. Send promos to: PO Box 885, Morgantown, WV 26505.

Greater WV

WVMR 1370 AM
Rte. 1, Box 139
Dunmore, WV 24934
watts: 5000
main: 304-799-6004
request: 800-297-2346
e: amr@frontiernet.net
www.allegheny mountainradio.org
genres: Americana, Gospel, Alt. Country, Blues, Pop, Jazz
format: Public
reports to: AMA, Roots Music Report, Living Blues, Bluegrass Unlimited
pd: Bart Perdue
e: bpamr@frontiernet.net
The only broadcast in 40 miles reaches parts of VA until 6pm. Airs specialty shows, indie releases & on-air opps.

Wisconsin

Madison

WMMM 105.5 FM
7601 Ganser Way
Madison, WI 53719
watts: 2000
main: 608-826-0077
request: 608-281-1055
e: triplem@entercom.com
www.1055triplem.com
webcast: Yes **podcast:** Yes
format: Commercial/AAA
reports to: R&R, FMQB, Album Network
pd: Pat Gallagher
ext: 608-826-0077 x237
e: pgallagher@entercom.com
md: Gabby Parsons
e: gparsons@entercom.com
Weekly in-studio performances which may be included on annual compilation CD. Spins some indies to a 45-mile radius.

WORT 89.9 FM
118 S Bedford St.
Madison, WI
53703
watts: 2000
main: 608-256-2001
e: wort@wort-fm.org
www.wort-fm.org
webcast: Yes **podcast:** Yes
genres: Jazz, Folk, Alt., Techno, Reggae, Hard Rock, Alt. Country, Classical, World, Blues, Spoken Word
format: Public
reports to: CMJ, Living Blues, Jazziz
pd: K.P. Whaley
ext: 608-256-2001 x227
e: newsfac@wort-fm.org
md: Sybil Augustine
e: musicdir@wort-fm.org
Focused on non-mainstream releases & airs many in-studio opps. & specialty shows. Signal reaches a 50-100-mile radius around Madison & south central WI & into IL.

Milwaukee/Appleton

WLUM 102.1 FM
N72 W192922 Good Hope Rd.
Menomonee Falls, WI
53051
watts: 20,000
main: 414-771-1021
request: 414-799-1021
e: info@milwaukeeradio.com
www.fm1021milwaukee.com
genres: Alt., New Rock
format: Commercial/Alt.
reports to: R&R, FMQB, Billboard
pd: Jacent Jackson
e: jjackson@ milwaukeeradio.com
md: Chris Calef
e: chris@milwaukeeradio.com
Covers the metro Milwaukee area: "The Scene" w/ Suzanne Sando, Sun 10pm, features Local & Reg'l acts. "Indie Soundcheck" w/ Ryan Miller, ryan@milwaukeeradio.com, Sun-Thu 11pm, focuses on indie Rock.

WMSE 91.7 FM
820 N Milwaukee
Milwaukee, WI
53202
watts: 3200
main: 414-277-7247
request: 414-799-1917
e: crawford@msoe.edu
www.wmse.org
webcast: Yes
genres: Alt., Blues, World, Jazz, Hip-Hop
format: Public/Alt.
reports to: CMJ, Living Blues
pd: Mike Bereiter
ext: 414-277-6942
e: bereiter@msoe.edu
Send promos to: 1025 N Broadway, Milwaukee, WI 53202.

WZOR 94.7 FM
2800 E College Ave.
Appleton, WI
54915
watts: 25,000
main: 920-734-9226
request: 920-281-0947
e: razor@wcinet.com
www.razor947.com
format: Commercial/Active Rock
reports to: FMQB, R&R
pd: Joe Calgaro
e: jcalgaro@wcinet.com
md: Borna Velic
e: bvelic@wcinet.com
Blasts Metal & Reg'l shows into northeast WI. For "Over the Edge" & "Local Edge," contact: Cutter at cutter@wcinet.com. No unsolicited material.

Greater WI

KUWS 91.3/102.9 FM
Holden Fine Arts Ctr.
1805 Catlin Ave.
Superior, WI
54880
watts: 83,000
main: 715-394-8530
request: 715-395-1790
www.kuws.fm
podcast: Yes
genres: Jazz, Alt.
format: Public
reports to: CMJ
pd: John Munson
e: jmunson@uwsuper.edu
md: Brandie Smith
e: kuwsmd@yahoo.com
Specialty shows heard throughout NW WI & NE MN. Send promos w/ genre marked on envelope to: PO Box 2000, Superior, WI 54880.

WXPR 91.7 FM
303 W Prospect St.
Rhinelander, WI 54501
watts: 100,000
main: 715-362-6000
e: wxpr@wxpr.org
www.wxpr.org
webcast: Yes
genres: Big Band, Folk, Blues, New Age, Bluegrass, Polka, Jazz, Classical
format: Public
pd: Jeff Dabel
e: jeff@wxpr.org
NPR outlet plays some indies. Signal covers central & northern WI & parts of MI.

Wyoming

Casper/Laramie

KUWR 91.9 FM
1000 E University Ave.
Dept. 3984
Laramie, WY
82071
watts: 100,000
main: 307-766-4240
request: 307-766-4255
www.uwyo.edu/wpr
webcast: Yes
genres: Classical, Jazz, Bluegrass
format: Public/AAA
reports to: CMJ, FMQB, Album Network
pd: Roger Adams
ext: 307-766-3587
e: radams@uwyo.edu
md: Grady Kirkpatrick
ext: 307-766-6624
e: wkirkpa1@uwyo.edu
Indie music in rotation, along w/ in-studio performances & a variety of specialty shows. Broadcast covers 85% of WY & about 100 miles into CO.

Jackson

KMTN 96.9 FM
1140 W Hwy. 22
Jackson, WY
83001
watts: 50,000
main: 307-733-4500
request: 307-733-5686
e: jacksonholeradio@aol.com
www.jacksonholeradio.com/ kmtn.htm
webcast: Yes
format: Commercial/AAA
reports to: Album Network, R&R, Hits
pd: Mark Fishman
ext: 307-733-4500 x114
Indie tunes in rotation & on Sun specialty shows. Broadcasts to northwest WY & into MT. Send promos to: PO Box 100, Jackson, WY 83001.

Online Radio

3WK Undergroundradio
www.3wk.com
genres: Indie Rock, Classic Rock, 80s, 90s, Alt.
md: Wanda Atkinson
e: wandagm@3wk.com
pd: Jim Atkinson
e: jim@3wk.com
Streams indie, underground & classic Rock for mostly male audiences, 25-44yrs. Email music links or send CDs & contact info only to: Box 16016, St. Louis, MO 63116. No folders, biogs, photos, press kits, etc.

AccuRadio
e: feedback@accuradio.com
www.accuradio.com
genres: All Styles
md: Kurt Hanson
e: kurt@accuradio.com
pd: Paul Maloney
e: paul@accuradio.com
Listener-supported station w/ diverse programming & customizable channels attracts adults 25-50+, mostly males. Claims to sell $40,000 of CDs/mo via its Amazon link. Send CDs to: 400 N Wells St., Ste. 404, Chicago, IL 60610.

Adrenaline Radio
e: info@adrenalineradio.com
www.adrenalineradio.com
genres: All Styles
md: George Peterson
pd: Dan Stevens
e: danstevens@adrenalineradio.com
Will not consider any songs w/ foul language. Broadcast is avail. via cell phone. Send promos & lyrics to: Box 5832, Whittier, CA 90607.

BBC 6 Music
e: 6music@bbc.co.uk
www.bbc.co.uk/6music
genres: All Styles
Web aspect of famed BBC radio broadcasts wide range of music & on-air opps. on digital radio, digital TV & online.

Beta Lounge
e: feedback@betalounge.com
www.betalounge.com
genres: Electronic
md: Ian Raikow
e: raikow@betalounge.com
Weekly live broadcasts showcase Electronic & related styles that are archived at site. Primarily German, UK & Russian listeners. Submit to: 1072 Illinois St., San Francisco, CA 94107 or: Sternstrausse 67, 20357 Hamburg, Germany. Also runs Beta Lounge Record Club.

BreakThru Radio
e: info@breakthruradio.com
www.breakthruradio.com
genres: Rock, Indie, Alt.
md: Jeff Kuprycz
e: jeff@breakthruradio.com
Indie format w/ DJs has on-demand programming. Over 1million music fans 19-24yrs tune in.

CollegeMusicRadio.com
e: management@collegemusicradio.com
www.collegemusicradio.com
genres: Hip-Hop, Rock, Alt.
md: Michael Knox
e: michael.knox@comcast.net
Indie bands upload Hip-Hop, Rock & Alt. songs & listeners customize radio stations. Also features 83¢ downloads.

Deeper Into Music
e: dim@deeperintomusic.net
www.deeperintomusic.net
genres: Alt., Experimental, Rock, Oldies, Indie
md: Keith Weston
pd: Keith Weston
24-hr freeform station features pop articles & web-only content. Promos to: 101 S Peak Dr., Carrboro, NC 27510.

DefJay.com
e: info@defjay.com
www.defjay.com
genres: R&B, Hip-Hop
Spins the best w/o explicit lyrics to a worldwide audience. Seeking new material from DJs & labels. Email MP3s only to demo@defjay.com.

Destroyer.net
e: info@destroyer.net
www.destroyer.net
genres: Breakbeat, Jungle, Drum n Bass
Public station is an outlet for Breakbeat & similar genres.

DubLab.com
e: info@dublab.com
www.dublab.com
genres: Future Roots
md: Frosty
LA-based DJ collective broadcasts live to 2500 worldwide listeners per day. Feat. music reviews, & links to everything in DJ culture. Submit to: 4519 Santa Monica Blvd., Los Angeles, CA 90029.

Free Radio SAIC
e: freeradio@saic.edu
www.freeradiosaic.org
genres: Punk, Urban, Indie Emo, Rock, Electronic
pd: Nick Williams
Art Instit. of Chicago students experiment w/ live radio & annual music festival.

Freight Train Boogie Radio
www.freighttrainboogie.com
genres: Americana, Alt. Roots, Country, Folk, S/S, Bluegrass
md: Bill Frater
e: frater@freighttrainboogie.com
Broadcasts via Live365 plus a 2hr weekly radio show on KRCB. Send 2 copies w/ press to: Box 4262, Santa Rosa, CA 95402.

GrooveRadio
e: groove@grooveradio.com
www.grooveradio.com
genres: Electronic, Dance, House, Trance, Drum n Bass
md: Ena Aalvik
e: ena@grooveradio.com
Pioneer station celebrates Electronic music & culture. Send mixes, vinyl tracks & CDs to: Box 11268, Whittier, CA 90603.

HardRadio
e: feedback@hardradio.com
www.hardradio.com
genres: Hard Rock, Metal
pd: Tracy Barnes
Headbanger radio features news, interviews, release dates, videos & forums. Email first.

HomeGrownRadioNJ
e: contact@homegrownradionj.com
www.homegrownradionj.com
genres: Rock, Roots, Jazz, Bluegrass, Alt. Country, Jam
md: Sher Stec
Freeform station w/ over 50 volunteer DJs exposes listeners to diverse & obscure music via 24/7 broadcasts, live remotes & festivals. Send 2 copies of CD to: Music Dept., 1077A Rte. 94, Blairstown, NJ 07825.

Live365
e: 365music@live365.com
www.live365.com
genres: All Styles
Create your own interactive Internet radio station or listen to 10,000 stations created by others, in 260+ genres. Over 4 million listeners/month.

Midnight Special Blues Radio
e: support@ms-blues.com
www.ms-blues.com
genres: Contemporary Blues, Blues Rock, Jam
md: Paul Bondarovski
Non-commercial station promotes indie artists & releases to worldwide audience.

Music Choice
e: comments@musicchoice.com
www.musicchoice.com
genres: All Styles
Cable & satellite TV provider w/ 50+ channels of a variety of commercial-free music for listeners of all ages & interests. ATTN: Unsigned Material, 328 W 34th St., New York, NY 10001.

mvyradio
www.mvyradio.com
genres: Rock, Alt., S/S, Blues, Roots
md: Barbara Dacey
e: bdacey@mvyradio.com
pd: PJ Finn
e: pj@mvyradio.com
Terrestrial & web station focuses on hi-quality music that tells a story. Submit music for airplay on Local MusiCafe thru Sonicbids.

Proton Radio
e: info@protonradio.com
www.protonradio.com
genres: Prog, Tech House, Minimal, Breaks, Techno
md: Jason Wohlstadter
e: jason@protonradio.com
Well-known station & label, w/ 100+ shows for DJs around the world w/ emphasis on lesser-known talent. Promos (w/ bio & photo) to: info@protonradio.com. Will contact if interested.

Punk Radio Cast
e: info@punkradiocast.com
www.punkradiocast.com
genres: Punk Rock
md: Danny Keyes
e: danny@punkradiocast.com
Has 20+ million unique listeners/mo. Material ATTN: Music Sorting, 6-295 Queen St. E, Ste. #388, Brampton, ON L6W 4S6.

Radio Free Satan
www.radiofreesatan.com
genres: All Styles
md: Shane Bugbee
e: shane@evilnow.com
pd: Tiberia Nine
e: tiberia_nine@yahoo.com
Actively promotes releases & demos w/ live streams, podcast & affordable ad rates. Include band name, location, tracks & English translation of lyrics. Mail to: Box 2925, St. Paul, MN 55102; MP3s to: mp3@radiofreesatan.com w/ band name as subject.

Radio Free World
e: radiofreeworld@gmail.com
www.radiofreeworld.com
genres: All Indie Styles
Send CDs to: Radio Free World, Box 444, Idyllwild, CA 92549.

Radio Paradise
www.radioparadise.com
genres: Alt., Rock
md: Rebecca
e: rebecca@radioparadise.com
pd: Bill Goldsmith
e: bill@radioparadise.com
Anti-commercial station supports eclectic Rock. For consideration, best to upload 2-3 songs on Listener Review Channel or send CDs only to: Box 3008, Paradise, CA 95967.

Radio Wazee
e: radio@wazee.org
www.wazee.org
genres: Punk, Metal, Industrial, Electronica
pd: Mike Baynton
e: mike@wazee.org
Artists can add their music to the Wire Music Database for listener review. Popular songs added to playlist. For more info, contact: Mike Baynton at mike@wazee.org.

radioIO
e: customercare@radioio.com
www.radioio.com
genres: All Styles
md: Mike Roe
e: mike@radioio.com
Indie-friendly multi-channel station airs eclectic mix. Use contact page to email genre MD before submitting.

SomaFM
e: dj@somafm.com
www.somafm.com
genres: Ambient, Jazz, Dance, Indie, House, Trance, Lounge, Industrial
pd: Rusty Hodge
Influential listener-supported station has 14 channels. 'Groove Salad' channel airs on NPR HD. Check site for DJ submission preferences.

record labels

1-2-3-4 Go!!!!
419 40th St.
Oakland, CA 94609
e: stevo@1234gorecords.com
www.1234gorecords.com
genres: Punk, Hardcore, Crust, Garage, Indie
artists: Steve E. Nix & the Cute Lepers, J Church, Off With Their Heads, Drunken Boat, Hickey, Ringers
See site for submission policy.

215 Execs Entertainment
656 Romford Dr., Ste. 118
Landover, MD 20785
p: 240-398-6078
www.215execs.com
genres: Urban, Rock, Jazz
artists: Thugz Nation, Kove, Diamond District Cartel, Swear EN Gin, Saddam Oakain
contact: Graylin McClary/ A&R - Urban, R&B, Rock
e: gmcclary@215execs.com
contact2: Robert Garrett/ A&R - Jazz, AC
ext: 443-570-1653
e: rgarrett@215execs.com
Include contact info.

2B1 Multimedia
3075 17th St.
San Francisco, CA 94110
p: 415-861-1520
f: 415-861-1519
e: info@2b1records.com
www.2b1records.com
genres: Reggae, Hip-Hop, Dance, Rock, Metal
artists: Gregory Isaacs, Yellowman, Frankie Paul, The Congos, Dub Syndicate
contact: Fritz Sieg/A&R
e: riskarmy@gmail.com
contact2: Boots R. Hughston
ext: 415-861-1519
Include cover letter & contact info.

785 Records & Publishing
785 Fifth Ave.
New York, NY 10022
p: 212-644-1955
f: 646-840-1049
e: info@785records.com
www.785records.com
genres: All Styles
artists: Tiffany Giardina, Article A, Epiphany
contact: Mark Eichner/ Pres.
e: marke@785records.com
contact2: Mike Beck
e: mikeb@785records.com
No unsolicited material.

A to Y Productions
PO Box 5766
Irvine, CA 92616
e: spradio1@aol.com
www.skaparade.com
artists: The Donkey Show, The Equators
contact: Tazy Phyllipz/ Pres.
e: skaparade@aol.com
CDs only.

A&G Records
5 Ching Ct., 61-63 Monmouth St.
London, UK WC2H 9E7 UK
p: 44-207-845-9880
www.agrecords.co.uk
genres: Indie, Alt., Rock, Acoustic, Folk
artists: Lou Rhodes, Bowling for Soup, Sohodolls, The Cloud Room, Gloria Cycles
contact: Sarah Bridge
e: sarah@agrecords.co.uk
contact2: Roy Jackson
e: roy@aegweb.com
Affiliated w/ A&G Songs & A&G Sync.

A.P.O.
1500 S 9th St.
Salina, KS 67402
p: 785-825-8609
f: 785-825-0156
www.aporecords.com; www.acousticsounds.com
genres: Blues, Jazz
artists: Hubert Sumlin, Honeyboy Edwards, Jimmie Lee Robinson, Jimmy D. Lane, Harry Hypolite
contact: Marc Sheforgen/ A&R - Blues
e: marc@acousticsounds.com
contact2: Chad Kassem/ A&R - Blues, Jazz
e: chad@acousticsounds.com
Owned by Acoustic Sounds.

Aaron Ave. Records
2205 W Division St., #1C
Arlington, TX 76012
p: 817-274-5010
f: 817-274-6403
e: aaronave@aaronave.com
www.aaronave.com
genres: Rock, Pop, Country
artists: Brad Thompson, Velvet Love Box, The E.P.'s, Brenton Scott, Emily Rogers
contact: Matt Key/GM
ext: 817-274-5010 x3
No unsolicited material.

ABB Records/ ABB Soul
2201 Broadway, Ste. 506
Oakland, CA 94612
p: 510-419-0396
f: 510-419-0398
e: info@abbrecords.com
www.abbrecords.com
genres: Hip-Hop, Soul, Electronica, Rock
artists: Little Brother, Dilated Peoples, Defari, Likwit Junkies, Evidence
Send submissions to: demos@abbrecords.com

Abet Music
11119 Daines Dr.
Arcadia, CA 91006
p: 626-303-4114; 866-574-0275
e: aeron@abetmusic.com
www.abetmusic.com
genres: Rock, Pop, Easy Listening, World, Smooth Jazz
artists: Effusion, Aeron, 5th Element
contact: Tony Nersoyan/ A&R - World
e: tony@abetmusic.com
contact2: Cindy Wong/ A&R - Pop/Rock
e: cindy@abetmusic.com

Abrad Media
8033 Sunset Blvd.
Los Angeles, CA 90046
p: 323-924-9052
f: 323-924-9047
e: unsigned@abrad.com
genres: Rock, Alt., Pop
artists: Bradford, Cory Brusseau, Lisa Donnelly, Lennard Donnovan
contact: Brian Redding
contact2: Julian Meiojas
e: julian@abrad.com
No calls or faxes.

Ace Fu Records
PO Box 552
New York, NY 10009
p: 212-352-8052
f: 212-352-8052
e: office@acefu.com
www.acefu.com
genres: Punk, Pop, Rock
artists: Acid Mothers Temple, Aqui, Oneida, Kaiser Chiefs, The Dears
contact: Eric Speck/A&R

Acid Jazz Records
146 Bethnal Green Rd.
London, E2 6DG UK
p: 44-207-613-1100
e: info@acidjazz.co.uk
www.acidjazz.co.uk
genres: Jazz, Dance, Rock, Soul
artists: Smoove, Andy Lewis & Paul Weller, Lord Large, Speak Low
contact: Richard Searle/A&R
e: rich@acidjazz.co.uk
Snail mail submissions.

Acoustic Disc
PO Box 4143
San Rafael, CA 94913
p: 415-454-1187
f: 415-459-2815
e: sales@acousticdisc.com
www.acousticdisc.com
genres: Folk, Bluegrass, Acoustic, Latin, Swing
artists: David Grisman Quintet, Old School Freight Train, Riders in the Sky, Enrique Coria, Old & in the Gray
contact: Harriet Rose/A&R
contact2: Craig Miller/A&R
ext: 818-704-7800
e: business@acousticdisc.com
No unsolicited material.

Activate Entertainment
11504 Ventura Blvd., #333
Studio City, CA 91604
p: 818-505-0669
www.activate1.com
genres: Urban, Pop, Rock, Alt., Club
artists: Spice 1, Above the Law/Big Hutch, Poo Poo feat. George Clinton, Mopreme Shakur
contact: Jay Warsinske/A&R
e: jay@2activate.com

AERIA Records
305 Bond St.
Asbury Park, NJ 07712
p: 732-361-2751
www.aeriarecords.com
genres: Pop, Indie, Jam, S/S, Hard Rock, Folk
artists: Joe Harvard, Agency, Candyland Riots!, Juggling Suns, Rick Barry
contact: Colie Brice/A&R
e: colie.brice@aeriarecords.com
contact2: Adam Jones/ A&R - S/S, Hard Rock, Pop
ext: 732-361-4581
e: adam.jones@aeriarecords.com
Runs Princetone, Rewind & Song Haus Records. Send CDs or Vinyl.

A-F Records
1312 Rte. 8, Ste. B
Glenshaw, PA 15116
p: 412-487-7830
f: 412-487-7830
e: orders@a-frecords.com
www.a-frecords.com
genres: Punk, Alt., Rock
artists: Tabula Rasa, Anti Flag, Pipedown, Thought Riot, Destruction Made Simple
contact: Jorge Orsovay/A&R
e: jorge@a-frecords.com
No unsolicited material.

Alert Music
51 Hillsview Ave.
Toronto, ON M6P 1J4
Canada
p: 416-364-4200
f: 416-364-8632

e: contact@alertmusic.com
www.alertmusic.com
genres: Blues, Pop, Folk, Jazz, Rock
artists: Holly Cole, Michael Kaeshammer, Kim Mitchell, Roxanne Potvin
contact: Dan Erison/A&R
e: dan@alertmusic.com
No unsolicited material.

All Things Ordinary
71 Custer St.
Buffalo, NY 14214
p: 716-213-8368
genres: Indie Rock, Punk, Synthpop
artists: La Cacahouette, Lemuria, Team Chocolate, Dasha, White York
contact: Derek Neuland/A&R
ext: 716-799-2384
e: derek@allthingsordinary.com
Snail mail submissions.

Allegro Music
20048 NE San Rafael St .
Portland, OR 97230
p: 503-257-8480
f: 503-257-9061
e: webmast@allegro-music.com
www.allegro-music.com
genres: All Styles
contact: Bryan Huitt/A&R
ext: 503-257-8480 x2037
e: bryan.huitt@allegromediagroup.com
contact2: Patricia Price
ext: 503-257-8480 x2137
e: patricia.price@allegromediagroup.com
Runs Sideburn, Burnside & Alula Records. Submit online.

Allied Artists Records
15810 E Gale, Ste. 133
Hacienda Heights, CA 91745
p: 626-330-0600
f: 626-961-0411
e: info@alliedartists.net
www.alliedartists.net
genres: Pop, Rock, Hip-Hop, Country, Alt., R&B, Latin
artists: Renegade, Eek-A-Mouse, David Burrill, Coolio, Luis Cardenas
contact: Robert Fitzpatrick/President
contact2: Danny Ramos/A&R
Runs Allied Artists Classics, Allied Artists Music Group & Brimstone. Material to: PO Box 2035, Industry, CA 91746.

Alligator Records
PO Box 60234
Chicago, IL 60660
p: 773-973-7736
f: 773-973-2088
e: info@allig.com
www.alligator.com
genres: Blues
artists: Lonnie Brooks, Koko Taylor, JJ Grey & Mofro, The Holmes Brothers, Marcia Ball
ext: 773-973-7736 x221
Blues-based acts send up to 4 songs & contact info (all submissions responded to via mail). No calls or emails.

AlliKat Records
24 Roy St., Ste. 328
Seattle, WA 98109
p: 206-245-2694
e: info@allikats.com
www.allikats.com
genres: Rock, Pop, Roots, S/S, Alt., Jazz, World, Ambient
artists: Leroy White, Rune, Kris Orlowski, Koralee Nickarz
contact: Gwen Jones/A&R
e: gwen@allikats.com
Also does booking for Choochokam Music Festival.

Allure Media Entertainment
PO Box 648
Conshohocken, PA 19428
f: 484-412-8221
www.allureinc.com
genres: Rock, Alt. Rock, Adult Rock, Pop, Urban
artists: Greg Howe, Uncle Plum, Love Jones, Thoroughfare, Wonder Years
contact: Kenny Charles/A&R - Alt., Rock, Pop
contact2: Casey Alrich, A&R
See site for submission policy before sending material.

Alternative Tentacles Records
PO Box 419092
San Francisco, CA 94141
p: 510-596-8981
f: 510-596-8982
e: jesse@alternativetentacles.com
www.alternativetentacles.com
genres: Punk, Rock, Hardcore, Spoken Word
artists: The Bellrays, Jello Biafra, False Prophets, The Subhumans, Alice Donut
contact: Jello Biafra/A&R, Owner
e: jello@alternativetentacles.com; anr@alternativetentacles.com
Snail mail CD, vinyl or tapes.

Amathus Music
PO Box 95
Hewlett, NY 11557
p: 516-561-8622
f: 516-561-8814
e: amathusmusic@aol.com
www.amathusmusic.com
genres: House, Club, Pop, Dance, Electronic, Urban
artists: Platinum Project, Ava Dayton, Darren Round, Collage
contact: Chris Panaghi/A&R
Runs Amathus Urban, Amathus Electro & Amathus Traditions. Mail submissions.

American Eagle Recordings
13001 Dieterle Ln.
St. Louis, MO 63127
p: 888-521-8146
e: info@americaneaglerecordings.com
www.americaneaglerecordings.com
genres: All Styles
artists: Well Hungarians, Sable, Stephen Burns, Kessler
contact: Dr. Charles 'Max' Million/A&R, President
ext: 314-965-5648
contact2: Miami Flynn/A&R - Soul, Funk, R&B, Jam
e: soulsailin@yahoo.com
Runs Soulsailin' Records & MaXam Records. Contact before sending CDs, DVDs, bio, photos & filled out online questionnaire. No links.

American Laundromat Records
PO Box 1428
Pawcatuck, CT 06379
p: 860-460-8903
e: americanlaundromat@hotmail.com
www.americanlaundromatrecords.com
genres: Indie Rock
artists: The Caulfield Sisters, Elizabeth Harper, Julie Peel, Dylan in the Movies
No unsolicited material.

Amherst Records
1762 Main St.
Buffalo, NY 14208
p: 716-883-9520
f: 716-884-1432
e: info@amherstrecords.com
www.amherstrecords.com
genres: Country, Blues, Big Band, Jazz, Rock, Swing
artists: Jeff Jarvis, Kef, A Thousand Shades of Cold, Glenn Medeiros, Doc Severinson
contact: Yusef Jackson
ext: 716-883-9520 x100
e: yusef@amherstrecords.com

Amp Records
153 Balsam Ave. S
Hamilton, ON L8M 3B6
Canada
p: 905-545-8617
e: amprec1@cogeco.ca
www.amprecords.com
genres: Punk
artists: The Bullys, Anna & The Psychomen, Carbona, The Manges, LaTense
contact: Larry/A&R
e: larry@amprecords.com

Analekta
1713 St. Patrick St., Rm. 101
Montreal, QC H3K 3G9
Canada
p: 514-939-0559
e: info@analekta.com
www.analekta.com
genres: Classical
artists: James Ehnes, Angele Dubeau, Marie-Nicole Lemieux, Alain Lefevre, Tafelmusik
contact: Mario Labbe/Pres.
No unsolicited material.

Angelic Music
PO Box 61
East Molesey, Surrey KT8 0HR
UK
p: 44-208-979-1732
e: info@angelicmusic.co.uk
www.angelicmusic.co.uk
genres: Female Artists
artists: Liz Simcock, Abbie Lathe, Janis Haves
contact: Janis Haves
Submit CDs only.

API Records
PO Box 7041
Watchung, NJ 07069
p: 908-753-1601
f: 908-753-3724
e: apirecords@comcast.net
www.apirecords.com
genres: Pop, Rock, Classical
artists: Tim Keyes, Bait-Oven, Funhaus, Frenchman's Hill Band, Merynda Adams
contact: Meg Poltorak/A&R
No unsolicited material.

Appleseed Records
PO Box 2593
West Chester, PA 19380
p: 610-701-5755
f: 610-701-9599
e: info@appleseedrec.com
www.appleseedrec.com
genres: Folk, S/S, World
artists: Pete Seeger, Roger McGuinn, Tom Paxton, David Bromberg, Sweet Honey in the Rock
contact: Jim Musselman/A&R
e: jim@appleseedrec.com

Arabesque Recordings
501 5th Ave., Ste. 805
New York, NY 10017
p: 212-730-5000
f: 212-730-8316
e: info@arabesquerecords.com
www.arabesquerecordings.com
genres: Jazz, Classical
artists: Radam Schwartz, Norberto Tamburrino, Steve Weist, Bruce Brubaker, Gabriela Imreh
contact: Chaim Roberts/A&R
e: chaim@arabesquerecords.com

Ardent Records
2000 Madison Ave.
Memphis, TN 38104
p: 901-725-0855
f: 901-725-7011
e: info@ardentrecords.com
www.ardentrecords.com
genres: CCM, Rock, Pop, Alt.
artists: Todd Agnew, Skillet, Joy Whitlock
contact: Jody Stephens/A&R
e: jstephens@ardentmusic.com
contact2: Aislynn Rappe/A&R
e: arappe@ardentmusic.com
No unsolicited material.

Arena Rock Recording Co.
17 SE 3rd Ave.
#405
Portland, OR 97214
p: 503-233-3775
e: takinaride@aol.com
www.arenarock.com
genres: Rock, Alt., Indie
artists: The Boggs, Carnival Season, The Ecclesia, Larry Norman, Pilot to Gunner
contact: Greg Glover/A&R
e: greg@arenarockrecordingco.com
No unsolicited material.

Arista Records
1400 18th Ave. S
Nashville, TN 37212
p: 615-301-4300
f: 615-301-4438
www.sonybmg.com
genres: Country
artists: Keith Anderson, Brooks & Dunn, Alan Jackson, Brad Paisley, Carrie Underwood
contact: Renee Bell/Sr. VP of A&R
ext: 615-301-4309
e: renee.bell@sonybmg.com
contact2: Carole Ann Mobley/Sr. Director of A&R
ext: 615-301-4337
e: carole-ann.mobley@sonybmg.com
Part of Sony/BMG & runs RCA, BNA & Columbia Records. No unsolicited material.

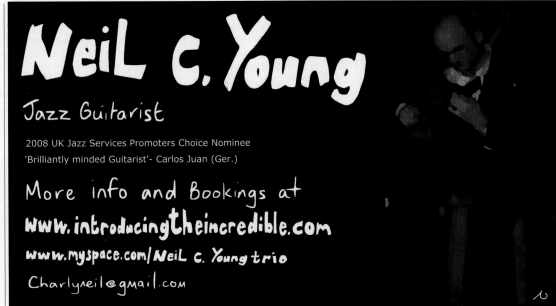

Arkadia Entertainment
34 E 23rd St., 3rd Fl.
New York, NY 10010
p: 212-533-0007
f: 212-979-0266
e: arkadiany@aol.com
www.arkadiarecords.com
genres: Jazz, World, Classical
artists: T.K. Blue, Billy Taylor, Christian Howes, Benny Bolson, Joanne Brackeen
contact: Bob Karcy/A&R
e: bob@view.com
Runs Arkadia Jazz, Arkadia Chansons, Arkadia DVD & Postcards. Send video only.

Armadillo Music
PO Box 3055
Sturminster Newton
DT10 2XA UK
p: 44-196-336-4504
www.bluearmadillo.com
genres: Blues, Americana, Roots, Rock
artists: Daryl Davis, The Rocky Athas Group, Eugene Hideaway Bridges, Beth Garner, Larry Johnson
contact: Hannah Sweet
e: hannah@bluearmadillo.com
No unsolicited material.

Arts & Crafts Productions
460 Richmond St. W, #402
Toronto, ON M5V 1Y1
Canada
p: 416-203-2203
f: 416-203-2208
www.arts-crafts.ca
genres: Indie
artists: Broken Social Scene, Stars, Feist, Jason Collett, The Most Serene Republic
contact: Jeffrey Remedios/A&R
e: raiseyourhands@arts-crafts.ca

Artscope Music
PO Box 121
The Oaks, Sydney, NSW 2570
Australia
p: 61-24-657-2863
e: artscope@artscopemusic.com.au
www.artscopemusic.com.au
genres: New Age, Children's, Jazz, Classical, Funk, Alt., Experimental
contact: Tania Rose
contact2: Jean M.

Asian Man Records
PO Box 35585
Monte Sereno, CA 95030
p: 408-395-0662
e: skylar@asianmanrecords.com
www.asianmanrecords.com
genres: Punk, Ska, Indie Rock
artists: The Broadways, Bomb the Music Industry, Let's Go Bowling, Link 80, The Queers
contact: Mike Park
e: mikeasianman@aol.com
No unsolicited material.

Asphodel
763 Brannan St.
San Francisco, CA 94103
p: 415-863-3068
f: 415-863-4973
e: inform@asphodel.com
www.asphodel.com
genres: Electronic, Hip-Hop, Experimental, Noise, Eclectic
artists: Rhythm & Sound, Alien, Christian Marclay, Tipsy
contact: Mitzi Johnson/Pres.
ext: 415-863-3068 x13
e: mitzi@asphodel.com
No unsolicited material.

Astonish Records
7512 Dr. Phillips Blvd., Ste. 50, PMB 347
Orlando, FL 32819
p: 877-465-6015
www.astonish.com
genres: Rock, Pop
artists: No More Kings, Aranda, David Martin, Soular, Dirt Poor Robins
contact: Topher Grant
e: topher@astonish.com

Astralwerks
101 Ave. of the Americas
4th Fl.
New York, NY 10013
p: 212-886-7500
f: 212-643-5573
e: feedback@astralwerks.net
www.astralwerks.com
genres: Rock, Alt., Electronic, Punk, World, Dance
artists: Beth Orton, Chemical Brothers, Kooks, Pacific!, We Are Scientists
contact: Andy Hsueh/A&R
e: andy.hsueh@astralwerks.com
Part of EMI.
No unsolicited material.

Atlantic Records
1290 Ave. of the Americas
27th Fl.
New York, NY 10104
p: 212-707-2000
f: 212-405-5477
e: info@atlanticrecords.com
www.atlanticrecords.com
genres: Pop, Rock, Urban
artists: Tracy Chapman, T.I. Bjork, Jason Mraz, James Blunt
contact: Julie Greenwald/ Pres.
ext: 212-707-2232
e: julie.greenwald@atlanticrecords.com
Part of Warner Music Group & runs Photo Finish Records, Chop Chop & Fueled By Ramen. ***CA office:*** *Michael Caren, 818-238-6811; mike.caren@atlanticrecords.com. No unsolicited material.*

Audiogram Records
355 St. Catherine W, Ste. 600
Montreal, QC H3B 1A5
Canada
p: 514-285-4453
f: 514-285-4413
e: info@audiogram.com
www.audiogram.com
genres: Pop
artists: Lhasa De Sela, Daniel Belanger, Ariane Moffatt, Jean Leloup, Pierre LaPointe
contact: Mathieu Houde/A&R
e: math@audiogram.com
No unsolicited material.

Authentik Artists
10061 Riverside Dr., #618
Toluca Lake, CA 91602
p: 714-321-1471
e: info@authentikartists.com
www.authentikartists.com
genres: Rock, Pop, R&B, Alt.
artists: Big City Kids, Brandon Rogers, Civalias
contact: Scott Austin/CEO
Digital press kits preferred.

AV8 Records
630 Ninth Ave., Ste. 906
New York, NY 10036
p: 212-397-4696
f: 212-397-4697
e: av8info@yahoo.com
www.av8records.com
genres: Hip-Hop, R&B
artists: Fatman Scoop, Stik-e & the Hoods, DJ Kurupt, Crooklyn Clan, Team Jedi
contact: Brian P./A&R
ext: 212-397-4696 x102
e: brianp47@aol.com
contact2: Marc Petricone/ President
e: marcav8records@aol.com
Send MP3s (smaller than 10MB) w/ demo in subject line to: marcav8records@aol.com.

Avatar Records
2029 N Hyperion
Los Angeles, CA 90027
p: 323-906-1500
f: 323-906-1591
www.avatarrecords.com
genres: Urban, Reggaeton
artists: Planet Asia, One Block Radius, Bishop Don Magic Juan, Rosalia de Souza, Deux Process
contact: Bo Sibley/A&R
e: bo@avatarrecords.com
Mail submissions.

Avenue Records
1801 Ave. of the Stars, Ste. 421
Los Angeles, CA 90067
p: 310-824-6393
f: 310-479-1356
e: avenuemusicgroup@yahoo.com
www.avenuerecords.com
genres: Jazz, R&B, Pop, Rock
artists: War, Sly Stone, Tricky, The Lost Trailers, Will Downing
contact: Rich March/ A&R - Jazz
e: musicman90024@aol.com
No unsolicited material.

Aware Records
624 Davis St., 2nd Fl.
Evanston, IL 60201
p: 847-424-2000
f: 847-424-2001
e: awareinfo@awaremusic.com
www.awaremusic.com
genres: Pop, Alt., Hot AC
artists: Five For Fighting, John Mayer, Mat Kearney, Kyle Riabko, Newton Faulkner
contact: Steve Smith/A&R
e: steve@awaremusic.com
No unsolicited material.

BabyBoom Records
PO Box 512
Stockport, SK2 6WR UK
p: 44-793-962-0751
f: 44-161-279-7302
e: cwilliams@ccm.ac.uk

www.myspace.com/babyboomrecordsuk
genres: Indie, Lo-Fi, Electronica, Alt., Metal
artists: SuperFudgeChunk (France), Prince Edward Island
contact: Chris Williams/Label Manager
Runs BabyBoom Records in France, Canada, Japan & Scandinavia. Send bio, pics & CD or MP3s.

Bad Boy Worldwide Entertainment Group
1710 Broadway
New York, NY 10019
p: 212-381-1540
f: 212-381-1599
www.badboyonline.com
genres: Urban, Pop
artists: Diddy, Danity Kane, Elephant Man, Mario Winans, Yung Joc
contact: Harve Pierre/VP of A&R
e: hpierre@badboyworldwide.com
contact2: Gwen Niles/A&R
ext: 212-381-2095
e: gniles@badboyworldwide.com
Part of Warner Music Group. No unsolicited material.

Bar/None Records
PO Box 1704
Hoboken, NJ 07030
p: 201-770-9090
e: info@bar-none.com
www.bar-none.com
genres: Rock, Pop, Alt.
artists: The Sharp Things, Michael Hearst, Birdie Busch, Esquivel, Spinto Band
contact: Glenn Morrow/A&R
Email MySpace link or site. No MP3's or CDs.

Base 9
22324 Golden Springs Dr.
Diamond Bar, CA 91765
p: 909-859-6563
f: 909-396-0553
e: base009@aol.com
www.base009.com
genres: Drum N Bass, House, Techno, Hip-Hop, Neo-Soul
artists: Dr. Onionskin, Alfa One Seven, Moonraker, Fhonic, Rebirth
contact: Christine Propster/A&R
Accepts CDs only.

Basement Boys Records
500 St. Mary St.
Baltimore, MD 21201
p: 410-383-9103
f: 410-383-9103
e: basementboys@att.net
www.basementboys.com
genres: Dance, R&B, Jazz, Soul, Gospel
artists: Mudfoot Jones, Jasper Street Co., Marcell & the Truth
contact: Teddy Douglas/A&R
e: teddancing1@verizon.net
Runs God's House & Elephunk Records. Send CDs or links. No MP3s w/o permission.

The Beautiful Music
207 Bank St., #129
Ottawa, ON K2P 2N2 Canada
e: admin@thebeautifulmusic.com
www.thebeautifulmusic.com
genres: Mod, Surf, Pop, Alt., Folk, Americana
artists: Skytone, The Mules, Nick Danger & The DCR, Tremolo, The Higher Elevations
contact: Wally Salem/A&R
e: wsalem@cyberus.ca
contact2: Jamie Spacecat/A&R
e: jamie@spacecatmedia.ca

Beggars Group
304 Hudson St., 7th Fl.
New York, NY 10013
p: 212-995-5882
e: banquet@beggars.com
www.beggars.com/us
genres: Rock, Pop, Electronic
artists: Pixies, Belle & Sebastian, Gotan Project, Dead Can Dance, Vampire Weekend
contact: Lesley Bleakley/CEO
ext: 212-995-5882 x1105; 646-218-1105
e: lesleybleakley@beggars.com
contact2: Liz Hart/A&R
ext: 212-995-5882 x1116
Runs 4AD, XL Recording, Rough Trade & Matador Records. No unsolicited material.

Better Looking Records
11041 Santa Monica Blvd., #302
Los Angeles, CA 90025
e: info@betterlookingrecords.com
www.betterlookingrecords.com
genres: Indie Rock, Alt., Indie-tronic
artists: Aberdeen, Boilermaker, Goldrush, Ides Of Space, Maquiladora
contact: David Brown
No unsolicited material.

Big Fuss Records
PO Box 1556
Campbell, CA 95009
p: 408-871-9135
e: info@bigfussrecords.com
www.bigfussrecords.com
genres: Pop, Rock, Folk Rock, Spiritual, Latin
artists: Miss Kristin, Tom Landry, Donnie Woodruff, Adrienne Lawton, Marcel de Marco
contact: K. Pedderson
Snail mail submissions. No EPKs.

Big Mo Records
2002 Gove Hill Rd.
Thetford, VT 05075
p: 802-785-4221
e: bigmo@empire.net
www.bigmo.com
genres: Blues, Jazz
artists: Danny Gatton, Joey DeFrancesco, Rob Piazza, Johnny Neel, Tommy Lepson
contact: Ed Eastridge/A&R
contact2: Dixie Eastridge/A&R

Big Noise
11 S Angell St., Ste. 336
Providence, RI 02906
p: 401-274-4770
www.bignoisenow.com
genres: Pop, Rock, R&B, Metal, Jazz, Acoustic, Blues, Punk, Techno
artists: Christina Aguilera, Katharine McPhee, Paul Doucette (Matchbox 20), Little Anthony & The Imperials, Billy Gilman, Patti Rothberg
contact: Al Gomes/A&R
e: al@bignoisenow.com
contact2: A. Michelle/A&R
e: artists@bignoisenow.com
Seeking new artists. Call or email before sending material.
See Ad On Page 217

black & blue star
3554 Vinton Ave., Ste. 109
Los Angeles, CA 90034
p: 310-924-5651
e: mindi@blackandbluestar.com
www.blackandbluestar.com
genres: Alt., S/S, Rock
artists: Stacy Rasfeld, Year of the White Buffalo, Antonia Bath, Rene Reyes, Spacecow 9000
contact: Otis Smith/A&R
Email before sending material.

Black & Tan Records
PO Box 10168
Apeldoorn
Gelderland 7301 GD
Netherlands
p: 31-55-521-4757
e: info@black-and-tan.com
www.black-and-tan.com
genres: Blues, Roots
artists: Billy Jones, Teresa James, Boo Boo Davis, Doug MacLeod, Big George Jackson
contact: Jan Mittendorp
Send site or MySpace link.

Black Rose
PO Box 970
Pt. Jefferson Station, NY 11776
p: 631-928-0660
www.bulldogevansrecords.com
genres: Urban, Jazz, R&B, Pop, Rock
artists: Catherine, Lay-Away, Doug Gordon Band, Roger Evans, Split Leaf
contact: Robin Evans/A&R
e: bulldogrecords@blackroseproductions.com
Also runs Bull Dog Evans Records. Material must be copyrighted.

Blackbird Music
1531 Reasor Rd., #F
McKinleyville, CA 95519
p: 707-832-9241
e: blackbirdmusicrecords@hotmail.com
www.blackbirdmusic.com
genres: Pop, Rock, Alt.
artists: Franklin For Short, Le Meu Le Purr, The Missing 23rd, Hail the Black Market, The Shape
contact: Travis Whitlock/A&R
e: blackbirdtravis@hotmail.com
Mail demo, one sheet or bio & photo. No calls.

Blackheart Records Group
636 Broadway
New York, NY 10012
p: 212-353-9600
f: 212-353-8300
e: blackheart@blackheart.com
www.blackheart.com
genres: Punk, Indie
artists: The Cute Lepers, Joan Jett & The Blackhearts, The Vacancies, The Dollyrots, Girl in a Coma
contact: Xander Wolff/A&R
e: ar@blackheart.com
Must be copyrighted material. Include contact info.

Blind Pig Records
PO Box 2344
San Francisco, CA 94126
p: 415-550-6484
f: 415-550-6485
e: info@blindpigrecords.com
www.blindpigrecords.com
genres: Blues, Roots
artists: Webb Wilder, Nappy Brown, Peter Karp, Harper, Hamilton Loomis
contact: Ben Nicastro/A&R
e: pigpen@blindpigrecords.com
No unsolicited material.

Blocks Recording Club
280 Spadina Ave., PO Box 67613, Dundsa/Spadina RPO
Toronto, ON M5T 3B8
Canada
p: 416-593-4195
e: blocks.recording.club@gmail.com
www.blocksblocksblocks.com
genres: Indie
artists: The Diskettes, Final Fantasy, Ninja High School, The Creeping Nobodies, Animal Monster
Toronto-based acts.

Bloodshot Records
3039 W Irving Park Rd.
Chicago, IL 60618
p: 773-604-5300
f: 773-604-5019
e: bshq@bloodshotrecords.com
www.bloodshotrecords.com
genres: Roots, Punk, Garage, R&B
artists: Firewater, Ha Ha Tonka, Justin Townes Earle, Bottle Rockets, Mark Pickerel & His Praying Hands
contact: Demo/A&R
Runs Bloodshot Revival. Must be actively touring in the US.

Blue Note Records
150 5th Ave., 6th Fl.
New York, NY 10011
p: 212-786-8600
f: 212-786-8668
www.bluenote.com
genres: Jazz, World, S/S, Blues
artists: Norah Jones, Terence Blanchard, Amos Lee, Dr. John, Wynton Marsalis
contact: Eli Wolf/A&R
e: eli.wolf@emicap.com
contact2: Keith Karwelies/A&R
e: keith.karwelies@emicap.com
Part of EMI & runs Narada Jazz & Metro Blue. No unsolicited material.

Blue November/ GAG Order Records
PO Box 1245
New York, NY 10159
p: 212-686-0902
e: go@gagorder.com
www.bluenovemberrecords.com
genres: Rock, Pop, Alt. Country, Contemporary Folk, World, Classical Crossover
artists: Frederik Doci, Jim Barbaro, GGP, Dusty Blue
contact: George Gesner/A&R
Send CDs or web links.

Blue Skunk Music
12400 Russett Ln.
Huntley, IL 60142
p: 847-275-8378
www.blueskunkmusic.com
genres: Jazz, Blues, Folk, Country
artists: Cleveland Fats, Dan Hayes, Ross Hubbell Trio, Rusty Evans, Devil In A Woodpile

contact: Joe Rutan
e: jrutan@blueskunkmusic.com

Blue Star Entertainment
PO Box 580051
Houston, TX 77258
p: 210-833-4094
genres: All Styles
artists: Lady V., Blackstone, Bon Ton Mickey, Trudy Lynn, Fay Robinson
contact: Ronald Drummer/ A&R, CEO
e: rdrumm2@aol.com; ronalddrummer@yahoo.com
contact2: Marcellus Jones/A&R
Send EPKs.

Blue Storm Music
PO Box 940179
Rockaway Park, NY 11694
p: 718-474-1546
f: 718-474-2001
e: info@bluestormmusic.com
www.bluestormmusic.com
genres: Roots, Rock, Blues
artists: Vince Converse, Scott Holt, Dick Hecktal-Smith, Peter Green, Blue Cheer
contact: Arnie Goodman/A&R
No unsolicited material.

bluhammock music
227 W 29th St., 6th Fl.
New York, NY 10001
p: 212-239-3440
f: 212-239-3442
e: info@bluhammock.com
www.bluhammock.com
genres: Honest, Evocative Music
artists: Jim Boggia, The Break & Repair Method, KaiserCartel, Val Emmich, Kristoffer Ragnstam
contact: Rachel Reiter
ext: 212-239-3444
e: rachel@bluhammock.com
Runs Procrastination Records. Must get approval from Rachel before sending material.

Boa Records
223, 5512 Fourth St., NW
Calgary, AB T2K 6J0 Canada
p: 403-274-1654
e: boa@boarecords.ca
www.boarecords.ca
genres: Rock, Pop, Country, S/S
artists: Dan Nash, Brian Cline, Dex, Ian Earl, Jim Banning
contact: Bob James/Mngr.
e: bobjames@boarecords.ca
Run by Zamie Songs. Email first.

Bomp Records
PO Box 7112
Burbank, CA 91510
e: promo@bomprecords.com
www.bomp.com
genres: Punk, Psychedelic
artists: Stiv Bators, Black Lips, BBQ, Brian Jonestown Massacre, Iggy & The Stooges
contact: Patrick Boissel/A&R
e: patrick@bomprecords.com
Runs AIP, Alive & Voxx. No unsolicited material.

Bridge 9 Records
119 Foster St., Bldg. 4, Ste. 3
Peabody, MA 01960
p: 978-532-0666
f: 978-532-3806
e: info@bridge9.com
www.bridge9.com
genres: Punk, Hardcore
artists: Agnostic Front, New Found Glory, Triple Threat, Panic, Stand & Fight
Send demos. No calls.

Broken Records
198 E Park Ave.
Flushing, MI 48433
p: 810-624-8310
e: info@brokenrecordsmusic.com
www.brokenrecordsmusic.com
genres: Rock, Pop, Country, R&B
artists: After the Ashes, Crop Circle, Letters for Thursday
contact: Norm Coleman/ A&R - Pop, Rock, R&B
e: norm@brokenrecordsmusic.com
contact2: Joe Boettger/ A&R - Pop, Country
e: joe@brokenrecordsmusic.com
No calls regarding submissions.

Broken Star Records
2435 Hwy. 34, #295
Manasquan, NJ 08736
p: 732-701-9044
f: 732-701-9777
e: info@brokenstarrecords.com
www.brokenstarrecords.com
genres: Rock, Punk, Emo, Hardcore, Acoustic, Indie, Experimental
artists: The Youth Ahead, Weak At Best
contact: Thom Zarra/A&R
e: thom@brokenstarrecords.com
contact2: Meara Jones/A&R
e: meara@brokenstarrecords.com
No Sonicbids EPKs.

Buckyball Music
PO Box 2034
New York, NY 10101
p: 212-333-5812
f: 212-333-5813
e: records@buckyballmusic.com; info@buckyballmusic.com
www.buckyballmusic.com
genres: Jazz, Fusion, Crossover
artists: Sarah Pillow, Brand X, Tunnels, Marc Wagnon, Nicholas D'Amato
contact: Lynn Huyett/A&R
e: lynn@buckyballmusic.com
No unsolicited material.

Bug House Records
6311 N Neenah
Chicago, IL 60631
p: 773-763-7509
f: 773-763-3252
e: pravdausa@aol.com
www.pravdamusic.com
genres: Rock, Rockabilly, Alt., Experimental
artists: Hasil Adkins, Cordell Jackson, Tiny Tim, The Legendary Stardust Cowboy
contact: Matt Favazza/A&R
Owned by Pravda Records.

Bullseye Records of Canada
180 Station St., Ste. 53
Ajax, ON L1S 1R9 Canada
p: 905-523-5999
www.bullseyecanada.com
genres: Rock, Pop
artists: Glen Foster, Bill Culp, Honeymoon Suite, Dave Rave, Creighton Doane
contact: Jaimie Vernon
e: president@bullseyecanada.com
Runs Frontline Records. No unsolicited material.

Burning Heart Records
PO Box 441
Orebro, 701 48 Sweden
p: 46-1-917-4690
f: 46-1-917-4699
e: info@burningheart.com
www.burningheart.com
genres: Punk, Rock, Pop, Hip-Hop
artists: Refused, Millencolin, The Weakerthans, Franky Lee, Sounds Like Violence
contact: Peter Ahlqvist/A&R
e: peter@burningheart.com
Germany office: 49-307-261-9840. Send CD, DAT or Vinyl.

Canyon Records
3131 W Clarendon Ave.
Phoenix, AZ 85017
p: 800-268-1141
f: 602-279-9233
e: canyon@canyonrecords.com
www.canyonrecords.com
genres: Native American, World, New Age
artists: R. Carlos Nakai, Northern Cree, Robert Tree Cody, Randy Wood, Radmilla Cody
contact: Stephen Butler/A&R
ext: 602-266-7835
e: stephen@canyonrecords.com
contact2: Kathy Norris/A&R
e: kathy@canyonrecords.com

Capitol/EMI Records
1750 N Vine St., 10th Fl.
Los Angeles, CA 90028
www.capitolrecords.com
genres: Rock, Pop, Alt., Urban
artists: Coldplay, Saosin, Interpol, The Decemberists, Lily Allen
contact: Louie Bandak/ VP of A&R
ext: 323-871-5101
e: louie.bandak@capitolmusic.com
contact2: Marc Nathan/ Sr. Director of A&R
ext: 323-871-5747
e: marc.nathan@capitolmusic.com
*Part of EMI. Other location in **TN:** Larry Willoughby, 615-269-2037; larry.willoughby@emicap.com. No unsolicited material.*

Carbon 7
85 Rue Froissart
Brussels, 1040
Belgium
p: 32-2-242-9703
f: 32-2-245-3885
e: carbon7records@skynet.be
www.carbon-7.com
genres: Jazz, Rock, World, New Music, Indie
artists: Aka Moon, Attica, Present, Lula Pena, Hilliard Ensemble
contact: Guy Segers/Pres.

Castle Records
30 Music Sq. W, Ste. 103
Nashville, TN 37203
p: 615-401-7111
f: 615-320-7006
e: castlerecords@castlerecords.com
www.castlerecords.com
genres: Country, R&B, Pop, AC, Gospel
artists: Carl Butler, Kebo Cyrus, Eddie Ray, Shane Keane, Shooter
contact: Dave Sullivan/A&R
ext: 615-320-7003
e: davesullivan@castlerecords.com
contact2: Deb Wallin/A&R
ext: 615-320-9501
e: debwallin@castlerecords.com

Century Media Records
2323 W El Segundo Blvd.
Hawthorne, CA 90250
p: 323-418-1400
f: 323-418-0118
e: mail@centurymedia.com
www.centurymedia.com
genres: Metal, Hard Rock, Hardcore, Black Metal
artists: Arch Enemy, Lacuna Coil, God Forbid, In This Moment, Suicide Silence
contact: Phil Hinkle/A&R
e: phil@centurymedia.com
contact2: Steve Joh/A&R
e: steve@centurymedia.com
Runs US Nuclear Blast Records.

Chesky Records
PO Box 1268
Radio City Station
New York, NY 10101
p: 212-586-7799
f: 212-262-0814
e: info@chesky.com
www.chesky.com
genres: Jazz, Pop, World, Classical
artists: Alexander Gibson, Bruce Dunlap, Chuck Mangione, John Pizzarelli, Paquito D'Rivera
contact: Lisa Hershfield/A&R
e: chesky2@pipeline.com

CIA (Copeland Int'l Arts)
1830 N Sierra Benita
Los Angeles, CA 90046
p: 323-512-4080
f: 323-512-4089
www.cialabel.com
genres: World Music, Arab/Middle Eastern Music
artists: Bellydance Superstars, Baghdad Heavy Metal, Hoda
contact: Miles A. Copeland/ A&R - World
e: miles@milescopeland.net
contact2: John Bevilacqua/ A&R - World, Arab
e: john@milescopeland.net
Also see www.ciaweb.us. No unsolicited material.

CIMP/ Creative Improvised Music Productions
Cadence Bldg.
Redwood, NY 13679
p: 315-287-2852
f: 315-287-2860
e: cimp@cadencebuilding.com
www.cadencebuilding.com
genres: Jazz, Improv
artists: Anthony Braxton, Kahil El' Zabar, Paul Smoker, Joe McPhee, Odean Pope
contact: Bob Rusch/A&R
contact2: Larry Raye/A&R
Runs CadenceJazz Records, Quixotic Records, CIMPoL Records & CIMPview. Send CDRs or cassettes.

Cleopatra Records
11041 Santa Monica Blvd.
PMB #703

Los Angeles, CA 90025
p: 310-477-4000
f: 310-312-5653
e: cleoinfo@cleorecs.com
www.cleopatrarecords.com
genres: Rock, Metal, Gothic, Darkwave, Rap
artists: L.A. Guns, Great White, Stephen Pearcy, New Skin, Lonesome Spurs
Runs Hypnotic Records, Master Classics, Purple Pryamid, Stardust Records, X-Ray Records, Deadline Records, Goldenlane & Soundtracks. Email before sending CD, bio, press & tour schedule.

Clickpop Records
PO Box 5765
Bellingham, WA 98227
p: 360-961-9759
e: clickpop@mac.com
www.clickpoprecords.com
genres: Rock, Folk, Pop, Electronic, Ambient, Punk
artists: Idiot Pilot, Kristin Allen-Zito, Hakea, Delay, The Trucks
contact: Dave Richards/A&R
Runs Memex Records & De La Creme Soundsystem. Snail mail submissions.

CMH Records
PO Box 39439
Los Angeles, CA 90039
p: 323-663-8073
f: 323-669-1470
e: info@cmhrecords.com
www.cmhrecords.com
genres: Bluegrass, Country, Rock, Tributes
artists: Wanda Jackson, Mac Wiseman, Merle Haggard, Raol Malo, Lester Flatt
contact: James Curtis/A&R
e: jamesc@cmhrecords.com
Runs Dwell, Vitamin, Crosscheck, Urabon & Scufflin' Records. Send CDs to: 2898 Rowena Ave., Los Angeles, CA 90039.

Coach House Records
3503 S Harbor Blvd.
Santa Ana, CA 92704
p: 714-545-2622
f: 714-545-3490
e: chr@thecoachhouse.com
www.coachhouserecords.com
genres: All Styles
artists: Ambrosia, Dada, Hellbound Hayride, Ashley Matte, Buck Bros
contact: Andrella Christopher/A&R
e: andrella@thecoachhouse.com
See site for submission policy.

Columbia Records
550 Madison Ave., 26th Fl.
New York, NY 10022
p: 212-833-8000
f: 212-833-5607
e: feedback@sonymusic.com
www.columbiarecords.com
genres: Rock, Pop, R&B, Funk, Punk, Alt.
artists: Prince, Beyonce, Bruce Springsteen, Nellie McKay, Coheed & Cambria
contact: John Doelp/ Sr. VP of A&R
ext: 212-833-4623
e: john.doelp@sonybmg.com
Part of Sony/BMG. No unsolicited material.

Compass Records
916 19th Ave. S
Nashville, TN 37212
p: 615-320-7672
f: 615-320-7378
e: info@compassrecords.com
www.compassrecords.com
genres: Contemporary Folk, Celtic, Americana, Bluegrass, Adult Pop
artists: Solas, Colin Hay, Catie Curtis, The Waifs, Paul Brady
contact: Garry West/A&R
e: garry@compassrecords.com
No unsolicited material.

Concord Records
100 N Crescent Dr.
Beverly Hills, CA 90210
p: 310-385-4455
f: 310-382-4142
e: info@concordrecords.com
www.concordmusicgroup.com
genres: Jazz, Rock, Adult Standard,
artists: Michael Feinstein, The Rippingtons, Ozomatli, Poncho Sanchez, Chick Corea
contact: John Burk/A&R
contact2: Nick Phillips/A&R
Runs Concord Records, Concord Jazz, Concord Picante, Contemporary, Fantasy, Good Time Jazz, Heads Up, Hear Music, Milestone, Monterey Jazz Festival Records, Original Blues Classics, Original Jazz Classics, Pablo, Peak Records, Riverside, Specialty & Stax.

Cooking Vinyl
10 Allied Way
London, W3 0RQ UK
p: 44-208-600-9200
f: 44-208-743-7448
e: info@cookingvinyl.com
www.cookingvinyl.com
genres: Rock, Folk, World, Americana, Alt.
artists: Frank Black, AM/FM, Echo & The Bunnymen, They Might Be Giants, Billy Bragg
contact: Leyla Leonard/A&R
e: leyla@cookingvinyl.com

COP Int'l
851 81st Ave., Ste. 226
Oakland, CA 94621
f: 510-633-9028
www.copint.com
genres: Industrial, Goth, Electro
artists: Tactical Sekt, Reaper, Heimataerdre, Soil & Eclipse, Psychobitch
contact: Christian Petke/A&R
e: christian@copint.com
Email for submission policy. No calls.

Cordova Bay Records
2750 Quadra St., Ste. 209
Victoria, BC V8T 4E8 Canada
p: 250-361-1444
f: 250-361-1570
e: info@cordovabay.com
www.cordovabay.com
genres: Rock, Pop, Blues, Jazz, Country, Folk
artists: State of Shock, David Gogo, Bill Bourne, Wyckham Porteous
contact: Jocelyn Greenwood/ A&R
e: jocelyn@cordovabay.com
contact2: Alfie Williams/A&R
ext: 604-320-0044
e: alfie@cordovabay.com
Runs Fierce Panda Canada. See site for submission policy. No Sonicbids EPKs.

Core-Upt Records
3837 Park Hill St.
Calgary, AB T2S 2Z5 Canada
p: 403-803-7899
e: coreuptrec@hotmail.com
www.core-uptrecords.com
genres: Punk, Ska, Emo, Pop, Metal, Hardcore, Screamo
artists: Joule, Angry Agency
contact: Mike Condic/A&R

Courthouse Records
PO Box 8462
Richmond, VA 23226
p: 804-320-7067
f: 804-320-7067
www.courthousecds.com
genres: Acoustic, Bluegrass, Jazz, Newgrass, R&B, S/S
artists: Jackie Frost Trio, Daniel Clarke, Among Friends, Modern Groove Syndicate, Old School Freight Train
contact: W.B. 'Wally' Thulin/ A&R
e: fcrestmus@aol.com
Run by Fieldcrest Music. Email before sending material.

CrackNation
306 W St. Charles
Lombard, IL 60148
p: 773-793-0119
e: info@cracknation.com
www.cracknation.com
genres: Drum n Bass, Metal, Industrial, Shoegazer
artists: DJ? Acucrack, Acumen Nation, Fawn, Headcase, Iron Lung Corp
contact: Jason Novak/Pres.
No unsolicited material.

Crossroads Entertainment
PO Box 829
Arden, NC 28704
p: 828-684-3066
f: 828-684-4495
e: info@crossroadsmusic.com
www.crossroadsmusic.com
genres: Southern Gospel, Bluegrass, Gospel
artists: Talley Trio, McKamey's, Kingsmen, Kingdom Heirs, Doyle Lawson & Quicksilver
contact: Chris White/A&R
e: chris.white@crossroadsmusic.com
contact2: Mickey Gamble/A&R
e: mickey.gamble@crossroadsmusic.com
Runs Horizon Records, Sonlite Records, Mountain Home Music, Organic Records, Preferred Records, Crossroads Records & Pinnacle Records. No unsolicited material.

CTA Records
609 Kappock St., Ste. 8A
Bronx, NY 10463
p: 646-207-7743
e: info@ctarecords.com
www.ctarecords.com
genres: Jazz, World, Gospel
artists: Alma Micic, Rale Micic, Riley Bandy, Uros Markovic Gospel Jazz Trio
contact: John Summers
Send Sonicbids EPKs.

CTI Records
10 Waterside Plaza
New York, NY 10010
p: 212-645-9302
f: 212-727-0415
e: ctirecords@aol.com
www.ctijazz.com
genres: Jazz, R&B, Crossover, Blues, Pop
artists: Chet Baker, Chris Botti, George Benson, Michael Buble, Wynton Marsalis
contact: Creed Taylor/A&R

Curb Records
48 Music Sq. E
Nashville, TN 37203
p: 615-321-5080
f: 615-321-9511
www.curb.com
genres: Country, Pop, Christian, Gospel
artists: Tim McGraw, Hank III, LeAnn Rimes, Kimberley Locke, Natalie Grant
contact: Doug Johnson/A&R
e: djohnson@curb.com
contact2: John Ozier/A&R
e: jozier@curb.com
No unsolicited material.

Cutting Records
190 Main St., Ste. 403
Hackensack, NJ 07601
p: 212-868-3154; 201-488-8444
f: 201-488-8444
e: info@cuttingnyc.com
www.cuttingnyc.com
genres: Latin House, Industrial, Dance, Reggaeton, Alt., Urban
artists: Fulanito, Alexa, Las Guanabanas, Ereal, KHZ
contact: Aldo Marin/ A&R - Latin
e: aldo@cuttingnyc.com

Cyclone Records
PO Box 71550
Aurora, ON L4G 6S9 Canada
p: 416-738-5022
f: 905-841-7463
e: info@cyclonerecords.ca
www.cyclonerecords.ca
artists: Allen Christie, BlackSky, Caveat, Eternal Infidels, Holly Woods
contact: Brad Trew/Pres.
e: btrew@cyclonerecords.ca

Dancing Ferret Discs
732 S 4th St.
Philadelphia, PA 19147
p: 215-477-6631
f: 215-477-7408
e: contact@dancing-ferret.com
www.dancing-ferret.com
genres: Goth, Industrial, Electronic, Synth-Pop
artists: Absurd Minds, Behind The Scenes, DJ Ferret, Qntal, Subway to Sally
contact: Carsten Tripscha/A&R
e: office@dancing-ferret.com
Owns Philadelphia record store Dancing Ferret, runs Noir Records & books area gigs. No unsolicited material.

Dare to Care Records
PO Box 463, Stn. C
Montreal, QC H2L 4K4 Canada
p: 514-271-2273
f: 514-844-8211
e: info@daretocarerecords.com
www.daretocarerecords.com
genres: Punk, Rock, Folk, Ska, Indie Pop, Country, Hardcore
artists: Malajube, Ann Beretta, Avec Pas D'Casque, Pawa Up First, We Are Wolves,

Les Georges Leningrad
contact: Demos
e: eli@daretocarerecords.com
Affiliate w/ Grosse Boite.

Dead Truth Recordings
9238 NW 13th Pl.
Coral Springs, FL 33071
p: 954-608-4584
e: deadtruthrecordings@gmail.com
www.deadtruthrecordings.com
genres: Hardcore
artists: Remembering Never, XbishopX, Jump the Shark, Alarmed, Hours
contact: Derek Zipp
e: derek@deadtruthrecordings.com
contact2: Peter Kowalsky
e: peter@deadtruthrecordings.com
Snail mail submissions.

Decon
84 Wooster St., #503
New York, NY 10012
p: 212-343-8486 x16
f: 212-343-3934
e: info@deconmedia.com
www.deconrecords.com
genres: Hip-Hop
artists: Aceyalone, Evidence, 88-Keys, Izza Kizza, Jurrasic 5
contact: Laurent Masset
e: laurent@deconmedia.com
Snail mail CDs.

Deep Elm Records
210 N Church St., #2502
Charlotte, NC 28202
p: 704-322-3042
e: info@deepelm.com
www.deepelm.com
genres: Indie Rock, Punk, Hardcore, Emo
artists: Moving Mountains, Desoto Jones, Track A Tiger, Ride Your Bike, Dartz!
contact: John Szuch/A&R
Send completed full-length album (un-shrink-wrapped) w/ band name, phone & email written on CD via First Class US Post only. No FedX, UPS or DHL. No calls or emails.

Definitive Jux
147 W 24th St., #5
New York, NY 10011
e: info@definitivejux.net
www.definitivejux.net
genres: Hip-Hop
artists: Aesop Rock, C Rayz, Cage, Calm Pete, Camutao
No unsolicited material.

Dekkor Records
5 Denmark St.
London, WC2H 8LP UK
p: 44-207-836-1717
f: 44-207-836-1715
www.dekkorrecords.com
genres: Pop, Rock, Jazz, Indie
artists: James Harries, Terri Walker, Eva Walker, Eva Katzler, David Migden
contact: Corina Casu
e: corina@dekkorrecords.com

Delicious Vinyl Records
6607 Sunset Blvd.
Los Angeles, CA 90028
p: 323-465-2700
f: 323-465-8926
e: contact@deliciousvinyl.com
www.deliciousvinyl.com
genres: Funk, R&B, Hip-Hop, Rock, Alt.
artists: Fatlip, Chop Black, Bucwheed, Brand New Heavies, Mr. Vegas
contact: Michael Ross/A&R
ext: 323-465-2700 x200
contact2: Rick Ross/A&R
ext: 323-465-2700 x112
e: rickross18@mac.com
No unsolicited material.

Delirium Records
PMB 330,
1042 N Mountain, #B
Upland, CA 91786
www.deliriumrecords.com
genres: Power Pop, Punk, Rockabilly
artists: Danny Dean & the Homewreckers, The Relatives, Lift Off, Statica, Youth Authority
contact: Curt Sautter/A&R
e: curt@deliriumrecords.com
Email before sending material.

Delmark Records
4121 N Rockwell
Chicago, IL 60618
p: 773-539-5001
f: 773-539-5004
e: delmark@delmark.com
www.delmark.com
genres: Jazz, Blues
artists: Junior Wells, Sun Ra, Otis Rush, Fred Anderson, Lurri Bell
contact: Steve Wagner/A&R
e: wagadelic@delmark.com
Mail CDs ATTN: Robert Koester.

Detach Records
PO Box 4058
Albuquerque, NM 87196
p: 505-265-0949
e: incoming@detachrecords.com
www.detachrecords.com
genres: Rock, Pop, Alt.
artists: Of God & Science, The Onlys, The Mindyset, Weapons of Mass Destruction
contact: Jeremy Fine
e: jerfine@detachrecords.com
contact2: Jason Chenoweth
e: jason@detachrecords.com
No unsolicited material.

DFA Records
43 Brook Green
London, W6 7EF UK
p: 44-207-605-5000
f: 44-207-605-5182
e: webmail@dfarecords.com; dfaweb@dfarecords.com
www.dfarecords.com
genres: Funk, Punk, Rock, Groove
artists: LCD Soundsystem, Black Dice, The Juan McLean, The Rapture, Delia Gonzalez & Gavin Russom
contact: Matthew Rumbold/A&R
e: matthew.rumbold@emimusic.com
Part of EMI.
No unsolicited material.

Digitone Records
9507 Hull Street Rd., Ste. A
Richmond, VA 23236
p: 800-595-4937
f: 804-745-7772
e: info@digitonerecords.com
www.digitonerecords.com
genres: All Styles
artists: Cinema Cinema, Cy Taggart, Alizon Device, Diafanes, Guilty Method, Red Metric
contact: Gary Gaskin/A&R
e: g@digitonerecords.com
Submit w/ band & gig history, contact info, photos & distribution info to: PO Box 3834, Chester, VA 23831.

Dischord Records
3819 Beecher St. NW
Washington, DC 20007
p: 703-351-7506
f: 703-351-7582
e: dischord@dischord.com
www.dischord.com
genres: DC Punk Rock
artists: Antelope, Beauty Pill, The Evens, French Toast, Fugazi
Runs Peterbilt Records. Only underground DC Punk acts.

Distinctive Records
229 Shoreditch High St.
London, E1 6PJ UK
p: 44-207-650-7964
e: info@distinctiverecords.com
www.distinctiverecords.com
genres: House, Breakbeat
artists: Hybrid, ils, General Midi, Way Out West, Dub Pistols, Chris Coco
contact: Richard Ford/A&R
ext: 44-207-240-1399
e: richard@distinctiverecords.com
Also runs Ink Records.

Doghouse Records
520 8th Ave., Ste. 2001
New York, NY 10018
p: 212-594-2411
f: 212-594-4206
e: info@doghouserecords.com
www.doghouserecords.com
genres: Punk, Emo, Indie
artists: Weatherbox, Paulson, Army of Me, Jet Lag Gemini
contact: Dirk Hemsath/A&R
ext: 212-594-2411 x123
e: dirk@doghouserecords.com
contact2: Dave Conway/A&R
ext: 212-594-2411 x125
e: conway@doghouserecords.com
Send 7', 10' or 12' vinyl only.
No calls.

Downtown Sound
830 Broadway, 3rd Fl.
New York, NY 10003
p: 212-473-0479
f: 212-475-1567
e: info@downtown-sound.com
www.downtown-sound.com
genres: Modern Jazz, Avant Garde, Fusion, World Beat
artists: Abdullah Ibrahim, Tarika Blue, Antonio Hart, James Mason
contact: Dina Sereyka
ext: 845-279-4828
e: chiaro@epix.net
contact2: Hank O'Neal/Pres.
e: hank@chiaroscurojazz.com
Also runs Chiaroscuro Records.

Drive-Thru Records
PO Box 55234
Sherman Oaks, CA 91413
p: 310-473-4889
f: 310-473-4889
e: info@drivethrurecords.com
www.drivethrurecords.com
genres: Rock, Punk, Indie
artists: Hellogoodbye, Halifax, Steel Train, House of Fools, I Am The Avalanche
contact: Richard Reines/A&R
e: richard@drivethrurecords.com
contact2: Stephanie Reines/A&R
e: stephanie@drivethrurecords.com

DSBP
237 Cagua NE
Albuquerque, NM 87108
p: 505-266-8274
f: 505-277-8919
e: dsbp@dsbp.cx
www.dsbp.cx
genres: Electro-Industrial, EBM, Cyber
artists: Aghast View, Diverje, Electro Synthetic Rebellion, Penal Colony, Type001
contact: Tommy T. Rapisardi/A&R
e: tommyt@dsbp.cx
Accepts CDs or CD-Rs only.

DTR/ DeepThinka Records
604 Hertel Ave.
Buffalo, NY 14207
p: 716-873-2151
f: 716-873-2151
e: information@deepthinka.com
www.deepthinka.com
genres: Hip-Hop, Prog
artists: Edreys, Constant Climax, [ONE] Nation
contact: Andy Duwe
ext: 716-536-5110
e: gduwe@deepthinka.com
contact2: Chris Rodgers/Demo Review
e: demos@deepthinka.com
Mail material or drop-off.
No MP3s.

Earache Records
43 W 38th St., 2nd Fl.
New York, NY 10018
p: 212-840-9090
f: 212-840-4033
e: usamail@earache.com
www.earache.com
genres: Rock, Metal, Death Metal, Grind Metal
artists: Akercocke, Evile, At the Gates, Gama Bomb, The Berzerker
contact: Al Dawson/A&R
Also runs Wicked World Records.

EarthBeat Records/ Music for Little People
PO Box 1429
Redway, CA 95560
p: 707-923-3991
f: 707-923-3241
www.mflp.com; www.earthbeatrecords.com
genres: Children's, World, Folk, Blues, Vocal, Native American, Instrumental, Jazz
artists: Catfish Hodge, Donovan, Eric Bibb, Taj Mahal, Maria Muldaur
contact: Leib Ostrow/A&R
ext: 707-923-3991 x112
e: leib@mflp.com
No unsolicited material.

Earwig Music Co.
2054 W Farwell Ave.
Chicago, IL 60645
p: 773-262-0278
f: 773-262-0285
e: info@earwigmusic.com
www.earwigmusic.com
genres: Blues
artists: Liz Mandeville, David 'Honeyboy' Edwards, Johnny Drummer, Sunnyland

Slim, Big Jack Johnson
contact: Michael Frank/ President, CEO
e: mfrank@earwigmusic.com
Also runs Bea & Baby Records. Estab touring artists only email material.

East Coast Records
PO Box 40031
Studio City, CA 91614
p: 310-702-1600
e: eastcoastrec@yahoo.com
www.eastcoastrecords.com
genres: Rock, Pop, Alt., Punk, Metal
artists: Simon Stinger, Suffocate, Tre Props, Logan's Heroes, Alestar Digby
Snail mail submissions only.

East Side Digital
PO Box 7367
Minneapolis, MN 55407
p: 612-375-0233
f: 612-359-9580
e: chill@noside.com
www.e-s-d.com
genres: Prog., Spoken Word
artists: Wendy Carlos, Kevin Kling, Bottle Rockets, Halloween Alaska
contact: Rob Simonds/A&R
Also runs North Side & Omnium.
No unsolicited material.

Elevator Music
PO Box 143
Hibbs, PA 15443
p: 914-509-5870
f: 914-779-2389
www.elevatormusic.com
genres: Indie, Punk, Garage, Prog, Soul, Avant-Garde
artists: 77, Tedio Boys, Les Baton Rouge, The Parkinsons, Showcase Showdown
contact: Fernando Pinto/A&R
e: fernando@elevatormusic.com
No unsolicited material.

Eleven Seven Music
700 San Vicente Blvd. #G410
Hollywood, CA 90069
p: 310-385-4700
f: 310-385-4742
e: sama@10thst.com
www.elevenseven.net
genres: Rock, Glam Metal, Alt.
contact: Allen Kovac/CEO
artists: Nikki Sixx
Artist friendly label part of 10th St. Ent. & associated w/ ADA/Warner Music Group.
***NYC office:** 212-334-3160.*

EMI Music Group
150 5th Ave. 8th Fl.
New York, NY 10011
p: 212-786-8000
f: 212-245-4115
e: info@emimusicgroup.com
www.emigroup.com
genres: All Styles
artists: Chemical Brothers, Coldplay, 30 Seconds to Mars, Jamie Cullum, KT Tunstall
contact: Eric Nicolai/CEO
e: eric.nicolai@virgin-records.com
contact2: David Wolter
ext: 212-786-8900
e: david.wolter@virgin-records.com
Also runs Blue Note, Astralwerks, Heavenly Records, Additive Records, Mute Records, DFA Records, Capitol Records, Narada Jazz & Metro Blue.
Canadian office:
Fraser Hill, 905-364-3149, fraser.hill@emimusic.ca.
***TN:** Brad O'Donnell, 615-371-6800, bodonnell@emicmg.com*
No unsolicited material.

Endearing Records
PO Box 95075, RPO Kingsgate
Vancouver, BC V5T 4T8
Canada
e: info@endearing.com
www.endearing.com
genres: Indie Pop, Indie Rock, Power Pop, Space Rock, S/S, Alt. Country
artists: Radiogram, Julie Doiron, The Heavy Blinkers, Paper Moon
contact: Blair Purda/Pres.
e: blair@endearing.com
No unsolicited material.

EO Music
7762 Beechmont, Ste. B
Cincinnati, OH 45255
p: 513-474-4904
f: 513-474-4905
e: eomusic@yahoo.com
genres: Pop, Hot AC, Alt., Rhythm, Indie, Rock, Hip-Hop
artists: Lorenzo, Kasper, 500 Miles
contact: Mike Landis/A&R
contact2: Bill Scull/President
e: wscull@tspromo.com

Epic Records
550 Madison Ave.
New York, NY 10022
p: 212-833-8000
www.epicrecords.com
genres: Rock, Pop, Urban, Latin, Gospel
artists: Tori Amos, Fiona Apple, Modest Mouse, Franz Ferdinand, Good Charlotte
contact: Farra Matthews/A&R
ext: 212-833-4188
e: farra.matthews@sonybmg.com
contact2: Scott Graves/Sr. Director of A&R
e: scott.graves@sonybmg.com
Part of Sony/BMG. CA office: Mike Flynn, 310-449-2100.
No unsolicited material.

Epitaph Records
2798 Sunset Blvd.
Los Angeles, CA 90026
p: 213-413-7353
f: 213-413-9678
e: faq@epitaph.com
www.epitaph.com
genres: Punk, Rock, Emo, Post Hardcore
artists: Bouncing Souls, Death By Stereo, The Matches, Rancid, The Weakerthans
contact: Brett Gurewitz/CEO
e: brett@epitaph.com
contact2: Andy Kaulkin/Pres.
e: andy@epitaph.com
Also runs Hellcat & Anti Records.

Equal Vision Records
PO Box 38202
Albany, NY 12203
p: 518-458-8250
f: 518-458-1312
e: info@equalvision.com
www.equalvision.com
genres: Indie Rock, Hardcore, Punk, Rock, Alt.
artists: ActionReaction, Fear Before, Pierce The Veil, Olympia, Modern Life Is War
Email links to: music@equalvision.com. No CDs.

Everfine Records
44 Wall St., 22nd Fl.
New York, NY 10005
p: 212-213-6101
www.everfinerecords.com
genres: Rock
artists: O.A.R., Stephen Kellogg & The Sixers
contact: Dave Roberge/Pres.
ext: 212-213-6101 x12
e: dave@everfinerecords.com
Snail mail submissions.

Eyeball Records
PO Box 400
Ridgewood, NJ 07451
p: 201-997-7664
e: info@eyeballrecords.com
www.eyeballrecords.com
artists: The #12 Looks Like You, Kiss Kiss, New Atlantic, Baumer, Pompeii
contact: Alex Saavedra
e: alex@eyeballrecords.com
contact2: Marc Debiak
e: marc@eyeballrecords.com
Also runs AstroMagnetics.

Fake Chapter Records
115 Romaine Ave.
Maywood, NJ 07607
p: 201-745-2145
e: info@fakechapter.com
www.fakechapter.com
genres: Rock, Pop, Punk, Emo, Acoustic
artists: Green To Think, The House Lights, CJ Grogan, The Trauma Queens, The Sixfifteens
contact: Michael Gilligan/A&R
Email before sending material.

Family Records
242 E 3rd St., Ste. 11
New York, NY 10009
www.thefamilyrecords.com
artists: The Undisputed Heavyweights, Jeff Jacobson, Pearl & the Beard, Wakey!Wakey!, Casey Shea
contact: Wesley Verhoeve/ Label Manager
e: wes@liberatedmatter.com
contact2: Lisa Box/A&R
e: lisa@thefamilyrecords.com

Fat Possum Records
PO Box 1923
Oxford, MS 38655
p: 662-473-9994
f: 662-473-9090
e: justin@fatpossum.com
www.fatpossum.com
genres: Rock, Blues, Alt.
artists: Heartless Bastards, Deadboy & The Elephantmen, We Are Wolves, The Black Keys, The Fiery Furnaces
contact: Matthew Johnson
e: matthew@fatpossum.com
Snail mail submissions.

Fat Wreck Chords
PO Box 193690
San Francisco, CA 94119
e: mailbag@fatwreck.com
www.fatwreck.com
genres: Punk, Hardcore
artists: NoFX, Lagwagon, Me First & The Gimmie Gimmies, No Use For A Name, Strike Anywhere
No unsolicited material.

Favored Nations
17328 Ventura Blvd., #165
Encino, CA 91316
p: 818-385-1989
f: 818-385-1070
e: fn@favorednations.com
www.favorednations.com
genres: Instrumental, Rock, Jazz
artists: Tommy Emmanuel, Eric Johnson, Andy Timmons, Eric Sardinas, Steve Vai
contact: Jason Scherr/A&R
e: jasonscherr@favorednations.com
Also runs Favored Nations Acoustic & Favored Nations Cool.
No unsolicited material.

Fearless Records
13772 Goldenwest St., #545
Westminster, CA 92683
p: 562-592-3438
e: info@fearlessrecords.com
www.fearlessrecords.com
genres: Punk, Rock, Indie, Hardcore, Emo, Alt.
artists: Plain White T's, At The Drive-In, Sugarcult, A Static Lullaby, Alesana
contact: Bob Becker/A&R
e: bob@fearlessrecords.com
No emails.

Fenway Recordings
PO Box 15709
Kenmore Station
Boston, MA 02115
p: 617-497-2012
f: 617-497-9988
e: info@fenwayrecordings.com
www.fenwayrecordings.com
genres: Alt., Rock
artists: Consonant, Read Yellow, The Love Scene, The Kickovers, Gerling
contact: Mark Kates/A&R
e: mark@fenwayrecordings.com
contact2: Nick Palmacci/A&R
e: nick@fenwayrecordings.com
No calls.

Fonovisa
8200 NW 52nd Terr., 2nd Fl.
Miami, FL 33166
p: 305-487-5500
f: 305-487-5501
www.fonovisa.com
genres: Latin
artists: Conjunto Primavera, Los Tigres Del Norte, Marco Antonio Solis, Los Temperarios, Banda El Recodo
contact: Carlos Maharbiz/A&R
e: cmaharbiz@univision.net
Affiliated w/ Univision Music Group.

Foodchain Records
6464 Sunset Blvd., Ste. 920
Hollywood, CA 90028
p: 323-957-7900
f: 323-957-7911
e: info@foodchainrecords.com
www.foodchainrecords.com
genres: Rock, Alt.
artists: Supagroup, Betty Blowtorch, Minibar, Coyote Shivers, Garageland
contact: Kelly Spencer/A&R
ext: 323-957-7900 x14
contact2: Scott Milano
ext: 323-957-7900 x12
No unsolicited material.

Fore Reel Entertainment
201 E 87th St., #21C
New York, NY 10128
p: 212-410-9055
f: 212-831-0823
e: forereelent@aol.com
www.forereelent.com
genres: Indie female artists/female-fronted groups
artists: NooVooDoo, Hanna, Deena Miller, Its About Eve
contact: Hernando Courtright/President
Only female artists/groups.

Frenchkiss Records
111 E 14 St., Ste. 229
New York, NY 10003
p: 212-414-4533
f: 212-719-9396
e: info@frenchkissrecords.com
www.frenchkissrecords.com
genres: Rock, Indie Rock
artists: Les Savy Fav, Rahim, Ex-Models, The Hold Steady, Thunderbirds Are Now!
contact: Syd Butler/A&R
ext: 212-414-4533 x1
contact2: Paul Hanly
ext: 212-414-4533 x2
e: paul@frenchkissrecords.com
Also runs Fifty Fifty Music. Send 4 best songs on CD w/ contact info & pics.

Frontier Records
PO Box 22
Sun Valley, CA 91353
p: 818-759-8279
e: info@frontierrecords.com
www.frontierrecords.com
genres: Punk, Alt.
artists: The Adolescents, Middle Class
contact: Lisa Fancher/Pres.
No unsolicited material.

Frontline Records of Canada
2-431 Barton St., East Unit 2
Hamilton, ON L8L 2Y5
Canada
p: 905-523-5999
artists: Dave Rave, The First Time, Geoff Gibbons, Jamie Dart, Melanie Joy
contact: Lisa Millar/President
e: lmillar@bullseyecanada.com
Run by Bullseye Records.

Fueled By Ramen
PO Box 1803
Tampa, FL 33601
p: 813-887-4240
f: 813-887-4290
e: info@fueledbyramen.net
www.fueledbyramen.com
genres: Rock
artists: Paramore, The Cab, Gym Class Heroes, The Academy Is..., Panic at the Disco
contact: John Janick/Pres.
contact2: Johnny Minardi/A&R
Also runs Decaydance Records.

Gearhead Records
PO Box 1386
Woodland, CA 95776
p: 530-662-7877
f: 530-662-7977
e: info@gearheadrecords.com
www.gearheadrecords.com
genres: Garage Rock, Punk, Alt. Country
artists: Black Furies, The Spunks, The Hellacopters, Hellbound Glory, Million Dollar Marxists,
No unsolicited material.

Get Hip Records
1800 Columbus & Preble Ave.
Pittsburgh, PA 15233
p: 412-231-4766
www.gethip.com
genres: Garage, Punk, Pop
artists: Breakup Society, Candy Snatchers, Jet Lag, Ugly Beats, The Chains
contact: Gregg Kostelich/Pres.
Vinyl & CD label for above genres only. No Hip-Hop & No unsolicited material.

Gig Records
520 Butler Ave.
Pt. Pleasant, NJ 08742
p: 732-701-9044
f: 732-701-9777
e: info@gigrecords.com
www.gigrecords.com
genres: Rock, Pop, Punk, Alt., S/S, Acoustic
artists: Dead 50s, Miles Hunt, Ned's Atomic Dustbin, The Vibrators, The Youth Ahead
contact: Lenny Hipp/A&R
e: lenny@gigrecords.com
contact2: Indian/President
e: indian@gigrecords.com
Also runs Ear Raid, Mothership, DRP & Motor Marketing. Snail mail submissions - No EPKs.

Go-Kart Records
PO Box 20, Prince St. Station
New York, NY 10012
e: info@gokartrecords.com
www.gokartrecords.com
genres: Punk, Rock, Hardcore, Pop
artists: Bambix, Cougars, Guff, I Farm, Ira
contact: Greg Ross/CEO
e: greg@gokartrecords.com
Supports music, not trends. No calls.

Gossip Records
1 Harding Rd., Ste. 103B
Red Bank, NJ 07701
p: 732-933-9229
f: 732-933-9622
e: info@gossiprecords.com
www.gossiprecords.com
genres: Dance, Electronic, Rap, R&B, World
artists: Live Element, Hott 22, Pure Dynamite, Richard Grey, Christian Alvarez
contact: Greg Bahary/A&R
ext: 732-933-9229 x3
e: greg@gossiprecords.com
Also runs Blazin & Undo Records.

Gotee Records
401 Church St.
Franklin, TN 37067
p: 615-370-2980
f: 615-370-2990
www.gotee.com
genres: Pop, Rock, Hip-Hop
artists: Ayiesha Woods, Family Force 5, John Reuben, Relient K, Sarah Kelly
contact: Tobin Hyman/A&R
e: tobin@gotee.com
Also runs Mono vs. Stereo Records. No unsolicited material.

Gotham Records
PO Box 7185
Santa Monica, CA 90406
p: 310-393-0828
f: 310-393-0829
e: info@gothamrecords.com
www.gothamrecords.com
genres: Rock, Metal, Alt.
artists: The Day After, Chiba-Ken, Red Horizon, Mike Rocket, The Vicious Martinis
contact: Patrick Arn/Pres.
e: patrick@gothamrecords.com
contact2: Cory Dunbar/A&R
Prefers finished albums. No calls or MP3s.

GrayRose Records
717 El Medio Ave.
Pacific Palisades, CA 90272
p: 310-230-6040
f: 310-230-6038
e: assistant@rosenmusiccorp.com
www.rosenmusiccorp.com
genres: All Styles
artists: Bret Ryan, The KillerHeels, Alex Cartana
No unsolicited material.

Hacienda Records & Recording Studios
1236 S Staples St.
Corpus Christi, TX 78404
p: 361-882-7066
f: 361-882-3943
e: info@haciendarecords.com
www.haciendarecords.com; www.haciendaradio.com
genres: Tex Mex, Tejano, Latin Rap, Spanish, Country, Rock en Espanol
artists: The Hometown Boys, Michelle, Gary Hobbs, Ruben Vela, Steve Jordan
contact: Rick Garcia
e: rick.garcia@haciendarecords.com
contact2: Roland Garcia
e: roland.garcia@haciendarecords.com
Also runs Las Brisas Records. Send CD & SASE.

Harmonized Records
6520 Oak Grove Church Rd.
Mebane, NC 27302
p: 828-252-3678
f: 828-252-3614
www.harmonizedrecords.com
genres: Jam, Rock, Jazz, World
artists: Garaj Mahal, Perpetual Groove, Lotus, Modereko, Raq
contact: Brian Asplin/A&R
e: brian@harmonizedrecords.com; asplin@homegrownmusic.net
contact2: Lee Crumpton/A&R
e: lee@homegrownmusic.net
No unsolicited material.

Heads Up/Telarc
23309 Commerce Park Rd.
Cleveland, OH 44122
p: 216-765-7381
f: 216-464-6037
e: headsup@headsup.com
www.headsup.com
genres: Jazz, World, Latin, Blues, Crossover, Smooth Jazz
artists: Yellowjackets, Michael Brecker, Spyro Gyra, Ladysmith Black Mambazo, Pieces of a Dream
contact: Dave Love/Pres.
ext: 216-765-7381 x262
e: dave@headsup.com
contact2: Robert Woods
ext: 216-464-2313
Part of Concord Music Group. No unsolicited material.

Heart Music
PO Box 160326
Austin, TX 78716
p: 512-795-2375
f: 512-795-9573
e: info@heartmusic.com
www.heartmusic.com
genres: Jazz, Folk, Pop, Rock
artists: Monte Montgomery, Will Taylor, Libby Kirkpatrick, Tony Campise, Doug Hall Quartet
contact: Tab Bartling/A&R
e: tab@heartmusic.com
contact2: Mimi
e: mimi@heartmusic.com
No unsolicited material.

Heavenly Records
47 Frith St.
London, W1K 4SE UK
p: 44-207-605-5000
f: 44-207-605-5182
e: info@heavenlyrecordings.com
www.heavenly100.com
genres: Rock, Pop, S/S
artists: The Magic Numbers, The Vines, Beggars, Cherry Ghost, Clarky Cat
contact: Matthew Rumbold/A&R
e: matthew.rumbold@emimusic.com
Part of EMI. No unsolicited material.

Heyday Records
PO Box 757
Temecula, CA 92593
p: 877-323-7639
e: heyday@heyday.com
www.heyday.com
genres: Pop, Surf, Rockabilly, Punk, Acoustic
artists: David J, Marty Willson-Piper, Noctorum, The Duo-Tones, The Nerve!
contact: Robert Rankin Walker/A&R
Send Sonicbids EPKs.

Hi-Bias Records
20 Hudson Dr.
Maple, ON L6A 1X3 Canada
p: 905-303-9611
f: 905-303-6611
e: support@hibias.ca
www.hibias.com
genres: House, Trance, Retro, New Wave, Old School, Chill, Lounge, Dance, Electronica
contact: Nick Fiorucci/A&R
e: nick@hibias.ca
No calls.

Hidden Beach Recordings
3030 Nebraska Ave.
Santa Monica, CA 90404
p: 310-453-1400
f: 310-453-6760
e: steve@hiddenbeach.com
www.hiddenbeach.com
genres: Jazz, R&B, Gospel
artists: Jill Scott, Mike Phillips, Keite Young, Onitsha, Sunny Hawkins
contact: Jerrold Thompson
e: jerrold@hiddenbeach.com

Higher Realm Entertainment
501 MaClay St., Ste. 43
Harrisburg, PA 17110
p: 717-213-4282
f: 717-213-4181
e: higherrealmentertainment@yahoo.com

genres: R&B, Hip-Hop
artists: Penhead, Grip, Jay Allen, Phene, Weezy Pipes
contact: Tyrone J. Allen/A&R
e: heistpro@yahoo.com
contact2: Tyson Singletary
e: tysonsingletary@hotmail.com
Snail mail submissions.

HIGHnote Records
106 W 71st St.
New York, NY 10023
p: 212-873-2020
f: 212-877-0407
e: jazzdepo@ix.netcom.com
www.jazzdepot.com
genres: Blues
artists: Homesick James, Arthur Williams, Jimmy Dawkins, Fillmore Slim, Dave Riley
contact: Barney Fields/A&R
Also runs Savant Records.

Hi-Octane Records
2808 Azalea Pl.
Nashville, TN 37204
p: 615-297-0700
f: 615-297-6959
www.treasureislenashville.com
genres: Americana, Mainstream Country, AC, Rock, Folk, CCM, S/S
artists: Jason Eastman, Jaymi Galpin, Amanda Corriher, Todd Rash, Jody Lineberry
contact: Fred Vail/A&R
e: fredvail@treasureislenashville.com
contact2: Sam Martin/A&R - Acoustic, Folk, Rock
Affilliated w/ Treasure Isle Recorders. Contact first.

Hit Track Records
1655 S Mojave Rd.
Las Vegas, NV 89104
p: 702-735-4283
f: 702-207-4965
www.hittrackrecords.com
genres: Rock, Metal, Alt.
artists: 187, Cheva, ByDeathsDesign, Epicedium, Drainage X
contact: Tom Parham/A&R
ext: 702-481-1663
e: tom@hittrackrecords.com
contact2: Sheila Zinn Parham/A&R
e: sheila@hittrackrecords.com

Hollywood Records
500 S Buena Vista St.
Burbank, CA 91521
p: 818-560-7084
f: 818-841-5140
www.hollywoodrecords.com
genres: Rock, Pop
artists: Hillary Duff, Jesse McCartney, Josh Kelley, Breaking Benjamin, Ingram Hill
contact: Geoffrey Weiss
ext: 818-560-2017
e: geoffrey.weiss@disney.com
contact2: Jon Lind/A&R
ext: 818-560-5670
e: jon.lind@disney.com
Part of Walt Disney. No unsolicited material.

Holographic Records
700 W Pete Rose Way
Lobby B, 3rd Fl.
Cincinnati, OH 45203
p: 513-542-9525
f: 513-542-9545
e: info@holographicrecords.com
www.holographicrecords.com
genres: Prog, Rock, Jazz, Fusion
artists: Acumen, Mads Eriksen, John Novello, Alex Skolnick Trio, Jeff Berlin
contact: Richard Waring/A&R - Jazz, Fusion
ext: 513-542-9525 x3
e: rickw@holographicrecords.com
contact2: Brooks Jordan/A&R - Rock
e: bwj@holographicrecords.com
Call before sending material.

Honest Jons
278 Portobello Rd.
London, W10 5TE UK
p: 44-208-969-9822
f: 44-208-969-5395
e: mail@honestjons.com
www.honestjons.com
genres: Rock, Alt., Electronic, Punk, World, Dance
artists: Damon Albarn, Cedric Im Brooks, Candi Staton, Terry Hall & Mushtaq, Bettye Swann
contact: Mark Ainley/A&R

Hopeless Records/Sub City
PO Box 7495
Van Nuys, CA 91409
p: 818-997-0444
f: 818-997-6445
e: info@hopelessrecords.com
www.hopelessrecords.com
genres: Punk, Rock, Indie, Emo, Metal, Ska
artists: The Human Abstract, All Time Low, Nural, Kaddisfly, Amber Pacific
contact: Louis Posen/A&R

Hybrid Recordings
100 5th Ave., 11th Fl.
New York, NY 10011
p: 212-277-7171
f: 212-719-9396
e: info@hybridrecordings.com
www.hybridrecordings.com
genres: Rock, Pop, S/S
artists: Johnette Napolitano, Gin Blossoms, Assembly of Dust
contact: Joe Augustine/A&R - Rock
e: joe@metrohybrid.com
Run by Metropolitan Talent. No unsolicited material.

Hyena Records
105 15th St., Ste. 3L
Brooklyn, NY 11215
p: 718-369-6567
www.hyenarecords.com
genres: Jazz, Blues, Rock, Alt. Country
artists: James Blood Ulmer, Skerik's Syncopated Taint Septet, John Ellis, Lafayette Gilchrist, Jacob Fred Jazz Odyssey
contact: Kevin Calabro/A&R
e: hyenarecords@aol.com
No unsolicited material.

Icehouse
1981 Fletcher Creek Dr.
Memphis, TN 38133
p: 901-388-1190
f: 901-382-7556
www.icehouserecords.com
genres: Blues, Roots, Rock, Jazz, Contemporary Classical
artists: Wes Jeans, Mark May, Voodoo Village, Toler Brothers, The Cate Brothers
contact: John Phillips/A&R
e: jp@selectohits.com
Runs 40 West Records. Email before sending material.

Idol Records
PO Box 720043
Dallas, TX 75372
p: 214-321-8890
f: 214-321-8889
e: info@idolrecords.com
www.idolrecords.com
genres: Rock, Pop, Punk
artists: Black Tie Dynasty, Watershed, PPT, The Crash That Took Me, Mitra
contact: Erv Karwelis/A&R
e: erv@idolrecords.com
Snail mail submissions.

Inpop Records
7106 Crossroads Blvd.
Ste. 215
Brentwood, TN 37027
p: 615-377-7857
f: 615-377-7860
e: info@inpop.com
www.inpop.com
genres: CCM
artists: Newsboys, Superchick, Tree63, Mat Kearney, Shane & Shane
contact: Shara Katerberg/A&R
contact2: Dale Bray/A&R
No unsolicited material.

Integrity Label Group
1000 Cody Rd.
Mobile, AL 36695
p: 251-633-9000
f: 251-776-5014
e: info@integritymusic.com
www.integritymusic.com
genres: Gospel, Praise, Worship
artists: Michael Neale, Jason Morant, Travis Cottrell, Joe Pace, Israel Houghton
Also runs Integrity Gospel & INO Records. No unsolicited material.

Interchill Records
PO Box 239
Salt Spring Island
BC V8K 2V9 Canada
p: 250-537-8948
e: info@interchill.com
www.interchill.com
genres: Electronica, Downtempo, Dub, World Fusion, Chill, Ambient
artists: Eat Static, Pushmipulyu, Mauxuam, Umberloid, Ashtech
contact: Andrew Ross Collins/A&R, President
e: andrew@interchill.com
contact2: Naasko/A&R
ext: 250-505-2433
e: naasko@interchill.com
Also runs Sub Signal Records.

Internet Records
PO Box 92
Oceanside, NY 11572
p: 516-425-1728
e: internetrecords@mac.com
www.internetrecords.tv
genres: Dance, Pop, R&B, Hip-Hop, Rock
artists: Lifeline, Andrejack
contact: Tyrone Williamson
e: twilliamson@internetrecords.biz
contact2: Kenneth Williamson
e: kwilliamson@internetrecords.biz
Email before sending bio, full CD or 4 song demo.

Interscope-Geffen-A&M
1755 Broadway, 8th Fl.
New York, NY 10019
p: 212-333-8000
f: 212-445-3689
www.amrecords.com; www.interscope.com
genres: Rock, Pop, Urban, S/S
artists: 50 Cent, Beck, Black Eyed Peas, AFI, The Yeah Yeah Yeahs
contact: Thom Panuzio
e: thom.panuzio@umusic.com
contact2: Luke Wood
e: luke.wood@umusic.com
Part of Universal Music Group runs G-Unit, Shady, Aftermath, Octone, Mosley Music, Cherry Tree, MySpace Music & VuRecords. CA office: Ben Gordon, 310-865-451; ben.gordon@umusic.com. No unsolicited material & No calls.

Intr_Version Recordings
4704 Rue Parthenais
Montreal, QC H2H 2G7
Canada
p: 514-528-8260
e: info@intr-version.com
www.intr-version.com
genres: Electronic, Post-Rock, Experimental
artists: Ghislain Poirier, Desormais, Vitaminsforyou, Joshua Treble, The Beans
contact: Mitchell Akiyama
Accepts CDs only.

Invisible Records
PO Box 16008
Chicago, IL 60616
p: 773-523-8316
e: info@invisiblerecords.com
www.invisiblerecords.com
genres: Industrial, Rock, Electronic
artists: Pigface, Chris Connelly, My Life With the Thrill Kill Kult, Bile, Hellbent
contact: Mike Johnson/A&R
e: mike@invisiblerecords.com
Affiliated w/ Underground Inc., Deezal, Crack Nation, Tone Zone & Diva Nation. No unsolicited material.

Ipecac Recordings
PO Box 1778
Orinda, CA 94563
e: info@ipecac.com
www.ipecac.com
genres: Heavy Metal, Experimental, Hip-Hop, Jazz, Electronica, Classical, Rock
artists: A Perfect Place, Isis, Imani Coppola, Dub Trio, Venomous Concept
No unsolicited material.

Island Records/Def Jam Music Group
825 8th Ave., 28th Fl.
New York, NY 10019
p: 212-333-8000
f: 212-603-7654
www.islanddefjam.com
genres: Pop, Rock
artists: Lionel Richie, The Roots, Fall Out Boy, Kanye West
contact: Steve Bartels/Pres.
e: steve.bartels@umusic.com
Part of Universal Music Group. CA office: Brian Postelle, 310-865-5371; brian.postelle@umusic.com. No unsolicited material.

It's Alive Records
11411 Hewes St.
Orange, CA 92869
e: info@itsaliverecords.com
www.itsaliverecords.com
genres: Punk, Pop Punk, Rock n Roll
artists: The Copyrights, Teenage Bottlerocket, Prototipes, Kitty & The Manges, The Popsters

J Curve Records
PO Box 43209
Cincinnati, OH 45243
p: 513-272-8004
f: 513-530-0229
e: jcurverecords@hotmail.com
www.jcurverecords.com
genres: Jazz, Roots, R&B, Blues, Latin
artists: Aaron Goldberg, Darren Barrent, Phil DeGreg, Mark Gross, Randy Johnston
contact: Dale Rabiner/A&R
No unsolicited material.

J Records
745 5th Ave., 6th Fl.
New York, NY 10151
p: 646-840-5600
f: 646-840-5791
www.jrecords.com
genres: Hip-Hop, Pop, Rock
artists: Alicia Keys, Babyface, Sarah McLachlan, Dido, Annie Lennox
contact: Peter Edge/Exec. VP of A&R
ext: 646-840-5602
e: peter.edge@sonybmg.com
contact2: Rani Hancock/VP of A&R
ext: 646-840-5740
e: rani.hancock@sonybmg.com
Part of Sony/BMG. No unsolicited material.

JaThom Records
PO Box 1579
New York, NY 10025
p: 212-864-9937
www.jathomfamily.com
genres: Hip-Hop, R&B, Neo-Soul, Alt. Rap, Alt. Rock
artists: Az-One, Candi Girl Steph, Nini, Mr. Glenn, Count Coolout
contact: J. Minor/A&R
e: justthemusic@att.net
contact2: Fred Sutton III/A&R
ext: 215-913-2007
e: fsutt2@aol.com
Send photo, bio & CD.

Jive/ Silvertone Records
550 Madison Ave., 13th Fl.
New York, NY 10022
p: 212-833-5243
www.jiverecords.com
genres: Pop, Rock, R&B, Hip-Hop, Afro-Latin
artists: Justin Timberlake, Mystikal, Charlie Wilson, R.Kelly, Ciara
contact: Peter Thea/Exec. VP of A&R
ext: 212-833-5445
e: peter.thea@sonybmg.com
contact2: Wayne Williams/VP of A&R - Urban
ext: 212-833-5502
e: wayne.williams@jiverecords.com
Part of Sony/BMG & runs Zomba & Battery Records. No unsolicited material.

Justin Time Records
5485 Chemin Cote-de-Liesse
Ville St. Laurent, QC H4P 1A4
Canada
p: 514-738-9533
f: 514-737-9780
e: info@justin-time.com
www.justin-time.com
genres: Jazz, Blues, World, Rock, Gospel
artists: Odd Jazz Group, Carmen Lundy, Thomas Hellman, Frank Marino & Mahogany Rush, Bryan Lee
contact: J.P. Leduc/A&R - Int'l
ext: 514-738-9533 x117
e: jp@justin-time.com
contact2: Laval Cote/A&R - Canada
ext: 514-738-9533 x134
e: laval@fusion3.com
Also runs Secret City Records.

Kemado Records
601 W 26th St., Ste. 1175
New York, NY 10001
p: 212-242-8883
f: 212-242-8257
e: info@kemado.com
www.kemado.com
genres: Rock, Metal, Punk, Indie, Folk, S/S, Psychedelic
artists: The Sword, Cheeseburger, Saviours, Danova, Diamond Nights
contact: Andres Santo Domingo/A&R, President
e: andres@kemado.com
contact2: Keith Abrahamsson/Director of A&R
e: keith@kemado.com
Send CD, will contact if interested.

Kill Rock Stars
120 NE State Ave., PMB 418
Olympia, WA 98501
p: 360-357-9732
f: 360-357-6408
e: demos@killrockstars.com
www.killrockstars.com
genres: Punk, Rock, Folk, Spoken Word, Alt.
artists: Deerhoof, Gossip, Xiu Xiu, Jeff Hanson, Erase Errata
contact: Maggie Vail/VP
ext: 360-357-9732 x11
e: maggie@killrockstars.com
contact2: Portia Sabin
e: portia@killrockstars.com
No unsolicited material.

King Street Sounds/ Nite Grooves
139 Fulton St., Ste. 508
New York, NY 10038
p: 212-594-3737
f: 212-594-3636
e: robw@kingstreetsounds.com
www.kingstreetsounds.com
genres: House, Tribal, Vocal, Deep, Afro, Jazz, Downtempo
artists: Ananda Project, Kerri Chandler, Dennis Ferrer, Louie Vega, David Morales
contact: Roman Shelepanov
e: romans@kingstreetsounds.com
contact2: Joe B./A&R
e: joeb@kingstreetsounds.com

Kinky Star Records
Vlasmarkt 9
Ghent, Oost Vlaanderen
B-9000 Belgium
p: 32-9-223-4845
f: 32-9-223-4845
e: info@kinkystar.com
www.kinkystar.com
genres: Indie Rock
artists: Needle & The Pain Reaction, Dr. Pepper Family, Indigenous, Waldorf
contact: Luc Waegeman

Koch Entertainment
740 Broadway, 7th Fl.
New York, NY 10003
p: 212-353-8800
f: 212-228-0660
www.kochentertainment.com
genres: All Styles
artists: AZ, In Flames, Ray J, Anew Revolution
contact: Cliff Cultreri/Sr. VP
ext: 212-353-8800 x229
e: cliff.cultreri@kochent.com
contact2: Dave Wilkes/VP
ext: 212-353-8800 x222
e: david.wilkes@kochent.com
Also runs Floodgate Records.

Lamon Records/ Nashville
PO Box 1907
Mt. Juliet, TN 37121
p: 615-379-2121
f: 615-379-2122
e: info@lamonrecords.com
www.lamonrecords.com
genres: Country, Acoustic, Bluegrass, Christian
artists: George Hamilton IV, Chris Berardo & the DesBarardos, Jesse McReynolds, Dave Moody, PraiseStreet Worship Band
contact: Dave Moody/Pres.
ext: 615-379-2121 x101
e: dave@lamonrecords.com
contact2: Josh Moody/A&R
ext: 615-379-2121 x102
e: josh@lamonrecords.com
Runs AmericanaStreet, PraiseStreet, Bluegrass Boulevard, Tabernacle Records, Southern Crossroad & Lion & Lamb. CDs only w/ bio, photos & online submission form.

Latin Music Entertainment/ Dimelo Records
10835 Chandler Blvd.
North Hollywood, CA 91601
p: 818-508-0337
f: 818-508-0338
e: webinfo@dimelorecords.com
www.dimelorecords.com
genres: Latin
artists: Chino Espinoza, Orquesta Tabaco Y Ron, Kuero, Lacharanga Cubana
contact: Nissim J. Baly/A&R
e: nissim@dimelorecords.com
contact2: Valerie Guzman/A&R
ext: 818-508-0337 x103
Mail CDs to: PO Box 33251, Granada Hills, CA 91394.

Lazy Bones Recordings
9594 First Ave. NE, #449
Seattle, WA 98115
p: 310-281-6232; 206-447-0712
f: 425-821-5720
e: lbrinc@earthlink.net
www.lazybones.com
genres: All Styles of Indie except Country & R&B
artists: Tony Levin, Living In Question, Mackabella, Headland, I Want My Mommy
contact: Scott Schorr/A&R
No unsolicited material.

Lazy S.O.B. Recordings
PO Box 4084
Austin, TX 78765
p: 512-480-0765
f: 512-499-0207
e: info@lazysob.com
www.lazysob.com
genres: Americana, Honky-Tonk, Country, S/S
artists: Bradley Jaye Williams, Red Dirt Ranger, The Lucky Strikes, The Wandering Eye, Ana Egge
contact: David Sanger/Pres.
e: lazysob1@aol.com
Affiliated Freedom Records & TX Music Round-Up Records. TX musicians only.

Lens Records
2020 N California Ave.
Ste. 7-119
Chicago, IL 60647
p: 773-704-8044
e: info@lensrecords.com
www.lensrecords.com
genres: Ambient, Experimental, Electronic, Rock, Modern Classical
artists: Beehatch, Rapoon, Encomiast, Matt Schultz, Robert Scott Thompson
contact: Robert Hyman
e: rob@lensrecords.com
Prefers CDs or links to MySpace.

Leviathan Records
PO Box 745
Tyrone, GA 30290
p: 770-502-2396
e: general@leviathanrecords.com
www.leviathanrecords.com
genres: Hard Rock, Heavy Metal, Blues Rock
artists: Joe Stump, Chastain, Southern Gentleman, Stephen Frederick, Firewind
contact: David Chastain/A&R
Email before sending material.

Little Dog Records
2219 W Olive Ave., #150
Burbank, CA 91506
p: 818-557-1595
f: 818-557-0524
e: info@littledogrecords.com
www.littledogrecords.com
genres: Blues, Alt., Country, Americana, S/S, Roots
artists: Moot Davis, Curt Kirkwood, The Blazers, Pete Anderson, Chris Jones
Touring acts only. No calls, will contact if interested.

Little Fish Records
PO Box 19164
Cleveland, OH 44119
p: 216-481-1634
f: 216-481-5667
e: lkoval@littlefishrecords.com
www.littlefishrecords.com
genres: Reggae, World, Roots, Blues, Americana, Rock, Folk, Jazz, Latin, S/S
artists: Cletus Black, Robin Stone, Mike Calzone, Alexus Antes, Public Property
contact: Stephen McCullagh/A&R
e: mac@littlefishrecords.com
Run by Cross Track Music. Send bio, press kit & full CD.

Livid Records
PO Box 276132

Boca Raton, FL 33427
p: 866-819-2294
f: 561-674-9038
www.lividrecords.com
genres: Punk, Indie, Experimental
artists: Daze, The Ilustrated, I Die You Die, The Shrubs
contact: Charles Furment/A&R
e: chuck@lividrecords.com
Snail mail submissions.

Lobster Records
PO Box 1473
Santa Barbara, CA 93102
p: 805-899-2627
f: 805-899-2995
www.lobsterrecords.com
genres: Modern Rock, Punk
artists: Anchors for Arms, Lorene Drive, First to Leave, Mock Orange, Yellowcard
contact: Steve Lubarsky/A&R
e: steve@lobsterrecords.com
Promos must be unwrapped.

Lofton Creek Records
PO Box 1124
Mt. Juliet, TN 37122
p: 615-726-0099
f: 615-726-0096
e: info@loftoncreekrecords.com
www.loftoncreekrecords.com
genres: Country
artists: Doug Stone, Shane Sellers, Jeffrey Steele, Keith Byrant, Shawn King
contact: Mike Borchetta/A&R
ext: 615-726-0099 x101
e: mikeborchetta@loftoncreekrecords.com
No unsolicited material.

Lost Highway Records
401 Commerce St., #1100
Nashville, TN 37219
p: 615-524-7500
f: 615-524-7600
www.losthighwayrecords.com
genres: Country, Blues, S/S, Alt. Country, Rock
artists: Ryan Adams, Elvis Costello, Mary Gauthier, Lyle Lovett, Willie Nelson
contact: Luke Lewis/Chairman
ext: 615-524-7524
e: luke.lewis@umusic.com
contact2: Kim Buie/VP A&R
ext: 615-524-7811
e: kim.buie@umusic.com
Part of Universal Music Group. No unsolicited material.

Malaco Records
3023 W Northside Dr.
Jackson, MS 39286
p: 601-982-4522
f: 601-982-2944
e: malaco@malaco.com
www.malaco.com
genres: Urban, R&B, Gospel
contact: Tommy Couch, Jr./A&R - R&B, President
ext: 601-982-4522 x231
e: tcouchjr@malaco.com
contact2: Wolf Stephenson/VP of A&R
ext: 601-982-4522 x203
e: wstephenson@malaco.com
Runs 601 Records, Savoy Records, Waldoxy Records, Malaco Jazz, Freedom Records, J Town Records, Muscle Shoals/Muscle Shoals Sound Gospel, Fame Records & Chimneyville Records. No unsolicited material.

Marsalis Music
323 Broadway
Cambridge, MA 02139
p: 617-354-2736
f: 617-354-2396
e: info@marsalismusic.com
www.marsalismusic.com
genres: Jazz
artists: Harry Connick Jr., Branford Marsalis Quartet, Doug Wamble, Miguel Zenon, Joey Calderazzo
contact: Bob Blumenthal/A&R
Copyrighted material only.

MAXJAZZ
115 W Lockwood Ave.
St. Louis, MO 63119
p: 800-875-8331; 314-918-9170
f: 314-961-6074
e: info@maxjazz.com
www.maxjazz.com
genres: Jazz
artists: Jeremy Pelt, Russell Malone, Mulgrew Miller, Dena DeRose, John Proulx
contact: Clayton McDonnell
e: cmcdonnell@maxjazz.com

MC Records
PO Box 1788
Huntington Station, NY 11746
p: 631-754-8725
f: 631-262-9274
www.mc-records.com
genres: Blues, Folk, Americana
artists: Katharine Whalen, Kim Wilson, Pinetop Perkins, Odetta, Gary U.S. Bonds
contact: Mark Carpentieri/President
e: mc@mc-records.com
No unsolicited material.

Megaforce Records
PO Box 1955
New York, NY 10113
p: 212-741-8861
e: info@megaforcerecords.com
www.megaforcerecords.com
genres: All Styles
artists: Clutch, Delgados, S.O.D., Wellwater Conspiracy, Mushroomhead
contact: Greg Caputo/A&R
e: gregaforce@aol.com
No unsolicited material.

Merge Records
PO Box 1235
Chapel Hill, NC 27514
p: 919-688-9969
f: 919-688-9970
e: merge@mergerecords.com
www.mergerecords.com
genres: Rock, Pop
artists: Arcade Fire, Spoon, Superchunk, M. Ward, Camera Obscura,
contact: Spott/A&R
No unsolicited material.

Metal Blade Records
2828 Cochran St., Ste. 302
Simi Valley, CA 93065
p: 805-522-9111
f: 805-522-9380
e: metalblade@metalblade.com
www.metalblade.com
genres: Hard Rock, Metal
artists: As I Lay Dying, Unearth, Soilent Green, The Black Dahlia Murder, Job for a Cowboy
contact: A&R
e: ar@metalblade.com
Mail CDs or email links to MySpace page.

Metropolis Records
PO Box 974
Media, PA 19063
p: 610-595-9940
f: 610-595-9944
e: label@metropolis-records.com
www.metropolis-records.com
genres: Industrial, Goth, EBM, Synthpop, Electronic
artists: Front Line Assembly, Electric Six, VNV Nation, Mindless Self Indulgence
contact: Joe Schulthise/A&R
e: demo@metropolis-records.com
No unsolicited material.

Miami Records & Discos Fuentes
PO Box 454008
Miami, FL 33245
p: 305-269-9323
f: 305-269-0223
e: sales@miami-records.com
www.miami-records.com
genres: Latin, Tropical, Salsa
artists: Sonora Carruseles, La Sonora Dinamita, Fruko Y Sus Tesos, Joe Arroyo
contact: Jorge Fuentes/A&R
ext: 305-269-9323 x11
e: jorgef@miami-records.com
Send promos to: 7001 N Waterway Dr., #108, Miami, FL 33155.

Mighty Peace Records
9408 Eighth St.
Dawson Creek, BC V1G 3N9
Canada
e: mightypeacerecords@hotmail.com
www.mightypeacerecords.com
genres: Country, Metal
artists: The Dick Twang Band, Jess Lee, Inspected by 40, Brian Anger, Skull Dozer
contact: Marty Peterson
ext: 250-219-7088
contact2: Diane Horseman
ext: 250-782-6755
Contact before sending material.

Mint Records
PO Box 3613
Main Post Office
Vancouver, BC V6B 3Y6
Canada
p: 604-669-6468
f: 604-669-6478
e: mint@mintrecs.com
www.mintrecs.com
genres: Pop, Alt. Country, Rock N Roll, Garage, Surf
artists: Carolyn Mark, The Organ, Immaculate Machine, Bella, The Awkward Stage
contact: Kevin Beesley/A&R
e: kbh@mintrecs.com
No unsolicited material.

Minty Fresh
PO Box 577400
Chicago, IL 60657
p: 773-665-0289
f: 773-665-0215
e: info@mintyfresh.com
www.mintyfresh.com
genres: Pop, Rock, Alt., Folk, Indie, Children's, Electronica
artists: Prototypes, Tahiti 80, Alamo Race Track, White Shoes & the Couples Company, The Cardigans
contact: Anthony Musiala/A&R
e: musiala@mintyfresh.com
contact2: Jim Powers/Pres.
Runs Mini Fresh & Steady Records.

Mohican Records
99 Rochester Ave.
London, Middlesex TW13 4EF
UK
p: 44-208-751-6401
e: david.hughes55@btinternet.com
www.mohicanrecords.co.uk
genres: Indie, Rock, Electronic
artists: Vee Nex, Sound Horn, Kama Linden, Munkie, The Final Hour
contact: Dave Mohican/A&R - Indie, Electronic
e: davemohican@mohicanrecords.co.uk

Morphius Records
100 E 23rd St.
Baltimore, MD 21218
p: 410-662-0112
f: 410-662-0116
e: info@morphius.com
www.morphius.com
genres: Rock, Punk, Hip-Hop, Jazz, Experimental, Metal, Club
artists: Bang! Bang!, Pietasters, Death Set, X, Little Clayway
contact: Matt Selander/A&R
e: matt@morphius.com
Runs Morphius, Revolver, Choke, Cargo, Stick Figure, Carrot Top, AEC, Revelation, Sonic Unyon, Rockbottom, Liaison, VMS, Rabbit Foot Records, Morphius Urban, Morphius Archives, Party Hair Records & What Else Records. Email submissions.

Motown Records
1755 Broadway, 6th Fl.
New York, NY 10019
p: 212-373-0750
www.motown.com
genres: Urban, Soul, Pop
artists: Erykah Badu, India.Arie, Stevie Wonder, The Temptations, Diana Ross
contact: Bruce Carbone/A&R
e: bruce.carbone@umusic.com
Part of Universal Music Group. No unsolicited material.

Music World Music
1505 Hadley St.
Houston, TX 77002
p: 713-772-5175
f: 713-772-3034
e: hr@musicworldent.com
www.musicworldent.com
genres: Gospel, Pop, R&B, Country
artists: Solange, Ramiyah, Michele Williams, Beyonce, Destiny's Child, Mary Mary
No unsolicited material.

Mute Records
101 Ave. of the Americas
4th Fl.
New York, NY 10013
p: 212-255-7670
f: 212-255-6056
e: mute@mute.com
www.mute.com
genres: Electronic, Rock, Avant Garde, Alt.
artists: Goldfrapp, Erasure, Jose Gonazalez, The Knife, Motor
contact: Adrian Janssens/A&R
ext: 212-255-7670 x233
e: aj@mute.com
Part of EMI. No unsolicited material.

My Pal God Records
47 Hardy Dr.
Princeton, NJ 08540
p: 609-989-8066
f: 609-924-6459
e: info@mypalgodrecords.com
www.mypalgodrecords.com
genres: Rock, Alt.
artists: Del Rey, The Quick Fix Kills, Bitter Bitter Weeks, Eyeball Skeleton, The Yah Mos Def
contact: Jon Solomon/A&R
e: jon@mypalgodrecords.com
No unsolicited material.

Negative Gain Productions
PMB 171, Ste. A.
1770 S Randall Rd.
Geneva, IL 60134
p: 630-208-5088
f: 630-443-0103
e: info@negativegain.com
www.negativegain.com
genres: Electronic, Industrial, Gothic, Darkwave
artists: Cruciform Injection, Kevorkian Death Cycle, HexRx, Filament 38, Emergence
contact: Micah Skaritka/A&R
ext: 630-417-3075
e: micah@negativegain.com
Run by Apophis Consortium Snail mail submissions.

NEH Records
7915 Oxford Rd.
Niwot, CO 80503
p: 303-652-0199
f: 303-652-2279
www.nehrecords.com
genres: Melodic Rock, AOR, Southern Rock, Hard Rock, Prog, Metal
artists: Axe, Guild of Ages, Blister 66, Red Rock Roosters, Michael McPherson
contact: Michael McPherson
e: mmcpherson@nehrecords.com
No unsolicited material.

Nettwerk Productions
1650 W 2nd Ave.
Vancouver, BC V6J 4R3
Canada
p: 604-654-2929
f: 604-654-1993
e: info@nettwekamerica.com
www.nettwerk.com
genres: Alt., Electronic, Roots
artists: Delerium, Be Good Tanyas, Old Crow Medicine Show, Erin McKeown, MC Lars
contact: Mark Jowett/A&R
ext: 604-654-2929 x208
e: mark@nettwerk.com
contact2: Blair McDonald/A&R
ext: 44-207-424-7500 x517
e: blair@nettwerk.com
*Also runs NuTone Records. Other offices in **CA**: 323-301-4200; **Boston**: 617-497-8200; **London**: 44-207-424-7500; **Nashville**: 615-320-1200; **New York**: 212-760-9711 & **Hamburg**: 49-404-318-4650. Mail demos to: Polly Greenwood.*

Neurodisc Records
3801 N University Dr.
Ste. #403
Ft. Lauderdale, FL 33351
p: 954-572-0289
f: 954-572-2874
e: info@neurodisc.com
genres: Electronic, Dance, World, Lounge, Pop
artists: Blue Stone, Amethystium, Deviations Project, Sleepthief, Etro Anime
contact: Troy Kelley/A&R
e: troy@neurodisc.com
contact2: Tom O'Keefe/A&R
e: tom@neurodisc.com
Runs Spectacle Entertainment. Send w/ full contact info.

New Vision Records
PO Box 4738
Cary, NC 27519
p: 404-462-7445
e: corporate@newvisionrecords.com
www.newvisionrecords.com
genres: Gospel, R&B
artists: Darryl Peavy & Israel, Rising Stars, Mary Lowery & Company
contact: Cecil Wilson/A&R
contact2: Lamont Crump/Song Acquisitions
ext: 919-434-9948
e: crumpcakes@newvisionrecords.com
Offers an artist development & distribution program.

New West Records
9215 W Olympic Blvd.
Beverly Hills, CA 90212
p: 310-246-5766
f: 310-246-5767
e: katelyn@newwestrecords.com
www.newwestrecords.com
genres: Rock, Americana, S/S, Alt. Country, Folk, Pop
artists: Alice Cooper, Drive-By Truckers, Old 97s, The Flatlanders, Steve Earle
contact: Peter Jesperson/A&R
e: peter@newwestrecords.com
Runs Soft Drive & Ammal Records. No unsolicited material.

Nitro Records
7071 Warner Ave., Ste. F-736
Huntington Beach, CA 92647
p: 714-842-8897
f: 714-842-8609
e: info@nitrorecords.com
www.nitrorecords.com
genres: Punk, Rock
artists: Rufio, The Letters Organize, A Wilhelm Scream, The Aquabats, T.S.O.L.
contact: Sean Ziebarth/A&R
e: senaboy@nitrorecords.com
Send MySpace link to demoman@nitrorecords.com. No calls.

No Alternative Music Group
3148 Bryant Ave. S
Minneapolis, MN 55408
p: 612-375-1113
f: 612-341-3330
www.noalternative.com
genres: Indie Rock
artists: The Silent Years, Model One, James Apollo
contact: Jon Delange, A&R
e: jon@tinderboxmusic.com
contact2: Wes Schuck
ext: 507-344-8985
e: wes@noalternative.com
Accepts CDs only.

No Idea Records
PO Box 14636
Gainesville, FL 32604
p: 352-379-0502
f: 352-375-9041
e: noideanerds@earthlink.net
www.noidearecords.com
genres: Punk, Hardcore
artists: Glass & Ashes, The Tim Version, North Lincoln, I Hate Myself, Assholeparade

No Type
4580 Ave. de Lorimier
Montreal, QC H2H 2B5
Canada
p: 514-526-4096 x1
f: 514-526-4487
www.notype.com
genres: Electronic, Experimental
artists: Books on Tape, Tomas Jirku, The Unireverse, Morceaux de Machines, Magali Babin
contact: David Turgeon/Director of A&R
ext: 514-526-4096 x1
e: dt@electrocd.com
Affiliated w/ Empreintes Digitales & Diffusion i Media. Snail mail CDRs; No calls.

Nomadic Wax
486 Jefferson Ave., Ste. 100
Brooklyn, NY 11221
e: info@nomadicwax.com
www.nomadicwax.com
genres: All Styles of Hip-Hop, African, Dub, World, Dancehall
artists: Chosan, Omzo, African Underground Allstars, Nomadic Wax Allstars, BMG 44
contact: Ben Herson/A&R
e: ben@nomadicwax.com
contact2: Dan Cantor/A&R
e: dan@nomadicwax.com
No MP3s.

Nonesuch Records
1290 Ave. of the Americas
23rd Fl.
New York, NY 10104
p: 212-707-2900
f: 212-707-3205
e: info@nonesuch.com
www.nonesuch.com
genres: Jazz, Pop, World, Classical, Musical Theatre
artists: Laurie Anderson, John Adams, The Black Keys, Philip Glass, Chris Thile
Part of Warner Music Group. No unsolicited material.

North Star Music
338 Compass Cir., A1
North Kingstown, RI 02852
p: 401-886-8888
f: 401-886-8880
e: info@northstarmusic.com
www.northstarmusic.com
genres: World Beat, Celtic, Jazz, S/S, Instrumental, New Age
artists: Robin Spielberg, David Osborne, Chris Caswell & Friends, Steve Schuch & The Night Heron Consort, CommonGround
contact: Sue Waterman/A&R
ext: 401-886-8888 x104
e: sue@northstarmusic.com
Markets music to nat'l specialty stores & bookstores. Email before sending material.

Northern Blues Music
290 Shuter St.
Toronto, ON M5A 1W7
Canada
p: 866-540-0003; 416-536-4892
f: 416-536-1494
e: info@northernblues.com
www.northernblues.com
genres: Blues, Roots
artists: Watermelon Slim, Homemade Jamz Blues Band, Carlos Del Junco, Paul Reddick, Moreland & Arbuckle
contact: Fred Litwin/Pres.
e: fred@northernblues.com

Northern Records
Yorba Linda, CA
p: 714-528-7625
f: 714-528-7626
e: info@northernrecords.com
www.northernrecords.com
genres: All Styles
artists: The Lassie Foundation, Cush, Monarch, Holly Nelson, They Sang As They Slew
contact: Eric Campuzano/A&R
e: eric@northernrecords.com
Email link to site & MySpace page.

Nu Jazz Records
PO Box 197
New York, NY 10116
p: 212-251-1936
e: info@nujazzentertainment.com
www.nujazzentertainment.com
genres: Jazz
artists: Jimmy Greene, Kendrick Scott, Xavier Davis, Walter Blanding Jr., Geoff Clapp
contact: Jerald Miller
No unsolicited material.

NYC Records
175 W 72nd St., Apt. 10H
New York, NY 10023
p: 212-496-1625
www.nycrecords.com
genres: Jazz, S/S
artists: Mike Mainieri, Zachary Breaux, Kenneth Silvertsen, Steps Ahead
contact: Mike Mainieri/A&R
e: mmvibe@aol.com
Also runs Exit 9 Records. No unsolicited material.

Oh Boy Records
33 Music Sq. W, Ste. 102B
Nashville, TN 37203
p: 615-742-1250
f: 615-742-1360
e: ohboy@ohboy.com
www.ohboy.com
genres: Americana, Folk, Country, Bluegrass, Rock
artists: John Prine, Todd Snider, Dan Reeder
Also runs Red Pajamas Records & Blue Plate Music. No unsolicited material.

One Little Indian
2087 Union St., #2
San Francisco, CA 94123
p: 415-567-5652
f: 415-567-5990
e: info@onelittleindian-us.com
www.onelittleindian-us.com
genres: Rock, Pop, Electronic, S/S
artists: Bjork, Lloyd Cole, Pieta Brown
contact: Johnny Igaz/A&R
e: johnny@onelittleindian-us.com
contact2: Celia Hirschman
e: celia@onelittleindian-us.com
Snail mail submissions.

Organik Rekords
2238 Dundas St. W
PO Box 59009
Toronto, ON M6R 3B5
Canada
p: 416-535-5110
e: info@organik.ca
www.organik.ca
genres: Rock, Ambient, Alt., Prog, Electronic, Acoustic
artists: 5th Projekt, Night Flowers, Tara Rice, Knell
contact: Tara Rice/ A&R - Acoustic, Rock
contact2: Skodt D. McNalty/ A&R - Electronic, Ambient, Rock
No Metal, Punk, Rap or Pop

Ovum Recordings
1528 Walnut St., Ste. 202
Philadelphia, PA 19102
p: 215-735-8900
f: 215-735-2911
www.ovum-rec.com
genres: Dance, Electronic
artists: Josh Wink, Loco Dice, David Alvardo, Stefan Goldmann, Nick & Danny Chatelain
contact: Matt Brookman/A&R
ext: 215-735-8900 x11
e: mattb@ovum-rec.com
Dance & Electronic music only.

Pandisc Music
247 SW 8th St., #349
Miami, FL 33130
p: 305-557-1914
e: info@pandisc.com
www.pandisc.com
genres: Urban, Bass, Dance
artists: Bass Mekanik, Beat Dominator, Blowfly, DJ Laz, DJ Baby Anne
contact: Bo Crane/Pres.
ext: 305-557-1914 x128
e: bocrane@pandisc.com
contact2: Beth Sereni/A&R
ext: 305-557-1914 x125
e: beth@kriztal.com
Also runs Kriztal Entertainment, StreetBeat Records & NuVision. Only artists w/ buzz or track record.

Paper Bag Records
455 Spadina Ave., Ste. 212
Toronto, ON M5S 2G8
Canada
p: 416-260-1515
e: info@paperbagrecords.com
www.paperbagrecords.com
genres: Indie Rock, Alt. Rock, Electronic, Pop
artists: Tokyo Police Club, You Say Party! We Say Die!, The Acorn, Winter Gloves
contact: Trevor Larocque/A&R

Paper Garden Records
1900 Belmont Blvd., BMH 431
Nashville, TN 37212
p: 615-473-0096
www.papergardenrecords.com
genres: Indie Rock, Indie Pop
artists: Eagle Seagull, Peasant, Darla Farmer
contact: Bryan Vaughan/CEO
e: bryan@papergardenrecords.com
Green label accepts high quality CDs ATTN: Bryan Vaughan, 205 Lexington Ave., 2nd Fl., New York, NY 10016.

Parma Recordings
861 Lafayette Rd., Ste. 6B
Hampton, NH 03842
p: 603-967-4712
e: info@parmarecordings.com
www.parmarecordings.com
genres: Modern Classical
artists: Richard Stoltzman, Gerard Schwartz, Carl Vollrath, Vit Micka
contact: Bob Lord
e: bob.lord@parmarecordings.com
contact2: Renee Dupuis
e: renee.dupuis@parmarecordings.com
Also runs Navona Records. Email submissions.

Plug Research Music/ Sofa Disk
4519 Santa Monica Blvd.
Los Angeles, CA 90029
p: 323-662-1435
f: 818-773-1754
e: info@plugresearch.com
www.plugresearch.com
genres: Electronica, Hip-Hop, Alt., Jazz, Funk, Rock, Afrobeat
artists: Camping, Chessie, Flying Lotus, Life Force Trio, Mia Doi Todd
contact: Allen Avanessian
e: allen@plugresearch.com
No unsolicited material.

PRA Records
1255 5th Ave., #7K
New York, NY 10029
p: 212-860-3233
f: 212-860-5556
www.prarecords.com
genres: Contemporary Jazz, Pop, Rock
artists: Joe Sample, The Crusaders
contact: Patrick Rains/A&R
e: pra@prarecords.com
No unsolicited material.

Putumayo World Music
411 Lafayette St., 4th Fl.
New York, NY 10003
p: 212-625-1400
f: 212-460-0095
e: info@putumayo.com
www.putumayo.com
genres: World Beat, Folk, Latin, Americana, Blues, Electronica
artists: Oliver Mtukudzi, Habib Koite, Andy Palacio, Dobet Gnahore, Angelique Kidjo
contact: Jacob Edgar/A&R
ext: 212-625-1400 x209
e: jacob@putumayo.com
Also runs Cumbancha Records. Send CD & contact info.

Q Division Records
363 Highland Ave.
Somerville, MA 02144
p: 617-625-9900
f: 617-625-2224
e: info@qdivision.com
www.qdivision.com
genres: Rock, Pop
artists: Loveless, Francine, Gigolo Aunts, Senor Happy, Bill Janovitz & Crown Victoria
contact: Mike Denneen/A&R
contact2: Jon Lupfer/A&R
Also runs Q-Dee Records. northeast US-based artist email before sending material. No calls.

Radical Records
77 Bleecker St.
New York, NY 10012
p: 212-475-1111
f: 212-475-3676
e: info@radicalrecords.com
www.radicalrecords.com
genres: Punk, Hardcore, Rock, Glam, Cool Rock
artists: Sex Slaves, Blanks 77, Inspecter 7, ICU
contact: Yoon/A&R
e: yoon@radicalrecords.com
Seeking touring Rock bands.

Radikal
PO Box 186
Teaneck, NJ 07666
p: 201-836-5116
f: 201-836-0661
e: info@radikal.com
www.radikal.com
genres: Dance, Electronic, Trance
artists: Yello, Galleon, Voodoo & Serano, Snap, Havochate
contact: Jurgen Korduletsch
e: contact@radikal.com
Affiliated w/ 4 West Records. Send CDs, webform & letter w/ contact info.

Rap-A-Lot
2141 W Governors Cir.
Houston, TX 77092
p: 713-680-8588
f: 713-335-1638
e: info@rapalotrecords.com
www.rapalotrecords.com
genres: Rap
artists: Z-ro, Damm D, Bun B, ABN, Devin the Dude
contact: James Prince/A&R
contact2: Thomas Randall/A&R
ext: 713-335-1624
Seeking 'raw talent.' Send demos to: PO Box 924190, Houston, TX 77292.

Razor & Tie Music
214 Sullivan St., Ste. 4A
New York, NY 10012
p: 212-473-9173
f: 212-473-9174
e: info@razorandtie.com
www.razorandtie.com
genres: Rock, S/S, Hip-Hop, World, Electronic, Folk, Metal
artists: All That Remains, Dar Williams, Angelique Kidjo, Semi Precious Weapons, Ryan Shaw
contact: Beka Callaway/A&R
e: bcallaway@razorandtie.com
contact2: Michael Caplan/ Exec. Sr. VP of A&R
e: mcaplan@razorandtie.com
Also runs Ghostlight, Prosthetic Records & The Militia Group. Snail mail submissions.

Real Music
85 Liberty Ship Way, Ste. 207
Sausalito, CA 94965
p: 415-331-8273
f: 415-331-8278
e: realmusic@realmusic.com
www.realmusic.com
genres: New Age
artists: Liquid Mind, Karunesh, Gandalf, Bernward Koch, Kevin Kern
contact: Terence Yallop/A&R
e: tyallop@realmusic.com
Also runs iRelax & Real Mystic.

Rebel Records
PO Box 7405
Charlottesville, VA 22906
p: 434-973-5151
f: 434-973-6655
e: questions@rebelrecords.com
www.rebelrecords.com
genres: Bluegrass
artists: Steep Canyon Rangers, Kenny & Amanda Smith Band, Junior Sisk & Ramblers Choice, David Davis & The Warrior River Boys
contact: Mark Freeman/A&R
e: mfreeman@rebelrecords.com
Also runs County Records.

Red House Records
501 W Lynnhurst Ave.
St. Paul, MN 55104
p: 651-644-4161
f: 651-644-4248
e: customerservice@redhouserecords.com
www.redhouserecords.com
genres: Folk, S/S, Acoustic
artists: Bill Staines, Greg Brown, Lucy Kaplansky, Jimmy Lafave, Eliza Gilkyson
contact: Ellen Stanley/A&R
e: promotions@redhouserecords.com
No unsolicited material.

Redrum Productions
14737 McCormick St.
Van Nuys, CA 91411
p: 323-556-1172
e: info@redrumproductions.net
www.redrumproductions.net
genres: Indie Rock, Rock n Roll
artists: Mishavonna, Slaamd, The Fabulous Miss Wendy
contact: Boi/A&R
e: boi@redrumproductions.net
contact2: Simone Sello/A&R
ext: 323-428-6209
e: simone@redrumproductions.net
No calls.

Regain Records (Sweden)
Lommavägen 53
Hjärups Gård
Hjarup, 245 62 Sweden
p: 464-030-2173
f: 464-030-2174
e: info@regainrecords.com
www.regainrecords.com
genres: Metal
artists: Behemoth, Bewitched, Centinex, Devils Whorehouse, Time Requiem
contact: Dennis Clapp/ US Label Manager
e: per@regainrecords.com
contact2: Jörg "Jarne" Brauns/ A&R
e: jarne@regainrecords.com
Promos to: PO Box 12026, 245 02 Hjarup, Sweden.

Relapse Records
PO Box 2060
Upper Darby, PA 19082
p: 610-734-1000
f: 610-734-3719
e: relapse@relapse.com
www.relapse.com
genres: Metal, Punk, Hardcore, Experimental
artists: Zeke, Alchemist, Alabama Thunderpussy, High on Fire, Pig Destroyer
Send demo & tour history.

Revelation Records
PO Box 5232
Huntington Beach, CA 92615
p: 714-375-4264
f: 714-375-4266

e: info@revhq.com
www.revhq.com;
www.revelationrecords.com
genres: Hardcore, Punk, Rock
artists: Down To Nothing, End Of A Year, Gracer
No unsolicited material.

RF Records
Rm. A30, City College Manchester
Manchester, M1 3HB UK
p: 44-161-279-7302
f: 44-161-279-7225
www.rfrecords.com
genres: Multi-Genre
artists: Compilations & Samplers
contact: Chris Williams, A&R
e: cwilliams@ccm.ac.uk
contact2: Phil Ellis, A&R
e: pellis@ccm.ac.uk
Also runs D6 Records, Bass Foundation, Coarse Recordings, Redline Records, Raw Strings & Babyboom Records.
Send CDs, Sonicbids EPKs or MySpace links.

Rhymesayers Entertainment
2409 Hennepin Ave.
Minneapolis, MN 55405
p: 612-977-9870
f: 612-977-9871
e: info@rhymesayers.com
www.rhymesayers.com
genres: Hip-Hop
artists: DJ Abilities, POS, Atmosphere, Brother Ali, Boom Bap Project
contact: Siddiq/CEO
e: siddiq@rhymesayers.com
No unsolicited material.

Righteous Babe Records
PO Box 95, Ellicott Station
Buffalo, NY 14205
p: 716-852-8020
f: 716-852-2741
e: info@righteousbabe.com
www.righteousbabe.com
genres: Alt., Folk
artists: Ani DiFranco, Toshi Reagon, Hamell On Trial, Anais Mitchell
No unsolicited material.

Roadrunner Records
902 Broadway, 8th Fl.
New York, NY 10010
p: 212-274-7500
f: 212-505-7469
e: webmaster@roadrunnerrecords.com
www.roadrunnerrecords.com
genres: Metal, Rock
artists: Slipknot, Nickelback, Cradle of Filth, Killswitch Engage, StoneSour
contact: Mike Gitter/A&R
e: gitter@roadrunnerrecords.com
contact2: Ron Burman/A&R
e: burman@roadrunnerrecords.com
No unsolicited material.

Robbins Entertainment
159 W 25th St., 4th Fl.
New York, NY 10001
p: 212-675-4321
f: 212-675-4441
e: info@robbinsent.com
www.robbinsent.com
genres: Dance, Pop
artists: Cascada, DHT, DJ Sammy, Lasgo, Ian Van Dahl
contact: John Parker/A&R
e: jparker@robbinsent.com
contact2: Stephanie Karten/A&R, New Media
e: skarten@robbinsent.com
Also runs Robbins Nashville.
Snail mail Dance music only.
No FedX.

Roc-A-Fella
825 8th Ave., 29th Fl.
New York, NY 10019
p: 212-333-8000
f: 212-445-3616
www.rocafellarecords.com
genres: Rap, Hip-Hop
artists: Jay-Z, Kanye West, Young Gunz, DJ Clue
contact: Shawn Carter/CEO
contact2: Shaliek Berry/A&R
e: shaliek.berry@umusic.com
Part of Universal Music Group.
No unsolicited material.

ROIR (Reachout Int'l Records)
PO Box 501, Prince St. Station
New York, NY 10012
p: 212-477-0563
f: 212-505-9908
e: info@roir-usa.com
www.roir-usa.com
genres: Punk, Reggae, Rock, Electronic, Experimental
artists: Bad Brains, Television, Jon Langford, Asphalt Jungle, Styreens
contact: Lucas Cooper/A&R

Ropeadope Records
417 B Boot Rd.
Downingtown, PA 19335
p: 800-786-1062
f: 610-873-6882
e: licensing@ropeadope.com
www.ropeadope.com
genres: Funk, Jazz, Hip-Hop, Rock
artists: Antibalas Afrobeat Orchestra, Charlie Hunter, DJ Logic, Marco Benevento, Medeski, Martin & Wood
contact: Jerome Brown/A&R
e: jerome@ropeadope.com
contact2: Andy Blackman Hurwitz/President
e: andy@ropeadope.com

Rounder Records
1 Rounder Way
Burlington, MA 01803
p: 617-354-0700
f: 617-354-4840
e: info@rounder.com
www.rounder.com
genres: Pop, Roots, Folk, Country, Bluegrass
contact: Troy Hansbrough/A&R
e: thansbrough@rounder.com
contact2: Scott Billington/A&R
e: sbillington@rounder.com
Also runs Zoe, Philo & Heartbeat.
No unsolicited material.

Rykodisc
30 Irving Pl., 3rd Fl.
New York, NY 10003
p: 212-287-6100
f: 212-287-6139
e: info@rykodisc.com
www.rykodisc.com
genres: Rock, Jazz, Folk, S/S, Eclectic, Country, Blues, Reggae
artists: Brian Eno, Elf Power, Freezepop, Matt Duke, Was (Not Was)
contact: Beth Tallman/VP
contact2: Ruby Marchand/A&R
Snail mail CDs. No emails.

Shanachie Entertainment
37 E Clinton St.
Newton, NJ 07860
p: 973-579-7763
f: 973-579-7083
e: lkowalski@shanachie.com
www.shanachie.com
genres: Jazz, Folk, Ska, World, Blues, Groove, R&B
artists: Kim Waters, Third World, Hill St. Soul, Sax Pack, Everette Harp
contact: Randall Grass/A&R
e: rgrass@shanachie.com
contact2: Danny Weiss/A&R - Jazz
Also runs Yazoo Records.
Snail mail submissions.

Sheridan Square Entertainment
210 25th Ave. N, Ste. 1200
Nashville, TN 37203
p: 615-277-1800
f: 615-277-1801
www.sheridansquaremusic.com
genres: Pop, Rock, Blues, Country, World, New Age, Urban, Classical, Jazz, Christian, Dance, Electronica, Children's
artists: Shirley Caesar, Joan Osborne, Moby, Susan Tedeschi
contact: Mick Lloyd/A&R
ext: 615-277-1825
e: mlloyd@sheridansq.com
contact2: Paul Colson/A&R
ext: 615-277-1133
e: pcolson@sheridansq.com
Runs V2 Records, Intersound, Tone Cool, Triloka/Karma, Sheridan Square Records, Compendia, Light, Spitfire & Artemis Records.
No unsolicited material.

Sh-K-Boom
630 9th Ave., #407
New York, NY 10036
p: 212-581-6100
f: 212-581-0610
e: info@sh-k-boom.com
www.sh-k-boom.com
genres: Pop, Rock, Folk, Gospel
artists: Sherie Rene Scott, Adam Pascal, Alice Ripley, Billy Porter, Klea Blackhurst
contact: Kurt Deutsch/A&R
e: kurt@sh-k-boom.com
contact2: Noah Cornman/A&R
e: noah@sh-k-boom.com
Also runs Ghost Light Records.
No unsolicited material.

Shut Eye Records & Agency
1180 Vickers St., 2nd Fl.
Atlanta, GA 30316
p: 678-986-4931
f: 404-584-5171
e: hello@shuteyerecords.com
www.shuteyerecords.com
genres: Americana, Roots Rock, Folk, Alt. Country
artists: Wrinkle Neck Mules, The Whipsaws, Hayshaker
contact: Peter Knapp/A&R
e: knapp@shuteyerecords.com

SiAn Records
Camelot Studios
Tyrrelstown House
Dublin, 15 Ireland
p: 35-387-241-2000
www.sianrecords.com
genres: Rock, Pop, Indie
artists: Jaded Sun, Simon Fagan, Hogan
contact: Andrew Wilkinson/A&R - Rock, Pop, Indie
e: andrew@sianrecords.com

Signature Sounds Recording
PO Box 106
Whatley, MA 01093
p: 413-665-4036
f: 509-691-0457
e: info@signaturesounds.com
www.signaturesounds.com
genres: S/S, Acoustic, Americana
artists: Chris Smither, Crooked Still, Winterpills, Kris Delmhorst, Tracy Grammer
contact: Jim Olsen/A&R
ext: 413-665-4036 x1
e: jim@signaturesounds.com
contact2: Mark Thayer/VP
ext: 860-974-2016
e: mthayer814@aol.com
No unsolicited material.

Silver Wave Records
PO Box 7943
Boulder, CO 80306
p: 303-443-5617
f: 303-443-0877
e: info@silverwave.com
www.silverwave.com
genres: Native American, World, New Age
artists: Joanne Shennandoah, Mary Youngblood, Robert Mirabal, Peter Kater, R. Carlos Nakai
contact: Tessalin Green, Initial Music Review
Contact before sending material.

Sire Records
1290 Ave. of the Americas
23rd Fl.
New York, NY 10104
p: 212-707-3200
f: 212-707-3233
www.sirerecords.com
genres: Punk, Rock, Alt., Dance, International
artists: Depeche Mode, Tegan & Sara, Regina Spektor, HIM, The Veronicas
contact: Seymour Stein/Chairman
e: seymour.stein@wmg.com
Part of Warner Music Group.
Call before sending material.

Six Degrees Records
540 Hampshire St.
San Francisco, CA 94110
p: 415-626-6334
f: 415-626-6167
e: info@sixdegreesrecords.com
www.sixdegreesrecords.com
genres: World, Dance, Grooves, Electronic, Pop
artists: Bebel Gilberto, CeU, Spanish Harlem Orchestra, Cheb i Sabbah, Karsh Kale
contact: Bob Duskis/Pres.
ext: 415-626-6334 x12
e: bobd@sixdegreesrecords.com
contact2: Doug Major/A&R
ext: 415-626-6334 x14
e: doug@sixdegreesrecords.com
No unsolicited material.

Smallman Records
PO Box 352, RPO Corydon
Winnipeg, MB R3M 3V3
Canada

p: 204-452-5627
f: 204-480-4309
www.smallmanrecords.com
genres: Punk, Alt.
artists: Comeback Kid, The Reason, Sick City, Broadway Calls, Sights & Sounds
contact: Rob Krause/A&R
ext: 204-284-1256
e: rob@smallmanrecords.com
No unsolicited material.

Smithsonian Folkways Recordings
600 Maryland Ave. Ste. 2001
Washington, DC 20024
p: 202-275-1143
f: 202-275-1165
e: mailorder@si.edu
www.folkways.si.edu
genres: Blues, Bluegrass, World, Jazz, Children's, Classical, Instrumental, Rock, Folk
artists: Lead Belly, Pete Seeger, Woody Guthrie, Bill Monroe, Lucinda Williams
contact: D.A. Sonneborn/ Director of A&R
e: sonneborna@si.edu
No unsolicited material.

Smogveil Records
1658 N Milwaukee Ave., #284
Chicago, IL 60647
p: 773-706-0450
f: 312-276-8519
e: smogveil@mac.com
www.smogveil.com
genres: Rock n Roll, Punk, Experimental, Avant-Garde
artists: Pere Ubu, David Thomas, Peter Laughner, The Pagans, Thor
contact: Frank Mauceri
e: info@smogveil.com

Songlines Recordings
3036 W 6th Ave.
Vancouver, BC V6K 1X3
Canada
p: 604-737-1632
f: 604-737-1678
www.songlines.com
genres: Jazz, World, Avant-Garde
artists: Dave Douglas, Bill Frisell, Misha Mengelberg, Wayne Horvitz, Robin Holcomb
contact: Tony Reif/A&R
e: treif@songlines.com
No unsolicited material.

Sony BMG
550 Madison Ave.
New York, NY 10022
p: 212-833-8000
f: 212-833-4732
www.sonybmg.com
genres: Rock, Pop, Urban
artists: Incubus, John Mayer, Indigo Girls, Harry Connick, Wyclef Jean
contact: Lisa Ellis/Sr. VP
ext: 212-833-4141
e: lisa.ellis@sonybmg.com
contact2: Hip-Hop/GM
ext: 212-833-6000
e: hiphop@sonybmg.com
Runs, Jive/Silvertone Records, Epic Records, RCA Records, Columbia Records, Zomba, Battery Records, Arista, Legacy, J Records, Volcano Records & Loud Records.
No unsolicited material.

Sound Barrier Records
1920 Benson Ave.
St. Paul, MN 55116
p: 651-699-1155
f: 651-699-1536
genres: R&B, Rock
artists: The Commodores, Debra Laws, Grade 8
contact: David Fish/A&R
e: davidlfish@1155msp.com
contact2: Jono Tearle/A&R
e: grade8@1155msp.com
Snail mail submissions.

Sound Gizmo Audio
1818 Newkirk Ave., #3L
Brooklyn, NY 11226
p: 718-832-1806
e: info@earthprogram.com
www.soundgizmo.com
genres: House, Drum n Bass, Electronic, Indie Rock
artists: Ming+FS, Dune, GFS, Sky City, Dave Hodge
contact: Nick Cain, A&R
ext: 718-832-1806 x201
e: nick@earthprogram.com
contact2: Joel Jordan
ext: 718-832-1806 x202
e: joel@earthprogram.com
Also runs Warmth & Savant Guard Records.

Springman Records
2308 P St., Apt. 9
Sacramento, CA 95816
e: info@springmanrecords.com
www.springmanrecords.com
genres: Punk, Ska, Rock
artists: The Phenomenauts, River City Rebels, Ashtray, The Teenage Harlets, Mitch Clem
Also runs Facepalm Records.
No unsolicited material.

SST Records
406 Talbot St.
Taylor, TX 76574
p: 512-352-8165
f: 512-352-8178
e: orders@sstsuperstore.com
www.sstsuperstore.com
genres: Rock, Punk
artists: Mojack, Jambang, Greg Ginn & the Taylor Texas Corrugators, Gone
contact: Greg Ginn/A&R
e: ginn@sstsuperstore.com
Affiliated w/ Cruz Records.

Stony Plain Records
PO Box 861
Edmonton, AB T5J 2L8
Canada
p: 780-468-6423
f: 780-465-8941
e: info@stonyplainrecords.com
www.stonyplainrecords.com
genres: Blues, Roots, Rock, Folk
artists: Ian Tyson, Corb Lund, Duke Robillard, Ronnie Earl, Maria Muldaur
contact: Zoe Hawnt/A&R
e: zoe@stonyplainrecords.com

Sub Pop
2013 4th Ave., 3rd Fl.
Seattle, WA 98121
p: 206-441-8441
f: 206-441-8245
e: info@subpop.com
www.subpop.com
genres: Alt., Pop, Rock
artists: Flight of the Conchords, The Go! Team, The Shins, The Postal Service, Wolf Parade
contact: Tony Kiewel/A&R
e: tonyk@subpop.com
contact2: Andy Kotowicz/A&R
e: andyk@subpop.com
No unsolicited material.

Subliminal
199 Hackensack Plank Rd.
Weehawken, NJ 07087
p: 201-866-5340
f: 201-866-5444
e: info@subliminalrecords.com
www.subliminalrecords.com
genres: House
artists: Erick Morillo, Harry Romero, Monkey Bars, Monkey Bars, Jose Nunez
contact: Tim Waugh, A&R
e: tim@subliminalrecords.com
Also runs Bambossa, Sondos, Subliminal Soul & Subusa.
No Prog or Trance.

Sudden Death Records
Moscrop, PO Box 43001
Burnaby, BC V5G 3H0
Canada
p: 604-777-6972
f: 604-777-6974
e: info@suddendeath.com
www.suddendeath.com
genres: Punk, Alt., Acoustic
artists: Agriculture Club, Apt 3G, The Honeymans, The Vibrators, Young Canadians
contact: Bill Brown/A&R
contact2: Joe Keithley
Also runs Taboo Records & JSK Media. Accepts CDs or Sonicbids EPKs.

Sugar Hill Records
2700 Pennsylvania Ave.
Ste. 100
Santa Monica, CA 90404
p: 615-297-6890
f: 615-297-9945
e: info@sugarhillrecords.com
www.sugarhillrecords.com
genres: Roots, Americana, Bluegrass, Folk
artists: Sam Bush, Nickel Creek, The Duhks, Scott Miller, Casey Driessen
contact: Gary Paczosa/A&R
ext: 615-463-9556
e: garyp@sugarhillrecords.com
Affiliated w/ Welk Music Group.
No unsolicited material.

Sunset Records
1133 Broadway, #708
New York, NY 10010
p: 877-542-6664
e: corporate@sunsetholding.com
www.sunsetrecordings.com
genres: All Styles
artists: Kan 'Nal, Zamza, Grayscale, Clayton Road, Obka
contact: Don Lichterman/CEO
ext: 877-542-6664 x3178
e: don.lichterman@sunsetrecordings.com
contact2: Ronald C. Bullock/ A&R - Urban
e: ronald.bullock@sunseturban.com
Runs Alamo Records, Lanark Records, Sunset Urban, Sunset Jazz, Sunset Classical, Sunset Strategic Marketing, Sunset Home Visual Entertainment, Tropical Records & Blue Mountain Records. Submit w/ online A&R submittal tool.

Tantrum Records
PO Box 5828
Santa Barbara, CA 93150
p: 805-275-4295
f: 814-295-2988
e: info@tantrumrecords.org
www.tantrumrecords.org
genres: Rock, World, Hip-Hop, Jazz, Pop, Classical
artists: Aynsley Dunbar, Uru, Bara M'Boup, Izayu, Oliver
contact: Oliver Koppert/ A&R - Punk, Alt., Rock
ext: 805-695-8553
e: oliver@tantrumrecords.org
contact2: Sjoerd "Sjoko" Koppert/A&R - Punk, Alt., Rock
e: sjoko@tantrumrecords.org
No unsolicited material.

Team Love Records
New York, NY
e: info@team-love.com
www.team-love.com
genres: Indie, S/S
artists: A Weather, Mars Black, The Berg Sans Nipple, Capgun Coup
Affiliated w/ Saddle Creek Records. Submit digital material at site.

Texas Music Group
805 West Ave., Ste. 1
Austin, TX 78701
p: 512-322-0617
e: info@txmusicgroup.com
www.txmusicgroup.com
genres: Blues, Country, Texas Rock, Alt.
artists: Johnny Bush, Guy Forsyth, Michael Fracasso, The Derailers, Alejandro Escovedo
contact: Randolph Clendenen/ Pres.
e: randolph@txmusicgroup.com
contact2: Heinz Geissler/A&R
e: heinz@txmusicgroup.com
Runs Lone Star Records & Antone's Records.
No unsolicited material.

Thick Records
PO Box 27506
Los Angeles, CA 90027
p: 323-666-5448
e: info@thickrecords.com
www.thickrecords.com
genres: Punk, Indie Rock
artists: The Brokedowns, Seven Storey Mountain, The Bomb, Four Star Alarm
contact: Zak Einstein/A&R
e: zak@thickrecords.com
No unsolicited material.

Thirsty Ear Recordings
22 Knight St.
Norwalk, CT 06851
p: 203-838-0099
f: 203-838-0006
e: info@thirstyear.com
www.thirstyear.com
genres: Jazz, Electronica
artists: DJ Spooky, Mike Ladd, The Free Zen Society, Mat Maneri, Eri Yamamoto
contact: Hope Kramer/A&R
e: hope@thirstyear.com
Fit the genres before sending CD w/ SASE.

Thrill Jockey Records
PO Box 08038
Chicago, IL 60608
p: 312-492-9634
f: 312-492-9640
e: info@thrilljockey.com
www.thrilljockey.com
genres: Alt., Rock, Country, Bluegrass, Electronic, Jazz
artists: The Sea & Cake, Trans Am, Thank You, Exploding Star Orchestra,

The Fiery Furnaces,
contact: Bettina Richards/A&R
No unsolicited material.

Time Value Records
1905 W Thomas St., Ste. D-109
Hammond, LA 70401
e: info@timevaluerecords.com
www.timevaluerecords.com
genres: Modern Rock, Urban, Hardcore, Industrial, Punk, Electronic, S/S, Acoustic
artists: Murder Capital AllStars, Afterhuman, Scumbag, Many More Graveyards, Goldee
contact: Craig Santicola/A&R
e: csanticola@timevaluerecords.com
Send full kits & contact info or email MP3s to: submissions@timevaluerecords.com.

TKO Records
8941 Atlanta Ave., #505
Huntington Beach, CA 92646
p: 714-961-0500
e: info@tkorecords.com
www.tkorecords.com
genres: Punk
artists: Smut Peddlers, The Stitches, The Boils, Lower Class Brats, Poison Idea
contact: Mark Rainey/A&R
ext: 714-540-0800
No unsolicited material.

To The Fallen Records
PO Box 3369
Newport, RI 02840
p: 401-608-2312
f: 866-843-5101
e: info@tothefallenrecords.com
www.tothefallenrecords.com
genres: Rock, Hip-Hop, Country
artists: Citizen Reign, Logic, Keni Thomas, Dirty Boi Vets, Cutler Spur
contact: Mason James/A&R
e: mason@tothefallenrecords.com
contact2: Sean Gilfillan/CEO
e: sean@tothefallenrecords.com
Non-partisan label devoted to original music by veteran & active duty military artists. Email tothefallenrecords@gmail.com.

Tommy Boy
120 5th Ave., 7th Fl.
New York, NY 10011
p: 212-388-8300
f: 212-388-8431
e: info@tommyboy.com
www.tommyboy.com
genres: Dance, Electronic, Hip-Hop, Alt., Soundtracks
artists: The Cliks, Bob Sinclair, Danny Tenaglia, Plushgun, Bimbo Jones
contact: Rosie Lopez/VP
ext: 212-388-8475
e: rosie@tommyboy.com
Runs Big Cat, Gargamel, Rasa & Silver Label. Email low-bit rate MP3s, links to MySpace to info@tommyboy.com or mail CDs.

Tooth & Nail Records
PO Box 12698
Seattle, WA 98111
p: 206-691-9831
f: 206-691-9776
e: webmaster@toothandnail.com
www.toothandnail.com
genres: Punk, Hardcore, Rock, Pop
artists: The Almost, Anberlin, As Cities Burn, The Becoming, Bon Voyage
contact: Brandon Ebel/A&R
contact2: Chad Johnson/Director of A&R
Runs Solid State & BEC Records. Snail mail CDs; No emails.

Touch & Go/ Quarterstick Records
PO Box 25520
Chicago, IL 60655
p: 773-388-8888
f: 773-388-3888
e: info@tgrec.com
www.touchandgorecords.com
genres: Rock, Punk
artists: Ted Leo & Pharmacists, Pinback, Enon, Calexico, The Black Heart Procession
contact: Chad Nelson/A&R
e: chad@tgrec.com

Transdreamer Records
PO Box 1955
New York, NY 10113
p: 212-741-8861
www.transdreamer.com
genres: Pop, Indie
artists: Arab Strap, Dressy Bessy, A Whisper in the Noise, The Delgados
Will contact if interested. No calls.

Triple Crown Records
331 W 57th St., #472
New York, NY 10019
e: info@triplecrownrecords.com
www.triplecrownrecords.com
genres: Punk, Emo, Ska, Hardcore, Electro
artists: As Tall As Lions, The Gay Blades, The Dear Hunter, The Receiving End of Sirens
contact: Fred Feldman/A&R

Triple Threat Records
205 Copperfield Common SE
Calgary, AB T2Z 4W8 Canada
p: 403-870-6556
e: info@triplethreatrecords.com
www.triplethreatrecords.com
genres: Punk
artists: A Common Ground, Deville, No Coast Hardcore, The Amazing Larrys
contact: Chris Holman/A&R
e: chris@triplethreatrecords.com
Snail mail submissions.

True North Records/ Linus Entertainment
113 Lakeshore Rd. W
Mississauga, ON L5H 1E9
Canada
p: 905-278-8883
f: 905-278-8803
www.truenorthrecords.com; www.linusentertainment.com
genres: Roots, Americana, Rock, Alt Rock, S/S
artists: The Golden Dogs, Blackie & The Rodeo Kings, Stephen Fearing, Colin Linden, Tom Wilson

U & L Records
1617 Cosmo St., Ste. 310
Los Angeles, CA 90028
p: 323-230-6592
f: 323-924-2352
www.urbandlazar.com
genres: Alt., Indie, Acoustic
contact: Jonathan Lazar
e: jonathan@urbandlazar.com
contact2: Zach Urband
e: zach@urbandlazar.com
No unsolicited material.

Ubiquity Records
1010 W 17th St.
Costa Mesa, CA 92627
p: 949-764-9012
f: 949-764-9013
e: mail@ubiquityrecords.com
www.ubiquityrecords.com
genres: Soul, Jazz Re-Issues, Funk, Hip-Hop, Reggae
artists: Darondo, Orgone, PPP, NOMO, Blank Blue
contact: Andrew Jervis/VP
e: andrew@ubiquityrecords.com
contact2: Jody McFadin/Co-Founder
e: jodym@ubiquityrecords.com
Runs Luv N' Haight & CuBop Records. Snail mail submissions. No calls or MP3s.

Undercurrent Records
PO Box 3446
Alpharetta, GA 30023
p: 678-887-2700
e: undercurrent@inspiremedia.info
www.undercurrentrecords.com
genres: Alt., Rock, Dance, Electronic, Holy Hip-Hop, Urban, Inspirational, Gospel
contact: Sean Irvin/A&R
e: submissions@undercurrentrecords.com
Email before sending material.

United for Opportunity
133 W 25th St., 5th Fl.
New York, NY 10001
p: 212-414-0505
f: 212-414-0525
e: info@ufomusic.com
www.ufomusic.com
genres: Pop, S/S, Rock, Alt., World, R&B
artists: Gail Ann Dorsey, Enter The Haggis, Mark Gardener, Sleeptalker, The Guggenheim Grotto
Runs Modern Imperial, Modiba Records, Douglas Records, Innerhythmic Records & Wheat Recording Company. Material must be accompanied by online submission form.

Universal Motown Republic Group
1755 Broadway, 7th Fl.
New York, NY 10019
p: 212-373-0600
f: 212-373-0688
www.umrg.com
genres: Alt., Rock, Pop, Urban, Latin, Country, Jazz
artists: Nelly, Akon, Chamillionaire, Amy Winehouse, Godsmack
contact: Monte Lipman/Pres.
ext: 212-373-0717
e: monte.lipman@umusic.com
contact2: Bruce Carbone/Exec. VP of A&R
ext: 212-841-8677
e: bruce.carbone@umusic.com
Runs Interscope-Geffen-A&M, Island Records/Def Jam, Lost Highway Records, Motown Records, Roc-A-Fella, G-Unit, Shady, Aftermath, Octone, Mosley Music, Cherry Tree, MySpace Music, VuRecords, Verve Records & Verve Forecast. No unsolicited material.

Universal Music Group Nashville
401 Commerce St., Ste. 1100
Nashville, TN 37219
p: 615-524-7500
e: info@umgnashville.com
www.umgnashville.com
genres: Country, Rock
artists: Billy Currington, Halfway to Hazard, Sugarland, Shania Twain, Vince Gill
contact: Brian Wright/VP
e: brian.wright@umusic.com
No unsolicited material.

Vagrant Records
2118 Wilshire Blvd., #361
Santa Monica, CA 90403
e: info@vagrant.com
www.vagrant.com
genres: Indie Rock, Emo, Punk, Alt.
artists: Protest The Hero, Saves The Day, Thrice, Dashboard Confessional, The Hold Steady, Alexisonfire
London office: vagrantuk@vagrant.com. Snail mail CDs.

Valley Entertainment
305 W 71st St.
New York, NY 10023
p: 212-580-9200
e: info@valley-entertainment.com
www.valley-entertainment.com
genres: Pop, Americana, New Age, World, Blues
artists: Michelle Malone, Danielle Howie, Pieta Brown, Jules Shear
contact: Jon Birge/A&R
ext: 212-580-9200 x15
e: jon@valley-entertainment.com
contact2: Sue Stillwagon
ext: 212-580-9200 x11
Also runs Sledgehammer Blues & Hearts of Space.

Van Richter Records
100 S Sunrise Way, Ste. 219
Palm Springs, CA 92262
p: 760-320-5577
www.vanrichter.net
genres: Industrial, Gothic, Metal, Electronica
artists: Testify, The Fair Sex, Girls Under Glass, Sielwolf, DHI
contact: Paul Abramson/A&R - Industrial
e: manager@vanrichter.net

Vanguard Records
2700 Pennsylvania Ave.
Ste. 1100
Santa Monica, CA 90404
p: 310-829-9355
e: info@vanguardrecords.com
www.vanguardrecords.com
genres: Folk, AAA, Blues, Rock, Jazz
artists: Watson Twins, Matt Nathanson, Greg Laswell, Mindy Smith, Alternate Routes
contact: Steve Buckingham/A&R
ext: 615-297-6890
e: steve@vanguardrecords.com
Affiliated w/ WelkMusic Group. No unsolicited material.

Vapor Records
1460 4th St., Ste. 300

Santa Monica, CA 90401
p: 310-393-8442
e: webstar@vaporrecords.com
www.vaporrecords.com
genres: Alt., Rock
artists: Jason Yates, Cake Like, Jonathan Richman, Acetone, Tegan & Sara
contact: Elliot Roberts/A&R
e: elliot@lookoutmgmt.com
contact2: Bonnie Levetin/A&R
e: bonnie@vaporrecords.com
No calls.

Verve Music Group
1755 Broadway, 3rd Fl.
New York, NY 10019
p: 212-331-2000
www.vervemusicgroup.com
genres: S/S, Rock, Jazz, Pop, Blues, Urban, Electronic, Alt.
artists: Diana Krall, Jamie Cullum, Brazilian Girls, Jessie Baylin, The Bridges
contact: Mitchell Cohen/VP
ext: 212-331-2016
e: mitchell.cohen@umusic.com
contact2: Dahlia Ambach-Caplin/Director of A&R
e: dahlia.ambach-caplin@umusic.com
Part of Universal Music Group, Verve Records & Verve Forecast. No unsolicited material.

Victory Records
346 N Justine St., Ste. 504
Chicago, IL 60607
p: 312-666-8661
f: 312-666-8665
e: tony@victoryrecords.com
www.victoryrecords.com
genres: Rock, Punk, Metal
artists: 1997, A Day To Remember, Atreyu, The Junior Varsity, Streetlight Manifesto
contact: Brian Kucharski
ext: 888-447-3267
e: brian@victoryrecords.com

Violator Records
36 W 25th St., 11th Fl.
New York, NY 10016
p: 646-486-8900
f: 646-486-8929
www.violator.com
genres: Rap, Hip-Hop, R&B
artists: 50 Cent, Busta Rhymes, LL Cool J, Macy Gray, Q-Tip
contact: Shaun Copeland/A&R
e: scopeland@violator.com
contact2: Ray Edwards/Director of Operations
e: redwards@violator.com

Warner Bros.
75 Rockefeller Plaza, 8th Fl.
New York, NY 10019
p: 212-275-4500
www.wbr.com; www.wmg.com
genres: Alt., Rock, Pop, Urban, Jazz
artists: Talib Kweli, R.E.M., Flaming Lips, Josh Groban, Avenged Sevenfold
contact: Thomas Whalley/Chairman
ext: 818-953-3456
e: thomas.whalley@wbr.com
contact2: James Dowdall/Sr. VP of A&R
ext: 212-275-4816
e: james.dowdall@wbr.com
Runs Sire Records, Atlantic Records, Bad Boy Ent., Nonesuch Records, Chop Chop, Word Ent., Photo Finish Records, & Fueled By Ramen.
Other locations:
***CA:** Tom Whalley, 818-953-3456, tom.whalley@wbr.com;*
***Nashville:** Paul Worley, 615-214-1553, paul.worley@wbr.com;*
***Canada:** Steve Blair, 416-458-1113, steve.blair@warnermusic.com & for Warner Music Latina, call 305-702-2200.*
No unsolicited material.

Waterdog Music
329 W 18th St., #313
Chicago, IL 60616
p: 312-421-7499
e: waterdog@waterdogmusic.com
www.waterdogmusic.com
genres: Rock, Children's
artists: Ralph Covert, The Bad Examples, Middle 8, Matt Tiegler, Tomorrow the Moon
contact: Rob Gillis/A&R
Also runs Whitehouse & Absolute Records.
No unsolicited material.

Waxploitation
201 S Santa Fe Ave., Ste. 100
Los Angeles, CA 90012
p: 213-687-9563
f: 213-687-9569
e: music@waxploitation.com
www.waxploitation.com
genres: Rock, Hip-Hop, Electronic, Soul
artists: Tweaker, Teargass & Plateglass, DangerDoom, Gnarls Barkley, Danger Mouse
contact: Jeff Antebi/A&R - Rock
No unsolicited material.

WC Music
12718 Greene Ave.
Los Angeles, CA 90066
p: 310-488-5431
e: carlosc@wc-music.com
www.wc-music.com
genres: All Styles of Electronic music
artists: Palenke Soultribe, Insectosound, Sismo, Giovanny DJ, Pytto DJ
contact: Juan Diego Borda/A&R - Electronic
ext: 310-985-4107
e: juandiego@wc-music.com
No unsolicited material.

What Are Records?
2401 Broadway
Boulder, CO 80304
p: 303-440-0666
f: 303-447-2484
e: info@whatarerecords.com
www.whatarerecords.com
genres: Rock, Folk, Funk, Soul
artists: Stephen Lynch, Fancey, Maceo Parker, David Wilcox, The Samples
contact: Kyle Wofford/A&R
ext: 303-440-0666 x202
e: kyle@whatarerecords.com
contact2: Matthew Wilkening/A&R
e: mw@whatarerecords.com

Where Are My Records
PO Box 91, Stn. R
Montreal, QC H2S 3K6
Canada
p: 514-495-0880
e: wamrecords@videotron.ca
www.wherearemyrecords.com
genres: Experimental, Ambient, Electro, Post-Rock, Slow-Core, Shoegaze, Rock
artists: DestroyAllDreamers, Below the Sea, Barzin, Readymade, epic45
contact: Jeff Rioux/Owner
contact2: Patrick Lacharite/A&R
Email before sending material.

Wild Oats Records
PO Box 210982
Nashville, TN 37221
p: 615-673-2860
e: info@wildoatsrecords.com
www.wildoatsrecords.com
genres: Country, Americana, Blues, Folk, Roots Rock, Rock, Bluegrass
artists: Steve Haggard, Gail & The Tricksters, Joel Alan Lehman, Pat DiNizio, Frank 'Andy' Starr
contact: Glen Edwards
e: glen@wildoatsrecords.com
Email before sending material.

Wind River Records
705 S Washington St.
Naperville, IL 60540
p: 630-637-2303
e: karen@folkera.com
www.folkera.com/windriver
genres: S/S, Acoustic, Folk
artists: Rod MacDonald, Kate MacLeod, Jack Williams, Danny Santos, David Roth
Affiliated w/ Folk Era Records. No unsolicited material.

Wind-Up Records
79 Madison Ave., 7th Fl.
New York, NY 10016
p: 212-895-3100
e: windup@winduprecords.com
www.winduprecords.com
genres: Rock, Pop
artists: 12 Stones, Evanescence, The Februaries, Papercut Massacre, Tickle Me Pink
contact: Diana Meltzer/Sr. VP of A&R
e: dmeltzer@winduprecords.com
contact2: Mike Khan/VP of A&R
e: mkahn@winduprecords.com
No unsolicited material.

Word Entertainment
25 Music Sq. W
Nashville, TN 37203
p: 615-251-0600
e: wordtech@wbr.com; info@wordlabelgroup.com
www.wordlabelgroup.com
genres: Gospel, CCM
artists: Point of Grace, Mark Schultz, Barlowgirl, Big Daddy Weave, Diamond Rio
contact: Jim VanHook/Pres.
ext: 615-726-7932
e: jim.vanhook@wbr.com
contact2: Susan Riley/A&R
e: susan.heard@wbr.com
Part of Warner Music Group. No unsolicited material.

XS Records
PO Box 272410
Boca Raton, FL 33427
p: 561-756-1642
f: 561-361-8242
e: info@xsrecords.com
www.xsrecords.com
genres: Rock, Pop, Punk
artists: Josh Todd, The Kicks, Stavesacre, Embodyment
contact: Ed Phillips/A&R
e: efp@xsrecords.com
contact2: Greg Brennen/A&R
e: ggb@xsrecords.com

Yep Roc Records
449-A Trollingwood Rd.
Haw River, NC 27258
p: 336-578-7300
e: info@yeproc.com
www.yeproc.com
genres: Rock, Pop, Indie Rock, Country, Bluegrass, S/S, Americana
artists: Nick Lowe, Robyn Hitchcock, Apples in Stereo, Loudon Wainwright III,
contact: Tor Hansen/A&R
e: tor@redeyeusa.com
contact2: Ryan Dimock/A&R
ext: 336-578-7300 x204
e: ryan@redeyeusa.com
Affiliated w/ Eleven Thirty Records & Redeye. Mail submissions to: PO Box 4821, Chapel Hill, NC 27515.

Zebra Records
PO Box 9178
Calabasas, CA 91372
p: 818-988-6285
e: zebradisc@aol.com
genres: Jazz, Fusion, Jam, Blues
contact: Ricky Schultz/A&R
contact2: Sean Green
Runs Zebra Acoustic. Only accepts submissions from bands w/ significant fan-base.

regional promoters

2nd Street Entertainment
117 W Liberty St.
Louisville, KY
40202
p: 502-561-7050
f: 502-589-3875
www.2ndstreet.com
contact: Eric Wiegel
e: emwiegel@aol.com
genres: All Styles
regions: Mostly KY & surrounding region
venues: Festivals, Clubs, Arenas, Theaters
Books Local-Nat'l acts for all ages shows.

462 Inc.
1825a Abrams Pkwy.
Dallas, TX 75214
p: 214-526-8077
f: 214-526-8242
e: 462inc@earthlink.net
www.462concerts.com
contact: Mark Lee
e: mark462inc@earthlink.net; mlee@462concerts.com
genres: Rock, CCM, Alt., Pop, Jazz
regions: TX
venues: Clubs, Festivals, Fairs, Private Events
Large CCM promoter books original acts; some shows all ages.

AC Entertainment
507 S Gay St.
Ste. 1100
Knoxville, TN
37902
p: 865-523-2665
f: 865-637-2141
e: info@concertwire.com
www.concertwire.com
contact: Ted Heinig
e: ted@acentertainment.com
genres: All Styles
regions: USA
venues: Clubs, Theaters, Corporate/Special Events, Festivals
Prime outfit w/ emphasis on southeast USA. Promotes mostly original Local-Int'l acts; some shows all ages. Co-produces Bonnaroo & Vegoose Music Festivals. Snail mail promos; 3wk follow-up.

AEG Live (CA)
5750 Wilshire Blvd., Ste. 501
Los Angeles, CA 90036
p: 323-930-5700
f: 323-930-5799
www.aeglive.com
contact: Larry Vallon
ext: 323-930-5777
e: lvallon@aeglive.com
genres: Rock, Pop, Country, Americana, Hip-Hop, R&B, Gospel, CCM
regions: USA
venues: Arenas, Theatres
Top event & touring company, subsidiary of global Anschutz Ent. Group, promotes Local-Int'l acts for all ages events. Also produces Coachella & New Orleans Jazz Festival.

AEG Live (TX)
3001 Maple Ave.
Ste. 201
Dallas, TX 75201
p: 972-343-2424
f: 972-343-2401
www.aeglive.com; www.aeg-sw.com
contact: Danny Eaton
ext: 972-343-2424
e: danny@aeglive.com
genres: Rock, Country, Alt.
regions: southwestern USA
venues: PACs, Clubs, Arenas
Southwest branch of top event & touring co. promotes original Reg'l-Int'l talent for all ages shows.

Alabama Concerts/ High Cotton Productions
8013 Parkridge Cir.
Morris, AL 35116
p: 205-590-2444
f: 205-590-0776
contact: Jerry Motte
e: j1035@bellsouth.net
genres: Country, Classic Rock
regions: Southern USA
venues: Civic Centers, Fairs, Festivals, PACs,
Mainly established Reg'l & Nat'l original & tribute acts for sheds 10,000 & less. Snail mail full kits.

AM Productions
16 Mount Vernon Rd.
Manalapan, NJ
07726
p: 732-264-2111
f: 732-264-0081
e: amprod@aol.com
www.amprod.net
contact: Stanley Andrucyk
e: amprodsa@aol.com
genres: AC, Country, Classic Rock
regions: northeastern USA
venues: Theaters, PACs, Colleges, Outdoor Stages
Primarily books legends & tribute acts for mostly NJ area all ages gigs. Email only; No calls.

Apex Entertainment
Oshkosh, WI 54902
p: 920-216-2764
e: apexentpro@gmail.com
www.myspace.com/ apex1promotions
contact: Angela
genres: Hip-Hop, R&B, Rock, Country
regions: USA
venues: All Types
Books Local-Int'l acts & some DJs for an all ages crowd. Prefers press kits.

Austin Universal Entertainment
1701 Directors Blvd.
Ste. 350
Austin, TX 78744
p: 512-452-6856
f: 512-452-7257
e: samantha@aueonline.com
www.aueonline.com
contact: Greg Henry
ext: 512-452-6856 x12
e: greg@aueonline.com
genres: Country, Rock, Alt.
regions: USA, France
venues: All Types
Books Local-Int'l acts for all ages gigs. No unsolicited kits.

Big Easy Concerts/ Bravo Entertainment
416 S 9th St., Ste. 306
Boise, ID 83702
p: 208-367-1212
e: info@bravobsp.com
www.bravopresents.com
contact: Greg Marchant
ext: 208-343-8833
genres: All Styles
regions: northwest thru midwest USA
venues: Clubs thru Arenas
Part of Knitting Factory Entertainment, promotes top original Touring acts & polished emerging talent in secondary markets in 19 states.

Bignote Ent.
87 Tuscany Springs Way NW
Calgary, AB T3L 2N4
p: 403-668-0880
f: 403-668-74411
contact: Jim Samuelson
e: jim@bignote.net
genres: Folk, Blues, Jazz
regions: Canada, some USA
venues: Clubs, Festivals
Books original Local-Int'l acts for all ages. Also plays Folk, New Wave, Alt. Country & S/S on live365 radio show, "Jim's Basement".
Contact before sending materials.

Big Productions
PO Box 460386
Houston, TX 77056
p: 713-622-1518; 713-516-3437
f: 713-664-9678
contact: Don Gomez
ext: 713-351-9131
e: donflashgomez@ yahoo.com
genres: Country, Pop, Rock, Hip-Hop, Latin
regions: Reg'l, USA
venues: Clubs, Festivals, Rodeos
Maily Nat'l Touring acts w/ some Local/Reg'l openers for Houston area events. Snail mail; call 10 days later to follow up.

Box Talent Agency
6305 Waterford Blvd., Ste. 480
Oklahoma City, OK 73118
p: 405-858-2263
f: 405-418-2157
e: talent@boxtalent.com
www.boxtalent.com
contact: Kym Johnston
e: kymjohnston@ boxtalent.com
genres: Alt., Rock, Pop, Top 40, Country
regions: OK, TX, KS, AR, MD, DC, AZ
venues: Clubs, Casinos, Corporate & Special Events
Books some original Local-Int'l acts, but mainly cover bands. Offices in Tulsa: 918-743-2263 & Dallas: 214-755-7526.

C 3 Presents
98 San Jacinto Blvd., Ste. 400
Austin, TX 78701
p: 512-478-7211
f: 512-476-0611
e: hello@c3presents.com
www.c3presents.com
contact: Sarah McGoldrick
e: smcgoldrick@ c3presents.com
genres: All Styles
regions: TX, USA
venues: Clubs, PACs, Arenas, Festivals, Theaters, Events
Formerly Charles Attal Presents, works w/mostly original Local-Int'l act & some DJs for all ages shows.
Write venue/event on package.

Chris Ricci Presents
930 11th St.
Modesto, CA 95354
p: 209-312-3463; 916-812-7625
www.chrisriccipresents.com
contact: Chris Ricci
e: chris@ chrisriccipresents.com
genres: All Styles
regions: western CA
venues: The Fat Cat Music House in Modesto, CA, X-Fest
Books original Local-Nat'l acts

for 21+ shows & X-Fest. Email kits, then call to follow up.

Concert Ideas
73 Ratterman Rd.
Woodstock, NY
12498
p: 800-836-2000
f: 845-679-9022
e: info@concertideas.com
www.concertideas.com
contact: Harris Goldberg
e: harrisg@concertideas.com
genres: Alt., Rock, Pop, Hip-Hop, World, S/S
regions: USA
venues: Colleges
Presents A-list & polished talent & DJs for all ages campus gigs. Also contact: adam@concertideas.com, mike@concertideas.com & taylor@concertideas.com. ***OH office:*** *888-832-0808; dave@concertideas.com.* ***NYC office:*** *800-268-1201; brian@concertideas.com. No unsolicited material.*

Create A Vibe
1 Crest Dr.
Long Valley, NJ
07853
p: 908-876-3884
f: 908-876-3850
e: booking@createavibe.com
www.createavibe.com
contact: Rob Ortiz
ext: 973-448-3977
e: rob@createavibe.com
genres: Jam, Jazz, Blues, Rock, Acoustic, Country, Pop
regions: NJ
venues: Mexicali Blues Cafe
Eatery & listening room books original Local-Int'l acts for 18+. Contact first.

Creative Entertainment Group
505 8th Ave.
Ste. 805
New York, NY 10018
p: 212-634-0427
f: 212-634-0432
e: info@cegmusic.com
www.cegmusic.com
contact: Howie Schnee
ext: 212-634-0427 x6
e: howie@cegmusic.com
genres: Rock, Pop, Jam, Jazz, Hip-Hop, Reggae
regions: NY, NJ
venues: NYC: Sullivan Hall, BB Kings, Canal Room, Irving Plaza, Knitting Factory, Crash Mansion, Fontana's, Highline Ballroom, Maxwell's
Prime promotions & mgmt. company presents A-list & polished acts for all ages. Prefers Sonicbids or email Howie kits w/ NYC gig history (incl. draw) & music links.

CrossCurrents/ KC Folk Music
PO Box 10104
Kansas City, MO 64171
p: 816-292-2887
f: 913-344-6777
e: ccurrent@crosscurrentsculture.org
www.crosscurrentsculture.org
contact: Diana Suckiel
e: bob-diana73@sbcglobal.net
genres: Folk, Acoustic, Womyn's, Theater
Non-profit uses several venues to book original Local-Int'l acts for all ages.

Detached Entertainment
9651 E 28th St.
Tulsa, OK 74129
p: 918-855-2725
www.myspace.com/detachedentertainment
contact: Brandon Young
e: hateuponvirtue@yahoo.com
genres: Hardcore, Punk, Pop, Metal, Emo, Indie, Hip-Hop
regions: OK
venues: Clubs
Original, mostly Local/Reg'l acts for all ages gigs. Seeking new acts.

Direct Events
13101 Hwy. 71 W
Austin, TX 78738
p: 512-263-4240
f: 512-263-4194
e: info@directevents.net
www.directevents.net
contact: Georgia Clarke
e: booking@directevents.net
genres: All Styles
regions: USA
venues: Clubs, Theaters, Private Events
Books original recording acts & polished Local-Int'l bands & DJs for area's top venues. Shows mostly all ages.

Double Tee Promotions
10 NW 6th Ave.
Portland, OR 97209
p: 503-221-0288
f: 503-227-4418
www.doubletee.com
contact: David Leiken
genres: All Styles
regions: northwestern USA
venues: Clubs thru Arenas, Festivals
Top area agency promotes original A-list Touring acts & buzz bands; some DJs. Shows mostly all ages. Contact first.

EvilGirl Entertainment
624 Palmer Ave.
Maywood, NJ
07607
p: 201-926-2677
e: evilgirlent@yahoo.com
www.myspace.com/evilgirlentertainment
contact: Paige Davis
genres: Mostly Rock & Metal
regions: NJ, NY & PA
venues: Clubs, Events
Promotes Local-Int'l bands & DJs at area venues & all ages events. Oversees promo materials & mailing list on site. Acts must draw min. of 25-30.

Excess dB Entertainment
100 5th Ave., 11th Fl.
New York, NY 10011
p: 212-277-7171
f: 212-840-7006
www.excessdb.com
contact: Heath Miller
ext: 201-567-9771
e: heath@metrohybrid.com
genres: Rock, Pop, Punk, Alt.
regions: northeastern USA
venues: Clubs
Prime agency, part of Metropolitan Talent, books top original Touring acts & buzz bands for all ages. Send email links only to Casey McCabe: casey@metrohybrid.com. No MP3s or attachments. Don't call; will contact if interested.

Fat Lip Entertainment
PO Box 700803
Tulsa, OK 74170
p: 918-281-9825
f: 918-270-1009
e: info@fatlipmusic.com
www.fatlipmusic.com
contact: Matt Lip
genres: Hip-Hop, Alt., Pop, Rock
regions: OK, TX, FL
venues: Festivals, Clubs: The Pink Eye, The Otherside, Blue Dome Roadhouse, Plan B, Exit 6C, The Blank State
Original Local-Int'l acts for an all ages crowd. Contact via MySpace before sending kits.

FCM Productions
PO Box 93
Waterloo, NY 13165
p: 800-675-9123
f: 315-539-0865
www.fcmproductions.com
contact: Cliff Maus
e: fcmaus@fcmproductions.com
genres: Country
regions: NY State Finger Lakes Region
venues: Clubs thru Arenas
Only signed, Nat'l-Int'l artists considered; all ages shows.

Fusion Shows
420 Northlawn Ave.
East Lansing, MI 48823
www.fusionshows.com
contact: Irving Ronk
e: irving@fusionshows.com
genres: Indie, Rock, S/S
regions: central MI
venues: Bars, PACs
Formerly Northlawn Music Group, books Local-Int'l acts for some all ages gigs. Send kits.

Graverot Promotions
1107 N First St.
El Cajon, CA 92021
p: 619-277-6751
e: reekngraverot@yahoo.com
www.myspace.com/graverotbookings
contact: Trish Barclay
genres: All Styles of Metal
regions: USA, Int'l
venues: 21+ Clubs
Books Local-Nat'l bands in SoCal clubs, now seeking Int'l acts. Mail or email promos.

Great Northeast Productions
PO Box 1010
Townsend, MA
01469
p: 978-597-3289
f: 978-597-5576
www.greatnortheast.com
contact: Dave Werlin
e: dave@greatnortheast.com
genres: Roots, Rock, Pop, Alt., Blues, Jazz, Folk
regions: northeastern USA
venues: Festivals, Clubs, Events
Books Reg'l buzz bands, Nat'l Touring talent & DJs for some all ages shows. Contact: Ben, ben@greatnortheast.com, before sending material.

High Street Concerts
PO Box 668
Lyons, CO 80540
p: 303-817-6433
e: info@highstreetconcerts.com
www.highstreetconcerts.com
contact: Annie Sirontniak
genres: Acoustic, Americana, Bluegrass, Folk
regions: Boulder, CO
venues: Rogers Hall, Events
Series presents Local-Int'l talent May-Oct at Rogers Hall. Slots avail. & shows are all ages.

Jab Productions
5212 S 156th St., Apt. 134
Omaha, NE 68135
p: 402-990-2109
e: jab@eventsomaha.com
www.eventsomaha.com
contact: Chris Jones
genres: All Styles, mostly DJs
regions: midwestern USA
venues: Club Miko, Citrus Ultra Lounge
Mostly DJs for 18 & 21+ shows.

Jade Presents
3014 26th Ave. SW
Fargo, ND 58103
p: 701-298-0071
f: 701-298-0072
www.jadepresents.com
contact: Jade Nielson
e: jade@jadepresents.com
genres: Rock, Pop, Americana, S/S, Hip-Hop
regions: ND
venues: Concerts, Festivals, Casinos, Events
Books Reg'l & Nat'l acts for all ages shows & provides event production, media relations & consultation.

Jam Productions
205 W Goethe St.
Chicago, IL 60610
p: 312-440-9191
f: 312-266-9568
www.jamusa.com
contact: Jerry Mikelson
genres: All Styles
regions: Chicago
venues: Festivals, Clubs thru Arenas
Full svc. concert & event producer works w/ original A-list & polished bands & DJs for all ages gigs. Call only - NO unsolicited material.

Jay Goldberg Events & Entertainment
1115 W Oregon
Ste. A
Urbana, IL 61801
p: 217-278-7400
f: 217-367-3142
www.jaytv.com
contact: Ian Goldberg
e: ian@jaytv.com
genres: Alt., Rock, Pop, Roots, Blues, Jam, Country
regions: midwestern USA
venues: Clubs, Festivals, Corporate, College
Partners w/ Jam Prod. to present mostly original buzz bands, DJs & top recording acts. Some shows all ages. Submit EPKs only.

Jersey Shows
275 Main St.
Matawan, NJ
07747
p: 866-374-7862
f: 732-696-1032
e: info@jerseyshows.com
www.jerseyshows.com
contact: Dan Fulton
e: dan@jerseyshows.com
genres: Rock, Pop, Ska, Alt., Metal, Hardcore, Emo
regions: NJ, NY, PA
venues: The Saint, Chubby's, Room 2858, Court Tavern, Marlboro Rec Center, Station 36 (at Waretown Firehall) & Mainstage
Books Local-Int'l acts; some all ages shows. Hosts Tri-State area Battle of the Bands w/ $20,000 prize. No unsolicited material.

John Harris Group
PO Box 1012
Federal Sq. Stn.
Harrisburg, PA 17108
p: 717-221-1124
e: info@johnharris.com
www.johnharris.com
contact: John Harris
e: johnharris@johnharris.com
genres: All Styles
regions: PA, NJ, DE, MD
venues: Clubs, Theaters, Colleges, Fairs, Festivals
Presents Local-Nat'l Touring bands for all ages shows. Also produces Millennium Music Conference & Singer Songwriter of Cape May. Prefers EPKs.

Kendall West Agency
PO Box 173776
Arlington, TX
76003
p: 817-468-7800; 336-940-3356
f: 336-940-3356
e: kendallwestagency@roadrunnner.com
www.myspace.com/kendallwestagency
contact: Michelle Vellucci
genres: Country, Rock, Jazz, Dance
regions: USA
venues: Clubs, Festivals, Fairs, Corporate/Private Events
Presents Local-Int'l bands for all ages shows. No unsolicited material.

Latin Spectrum Entertainment
28 Marion St.
Roslindale, MA 02131
p: 617-325-8900
f: 617-325-8901
www.latinspectrum.com
contact: Rafael Jaimes
e: bookings@latinspectrum.com
genres: All Styles of Latin
regions: New England
venues: Clubs, Events
Region's top Latin promoter books Local-Int'l bands.

Live Nation (NY)
220 W 42nd St.
New York, NY
10036
p: 917-421-5100
www.livenation.com
contact: Rebecca Novak
ext: 917-421-5130
e: rebeccanovak@livenation.com
genres: All Styles
regions: metro NY
venues: Clubs, Theaters, Stadiums
Leading agency & Clear Channel spinoff presents A-list artists, DJs & buzz bands for all ages NYC area gigs. Nat'l & Int'l acts contact CA office: 415-371-5500. No unsolicited material.

Lommori Productions
1415 Arnold Dr.
Martinez, CA 94553
p: 925-858-6650
f: 925-676-0699
www.myspace.com/lommoriproductions
contact: Chris Lommori
e: chrislommori@aol.com
genres: Rock, Pop, Dance, Metal, Punk, Ska, Blues, R&B
regions: northern CA
venues: Clubs: Bourbon St. Bar/Grill & Tommy T's
Books Local-Touring up & comers & some estab. acts; some all ages shows.

Love-Sexy
307 2nd St.
Hoboken, NJ
07030
p: 201-795-1878
f: 201-795-0791
www.love-sexy.com
contact: John Vargas
e: vinvarg1@aol.com
genres: Pop, Rock, Alt., Latin, Hip-Hop, World, Electronic, Metal, Punk, Neo-Soul, Avant Garde, Electro, Dance
regions: Metro NYC, LA, San Francisco, Boston, Austin & PA
venues: Clubs, Events
Books Local-Nat'l acts for the 21-40/yr old market. Prefers electronic submissions.

Luckyman Concerts
730 N Mill Ave.
Tempe, AZ 85281
p: 480-829-0607
e: james@luckymanonline.com
www.luckymanonline.com
contact: Tom Lapenna
ext: 480-829-0727
e: tom@luckymanonline.com
regions: AZ, NM
venues: Clubs, Theatres
Promotes buzz bands & top acts for all ages shows. Local Talent contact: James Nicoll: james@luckymanonline.com.

MassConcerts
261 Main St.
Worcester, MA
01608
p: 978-440-9860
f: 978-275-9527
e: massmediagirl@aol.com
www.massconcerts.com
contact: John Peters
genres: Alt., Rock, Punk, Metal, Pop, Rap, DJ
regions: New England, NY
venues: Clubs thru Arenas
Presents buzz bands, top recording acts & Touring DJs for an all ages crowd. Send CD, photo, bio & touring history.

McMillan Associates
1929 3rd Ave. N
Ste. 900
Birmingham, AL
35203
p: 205-324-6881
f: 205-323-7074
www.mcmillan-associates.com
contact: George McMillan
ext: 205-324-6881 x104
e: george@mcmillan-associates.com
genres: All Styles
regions: southeast USA
venues: Sloss Furnace, City Stages, Corporate Events
Books Local-Int'l bands for all ages crowd. Submissions thru Sonicbids.com only.

Mike Thrasher Presents
525 SE 11th, Ste. C
Portland, OR 97214
p: 503-231-1530
f: 503-231-1597
e: info@mikethrasherpresents.com
www.mikethrasherpresents.com
contact: Mike Thrasher
e: mike@mikethrasherpresents.com
genres: Rock, Punk, Metal, Hip-Hop, S/S, Jazz, AC, Electronica, World, Indie
regions: OR, WA, UT, CA & BC, Canada
venues: The Hawthorne Theater, Roseland, The Crystal Ballroom, Tacoma Dome, Loveland
Works w/ buzz bands, Nat'l Touring acts & DJs; some all ages shows. Email first.

Monqui Events
PO Box 5908
Portland, OR 97228
p: 503-223-5833
f: 503-223-5960
e: web@monqui.com
www.monqui.com
contact: Keith Buckingham
e: keith@monqui.com
genres: Alt., Rock, Indie, Pop, Country
regions: northwest USA
venues: The Wonder Ballroom, Dante's, Roseland Theater, Crystal Ballroom, Doug Fir Lounge, Berbati's Pan.
Key area promoter for NW area's top clubs. Presents original rising stars & estab. acts. Most shows all ages. Snail mail materials.

Nitelite
500 Park Blvd.
Ste. 160C
Itasca, IL 60143
p: 630-773-5552
f: 630-773-3370
e: info@nitelite.com
www.nitelite.com
contact: Don Kronberg
e: don@nitelite.com
genres: All Styles
regions: USA
venues: Corporate Events, Colleges, Fairs, Festivals
Works w/ Reg'l-Int'l acts for some all ages shows. No unsolicited material.

Nomad Artists
PO Box 1186
Athens, GA 30603
p: 706-354-6107
f: 706-316-0752
e: nomadartists@msn.com
www.nomadartists.com
contact: Troy Aubrey
genres: Rock, Roots, Pop-Punk, Hip-Hop, Tribute, Americana
regions: Atlanta, Athens, GA
venues: Clubs (Melting Point), Theaters, Festivals (AthFest), Special Events
Works w/ Local-Int'l bands.

Numbskull Productions
2490 Deerfield Ct., Ste. P
Camarillo, CA 93010
p: 805-987-2026
f: 805-987-7806
e: info@numbskullshows.com
www.numbskullshows.com
contact: Eddy
e: eddy@numbskullshows.com
genres: Hardcore, Punk, Rock, Indie, Reggae, Metal, Ska, Hip-Hop, Alt., Rockabilly
regions: CA
venues: Clubs, Resorts, Lounges, Bars, Pubs, PACs
Prime indie promoter for all levels of original Local-Touring acts. All ages shows.

People Productions
PO Box 962
Redway, CA 95560
p: 707-923-4599
f: 707-923-4509
e: people@peopleproductions.net
www.peopleproductions.net
contact: Carol Bruno
genres: All Styles
regions: CA
venues: Clubs, Fairs, Festivals, Tours
Presents Local-Int'l musicians & DJs for all ages shows.

Pioneer Music
2638 24th Ave. NE
Olympia, WA
98506
p: 360-753-5463
f: 360-753-5463
www.pioneermusic.org
contact: Audrey Henley
e: audrey@pioneermusic.org
genres: All Styles
regions: Olympia, WA
venues: The Capitol Theater, The Backstage
Outfit w/ DIY sensibility pairs original Touring acts w/ Local bands for all ages gigs. Call first.

Pipeline Productions
123 W 8th St.
Ste. 309
Lawrence, KS
66044
p: 785-749-3655
f: 785-749-3036
e: music@pipelineproductions.com
www.pipelineproductions.com
contact: Brett Mosiman
e: brettm@pipelineproductions.com
genres: Alt., Rock, S/S, Pop, Punk
regions: Lawrence, KS & Kansas City, MO
venues: Clubs, Theaters
Local-Int'l bands & DJs for all ages gigs. Submit via site or

mail Attn: Julia, The Bottleneck, 737 New Hampshire, Lawrence, KS 66044. 1st time acts email: music@pipelineprodutions.com.

Promoter Line
4218 Gateway Dr.
Ste. 140
Colleyville, TX
76034
p: 817-557-1009
f: 817-557-6155
www.promoterline.com
contact: Jerry Thompson
ext: 817-557-1009 x1
e: jtpresents@aol.com
genres: Country, Blues, Folk, Rock
regions: Reg'l, USA
venues: Festivals, Events
Works w/ original Local-Int'l bands for all ages gigs. No unsolicited material.

PromoWest Productions
405 Neil Ave.
Columbus, OH
43215
p: 614-461-5483
f: 614-461-0297
e: contact@promowestlive.com
www.promowestlive.com
contact: Scott Stienecker
ext: 614-461-5483 x201
e: scotts@promo-west.com
genres: All Styles
regions: OH
venues: Newport Music Hall, The Basement, Lifestyle Communities Pavilion, House of Crave
Locals contact: sboyer@promowestlive.com; Nat'ls contact: adam@promowestlive.com. Books some DJs & all ages shows.

Pulse Productions
120 Pearl Alley
Santa Cruz, CA 95060
p: 831-423-7970
f: 831-423-3238
www.pulseproductions.net
contact: Michael Horne
e: michael@pulseproductions.net
genres: Jazz, Folk, Rock, Jam, World, Country, S/S, Americana
regions: northern CA
venues: Clubs, PACs
Presents mostly Nat'l Touring acts; some all ages shows.

RipStar
806 Moultrie St.
San Francisco, CA
94110
p: 415-867-5383
e: bandsthatrock@gmail.com
www.ripstar.cfsites.org
contact: Rob Jackson
genres: Indie, Alt., Rock, Folk, Blues, World, Jazz
regions: San Francisco, CA
venues: Clubs
Produces monthly, 18+ showcases for Local-Int'l acts. Snail mail 2-4 CDs (with phone # written on CD), will contact if interested.

Rising Tide Productions
317 Monticello Ave.
Norfolk, VA
23510
p: 757-622-9877
f: 757-622-2829
e: kara@rtconcerts.com
www.rtconcerts.com
contact: Rick Mersel
e: bayourick@aol.com
genres: All Styles
regions: Virginia Beach, Norfolk & Richmond, VA
venues: Clubs, Pavilions
Books original Local-Int'l buzz bands, DJs & top recording acts for mostly all ages shows. No unsolicited material.

S.T.A.R.S. Productions (East)
91 High St.
Newton, NJ 07860
p: 973-300-9123
f: 973-300-5857
e: info@stars-productions.com
www.stars-productions.com
contact: Steve Tarkanish
genres: All Styles
regions: NJ, NY, PA
venues: Clubs, Events
East coast arm books Local-Nat'l bands & DJs. West coast bookings contact: Scott Stimpson: bigmountainllc@comcast.net. No unsolicited material.

Sings Like Hell
3509 Socorro Tr.
Austin, TX 78739
p: 512-282-5082
f: 512-291-8164
e: hellgirlsb@aol.com
www.singslikehell.com
contact: Peggie Jones
genres: Pop, Rock, S/S, Jazz, World, Reggae, Folk
regions: Santa Barbara, CA
venues: The Lobero Theater
Non-profit subscription series presents original Local-Int'l acts to upscale, hip audiences. Send CDs only & wait for reply.

Spune Productions
1009 Andrew Dr.
Burleson, TX 76028
p: 817-637-8199
e: booking@spune.com
www.spune.com
contact: Lance Yocom
e: lance@spune.com
genres: Indie, Acoustic, Folk, Alt., Rock, S/S
regions: Local, Reg'l, USA
venues: Clubs, Festivals
Works w/ original Local-Nat'l bands & DJs for some all ages shows. Mail kits. Also a label, booking agent & mgmt. co.

Stardate Concerts
10480 Shady Tr.
Ste. 104
Dallas, TX 75220
p: 940-497-2200
f: 940-497-6677
e: starconkw@cs.com
contact: Randy Shelton
genres: Rock, Country
regions: TX, NM
venues: Clubs thru Arenas, Festivals
Local-Int'l acts for mostly all ages shows.

Stars & Scars
149 7th St.
Belford, NJ
07718
e: starsxscars@yahoo.com
www.starsandscars.com
contact: Elyse Jankoski
genres: Rock, Pop, Emo, Ska, Indie, Alt., Acoustic, Hip-Hop
regions: NJ
venues: Christ Church, Old First Church
Supports Indie bands & communities by organizing shows w/ door prizes & fair payment policies. Books secular Local & Reg'l acts for all ages gigs. Contact via MySpace or snail mail CDs. No Metal, Screamo or Hardcore.

Trans-Fusion Entertainment
PO Box 342
Hamersville, OH 45130
p: 513-545-3142
e: transfusionrec@aol.com
www.myspace.com/cincytransfusion
contact: Paul
genres: Rock, Tribute
regions: OH, MI, KY, WV, MA, NJ, NC, MO
venues: Clubs, Theaters
Original Local-Nat'l bands w/ pro look & sound for all ages shows. Promos: 237 Main St., Hamersville, OH 45130.

Trey Merrill Presents
335 Coffee St.
Mandeville, LA
70448
p: 985-789-0001
f: 985-727-0084
www.treymerrillpresents.com
contact: Trey Merrill
e: treymerrillpresents@gmail.com
genres: Rock, Indie, Country, Folk, Blues, Gospel, Metal
regions: statewide
venues: Clubs, Festivals
Local-Int'l acts for some all ages shows.

Triangle Talent
10424 Watterson Tr.
Louisville, KY 40299
p: 502-267-5466
f: 502-267-8244
e: info@triangletalent.com
www.triangletalent.com
contact: David Snowden
e: dsnowden@triangletalent.com
genres: Rock, Country, Dance, Blues, Jazz, Pop
regions: USA, Canada
venues: Clubs, Colleges, Fairs, Festivals, Special Events
Books original Local-Nat'l bands for all ages shows. For club bookings contact Tom Nutgrass: nutgrass@triangletalent.com.

Vootie Productions
317 N Bozeman Ave.
Bozeman, MT
59715
p: 406-586-1922
f: 406-586-2021
e: info@vootie.com
www.vootie.com
contact: Tom
genres: Americana, Folk, Reggae, Country, Bluegrass
regions: western USA
venues: Clubs, Festivals, Corporate/Special Events
Polished & estab. artists. No unsolicited material.

Washington Ave.
Washington, NJ
p: 908-268-9294
f: 908-453-4286
contact: Mike Lavalle
e: lavalleindustries@gmail.com
genres: Rock, Punk, Alt.
regions: north & central NJ, eastern PA
Presents cheap shows w/ amazing Local-Int'l bands for all ages. Bands sell tix at door. Promos to: 77 Shippen Rdg., Oxford, NJ 07863 - ATTN: Michael Lavalle.

The Wheel Company
2995 Woodside Rd.,
Ste. 400-364
Woodside, CA 94062
p: 650-368-9225
f: 650-368-0920
www.thewheelcompany.com
contact: Jay Saber
e: jaysaber@thewheelcompany.com
genres: Jam, Rock, Acoustic, Bluegrass, Blues
regions: Santa Cruz & San Francisco, CA
venues: Clubs, Festivals, Events
Books Local-Nat'l acts for an all ages crowd. Seeks Touring bands w/ draw of 200+.

advertiser index

FROM THE PAGES OF THE atlas plugged eNEWSLETTER

FUEL FOR THOUGHT

A songstress with talent, wit and a heart of green, Brooklyn-based April Smith converted a diesel bus to run on veggie oil to save money and the planet. April may be pulling up to re-fuel at a fast-food joint near you, but we were lucky to catch up with her just before she and her tour bus, "Mr. Belvedere" set off on their eco-friendly cross-country tour.

Atlas Plugged: When & why did you decide to use vegetable oil for your tour bus?

April Smith: I did this because I was shocked at how much gas we burned traveling to Austin in 2007. It really seemed a shame to me that we didn't have a better alternative. I decided that the only way I would tour was if I could do it on veggie oil. And once I decide to do something, there's pretty much no changing my mind. I had wanted to do this for a few years, but I needed a diesel bus to convert. It's not easy to find an inexpensive diesel bus in good condition. And the bigger, full-size buses are harder to maintain so I wanted a smaller bus. But I'll probably move on to a diesel RV next. For now, Mr. Belvedere will do just fine.

AP: Mr. Belvedere?

AS: Our last tour vehicle was Mrs. Garrett, an 86 Vandura. We outgrew her pretty quickly and she used a lot of gas. So we had to get rid of her. We figured we'd stick with the 80's sitcom names. We hope Mr. Belvedere will take care of us as well as Mrs. G, may she rest in pieces.

AP: Where did you find an inexpensive diesel bus in good enough condition?

AS: I just searched ebay and Craigslist for months until I found the right bus. You just have to know what you want and make sure that you don't buy something on impulse.

AP: How did you determine what you would need to outfit your bus – is there a kit or an organization that supplies a list or instructions?

AS: I connected with a friend who is actually a wiz when it comes to this stuff. He converted his own car and was up for the challenge of a bus. He's seriously one of the smartest people I've ever met. He's currently designing an on-board filtering system for me.

AP: From start to finish - how long did it take you to find & retro-fit?

AS: Just a week or 2 really. The hardest part is getting all of the parts you need and getting them to arrive on time. A lot of this stuff is specialized so the parts often need to be made before they're shipped.

AP: How large of a container will it take to fill your tank & what does that usually cost?

AS: Our veggie tank hold 32 gallons. So we can probably get about 320 – 375 miles from one veggie tank, depending on how many people and how much equipment we have with us. We also plan on taking two 30 gallon drums of oil as backup. It will probably wind up costing about 1-2 bucks a gallon, which is great.

AP: What brand of vegetable oil will you use - does it matter if it's a name brand or generic? Or will you be using used restaurant oil?

AS: I'd love to be sponsored by Wesson because then it would be "Smith & Wesson" which would be pretty funny. In all seriousness, it doesn't matter what brand but more what type of oil you use. Canola is the best. And the less it has been used for cooking, the better it is for your tank. We're hoping restaurants here in Williamsburg will be kind and give us whatever they can.

AP: If restaurant oil - do you get it from a dealer or do you pull up to the drive-thru window? Is that free? Do you think a fast food chain might fund your tour?

AS: No, you have to give the restaurant containers and they will fill them for you. Then you pick them up every few days and filter them before using them for fuel.

AP: Apparently converting a car engine to burn vegetable oil is not officially legal, though the EPA & Government haven't charged anyone with a crime. Are you concerned about that or do you think, with gas prices so high & the economy so low that they won't bother self-sufficient, eco-friendly artists?

AS: It's not legal, but I don't know that the government is all that hard on veggie car owners. I think that as long as you pay a road tax, you should be fine. And we're still using diesel, just significantly less than we would if we couldn't run on veggie oil. We can also run the bus on biodiesel so if they do crack down, at least we've got that. I'm sure it won't be long before the government gets involved, which is unfortunate. But at least we can feel good about what we're doing for the time being.

AP: How much did it cost to retro-fit your bus?

AS: About $2,000 after all is said and done.

AP: How much do you expect to save?

AS: Thousands of dollars and millions of people!

AP: Do you have any other green initiatives – packaging, sign up sheets for environmental causes, etc?

AS: We're looking for like-minded groups and companies to team up with. Ideally, we'd love to be sponsored by companies that are really trying to reduce their carbon footprints and green up. We also want to have solar panels installed on the bus so we can charge phones and run small things like laptops and GPS devices. I'd also like to introduce more green merch..but that's coming soon so you'll find out!

AP: Describe your music & your fan base?

AS: I'd say that my music is like a retro pop sounds...sort of like the Beatles meets the Andrews Sisters. My fan base is really diverse and sort of all over the place. I met this guy recently who was all inked up and built like a tank and he was like, "Colors is the best song ever!". I was so floored by that!

AP: How have other artists responded?

AS: Other artists have expressed interest in doing the same thing, which is really great. When I have the money, I'd like to buy an RV and convert it to be super green. Then I'll sell the bus to a band who promises to carry the torch for me.

AP: Do you think that all artists can easily turn more green?

AS: Yes, it's actually not that hard. You don't need a diesel bus with an extra tank. You can limit your waste as a band...don't drink bottled water. Get a brita pitcher and some plastic tumblers. Start composting. Ask for green packaging when you order CDs. Print on recycled paper. The list is endless!

AP: Where should artists go to learn more about your efforts & learn how they can be more eco-friendly?

AS: Just go to my Myspace page (**www.myspace.com/aprilsmithmusic**) and read my blogs. I'm trying to keep them current so that everyone can watch Mr. Belvedere's transition. He's going to be such a ladykiller.